Black
OF
3D Game
Programming

André LaMothe

WAITE GROUP PRESS™
CORTE MADERA, CA

PUBLISHER Mitchell Waite
EDITOR-IN-CHIEF Charles Drucker
ACQUISITIONS EDITOR Jill Pisoni
EDITORIAL DIRECTOR John Crudo
MANAGING EDITOR Kurt Stephan
CONTENT EDITOR Heidi Brumbaugh
TECHNICAL REVIEWER Jeff Bankston
COPY EDITOR Judith Brown
PRODUCTION DIRECTOR Julianne Ososke
PRODUCTION MANAGER Cecile Kaufman
PRODUCTION TRAFFIC COORDINATOR Ingrid Owen
DESIGN Sestina Quarequio, Christi Fryday
PRODUCTION Jude Levinson
ILLUSTRATIONS Kristin Peterson, Pat Rogondino, Larry Wilson
COVER ILLUSTRATION James Dowlen
APPENDIX A ILLUSTRATION Barclay Shaw

        98 •   10 9 8 7 6 5 4

Library of Congress Cataloging-in-Publication Data

LaMothe, André.
        Black art of 3D game programming / André LaMothe.
                p.   cm.
        Includes index.
        ISBN 1-57169-004-2
        1. Computer games--Programming. 2. Three-dimensional display systems. I. Title.
        QA76.76.C672L36 1995
        794.8′16765--dc20   95-32976
                                                                                 CIP

Dedication

I dedicate this book to all the children of the world; may you take us boldly into the 21st century and beyond...

Message from the
Publisher

WELCOME TO OUR NERVOUS SYSTEM

Some people say that the World Wide Web is a graphical extension of the information superhighway, just a network of humans and machines sending each other long lists of the equivalent of digital junk mail.

I think it is much more than that. To me the Web is nothing less than the nervous system of the entire planet—not just a collection of computer brains connected together, but more like a billion silicon neurons entangled and recirculating electro-chemical signals of information and data, each contributing to the birth of another CPU and another Web site.

Think of each person's hard disk connected at once to every other hard disk on earth, driven by human navigators searching like Columbus for the New World. Seen this way the Web is more of a super entity, a growing, living thing, controlled by the universal human will to expand, to be more. Yet unlike a purposeful business plan with rigid rules, the Web expands in a nonlinear, unpredictable, creative way that echoes natural evolution.

We created our Web site not just to extend the reach of our computer book products but to be part of this synaptic neural network, to experience, like a nerve in the body, the flow of ideas and then to pass those ideas up the food chain of the mind. Your mind. Even more, we wanted to pump some of our own creative juices into this rich wine of technology.

TASTE OUR DIGITAL WINE

And so we ask you to taste our wine by visiting the body of our business. Begin by understanding the metaphor we have created for our Web site—a universal learning center, situated in outer space in the form of a space station. A place where you can journey to study any topic from the convenience of your own screen. Right now we are focusing on computer topics, but the stars are the limit on the Web.

If you are interested in discussing this Web site, or finding out more about the Waite Group, please send me email with your comments and I will be happy to respond. Being a programmer myself, I love to talk about technology and find out what our readers are looking for.

Sincerely,

Mitchell Waite

Mitchell Waite, C.E.O. and Publisher

200 Tamal Plaza
Corte Madera CA 94925
415 924 2575
415 924 2576 fax

Internet email:
mwaite@waite.com

CompuServe email:
75146,3515

Website:
http://www.waite.com/waite

CREATING THE HIGHEST QUALITY COMPUTER BOOKS IN THE INDUSTRY

Waite Group Press
Waite Group New Media

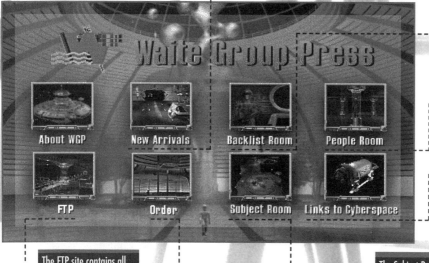

About the Author

André LaMothe has worked in many areas of the computing industry, including neural networks, 3D graphics, virtual reality, and robotics. He holds degrees in Math, Computer Science, and Electrical Engineering. You'll find articles by André published in *Computer Language, Circuit Cellar,* and *Game Developer.* André has previously written two best-selling books: *Tricks of the Game Programming Gurus* and *Teach Yourself Game Programming in 21 Days.*

Table of Contents

Foreword by Steve Wozniak . . . . *xxiv*
Preface . . . . *xxvii*
Installation . . . . *xxviii*

Part I: Incantations   1
Chapter 1: The Genesis of 3D Games 3
Chapter 2: Elements of the Game 21

Part II: Alchemy   45
Chapter 3: The Mysterious VGA Card 47
Chapter 4: Waking the Dead with Animation 105
Chapter 5: Communicating with the Outside World 205
Chapter 6: Dancing with Cyberdemons 267
Chapter 7: The Magick of Thought 345
Chapter 8: The Art of Possession 401
Chapter 9: Multiplayer Game Techniques 453
Chapter 10: 3D Fundamentals 543
Chapter 11: Building a 3D Graphics Engine 631
Chapter 12: Solid Modeling and Shading 701
Chapter 13: Universal Transformations 783
Chapter 14: Hidden Surface and Object Removal 803
Chapter 15: Clipping and Rendering the Final View 827
Chapter 16: Voxel Graphics 933

Part III: Spells   991
Chapter 17: Optimizing the 3D Engine 993
Chapter 18: Kill or Be Killed 1115
Appendix A: Cybersorcerer and Cyberwizard Contests 1155
Index 1159

Contents

Part I: Incantations   1

Chapter 1: The Genesis of 3D Games 3

Of Cyberspace and 3D Games 5
Evolving from 2D to 3D 6
    Vector Graphics 8
    Raster Graphics 9
    Parallax Scrolling 10
    Wireframe Polygon Engines 12
Trends in Sorcery 13
    Solid Polygon Rendering 13
    Ray Casting 14
    Voxel Graphics 15
    Ellipsoidal Technology 16
Journeys into the Mind's Eye 18
The Black Box 18
Summary 20

Chapter 2: Elements of the Game 21

The Sequence of a Game 23
    The Installation and Setup Phase 24
    Introducing the Player to the Game 25
    Run Time 26
    The Concluding Sequence 26
The Input Channel 27
Event Driven Programming 30
    Input Driven Event Loops 30
    Real-Time Event Loops 32
    Typical 3D Game Loops 34
Autonomous Functions and Auto-Logic 40

Temporal and Video Synchronization 41
The Sound System. 43
Summary 44

Part II: Alchemy   45

Chapter 3: The Mysterious VGA Card. 47

Raster Graphics Primer 49
VGA Internals. 54
    Graphics Controller. 54
    Display Memory 55
    Serializer 56
    Attribute Controller. 56
    CRT Controller 56
    Sequencer 56
Using BIOS and the C Library Functions. 57
Screen Coordinates 57
The Lay of the Land 60
Summoning Mode 13h 61
Clearing the Screen 63
Rendering Images on the Screen 65
    Plotting Pixels 66
    Drawing Lines 69
    Horizontal Lines 71
    Vertical Lines 71
    Filling Rectangles 73
Restoring the Video Mode 74
Optimizing Screen Access 75
The Color Lookup Table 76
    Writing to a Color Register 77
    Reading a Color Register 79
    Saving and Restoring the Palette 80
Bitmapped Graphics Fundamentals 82
Drawing Text with Dots 84
Mode 13h in Action 88
The Dark Secrets of the *X-tended* Graphics Modes 91
Introduction to Mode Z 92
The Memory Configuration 92
Switching to Mode Z 95
Clearing the Mode Z Screen 98
Plotting Z Pixels 99
Page Flipping 100
Mode Z in Action 101
Summary 103

Chapter 4: *Waking the Dead with Animation* 105

Introduction to Animation 107
The Animation Cycle 108
Cutting to Another Screen 111
Double Buffering. 115
Simple Bitmapped Graphics 122
A Simple Bitmap Engine 125
    Drawing a Bitmap 126
    Scanning a Bitmap. 129
Loading Images from Outside Sources 131
Reading PCX Files 131
A Sprite Structure 140
Drawing Sprites 149
Scanning Under Sprites 151
Erasing Sprites 153
Putting Sprites in Motion 155
Sprite Clipping. 161
Testing for Collisions. 171
Scrolling the World Around Us. 175
Parallax Scrolling 175
The Layers System 179
    Creating a Layer 180
    Deleting a Layer 181
    Building a Layer 182
    Drawing a Layer 183
Surfing on Alien Worlds 186
Locking onto the Signals from Cyberspace 191
3D Palette Animation 193
Flipping Out 197
Odds and Ends. 204
Summary 204

Chapter 5: *Communicating with the Outside World* 205

The Ins and Outs of Input Devices 207
The Keyboard 208
Reading Keys with BIOS and C. 209
Scan Codes 211
Make and Break Codes. 214
The Shift State 216
Tracking Multiple Keypresses 218
Writing the Keyboard Driver 220
    Installing the Driver 221
    Removing the Driver. 222

The New Keyboard Driver 223
Keying in the Right Combination 227
Joysticks 230
Reading the Buttons 232
Computing the Position of the Stick 234
Calibrating the Joystick 239
Joystick Detection Techniques 245
Driving the Stick Crazy 246
The Mouse 251
Talking to the Mouse 253
A Mouse Interface Function 254
Point and Squash! 258
Creating an Input System 264
Input Device Conditioning 264
Summary 265

Chapter 6: *Dancing with Cyberdemons* 267

Fundamentals of Sound 269
Digitized Sound 273
MIDI Music 277
    FM Synthesis 278
    Wave Table Synthesis 280
The Audio Solution 281
    Creating the Drivers 283
    Installing the Drivers 284
Playing Digitized Sounds with DIGPAK 284
    The DIGPAK Interface 285
    Accessing DIGPAK from C 288
    Digital Recording Techniques 303
Making Music with MIDPAK 303
    Creating Extended MIDI Files 303
    The MIDPAK Interface 305
    Accessing MIDPAK from C 307
Real-Time Sound Processing 316
    Amplification and Attenuation 317
    Mixing Sounds 318
Sound Scheduling 320
    Fully Preemptive 321
    Priority-Based Preemption 321
    Queued Priority-Based Preemption 322
    Real-Time Queued Priority-Based Multiple Synthesized Digital Channels 322
Building Your Own Digital Sound Device—DIGIBLASTER 323
    The Hardware 325

The Software 329
Implementing 3D Sound 335
Remote Sound FX 339
Voice Recognition 340
Summary 344

Chapter 7: The Magick of Thought 345
Introduction to Artificial and Synthetic Intelligence 347
Tracking Techniques 348
    Chasing Algorithms 349
    Evasion Tactics 350
Random Variables 358
Teaming Up the Enemies 363
    Convergence 363
    Divergence 372
    Moving in Patterns 372
    Synchronous Motion 379
State Machines 380
    Probabilistic State Selection 385
    Rule-Based State Selection 386
    State Machine Probability Tables 387
Terrain Following 389
Implementing Vision 394
Building the Perfect Predator 398
Extending to the Third Dimension 398
Summary 399

Chapter 8: The Art of Possession 401
Multitasking Fundamentals 403
PC Interrupts 405
Software Interrupts 407
Hardware Interrupts 408
The Programmable Interrupt Controller (PIC) 408
The Interrupt Vector Table 411
Writing an Interrupt Service Routine in C 413
    Installing an Interrupt Service Routine 415
    Restoring an Interrupt Service Routine 416
    Chaining Interrupt Service Routines 421
The Issues of Re-Entrancy and DOS Calls 424
The Vertical Blank Interrupt 425
The Internal Timer 430
Programming the Timer 434
Time Tracking 437
Background Processing 439
Autonomous Functions and Programming Techniques 441

Processing Multiple Data Objects. 444
Summary 452

Chapter 9: *Multiplayer Game Techniques* **453**

Introduction to Multiplayer Games. 455
Multiple Players—One at a Time 458
Multiple Players—Same Time, Same Screen 459
Multiple Players—Split Screen 460
Linking Two PCs. 460
The Serial Communications System 463
  Overview of the Serial System 470
  Writing a Serial Communications Library 473
  An Example of Serial Communications. 482
Making Contact with Modems 483
  The AT Command Set 486
  Sending Multiple AT Commands. 495
The Modem Interface Library 496
Game Synchronization Techniques 512
  Input Device Reflection 512
  Universe Reflection 515
  Sending Tokens to Stay Locked 518
  The Master-Slave Setup 519
  The Master-Master Setup 521
Protocol Modems 523
On-Line Games 524
  Common Games. 525
  The Basic Model 525
  The Master and the Database 526
  Keeping in Sync 527
Starblazer 527
  The Idea. 529
  Playing the Game 529
  Minimum Requirements 531
  Loading MIDPAK and DIGPAK 531
  Making a Modem-2-Modem Connection 532
  The Game Universe 533
  Introduction and Control Panel 534
  The Star Field 534
  The Asteroid Belt 535
  The Alien 536
  The Wormhole 536
  The Ship and Its Equipment 536
  Shields 536
  Photon Cannon 537
  Cloaking Device 537

Scanners. 537
Heads-Up Display 538
Making the Music 538
The Digital FX System 539
The Explosions 540
Modem Communications Strategy 540
End of Game Sequence 540
The Game Loop 541
The Cybersorcerer Contest. 541
Summary 542

Chapter 10: 3D Fundamentals **543**

Starting with the Flatlands 545
Points, Lines, and Polygons in 2D 546
Transformations in the 2D Plane 549
Translation 549
Scaling 550
Rotation. 552
Introduction to 3D Space. 556
The Left-Handed System. 557
The Right-Handed System 557
Vectors and Vector Operations 559
Addition of Vectors 562
Subtraction of Vectors 562
Scalar Multiplication. 564
The Dot Product. 566
The Cross Product and Normal Vectors 567
Unit Vectors 569
Generating Vectors from Points 571
Matrices and Matrix Operations 574
Matrix Addition and Subtraction. 576
Matrix Multiplying 577
The Identity Matrix 578
Computing the Inverse 580
Concatenation. 581
Fixed Point Mathematics. 581
Making the Quantum Leap to 3D. 586
Points, Lines, and Polygons in 3D 587
Data Structures 588
Coordinate Systems 591
Local Coordinates 592
World Coordinates 594
Camera Coordinates 597
Transformations in 3D 599

Translation 601
Scaling 602
Rotation 603
Projecting the Image 606
Parallel Projections 606
Perspective Projections 607
Clipping the Image 609
Object Space Clipping 611
Image Space Clipping 615
Hidden Surface Removal and Rendering 617
Depth Sorting and the Painter's Algorithm 619
Z-Buffer Algorithms 622
Illumination 625
Ambient Lighting 625
Point Light Sources 626
Directional Light Sources 628
The Graphics Pipeline 629
Summary 630

Chapter 11: *Building a 3D Graphics Engine* 631

Engine Data Structures 634
Math Functions 639
Defining Objects 646
DXF Files 647
PLG Files 648
Importing Objects with PLG Files 651
Wireframe Graphics—Drawing Lines 660
Bresenham's Algorithm 661
Speeding Up Line Drawing 665
Using Projection to Draw Lines in 3D 668
Parallel Projection 669
Perspective Projection 670
2D Clipping to the Viewport 673
Transforming Objects 682
Positioning and Translation 684
Scaling Objects 686
Rotation and Matrix Concatenation 687
Viewing a 3D Wireframe Object 693
Positioning the Viewer 700
Summary 700

Chapter 12: *Solid Modeling and Shading* 701

Introduction to Solid Modeling 703
Vertex Ordering 704

Two-Sided Polygons 706
The Surface Normal of a Polygon and Visibility 707
Concave and Convex Polygons 708
The Plane Equation of a Polygon 709
Building Objects from Triangles and Quadrilaterals 711
Filled Polygons 712
Scan Conversion 713
Drawing Triangles 716
Clipping the Triangles 727
Drawing Quads 730
Lighting Models 730
    Ambient Light 730
    Directional Light 731
    Point Light Sources 734
Building a Flat Shader 735
Gouraud Shading 749
Texture Mapping 762
Modeling Special FX 774
    Transparency 774
    Morphing 778
Summary 781

Chapter 13: *Universal Transformations* 783
The Player and the Universe 785
Moving the Player and the Camera 787
Positioning the Virtual Viewpoint at the Origin 789
The Local to World Transformation 790
The World to Camera Transformation 792
Implementing the Global Transformation Matrix 794
Projecting the Universe on the Screen 796
Order of Operations 802
Summary 802

Chapter 14: *Hidden Surface and Object Removal* 803
The Hidden Surface Removal Problem 805
Back-Face Culling 806
    Computing the Normal 807
    Crossing the Edges 809
    Finding the Angle 809
    Removing the Surface 810
Precomputing the Normal 810
The Limits of Back-Face Removal 811
    Convex Objects 812
    Concave Objects 813

Object Level Culling 813
  Projecting the Object's Sphere 814
  The Trivial Rejection Tests 816
Summary 825

Chapter 15: *Clipping and Rendering the Final View* 827

Clipping to the 3D Viewing Volume 829
Generating the Polygon List 837
Rendering vs. Hidden Surface Removal 842
The Painter's Algorithm and Depth Sorting 842
  Rendering the Final Image with Perspective 850
The Z-Buffer Algorithm 859
  The Vertical Scan Line Z-Buffer 892
The Binary Space Partition 893
  The BSP Tree Functions and Data Structures 900
  Creating the BSP Tree 901
  Traversing the BSP Tree 917
  Adding the BSP Tree to the Graphics Pipeline 925
  The BSP Demo 928
  Limitations of the BSP 929
Comparative Analysis of Techniques 930
Adding Other Entities to the 3D World 931
  Adding Points 931
  Adding Lines 932
The 3D Animation Model for Games 932
Summary 932

Chapter 16: *Voxel Graphics* 933

Voxel Primer 935
Generating the Voxel Database 936
  Using Scanned Terrain Maps 938
  Fractal and Random Terrain Maps 939
Ray Casting 941
Height Mapping 943
  Rotating the Ray 946
  Fixing the Distortion 948
  Finding the Height of the Voxel 950
  Scaling the Strips 952
Putting It All to Work 953
A Tile-Based Voxel Engine 963
  Finding the Correct Cell 965
  Finding the Exact Pixel 965
  The Tile-Based Demo 966
Optimizations 976

Code Analysis 976
Inlining Everything 977
Drawing Less Is More 978
Using Shifts and Logical Operations 978
Using Look-Up Tables 980
The Optimized Voxel Engine. 980
Adding Foreground Objects 989
Summary 989

Part III: Spells   991

Chapter 17: Optimizing the 3D Engine 993

Updating the PLG File Format 995
More Efficient Data Structures 1003
Multiple Levels of Detail 1004
Revised Matrix Mathematics 1005
    Matrix Multiplication Analysis 1006
    Manual Matrix Multiplication 1006
    Sparse Matrices and Zeros 1008
    Floating Point Data Assignments via Memory Movements. 1011
Minimizing the Degrees of Freedom. 1013
    Faster Object Rotation 1013
    Speeding Up the World to Camera Transformation . . . 1024
Clipping Time from the 3D Clipper 1034
A Faster Z-Sort 1040
The 80387 Math Coprocessor. 1043
    The 80387 Architecture 1044
    The 80387 Instruction Set 1047
        Classical Instruction Format 1052
        Memory Instruction Format 1052
        Register Instruction Format 1053
        Register Pop Instruction Format 1054
    Popular 80387 Examples 1054
        FLD Examples 1055
        FST Examples 1055
        FADD Examples 1058
        FSUB Examples 1060
        FMUL Examples 1062
        FDIV Examples 1063
Using an External Assembler and the 80387. 1064
    Passing Floating Point Values to an External
    Assembly Function. 1065
    Returning Floating Point Values from an External
    Assembly Function. 1067

Defining Floating Point Constants Within an External
Assembly Function 1068
Mixing Assembly Language and C 1069
Advanced Fixed Point Math 1070
Multiplication of Fixed Point Numbers 1074
Division of Fixed Point Numbers 1077
Transcendental Functions 1080
Accuracy Analysis 1080
External 32-Bit Assembly Language Functions 1081
Data Filling 1081
Data Movement 1082
Clearing the Screen 1083
Copying the Double Buffer to the Video Buffer 1084
Faster Triangle Scan Conversion 1084
Back-Face Removal and Shading Tricks 1093
Eliminating the Back-Face Removal Step 1093
Faster Shading 1094
32-Bit Programming and DOS Extenders 1100
Making More Optimizations 1101
Starblazer 3D 1101
Summary 1113

Chapter 18: Kill or Be Killed **1115**
The Story 1117
The Design and Creation of KRK 1120
Components of the Game 1121
The New 3D Library Module 1122
The Introductory Screens 1128
The Main Menu 1128
Selecting a Mech 1129
The Rules Dialog 1129
Entering the Game 1129
Leaving the Planet 1129
The Player's View 1130
The Sky 1130
The Background Mountainscape 1131
The Ground 1131
The Instrument Panel 1131
The Scanner 1132
The Multifunction Display 1132
System Meters 1133
Hull Damage System 1133
The Heads-Up Display 1133
The Objects in the Game 1133

Static Objects. 1136
Alien Ships 1140
The Missiles 1146
Collision Detection 1147
Explosions 1147
Terrain Following. 1149
Music and Sound FX 1150
Loading the Game 1150
Playing the Game 1151
Problems with the Game 1151
The Cybersorcerer Contest 1151
Looking Toward the Future 1152
The Final Spell 1153
Appendix A: Cybersorcerer and Cyberwizard Contests **1155**
Index **1159**

Acknowledgments

The acknowledgments of any piece of work, whether it be a book, a movie, or a song, is always one of the hardest parts to write. *Black Art of 3D Game Programming* is the largest project I have ever undertaken, and dealing with the sheer magnitude of it wouldn't have been possible without dozens of other people working behind the scenes. I hope I will remember all the wonderful and talented people that contributed, but if I've left anyone out, let me say thank you now.

First, I would like to thank Monique Parker for introducing me to Mitch Waite. The introduction was right out of an episode of "Beverly Hills 90210." We were introduced on a car phone, which was followed by me reading my first few paragraphs of the book to Mitch. I guess deals aren't made on golf courses anymore, but on Highway 101 at 85 mph! Thanks to Mitch Waite for allowing me total artistic freedom with the book and letting me have my way in *most* cases. I tried very hard to write a book like you would, Mitch; I hope I have at least come close. Next, I'd like to thank Jacqueline Berry for always keeping me up when I was down and making sure I didn't stay up more than 20 hours a day. May all your dreams come true. And by the way, I think I saw your monkey over here again!

Black Art of 3D Game Programming took many months to complete; during this time many souls crossed my path. Each of them had a slight effect on my mood, my views, and, of course, my writing. First, thanks to my training partner, Armand Delgado, for making sure that I didn't turn into a jello mold while writing this book, and for his assistance in editing its last chapters. Next, I'd like to thank Dion Phillips and Mark Bell for keeping me on my toes and always arguing with me (what are friends for?). By the way, Mark, I *am* always right! Thanks also to Lloyd Richman for taking me jet skiing and making me come out of my dungeon occasionally. Thank you to networking master Ash Patel for always getting me that little item that I needed, no matter what it was. Thanks to my cousin Dennis Duarte for making sure I

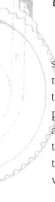

stayed alive and ate once in a while, and to Danny of Dry Creek Liquors for letting me hang out and watch all those good cable channels at his store. I also would like to thank Jim Valentine, the CEO of my new company, Andromeda FX, for his support. Thank you Steve Wozniak for making an old dream come true—that is, sitting around eating pizza and talking to the "Woz" about the old days of Apple. And thanks to the producers of the *Enigma* CDs and the Cirque Du Soleil *Alegria* CD for the wonderful music. I listened solely to these CDs while writing this book, so my words and thoughts have your music within them.

The next group of people I'd like to thank are those that had a direct or indirect input into this book in one way or another. First, I want to thank all the hard-working editors, artists, and production staff at Waite Group Press; you have done an incredible job, better than I could have ever expected. Thanks to Kurt Stephan, my managing editor, for understanding that good things take time—sometimes it's worth a slip or two (or three or four...) in a schedule to ensure the very best work. I want to thank acquisitions editor Jill Pisoni for obtaining compilers, books, and various other items that helped make this book happen. Thank you to Heidi Brumbaugh for her developmental edit to the book. Also, thanks to Lisa Anderson Mann for helping put together the final marketing touches. Thank you to WGP editorial assistants Joanne Miller and Laura Brown for sending me all those nice letters, directing me to the right person all the time, and for getting all the permissions for the games on the CD. Finally, thanks to 3D modeling guru James Dowlen for creating the perfect cover for the book.

I'd like to mention some of the companies that gave me access to their products to help create the content of this book. Tenberry Software (formerly Rational Systems) provided its killer DOS Extender. Theresa Pulido of Creative Labs loaned me some of the company's most advanced products, such as the AWE32 sound card and Video Blaster. By the way, Theresa I'm still, uh, using the cards. Borland and Microsoft supplied copies of their C/C++ compilers. Watcom provided a copy of its latest C/C++ 32-bit development system, which I must say is the coolest and most widely used DOS-based protected-mode compiler available for game programming. Finally, I want to thank Bill Dunlap, an old college buddy and a head honcho at Borland, for getting me a copy of TASM on an hour's notice!

Next, I want to thank some other friends that took time out from their busy schedules to help me out with the book. Thanks to musical genius Dean Hudson of Eclipse Productions for creating the music for this book within hours, and to Rob Wallace for lending a helping hand in converting MIDI to MIDPAK files. I want to thank Richard Benson for flying here from Los Angeles to assist me in converting all the software from Microsoft C/C++ to Borland C/C++ to make all you Borland users happy! (And don't feel bad that I beat you 11 times in Descent, Rich!) Also, I'd like to thank the 3D Studio guru Joe Font for creating the PLANETS.FLI animation for Kill or Be Killed.

Finally, thanks to all my family, especially my mother and father, for the support they gave me during this adventure. And last but not least, I want to thank God in the skies above, because when I was exhausted from lack of sleep and pushed beyond the limits of human endurance, it was He that gave me the strength to finish this book and begin this most excellent adventure...

André J. LaMothe
Sometime in the late 20th Century
Silicon Valley, U.S.A.
Third Planet from the Sun, Milky Way Galaxy
CompuServe: 75541,2455

Foreword

By Steve Wozniak

In the '50s and '60s computers were so expensive that only the largest corporations owned them...so expensive that computers gave corporations invincibility. Computers occupied gigantic lairs requiring dozens of Superman technicians. This kept computers shrouded in mystery from the rest of us. But advances in photographic reduction have reduced the cost of computers hundreds of times during my life. Each year, computer chips cost less and less, and this phenomenon will continue until we reach atomic limits.

In 1969, Apple was just a glimmer in my eye. I told my father that someday I'd own a computer. He pointed out that they cost as much as a house, so I told him that I'd live in an apartment! However, by 1975 it was feasible to build or buy a tiny computer for roughly the cost of a good electric typewriter. The first small computers could do nothing more than blink a few lights, but they *were* in fact computers...mostly kits containing LEDs and switches that made little sense to most people. But to me a computer was complete when it could be programmed with a set of logical decisions in order to play a game. Once that was possible, every conceivable application involving procedures, inputs, responses, and decision-making was possible. Hence, if a computer could be used to write a game, then any other application could be written.

In the early days of arcade video games (shortly before Apple), I had designed the game Breakout for Atari. Games then were not computers; they were made purely of hardwired logic built from TTL and CMOS chips with the single task of generating simple graphics on a TV display. When I designed the Apple, I wanted it to be able to play games. Most computer games in 1975 were written in BASIC. The Apple II was the first computer ever to come with a programming language in ROM, which I called GAME BASIC. The Apple II was also the first with sound, paddles, high-resolution color graphics, and extensions to the ROM BASIC to utilize these capabilities.

Having the Apple II in hand, I set out for the ultimate test. My test was to write Breakout as a software program instead of a collection of hard-wired logic, as I had done for Atari. In less than an hour, I had a working version of Breakout and within the next couple hours I was able to try a multitude of options that would be virtually impossible if the game were based on pure hardware. At that instant I realized that game design would change forever—that games would be software programs and not made of hard-wired logic designs.

Today, game programming is much more difficult than it was in the '70s and '80s. For a game to be popular, it must strive for levels of graphics, sound, and response that are common for the day—in 1995, this means digital sound and full 3D graphics. So how did game programming evolve from the 8-bit days of Apple? Well, we started with a low resolution Breakout game. Soon a few programmers used high-res graphics for finer detail. They developed techniques to play sound simultaneously. Very often they were able to accomplish what even I felt the computer was too slow to do. Each game took a single programmer a month or more to write.

Then something happened: games became valuable and a multimillion dollar industry overnight! Soon more effort went into them. Programmers found it useful to construct reuseable "parts" that could be pieced together to make a game. One of the experiments in this reuseable-parts technology was a game called the Pinball Construction Set. It allowed the player to build his or her own pinball game by adding bouncers, gadgets, and various other pinball-related components until the desired custom game was complete. This open-ended technology was complex and took more time than usual for the software engineers to implement, but once it was complete, new pinball games could be constructed in a matter of minutes to hours!

This was the beginning of the age of "tools." Various individuals realized that there are many aspects to a game that the game programmer shouldn't have to worry about—such as paint and sound programs—so many manufacturers started supplying these tools to the game programmers. Then something else happened. Game programmers realized that for each game they were rewriting many low-level functions for pixel plotting, sound, and so on, so graphic and sound software toolboxes full of useful and expertly prewritten programs emerged. The world advanced and 2D games improved. By the mid-'80s, game creation typically involved up to a dozen key parties. But now in the '90s, 3D games are by far the most exciting and popular, and unfortunately can be created by only a handful of individuals. Moreover, almost no serious business program can compete with a game when it comes to complexity and speed.

Writing a good game today requires more computer knowledge than was available in all the college courses offered when I attended school. There are literally hundreds of different topics that cover programming alone, and hundreds more topics for writing games. It's an amazing feat that anyone has been able to collect all this knowledge and focus it in one place at one time for others. I've never met a

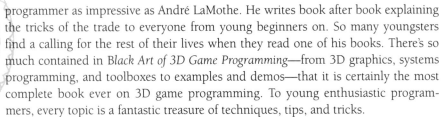
programmer as impressive as André LaMothe. He writes book after book explaining the tricks of the trade to everyone from young beginners on. So many youngsters find a calling for the rest of their lives when they read one of his books. There's so much contained in B*lack Art of 3D Game Programming*—from 3D graphics, systems programming, and toolboxes to examples and demos—that it is certainly the most complete book ever on 3D game programming. To young enthusiastic programmers, every topic is a fantastic treasure of techniques, tips, and tricks.

I feel a huge sadness when I meet someone like André and see how much he cares about a program feeling right to the final user, and when I see such a wonderful book. Sadness because I am frustrated by most programs written today (not games!) being so slow, full of bugs, not doing what's expected, giving misleading or incorrect messages, etc. Sadness because I'm not 10 years old, with all the greatest treasures of the world awaiting me in *Black Art of 3D Game Programming,* a book written with the single goal of helping others begin a fantastic journey.

Sincerely,

Woz

Steve Wozniak
(Inventor of the Apple Computer)

Preface

Within these pages are the descriptions of ancient spells and incantations. If mastered, these ancient rites foretell the techniques of creating full 3D virtual worlds existing within a parallel "electrical" dimension. With this knowledge, you will be able to create hordes of alien creatures, living machines, and universes where the laws of physics and gravity are yours to toy with. You will become a master with powers beyond bound and reason. After completing this Necronomicon, you will have reached the level of Cybersorcerer. Read on, mortal, if you dare...

For years, video game design has been a "Black Art" passed on from one master to another. Many people affiliated with the world of software engineering and computer science think that video games are child's play and not serious programming challenges. They are most incorrect in those assumptions. I can attest that never in all my years of programming have I written anything as challenging as a video game. A video game is more than a program; it is a conduit into another dimension, a dimension synthesized by the imagination and realized by sheer will. Technically, a video game is nothing less than a work of art. It must be incredibly efficient, it must control every aspect of the computer it is running on, and it must be perfect. To create such a work, the Cybersorcerer must be resourceful and highly creative. He must know every dark secret about the system he is using, so as to exploit it in a way that has never been seen before.

Black Art of 3D Game Programming unlocks the mysteries of how 3D games are created. This book will show you the details, the logic, and the "magick" of creation. It will teach the philosophy behind game algorithm design, and it will teach the most important thing of all: the essence of what makes games fun to play. After reading this book, you will be able to create 3D games of your own. However, this knowledge comes at a price and the price is this: you must use what you learn and create the best games you possibly can. With that in mind, you are now an apprentice Cybersorcerer. Turn the page and begin your training...

Installation

The software and tools for *Black Art of 3D Game Programming* are located on the CD-ROM bundled with the book. To make the installation of the CD simple, I have included a menu-driven installation program that will query you as to the files you wish loaded. The CD contains both Microsoft and Borland versions of the source code along with various graphic and sound tools. Be sure to explore the GRAPHICS and SOUND directories to discover such valuable bonuses as the NorthCAD-3D wireframe CAD program, the NeoPaint painting program, DiamondWare's Sound ToolKit, and the BLASTER Master audio toolkit.

To load the CD onto your computer, follow these steps:

1. Place the CD into your CD-ROM drive.

2. Make the CD-ROM drive the current drive by typing **E:** or **F:** (or whatever the CD-ROM drive letter is).

3. Type in **INSTALL.EXE** at the DOS prompt—this will launch the installer program.

4. Once in the installation program, follow the on-line help and instructions.

VERY IMPORTANT: Please note that the installation program installs whole directories and not individual files. If you wish to replace a file, you will have to copy it using the DOS Copy command or Windows File Manager. Also, if you do not use the installer program and decide to copy the files instead, be sure to change the Read Only attribute on all the files you copy.

After you have loaded the software onto your computer's hard drive, you are ready to begin the book. You will find all the files under the main directory BLACK3D. I suggest that you load at least one version of the source code (either Microsoft or Borland), and both the graphics and sound programs. You might want to hold off on loading all the bonus games since they take up quite a bit of disk space. Instead, I suggest you try to play them directly off the CD first, or load only the games you want to check out onto your computer one at a time. Games that will not play off the CD will need to be installed to your hard drive.

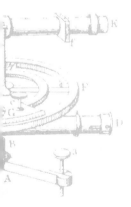

Part I

Incantations

1

The Genesis of 3D Games

come tuele fare le manovelle e le quali prmovano e la ga
e gra pe si come le mano te o bone e sa go rano di bone
ryare nella mano e la permanela della mano bella pegi que n
forga e più ssomo pobibal.

al poco como le bi e e no mg lo
el li e le mago a no us so de m
no de o como a co

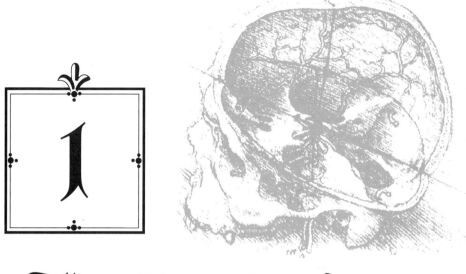

The Genesis of 3D Games

We have all played video games, but do we really know what they are? Do we really understand how they are created? Within this chapter the secrets of the technology used to create games is going to be uncovered for all to see. We'll begin by understanding the Black Art of Cybersorcery and what it means. Then we will discuss the history of games and their advancement through the ages. Finally, we'll cover the details of the 3D game library that we are going to construct throughout the pages of the book. Beware, if you read on there is no turning back…

Of Cyberspace and 3D Games

The time has arrived when the machines known as computers can finally open up the gateway into the parallel universe known as Cyberspace. This gateway, depicted in Figure 1-1, was closed many eons ago by the ancient ones. Before that time, these ancient ones (alchemists and sorcerers) manipulated and traversed the gateway to manifest unbelievable creatures and forces to do their bidding. Unfortunately, after many millenniums the ancient technology of Cybersorcery has been lost. However, using computers as tools, once again we have established a link to the gateway that separates our universe from Cyberspace. Due to the primitive nature of our machines, we can't yet teleport objects from Cyberspace back into our

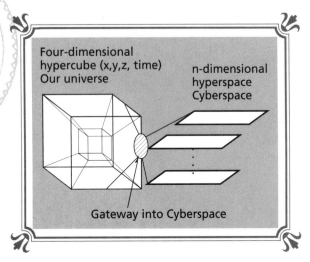

Four-dimensional hypercube (x,y,z, time) Our universe

n-dimensional hyperspace Cyberspace

Gateway into Cyberspace

world, as the ancient ones could. We can only view them, as shown in Figure 1-2. But this isn't too bad. Since it's possible to control and manipulate the creatures beyond the gateway, we can force them to participate in games of fantasy, fiction, and destruction. This is our goal.

An entire science based on the ancient techniques of Cybersorcery has been formed to create small windows into the gateway. These small windows are called video games. The first video games only projected two-dimensional images from the gateway onto the screen. These two-dimensional games sufficed for many years and will probably still be around for more to come. But now, a far better communications channel between us and the gateway is possible. This new communications channel is made possible by the faster processing ability and increased memory capacity of our computers. With it we can truly see into Cyberspace and control the beings within it to participate in full, three-dimensional video games.

Although it is impossible to draw a 3D image on a 2D surface (such as a video screen), a 3D image can be "projected" onto a 2D surface, as shown in Figure 1-3. Cybersorcerers use this technique to create the illusion of three dimensions on a two-dimensional surface. Hence, when the term 3D is used to describe a game, it means a projection of a 3D world. The technology of Virtual Reality (another branch of Cybersorcery) is committed to allowing humans to project their consciousness into Cyberspace, but this technology is still in its infancy.

Evolving from 2D to 3D

The evolution of 3D games has taken many years. Even today they continue to evolve and progress as new technologies emerge. However, there were specific

FIGURE 1-2
◉ ◉ ◉ ◉ ◉ ◉
*The mechanics of
projecting
Cyberspace into
our universe*

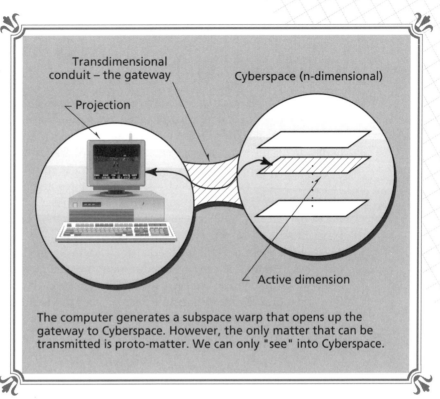

Transdimensional
conduit – the gateway

Cyberspace (n-dimensional)

Projection

Active dimension

The computer generates a subspace warp that opens up the
gateway to Cyberspace. However, the only matter that can be
transmitted is proto-matter. We can only "see" into Cyberspace.

FIGURE 1-3
◉ ◉ ◉ ◉ ◉ ◉
*Projecting a 3D
image onto the
computer
screen*

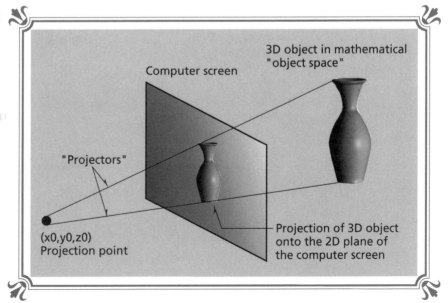

3D object in mathematical
"object space"

Computer screen

"Projectors"

$(x0,y0,z0)$
Projection point

Projection of 3D object
onto the 2D plane of
the computer screen

transitional stages to this evolution that we should recall and study in order to better understand the problems associated with 3D games.

Vector Graphics

Rendering 3D graphics was too much for the computers of the early eighties. Thus other techniques had to be used, allowing visualization of the 3D entities at a rate that was acceptable for such a demanding application as a video game. The solution to this problem was initially solved by using vector display systems much like that found in an oscilloscope. An example is shown in Figure 1-4. Vector displays draw video images by positioning an electron gun (mounted in the rear of the vector display) to different (x,y) locations on the video screen. Then by modulating the intensity of the electron beam, straight lines can be drawn from one point to another in very rapid succession. Figure 1-5 illustrates this process.

Since the only geometrical entities that could be drawn effectively by the vector display were lines, the games created using this technique were all wireframe. In other words, the objects were not solid. Video games of this type were acceptable for a while (*Battlezone* and *Stars Wars* by Atari used this technology), but the public wanted more. Furthermore, vector graphics systems weren't available on personal computers, so this made it difficult for PC Cybersorcerers to implement this technology. In time, the idea of vector graphics died, and the current technology of raster displays reigned supreme.

FIGURE 1-4

◎ ◎ ◎ ◎ ◎ ◎

Typical vector graphics display

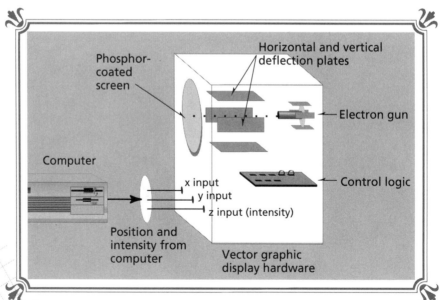

FIGURE 1-5

◉ ◉ ◉ ◉ ◉ ◉

*Rendering a
vector image*

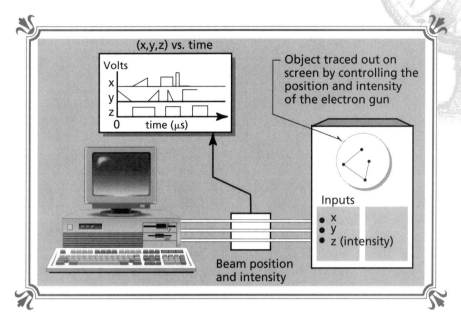

Raster Graphics

A raster display is generated in much the same way as a vector display, except for a few aspects of the rendering and hardware. First, the video screen itself is composed of thousands of small pixels that are each addressable as a single (x,y) location. These pixels (picture elements) are used to generate the image on the video screen by energizing a subset of them while leaving the others off. Furthermore, each pixel can be illuminated in a multitude of colors, unlike the vector displays that were usually in monochrome. This is possible since each pixel is composed of three separate subelements that can illuminate in red, green, and blue, respectively.

The video image of a raster display is drawn row-by-row by the electron gun, as shown in Figure 1-6. When all the lines of the display have been drawn, the gun retraces to the top of the screen and the process starts over. On average, the video display of a typical computer monitor is redrawn 60 times a second. This is more than enough for smooth animation and graphics to take place. Also, raster graphic displays look much better than vector displays. But there is one problem: Every 3D image on the screen has to be drawn a pixel at a time instead of a line at a time. This was a serious bottleneck for early processors since images could have thousands of illuminated pixels in each frame. And there are many calculations for each pixel. This problem slowed the development of 3D games to a crawl. Cybersorcerers had to wait for the hardware to catch up with the software they wanted to create.

FIGURE 1-6

◉ ◉ ◉ ◉ ◉ ◉

Generating a raster display

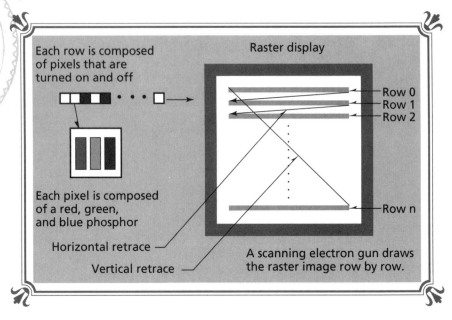

Each row is composed of pixels that are turned on and off

Each pixel is composed of a red, green, and blue phosphor

Horizontal retrace

Vertical retrace

Raster display

Row 0
Row 1
Row 2

Row n

A scanning electron gun draws the raster image row by row.

Parallax Scrolling

The first 3D games weren't 3D at all. Instead they used 3D illusions to trick the player into thinking the universe being projected was in some way three-dimensional. One of the first techniques that was used to accomplish this trickery was called *parallax scrolling*. Parallax scrolling is a modeling of what happens in the real world when you're in motion and look out to the horizon. The objects in the distance move very slowly while the objects nearer move very rapidly. Figure 1-7 shows this. The parallax effect is due to the properties of light and relative motion. In any case, it is easy to simulate. It can be done by taking a few different backgrounds and moving them at different rates to create the illusion of depth.

The only drawback to this technique was that all the games made with it had to be side views, and thus the games were still locked into a 2D environment. Even though the player could see parallax in the distance, it was only an illusion, and the player couldn't move there.

Bitmap Scaling

Next, Cybersorcerers created 3D environments that simulated many 3D effects by means of one of the most important 3D cues that our brains use: perspective. As you know, when an object moves nearer it becomes larger, and when it moves away it becomes smaller. An example of this is shown in Figure 1-8. This effect is created by the light rays converging to the viewpoint of the observer.

FIGURE 1-7
◎ ◎ ◎ ◎ ◎ ◎

*Scrolling layers
of scenery to
create parallax*

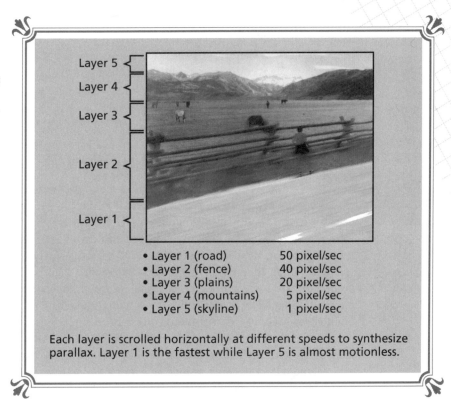

Layer 5
Layer 4
Layer 3
Layer 2
Layer 1

- Layer 1 (road)   50 pixel/sec
- Layer 2 (fence)   40 pixel/sec
- Layer 3 (plains)   20 pixel/sec
- Layer 4 (mountains)   5 pixel/sec
- Layer 5 (skyline)   1 pixel/sec

Each layer is scrolled horizontally at different speeds to synthesize parallax. Layer 1 is the fastest while Layer 5 is almost motionless.

Perspective was implemented in games by drawing flat rectangular objects composed of pixels (usually referred to as bitmaps) that were made larger or smaller depending on their distance from the player's viewing position. The size of the bitmaps can be computed using the formula

Object size = K/distance

where K is a constant based on the original size of the object.

FIGURE 1-8
◎ ◎ ◎ ◎ ◎ ◎

*Bitmap scaling
used to simulate
perspective*

Drawing the objects on the video screen in different sizes is implemented with a technique called *bitmap scaling*. Bitmap scaling is performed by multiplying the size of an object by a factor called the scale factor. However, using bitmap scaling to synthesize a 3D world has its problems. Scaling bitmaps isn't as easy as it seems; furthermore, all the objects in the game universe are still flat! They only look like they have volume. Hence, the worlds constructed using this technique are still not truly three-dimensional.

Wireframe Polygon Engines

At some point, Cybersorcerers looked back at what was previously done with vector graphics and wireframe worlds and then tried to implement wireframe 3D graphics using raster hardware. This technique was successful, and the first truly 3D games were born on the PC. These wireframe games existed in real 3-space and were viewed by projecting the 3D images on the 2D video screen, as shown in Figure 1-9.

Even though they were the first real 3D games, they looked primitive. They needed to look more realistic because games using the techniques of parallax and bitmap scaling, though not truly 3D, actually looked better! At last, some real brainpower was put into the problem of rendering 3D graphics using a PC, and many techniques were thought up that are all good for some specific purpose or game type. Since Cybersorcerers are only interested in making games, we can use any technique that we want as long as it works. Well, so much for the history lesson. Now let's learn about the latest 3D techniques and what they offer.

FIGURE 1-9

◉ ◉ ◉ ◉ ◉ ◉

Wireframe projection on a raster display

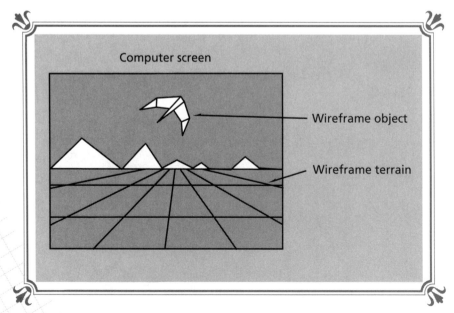

Computer screen

Wireframe object

Wireframe terrain

Trends in Sorcery

Today, a handful of techniques are being used to create 3D games. These techniques all have their strengths and weaknesses, but they are all interesting and solve different kinds of game problems. By understanding all of them, or at least being acquainted with them, we will be better prepared for all of the difficult spells we must cast to create 3D games.

Solid Polygon Rendering

The technique that we will be using to create our games is based on polygons—more precisely, filled polygons. Filled polygon graphics are the next step up from the wireframe techniques described earlier. The only real difference is that the images are solid and composed of flat facets instead of lines, as shown in Figure 1-10. Polygon rendering is one of the most prominent techniques used in the flight-simulation industry and is becoming very popular among PC games as the speed of PCs increases.

The computational expense of rendering solid polygon-based worlds is high, but since we are making games and not modeling packages or military-quality flight simulators, we can use tricks and shortcuts to get the performance we need. The most common examples of polygon-based 3D games are flight simulators and racing simulators. For example, the *Falcon* series from Spectrum Holobyte uses poly-

FIGURE 1-10

◉ ◉ ◉ ◉ ◉ ◉

A solid model based on polygons

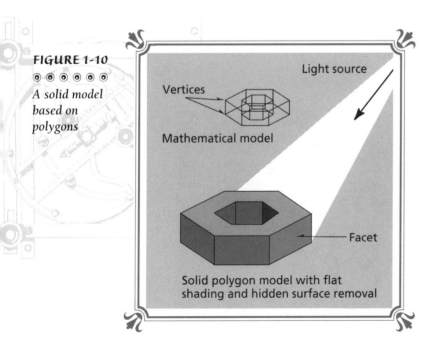

Light source

Vertices

Mathematical model

Facet

Solid polygon model with flat shading and hidden surface removal

gon-based graphics to render the world and the planes. It also uses bitmaps in special cases of the game, such as explosions.

In general, polygon-based graphics are probably going to be either the most successful method of rendering 3D games or come in a close second. Solid polygon worlds with texture mapping produce startlingly real images, and this technology has already been used in some of the most successful video games.

Ray Casting

Ray casting is based on ray tracing, which is a method of rendering three-dimensional worlds by modeling the interaction of light with the geometry of the world. This method of rendering is one of the most realistic to date. Ray casting, on the other hand, is simply a subset of this technique that is used to render special types of worlds. Ray casting is used in *Wolfenstein 3D*, by id Software, to create a realistic looking textured environment that moves quickly, as shown in Figure 1-11.

Ray casting works by casting out a collection of mathematical rays (one for each column of the screen) from the player's virtual viewpoint and recording the intersections with the objects in the world (which are usually flat walls on a cube). Based on these collisions, the final view is generated by using the distance between the player's viewpoint along with the point of the collisions to render thin vertical strips of texture (one for each column). This process is shown in Figure 1-12.

This technique is so popular that about a million ray-casted games have been released. The only downfall to ray casting is that there are limits on the kinds of worlds that can be rendered. In general, the worlds must be composed of regular cubes, and the angles between walls must either be parallel or perpendicular. Nevertheless, ray casting is a 3D technique that can generate a 3D image with texture mapping and hidden surface removal at an unbelievable rate.

FIGURE 1-11

◎ ◎ ◎ ◎ ◎ ◎

The ray-casted world of Wolfenstein 3D

FIGURE 1-12

◎ ◎ ◎ ◎ ◎ ◎

The principles of
ray casting

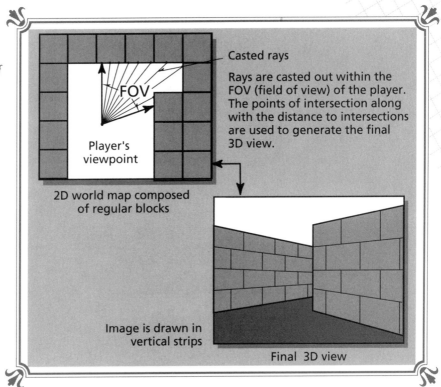

Casted rays

Rays are casted out within the
FOV (field of view) of the player.
The points of intersection along
with the distance to intersections
are used to generate the final
3D view.

FOV

Player's
viewpoint

2D world map composed
of regular blocks

Image is drawn in
vertical strips

Final 3D view

Voxel Graphics

Voxel graphics is a bit of a misnomer that I think the originator (Nova Logic) isn't
going to bother correcting because they don't want the whole world knowing exactly how it works! It is more of a data structure and mathematical representation of a
volume using voxels than a technique. The word *voxel* itself comes from volume
and pixel. Voxels are 3D entities that are cubic in nature and fill space. Each voxel
has eight neighbors, which are usually connected using some kind of data structure, as shown in Figure 1-13.

Well, that's all fine and dandy, but whatever voxel graphics really is, isn't important to game makers. At this point, in the context of game development, it means
using collections of single pixels or simple lines to generate a 3D view. These views
are mostly of terrain; hence voxel graphics are best suited for making games that
are in some kind of outside environment.

The basic technique behind voxel rendering is as follows: A height map is generated (or input from a database) in the form of a 2D matrix of integers. Each element
in the matrix is the height above sea level or the "floor," as shown in Figure 1-14.
Then a rendering engine uses this data and the perspective transforms (we'll get to

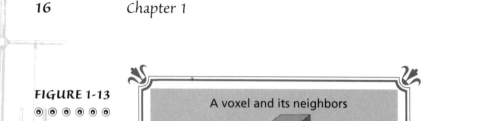

FIGURE 1-13

An abstract representation of voxels

that later) to draw the voxel data line-by-line, starting from the horizon and ending at the viewpoint of the player. While the rendering is being done, the voxels are either shaded, using a light source, or colored, using a database. It's even possible to texture them, but the results can be quite distorted. A groundbreaking voxel-based game is *Commanche*, by Nova Logic, which allows a helicopter pilot to fly around a mountain range and shoot down enemies. The environment of the game was generated using voxel graphics, and the enemies were done with bitmap scaling; so you see that sometimes techniques are mixed to create the best overall game.

Ellipsoidal Technology

Using ellipsoids is a relatively new technology somewhere between polygon graphics and voxel graphics. Ellipsoids are similar to spheres except that they can be elongated in each direction X, Y, or Z. Figure 1-15 shows an example of an ellipsoidal man. The attractive feature of using small ellipsoids to generate a 3D world is that ellipsoids are convex objects (have no dents), and this makes hidden surface removal easier. Also, ellipsoids are very regular and symmetrical, and this can be used to make certain optimizations during rendering. Finally, ellipsoidal games tend to have a natural look when coupled with advanced shading techniques.

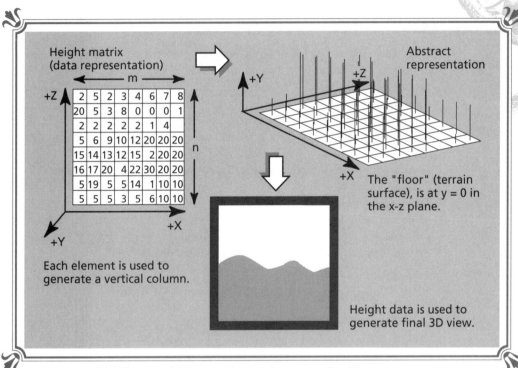

FIGURE 1-14 ⊙ *The transformation of voxel data into a final image*

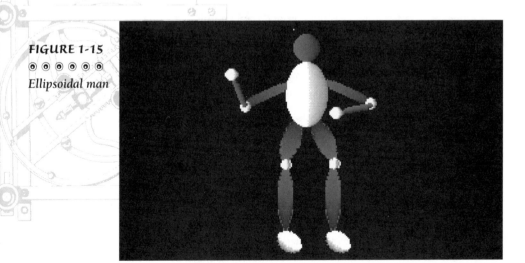

FIGURE 1-15

⊙ ⊙ ⊙ ⊙ ⊙ ⊙

Ellipsoidal man

Journeys into the Mind's Eye

Well, well, well ... Now that we have acquainted ourselves with the origins and techniques of Cybersorcery, it's time to talk about why you are reading this book. You are reading this book to learn how to create 3D video games. Within these pages you will find the magick and sorcery to do this, but there is something else that you need in order to create games. Something that can't be taught. This is creativity. Everyone is creative; the problem is allowing yourself to be creative with all the pressures of everyday life on your mind.

Allowing yourself to be creative is the single most important thing you need to learn about writing video games. Cybersorcerers are a unique group of people. They believe in the impossible and look at video games as a form of expression. Make no doubt, a video game is a piece of art. But, unlike a painting that is static and unlike a song that is only heard, a video game is in flux, it is art in motion. To get your creative juices flowing, here are some suggestions:

✤ Play lots of games and try to determine what makes them fun and addictive.

✤ Read science fiction and fantasy novels.

✤ Rent some science fiction movies and, especially, some Japanese animated films (lots of good ideas in them).

✤ Don't limit yourself to reality; remember, anything is possible in Cyberspace.

✤ When writing your games don't think that something can't be done. Just assume it is possible and then figure it out.

✤ When trying to figure out what people like, think in terms of primal needs. Use analogies of the needs as goals in your games.

✤ When you work, surround yourself with interesting imagery, books, and music. They will help you make contact with your inner creativity.

✤ Finally, keep the lights on, because things are going to get really weird!

The Black Box

The main goal of this book is to teach you how to create 3D games on the PC. As we near this goal, chapter by chapter, we will be creating many functions that will be used to produce the final game library, called the Black Box. Within the Black Box will be all the sorcery needed to generate 3D worlds, play music, obtain input, and so forth. To produce this library in an organized manner, we're going to create a module in each chapter (if there are any programs in the respective chapter) and then add each module to the main library as the book proceeds.

We will name each module with the prefix BLACK followed by the number of the chapter. For example, the module for Chapter 3 will be named BLACK3.C, and if there is a header file, it will be named BLACK3.H. By the end of the book you will have a collection of these modules that together form the foundation of the 3D game library. Also, as the chapters proceed, you should build a library that contains the modules up to that point. Name the library BLACKLIB.LIB and build it in the Microsoft Library Manager or, if you are using Borland's compiler, include each module in the current project. Then instead of individually linking all the modules from each chapter, you can simply link to the growing library, BLACKLIB.LIB.

As far as compiler selection goes, you can use anything you like, but I suggest Microsoft or Borland compilers. The code for this book was developed and compiled using Microsoft C/C++ 7.0, but to be fair, there are Borland 4.5 versions of everything on the CD. However, the listings in the book are the Microsoft versions. The following Microsoft compile line was used to create most of the objects:

```
CL -C -AM -G2 -Gs -Zi -W4 FILENAME.C
```

Here are the meanings of the compiler options:

- **-C** This instructs the compiler not to invoke the linker.

- **-AM** Use the MEDIUM memory model, which has one 64K data segment and multiple 64K code segments.

- **-G2** This allows 80286 instructions in inline assembly language and also tells the compiler to use the 80286 instruction set when compiling programs.

- **-Gs** This removes *stack probes*. Stack probes are a run-time stack testing system that makes sure there's enough space on the stack to allocate the variables for a function before calling the function. This is an unnecessary waste of time since we will make sure the stack is big enough by setting its size during the linking process.

- **-Zi** This directive is used to allow the Codeview debugger, or any other Codeview-compatible debugger, to have access to the symbol table and source of the program. It inserts debugger information into the final executable, making it a bit larger and slower.

- **-W4** This turns the warning level up to maximum and will flag everything as a warning. We will ignore most of the warnings, but it's nice to be aware of every little potential problem in our programs.

The compiler directives should all seem reasonable to you except the inclusion of debugger information and the MEDIUM memory model. The debugger information is needed only during development, and you should recompile everything when you are ready to generate the final version of your game(s). A good idea is to have multiple batch files or *make* files that compile with and without debugger

information inserted into the executables. This way you can quickly create a final executable once you have found all the bugs.

We will be using the MEDIUM memory model for two reasons. First, the data segment will always be accessible in the *DS* register, thus making assembly language interfacing and variable access simple. Second, if we need more than one 64K data segment, we will use the memory allocation functions to allocate the memory from the FAR heap. In general, SMALL or MEDIUM are the best memory models to write games in when working with DOS, but for this book we will use the MEDIUM model.

After you have compiled each module and are ready to link it to your program, or one of the programs in the book that use the game library, you will need to invoke the linker. The link line that I use for Microsoft's Segment Executable Linker is as follows:

```
LINK /ST:8192 /CO SOURCE.OBJ+OBJECTS.OBJ,,,BLACKLIB..LIB,,
```

This informs the linker to link SOURCE.OBJ with OBJECTS.OBJ (optional) and link to the library BLACKLIB.LIB. Also, the stack is set to 8192 BYTES (/ST:8192), and the linker is told to add in the debugger information (/CO).

If you use the preceding compile and link lines, you should have no trouble getting everything to work. However, just to make sure, the CD includes the compiled version of each chapter's module, along with all C programs compiled into executables, along with a version of the game library containing each chapter's module up to that point in the book. For example, in the directory for Chapter 5, you would find all the source and executables for that chapter, the library module BLACK5.C, and BLACK5.OBJ. Finally, there will be a partial version of the game library that has all the modules from Chapters 1 through 5 within it.

Summary

Within the pages of this chapter we discussed the source of all games and the techniques used throughout the years to make games more and more realistic. Then we covered the most popular techniques used today and selected polygon-based graphics as our chosen Cybersorcery. Finally, we described the Black Box game library, which we will construct as the days pass. With all that in mind, you are now an apprentice Cybersorcerer. Turn to the next chapter and open your mind: we are about to embark on a most excellent adventure…

2

Elements of the Game

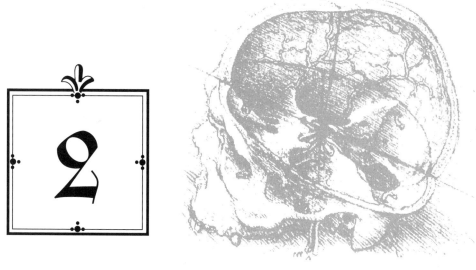

2

Elements of the Game

We've discussed the principles underlying 3D games and the relationship between Cyberspace and our own dimension. Now it's time to cover the basic architecture of 3D games and how to implement them. We need to know this so we can conjure up the subspace field that links us to the world of Cyberspace. Although the most important part of 3D games is the graphics that are transmitted from Cyberspace to the PC, we must abide by a set of universal rules when designing the overall structure of a game. These rules, along with the details such as setup and installation, are what we'll cover in this chapter.

The Sequence of a Game

A 3D video game, like any other program, has a sequence of steps that must be executed in some specific order. The most complex components of a game are the graphics and animation, which are executed in the main loop of the game. However, there are other aspects of the game, such as setup and installation, that are just as important and must be performed.

The Installation and Setup Phase

All video games written on the PC have some type of installation and setup phase that allows the user to install the game on the hard drive and start the game properly. As a rule, you should have a very simple installation program, preferably named INSTALL.EXE. When the user runs this program, the game will load itself off the floppy disk(s) to the hard drive and create whatever directories are necessary for the file structure of the game. Also, this installation process should query the user as to his destination drive preference.

Information about the current drive(s) installed on the PC can be determined using DOS and BIOS calls. With this information you can create an attractive menu that states the available drives and the amount of space on each drive. For example, you wouldn't want to start loading the game on drive C:\> if there wasn't enough space on the drive to fit the entire game!

Once the user has installed the software, the installation program should either allow the user to configure the game at that point, or it should emit a message telling the user to run a setup program named, preferably, SETUP.EXE.

Following the setup program, the user can configure all the programmable aspects of the game, such as the input device he wishes to use, the sound and music card(s), and the availability of extra memory. Figure 2-1 shows a sample setup interface. Don't assume the user knows what he's doing during the setup process. He may misunderstand something and make an incorrect entry. To protect your game against incorrect setups, the configuration data should be tested as it's entered, and the user should be asked at the end of the sequence whether the settings are acceptable. This gives him a chance to make corrections before playing the game and possibly crashing the computer.

After the setup process is complete the setup information should be written as a file out to the disk. The game will use this file during run-time to set the proper hardware and software configurations. Finally, when writing the installation and setup programs, make the interfaces as simple and intuitive as possible. Granted,

FIGURE 2-1

Typical game setup screen

it's impossible to make interfaces too simple because of the complexity of the setup and installation process, but try to minimize the amount of information shown on the screen at once. As a rule, don't overload the user with too many decisions; use menus or some similar technique to make the process incremental..

Introducing the Player to the Game

The player will be anxious to play your game, but before letting him play, always include an introductory sequence with a storytelling phase. Introductions to 3D games are usually rendered using a high-end modeling system such as Autodesk 3D Studio. Your purpose is to set the scene and introduce some of the elements of the game in a passive manner. The player will only be watching at this point and not interacting.

Along with the introductory sequence and animation, provide some form of online instructions that the user can view. The instructions don't have to be complete (complete instructions can be on disk or hard copy), but the minimum information needed to play the game should be displayed in some form, whether it's visual, auditory, or both.

FIGURE 2-2

◎ ◎ ◎ ◎ ◎ ◎

Using a data file for a demo mode source

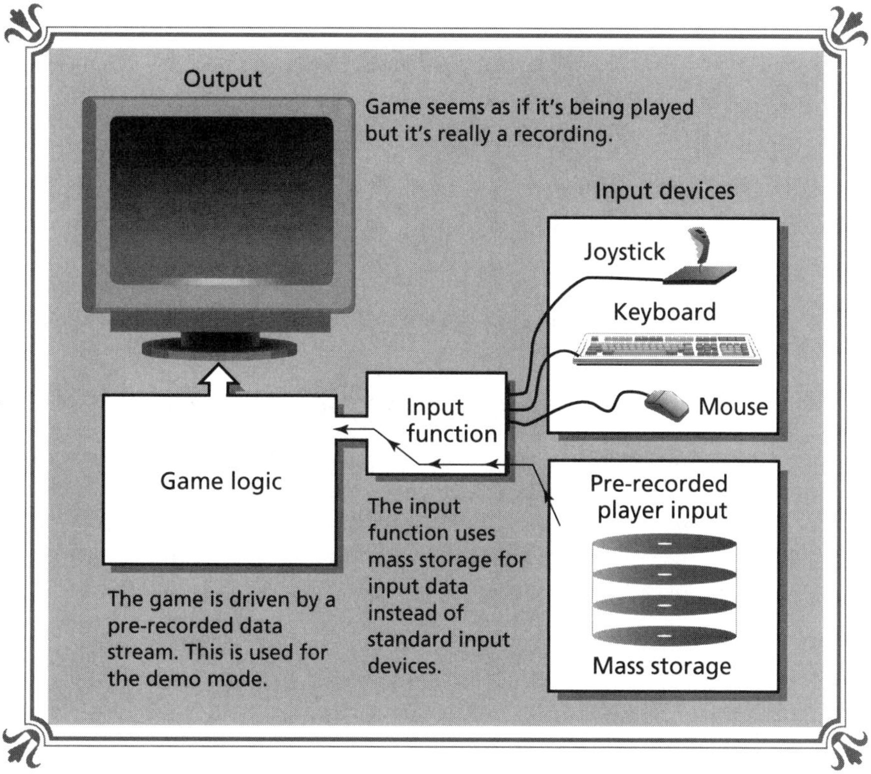

Output

Game seems as if it's being played but it's really a recording.

Input devices

Joystick

Keyboard

Mouse

Input function

Game logic

Pre-recorded player input

The input function uses mass storage for input data instead of standard input devices.

The game is driven by a pre-recorded data stream. This is used for the demo mode.

Mass storage

Last of all, the introductory phase should put the game into a demo loop or wait state that allows the player to begin at his leisure. This can be accomplished with more prerecorded animation or by actually running the game in a special mode that uses previously digitized input to control the character in the game. Figure 2-2 shows a bit of the software logic to implement something like this. When the player is ready he can press the start button (whatever it may be), and the game should begin.

Run Time

The run-time portion of the game consists mostly of the active game logic and animation in contrast to the passive introductory scenes. The single most important factor of the run-time portion of any game, and especially that of a 3D game, is *speed*. The game must execute at a rate that can sustain a constant frame rate of at least 12 FPS (frames per second). If the frame rate drops below this, the video image will begin to look jerky, and the player will start to get upset! In general, a game loop will have the following minimum set of steps:

- ✤ Obtain the user's input.
- ✤ Perform the logic on the objects in the game and the environment.
- ✤ Transform the objects and the game world.
- ✤ Render the current video image.
- ✤ Synchronize to some time base.
- ✤ Play music and sound effects.
- ✤ Repeat the process.

We'll cover each of these steps in detail throughout the book, but for now we simply want to get an overall picture of what goes on in a typical 3D game.

The Concluding Sequence

At some point in the game the player will either exhaust his life force or simply want to quit. In each case you should end the game with a concluding scene or animation that shows what has happened, or what would have happened (you get what I mean). After this sequence, a high score screen should display, allowing the player to input his name (if applicable), and the game should return to the demo mode or setup screen.

Make the concluding sequence very intense, much like that of the introduction. If possible, it should have a lot of sound effects, graphics, and personally directed comments to the player about his performance. This contributes to the illusion that the player is actually part of the game. This important factor is missing from many games on the market today; the games aren't personalized enough. For example, wouldn't it be cool if the player could supply a PCX or BMP file that contained an image of himself, and this image would be used during the game to help personalize it?

The Input Channel

The player will be communicating with your game via a communications channel. This communications channel will normally consist of one or more input devices, such as a joystick, mouse, keyboard, bat (a flying mouse), flight sticks, and—soon—mind control. In any case, as a Cybersorcerer, you must condition the input device data into a form that controls the aspects of the player's character or ship in the game. This means that you might have to write special logic to make the input of a specific device more palatable to your game logic in addition to simply obtaining the input.

FIGURE 2-3

◎ ◎ ◎ ◎ ◎ ◎

Input time lag

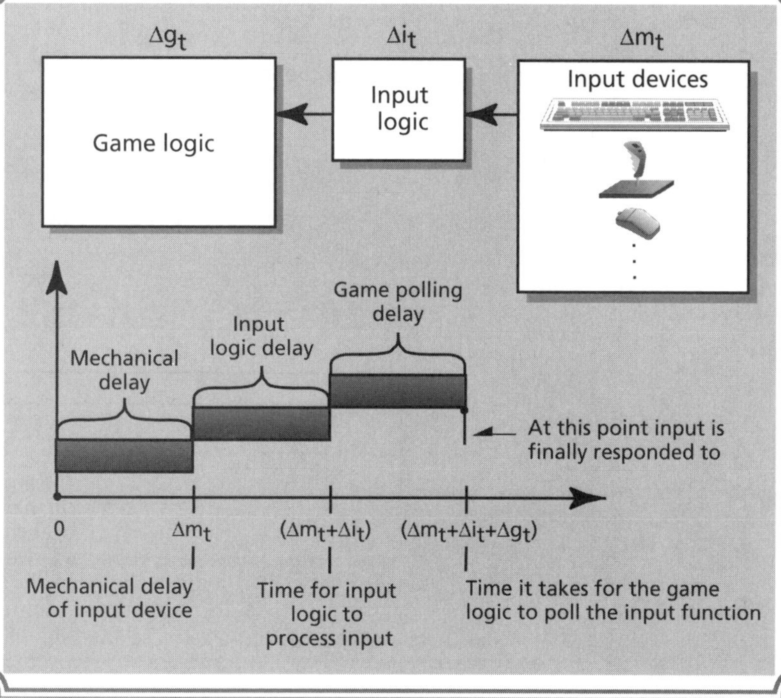

Δg_t Δi_t Δm_t

Game logic   Input logic   Input devices

Game polling delay

Input logic delay

Mechanical delay

At this point input is finally responded to

0   Δm_t $(\Delta m_t + \Delta i_t)$ $(\Delta m_t + \Delta i_t + \Delta g_t)$

Mechanical delay of input device   Time for input logic to process input   Time it takes for the game logic to poll the input function

It's not that hard to obtain input from the keyboard, mouse, and joystick, but controlling the character in the game the way the player actually meant rather than what the player input is a bit of problem. For example, if a game was originally designed for a mouse and the player uses a keyboard or joystick, you'll need special software to help the keyboard and joystick act more like the mouse.

Another important aspect of the input channel is *time lag*. Time lag is the amount of time from the player's input command to when the input acts on the game logic. Figure 2-3 shows this graphically. Ideally, time lag should be zero. However, in practice this is impossible to achieve because of physical limitations of the input device and its data rate. For example, the keyboard as currently set up by DOS will produce a maximum key repeat rate of 18 characters per second. It is possible that a player could input faster than that (improbable as it may be), and these inputs would be lost. For another example, imagine that a particular game's frame rate is only 10 FPS and the player fires a missile. In the worst case, the player will have to wait one frame before the missile is fired. Therefore, it's possible for the

FIGURE 2-4

◎ ◎ ◎ ◎ ◎ ◎

An input event is missed

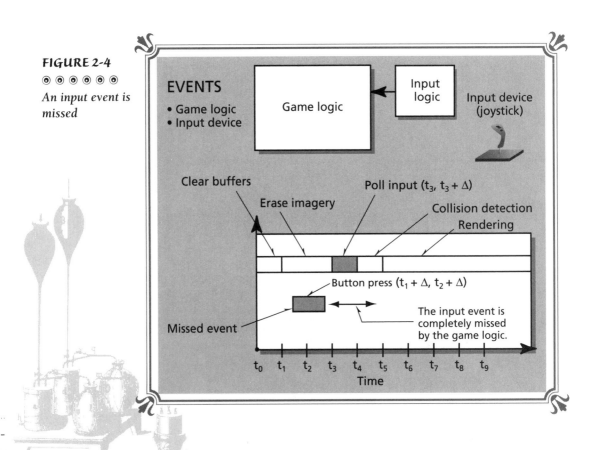

player to fire the missile by pressing the fire button and then release the button before the game has time to detect the input. This is called *input loss* and is shown in Figure 2-4.

This type of input loss can affect the score because the player was probably in a moment of decision, made the decision, but the game didn't register it. Hence, the player might be penalized even though he made the correct decision. If the game misses inputs due to slow frame rate, it might be wise to buffer inputs in some way so they aren't lost when a player drives an input for too short a period. You have two ways to do this. You could write an interrupt routine that continually queries and buffers the inputs faster than any human could change them. Or you could perform input testing at more than one place in the main loop, average what the player did, and use that as the final input for the game cycle. This is shown in Figure 2-5.

Although the issues just discussed are important and do arise, as long as the frame rate stays at a reasonable rate (12 FPS), the input devices can be polled and nothing will be lost.

FIGURE 2-5

◎ ◎ ◎ ◎ ◎ ◎

Averaging the player's input

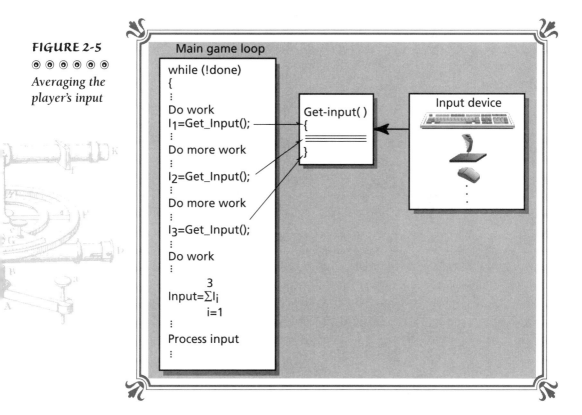

Event Driven Programming

We've been talking about inputs, event loops, and the general architecture of a game, but we really need to understand how video games differ from normal programs and why this is so. Video games are real-time programs that are event driven by time instead of user input. Event driven programming, in general, is a method of waiting for an event to occur and then acting upon the event. For example, when you are typing at the command line in DOS, DOS is waiting for you to enter another character (the event).

A video game, on the other hand, doesn't wait for the user (player) to input an event. The game continues its processing with or without the input of the player. This is the real-time aspect of a video game that must be implemented by the software. Let's take a more detailed look at standard input event driven programming and that of real-time video games.

Input Driven Event Loops

Most commercial and business applications written today are input driven event systems. A word processor is a perfect example. The word processor can print, search, type on the screen, load files, and so forth; however, once launched, the word processor will just sit there waiting for the user to do something. A typical main loop for an input driven event system looks something like this:

```
while(!done)
        {
        Wait_For_User_Input();

        Switch(user_input)
            {
            case ACTION_1:
            .
            .
            .
            case ACTION_N:

            } // end switch

        Update_Data_Structures();

        } // end main event loop while
```

The key to the input driven nature of this fragment is the call to the function *Wait_For_User_Input()*. This call forces the system to wait for the user to do something before proceeding. Hence, it's possible that the *switch* statement and data structure update sections won't be executed for a long time.

Listing 2-1 shows an example of a real program that uses an input driven event loop for a simple game. The game queries the player to guess a number between 1 and 100. You can type this program in or find it on the CD-ROM. The name of the program is GUESS.C and the executable is GUESS.EXE.

LISTING 2-1 A number guessing game that uses an input driven event loop

```c
// GUESS.C - An example of input driven event loops

// I N C L U D E S ////////////////////////////////////////////////////////////

#include <stdio.h>
#include <stdlib.h>
#include <math.h>
#include <graph.h>

// M A I N ////////////////////////////////////////////////////////////////////

void main(void)
{
int done=0,          // exit flag
    number,          // the random nunber
    num_tries=0,     // number of tries
    guess;           // the players guess

unsigned int far *clock = (unsigned int far *)0x0000046CL; // pointer to clock

// SECTION 1 ////////////////////////////////////////////////////////////////
// print out introductory instructions
printf("\nI'm thinking of a number from 1-100.");
printf("\nTry and guess it!\n");

// seed the random number generator with the time
srand(*clock);

// choose a random number from 1-100
number = 1 + rand() % 100;

// SECTION 2 ////////////////////////////////////////////////////////////////
// main event loop

while(!done)
    {

// SECTION 3 ////////////////////////////////////////////////////////////////
    // query user for input (the event)

    printf("\nWhat's your guess?");
    scanf("%d",&guess);
```

continued on next page

continued from previous page

```
// SECTION 4 //////////////////////////////////////////////////////////////////
    // increment number of tries
    num_tries++;

    // process the event
    if (guess > number)
       printf("\nToo big!\n");
    else
    if (guess < number)
       printf("\nToo small!\n");
    else
       {
       // the user must have guessed the number
       printf("\nYou guessed the number in %d tries!!!\n",num_tries);

       // set the exit flag
       done=1;

       } // end else
    } // end while
} // end main
```

Let's take a look at what each section of the code does.

Section 1: This is the initialization section of the program. It seeds the random number generator with the current time, selects a random number, and then prints out a message to the player.

Section 2: This is the entrance to the main event loop.

Section 3: Here's where the input driven event system waits for an event. In this case, the event is a character string that represents an integer. Note that the program will not proceed until the integer is entered.

Section 4: Once the input has been entered, this section is executed. The number that the player enters is tested against the computer's selection, and messages are displayed telling the player if the guess is too high or too low.

As you can see, this type of main loop is totally unacceptable for a 3D video game. We need something that will execute the remainder of the code elements in the main loop regardless of the user's input status!

Real-Time Event Loops

A real-time event loop is the best way to implement a video game's main loop. The computer science definition of real-time is: a program that responds to inputs as they occur. For example, military fighter jets have real-time computers onboard that will respond to inputs and act upon them within microseconds in most cases.

This definition of real-time is not really appropriate in the context of 3D video games, since we have already concluded that our input channel may be sluggish, and it may take an entire video frame to recognize specific inputs. Real-time in our context means this: The image of the game is continually changing, the objects in the game will function on their own, and finally, the game won't wait for user input. This definition is a bit broad, but it satisfies our needs.

The difference between an input driven event loop and a real-time event loop is very simple: The real-time loop won't wait for input. Therefore, the main loop will execute very quickly and process all the functions and logic within it repeatedly. Here is the structure of a real-time event loop:

```
while(!done)
        {
        if (User_Input_Ready())
            {
            Get_User_Input();

            Switch(user_input)
                    {
              case ACTION_1:
              .

              .

              .

              case ACTION_N:

               } // end switch

           } // end if user had an input

        Update_Data_Structures();

  } // end main event loop while
```

Let's analyze the new main loop by beginning with the *if* statement that leads the code fragment. Instead of waiting for user input, the system is polled to see if there is an input waiting. If there is an input waiting, it is retrieved and acted upon by the *switch* statement. Note that the *switch* statement is within the body of the *if* statement. This is because there is no reason to act upon the user's input if there hasn't been any. Finally, at the end of the loop, there is the call to the data structure update function, which could be anything and simply represents the game logic.

We have covered the difference between input driven event programming and real-time event programming. Now, let's see what the main loop of a video game looks like.

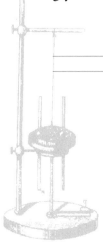

Typical 3D Game Loops

As we discussed in the section on run-time, a video game is mostly composed of a small set of actions that are performed each game cycle or frame. When writing games, think of each iteration through the main loop as a frame, and use this as the standard by which to gauge your game's performance. The question is, what should be in the game loop? The answer to this depends on many factors that you will learn as we go, but as a first attempt at a game loop, here is the typical functionality of one:

```
while(!game_over)
     {

     // erase all the imagery
     Erase_Objects();
     Erase_Player();

     // is the player trying to do something?
     Get_User_Input();

     // perform game logic on player and AI on objects

     Do_Players_Logic();
     Do_Objects_Logic();

     // test for all possible collisions
     Do_Collision_Detection();


     // scale, rotate, translate all the objects and player to render them
     Transform_Player();
     Transform_Objects();

     // draw everything
     Draw_Objects();
     Draw_Player();

     // lock onto the video display and update the screen with the next frame
     Synchronize_To_Video_Display();
     Display_New_Frame();

     // play music and sound FX
     Do_Sounds_And_Music();

     // update any miscellaneous data structures and do housekeeping
     Do_Misc();

     } // end main game loop
```

The main event loop executes over and over, continually updating the screen image regardless of the player's input (or lack of input). The function names in the loop should help you understand what's going on; however, the main concept of a video game loop is very simple: All the objects are erased in the world, the user's inputs are retrieved, the game logic is performed, and finally, the next frame of animation is drawn. That's really all there is to it. Of course, this example is a bit synthetic, and many of the functions would be performed in different orders or even be combined.

To give another example, Listing 2-2 is a small demo that uses a real-time event loop. It depicts a small light cycle (from the movie *TRON*) moving on a game grid. The light cycle is turned by using the keys Ⓐ for left and Ⓢ for right. If the player turns the light cycle, then it will turn; otherwise it will continue moving in the direction it is pointing. This is the real-time aspect of the demo. The name of the program is LIGHT.C and the executable is named LIGHT.EXE. If you wish to build your own executable, compile it using the medium memory model and link it to the Microsoft graphics library, or to Borland's, depending on the compiler you are using.

The program uses mode 13h (320x200 with 256 colors), which we will learn about in great detail in the next chapter. The graphics are implemented with Microsoft's library since we don't yet know how to change video modes, plot pixels, and so forth. Anyway, don't worry too much about how the graphics are done. Focus on the real-time aspects of the event loop. Let's look at the code.

LISTING 2-2 *A light cycle demo of real-time event loops*

```
// LIGHT.C - An example of real-time event loops

// I N C L U D E S ///////////////////////////////////////////////////////////

#include <stdio.h>
#include <stdlib.h>
#include <conio.h>
#include <math.h>
#include <graph.h>


// D E F I N E S ///////////////////////////////////////////////////////////


// directions
#define NORTH   0
#define EAST    1
#define SOUTH   2
#define WEST    3

// F U N C T I O N S ///////////////////////////////////////////////////////////

void Delay(int clicks)
```

continued on next page

continued from previous page

```c
{
// this function uses the internal timer to delay a number of clock ticks
unsigned long far *clock = (unsigned long far *)0x0000046CL;
unsigned long now;

// get current time
now = *clock;

// wait for number of click to pass
while(abs(*clock - now) < clicks){}

} // end Delay

///////////////////////////////////////////////////////////////////////////

void Draw_Game_Grid(void)
{
// this function draws a game grid out of horizontal and vertical lines
short x,y;

// set the line color to white
_setcolor(15);

// draw the vertical lines
for (x=0; x<320; x+=20)
    {
    // position the pen and draw the line
    _moveto(x,0);
    _lineto(x,199);
    } // end for x

// draw the horizontal lines
for (y=0; y<200; y+=20)
    {
    // position the pen and draw the line
    _moveto(0,y);
    _lineto(319,y);

    } // end for y

} // end Draw_Game_Grid

// M A I N ///////////////////////////////////////////////////////////////

void main(void)
{
int done=0,                       // main event loop exit flag
    player_x        = 160,        // starting position and direction of player
    player_y        = 150,
    player_direction = NORTH;
```

```
// SECTION 1 /////////////////////////////////////////////////////////////

// set the graphics mode to mode 13h 320x200x256
_setvideomode(_MRES256COLOR);

// draw the game grid
Draw_Game_Grid();

// SECTION 2 /////////////////////////////////////////////////////////////

// begin real time event loop
while(!done)
    {
// SECTION 3 /////////////////////////////////////////////////////////////
    // is the player steering his light cycle or trying to exit?
    if (kbhit())
       {
       // test for <A>, <S> or <Q>
       switch(getch())
            {
            case 'a': // turn left
                 {
                 // turn 90 to the left
                 if (--player_direction<NORTH)
                    player_direction=WEST;
                 } break;

            case 's': // turn right
                 {
                 // turn 90 to the right
                 if (++player_direction>WEST)
                    player_direction=NORTH;
                 } break;

            case 'q': // quit game
                 {
                 // set exit flag to true
                 done=1;
                 } break;

            default:break; // do nothing

            } // end switch

       } // end if kbhit

// SECTION 4 /////////////////////////////////////////////////////////////

    // at this point we need to move the light cycle in the direction it's
    // currently pointing
```

continued on next page

continued from previous page

```
switch(player_direction)
    {
    case NORTH:
        {
        if (--player_y<0)
            player_y = 199;
        } break;

    case SOUTH:
        {
        if (++player_y>199)
            player_y = 0;
        } break;

    case EAST:
        {
        if (++player_x>319)
            player_x = 0;
        } break;

    case WEST:
        {
        if (--player_x<0)
            player_y = 319;
        } break;

    default:break;

    } // end switch direction

// SECTION 5 /////////////////////////////////////////////////////////////////

    // render the lightcyle
    _setcolor((short)9);
    _setpixel((short)player_x,(short)player_y);

    // wait a moment and lock the game to 18 fps
    Delay(1);

    } // end while

// SECTION 6 /////////////////////////////////////////////////////////////////

// restore the video mode back to text
_setvideomode(_DEFAULTMODE);

} // end main
```

   The light cycle demo has a lot of interesting lessons within it. The program has animation, collision detection, real-time input, and temporal synchronization (which we'll learn about in detail in a few moments). Let's discuss the program section by section and see what we can learn from it.

Section 1: This is the initialization section. In this case, it sets the graphics mode to 320x200 with 256 colors (mode 13h) and draws the game grid by calling the function *Draw_Game_Grid()*.

Section 2: This is the entrance to the main event loop. Notice the usage of the variable *done* as the exit flag for the while loop.

Section 3: Here's where the real-time aspect of the loop is apparent. A test using the library function *kbhit()* is performed to see if the player has pressed a key. If the function returns *true*, then the keypress is processed and the direction of the player is changed. If the function returns *false*, then the code jumps to the next section and continues processing. Hence, if there is input, it will be processed, but if there isn't, then the program won't wait, the logic will continue onward.

Section 4: Based on the current direction of the player's light cycle, the position of the light cycle is moved forward one pixel in that direction. Moreover, collision detection is performed to test whether the light cycle has moved past one of the four screen boundaries. If so, then the light cycle is "warped" to the other side of the screen. This logic is shown on Figure 2-6.

FIGURE 2-6

◎ ◎ ◎ ◎ ◎ ◎

Warping the light cycle to keep it on the game grid

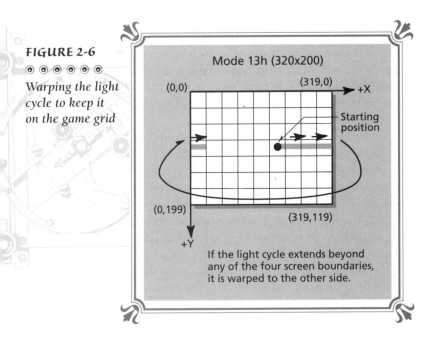

Mode 13h (320x200)

(0,0)   (319,0)   ▸ +X

Starting position

(0,199)   (319,119)

+Y

If the light cycle extends beyond any of the four screen boundaries, it is warped to the other side.

Section 5: At this point the light cycle has been moved and collision detection has been performed, so it's time to draw the actual light cycle. This is done by plotting a single pixel at the current location of the light cycle, which is at *(player_x, player_y)*. After the light cycle is drawn, a call to a time delay function is made to slow down the game; otherwise, the light cycle would move at light speed!

Section 6: This is the end of the game, and the computer is placed back into text mode.

That concludes the analysis of the program. If you're feeling ambitious, add another light cycle that is controlled by the computer. Place the logic for this right after the logic for the player's light cycle, but before the rendering section.

I hope you're starting to get a feel for the complexity of a video game. You just saw how much code it took to make a little dot move around on the screen—but we have to start somewhere! To become successful Cybersorcerers, we will master many new programming techniques that are more acclimated to real-time environments. Let's briefly touch on some of them.

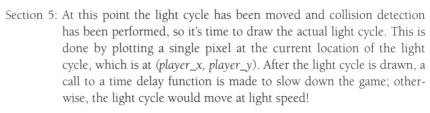

Autonomous Functions and Auto-Logic

If you've ever written a program, you know that you start off with a big problem, then break it into smaller pieces, and write functions for all these smaller pieces (or something close to this). Video game programming is similar, but the functions that control major aspects of the game must be powerful and have memory. The functions must be *autonomous*. We'll cover this topic in more detail in Chapter 8, *The Art of Possession,* when we talk about interrupts and multitasking, but for now let's take a few moments to get acquainted with the subject.

A video game has many creatures and objects that are doing their thing, along with other events, such as user input, that are occurring while the game is running. If the link to Cyberspace is to be sustained, we need a method of programming that simplifies the creation and operation of the creatures, objects, and events within the game. For example, say you make an underwater submarine game with moving subs that the player tries to shoot. Each submarine in the game needs its own set of functions and control logic that perform the necessary operations to keep the sub doing what it's supposed to do. This means that the functions you write for the submarine control must be very smart. They need to know when they are called for the first time, so they can create and set up any data structures, and they need to know when they are being called to implement the normal functions for which they are designed.

This autonomy is implemented by using static variables. Since the static variables are within the scope of the autonomous functions, they can be used to track the state of the function from call to call, as shown in Figure 2-7. State tracking is simply a method of determining what happened last cycle—it's a system of memory. In general, we want game functions that are as self-contained as possible and perform a great deal of their own logic. We don't want to burden the *main()* of the game program with all kinds of work, since this will obscure and complicate the delineation between the functions of each of the objects in the game and their control logic.

Temporal and Video Synchronization

Video games are basically free-running programs that run as fast as possible on the hardware they are running on. This can be a problem, since a game may run too fast on a 486DX4 and just right on a 486SX. To solve this problem, we must synchronize the game using some kind of time base at which to lock the frame rate. This is usually accomplished by placing a function call or a wait loop at the end of the main game loop right before it repeats. For example, a simple technique is to make a delay function that will wait one system clock tick or roughly 1/18th of a

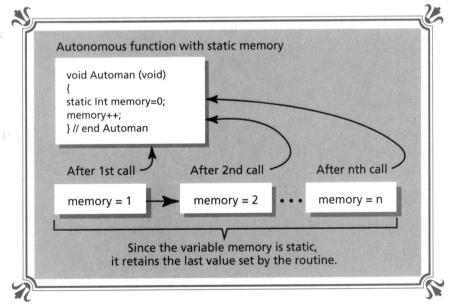

Autonomous function with static memory

```
void Automan (void)
{
static Int memory=0;
memory++;
} // end Automan
```

After 1st call   After 2nd call   After nth call

memory = 1   →   memory = 2   • • •   memory = n

Since the variable memory is static,
it retains the last value set by the routine.

second. This guarantees that the game will never run faster than 18 FPS no matter what machine it runs on.

The only downfall to this technique is that it may severely impede the performance of the machines that can barely sustain 18 FPS on their own. For example, if there was no time delay at the end of the game and it ran at 18 FPS, and then we placed a time delay in for one clock tick, the total time delay would be 2/18ths of a second, making the maximum frame rate 9 FPS on a machine that can actually do 18 FPS! To solve this problem, we can record the current system's timer value at the beginning of the game loop, and then at the end of the game loop test whether one clock tick (or more) transpired. If so, then the game is running at less than 18 FPS, and there should be no delay. On the other hand, if the timer value hasn't changed yet, then the game logic has executed in less than 1/18th of a second, and a *while* loop or other similar logic should be used to wait for a complete tick to occur before repeating the game loop.

Reading the internal timer and reprogramming it isn't difficult, and we'll learn about it in Chapter 8 (you can take a peek at the *Delay()* function in LIGHT.C). But for now here's a code fragment that will guarantee that the game runs at 18 FPS maximum, and slow machines will not be penalized:

```
// main game event loop

while(!game_over)
        {
        current_time = Get_Timer();

        // perform game logic

        // has one tick already passed?, if not wait until it does.

        while(Get_Timer() - current_time<1);

        } // end while
```

The synchronization is accomplished by recording the current value of the internal timer (we'll learn about this later) and then performing the game logic. When the game logic is complete, the saved timer value is subtracted from the current timer value. If the difference is less than 1, we can deduce that 1/18th of a second hasn't passed, so we should wait until it does. This is exactly what the *while* loop does.

There are several kinds of synchronizations used in 3D games other than temporal ones. Many times it's desirable to perform video updating while the video screen is in the vertical retrace phase (see Figure 2-8). During this time, the video hardware isn't accessing the VGA card's video buffer and any updates to the buffer will be much faster, since there won't be a data *bus contingency* (as it's called) between the system processor and the VGA card. When they both try to access the video RAM, access slows and image sheering results, as shown in Figure 2-9.

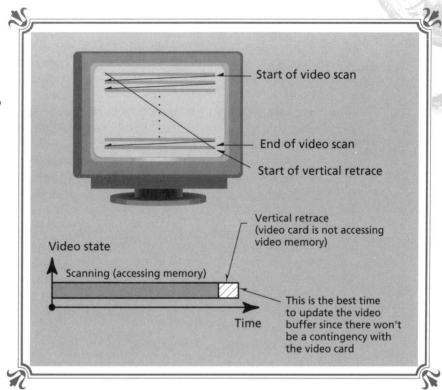

The Sound System

If 3D video games are a Black Art, then sound has got to be the Blackest Art! Two kinds of sounds can be played on the PC equipped with a Sound Blaster or similar card. The first kind is digitized samples. These sounds are played using a digital to analog converter within the sound card. Implementing digitized playback isn't too

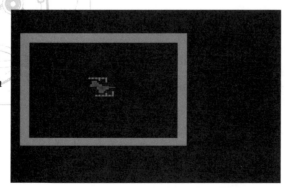

hard. Sounds can be played back with a couple hundred lines of code along with the drivers supplied with the card. However, playing music is another story! Although Sound Blaster and most popular cards come with drivers to play music, and documentation can be found to use them, it is complex, to say the least. Moreover, if you get one specific card to play digitized sounds and music, what about the rest?

In most cases, Cybersorcerers use other software libraries that can play digitized sound and music on any sound card. These libraries have relatively easy-to-understand interfaces and take care of all the details of playing the sound FX for you. Of course, you'll still have to supply the raw digital samples and music files, but that's life. As for operation of the sound system, it is usually done in the background of the game, and the game logic doesn't need to do anything with the sound card in the foreground. For example, Sound Blaster can play a digital sample using DMA, and the computer doesn't have to do anything except start the sound. Music, on the other hand, does need the main CPU's time. But the music drivers are usually implemented as interrupts or TSRs (terminate and stay resident programs) that latch onto the timer interrupt and update the music output every system timer tick—again, relieving the main CPU from any chores. However, there will be a slight degradation in overall system performance, since the timer interrupt will be servicing the sound card.

More detailed discussion of sound can be found in Chapter 6, *Dancing with Cyberdemons*.

Summary

In this chapter we covered the overall structure of 3D games and their major components. We also discussed real-time programming and synchronization techniques used in games. Finally, we touched on one of the most important elements of a game, and that's sound! You probably have a lot of questions now—more than you began with. But that's good. A lot of topics were introduced without going into much detail, but that will change as soon as you turn the page ...

Part II

Alchemy

3

The Mysterious VGA Card

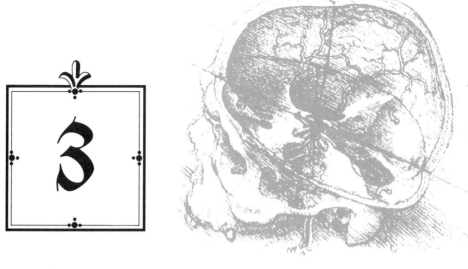

The Mysterious VGA Card

The VGA card is the heart of the PC's graphics abilities. It alone creates the subspace field that opens the gate to Cyberspace and allows us to view the projection of the virtual worlds on the video display. In this chapter we will delve into the intricacies of the VGA's hardware. By the end of this chapter we'll be able to place the PC into mode 13h (a popular 3D game graphics mode) and manipulate the images on the screen. We'll learn how to plot pixels, draw lines, change colors, and print text. Finally, we'll uncover a secret spell. The spell and its incantations transform the VGA by altering its internal registers to create a new mode of operation. This mode has twice the vertical resolution of mode 13h. We will refer to this new mode as *mode Z*.

Mode Z isn't well documented, but it is becoming more and more popular with Cybersorcerers. By mastering it now, we'll have an edge on the competition. So dim the lights and let's begin studying the VGA card.

Raster Graphics Primer

As we learned earlier, the PC's VGA card generates a raster image composed of pixels. Pixels are the basic elements used to draw images on the video screen. But before discussing the VGA card, we need to learn a small vocabulary that we'll use to communicate the concepts. This vocabulary will help us understand all the different modes of the VGA and how to gauge their attributes in an objective manner.

The first term in our vocabulary is *resolution*. Resolution is a measure of how many pixels can be displayed on the video screen in a particular graphics mode. For example, Figure 3-1 shows two possible resolutions of the VGA card. Two common resolutions are 320x200 and 640x480. With twice the number of pixels in both the horizontal and vertical direction, the 640x480 resolution is more than four times that of the 320x200 resolution. Ideally, we would like to have a resolution of about 1280x1024 (which is actually a Super VGA mode). With a resolution that high, the images will look photorealistic if there are enough colors, which brings us to the next topic, *color depth*.

Color depth is a measure of how many colors can be on the screen at one time. The human eye is capable of differentiating millions of different colors, so the more colors available the better. The VGA can display from 16 to 256 colors at a time. However, these colors are selected from a larger subset of 262,144 colors. The number 256 is the color depth. In binary, 256 is equal to 2^8, meaning that there are 8 color planes or 8 bits per pixel that define the color. Figure 3-2 shows the relationship between the screen pixels and the color depth. Compared to the millions of colors we can see, 256 may not seem like many; but surprisingly enough, if the proper set of 256 are selected, photorealistic images of excellent quality can be created.

The next important factor relating to raster graphics is the configuration of the screen memory. The pixels that are displayed by the VGA card must be represented

FIGURE 3-1

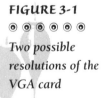

Two possible resolutions of the VGA card

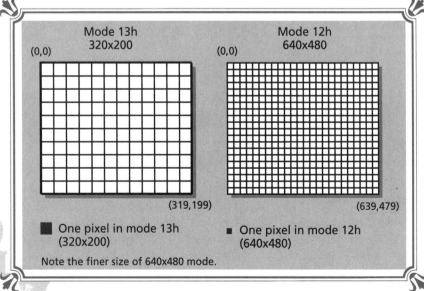

FIGURE 3-2
◎ ◎ ◎ ◎ ◎ ◎
The relationship between pixels and color depth

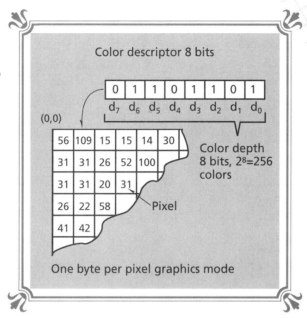

somewhere in memory with some reasonably efficient encoding. The best possible representation is called a *frame buffer*, which maps each pixel to a byte or word in the frame buffer. Moreover, this mapping is done in a contiguous manner so that the frame buffer can be accessed as if it were a large array. Figure 3-3 shows a mem-

FIGURE 3-3
◎ ◎ ◎ ◎ ◎ ◎
Linear memory mapping of display memory

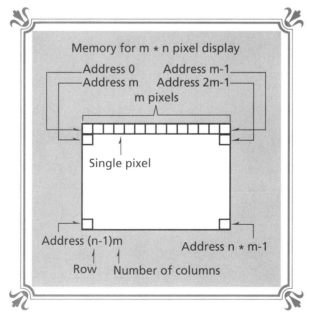

ory mapping that is completely linear. This makes drawing routines easy to write and very fast—the two most important considerations in graphics functions. A second, less popular method of representing video memory is called *planar* memory mapping. Actually the VGA always uses this method in hardware, but luckily, with some clever programming, we can make the memory look as if it were a single contiguous memory map similar to a frame buffer.

The problem with planar memory configurations is that they require multiple steps to draw pixels, lines, or any object. Not only must the actual points of the object be determined in Cartesian Space (mathematical space), but there is usually a complex rule to map the pixels into the planar memory map. For example, pixels with odd X components might be drawn in one plane and those with even ones in another. Or maybe, each plane represents one pixel that makes up the color of each pixel and all the planes must be written in parallel to draw a single point. Take a look at Figure 3-4 to see two possible planar memory configurations.

The last two terms that we'll consider—*refresh rate* and *aspect ratio*—relate to output issues. The refresh rate of a display system is the rate at which the screen is

FIGURE 3-4

⊙ ⊙ ⊙ ⊙ ⊙ ⊙

Two possible planar memory mappings

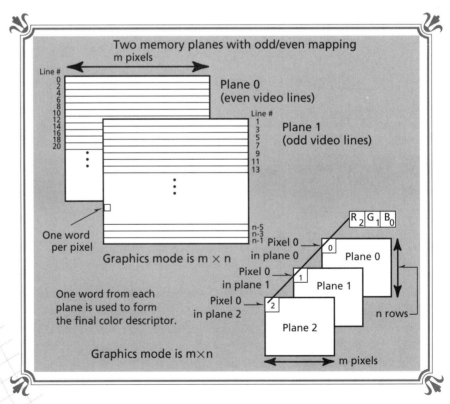

redrawn as a function of time. For example, movies have a refresh rate of 24 FPS (frames per second). On the other hand, TV has a refresh rate of 30 FPS. The actual TV transmission is coming in at 60 FPS, but there are two display fields—one for the even lines of the image and one for the odd lines. Merging the two images results in an effective refresh rate of 30 FPS.

In general, the refresh rate of the computer monitor is 50 to 70 FPS or 50 to 70 hertz (Hz). Hertz is a measurement of frequency. The human eye will start to detect flicker if the refresh rate drops much below 60 Hz. This critical frequency (called the frequency of fusion) can differ widely among people, but a minimum refresh rate of 60 Hz will suffice. The VGA card in most high-resolution modes has a refresh rate of 60 to 70 Hz, which is more than enough for a rock-solid display.

Aspect ratio is a measure of the relative width and height of a display. For example, Figure 3-5 shows a typical VGA monitor. Notice that the display screen is slightly rectangular (it is wider than it is tall). This creates a non-uniform display aspect that can make images longer or shorter in one of the axial directions. Imagine that the screen has a resolution of 100x100 pixels. That would mean that each pixel is a little wider than it is tall. Thus, if we were to draw a 10x10-pixel square, it would look like a rectangle! This is a side effect of aspect ratio. The standard computer monitor has an aspect ratio of 4:3, which means that the screen is 4/3 or 1.33 times wider than it is tall. Hence, if a square is to be square, the screen resolution can't be *nxn*. The resolution must have the same aspect ratio as the screen.

For example, a resolution of 640x400 has an aspect ratio of 640/400 or 1.6, which is slightly larger than the screen's 1.33. This will have the effect of making squares tall. On the other hand, the resolution of 640x480 has an aspect of

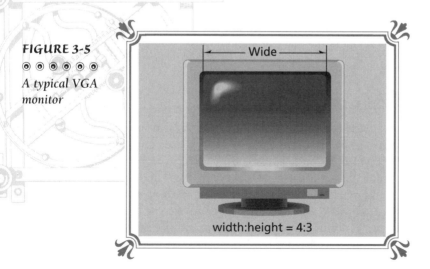

FIGURE 3-5

◎ ◎ ◎ ◎ ◎ ◎

A typical VGA monitor

640/480 or 1.33, which is equal to the screen's aspect ratio, and thus squares will be squares! When writing 3D games it's important to use a video mode that has an aspect as close as possible to that of the screen. This helps objects keep their proper dimensions when they are rotated; otherwise, as objects are transformed, they will get taller and wider, or vice versa.

VGA Internals

As Cybersorcerers of the late twentieth century (indigenous to Earth), we shouldn't have to concern ourselves with the internal operations of the VGA card. Knowing this kind of low-level detailed information just isn't worth it anymore. In the mid to early eighties writing a video game was so intense that the Cybersorcerer had to know everything about the EGA/VGA. Games were written in 100 percent assembly most of the time. The gains Cybersorcerers achieved from custom register programming and tricks is nothing in comparison to the new processing capabilities of the 486 and Pentium chips. Today all that is needed is a basic understanding of the VGA's internal structure. The main points to master are how to place the VGA into graphics modes, change colors, plot pixels, and so forth. With all that in mind, let's take a quick tour of the VGA card to be complete!

The VGA card is a totally reprogrammable display controller, unlike the EGA card that was locked into a specific architecture. The timing, memory addressing, color schemes, and resolution of the VGA can all be reprogrammed. There are dozens, possibly hundreds, of valid modes of operation that the VGA can be placed into. This programmability is a result of the modular design of the VGA's logic and data paths. Each section within the VGA has a specific task assigned to it. Although some of the sections have a bit of overlap, this separation of logic and control allows the VGA to be a versatile and "liquid" video card. Take a look at Figure 3-6 to see a block diagram of the different sections of the VGA card and their interconnections.

Graphics Controller

The *graphics controller* is a link between the CPU and the display memory. It can be totally transparent to the data path or it can perform operations to improve the performance of the video memory access and updating. The graphics controller has both a logic unit and a set of memory latches. The logic unit or LU is used to perform logical transformations on the CPU data and video memory. Operations such as logical *OR*, *AND*, *XOR*, and *ROTATE* can all be accomplished. However, these operations are not performed on the display memory directly, but to a set of memory latches. These memory latches latch the data from each of the four memory

FIGURE 3-6

◎ ◎ ◎ ◎ ◎ ◎

Layout of the VGA card

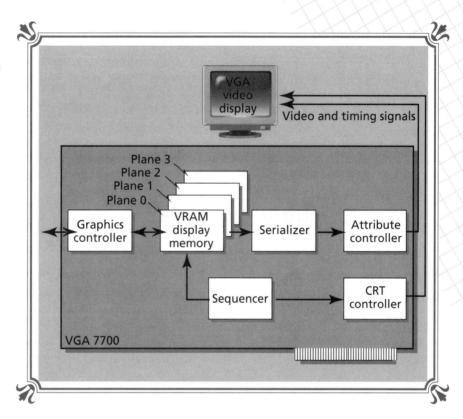

planes that make up the VGA memory (yes, the VGA has a planar memory configuration... yuk).

You see, when the processor writes to the display memory, it can only write one byte or word in some cases, but the graphics controller can read all four planes simultaneously and latch them into local byte-wide latches. Then the processor can read any of these latches it desires with a latch select. Hence, display memory to display memory copying can be performed four bytes at a time!

Display Memory

The *display memory* is a collection of VRAM (Video RAM) chips that make up the memory planes that the VGA accesses. The display memory can be accessed by the CPU as if it were normal memory in the address space of the PC. However, accesses will be slower since the VGA's rasterizing hardware and the CPU will both try to access the same memory locations, potentially at the same time, thus causing bus contingencies and wait states to be inserted. Moreover, since the display memory is

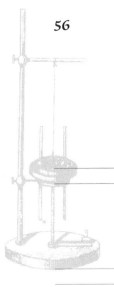

planar, when a write or read operation is performed, all four planes might be involved. Therefore, the programmer must take care to ensure that the proper memory planes are written to or read from. The VGA is supposed to be equipped with a minimum 256K of VRAM, but some cards have less (or more).

Serializer

The *serializer* is responsible for taking the video data and converting it into a single stream of data instead of a stream of bytes or words. Basically it is a very fast shift register that feeds the next stage of the video pipeline, the attribute controller.

Attribute Controller

The *attribute controller* is responsible for controlling the color of the video image. As you will learn later, the VGA card uses *color indirection*. As an example of this, imagine a pixel has the value 23. The value of 23 isn't interpreted in some manner as the RGB components of the desired color, but used as an index into a table that does have separate RGB components for each color index. This table is called the *color lookup table*, and it holds all the color information for the 256 possible colors that the VGA can display at one time. Hence, the main function of the attribute controller is to take the serial stream from the serializer and use it to convert the requested colored pixels into actual video signals for red, green, and blue.

CRT Controller

The *CRT controller* is perhaps the most complex piece of hardware in the VGA card. It is responsible for generating the sophisticated timing signals that drive the video display. These signals include the vertical and horizontal synchronization pulses. Also, the CRT controller dictates how many pixels per line and the number of lines that will be drawn on the video display. Other operations that the CRT controller performs are video refresh timing, cursor control, and scrolling. Interestingly enough, the CRT controller in the VGA is very similar to that of the CGA's display controller, which was a single chip named the 6845 CRT Controller. This was a very popular chip in the seventies and eighties for producing a reasonably high-resolution memory-mapped video signal (and used by a lot of computer hackers to build video displays for their homemade computers).

Sequencer

The ringmaster of the circus is the *sequencer.* It is responsible for controlling the overall timing and communication between each of the sections of the VGA card. The sequencer also has a close relationship to the memory accessing of the VGA and the memory path between the CPU and the display memory. Thus the sequencer is used to tightly control the way video memory is accessed by the programmer and the other VGA sections.

Using BIOS and the C Library Functions

The first question you should always ask yourself before doing anything is, "Why am I doing this?" This philosophy can be applied to everything in life. For example, I still don't know why I took that Elizabethan history class in college, but, oh well. The point is, why write all of our own functions and program the VGA card when the BIOS and C libraries already have a complete set of functions to do just about everything we need? The answer is that both BIOS and the standard C graphics libraries that come with any compiler are just too slow. Although they are getting faster and more robust as time marches on, they will never be as fast as custom code. I admit that WinG is impressive, but there's still a separation between the hardware and the programmer via APIs and low-level device drivers. And if we are to achieve the high performance needed in 3D games, we must communicate with the video hardware ourselves and not use library functions or BIOS calls to accomplish time-critical processing.

Using BIOS or C functions to set video modes, do equipment checks, and so forth, is fine. I strongly recommend that you use BIOS and C functions for these kinds of functions. But operations such as pixel plotting, line drawing, and polygon rendering must be performed with highly optimized code that communicates directly with the video hardware.

Screen Coordinates

Before we place the PC into graphics mode and blast pixels onto the screen, we need to understand what *screen coordinates* are relative to a standard Cartesian coordinate system. Figure 3-7 shows the standard 2D plane. The origin of the system is at the center where the two axes intersect. This point has coordinates (0,0). The positive X axis varies from the origin to the right, and the negative X axis varies from the origin to the left. The Y axis runs vertically, with positive values in the upward direction and negative values in the downward direction.

Using a pair of coordinates (one for the X position and one for the Y position), any point on the 2D plane can be located. For example, in Figure 3-8 the points (5,7), (3,–4), and (1,1) are labeled. Also, the different regions of the Cartesian system are broken up into four quadrants named I, II, III, IV. Referring to Figure 3-8,

FIGURE 3-7

◎ ◎ ◎ ◎ ◎ ◎

The Cartesian 2D plane

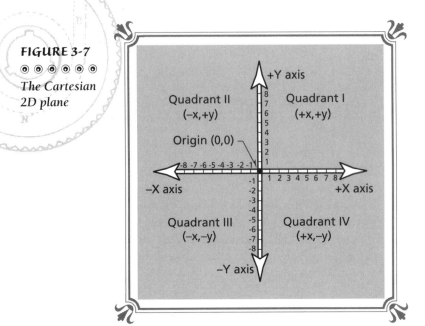

FIGURE 3-8

◎ ◎ ◎ ◎ ◎ ◎

Plotting points in the plane

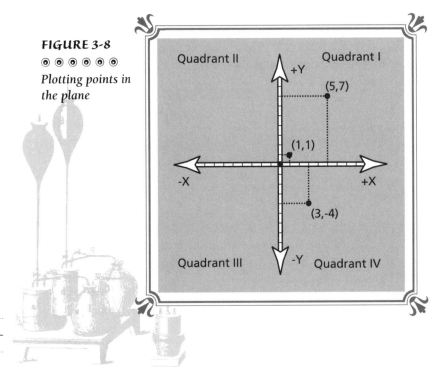

the region that contains all points (x,y) where (x,y) are positive is called Quadrant I. Similarly, Quadrant II contains all points (x,y) where the X component is negative and the Y component is positive.

So, what's the big deal about the Cartesian coordinate system and the 2D plane? Well, they are important because the video screen's raster nature and pixel address-able format is basically a type of integer coordinate system. In fact, the screen is similar to Quadrant I of a 2D Cartesian coordinate system. This is true on about 99 percent of the graphics hardware in the world and is definitely true for the PC and the VGA card. Figure 3-9 shows how the coordinates are laid out on the display screen. However, you should notice one little peculiarity about the layout of the X and Y axis. The positive Y axis is pointing downward, while the positive X axis is pointing to the right. This is similar to Quadrant I of the Cartesian coordinate system except that the Y axis is inverted. This isn't a problem since we can always transform the screen coordinates into anything we want by using simple mathematical transformations, but we'll get to that later.

As an example, let's say we instructed the computer to plot the point (0,0) on the computer screen or, in other words, to illuminate the pixel at location x=0,y=0 with some color, say blue. The result would be a blue dot in the upper-left corner of the screen, since this is the origin of the screen coordinate system. At this point, we have a lot of power. By turning on pixels at any position on the screen we can draw an image and animate it. But of course, the resolution of the screen, its color

FIGURE 3-9

◉ ◉ ◉ ◉ ◉ ◉

Mapping screen coordinates

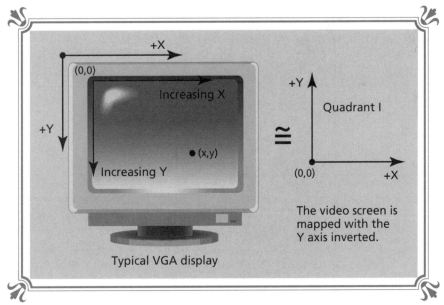

depth, and memory mapping will dictate the types of images that can be drawn and how efficiently they can be drawn.

The next piece in the puzzle is learning how the graphics memory is laid out for the modes we are interested in and how to plot pixels at any screen coordinate we wish.

The Lay of the Land

For purposes of this book and the graphics engine, we want to select a graphics mode that is easy to use, has a lot of color (for 3D shading), has a decent resolution, and is readily available on all VGA cards. The one mode that meets all these criteria is called mode 13h or mode 19. Mode 13h has a resolution of 320x200 pixels with a color depth of 8 bits or 256 colors. The 256 colors are selected using a color palette and color indirection from a total set of 262,144. Figure 3-10 shows the memory layout of mode 13h along with its screen coordinates. If you study the figure closely you should notice something. There is exactly one byte for every pixel on each line, and the memory addresses are linear as a function of X. This means that mode 13h has a linear memory mapping. This is almost too good to be true! In essence, we can assign a pointer to the video segment (which is the address of the display memory on the VGA card) and then plot pixels (and read them) by indexing into the video memory as if it were an array.

FIGURE 3-10

⊙ ⊙ ⊙ ⊙ ⊙ ⊙

The layout of mode 13h

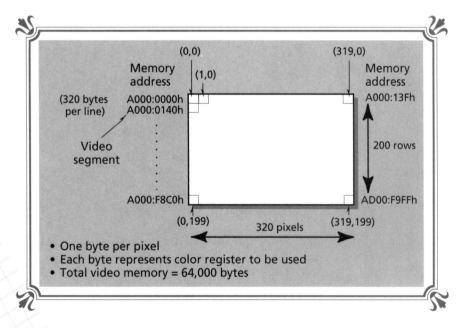

- One byte per pixel
- Each byte represents color register to be used
- Total video memory = 64,000 bytes

This is a much better memory configuration than the other modes of the VGA card, which usually have a planar configuration. These planar modes are difficult to deal with because there isn't an easy rule for locating any (x,y) screen coordinate in display memory. Anyway, we won't need to worry about all that when using mode 13h! The next thing we need to know how to do is place the VGA into mode 13h. But before we do that, let's see how easy it is to access the video buffer and write a pixel into it.

The video buffer or display memory can be found at segment 0xA000h. The resolution of mode 13h is 320x200, and there is exactly one byte for each pixel; hence there are 320*200=64,000 bytes that are required to support the graphics mode. This means that the video buffer (more commonly known as the frame buffer) is located from 0xA000:0000h – 0xA000:F9FFh. We access this memory with a simple FAR pointer like this:

```
video_buffer =(unsigned char far *)0xA0000000L;
```

The preceding code fragment creates a pointer named *video_buffer* that will point to the beginning of the video buffer. To access a location in video memory, it's as simple as this:

```
video_buffer[100] = 25;
```

This places a 25 into memory location 100, resulting in a pixel being displayed at 100 pixels from the left edge on the first row. We will learn the exact relationship between screen coordinates and memory later, but hopefully you see that this mode is a dream come true!

Summoning Mode 13h

I'm getting excited about mode 13h, so let's see how to place the VGA into it. This can be done in myriad ways. For starters, we could manually reprogram the VGA card. But by doing this we might distort the subspace link between the VGA and Cyberspace and damage the VGA (not to mention how complex this process would be). As a second method we could use a C graphics library function to place the VGA into mode 13h, but this would be compiler dependent. Alas, we will use the ROM BIOS video interrupt to do our bidding. Using BIOS in this case is perfectly legitimate since setting the video mode isn't a time-critical function; moreover, the BIOS functions will work properly with any VGA card on Earth.

Video BIOS can be accessed in two ways. We could use inline assembly (which we will use from time to time in the book for speed) or use a C library call to invoke an interrupt. Let's use the C interrupt function this time. The code is shown in Listing 3-1.

LISTING 3-1 A function to place the VGA into any supported video mode

```
void Set_Graphics_Mode(int mode)
{

// use the video interrupt 10h and the C interrupt function to set
// the video mode

union REGS inregs,outregs;

inregs.h.ah = 0;                    // set video mode subfunction
inregs.h.al = (unsigned char)mode;  // video mode to change to

_int86(0x10, &inregs, &outregs);

} // end Set_Graphics_Mode
```

The function works by calling the video BIOS interrupt, which happens to be *INT 10h*. The code places the proper parameters into the registers and makes the interrupt call. In the case of video BIOS functions it is standard to place the video subfunction in the *AH* register and any other parameters in other registers. Subfunction 0, which is Set Video Mode, is therefore placed in the *AH* register and the mode is placed into the *AL* register. Once the registers are set, the call to the C function *_int86()* is made and the video BIOS does its job.

The function *Set_Graphics_Mode()* is general and can be used to place the VGA into any of the standard modes. Table 3-1 lists all of the possible modes along with the constants that represent them. Since we're only interested in mode 13h, the constant sent to *Set_Graphics_Mode()* will usually be 0x13h.

TABLE 3-1

◇◇◇◇◇◇

Interesting video modes supported by video BIOS

Mode(hex)	Resolution	Colors
1	40x25 (text)	16
3	80x25 (text)	16
4	320x200	4
6	640x200	2
7	80x25 (text)	monochrome
D	320x200	16
E	640x200	16
F	640x350	monochrome
10	640x350	16
11	640x480	2
12	640x480	16
13	320x200	256

Note: Modes not listed have color burst disabled or work only on the PCjr.

Now before we get too far, let me break off and tell you what you will find on the CD-ROM included with this book. Within the directory for this chapter you will find the library module for all of this chapter's software. There are two main files of interest, BLACK3.C and BLACK3.H. They are the source and header file that contain all of the functions covered in this chapter. So, if you want to skip ahead at any time, feel free to look inside them. For example, I have defined the following constants to be used in the *Set_Graphics_Mode()* function:

```
#define GRAPHICS_MODE13    0x13  // 320x200x256
#define TEXT_MODE          0x03  // 80x25 text mode
```

These are used to place the VGA into mode 13h and then restore it to text mode. For example, to place the VGA into mode 13h, you could use the following code fragment:

```
Set_Graphics_Mode(GRAPHICS_MODE13);
```

In general, if a piece of code or function has something that isn't defined within the text it will be in the header file for the chapter... just wanted you to know where everything is.

Clearing the Screen

Once the VGA is placed into mode 13h the first operation to be mastered is filling the video buffer with a single value. This value is usually the background color of the screen. Whatever color we decide to fill the screen with, we need to write a function that does it very quickly. Since the video buffer is just an array, we could do something like this:

```
for (index=0; index<64000; index++)
        video_buffer[index]=color;
```

This would fill the video buffer with the value of *color*. The preceding fragment will work, but we need to be able to fill the screen quickly. This only writes bytes at a time instead of words, which would be twice as fast. Sure, we could make *video_buffer* a word pointer. But then there's still the overhead of the *for* loop that will slow down the fill. We might be tempted to use one of the *memset()* functions to do the clear. But *memset()* still only uses byte writes, which just won't do. Filling and clearing the screen is something that has to be done very quickly, so we're going to use inline assembly to do it.

We'll use the inline assembler for 99 percent of the assembly in this book since it is easy to use and most compilers have one. It's a real pain creating external assembly modules and then linking them in. In addition, the inline assembler allows you to access variables in the scope of the C program just as if they were in the scope of the inline assembly. This makes writing functions a snap.

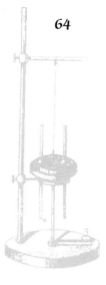

If you're one of those people who hates assembly language, don't worry. If you don't totally understand how the inline function(s) work on a line-by-line basis, that's not as important as understanding the general purpose of the inline functions. Anyway, I'll try to overcomment all assembly language listings, so that even if you've never seen a line of assembly in your life, you'll get the general idea of the function. To begin an inline assembly block in C most compilers use the keyword *asm* in some way. For example, the Microsoft C/C++ compiler uses the following syntax:

```
_asm
    {   ; this is the beginning


    }   ; this is the end
```

The Borland compilers like the first brace to be on the same line (and comments are the same as C/C++), like this:

```
_asm {   // this is the beginning


    }  // this is the end
```

Notice that the semicolon (;) is used as a comment. Anyway, that's all there is to adding inline assembly to C/C++ programs. As far as corrupting registers goes, everything is stacked on entrance to an inline section except *SI, DI, DS, SS, SP, BP*. Hence, if you change those registers, you must save and restore them on exiting the inline section. For a more in-depth review of your particular inline assembler, read the documentation that came with your C/C++ compiler. In general, we won't be doing much inline assembly, but the functions we do write will be straightforward and simple (lots of room for assembly gurus to tweak them). Let's create our first inline assembly function that can be used to clear the screen by filling it with any color. We'll call it *Fill_Screen()*, and the source for it is shown in Listing 3-2.

LISTING 3-2 A screen filling function

```
void Fill_Screen(int color)
{
// this function will fill the entire screen with the sent color

// use the inline assembler for speed

_asm
   {
   les di,video_buffer    ; point es:di to video buffer
   mov al,BYTE PTR color  ; move the color into al
   mov ah,al              ; replicate color into ah
   mov cx,320*200/2       ; number of words to fill(using word is faster
                              than bytes)
```

```
rep stosw               ; move the color into the video buffer really fast!
                        } // end inline asm
```

```
} // end Fill_Screen
```

The *Fill_Screen()* function takes one parameter—the color to fill the screen with. The function then proceeds to point *ES:DI* to the video buffer and then use a string operation to move 32,000 words into the video buffer of the sent color. Remember the video buffer is 64,000 bytes, which is 32,000 words. As you can see, using inline isn't that bad. Actually it's kinda fun. I have to admit that I'm starting to use more and more inline instead of external assembly modules. The trend in game programming is to get away completely from external assembly language and use the inline assembler when speed is absolutely necessary.

We've learned that the video buffer can be accessed as if it were a continuous array of bytes. This isn't really true, but mode 13h chains the display memory planes in such a way that from our point of view it's true. The next step is to figure out the exact relationship between screen coordinates and video memory so we can plot pixels, draw lines, and create objects on the screen.

Rendering Images on the Screen

Ultimately a video game is a sequence of frames representing the image that is being transported from Cyberspace through the gateway to your PC. Each of these frames is composed of a set of colored pixels. We learned earlier that the origin of the screen coordinate system is in the upper-left corner of the screen, but we haven't yet discussed the exact relationship between the screen coordinates and the video buffer. Once we have this information, writing graphics functions is a relatively straightforward process. The only problem is making them really fast!

The relationship between screen coordinates and video memory can be derived by looking at the representation of the video buffer. Referring back to Figure 3-10, we see that there are 320 bytes per line and a total of 200 lines. We also know that the video buffer starts at 0xA000:0000h. Taking a moment to think about it, the following mathematical formula comes to mind to plot a pixel:

```
memory_location  = screen_y * 320 + screen_x;
```

Where (*screen_x,screen_y*) are the X and Y components of the point to be plotted on the video screen.

Therefore, if we want to plot a point at (50,60), we can write:

```
video_buffer[60*320+50] = color;
```

And miraculously a point would appear on the screen. We still need to cover how color indirection works, but for now just pretend that there's a palette of 256 colors, numbered 0 through 255, which can be placed into the video buffer. Each one of these values represents a different color. With all this knowledge we can finally write some of the simpler graphics functions. Let's begin with pixel plotting.

Plotting Pixels

To plot a point all we need to know are the coordinates of the point and the desired color. We just learned that the transformation to video memory from screen coordinates is a single multiplication and addition. Right now we could write a pixel-plotting function that takes the Y component of the desired point, multiplies it by 320, and then adds the X component to find the final memory offset from the beginning of the video buffer. Although this technique is mathematically correct, it isn't as fast as it could be.

Pixel plotting must be done very rapidly, and multiplication and division are generally avoided because they are more complex than addition or subtraction. Therefore, we will invoke a bit of Cybersorcery to solve the problem. We need to transform the sum,

y*320+x

into something that has no multiplication. We can do this using binary shifting, which is about five to eight times faster than using the CPU to do the integer multi-

FIGURE 3-11

⊙ ⊙ ⊙ ⊙ ⊙ ⊙

Binary representation of a decimal number

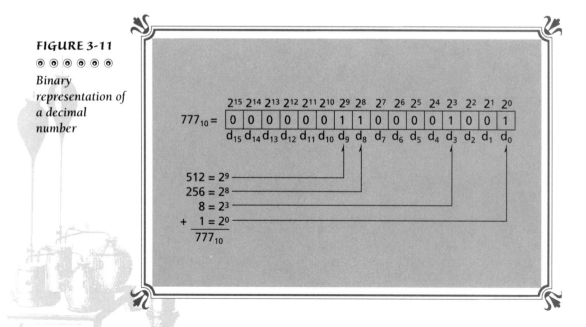

plication! The basis of the trick is to recall that all numbers in the computer are represented in base 2. Figure 3-11 shows a typical 16-bit integer represented as a binary number. The next thing to recall is that when a number represented in any base system is shifted to the right or left by one digit, the number is divided or multiplied (depending on the direction of the shift) by the base. We can use this fact to multiply binary numbers by powers of 2 to arrive at a final sum of products that can be made to equal any desired product. The only catch to this is that we can only multiply a number by a power of 2. Figure 3-12 shows the different multiplications for different binary shifts.

To multiply the Y coordinate by 320 we must break 320 down into a sum of powers of 2. Luckily 320=256+64. Therefore, to multiply Y by 320 the following code fragment can be used:

```
(y<<8)+(y<<6)
```

Then to find the final address in video memory, do this:

```
video_buffer[(y<<8)+(y<<6)+x] = color;
```

FIGURE 3-12

◎ ◎ ◎ ◎ ◎ ◎

Using shifts to multiply by powers of 2

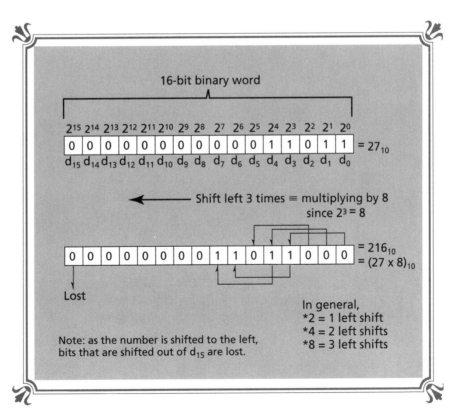

This would result in setting the pixel at (x,y) to the specified color; the speed of which is about three times faster than standard multiplying. Not bad for a quickie!

Using the binary multiplication technique, we can now write a function to plot a pixel on the screen in mode 13h at any desired screen coordinate (x,y). The function in Listing 3-3 does the job.

LISTING 3-3 Plotting a pixel in mode 13h

```
void Write_Pixel(int x,int y,int color)
{

// plots the pixel in the desired color a little quicker using binary shifting
// to accomplish the multiplications

// use the fact that 320*y = 256*y + 64*y = y<<8 + y<<6

video_buffer[((y<<8) + (y<<6)) + x] = (unsigned char )color;

} // end Write_Pixel
```

The converse of plotting a pixel is reading a pixel. This is done by returning the value from the video buffer. Although pixel reading won't be that necessary in the type of game we'll be making, it does come in handy with various types of collision detection algorithms, so we'll add it to our repertoire. Listing 3-4 contains the code to read a pixel.

LISTING 3-4 Reading the value of a pixel

```
int Read_Pixel(int x,int y)
{
// this function reads a pixel from the screen buffer

// use the fact that 320*y = 256*y + 64*y = y<<8 + y<<6

return((int)(video_buffer[((y<<8) + (y<<6)) + x]));

} // end Read_Pixel
```

You'll notice that the function returns an integer even though the pixel is a byte. This is a common practice throughout the book, and it makes things a bit easier. As long as the proper casts are done in the functions, it's a good idea to use integers as coordinates and pixel values rather than bytes. In many cases bytes can actually be slower to process than words due to memory-accessing schemes, and, of course, they have much less range.

Drawing Lines

A line is the collection of points that connects two points in space. In our case a line connects two points in the 2D plane. Figure 3-13 shows a line drawn between two points on the screen. Drawing the points between two lines is called *rasterization*. Basically, a line on the computer screen is composed of a finite set of pixels that only approximate the true line. Figure 3-14 shows the relationship between a true line and the rasterized one. Determining the points that most closely fit the true line is not an easy problem. We will cover this later when we learn about wireframe graphics. For now let's see if we can draw a couple special cases of lines. These are horizontal and vertical lines. Figure 3-15 shows the relationship between the adjacent pixels and the endpoint coordinates of these kinds of lines.

Of the two special cases, horizontal lines are the easiest and fastest since the points on a horizontal line, when converted from screen coordinates to memory addresses, are all continuous. This means that a *memset()* or other similar technique can be used to draw them. Vertical lines, on the other hand, are generated by illuminating pixels in a single column, where each pixel is on a different row. Accomplishing this is more complex since each pixel is exactly 320 bytes from the last. Alas, vertical lines can't be drawn as fast as horizontal ones; however, with a tight loop, performing the additions isn't bad.

FIGURE 3-13

◎ ◎ ◎ ◎ ◎ ◎

Line drawn between two points

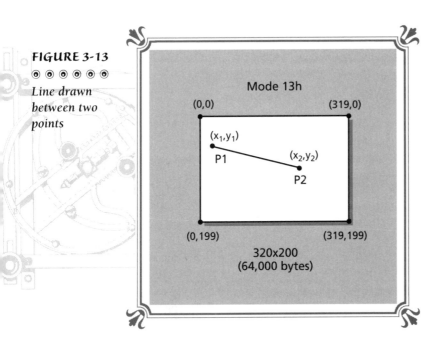

Mode 13h

(0,0)　　　　　　　　　　(319,0)

(x_1,y_1)

P1　　　　(x_2,y_2)

P2

(0,199)　　　　　　　　(319,199)

320x200
(64,000 bytes)

FIGURE 3-14

◉ ◉ ◉ ◉ ◉ ◉

The rasterization of a line

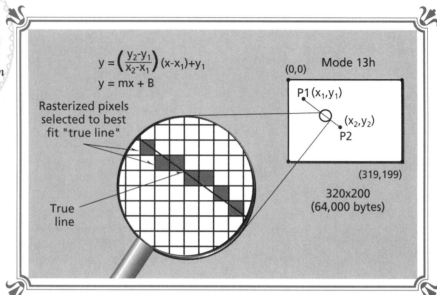

FIGURE 3-15

◉ ◉ ◉ ◉ ◉ ◉

Special cases of lines

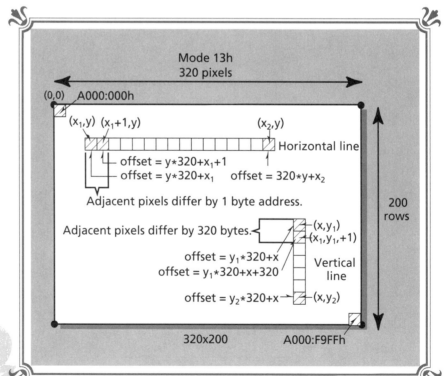

Horizontal Lines

Drawing horizontal lines is as easy as making a single call to the *memset()* function
with the proper parameters. A horizontal line has two endpoints, each with the
same Y position; therefore, the function that draws a horizontal line will need a
total of four parameters (one for the color). Listing 3-5 shows a function that draws
a horizontal line in the video buffer with a specific color.

LISTING 3-5 Horizontal line drawing function

```
void Line_H(int x1,int x2,int y,int color)
{
// draw a horizontal line using the memset function
// this function does not do clipping hence x1,x2 and y must all be within
// the bounds of the screen

int temp; // used for temporary storage during endpoint swap

// sort x1 and x2, so that x2 > x1

if (x1>x2)
   {
   temp = x1;
   x1   = x2;
   x2   = temp;
   } // end swap

// draw the row of pixels

_fmemset((char far *)(video_buffer + ((y<<8) + (y<<6)) + x1),
        (unsigned char)color,x2-x1+1);

} // end Line_H
```

The only interesting points about the function are that it sorts the input X coordinates and makes sure that *x1* is less than or equal to *x2*, and it calls the memory
function *_fmemset()* (which is the *FAR* version of the function). The latter point is a
very important factor to note. Since we are using the MEDIUM memory model, we
need to use the *FAR* versions of some C functions, and *memset()* is one of them.
Finally, the function uses the binary shifting technique to compute the starting row
address in the video buffer.

Vertical Lines

Vertical lines can't be drawn as fast as horizontal ones because the pixels are on separate video rows, each separated by 320 bytes. It would be cool if the Intel processors had a memory move function that could increment by any value—then we

could use another *memset()* type function. But that's not the case, so the only thing we can do is write a *for* loop to do the job. The basic idea of the vertical line function is to start at a point $(x,y1)$ and draw pixels until the point $(x,y2)$ is reached. So, a *for* loop can be used that iterates from $y1$ to $y2$ within the column of x. The function to do this is shown in Listing 3-6.

LISTING 3-6 *Vertical line drawing function*

```
void Line_V(int y1,int y2,int x,int color)
{
// draw a vertical line, note that a memset function can no longer be
// used since the pixel addresses are no longer contiguous in memory
// note that the end points of the line must be on the screen

unsigned char far *start_offset; // starting memory offset of line

int index, // loop index
    temp,  // used for temporary storage during swap
    length; //   length of line

// make sure y2 > y1

if (y1>y2)
   {
   temp = y1;
   y1   = y2;
   y2   = temp;
   } // end swap

// compute starting position

start_offset = video_buffer + ((y1<<8) + (y1<<6)) + x;

// pre-compute length of line
length = y2-y1;

for (index=0; index<=length; index++)
   {
   // set the pixel

   *start_offset = (unsigned char)color;

   // move downward to next line

   start_offset+=320;

   } // end for index

} // end Line_V
```

The function begins by sorting the Y coordinates to make sure $y2$ is greater than or equal to $y1$. Then it computes the starting address of the line in the video buffer, which is at *(x,y1)*. Next the function uses a *for* loop to iterate from *y1* to *y2* while adding 320 to the current address every cycle in order to compute the proper video address each cycle. The function could have accessed the array *video_buffer[]*, but using a precomputed video address that is updated each cycle without an array index is much faster. The key to this is equating *start_offset* to the starting address of the line in the video buffer memory.

Filling Rectangles

Once horizontal and vertical lines have been mastered, we can use them as the basis for drawing filled rectangles with horizontal or vertical strips. However, we just learned that horizontal lines are much faster than vertical ones, so we'll base our rectangle fill on them. Figure 3-16 shows a rectangle that has corner points *(x1,y1)* and *(x2,y2)*. To fill in the rectangle, we must draw a set of horizontal lines that have width *(x2–x1)* from the starting row of *y1* and ending at *y2*. This can be accomplished by a simple *for* loop. Listing 3-7 shows the code.

LISTING 3-7 Drawing a rectangle with lines

```
void Draw_Rectangle(int x1,int y1,int x2,int y2,int color)
{
// this function will draw a rectangle from (x1,y1) - (x2,y2)
// it is assumed that each endpoint is within the screen boundaries
```

continued on next page

FIGURE 3-16
◎ ◎ ◎ ◎ ◎ ◎
A rectangle

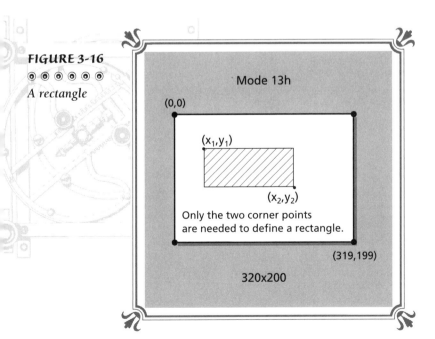

continued from previous page

```
// and (x1,y1) is the upper left hand corner and (x2,y2) is the lower
// right hand corner

unsigned char far *start_offset;   // starting memory offset of first row

int width;   // width of rectangle

// compute starting offset of first row

start_offset = video_buffer + ((y1<<8) + (y1<<6)) + x1;

// compute width of rectangle

width  = 1 + x2 - x1; // the "1" to reflect the true width in pixels

// draw the rectangle row by row

while(y1++<=y2)
    {
    // draw the line

    _fmemset((char far *)start_offset,(unsigned char)color,width);

    // move the memory pointer to the next line

    start_offset+=320;

    } // end while

} // end Draw_Rectangle
```

The function takes as parameters the two corner points of the rectangle and the color of the rectangle and then proceeds to draw it. The function *Draw_Rectangle()* doesn't do any vertex sorting, so the endpoints should be set such that the point (*x1,y1*) is above and to the left of (*x2,y2*) in screen coordinates. Note that the function doesn't explicitly make a call to the line function, but draws each line within the function body. This is a standard technique in graphics functions. The number of function calls should always be minimized within the body of a time critical graphics function. For instance, in this case, if a rectangle 100 pixels high was drawn and a call was made to the *Line_H()* function each time, there would be 100 function calls and something like 500 to 1000 extra instructions executed!

Restoring the Video Mode

The function that we made *Set_Graphics_Mode()* is very general since it calls the video BIOS interrupt *INT 10h*. If we want to restore the video mode to standard 80x25 text, all we need to do is send the function the proper mode number. Look back a few sections to Table 3-1, where we see that the mode we are looking for is numbered 0x03 or mode 3. Hence, if we make the call *Set_Graphics_Mode*(3), the VGA will be placed back into the standard DOS text mode. But we have already defined these constants, so we can use them instead. Anyway, a complete program that enters into mode 13h and exits might look something like this:

```
void main(void)
{
// place VGA into mode 13h
Set_Graphics_Mode(GRAPHICS_MODE13)

..game goes here!!!

// restore graphics mode back to text
Set_Graphics_Mode(TEXT_MODE);

} // end main
```

Of course, you can use the constants that are defined in BLACK3.H instead of those ugly numbers, but you get the idea.

Optimizing Screen Access

Before moving on to more colorful pastures, let's talk a moment about video access optimization. In general, the CPU can't access the video memory at all times. The video memory is constantly being accessed by the display hardware to render the actual video image. This means that if the CPU tries to read or write the video memory at the wrong time (when the display hardware is accessing it), the CPU will be halted and memory wait states will be placed on the system bus. The result is wasted computing time. It is possible to access the screen memory at times when the video hardware isn't working with it, and this is the optimal situation; otherwise, the condition of a bus contingency, as you read in Chapter 2, will occur.

We can't stop the CPU from having to wait at times for the video memory, but we can make this wait worth the CPU's while. Most new VGA cards can handle word-size writes (and some can even handle double word or quad-byte). This means that we can write a word at a time or two pixels at a time. This doesn't help much if we want to plot a single pixel, but if we want to draw a horizontal line or a rectangle, it can speed video access up by about 90 percent.

For example, if a line to be drawn is 100 pixels, the video buffer would be accessed 100 times if byte writes were done. On the other hand, if word-size writes were done, only 50 accesses would be required. Granted, there is a bit of overhead to make sure the endpoints of the line are drawn correctly, but this method is still very important and will be of use many times. (Note that the video fill function uses word-size writes.) Writing words will come in handy when we draw objects that have a lot of horizontal symmetry and long runs of the same color.

The Color Lookup Table

We've discussed plotting pixels and accessing the video buffer. Now we're going to focus on color control in more detail. Thus far we have been writing values into the video buffer that represent the colors to be displayed. In actuality, these values weren't the true colors, but indices into a table called the color lookup table. Each element in this table contains a 3-byte value that represents the final color. Figure 3-17 shows how these indices and the values in the table are used to arrive at a final color. Also, remember that the attribute controller is responsible for the final color translation.

We see that there are 3 bytes for each color register—1 byte for each of the components red, green, and blue. Hence, you might think that there would be a total of 256^3 total colors. Unfortunately, this is not true for standard VGA cards. The standard vanilla VGA only uses the first 6 bits of each color register element, therefore only a total of 2^6 or 64 shades of each primary color can be selected. This formulation gives a grand total of $64^3 = 262,144$ different colors. Granted, it's not as good as $256^3 = 16,777,216$. But it's more than enough to make images look photorealistic.

The first question that comes to mind is, how are the 256 color registers programmed when the VGA is first placed into mode 13h? In other words, what is the default palette? The default palette contains all kinds of colors, including shades of the most popular colors along with flesh and earth colors. But most of the time we

FIGURE 3-17

⊚ ⊚ ⊚ ⊚ ⊚ ⊚

Pixel being translated into an RGB triple

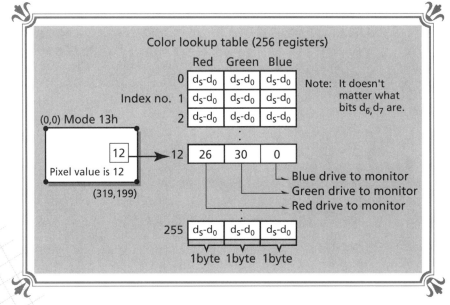

won't use the default palette; we'll load one of our own that is based on the imagery and color schemes of our games. About the only thing that's worth noting about the standard mode 13h palette is that the first 16 colors are similar to the 16 colors of the EGA palette. I suspect this is for compatibility, allowing programs written for EGA modes to be easily ported to mode 13h. For example, if you want to see all the colors, you can write a little program that iterates through all 256 colors and draws a line with the color, something like this:

```
for (color=0; color<256; color++)
    Line_V(0,199,color,color);
```

Of course, the VGA would have to be placed into mode 13h, and so forth, but the above fragment would display all the colors from 0 to 255.

Alrighty then! Back to the problem at hand. How do we read and write the color registers? This is actually very easy to do once we know how to communicate with the palette registers onboard the VGA. We accomplish this through four ports. One of them is called the palette data port, and it is used to read and write data to the selected color register. The next pair of ports are used to select the color register that is going to be read or written to. There is one port to select the index for reading and one port to select the index for writing. The last port is used as a bit mask to select which bits of the data are used for writing pixels. In most cases this port defaults to 0xFFh to allow all bits to be used as the pixel data. Figure 3-18 shows a diagram of the data paths for the color register ports.

To make accessing the color lookup table easy, BLACK3.H defines the following constants:

```
#define COLOR_MASK          0x3C6   // the bit mask register
#define COLOR_REGISTER_RD   0x3C7   // set read index at this I/O
#define COLOR_REGISTER_WR   0x3C8   // set write index at this I/O
#define COLOR_DATA          0x3C9   // the R/W data is here
```

Writing to a Color Register

Writing to a color register can be done in a couple lines. Simply select the color register to be written to with the color register write port at 0x3C8 and write the data for the red, green, and blue components to the data port at 0x3C9h. The only catch is, there are three bytes to be written and only one data port! So how does that work? It works based on a specific order. A counter in the VGA color lookup table is incremented every time you write one byte to the data port. Thus the first byte will be interpreted as the red component, the second byte as the green component, and the third as the blue component. This isn't much of a problem once you know this. The only drawback to this arrangement is that we can't select one component of the color register (red, green, or blue) and write specifically to it. We must write to all three.

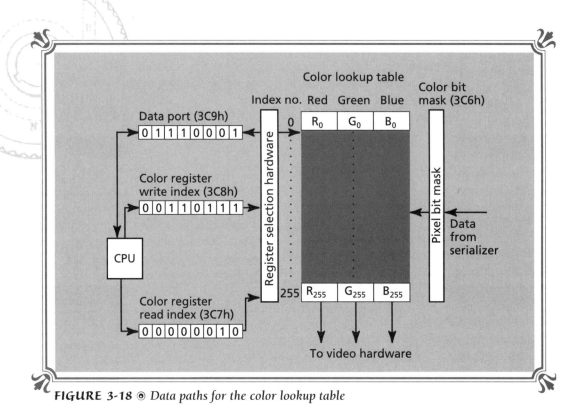

FIGURE 3-18 ⊚ *Data paths for the color lookup table*

Let's write a little function that takes as parameters the new RGB values of the color and the color register we wish reprogrammed. But before we do this, let's create a color structure that contains all the RGB components in a single entity, so we don't have to carry around three values all over the place. The name of the structure is *RGB_color* and it is defined in BLACK3.H. The definition follows:

```
// this structure holds a RGB triple in three unsigned bytes
typedef struct RGB_color_typ
        {
        unsigned char red;     // red   component of color 0-63
        unsigned char green;   // green component of color 0-63
        unsigned char blue;    // blue  component of color 0-63
        } RGB_color, *RGB_color_ptr;
```

Notice that each field is an *unsigned char*. This is because each color register component is interpreted as an unsigned number. There is another detail we should review, which is that each color register component is only 6 bits wide. This means that the upper 2 bits of each primary component are meaningless. Only the numbers 0 through 63 will make a difference to the color's shade. It's perfectly legitimate to place values ranging from 0 to 255 into any color register component, but the last 2 bits are simply ignored unless you have a 24-bit VGA card.

Now that we've taken care of the preliminaries, Listing 3-8 contains the function to write a new RGB value into a color register.

LISTING 3-8 Function to write a color register

```
void Write_Color_Reg(int index, RGB_color_ptr color)
{

// this function is used to write a color register with the RGB value
// within "color"

// tell vga card which color register to update

_outp(COLOR_REGISTER_WR, index);

// update the color register RGB triple, note the same port is used each time
// the hardware will make sure each of the components is stored in the
// proper location

_outp(COLOR_DATA,color->red);
_outp(COLOR_DATA,color->green);
_outp(COLOR_DATA,color->blue);

} // end Write_Color_Reg
```

As an example, if we wanted to change color register 55 to a bright green, we could write the following code:

```
RGB_color color; // the color that we will work with

// set the color to bright green
color.red    = 0;
color.green  = 63;
color.blue   = 0;

// update the color register
Write_Color_Reg(55,(RGB_color_ptr)&color);
```

Note that a pointer to the color structure is sent rather than the actual color structure. In general you should always send pointers as parameters to functions, rather than values, when the structures are involved.

Reading a Color Register

The opposite of writing is reading, and the process is almost identical. The color register is selected using the read port instead of the write port. Then the three values, red, green, and blue, are read from the data port. Listing 3-9 contains the function to read a color register.

LISTING 3-9 Reading the value of a color register

```
RGB_color_ptr Read_Color_Reg(int index, RGB_color_ptr color)
{

// this function reads the RGB triple out of a palette register and places it
// into "color"

// tell vga card which register to read

_outp(COLOR_REGISTER_RD, index);

// now extract the data

color->red   = (unsigned char)_inp(COLOR_DATA);
color->green = (unsigned char)_inp(COLOR_DATA);
color->blue  = (unsigned char)_inp(COLOR_DATA);

// return a pointer to color so that the function can be used as an RVALUE

return(color);

} // end Read_Color_Reg
```

The function places the selected RGB values of the color register into the sent color structure and also returns a pointer to this structure. This allows the function to be used as an *lvalue* or, in other words, as a parameter to another function. For example, imagine we wanted to write color register 50 with the value in color register 51. We could do something like this:

```
RGB_color color; // our working color
Write_Color_Reg(50,Read_Color_Register(51,(RGB_color_ptr)&51);
```

By using this technique on large runs of color registers, a technique of color register animation can be achieved; but we'll talk about that in the next chapter.

Saving and Restoring the Palette

Many times during a game we may want to manipulate the color palette to achieve some effect. However, after this effect, we want the original color palette restored with its previous values. We have the functionality to do this. We only need to create functions that can read and write a set or range of color registers. To facilitate this we are going to add another data structure to our library, called *RGB_palette*. The structure will be used as a holding place for the RGB values of the color registers. Using the *RGB_palette* structure many palettes can be saved, loaded, and swapped in and out very rapidly. Being able to change palettes is very important in 3D games, especially when lighting effects are introduced. Here's what the *RGB_palette* structure looks like:

```
typedef struct RGB_palette_typ
      {
      int start_reg;   // index of the starting register that is saved
      int end_reg;     // index of the ending register that is saved
      RGB_color colors[256];   // the storage area for the palette
      } RGB_palette, *RGB_palette_ptr;
```

We're going to create two functions. One function will save a range of color registers from the VGA card and store them in the *RGB_palette* structure, and one function will restore or write a range of color registers from the *RGB_palette* structure to the VGA card. Let's take a look at the first function to save the color registers, shown in Listing 3-10.

LISTING 3-10 Function to save the color palette

```
void Read_Palette(int start_reg,int end_reg, RGB_palette_ptr the_palette)
{
// this function reads the palette registers in the range start_reg to
// end_reg and saves them into the appropriate positions in the_palette

int index; // used for looping

RGB_color color;

// read all the registers

for (index=start_reg; index<=end_reg; index++)
    {
    // read the color register

    Read_Color_Reg(index,(RGB_color_ptr)&color);

    // save it in database

    the_palette->colors[index].red   = color.red;
    the_palette->colors[index].green = color.green;
    the_palette->colors[index].blue  = color.blue;

    } // end for index

// save the interval of registers that were saved

the_palette->start_reg = start_reg;
the_palette->end_reg   = end_reg;

} // end Read_Palette
```

The *Read_Palette()* function takes as parameters the range of color registers to be saved and the palette structure that they should be stored in. The addition of a range to qualify a particular set of color registers allows the function to save only what it needs instead of the entire palette. For example, to save the first 128 color registers, we could write:

```
RGB_palette save;    // the palette that will hold the saved values
Read_Palette(0,127,(RGB_palette_ptr)&save);
```

To restore the palette we need a function to index through the range and then write each of the color registers with the saved data. This can be done by changing a couple lines in the *Read_Palette()* function to come up with the function in Listing 3-11.

LISTING 3-11 Function to restore a saved palette

```
void Write_Palette(int start_reg,int end_reg, RGB_palette_ptr the_palette)
{
// this function will write to the color registers using the data in the
// sent palette structure

int index; // used for looping

// write all the registers

for (index=start_reg; index<=end_reg; index++)
    {
    // write the color registers using the data from the sent palette

    Write_Color_Reg(index,(RGB_color_ptr)&(the_palette->colors[index]));

    } // end for index

} // end Write_Palette
```

As you can see, the *Write_Palette()* function is even simpler than the *Read_Palette()* function. Moreover, there is no reason why the *Write_Palette()* function needs to restore a previously saved palette. If you wish, you can simply create an artificial palette and use *Write_Palette()* to update the VGA's color registers.

Bitmapped Graphics Fundamentals

Using points and lines is fine for drawing very simple visual representations, but we need to evolve to something else if we're going to draw objects on the screen that have any complexity. The technique of *bitmapping* is well suited for this application. Bitmapping involves the translation of a matrix of cells into an image. For example, we might define a bitmapped object to be a matrix of 8x8 cells where each cell represents exactly one pixel. Therefore, the bitmapped object would contain a total of 8*8=64 pixels. In mode 13h, where each pixel is exactly 1 byte, we might have the following definition:

```
unsigned char bitmap[8][8]; // a 8x8 bitmap of bytes
```

FIGURE 3-19

An 8x8 bitmap representation of a man

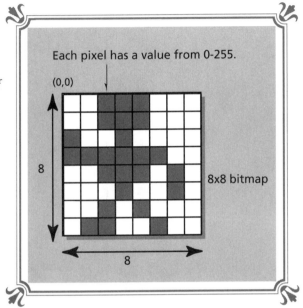

Each element of the bitmap represents the color of the pixel in that position. Figure 3-19 is an 8x8 bitmapped representation of a little man. To draw the bitmap, we construct a loop that will index into the bitmap array and, using the bitmap information, we can draw the image at any given (x,y) screen location. The following fragment of code will do just this.

```
for (y1=0; y1<8; y1++)
    for (x1=0; x1<8; x1++)
        if (bitmap[y1][x1]!=0)
            Write_Pixel(x+x1,y+y1,bitmap[y1][x1]);
```

The *if* statement takes care of transparency. This is needed since pixel values of 0 usually mean background or transparent. Hence, the areas of the bitmap that have 0's in them shouldn't be drawn. This is done by testing for 0's and not drawing anything if a cell location has a 0 within it. By doing this the background will show through the transparent portions of the bitmap being drawn. Figure 3-20 shows the results of bitmapping with and without transparency.

The preceding code fragment is theoretically correct and will work fine; however, it isn't the optimal way of doing things. For example, there is no need to call the *Write_Pixel()* function every iteration. The video buffer accessing could be done inline with the function.

Again, we will cover these aspects more closely in the next chapter. For now, at least we have the main idea behind bitmapped graphics. As an exercise using bitmapped techniques, let's see if we can draw some text on the screen.

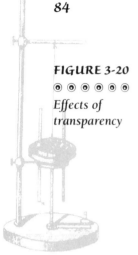

FIGURE 3-20

◉ ◉ ◉ ◉ ◉ ◉

Effects of
transparency

Drawing Text with Dots

The problem with drawing text in a video mode is that the text is drawn using hardware, as it is in the text modes. We must draw each character with individual pixels. These pixels are placed in such a way that they look like characters. Figure 3-21 shows the actual bitmap of a character *A*. To draw characters we are really drawing small bitmaps on the screen, where the bitmaps look like the characters in the ASCII character set. The only problem is, where do we get these bitmaps? We could draw them by hand. And this is a common practice, but very time consuming. Actually, in the games we'll make later, a hand-drawn, high tech-looking character set will be used along with an advanced text drawing engine. But for now let's see if we can't find any standard character bitmaps hiding anywhere in the PC.

The PC is full of wonderful data if you know where to look. Luckily for us there is a place deep within the id of the PC that the data for the character set can be found. One such data set is for the 8x8-pixel font and thus is fairly simplistic; but then again most games don't use complex fonts for text output. The format of the data is slightly compressed but nothing we can't handle. Since text fonts are monochrome, there is no reason to represent each pixel with a color descriptor or a whole byte. The PC's font engine only needs to know whether the pixel is on or off. Hence, each character is defined by 8 bytes where each byte is 1 row. Furthermore, the bits in the byte represent the pixels in the row, as shown in Figure 3-21. This bitwise compression isn't a problem, since we can use a bit mask to determine which bits are on and off and then use the results to draw the character pixel by pixel.

The actual data for the character set can be found at 0xF000:FA6Eh. The data is in ASCII order. Therefore, to find the 8 bytes that make up any character, you must

FIGURE 3-21

◎ ◎ ◎ ◎ ◎ ◎

Internal representation of the character A in the PC

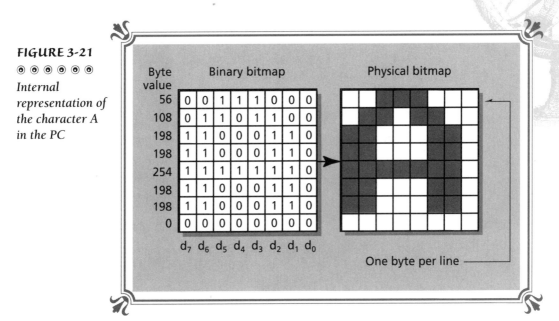

multiply the character's ASCII code by 8, and then add it to the starting point of the character bitmap data at 0xF000:FA6Eh to find the first row (byte) of character data for the character in question. Figure 3-22 is a visualization of the data layout of the PC's character set.

FIGURE 3-22

◎ ◎ ◎ ◎ ◎ ◎

Memory layout of the PC's character set

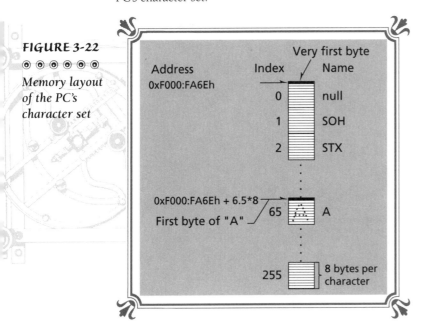

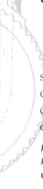

We know that each character is represented by 8 bytes and that each byte represents the 8 pixels on a row (each bit is 1 pixel). We also know the location in memory where the PC's ROM character set is; so let's write a function to draw text in any color at a given (x,y) screen location. First, here are a couple constants and a pointer to the ROM character set to make things more readable:

```
#define ROM_CHAR_SET_SEG 0xF000   // segment of 8x8 ROM character set
#define ROM_CHAR_SET_OFF 0xFA6E   // beginning offset of 8x8 ROM character set
unsigned char far *rom_char_set = (unsigned char far *)0xF000FA6EL;
```

Before we write the function, let's design its functionality. The function should take as parameters the character to print, its position on the screen, its color, and finally, a flag for whether the character should be drawn with black being transparent. The function that does the job is shown in Listing 3-12.

LISTING 3-12 Function to draw a character on the video screen using the ROM character set

```
void Print_Char(int xc,int yc,char c,int color,int transparent)
{
// this function is used to print a character on the screen. It uses the
// internal 8x8 character set to do this. Note that each character is
// 8 bytes where each byte represents the 8 pixels that make up the row
// of pixels

int offset,             // offset into video memory
    x,                  // loop variable
    y;                  // loop variable

unsigned char far *work_char; // pointer to character being printed

unsigned char bit_mask;       // bit mask used to extract proper bit

// compute starting offset in rom character lookup table
// multiply the character by 8 and add the result to the starting address
// of the ROM character set

work_char = rom_char_set + c * ROM_CHAR_HEIGHT;
// compute offset of character in video buffer, use shifting to multiply

offset = (yc << 8) + (yc << 6) + xc;

// draw the character row by row

for (y=0; y<ROM_CHAR_HEIGHT; y++)
    {
    // reset bit mask

    bit_mask = 0x80;

    // draw each pixel of this row
```

```
for (x=0; x<ROM_CHAR_WIDTH; x++)
    {
    // test for transparent pixel i.e. 0, if not transparent then draw

    if ((*work_char & bit_mask))
        video_buffer[offset+x] = (unsigned char)color;

    else
    if (!transparent)                    // takes care of transparency
        video_buffer[offset+x] = 0; // make black part opaque

    // shift bit mask

    bit_mask = (bit_mask>>1);

    } // end for x

// move to next line in video buffer and in rom character data area

offset      += MODE13_WIDTH;
work_char++;

    } // end for y

} // end Print_Char
```

The function begins by finding the data for the character to be printed in the PC's memory. Then the starting location for the character is computed in video memory. At this point, the rendering loop begins. The loop simply masks the current character row with a shifting bit mask that extracts a single bit and tests whether it's on and needs to be drawn. This is done eight times (once for each bit); then the data pointer moves to the next byte of the character. Then the video starting address is bumped down 320 bytes to the next line. This process is repeated eight times (once for each row of the character) and then terminates. Finally, as the rendering of the character is performed, each pixel is tested, based on the transparency flag, and the pixel is either drawn or ignored. This is a nice feature that allows you to draw text with an opaque background color or with a transparent background.

Drawing characters is good, but we can do better. Most of the time when text is printed it is printed in a string of characters; so let's put a shell around the *Print_Char()* function, allowing it to print out an entire string. Listing 3-13 shows a function to do just that.

LISTING 3-13 Printing an entire string one character at a time

```
void Print_String(int x,int y,int color, char *string,int transparent)
{
// this function prints an entire string on the screen with fixed spacing
// between each character by calling the Print_Char() function
```

continued on next page

continued from previous page

```
int index,    // loop index
    length;   // length of string

// compute length of string

length = strlen(string);

// print the string a character at a time

for (index=0; index<length; index++)
    Print_Char(x+(index<<3),y,string[index],color,transparent);

} // end Print_String
```

The *Print_String()* function has almost the same interface as the *Print_Char()* function, except that *Print_String()* takes as a parameter a pointer to a *NULL* terminated string instead of a single character. As usual these functions are in the library module of BLACK3.C, and any header information is in BLACK3.H.

Mode 13h in Action

We've learned about the memory configuration of mode 13h, its color abilities, and how to draw on the screen. Now it's time to see a demo of all the functions we've created thus far. As I said before, all the source for this chapter is on the CD-ROM, within the directory for this chapter. The files for today are named BLACK3.C and BLACK3.H. You'll need to compile BLACK3.C and create an object with it, or you can use the precompiled object on the disk to add to your growing library, BLACK-LIB.LIB. Do what makes you happy, but you will have to link the code in BLACK3.C to the following demo program to make it work. To run the demo, you can compile the code shown in Listing 3-14 (MODE13.C), or you can just use the precompiled executable on the disk named MODE13.EXE.

LISTING 3-14 *Demonstration of all the graphics calls*

```
// MODE13.C - A demo of all the mode 13h functions for this chapter

// I N C L U D E S //////////////////////////////////////////////////////////

#include <io.h>
#include <conio.h>
#include <stdio.h>
#include <stdlib.h>
#include <dos.h>
#include <bios.h>
#include <fcntl.h>
#include <memory.h>
#include <malloc.h>
```

```
#include <math.h>
#include <string.h>

#include "black3.h"    // the header file for this module

// M A I N /////////////////////////////////////////////////////////////////

void main(int argc, char **argv)
{

RGB_color color;  // used as temporary color variable
int index;        // used for looping
RGB_palette save_palette;  // used to save the palette
printf("/nHit any key to switch to mode 13h");
getch();

// set the graphics mode to mode 13h

Set_Graphics_Mode(GRAPHICS_MODE13);

// show some text

Print_String(0,0,15,"Hit a key to see text printing          ",0);
getch();

// print a few hundred strings on the screen

for (index=0; index<1000; index++)
    Print_String(rand()%(320-256),rand()%190,rand()%256,
                 "This is a demo of text printing",1);

Print_String(0,0,15,"Hit a key to see screen filling         ",0);
getch();

// fill the screen dark grey

Fill_Screen(8);
Print_String(0,0,15,"Hit a key to see pixel plotting         ",0);
getch();

// plot 10000 random pixels

for (index=0; index<10000; index++)
    Write_Pixel(rand()%320,rand()%200,12);

Print_String(0,0,15,"Hit a key to see lines                  ",0);
getch();

// draw 1000 randomly positioned horizontal and vertical lines

for (index=0; index<1000; index++)
    {
```

continued on next page

continued from previous page

```
    Line_H(rand()%320,rand()%320,rand()%200,rand()%256);
    Line_V(rand()%200,rand()%200,rand()%320,rand()%256);
    } // end for index

Print_String(0,0,15,"Hit a key to change color registers   ",0);
getch();

// save the palette

Read_Palette(0,255,(RGB_palette_ptr)&save_palette);

// change the palette

for (index=0; index<256; index++)
    {
    // set the color to bright green

    color.red   = 0;
    color.green = 63;
    color.blue  = 0;

    // change the currently indexed color register

    Write_Color_Reg(index,(RGB_color_ptr)&color);

    // let user see it happen

    Time_Delay(1);

    } // end for index

// make color 15 visible so user can read text

color.red   = 63;
color.green = 63;
color.blue  = 63;
Write_Color_Reg(15,(RGB_color_ptr)&color);

Print_String(0,0,15,"Hit a key to restore palette           ",0);
getch();

// restore the palette

Write_Palette(0,255,(RGB_palette_ptr)&save_palette);

Print_String(0,0,15,"Hit a key to switch back to text mode  ",0);
getch();

// restore graphics mode to text

Set_Graphics_Mode(TEXT_MODE);

} // end main
```

The program will query you to hit any key to progress through the different parts of the demo. Admittedly, the demo doesn't do much, but then again we're just getting started. Its main purpose is to let you play with the functions and see how they're used in the context of a program.

The Dark Secrets of the
X-tended Graphics Modes

At the writing of this book a nonstandard video mode named *mode X* was very popular. Although there are a couple of video modes referred to as mode X, the most accepted one is the 320x240 version with 256 colors. Of course, mode X and any other mutations of the VGA card's standard graphics modes are not supported by BIOS or the standard C/C++ libraries. We must reprogram that VGA ourselves to make it work.

The beauty of mode X is its 1:1 aspect ratio, meaning that pixels are square. This is true since the ratio of the X axis resolution to the Y axis resolution is 320/240=1.33, which is equal to the video screen's aspect ratio of 4:3=1.33. Square pixels make everything look better, especially when rotating objects. When a 1:1 aspect ratio exists, there isn't any stretching in a single axis during rotation. The second attractive feature of mode X is that it allows for multiple video pages (unlike mode 13h, which only has one video page). Having multiple video pages allows for flicker-free animation using a technique called *page flipping* (which we'll cover later).

The only downfall of mode X (other than the difficulty in finding information on how to generate it) is its inherent planar configuration. There are four memory planes, each containing a different portion of the final image. Luckily there is still a single byte per pixel, and the color descriptors aren't strewn about over all the planes; but the planar architecture makes mode X slower than mode 13h as far as access time is concerned. The major difference is that the proper plane must be selected before the video buffer is accessed. This added step can be optimized and, if done sparingly, it is almost transparent; but nevertheless it's still there.

Mode X and most other 256-color mutations of the VGA card use the standard settings of mode 13h as a foundation. Modifications are made to the configurations of the graphics controller, CRT controller, and sequencer to generate the proper memory configuration, addressing, and timing of the desired mode. We aren't going to learn all the intricacies of VGA programming. But we are going to learn how to specifically reprogram the VGA for a mode I call mode Z. For example, when using the video BIOS *INT 10h* to place the VGA into mode 13h, we don't worry too much about how it works; so let's keep the same point of view with the extended mode Z.

With that in mind we're going to learn how to tweak the VGA into a graphics mode that is similar to mode X except that it has 400 lines of resolution.

Introduction to Mode Z

In the near future people are going to want still higher resolutions than the 320x240 of mode X. The next step is to push the VGA to 320x400 in 256 colors. This is easy to do using mode 13h as a starting point and then making some modifications to the VGA to support the mode. The major problem with a 320x400-resolution graphics mode is that the amount of memory necessary to support this resolution is 320*400=128,000 bytes. This is far too much to be addressed by the standard VGA's hardware without using a planar memory configuration. Remember, the largest amount of memory that the VGA can address in a single plane is 64,000 bytes, which is what mode 13h uses.

Hence, mode 13h is the best possible resolution we can get out of the VGA with 256 colors and a totally linear address space. We can implement mode Z by reprogramming some of the registers in the VGA to coerce mode 13h into a 320x400, 256 color mode with multiple planes. This is actually quite easy since mode 13h is really a 400-line mode already! The fact of the matter is that the VGA has been told to double-scan each line. In essence, every two scan lines have been tied together to decrease the vertical resolution. Figure 3-23 shows the relationship between the number of video scan lines and screen scan lines in mode 13h. Placing the VGA into mode Z is accomplished in two steps:

1. Place the VGA into the standard mode 13h using BIOS.

2. Reprogram the VGA registers to change the addressing, number of scan lines, and memory configuration for four planes with 256 colors.

Placing the VGA into mode 13h is easy—it's done with a call to BIOS via our function *Set_Graphics_Mode()*. The hard part is reprogramming the VGA's registers in the proper way to generate mode Z. A full explanation of the changes that must be made to the VGA's registers are far beyond the scope of this book. But not to worry, the function we'll see in a minute will take care of the details of placing the VGA into mode Z.

The Memory Configuration

Before we place the PC into mode Z, let's discuss the actual memory configuration and see how to plot pixels. Mode Z is composed of four planes. Each plane holds one-quarter of the final image that will be displayed. Moreover, each pixel in each plane is defined by a single byte, so there is a one-to-one relationship between pixels and bytes. Figure 3-24 shows a visual representation of the four planes and their interrelationships. Each memory plane can be accessed at segment 0xA000:0000 - 0xA000:7CFFh; in other words, each plane spans 32,000 bytes. However, all the

FIGURE 3-23

◉ ◉ ◉ ◉ ◉ ◉

*Relationship
between screen
scan lines and
video scan lines*

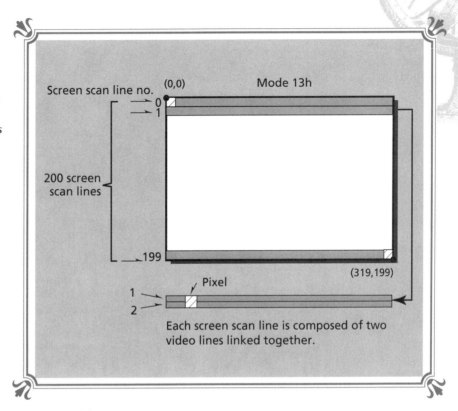

planes are accessed in the same address range. Writing to one memory location in the range of 0xA000:0000 – 0xA000:7CFFh writes to all four planes in parallel! This means that we must select which planes the CPU has access to using some aspect of the VGA's hardware. This is called *plane selection* and can be accomplished with the sequencer on the VGA. There is a register called the *plane select register* or *plane enable register*, depending on what reference you read. This register uses a bit pattern to select which planes will be written to by the CPU. Figure 3-25 shows the bitmapping of the plane select register. By controlling the plane select register (which exists at I/O port 0x3C4h index 0x02), we can control the plane that the CPU writes to.

The final question is, what's the relationship between screen coordinates and memory? The relationship is similar to the one in mode 13h with a couple differences. If you recall, given a point (x,y) in screen coordinates, the memory offset for mode 13h can be computed using this formula:

offset=y*320+x

FIGURE 3-24
◎ ◎ ◎ ◎ ◎ ◎
*Memory mapping
of mode Z*

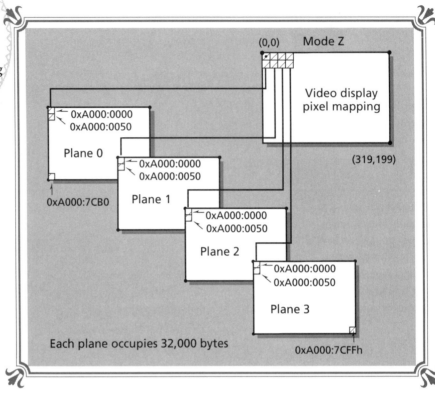

Of course, this offset is relative to the beginning of the video memory at 0xA000:0000h. To arrive at the formula for mode Z we must understand how pixels are mapped in mode Z. Referring to Figure 3-24, we see that each plane consists of a specific group of pixels. Here are the pixel distributions for the four memory planes:

Plane 0 contains the pixels that have X coordinates 0, 4, 8, 12, 16, and so forth.
Plane 1 contains the pixels that have X coordinates 1, 5, 9, 13, 17, and so forth.
Plane 2 contains the pixels that have X coordinates 2, 6, 10, 14, 18, and so forth.
Plane 3 contains the pixels that have X coordinates 3, 7, 11,15, 19, and so forth.

Even though there are 320 columns or pixels per row, there are only 80 pixels per memory plane row. Therefore the Y coordinate, instead of being multiplied by 320 (as it was for mode 13h), must be multiplied by 80. Furthermore, the X coordinate needs to be divided by 4. Taking these two factors into consideration, the final offset address in the video buffer for a point with screen coordinates (x,y) is:

offset=y*80+x/4

FIGURE 3-25

◎ ◎ ◎ ◎ ◎ ◎

*Bit definition for
the color plane
select register*

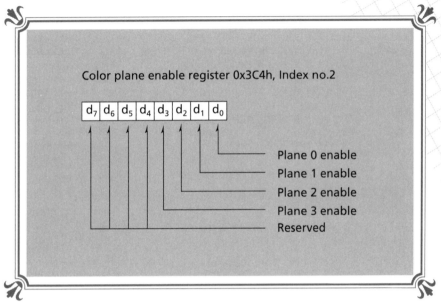

FIGURE 3-25

◎ ◎ ◎ ◎ ◎ ◎

*Bit definition for
the color plane
select register*

Now if we were to write a pixel into memory at this location relative to the start of video memory, we would have one slight problem—up to four pixels would be drawn! This is because we must first select the proper memory plane. This is done by using the X coordinate in the following formula to find the proper plane:

plane = X MOD 4

Then *plane* is used to set the bit in the plane select register, and the CPU write can take place.

To recapitulate the process, you take the screen location (x,y) and find the offset from video memory by multiplying Y by 80 and then adding that to X divided by 4. Then the proper plane is selected by turning on the appropriate bit in the sequencer's plane select register, which was found by *MOD*ing X by 4. That's about it.

Switching to Mode Z

It's time for some action! Let's see how to put the VGA into mode Z. To do this, I have created a function called *Set_Mode_Z()*. The function is only a few lines long but uses quite a few constants and identifiers to access the registers in the VGA card. To eliminate confusion as you analyze the function, here are the constants that have been defined in BLACK3.H to make the function body clearer:

```
// the VGA card controller ports

#define SEQUENCER              0x3C4    // the sequencer's index port
#define CRT_CONTROLLER         0x3D4    // the crt controller's index port
#define GFX_CONTROLLER         0x3CE    // the graphics controller's index port
#define ATTR_CONTROLLER_FF     0x3DA    // the attribute controller's Flip Flop
#define ATTR_CONTROLLER_DATA   0x3C0    // the attribute controller's data port

// defines for the CRT controller registers of interest

#define CRT_MAX_SCANLINE       0x09    // the maximum scanline register
                                       // used to select how many scanlines
                                       // per row

#define CRT_ADDR_MODE          0x14    // the address mode register
                                       // used to select byte addressing
                                       // for VGA
                                       // also known as the underline register

#define CRT_MODE_CONTROL       0x17    // the mode control register
                                       // used to select single byte addressing


// defines for the GFX controller registers of interest
#define GFX_WRITE_MODE         0x05    // the memory write mode register
                                       // used to deselect even/odd plane
                                       // addressing

#define GFX_MISC               0x06    // the miscellaneous register
                                       // used to deselect the chaining
                                       // of memory

// defines for the SEQUENCER registers of interest

#define SEQ_PLANE_ENABLE       0x02    // plane enable register, used to select
                                       // which planes are written to by a
                                       // CPU write

#define SEQ_MEMORY_MODE        0x04    // the memory mode register
                                       // used to deselect memory chain mode
                                       // and odd/even memory addressing

// M A C R O S /////////////////////////////////////////////////////////////

#define SET_BITS(x,bits)   (x | bits)  // used to set bits in word
#define RESET_BITS(x,bits) (x & ~bits) // used to reset bits in a word
```

Based on these defines and macros, Listing 3-15 contains the function that will put the VGA into mode Z.

LISTING 3-15 Function to place the VGA in mode Z

```
void Set_Mode_Z(void)
{
// this function will set the video mode to 320x400x256
int data;   // used to store data

// set system to mode 13h and use it as a foundation to base 320x400 mode on
_asm
   {
   mov ax,0013h  ; ah=function number 00(set graphics mode), al=13h
   int 10h       ; video interrupt 10h
   } // end asm

// make changes to the crt controller first

// set number of scanlines to 1
_outp(CRT_CONTROLLER,CRT_MAX_SCANLINE);
data=_inp(CRT_CONTROLLER+1);
_outp(CRT_CONTROLLER+1,RESET_BITS(data,0x0f));

// use byte addressing instead of word
_outp(CRT_CONTROLLER,CRT_ADDR_MODE);
data=_inp(CRT_CONTROLLER+1);
_outp(CRT_CONTROLLER+1,RESET_BITS(data,0x40));
// second register that needs to reflect byte addressing
_outp(CRT_CONTROLLER,CRT_MODE_CONTROL);
data=_inp(CRT_CONTROLLER+1);
_outp(CRT_CONTROLLER+1,SET_BITS(data,0x40));

// make changes to graphics controller

// set addressing to not use odd/even memory writes
_outp(GFX_CONTROLLER,GFX_WRITE_MODE);
data=_inp(GFX_CONTROLLER+1);
_outp(GFX_CONTROLLER+1,RESET_BITS(data,0x10));

// don't chain the memory maps together
_outp(GFX_CONTROLLER,GFX_MISC);
data=_inp(GFX_CONTROLLER+1);
_outp(GFX_CONTROLLER+1,RESET_BITS(data,0x02));

// make changes to sequencer

// again we must select no chaining and no odd/even memory addressing
_outp(SEQUENCER,SEQ_MEMORY_MODE);
data =_inp(SEQUENCER+1);
data = RESET_BITS(data,0x08);
data = SET_BITS(data,0x04);
_outp(SEQUENCER+1,data);
```

continued on next page

continued from previous page

```
// now clear the screen
_outp(SEQUENCER,SEQ_PLANE_ENABLE);
_outp(SEQUENCER+1,0x0f);

// clear the screen, remember it is 320x400, but that is divided into four
// planes, hence we need only to clear 32k out since there are four planes
// each being cleared in parallel for a total of 4*32k or 128 = 320x400
// note: "k" in this example means 1000 not 1024

_asm
   {
   les di,video_buffer      ; point es:di to video buffer, same address for mode Z
   xor ax,ax                ; move a zero into al and ah
   mov cx,320*400/8         ; number of words to fill(using word is faster than bytes)
   rep stosw                ; move the color into the video buffer really fast!
   } // end inline asm

} // end Set_Mode_Z
```

The function has three specific phases of operation. The first phase uses the video BIOS interrupt to place the VGA into mode 13h. Then the necessary changes are made to the VGA's registers to place the VGA into mode Z, and finally, the video memory is cleared. You will notice that only 32,000 bytes of memory are cleared. In actuality a total of 128,000 bytes are cleared since all four planes are accessed in parallel, but only 32,000 bytes are written (or 16,000 words). This is made possible by the VGA's hardware assistance in memory addressing! So, you see that mode Z's video memory can be cleared twice as fast as mode 13h's, which is another advantage of mode Z over mode 13h.

Although we'll be using mode 13h as the primary graphics mode for this book (due to its overall simplicity), mode Z will be discussed from time to time. To facilitate these discussions, we're going to write a few basic routines for mode Z. You can use them to experiment with it and get an overall idea of its appearance and performance.

Clearing the Mode Z Screen

Clearing the screen in mode Z is similar to mode 13h. A region of memory will be cleared (actually filled with a value) using a memory movement operation. The only difference is that the plane select register within the sequencer must be set to enable access to all four planes simultaneously. This is done by writing a 0x0Fh into the plane select register. Actually, this was done at the end of the *Set_Mode_Z()* function to clear out the video buffer. The only difference is that *Set_Mode_Z()* filled the video buffer with 0's. A general clear screen function should clear the screen with any value from 0 to 255. The function is shown in Listing 3-16.

LISTING 3-16 Screen filling function for mode Z

```
void Fill_Screen_Z(int color)
{
// this function will fill the mode Z video buffer with the sent color

// use the inline assembler for speed
_asm
   {
   mov dx,SEQUENCER              ; address the sequencer
   mov al,SEQ_PLANE_ENABLE       ; select the plane enable register
   mov ah,0fh                    ; enable all four planes
   out dx,ax                     ; do it baby!
   les di,video_buffer      ; point es:di to video buffer
   mov al,BYTE PTR color    ; move the color into al and ah
   mov ah,al                     ; replicate color into ah
   mov cx,320*400/8              ; number of words to fill(using word is faster than bytes)
   rep stosw                     ; move the color into the video buffer really fast!
   } // end inline asm

} // end Fill_Screen_Z
```

Plotting Z Pixels

We already have all the information we need to plot a pixel in mode Z. Let's review the algorithm.

1. Compute the video offset by multiplying Y by 80 and adding that to X divided by 4.

2. Select the proper plane in the plane select register. The plane 0-3 can be computed as X *MOD* 4.

3. Write the desired value into video memory.

The function we will write will have a couple tricks in it, such as quick shifting to do multiplication and using logical *AND* to perform the *MOD*. Listing 3-17 shows the function to plot a pixel in any color.

LISTING 3-17 Plotting a pixel in mode Z

```
void Write_Pixel_Z(int x,int y,int color)
{

// this function will write a pixel to screen in mode Z

// first select the proper color plane. Use inline for speed.
// if we used C then there would be a function call and about 10-15 more
// instructions!
```

continued on next page

continued from previous page

```asm
_asm
   {
   mov dx,SEQUENCER           ; address the sequencer
   mov al,SEQ_PLANE_ENABLE    ; select the plane enable register
   mov cl,BYTE PTR x          ; extract lower byte from x
   and cl,03h                 ; extract the plane number = x MOD 4
   mov ah,1                   ; a "1" selects the plane in the plane enable
   shl ah,cl                  ; shift the "1" bit proper number of times
   out dx,ax                  ; do it baby!
   } // end asm
// write the pixel, offset = (y*320+x)/4

video_buffer[(y<<6)+(y<<4)+(x>>2)] = (unsigned char )color;

} // end Write_Pixel_Z
```

The first part of the function selects the proper memory plane, and the second part writes into video memory. The inline assembly is the only part that could be a source of confusion, so let's see what it's doing. First, the sequencer's I/O port address is placed into *DX*, and the register index of the plane select register is placed in *AL*. Then we perform a bit of sorcery. The lower byte of x is placed into *CL* and then logically *AND*ed with 0x03h. This is equivalent to *MOD*ing X by 4. The result in *CL* is then used to shift a "1" bit to the left a number of times equal to the result of the *MOD* operation. The result of the shift is used to select which plane is written to. Remember, when selecting a plane, it is not the number of the plane that is placed in the plane select register, but the bit number from 0 to 3 is enabled to write to planes 0 to 3. This bit configuration allows more than one plane to be enabled at once. Hence, only the bits d0 through d3 are of importance in the plane select register.

We take two performance hits when writing directly to mode Z. The first hit is dividing X by 4 and shifting the plane select mask. The second hit is the actual I/O write to the plane select register, which is very slow. Therefore, as far as writing single pixels, mode Z is a bit slower. However, when performing bitmapped graphics, mode Z is almost as fast as mode 13h (as long as each plane is written to in an intelligent manner). If functions are written properly, the plane select mask need only be changed four times per bitmapped object.

We'll be making observations throughout the book on how mode 13h and mode Z compare in different operations, to come up with an overall best solution depending on the application.

Page Flipping

The other very important asset of mode Z is that it can support two video pages. This allows us to update one page while the other is being displayed. With page flipping we can display one screen while preparing the next frame on the invisible page, and then swap pages. This swap occurs instantaneously, and the result is flicker-free animation—a vital feature of 3D video games. The user must never see the video image being drawn! Figure 3-26 is a pictorial representation of page flipping. It shows one page being updated while another is being drawn. Then the pages are flipped and their roles are reversed.

Mode 13h doesn't support page flipping. Only one video page can be accessed by the VGA hardware since the size of the video buffer is 64,000 bytes. On the other hand, mode Z's video buffer of 32,000 bytes (times 4 planes) allows two pages to fit nicely in the 64K video memory region of 0xA000:0000–0xA000:FFFFh. Figure 3-27 shows the memory layout of a two-page mode Z system. In the next chapter, we will cover page flipping in more detail and see an actual example, but for now you just need to know the basic idea behind it.

Mode Z in Action

We didn't write many functions for mode Z (only a couple of them). To be complete, the program in Listing 3-18 clears the screen, fills it with colored dots, and then swipes the screen image to blackness. The name of the program is MODEZ.C, and the precompiled executable is called MODEZ.EXE. The program uses the library module BLACK3.C and the related header file BLACK3.H.

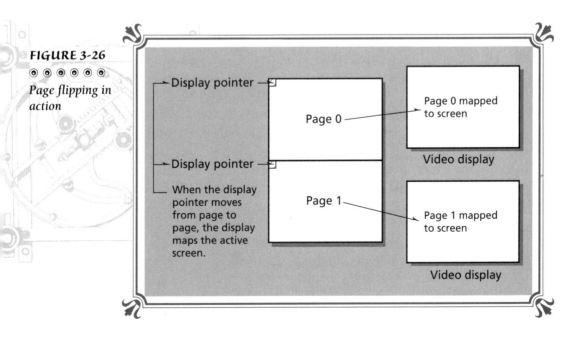

FIGURE 3-26
◉ ◉ ◉ ◉ ◉ ◉
Page flipping in action

FIGURE 3-27

◉ ◉ ◉ ◉ ◉ ◉

The two pages of mode Z

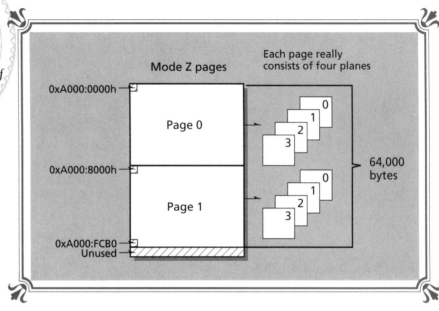

LISTING 3-18 Demo of mode Z (320x400 in 256 colors)

```c
// MODEZ.C - A demo of mode Z (320x400x256)

// I N C L U D E S /////////////////////////////////////////////////////////////

#include <io.h>
#include <conio.h>
#include <stdio.h>
#include <stdlib.h>
#include <dos.h>
#include <bios.h>
#include <fcntl.h>
#include <memory.h>
#include <malloc.h>
#include <math.h>
#include <string.h>

#include "black3.h"

// M A I N /////////////////////////////////////////////////////////////////////

void main(int argc, char **argv)
{
int index, // loop variables
    x,y,
    color; // holds the current color
```

```
// set the graphics mode to mode Z 320x400x256

Set_Mode_Z();

// fill the screen with dark grey

Fill_Screen_Z(8);

// plot 1000 pixels in each of the colors

for (color=1; color<256; color++)
    for (index=0; index<1000; index++)
        Write_Pixel_Z(rand()%320,rand()%400,color);
// wipe screen

for (index=320; index>=0; index--)
    for (y=0; y<400; y++)
        Write_Pixel_Z(index,y,0);

// restore the video system to text

Set_Graphics_Mode(TEXT_MODE);

} // end main
```

As a final note, the imagery produced using mode Z can be strikingly realistic. This is due to the strong connection made with Cyberspace through the reprogramming of the VGA card. So, caution must be used with this mode to make sure that it doesn't fall into the wrong hands! GIF files look really real, if you know what I mean.

Summary

In this chapter we learned about the most important link to Cyberspace that a Cybersorcerer can master, and that is the control of the VGA card. We learned how to place the VGA into mode 13h and manipulate the video buffer. Then we discussed some possible optimizations that should be taken into consideration when performing graphics, such as word-size writes and fast multiplies. Finally, we covered a new mode of operation of the VGA deemed mode Z. It supports 256 colors and has a resolution of 320x400, twice that of mode 13h! Moreover, it supports two video pages, making the animation technique of page flipping possible. Now we're ready to delve deeper into the darkness of bitmapped graphics and animation. Put another dash of bats' brains into the cauldron and turn the page …

4

Waking the Dead with Animation

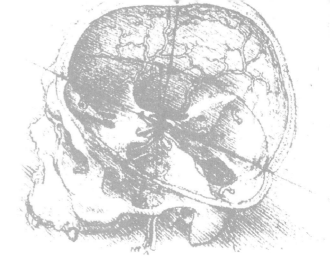

Waking the Dead with Animation

We now have the power to open the gateway to Cyberspace using the VGA card to create a subspace distortion field. We can project images from Cyberspace to the PC and display them on the monitor. The next step in our evolution of Cybersorcery is to learn how to animate these objects—or in other words, how to bring them to life. Animation is the technique of moving objects around on the screen and changing their form as a function of time. In the 3D games we'll create, most of these objects will be polygon based. However, as an introduction to animation, we will start with 2D objects and bitmaps to gain a firm grasp on the basic concepts. Moreover, there are many uses for 2D animation in a 3D game. Bitmapped animation is commonly mixed with 3D graphics to create special effects such as explosions, instrument panels, and more.

Introduction to Animation

Animation is a broad term and has many meanings. In the context of video games it generally means to move objects around on the screen in real-time. The objects can be 2D, 3D, or a mixture of both. However, the steps you take to accomplish animation are relatively the same regardless of dimensionality. Animation for computer

FIGURE 4-1

◎ ◎ ◎ ◎ ◎ ◎

*The logical
screen layout*

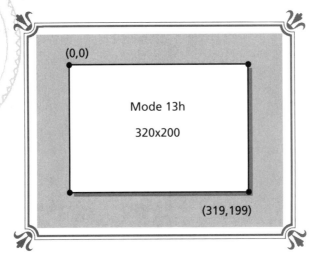

games is performed a frame at a time. The position and state of the player and the other elements of the game are used to draw the view of the universe a number of times a second, similar to a movie. Most games have a frame rate of 15 to 30 FPS (frames per second). As the frames are displayed, the objects in the universe move and change. This is what we call *animation.*

In a 3D game the images we draw will represent the player's universe and objects within it. We will render these images using polygons or flat facets to approximate the objects in the universe. But before we learn about 3D animation, we will start off with something that is a bit easier to understand such as 2D bitmapped graphics. The concepts we learn for 2D animation will all transfer over to 3D. Moreover, we're going to need 2D bitmapped graphics in our 3D games anyway, so now is a good time to learn.

For our discussions of animation we will always refer to the computer display in screen coordinates. In other words, the origin of the screen is at (0,0) located at the upper-left corner of the screen, and the bottom-right corner of the screen is (319,199). Figure 4-1 shows a representation of this. Note that 320x200 is the resolution of mode 13h, which is what we'll be working with for the most part.

The Animation Cycle

We have learned how to plot pixels and perform simple text bitmapped graphics, but how are objects moved and animated? Like anything else in life, objects are moved and animated by following a sequence of steps:

Method I: Animation Cycle for Backgrounds of Solid Color

1. Erase the object.

2. Move the object to another location.

3. Draw the object.

4. Repeat process.

Figure 4-2 shows a small ship being moved using this technique. Now there are some details we should discuss. For example, the first step of erasing the object can be accomplished in many ways. The object could be drawn in the background color and that would erase it, but it would erase any image in the background! Say we want to animate a little man walking across a street scene. The street scene would be drawn on the screen and should be static. When we went to animate the little man, the first step of the animation cycle would erase the object. During this erasure, the image of the street at the location of the man would be obliterated. To solve this problem, we must refine what we mean by erase.

If objects are going to be animated on top of a predrawn background, then whenever the objects are drawn, the imagery under them must be saved. During the erasure phase, instead of drawing the object with background color, the imagery that was previously under the object is restored, and in one operation the object is erased and the background is replaced. This is the way nondestructive animation works. The background under an object is scanned, and then the object is

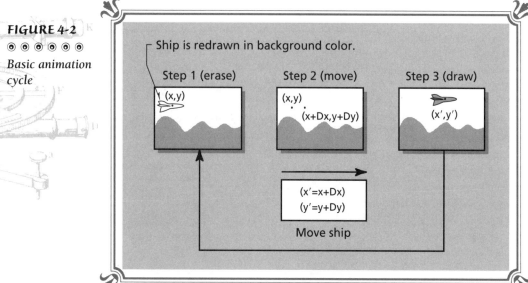

FIGURE 4-2

◎ ◎ ◎ ◎ ◎ ◎

Basic animation cycle

drawn at its new position. When it's time to move the object, the background is replaced and the cycle starts over. Hence, the new sequence of steps to perform proper animation:

Method II: Animation Cycle for Backgrounds with Images

1. Replace background previously scanned where object was drawn.

2. Move the object.

3. Scan background under object.

4. Draw object.

5. Repeat the process.

The only unanswered detail is, how can we replace the background on the first cycle when the background hasn't been scanned? Well, it's performed as part of the startup or initialization of the object's animation. Before the object is animated and the loop is entered, the background is scanned. You can think of this as step 0. Figure 4-3 shows the new animation process in action.

In general, Method II is usually used in games that have some kind of predrawn background. However, in 3D games, there isn't a background most of the time since the entire world is redrawn every frame. There is no compelling reason to scan the background, since it is continually changing. If the background changes every frame, steps 0, 1, and 3 can be deleted. All that must be done to move and animate the object is to draw it over the newly drawn background every frame. This is a

FIGURE 4-3

◎ ◎ ◎ ◎ ◎ ◎

Complete animation cycle

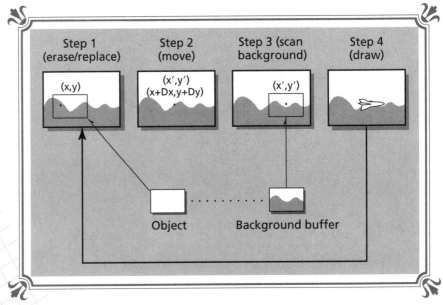

very important factor because deleting those three steps speeds up the rendering quite a bit. We will see demonstrations of both of these techniques later in the chapter.

Another aspect of animation we need to consider here is *flicker.* Flicker is a term used in computer graphics to describe an annoying aspect of animation: seeing the objects being drawn and erased. If you animate the objects in the video buffer itself, it's possible that the user will "see" the objects being erased and drawn since the VGA hardware is constantly accessing the video buffer and using it to draw the screen. The solution is to draw each frame of animation in an invisible work. There are two main ways to do this. The first is with *double buffering,* which we will use for the remainder of the book and discuss shortly. The second method is page flipping, which is very similar but a bit more hardware dependent (as we saw using mode Z). We won't be using page flipping for the animation in this book; but as I promised, there will be a demo of it supporting mode Z at the end of the chapter, so you can see what it is.

Before we dive off the deep end and get into a mega high-tech discussion, let's digress for a second and talk about some of the more aesthetic aspects of a video game.

Cutting to Another Screen

You've just written a cool game and it's almost ready to put on the market, but it has one flaw: every time the scenery changes or a new display comes up, there is an abrupt change instead of a smooth transition. Just as movies have screen fades, wipes, and other special effects, a game should too. These screen transitions are used when there is a change of universe or environment, for example. They're just a nice way to make an entrance or an exit. Screen transitions usually operate directly in the video buffer and manipulate the image that's within it. For example, you can dissolve the image in the video buffer by plotting colored pixels randomly, fade the lights by decreasing the values in the color registers slowly, or do something else more creative.

With that in mind, let's write a function that takes as a parameter the screen transition that we want it to perform. The function will then perform the screen transition and return. We'll use the screen transition function in the demos for this chapter, allowing them to make graceful exits when complete. We'll name the function *Screen_Transition(),* and it will take a single parameter that commands it to do a specific effect. The effects supported are defined below:

```
// screen transition commands

#define SCREEN_DARKNESS    0      // fade to black
#define SCREEN_WHITENESS   1      // fade to white
#define SCREEN_WARP        2      // warp the screen image
```

continued on next page

continued from previous page

```
#define SCREEN_SWIPE_X    3        // do a horizontal swipe
#define SCREEN_SWIPE_Y    4        // do a vertical swipe
#define SCREEN_DISSOLVE   5        // a pixel dissolve
```

The result of each of the effects should be obvious from the names given to them except for *SCREEN_WARP*. The code for this one has been left blank, and you get to put in your own transition! Listing 4-1 shows the code for the screen transition function.

LISTING 4-1 A screen transition function

```
void Screen_Transition(int effect)
{
// this function can be called to perform a myriad of screen transitions
// to the video buffer, note I have left one for you to create!

int pal_reg;       //  used as loop counter
long index;        // used as loop counter
RGB_color color;   // temporary color

// test which screen effect is being selected

switch(effect)
     {
     case SCREEN_DARKNESS:
          {
          // fade to black
          for (index=0; index<20; index++)
               {
               // loop thru all palette registers

               for (pal_reg=1; pal_reg<255; pal_reg++)
                    {
                    // get the next color to fade
                    Read_Color_Reg(pal_reg,(RGB_color_ptr)&color);

                    // test if this color register is already black
                    if (color.red > 4) color.red-=3;
                    else
                       color.red = 0;

                    if (color.green > 4) color.green-=3;
                    else
                       color.green = 0;

                    if (color.blue  > 4) color.blue-=3;
                    else
                       color.blue = 0;

                    // set the color to a diminished intensity
                    Write_Color_Reg(pal_reg,(RGB_color_ptr)&color);
```

```
                    } // end for pal_reg

            // wait a bit
            Time_Delay(1);

            } // end for index

        } break;

case SCREEN_WHITENESS:
        {
        // fade to white

        for (index=0; index<20; index++)
            {
            // loop thru all palette registers
            for (pal_reg=0; pal_reg<255; pal_reg++)
                {
                // get the color to fade
                Read_Color_Reg(pal_reg,(RGB_color_ptr)&color);
                color.red+=4;

                if (color.red > 63)
                   color.red = 63;

                color.green+=4;

                if (color.green > 63)
                   color.green = 63;

                color.blue+=4;

                if (color.blue >63)
                   color.blue = 63;

                // set the color to a brighter intensity
                Write_Color_Reg(pal_reg,(RGB_color_ptr)&color);

                } // end for pal_reg

            // wait a bit
            Time_Delay(1);

            } // end for index

        } break;
case SCREEN_WARP:
        {
        // this one you do!!!!
        } break;

case SCREEN_SWIPE_X:
```

continued on next page

continued from previous page

```
        {
        // do a screen swipe from right to left, left to right
        for (index=0; index<160; index+=2)
            {
            // use this as a 1/70th of second time delay
            Wait_For_Vertical_Retrace();

            // draw two vertical lines at opposite ends of the screen
            Line_V(0,199,319-index,0);
            Line_V(0,199,index,0);
            Line_V(0,199,319-(index+1),0);
            Line_V(0,199,index+1,0);
            } // end for index

        } break;

case SCREEN_SWIPE_Y:
        {
        // do a screen swipe from top to bottom, bottom to top
        for (index=0; index<100; index+=2)
            {
            // use this as a 1/70th of second time delay
            Wait_For_Vertical_Retrace();

            // draw two horizontal lines at opposite ends of the screen
            Line_H(0,319,199-index,0);
            Line_H(0,319,index,0);
            Line_H(0,319,199-(index+1),0);
            Line_H(0,319,index+1,0);

            } // end for index

        } break;


case SCREEN_DISSOLVE:
        {
        // dissolve the screen by plotting zillions of little black dots
        for (index=0; index<=300000; index++)
            Write_Pixel(rand()%320,rand()%200, 0);
        } break;

default:break;

} // end switch

} // end Screen_Transition
```

You will find the function code and header information in the library modules BLACK4.C and BLACK4.H. Let's take a quick look at how each of the transitions works.

SCREEN_DARKNESS—This screen transition works by decrementing the RGB values of all the color registers repeatedly until each color register has a value that is near black (0,0,0). This has the effect of dimming the lights.

SCREEN_WHITENESS—The effect is the opposite of the fade to black transition. Instead of decrementing the RGB values of each color register, this transition increments them until they reach a maximum of pure white (63,63,63). This transition has the effect of being blinded by light.

SCREEN_WARP—This transition is meant for you to implement. Try to implement a kind of vortex that sucks the screen image into a single point.

SCREEN_SWIPE_X—This simple effect is achieved by performing a slow clear screen using vertical black lines that move toward the center from the edges of the screen. The function uses the *Line_V()* call and looks like a black door is being closed, obscuring the image.

SCREEN_SWIPE_Y—This is identical to the previous transition except it is done in the vertical direction instead of the horizontal by use of *Line_H()*.

SCREEN_DISSOLVE—This is a favorite of mine, probably because it's so easy to implement and looks cool. The effect is achieved by plotting 300,000 black pixels. As the pixels are drawn, the screen image is slowly "eroded" and finally disappears.

Now that we have a cool way to exit our animation demos and games let's see how to actually implement animation.

Double Buffering

As I said, we will be using a double buffer animation system. In essence this means that we will build the next frame of animation in an invisible buffer offscreen. Then to draw the next video frame, we will copy the data from the double buffer to the video buffer using a high-speed *memcpy()* function. Although this means that we need an extra buffer of 64,000 bytes to hold the offscreen buffer, it is well worth it since using a double buffer is absolutely necessary to alleviate flicker. And 64,000 bytes isn't going to kill us! Figure 4-4 shows the relationship between the double buffer and the video buffer. Creating a double buffer is as easy as defining a pointer and allocating 64,000 bytes to it. For example, we can define a double buffer area like this:

```
unsigned char far *double_buffer=NULL;
```

Then we use a memory allocation function to allocate 64,000 bytes for the buffer and point the pointer to it. Actually, we want to allocate the memory from the *FAR* heap, so we have to use *_fmalloc()* (or *farmalloc()* for Borland users).

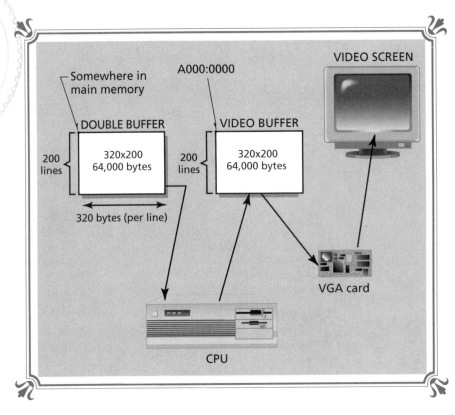

FIGURE 4-4

◎ ◎ ◎ ◎ ◎ ◎

*The double
buffer*

Once the double buffer is allocated, we can access it as if it were the video buffer. We simply pretend that it has the same layout as the video buffer (which is 320 pixels per row with 200 rows). For instance, if we wanted to convert the pixel plotting function we wrote previously to work with a double buffer, we need to change only one variable in the *Write_Pixel()* function. See if you can find the change in the function in Listing 4-2.

LISTING 4-2 A double buffer version of the pixel plotting function

```
void Write_Pixel_DB(int x,int y,int color)
{

// plots the pixel in the desired color to the double buffer
// to accomplish the multiplications
// use the fact that 320*y = 256*y + 64*y = y<<8 + y<<6
double_buffer[((y<<8) + (y<<6)) + x] = (unsigned char )color;

} // end Write_Pixel_DB
```

Since there's only one line of code in the whole function, it's easy to see that the reference to *video_buffer* has been changed to *double_buffer*. That's all you need to do. If you wish, you can change every function written thus far to work with a double buffer instead of the video buffer. We won't really need to change every function, but the ones we do change will have _DB added to their names and can be found in the library modules for this chapter.

Performing double buffer animation is very easy. You create the double buffer, do all your rendering in it, and then when the time is right, copy the double buffer into the video buffer and repeat the process each frame. By doing this you can get rid of flicker. As a second bonus, accessing normal memory is much faster than video memory, so the screen can be built up much faster. The only downside to the double buffer is that it must be copied to the video buffer to be seen by the user. But this can be done very quickly using a *memcpy()* function or, better yet, some inline assembly that moves *WORDs* or *LONGs* instead of *BYTEs* as *memcpy()* does.

So what do we need to create a double buffer animation system? Not much really. We need to write some functions that will create a double buffer, clear it, fill it with a color, and copy it to the video buffer. That's about it. However, before we do this, let's add a little bit of functionality to the double buffer system. Let's allow it to be different heights, up to a maximum of 200 lines. For example, say we wrote a game that used the upper 180 lines of the screen for the game and the lower 20 lines for instruments. We would probably want to double buffer only the active part of the screen (the upper 180 lines) and draw directly to the video buffer to implement the instruments. Thus, our double buffer system will have a height associated with it.

We already defined the double buffer itself, but there are a couple more variables we need to keep everything straight. Here they are:

```
// the default dimensions of the double buffer

unsigned int double_buffer_height = SCREEN_HEIGHT;

// size of double buffer in WORDS

unsigned int double_buffer_size   = SCREEN_WIDTH*SCREEN_HEIGHT/2;
```

You will notice that the *double_buffer_size* variable tracks the size of the double buffer in *WORDs* instead of *BYTEs*. This is because the function that copies the double buffer's image into the video buffer will use a *WORD*-size memory copy for speed. We're ready to start writing. Let's begin with a function to create a double buffer, shown in Listing 4-3.

LISTING 4-3 *Function to create a double buffer*

```
int Create_Double_Buffer(int num_lines)
{
// allocate enough memory to hold the double buffer

if ((double_buffer = (unsigned char far *)_fmalloc(SCREEN_WIDTH *
    (num_lines + 1)))==NULL)
    {
```

continued on next page

continued from previous page

```
   printf("\nCouldn't allocate double buffer.");
   return(0);
   } // end if couldn't allocate

// set the height of the buffer and compute its size
double_buffer_height = num_lines;
double_buffer_size = SCREEN_WIDTH * num_lines/2;

// fill the buffer with black
_fmemset(double_buffer, 0, SCREEN_WIDTH * num_lines);

// everything was ok
return(1);

} // end Create_Double_Buffer
```

The function is really a memory allocation shell coupled with a few variable initializations. The function first tries to allocate a double buffer of the requested line size, and if successful, will set the global size and height variables and return success. In the case that there isn't enough memory available to allocate the double buffer, an error will be printed and the function will return failure. Once the double buffer has been allocated, the next step is to fill or clear it with a value. This can be accomplished by writing a value from 0 to 255, representing the desired fill color, into the double buffer's memory. To do this we could write something like this:

```
for (index=0; index<double_buffer_size*2; index++)
    double_buffer[index] = fill_color;
```

This will work, but it's a bit slow. A better method would be to use some inline assembly language to make the process as fast as possible since clearing the screen (as we will later see) is a critical operation in 3D graphics. With that in mind, take a look at Listing 4-4 for a faster inline version.

LISTING 4-4 *Clearing the double buffer with inline assembly*

```
void Fill_Double_Buffer(int color)
{
// this function fills in the double buffer with the sent color a WORD at
// a time
_asm
   {
   mov cx,double_buffer_size  ; this is the size of buffer in WORDS
   mov al, BYTE PTR color     ; move the color into al
   mov ah,al                  ; move the color in ah
   les di,double_buffer       ; es:di points to the double buffer
   rep stosw                  ; fill all the words
   } // end asm

} // end Fill_Double_Buffer
```

The function is simple if you know assembly, but if you don't, it may seem a bit mysterious. Rule one: Never be intimidated by assembly language. It's very simple once you get a handle on it. Let's take a moment to see how the *Fill_Double_Buffer()* function works. The Intel processor has a set of memory movement instructions, and most of these instructions (I think all of them) use *DS:SI* to point to the source data, *ES:DI* to point to the destination data area, and *CX* to hold the number of BYTEs, WORDs, or LONGs to move. Finally, if the operation is a fill, then *AX* holds the data to be used as the filler. In our case we want to move WORDs, so in *CX* we place the size of the double buffer in WORDs. Then in *AX* we place the color value in *AH* and *AL*. Finally, we point *ES:DI* at the double buffer area and then use the instruction *rep stosw*, which roughly translates to "repeat the store word operation." When the function is complete, the double buffer will be filled with the desired color, or cleared to black if the fill color was 0.

The next function we need to write is one that will copy the double buffer to the video buffer. Again, we could accomplish this by using a simple *for* loop, or even with a *memcpy()* function such as:

```
_fmemcpy((void far *)video_buffer, (void far *)double_buffer,double_buffer_size/2);
```

This would work and would be faster than the *for* loop, but it still only copies BYTEs. We need to use inline again to copy WORDs as fast as possible. And this is absolutely necessary since the double buffer must be literally blasted to the video buffer! Listing 4-5 contains the code to copy the double buffer to the video buffer.

LISTING 4-5 Function to copy the double buffer to the video buffer

```
void Display_Double_Buffer(unsigned char far *buffer,int y)
{
// this function copies the double buffer into the video buffer at the
// starting y location

_asm
  {
  push ds                        ; save DS on stack
  mov cx,double_buffer_size       ; this is the size of buffer in WORDS
  les di,video_buffer             ; es:di is destination of memory move
  mov ax,320                      ; multiply y by 320 i.e. screen width
  mul y
  add di,ax                       ; add result to es:di
  lds si,buffer                   ; ds:si is source of memory move
  rep movsw                       ; move all the words
  pop ds                          ; restore the data segment
  } // end asm

} // end Display_Double_Buffer
```

The function *Display_Double_Buffer()* has a bit more functionality than it needs as a minimum, but this extra functionality will allow us to do a lot with the function. First, you will notice that the function takes a pointer to a buffer as a parameter. This will in most cases be *double_buffer*; but in the event that we want to copy another buffer to the video buffer, we will have the ability to do so. The second parameter is a positioning parameter. In the case that the double buffer is smaller than 200 lines, it is possible to position it on the video buffer at a location other than line 0.

Figure 4-5 shows this pictorially. We can map the double buffer down at different positions in the video buffer as long as the bottom of the double buffer doesn't extend farther than the video buffer. This will allow us to do some cool effects. For example, if we make the double buffer 190 lines and then map it to the video buffer with each frame at a different starting y position, where 0<=y<=9, then the screen will look like it's shaking. This technique can be used to simulate an earthquake or being hit by photon torpedoes. Also, we may wish to put the instrument panel at the top of the screen and the double buffer at the bottom, as in Figure 4-6. Therefore, sending the starting y position as a parameter allows all this to be implemented with ease.

The inline assembly is roughly the same as what was used in the fill screen, except this time around the source pointer *DS:SI* is used, and the memory movement instruction is changed to *movsw*, which means "move words." And of course, the starting offset in the video buffer is computed based on the sent y parameter

FIGURE 4-5

◉ ◉ ◉ ◉ ◉ ◉

Mapping a variable-height double buffer into the video buffer

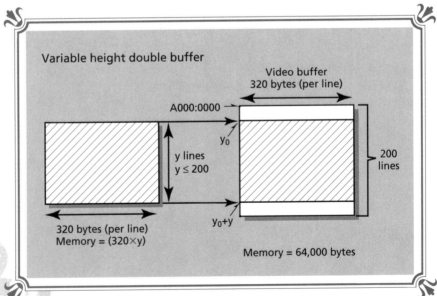

Variable height double buffer

Video buffer
320 bytes (per line)

A000:0000 →

y_0

y lines
y ≤ 200

200 lines

320 bytes (per line)
Memory = (320×y)

y_0+y

Memory = 64,000 bytes

FIGURE 4-6

◎ ◎ ◎ ◎ ◎ ◎

Building a display with a double buffer and direct video access

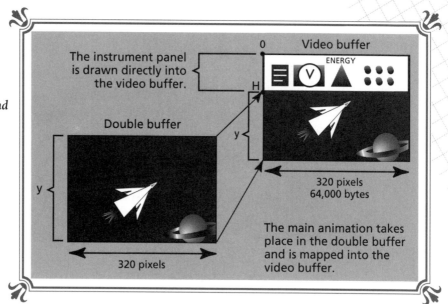

and added to the destination buffer start address in *ES:DI*. Basically, if you can understand how to set up the memory movement instructions in assembly, that's about 99 percent of all the assembly language you'll ever need to write games!

The final function needed to complete the system is a double buffer memory deallocation function that "frees" the memory used by the double buffer back to the operating system. This can be done in a couple lines, as shown in Listing 4-6.

LISTING 4-6 Function to free up the memory used by the double buffer

```
void Delete_Double_Buffer(void)
{
// this function frees up the memory allocated by the double buffer
// make sure to use FAR version

if (double_buffer)
  _ffree(double_buffer);

} // end Delete_Double_Buffer
```

That completes the software we need to implement a double buffer. Once we have a collection of functions to draw in the double buffer, we can write a game loop that looks like this:

```
//...initialize game

// create a 200 line full screen double buffer
```

continued on next page

continued from previous page

```
Create_Double_Buffer(200)

// scan under all objects in game (if needed)

While(!game_over)
        {
        // erase all objects in double buffer

        // process game logic

        // scan background under all objects (if needed)

        // draw all objects in double buffer

        // display the next frame starting at line 0

        Display_Double_Buffer(video_buffer,0);

        // synchronize to some time base

        Time_Delay(1);  // wait 1/18th of a second

        } // end main loop
```

Of course, we have a long way to go to add the functionality of all those little comments, but we're getting there! Let's move on to simple bitmapped graphics.

Simple Bitmapped Graphics

We learned in Chapter 3 that a bitmap is a rectangular matrix of pixels that can be drawn on the video screen (or double buffer) by copying the pixels from the source bitmap to the destination position on the screen. Figure 4-7 shows this process of mapping a bitmap onto the video screen. We actually implemented a crude form of bitmapping with the text blitter that drew text on the screen based on the ROM character set. However, this bitmapping wasn't really bitmapping since there wasn't a one-to-one correlation between the data of the characters and the images they represented. If you recall, we had to translate the bit pattern of each row into a byte pattern. Now we are going to do real bitmapping. This will provide us with the basic techniques to implement animation objects referred to as *sprites*.

Each pixel in the collection of pixels that makes up a bitmap is represented by a single byte. This collection of pixels is usually stored in a one-dimensional array. Although it may seem more logical to use a two-dimensional array, this is a bit slower than a one-dimensional array due to memory accessing. Therefore we'll be using one-dimensional arrays to represent all bitmaps in the book.

FIGURE 4-7

◎ ◎ ◎ ◎ ◎ ◎

*Drawing a
bitmap on the
screen*

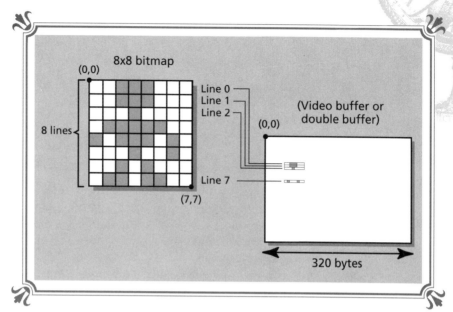

Alrighty then. Let's say we wanted to define a bitmap that was 8x8 pixels. This would take a total of 8*8=64 bytes of memory, so we could use a definition such as:

```
unsigned char bit_creature[64];
```

And we would use the convention that each row of the bitmap would be represented by 16 elements in the array, so the object would have an abstract data structure like this:

Row 0—Elements 0–7
Row 1—Elements 8–15
Row 2—Elements 16–23
Row 3—Elements 24–31
Row 4—Elements 32–39
Row 5—Elements 40–47
Row 6—Elements 48–53
Row 7—Elements 54–63

Hence, to locate a single pixel in the bitmap at a location (x,y), where (x,y) can each range from 0 through 7, the array location would be calculated as follows:

```
offset = y*8 + x;
```

That seems reasonable since there are 8 bytes per row. In essence, we are emulating the compiler's 2D arrays with a one-dimensional array. Figure 4-8 depicts a bitmap and the offset location of some pixels within the image for an 8x8 bitmap. To draw a bitmap on the video screen or double buffer, we can use a pair of simple *for* loops to copy each line of the image into the designation buffer. For example, if *bit_creature[]* had an image in it and we wanted to map it into the video buffer at (x,y), we could use the following code:

```
for (row=0; row<8; row++)
    for (column=0; column<8; column++)
        video_buffer[(y+row)*320+x+column] = bit_creature[row*8+column];
```

The above fragment will work perfectly, but there is one little problem. It's just about the slowest way that a bitmapped image can be drawn. Also, it doesn't take transparency into consideration. Remember that some portions of an image should be opaque and some shouldn't. The opaque portions of a bitmap should be drawn while the transparent portions (usually represented by black in the bitmaps) should not be drawn so the background can be seen through them. To take this point into consideration, an *if* statement must be used in the loop to test whether the pixel is transparent before drawing.

```
for (row=0; row<8; row++)
    for (column=0; column<8; column++)
        {
```

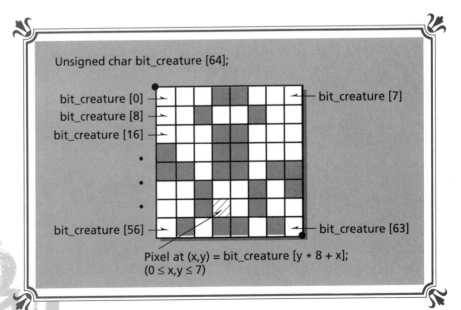

Unsigned char bit_creature [64];

bit_creature [0] →
bit_creature [8] →
bit_creature [16] →

bit_creature [7]

bit_creature [56] →
bit_creature [63]

Pixel at (x,y) = bit_creature [y * 8 + x];
(0 ≤ x,y ≤ 7)

```
// get next pixel of this row
 pixel  = bit_creature[row*8+column];

// test for transparency
 if (pixel)
        video_buffer[(y+row)*320+x+column] =pixel;

} // end for
```

There are times when transparency isn't important, for example, if the bitmap being drawn is part of the background. But in general, a transparency option should be implemented in the loop. In any case, neither of the above functions is going to work. They both have too much math involved and, with some optimizations, you can speed them up about 10 to 50 times (depending on your processor). The main optimization is to get rid of the multiplications (yuk) and precompute the starting offset at the entrance to the loop; then use simple additions to move the pointers in the source bitmap and destination buffer. We will see this shortly when we implement an actual bitmap engine, but for now keep those factors in mind.

The two previous fragments draw in the video buffer, which as we already learned isn't going to be done all that much. We will be using the double buffer most of the time, but making the fragments work in the double buffer is as easy as changing a single variable from *video_buffer* to *double_buffer*. Hence, most of the functions we'll write from now on will take as a parameter a pointer to the destination buffer, which could be the video buffer or a double buffer. This level of indirection allows a little more flexibility in the routines. Otherwise, we would have to make two copies of all the routines, one for the video buffer and one for the double buffer (which is actually quite common in real designs). Even passing a single variable to a function is sometimes unwise in time-critical graphics functions!

A Simple Bitmap Engine

At this point, we're ready to take a first stab at writing some bitmapping functions that will pave the way for the more advanced functions later in the chapter. The functions that we are about to write will serve as a good exercise to see just how simple bitmapped graphics really are. Let's begin by designing a minimal data structure that will suffice to track a bitmap. We will need a buffer to hold the memory for the bitmap image, a pair of (x,y) coordinates to locate its position, and a final pair of variables that record the size of the bitmap in pixels. A data structure that meets these criteria is:

```
// this is the typedef for a bitmap

typedef struct bitmap_typ
        {
```

continued on next page

continued from previous page

```
    int x,y;                    // position of bitmap
    int width,height;           // size of bitmap
    unsigned char far *buffer;  // buffer holding image

} bitmap, *bitmap_ptr;
```

The bitmap structure has all the elements we need. Pay close attention to the way the buffer is defined as an *(unsigned char far *)*. This is to alleviate casting problems when an element of a bitmap is assigned to a signed integer. If the bitmap buffer was not *unsigned*, there would be a sign extension, and a pixel value of 200 would be interpreted as a negative number when assigned to an *int*. Of course, this won't be an issue if the integer that the pixel value is being assigned to is *unsigned*, but many times it is, hence this definition gives us a little insurance.

Drawing a Bitmap

Now that we have the bitmap structure in place, let's write a function that will map it down into a destination buffer. The destination buffer will be sent as a parameter, so we can use the same bitmap functions for both video buffer output and double buffer output. Figure 4-9 depicts the function we wish to perform. The source

FIGURE 4-9

◉ ◉ ◉ ◉ ◉ ◉

Bitmap drawing function

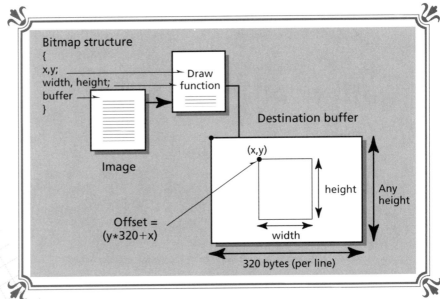

image is contained within the bitmap structure, and it is mapped down at the desired (x,y) coordinates of the destination buffer. Of course, the width of the destination buffer must always be 320 bytes, but the height can be any size.

Before writing the function, let's add one more feature to it. We have been talking about transparency from time to time and have learned that a test must be made for every pixel in the rendering loop to test for transparency. However, if a bitmap or object doesn't have any transparent portions, this test can be thrown out, and a very fast *memcpy()* function can be used to transfer the bitmap data to the destination buffer. Therefore, we are going to add this ability to our bitmap drawing function to allow it to select whether transparency is on or off. This gives us more speed in the cases that we don't need to test for transparency. Taking all of the previous requirements into consideration, our bitmap drawing function is shown in Listing 4-7.

LISTING 4-7 Bitmap drawing function

```
void Bitmap_Put(bitmap_ptr image, unsigned char far *destination,int transparent)
{
// this function draws a bitmap on the destination buffer which can
// be a double buffer or the video buffer

int x,y,                       // looping variables
    width,height;              // size of bitmap

unsigned char far *bitmap_data; // pointer to bitmap buffer
unsigned char far *dest_buffer; // pointer to destination buffer

unsigned char pixel;            // current pixel value being processed

// compute offset of bitmap in destination buffer. Note: all video or
// double buffers must be 320 bytes wide!

dest_buffer = destination + (image->y << 8) + (image->y << 6) + image->x;

// create aliases to variables so the structure doesn't need to be
// dereferenced continually

height      = image->height;
width       = image->width;
bitmap_data = image->buffer;

// test if transparency is on or off

if (transparent)
   {
   // use version that will draw a transparent bitmap (slightly slower)
   // draw each line of the bitmap
```

continued on next page

continued from previous page

```
for (y=0; y<height; y++)
    {
    // copy the next row into the destination buffer

    for (x=0; x<width; x++)
        {
        // test for transparent pixel i.e. 0, if not transparent then draw

        if ((pixel=bitmap_data[x]))
            dest_buffer[x] = pixel;

        } // end for x

    // move to next line in double buffer and in bitmap buffer

    dest_buffer += SCREEN_WIDTH;
    bitmap_data += width;

    } // end for y

} // end if transparent
else
    {

    // draw each line of the bitmap, note how each pixel doesn't need to be
    // tested for transparency hence a memcpy can be used (very fast!)

    for (y=0; y<height; y++)
        {
        // copy the next row into the destination buffer using memcpy for speed

        _fmemcpy((void far *)dest_buffer,
                 (void far *)bitmap_data,width);

        // move to next line in destination buffer and in bitmap buffer

        dest_buffer += SCREEN_WIDTH;
        bitmap_data += width;

        } // end for y

} // end else non-transparent version

} // end Bitmap_Put
```

The function has three distinct phases of operation. During the initialization phase, the starting memory location in the destination buffer where the bitmap will be placed is computed. This starting address is stored in *dest_buffer*. Similarly, *bitmap_data* is aliased to the buffer region within the bitmap structure so that a pointer dereference isn't needed every cycle to access the bitmap data. This is a typical technique used to cache variables that are within structures to gain speed. The next phase of the function tests the *transparent* flag to determine whether the bitmap should be drawn with or without transparency. Then a jump is made to either the transparent version of the drawing code or the nontransparent version. In either case, each pixel of the source bitmap is transferred to the destination buffer (which is usually the double buffer), and the address of the next line of the source bitmap and destination bitmap is recomputed for the next cycle.

Scanning a Bitmap

When writing bitmapping functions, it's always a good idea to make the function set orthogonal. In other words, for every function there's an antifunction (kinda like antimatter, but different). In the case of *Bitmap_Put()*, its inverse function would be *Bitmap_Get()*, which would extract or scan a region from a source buffer. This source buffer could be the video buffer, the double buffer, or whatever. Both the put and get functions are absolutely necessary if animation is to take place, since part of the animation cycle needs to scan the background under an image before it is drawn so that the background can be replaced. This is the motivation behind the *Bitmap_Get()* function. Another motivation is that we need to have some method to load in bitmaps themselves, otherwise how are we going to get the actual bitmaps for the objects to animate? Later we'll learn to scan objects from PCX files loaded from disk, but the point is we need to be able to scan objects.

Writing a *Bitmap_Get()* function is about half as hard as the put function. This is because we don't need to have two versions of the code to scan for transparent and nontransparent. In all cases, we want to extract a rectangular region that has dimensions *width* by *height* as defined in the structure. And there is no transparency test, so we can use the faster *memcpy()* type function to extract each line of the source bitmap. Listing 4-8 contains the code we need to do just that.

LISTING 4-8 *Function to extract a bitmap from a source image buffer*

```
void Bitmap_Get(bitmap_ptr image, unsigned char far *source)
{
// this function will scan a bitmap from the source buffer
// could be a double buffer, video buffer or any other buffer with a
// logical row width of 320 bytes

unsigned int source_off,        // offsets into destination and source buffers
            bitmap_off;
int y,                          // looping variable
    width,height;               // size of bitmap

unsigned char far *bitmap_data; // pointer to bitmap buffer
```

continued on next page

continued from previous page

```
// compute offset of bitmap in source buffer. Note: all video or double
// buffers must be 320 bytes wide!

source_off   = (image->y << 8) + (image->y << 6) + image->x;

bitmap_off = 0;

// create aliases to variables so the structure doesn't need to be
// dereferenced continually

height       = image->height;
width        = image->width;
bitmap_data = image->buffer;

// draw each line of the bitmap, note how each pixel doesn't need to be
// tested for transparency hence a memcpy can be used (very fast!)

for (y=0; y<height; y++)
    {
    // copy the next row into the bitmap buffer using memcpy for speed

    _fmemcpy((void far *)&bitmap_data[bitmap_off],
            (void far *)&source[source_off],width);

    // move to next line in source buffer and in bitmap buffer

    source_off += SCREEN_WIDTH;
    bitmap_off += width;

    } // end for y

} // end Bitmap_Get
```

The function works in much the same way as *Bitmap_Put()* does. First the
source memory offset and bitmap image buffer are aliased, then a *for* loop scans
each line of the source image into the bitmap image buffer, and that's about it.

Using *Bitmap_Put()* and *Bitmap_Get()*, we could write a simple animation program that moves an object around the screen and so forth; however, at this point
the functions we have aren't really designed for the purpose of animation. We need
a more robust data structure and a couple more functions to really do animation
right. This is where the concept of sprites comes in. We will learn about them
shortly and the power that they offer for 2D animation. But before that, let's discuss
where on Earth we're going to get all the artwork and imagery for our games.

Loading Images from Outside Sources

I'm sure you've seen or heard of many different paint and illustration programs for the PC. These programs are used to create artwork for many purposes. In our case, we need a source of artwork and bitmapped images that we can import into our games. Standards are hard to come by in the graphics world, and there are probably as many different graphics file formats as there are graphic paint programs; however, over time a few formats have become popular and are used the most. These are GIF, TIFF, TARGA, PCX, and BMP. The only one we need to concern ourselves with is PCX. The PCX standard was invented by ZSoft as part of the paint program, PC-Paintbrush, which they made years ago. At the time they wrote the program, there wasn't a good bitmapped file format, so they invented one.

The PCX format is very easy to decode and supports all kinds of resolutions and color depths; moreover, it supports a simple data compression method, so that the image files take as little space as possible. We will be working primarily with PCX files, but there is no reason you can't write other file readers if you wish. PCX files are generated by PC-Paintbrush, but where else can they be found? The fact of the matter is that it doesn't really matter what paint program you use because there are hundreds of programs that will convert from one format to another.

Most paint programs themselves allow you to save and load images in most of the popular formats. However, I suggest that you use a paint program that supports 256 colors and one that can function in mode 13h. It is very important that you can see what your artwork looks like in the native mode it will be used in. For example, if you draw objects for a game in 640x480 and then import them into your game that runs in 320x200, the images are not going to look right. So the moral of the story is: Use a paint program that supports mode 13h. I have worked with DPaint and Deluxe Animation (Electronic Arts) and PC-Paintbrush (ZSoft). They are all excellent paint programs and all support mode 13h. I suggest you use one of these as a start.

Reading PCX Files

Once you have selected a paint program or have artwork that is in the 320x200, PCX file format, the next step is to figure out how to read the data in the file. PCX files consist of three main parts:

- ✛ Header section
- ✛ Image data
- ✛ Color palette

The header section is a typical header with information describing the kind of image that is contained within the image section. In our case, we will just skip the header since we already know that the image is a 320x200, 256-color image; but to be complete, here is the C version of the header for a PCX file:

```
// the PCX file structure

typedef struct pcx_header_typ
        {
        char manufacturer;          // the manufacturer of the file
        char version;               // the file format version
        char encoding;              // type of compression
        char bits_per_pixel;        // number of bits per pixel
        int x,y;                    // starting location of image
        int width,height;           // size of image
        int horz_res;               // resolution in DPI (dots per inch)
        int vert_res;
        char ega_palette[48];       // the old EGA palette (usually ignored)
        char reserved;              // don't care
        char num_color_planes;      // number of color planes
        int bytes_per_line;         // number of bytes per line of the image
        int palette_type;           // 1 for color, 2 for grey scale palette
        char padding[58];           // extra bytes

        } pcx_header, *pcx_header_ptr;
```

If you count the number of bytes that make up the entire header file, you will come up with a grand total of 128 bytes. Hence, the header section is always the first 128 bytes of a PCX file.

The next section of the PCX file is the compressed image that represents the full 320x200-pixel image. In actuality the image data can be any size. It may be 50 bytes or it may be 50,000 bytes, but when it's decompressed and translated into pixels, there will be exactly 64,000 pixels or bytes that are generated from the file. This creates a little problem. We don't know how big the image section is, so how can we find the start of the color palette information? We will use the file seeking function supported by C to move the file pointer to the end of the PCX file and back up to the color palette section without knowing how big the image section is. Let's talk about how the image is compressed.

PCX files use a simple compression method that is based in *run length encoding (RLE)*. It is very common for bitmapped images to have long runs of the same color. In the best case an entire screen could be filled with a single color. Thus, we could encode this as the number of bytes that the color ran (64,000 in this case) and the color. This is the basis of run length encoding. It works by scanning the image and looking for runs of pixels that have the same value. When a run is found, the RLE algorithm computes how many pixels have the same color; then the color itself along with the length of the run are written to the compressed output file. That's the basic idea behind textbook RLE. However, ZSoft made a couple changes to it.

I'm not sure why, but my intuition tells me that there was some kind of color palette motivation. Anyway, here's how RLE works for PCX files. The first byte of the image data is read. If it is in the range of 0 to 191, it is written to the decompression buffer or destination buffer without change. However, if the value read is between 192 and 255, it's a pixel run and should be decompressed. To decompress the run, the value of 192 is subtracted from the previously read value. The result is the number of bytes or pixels that need to be replicated. The value of the pixel can be found by reading the next byte in the file.

For example, take a look at Figure 4-10 to see the decompression of a few values in the beginning of a PCX file. Referring to the figure, the first three values are between 0 and 191, so they aren't changed, they are copied directly into the decompression buffer. But the fourth number (200) is between 192 and 255; therefore, 192 is subtracted from 200 resulting in 8, and then the next data value (5) is copied 8 times into the destination buffer. Hence, the 200 described the run length and the 5 was the data to replicate. The last value is 26 and is less than 192; thus, it is directly copied to the decompression buffer.

The question is, how do we know when the PCX image has been totally decompressed? The best way is to keep a count of the number of bytes written to the destination decompression buffer. When it equals 64,000 we know that an entire file has been decompressed. But remember, the number of bytes read may only be a few, which when decompressed make up the total of 64,000!

FIGURE 4-10

◉ ◉ ◉ ◉ ◉ ◉

Decompressing a
PCX file

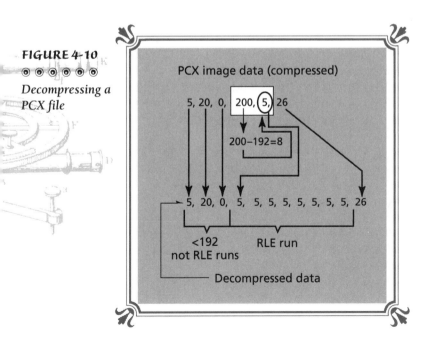

The last section of the PCX file contains the color palette information. This section contains 256 descriptors that each have 3 bytes (one for red, green, and blue), for a total of 256∗3=768 bytes in the color palette. Therefore, to read the color palette information for the PCX image, we can move the random access file pointer to the end of the PCX file and then read 768 bytes in 3-byte chunks. Figure 4-11 shows the relationship between the header, image data, and palette information. You see that the first 3 bytes define color register zero, the next 3 bytes define color register one, and so on. However, you'll also note that each RGB value needs to be scaled down by a factor of 4. This is because the PCX file format uses "Truecolor" or 24-bit color descriptors, and if you remember, the VGA only uses 6 bits per channel or a total of 18-bit color. Alas, we must divide each RGB set by a factor of 4 or shift to the right 2 bits to scale the values down.

We now know all the little secrets of PCX files, so let's write some functions to load them into the computer. First, let's add another data structure that will contain the header of a PCX file, the full 64,000 bytes of image data, and the color palette. Here's a structure that will work:

FIGURE 4-11
◉ ◉ ◉ ◉ ◉ ◉
*Layout of a ZSoft
PCX file*

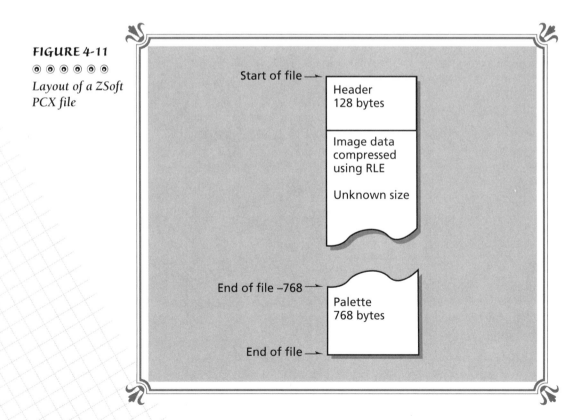

```
// this holds the PCX header and the actual image

typedef struct pcx_picture_typ
        {
        pcx_header header;          // the header of the PCX file
        RGB_color palette[256];     // the palette data
        unsigned char far *buffer;  // a pointer to the 64,000 byte buffer
                                    // holding the decompressed image


        } pcx_picture, *pcx_picture_ptr;
```

The *pcx_picture* structure will be used to encapsulate an entire PCX image, so we can load more than one image at a time. Now we're ready to write a function that will load a PCX file. But first let's write a pair of functions that will allocate the memory for a *pcx_picture* and release it. This will make the application programming a little cleaner. Listing 4-9 contains the functions to allocate and deallocate the memory for a *pcx_picture*.

LISTING 4-9 Memory allocation functions for PCX file structures

```
int PCX_Init(pcx_picture_ptr image)
{
// this function allocates the buffer that the image data will be loaded into
// when a PCX file is decompressed

if (!(image->buffer = (unsigned char far *)_fmalloc(SCREEN_WIDTH * SCREEN_HEIGHT + 1)))
        {
        printf("\nPCX SYSTEM - Couldn't allocate PCX image buffer");
        return(0);
        } // end if

// success

return(1);

} // end PCX_Init


void PCX_Delete(pcx_picture_ptr image)
{
// this function de-allocates the buffer region used for the pcx file load

_ffree(image->buffer);

} // end PCX_Delete
```

The functions don't do much except take a pointer to a *pcx_picture* and allocate memory from the *FAR* heap or deallocate it, but they make the process easier than doing it inline in the game code all the time. Thus, we can load a PCX file, work with it, and then delete it. You now have everything you need to load and decompress the PCX image data, so I'll leave this function to you. The next thing we are going... Just kidding! The final function we need is a loader function that will open the PCX file on disk, load the header, image, and palette, and then close the file. The function to do this is called *PCX_Load()* and it's shown in Listing 4-10.

LISTING 4-10 Loading a PCX file

```c
int PCX_Load(char *filename, pcx_picture_ptr image,int load_palette)
{

// this function loads a PCX file into the image structure. The function
// has three main parts: 1. load the PCX header, 2. load the image data and
// decompress it and 3. load the palette data and update the VGA palette
// note: the palette will only be loaded if the load_palette flag is 1

FILE *fp;                   // the file pointer used to open the PCX file

int num_bytes,             // number of bytes in current RLE run
    index;                 // loop variable

long count;                // the total number of bytes decompressed
unsigned char data;        // the current pixel data
char far *temp_buffer;     // working buffer

// open the file, test if it exists
if ((fp = fopen(filename,"rb"))==NULL)
   {
   printf("\nPCX SYSTEM - Couldn't find file: %s",filename);
   return(0);
   } // end if couldn't find file

// load the header
temp_buffer = (char far *)image;

for (index=0; index<128; index++)
   {
   temp_buffer[index] = (char)getc(fp);
   } // end for index

// load the data and decompress into buffer, we need a total of 64,000 bytes

count=0;

// loop while 64,000 bytes haven't been decompressed

while(count<=SCREEN_WIDTH * SCREEN_HEIGHT)
   {
   // get the first piece of data
   data = (unsigned char)getc(fp);
```

```
                    // is this a RLE run?
                    if (data>=192 && data<=255)
                        {
                        // compute number of bytes in run
                        num_bytes = data-192;

                        // get the actual data for the run
                        data  = (unsigned char)getc(fp);

                        // replicate data in buffer num_bytes times
                        while(num_bytes-->0)
                            {
                            image->buffer[count++] = data;
                            } // end while

                        } // end if rle
                    else
                        {
                        // actual data, just copy it into buffer at next location
                        image->buffer[count++] = data;
                        } // end else not rle

                    } // end while

            // load color palete

            // move to end of file then back up 768 bytes i.e. to beginning of palette
            fseek(fp,-768L,SEEK_END);

            // load the PCX palette into the VGA color registers
            for (index=0; index<256; index++)
                {
                // get the red component
                image->palette[index].red   = (unsigned char)(getc(fp) >> 2);

                // get the green component
                image->palette[index].green = (unsigned char)(getc(fp) >> 2);

                // get the blue component
                image->palette[index].blue  = (unsigned char)(getc(fp) >> 2);

                } // end for index

            // time to close the file
            fclose(fp);

            // change the palette to newly loaded palette if commanded to do so

            if (load_palette)
                {
                // for each palette register set to the new color values
```

continued on next page

continued from previous page

```
for (index=0; index<256; index++)
    {
    Write_Color_Reg(index,(RGB_color_ptr)&image->palette[index]);
    } // end for index

} // end if load palette data into VGA

// success
return(1);

} // end PCX_Load
```

The function takes as parameters the file name of the PCX file to load, a pointer to the previously initialized *pcx_picture* that the information should be loaded into, and finally, a flag that determines whether the palette information should be loaded into the palette registers of the VGA. Many times when you create imagery in a paint program, the paint program will have its own palette or maybe a palette that you created. In either case, you have to load that palette if the images are to be colored correctly. Otherwise, when you view or manipulate the images from the PCX file, they will have the wrong colors. This is the purpose of the *load_palette* flag. It tells the *PCX_Load()* function that it should reprogram all the color registers in the VGA to the values within the PCX file's palette.

We are almost ready to see the PCX functions in action, but we need one more very simple function. And that's to copy the image in the *pcx_picture* buffer to the video buffer so we can see it. A function to do this is as easy as a single *memcpy()* function, but we'll use inline assembly for speed. Take a look at Listing 4-11.

LISTING 4-11 Copying the image from a PCX file in the video buffer

```
void PCX_Show_Buffer(pcx_picture_ptr image)
{
// copy the pcx buffer into the video buffer

char far *data; // temp variable used for aliasing

// alias image buffer

data = image->buffer;

// use inline assembly for speed

_asm
    {
    push ds                 ; save the data segment
    les di, video_buffer    ; point es:di to video buffer
    lds si, data            ; point ds:si to data area
    mov cx,320*200/2        ; move 32000 words
```

```
cld                     ; set direction to forward
rep movsw               ; do the string operation
pop ds                  ; restore the data segment
} // end inline

} // end PCX_Show_Buffer
```

I admit that it could have been done with a *memcpy()* instead of inline assembly, but this is a bit faster, and I really want you to feel comfortable with the inline assembler to do tasks such as this. At this point, we are ready for a demo to see all the PCX functions in action. The name of the demo is PCXDEMO.EXE and can be found in this chapter's directory along with the source file PCXDEMO.C. If you want to compile it yourself, you will need to add the library module BLACK4.C and its header file BLACK4.H. The demo loads a picture of a really scary monster and then displays it. To exit the program, press any key and one of the transitions will fade the image away. Listing 4-12 contains the code.

LISTING 4-12 PCX file demo

```
// PCXDEMO.C - A pcx file demo that loads a pcx file and displays it

// I N C L U D E S ///////////////////////////////////////////////////////////

#include <io.h>
#include <conio.h>
#include <stdio.h>
#include <stdlib.h>
#include <dos.h>
#include <bios.h>
#include <fcntl.h>
#include <memory.h>
#include <malloc.h>
#include <math.h>
#include <string.h>

#include "black3.h"
#include "black4.h"

// G L O B A L S ///////////////////////////////////////////////////////////

pcx_picture image_pcx; // general PCX image used to load background and imagery

// M A I N ///////////////////////////////////////////////////////////////////

void main(int argc, char **argv)
{
// set the graphics mode to mode 13h
```

continued on next page

continued from previous page

```
Set_Graphics_Mode(GRAPHICS_MODE13);
// load the screen image
PCX_Init((pcx_picture_ptr)&image_pcx);

// load a PCX file (make sure it's there)
if (PCX_Load("andre.pcx", (pcx_picture_ptr)&image_pcx,1))
   {
   // copy the image to the display buffer
   PCX_Show_Buffer((pcx_picture_ptr)&image_pcx);

   // delete the PCX buffer
   PCX_Delete((pcx_picture_ptr)&image_pcx);

   // wait for a keyboard press
   while(!kbhit()){}

   // use a screen transition to exit
   Screen_Transition(SCREEN_DARKNESS);

   } // end if pcx file found

// reset graphics to text mode
Set_Graphics_Mode(TEXT_MODE);

} // end main
```

Pay close attention to the simplicity of our PCX file functions. This is the key to writing games that create a strong link to Cyberspace. The functions must be simple, compact, and fast. And if they are slightly specialized that's not a big deal.

A Sprite Structure

We have covered animation, bitmaps, and PCX files. Now we're ready to design and implement a fairly complex 2D bitmapped graphics engine. Although the focus of this book is 3D, a majority of displays and animation will still be done in 2D, so having the functionality is an integral part of the overall 3D package. The animation objects that we're going to focus on are called sprites. I personally don't know the origin of the word, but it started back in the days of the Atari 800 and Commodore 64. We will continue the tradition and refer to them as sprites also.

Roughly defined, a sprite is an object that can move around on the screen without disturbing the background under it. That's easy enough to implement. However, we are going to be using sprites to represent objects and possibly creatures in our games; thus, we are going to add many features to them to make them more powerful. For one thing, each sprite will have multiple frames of animation or multiple images that can all be used to represent the sprite. For example, Figure 4-12 shows an abstract representation of a walking alien sprite. The alien has a posi-

FIGURE 4-12

◎ ◎ ◎ ◎ ◎ ◎

A sprite

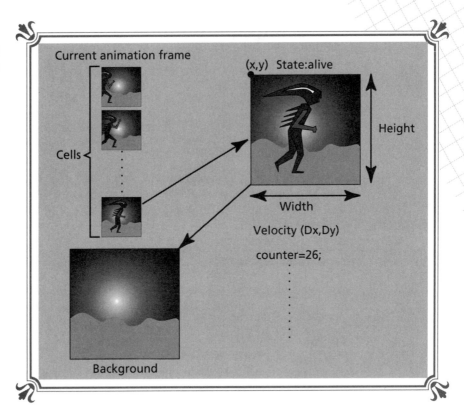

tion, timing variables, counters, a buffer for the background under it, and finally, an array of images that can be used to animate it.

There is no single best way to implement a sprite engine. We just want to make sure that the sprites can do what we need them to do. Therefore, why don't we start by designing the data structure we'll be using for our sprites. If we add all the attributes we've spoken of plus a few more to round out the sprite definition, the results are something like this:

```
// this is a sprite structure

typedef struct sprite_typ
        {
        int x,y;            // position of sprite
        int width,height;   // dimensions of sprite in pixels

        int counter_1;      // some counters for timing and animation
        int counter_2;
        int counter_3;
```

continued on next page

continued from previous page

```
        int threshold_1;    // thresholds for the counters (if needed)
        int threshold_2;
        int threshold_3;
        unsigned char far *frames[MAX_SPRITE_FRAMES]; // array of pointers to
                                                      // the images

        int curr_frame;              // current frame being displayed
        int num_frames;              // total number of frames
        int state;                   // state of sprite, alive, dead...
        unsigned char far *background; // image under the sprite

        int x_clip,y_clip;           // clipped position of sprite
        int width_clip,height_clip;  // clipped size of sprite used
        int visible;                 // by sprite engine to flag
                                     // if a sprite was invisible last
                                     // time it was drawn hence the background
                                     // need not be replaced

    } sprite, *sprite_ptr;
```

The function of each field is rather important, so let's take the time to understand the motivation for each of them. The variables x and y track the absolute position of the sprite on the display buffer itself (which could be a double buffer or the video memory); therefore, if the sprite's position was (160,100), the sprite would be drawn in the middle of the screen (or double buffer). The next variables, *width* and *height*, are similar to the ones in the bitmap structure. A sprite also will be defined by a rectangular bitmap, hence *width* and *height* are needed to track its size. The variables named *counter_1*, *counter_2*, and *counter_3* work in conjunction with *threshold_1*, *threshold_2*, and *threshold_3* as timing variables. They can be used for anything we wish. As you program games, you will find that there are a lot of little details that need to be tracked, and that's the function of these variables. Next is an array of pointers that contain pointers to the cells of animation that make up the sprite. For example, a particular sprite may have five frames of animation; therefore, the first five pointers in this array would be pointing to the bitmaps for these images.

The next set of variables track the "state" of the sprite. The *curr_frame* variable is used to hold the current frame of animation that the sprite is displaying. Again, this is just a place holder, so our functions don't have to keep track of these items. The next variable, *num_frames*, contains the number of animation cells that are within the sprite. Some sprites may have one animation cell, some may have ten, but in any case there is a record of this information. The next variable is a bit hard to explain at this point, but let's see if we can get a good handle on it. In a game, whether it is 2D, 3D, or something else, the objects in the game must have some kind of "state" associated with them. There must be a record of whether the object is hunting down the player, exploding, dead, teleporting, or whatever. That is what the *state* field is for. It is a completely definable record of the concept of "state." For example, in one game it may take on only a couple values: one value to mark a sprite as "alive" and another to mark it as "dead." It's up to you and your design, but this field gives you the ability to record that kind of information.

The next field, *background*, holds the background image under the sprite and is very important. If you remember, one of the most important aspects of a sprite is that it can move around the screen without destroying the background. This is accomplished by saving the background under a sprite (at the right moment) into the background buffer. Finally, the last few fields of the sprite structure are for clipping, which we will get to later in the chapter. For now we know all we need to, so let's get cracking!

We could begin by writing functions to draw, erase, and scan under sprites, but this time we are going to consider a very important detail. And that's the images that represent the sprite! In the bitmap examples, we learned the mechanics of creating the bitmaps, drawing them, and deallocating them, but we never really had a source of the artwork from which to extract the bitmaps in the first place. Now we are in a much better position. We can draw a set of animation cells for our sprites and then load them as PCX files. We can then access the image buffer field of the *pcx_picture* structure and extract bitmaps for the sprites from there. So what we need to do is write a function that takes as parameters a sprite, a PCX file, the desired (x,y) position from which to extract the bitmap, and the frame number of the bitmap. Figure 4-13 shows this process graphically. The data from a PCX file is used to load up the *frames[]* array of the sprite structure.

To write the function, we need to make a couple decisions about the way bitmaps will be extracted from the buffer of the *pcx_picture* (which is simply a 320x200-byte buffer). Since size of a sprite is *widthxheight* in the sprite structure, the bitmap that is extracted must be the exact same size. Hence, one way to do the extraction would be to send an (x,y) coordinate for the desired location of where to extract the bitmap from the *pcx_picture* buffer. This would do the trick since the function would know how big of a bitmap to scan by referring to the *width* and *height* fields in the sent sprite structure.

This will work, but the drawback is that the caller must continually recompute the (x,y) position of all the desired bitmaps, which can be a pain. A much easier method would be to create a template that has cells in it. For example, if you knew that all the bitmaps in your artwork were going to be 16x16 pixels, you could create a template of 16x16 place holders and put your bitmaps into them in your original artwork file. Then the extraction function would locate a bitmap by referring to it by its cell location in the template instead of its screen coordinates. This is the method that we are going to use for our sprite engine. To make sure that you really understand this, take a look at Figure 4-14, which is a representation of some artwork that has been laid out into cells. The original artwork was drawn with DPaint,

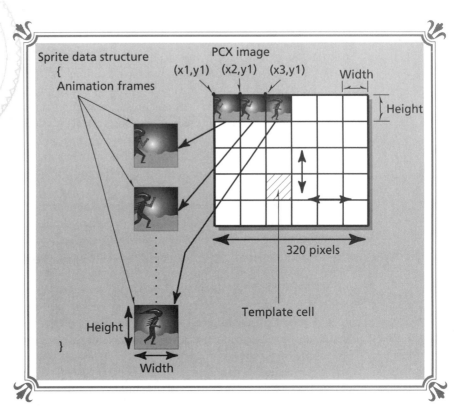

FIGURE 4-13

Extracting bitmaps from a PCX image

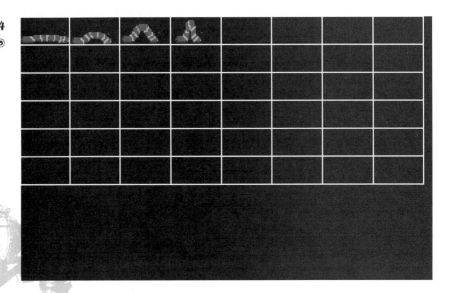

FIGURE 4-14

Bitmaps in a template

and then each bitmap was picked up and placed into one of the cell locations using the painting tools.

As you see from the figure, each bitmap region is bounded by a rectangle which actually has a thickness of one pixel. Therefore, to locate a bitmap that has cell location (cx,cy), we would multiply each component by the *width* and the *height* of the sprite plus one. For example, to convert from cell coordinates to image coordinates in the PCX buffer, we would do this:

```
screen_x = (sprite_width+1) * cell_x;
screen_y = (sprite_height+1) * cell_y;
```

The "+1" is to take into account the borders around each cell. These borders serve no purpose other than to help the artist position the bitmaps in the template and can be taken out if we wish.

Once the coordinates of the actual bitmap are computed, extracting the bitmap data is as simple as a *for* loop that scans each line of the source bitmap into one of the animation frames of the sprite structure. Before we write a function to do this, let's take care of a little housekeeping and write sprite initialization and deletion functions similar to what we did with the bitmaps. The sprite initialization function will take a set of parameters to fill up the fields of the sprite, and then it will allocate the background buffer. It won't allocate any memory for the animation cells since during initialization, we don't know how many cells are going to represent the sprite (most of the time). The function is shown in Listing 4-13.

LISTING 4-13 Sprite initialization function

```
void Sprite_Init(sprite_ptr sprite,int x,int y,int width,int height,
                                 int c1,int c2,int c3,
                                 int t1,int t2,int t3)
{
// this function initializes a sprite

int index;

sprite->x            = x;
sprite->y            = y;
sprite->width        = width;
sprite->height       = height;
sprite->visible      = 1;
sprite->counter_1    = c1;
sprite->counter_2    = c2;
sprite->counter_3    = c3;
sprite->threshold_1  = t1;
sprite->threshold_2  = t2;
sprite->threshold_3  = t3;
sprite->curr_frame   = 0;
sprite->state        = SPRITE_DEAD;
sprite->num_frames   = 0;
```

continued on next page

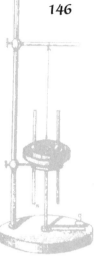

continued from previous page

```
sprite->background    = (unsigned char far *)_fmalloc(width * height+1);
// set all bitmap pointers to null

for (index=0; index<MAX_SPRITE_FRAMES; index++)
    sprite->frames[index] = NULL;

} // end Sprite_Init
```

You're probably starting to notice the use of some defines in the sprite functions and associated code. These are all defined in the file BLACK4.H and are named after what they do. For example, *MAX_SPRITE_FRAMES* is a constant that marks the upper limit on the number of frames of any sprite. Feel free to change these, but I have set everything up to give us more than what we need, so changes probably won't be needed. All right, now let's write a function that will delete or deallocate all the resources used by a sprite. This can be done by freeing all the memory used by the background and the sprite animation frames. Listing 4-14 contains the function to do just that.

LISTING 4-14 Function to delete a sprite

```
void Sprite_Delete(sprite_ptr sprite)
{
// this function deletes all the memory associated with a sprite

int index;

_ffree(sprite->background);

// now de-allocate all the animation frames

for (index=0; index<MAX_SPRITE_FRAMES; index++)
    _ffree(sprite->frames[index]);

} // end Sprite_Delete
```

We can now create and destroy a sprite. It's time to write the function that will extract the images for the animation cells of the sprite. The function only needs a few parameters. It needs the sprite itself (which we'll send a pointer to), the cell coordinates from which to extract the bitmap, and finally, the frame number to place the bitmap into (which is just an array index into *frames[]*). The function to do this is shown in Listing 4-15.

LISTING 4-15 Function to extract a sprite bitmap image from a PCX file

```
void PCX_Get_Sprite(pcx_picture_ptr image,
                    sprite_ptr sprite,
```

```
                     int sprite_frame,
                     int cell_x, int cell_y)
{
// this function is used to load the images for a sprite into the sprite
// frames array. It functions by using the size of the sprite and the
// position of the requested cell to compute the proper location in the
// pcx image buffer to extract the data from.

int x_off,  // position of sprite cell in PCX image buffer
    y_off,
    y,         // looping variable
    width,  // size of sprite
    height;

unsigned char far *sprite_data;

// extract width and height of sprite
width  = sprite->width;
height = sprite->height;

// first allocate the memory for the sprite in the sprite structure
sprite->frames[sprite_frame] = (unsigned char far *)_fmalloc(width * height + 1);

// create an alias to the sprite frame for ease of access
sprite_data = sprite->frames[sprite_frame];

// now load the sprite data into the sprite frame array from the pcx
// picture
x_off = (width+1)  * cell_x + 1;
y_off = (height+1) * cell_y + 1;

// compute starting y address
y_off = y_off * 320; // 320 bytes per line

// scan the data row by row
for (y=0; y<height; y++,y_off+=320)
    {
    // copy the row of pixels
    _fmemcpy((void far *)&sprite_data[y*width],
             (void far *)&(image->buffer[y_off + x_off]),
             width);
    } // end for y

// increment number of frames
sprite->num_frames++;

// done!, let's bail!

} // end PCX_Get_Sprite
```

The function doesn't do much except compute the position of the desired bitmap in the *pcx_picture* buffer, allocate the memory to hold the bitmap, and then copy the bitmap into the storage area. You will see more and more that game programming is mostly moving memory from one place to another. If you learn to do this efficiently, your games will be wickedly fast and make lots of money! Back to the function... As you can see, it does very little error checking; as a matter of fact, it doesn't do any. If you want error checking (which in general you should), you will have to put it in yourself. I have omitted error checking in most functions so we can concentrate on the mechanics of the functions and their operation. Error checking is basic stuff and in most cases is implemented with a couple lines of code, so I'll leave that up to you.

Let's take the functions we have and create a sprite. Although we can't draw or move the sprite, it will be a good exercise to see how the functions are used. With that in mind, imagine that we want to create a sprite that is 24x24 pixels and load it with some animation frames from a PCX file on disk called SHIPS.PCX. The images are placed in template form within the upper-left corner of the PCX file and there are four of them. To load the bitmaps into the sprite, we must first create a PCX structure, a sprite, load the PCX file off disk, initialize the sprite, and then extract the four bitmaps from the PCX image. The code to do this follows:

```
pcx_picture imagery; // this will hold the artwork
sprite ship;              // our little spaceship sprite

// initialize and load PCX file

PCX_Init((pcx_picture_ptr)&imagery);

PCX_Load((pcx_picture_ptr)&imagery,1);

// initialize the sprite to be 24x24 pixels at location (160,100)

Sprite_Init((sprite_ptr)&ship,160,100,24,24,0,0,0,0,0,0);

// extract the four bitmaps for sprite from row 0, columns 0,1,2,3

for (frame=0; frame<4; frame++)

        PCX_Get_Sprite((pcx_picture_ptr)&imagery,
        (sprite_ptr)&ship,frame,frame,0);

// done with PCX file so delete it

PCX_Delete((pcx_picture_ptr)&imagery);
```

The above fragment is all we need to create a sprite and load in the animation images. Now let's learn how to display these phantom sprites!

Drawing Sprites

We draw sprites the same way we draw bitmaps. The source data is copied pixel by pixel to the destination buffer at some (x,y) screen position. Moreover, the pixel-by-pixel copy may or may not take transparency into consideration. Hence, our sprite drawing function will have two sections within it to handle these two cases at the fastest possible speed. As an exercise, let's discuss the logical steps to draw a sprite on the screen or in a double buffer. First, the sprite could possibly have multiple bitmaps that define it (unlike the simple bitmap structure). The sprite drawing function will use one of the bitmaps within the *frames[]* array as the source bitmap image. To draw any bitmap of the sprite, all we need is the bitmap, the position at which to draw it, and its size. We indeed have all of these variables within the sprite structure.

The function uses this information along with a destination buffer to draw the sprite. The function we'll write will take only three parameters. The first parameter is a pointer to the sprite to be drawn, the second parameter is the destination memory buffer (destination memory context), and the third variable is a transparency flag used to direct the function to take transparent (black) pixels into consideration or not. Now that we have all the particulars down, let's put it all together in Listing 4-16.

LISTING 4-16 *Function to draw a sprite*

```
void Sprite_Draw(sprite_ptr sprite, unsigned char far *buffer,
                 int transparent)
{

// this function draws a sprite on the screen row by row very quickly
// note the use of shifting to implement multiplication
// if the transparent flag is true then pixels will be drawn one by one
// else a memcpy will be used to draw each line

unsigned char far *sprite_data; // pointer to sprite data
unsigned char far *dest_buffer; // pointer to destination buffer

int x,y,                        // looping variables
    width,                      // width of sprite
    height;                     // height of sprite

unsigned char pixel;            // the current pixel being processed

// alias a pointer to sprite for ease of access
sprite_data = sprite->frames[sprite->curr_frame];
```

continued on next page

continued from previous page

```c
// alias a variable to sprite size
width  = sprite->width;
height = sprite->height;

// compute number of bytes between adjacent video lines after a row of pixels
// has been drawn

// compute offset of sprite in destination buffer
dest_buffer = buffer + (sprite->y << 8) + (sprite->y << 6) + sprite->x;

// copy each line of the sprite data into destination buffer
if (transparent)
   {
   for (y=0; y<height; y++)
       {
       // copy the next row into the destination buffer
       for (x=0; x<width; x++)
           {
           // test for transparent pixel i.e. 0, if not transparent then draw
           if ((pixel=sprite_data[x]))
               dest_buffer[x] = pixel;

           } // end for x

       // move to next line in destination buffer and sprite image buffer
       dest_buffer += SCREEN_WIDTH;
       sprite_data += width;

       } // end for y

   } // end if transparent
else
   {
   // draw sprite with transparency off

   for (y=0; y<height; y++)
       {
       // copy the next row into the destination buffer

       _fmemcpy((void far *)dest_buffer,(void far *)sprite_data,width);

       // move to next line in destination buffer and sprite image buffer
       dest_buffer += SCREEN_WIDTH;
       sprite_data += width;

       } // end for y

   } // end else

} // end Sprite_Draw
```

The *Sprite_Draw()* function is simple but fast. Typically, a video game will spend 99 percent of the time drawing the screen; therefore, we want to make the drawing operations as fast as possible. The function begins by computing some values and assigning them to a pair of pointers. These pointers are *dest_buffer* and *sprite_data,* which refer to the sprite's position in the destination buffer and the sprite bitmap itself. You will also notice that the width and height of the sprite are cached or aliased to local variables–this is for speed purposes. Remember, dereferencing a variable takes more time than accessing a simple type. The main body of the function begins and decides which subfunction will be used based on the transparency flag.

If the sprite is to be drawn with transparency, each pixel from the source bitmap must be tested to see if it's 0 (which is black in most cases). Depending on the results of this test, the pixel will be copied to the next position in the destination buffer. The process is repeated on a line-by-line basis. Hence, in the function you see a loop that iterates through X values. When the inner loop completes, the outer Y loop adds the constants *SCREEN_WIDTH* and *width* (the width of the sprite) to the data pointers to ready them for the next iteration. Therefore, we can deduce that a sprite that is MxN pixels will run through the *if* statement M*N times! This is unavoidable if transparency is going to be used.

If transparency is turned off, we can simply blast the sprite bitmap line-by-line to the destination buffer using a *memcpy()* function. This is possible since we don't need the inner X *for* loop to iterate through each pixel anymore. Therefore, the second section of the code takes care of the nontransparent case, and the whole operation takes place about three times faster. Consequently, use transparent sprites only when you must. You will usually only need transparency when a static background has sprites running around on it. The next function we need for the sprite animation system is a way to scan the background under a sprite before we draw it. The background under a sprite must be saved in many cases before it's drawn so that the background image can later be restored.

Scanning Under Sprites

The function to scan the background works in much the same way as the drawing function does except that the destination buffer is now the background field within the sprite structure, and the source data is now the video buffer or a double buffer. Line by line, the source buffer is scanned into the background buffer of the sprite. Also, the scanned image has the same dimensions as the sprite image since, at worst, the sprite will corrupt an area defined by its own width and height. The function to scan an image from a source buffer into the sprite background is defined in Listing 4-17.

LISTING 4-17 Function to scan the background under a sprite

```
void Sprite_Under(sprite_ptr sprite, unsigned char far *buffer)
{

// this function scans the background under a sprite so that when the sprite
// is drawn the background isn't obliterated

unsigned char far *back_buffer; // background buffer for sprite

int y,                          // current line being scanned
    width,                      // size of sprite
    height;

// alias a pointer to sprite background for ease of access
back_buffer = sprite->background;

// alias width and height
width  = sprite->width;
height = sprite->height;

// compute offset of background in source buffer
buffer = buffer + (sprite->y << 8) + (sprite->y << 6) + sprite->x;

for (y=0; y<height; y++)
    {
    // copy the next row out of image buffer into sprite background buffer
    _fmemcpy((void far *)back_buffer,
             (void far *)buffer,
             width);

    // move to next line in source buffer and in sprite background buffer
    buffer      += SCREEN_WIDTH;
    back_buffer += width;

    } // end for y

} // end Sprite_Under
```

The function begins the same way as the sprite drawing function does except that there is no need for a transparency flag, and thus, there is only one section of scanner code. The scanner code retrieves the data from the memory pointed to by *buffer* and stores it into the sprite's background buffer. This operation is done a line at a time via *memcpy*(). (Note: *_fmemcpy*() is the *FAR* version, but conceptually they are the same.)

We are almost ready to make a small animation system; we simply need to write a function to replace the scanned background.

Erasing Sprites

The concept of erasing a sprite is a bit of a misnomer. We usually think of erasure as painting black or the background color on top of something. In the case of our sprite engine however, we will erase a sprite by replacing the previously scanned background. Therefore, the erasure function will use the bitmap in the background field of the sprite as the source data, and the destination will be either the video buffer or a double buffer.

The function that replaces the background also doesn't suffer from the affliction of having to test for transparency; it can just blast the image back down line by line. In fact, there isn't much difference between the scan function and the erase function other than the fact that the roles of the source and destination memory have been switched. Listing 4-18 shows the erasure function.

LISTING 4-18 Function to erase a sprite

```
void Sprite_Erase(sprite_ptr sprite,unsigned char far *buffer)
{
// replace the background that was behind the sprite
// this function replaces the background that was saved from where a sprite
// was going to be placed

unsigned char far *back_buffer; // background buffer for sprite

int y,                          // current line being scanned
    width,                      // size of sprite
    height;

// alias a pointer to sprite background for ease of access
back_buffer = sprite->background;

// alias width and height
width  = sprite->width;
height = sprite->height;

// compute offset in destination buffer
buffer = buffer + (sprite->y << 8) + (sprite->y << 6) + sprite->x;

for (y=0; y<height; y++)
    {
    // copy the next from sprite background buffer to destination buffer
    _fmemcpy((void far *)buffer,
             (void far *)back_buffer,
             width);

    // move to next line in destination buffer and in sprite background buffer
    buffer      += SCREEN_WIDTH;
    back_buffer += width;
```

continued on next page

continued from previous page

```
        } // end for y

} // end Sprite_Erase
```

We are just about ready to see the whole sprite animation system in action, but before we write a demo, let's address an issue that will be important later on in the development of our games. We will need a way to copy the image from a PCX file into the double buffer, allowing us to use the double buffer as an offscreen animation page with a colorful background. To accomplish this simple task we could write the following loop:

```
for (index=0; index<double_buffer_size; index++)
    double_buffer[index] = pcx_image->buffer[index];
```

The above fragment would do the job, but *for* loops are ugly and *memcpy()* works faster. Also, we may want to copy the image from the PCX file into a myriad of destinations; therefore, we shouldn't lock ourselves into a hardcoded destination. With those factors in mind, Listing 4-19 contains a function that will take as parameters both a *pcx_picture_ptr* and a destination buffer.

LISTING 4-19 Function to copy the data from a PCX file into a destination buffer

```
void PCX_Copy_To_Buffer(pcx_picture_ptr image,unsigned char far *buffer)
{
// this function is used to copy the data in the PCX buffer to another buffer
// usually the double buffer

// use the word copy function, note: double_buffer_size is in WORDS

fwordcpy((void far *)buffer,(void far *)image->buffer,double_buffer_size);

} // end PCX_Copy_To_Buffer
```

You will notice something if you look close enough—the memory movement function is called *fwordcpy()*. This is not a C function (although it should be). I have created it manually to move *WORDs* at a time instead of *BYTEs*. The function has the same interface as *memcpy()*, but it will use the assembly language equivalent of a 16-bit memory move instead of an 8-bit memory move. The code for the function is shown in Listing 4-20.

LISTING 4-20 A 16-bit WORD-based memory move function

```
void fwordcpy(void far *destination, void far *source,int num_words)
{
// this function is similar to fmemcpy except that it moves data in words
// it is about 25% faster than memcpy which uses bytes
```

```
_asm
  {
    push ds                ; need to save segment registers i.e. ds
    les di,destination     ; point es:di to destination of memory move
    lds si,source          ; point ds:si to source of memory move
    mov cx,num_words       ; move into cx the number of words to be moved
    rep movsw              ; let the processor do the memory move
    pop ds                 ; restore the ds segment register

  } // end inline asm

} // end fwordcpy
```

The function takes as parameters a *(void far *)* pointer to both the source and destination memory buffer and then an integer representing the number of words to copy. The function is a general utility function and can be used anytime that we wish to move a large amount of memory a *WORD* at a time.

Putting Sprites in Motion

As an example of using the sprite engine, we're going to write a demo that will load in a PCX file for a background, load PCX files for the sprite images, and then create a couple of sprites. The sprites will then be moved and animated on the video screen. The animation is achieved by displaying different frames of the sprites as a function of time. In most cases, the *curr_frame* element of the sprite structure will be updated each video frame, and as the frames are drawn, the sprites will animate. The question is, how do we move the sprites or *translate* them around the screen?

Translation is a simple concept in computer graphics and can be done in a couple lines of code. In the case of the sprite engine, we know that each sprite is drawn at its (x,y) position, which is recorded in the sprite structure. Hence, if we change these (x,y) coordinates, the sprite will move. To put it mathematically, if you wish to translate an object positioned at (xo,yo) by the values of (dx,dy), you would write:

```
xo = xo + dx;
yo = yo + dy;
```

That's all there is to it. The result of the transformation is graphically illustrated in Figure 4-15. Here we see a ship being moved 2 units in the X direction and 1 unit in the Y direction. If this translation operation is performed every game cycle or frame, the object (whatever it is) will move at a constant rate.

There are of course other transformations that can be applied to objects, such as rotation and scaling. However, since the only objects we are considering right now are sprites, the only transformation that is simple enough to implement at this

FIGURE 4-15

◎ ◎ ◎ ◎ ◎ ◎

Translation in action

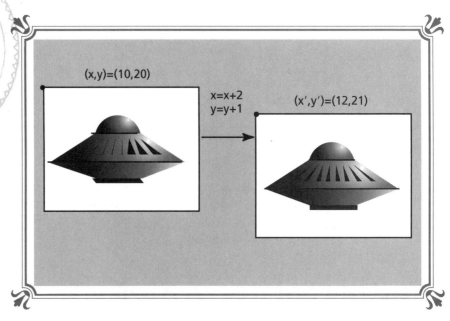

point is translation. Later in the book when we cover 3D graphics, we'll cover all the complex transformations in grueling detail. But for now, let's not get too carried away!

Now for the demo that I promised. The name of the demo is WORMS.EXE and the C source is called WORMS.C. The program must be linked with BLACK3.OBJ and BLACK4.OBJ, and of course, the program will need the header files BLACK3.H and BLACK4.H. To run the program, type WORMS at the command line, and you will see a mushroom patch with a worm and an ant crawling in it. Press any key to exit the demo. Listing 4-21 contains the source for the demo.

LISTING 4-21 Sprite animation demo program

```
// WORMS.C - A demo of sprites, clipping and double buffering

// I N C L U D E S ////////////////////////////////////////////////////////

#include <io.h>
#include <conio.h>
#include <stdio.h>
#include <stdlib.h>
#include <dos.h>
#include <bios.h>
#include <fcntl.h>
#include <memory.h>
```

```c
#include <malloc.h>
#include <math.h>
#include <string.h>

#include "black3.h"
#include "black4.h"

// G L O B A L S ////////////////////////////////////////////////////////////

pcx_picture image_pcx;  // general PCX image used to load background and
                        // imagery

sprite worm,ant;        // the worm and ant

// M A I N ////////////////////////////////////////////////////////////////

void main(int argc, char **argv)
{
int index;  // loop variable

// set the graphics mode to mode 13h
Set_Graphics_Mode(GRAPHICS_MODE13);

// create the double buffer
Create_Double_Buffer(200);

// load the imagery for worm
PCX_Init((pcx_picture_ptr)&image_pcx);
PCX_Load("wormimg.pcx", (pcx_picture_ptr)&image_pcx,1);

// intialize the worm sprite
Sprite_Init((sprite_ptr)&worm,160,100,38,20,0,0,0,0,0,0);

// extract the bitmaps for the worm, there are 4 animation cells
for (index=0; index<4; index++)
    PCX_Get_Sprite((pcx_picture_ptr)&image_pcx,
    (sprite_ptr)&worm,index,index,0);

// done with this PCX file so delete memory associated with it
PCX_Delete((pcx_picture_ptr)&image_pcx);

// load the imagery for ant
PCX_Init((pcx_picture_ptr)&image_pcx);
PCX_Load("antimg.pcx", (pcx_picture_ptr)&image_pcx,1);

// intialize the ant sprite
Sprite_Init((sprite_ptr)&ant,160,180,12,6,0,0,0,0,0,0);

// extract the bitmaps for the ant, there are 3 animation cells
for (index=0; index<3; index++)
    PCX_Get_Sprite((pcx_picture_ptr)&image_pcx,
    (sprite_ptr)&ant,index,index,0);
```

continued on next page

continued from previous page

```
// done with this PCX file so delete memory associated with it
PCX_Delete((pcx_picture_ptr)&image_pcx);

// now load the background that the worm and ant will run around in
PCX_Init((pcx_picture_ptr)&image_pcx);
PCX_Load("mushroom.pcx",(pcx_picture_ptr)&image_pcx,1);

// copy PCX image to double buffer
PCX_Copy_To_Buffer((pcx_picture_ptr)&image_pcx,double_buffer);

PCX_Delete((pcx_picture_ptr)&image_pcx);

// scan under ant and worm before entering the event loop, this must be
// done or else on the first cycle the "erase" function will draw garbage
Sprite_Under((sprite_ptr)&ant,double_buffer);
Sprite_Under_Clip((sprite_ptr)&worm,double_buffer);

// main event loop, process until keyboard hit
while(!kbhit())
    {
    // do animation cycle, erase, move draw...

    // erase all objects by replacing what was under them

    Sprite_Erase((sprite_ptr)&ant,double_buffer);
    Sprite_Erase_Clip((sprite_ptr)&worm,double_buffer);

    // move objects, test if they have run off right edge of screen
    if ((ant.x+=1) > 320-12)
       ant.x = 0;

    if ((worm.x+=6) > 320)
       worm.x = -40;    // start worm back one length beyond the
                        // left edge of screen

    // do animation for objects

    if (++ant.curr_frame==3)    // if all frames have been displayed then
       ant.curr_frame = 0;      // reset back to frame 0

    if (++worm.curr_frame==4)   // if all frames have been displayed then
       worm.curr_frame = 0;     // reset back to frame 0

    // ready to draw objects, but first scan background under them
    Sprite_Under((sprite_ptr)&ant,double_buffer);
    Sprite_Under_Clip((sprite_ptr)&worm,double_buffer);

    Sprite_Draw((sprite_ptr)&ant,double_buffer,1);
    Sprite_Draw_Clip((sprite_ptr)&worm,double_buffer,1);
    // display double buffer
    Display_Double_Buffer(double_buffer,0);
```

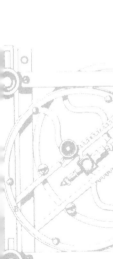

```
        // lock onto 18 frames per second max
        Time_Delay(1);

        } // end while

// exit in a very cool way
Screen_Transition(SCREEN_SWIPE_X);

// free up all resources
Sprite_Delete((sprite_ptr)&worm);
Sprite_Delete((sprite_ptr)&ant);
Delete_Double_Buffer();
Set_Graphics_Mode(TEXT_MODE);

} // end main
```

Let's analyze the program. First the VGA is placed into mode 13h and the double buffer is created. Then the PCX file containing the worm imagery is loaded, and the worm is initialized and loaded with the four animation frames. Then the PCX buffer is deleted. The process is repeated for the ant, except this time the images for the ant are 12x6 pixels instead of 38x20 pixels as the worm was. The ant animation frames are loaded and the PCX memory is deleted. Finally, the program loads the last PCX file, which is the background for the demo, and copies the image into the double buffer.

At this point, the main game loop is ready to be entered, but first we must scan the backgrounds under the sprites. Remember, on the very first cycle the backgrounds must be scanned so they can be replaced. This is done right before the *while* loop. Once the *while* loop is entered, the animation cycle begins. First the sprites are erased (which is accomplished by replacing the background under them), then the sprites are moved, and their positions are tested against the right edge of the screen. If either of them has moved off the right edge, they are "warped" back to the left edge by resetting their respective X positions in their sprite structures. The next step of the program animates the sprites by incrementing the *curr_frame* element of each sprite structure. If the logic detects that the last frame has been reached, the *curr_frame* field is reset to 0.

The sprites are almost ready to be drawn, but before drawing them, we must scan under them with the *Sprite_Under()* functions. After this operation, the sprites are drawn and the double buffer is copied to the video buffer for viewing.

Once the video frame is displayed, a short period is allowed for the user to view it, so there is a call to *Time_Delay(1)*. This will also synchronize the system to 18 FPS, and the animation will look smooth. Without this synchronization phase, the animation would run so fast it would be a blur. As an exercise, comment out the delay and see what I'm talking about. Anyway, after the delay completes its cycle, the process continues again until a key is pressed.

Now I want you to study the animation program's code and running program. You should notice something that seems a bit odd. The sprite manipulation functions that draw the worm have an _Clip after them. These versions of the sprite functions perform clipping. I have placed them in the program to let you see clipping in action before we discuss it. You see, when the worm sprite is drawn on the screen, it is so big that if we draw it near the right edge of the screen it would extend past the last column, which is at X position 319. Hence, the standard sprite drawing program would crash or draw something incorrectly if a sprite was drawn that extended past the edges of the screen. Figure 4-16 shows this problem graphically. In the figure a bounding box represents the sprite (or any other game object) drawn at different positions on the screen. We can see that something has to be done to allow sprites to be drawn correctly in these cases. Otherwise, we will never be able to draw sprites that are partially visible. We will always have to stop them before their bounding boxes extend past a screen edge. This isn't acceptable if the sprites are large. Alas, we must learn how to clip—guess what's next!

FIGURE 4-16

◎ ◎ ◎ ◎ ◎ ◎

The clipping problem

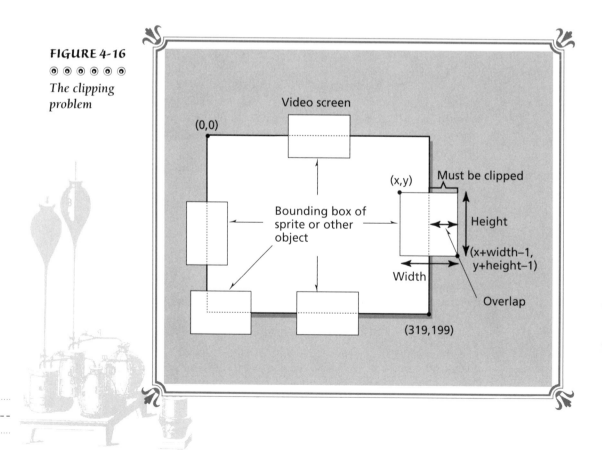

Sprite Clipping

I know that I cheated a bit by using the clipped versions of the sprite functions in the demo program WORMS.EXE, but sometimes it's better to see something and then try to explain it. Anyway, we need to rewrite the three main sprite functions to take clipping into consideration. If you recall, the original sprite structure had some elements at the end that looked like they had something to do with clipping. Here are those particular fields again for review:

```
int x_clip,y_clip;              // clipped position of sprite
int width_clip,height_clip;     // clipped size of sprite
int visible;                    // used by sprite engine to flag
                                // if a sprite was invisible last
                                // time it was drawn hence the background
                                // need not be replaced
```

These variables will help us write a new set of sprite functions that can clip the sprite image to the boundaries of the screen.

Sprites can be abstracted geometrically to rectangles that have size (*width*x*height*), where *width* and *height* are the width and height of the sprite. Therefore, we can assume that clipping sprites to the screen (which is a rectangle) is equivalent to clipping rectangles against a larger rectangle. Refer to Figure 4-16 again, which shows the different cases of clipping. The numerous cases in the figure can be boiled down to the following main cases:

1. A sprite is completely invisible, that is, no portion of it overlaps the view screen.

2. A sprite is completely visible, that is, the entire portion of it is within the view screen.

3. The sprite's X extents overlap either the right or left edge of the screen.

4. The sprite's Y extents overlap either the top or bottom edge of the screen.

5. The sprite's extents overlap both the X and Y edges of the screen, such as a corner.

Case 1 is easily taken care of by not drawing the sprite at all. Case 2 is accomplished by drawing the sprite as usual without any clipping. Cases 3 through 5 are the hard part, and that's what we're going to concentrate on. For our discussion we are going to use the following conventions to make the process easier to understand. First, the screen will be used as a clipping rectangle; thus its dimensions are 320x200. Second, we will use a rectangle as the object to be clipped. The rectangle will be defined by its upper-left corner (x1,y1) and its lower-right corner (x2,y2). The rectangle will have size (*width*x*height*). Figure 4-17 is a representation of this setup.

FIGURE 4-17

◎ ◎ ◎ ◎ ◎ ◎

*Abstract of the
clipping problem*

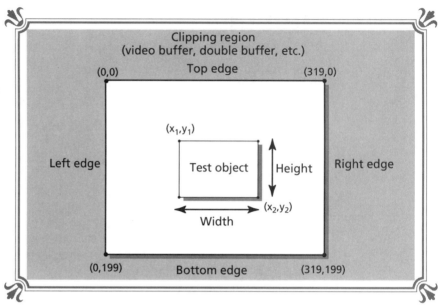

Using our geometrical conventions, let's see if we can't come up with an algorithm that will clip the object to the screen boundary. First let's implement cases 1 and 2. We do this by testing the corner points of the rectangle.

```
// Case 1
if  ((x1<0 and x2<0) or (x1>319 and x2>319) or
     (y1<0 and y2<0) or (y1>199 and y2>199) then invisible, do nothing
```

```
// Case 2
if (x1>0 and x2<319 and y1>0 and y2<199) then totally visible, draw as usual
```

Cases 3, 4, and 5 can all be taken care of at the same time. In essence, if cases 1 and 2 fail, the object (a rectangle) must be partially visible and overlaps the X edges of the screen, the Y edges of the screen, or both. Therefore, we will simply test to see if either of the endpoints of the rectangle do indeed extend past the edges of the screen, and if so, we will shrink them back to make them fit. Here's the algorithm to do it:

```
// test X extents first
if (x1<0) x1=0;
if (x2>319) x2=319;

// now test Y extents
if (y1<0) y1=0;
if (y2>199) y2=199;
```

Let's test the algorithm on a couple examples and see if it works. Take a look at Figure 4-18, which shows the results of three different rectangles being drawn on the screen after being processed with the clipping algorithm. Rectangle 1 is completely invisible and would fail the test for case 1; therefore, it isn't drawn. Rectangle 2 is totally visible since both endpoints are within the screen boundaries, and hence it's drawn unscathed. Rectangle 3 fails the tests for both cases 1 and 2 and must therefore need clipping. We see that the endpoints for rectangle 3 are $(-5,-4)$ and $(10,20)$. The upper-left corner will be recomputed as $(0,0)$ since both -5 and -4 are beyond left and top edges of the screen. The final clipped rectangle is defined by the endpoints $(0,0)$ and $(10,20)$.

We now have a complete algorithm that will clip a rectangular object to a rectangular clipping region such as the screen or double buffer. The next step is to implement this algorithm into our sprite engine so that the bitmaps of the sprites are drawn in a clipped manner. This is a bit tricky, but in essence the clipping of the sprite's bounding box or rectangle is performed first. Then, based on the results of this, the proper sub-bitmap is drawn in the clipped rectangle that is representative of the visible portion of the sprite when drawn on the screen.

FIGURE 4-18

◎ ◎ ◎ ◎ ◎ ◎

The cases of clipping

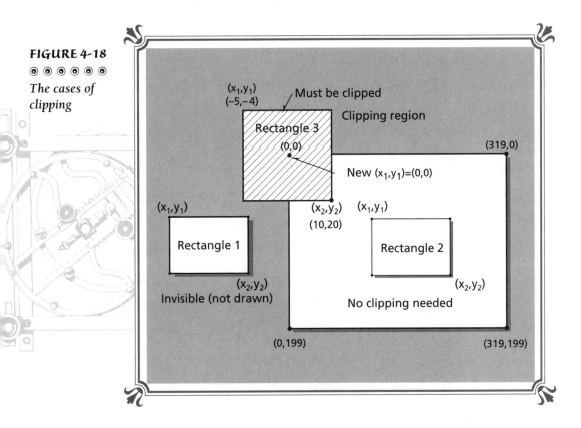

Figure 4-19 shows an example of a sprite being drawn with its bitmap clipped. First, the new clipped rectangle is computed, and then the proper subportion of the bitmap within the bitmap of the sprite is mapped down. The extra operations to implement clipping are nothing more than a couple of additions and multiplications. Hence, clipped sprites perform almost as well as nonclipped sprites. As a rule of thumb, the larger the sprite, the smaller the performance penalty for clipping it will be.

Now that we have all the technicalities of clipping down, let's rewrite the sprite functions. First, the drawing function is shown in Listing 4-22.

LISTING 4-22 Sprite drawing function that clips to the screen boundaries

```
void Sprite_Draw_Clip(sprite_ptr sprite, unsigned char far *buffer,
                      int transparent)
{

// this function draws a sprite on the screen row by row very quickly
// note the use of shifting to implement multiplication
// if the transparent flag is true then pixels will be drawn one by one
// else a memcpy will be used to draw each line
// this function also performs clipping. It will test if the sprite
// is totally visible/invisible and will only draw the portions that are visible

unsigned char far *sprite_data; // pointer to sprite data
unsigned char far *dest_buffer; // pointer to destination buffer
```

FIGURE 4-19

◉ ◉ ◉ ◉ ◉ ◉

A sprite getting clipped

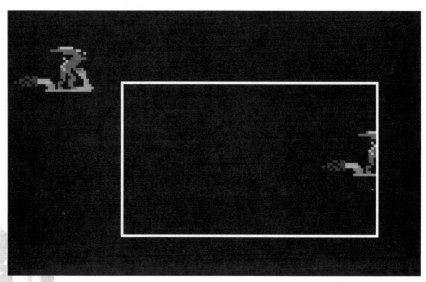

```
int x,y,                          // looping variables
    sx,sy,                        // position of sprite
    width,                        // width of sprite
    bitmap_x      =0,             // starting upper left corner of sub-bitmap
    bitmap_y      =0,             // to be drawn after clipping
    bitmap_width  =0,             // width and height of sub-bitmap
    bitmap_height =0;

unsigned char pixel;              // the current pixel being processed

// alias a variable to sprite size

width         = sprite->width;
bitmap_width  = width;
bitmap_height = sprite->height;
sx            = sprite->x;
sy            = sprite->y;

// perform trivial rejection tests

if (sx >= (int)SCREEN_WIDTH || sy >= (int)double_buffer_height ||
    (sx+width) <= 0          || (sy+bitmap_height) <= 0 || !sprite->visible)
    {
    // sprite is totally invisible therefore don't draw

    // set invisible flag in structure so that the erase sub-function
    // doesn't do anything
    sprite->visible = 0;
    return;

    } // end if invisible

// the sprite needs some clipping or no clipping at all, so compute
// visible portion of sprite rectangle

// first compute upper left hand corner of clipped sprite
if (sx<0)
    {

    bitmap_x      = -sx;
    sx            = 0;
    bitmap_width -= bitmap_x;

    } // end off left edge
else
if (sx+width>=(int)SCREEN_WIDTH)
    {
    bitmap_x      = 0;
    bitmap_width  = (int)SCREEN_WIDTH-sx;

    } // end off right edge
```

continued on next page

continued from previous page

```
// now process y

if (sy<0)
   {
   bitmap_y        = -sy;
   sy              = 0;
   bitmap_height -= bitmap_y;
   } // end off top edge
else
if (sy+bitmap_height>=(int)double_buffer_height)
   {
   bitmap_y        = 0;
   bitmap_height   = (int)double_buffer_height - sy;
   } // end off lower edge

// this point we know where to start drawing the bitmap i.e.
// sx,sy
// and we know where in the data to extract the bitmap i.e.
// bitmap_x, bitmap_y,
// and finally we know the size of the bitmap to be drawn i.e.
// width,height, so plug it all into the rest of function

// compute number of bytes between adjacent video lines after a row of
// pixels has been drawn

// compute offset of sprite in destination buffer

dest_buffer = buffer + (sy << 8) + (sy << 6) + sx;

// alias a pointer to sprite for ease of access and locate starting sub
// bitmap that will be drawn

sprite_data = sprite->frames[sprite->curr_frame] + (bitmap_y*width) +
bitmap_x;

// copy each line of the sprite data into destination buffer

if (transparent)
   {
   for (y=0; y<bitmap_height; y++)
       {
       // copy the next row into the destination buffer

       for (x=0; x<bitmap_width; x++)
           {
           // test for transparent pixel i.e. 0, if not transparent then draw
           if ((pixel=sprite_data[x]))
               dest_buffer[x] = pixel;

           } // end for x
       // move to next line in destintation buffer and sprite image buffer
```

```
                dest_buffer += SCREEN_WIDTH;
                sprite_data += width;   // note this width is the actual width of the
                                        // entire bitmap NOT the visible portion

                } // end for y

        } // end if transparent
else
    {
    // draw sprite with transparency off

    for (y=0; y<bitmap_height; y++)
        {
        // copy the next row into the destination buffer
        _fmemcpy((void far *)dest_buffer,(void far *)sprite_data,bitmap_width);

        // move to next line in destintation buffer and sprite image buffer
        dest_buffer += SCREEN_WIDTH;
        sprite_data += width;  // note this width is the actual width of the
                               // entire bitmap NOT the visible portion
        } // end for y

    } // end else

// set variables in structure so that the erase sub-function can operate
// faster

sprite->x_clip      = sx;
sprite->y_clip      = sy;
sprite->width_clip  = bitmap_width;
sprite->height_clip = bitmap_height;
sprite->visible     = 1;

} // end Sprite_Draw_Clip
```

The function *Sprite_Draw_Clip()* is roughly the same as *Sprite_Draw()* except that two extra steps are performed. First the clipping is performed, which computes the proper sub-bitmap and its position and passes them to the next step of the function that draws the bitmap. Second, during the end of the function, the clipping information that was computed during this function is stored in those mystery variables in the sprite structure (*x_clip, y_clip, width_clip, height_clip*). This is so the *Sprite_Erase_Clip()* function (which we'll see in a moment) doesn't have to recompute all the clipping information. This is an important optimization and is possible because the position of a sprite won't change in the time between drawing and erasing. Also, a very important flag that is set is the visibility flag named *visible*. If this flag is false, the erasure function will simply return to the caller, since it is being notified that the sprite wasn't even drawn on the screen! This is another good optimization. There is no reason to replace the background if there was nothing drawn.

The erasure function works similarly in the nonclipped version except that the size of the region to be replaced is recorded in the variables *width_clip* and *height_clip*, and the position where the bitmap is to be replaced is recorded in *x_clip* and *y_clip*. Since *x_clip* and *y_clip* are computed by the drawing function, we can simply access them within the sprite structure without computing them. Listing 4-23 contains the code for the clipped erasure function.

LISTING 4-23 *A clipped sprite erasure function*

```
void Sprite_Erase_Clip(sprite_ptr sprite,unsigned char far *buffer)
{
// replace the background that was behind the sprite
// this function replaces the background that was saved from where a sprite
// was going to be placed

unsigned char far *back_buffer; // background buffer for sprite

int y,                          // current line being scanned
    width,                      // size of sprite background buffer
    bitmap_height,              // size of clipped bitmap
    bitmap_width;

// make sure sprite was visible
if (!sprite->visible)
   return;

// alias a pointer to sprite background for ease of access
back_buffer = sprite->background;

// alias width and height
bitmap_width  = sprite->width_clip;
bitmap_height = sprite->height_clip;
width         = sprite->width;

// compute offset in destination buffer
buffer = buffer + (sprite->y_clip << 8) + (sprite->y_clip << 6)
                + sprite->x_clip;

for (y=0; y<bitmap_height; y++)
   {
   // copy the next row from sprite background buffer to destination buffer
   _fmemcpy((void far *)buffer,
            (void far *)back_buffer,
            bitmap_width);
   // move to next line in destination buffer and in sprite background buffer
   buffer      += SCREEN_WIDTH;
   back_buffer += width;

   } // end for y

} // end Sprite_Erase_Clip
```

As you can see, the function is very simple and almost identical to the non-clipped version except for the computation of position and size of the bitmap to replace.

The final function that we need to complete our bag of spells is the background scanning function. This function is very similar to the drawing function; that is, it will perform all the clipping calculations and then scan the visible portion of the screen that the sprite will disturb when drawn. You could argue that there was no reason to redo the calculations in the drawing function, and you would almost be correct. But in the case that the background doesn't need to be scanned, such as a dynamic background game, the *Sprite_Draw_Clip()* wouldn't have clipping information sent to it. Hence, there is a bit of redundancy here, but that's life! Listing 4-24 shows the code for the function.

LISTING 4-24 *A sprite background scanner that clips to the screen boundaries*

```
void Sprite_Under_Clip(sprite_ptr sprite, unsigned char far *buffer)
{

// this function scans the background under a sprite, but only those
// portions that are visible

unsigned char far *back_buffer;   // pointer to sprite background buffer
unsigned char far *source_buffer; // pointer to source buffer

int x,y,                       // looping variables
    sx,sy,                     // position of sprite
    width,                     // width of sprite
    bitmap_width  =0,          // width and height of sub-bitmap
    bitmap_height =0;

unsigned char pixel;           // the current pixel being processed

// alias a variable to sprite size
width         = sprite->width;
bitmap_width  = width;
bitmap_height = sprite->height;
sx            = sprite->x;
sy            = sprite->y;

// perform trivial rejection tests
if (sx >= (int)SCREEN_WIDTH || sy >= (int)double_buffer_height ||
    (sx+width) <= 0          || (sy+bitmap_height) <= 0)
    {
    // sprite is totally invisible therefore don't scan

    // set invisible flag in structure so that the draw sub-function
    // doesn't do anything
    sprite->visible = 0;
```

continued on next page

continued from previous page

```
    return;

    } // end if invisible

// the sprite background region must be clipped before scanning
// therefore compute visible portion

// first compute upper left hand corner of clipped sprite background

if (sx<0)
   {
   bitmap_width += sx;
   sx           = 0;
   } // end off left edge
else
if (sx+width>=(int)SCREEN_WIDTH)
   {
   bitmap_width = (int)SCREEN_WIDTH-sx;
   } // end off right edge

// now process y

if (sy<0)
   {
   bitmap_height += sy;
   sy            = 0;
   } // end off top edge
else
if (sy+bitmap_height>=(int)double_buffer_height)
   {
   bitmap_height = (int)double_buffer_height - sy;
   } // end off lower edge

// this point we know where to start scanning the bitmap i.e.
// sx,sy
// and we know the size of the bitmap to be scanned i.e.
// width,height, so plug it all into the rest of function

// compute number of bytes between adjacent video lines after a row of pixels
// has been drawn

// compute offset of sprite background in source buffer
source_buffer = buffer + (sy << 8) + (sy << 6) + sx;

// alias a pointer to sprite background
back_buffer = sprite->background;

for (y=0; y<bitmap_height; y++)
    {
    // copy the next row into the destination buffer
    _fmemcpy((void far *)back_buffer,(void far *)source_buffer,bitmap_width);
```

```
        // move to next line in destination buffer and sprite image buffer
        source_buffer += SCREEN_WIDTH;
        back_buffer   += width;  // note this width is the actual width of the
                                 // entire bitmap NOT the visible portion

        } // end for y

// set variables in structure so that the erase sub-function can operate
// faster
sprite->x_clip      = sx;
sprite->y_clip      = sy;
sprite->width_clip  = bitmap_width;
sprite->height_clip = bitmap_height;
sprite->visible     = 1;

} // end Sprite_Under_Clip
```

The question is, do we always need to clip? Not really. For example, if we already know that a sprite or object can never get near a screen edge, there is no reason to clip. Also, if the objects are very small, simply making them disappear won't upset the player too much. For example, if an 8x8 sprite were about to cross an edge and you made it disappear, that's not a big deal; but a 100x100 starship disappearing would be suspicious at the very least! When we implement the 3D graphics engine, clipping will be an absolute necessity, so get a grip on it, baby!

Now that we have a complete, basic animation package, let's start thinking about some game-related topics such as *collision detection*. For example, how can we detect if two sprites have collided? Good question, guess what's next?

Testing for Collisions

During the course of a video game, one of the main functions that the game code must perform each frame is collision detection. Collision detection is the technique of deciding if an object has collided with another object or some aspect of the environment. Since we are concentrating at this point on sprites and 2D space, we are only going to detect collision of 2D objects. When we make the leap to 3D space later in the book, we will extend these concepts to full 3D space.

Detecting a collision between two sprites can be done in a couple of ways. The first method, *binary image overlap testing* (BIOT), tests for a collision between two sprites by logically *AND*ing their bitmaps together in image space. Figure 4-20 shows this graphically. If there is a region that both sprites are occupying at the same time, the result of the logical *AND* operation will be a non-zero area of pixels. If any such area exists during the test, the sprites have collided and the proper action(s) should be taken.

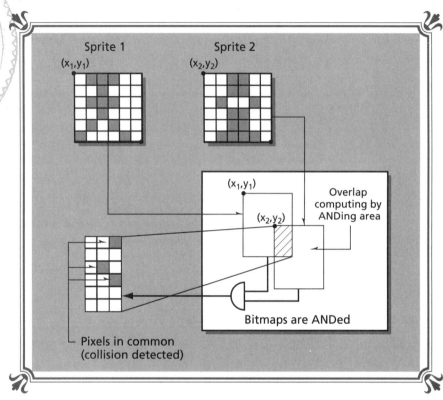

BIOT is the most precise method of collision detection between bitmapped images. However, there is one drawback: the test will probably take more time than drawing the sprites! This is because a logical operation must be done for every single pixel in the sprites, and this is just too much computation to waste on collision detection. There are computer systems that actually perform these kinds of tests in hardware, but implementing them in software is too intensive. The solution is to simplify the collision detection by approximating the object's geometry with a shape that can be more easily tested. The problem with a sprite's bitmap is that it could be anything; but what if we were to use the bounding box of a sprite as the test shape?

Using the bounding box of a bitmap or sprite object for collision detection is a popular technique that gives good results most of the time and is orders of magnitude faster than BIOT. Here's how it works: Say we have two sprites and we wish to test if they have collided. What we can do is represent them with their respective bounding boxes. Then instead of testing the sprite images for overlap, we test if the bounding boxes have overlapped. Figure 4-21 shows this process graphically. Sprite 1 is positioned at $(x1,y1)$ and has dimensions (*width_1xheight_1*); sprite 2 is posi-

FIGURE 4-21

◎ ◎ ◎ ◎ ◎ ◎

*The bounding
box collision test*

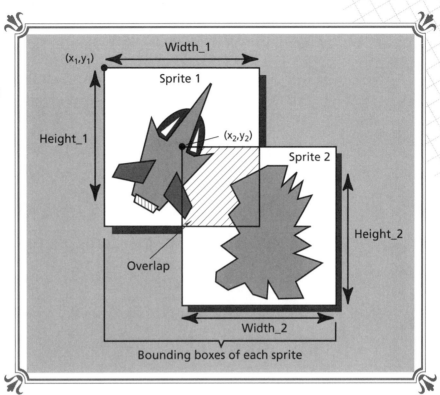

tioned at (*x2,y2*) and has dimensions (*width_2xheight_2*). To test if the bounding
boxes have overlapped, we use the following algorithm:

```
if ( x1>= x2 and x1<x2+width_2 ) or
( x1+width_1 >= x2 and x1+width_1<x2+width_2) or
( y1>= y2 and y1<y2+height_2 ) or
( y1+height_1 >= y2 and y1+height_1<y2+height_2) then they have collided
```

Basically, the pseudocode tests the four corner points of object 1 to see if they
are within object 2's rectangular bounding box. The above algorithm can be optimized in many situations to increase the speed of collision testing even further. For
example, if the width and height of the objects (sprites or whatever) are the same,
another more clever technique can be used. Here's such a test in real C code:

```
// compute amount of overlap in x and y

dx = abs(x2-x1);
dy = abs(y2-y1);

// test if overalap region is within sprite bounding box
```

continued on next page

continued from previous page

```
if (dx<width && dy<height)
   {
   // a collision has occurred process it
   } // end if collision detected
```

Of course, the *abs()* function isn't free, but the above technique is a bit cleaner than testing all four points of object 1 against object 2. Anyway, you get the basic idea behind the different collision techniques. These techniques will be applicable to 3D. For example, when we evolve to 3D, we will use bounding spheres instead of bounding boxes for the collision detection.

Before moving on, let's briefly discuss the accuracy of bounding box collision detection. In general, the technique works fine, and the player will never notice when the game is or isn't detecting a proper collision. I always get a kick out of watching someone play a game and say, "I hit that!" They probably did, but what they don't know is that sometimes collisions are miscalculated. When using the bounding box technique, the program will sometimes detect collisions that didn't occur. This happens when the bounding boxes of the sprites or 2D game's objects overlap, but the actual bitmaps don't. Take a look at Figure 4-22 for a classic example. In the figure an alien ship and a missile are both within range of each other. Moreover, the missile's bounding box has definitely encroached upon the alien's bounding box. However, the missile hasn't actually hit the alien yet. Granted, in a couple of cycles the alien will probably meet its maker, but at this point a collision should not be flagged.

FIGURE 4-22

◎ ◎ ◎ ◎ ◎ ◎

A classic miscalculation

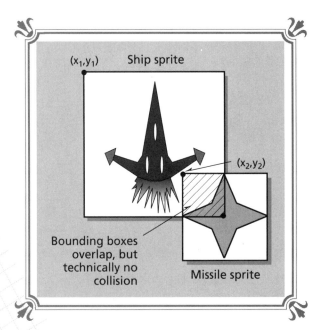

(x_1,y_1) Ship sprite

(x_2,y_2)

Bounding boxes overlap, but technically no collision

Missile sprite

However, with our technique a collision would be detected. This is the typical situation that occurs and can really upset a player. If the player is the alien, it's possible that he might have the dexterity to move out of the way fast enough to evade the missile, but since the bounding boxes have intersected, it's all over.

The only workable solution to this problem is to shrink the bounding box of the alien a bit to make sure that the box contains most of the "mass" of the alien and when a collision is detected it is a solid collision and not just an arm or grazing hit. To do this we compute the size of the bounding box and then shrink it by multiplying it by a factor less than 1.0. For example, most sprites take up from 70 to 100 percent of their bitmap area, so a multiplication factor of .75 is usually a good bet.

We have covered a lot of ground and have a complete sprite and animation system. I bet that we could write some decent 2D bitmapped games at this point if we really worked at it, but it's time to get a taste of 3D graphics–at least simulated 3D.

Scrolling the World Around Us

One of the most popular genres of video games are scrolling games. A scrolling game is based on the concept of allowing the player to move around in an environment that is larger than the screen. In other words, the screen is a window to a larger universe. This is illustrated in Figure 4-23. Here we see a large universe that is 4000x4000 pixels large, but only a 320x200-pixel window of it is visible at any time. The player moves the window around the larger environment, and the contents of the window are mapped to the video screen or video buffer. Using this technique, a player can immerse himself in a huge environment.

As you might imagine, the memory requirements of a scrolling game can be intense. With a single 320x200-pixel window costing 64,000 bytes, a 10x10 screen universe would take 6.4 megabytes! Obviously, there must be other techniques used to create large scrolling universes that are based on more efficient memory models. And of course there are, but for now, we are going to concentrate on the method that uses one byte to represent one pixel. The reason for this is that we aren't interested in making a general scrolling engine like the one you see in side scrolling games such as *Mario Brothers* or *Sonic The Hedgehog*. We are more interested in using scrolling to create background mountainscapes or cloud formations that will be backdrops for our 3D games. We will primarily be using scrolling to implement a special type of scrolling that is usually referred to as parallax scrolling.

Parallax Scrolling

Parallax scrolling is the technique of creating a scrolling environment (usually horizontally oriented) that has one or more layers in the vertical direction. Each one of

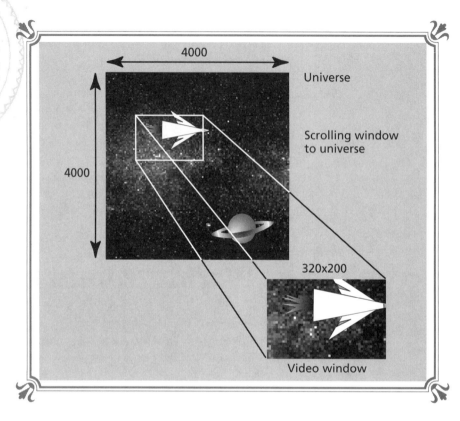

these layers scrolls at different speeds to synthesize the effects of perspective at various distances. The result of scrolling layers of an image at different rates will be the simulation of motion in the plane where the viewer is looking perpendicular to the direction of motion. Figure 4-24 shows this setup graphically. We had a brief introduction to parallax scrolling in Chapter 1 when we discussed the evolution of 3D games. We learned that parallax scrolling was one of the first methods to "cheat" a 3D view.

We'll be using parallax scrolling to create a simulated 3D view, but when coupled with foreground objects that are really 3D, the results will be quite impressive. So how do we create a parallax scrolling engine? Well, we should start off by thinking of the capabilities that we want it to have. If you take a look at Figure 4-25, you will see an eerie landscape of a distant world. If we were to drive a landspeeder across this landscape, the mountains would move slowly, and the grass and terrain close to us would move swiftly. Thus, if we could break the image into a collection of "layers" and then scroll each layer at different velocities, the illusion of parallax would be attained.

FIGURE 4-24

◎ ◎ ◎ ◎ ◎ ◎

The mechanics of parallax scrolling

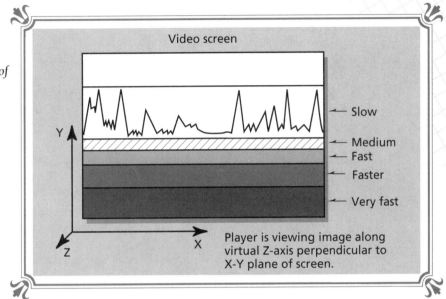

To accomplish the scrolling, we need to extract a layer of a given width and height and store it in some kind of bitmap structure. Then we draw the layer on the screen or double buffer at different horizontal positions while wrapping the region that extends beyond the right edge around to the other side. For example, say we defined the mountains as a single layer and extracted them as a single bitmap

FIGURE 4-25

◎ ◎ ◎ ◎ ◎ ◎

Alien landscape

320x45 pixels. Then we could draw this bitmap at some starting X position and some Y position, but there's a problem. The bitmap is so big (320 pixels horizontally) that it would extend beyond the right edge of the screen or double buffer. We could clip it, but this would lose information. What we want to do is wrap the portion that extends beyond the right edge of the screen back to the left side and create a seamless image. Figure 4-26 shows this process graphically. The portion of the image that extends beyond the right edge of the screen is simply drawn at the left edge of the screen.

Now, there's a little artistic problem with this method. The right and left edges must match or be able to wrap around. If they don't, there will be a perceivable discontinuity. So we need to draw the artwork so that the right and left edge of a layer mesh together.

The parallax engine we create should be able to handle layers that are wider than 320 pixels just in case we want to have a large universe, but this isn't a problem. If we wanted to make a layer that was, say 640x50, we could draw two mountainscapes and make sure they form a seamless connection. Then we would place the

FIGURE 4-26

◎ ◎ ◎ ◎ ◎ ◎

The proper way to draw a layer

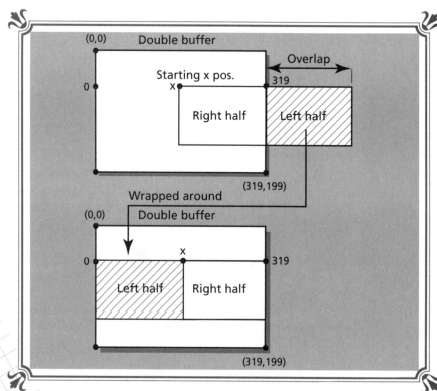

FIGURE 4-27

◎ ◎ ◎ ◎ ◎ ◎

Building a large layer from smaller pieces

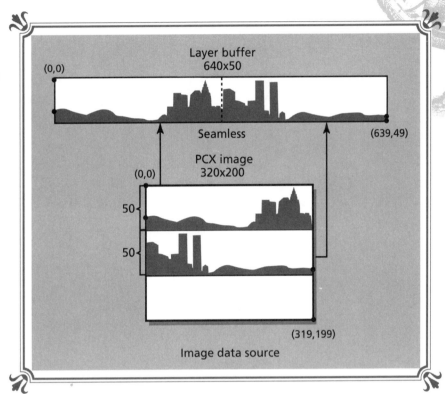

two layers in a PCX file and extract the first 320x50 section, and then connect the second 320x50 section to the right of the first section. This is shown in Figure 4-27. With this, we'll have the power to create large scrolling universes.

Once we can extract a single layer from a PCX image we can create a group of layers by stacking them on top of each other in the vertical direction. Then by moving the layers horizontally while wrapping them, it will seem as if the viewpoint of the player is moving. And if each layer is moved at different velocities, perspective parallax will take place and the illusion will become a reality.

The Layers System

Now that we have a basic inventory of the capabilities that a parallax scrolling engine needs, let's begin implementing it. In reality we need but a few functions to make a very robust system. The working set should include a pair of functions to create and delete a layer. These functions will do little more than allocate and deallocate memory and set a few variables. Next we need a function to build up a layer from smaller pieces. As we talked about a few moments ago, we may want to create a layer that is larger or smaller than the width of the screen; hence, we will "tile" pieces together to create a final layer. And finally, we need a function to draw the layer on the screen or double buffer. The function should take only a few parameters, such as the position to start drawing the layer (which will always wrap around), a transparency flag to allow for overlapping layers, and the layer to be used as a data source.

The data structure that we'll use is hardly more complex than our first bitmap structure at the beginning of the chapter. As a matter of fact, the layer structure is identical (at this point in the game—but this may change later). Take a look:

```
// this is a typedef used for the layers in parallax scrolling
// note it is identical to a bitmap, but we'll make a separate typedef
// in the event we later need to add fields to it

typedef struct layer_typ
        {
        int x,y;                   // used to hold position information
                                   // no specific function
        int width,height;          // size of layer, note:width must
                                   // be divisible by 2
        unsigned char far *buffer; // the layer buffer

        } layer, *layer_ptr;
```

You will note one attribute of the structure definition that seems a bit stringent, and that's the need for the width of the layer to be divisible by two. In other words, a layer must have an even number of bytes. This will allow us later to use *WORD*-size moves to render a layer if we need the extra speed. For now, this is just a suggestion, and layers don't have to have a width that is a multiple of two.

We are now ready to implement the functions that create and render layers. Let's begin with the simple functions to create and destroy a layer.

Creating a Layer

To create a layer, we must allocate the proper amount of memory to hold the entire bitmap, which could be quite large. In fact, we have set no upper limit for the size of these layers. However, there is a memory model and PC-related limit that is in flux in a subtle way. And that's the fact that we can't allocate a single chunk of memory larger than 64K in any of the memory models other than *HUGE*. Hence, we must insure that the dimensions of a layer when multiplied together do not exceed 65,536 bytes, or else there will be trouble! The function to create a layer is shown in Listing 4-25.

LISTING 4-25 The layer creation function

```
int Layer_Create(layer_ptr dest_layer, int width, int height)
{
// this function can be used to allocate the memory needed for a layer
// the width must be divisible by two.

if ((dest_layer->buffer = (unsigned char far *)_fmalloc(width*height+2))==NULL)
   return(0);
else
   {
   // save the dimensions of layer
   dest_layer->width  = width;
   dest_layer->height = height;

   return(1);

   } // end else

} // end Layer_Create
```

The function takes as parameters a pointer to the layer to create and the desired width and height. The function will then allocate the necessary memory and return a 0 if there isn't enough RAM available for the operation (one of my few error checks!).

Deleting a Layer

It's always easier to destroy than to create, and that's what we'll do next. We simply need to deallocate the memory that was previously allocated to a layer and release it back to DOS. Listing 4-26 contains the code to do that.

LISTING 4-26 Function to delete a layer

```
void Layer_Delete(layer_ptr the_layer)
{
// this function deletes the memory used by a layer

if (the_layer->buffer)
   _ffree(the_layer->buffer);

} // end Layer_Delete
```

The function takes a single parameter, which surprisingly enough is the layer to delete. Note that the *FAR* version of *free()* is used to deallocate the memory. Remember always to be on your toes when allocating and deallocating memory if you are using mixed memory models—that is, mixing *FAR* and *NEAR* pointers in the same program.

Building a Layer

The next function we need in order to finish creating a layer is a function that builds up the layer's bitmap. The function should work relatively the same as the functions that extract bitmaps for both the sprites and the primitive bitmap type, but it should allow multiple rectangular chunks of bitmapped images to be chained together to create a larger overall bitmap. The source of the bitmap image can be any memory context that has a width of 320 bytes or pixels. Therefore, a PCX buffer, the video buffer, or a double buffer are all possible source data buffers. The code to implement such a function is shown in Listing 4-27.

LISTING 4-27 Function to build a layer out of smaller bitmaps

```
void Layer_Build(layer_ptr dest_layer,int dest_x, int dest_y,
                unsigned char far *source_buffer,int source_x,int source_y,
                int width,int height)
{
// this function is used to build up the layer out of smaller pieces
// this allows a layer to be very long, tall etc. also the source data buffer
// must be constructed such that there are 320 bytes per row

int y,                          // looping variable
    layer_width;                // the width of the layer

unsigned char far *source_data;  // pointer to start of source bitmap image
unsigned char far *layer_buffer;  // pointer to layer buffer

// extract width of layer
layer_width  = dest_layer->width;

// compute starting location in layer buffer
layer_buffer = dest_layer->buffer + layer_width*dest_y + dest_x;

// compute starting location in source image buffer
source_data = source_buffer + (source_y << 8) + (source_y << 6) + source_x;

// scan each line of source image into layer buffer
for (y=0; y<height; y++)
    {
    // copy the next row into the layer buffer using memcpy for speed
    _fmemcpy((void far *)layer_buffer,
            (void far *)source_data,width);

    // move to next line in source buffer and in layer buffer
    source_data  += SCREEN_WIDTH;
    layer_buffer += layer_width;

    } // end for y

} // end Layer_Build
```

Remember that this function may be called one or more times by the game code. It will continually build up the image as directed. The function takes quite a few parameters. It takes a pointer to the layer to build, a position in the layer buffer where the source image should be mapped, a pointer to a source buffer, and the position and size of the region to scan. You will notice that the function is basically the core code from the *PCX_Get_Sprite()* function with a few simplifications.

Drawing a Layer

The final ingredient of the layers system is a function to draw the layer! This is the most complex function of all. The reason for the complexity is that the layer's bitmap must be drawn on the screen at some starting X position, but the portion that extends off the right edge of the screen must be wrapped around to the left to create a seamless image. This isn't that hard to do, but *off-by-one errors* have to be paid attention to, or else! An off-by-one error is a common problem that plagues programmers and Cybersorcerers alike. A quick example will illustrate the point. If there are 100 parking spaces, how many lines divide the spaces? Your first response might be 100, but that would be wrong. There are 101! This is the basis of the off-by-one problem. And to avoid it, take your time when doing simple calculations.

Anyway, back to the problem at hand. Our basic plan of attack to draw a layer is the following:

1. Based on the destination position of the layer, compute the starting position in the destination buffer.

2. Based on the current (x,y) position of the layer, compute the starting address of the bitmap that should be mapped onto the destination area.

3. Compute the width of the bitmap that will extend off the right-hand portion of the screen.

4. Draw the right-hand portion from the starting X location. Then, starting from 0, draw the remaining left-hand portion that was previously computed to overlap the right edge of the screen.

I agree, the explanation seems a bit hard to grasp, but the actual code should help iron out the details. So without further ado, the final function to complete our layer system is shown in Listing 4-28.

LISTING 4-28 Function to draw a layer

```
void Layer_Draw(layer_ptr source_layer, int source_x, int source_y,
            unsigned char far *dest_buffer,int dest_y,int dest_height,
            int transparent)
{
// this function will map down a section of the layer onto the destination
// buffer at the desired location, note the width of the destination buffer
// is always assumed to be 320 bytes width. Also, the function will always
// wrap around the layer
```

continued on next page

continued from previous page

```
int x,y,                        // looping variables
    layer_width,                // the width of the layer
    right_width,                // the width of the right and left half of
    left_width;                 // the layer to be drawn

unsigned char far *layer_buffer_l; // pointers to the left and right halves
unsigned char far *dest_buffer_l;  // of the layer buffer and destination
unsigned char far *layer_buffer_r; // buffer
unsigned char far *dest_buffer_r;

unsigned char pixel;            // current pixel value being processed

layer_width = source_layer->width;
dest_buffer_l  = dest_buffer + (dest_y << 8) + (dest_y << 6);
layer_buffer_l = source_layer->buffer + layer_width*source_y + source_x;

// test if wrapping is needed
if ( ( (layer_width-source_x)-(int)SCREEN_WIDTH ) >= 0)
   {
   // there's enough data in layer to draw a complete line, no wrapping needed
   left_width  = SCREEN_WIDTH;
   right_width = 0; // no wrapping flag
   } // end if
else
   {
   // wrapping needed
   left_width  = layer_width - source_x;
   right_width = SCREEN_WIDTH - left_width;
   dest_buffer_r  = dest_buffer_l + left_width;
   layer_buffer_r = layer_buffer_l - source_x; // move to far left end of layer
   } // end else need to wrap

// test if transparency is on or off
if (transparent)
   {
   // use version that will draw a transparent bitmap(slightly slower)
   // first draw left half then right half
   // draw each line of the bitmap
   for (y=0; y<dest_height; y++)
       {
       // copy the next row into the destination buffer
       for (x=0; x<left_width; x++)
           {
           // test for transparent pixel i.e. 0, if not transparent then draw
           if ((pixel=layer_buffer_l[x]))
               dest_buffer_l[x] = pixel;

           } // end for x

       // move to next line in destination buffer and in layer buffer

       dest_buffer_l  += SCREEN_WIDTH;
       layer_buffer_l += layer_width;
```

```
            } // end for y

    // now right half

    // draw each line of the bitmap
    if (right_width)
        {
        for (y=0; y<dest_height; y++)
            {
            // copy the next row into the destination buffer
            for (x=0; x<right_width; x++)
                {
                // test for transparent pixel i.e. 0, if not transparent then draw
                if ((pixel=layer_buffer_r[x]))
                     dest_buffer_r[x] = pixel;

                } // end for x

            // move to next line in destination buffer and in layer buffer
            dest_buffer_r  += SCREEN_WIDTH;
            layer_buffer_r += layer_width;
            } // end for y

        } // end if right side needs to be drawn

    } // end if transparent
else
    {
    // draw each line of the bitmap, note how each pixel doesn't need to be
    // tested for transparency hence a memcpy can be used (very fast!)
    for (y=0; y<dest_height; y++)
        {
        // copy the next row into the destination buffer using memcpy for speed

        _fmemcpy((void far *)dest_buffer_l,
                 (void far *)layer_buffer_l,left_width);

        // move to next line in double buffer and in bitmap buffer
        dest_buffer_l  += SCREEN_WIDTH;
        layer_buffer_l += layer_width;

        } // end for y

    // now right half if needed
    if (right_width)
        {
        for (y=0; y<dest_height; y++)
            {
            // copy the next row into the destination buffer using memcpy for speed
            _fmemcpy((void far *)dest_buffer_r,
                     (void far *)layer_buffer_r,right_width);

            // move to next line in double buffer and in bitmap buffer
```

continued on next page

continued from previous page

```
        dest_buffer_r  += SCREEN_WIDTH;
        layer_buffer_r += layer_width;

        } // end for y
    } // end if right half

    } // end else non-transparent version

} // end Layer_Draw
```

The function's interface is very similar to *Layer_Build()* except that the roles of the parameters are reversed. In the case of the *Layer_Draw()* function, the source parameters describe the bitmap in the layer that is to be mapped to the destination buffer (which in most cases will be the double buffer).

The only new parameter needed for the drawing function is the transparency flag. As in the sprite engine, this flag is used to select between the sections of code that take transparent pixels into account or simply blast the bits without hesitation. Of course, the second method is preferred since it's faster, but in some cases the transparent version of the code will be used if we wish to have trees or other objects that extend into other layers and overlap. The example program that follows doesn't need to use transparency since it cuts all the layers into nice horizontal strips that don't overlap, but in general, transparency is a good feature to keep in place.

We are now ready to wave our hands (or claws) and perform some Cybersorcery. Let's use the layers system to create an impressive demo in a couple dozen lines of code.

Surfing on Alien Worlds

After I wrote the layers system, I was trying to think of something cool for the demo of it, and at about 3:00 A.M., after watching the movie *Aliens II* for the zillionth time, I came up with the demo you will soon see. It uses the landscape pictured earlier, in Figure 4-25, as the background along with a small alien I drew with Deluxe Animation. Six layers are created and then moved at different velocities to simulate parallax. The details of the layers are listed in Table 4-1.

TABLE 4-1
◇◇◇◇◇◇

The layers and their attributes in the alien world demo

Number	Description	Height (in Pixels)	Scrolling Velocity
Layer 1	Mountains	44	1 pixel/frame
Layer 2	First section of grass	5	2 pixels/frame
Layer 3	Second section of grass	8	4 pixels/frame
Layer 4	Third section of grass	9	8 pixels/frame
Layer 5	Fourth section of grass	16	14 pixels/frame
Layer 6	Fifth section of grass	12	24 pixels/frame

The heights of each layer are determined by making sections of the grass that are nearer to the viewpoint larger and larger. I arrived at the layer velocities experimentally based on the motivation that the farther the layer from the viewpoint, the slower it should scroll.

Finally, an alien on a jet board is surfing on the surface of the grass. The alien has no animation frames, but a scarf fluttering in the wind would be a nice touch. The alien moves at a constant velocity of two pixels per frame. The code that draws him uses the clipped versions of the sprite engine. When the alien has completely moved off the right edge of the screen, he is warped back to the left edge. The animation in this demo uses the double buffer and hence is flicker free.

The name of the demo is ALIEN.EXE and the source is called ALIEN.C. As usual, to create an executable, you'll need both BLACK3.OBJ and BLACK4.OBJ and their respective header files. Run the demo and check it out. To exit, just press a key. The source for the demo is shown in Listing 4-29.

LISTING 4-29 A parallax scrolling demo

```c
// ALIEN.C - A demo of parallax scrolling

// I N C L U D E S ///////////////////////////////////////////////////////////

#include <io.h>
#include <conio.h>
#include <stdio.h>
#include <stdlib.h>
#include <dos.h>
#include <bios.h>
#include <fcntl.h>
#include <memory.h>
#include <malloc.h>
#include <math.h>
#include <string.h>


#include "black3.h"
#include "black4.h"


// D E F I N E S ///////////////////////////////////////////////////////////

#define MOUNTAIN_Y       106     // the starting vertical position of the mountains

#define GRASS_1_Y        150     // the starting vertical positions of the
                                 // grass layers
#define GRASS_2_Y        155
#define GRASS_3_Y        163
#define GRASS_4_Y        172
#define GRASS_5_Y        188

#define MOUNTAIN_HEIGHT  (1+149-106)   // the height of each layer

#define GRASS_1_HEIGHT   (1+154-150)
```

continued on next page

continued from previous page

```
#define GRASS_2_HEIGHT   (1+162-155)
#define GRASS_3_HEIGHT   (1+171-163)
#define GRASS_4_HEIGHT   (1+187-172)
#define GRASS_5_HEIGHT   (1+199-188)

// G L O B A L S ///////////////////////////////////////////////////////

pcx_picture image_pcx;  // general PCX image used to load background and
                        // imagery

sprite alien;        // our rocket sledding alien

layer mountains,    // the layers for the mountains and grass
      grass_1,
      grass_2,
      grass_3,
      grass_4,
      grass_5;

int mountain_x=0,   // positions of scan window in each layer
    grass_1_x=0,
    grass_2_x=0,
    grass_3_x=0,
    grass_4_x=0,
    grass_5_x=0;

RGB_color fire_color = {63,0,0};    // used for engines

// M A I N ///////////////////////////////////////////////////////////////

void main(int argc, char **argv)
{
int done=0;  // main event loop exit flag

// set the graphics mode to mode 13h
Set_Graphics_Mode(GRAPHICS_MODE13);

// create the double buffer
Create_Double_Buffer(200);

// load the imagery
PCX_Init((pcx_picture_ptr)&image_pcx);
PCX_Load("alienimg.pcx", (pcx_picture_ptr)&image_pcx,1);

// intialize the alien sprite
Sprite_Init((sprite_ptr)&alien,160,160,32,18,0,0,0,0,0,0);

// extract the bitmap for the alien

PCX_Get_Sprite((pcx_picture_ptr)&image_pcx,(sprite_ptr)&alien,0,0,0);

// done with this PCX file so delete memory associated with it
```

```
PCX_Delete((pcx_picture_ptr)&image_pcx);

// now load the background that will be scrolled
PCX_Init((pcx_picture_ptr)&image_pcx);
PCX_Load("alienwld.pcx",(pcx_picture_ptr)&image_pcx,1);
PCX_Copy_To_Buffer((pcx_picture_ptr)&image_pcx,double_buffer);
PCX_Delete((pcx_picture_ptr)&image_pcx);

// create the layers
Layer_Create((layer_ptr)&mountains,SCREEN_WIDTH,MOUNTAIN_HEIGHT);
Layer_Create((layer_ptr)&grass_1,  SCREEN_WIDTH,GRASS_1_HEIGHT);
Layer_Create((layer_ptr)&grass_2,  SCREEN_WIDTH,GRASS_2_HEIGHT);
Layer_Create((layer_ptr)&grass_3,  SCREEN_WIDTH,GRASS_3_HEIGHT);
Layer_Create((layer_ptr)&grass_4,  SCREEN_WIDTH,GRASS_4_HEIGHT);
Layer_Create((layer_ptr)&grass_5,  SCREEN_WIDTH,GRASS_5_HEIGHT);

// scan layers out of double buffer, could have easily scanned from PCX
// file...just personal taste

Layer_Build((layer_ptr)&mountains,0,0,
            double_buffer,0,MOUNTAIN_Y,SCREEN_WIDTH,MOUNTAIN_HEIGHT);

Layer_Build((layer_ptr)&grass_1,0,0,
            double_buffer,0,GRASS_1_Y,SCREEN_WIDTH,GRASS_1_HEIGHT);

Layer_Build((layer_ptr)&grass_2,0,0,
            double_buffer,0,GRASS_2_Y,SCREEN_WIDTH,GRASS_2_HEIGHT);

Layer_Build((layer_ptr)&grass_3,0,0,
            double_buffer,0,GRASS_3_Y,SCREEN_WIDTH,GRASS_3_HEIGHT);

Layer_Build((layer_ptr)&grass_4,0,0,
            double_buffer,0,GRASS_4_Y,SCREEN_WIDTH,GRASS_4_HEIGHT);

Layer_Build((layer_ptr)&grass_5,0,0,
            double_buffer,0,GRASS_5_Y,SCREEN_WIDTH,GRASS_5_HEIGHT);

// main event loop, process until keyboard hit

while(!kbhit())
    {
    // move the alien
    if ( (alien.x+=2) > 320)
      alien.x = -32;

    // move each layer

    if ((mountain_x+=1) >= 319)
        mountain_x -= 320;

    if ((grass_1_x+=2) > 319)
        grass_1_x -= 320;
```

continued on next page

continued from previous page

```
        if ((grass_2_x+=4) > 319)
            grass_2_x -= 320;

        if ((grass_3_x+=8) > 319)
            grass_3_x -= 320;

        if ((grass_4_x+=14) > 319)
            grass_4_x -= 320;

        if ((grass_5_x+=24) > 319)
            grass_5_x -= 320;

        // draw layers
        Layer_Draw((layer_ptr)&mountains,mountain_x,0,
                double_buffer,MOUNTAIN_Y,MOUNTAIN_HEIGHT,0);

        // update background layer positions
        Layer_Draw((layer_ptr)&grass_1,grass_1_x,0,
                double_buffer,GRASS_1_Y,GRASS_1_HEIGHT,0);

        Layer_Draw((layer_ptr)&grass_2,grass_2_x,0,
                double_buffer,GRASS_2_Y,GRASS_2_HEIGHT,0);

        Layer_Draw((layer_ptr)&grass_3,grass_3_x,0,
                double_buffer,GRASS_3_Y,GRASS_3_HEIGHT,0);

        Layer_Draw((layer_ptr)&grass_4,grass_4_x,0,
                double_buffer,GRASS_4_Y,GRASS_4_HEIGHT,0);

        Layer_Draw((layer_ptr)&grass_5,grass_5_x,0,
                double_buffer,GRASS_5_Y,GRASS_5_HEIGHT,0);

        // draw the sprite on top of layers

        alien.visible = 1;
        Sprite_Draw_Clip((sprite_ptr)&alien,double_buffer,1);

        // change color of fire
        fire_color.red = 20 + rand() % 44;
        Write_Color_Reg(32,(RGB_color_ptr)&fire_color);

        // display double buffer
        Display_Double_Buffer(double_buffer,0);

        // lock onto 18 frames per second max
        Time_Delay(1);

        } // end while

// exit in a very cool way
Screen_Transition(SCREEN_SWIPE_Y);
```

```
// free up all resources
Sprite_Delete((sprite_ptr)&alien);
Delete_Double_Buffer();
Set_Graphics_Mode(TEXT_MODE);

} // end main
```

The program is quite short for all that it does. And most of the code is for initialization purposes. There is a good point to be made here about game design. You should always try to make your support functions very powerful and self-contained; this will alleviate pressure from the *main()* and general game logic.

Let's briefly cover the steps of the program to make sure we are both in the same Cyberdimension! The program begins by creating the double buffer and loading the imagery for the alien and layers. The alien image and the layers are then extracted from the PCX files. Then the main loop of the program begins by translating the alien and scrolling the layers. You will note that there is no erasure phase. This is unnecessary here because the background is dynamic–it is redrawn every frame and the sprite is drawn on the background. Hence, it would be a waste to scan the background and replace it under the sprite each frame. Next, the layers are drawn and the alien is drawn on top of the scenery. Since the rendering is done in the double buffer, the double buffer is copied into the video buffer for viewing followed by a short delay, and the process repeats. When the player presses a key, the program terminates with a screen transition and releases all the resources back to DOS.

Locking onto the Signals from Cyberspace

Animation and timing go hand in hand when implementing a video game. We have already seen a delay technique used at the end of the game loop for most of the demos. A call is made to *Time_Delay()* to synchronize the PC to an 18 FPS rate. However, this technique is not the only synchronization technique, and there are better ways to synchronize a game to a time source. One such method is synchronizing to the vertical blank period.

We learned that the VGA card displays 70 frames a second, or in other words, the video memory is rasterized 70 times a second. In most cases we can't possibly update video memory at a rate this high; but no matter what we do to the video memory image, it will be redrawn 70 times a second when in mode 13h or, for that matter, mode Z. This means that there is an opportunity to track this event and use it to our advantage. The video image is drawn from top to bottom; then the electron gun turns off and retraces to the top-left corner of the video screen, and the process repeats.

During this retrace period, we have two things going for us. First, the video memory buffer is not being accessed, and this is probably the best time to copy the double buffer into video memory with the least amount of wait states. Second, if we write a function that waits for a vertical retrace to occur, we can create a time source that has a resolution of 1/70th of a second, which is much better than the system clock's resolution of 1/18th of a second.

The question is, how do we track the start of a vertical retrace? Well, the VGA card has many internal flags and registers that reflect the state of the VGA as a function of time. And since the VGA is responsible for drawing the video image on the screen, you can bet that somewhere within the VGA card's many registers there is a bit that describes the state of the vertical retrace. The name of this bit is the *vertical retrace flag*, and it can be found within one of the VGA's input status registers, actually, number one. By testing the vertical retrace flag, we can detect whether a retrace is in progress or video is being displayed. Using this fact, we can write a function that tracks the beginning and end of a vertical retrace period, and hence, use this to synchronize the transfer of the double buffer to the video buffer. Or if we wish, we can use it for a general high-resolution time source.

The register containing the vertical retrace flag is called the *VGA input status register 1*. It is located at I/O port 0x3DAh. Table 4-2 lists the bit definitions of the register.

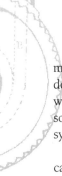

TABLE 4-2
◇◇◇◇◇◇
The bit definitions for the VGA input status register 1

Bit Number	Purpose
bit 7	Unused
bit 6	Unused
bit 5	Diagnostic
bit 4	Diagnostic
bit 3	Vertical retrace, 1—VGA is in retrace, 0—VGA is not in retrace
bit 2	Light pen
bit 1	Light pen strobe
bit 0	Display enable

The bit we are interested in is of course bit 3, which is the retrace bit. Actually, bit 0 looks kind of interesting, but we'll leave that alone in this lifetime. Referring to the table, we see that the retrace is in progress when bit 3 is a 1; hence, we can write a simple procedure that waits for the start of a vertical retrace by polling this bit. The function is shown in Listing 4-30.

LISTING 4-30 A vertical retrace tracking function

```
void Wait_For_Vertical_Retrace(void)
{
// this function waits for the start of a vertical retrace, if a vertical
// retrace is in progress then it waits until the next one
// therefore the function can wait a maximum of 2/70ths of a second
// before returning
// this function can be used to synchronize video updates to the vertical blank
// or as a high resolution time reference

while(_inp(VGA_INPUT_STATUS_1) & VGA_VRETRACE_MASK)
    {
    // do nothing, vga is already in retrace
    } // end while
// now wait for start of vertical retrace and exit

while(!(_inp(VGA_INPUT_STATUS_1) & VGA_VRETRACE_MASK))
    {
    // do nothing, wait for start of retrace
    } // end while

// at this point a vertical retrace is occurring, so return back to caller

} // end Wait_For_Vertical_Retrace
```

The *Wait_For_Vertical_Retrace()* will perform the function of tracking the start of a vertical retrace and then returning to the caller. Therefore, if a retrace is in progress, the function waits until the start of the next retrace. You might decide to take out this wait and just have the function return if a retrace is in progress, but this way, we know the exact state of the retrace instead of having a general idea that it's somewhere between starting and finishing.

In most cases, we'll be using the vertical retrace as the synchronization to copy the double buffer to the video buffer or as a high-resolution timer source. However, the latter purpose won't be as important when we learn, later on in the book, to reprogram the PC's internal timer to any time base we wish.

3D Palette Animation

Although the use of color register animation has died out in the past few years, it is still a viable method to create a plethora of special effects, such as lighting and motion. For example, in the classic game *Doom*, by id Software, palette animation is used to create the most excellent lighting effects that occur when a weapon is fired or when a bad guy is blasted, not to mention all those scary hallways with flickering lights.

Palette animation is the technique of drawing images on the screen in specific colors and then changing the values of the color registers that the images are drawn

with to create some effect. For example, the screen transition functions that we wrote used palette animation to fade the lights. Hence, by changing values of color registers, we can make it seem as though we are updating the video buffer at incredible rates. As another example, imagine that you wish to make something look like it's moving when it's not. You can do this by drawing the image in a set of adjacent color registers and then rotating the colors from register to register. Say we drew a waterfall with the three color registers indexed by 10, 11, and 12. Then we could make the water look like it's moving by rotating these colors using the following algorithm:

temp = color register 10

color register 10 = color register 11
color register 11 = color register 12
color register 12 = temp

In essence we have animated the colors, which will make the water look like it's moving. Although creating motion in this way is a bit old-fashioned, it still has its uses and is a valid technique to add to our list of spells. As a matter of fact, color rotation and palette animation were used (and still are) to synthesize 3D motion. As an example of this, I have created a program that uses color register animation to make a PCX file of a 3D road look like it's moving. The program is called SPEED.EXE and the C source is called SPEED.C. The program is shown in Listing 4-31.

LISTING 4-31 A 3D palette animation demo

```
// SPEED.C - A demo of 3-D palette animation

// I N C L U D E S ///////////////////////////////////////////////////////////

#include <io.h>
#include <conio.h>
#include <stdio.h>
#include <stdlib.h>
#include <dos.h>
#include <bios.h>
#include <fcntl.h>
#include <memory.h>
#include <malloc.h>
#include <math.h>
#include <string.h>

#include "black3.h"
#include "black4.h"

// D E F I N E S ///////////////////////////////////////////////////////////

// the color register ranges used by the road and side markers
```

```
#define START_ROAD_REG      16
#define END_ROAD_REG        23

#define START_MARKER_REG  32
#define END_MARKER_REG    34

// G L O B A L S  //////////////////////////////////////////////////////////

pcx_picture image_pcx;  // general PCX image used to load background and
                        // imagery

// M A I N ////////////////////////////////////////////////////////////////

void main(int argc, char **argv)
{
RGB_color color_1, color_2;  // used to perform the color rotation

int index;                   // looping variable

// set the graphics mode to mode 13h
Set_Graphics_Mode(GRAPHICS_MODE13);

// load the screen image
PCX_Init((pcx_picture_ptr)&image_pcx);

// load a PCX file (make sure it's there)
if (PCX_Load("speed.pcx", (pcx_picture_ptr)&image_pcx,1))
   {
   // copy the image to the display buffer
   PCX_Show_Buffer((pcx_picture_ptr)&image_pcx);

   // delete the PCX buffer
   PCX_Delete((pcx_picture_ptr)&image_pcx);

   // remap color registers to more appropriate values

   // remap the side marker colors to red, red, white
   color_1.red   = 63;
   color_1.green = 0;
   color_1.blue  = 0;

   Write_Color_Reg(START_MARKER_REG,   (RGB_color_ptr)&color_1);
   Write_Color_Reg(START_MARKER_REG+1,(RGB_color_ptr)&color_1);

   color_1.green = 63;
   color_1.blue  = 63;

   Write_Color_Reg(START_MARKER_REG+2,(RGB_color_ptr)&color_1);

   // now color the road all grey except for three slices
   color_1.red   = 20;
   color_1.green = 20;
```

continued on next page

continued from previous page

```
color_1.blue   = 20;

for (index=START_ROAD_REG; index<=END_ROAD_REG; index++)
    Write_Color_Reg(index,(RGB_color_ptr)&color_1);

// now color three of the slices a slightly brighter grey
color_1.red    = 30;
color_1.green  = 30;
color_1.blue   = 30;

for (index=START_ROAD_REG; index<=END_ROAD_REG; index+=4)
    Write_Color_Reg(index,(RGB_color_ptr)&color_1);

// wait for a keyboard press
while(!kbhit())
    {
    // rotate road colors

    // temp = r1
    // r1 <--- r2 <---- r3 <---- ... ri-1 <---- ri
    // ri = temp


    Read_Color_Reg(END_ROAD_REG, (RGB_color_ptr)&color_1);
    for (index=END_ROAD_REG; index>START_ROAD_REG; index--)
        {
        // read the (i-1)th register
        Read_Color_Reg(index-1, (RGB_color_ptr)&color_2);

        // assign it to the ith
        Write_Color_Reg(index, (RGB_color_ptr)&color_2);

        } // end rotate loop

     // place the value of the first color register into the last to
     // complete the rotation
     Write_Color_Reg(START_ROAD_REG, (RGB_color_ptr)&color_1);

    // rotate side marker colors
    Read_Color_Reg(END_MARKER_REG, (RGB_color_ptr)&color_1);

    for (index=END_MARKER_REG; index>START_MARKER_REG; index--)
        {
        // read the (i-1)th register
        Read_Color_Reg(index-1, (RGB_color_ptr)&color_2);

        // assign it to the ith
        Write_Color_Reg(index, (RGB_color_ptr)&color_2);

        } // end rotate loop

    // place the value of the first color register into the last to
    // complete the rotation
```

```
        Write_Color_Reg(START_MARKER_REG, (RGB_color_ptr)&color_1);

        // synchronize to 2/18th of second or 9 FPS
        Time_Delay(2);
        } // end main loop

    // use a screen transition to exit
    Screen_Transition(SCREEN_WHITENESS);

    } // end if pcx file found

// reset graphics to text mode
Set_Graphics_Mode(TEXT_MODE);

} // end main
```

The program is trivial, but it looks impressive! The program begins by loading in the PCX image of the road. Next, the color registers that make up the road and edges of the road are remapped with better colors. At this point, the main event loop is entered and each set of colors is rotated. This makes the road look like it's moving.

You could actually make a little 3D race game with this technique. You could draw about ten different angles of the road with a paint program, and then as the road conditions changed, you would display each different view while performing the color rotation. The overall effect would be a seamless racing game. Moreover, by changing the color rotation rate, you could speed up or slow down the virtual car.

For the real 3D games, palette animation finds its best use in lighting effects, but who knows, maybe there are some other effects we can implement with this technique?

Flipping Out

We're almost ready to complete this chapter's material, but as I promised, we are going to cover page flipping using mode Z as the example mode. Double buffering is used primarily with mode 13h, since most of the other video modes supported by the VGA used a planar memory configuration with multiple display pages. If you recall, mode Z is 320x400 and uses four memory planes, where each plane holds a different subset of the final image. Hence, the amount of memory used by mode Z is 128K; but since it is divided into four planes, the video buffer is addressed at locations A000:0000h to A000:7CFFh, which is only the first 32,000 bytes of the buffer. There is another 32,000 bytes waiting to be exploited. Figure 4-28 shows the layout of the two display pages for mode Z.

We're going to add a couple functions to our mode Z library, allowing us to write to the second video page and to select which page is displayed at any time. The motivation behind page flipping is similar to double buffering. By having two memory pages to draw on, we can display one page while updating the other; then we

FIGURE 4-28

◎ ◎ ◎ ◎ ◎ ◎

*Layout of the two
video pages in
mode Z*

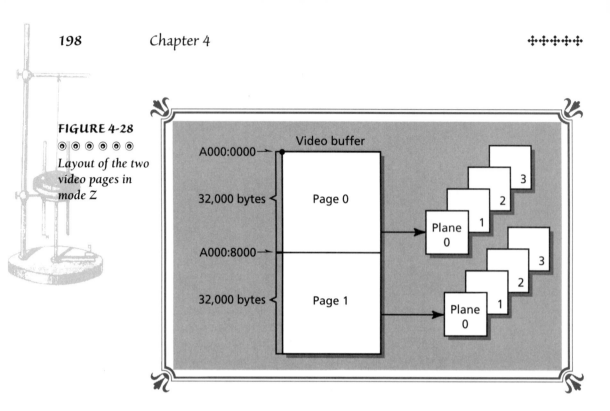

can display the other. This process is repeated frame by frame, and since the player will never see the screen being updated, flicker won't occur.

What is the main difference between page flipping and double buffering? Well, conceptually they are the same, but in implementation page flipping uses memory on the VGA for both video pages, and there isn't a secondary step of copying the image from the double buffer into the video buffer as there is in a double buffer system. Hence, page flipping can be a bit faster than double buffer systems since the copying step is no longer necessary. However, doing all the drawing in video memory will be a bit slower than standard memory since there is the possibility of wait states. Remember, if the VGA rasterizer wants to access video memory at the same time the CPU does, the CPU will be told to wait a cycle or two. But all in all, page flipping is a good way to implement smooth animation in a planar video mode on the VGA. Furthermore, if you wish to write a game using a higher resolution, such as 640x480, you will undoubtedly use a page flipping system instead of a double buffer system, so the knowledge gained by page flipping mode Z is useful.

Page flipping mode Z takes only two functions, a couple of defines, and a global variable or two. Let's begin by defining the problem. First, to be able to draw in the second half of the video buffer's 64,000 bytes is very simple. We could add a constant of 32,000 to all our video buffer operations. Or we can simply advance the video pointer by 32,000 bytes (the method we'll use) so all of our current functions work without change. For example, mode Z is accessed via a pointer to the video buffer that is aliased to A000:0000h. We could do something like this to access both pages,

```
Page_0 = 0;
Page_1 = 32000;

// to access video page zero
video_buffer[Page_0 + offset] = value;

// to access video page one
video_buffer[Page_1 + offset] = value;
```

where *offset* is the standard offset in the video buffer that we calculate based on the (x,y) coordinate of the desired pixel.

The above method will work, but we would have to rewrite the *Write_Pixel_Z()* function to take this into consideration. A better method would be to adjust the *video_buffer* pointer itself to point to either page. This is the method that we'll use along with a secondary global variable to track the page that *video_buffer* is pointing to. Here are the defines and variables needed to implement the tracking system:

```
// mode Z page stuff

#define PAGE_0              0
#define PAGE_1              1

unsigned char far *page_0_buffer  = (unsigned char far *)0xA0000000L;
unsigned char far *page_1_buffer  = (unsigned char far *)0xA0008000L;
int mode_z_page                   = PAGE_0;
```

You see, we have a separate pointer to both pages of video memory. To switch active pages, we simply assign one of the page pointers to the global *video_buffer* pointer. Magically, all video updates occur in the proper page. For example, to change the active page to page 0, we would do the following:

```
video_buffer = page_0_buffer;
```

And we would record this in the variable *mode_z_page* like this:

```
mode_z_page = PAGE_0;
```

That's the basic idea behind setting the active page for video updates. Listing 4-32 shows the function to do all this.

LISTING 4-32 *Setting the active work page for mode Z*

```
void Set_Working_Page_Mode_Z(int page)
{
// this function sets the page that all mode Z functions will update when
// called
if (page==PAGE_0)
   video_buffer = page_0_buffer;
```

continued on next page

continued from previous page

```
else
    video_buffer = page_1_buffer;

} // end Set_Working_Page_Mode_Z
```

The function takes a single parameter, which is the page to set the video system to. And the possible choices have been defined in the header file as *PAGE_0* or *PAGE_1*. We can then use the remaining mode Z functions since they all function relative to the video pointer, which has been changed by the above function to the desired video page.

The next question is, how do we tell the VGA to display the second page? That's a good question and takes a bit more research. But luckily, there is a register in the VGA that is designed for just such a purpose. The VGA has a pair of registers that define the start address of the video memory that should be mapped to the video screen. These registers are within the CRT controller at locations 0X0Dh and 0X0Ch. Figure 4-29 shows the details of this mapping. All we need to do is reprogram these registers to point to the second 32,000 bytes of the video memory, and instantly the second page will be displayed. I have defined the I/O port of theses registers for ease of access. Here's the definition:

```
// these are used to change the visual page of the VGA

#define CRT_ADDR_LOW    0x0D // the index of the low byte of the start address
#define CRT_ADDR_HI     0x0C // the index of the hi byte of the start address
```

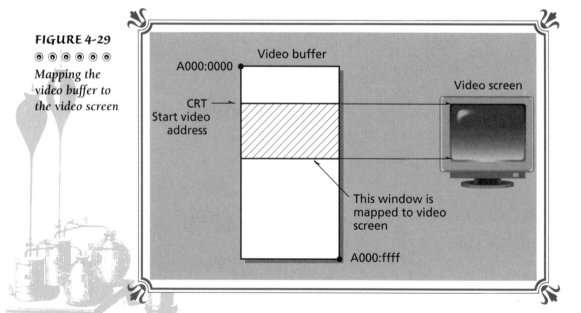

FIGURE 4-29

◎ ◎ ◎ ◎ ◎ ◎

Mapping the video buffer to the video screen

Using this information, let's write a function that will write the value of 0 or 32,000 into these registers depending on whether or not we want to view page 0 or page 1. Listing 4-33 contains the function's code.

LISTING 4-33 Function to change the start address of video memory in the CRT controller

```c
void Set_Visual_Page_Mode_Z(int page)
{
// this function sets the visual page that will be displayed by the VGA

if (page==PAGE_0)
   {
   // re-program the start address registers in the CRT controller
   // to point at page 0 @ 0xA000:0000

   // first low byte of address

   _outp(CRT_CONTROLLER,CRT_ADDR_LOW);
   _outp(CRT_CONTROLLER+1,0x00);

   // now high byte

   _outp(CRT_CONTROLLER,CRT_ADDR_HI);
   _outp(CRT_CONTROLLER+1,0x00);

   } // end if page 0
else
if (page==PAGE_1)
   {
   // re-program the start address registers in the CRT controller
   // to point at page 1 @ 0xA000:8000

   // first low byte of address

   _outp(CRT_CONTROLLER,CRT_ADDR_LOW);
   _outp(CRT_CONTROLLER+1,0x00);

   // now high byte

   _outp(CRT_CONTROLLER,CRT_ADDR_HI);
   _outp(CRT_CONTROLLER+1,0x80);
   } // end else page 1

// note: we could use WORD, but this is clearer, feel free to change them

} // end Set_Visual_Page_Mode_Z
```

The function takes a single parameter, which is the page to be displayed. You might think, why do we have two functions? Shouldn't we always be viewing the page that is the working or active page? The answer is no! The whole reason for page flipping is to allow us to show the user one page while manipulating the other out of view.

As a demo of page flipping, the following program draws some spheres in each video page and then toggles between the two pages. Granted, the demo isn't as cool as ALIENS.EXE, but it gets the concept across and that's the important part. The name of the demo is SPHERES.EXE and the source is called SPHERES.C. It's shown in Listing 4-34.

LISTING 4-34 Page flipping demo

```
// SPHERES.C - A demo of mode Z page flipping

// I N C L U D E S ///////////////////////////////////////////////////////////

#include <io.h>
#include <conio.h>
#include <stdio.h>
#include <stdlib.h>
#include <dos.h>
#include <bios.h>
#include <fcntl.h>
#include <memory.h>
#include <malloc.h>
#include <math.h>
#include <string.h>

#include "black3.h"
#include "black4.h"

// F U N C T I O N S ///////////////////////////////////////////////////////////

void Draw_Sphere(int x0,int y0,int radius, int color)
{
// this function draws a sphere in the active video page

int x1,y1,y2, // location coordinates
    angle;    // used to track current angle

// iterate thru 90 degrees and use symmetry to draw circle
for (angle=0; angle<90; angle++)
    {
    // draw the sphere as a collection of vertical strips
    x1 = radius*cos(3.14159*(float)angle/(float)180);
    y1 = -radius*sin(3.14159*(float)angle/(float)180)*1.66;

    // draw the next vertical strip
    for (y2=y0+y1; y2<y0-y1; y2++)
        {
        Write_Pixel_Z(x0+x1,y2,color);
        Write_Pixel_Z(x0-x1,y2,color);
```

```
        } // end for y2

    } // end for angle

} // end Draw_Sphere

// M A I N ///////////////////////////////////////////////////////////////////

void main(int argc, char **argv)
{
int index; // loop variables

// set the graphics mode to mode Z 320x400x256
Set_Mode_Z();

// clear out all of display memory, only page 1 was cleared during set_mode_z
Set_Working_Page_Mode_Z(PAGE_1);
Fill_Screen_Z(0);

// set visual and working page to page 0
Set_Visual_Page_Mode_Z(PAGE_0);
Set_Working_Page_Mode_Z(PAGE_0);

// draw some colored spheres on this page
for (index=0; index<50; index++)
    {
    Draw_Sphere(20+rand()%280,20+rand()%360,rand()%15, 34 + rand()%6);
    } // end for index

// now draw grey spheres on page 1
Set_Working_Page_Mode_Z(PAGE_1);

for (index=0; index<50; index++)
    {
    Draw_Sphere(20+rand()%280,20+rand()%360,rand()%15, 16 + rand()%16);
    } // end for index

// now toggle between pages
while(!kbhit())
    {
    Set_Visual_Page_Mode_Z(PAGE_0);
    Time_Delay(5);

    Set_Visual_Page_Mode_Z(PAGE_1);
    Time_Delay(5);

    } // end while

// restore the video system to text
Set_Graphics_Mode(TEXT_MODE);

} // end main
```

Odds and Ends

We are at the end of our 2D animation journey. But before we leave and learn about input devices in the next chapter, I want to add a couple of functions to our repertoire that can be used with a double buffer system. The function listings and source are in BLACK4.C and BLACK4.H, but I want you to at least see the function prototypes so you won't be surprised by them when we use them later. The double buffer modified functions are:

```
void Print_Char_DB(int xc,int yc,char c,int color,int transparent);

void Print_String_DB(int x,int y,int color, char *string,int transparent);

void Write_Pixel_DB(int x,int y,int color);

int Read_Pixel_DB(int x,int y);
```

They are identical to the video buffer versions except the reference to *video_buffer* has been changed to *double_buffer*.

Summary

In this chapter we covered so many topics it's amazing that we're both still breathing! We learned about double buffer animation systems and implemented a sprite engine complete with clipping. We also learned how to load PCX images off disk. Furthermore, we got a taste of collision detection using bounding boxes. Also along the way, we created a multilayer scrolling system, which can be used to create a parallax scrolling environment that mimics 3D perspective of a moving viewpoint. Next, we learned how to synchronize our game to the heartbeat of Cyberspace via the vertical retrace period. Finally, we took another look at the new mode Z and did a little page flipping. Along the way, we got to see a multitude of demos that used all the techniques and code we've built up to this chapter. Now it's time to let the users of our games have a bit of control, but not too much!

5

Communicating with the Outside World

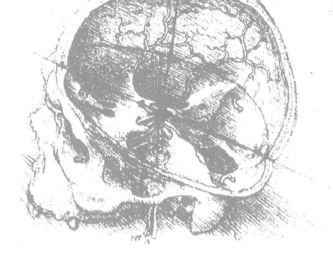

Communicating with the Outside World

At this point in the game we've learned how to control the PC and the VGA to do our bidding. We can generate incredible imagery that links us to the netherworld of Cyberspace. However, we are missing one crucial element, and that is the ability to communicate with the world of the living. In other words, we must learn how to interpret and control the various input devices that the humans playing our games may connect to their PCs. In this chapter we'll cover the keyboard, joystick, and mouse and write a complete software library to communicate with each device in an effortless manner.

The Ins and Outs of Input Devices

There are so many input devices today that it would be practically impossible to list and explain all of them. Nevertheless, they have many attributes in common and hence can be collected into distinct groups. Each group has a device or two that can be thought of as the most representative of that grouping. Thus, we will focus on the most common input devices used in games on the PC. Granted, many people may have flight sticks, track balls, or flying mice, but each of these devices functions similarly to the devices that we will cover.

As the player manipulates an input device, he is trying to tell the computer to do what he is thinking. Of course, much is lost in the translation. Many input devices are fairly crude in design and can't translate concepts such as "english" or finesse. This will improve as time marches forward; however, we must make the best use of the input devices that we have at our disposal to allow the player to control the game as closely as possible.

The keyboard is the most common of all input devices, and you can be almost certain that every PC has one. Amazingly enough, the keyboard is the most complex input device of all. It contains a simple processor and has a very complex design. The next and probably simplest input device is the joystick. It's uncomplicated in construction and is used mostly in simulations or flight games. Today, you can bet that most game players have a joystick, but it's still not guaranteed like the keyboard. Therefore, don't write a game that only uses the joystick for input, or else you'll be in trouble! The final and most un-game-like input device is the mouse. The mouse has no real mapping to the world of video game inputs other than a pointing device. And since pointing at something to select it is not frequently done in most games (except for targeting maybe), mice usually find their best use in games as user interface controllers and pseudotrackballs. As far as betting on a PC having a mouse, it's probably a good bet. Most people on Earth now have MS Windows/Windows 95 or some other window-based GUI, and these GUIs commonly use a mouse; so writing a game that is specifically targeted for a mouse is safer than a joystick, but still not wise in all cases. Now let's discuss each input device in detail.

The Keyboard

We're going to begin with the hardest input device and finish with the easiest input device, so let's begin with the keyboard. The keyboard is such a complex input device, I'm surprised there aren't a million reference books on the topic. However, the truth is, there aren't. Maybe the reason for this is that the PC keyboard is used commonly as a text input device for programs and not a real-time video game input device. Using the keyboard for a text input device is easily accomplished with C or BIOS calls and, accordingly, there's not much to it. The problems arise when we wish to take the keyboard over and use it as a set of mutually exclusive switches, much like a control panel on an arcade or console game machine.

The keyboard is basically a small computer with the single mission in life of detecting keypresses, encoding them, and sending the information serially to the host PC. Figure 5-1 shows the hardware layout of the keyboard setup. When the keyboard detects a keypress, the keyboard processor looks up the key's *scan code* in a table and encodes it with some extra information. (The scan code is a unique bit pattern representing the key; it is different from the ASCII code.) The information is

FIGURE 5-1

◉ ◉ ◉ ◉ ◉ ◉

The hardware layout of the keyboard

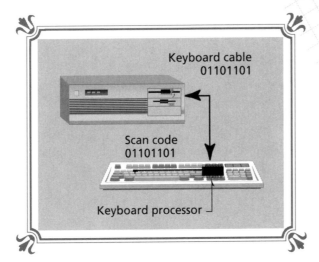

then sent to the PC serially over the keyboard cable into a buffer area within the PC. Furthermore, this event causes an interrupt to occur. The processor, in response to the interrupt signal, reads the scan code from the keyboard buffer area, converts the scan code to ASCII, and stores the results in a larger software buffer. This buffer is the standard DOS 13-character look-ahead buffer that I'm sure you're used to.

The translation from scan code to ASCII code is very important. Many people don't realize that the keyboard doesn't send ASCII codes, but it sends low-level raw information called scan codes. These scan codes are what our keyboard driver will be primarily interested in obtaining. Also, a keypress is really two events. A scan code is sent when a key is pressed, and another related scan code is sent when the key is released. These two codes are referred to as the *make code* and *break code* and are both required to determine when a key is being held down and released and so forth.

This will all make sense in a while, but now you have the big picture, so let's start painting finer strokes.

Reading Keys with BIOS and C

For a real-time video game to obtain keyboard input and player commands in a clean and crisp manner, the C and BIOS input functions are hardly appropriate. However, they do have their uses in simple situations where real-time or multiple keypresses aren't necessary, so it's worthwhile to see how they work. The first and simplest input technique is to use *getch()*. This function allows the user to input a

character without pressing ENTER An example use of *getch()* could be to control the direction of a ship. Take a look at this fragment:

```
direction = getch();

if (direction=='R')
   x++;
if (direction=='L')
   x--;
```

The above fragment is conceptually in the ballpark, but it lacks many important features. Obviously, we are trying to move a ship or something that uses the variable *x* as one of its coordinates. The user's input is obtained via *getch()* followed by a conditional statement on the result of the function call. But there are two glaring problems. First, the *getch()* function waits for an input, and hence the game will get stuck at *getch()* if there isn't an input key ready. This isn't acceptable because the whole game would stop. The second problem is that the *getch()* function retrieves the ASCII code of the key pressed and not the scan code; hence, depending on the state of the CAPSLOCK key, the program may or may not work since the test is done using the uppercase version of the ℝ and 𝕃 keys.

Let's see if we can improve our dilemma a bit. There are a couple of ways supported by most C libraries to detect whether a key has been pressed. One such way is the function called *kbhit()*, which returns a true if there is a key buffered and ready to be retrieved. Let's add this function, along with tests for both upper and lowercase characters, to our little program and see what we gain.

```
if (kbhit())
  {
  direction = getch();

  if (direction=='R' || direction=='r')
     x++;
  if (direction=='L' || direction=='l')
     x--;

  } // end if keyboard hit
```

The above fragment indeed solves two of our problems. It will not lock up the system if there isn't a key waiting, and both the uppercase and lowercase versions of the input characters are tested, so the state of the CAPSLOCK key is no longer a problem. However, a problem still exists that may not seem obvious, but is nevertheless there. The problem is that only one key can be pressed at once! In other words, what happens if the player is turning and firing at the same time? Well, the program we wrote wouldn't work and the player would either turn or fire, but not both. We need a way to read multiple keypresses as if the keyboard were a set of switches indexed by a table. With this structure, simple tests can be made to see if any key is currently active.

We have just seen how C functions can be used to access the keyboard, but doesn't BIOS have a better interface or something that can help us with the above problems? Not really–the C functions are based on the BIOS functions. Alas, there is nothing new, but we might as well create a clean function to retrieve a single key from the keyboard before we move on. The function will use a couple C functions that are based on BIOS functions. These functions have similar functionality to the *kbhit()* and *getch()*, but are implemented using a direct interface to BIOS via C. Listing 5-1 contains a function to read a single key.

LISTING 5-1 Reading an ASCII key using C and BIOS

```
unsigned char Get_Key(void)
{
// test if a key press has been buffered by system and if so, return the ASCII
// value of the key, otherwise return 0

if (_bios_keybrd(_KEYBRD_READY))
 return((unsigned char)_bios_keybrd(_KEYBRD_READ));
else return(0);

} // end Get_Key
```

First off, the above function and everything else in this chapter are in the files BLACK5.C and BLACK5.H, which can be found in the directory for this chapter. The above function is based on the *_bios_keybrd()* C function, which is a clean interface to the BIOS keyboard interrupt *INT 16h* through C. We can use *Get_Key()* in the main event loop of a game as long as we aren't expecting multiple keypresses. However, the function is still a bit compiler dependent and uses BIOS, which is slow.

Scan Codes

We've learned how to retrieve and test a key. However, we saw that there can be a bit of a problem testing the upper or lowercase version of a key without extra logic. There is another more elegant solution to the problem: take out the middle man and retrieve the actual scan code of a key before it has been translated by the PC's software into an ASCII code. By reading scan codes instead of ASCII codes, we are in essence reading the lowest level of keyboard information, and since there is a one-to-one correspondence between scan codes and keyboard keys, the concept of upper and lowercase is irrelevant. For example, if the scan code for the Ⓙ key is sent, regardless of the state of the SHIFT keys or CAPSLOCK, the scan code will always be 36. This level of abstraction is much closer to our final goal of creating a set of switches like that of an arcade or console machine. We can think of a key's scan code as the value that represents that physical key instead of a value that represents the symbol on the key.

So how do we read scan codes? The easiest way is to again use BIOS and make a couple function calls that test if a key is ready and retrieve the scan code of the sent key. The BIOS keyboard interrupt we'll use is *INT 16h* and has the subfunctions as shown in Table 5-1.

TABLE 5-1

◇◇◇◇◇◇

The BIOS keyboard interrupt 16h functions

Function 00h: Read character from keyboard buffer.

    Entry: AH = 00h

    Exit: AH—Contains the keyboard scan code.

            AL—Contains the keyboard ASCII code.

Function 01h: Get keyboard buffer status.

    Entry: AH = 01h

    Exit: ZF, Zero Flag = 1 means character ready else none ready.

            AH—Contains the keyboard scan code.

            AL—Contains the keyboard ASCII code.

Function 02h: Get keyboard shift byte.

    Entry: AH = 02h

    Exit: AL = Status of shift state as detailed below:

Bit Number	Meaning
0	Right SHIFT is down.
1	Left SHIFT is down.
2	CONTROL is down.
3	ALTERNATE is down.
4	SCROLLLOCK is on.
5	NUMLOCK is on.
6	CAPSLOCK is on.
7	INSERT is on.

We'll use function 0 to determine if a key is ready and function 1 to actually read the scan code of the key. A complete C function to do this is shown in Listing 5-2.

LISTING 5-2 *Reading the scan code of a key*

```
unsigned char Get_Scan_Code(void)
{
// use BIOS functions to retrieve the scan code of the last pressed key
// if a key was pressed at all, otherwise return 0

_asm
   {
   mov ah,01h        ; function #1 which is "key ready"
   int 16h           ; call the BIOS keyboard interrupt
   jz buffer_empty   ; if there was no key ready then exit
   mov ah,00h        ; function #0: retrieve raw scan code
   int 16h           ; call the BIOS keyboard interrupt
   mov al,ah         ; result is placed by BIOS in ah, copy it to al
   xor ah,ah         ; zero out ah
   jmp done          ; jump to end so ax doesn't get reset

buffer_empty:
      xor ax,ax      ; a key was retrieved so write a 0 into ax to reflect this
done:
     } // end asm

// 8 or 16 bit data is returned in AX, hence no need to explicitly say return()

} // end Get_Scan_Code
```

The *Get_Scan_Code()* function works similarly to the *Get_Key()* function as far as the interface goes. If a key is ready, the scan code of the key will be retrieved, otherwise, a 0 will be returned. The function has two distinct phases to it. The first phase sets up the parameters for the function 1 call of *INT 16h* (which tests if a key is ready) and then makes a call to the function. Then, based on the results of function 0 (which are placed in the *ZF* flag), a jump is either made to exit the program returning 0, or the remainder of the function executes, retrieving the scan code of the buffered key.

Now that we have a function to read scan codes from the keyboard, we can use these scan codes in the game logic to determine which key(s) is being pressed. However, what are the scan codes for all the keys of the PC's keyboard? This is a good question and deserves a good answer. All the scan codes can be found either by looking in some reference or by pressing each key on the keyboard to produce its scan code and making a list of the codes. The latter method is a bit primitive, and I do indeed have a list for you; but let's wait a moment before reviewing it, so we can see the scan codes for both the make codes and the break codes.

At this point, we have addressed all the issues associated with reading single keys, but we still need to solve the problem of reading multiple keys. This is an absolute must in a video game. It's now time to cast the Cybersorcery spell to solve it!

Make and Break Codes

At the beginning of the chapter we discussed that when a key is pressed, a scan code called the make code is produced, and when the key is released, a break code is produced (it is related to the make code by setting one bit). By tracking make and break codes, we can create a table in memory that contains the state of each key on the keyboard. The make codes produced by the PC's keyboard are probably arbitrary, but they are the same on every keyboard. They are set up in a way that if you were to scan across the keyboard from top to bottom, left to right, the make codes in most cases increment numerically. But we don't need to know the rhyme or reason behind the selection of the values of the make codes for each key, we just need to know them and store them in a table.

The break codes are the interesting part. When a key is released, the keyboard sends a break code. The break code is related to the make code for the particular key by changing the high bit of the make code. Specifically, break codes are make codes with the number 128 added to them. Figure 5-2 shows this graphically. When a key is pressed, a make code is sent, and then when the same key is released (sometime in the future), the break code is sent. Hence, if we have a table of the make codes for the keyboard, we can build or compute any break code with the simple rule of adding 128. In the BLACK5.H header file there is a complete list of all the make codes and break codes. Here are the make codes for you to review:

```
// these are the scan codes for the keys on the keyboard, note they are all
// from 0-127 and hence are the "make" scan codes, 128-255 are for the break
// scan codes and are computed simply by adding 128 to each of the make codes
```

FIGURE 5-2

◎ ◎ ◎ ◎ ◎ ◎

The relationship between make codes and break codes

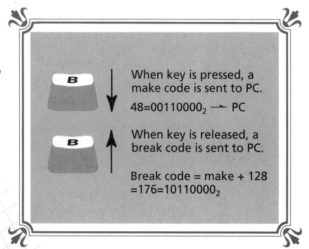

When key is pressed, a make code is sent to PC.
$48 = 00110000_2 \rightarrow$ PC

When key is released, a break code is sent to PC.

Break code = make + 128
$= 176 = 10110000_2$

```
#define MAKE_ESC              1
#define MAKE_1                2
#define MAKE_2                3
#define MAKE_3                4
#define MAKE_4                5
#define MAKE_5                6
#define MAKE_6                7
#define MAKE_7                8
#define MAKE_8                9
#define MAKE_9                10
#define MAKE_0                11
#define MAKE_MINUS            12
#define MAKE_EQUALS           13
#define MAKE_BKSP             14
#define MAKE_TAB              15
#define MAKE_Q                16
#define MAKE_W                17
#define MAKE_E                18
#define MAKE_R                19
#define MAKE_T                20
#define MAKE_Y                21
#define MAKE_U                22
#define MAKE_I                23
#define MAKE_O                24
#define MAKE_P                25
#define MAKE_LFT_BRACKET      26
#define MAKE_RGT_BRACKET      27
#define MAKE_ENTER            28
#define MAKE_CTRL             29
#define MAKE_A                30
#define MAKE_S                31
#define MAKE_D                32
#define MAKE_F                33
#define MAKE_G                34
#define MAKE_H                35
#define MAKE_J                36
#define MAKE_K                37
#define MAKE_L                38
#define MAKE_SEMI             39
#define MAKE_APOS             40
#define MAKE_TILDE            41
#define MAKE_LEFT_SHIFT       42
#define MAKE_BACK_SLASH       43
#define MAKE_Z                44
#define MAKE_X                45
#define MAKE_C                46
#define MAKE_V                47
#define MAKE_B                48
#define MAKE_N                49
#define MAKE_M                50
#define MAKE_COMMA            51
#define MAKE_PERIOD           52
```

continued on next page

continued from previous page

```
#define MAKE_FORWARD_SLASH          53
#define MAKE_RIGHT_SHIFT            54
#define MAKE_PRT_SCRN              55
#define MAKE_ALT                   56
#define MAKE_SPACE                 57
#define MAKE_CAPS_LOCK             58
#define MAKE_F1                    59
#define MAKE_F2                    60
#define MAKE_F3                    61
#define MAKE_F4                    62
#define MAKE_F5                    63
#define MAKE_F6                    64
#define MAKE_F7                    65
#define MAKE_F8                    66
#define MAKE_F9                    67
#define MAKE_F10                   68
#define MAKE_F11                   87
#define MAKE_F12                   88
#define MAKE_NUM_LOCK              69
#define MAKE_SCROLL_LOCK           70
#define MAKE_HOME                  71
#define MAKE_UP                    72
#define MAKE_PGUP                  73
#define MAKE_KEYPAD_MINUS          74
#define MAKE_LEFT                  75
#define MAKE_CENTER                76
#define MAKE_RIGHT                 77
#define MAKE_KEYPAD_PLUS           78
#define MAKE_END                   79
#define MAKE_DOWN                  80
#define MAKE_PGDWN                 81
#define MAKE_INS                   82
#define MAKE_DEL                   83
```

There is a similar table in BLACK5.H that contains the break codes. The defines are all prefixed by BREAK.

Using the above table along with the break code table we can now compute whether any key is down or up, but we still can only gain access to one keypress. The problem is we need to get closer to the hardware and talk directly to the keyboard. This means that we must install a new keyboard interrupt service routine to take over the information transport from the keyboard to the PC. But before we do this, we need to take a look at a possible problem with using scan codes instead of ASCII codes.

The Shift State

Scan codes are great, and the make and break codes will give us all the information we need to track whether any key is down or up. However, what if we want to know the difference between an uppercase or lowercase letter? Or what if the user wants to type * instead of 8? This level of differentiation can only be achieved with the shift keys. In general, the PC has a few keys that further qualify the meaning of the standard keys on the keyboard, such as the shift keys (SHIFT), control keys (CTRL), the alternate keys (ALT), and other miscellaneous keys such as (SCROLL LOCK), (NUM LOCK), (SYS REQ), and so forth. Many times, these keys are pressed simultaneously with the standard keyboard keys to arrive at some desired combination.

The keyboard takes care of these keys in a special way and places the state of the keys in a bitmapped register called the *shift state*. By reading the shift state and the scan codes, a program can determine the key that is being pressed and whether it's being further qualified by a special control key. The shift state can be read in two ways: using a C call or directly with BIOS. If you look back a couple pages to Table 5-1, you'll notice that Function 02h reads the shift state of the keyboard. If you wish, you can use this technique. However, the C compiler provides a clean interface to this function, so we will write a quick function that can retrieve the shift state of the keyboard and test if any particular key is down or activated, such as (NUM LOCK). The function will simply retrieve the shift state from the keyboard by using the _bios_keybrd() function. However, it would be nice to have a set of defines that make the decoding of the bit vector easy. Hence, I have created a set of defines in BLACK5.H that have the following values:

```
// bitmasks for the "shift state"

// note there is a difference between "on" and "down"
```

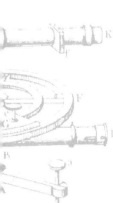

```
#define SHIFT_RIGHT        0x0001    // right shift
#define SHIFT_LEFT         0x0002    // left shift
#define CTRL               0x0004    // control key
#define ALT                0x0008    // alternate key
#define SCROLL_LOCK_ON     0x0010    // the scroll lock is on
#define NUM_LOCK_ON        0x0020    // the numeric lock is on
#define CAPS_LOCK_ON       0x0040    // the capitals lock is on
#define INSERT_MODE        0x0080    // insert or overlay mode
#define CTRL_LEFT          0x0100    // the left control key is pressed
#define ALT_LEFT           0x0200    // the left alternate key is pressed
#define CTRL_RIGHT         0x0400    // the right control key is pressed
#define ALT_RIGHT          0x0800    // the right alternate key is pressed
#define SCROLL_LOCK_DOWN   0x1000    // the scroll lock key is pressed
#define NUM_LOCK_DOWN      0x2000    // the numeric lock is pressed
#define CAPS_LOCK_DOWN     0x4000    // the capitals lock key is pressed
#define SYS_REQ_DOWN       0x8000    // the system request key is pressed
```

If you refer back to the BIOS *INT 16h* function and take a look at Function 03h, you'll notice that there are only eight bits defined; hence, the C version of the shift state function has quite a bit more functionality. It accomplishes this by looking a little deeper than the BIOS function does to compute the complete shift state of the PC.

Now let's write a function that takes as a parameter one of the above constants and then returns a true if that particular bit is on. Listing 5-3 contains the function to do this.

LISTING 5-3 Function to read the shift state of the keyboard

```
unsigned int Get_Shift_State(unsigned int mask)
{
// return the shift state of the keyboard logically ANDed with the sent mask

return(mask & _bios_keybrd(_KEYBRD_SHIFTSTATUS));

} // end Get_Shift_State
```

As you can see, the function is hardly complex since it is based on the C function _bios_keybrd(). In any case, if we wanted to use the function to test whether the right alternate key was on, we could write something like this:

```
if (Get_Shift_State(ALT_RIGHT))
   {
   //.. do whatever
   } // end if right alternate on
```

We can test the other shift states in a similar manner.

We are getting very close to our final goal. We can read scan codes and make codes, compute break codes, and read the shift state to figure out exactly what the player intends. Now it's time to write a complete keyboard driver!

Tracking Multiple Keypresses

Tracking multiple keys is not complicated as long as we know where to look for the keys. Unfortunately, we can't wait for DOS to respond to a keypress, we must remove the DOS keyboard handler and install one of our own. This is necessary because we must know when a keypress or release occurs. This can only be done effectively if the interrupt that is generated during a keyboard event is used to call our new keyboard handler. Interrupt service routines and device drivers is a topic we will cover in depth later in the book, but for now we are going to at the very least install a new keyboard driver that will do the following:

✛ When a key is pressed or released, the keyboard driver will update a global table and set the appropriate table element to true or false reflecting the state of the key.

✛ After the update is complete, the driver will reset the interrupt controller and return to the caller of the interrupt (usually DOS).

❖ During the process, the number of active keys will be tracked in a variable. This variable will be used to facilitate more efficient keyboard testing logic.

The hard part of all this is writing an interrupt service routine (ISR) to replace the standard DOS keyboard ISR. Figure 5-3 shows what needs to be done. How do we replace the standard DOS keyboard interrupt with ours? Well, there is a table located in the first 400 bytes of the PC's memory that contains the interrupt vectors for all the interrupts the PC can respond to. All we need to know now is that the keyboard interrupt is *INT 09h* and can be found at offsets 24h to 27h in the table (each interrupt vector is 4 bytes).

By pointing the keyboard vector to a new function (such as ours), we can take over the keyboard completely and do whatever we wish with the data. Let's review the game plan to install a new keyboard driver ISR. We will first write a new keyboard driver that will retrieve a key from the proper data port and then update a global table that can be accessed by other functions. We will then save the old keyboard ISR at interrupt vector 09h in the interrupt table and install our own. Then to test if a key or keys are pressed, we won't make a call to any keyboard function, we will simply refer to the table. Figure 5-4 shows the architecture of our new keyboard driver and its relationship to the game application.

FIGURE 5-3

◎ ◎ ◎ ◎ ◎ ◎

Replacing the system keyboard interrupt

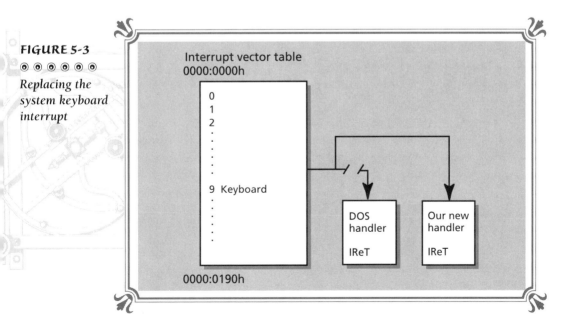

FIGURE 5-4
◎ ◎ ◎ ◎ ◎ ◎
Architecture of
the keyboard
system

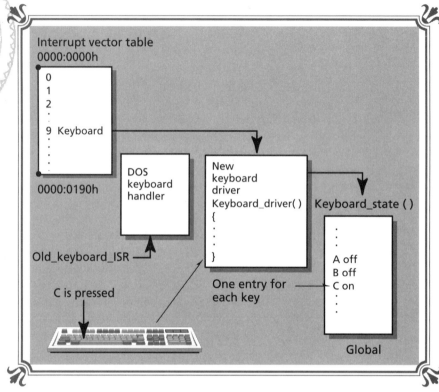

Writing the Keyboard Driver

There are a lot of details that we need to consider when writing a new keyboard driver ISR, such as how to begin, where to look for the keyboard data, the control of the interrupt controller, and so forth. However, it turns out that all of these details aren't too bad if we tackle them one at a time. Let's begin with how to write an interrupt handler in C.

Luckily for us, the C language has had a few extensions added to it, allowing us to change interrupt vectors in the interrupt table, read any particular interrupt vector, and finally, to write complete ISRs in C! Let's begin with the latter. To write an interrupt function, we must heed a couple of rules: the interrupt handler must be short, and it must have the proper prolog and epilog code to save the CPU registers and set up the stack. The C language has a new keyword that makes this easy, and it's called _interrupt. If we place this keyword in the definition of a function, it directs the compiler to make the function an interrupt and will force the proper prolog, epilog, and return code to make the function perform as a standard ISR. For example, a simple ISR that does nothing can be defined as:

```
void _interrupt _far ISR()
{
// ... interrupt code

} // end ISR
```

That's it! The function takes no parameters, but when installed in the interrupt table, it will be called when the appropriate interrupt occurs. Of course, the hard part of writing the driver is the code in between the braces, but we're getting there! We will hold off on writing the function for a bit; first, let's see exactly how we will install and remove the new driver from the interrupt table.

Installing the Driver

Before we install the new keyboard driver, we need a place to save the old interrupt vector that points to the standard DOS keyboard interrupt. Later, we will use this saved vector to restore the DOS keyboard handler when our game or program has completed. The variable that will hold the old keyboard handler is defined below:

```
void (_interrupt _far *Old_Keyboard_ISR)();  // holds old keyboard
                                             // interrupt handler
```

As you can see, it is a pointer to a function that is both *FAR* and *_interrupt*. You will also note that the function takes no parameters. To further facilitate the installation of our new keyboard driver, here are a few defines to make the code more readable:

```
// defines for the keyboard interface

#define KEYBOARD_INTERRUPT      0x09  // the keyboard interrupt number
#define KEY_BUFFER              0x60  // the port of the keyboard buffer
#define KEY_CONTROL             0x61  // the port of the keyboard controller
#define PIC_PORT                0x20  // the port of the peripheral
                                      // interrupt controller (PIC)
```

Only *KEYBOARD_INTERRUPT* is of interest at this point. It is simply aliased to the number 09h, which is the keyboard interrupt vector number that is the 9th entry in the interrupt table. The remaining defines are to communicate with the keyboard buffer and control logic, which we'll get to shortly.

We're about ready to write a function to install the new keyboard driver, but we don't know its name yet! So we'll call it *Keyboard_Driver()*, and here's its formal prototype:

```
void _interrupt _far Keyboard_Driver();
```

Notice it has no parameters. This is typical of ISRs since they are not called by an application, but started by an event; therefore, there's really no need for parameters. We now have all the elements to install the new keyboard driver. To install it, we'll use the C function *_dos_getvect()* to first save the old DOS keyboard handler, and then we'll install our new handler with _dos_setvect(). Listing 5-4 contains the function to install the new keyboard driver.

LISTING 5-4 Function to install the new keyboard driver

```
void Keyboard_Install_Driver(void)
{
// this function installs the new keyboard driver

int index;

// clear out keyboard state table
for (index=0; index<128; index++)
    keyboard_state[index]=0;

// save the old keyboard driver
Old_Keyboard_ISR = _dos_getvect(KEYBOARD_INTERRUPT);

// install the new keyboard driver
_dos_setvect(KEYBOARD_INTERRUPT, Keyboard_Driver);

} // end Keyboard_Install_Driver
```

The C interrupt functions need a little explanation. The _dos_setvect() function takes as parameters the interrupt number to change along with a pointer to the new interrupt. Likewise, _dos_getvect() takes as a parameter the interrupt number to retrieve and returns a pointer to it. You can refer to your C compiler's run-time library reference for a more complete explanation of these and other related functions. About the only question we should be asking is, why are we using a C function to install the driver at all? Why not index into the memory from 0000:0000h to 0000:0190h and do it ourselves? The answer is a very important one. The problem is: it's possible that during the vector change an interrupt could occur and the half-changed interrupt vector might be the one that is called! The result would be a crash, so instead of taking a chance by doing it ourselves, we can rest assured that the C version performs the vector update in an "atomic" fashion that can't be interrupted. (Actually, it inhibits all interrupts and performs a 32-bit write, but let's just pretend it's magick.)

We're ready to move on to the next step, which is removing the driver (which doesn't exist yet) from the system when our game is complete.

Removing the Driver

To remove the new keyboard driver and replace or restore the old DOS one, we only need to do a single _dos_setvect() with the old keyboard handler that was saved in the variable Old_Keyboard_ISR. Listing 5-5 contains a function to do this.

LISTING 5-5 Function to remove the keyboard driver

```
void Keyboard_Remove_Driver(void)
{

// this function restores the old keyboard driver (DOS version) with the
// previously saved vector

_dos_setvect(KEYBOARD_INTERRUPT, Old_Keyboard_ISR);

} // end Keyboard_Remove_Driver
```

The only function we are missing at this point is the most important one, which, of course, is the new keyboard driver. Let's discuss it.

The New Keyboard Driver

The new keyboard driver will be called whenever the user presses or releases a key. Basically, when the keyboard hardware retrieves a key, the keyboard tells the PC to initiate an interrupt to service the keyboard event. This interrupt service routine can do whatever it wants to, but at the very least, it should read the scan code out of the PC keyboard buffer and reset the PC's keyboard buffer logic, so another key can be retrieved. This reset involves a couple steps. The first step is to reset the keyboard buffer flip-flop, which is used as a single memory bit to track that a key is in the buffer. Second, the *peripheral interrupt controller* or PIC must be reset so that another interrupt can be processed by the PC. The first step is achieved by writing to one of the keyboard controller ports, and similarly, the second step is done by writing a 20h to the PIC's control register, which is at port 20h (yes a 20h to 20h—coincidence?).

Resetting the PIC is easy enough and can be done in a single line, but reading the key from the keyboard and resetting the keyboard logic is a bit complex, so let's cover it before we continue. The keyboard buffer is at I/O port 60h and has been defined in our software as *KEYBOARD_BUFFER*. The keyboard control register exists at port 61h and is defined in our software as *KEYBOARD_CONTROL*. When the keyboard detects a keypress, the scan code will be stored in the *KEYBOARD_BUFFER* port and can be retrieved with a simple read. However, after the scan code is retrieved, a specific sequence of operations must be performed to the keyboard control registers to reset the keyboard and indicate to the logic that the key has been processed. This is done by the following steps:

1. The *KEYBOARD_CONTROL* register is read and logically ORed with 82h.

2. The result is written back out to the *KEYBOARD_CONTROL* port.

3. The result is then again logically ANDed with 7Fh, and the result is again written out to the KEYBOARD_CONTROL port.

4. Finally, a value of 20h is written to the PIC control register at 20h, and this completes the keyboard reset and interrupt re-enable.

Of course, before all this happens, the scan code will be read into some variable for processing. In our case, this variable is named *raw_scan_code* and is defined below:

```
int raw_scan_code=0;  // the global keyboard scan code
```

This value is used to update the global keyboard state table, which tracks all keys. The name of the table is *keyboard_state[]* and is defined like this:

```
int keyboard_state[128];
```

Now here's the tricky part. The function must place either a 1 or a 0 into each location of the keyboard state table that is indexed by the *raw_scan_code*. The value in *raw_scan_code* can either be a make code or a break code. We know that all make codes are from 0 to 127, so we can use this information to conclude that if a scan code is retrieved from 0 to 127, it must be a make code, and hence, a 1 will be placed into the *keyboard_state[]* table at the location indexed by the scan code. On the other hand, if the scan code is greater than 127, it must be a break code; thus, 128 is subtracted from the *raw_scan_code* value and this is used as an index into the *keyboard_state[]* table, and a 0 is placed into the position to reflect that the key has been released.

That completes the steps to write a minimal keyboard handler that can detect and track multiple keypresses in real-time. The function that does all this is shown in Listing 5-6.

LISTING 5-6 *The new keyboard driver*

```
void _interrupt _far Keyboard_Driver()
{
// this function is used as the new keyboard driver. once it is installed
// it will continually update a keyboard state table that has an entry for
// every key on the keyboard, when a key is down the appropriate entry will be
// set to 1, when released the entry will be reset. any key can be queried by
// accessing the keyboard_state[] table with the make code of the key as the
// index

// need to use assembly for speed since this is an interrupt

_asm
   {
   sti                        ; re-enable interrupts
   in al, KEY_BUFFER          ; get the key that was pressed from the keyboard
   xor ah,ah                  ; zero out upper 8 bits of AX
   mov raw_scan_code, ax      ; store the key in global variable
   in al, KEY_CONTROL         ; set the control register to reflect key was read
```

```
    or al, 82h              ; set the proper bits to reset the keyboard flip flop
    out KEY_CONTROL,al      ; send the new data back to the control register
    and al,7fh              ; mask off high bit
    out KEY_CONTROL,al      ; complete the reset
    mov al,20h              ; reset command
    out PIC_PORT,al         ; tell PIC to re-enable interrupts

    } // end inline assembly

// update the keyboard table

// test if the scan code was a make code or a break code
if (raw_scan_code <128)
    {
    // index into table and set this key to the "on" state if it already isn't
    // on

    if (keyboard_state[raw_scan_code]==KEY_UP)
        {
        // there is one more active key
        keys_active++;

        // update the state table
        keyboard_state[raw_scan_code] = KEY_DOWN;

        } // end if key wasn't already pressed

    } // end if a make code
else
    {
    // must be a break code, therefore turn the key "off"
    // note that 128 must be subtracted from the raw key to access the correct
    // element of the state table

    if (keyboard_state[raw_scan_code-128]==KEY_DOWN)
        {
        // there is one less active key
        keys_active--;

        // update the state table
        keyboard_state[raw_scan_code-128] = KEY_UP;

        } // end if key wasn't already pressed

    } // end else

} // end Keyboard_Driver
```

The *Keyboard_Driver()* works more or less as we have described except for a little twist at the end. When a scan code has been determined to be either a make

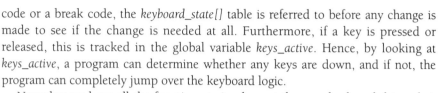

code or a break code, the *keyboard_state[]* table is referred to before any change is made to see if the change is needed at all. Furthermore, if a key is pressed or released, this is tracked in the global variable *keys_active*. Hence, by looking at *keys_active*, a program can determine whether any keys are down, and if not, the program can completely jump over the keyboard logic.

Now that we have all the functions to implement the new keyboard driver, let's rewrite our original program that tested to see if the Ⓡ or Ⓛ keys were down. The code would look like this:

```
// first install our new driver

Keyboard_Install_Driver();

while(!done)
     {
     // test if any keys are active

     if (keys_active)
        {
        // test for the 'R' key
        if (keyboard_state[MAKE_R])
           x++;

        // test for the 'L' key
        if (keyboard_state[MAKE_L])
           x--;
        } // end if keys active
     } // end main event loop

// remove the driver when done

Keyboard_Remove_Driver();
```

The beauty of the above fragment is that it can handle multiple keypresses at once. In this case, the player can press both Ⓡ and Ⓛ simultaneously. If this occurs, the result will be that *x* doesn't change, since it will be both incremented and decremented! This is exactly what we're trying to achieve, and we have done it with a few dozen lines of code and three relatively simple functions. In general, the new keyboard system is practically transparent to use. We load it, use it, and then remove it when we are done.

There is one drawback, and that's the fact that none of the BIOS or C functions will work anymore since we have taken over the keyboard completely and thrown out the old driver. But that's life. Although it's possible to chain interrupts and link the DOS keyboard driver on top of ours, we won't be chaining the keyboard at this time. We'll learn how to do that later in the book.

Keying in the Right Combination

As a demo of the keyboard driver, I have put together a program that loads a PCX file with the image of a numeric keypad. When you run the program, press the keys 1 through 9 on the keyboard and the virtual keys on the screen will light up. The main point of the program is to demonstrate that multiple, simultaneous keypresses can be detected with the new keyboard driver. The name of the demo is KEYTEST.EXE. If you wish to make your own executable from the source KEYTEST.C, you will have to link it to all the previous library modules, including BLACK5.C. Listing 5-7 shows the source for your review.

LISTING 5-7 A program to demonstrate the keyboard driver

```
// KEYTEST.C - A demo of the keyboard driver

// I N C L U D E S ///////////////////////////////////////////////////////

#include <io.h>
#include <conio.h>
#include <stdio.h>
#include <stdlib.h>
#include <dos.h>
#include <bios.h>
#include <fcntl.h>
#include <memory.h>
#include <malloc.h>
#include <math.h>
#include <string.h>

// include our graphics library

#include "black3.h"
#include "black4.h"
#include "black5.h"

// D E F I N E S //////////////////////////////////////////////////////////

#define START_NUMERIC_COLOR 6*16      // start of color register bank that
                                      // keys are drawn with

// G L O B A L S ////////////////////////////////////////////////////////

pcx_picture image_pcx; // general PCX image used to load background and
                       // imagery

// M A I N ////////////////////////////////////////////////////////////////

void main(int argc, char **argv)
```

continued on next page

continued from previous page

```
{

RGB_color on  = {0,63,0},    // the color values for the on and off buttons
          off = {0,20,0};

// set the graphics mode to mode 13h
Set_Graphics_Mode(GRAPHICS_MODE13);

// load the screen image
PCX_Init((pcx_picture_ptr)&image_pcx);

// load a PCX file (make sure it's there)
if (PCX_Load("keypad.pcx", (pcx_picture_ptr)&image_pcx,1))
   {
   // copy the image to the display buffer
   PCX_Show_Buffer((pcx_picture_ptr)&image_pcx);

   // delete the PCX buffer
   PCX_Delete((pcx_picture_ptr)&image_pcx);

   // install the keyboard driver
   Keyboard_Install_Driver();

   // enter main event loop
   while(!keyboard_state[MAKE_ESC])
       {
       // to avoid video snow wait for vertical retrace
       Wait_For_Vertical_Retrace();

       // now test all the keys to see if they are pressed or released
       // based on this turn the virtual light that illuminates each
       // button on or off

       if (keyboard_state[MAKE_1])
          Write_Color_Reg(START_NUMERIC_COLOR+0, (RGB_color_ptr)&on);
       else
          Write_Color_Reg(START_NUMERIC_COLOR+0, (RGB_color_ptr)&off);

       if (keyboard_state[MAKE_2])
          Write_Color_Reg(START_NUMERIC_COLOR+1, (RGB_color_ptr)&on);
       else
          Write_Color_Reg(START_NUMERIC_COLOR+1, (RGB_color_ptr)&off);

       if (keyboard_state[MAKE_3])
          Write_Color_Reg(START_NUMERIC_COLOR+2, (RGB_color_ptr)&on);
       else
          Write_Color_Reg(START_NUMERIC_COLOR+2, (RGB_color_ptr)&off);

       if (keyboard_state[MAKE_4])
          Write_Color_Reg(START_NUMERIC_COLOR+3, (RGB_color_ptr)&on);
       else
          Write_Color_Reg(START_NUMERIC_COLOR+3, (RGB_color_ptr)&off);
```

```
      if (keyboard_state[MAKE_5])
         Write_Color_Reg(START_NUMERIC_COLOR+4, (RGB_color_ptr)&on);
      else
         Write_Color_Reg(START_NUMERIC_COLOR+4, (RGB_color_ptr)&off);

      if (keyboard_state[MAKE_6])
         Write_Color_Reg(START_NUMERIC_COLOR+5, (RGB_color_ptr)&on);
      else
         Write_Color_Reg(START_NUMERIC_COLOR+5, (RGB_color_ptr)&off);

      if (keyboard_state[MAKE_7])
         Write_Color_Reg(START_NUMERIC_COLOR+6, (RGB_color_ptr)&on);
      else
         Write_Color_Reg(START_NUMERIC_COLOR+6, (RGB_color_ptr)&off);

      if (keyboard_state[MAKE_8])
         Write_Color_Reg(START_NUMERIC_COLOR+7, (RGB_color_ptr)&on);
      else
         Write_Color_Reg(START_NUMERIC_COLOR+7, (RGB_color_ptr)&off);

      if (keyboard_state[MAKE_9])
         Write_Color_Reg(START_NUMERIC_COLOR+8, (RGB_color_ptr)&on);
      else
         Write_Color_Reg(START_NUMERIC_COLOR+8, (RGB_color_ptr)&off);

      } // end main event loop

// remove the keyboard driver
Keyboard_Remove_Driver();
// use a screen transition to exit
Screen_Transition(SCREEN_WHITENESS);

   } // end if pcx file found

// reset graphics to text mode
Set_Graphics_Mode(TEXT_MODE);

} // end main
```

The program starts by loading the PCX image of the keypad and displaying it on the screen. Then the keyboard driver is installed and the main event loop is entered. The event loop contains a set of *if* statements that test whether each of the keys 1 through 9 are being pressed or not. If a key is being pressed, the virtual key on the screen is illuminated. This illumination is accomplished by using color register animation. Each one of the keys on the keypad was drawn using a different color register; then, by changing the values of the color registers, the keys look like they light up. Also, there is an interesting line of code that calls the *Wait_For_Vertical_Retrace()* function. This is necessary to avoid screen snow due to the continual updating of the color registers.

On some VGA cards, when the color registers are changed, the video image "snows." This problem can be minimized by making infrequent changes to the color registers or by updating them during the vertical retrace, as we have done here with the *Wait_For_Vertical_Retrace()* function. Finally, we exit the program by pressing (ESC), at which time the old keyboard driver is replaced and the program exits.

Joysticks

To evoke the strongest feeling of a true video game input device, you can't beat the joystick. The joystick has always been a common input device on home video game consoles and arcade machines alike. However, it's only been in the last few years that the PC has adopted the joystick as a main video game input device. Although the PC always had hardware to support joysticks, many people didn't like them because of their crude design and poor response. Today, things are different–joysticks are futuristic, with lights and rapid fire buttons that make them look like they're from a movie set!

Although there have been many changes in its design and construction, the basic operation of the PC joystick has remained the same. PC joysticks are controlled and interfaced by a joystick card. These days, most I/O cards or sound cards have a joystick port or two built in. Otherwise, you can still buy a separate joystick card and plug it in your PC. This isn't practical, however, since it's a bit of a waste using a whole slot for a joystick card. In any case, the interface card plugs into the PC and the joystick(s) plugs into the card.

The joysticks on the PC are of course analog, in contrast to the simpler digital models on video game consoles and arcade machines. This means that the joysticks can detect a range of values in both the X and Y directions. Figure 5-5 shows a typical joystick setup on the PC. Notice also that the joystick has two buttons. These buttons are placed in different positions depending on the joystick, but in general, the PC joystick design only supports two buttons. So how does the PC's analog joystick work? Well, first let's take a look at how a digital joystick works for some insight.

Basically, digital joysticks are a set of switches placed under some interface. When a digital joystick yoke is moved up, down, right, or left, one of the switches is activated. Figure 5-6 shows a digital joystick and its electrical configuration. The problem with a digital joystick is that it can only detect extreme values. It can't be used to go a little to the left or a lot to the right. It's either all or nothing! The analog joystick, on the other hand, uses a device called a *potentiometer* (a mechanically variable resistor) to measure the amount the joystick is deflected in either direction. Take a look at Figure 5-7. We see that each axis of the joystick is connected to a potentiometer, and these potentiometers are then used as the resistive elements in a

FIGURE 5-5

◎ ◎ ◎ ◎ ◎ ◎

A joystick and interface card

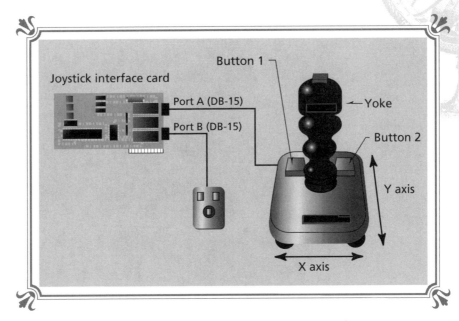

timing circuit on the joystick card. Also, there are a total of two joysticks, therefore, four timing circuits.

You might recall from high school physics, if you have a voltage source and you apply it to a resistor in series with a capacitor, the capacitor will take a certain

FIGURE 5-6

◎ ◎ ◎ ◎ ◎ ◎

Architecture of a digital joystick

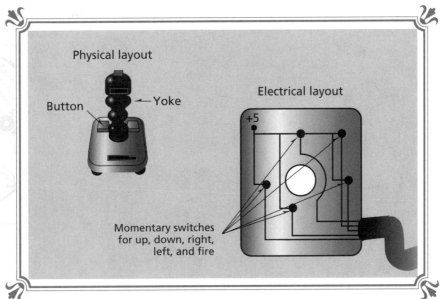

FIGURE 5-7

◎ ◎ ◎ ◎ ◎ ◎

The electronics in an analog joystick

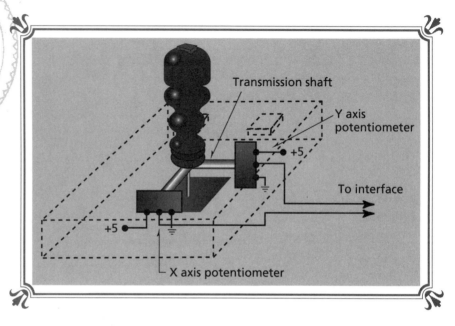

Transmission shaft

Y axis potentiometer

+5

To interface

+5

X axis potentiometer

amount of time to charge. This time is proportional to both the capacitor and the resistor. In the case of the PC's joystick design, the capacitors are a fixed value, as are the voltages. The only variables are the resistors. Hence, if we count the amount of time it takes for the charging circuits to charge the capacitors, we can compute the proportional value of the resistors, which in essence are the positions of the joystick potentiometers. The joystick cards don't have real A/D converters. And that's why it's necessary to use this timing method to compute the value of the joystick potentiometers (which are proportional to the X and Y axes deflection of the joystick yoke). In reality, the joystick potentiometers are part of the timing circuits of standard 555 timers–in case you're interested. But if you're not an electrical engineer, don't worry about it!

Reading the Buttons

Now that we know the basic premise behind the PC's joysticks, let's work our way through writing software to read the buttons and position of the sticks. Reading the buttons is the easy part, so we'll start there. A single port called the *joystick port* communicates with the joystick interface card. It is located at I/O port 201h and has been defined in BLACK5.H as:

```
#define JOYPORT          0x201  // joyport is at 201 hex
```

The joystick port is used to read both the buttons and the position of each joystick. Amazingly enough, all this information is somehow encoded in this single port. Table 5-2 shows the bit assignments for the port.

TABLE 5-2
◇◇◇◇◇◇

Bit assignments for the joystick port at 201h

Bit Number	Meaning
0	Joystick 1 X axis strobe
1	Joystick 1 Y axis strobe
2	Joystick 2 X axis strobe
3	Joystick 2 Y axis strobe
4	Joystick 1 Button 1
5	Joystick 1 Button 2
6	Joystick 2 Button 1
7	Joystick 2 Button 2

Let's ignore bits 0 through 3 for a moment, since they are used to read the positions of the joysticks, and focus on bits 4 through 7, which are used to read the buttons of the joysticks. They work in a straightforward manner. If a button is pressed on joystick 1 or 2, the appropriate bit will be set. The only glitch is that the bits are active low, meaning if no buttons are down, then bits 4 through 7 will all be 1's. Then when a button is pressed, the appropriate bit will revert to 0. This isn't a problem since we can invert the bits after we have read them so that a pressed button is a 1 and a released button is a 0.

Now let's write a function that can read either joystick's buttons. The function will take a single parameter, which is the bit mask to extract the proper bit from the joystick port. Also, the function will invert the result as we have discussed. Here are the defines for all the different buttons to make the function easier to call:

```
#define JOYSTICK_BUTTON_1_1    0x10    // joystick 1, button 1
#define JOYSTICK_BUTTON_1_2    0x20    // joystick 1, button 2
#define JOYSTICK_BUTTON_2_1    0x40    // joystick 2, button 1
#define JOYSTICK_BUTTON_2_2    0x80    // joystick 2, button 2
```

Before we write the function, there is one detail that I must tell you: the joystick port must be strobed before we can access it. This strobe tells the joystick port to sample the data and latch it into the joystick port buffer at 201h. To accomplish this strobe, all we have to do is write any data to the port itself. In essence, by writing a value to the port, the hardware is notified that it should take a sample of the joystick buttons. This is a bit crude, but it's not a big deal. However, if you didn't

know this little fact, you could read the joystick port until you're blue in the face with no results! Listing 5-8 contains the final function that does it all.

LISTING 5-8 Function to read the buttons of the joysticks

```
unsigned char Joystick_Buttons(unsigned char button)
{

// this function reads the state of the joystick buttons by retrieving the
// appropriate bit in the joystick port

outp(JOYPORT,0); // clear the joystick port and request a sample

// invert buttons then mask with request so that a button that is pressed
// returns a "1" instead of a "0"

return( (unsigned char)(~inp(JOYPORT) & button));

} // end Joystick_Buttons
```

Notice that the first line of the function strobes the port and directs it to sample; then the port is read and masked with the requested button, and the result is inverted and returned to the caller. Hence, if we wished to test if button 1 of joystick 1 was pressed, we could write:

```
if (Joystick_Buttons(JOYSTICK_BUTTON_1_1))
   {
   // fire photon torpedoes!
   } // end if joystick 1's first button is pressed
```

Pretty easy, huh? That's very important in video games. Make all your functions simple and to the point. Let's move on to reading the position of the joystick(s).

Computing the Position of the Stick

As we learned, each joystick consists of two potentiometers, which are each mechanically connected to both the X and Y axes of the joystick yoke. The potentiometers are in turn electrically connected to timing circuits within the joystick card and, based on their positions, change the charging time of the circuits. The value of the potentiometers (which is really the position of the joystick) can then be found by taking note of how long the charging took place. The question is, how do we make this whole process happen? Well, it's actually very easy. This is what we do:

1. Reset a counter.

2. Strobe the joystick port with any value. This starts the charging process and sets the joystick position bits all to 1's.

3. Increment the counter.

4. Test if the desired joystick bit has reverted to 0, and if so, the value in the counter is proportional to the position of the joystick axis; if not, return to step 3.

Basically, we start the charging process for all the joysticks by strobing the joystick port. Then we count how many cycles it takes for the desired bit to revert back to 0 in the joystick port. Of course the bits we are testing are the joystick strobe bits 0 through 3. The only problem with this method of testing the joystick position is that it's highly machine dependent. If we time how many cycles a joystick circuit takes to charge on an XT, it will be very different from how many cycles the same circuit will charge on a 586. Therefore, the values we retrieve must somehow be scaled or interpreted from a calibrated baseline. This is why many games have a joystick calibration phase. During this phase, the maximum and minimum values of the joystick's X and Y axes are computed, which can then be used to interpret the values retrieved from the joystick port during the game. Later we'll cover this, but keep the timing problem in mind.

We have all the information we need to read the position of either stick's X or Y axis. As usual, I've defined a few constants to make the calls to the function more readable:

```
#define JOYSTICK_1        0x01   // joystick 1
#define JOYSTICK_2        0x02   // joystick 2
#define JOYSTICK_1_X      0x01   // joystick 1, x axis
#define JOYSTICK_1_Y      0x02   // joystick 1, y axis
#define JOYSTICK_2_X      0x04   // joystick 2, x axis
#define JOYSTICK_2_Y      0x08   // joystick 2, y axis
```

There are defines for each axis of each joystick and a couple defines to represent either stick generically. Listing 5-9 contains the code to read a joystick on the PC.

LISTING 5-9 *Reading a joystick on the PC*

```
unsigned int Joystick(unsigned char stick)
{
// this function will read a joystick by starting the timing circuits connected
// to each joystick port, when the timing circuit has charged the joystick
// bit will revert to 0, the time this process takes is proportional to
// the joystick position and is returned as the result

_asm
    {
    cli                          ; disable interrupts for timing purposes
    mov ah, byte ptr stick       ; select joystick to read with bitmask
    xor al,al                    ; zero out al
    xor cx,cx                    ; clear cx i.e. set it to 0
    mov dx,JOYPORT               ; point dx to the joystick port
    out dx,al                    ; start the 555 timers charging
```

continued on next page

continued from previous page

```
charged:
    in al,dx                    ; read the joystick port and test if the bit
    test al,ah                  ; has reverted back to 0
    loopne charged              ; if the joystick circuit isn't charged then
                                ; decrement cx and loop


    xor ax,ax                   ; zero out ax
    sub ax,cx                   ; subtract cx from ax to get a number that increases
                                ; as the joystick position is moved away from
neutral

    sti                         ; re-enable interrupts

    } // end asm

// ax has the 16 result, so no need for an explicit return

} // end Joystick
```

The function is obviously in assembly language, but this is due to the tight timing constraints of the problem. I admit that I've never thought of writing one in pure C, but I bet a C version would work just as well on today's machines. Anyway, the function reads the requested joystick axis and returns the number of clicks or cycles that the charging took. The caller then must interpret this value. Remember, the same joystick on two machines may return very different values for the same position. The values may even be an entire order of magnitude off if the speed of the two machines is different enough.

The function literally implements the four steps we outlined at the beginning of this section except for a single change. The counter is decremented instead of incremented. This is done so the function will "time out" if it takes too long. This will occur if there isn't a joystick present. In any case, the final value returned to the caller is computed by subtracting the value in *CX* from 0, which will result in a number that becomes larger as the joystick is moved away from its neutral position and smaller as the joystick is moved toward its neutral position.

As an example of reading the joystick, we could write something like this:

```
x_pos = Joystick(JOYSTICK_1_X);
y_pos = Joystick(JOYSTICK_1_Y);
```

This fragment would read the X and Y axes of joystick 1 and place the values into the variables *x_pos* and *y_pos*. You might be wondering if BIOS has any joystick support? The answer is yes, but the functions are very slow. However, the BIOS routines are very accurate and they prescale the values of the joystick timings so that the results will always be from 0 to 512. This makes the calibration process almost unnecessary if the BIOS routines are used to read the joystick. The BIOS joystick interface is supported under universal interrupt *INT 15h*. The joystick function is 84h and has the subfunctions listed in Table 5-3.

TABLE 5-3
◇◇◇◇◇◇

The BIOS joystick interface INT 15h

Function 84h

Subfunction 00h: Read buttons.

    Entry: AH=84h

              DX=00h

    Exit: AL=Buttons as defined below:

Bit Number	Meaning
0	Don't care
1	Don't care
2	Don't care
3	Don't care
4	Joystick 1 button 1
5	Joystick 1 button 2
6	Joystick 2 button 1
7	Joystick 2 button 2

    Subfunction 01h: Read joystick positions.

        Entry: AH=84h

                 DX=01h

        Exit: AX = Joystick 1 X axis

                 BX = Joystick 1 Y axis

                 CX = Joystick 2 X axis

                 DX = Joystick 2 Y axis

Using the information in Table 5-3, we can create BIOS versions of the button function and the joystick function; however, it only makes sense to write a joystick position function since the BIOS button function does the same thing ours does. However, the BIOS version of the joystick position not only reads the desired joystick position but it autoscales it to a range of 0 to 255. This added functionality isn't free (it's very slow), but it's a quick way to write a very robust joystick interface if speed isn't an issue. Anyway, Listing 5-10 contains yet another version of the joystick position function that is based on BIOS. Notice that it uses the same interface as the previous low-level *Joystick()* function.

LISTING 5-10 A joystick position function based on BIOS

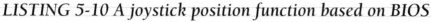

```
unsigned int Joystick_Bios(unsigned char stick)
{
// read the joystick using bios interrupt 15h with the joystick function 84h

union _REGS inregs, outregs; // used to hold CPU registers

inregs.h.ah = 0x84; // joystick function 84h
inregs.x.dx = 0x01; // read joysticks subfunction 1h

// call the BIOS joystick interrupt

_int86(0x15,&inregs, &outregs);

// return requested joystick

switch(stick)
      {
      case JOYSTICK_1_X:  // ax has joystick 1's X axis
          {
          return(outregs.x.ax);
          } break;

      case JOYSTICK_1_Y:  // bx has joystick 1's Y axis
          {
          return(outregs.x.bx);
          } break;

      case JOYSTICK_2_X:  // cx has joystick 2's X axis
          {
          return(outregs.x.cx);
          } break;

      case JOYSTICK_2_Y:  // dx has joystick 2's Y axis
          {
          return(outregs.x.dx);
          } break;
      default:break;

      } // end switch stick

} // end Joystick_Bios
```

The function doesn't do much more than respond to the request (which is the desired joystick and axis?) and return their proper value. We can literally replace any reference to the standard joystick function *Joystick()* with *Joystick_Bios()* in any of our programs if we wish to use the BIOS version. For example, the small fragment we wrote awhile back to compute the x and y positions of joystick 1 can be rewritten as:

```
x_pos = Joystick_Bios(JOYSTICK_1_X);
y_pos = Joystick_Bios(JOYSTICK_1_Y);
```

FIGURE 5-8
◎ ◎ ◎ ◎ ◎ ◎
*Typical
calibration
values for an
analog joystick*

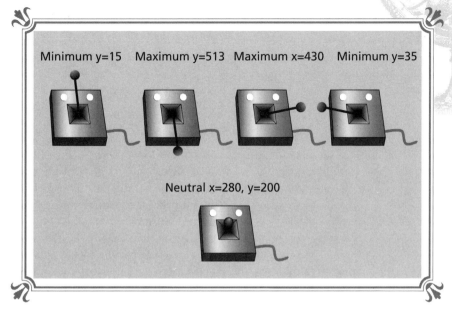

Remember though that the BIOS version is very slow and shouldn't be used in time-critical input processing. With that in mind, let's talk about calibration.

Calibrating the Joystick

If you've ever played a PC game, you've undoubtedly calibrated a joystick or two in your lifetime. The calibration process consists of moving the joystick to the extremes of its working envelope and pressing the fire button (or hitting a key) at different times. The purpose of this is to create a table that records the maximum and minimum values that the joystick can output. Take a look at Figure 5-8, which depicts a typical stick and some of the values that might be obtained during a calibration. Notice that the minimum and maximum X and Y values are recorded along with the neutral position.

The neutral position is needed since the center of the joystick may not be (0,0). It may be non-zero, such as (50,80); hence, the values retrieved by the *Joystick()* or *Joystick_Bios()* functions have to consider that (50,80) is the neutral position and not (0,0), as you might think. Anyway, we have everything we need to write a calibrator. All the calibrator needs to do is query the player to move the stick all around and record the maximum and minimum values in a table along with the neutral position. I have found that asking the user to swirl or move the joystick in a circle is a good method to obtain a full range of motion. We will record the data in the variables defined below:

```
unsigned int joystick_1_max_x,
             joystick_1_max_y,
```

continued on next page

continued from previous page

```
                    joystick_1_min_x,
                    joystick_1_min_y,
                    joystick_1_neutral_x,
                    joystick_1_neutral_y,
                    joystick_2_max_x,
                    joystick_2_max_y,
                    joystick_2_min_x,
                    joystick_2_min_y,
                    joystick_2_neutral_x,
                    joystick_2_neutral_y;
```

The names of the variables should give away each of their meanings, so let's write the function that does the actual calibration. The function will use standard I/O to print to the screen and query the user, but later you may want to make a more advanced joystick calibrator that has a graphical image of the joystick and prints out the values in real-time. Whatever you decide to do, the basic task of the function will be the same as our simple version. Tell the user to swirl the stick around, press fire after a cycle or two, center the stick, and press fire again. As the process takes place, the variables above are updated, and when the function exits, the calibration will be complete.

Also, we're going to add one more feature to our calibration function. We're going to allow it to use either the BIOS version of the joystick function or the low-level assembly version for the calibration process. This allows a little more flexibility because the method used to calibrate the joystick must be the same used to read the joystick during the game or else the data will be scaled incorrectly. We'll talk about how the calibration data is used in a moment, but let's take a look at the function in Listing 5-11.

LISTING 5-11 A joystick calibration function

```
void Joystick_Calibrate(int stick,int method)
{

// this function is used to calibrate a joystick. the function will
// query the user to move the joystick in circular motion and then release
// the stick back to the neutral position and press the fire button. using
// this information the function will compute the max,min and neutral
// values for both the X and Y axis of the joystick. these values will
// then be stored in global variables so they can be used by other
// functions, note the function can use either the BIOS joystick call
// or the low level one we made

unsigned int x_value, // used to read values of X and Y axis in real-time
             y_value;

// which stick does caller want to calibrate?
```

```
if (stick==JOYSTICK_1)
   {
   printf("\nCalibrating Joystick #1: Move the joystick in a circle, then");
   printf("\nplace the stick into its neutral position and press fire.");

   // set calibrations values to extremes

   joystick_1_max_x = 0;
   joystick_1_max_y = 0;
   joystick_1_min_x = 32000;
   joystick_1_min_y = 32000;

   // process X and Y values in real time

   while(!Joystick_Buttons(JOYSTICK_BUTTON_1_1 | JOYSTICK_BUTTON_1_2))
        {
        // get the new values and try to update calibration

        // test if user wants to use bios or low level
        if (method==USE_BIOS)
           {
           x_value = Joystick_Bios(JOYSTICK_1_X);
           y_value = Joystick_Bios(JOYSTICK_1_Y);
           }
        else
           {
           x_value = Joystick(JOYSTICK_1_X);
           y_value = Joystick(JOYSTICK_1_Y);
           }
        // update globals with new extremes

        // process X - axis
        if (x_value >= joystick_1_max_x)
           joystick_1_max_x = x_value;

        if (x_value <= joystick_1_min_x)
           joystick_1_min_x = x_value;

        // process Y - axis
        if (y_value >= joystick_1_max_y)
           joystick_1_max_y = y_value;

        if (y_value <= joystick_1_min_y)
           joystick_1_min_y = y_value;

        printf("\nx value = %d, y value = %d",x_value, y_value);

        } // end while

   // stick is now in neutral position so record the values here also
   joystick_1_neutral_x = x_value;
```

continued on next page

continued from previous page

```
            joystick_1_neutral_y = y_value;

    // notify user process is done
    printf("\nJoystick #1 Calibrated. Press the fire button to exit.");
    while(Joystick_Buttons(JOYSTICK_BUTTON_1_1 | JOYSTICK_BUTTON_1_2));
    while(!Joystick_Buttons(JOYSTICK_BUTTON_1_1 | JOYSTICK_BUTTON_1_2));

    } // end calibrate joystick #1

else
if (stick==JOYSTICK_2)
    {
    printf("\nCalibrating Joystick #2: Move the joystick in a circle, then");
    printf("\nplace the stick into its neutral position and press fire.");

    // set calibrations values to extremes
    joystick_2_max_x = 0;
    joystick_2_max_y = 0;
    joystick_2_min_x = 32000;
    joystick_2_min_y = 32000;

    // process X and Y axis values in real time
    while(!Joystick_Buttons(JOYSTICK_BUTTON_2_1 | JOYSTICK_BUTTON_2_2))
        {
        // get the new values and try to update calibration

        // test if user wants to use bios or low level
        if (method==USE_BIOS)
            {
            x_value = Joystick_Bios(JOYSTICK_1_X);
            y_value = Joystick_Bios(JOYSTICK_1_Y);
            }
        else
            {
            x_value = Joystick(JOYSTICK_1_X);
            y_value = Joystick(JOYSTICK_1_Y);
            }

        // update globals with new extremes

        // process X - axis
        if (x_value >= joystick_2_max_x)
            joystick_2_max_x = x_value;
        else
        if (x_value <= joystick_2_min_x)
            joystick_2_min_x = x_value;

        // process Y - axis
        if (y_value >= joystick_2_max_y)
            joystick_2_max_y = y_value;
        else
```

```
        if (y_value <= joystick_2_min_y)
            joystick_2_min_y = y_value;

        } // end while

        // stick is now in neutral position so record the values here also
        joystick_2_neutral_x = x_value;
        joystick_2_neutral_y = y_value;

    // notify user process is done
    printf("\nJoystick #2 Calibrated. Press the fire button to exit.");

    while(Joystick_Buttons(JOYSTICK_BUTTON_1_1 | JOYSTICK_BUTTON_1_2));
    while(!Joystick_Buttons(JOYSTICK_BUTTON_1_1 | JOYSTICK_BUTTON_1_2));

    } // end calibrate joystick #2

} // end Joystick_Calibrate
```

The joystick calibration function supports both joysticks and both low-level and BIOS reading methods. The function is self-contained but must be executed before the graphics of the game have started since the function uses standard *printf()* for output. The function uses a very simple algorithm to compute the maximum and minimum joystick values: first, the calibration variables are set to impossibly large and small values; then for each cycle, the new joystick values are tested against the current minimum and maximum values; then if the new values are smaller or larger, the last calibration values are overwritten with the new ones. Hence, by the end of the process, the variables "converge" to the actual minimum and maximum values for the joystick motion. The function itself is called with parameters representing the joystick to calibrate along with the method of calibration. The two methods are defined in BLACK5.H as:

```
#define USE_BIOS       0    // command to use BIOS version of something
#define USE_LOW_LEVEL  1    // command to use our own low level version
```

As an example, say we wanted to calibrate joystick 1 using the low-level method. We would call the calibration function like this:

```
Joystick_Calibrate(JOYSTICK_1, USE_LOW_LEVEL);
```

Of course, our entire game or application would have to use the joystick function called *Joystick()* for the calibration information to be valid.

The next burning question should be, how do we use this calibration information? The answer is, however we like! The calibration information simply gives us upper and lower bounds on the values we expect from the joystick function. Using these bounds, we can scale the joystick values to anything we wish, test if the joystick is in the neutral position, and so forth. A typical use of the calibration values is to test if the joystick is in the neutral position. For example, as a player moves his body around and gets excited, the joystick sometimes moves slightly, enough to make a change of values that wasn't really intended by the player. Hence, the software should implement a method that uses the possible range of values along with the neutral position to compute a "dead band" around the neutral position that is all considered neutral. As an example, let's use a joystick model that has only one axis, the X axis, and we have done the calibration and recorded the following:

⊹ The maximum X is *max_x*.

⊹ The minimum X is *min_x*.

⊹ The neutral or center position is *neutral_x*.

We could then write some pseudocode that wouldn't do anything if the joystick hadn't been moved enough to be considered an intentional movement. Here's the code:

```
// compute the possible range
range = max_x - min_x

// compute 10% of this range
delta = .1 * range;

// obtain the joystick position
value = Get_Joystick();

// test if the user really moved the joystick

if (value > neutral_x + delta   || value<neutral_x - delta)
   {
   // process motion
   } // end if user really moved the stick
else
   {
   // user must have bumped the stick a little, do nothing
   } // end else
```

The code fragment basically implements the following logic: if the joystick is moved farther than 10 percent of its range, then the movement was intended; otherwise, it was probably an accident. The value of 10 percent might be too high or too low, but this depends on the situation.

Now let's talk about a little detail that could really throw a monkey wrench in our whole program. What if there isn't a joystick connected and we execute these functions? This is definitely something to consider, so we should figure out a way to detect if a joystick(s) is present.

Joystick Detection Techniques

The joystick interface card has no clean way of detecting if a joystick is present that isn't hardware dependent. In the worst case, not only is the joystick missing, but there isn't even a joystick card! The best way to test for the existence of a joystick is to use the BIOS joystick routines to read the position of the stick. If both positions are 0, there's a 99 percent chance that the system is missing the joystick. You see, a value of (0,0) for the X and Y axes basically means infinite resistance, and that's definitely the case when the only thing connected to the joystick port is air! Therefore, we simply need to write a function that reads the X and Y axes of a joystick, adds the values together, and if the result is 0, there is no joystick attached. The function is shown in Listing 5-12.

LISTING 5-12 Detecting the presence of a joystick

```
int Joystick_Available(int stick_num)
{
// test if the joystick that the user is requesting is plugged in
// note the use of the BIOS joystick function, it is very reliable

if (stick_num == JOYSTICK_1)
   {
   // test if joystick 1 is plugged in by testing the port values
   // they will be 0,0 if there is no stick

   return(Joystick_Bios(JOYSTICK_1_X)+Joystick_Bios(JOYSTICK_1_Y));

   } // end if joystick 1
else
   {
   // test if joystick 2 is plugged in by testing the port values
   // they will be 0,0 if there is no stick
   return(Joystick_Bios(JOYSTICK_2_X)+Joystick_Bios(JOYSTICK_2_Y));

   } // end else joystick 2

} // end Joystick_Available
```

The function takes a single parameter, which is the joystick to try and detect. As an example, if we wanted to test if joystick 2 was available, we could write:

```
if (Joystick_Available(JOYSTICK_2))
   {
   // stick is connected
   } // end if
```

As a rule of thumb, it's always a good idea to first test if the joystick(s) is attached to the PC before allowing the user to calibrate it. Since the calibration function can only exit when the fire button is pressed, the lack of a joystick could present a problem, and an infinite loop would be the result!

Driving the Stick Crazy

For the joystick demo things have become a little more exciting. The joystick is used to control an alien ship on a starfield background. Not only do I want you to study the use of the joystick, but this demo is another good example of an event loop. The alien ship is erased, moved, and then drawn over and over. Remember, this is the standard technique we will be using throughout the book to create game loops and real-time event handling. In any case, the name of the demo is JOYTEST.EXE and the source is JOYTEST.C. Use the joystick to rotate the ship and move forward and backward. When the program starts, it will try to detect a joystick and calibrate it, so be sure to have one plugged in. Listing 5-13 contains the source.

LISTING 5-13 A joystick demonstration program

```
// JOYTEST.C - A demo of the joystick driver

// I N C L U D E S //////////////////////////////////////////////////////////////

#include <io.h>
#include <conio.h>
#include <stdio.h>
#include <stdlib.h>
#include <dos.h>
#include <bios.h>
#include <fcntl.h>
#include <memory.h>
#include <malloc.h>
#include <math.h>
#include <string.h>

#include "black3.h"
#include "black4.h"
#include "black5.h"

// D E F I N E S //////////////////////////////////////////////////////////////

#define SHIP_FRAMES 16  // number of animaton frames of ship

// G L O B A L S //////////////////////////////////////////////////////////////

pcx_picture image_pcx;  // general PCX image used to load background and imagery

sprite ship;            // the players ship
```

```c
// these are the velocity lookup tables, they have pre-computed velocities
// for each of the 16 directions the ship can point

int x_velocity[SHIP_FRAMES] = {0,2,4,4,6,4,4,2,0,-2,-4,-4,-6,-4,-4,-2};
int y_velocity[SHIP_FRAMES] = {-6,-4,-4,-2,0,2,4,4,6,4,4,2,0,-2,-4,-4};

// M A I N ////////////////////////////////////////////////////////////////

void main(int argc, char **argv)
{

int index,      // loop variable
    dx,         // use to hold roughly 15% of the range of each
    dy,         // joystick axis
    joy_x,      // the final normalized joystick position values
    joy_y;

// test if there is a joystick
if (!Joystick_Available(JOYSTICK_1))
   {
   printf("\nJoystick 1 not connected. Exiting.");
   return;
   } // end if

printf("\nJoystick 1 detected...");

// calibrate the stick
Joystick_Calibrate(JOYSTICK_1,USE_LOW_LEVEL);

// compute 15% of range
dx = (int)( (float).5 + (float).15 * (float)(joystick_1_max_x-joystick_1_min_x));
dy = (int)( (float).5 + (float).15 * (float)
     (joystick_1_max_y-joystick_1_min_y));

// set the graphics mode to mode 13h
Set_Graphics_Mode(GRAPHICS_MODE13);

// create the double buffer
Create_Double_Buffer(200);

// load the imagery for ship
PCX_Init((pcx_picture_ptr)&image_pcx);
PCX_Load("falcon.pcx", (pcx_picture_ptr)&image_pcx,1);

// intialize the ship sprite
Sprite_Init((sprite_ptr)&ship,160,100,24,20,0,0,0,0,0,0);

// extract the bitmaps for the ship, there are 16 of them, one for each
// pre-rotated angle

// get images off first row of template 0-11
for (index=0; index<12; index++)
```

continued on next page

continued from previous page

```
        PCX_Get_Sprite((pcx_picture_ptr)&image_pcx,(sprite_ptr)&ship,index,index,0);

// get images off second row of template 12-15
for (index=12; index<16; index++)
        PCX_Get_Sprite((pcx_picture_ptr)&image_pcx,(sprite_ptr)&ship,index,index-12,1);

// done with this PCX file so delete memory associated with it
PCX_Delete((pcx_picture_ptr)&image_pcx);

// now load the background starfield
PCX_Init((pcx_picture_ptr)&image_pcx);
PCX_Load("frontier.pcx",(pcx_picture_ptr)&image_pcx,1);

// copy PCX image to double buffer
PCX_Copy_To_Buffer((pcx_picture_ptr)&image_pcx,double_buffer);

// delete the pcx image
PCX_Delete((pcx_picture_ptr)&image_pcx);

// scan under the ship, so the first time through the event loop
// there is something to replace
Sprite_Under_Clip((sprite_ptr)&ship,double_buffer);

// main event loop, process until keyboard hit
while(!kbhit())
    {
    // do animation cycle: 1. erase, 2.game logic, 3. scan, 4. draw

    // erase the ship
    Sprite_Erase_Clip((sprite_ptr)&ship,double_buffer);

// PLAYERS SHIP LOGIC

    // get joystick position and subtract away center to
    // compute delta from center
    joy_x = Joystick(JOYSTICK_1_X) - joystick_1_neutral_x;
    joy_y = Joystick(JOYSTICK_1_Y) - joystick_1_neutral_y;

    // test if player has moved stick past the 10% mark, if so transform
    // ship
    if (joy_x > dx)
        {
        // rotate ship right
        if (++ship.curr_frame==SHIP_FRAMES)
            ship.curr_frame = 0;
        }
    else
    if (joy_x < -dx)
        {
        // rotate ship left
        if (--ship.curr_frame == -1)
            ship.curr_frame = SHIP_FRAMES-1;
```

```
    } // end if rotating left

// test if player is moving ship foward or backward
if (joy_y > dy)
    {
    // move ship backward

    // index into velocity table and translate ship with values

    ship.x -= x_velocity[ship.curr_frame];
    ship.y -= y_velocity[ship.curr_frame];

    }
else
if (joy_y < -dy)
    {
    // move ship foward
    ship.x += x_velocity[ship.curr_frame];
    ship.y += y_velocity[ship.curr_frame];

    } // end if forward

// clip ship to screen universe
if (ship.x > 319)
    ship.x = -24;
else
if (ship.x < -24)
    ship.x = 319;

if (ship.y > 199)
    ship.y = -20;
else
if (ship.y < -20)
    ship.y = 199;

// ready to draw ship, but first scan background under them
Sprite_Under_Clip((sprite_ptr)&ship,double_buffer);
Sprite_Draw_Clip((sprite_ptr)&ship,double_buffer,1);

// display double buffer
Display_Double_Buffer(double_buffer,0);

// lock onto 18 frames per second max
Time_Delay(1);

    } // end while

// exit in a very cool way

Screen_Transition(SCREEN_DARKNESS);

// free up all resources
```

continued on next page

continued from previous page
```
Sprite_Delete((sprite_ptr)&ship);
Delete_Double_Buffer();

Set_Graphics_Mode(TEXT_MODE);

} // end main
```

The demo JOYTEST.EXE is one of the most complex we have seen thus far (although the layer demo is probably the coolest!). The program begins by testing for a joystick and exiting if one isn't found. If a joystick is available, it is calibrated by the user and the main portion of initialization begins. First, the double buffer is allocated and the animation cells for the player's ship are loaded into a sprite. Notice that there are 16 frames of animation for the player's ship. This is because the ship can face one of the 16 directions. The 16 animation cells were predrawn using Deluxe Animation. This is a standard technique in 2D bitmapped games; that is, to prerotate the images and then load them into the game. Next, the background starfield frontier is copied into the double buffer.

The program is now ready to enter into the main event loop. At the mouth to the event loop is a call to *Sprite_Under_Clip()*. This is needed to scan the background under the player's ship so that when the event loop is entered for the first time, the call to *Sprite_Erase_Clip()* has an image to replace. Moving on, the event loop is entered and the ship is erased. Then the joystick's position is read and the deltas relative to the neutral position are calculated (this uses the precomputed calibration data). Then the joystick position is tested to see if the player is trying to rotate the ship or move. The logic will filter out any movements that don't exceed at least 15 percent of the joystick travel. This is to minimize the amount of accidental motion that is common with analog joysticks. Actually, your joystick may need a little trimming even after the demo starts. If you notice the ship drifting or rotating, adjust the joystick trimmers until the ship is motionless.

Rotation of the ship is performed by changing the *curr_frame* field of the ship sprite and using it as an index into the sprite animation cells, which are in 22.5 degree rotations. Hence, by incrementing or decrementing the *curr_frame* field of the sprite structure, it makes the ship look like it's rotating. However, if the player presses the joystick forward or backward, the ship will fly in the direction the ship is facing. This is accomplished by using the *curr_frame* field as an index in a pair of tables that contain precomputed velocities. Of course, we could have used the direction of the ship and sin and cos to compute the velocity for any given direction, but using look-up tables allows us to do computations primarily with integers instead of floating point numbers (which are slower).

The next portion of the ship logic tests whether the ship has flown off the screen; if so, the ship is warped back to the opposite edge. Finally, the ship is drawn and the double buffer is copied to the screen. We exit the demo by pressing any key, after which all the resources are released back to DOS and the demo exits. If you're feeling motivated, add some weapons and gravity to the ship!

The Mouse

Last but not least, it's time to mickey with the mouse (I couldn't resist). The mouse is a simple 2D input device that functions as a pointer. The user moves the mouse around on a flat surface, and the motion is tracked and sent to the PC via a serial transmission (although some mice, such as bus mice, have dedicated cards). This serial transmission is decoded by the mouse driver software, and the resulting information is used by the game or application to control something. Figure 5-9 shows a representation of a typical mechanical mouse. As the mouse moves in either the X or Y axis, the optical encoders are interrupted. This process is recorded and used to calculate the position and velocity of the mouse. We aren't interested in exactly how the mouse works and sends its information because we will be using a marvelous invention called a driver!

The mouse driver is a standard interface on PCs that is linked into interrupt *INT 33h*. We can query the state of the mouse and set its configuration using this interrupt. However, before we can do anything, the mouse driver must be installed during the game's startup process. Typically, the Microsoft mouse driver is called MOUSE.COM and is installed by entering **MOUSE.COM** at the command line, or as one of the programs loaded during the AUTOEXEC.BAT process. Similarly, there is another version of the driver called MOUSE.SYS, which can be loaded as one of the drivers in CONFIG.SYS. In any case, be sure you have a Microsoft-compatible mouse driver and mouse for the following demos and code.

FIGURE 5-9
◎ ◎ ◎ ◎ ◎ ◎
The insides of a mouse

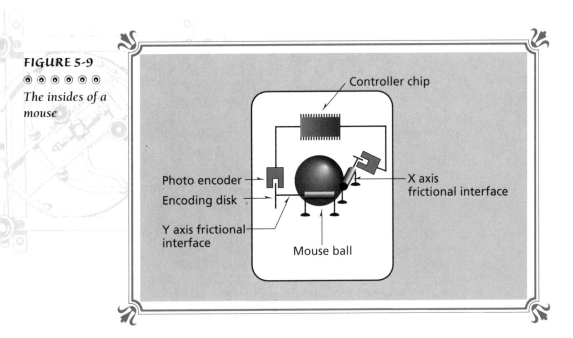

Communicating with the mouse is very easy and can be done in a single function. Even though the mouse interrupt 33h supports a lot of functions (enough to write a whole book on), we will only concern ourselves with a few. So, what do we want out of a mouse? We want to know its position, we want to be able to show or hide the mouse pointer, determine the state of the buttons, and finally, it would be nice to be able to set the sensitivity. The first items on our wish list are easy enough to understand, but what is sensitivity?

Sensitivity is a measure of how much physical mouse motion it takes to equal one virtual pixel on the screen. Take a look at Figure 5-10. Here we see a mouse, its work area, and the video screen. In most cases, we would like the mouse pointer to be able to move over the entire screen surface by moving the mouse within the bounds of its work area. This means that the 10x8-inch area (in this case) must be able to represent the entire screen without the user lifting up the mouse. This is achieved by setting the mouse sensitivity. The mouse has a finite resolution called a *mickey*, and each mickey is 1/200th of an inch, or 1/400th, depending on the mouse. Usually, the sensitivity of the mouse is set up to work with the surface area of most mouse pads quite well. However, in the case that you have a really small work area (or really large one), you may want to reprogram the sensitivity of the mouse. That's why we need the sensitivity setting. Personally, I have never in my life changed the sensitivity of a mouse except for the exercise of doing it, but you never know when you'll need it, so we'll support it.

FIGURE 5-10

◉ ◉ ◉ ◉ ◉ ◉

Mapping the mouse surface to the screen

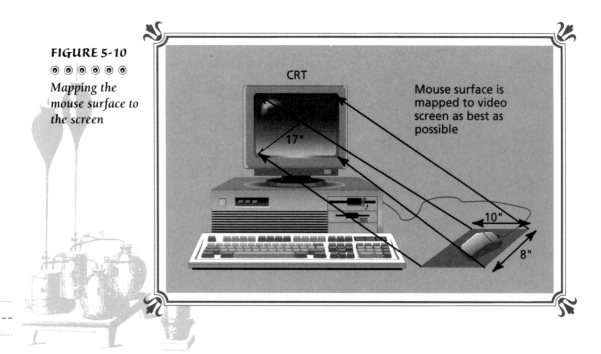

CRT

Mouse surface is mapped to video screen as best as possible

17"

10"

8"

Talking to the Mouse

The mouse functions through *INT 33h* can be called by setting up the appropriate registers and then making the call to interrupt 33h. The functions we're going to support are listed in Table 5-4.

TABLE 5-4
◇◇◇◇◇◇
Mouse interrupt 33h functions

Function 00h: Mouse reset and status.

    Entry: AX=0000h

    Exit: AX = FFFFh for success, 0000h is failure.

            BX = Number of buttons on mouse.

Function 01h: Show mouse cursor.

    Entry: AX=0001h

    Exit: Nothing

Function 02h: Hide mouse cursor.

    Entry: AX=0002h

    Exit: Nothing

Function 03h: Get button status and mouse position.

    Entry: AX=0003h

    Exit: BX = Button status as defined below:

Bit Number	Meaning
7-3	Don't care
2	Center mouse button, 1 if pressed, 0 otherwise.
1	Right mouse button, 1 if pressed, 0 otherwise.
0	Left mouse button, 1 if pressed, 0 otherwise.

CX = X absolute mouse position.

DX = Y absolute mouse position.

Function 0Bh: Read relative motion counters.

    Entry: AX=000Bh

    Exit: CX = Relative X axis motion in mickey units.

            DX = Relative Y axis motion in mickey units.

Function 1Ah: Set sensitivity.

    Entry: AX=001Ah

continued on next page

continued from previous page

BX = X axis sensitivity from 0–100.

CX = Y axis sensitivity from 0–100.

DX = Mouse double speed value from 0–100.

Exit: Nothing

Let's talk about what each function does before we write our mouse interface. The first function, 00h, is simple enough: it is used to reset the mouse driver. The next pair of functions, show mouse and hide mouse, are used to make the mouse pointer visible and invisible; however, they work in a funny way. When the system starts out, the mouse is visible. If we call the hide mouse function, the mouse pointer will become invisible. Then if we call the hide mouse function again, the mouse will still be invisible. But at this point, if we call the show mouse function, we would think the mouse would become visible, right? But it won't! The reason for this is that the mouse has a little internal counter that counts the number of times the mouse has been hidden and shown. When the count is positive, the mouse is visible; when the count is negative, the mouse is invisible. Hence, when writing routines, if you make ten calls to hide mouse, one after another, you had better make ten calls to show mouse if you want the mouse to become visible.

The next function, 03h, is the most important and most frequently used. It is responsible for tracking the mouse position and button state. The position values returned by the function are in screen pixels, not mickeys. However, sometimes (depending on the video mode) the mouse may have a different physical resolution, so you'll have to divide or multiply the mouse position by constants to arrive at a one-to-one mapping of mouse coordinates to screen coordinates.

The next function is useful in flight games and returns the relative motion of the mouse since the last call or, in other words, the delta of the mouse position. Unfortunately, these values are in mickeys, so there isn't an easy relationship between the motion and the screen. But relative motion detection is useful in many cases.

The last mouse function is the sensitivity and double speed control function. Three parameters are sent to the function, one for each setting. By changing these parameters from their default values, you can change the size of the physical-virtual mouse surface. Now let's take all this information and write a mouse interface function.

A Mouse Interface Function

Unlike the other interface devices such as the keyboard and joystick, the mouse interface consists of a single function that can be called upon to do different operations depending on a command code. These command codes direct the mouse driver to do one of the operations in Table 5-4. To make writing the function easier, here are some defines for the mouse interface to make it more readable:

```
// defines for mouse interface

#define MOUSE_INTERRUPT                 0x33 // mouse interrupt number
#define MOUSE_RESET                     0x00 // reset the mouse
#define MOUSE_SHOW                      0x01 // show the mouse
#define MOUSE_HIDE                      0x02 // hide the mouse
#define MOUSE_POSITION_BUTTONS          0x03 // get buttons and position
#define MOUSE_MOTION_REL                0x0B // query motion counters
                                             // to compute relative motion
#define MOUSE_SET_SENSITIVITY           0x1A // set the sensitivity of mouse

// mouse button bitmasks

#define MOUSE_LEFT_BUTTON               0x01 // left mouse button mask
#define MOUSE_MIDDLE_BUTTON             0x04 // middle mouse button mask
#define MOUSE_RIGHT_BUTTON              0x02 // right mouse button mask
```

The function we'll write in a moment should take only a few parameters, such as the command, parameters representing the X and Y axes, and the buttons. These latter variables will also be used as outputs when the function is requested to compute the position of the mouse or its status. Hence, some of the variables should be passed by reference so they can be changed by the function. Listing 5-14 contains the final mouse function that takes all these points into consideration.

LISTING 5-14 A mouse interface function

```
int Mouse_Control(int command, int *x, int *y,int *buttons)
{
union _REGS inregs,  // CPU register unions to be used by interrupts
            outregs;

// what is caller asking function to do?
switch(command)
    {
    case MOUSE_RESET: // this resets the mouse
        {
        // mouse subfunction 0: reset
        inregs.x.ax = 0x00;

        // call the mouse interrupt
        _int86(MOUSE_INTERRUPT, &inregs, &outregs);

        // return number of buttons on this mouse
        *buttons = outregs.x.bx;

        // return success/failure of function
        return(outregs.x.ax);
```

continued on next page

continued from previous page

```
        } break;

    case MOUSE_SHOW: // this shows the mouse
        {
        // this function increments the internal mouse visibility counter.
        // when it is equal to 0 then the mouse will be displayed.
        // mouse subfunction 1: increment show flag
        inregs.x.ax = 0x01;

        // call the mouse interrupt
        _int86(MOUSE_INTERRUPT, &inregs, &outregs);

        // return success always
        return(1);

        } break;

    case MOUSE_HIDE:  // this hides the mouse
        {
        // this function decrements the internal mouse visibility counter.
        // when it is equal to -1 then the mouse will be hidden.

        // mouse subfunction 2: decrement show flag
        inregs.x.ax = 0x02;

        // call the interrupt
        _int86(MOUSE_INTERRUPT, &inregs, &outregs);

        // return success
        return(1);

        } break;

    case MOUSE_POSITION_BUTTONS: // this gets both the position and
                                 // state of buttons
        {
        // this function computes the absolute position of the mouse
        // and the state of the mouse buttons

        // mouse subfunction 3: get position and buttons
        inregs.x.ax = 0x03;

        // call the mouse interrupt
        _int86(MOUSE_INTERRUPT, &inregs, &outregs);

        // extract the info and send back to caller via pointers
        *x       = outregs.x.cx;
        *y       = outregs.x.dx;
        *buttons = outregs.x.bx;

        // return success always
        return(1);
```

```
        } break;

case MOUSE_MOTION_REL:  // this gets the relative motion of mouse
        {
        // this function gets the relative mouse motions from the last
        // call, these values will range from -32768 to +32767 and
        // be in mickeys which are 1/200 of inch or 1/400 of inch
        // depending on the resolution of your mouse

        // subfunction 11: get relative motion
        inregs.x.ax = 0x0B;

        // call the interrupt
        _int86(MOUSE_INTERRUPT, &inregs, &outregs);

        // extract the info and send back to caller via pointers
        *x      = outregs.x.cx;
        *y      = outregs.x.dx;

        // return success
        return(1);

        } break;

case MOUSE_SET_SENSITIVITY:
        {
        // subfunction 26: set sensitivity
        inregs.x.ax = 0x1A;

        // place the desired sensitivity and double speed values in place
        inregs.x.bx = *x;
        inregs.x.cx = *y;
        inregs.x.dx = *buttons;

        // call the interrupt
        _int86(MOUSE_INTERRUPT, &inregs, &outregs);

        // always return success
        return(1);

        } break;

default:break;

} // end switch

} // end Mouse_Control
```

The function simply *cases* on the input command and calls the mouse interrupt with the proper parameters. If the function is retrieving data such as mouse
position, the input variables *x, y,* and *buttons* are overwritten. For example, to

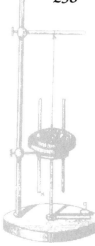

reset the mouse and print out its x and y position, we could write the following little program:

```
int x,y,buttons;

// reset the mouse

Mouse_Control(MOUSE_RESET, &x,&y,&buttons);

// main event loop

while(true)
        {
        // obtain the state of the mouse
        Mouse_Control(MOUSE_POSITION_BUTTONS,&x,&y,&buttons);

        // print results
        printf("\nMouse is at [%d,%d]",x,y);

        } // end infinite while
```

Point and Squash!

The final mouse demo is probably the closest thing to an actual game we have seen. A grassy area with a picnic blanket is being attacked by ants. Your mission is to use the mouse (which has a hammer attached to it) to squash the ants before they carry away all the food! If you smash an ant, you will see some graphic feedback that the ant has been exterminated. The name of the program is MOUSETST.EXE and the source code is MOUSETST.C. As usual, to create an executable, you will have to link all the library modules thus far to the final EXE file. The source code is shown in Listing 5-15.

LISTING 5-15 A demo that shows a good use of the mouse!

```
// MOUSETST.C - A demo of the mouse driver with some added fun

// I N C L U D E S ////////////////////////////////////////////////////////////

#include <io.h>
#include <conio.h>
#include <stdio.h>
#include <stdlib.h>
#include <dos.h>
#include <bios.h>
#include <fcntl.h>
#include <memory.h>
#include <malloc.h>
#include <math.h>
#include <string.h>
```

```
#include "black3.h"
#include "black4.h"
#include "black5.h"

// D E F I N E S /////////////////////////////////////////////////////////////

#define ANT_DEAD       0 // the ant is dead (smashed)
#define ANT_EAST       1 // the ant is moving east
#define ANT_WEST       2 // the ant is moving west

#define HAMMER_UP      0 // the hammer is in its resting position
#define HAMMER_MOVING  1 // the hammer is hammering!!!

// G L O B A L S ////////////////////////////////////////////////////////////

pcx_picture image_pcx;  // general PCX image used to load background and imagery

sprite ant,             // the ant
       hammer;          // the players hammer

// M A I N ///////////////////////////////////////////////////////////////////

void main(int argc, char **argv)
{
int index,      // loop variable
    mouse_x,    // mouse status
    mouse_y,
    buttons;

// set the graphics mode to mode 13h
Set_Graphics_Mode(GRAPHICS_MODE13);

// create the double buffer
Create_Double_Buffer(200);

// load the imagery for ant
PCX_Init((pcx_picture_ptr)&image_pcx);
PCX_Load("moreants.pcx", (pcx_picture_ptr)&image_pcx,1);

// intialize the ant sprite
Sprite_Init((sprite_ptr)&ant,0,0,12,6,0,0,0,0,0,0);

// extract the bitmaps for the ant, there are 3 animation cells for each
// direction thus 6 cells
for (index=0; index<6; index++)
    PCX_Get_Sprite((pcx_picture_ptr)&image_pcx,(sprite_ptr)&ant,index,index,0);

// done with this PCX file so delete memory associated with it
PCX_Delete((pcx_picture_ptr)&image_pcx);

// load the imagery for players hammer
PCX_Init((pcx_picture_ptr)&image_pcx);
PCX_Load("hammer.pcx", (pcx_picture_ptr)&image_pcx,1);
```

continued on next page

continued from previous page

```
// intialize the hammer sprite that will take the place of the mouse
// pointer
Sprite_Init((sprite_ptr)&hammer,0,0,22,20,0,0,0,0,0,0);

// extract the bitmaps for the hammer there are 5
for (index=0; index<5; index++)
    PCX_Get_Sprite((pcx_picture_ptr)&image_pcx,(sprite_ptr)&hammer,index,index,0);

// done with this PCX file so delete memory associated with it
PCX_Delete((pcx_picture_ptr)&image_pcx);

// now load the picnic area background
PCX_Init((pcx_picture_ptr)&image_pcx);
PCX_Load("grass.pcx",(pcx_picture_ptr)&image_pcx,1);

// copy PCX image to double buffer
PCX_Copy_To_Buffer((pcx_picture_ptr)&image_pcx,double_buffer);

// delete the pcx image
PCX_Delete((pcx_picture_ptr)&image_pcx);

// scan under ant and hammer before entering the event loop, this must be
// done or else on the first cycle the "erase" function will draw garbage
Sprite_Under_Clip((sprite_ptr)&ant,double_buffer);
Sprite_Under_Clip((sprite_ptr)&hammer,double_buffer);

// reset the mouse and hide the pointer
Mouse_Control(MOUSE_RESET,NULL,NULL,&buttons);
Mouse_Control(MOUSE_HIDE,NULL,NULL,NULL);

// main event loop, process until keyboard hit

while(!kbhit())
    {
    // do animation cycle: 1. erase, 2.game logic, 3. scan, 4. draw

    // erase all objects by replacing what was under them
    if (ant.state!=ANT_DEAD)
        Sprite_Erase_Clip((sprite_ptr)&ant,double_buffer);

    Sprite_Erase_Clip((sprite_ptr)&hammer,double_buffer);

// PLAYERS HAMMER LOGIC

    // obtain the new position of mouse and state of buttons
    Mouse_Control(MOUSE_POSITION_BUTTONS,&mouse_x,&mouse_y,&buttons);

    // map the mouse position to the screen and assign it to hammer
    hammer.x = (mouse_x >> 1)-16;
    hammer.y = mouse_y;

    // test if player is trying to use hammer
```

```
if (buttons==MOUSE_LEFT_BUTTON && hammer.state==HAMMER_UP)
   {
   // set state of hammer to moving
   hammer.state = HAMMER_MOVING;

   } // end if player trying to strike

// test if hammer is animating
if (hammer.state==HAMMER_MOVING)
   {
   // test if sequence complete
   if (++hammer.curr_frame==4)
      {
      hammer.state      = HAMMER_UP;
      hammer.curr_frame = 0;
      } // end if done

   // test if hammer is hitting ant
   if (hammer.curr_frame==3 && ant.state!=ANT_DEAD)
      {
      // do a collision test between the hammer and the ant

      if (ant.x > hammer.x && ant.x+12 < hammer.x+22 &&
         ant.y > hammer.y && ant.y+6 < hammer.y+20)
         {
         // kill ant
         ant.state = ANT_DEAD;

         // draw a smashed ant, use frame 5 of hammer
         // set current frame to blood splat
         hammer.curr_frame = 4;

         // draw the splat
         Sprite_Draw_Clip((sprite_ptr)&hammer,double_buffer,1);

         // restore the hammer frame
         hammer.curr_frame = 3;

         } // end if hammer hit ant

      } // end if smash test

   } // end if hammer moving

// ANT LOGIC

// test if it's time to start an ant
if (ant.state == ANT_DEAD && ((rand()%10)==0))
   {
   // which direction will ant move in
   if ((rand()%2)==0)
      {
```

continued on next page

continued from previous page

```
        // move ant east
        ant.y         = rand()%200;    // starting y position
        ant.x         = 0;             // starting x position
        ant.counter_1 = 2 + rand()%10; // ant speed
        ant.state     = ANT_EAST;      // ant direction
        ant.curr_frame= 0;             // starting animation frame

        }
    else
        {
        // move ant west
        ant.y         = rand()%200;    // starting y position
        ant.x         = 320;           // starting x position
        ant.counter_1 = -2 - rand()%10; // ant speed
        ant.state     = ANT_WEST;      // ant direction
        ant.curr_frame= 0;             // starting animation frame

        } // end else west

    } // end if an ant is started

// test if ant is alive

if (ant.state!=ANT_DEAD)
    {
    // process ant
    // move the ant
    ant.x+=ant.counter_1;

    // is ant off screen?

    if (ant.x <0 || ant.x > 320)
        ant.state = ANT_DEAD;

    // animate the ant use proper animation cells based on direction
    // cells 0-2 are for eastward motion, cells 3-5 are for westward motion

    if (ant.state==ANT_EAST)
        if (++ant.curr_frame>2)
            ant.curr_frame=0;

    if (ant.state==ANT_WEST)
        if (++ant.curr_frame>5)
            ant.curr_frame=3;

    } // end ant is alive
// ready to draw objects, but first scan background under them

if (ant.state!=ANT_DEAD)
    Sprite_Under_Clip((sprite_ptr)&ant,double_buffer);

Sprite_Under_Clip((sprite_ptr)&hammer,double_buffer);
```

```
        if (ant.state!=ANT_DEAD)
            Sprite_Draw_Clip((sprite_ptr)&ant,double_buffer,1);

        Sprite_Draw_Clip((sprite_ptr)&hammer,double_buffer,1);

        // display double buffer
        Display_Double_Buffer(double_buffer,0);

        // lock onto 18 frames per second max
        Time_Delay(1);

        } // end while

// exit in a very cool way
Screen_Transition(SCREEN_SWIPE_X);

// free up all resources
Sprite_Delete((sprite_ptr)&ant);
Sprite_Delete((sprite_ptr)&hammer);
Delete_Double_Buffer();

Set_Graphics_Mode(TEXT_MODE);

} // end main
```

The logic of the mouse demo is somewhat similar to that of the joystick demo except that a couple of elements have been added. There is an ant that moves by itself, and there is more animation. The program begins by allocating the double buffer and loading the imagery for the ant and player's hammer. Notice that there are multiple animation frames for both. Furthermore, the ant has animation cells for westward and eastward motion. After the imagery for the ant and hammer are loaded, the background picnic area is loaded and copied to the double buffer.

Once the graphics system is initialized, there are calls to the *Mouse_Control()* function before the main event loop. These calls are needed to reset the mouse and hide the mouse pointer (the mouse pointer is hidden so that it can be represented by a hammer instead of a pointer). Once we enter the main event loop, the standard animation cycle is followed, starting with the erasure of the ant and hammer. Notice that a test is made to see if the ant is dead or alive. This is because at times the ant won't be visible on the screen, and hence shouldn't be erased. The *ant.state* field is used to track this fact.

Anyway, the mouse position and buttons are read, and the mouse position is mapped to the screen. This is necessary because the mouse is in a different resolution than mode 13h, so the two lines,

```
hammer.x = (mouse_x >> 1)-16;
hammer.y = mouse_y;
```

make sure that the mouse pointer stays on the screen. Next, the logic for the hammer begins. The hammer can only do one thing and that's strike! Hence, if the player presses the left mouse button, the hammer will start its animation sequence for a strike. This will only occur if the sequence isn't already running. At the end of the hammer's logic is a collision test to see if the hammer has struck an ant. If so, the ant is killed–that is, its state field is set to *ANT_DEAD*, and a splat is drawn on the screen.

The next portion of code controls the ant and is fairly complex. The ant is tested to see if it's dead or alive. If the ant is dead, the program tries to start another ant. If an ant is started, the program selects a random position and velocity for the ant (west or east). On the other hand, if the ant is alive, it is moved, animated, and tested for collision with the screen boundaries. If the ant has walked off an edge of the screen, it is killed.

Finally, the ant and hammer are drawn and the double buffer is displayed. If the player presses a key, the program exits and the resources are released as usual. The game needs a score and more ants. See if you can add these features. The score is easy, but adding more ants is a bit harder. Here's a hint: use an array of ants …

Creating an Input System

Now that we know more about the keyboard, joystick, and mouse than we ever wanted to, let's talk about a higher level layer of software that can be created. This layer is called an *input event system*. In general, most games allow the user to select an input device, and the input device's data is filtered through an input handler. This input handler converts the messages or events into one common form and then passes them to the game logic. Figure 5-11 shows this process in action.

As game programmers, we don't want to write special code for each input device; we would much rather have all the input devices filtered through a single function that outputs a sort of generic structure that's the same for any input device. This level of indirection makes it easy to add input devices and debug the code since the input logic is not strewn all over, but is located in a single place.

Typically, the input event systems for each game are slightly different, so I don't have any code for you. The whole point is that the game logic should obtain its input from a virtual input source that could possibly be connected to a joystick, mouse, keyboard, or plug in the back of your head.

Input Device Conditioning

There is one final pseudophilosophical note that we should pay attention to: many input devices don't do what the player is trying to make them do, or in some cases,

FIGURE 5-11

◉ ◉ ◉ ◉ ◉ ◉

Filtering all inputs to a single function

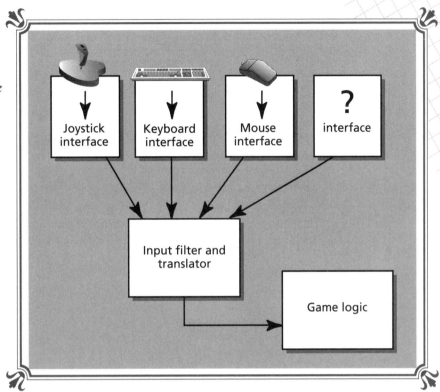

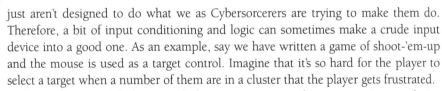

just aren't designed to do what we as Cybersorcerers are trying to make them do. Therefore, a bit of input conditioning and logic can sometimes make a crude input device into a good one. As an example, say we have written a game of shoot-'em-up and the mouse is used as a target control. Imagine that it's so hard for the player to select a target when a number of them are in a cluster that the player gets frustrated.

A nice feature might be to track the target nearest to the mouse pointer and give the player some help. In this case, he could just place the mouse near the object and the computer would lock onto it. That's the idea—give the player some help with the input devices to make them do what he is thinking, not what he's telling them to do!

Summary

In this chapter we covered the most popular input devices supported by the PC and Cybersorcerers alike. We covered the keyboard, joystick, and mouse. And

along the way, we created quite an extensive software library to read all of the input devices. The most complex of these is the keyboard driver that can track all the keys in the keyboard at once! Anyway, let me ask you a question: You like to dance, don't you? Well, it's time for a bit of music. Read on to see how to make the PC rock!

6

Dancing with Cyberdemons

...ome tuoti fione le manouelle... liquali fimodono e lalza
o igra pesi inuer lomo... e ... fadogeano dibono
re; are nella mano elaperunquella della manodella pegi quin
aforca... piu uomo pibiual.

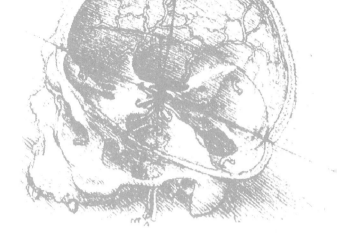

6

Dancing with Cyberdemons

The horrible creatures, living machines, and other manifestations transmitted through the gate of Cyberspace are not silent! In fact, with the right spells and incantations, we can listen to the eerie sounds and music transmitted to us. To do this, we must learn how to control the sound synthesis card within the PC and command it to couple its subspace field with that of the VGA card. The result: the unison of sight and sound creating the ultimate experience of reality.

Fundamentals of Sound

Sound is nothing more than mechanical waves traveling through air. These mechanical sound waves have a few simple properties that we shall discuss so that we have a common vocabulary to speak of them. For example, when you speak, your vocal cords *resonate* at different frequencies, and the sum of these resonations produces the final sound. Hence, the first concept we need to grasp is that of *frequency*. Simply put, frequency is the rate at which a particular waveform repeats itself as a function of time. For example, Figure 6-1 depicts two different waveforms with different frequencies. The first waveform is called a sine wave and is the purest of all waveforms. It has a frequency of 1000 Hz (Hz means cycles per second). The second waveform is more complex and has a frequency of 10 Hz.

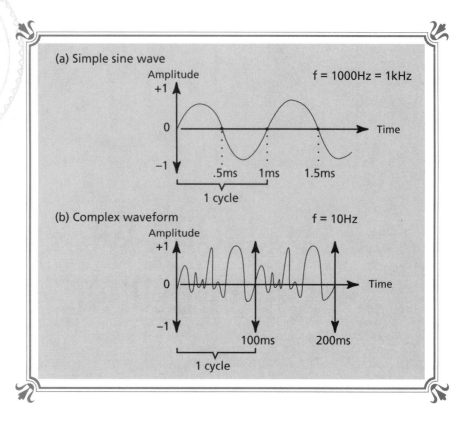

FIGURE 6-1

◎ ◎ ◎ ◎ ◎ ◎

Simple and complex waveforms

The interesting thing about complex waveforms is that they can all be generated using a sum of sine waves. This is because sine waves are mathematically the most fundamental waveforms. Hence, if we can synthesize a set of sine waves, then theoretically we can synthesize any sound. More on this later.

The next important quantity of sound is *amplitude* or *loudness*. This has to do with the size of the waveform or, in the physical world, the strength of the mechanical air wave. Amplitude can be measured in many units, such as volts, decibels (dB), and so forth. But musicians usually measure amplitude relative to some baseline, since they don't care how many volts or dBs a sound is. They simply need to know the loudest and softest sound that can be made with any particular piece of equipment and use those endpoints to scale all the sounds in between. For example, on your particular sound card, you may be able to set the loudness from 0 to 15. These values represent complete quiet (0) and full volume (15). The only way to get a feel for the loudness of the two extremes is to listen to them.

The next concept of importance is *frequency response*, which is the way we perceive different sounds. For example, most humans can only hear in the range of 20 Hz to 20,000 Hz. Anything beyond these two extremes will be highly attenuated.

FIGURE 6-2

◎ ◎ ◎ ◎ ◎ ◎

Frequency response of the garden variety human ear

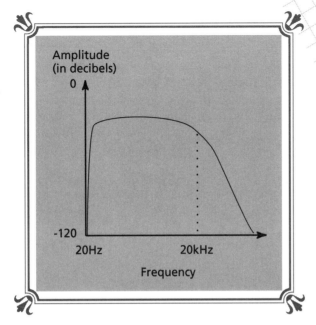

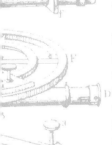

Figure 6-2 shows a diagram of the situation. As you can see, humans have a reasonable frequency response, well up to 20,000 Hz, and then the "response" falls off abruptly. Of course, some people have more range and some people have less, but 20 Hz to 20,000 Hz is the average. What does this mean? Well, it means the sounds that we produce must be within this range, or only insects and animals will hear them!

We have mentioned waveform a couple times, but let's pin the concept down a little better. Waveform means the shape of the sound wave. Figure 6-3 depicts some common waveforms, such as the sine wave, square wave, sawtooth wave, white noise, and human voice. The simplest of all, the sine wave, can't be broken down any further. Sine waves sound very simple and "electronic" when listened to. The square wave, on the other hand, is constructed out of a collection of sine waves, each a *subharmonic* of the fundamental frequency of the square wave. Harmonics are multiples of frequencies and subharmonics are submultiples. For example, the frequency 1000 Hz has its first harmonic at 2000 Hz, its second at 3000 Hz, and so forth. Similarly, its first subharmonic would be 500 Hz. Anyway, when you listen to a square wave it sounds "richer" than a sine wave; in other words, it has a bit of "texture." The reason of course is that the square wave is composed of hundreds, if not thousands, of sine waves, each with a smaller amplitude than the next.

The next waveform in Figure 6-3 is called a sawtooth wave and has a "brassy" sound to it. The sawtooth is also composed of sine waves. The human voice wave-

form is called *complex* and has no specific frequency since it doesn't repeat. However, the voice waveform is generated with thousands of sine waves that make up the final sound. Moreover, the amplitudes of these sine waves are modulated as a function of time while the word or phrase is being spoken. It's actually very complex, but we can deduce a couple of things from any voice waveform or *sample*: the overall loudness and the highest frequency. For example, my voice may have most of its spectral energy in the 3 to 4 kHz range, while a woman's voice may have most of the energy at a higher frequency, such as 6 kHz. This is important when sampling or digitizing voice. We must sample the voice at twice the highest frequency component if we want to reproduce the original sound perfectly.

The final waveform in Figure 6-3, white noise, has an equal distribution of all frequencies at all amplitudes up to some maximum. This is the sound of the ocean, wind, and other relaxing sounds. It's also the form of noise in electronic circuitry and is very difficult to filter. It's actually chaotic in nature—but that's a story for another book!

We now have the basic tools to discuss the two main types of sounds that we're going to create in this chapter, which are digital samples and synthetic music.

FIGURE 6-3

◎ ◎ ◎ ◎ ◎ ◎

The waveforms of sound

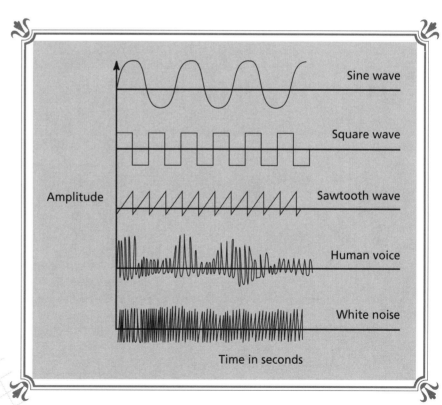

Digitized Sound

Digitized sound is probably the easiest to play because we don't need much hardware or software to do it. In essence, we must sample or record an analog signal (the sound) and convert it into digital form with an analog-to-digital converter. Figure 6-4 shows the conversion process in action. Note that the analog input waveform is sampled at some rate and then converted into binary words. There are two factors we must consider during the digitization process. First, the rate at which the sound is sampled must be high enough to capture the full spectral range of the input sound. This is called *frequency resolution.* Second, the analog-to-digital converter must have enough *amplitude resolution* to sample all the different amplitudes. If there's not enough of one or the other, errors will occur, such as frequency or amplitude aliasing.

The need for amplitude resolution is easy enough to understand. Simply put, if a sound has thousands of amplitude variations and our analog-to-digital converter only has 4 bits of resolution (16 values), then the sampled sound is going to lose a

FIGURE 6-4

◎ ◎ ◎ ◎ ◎ ◎

Conversion of voice to digital form

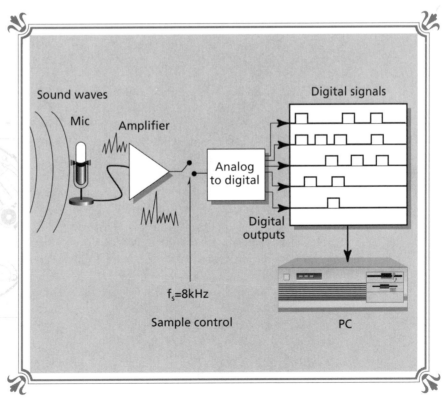

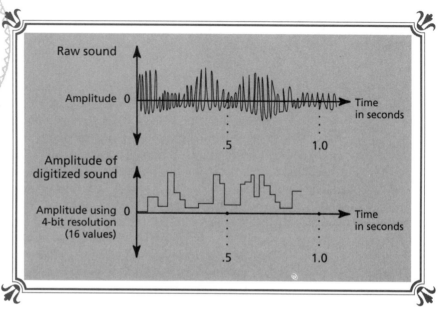

lot of its amplitude range (see Figure 6-5). The reasoning behind the double sample rate is less obvious, but let's see if we can derive it using common sense and fundamentals.

Recall that all sounds, simple and complex, are really a conglomeration of sine waves. Thus, even a sound such as a human voice is composed of sine waves. Therefore, it follows that any voice must have one component that contains the absolute highest frequency sine wave. For example, Figure 6-6 shows the average frequency spectrum of a man's voice saying "hello." You will notice that the largest spikes are centered around 700 Hz; however, there are also spikes all the way up to 12 kHz (as small as they may be). If we were to sample the voice at 2 Hz, we would get most of the information, but if we sampled it at 24 kHz, we would get it all. We'll get to the doubling in a second, but first listen to this. Have you ever heard yourself on a tape or other recording device? Have you ever noticed that it just doesn't sound like you? This is because some of those high or low frequencies are getting filtered. Even though the main portion of your voice is being sampled, some of the information gets lost during the recording. This occurs to different degrees depending on different voices. Some people sound perfect on the phone or tape, but others, because of the complex spectral content of their voices, sound weird. This is due to loss of information.

So why must we sample at twice the rate we are trying to record? The reason is this: if we want to sample a sound or voice that has 4 kHz as the highest frequency, we must sample at 8 kHz so that we can reconstruct the original sine wave. Take a

FIGURE 6-6

◎ ◎ ◎ ◎ ◎ ◎

Average frequency spectrum of a man saying "hello"

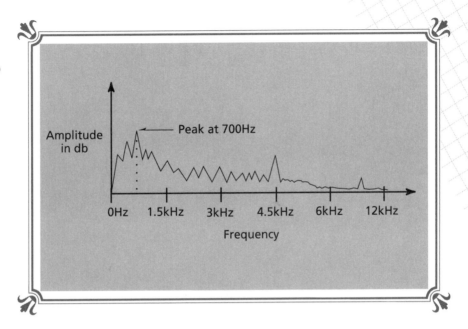

look at Figure 6-7. It shows the same waveform being sampled at two different rates, one rate half that of the other. You will notice that sometimes there aren't enough data points to reconstruct the sine wave, so an error occurs. This stems from the fact that we need two points on any sinusoidal curve to solve for the frequency of the wave, just like you need two points to define a circle. The whole thing is based on something called Shannon's Theorem, and the lowest possible sample rate before distortion is called the Nyquist Frequency, at which the sound when played back will be distorted. That's just for you sound buffs! Without going into all that, we have everything we need to sample and play back sound.

The moral of the story is that we should sample sounds at 6 kHz to 12 kHz (because of memory constraints) and use 8-bit samples unless high quality is necessary; then 16-bit samples will be more than ample. Personally, I get away with an 8 kHz sample rate with 8 bits of amplitude resolution all the time. The sound of cracking bones and photon torpedoes doesn't need the resolution of a Mozart symphony.

How do we record and play digitized samples on a sound card? First off, the sound card must have a digital sound channel or at least a digital-to-analog converter to play the sounds. Sound Blaster and similar cards all have the ability to play digital sounds. Some cards can play back at rates up to 44.1 kHz in 16 bits. In most cases, sounds can also be digitized by the sound card, so it must have an input analog-to-digital converter (A/D) to satisfy this need. If a particular card does not have the ability to record, most cards can still play back digitized sounds as long as the

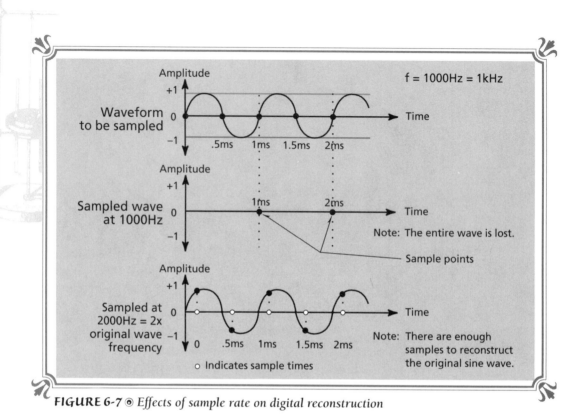

FIGURE 6-7 ◉ *Effects of sample rate on digital reconstruction*

sound is in some format that can be converted to the native format of the sound card. In the case of DOS games, the most widely used digital sound format is called VOC, which contains a header along with the data for the digital sample. VOC format supports multiple recording rates, stereo sound, and samples up to 16 bits, so it's more than enough for us. We'll learn how to read VOC files a bit later, but that's what we'll be using. Of course, there are other formats, such as WAV (Windows) and MOD (Amiga), but we'll stick to VOC for simplicity. However, there's no reason you can't write a reader for the others.

The main problem facing the world of sound and video games is lack of standardization. Even if I showed you how to record and play music on a Sound Blaster, you would be out of luck on a Gravis Ultrasound card. Hence, instead of depending on a particular sound card, we're going to use sound drivers from The Audio Solution and John Ratcliff for both digital samples and music. This will save us a great deal of time, and our code will work on any sound card without change.

Finally, most sound cards have onboard DMA logic and buffers that can play a sound from memory in parallel with the CPU, so the CPU isn't loaded with any work. In essence, playing a digital sound effect will impose very little computational load on the system CPU and will be practically transparent. The only computations and overhead for playing a digital sound will occur when the sound is started by the driver; after that, the sound card will usually take over. With that in mind, let's jam!

MIDI Music

Playing music on the computer is a daunting task. The nature of music itself is complex and mathematical. Music is basically a sequence of notes playing on different instruments as a function of time. However, there are about a million little details involved, such as velocity, aftertouch, and tempo, to name a few. Trying to concatenate all this information into a single standard is difficult to say the least, but a standard was finally arrived at in late 1982, and it is known as *MIDI*. MIDI stands for Musical Instrument Digital Interface, and you can find MIDI ports on most synthesizers and sound cards today. MIDI is a file format that describes a musical composition as a set of channels that are each playing a particular note of a particular instrument. The instruments are a generic collection of popular gadgets that the sound card or MIDI device tries to reproduce as best it can.

The standard MIDI specification states that there are 128 instruments, including pianos, guitars, percussion devices, and so forth. Hence, if a MIDI file indicates that an air guitar is to be played on channel 3, the sound card will do its best to output the sounds of an air guitar. Also, MIDI supports 16 different channels, or in essence, a MIDI stream can control 16 different instruments. So when MIDI music is played on a sound card, the sound card tries its best to support all 16 channels. For example, on the Sound Blaster channels 1 through 9 are usually used for normal instruments and channel 10 is allocated for the percussion device. The only problem with this is that each sound card and MIDI device has its own set of instrument "patches" that sound slightly different. For example, if you compose a song using a Sound Blaster and then play the MIDI file on a Turtle Beach card, the results might not sound totally correct. This is the reason why "instrument patches" came to be and Creative Labs created the CMF music format. CMF is similar to MIDI except that it has a header with instrument patches so that you can reprogram a Sound Blaster's default instruments with ones that are more appropriate for the composition.

The CMF format is the ultimate in MIDI music, since it allows new instruments to be loaded, but it isn't a standard, so we can't really use it. On the bright side, most sound cards do a good job of emulating all the default instruments in the MIDI specification, and most songs will sound decent to the untrained ear (like mine!). The question is, how do we create these MIDI files? Well, if you're a musician, it's easy. Using a sequencer and a computer, you can compose MIDI music on your computer and save the file as a *.MID file for use with any MIDI-compatible sound system. If you're not a musician, you're in serious trouble, and the only answer is to use premade MIDI files or hire a composer to create the music for you. For example, a friend of mine here in Silicon Valley will compose MIDI music for you at about $250 per minute of music. You can reach him at:

Andromeda/Eclipse Productions
Attn: Dean Hudson
P.O. Box 641744
San Jose, CA 95164-1744

Once we have the MIDI music, how do we play it on the sound card? We will play the music using someone else's drivers; that is, The Audio Solution's and John Ratcliff's, which are on the CD-ROM. Writing MIDI drivers for all the sound cards would take months to years, so we'll have to use their drivers. This isn't too bad since they are very complete, efficient, and sound great! Moreover, the interfaces are simple, and along with another layer that we will create on top of the standard Audio Solution/Ratcliff interface, playing music will be as easy as a few lines of code!

Now that we know what format the musical information is in, how is it synthesized? Good question! In most cases, music is synthesized using a technique referred to as *FM synthesis*, but a new technique that is becoming more affordable, called *wave table synthesis*, is much more realistic. Let's discuss FM synthesis first, since it's more common.

FM Synthesis

As we learned, all sounds are created with sine waves, and the more sine waves the more complex and rich the sound. Be warned, sound theory has a lot of words like rich, textured, brassy, hard, soft, and fluffy. They mean what they mean to you, get it? Anyway, generating sine waves, square waves, and sawtooth waves is easy, but the resulting sounds are artificial. A method had to be devised that would make it possible to add harmonics to some fundamental sine wave having varying amplitudes and then to modulate these harmonics as a function of time. The mathematical technique that accomplishes this is called *frequency modulation* or FM. It uses much the same technique that FM radio transmitters use to transmit a signal that encodes music on a specific carrier wave.

An FM synthesizer has two main components: the modulator and the carrier, as shown in Figure 6-8. The modulator modulates the base frequency of the carrier. Moreover, the output of this chain can be fed back into the input to create harmonics. Most low-cost sound cards use this technique. The cards have a set of FM synthesizers, usually 10 or 20 of them (combined to make channels), that are programmed with parameters to emulate a specific musical instrument. In addition,

FIGURE 6-8
◎ ◎ ◎ ◎ ◎ ◎
FM synthesis in action

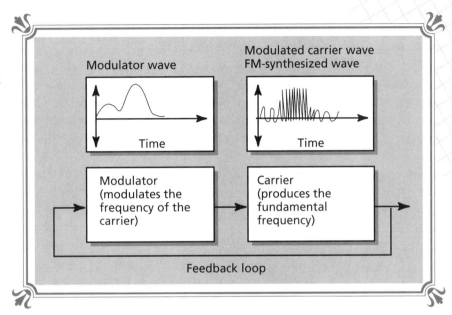

each channel has an ADSR amplitude control. ADSR stands for Attack Decay Sustain Release and controls the amplitude of the sound as a function of time. Figure 6-9 shows a typical ADSR envelope and the result of it on an FM synthesized instrument.

FIGURE 6-9
◎ ◎ ◎ ◎ ◎ ◎
Effects of ADSR amplitude modulation on sound

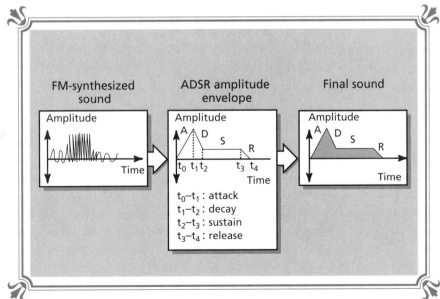

Using FM synthesis along with the concept of ADSR, we could write software to control a sound card to play a MIDI file. This isn't easy and takes thousands of lines of code, but nevertheless can be done. This is exactly what The Audio Solution has done for us; however, they have written drivers not just for the Sound Blaster, but for many sound cards! This relieves us from a ton of work. Once we know how to use both the digital and MIDI drivers, we're in business!

The only problem with FM synthesis is it's too perfect! That's right, real instruments and real people make slight mistakes in the music, little deviances. These deviances and "english" are lost in the translation since an FM synthesizer always reproduces the sound perfectly. Alas, sound engineers turned from FM synthesis and tried taking digital samples of instruments and using them to create music—with amazing results.

Wave Table Synthesis

Wave table synthesis is becoming very popular and is based on the concept of digitizing the actual sound output of each instrument and then playing back the sounds when called upon by a MIDI file. The basic hardware is shown in Figure 6-10. As you can see, a wave table holds short digital samples of each instrument. When a MIDI instruction indicates that a particular instrument should be played, the digital data is taken from the wave table, amplified, and played along with the other sounds to make the final musical note(s).

The problem with wave table synthesis is its complexity. It requires a DSP (digital signal processor) to perform the mathematics for pitch, amplitude, and envelope changes in real-time. This has been the main limiting factor for wave table-based sound cards in the past; but today, with the price of processors decreasing and their performance increasing, wave table synthesis is becoming more common. The Sound Blaster AWE32 is an example of a wave table synthesizer, and when you listen to it, you will notice a difference. Instead of sounding synthesized, the music sounds like it's being played by musicians in the next room.

The beauty of wave table synthesis is that MIDI composers don't need to do anything different. They can still compose as if they were writing for an FM synthesizer because the MIDI specification doesn't stipulate how the sounds are made, it only stipulates what the results should be. When wave table synthesis is coupled with instrument patches, its real power comes into play. I suspect a hundred dollar sound card will rival the performance of thousands of dollars of musical equipment in the near future.

Before we move on, there is one more new technology that I just want to hint at. It's actually possible to produce microsized wave guides, and using these wave guides, it's possible to synthesize physically the actual parameters of an instrument's acoustics. This is theoretical stuff, but I bet you by the time this book is out, you might be able to find "virtual wave guide synthesis" sound cards.

FIGURE 6-10
◉ ◉ ◉ ◉ ◉ ◉
*Layout of a wave
table synthesizer*

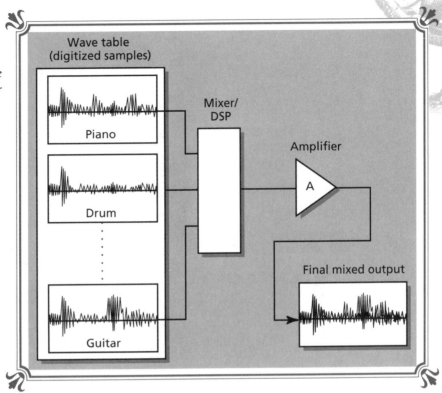

The Audio Solution

The main focus of this chapter is to learn how to play digitized sounds and music using the products DIGPAK and MIDPAK from The Audio Solution and John Ratcliff. The drivers were created by John Ratcliff and John Miles of Miles Design as solutions to playing digitized effects and music on myriad sound cards available. As Cybersorcerers, we only need to know two things about DIGPAK and MIDPAK: how they work and how to use them. Let's begin by seeing how everything fits together.

Both MIDPAK and DIGPAK are TSR (terminate and stay resident) drivers that latch on to interrupt 66h (*INT 66h*). These drivers are installed via COM files or loaded by the application software. MIDPAK plays music and DIGPAK plays digitized sounds. To communicate with MIDPAK and DIGPAK, interrupt calls are made with the proper parameters in various registers. Figure 6-11 is a graphical representation of the architecture of the system. As you can see, MIDPAK and DIGPAK are chained together, and when an *INT 66h* is invoked, one of the drivers either

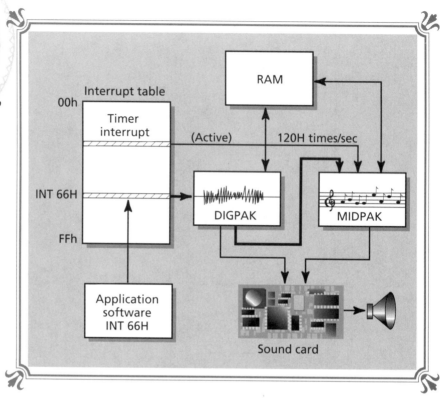

FIGURE 6-11
⊚ ⊚ ⊚ ⊚ ⊚ ⊚
*Sound system
architecture
under The Audio
Solution*

absorbs or transmits the command—that is, each driver will only listen to commands that are meant for it. This is how both drivers can be located at the same interrupt.

The interesting thing about the drivers is that the DIGPAK digital sound driver doesn't do much except direct the sound card to play a sound from memory or disk, and the sound card takes care of most of the work once the sound starts. The MIDPAK driver is different though. It must continually play MIDI music through the sound card and thus is called by an interrupt at a periodic rate. In essence, when we make a call to the MIDPAK driver using *INT 66h*, the driver does what we tell it, but another part of the driver (the active part) is continually called based on another interrupt that is hardware based.

The reason for this is that most sound cards can't play music; they must be programmed to do so in real-time. And the best way to do this is through an interrupt. Hence, MIDPAK uses the standard timer interrupt that usually occurs 18.2 times a second, but reprograms it to a rate of 288 Hz. This is so music can be played with a high enough resolution to catch all the pitch, velocity, and amplitude changes in real-time. This reprogramming is done by MIDPAK, but it's nice to know what's going on.

Let's review how everything works and add a little. First, both music and digital sound effects will be played using MIDPAK (music) and DIGPAK (digital effects). These drivers were written by The Audio Solution and are installed at interrupt 66h by running a COM file for each. In the case of MIDPAK, the COM file that loads the MIDI driver is called MIDPAK.COM. Also, it loads two other files called MIDPAK.ADV and MIDPAK.AD, which are the actual sound driver and instrument patches for your particular sound card. The digital sound driver is called DIGPAK and is loaded by running SOUNDRV.COM. Unlike the MIDPAK driver, the digital sound driver doesn't load any extra files. Here's a list of the files for each driver:

❖ MIDPAK - The MIDI Driver

❖ MIDPAK.COM - The interface to the low-level driver

❖ MIDPAK.ADV - The MIDI driver for your sound card

❖ MIDPAK.AD - The instrument patches for your sound card

❖ DIGPAK - The Digital Sound Driver

❖ SOUNDRV.COM

Of course, there is no law that states we must load both drivers. For example, we might want to use our own digital sound driver. In this case, we would only load the music driver. We can load one, the other, or both; but if both drivers are loaded, it's a good idea to first load the digital driver SOUNDRV.COM and then the MIDI driver MIDPAK.COM on top of it.

At this point, a couple of questions should come to mind: where do we get these drivers, and how do we communicate with them? Let's begin by answering the first question.

Creating the Drivers

Two programs are used to create the drivers. One program creates the digital sound driver SOUNDRV.COM, and the second program creates the MIDI driver MID-PAK.COM and its associated files MIDPAK.ADV and MIDPAK.AD. Both programs are in the subdirectory DRIVERS under this chapter, and they are called:

❖ SETM.EXE - A menu-driven program by John Ratcliff to create the MIDI drivers

❖ SETD.EXE - A menu-driven program by John Ratcliff to create the digital sound driver

To create the driver files for your particular sound card, you must run both of the programs SETM.EXE and SETD.EXE in the DRIVERS directory, which will output the files SOUNDRV.COM, MIDPAK.COM, MIDPAK.ADV, and MIDPAK.AD. Then take these output files and place them into your application's directory, so your game programs can access them.

If you view the contents of the DRIVERS directory, you will notice a lot of files that have various extensions along with familiar names of sound cards as the file names. These files generate the files for your particular card's sound drivers for both DIGPAK and MIDPAK. Another interesting thing about SETM.EXE and SETD.EXE is that each program allows you to configure the I/O port and interrupt of your sound card. This information is written right into the drivers themselves! So, the application doesn't ever have to change I/O ports or interrupts. The only downside to this is that the user of your game must run SETM.EXE and SETD.EXE, unless you are going to write a single installation program yourself.

Installing the Drivers

Once you have generated the driver files with SETM.EXE and SETD.EXE and copied them into your application's working directory, installing the drivers is simple. At the DOS prompt enter **SOUNDRV.COM** and **MIDPAK.COM**, and the drivers will load into memory as TSRs. Of course, MIDPAK.COM will also load the files MIDPAK.ADV and MIDPAK.AD, but this is transparent to us. Just make sure the files are in the working directory of the application, so the loader can find them.

Once the drivers are installed, they will wait for commands to be sent to them via interrupt 66h. Hence, we must learn how these commands work and how to interface to *INT 66h*.

Playing Digitized Sounds with DIGPAK

DIGPAK is the driver used to play raw digital samples from memory. The DIGPAK interface is rich and complex, but can be invoked through interrupt 66h. However, to make the digital driver even easier to use, we're going to write a single layer of software that sits on top of DIGPAK, creating a C interface. In most cases, the interface will simply call the appropriate DIGPAK function, but functions such as loading sound files and converting them to DIGPAK format aren't supported by DIGPAK; hence, we will add this functionality.

The DIGPAK Interface

The DIGPAK interface has about 25 functions, and each function can be invoked via *INT 66h*. DIGPAK plays unsigned 8- or 16-bit digital sound samples, but DIGPAK has no concept of WAV, VOC, MOD, or any other file format. We must parse any input sound files and send DIGPAK a structure that contains:

+ A pointer to the raw 8- or 16-bit sound data

+ The size of the data in bytes

+ The frequency at which the sample should be played

+ A few diagnostic bytes

For instance, the software interface we're going to create will read VOC files and create the proper DIGPAK structure to play the VOC file after it's loaded from memory.

The primary data structure that DIGPAK uses is called a *SNDSTRUC*. Here is its definition:

```
// the DIGPAK sound structure

typedef struct SNDSTRUC_typ
        {
        unsigned char far *sound;    // a pointer to the raw sound data
        unsigned short sndlen;       // the length of the sound data in bytes
        short far *IsPlaying;        // a pointer to a variable that will be
                                     // used to hold the status of a playing
                                     // sound
        short frequency;             // the frequency in hertz that the
                                     // sound should be played at

        } SNDSTRUC, *SNDSTRUC_PTR;
```

To play a sound, we must first build up this structure and send it to DIGPAK.

We're now ready to see the listing of the different functions that DIGPAK supports. But before we get to that, let's discuss a couple of points. First, DIGPAK supports real and protected modes; thus it can be used for 32-bit games. However, we are only going to support the 16-bit DOS real mode interface in our discussions. If you are interested in more detail, take a look in the DRIVERS directory at the document named DIGPKAPI.DOC, written by John Ratcliff, for a complete list of functions. The list of functions in Table 6-1 is a subset of DIGPAK, and we will only use a few of those listed, but these are the main functions and in most cases will suffice.

TABLE 6-1

◇◇◇◇◇◇

DIGPAK functions

Function 1: DigPlay - Play an 8-bit digitized sound.

    Input: AX = 688h - Command number.

              DS:SI - Pointer to the sound structure of the sound effect to be played.

    Output: None.

Function 2: SoundStatus - Check the status of sound driver and report the version number of the driver if greater than 3.1.

    Input: AX = 689h

    Output: AX = 0 - No sound is playing.

              = 1 - A sound is currently playing.

           DX = 0 - No sound is looping.

              = 1 - A sound is looping.

           BX = The version of the driver times 100; if the driver is less than version 3.1, a 0 will be returned.

Function 3: MassageAudio - Format the raw audio data into target output hardware format.

    Input: AX = 68Ah

              DS:SI - Pointer to sound structure of the sound effect to be played.

    Output: None.

Function 4: DigPlay2 - Play preformatted audio data.

    Input: AX = 68Bh

              DS:SI - Pointer to sound structure of sound effect to be played.

    Output: None.

Function 5: AudioCapabilities - Report the hardware capabilities of the sound card.

    Input: AX = 68Ch

    Output: AX = Hardware capabilities as defined in table below:

Bit Number	Function
0	1 - Driver supports background playback.
	0 - Driver only plays as a foreground process.
1	1 - The source data is reformatted for output device.
	0 - Device handles raw 8-bit unsigned audio.
2	1 - Device plays back at a fixed frequency, but the audio driver will downsample input data to fit.
	0 - Device plays back at user-specified frequency.
3	Device uses the timer interrupt vector during sound playback.
4	Driver supports timer sharing.
5	Device supports looped sounds and pending.
6	Device supports stereo panning.
7	Device supports 8-bit PCM stereo playback.
8	Supports audio recording.
9	Supports DMA backfilling.

DX = If the device only plays at a fixed frequency, DX will contain this playback frequency.

Function 8: StopSound - Stop the currently playing sound.

Input: AX = 68Fh

Output: None.

Function 17: SetPlayMode - Set the hardware to play specific data formats.

Input: AX = 698h

DX = Data format of play mode.

Bit Number	Function
0	8-bit PCM
1	8-bit stereo PCM (left/right)
2	16-bit PCM
3	16-bit PCM stereo

continued on next page

continued from previous page

Output: AX = 1 - Mode set.

0 - Mode not supported by this driver.

Function 24: Set PCM volume - Set the volume of the output device.

Input: AX = 69Fh

BX = Left channel volume (or both if mono) 0-100

CX = Right channel volume (or both if mono) 0-100

Output: AX = 1 - Volume was set.

0 - Device doesn't support volume setting.

To make using DIGPAK as easy as possible, we're going to create another API on top of the functions listed in Table 6-1. This will insulate us from making the *INT 66h* calls by using a clean C interface and a few extra housekeeping functions.

Accessing DIGPAK from C

To make calls to DIGPAK from C, we need to make an *INT 66h* call with the proper parameters set up in the CPU resistors. We can accomplish this using inline assembly or the *_int86()* function. Inline assembly is cleaner, so we'll use it. The API that we are going to write will in most cases just pass parameters into the proper registers and call DIGPAK with an *INT 66h*. However, we must write one function ourselves, and that's a function to load a VOC file, extract the sound data from it, and set up the DIGPAK sound structure properly. So we need to learn the format of VOC files and how to extract the different components from them.

As shown in Figure 6-12, a VOC file consists of two portions: a header section and a data section. The header section contains variable length information, so the length of the header can vary. Because of this, the 20th byte of the header is always the length of the header section. Using this information, we can always compute the start of the data section. Hence, the 20th byte of the header can be used as an offset from the beginning of the VOC file to find the data section (hey, I didn't make it up!).

The data section contains that actual raw digital data of the sample in either 8-bit or 16-bit form. Since we're only interested in 8-bit samples, all the VOC files we'll read will only contain 8-bit unsigned data. Loading a VOC file is similar to reading any other type of file:

1. The file is opened.

2. A buffer is allocated.

FIGURE 6-12

A VOC file

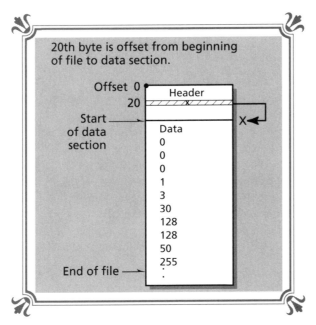

3   The data is read into the buffer.

4. The length of the header is computed using the 20th byte in the file.

5. The data is extracted and placed into the appropriate destination buffer.

6. The file is closed.

Or something like that...

Since we're using DIGPAK to play digital sound samples, we must extract a few pieces of information from the VOC file to place into the *SNDSTRUC* data structure. These are the size of the data portion of the VOC file and the playback frequency or sample rate of the file. These must then be placed, along with a pointer to the actual sound data, into a *SNDSTRUC* and passed to DIGPAK. To make life a little easier, we're going to create our own sound structure that will contain, among other things, a DIGPAK *SNDSTRUC*. The only reason for this is so that we can have a pointer to the start of the VOC file and add any fields in the future to the sound structure, such as information about what game object made the sound and so forth. The sound structure that we will use for our API is called *sound* and is defined below:

```
// our high level sound structure

typedef struct sound_typ
        {
        unsigned char far *buffer;  // pointer to the start of VOC file
```

continued on next page

continued from previous page

```
        short status;              // the current status of the sound
        SNDSTRUC SS;               // the DIGPAK sound structure

    } sound, *sound_ptr;
```

As you can see, it doesn't hold much except a DIGPAK *SNDSTRUC*, the VOC buffer, and a status variable. However, if we want to add to it in the future, we can; whereas adding to the DIGPAK structure might not be a good idea since adding fields could mess up DIGPAK's internal addressing! What do you think, John?

We are almost ready to write a program to load a VOC file, but first let's discuss a couple more details. For one, how do we compute the playback frequency of the VOC file? The sample rate can be found in the VOC file in the beginning of the data section in the "New Voice Block" section. You see, at the beginning of the digital data, there is actually a little header called the "New Voice Block." This header is only 6 bytes, but nevertheless has some interesting information, such as the sample rate, among other things. Here's the actual format of a VOC "New Voice Block":

Byte Number	Function
0	Block type
1-3	Block length
4	Sample rate (SR)
5	Pack bytes

The value we're interested in is located at the 4th byte and is called the sample rate. This byte has the following relationship to the original sample rate:

Sample rate in Hz = -1000000 / (SR - 256)

Hence, by retrieving the 4th byte of the data portion of the VOC file, which starts at an offset defined by the 20th byte in the header, we can compute the sample rate at which the sound effect should be played. This rate is then used to set up the DIGPAK *SNDSTRUC*. Figure 6-13 shows the relationship between the VOC headers and the VOC data. We are finally ready to write our first API function to load a VOC file off disk into memory and set up all the necessary data structures. Listing 6-1 contains the function.

LISTING 6-1 Function to load a VOC file

```
int Sound_Load(char *filename, sound_ptr the_sound,int translate)
{
// this function will load a sound from disk into memory and pre-format
// it in preparation to be played

unsigned char far *temp_ptr;    // temporary pointer used to load sound
```

FIGURE 6-13

◉ ◉ ◉ ◉ ◉ ◉

The complete VOC file

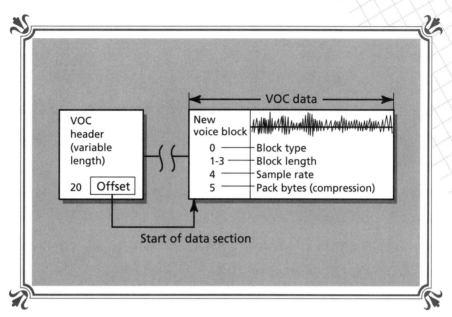

```c
unsigned char far *sound_ptr;   // pointer to sound data

unsigned int segment,           // segment of sound data memory
             paragraphs,        // number of 16 byte paragraphs sound takes up
             bytes_read,        // used to track number of bytes read by DOS
             size_of_file,      // the total size of the VOC file in bytes
             header_length;     // the length of the header portion of VOC file

int sound_handle;               // DOS file handle


// open the sound file, use DOS file and memory allocation to make sure
// memory is on a 16 byte or paragraph boundary

if (_dos_open(filename, _O_RDONLY, &sound_handle)!=0)
   {
   printf("\nSound System - Couldn't open %s",filename);
   return(0);
   } // end if file not found

// compute number of paragraphs that sound file needs
// size_of_file = _filelength(sound_handle);

paragraphs = 1 + (size_of_file)/16;

// allocate the memory on a paragraph boundary
_dos_allocmem(paragraphs,&segment);
```

continued on next page

continued from previous page

```c
// point data pointer to allocated data area
_FP_SEG(sound_ptr) = segment;
_FP_OFF(sound_ptr) = 0;

// alias pointer to memory storage area
temp_ptr = sound_ptr;

// read in blocks of 16k until file is loaded

do
 {
 // load next block
 _dos_read(sound_handle,temp_ptr, 0x4000, &bytes_read);

 // adjust pointer
 temp_ptr += bytes_read;

 } while(bytes_read==0x4000);

// close the file

_dos_close(sound_handle);

// make sure it's a voc file, test for "Creative"
if ((sound_ptr[0] != 'C') || (sound_ptr[1] != 'r'))
   {
   printf("\n%s is not a VOC file!",filename);

   // de-allocate the memory
   _dos_freemem(_FP_SEG(sound_ptr));

   // return failure
   return(0);

   } // end if voc file

   // compute start of sound data;
   header_length = (unsigned int)sound_ptr[20];

   // point buffer pointer to start of VOC file in memory
   the_sound->buffer        = sound_ptr;

   // set up the SNDSTRUC for DIGPAK
   the_sound->SS.sound      = (unsigned char far*)(sound_ptr+header_length+4);
   the_sound->SS.sndlen     = (unsigned short)(size_of_file - header_length);
   the_sound->SS.IsPlaying  = (short far *)&the_sound->status;
   the_sound->SS.frequency  = (short)((long)(-1000000) /
                               ((int)sound_ptr[header_length+4]-256));

   // now format data for sound card if requested
   if (translate)
       Sound_Translate(the_sound);
```

```
// return success
return(1);
```

```
} // end Sound_Load
```

The *Sound_Load()* function takes only three parameters: the file name, a pointer to the sound structure, and a flag indicating whether audio translation is needed. The function of the first two parameters is obvious, but the third parameter, *translate*, is a bit mysterious. Remember that DIGPAK doesn't know anything about VOC files; it only knows how to play raw 8- or 16-bit data. This means that if we want DIGPAK to play our audio data correctly and be able to play it more than once from memory without mangling it, then we must tell DIGPAK to translate the data using the *MassageAudio* function. Once we have done this, DIGPAK will be able to play the digital effect as many times as we wish, and it will sound right.

If you don't use the *MassageAudio* function, the original data buffer holding the VOC file in memory may be altered as the sound is played. Hence, you should always *MassageAudio* when loading a file unless you aren't going to use DIGPAK to play the sound (which will be the case when we make our own sound card synthesizer later in the chapter). Anyway, let's review the function.

The first thing you will notice about the function is that it uses DOS-level I/O and memory allocation. This is because it is easier to use DOS I/O than stream I/O to load large chunks into memory, and DOS memory allocation functions always allocate memory on paragraph boundaries, which is a good idea for sound files. Once the sound file is loaded, it's tested to see if it's a valid VOC file. This is accomplished by testing the first few characters of the file to see if the word "Creative" is there. If so, the remaining portion of the code computes the length of the sound data and the playback frequency rate, and finally, sets up the appropriate pointers to the sound data structures. Notice that the sound structure fields *IsPlaying* and *status* currently don't do much. The *status* field is part of our sound structure and can be used to track the status of the sound effect or whatever. The *IsPlaying* field of *SNDSTRUC* is used for a status semaphore issued by DIGPAK, but we won't be using it. The semaphore is used by DIGPAK as a status holder, so it needs to be defined even though we aren't going to use it.

At the very end of the *Sound_Load()* function is a call to *Sound_Translate()*, which is basically a wrapper for the *MassageAudio* function. The *Sound_Translate()* function is shown in Listing 6-2.

LISTING 6-2 *Function to translate and process a digital sound effect for playback by DIGPAK*

```
void Sound_Translate(sound_ptr the_sound)
{
// this function calls the DIGPAK function massage audio to translate
```

continued on next page

continued from previous page

```
// the raw audio data into the proper format for the sound card that
// the sound system is running on.

unsigned char far *buffer;

buffer = (unsigned char far*)&the_sound->SS;

_asm
  {
  push ds          ; save DS and SI on stack
  push si
  mov ax, 068Ah    ; function 3: MassageAudio
  lds si, buffer   ; move address of sound in DS:SI
  int 66h          ; call DIGPAK
  pop si           ; restore DS and SI from stack
  pop ds
                   ; have a nice day :)
  } // end inline assembly

} // end Sound_Translate
```

The function does nothing more than make a call to DIGPAK's Function 3, *MassageAudio*. The only parameter the function needs to send to DIGPAK is the starting address of the *SNDSTRUC* that contains the sound effect information. This is aliased to a pointer and passed in *DS:SI*. Notice how *SI* and *DS* are saved on the stack since we alter them during the function.

Next, we need a function to unload and deallocate the memory allocated by the *Sound_Load()* function to hold the VOC file. Listing 6-3 contains this function.

LISTING 6-3 Function to unload a VOC file

```
void Sound_Unload(sound_ptr the_sound)
{

// this function deletes the sound from memory

_dos_freemem(_FP_SEG(the_sound->buffer));
the_sound->buffer=NULL;

} // end Sound_Unload
```

The *Sound_Unload()* function simply releases the memory back to DOS. Notice how the *_dos_freemem()* function is used instead of *_ffree()* (which would normally be used if the memory were allocated by one of the *malloc()* functions rather than DOS). This is a very important point: if you allocate memory with DOS, you must use DOS to deallocate it. The same fact applies for memory allocated with C. However, you can use both types of memory for working buffers and so forth.

We can now load a sound, unload a sound, and translate it to DIGPAK format, so let's play it! The function to play a sound is one of the simplest, as shown in Listing 6-4.

LISTING 6-4 Function to play a digital sound effect

```
void Sound_Play(sound_ptr the_sound)
{
// this function plays the sound pointed to by the sound structure

unsigned char far *buffer;

// alias sound structure

buffer = (unsigned char far*)&the_sound->SS;

_asm
   {
   push ds            ; save DS and SI on stack
   push si
   mov ax, 068Bh      ; function 4: DigPlay2
   lds si, buffer     ; move address of sound in DS:SI
   int 66h            ; call DIGPAK
   pop si             ; restore DS and SI from stack
   pop ds

   } // end inline assembly

} // end Sound_Play
```

Interestingly enough, the function body is almost identical to that of *Sound_Translate()*. This is a direct result of The Audio Solution's clean interface to their driver. This function simply sends the pointer of the *SNDSTRUC*, places the proper command code in *AX*, and calls *INT 66h*. The sound will then begin playing. Once the sound begins to play, the next thing we'll want to do is track its status so we can detect when it's complete. Thus, a status function is in order. The status function will be based on DIGPAK's Function 2, *SoundStatus*, and the code is shown in Listing 6-5.

LISTING 6-5 Function to query the status of DIGPAK's digital sound channel

```
int Sound_Status(void)
{
// this function will return the status of DIGPAK i.e. is a sound playing
// or not

_asm
   {
   mov ax, 0689h      ; function 2: SoundStatus
   int 66h            ; call DIGPAK

   } // end inline assembly
// on exit AX will be used as the return value, if 1 then a sound is playing
```

continued on next page

continued from previous page
```
// 0 if a sound is not playing

} // end Sound_Status
```

The C function calls the *SoundStatus* function of DIGPAK and returns the result of digital sound channel back in *AX*. The result codes have been defined in BLACK6.H as:

```
#define SOUND_STOPPED    0      // no sound is playing
#define SOUND_PLAYING    1      // a sound is playing
```

For example, if we started a sound and wanted to wait for it to complete before continuing, the following line of code would suffice:

```
while(Sound_Status());
```

The final function we need is a way to stop a sound while it's playing so that we can start another or simply turn off all sound output. Stopping a sound while it's playing is accomplished using DIGPAK's Function 8, *StopSound*. Listing 6-6 contains our C version of the function.

LISTING 6-6 Function to stop a sound effect while it's playing

```
void Sound_Stop(void)
{
// this function will stop a currently playing sound

_asm
   {
   mov ax, 068Fh    ; function 8: StopSound
   int 66h          ; call DIGPAK

   } // end inline assembly

} // end Sound_Stop
```

The *Sound_Stop()* function stops a digital sound effect (if one is playing) and does nothing if a sound isn't playing. In general, DIGPAK is fairly forgiving about calling functions when their results can't possibly make sense, so our code doesn't have to be totally bulletproof!

We now have a complete C interface to play digital sounds using DIGPAK. You'll notice that we didn't implement a function for everything; for example, we left out volume control, but you can add these later, if you wish. Let's review how everything fits together. First, we use the SETD.EXE program to create the digital sound driver SOUNDRV.COM and then load it at the DOS prompt. Then DIGPAK installs itself and hooks into *INT 66h*. Next, to play a sound using C, we would include BLACK6.H and BLACK6.C and write a bit of code like this:

```
sound boom;  // the sound

// load the VOC file
```

```
Sound_Load("boom.voc",(sound_ptr)&boom,1);

// play the sound
Sound_Play((sound_ptr)&boom);

// wait for sound to complete
while(Sound_Status());

//  delete the sound
Sound_Unload((sound_ptr)&boom);
```

It doesn't get any better than that!

As an example, I have created a demo program that uses a technique called *digital concatenation* to create complete phrases out of smaller words. This technique is used when you call the operator for time and she tells you the time. The actual sounds you hear are concatenated. For example, we could digitize the vocalizations of:

0, 1, 2, 3, 4, 5, 6, 7, 8, 9, 10, 11, 12, 13, 14, 15, 16, 17, 18, 19, 20, 30, 40, 50, 60, 70, 80, 90, 100

Then we could concatenate the individual numerical vocalizations to create any number from 0 to 100. In essence, we can synthetically generate 101 numerical phrases from only 29 digital samples! For instance, 26 would be created by playing 20, then 6, in quick succession.

Anyway, the following demo uses this technique to create a verbal "Speak and Add" program that tests your skills of addition. The name of the program is DIGIDEMO.C and the executable is DIGIDEMO.EXE. To create the executable, you will need the previous library functions of BLACKLIB along with BLACK6.H and BLACK6.C. Moreover, you will have to generate the DIGPAK driver SOUNDRV.COM with the utility program SETD.EXE and load the driver from the command line before running DIGIDEMO.EXE. Listing 6-7 contains the source code.

LISTING 6-7 A digital sound demo program

```
// DIGIDEMO.C - Digital sound demo

// I N C L U D E S //////////////////////////////////////////////////////////

#include <io.h>
#include <conio.h>
#include <stdio.h>
#include <stdlib.h>
#include <dos.h>
#include <bios.h>
#include <fcntl.h>
#include <memory.h>
```

continued on next page

continued from previous page

```c
#include <malloc.h>
#include <math.h>
#include <string.h>

// include the sound library

#include "black3.h"
#include "black6.h"

// D E F I N E S //////////////////////////////////////////////////////////

// defines for the phrases

#define SOUND_WHAT       0
#define SOUND_WRONG      1
#define SOUND_CORRECT    2
#define SOUND_PLUS       3
#define SOUND_EQUAL      4

// G L O B A L S //////////////////////////////////////////////////////////

sound ones[11];   // this will hold the digital samples for 1..9
sound teens[11];  // this will hold the digital samples for 11-19
sound tens[11];   // this will hold the digital samples for 10,20,30,40...100
sound phrases[6]; // this will hold the phrases

// F U N C T I O N S //////////////////////////////////////////////////////

void Say_Number(int number)
{
// this function uses digitized samples to construct whole numbers
// note that the teens i.e. numbers from 11-19 have to be spoken as a
// special case and can't be concatenated as the numbers 20-100 can!

int ones_place,
    tens_place;

// compute place values, use simple logic, more complex logic can be
// derived that uses MODING and so forth, but better to see what's going
// on. However, the main point of this is to see the digital library
// in action, so focus on that aspect.

// test for 0..9

if (number<10)
   {
   Sound_Play((sound_ptr)&ones[number]);
   while(Sound_Status()==1);
   return;
   } // end if 0..9

// test for 11..19
```

```
if (number >= 11 && number <= 19)
   {
   Sound_Play((sound_ptr)&teens[number-11]);
   while(Sound_Status()==1);
   return;
   } // end if 11..19

// now break number down into tens and ones
tens_place = number / 10;
ones_place = number % 10;

// first say tens place
Sound_Play((sound_ptr)&tens[tens_place-1]);
while(Sound_Status()==1);

// now say ones place (if any)
if (ones_place)
   {
   Sound_Play((sound_ptr)&ones[ones_place]);
   while(Sound_Status()==1);
   } // end if

} // end Say_Number

// M A I N /////////////////////////////////////////////////////////////////

void main(int argc, char **argv)
{
char filename[16]; // used to build up filename

int number,     // loop variables
    number_1,
    number_2,
    answer,
    done=0;     // exit flag

float num_problems=0,  // used to track performance of player
      num_correct=0;

// load in the samples for the ones
for (number=1; number<=9; number++)
   {
   // build the filename
   sprintf(filename,"N%d.VOC",number);
   printf("\nLoading file %s",filename);

   // load the sound
   Sound_Load(filename,(sound_ptr)&ones[number],1);

   } // end for ones

// load in the samples for the teens
```

continued on next page

continued from previous page

```
for (number=11; number<=19; number++)
    {
    // build the filename
    sprintf(filename,"N%d.VOC",number);
    printf("\nLoading file %s",filename);

    // load the sound
    Sound_Load(filename,(sound_ptr)&teens[number-11],1);

    } // end for teens

// load in the samples for the tens
for (number=10; number<=100; number+=10)
    {
    // build the filename
    sprintf(filename,"N%d.VOC",number);
    printf("\nLoading file %s",filename);

    // load the sound
    Sound_Load(filename,(sound_ptr)&tens[-1+number/10],1);

    } // end for tens

// load the phrases
printf("\nLoading the phrases...");
Sound_Load("what.voc",    (sound_ptr)&phrases[SOUND_WHAT     ],1);
Sound_Load("wrong.voc",   (sound_ptr)&phrases[SOUND_WRONG    ],1);
Sound_Load("correct.voc",(sound_ptr)&phrases[SOUND_CORRECT  ],1);
Sound_Load("plus.voc",    (sound_ptr)&phrases[SOUND_PLUS     ],1);
Sound_Load("equal.voc",   (sound_ptr)&phrases[SOUND_EQUAL    ],1);

// main event loop, note this one is not real-time since it waits
// for user input!

printf("\n    S P E A K    N    A D D  !!!");
printf("\n\n\nThis program will test your skills of addition while
     demonstrating");
printf("\nthe digital sound channel in action!");

printf("\n\nJust answer each addition problem. To exit type in 0.\n");
printf("\n\nPress any key to begin!!!\n\n");

getch();

// the main event loop
while(!done)
    {

    // select two random numbers to add, but make sure their sum is less
    // than or equal to 100

    do
      {
```

```
   number_1 = 1 + rand()%99;
   number_2 = 1 + rand()%99;
   } while (number_1 + number_2 > 100);

// ask user question
printf("\nWhat is ");

Sound_Play((sound_ptr)&phrases[SOUND_WHAT]);
while(Sound_Status()==1);

printf("%d",number_1);
Say_Number(number_1);
printf(" + ");

Sound_Play((sound_ptr)&phrases[SOUND_PLUS]);
while(Sound_Status()==1);

Time_Delay(15);

printf("%d",number_2);
Say_Number(number_2);
printf(" = ?",number_2);

Sound_Play((sound_ptr)&phrases[SOUND_EQUAL]);
while(Sound_Status()==1);

scanf("%d",&answer);

// make sure user isn't exiting
if (answer!=0)
   {
   num_problems++;

   // test if user is correct
   if (answer == (number_1 + number_2))
      {
      Sound_Play((sound_ptr)&phrases[SOUND_CORRECT]);
      while(Sound_Status()==1);
      num_correct++;
      }
   else
      {
      // oops wrong answer!
      Sound_Play((sound_ptr)&phrases[SOUND_WRONG]);
      while(Sound_Status()==1);

      Say_Number(number_1+number_2);
      Time_Delay(25);

      } // end else wrong

   } // end if
else
```

continued on next page

continued from previous page

```
        {
        done = 1;
        } // end else user is exiting

    } // end main event loop

// unload all the sounds

for (number=1; number<=9; number++)
    Sound_Unload((sound_ptr)&ones[number]);

for (number=11; number<=19; number++)
    Sound_Unload((sound_ptr)&teens[number]);

for (number=10; number<=100; number+=10)
    Sound_Unload((sound_ptr)&tens[-1+number/10]);

for (number=0; number<=4; number++)
    Sound_Unload((sound_ptr)&phrases[number]);

// tell user their statistics

printf("\nYou got %.0 percent of the problems correct.",
        100*num_correct/num_problems);

} // end main
```

The program is actually very simple. It begins by loading all the prerecorded digital samples of the individual numbers along with a few phrases, such as "What Is?". After this, the program enters the main event loop and selects two random numbers such that their sum is less than or equal to 100. Then a complete sentence is concatenated, based on the individual numerical phrases, and spoken. Then the user must type in the correct answer. The heart of the program is the function *Say_Number()*, which basically computes the tens, ones, and teens places of the requested number, accesses the sound arrays and builds up the number, and plays the sounds. The main concepts to extract from the program are the ability to load multiple sounds, play sounds, and use digital sounds creatively.

Finally, we need to discuss the topic of memory consumption. Digital samples are notorious for eating memory alive. For example, if we were to sample 10 seconds at 44.1 kHz (CD-quality), we would eat up 440K of memory! What does this mean? It means that digital samples should be short, sweet, and to the point. Moreover, they should be sampled at a rate low enough so they don't use all of the system memory. Of course, you can always swap sounds in and out from disk and create a virtual sound buffer system, but if you want to fit everything into the DOS 640K model, don't get too crazy. Use a sample rate such as 6 to 8 kHz, which will be more than enough for most sound effects such as explosions, growls, and laser blasts.

Digital Recording Techniques

We now have a great digital sound library and interface, but where do we get the actual digital samples? That's a good question. There are many commercial products that can digitize samples. If you purchase a Sound Blaster for example, the distribution disks come with a couple utilities for DOS and a WAV player for Windows that allows you to take digital samples. The Windows WAV player also allows sound files to be written out in either VOC or WAV format.

Personally, for simple stuff, I use a program called Blaster Master. The program is Shareware and designed for a Sound Blaster. It allows you to digitize samples up to 25 seconds in 8-bit, 16-bit, mono, or stereo. Also, the program can read and write multiple sound formats. The program is on the CD-ROM under the directory called BMASTER. To digitize sounds, you'll need a sound source such as a mic or other input that is connected to the input of your sound. Using Blaster Master's menu-driven interface, you can digitize a sample and tweak it until it sounds good. Then you can write the sound file to disk and use it in your programs.

Looks like we've got digital sound down, but what about music? Well that's the hard part, so wave your hand in the air and prepare to conjure up some real Cybersorcery!

Making Music with MIDPAK

MIDPAK is the MIDI music interface that we will use to generate music. We use interrupt 66h to communicate with the interface, and just as we did for DIGPAK, we are going to create a software layer on top of MIDPAK to make the calls to it a bit simpler. Before we begin designing the software interface layer, there is a small detail about the MIDPAK file format that needs to be discussed. MIDPAK does not use standard MIDI files for its input, but a special file format designed by Miles Design called *Extended MIDI* or XMI files. Let's take a look at how these files are generated.

Creating Extended MIDI Files

Extended MIDI files are nothing more than a collection of MIDI files all concatenated in a single file. Using this format it becomes much easier to manipulate music in a game, since a single file contains all the music for the game. The XMI file is said to contain *sequences*. Each sequence is really a complete MIDI file. Hence, if we were to create an XMI file that had three MIDI songs within it, we would refer to the first one as sequence one, the second one as sequence two, and the third MIDI

file as sequence three. However, due to the numbering system of MIDPAK, they would really be 0, 1, and 2 in the program code.

So how do we create XMI files? The MIDPAK kit comes with a program named MIDIFORM.EXE. You'll find this program on the CD-ROM in the DRIVERS directory. Its syntax is very simple. In the most basic form it is used to create a single XMI file from a set of standard MIDI files. MIDIFORM has the following syntax:

MIDIFORM outputfile.XMI inputfile1.MID inputfile2.MID . . .

Figure 6-14 shows what's going on with the following command:

MIDIFORM MUSIC.XMI INTRO.MID BATTLE.MID END.MID

Here MIDIFORM is being used to make a single XMI file that contains all the music for a single game. The introduction music, the main game music, and the ending music are all placed in a single XMI file. MIDPAK refers to each of these compositions as a sequence. For example, if we wanted to play the ending music, that would be sequence 2. We will learn how to "register" an XMI file with MIDPAK and play a sequence, but now we know the overall structure of the system.

To reiterate, MIDPAK doesn't play MIDI files directly, we must convert the MIDI files into a single XMI file. The XMI file can contain one or more MIDI files, and each individual composition is referred to as a sequence and is numbered starting from 0. We are now in a position to write the interface, so let's see what MIDPAK has to offer.

FIGURE 6-14

⊚ ⊚ ⊚ ⊚ ⊚ ⊚

Operation of
MIDIFORM.EXE

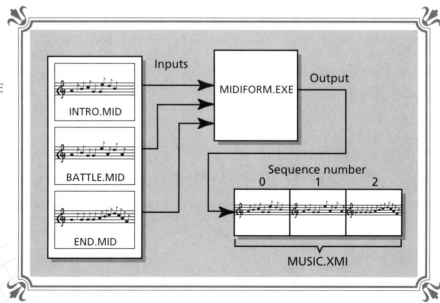

The MIDPAK Interface

MIDPAK contains a set of functions similar to DIGPAK except they are used to play music instead of digital sounds. There are about 23 functions in MIDPAK; some are obsolete and others we won't even be using. Table 6-2 lists the most important ones.

TABLE 6-2
❖❖❖❖❖

MIDPAK functions

Function 1: UnloadMidPak - Remove MIDPAK from memory but shouldn't be called by application software.

Input: AX = 700h - Command number.

Output: None.

Function 2: DigPakAvailable - Return the existence of the DIGPAK driver if it is loaded under MIDPAK.

Input: AX = 701h - Command number.

Output: AX = 0 - DIGPAK is not available.

                1 - DIGPAK is available.

Function 3: PlaySequence - Play a sequence from the currently registered XMI file.

Input: AX = 702h - Command number.

          BX = Sequence number to play starting from 0.

Output: AX = 1 - Sequence is being played.

                0 - The requested sequence is not available.

Function 5: RegisterXmidi - Used by the application software to register an XMI file by its memory address for playback.

Input: AX = 704h - Command number.

          BX = Offset portion of far address of XMI data in memory.

          CX = Segment portion of far address of XMI data.

          SI = Low word of length of XMI data in bytes.

          DI = High word of length of XMI data in bytes.

Output: AX = 0 - Unable to register XMI data.

                1 - XMI file registered and buffered by MIDPAK, so the application can delete the original XMI data from memory.

                2 - XMI file was registered to the application, but it couldn't be buffered, so the memory must stay intact.

continued on next page

continued from previous page

Function 6: MidiStop - Stop a currently playing XMI sequence.

Input: AX = 705h - Command.

Output: None.

Function 12: ResumePlaying - Used to resume a previously stopped sequence.

Input: AX = 70Bh - Command number.

Output: None.

Function 13: SequenceStatus - Used to report the status of a sequence.

Input: AX = 70Ch - Command number.

Output: AX = 0 - The sequence is stopped.

              1 - The sequence is playing.

              2 - The sequence has completed and is done.

Function 14: RegisterXmidiFile - Similar to Function 5 except it registers an XMI file by file name instead of memory address.

Input: AX = 70Dh - Command number.

        BX = Offset portion of file name address in memory.

        CX = Segment portion of file name address in memory.

Output: None.

Function 23: ReportSequenceNumber - Used to report the currently playing sequence number.

Input: AX = 716h - Command number.

Output: AX = The currently playing sequence number.

There are quite a few MIDPAK functions missing from the list, but they're used to implement advanced features such as a polled driver, event triggering, and related subfunctions. If you want more detail, feel free to review the file on the CD-ROM named MIDPKAPI.DOC, which contains the complete functional listing. Admittedly, the only thing I find of interest other than the functions in Table 6-2 are the event triggering functions. You see, many times in a game, we want to be able to determine where we are in the musical sequence so that an appropriate special effect can be displayed or logical decision can be made. Special MIDI commands called *SYSEXs* (system exclusive) take care of this. MIDPAK supports this, but it is beyond the scope of these pages. However, with some determination and a bit of detective work, you should be able to figure out how it works.

Now that we have the set of functions we are going to use, let's implement a C interface to access them in a simple manner.

Accessing MIDPAK from C

Unlike DIGPAK, MIDPAK has no "music structure." MIDPAK simply needs to know the starting address of the XMI data that represents the desired musical sequences in memory. Hence, all we need to do is write a function that loads an XMI file and implement some C shells around all the MIDPAK functions, and we're done! To play an XMI sequence is almost too easy–here are the steps:

1. An XMI file is generated with MIDIFORM.EXE.

2. The XMI file is loaded into memory.

3. The XMI file is "registered" to MIDPAK using Function 5, *RegisterXmidi*.

4. A selected sequence is played by calling Function 3, *PlaySequence*.

Step 2 is about the only thing we must write ourselves; the rest of the functions are simply calls to *INT 66h*.

We're ready to write the interface library, but let's add a data structure and some defines to make things easier. If you recall, MIDPAK doesn't support any data structure as does DIGPAK, but to make life easier, we'll create one that contains relevant information about a loaded XMI file. Here's the data structure we are going to use:

```
// this holds a midi file

typedef struct music_typ
        {

        unsigned char far *buffer;      // pointer to midi data
        long size;                      // size of midi file in bytes
        int status;                     // status of song
        int register_info;              // return value of RegisterXmidiFile

        } music, *music_ptr;
```

The structure holds a pointer to the loaded XMI file, its length, a status variable, and a field that holds the results when the XMI file is registered to MIDPAK. The structure is probably overkill, but better safe than sorry. To further facilitate the ease of writing the functions and determining their results, here are a few defines to make our code clearer:

```
// return values for the midi sequence status function

#define SEQUENCE_STOPPED      0    // the current sequence is stopped
#define SEQUENCE_PLAYING      1    // the current sequence is playing
#define SEQUENCE_COMPLETE     2    // the current sequence has completed
#define SEQUENCE_UNAVAILABLE  0    // this sequence is unavailable
```

continued on next page

continued from previous page

```
// these return values are used to determine what happened when a midi file
// has been registered

#define XMIDI_UNREGISTERED  0    // the midi file couldn't be registered at all
#define XMIDI_BUFFERED      1    // the midi file was registered and buffered
#define XMIDI_UNBUFFERED    2    // the midi file was registered, but was too
                                 // big to be buffered, hence, the caller
                                 // needs to keep the midi data resident
                                 // in memory
```

The first set of defines is used to determine the results of the *SequenceStatus* function, and the second set is to make sense of the results of the *RegisterXmidiFile* function.

All right, now that we have laid the groundwork, let's begin with the first and most important function, and that's to load the XMI file. We'll use DOS memory allocation and file functions as we did in the DIGPAK interface simply because I copied the functions and modified them! Listing 6-8 contains the function to load an XMI file off disk into memory and set up the *music* data structure appropriately.

LISTING 6-8 Function to load an XMI file into memory

```
int Music_Load(char *filename, music_ptr the_music)
{
// this function will load a xmidi file from disk into memory and register it

unsigned char far *temp_ptr;     // temporary pointer used to load music
unsigned char far *xmidi_ptr;    // pointer to xmidi data

unsigned int segment,            // segment of music data memory
             paragraphs,         // number of 16 byte paragraphs music takes up
             bytes_read;         // used to track number of bytes read by DOS

long         size_of_file;       // the total size of the xmidi file in bytes

int xmidi_handle;                // DOS file handle

// open the extended xmidi file, use DOS file and memory allocation to make sure
// memory is on a 16 byte or paragraph boundary
if (_dos_open(filename, _O_RDONLY, &xmidi_handle)!=0)
   {
   printf("\nMusic System - Couldn't open %s",filename);
   return(0);

   } // end if file not found

// compute number of paragraphs that sound file needs
size_of_file = _filelength(xmidi_handle);
paragraphs = 1 + (size_of_file)/16;

// allocate the memory on a paragraph boundary
_dos_allocmem(paragraphs,&segment);
```

```
// point data pointer to allocated data area
_FP_SEG(xmidi_ptr) = segment;
_FP_OFF(xmidi_ptr) = 0;

// alias pointer to memory storage area
temp_ptr = xmidi_ptr;

// read in blocks of 16k until file is loaded
do
 {
 // load next block
 _dos_read(xmidi_handle,temp_ptr, 0x4000, &bytes_read);

 // adjust pointer
 temp_ptr += bytes_read;

 } while(bytes_read==0x4000);

// close the file
_dos_close(xmidi_handle);

// set up the music structure
the_music->buffer = xmidi_ptr;
the_music->size   = size_of_file;
the_music->status = 0;

// now register the xmidi file with MIDPAK

if ((the_music->register_info = Music_Register(the_music))==XMIDI_UNREGISTERED)
   {
   // delete the memory
   Music_Unload(the_music);

   // return an error
   return(0);

   } // end if couldn't register xmidi file

// else return success
return(1);

} // end Music_Load
```

   The function takes two parameters, a file name and a pointer to a music structure. The function then proceeds to open the XMI file, determine its length, and
load the file into memory. If there are any problems during this phase, the function
returns an error. If all goes well, then the function sets the appropriate fields in the
music structure and registers the XMI file with MIDPAK. After that, the function
returns success. The registering of the XMI data is accomplished by a call to
Music_Register(), which simply calls the MIDPAK function to register an XMI file by
address. The code for *Music_Register()* is shown in Listing 6-9.

LISTING 6-9 Function to register an XMI file

```c
int Music_Register(music_ptr the_music)
{

// this function registers the xmidi music with MIDPAK, so that it can be
// played

unsigned int xmid_off,    // offset and segment of midi file
             xmid_seg,
             length_low,  // length of midi file in bytes
             length_hi;

// extract segment and offset of music buffer
xmid_off = _FP_OFF((the_music->buffer));
xmid_seg = _FP_SEG((the_music->buffer));

// extract the low word and high word of xmidi file length
length_low = the_music->size;
length_hi  = (the_music->size) >> 16;

// call MIDPAK

_asm
   {
   push si              ; save si and di
   push di
   mov ax,704h          ; function #5: RegisterXmidi
   mov bx,xmid_off      ; offset of xmidi data

   mov cx,xmid_seg      ; segment of xmidi data

   mov si,length_low       ; low word of xmidi length
   mov di,length_hi        ; hi word of xmidi length

   int 66h                 ; call MIDPAK
   pop di                  ; restore si and di
   pop si

   } // end inline assembly

// return value will be in AX

} // end Music_Register
```

Music_Register() is actually quite simple except for the few calculations done to extract the low and high words of the necessary parameters. There are cleaner ways to do this, but this is the clearest (I think). Feel free to simplify the function if you wish. Once an XMI file has been loaded into memory, sooner or later it must be unloaded. This is done with a simple call to deallocate the memory. But remember, we used DOS to allocate the memory, so DOS must be used to free it. Listing 6-10 contains the function to release the XMI memory and unload the file.

LISTING 6-10 Function to unload an XMI file

```
void Music_Unload(music_ptr the_music)
{
// this function deletes the xmidi file data from memory

_dos_freemem(_FP_SEG(the_music->buffer));
the_music->buffer=NULL;

} // end Music_Unload
```

Now that we can load, register, and unload an XMI file, let's learn to play one. We need only to implement the *PlaySequence* function in C. It's shown in Listing 6-11.

LISTING 6-11 Function to play a sequence from an XMI file

```
int Music_Play(music_ptr the_music,int sequence)
{
// this function plays an xmidi file from memory

_asm
   {
   mov ax,702h        ; function #3: PlaySequence
   mov bx, sequence   ; which sequence to play 0,1,2....
   int 66h            ; call MIDPAK

   } // end inline assembly

// return value is in AX, 1 success, 0 sequence not available

} // end Music_Play
```

The function takes as parameters a pointer to the music structure and the sequence number to play (starting from 0). The code makes a call to the *PlaySequence* function, and that's about it. Amazing, huh? Four lines of assembly language to play a MIDI song. But remember, there are thousands of lines under all this that are doing the real work, so be glad we are using MIDPAK!

Once a sequence is playing, we may wish to stop it. A function that accomplishes this task is shown in Listing 6-12.

LISTING 6-12 Function to stop a sequence

```
void Music_Stop(void)
{
// this function will stop the song currently playing

_asm
   {
   mov ax,705h     ; function #6: MidiStop
   int 66h         ; call MIDPAK

   } // end inline assembly

} // end Music_Stop
```

The function takes no parameters since only one sequence can be played at a time; therefore, it's obvious which one is to be stopped. After stopping a sequence, it's possible to resume the music with the function shown in Listing 6-13.

LISTING 6-13 Function to resume a stopped sequence

```
void Music_Resume(void)
{
// this function resumes a previously stopped xmidi sequence

_asm
  {
  mov ax,70Bh    ; function #12: ResumePlaying
  int 66h        ; call MIDPAK

  } // end inline assembly

} // end Music_Resume
```

Again, *Music_Resume()* needs no parameters since the sequence to resume is implied as the one that was stopped. The last function we need to implement is a status function so we can determine what's going on with a running sequence. Listing 6-14 contains the implementation of the *SequenceStatus* function.

LISTING 6-14 Function to determine the status of a sequence

```
int Music_Status(void)
{
// this function returns the status of a playing sequence

_asm
  {
  mov ax,70Ch    ; function #13: SequenceStatus
  int 66h        ; call MIDPAK

  } // end inline assembly

// return value is in AX

} // end Music_Status
```

The function takes no parameters, but returns a status code as defined by the status codes in BLACK6.H. This completes our music interface. As an example, let's use the functions in a pseudoprogram to load and play an XMI file. Here's the code:

```
music the_music; // the XMI structure

// load an XMI file
Music_Load("song.xmi",(music_ptr)&the_music);

// start the music playing, play sequence 0
```

```
Music_Play((music_ptr)&the_music,0);

// wait for song to end
while(Music_Status() == SEQUENCE_PLAYING);

// unload the XMI data i.e. release the memory
Music_Unload((music_ptr)&the_music);
```

Of course, we could stop the music and resume it with the extra function, but the above fragment indeed plays a song and exits when it's complete. As a real example of using MIDPAK, I have created a program called MIDIDEMO.EXE. The program is menu driven and allows you to load XMI files from DOS, play sequences, stop the music, and resume the sequences. The program and its source (MIDIDEMO.C) are on the CD-ROM. To create an executable, you'll have to link the program with the module BLACK6.C and all the previous modules accordingly. Listing 6-15 contains the source for the program.

LISTING 6-15 A complete program to load XMI files and manipulate sequences

```
// MIDIDEMO.C - MIDI Music Demo

// I N C L U D E S ///////////////////////////////////////////////////////

#include <io.h>
#include <conio.h>
#include <stdio.h>
#include <stdlib.h>
#include <dos.h>
#include <bios.h>
#include <fcntl.h>
#include <memory.h>
#include <malloc.h>
#include <math.h>
#include <string.h>


// include the sound library

#include "black3.h"
#include "black6.h"

// M A I N ///////////////////////////////////////////////////////////////

void main(int argc, char **argv)
{

char filename[16];  // the .XMI extended midi filename

int done=0,    // main loop exit flag
    loaded=0,  // tracks if a file has been loaded
```

continued on next page

continued from previous page

```
        sequence,   // sequence of XMI extended midi file to be played
        select;     // the users input

music song;         // the music structure

// main event loop
while(!done)
    {
    // print out menu

    printf("\n\nExtended MIDI Menu\n");
    printf("\n1. Load Extended MIDI file.");
    printf("\n2. Play Sequence.");
    printf("\n3. Stop Sequence.");
    printf("\n4. Resume Sequence.");
    printf("\n5. Unload Extended MIDI File from Memory.");
    printf("\n6. Print Status.");
    printf("\n7. Exit Program.");

    printf("\n\nSelect One ?");

    // get input
    scanf("%d",&select);

    // what does user want to do?
    switch(select)
        {
        case 1:  // Load Extended MIDI file
            {
            printf("\nEnter Filename of song ?");
            scanf("%s",filename);

            // if a song is already loaded then delete it
            if (loaded)
                {
                // stop music and unload sound
                Music_Stop();
                Music_Unload((music_ptr)&song);

                } // end if loaded

            // load the new file
            if (Music_Load(filename,(music_ptr)&song))
                {
                printf("\nMusic file successfully loaded...");

                // flag that a file is loaded
                loaded = 1;
                }
            else
                {
                // error
```

```
                       printf("\nSorry, the file %s couldn't be loaded!",filename);

                       } // end else

                  } break;

          case 2: // Play Sequence
              {
              // make sure a midi file has been loaded
              if (loaded)
                  {
                  printf("\nWhich Sequence 0..n ?");
                  scanf("%d",&sequence);

                  // play the requested sequence
                  Music_Play((music_ptr)&song,sequence);

                  } // end if loaded
              else
                  printf("\nYou must first load an extended MIDI file.");
              } break;

          case 3: // Stop Sequence
              {
              // make sure a midi file has been loaded
              if (loaded)
                  Music_Stop();
              else
                  printf("\nYou must first load an extended MIDI file.");

              } break;

          case 4: // Resume Sequence
              {
              // make sure a midi file has been loaded
              if (loaded)
                  Music_Resume();
              else
                  printf("\nYou must first load an extended MIDI file.");

              } break;

          case 5: // Unload Extended MIDI File from Memory
              {
              // make sure a midi file has been loaded
              if (loaded)
                  {
                  Music_Stop();
                  Music_Unload((music_ptr)&song);
                  loaded=0;
                  }
              else
```

continued on next page

continued from previous page

```
                    printf("\nYou must first load an extended MIDI file.");

            } break;

        case 6: // Print Status
            {
            printf("\nMIDPAK Status = %d",Music_Status());
            } break;

        case 7: // Exit Program
            {
            // delete music and stop
            if (loaded)
                {
                Music_Stop();
                Music_Unload((music_ptr)&song);
                loaded=0;
                }

            done=1;

            } break;
        default:
            {
            printf("\nInvalid Selection!");
            } break;

        } // end switch

    } // end while

// unload file if there is one
if (loaded)
    Music_Unload((music_ptr)&song);

} // end main
```

The program is nothing more than a menu system shell around our functions. To run the program, you'll have to use one of the XMI files on the CD-ROM or create one with some of the MIDI files of your own via MIDIFORM.EXE. I suggest you get a feel for the process. And of course, for the demo to operate, you must have loaded MIDPAK.COM into memory, which will in turn load MIDPAK.ADV and MIDPAK.AD.

Real-Time Sound Processing

At this point we're going to diverge a bit from creating sound and music and talk about how to manipulate and mix sounds. Sound cards exist that perform some of these operations for us, but then again, we will have to perform some of them ourselves, so it's nice to understand the underlying principles. We're going to study the two most basic sound processing operations, which are *amplitude amplification* and *mixing*.

Amplification and Attenuation

A digitized sound is sampled such that its amplitude spectrum is contained in either 8 or 16 bits. Hence, the sound has 8 or 16 bits of amplitude resolution. There are many times during a game that we might want to amplify or attenuate a digitized sound. For example, if an object is far away from the player's viewpoint and has a sound attached to it, the sound should be barely audible, but if the object closes nearer, the sound should become louder. Figure 6-15 shows this graphically. We see that the nearer sound has the same waveform as the more distant sound, but its amplitude is larger.

This amplitude amplification is accomplished simply by taking the original sound and multiplying each element of the data by a constant and placing the data in a destination buffer. Then the destination buffer contains the new amplified sound. For example, say that *buffer[]* contains a sound sample that is 8000 samples composed of *unsigned char*. To amplify the sound, we could do something like this,

```
unsigned char buffer[8000], destination[8000]; // these will hold the sounds

for (index=0; index<8000; index++)
    destination[index] = (unsigned char)( (float)buffer[index]* amplitude + .5);
```

where *amplitude* is a floating point number.

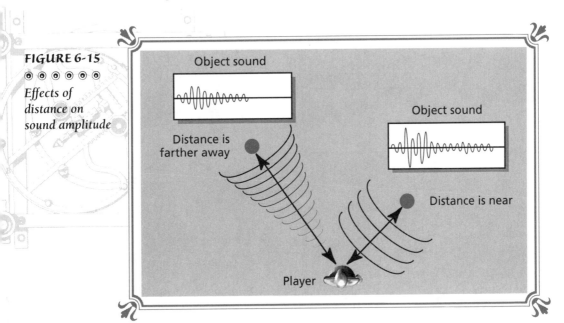

FIGURE 6-15
◉ ◉ ◉ ◉ ◉ ◉

*Effects of
distance on
sound amplitude*

The above fragment can be used to both amplify the sound if *amplitude* is greater than 1.0, or to attenuate it if *amplitude* is less than 1.0. The only problem with this method is that the calculations must be done with some precision; hence, floating point calculations of some sort must be used and the actual calculations may take a few milliseconds, which may be unacceptable in a game. Of course, if the amplification or attenuation factor is always a whole number, then floating point calculations can be avoided completely.

Using this amplification, we could write a function that uses a digitized sound as the input source and, based on an amplification factor, generates a new sound with the requested amplitude. A function of this sort would be useful in a 3D game to simulate 3D sounds occurring due to distance on sound cards that don't support hardware volume adjustments.

Mixing Sounds

Mixing is the next interesting operation that can be done to digital sounds. Mixing involves taking one or more inputs and summing them into a single output. Figure 6-16 shows this graphically. Here we see N input sounds all being summed and the

FIGURE 6-16

◉ ◉ ◉ ◉ ◉ ◉

Mixing sounds with software

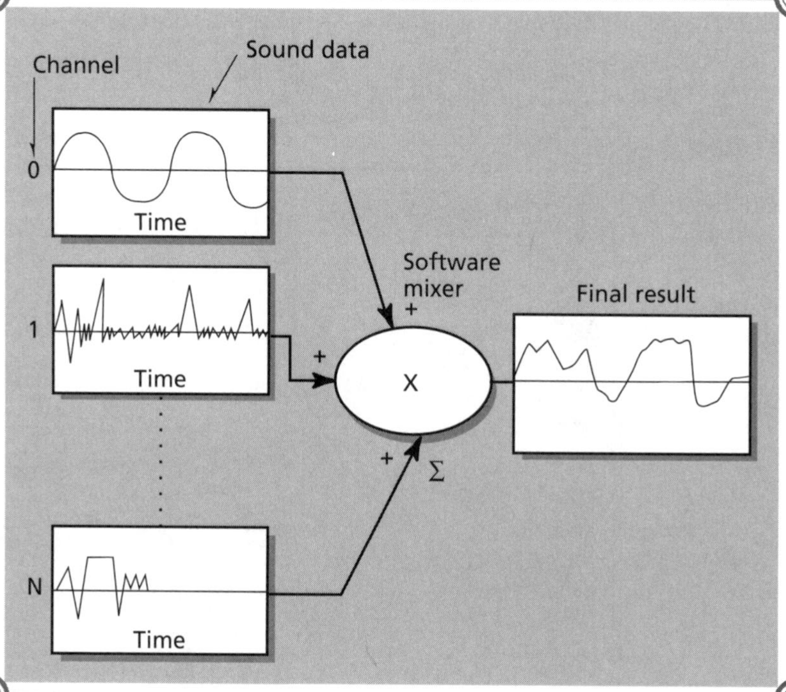

result placed into a single destination buffer. There are some factors to consider when summing or mixing sounds. The first is whether to use a weighted average or just blindly sum the sounds and clip the results to fit into bytes or words (depending on the sample rate).

Mathematically speaking, it may seem more correct to weigh each sound. For example, if two sounds were to be added together, the following code could be used to implement equal weighting:

```
for (index=0; index<length_of_sound; index++)
    destination[index] = (unsigned char)( (float)sound_1[index]*.5 +
                          (float)sound_2[index] * .5 + .5);
```

Since there are two sounds, each sound is weighted by 50 percent or 0.5. Even though this may seem like the correct thing to do, the result doesn't sound correct. Amazingly enough, to add two or more sounds together, the results are better if the sounds are simply added without weighting, for example:

```
for (index=0; index<length_of_sound; index++)
    destination[index] = (sound_1[index]+sound_2[index]);
```

Note that the length of the destination must be the size of the largest sound, and during the mixing of the two sounds, zeros should be used to pad for the shorter sound. This is shown in Figure 6-17. The length of the larger sound is determined, and then a *for* loop sums the two sounds together until the data for the shorter sound has been consumed. Then the remainder of the longer sound is simply copied into the end of the destination buffer. Here's a code fragment that adds two

FIGURE 6-17
◎ ◎ ◎ ◎ ◎ ◎

Mixing sounds of different lengths

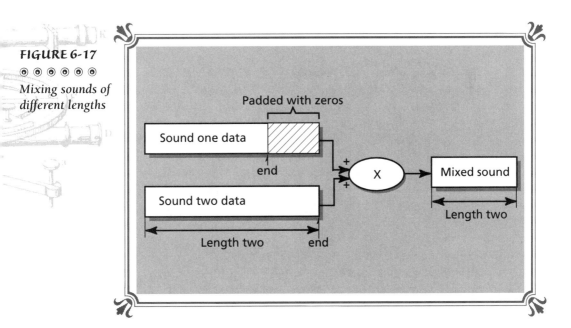

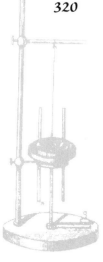

sounds together without weighting while it takes into consideration different lengths:

```
// test for same length

if (length_1==length_2)
    {
    for (index=0; index<length_1; index++)
        destination[index] = sound_1[index]+sound_2[index];
    } // end if equal lengths
else
if (length_1>length_2)
    {

    for (index=0; index<length_2; index++)
        destination[index] = sound_1[index] + sound_2[index];

    // now copy the rest of sound 1 into buffer

    for (; index<length_1; index++)
        destination[index] = sound_1[index];

    } // end if sound 1 is longer than sound 2
else
    {
    // sound 2 must be longer than sound 1

    for (index=0; index<length_1; index++)
        destination[index] = sound_1[index] + sound_2[index];

    // now copy the rest of sound 2 into buffer
    for (; index<length_2; index++)
        destination[index] = sound_2[index];

    } // end else sound 2 is longer than sound 1
```

Using the above techniques, you can create all kinds of interesting effects, such as echoes, reversing, and others. Digital sounds are a lot of fun to experiment with!

Sound Scheduling

We're getting closer to generating our own sound, but we need to cover the topic of *scheduling*. Simply put, the sound card is a finite resource, and it can only play one digital effect and one MIDI song at once (some cards have multiple digital and MIDI channels, but most don't). Hence, some sort of system must be devised to allow for contingencies and resource sharing among all the sounds and music in a game. For example, I'm sure you've played a game and blown something up, and just as the sound of the explosion was at its peak, it just stopped! This is because the sound was *preempted* by something else, maybe another object in the game or even your own laser blast. This situation is unfortunate, but it does happen.

To ease the amount of lost and preempted sounds, some sort of sound scheduler is used for both music and effects. This sound scheduler is something like a tiny operating system kernel that can queue up sounds, play sounds, preempt a playing sound for one of a higher priority, and "age" sounds that are waiting in the queue to determine if there's still enough time to play them anymore.

I'm not going to supply you with a sound scheduler, since the software will vary from game to game, but I will give you some ideas and a few designs so you can make your own. Here is a list of the different classes the schedulers fall into:

❖ Fully preemptive

❖ Priority-based preemption

❖ Queued priority-based preemption

❖ Real-time queued priority-based multiple synthesized digital channels

Fully Preemptive

A fully preemptive sound system is the simplest to implement. The basic idea is that when a new sound is to be played, the currently playing sound (if any) is stopped and the new sound is started. This technique is actually very common for low-end games. Implementing the system is as easy as playing the next sound with the *Sound_Play()* function, without any regard for the status of the sound system.

Priority-Based Preemption

A priority-based preemptive sound system operates under the premise that each sound has a specific priority attached to it. For example, the sound of a droning engine in the background may have a low priority, such as 10, while the sound of a laser blast may be a 5, and finally, the sound of an explosion may be a 1 (highest priority). Hence, as a sound is played, its priority is recorded in a global variable. Then when another effect is to be played, its priority is compared to that of the currently playing sound. If the new sound's priority is greater (that is, numerically less), the current sound is preempted and the new sound is started.

Using priority-based preemption is a vast improvement over total preemption, but still lacks any form of memory. For example, if a short sound is playing and one of slightly less priority is requested to be played, the second sound will be thrown away; even though in a few more cycles the initial shorter sound might have been completed. A solution to this is queuing up sounds and playing them when it's their turn.

Queued Priority-Based Preemption

We can improve the priority-based preemption by adding a small memory queue that queues up the requested sounds. For example, using the preemptive technique, if the program requests a sound to be played that has the same priority of the currently playing sound, then either the new sound is played or it isn't. A better solution would be to place the request in a queue and wait for the current sound to complete. After its completion, the queue is referred to and the waiting sound is played. The only problem with this technique is that a sound will be played some time in the future from when it was actually started. This can lead to *lag*. For example, if the player fires a missile, we surely can't queue up a missile sound and play it three seconds later!

To avoid this dilemma, a second part of the queue's logic should age each of the entries, and if they haven't been played within a specific number of game frames, remove them from the queue. For example, if a sound of a car driving in the distance was queued, it could be aged a long time without much trouble, but the sound of an explosion or something within view of the player must be started within a few frames of its initial request, otherwise, it must be removed from the queue.

A queued system supplemented with priority and aging performs very well, but the ultimate solution to the problem is to synthesize a set of virtual digital channels from the single channel that most sound cards are equipped with.

Real-Time Queued Priority-Based Multiple Synthesized Digital Channels

We have already seen how to mix sounds to create an output that is the sum of the input sounds. This concept can be taken to an extreme and used to synthesize a set of virtual digital channels from one physical channel. Basically the system is implemented by adding a sound to the currently playing sound; in other words, by adding the requested sound data in real-time to the data that is being played.

For example, imagine that a sample is played by the sound card and another effect is to be played. The system at this point determines where in the data stream the current sound is being played, say location 5300. Then the software takes the remainder of the currently playing sound and adds it to the newly requested sound in real-time. The result is placed into a buffer, and the buffer containing the mixed sounds is played. Thus, the buffer contains the data of the previously playing sound summed with the new sound. Hence, through software, we have synthetically created two channels from one.

The major drawback to this technique is that it does take time to mix the two sounds. This introduces a small time lag along with the possibility (depending on architecture) that the destination buffer will have to be replicated to juggle the memory properly. However, when we couple virtual channels along with queuing techniques, a complex and rich sound system can be created.

We have spoken of digital sound, MIDI music, The Audio Solution, and we have generated a complete library to do our bidding. Now it's time for some real Cybersorcery.

Building Your Own Digital Sound Device—DIGIBLASTER

A true Cybersorcerer not only knows the ways of software, but the ways of hardware. By understanding the hardware within a computer, we can better understand how to write software to take advantage of it. Therefore, we are going to build a little project that will plug into the PC's parallel ports and generate stereo digital sound! We'll call it DIGIBLASTER, and it will prove to be a fun project as well as an illuminating experience. Take a look at Figure 6-18 to see a general layout of DIGIBLASTER.

Referring to the figure, we see that the hardware is plugged into both parallel printer ports of the PC. If your particular PC doesn't have two ports, you will only need to build half of the hardware, but your DIGIBLASTER won't be stereo—but

FIGURE 6-18

⊚ ⊚ ⊚ ⊚ ⊚ ⊚

System layout of **DIGIBLASTER**

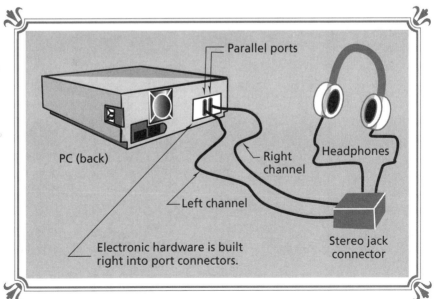

Parallel ports

PC (back)

Right channel

Headphones

Left channel

Stereo jack connector

Electronic hardware is built right into port connectors.

that's OK. DIGIBLASTER works by sending a stream of bytes through each of the parallel ports. These data streams are sent at the rate at which we wish the sound data to be played. The sound data is the standard 8-bit unsigned VOC data we have seen before. Hence, we will use the parallel ports as output devices to control our little synthesizer.

How will our synthesizer work? Here's the deal. We can communicate with each parallel port via a set of I/O ports. These I/O ports allow us to write bytes out to the parallel ports and receive status from each port. But we'll only be using the output abilities of each port. Take a look at Figure 6-19 to see a bitmap layout of the parallel port. Notice that each port can be accessed by retrieving the actual port address from location *[0000:0408 + parallel_port_number]*. We'll discuss this in more detail in a moment. However, the main point is that we can write a byte out to each parallel port. This byte will be represented by a set of voltages on pins 2 through 9 of the female DB-25 connector on the parallel port itself. Each one of these voltages will be relative to ground, which is on pins 18 through 25 (we will use pin 25).

FIGURE 6-19

Output bitmapping of parallel ports

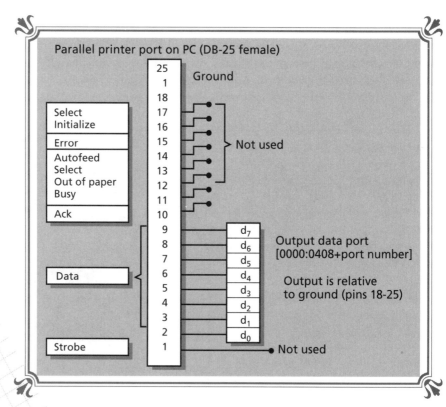

So what does all this mean? If you remember our discussion of digital sound generation, you will recall that digital sounds are generated by converting a stream of digital words into an analog signal using a digital-to-analog (D/A) converter. Therefore, if we place a D/A converter on the output of each parallel port and connect a pair of headphones to the outputs, any data we send to the parallel ports will be converted to analog voltages, and the headphones will vibrate accordingly. Now here comes the interesting part. If we send the data from a VOC file out to the parallel port at a high enough rate (the rate at which the VOC was sampled), we'll actually hear the sound recorded, and presto, we have a digital sound reproduction system!

Of course, the hard part of this design is the electronics to convert the digital 8-bit words into analog voltages, but as it turns out, it's not too difficult. Let's take a look.

The Hardware

To convert the digital outputs of each of the parallel ports, we are going to use a simple *resistive ladder network* of resistors. Figure 6-20 shows the complete design of the system and the values of all the components. The circuit works as follows: When a binary word is sent to the port, the bits d7 through d0 (pins 2 through 9) will either have a +5 or a +0 volts on them. These voltages will be converted into currents by each of the resistors R0 through R7. Each of the currents developed by the voltages is proportional to the resistor values. For example, the d7 bit has the highest magnitude weight; therefore, the resistor connected to it has the smallest value, since the smaller the resistor, the larger the current (which is what we want).

By connecting resistors to each of the outputs on the parallel port, we in essence generate a current that is proportional to the applied binary word (see Figure 6-21). This will be true only if the resistors themselves have values that are in powers of 2. In the case of DIGIBLASTER, I have selected resistors with values 100, 200, 400, 800, 1.6k, 3.2k, 6.4k, and 12.8k ohms. You won't actually be able to find most of these values unless you buy precision resistors, but purchase the values that are as close as possible.

The output currents that flow through each resistor are summed, and then the final current is passed through the diode D1, as shown in Figure 6-22. The diode is for protection. It allows current to flow only from the parallel port out, not the other way around. This is a good idea since the speaker or headphones that we connect the circuit to can develop a current (within the voice coil) and send it back through the port, and, as Bill Murray said in *Ghostbusters*, "This is a bad thing!"

The next stage of the circuit is the volume control and filter. The capacitor C1 is used to filter out the "hiss" and white noise that is normally heard with a circuit of this kind. Basically, the capacitor creates a low-pass filter network with a single pole

FIGURE 6-20
◎ ◎ ◎ ◎ ◎ ◎
Physical layout of DIGIBLASTER

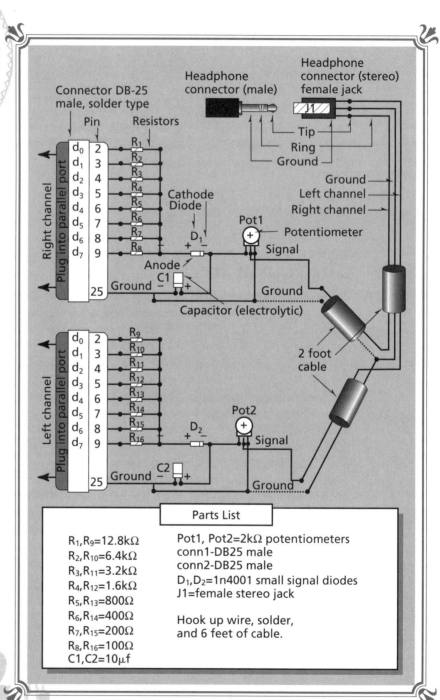

FIGURE 6-21

◎ ◎ ◎ ◎ ◎ ◎

The digital-to-analog conversion

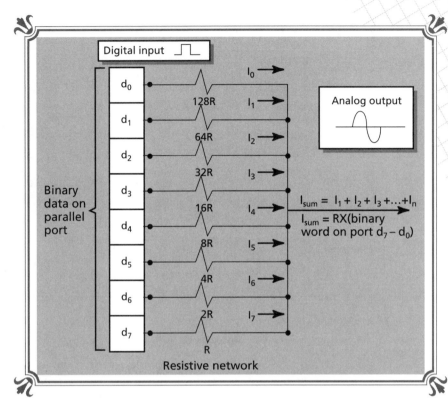

FIGURE 6-22

◎ ◎ ◎ ◎ ◎ ◎

Current feedback protection diode

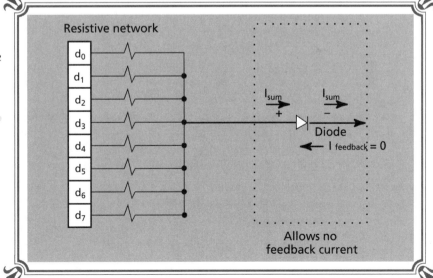

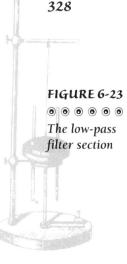

FIGURE 6-23

ⓞ ⓞ ⓞ ⓞ ⓞ ⓞ

The low-pass filter section

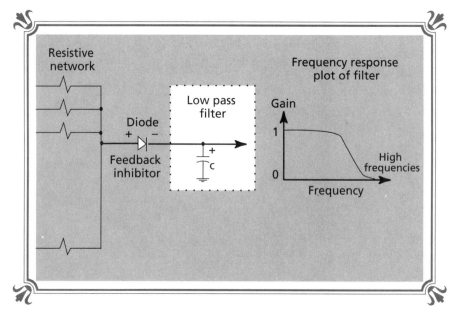

(for those of you who are EEs). Figure 6-23 shows the results of the filter on the sound's frequency spectrum. The final portion of the circuit is used to attenuate the signal into the headphones and is basically a variable resistor called a potentiometer. It functions by means of a conducting slider moving over a semicircular wedge of carbon. As the potentiometer knob is turned, the slider moves, making contact with the carbon wedge at different points. The overall effect is a change in resistance, since the resistance of any conductor is proportional to its length. Hence, as the potentiometer is adjusted, the output current will develop a larger or smaller voltage when applied to the headphones, thus acting as a volume control.

The final analog signal from each parallel port is received by the headphones by tying the commons (grounds) of each port together and into the ground of the headphones, along with connecting the right channel of the headphones to the output of one parallel port and the left channel to the output of the other parallel port.

As you build the hardware, take your time and be careful not to cause a short when you make connections to the male DB-25 connector. If you have never built anything in your life, you will need:

    ✛ A soldering iron (approximately $5.00)

    ✛ Some solder (approximately $3.00)

    ✛ Some 30-32 gauge wire (approximately $2.50)

    ✛ All the parts listed in Figure 6-20

The circuit and construction will take an hour or two and, with a bit of luck, should work on the first try. Once you have put the whole thing together, it should look something like Figure 6-24, which is my prototype.

Now that we have the hardware (hopefully), let's write some software to control the DIGIBLASTER.

The Software

Controlling the DIGIBLASTER is actually quite simple. We simply need to load a VOC file and send the audio data portion of it (a byte at a time) out to the parallel ports. However, to be intelligible, the data must be sent at the same rate at which the sample was taken. The major problem with all this is creating an exact time base with a resolution in kHz. You see, if the VOC file was sampled at 8 kHz, we have to write a function that sends the VOC data to the parallel port at the same rate. This can be done using tight timing loops or the internal timer, but is beyond the scope of this discussion. Hence, we will simply place a variable time delay in the function to slow it to any speed, and as the data is written to the port, the variable can be adjusted for reasonable results.

Since the DIGIBLASTER connects to two parallel ports, you will of course need two parallel ports. If you only have one, everything will still work, but the sound will be mono instead of stereo. The main function that we need to write is one that can write a byte to one of the four parallel ports defined in Table 6-3.

FIGURE 6-24

◎ ◎ ◎ ◎ ◎ ◎

Prototype of
DIGIBLASTER

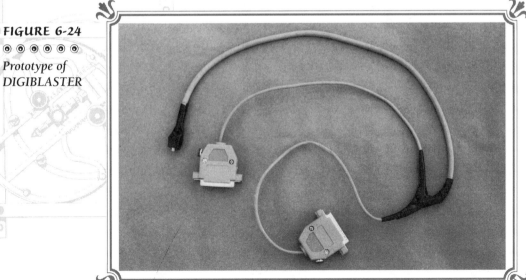

TABLE 6-3

◇◇◇◇◇◇

The parallel ports and their access numbers

DOS Port Name	parallel_port_number
LPT1:	0
LPT2:	1
LPT3:	2
LPT4:	3

A while ago we learned that each parallel port can be accessed by using the data at memory location *[0000:0408+parallel_port_number]* as the I/O port address. To make this access easy, we are going to define some constants and a parallel base pointer like this:

```
// the parallel port offsets

#define PAR_1_PORT    0
#define PAR_2_PORT    1
#define PAR_3_PORT    2
#define PAR_4_PORT    3
```

And we are going to define a pointer to access the I/O port of any parallel port:

```
unsigned int far *par_port = (unsigned int far*)0x00000408L;
```

Using the above declarations, let's write a function that takes as parameters the parallel port we wish to write to along with the data we want written:

```
void Par_Write(int port,unsigned char data)
{
// this function writes a byte to one of the parallel ports
_outp(*(par_port+port),data);

} // end Par_Write
```

That looks easy! The dereferencing may seem a bit confusing, but it basically says, "Look into location 0000:0408 - 0000:040B for the I/O address of the parallel port and then write *data* to it." With the above function in hand, we are 90 percent done. All we need now to play a VOC file is to load it and send the data out to both the right and left channels, which will be two of the possible parallel ports LPT1 through LPT4. For example, say that you have parallel ports LPT1: and LPT3: on your PC. In that case, a fragment that would blast a VOC file to those specific ports would look like this:

```
for (index=0; index<length_of_sound_data; index++)
    {
    Par_Write(PAR_1_PORT, buffer[index]);
    Par_Write(PAR_3_PORT, buffer[index]);
    } // end for
```

Of course, the above fragment would probably only be heard by ants since the data is written out too fast! To slow it down, we should place a delay into the loop that forces each byte to be written slower. Here is a possible solution:

```
for (index=0; index<length_of_sound_data; index++)
    {
    Par_Write(PAR_1_PORT, buffer[index]);
    Par_Write(PAR_3_PORT, buffer[index]);

    // wait a bit
    for (time=0; time<delay; time++);

    } // end for
```

Unfortunately, there is no hard-and-fast rule to relate the *delay* factor to the playback frequency, since it will be different depending on the speed of your particular PC. But you can always use another more complex technique to ensure the playback frequency. Also, just as a bit of trivia, I have found that the maximum bandwidth of the parallel port is about 100K per second, which is more than ample for CD-quality playback rates.

As an example of using the DIGIBLASTER, I have created a little demo that uses LPT1: for the right channel, LPT2: for the left channel, and plays a pair of VOC files through each channel into your headphones. The demo slowly pans the volume of each channel from right to left, simulating a moving sound source. This leads us into the next topic, 3D sound. The name of the demo is 3DIGI.EXE and its source is 3DIGI.C. The program uses the function *Sound_Load()* from our DIGPAK interface library to load the sound, so you will have to link BLACK6.C and the previous library modules to create an executable. In any case, the source code is shown in Listing 6-16.

LISTING 6-16 *Program to drive DIGIBLASTER*

```
// 3DIGI.C - A simple 3-D sound demo using the parallel ports and D/A
// convertors

// I N C L U D E S //////////////////////////////////////////////////////////////

#include <io.h>
#include <conio.h>
#include <stdio.h>
#include <stdlib.h>
#include <dos.h>
#include <bios.h>
#include <fcntl.h>
#include <memory.h>
#include <malloc.h>
#include <math.h>
#include <string.h>

#include "black3.h"
```

continued on next page

continued from previous page

```c
#include "black6.h"

// D E F I N E S //////////////////////////////////////////////////////////

// the parallel port offsets

#define PAR_1_PORT      0
#define PAR_2_PORT      1
#define PAR_3_PORT      2
#define PAR_4_PORT      3

// G L O B A L S //////////////////////////////////////////////////////////

// pointer to base parallel port
unsigned int far *par_port = (unsigned int far*)0x00000408L;

// the parallel ports to be used for right and left
int right_3D = PAR_1_PORT,
    left_3D  = PAR_2_PORT;

// the amount of power going to each channel (i.e. the volume)
float power_3D = .5; // each channel is at 50%, this will range 0..1

// F U N C T I O N S //////////////////////////////////////////////////////

void Par_Write(int port,unsigned char data)
{
// this writes a byte out to the parallel port
_outp(*(par_port+port),data);

} // end Par_Write

////////////////////////////////////////////////////////////////////////////

void Sound_Play_3D(sound_ptr the_sound,float power_right, float
                   power_left,int speed)
{

// this function will play a digitized sound through each of the parallel
// ports. Each channel's output is controlled by the input powers. Note that
// a local replica of the sound is made so that the attenuated version
// can be computed in real-time without destroying the original

unsigned int freq,        // used to slow or speed up playback rate
             index,       // looping variable
             size;        // size of sound data

unsigned char far *right_buffer; // working buffers
unsigned char far *left_buffer;

// create new sound based on right and left power
size   = the_sound->SS.sndlen;
```

```
right_buffer = (unsigned char far *)_fmalloc(size);
left_buffer  = (unsigned char far *)_fmalloc(size);

// create the new sounds, one for each channel
for (index=0; index<size; index++)
    {
    // compute proper value based on power level

    right_buffer[index] =
            (unsigned char)((float)the_sound->SS.sound[index] * power_right);

    left_buffer[index] =
            (unsigned char)((float)the_sound->SS.sound[index] * power_left);

    } // end for index

     // play the sound
     for (index=0; index<size; index++)
         {
         // delay a bit to slow frequency down
         for (freq=0; freq<speed; freq++)
             {
             // write left channel
             Par_Write(left_3D,left_buffer[index]);

             // write right channel
             Par_Write(right_3D,right_buffer[index]);

             } // end time delay frequency control

         } // end for index

// release the memory
_ffree((void far *)right_buffer);
_ffree((void far *)left_buffer);

} // end Sound_Play_3D

// M A I N /////////////////////////////////////////////////////////////////

void main(int argc, char **argv)
{
unsigned int index,    // looping variable
             done=0,   // exit flag
             delay=5;

sound effect_r,effect_l;  // the sound effects
float power_delta = .1;

// load the sound test sound effect into memory without translation
if (!Sound_Load("3dleft.voc",(sound_ptr)&effect_l,0))
    {
```

continued on next page

continued from previous page

```
    printf("\nCouldn't load test sound 3DLEFT.VOC");
    return;
    } // end if

if (!Sound_Load("3dright.voc",(sound_ptr)&effect_r,0))
    {
    printf("\nCouldn't load test sound 3DRIGHT.VOC");
    return;
    } // end if

// display menu
printf("\n3D DIGITAL SOUND DEMO\n");
printf("\nUse the <S> and <F> keys to slow down and speed up the sound.");
printf("\nPress <Q> to exit.\n");

// enter event loop

while(!done)
    {

    // test which size sound source is on
    if (power_3D > .5)
        Sound_Play_3D((sound_ptr)&effect_r,power_3D, (1-power_3D),delay);
    else
        Sound_Play_3D((sound_ptr)&effect_l,power_3D, (1-power_3D),delay);

    // pan sound from right to left left to right
    // make you dizzy!
    power_3D+=power_delta;

    if (power_3D > 1 || power_3D < 0)
        {
        power_delta=-power_delta;
        power_3D+=power_delta;
        } // end of reverse pan

    // test if user is hitting keyboard
    if (kbhit())
        {
        // what does user want to do
        switch(getch())
            {
            case 'f': // speed up the sound
                {
                if (--delay < 1)
                    delay=1;

                } break;

            case 's': // slow down the sound
                {
                ++delay;
```

```
            } break;

        case 'q': // exit
            {
            done=1;
            } break;

        } // end switch

    } // end if kbhit

    } // end while

// unload the sounds
Sound_Unload((sound_ptr)&effect_l);
Sound_Unload((sound_ptr)&effect_r);

} // end main
```

The program begins by loading the two VOC files 3DRIGHT.VOC and 3DLEFT.VOC. These are played depending on the virtual position of the sound source. The program then proceeds to print out a little menu and enters the main event loop. The event loop continually plays the sound and determines if the user has pressed any keys. The user can either speed up or slow down the rate at which the sounds are played. The main workhorse of the program is the function *Sound_Play_3D()*, which is a bit of a misnomer. It actually doesn't know anything about 3D space; it only knows how to amplify a sound and create two copies of it that are each amplified or attenuated versions of the original. This amplification is based on a variable called *power_3D*, which is the amount of power that is sent to each channel.

When *power_3D* is equal to 1, all the power goes to the right side; when *power_3D* is equal to 0, all the power goes to the left side. Therefore, by varying *power_3D* in a cyclical manner, it will seem as if the sound is "walking" around your head. The main point to get out of this demo is how the sounds are played and amplified. The 3D portion of it is rather simplistic and was added just for fun. A final note: if your PC doesn't support parallel LPT1: and LPT2:, simply change the variables *3d_right* and *3d_left* to the appropriate port constants.

With the DIGIBLASTER in hand, it is actually possible to create a 3D sound and play it! Let's see how...

Implementing 3D Sound

What is 3D sound? It is the sound that we hear in everyday life. When someone is behind us, we hear him differently than someone in front of us, or at any other position for that matter. Also, we can detect when sounds move closer or farther.

Unfortunately, the sounds produced by most video games are not 3D, but mono. Even if the sounds are stereo, each channel doesn't replicate the actual sound your right and left ears would hear if the sounds were 3D.

True 3D sound is so real, you can put on a pair of headphones and you'll think whatever you're listening to is right in front of you! The use of 3D sound is most prevalent in virtual reality systems. Since players must move around in Cyberspace, methods had to be devised to allow them to hear the objects as they would really be heard.

Implementing full 3D sound is complex at very best. An understanding of Fourier analysis, digital signal processing, and calculus is needed just to make a start! But in essence, 3D sound is created by synthesizing what a human's right and left ears would hear if the 3D world and sounds were real. Computing these sounds in the general case is much too complex, so we'll try for something a little less ambitious: 3D sound in a 2D plane.

Figure 6-25 shows a comparison between the two cases, general 3D sound and 3D sound in a plane. As you can see, the only information we need to determine

FIGURE 6-25

◉ ◉ ◉ ◉ ◉ ◉

Comparison of general 3D sound and 3D sound in a plane

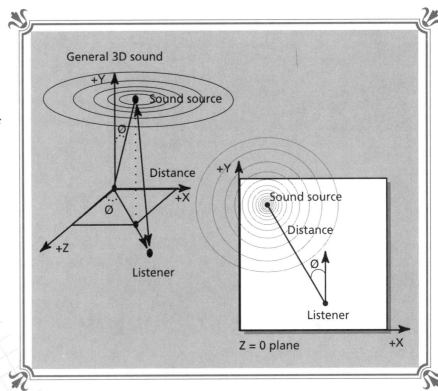

the position of a 3D sound (which is in the same plane as the listener) is the position of the sound (that is, the angle between the sound and the listener) and the distance between the sound and the listener. Using this information and basic physics, we should be able to come up with a crude model of the 3D sound as it would be heard by the listener for any position and distance, as long as both the sound and listener lie in the same plane.

The model we are going to create will be oversimplified but will produce decent results. Let's begin by taking another look at the system model, as depicted in Figure 6-26. The only data we have to go on are the angle between the listener's view direction (which is perpendicular to the direction of both ears) and the distance between the sound and the listener. Let's start with the distance.

In general, as a sound moves away, it becomes fainter. Therefore, we should attenuate the amplitude of the computed strength of the right and left channels proportional to the overall distance between the sound source and the listener. A first draft of the sound function might look like,

```
final_right_output_power = K*distance*right_power(angle);
final_left_output_power  = K*distance*left_power(angle);
```

where K is simply a constant, and the functions *right_power()* and *left power()* return the relative power that each ear hears as a function of the angle between the sound source and the listener.

FIGURE 6-26

◉ ◉ ◉ ◉ ◉ ◉

The planar 3D sound model

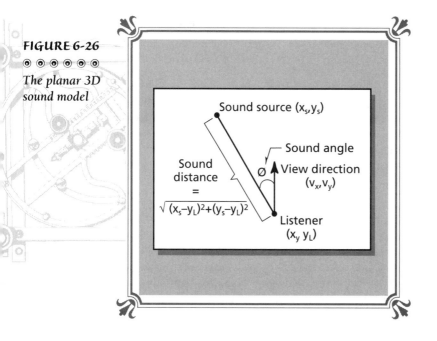

The determination of the functions *right_power()* and *left_power()*, if done correctly, would be enough to fill an entire chapter. Hence, we are going to make some approximations. First, we are going to assume that the listener is a single point and has no dimensional volume. Second, we are also going to assume that sounds behind the listener sound the same as sounds in front of the listener. These approximations are brutal, but necessary if we want to make any progress.

Now the problem boils down to computing the intensity of an energy wave on a single point. Furthermore, the point is modeled with two mutually opposing sound sensors that are directed perpendicularly to the listener's view direction. To compute the amount of energy, we will use the following hypothesis: If a sound is totally to the right of the listener, then only the right ear will be able to hear it; if a source is totally to left of the listener, then only the left ear will hear it. If the sound source is directly in front or behind the listener, then each ear will hear the sound equally well. Finally, if the sound source is somewhere in between, the power or loudness heard by each ear will be directly proportional to the angle of the sound with respect to the view direction of the listener.

Taking all this into consideration, we can write the following formulas to compute the right and left strengths of the sounds,

```
right_power(angle) = (angle/180)
left_power(angle) = (1 - (angle/180))
```

where *angle* varies from 0 to 180.

You will notice that each channel will vary from 0 to 1.0. Working the above formulas into the previous distance calculations, the final results are:

```
final_right_output_power = K*distance*(angle/180)
final_left_output_power  = K*distance*(1 - (angle/180))
```

Of course, constants must be computed as well as the angle and distance between the sound source and listener, but the results will yield quite impressive 3D planar response. At least it will be good enough so that the player can determine the relative distance of an object and its relative right or left position. Granted, the sounds may not really sound 3D, but they will have the elements of 3D sound. Just as a 3D game only looks 3D, our approximation will only give some 3D hints.

So what can we use 3D sound trapped in a plane for? We can use it for a whole lot! In a tank game for instance, we could use it to make the tanks and other objects seem like they are moving around not only visually, but auditorily. This adds a whole new dimension to games. In many 3D games sounds become louder as objects near, but few games implement 3D panning at all–even in a plane. The main reason for this is that the player must wear headphones or have a stereo with speakers directly behind him. However, I feel that requesting a player to plug a set of headphones into the sound card is a small price to pay for the added realism produced by 3D sound techniques.

Of course, the problems of amplifying or attenuating sound effects without hardware support is a time-consuming problem. Nevertheless, the amount of time needed to create the proper amplitude-modulated versions of a specific sound for each right and left channel is usually negligible on a fast machine.

Summing up, 3D sound in a plane can be modeled by a simplified approximation of the physical system using only the position and angle of the sound source relative to the listener. True, a real model would take into consideration details such as reflection, refraction, frequency response, group velocity, absorption, Doppler shift, resonance, and air density/temperature. But we're making video games not space shuttles, right?

Remote Sound FX

Remote sound FX only have meaning when two or more computers are linked by means of a modem or network of some kind. Imagine two players, each at a different location, playing a linked game of some sort (see Figure 6-27). Each local machine is running the same game software, and the games are running synchronously using techniques we will learn about later. Now imagine that the players want to talk to each other. How can they do this? Well, one solution would be to let them type to each other and send the message to the remote machine over the phone line along with the other game information.

FIGURE 6-27

◉ ◉ ◉ ◉ ◉ ◉

Setup for a linked game

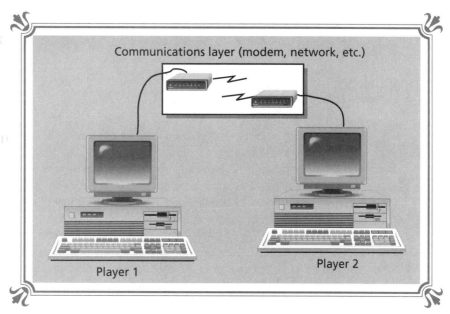

Wouldn't it be better if the players could actually hear each other talking or at least hear a voice that represented the opponent? This is the concept behind remote sound FX. Of course, there are many different levels we can take this concept to, but the simplest implementation has a set of sound FX on both machines. When the remote player presses a button, it directs the remote machine to play the effect. For example, each machine could have a set of evil phrases, such as "die alien," "eat photons," "there can be only one!", and so forth. Then by pressing a button on one machine, a message would be sent to the remote machine directing it to play one of the effects. Using this technique, the players could have a crude dialogue with a set of prerecorded phrases.

We can take the technology one step further and add personalization to the voice. For example, during the setup phase of the game, each player could be asked to speak a set of phrases. When complete, the data for the phrases would be sent to the remote machines, giving each remote machine a local copy of the digitized effects. Thus, when a player wanted to say something to the opponent, the opponent would hear the actual voice of his adversary!

Such techniques are good and make a game ten times more fun, but let's face it: the ultimate remote sound FX would have a voice recognition system on each machine that had a fairly large vocabulary (maybe 100 words). Then as a player spoke, messages would be sent to the remote machine directing it to play the digitized words. Hence, sentences could be spoken by each of the remote players. Of course, all these techniques use very little network bandwidth since each remote machine has a local copy of the sound effect in memory. However, if your network has a high enough bandwidth, it is feasible to send the actual voice signal!

In conclusion, remote sound FX are very cool and very easy to implement. You can rest assured that the game we construct at the end of the book will have them!

Voice Recognition

Before concluding the chapter, we should at least touch upon a technology that has been talked about for years, but never implemented well enough to be a valid input method. This is voice recognition technology. Voice recognition is basically a method of comparing a human's voice against a voice print of some kind that is in memory. For years this technology has been riddled with problems associated with the amount of memory needed for the voice samples, the inability to recognize any speaker's voice, and the advanced hardware needed to do voice recognition in real-time.

Now, however, voice recognition is a reality and can be done with most advanced sound cards containing onboard DSP processors. Both the Sound Blaster series and Media Vision products have add-on components that allow their cards to recognize speech in a fairly reasonable manner. The recognition still can't quite run in real-time and is speaker dependent, but it's a start. Hopefully, we'll start seeing games that use simple voice recognition, such as weapons commands, numbers, direction, and other small phrases, very soon.

As Cybersorcerers, we would like to use a library that performs voice recognition for us for the most popular sound cards, so we don't have to write the software ourselves. However, I haven't seen anything like this thus far (if you do, let me know). Hence, we're going to discuss some of the mathematics behind voice recognition and some of the problems, which should allow you to implement a crude voice recognizer yourself, or at least have an idea where to begin.

Recognizing voice in real-time is much too complex to start with; let's simply try to design a recognizer that first listens to the word and then decides if the word is in its vocabulary. We are going to make a single word recognizer.

Figure 6-28 shows the waveforms for a set of words that represent the four directions, north, south, east, and west. These waveforms were sampled at 12 kHz. Now all we have to do is record a user speaking a single word and then compare his input with the four voice prints. This is where the trouble begins. First, assuming that we sample at the same rate, what happens if the input word is slightly longer or shorter than any of the voice prints? There wouldn't be an easy way to

FIGURE 6-28

◉ ◉ ◉ ◉ ◉ ◉

Voice prints for the nautical directions

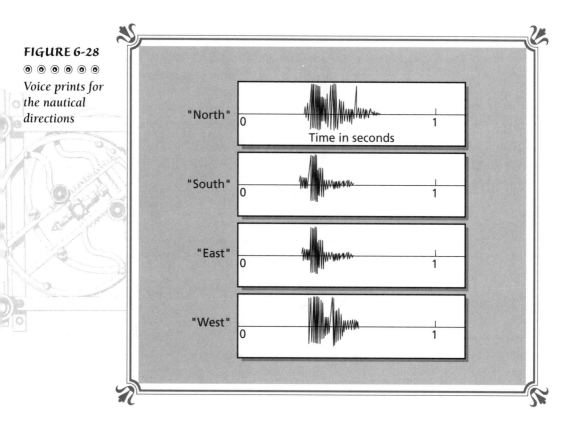

compare each value of the input word with the four voice prints. Moreover, this kind of comparison is practically futile.

When humans speak, they very seldom reproduce exactly the same word. There are always small anomalies. Therefore, we must use some sort of statistical approach to comparing the samples. For example, we could average the voice prints and average the input word and compare. However, this won't work because averaging time domain or time-dependent data loses the temporal aspects of the information, which is very important! Take a look at Figure 6-29. Here we see two voice prints of two words. The words themselves are irrelevant, but the fact of the matter is that the average of the data of each word is the same, so the words are no longer distinguishable.

A better solution would be to average smaller chunks of the voice print as a function of time. For example, if a voice print took .5 seconds, maybe we would average it in 50 millisecond sections. Figure 6-30 shows this process graphically. Now if an input voice print was averaged the same way, a comparison would make more sense. However, the problem of different length samples still exists. What if the speaker waits 100 milliseconds before speaking? The input voice sample would be averaged and the first chunk would average to zero. Even though the rest of the sample may be a perfect match with one of the voice prints, a match couldn't be found due to phase shifts. Thus, we must also take phase shifting into consideration and try to preprocess the input voice sample to make sure that we have the "meat" of it before we start the averaging process.

The above technique actually works if each voice print is very dissimilar and the input voice samples are spoken clearly and at the same rate as the voice prints. But

FIGURE 6-29

◎ ◎ ◎ ◎ ◎ ◎

The problem of averaging samples

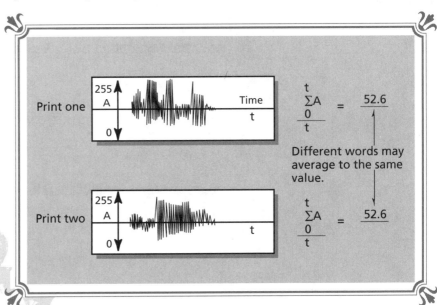

FIGURE 6-30
⊙ ⊙ ⊙ ⊙ ⊙ ⊙

Averaging sectors of a sound to maintain temporal information

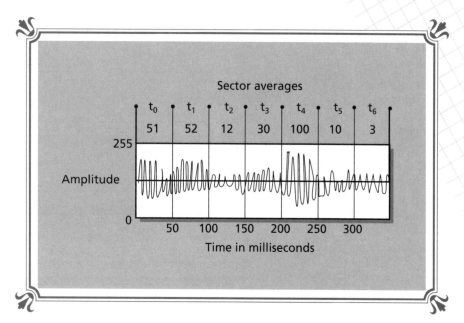

what about amplitude? This brings another whole dimension to our problems. The input voice print may be an exact match with one of the words in the vocabulary, but it may not have the same amplitude. How do we deal with this problem? The simplest solution is to first normalize the input data so that all voice prints have maximum amplitude relative to themselves. Then when a comparison is done, the amplitudes are already normalized to, say, 255 so that the averaging makes sense.

Using these techniques, I have implemented many voice recognizers that use a Sound Blaster or a simple A/D converter to listen to a word and then compare the input sample to a set of prerecorded voice prints (usually less than 10). The technique isn't perfect–it works about 50 to 80 percent of the time. To improve voice recognition matching, other techniques can be used that give more information about the sample. One such method is based on frequency spectrum analysis. You see, we have only been looking at the amplitude spectrum of the samples. However, frequency spectrum is much better since it's like a fingerprint. For example, Figure 6-31 shows what the average frequency spectrums of the words "north," "south," "east," and "west" might look like. Notice that they are different. The frequency spectrums will differ based on the speaker and the words; therefore, coupling frequency spectrum information along with amplitude information, a recognizer can be made that works consistently in the 90 percent range on a single voice.

Alas, everything we have tried so far is not very smart. A voice recognition system should try to figure out what you're saying even if you're not saying it correctly. Moreover, it should be able to learn as you speak. Implementing these techniques can be done with the help of neural nets, sparse distributed memory, and similar fuzzy technologies. This is where the final solution of real-time voice recognition

FIGURE 6-31

◎ ◎ ◎ ◎ ◎ ◎

*The frequency
spectrum of the
nautical
directions*

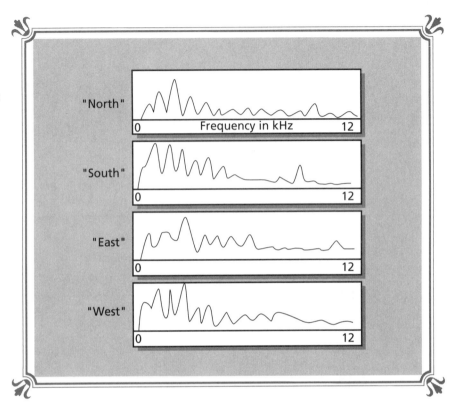

lies. However, with a Sound Blaster or similar card in hand and the basic techniques we have outlined, you should be able to write a simple recognizer that
understands a few words—at least enough to arm weapons and fire!

Summary

In this chapter we have covered topics that are truly mysterious to the world. We
can now command our sound cards to play digital samples and MIDI music as easily as we can plot a pixel. Furthermore, we learned some basic sound processing
techniques as well as how sounds should be scheduled in a game. After that, we
dove off the deep end and built some hardware. We used the elements of carbon,
aluminum, and copper (just as ancient alchemists used in their spells) to create a
sound synthesizer that plugs into the parallel ports of the PC! Then we used the
hardware to get a glimpse of 3D sound and its properties. Finally, we touched upon
a couple of concepts that aren't new, but aren't old either. Those, of course, are
remote sound FX and voice recognition—techniques that can turn a video game
into an engrossing auditory experience. Now it's time to play God and bring the
characters in our games to life.

7

The Magick of Thought

come tutti sono le manovelle e le quali primo buono e l'alça
o igra pesi invite le minute e ragione e la do prano di bone
orça re nella mano e la permana e tola alla mano bella pesi quin
força e più i tomo più vale

7

The Magick of Thought

The next step in our training is one of a difficult nature. We can project both sights and sounds from Cyberspace using our ancient techniques, but these projections are lifeless and without thought. Alas, in this chapter we are going to delve into areas that are forbidden to many. These areas are those of machine intelligence and synthetic thoughts. If we can master these sorcerous manipulations, we can indeed create games that are alive and interact with our world.

It would take many books to completely describe the magick of thought; hence, we're going to cover only the most basic of concepts as they apply to video games. However, using the simple techniques and algorithms within these pages, we can generate very complex "thinking models" that will be formidable adversaries.

Introduction to Artificial and Synthetic Intelligence

Artificial intelligence (AI) doesn't have to do with the science of making machines think; it has to do with the science of making machines look like they think. In many cases AI algorithms are more than enough for fairly deterministic problem

347

solving, but where AI sciences fail are in the fuzzy regions of computation and problem solving. This is where the sciences of *neural networks*, *fuzzy logic*, and *genetic algorithms* come into play. As game designers, we are interested in modeling thought, not simulating it.

For example, we could make a very complex knowledge base and then attach a natural language parser to it. If a user were to ask the knowledge base a question in its area of expertise, the knowledge base would seem almost human in its responses. However, the knowledge base is nothing more than text strings, rules, and algorithms. It isn't thinking, it's only responding. We are interested in the nature of thought. For example, if we study a human's mind or the mind of a bee, they both have a similar structure—that is, a collection of neurons with an interconnecting network. Both function by impulses transmitted (and inhibited) from neuron to neuron by means of electrochemical reactions induced by charge pumps.

In any case, the results of this process are autonomous beings that can work, use tools, and have a sense of existence (in one way or another). This brings us to the question: is the bee aware of its own existence? Does it think like we do, but on a smaller scale? Maybe, maybe not. However, that's irrelevant. The mind of a bee, spider, ant, or any small animal still performs computations that we don't yet fully understand. But if we can model a portion of these simple brains found in insects and animals, we can use these *wetware* models to implement simple thinking in our games.

In the near future games are going to use more and more complex intelligence models. The models are going to diverge from the standard rule-based AI systems, which are boring and predictable, to models that use software to implement neural networks and small cell-based thinking structures that use simple laws to create very complex systems. We won't have time to go into this kind of modeling in detail, but we will learn how to model certain types of responses and behaviors that simple creatures have. Then we can control the creatures in our games with these models and produce very complex ecosystems.

Before we begin discussing all the interesting concepts and techniques used to implement thinking machines, let me preface this by the following warning. This book is primarily designed to teach 3D polygon graphic techniques used in creating 3D games. However, using 3D graphics to illustrate many of these algorithms wouldn't be wise since we want to have a bird's-eye view in most cases. Hence, all the demos will be 2D, so we can see what's going on. At the end of the chapter, we will discuss how to extend the concepts into three dimensions for the techniques that are applicable.

Tracking Techniques

One of the simplest behaviors that can be implemented in a game is that of the enemy chasing or evading the player. We can implement this behavior in only a few lines of code, but the results are astounding. In general, if we know the coordinates of the player's character and the coordinates of the objects and creatures in the game, we can determine direction vectors that will direct a game creature either toward the player or away. Using these techniques, we can make a creature seem as if it is chasing or evading the player. Let's take a look at how algorithms are implemented.

Chasing Algorithms

Figure 7-1 shows the system we wish to model. Of course, we can extend this model into three dimensions, and add more creatures, and so forth. However, Figure 7-1 is the bare minimum we need in order to define a chasing algorithm. We see that the creature is located at a position (*creature_x,creature_y*) and the player is located at a position (*player_x,player_y*). The coordinates are in screen coordinates, so X increases to the right and Y increases downward.

The question is, how do we move the creature toward the player? The answer can be found by breaking the problem down into its component dimensions—meaning that we process the X- and Y-axis aspects of the problem separately. If the player and creature are at any given points on the screen or 2D plane, then the player is either to the right or left of the creature in the X axis and above or below the creature in the Y axis. If we create a conditional logic sequence that tests for these cases and then translate the creature

FIGURE 7-1
⊙ ⊙ ⊙ ⊙ ⊙ ⊙

Minimum model needed to chase down the player

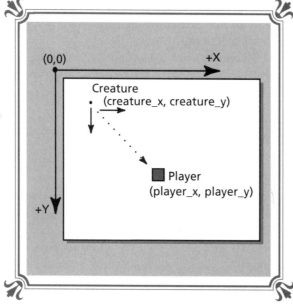

based on the results, then, as a function of time (each frame), the creature will move toward the player no matter what the player does.

Moreover, if we move the creature at a velocity (in units of pixels per frame) greater than that of the player, the player will be doomed at some point unless he can otherwise dispatch the creature! Algorithm 7-1 implements chasing with the model we have been discussing, where (dx,dy) are the rates at which we wish the creature to chase the player.

ALGORITHM 7-1 Chasing the player

```
// test X axis position
if (player_x > creature_x)
    creature_x+=dx;
else
if (player_x < creature_x)
    creature_x-=dx;

// test Y axis position
if (player_y > creature_y)
    creature_y+=dy;
else
if (player_y < creature_y)
    creature_y-=dy;
```

As you can see, the algorithm isn't something you would find on the Putnam Mathematics test, but nevertheless, it results in a creature that behaves much like the Terminator. It won't stop until it terminates its target! The only question that comes to mind is, what happens when the creature chases down and catches the player? Well, if you look at the logic, the case of equality isn't tested; hence, if the coordinates of the creature and player are equal, the creature will sit on top of the player (which is what we want).

The converse of chasing is of course evading (something we all wish we could do with the IRS!), which is implemented by inverting the conditional statements in Algorithm 7-1. Let's see how.

Evasion Tactics

A creature in a game might want to evade the player when it runs out of ammo, realizes that it's in a defensive position, or whatever. The best way to evade an approaching attacker (usually the player) is with an algorithm that looks at the positions of the player and creature and continually tries to move the creature in a direction away from the player. Therefore, if the player is to the right of the creature, the creature would move to the left. The implementation is a snap if we use the chasing algorithm as a foundation and reverse the logic. Take a look at Algorithm 7-2.

ALGORITHM 7-2 Evading the player

```
// test X axis position
if (player_x < creature_x)
   creature_x+=dx;
else
if (player_x > creature_x)
   creature_x-=dx;

// test Y axis position
if (player_y < creature_y)
   creature_y+=dy;
else
if (player_y > creature_y)
   creature_y-=dy;
```

You will notice the only difference between Algorithms 7-1 and 7-2 is that the conditional comparison signs are reversed.

As an example of the algorithms in action, I have created a program called LOCKON.EXE in which you use the arrow keys to move a little green alien around. However, the alien isn't alone; there's another, bigger, uglier alien in the same room. The second alien will either chase or run away from your alien depending on its internal logic state, which can be toggled by pressing SPACEBAR. The source for the program is called LOCKON.C, and it uses the library modules we have created thus far. You can review the source code in Listing 7-1.

LISTING 7-1 Demo of tracking algorithms

```
// LOCKON.C - A demo of tracking and evasion algorithms
// I N C L U D E S ///////////////////////////////////////////////////////

#include <io.h>
#include <conio.h>
#include <stdio.h>
#include <stdlib.h>
#include <dos.h>
#include <bios.h>
#include <fcntl.h>
#include <memory.h>
#include <malloc.h>
#include <math.h>
#include <string.h>

#include "black3.h"
#include "black4.h"
#include "black5.h"


// D E F I N E S ///////////////////////////////////////////////////////

// these are the animation cell indices for the alien walking in all the
// directions
```

continued on next page

continued from previous page

```c
#define ALIEN_START_RIGHT    0
#define ALIEN_START_LEFT     4
#define ALIEN_START_UP       8
#define ALIEN_START_DOWN    12

#define ALIEN_END_RIGHT      3
#define ALIEN_END_LEFT       7
#define ALIEN_END_UP        11
#define ALIEN_END_DOWN      15

// these are the directions the alien can move in

#define ALIEN_RIGHT          0
#define ALIEN_LEFT           1
#define ALIEN_UP             2
#define ALIEN_DOWN           3

// G L O B A L S /////////////////////////////////////////////////////////////

pcx_picture image_pcx;  // general PCX image used to load background and imagery

sprite alien, creature; // the players alien and the creature

// M A I N ////////////////////////////////////////////////////////////////////

void main(int argc, char **argv)
{
int index,      // loop variable
    chase=1,    // used to select creatures mode of operation, 1=chase, 0=evade
    done=0;     // event loop exit flag

char buffer[64]; // used to print strings

// set the graphics mode to mode 13h
Set_Graphics_Mode(GRAPHICS_MODE13);

// create the double buffer
Create_Double_Buffer(200);

// load the imagery for the players alien
PCX_Init((pcx_picture_ptr)&image_pcx);
PCX_Load("lockaln.pcx", (pcx_picture_ptr)&image_pcx,1);

// initialize the alien sprite
Sprite_Init((sprite_ptr)&alien,32,164,8,12,0,0,0,0,0,0);

// start the alien walking down
alien.state      = ALIEN_DOWN;
alien.curr_frame = ALIEN_START_DOWN;

// extract the bitmaps for the alien, there are 16 animation cells
for (index=0; index<16; index++)
```

```
        PCX_Get_Sprite((pcx_picture_ptr)&image_pcx,(sprite_ptr)&alien,index,index,0);

// done with this PCX file so delete memory associated with it
PCX_Delete((pcx_picture_ptr)&image_pcx);

// load the imagery for creature
PCX_Init((pcx_picture_ptr)&image_pcx);
PCX_Load("lockcrt.pcx", (pcx_picture_ptr)&image_pcx,1);

// intialize the creature sprite
Sprite_Init((sprite_ptr)&creature,160,100,24,12,0,0,0,0,0,0);

// extract the bitmaps for the creature, there are 4 animation cells
for (index=0; index<4; index++)
    PCX_Get_Sprite((pcx_picture_ptr)&image_pcx,(sprite_ptr)&creature,index,index,0);

// done with this PCX file so delete memory associated with it
PCX_Delete((pcx_picture_ptr)&image_pcx);

// now load the background image
PCX_Init((pcx_picture_ptr)&image_pcx);
PCX_Load("lockbak.pcx",(pcx_picture_ptr)&image_pcx,1);

// copy PCX image to double buffer
PCX_Copy_To_Buffer((pcx_picture_ptr)&image_pcx,double_buffer);
PCX_Delete((pcx_picture_ptr)&image_pcx);

// scan under alien and creature before entering the event loop, this must be
// done or else on the first cycle the "erase" function will draw garbage
Sprite_Under_Clip((sprite_ptr)&alien,double_buffer);
Sprite_Under_Clip((sprite_ptr)&creature,double_buffer);

// install new keyboard driver
Keyboard_Install_Driver();

// put up exit instructions
Print_String_DB(96,2,9,"Press Q to exit",0);

// main event loop, process until keyboard hit
while(!done)
    {

    // do animation cycle, erase, move draw...
    // erase all objects by replacing what was under them
    Sprite_Erase_Clip((sprite_ptr)&alien,double_buffer);
    Sprite_Erase_Clip((sprite_ptr)&creature,double_buffer);

    // move player
    // test for right motion
    if (keyboard_state[MAKE_RIGHT])
        {
        // move alien
```

continued on next page

continued from previous page

```
            if ((alien.x+=2)>320)
               alien.x=-8;

        // first test if alien was already moving right
        if (alien.state==ALIEN_RIGHT)
           {
           // animate and test for end of sequence
           if (++alien.curr_frame==ALIEN_END_RIGHT)
              alien.curr_frame = ALIEN_START_RIGHT;
           }
        else
           {
           // set state and current frame to right
           alien.state      = ALIEN_RIGHT;
           alien.curr_frame = ALIEN_START_RIGHT;

           } // end else

        } // end if right

    // test for left motion
    else
    if (keyboard_state[MAKE_LEFT])
       {
       // move alien
       if ((alien.x-=2)<-8)
            alien.x=320;

       // first test if alien was already moving left

       if (alien.state==ALIEN_LEFT)
          {
          // animate and test for end of sequence
          if (++alien.curr_frame==ALIEN_END_LEFT)
             alien.curr_frame = ALIEN_START_LEFT;
          }
       else
          {
          // set state and current frame to right
          alien.state      = ALIEN_LEFT;
          alien.curr_frame = ALIEN_START_LEFT;

          } // end else
       } // end if left
    // test for upward motion
    else
    if (keyboard_state[MAKE_UP])
       {
       // move alien
       if ((alien.y-=2) < -12)
          alien.y=200;
```

```
            // first test if alien was already moving up
            if (alien.state==ALIEN_UP)
               {
               // animate and test for end of sequence
               if (++alien.curr_frame==ALIEN_END_UP)
                  alien.curr_frame = ALIEN_START_UP;
               }
            else
               {
               // set state and current frame to right
               alien.state      = ALIEN_UP;
               alien.curr_frame = ALIEN_START_UP;

               } // end else
            } // end if up

        // test for downward motion
        else
        if (keyboard_state[MAKE_DOWN])
           {
           // move alien
           if ((alien.y+=2)>200)
              alien.y=-12;

           // first test if alien was already moving down
           if (alien.state==ALIEN_DOWN)
              {
              // animate and test for end of sequence

              if (++alien.curr_frame==ALIEN_END_DOWN)
                 alien.curr_frame = ALIEN_START_DOWN;

              }
           else
              {
              // set state and current frame to right
              alien.state      = ALIEN_DOWN;
              alien.curr_frame = ALIEN_START_DOWN;

              } // end else

           } // end if down

        // test for tracking toggle
        if (keyboard_state[MAKE_SPACE])
           {
           chase=-chase;
           while(keyboard_state[MAKE_SPACE]);
           }
        // test for exit key
        if (keyboard_state[MAKE_Q])
```

continued on next page

continued from previous page

```
          done=1;

// BEGIN TRACKING LOGIC /////////////////////////////////////////////////////

    // move creature, test if creature is chasing or evading player

    if (chase==1)
       {
       // track on x coordinate
       if (alien.x > creature.x)
          creature.x++;
       else
       if (alien.x < creature.x)
          creature.x--;

       // now track on y coordinate
       if (alien.y > creature.y)
          creature.y++;
       else
       if (alien.y < creature.y)
          creature.y--;

       } // end if chase
    else
       {
       // must be evading

       // evade on x coordinate
       if (alien.x < creature.x)
          creature.x++;
       else
       if (alien.x > creature.x)
          creature.x--;

       // now evade on y coordinate
       if (alien.y < creature.y)
          creature.y++;
       else
       if (alien.y > creature.y)
          creature.y--;

       } // end else

    // test if creature has moved off screen
    if (creature.x>310)
       creature.x = 310;
    else
    if (creature.x<-14)
       creature.x = -14;

    if (creature.y>190)
```

```
        creature.y = 190;
     else
     if (creature.y<-2)
        creature.y = -2;

// END TRACKING LOGIC ///////////////////////////////////////////////////////////

     // do animation for creature
     if (++creature.curr_frame==4)
        creature.curr_frame=0;

     // ready to draw objects, but first scan background under them
     Sprite_Under_Clip((sprite_ptr)&alien,double_buffer);
     Sprite_Under_Clip((sprite_ptr)&creature,double_buffer);
     Sprite_Draw_Clip((sprite_ptr)&alien,double_buffer,1);
     Sprite_Draw_Clip((sprite_ptr)&creature,double_buffer,1);

     // display text message of current tracking mode
     if (chase==1)
        sprintf(buffer,"Creature is Chasing!!!");
     else
        sprintf(buffer,"Creature is Evading!!!");

     Print_String_DB(64,190,12,buffer,0);

     // display double buffer
     Display_Double_Buffer(double_buffer,0);

     // lock onto 18 frames per second max
     Time_Delay(1);

     } // end while

// exit in a very cool way
Screen_Transition(SCREEN_WHITENESS);

// free up all resources
Sprite_Delete((sprite_ptr)&alien);
Sprite_Delete((sprite_ptr)&creature);
Delete_Double_Buffer();
Set_Graphics_Mode(TEXT_MODE);
Keyboard_Remove_Driver();

} // end main
```

The program begins by creating a double buffer and loading the animation cells for the two sprites that make up the demo: one sprite for the player and one for the computer-controlled tracker. Then the background is loaded and copied into the double buffer. Finally, the keyboard driver is loaded, the background image under each sprite is scanned, and the main event loop is entered.

Remember, the basic animation cycle in a game is erase, move, draw. This is exactly what this event loop does, except that the "move" section has the control logic for the creature in it. The control logic is separated into two sections, with each section implementing one of the algorithms (chase and evade). The algorithm executed depends on the value of *evade*, which is toggled by pressing SPACEBAR.

After the logic has been performed for both the player and the creature, the program draws the sprites into the double buffer and displays the double buffer on the video screen. Then the program waits 1/18th of a second and the process repeats. Although the main purpose of this demo is to show off tracking algorithms, there is always more that can be learned. For example, both the creature and player's alien are animated, and the clipped sprite routines are used. If you feel motivated, try adding a weapon allowing the player to shoot the creature.

Random Variables

Without random number generators, video games would be nearly impossible to make. At least they would be too predictable to be fun. Random numbers are used in many facets of game design to add a bit of uncertainty to anything. For example, random numbers can be used to select the direction a ship might fly, or its speed. On the other hand, random numbers may be used to compute random positions of aliens at the start of a game.

However, one of the most prevalent uses of random numbers is to select the direction and speed of a game object in shoot-'em-up or combat-based games. Given that a creature is at a position (*creature_x, creature_y*), as shown in Figure 7-2, we can create a direction vector and speed to move the creature for a short period of time. Furthermore, the actual amount of time may be fixed, or it may be another random value. For example, if we wanted to compute a random direction for the creature in Figure 7-2, we could write something like this,

```
creature_x_velocity = -max_speed + rand() % (2*max_speed+1);
creature_y_velocity = -max_speed + rand() % (2*max_speed+1);
```

where *max_speed* is the maximum positive or negative velocity that the creature will have in either the X or Y axis.

Then using the above values, we could translate the creature every game cycle with something like this:

```
creature_x+=creature_x_velocity;
creature_y+=creature_y_velocity;
```

Of course, moving an object around based solely on random decisions wouldn't be very interesting. The objects may be hard to hit, but they show no signs of intelligence. This is because the objects are not basing their decision making on past information or any logical premises at all. Nevertheless, random motion or logic does have its uses and is another spell to add to our bag of tricks.

FIGURE 7-2

◎ ◎ ◎ ◎ ◎ ◎

Translating an object with a random direction

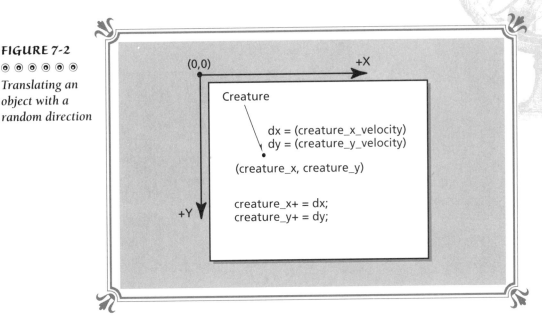

As an example of using random logic to control the motion of an object, I have created a program called LOSTNSPC.EXE. The demo is set in space and features a spaceship that moves around based on a random variable. Who's to say that the ship doesn't have some sort of primitive intelligence? The ship moves on its own and it isn't predictable. However, it's also oblivious to the world around it, but then again, most life forms are! The source code for the program is LOSTNSPC.C, which is shown in Listing 7-2 for review.

LISTING 7-2 Demo of random motion

```
// LOSTNSPC.C - A demo of random motion

// I N C L U D E S ///////////////////////////////////////////////////

#include <io.h>
#include <conio.h>
#include <stdio.h>
#include <stdlib.h>
#include <dos.h>
#include <bios.h>
#include <fcntl.h>
#include <memory.h>
#include <malloc.h>
#include <math.h>
#include <string.h>

#include "black3.h"
```

continued on next page

continued from previous page

```c
#include "black4.h"

// G L O B A L S //////////////////////////////////////////////////////////////

pcx_picture image_pcx;  // general PCX image used to load background and imagery

sprite ship;              // the alien ship

// M A I N //////////////////////////////////////////////////////////////////

void main(int argc, char **argv)
{
int index,           // loop variable
    velocity_x=0,  // used to control velocity of ship
    velocity_y=0;

// set the graphics mode to mode 13h
Set_Graphics_Mode(GRAPHICS_MODE13);
// create the double buffer
Create_Double_Buffer(200);

// load the imagery for the ship
PCX_Init((pcx_picture_ptr)&image_pcx);
PCX_Load("lostship.pcx", (pcx_picture_ptr)&image_pcx,1);

// initialize the ship
Sprite_Init((sprite_ptr)&ship,160,100,18,16,0,0,0,0,0,0);

// make ship sit for the first 1.5 seconds
ship.counter_1   = 0;
ship.threshold_1 = 25;

// extract the bitmaps for the ship, there are 2 animation cells
for (index=0; index<2; index++)
    PCX_Get_Sprite((pcx_picture_ptr)&image_pcx,
              (sprite_ptr)&ship,index,index,0);

// done with this PCX file so delete memory associated with it
PCX_Delete((pcx_picture_ptr)&image_pcx);

// now load the background image
PCX_Init((pcx_picture_ptr)&image_pcx);
PCX_Load("lostback.pcx",(pcx_picture_ptr)&image_pcx,1);

// copy PCX image to double buffer
PCX_Copy_To_Buffer((pcx_picture_ptr)&image_pcx,double_buffer);
PCX_Delete((pcx_picture_ptr)&image_pcx);

// scan background before entering event loop
Sprite_Under_Clip((sprite_ptr)&ship,double_buffer);

// put up exit instructions
```

```
Print_String_DB(80,2,9,"Hit any key to exit",1);

// main event loop, process until keyboard hit

while(!kbhit())
    {
    // do animation cycle, erase, move draw...

    // erase all objects by replacing what was under them
    Sprite_Erase_Clip((sprite_ptr)&ship,double_buffer);


// BEGIN RANDOM MOTION LOGIC //////////////////////////////////////////////////////////

    // test if ship is complete with current trajectory and
    // needs a new one selected
    if (++ship.counter_1 > ship.threshold_1)
        {
        // select new direction vector
        velocity_x = -5 + rand()%10;
        velocity_y = -5 + rand()%10;

        // select a random number of frames to stay on new heading
        ship.threshold_1 = 5 + rand()%50;

        // reset counter
        ship.counter_1   = 0;

        } // end if

    // move ship
    ship.x+=velocity_x;
    ship.y+=velocity_y;

    // test if ship went beyond screen edges
    if (ship.x > 320)
        ship.x = -18;
    else
    if (ship.x < -18)
        ship.x = 320;

    if (ship.y > 200)
        ship.y = -16;
    else
    if (ship.y < -16)
        ship.y = 200;


// END RANDOM MOTION LOGIC //////////////////////////////////////////////////////////

    // animate ship
    if (++ship.curr_frame == 2)
```

continued on next page

continued from previous page

```
          ship.curr_frame = 0;

     // add some special effects via a vapor trail
     if (rand()%10==1)
          Write_Pixel_DB(ship.x+rand()%20,ship.y+12+rand()%4,24+rand()%4);

     // ready to draw ship, but first scan background under it
     Sprite_Under_Clip((sprite_ptr)&ship,double_buffer);
     Sprite_Draw_Clip((sprite_ptr)&ship,double_buffer,1);

     // display double buffer
     Display_Double_Buffer(double_buffer,0);

     // lock onto 18 frames per second max
     Time_Delay(1);

     } // end while
// exit in a very cool way
Screen_Transition(SCREEN_DARKNESS);

// free up all resources
Sprite_Delete((sprite_ptr)&ship);
Delete_Double_Buffer();
Set_Graphics_Mode(TEXT_MODE);

} // end main
```

This program is a bit simpler than the previous one since there is no player interaction. As usual the double buffer is created, and the PCX files containing the spaceship and star background are loaded. The program initializes the ship sprite and enters the main event loop. Once the ship has been erased, the main portion of the control logic is performed and moves the ship in a random direction. However, the movement will only last for a finite period of time related to the values in *counter_1* and *threshold_1*.

If you recall, the sprite structure we originally came up with had some extra fields that were to be used as counters and so forth. This program is a perfect example of the use of the counter fields. In this case, *counter_1* and *threshold_1* are used to count the number of frames that the ship will travel in a single direction. When the counter reaches its threshold; that is, when *counter_1* is greater than *threshold_1*, a new trajectory is selected and the counter and threshold are reset to new values.

The counter allows the ship to move in random directions for random amounts of time instead of a fixed number of cycles. Moving on in the code, after the main portion of the logic executes, the standard screen boundary collision tests are performed and the ship is "warped" from edge to edge if it moves off the playing field. Finally, there is a vapor trail effect (cool!) implemented with another random variable. The following code fragment generates a vapor trail during run time:

```
if (rand()%10==1)
        Write_Pixel_DB(ship.x+rand()%20,ship.y+12+rand()%4,24+rand()%4);
```

FIGURE 7-3

◉ ◉ ◉ ◉ ◉ ◉

Directing objects toward a meeting place

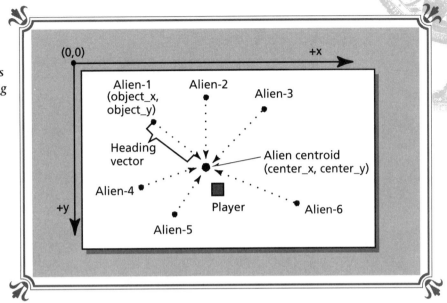

The fragment directs the system to draw a pixel within a small radius (centered about the exhaust nozzles) with a probability of 10 percent. Therefore, every 10 frames the ship expels a single vapor pixel. As an experiment, try decreasing the 10 in the *if* statement; this will increase the density of the vapor trail.

Random variables by themselves are useful, but when coupled with state machines they result in very complex thinking models. But we'll get to that later. At this point, let's see how to implement large-scale attacks (and retreats).

Teaming Up the Enemies

In many games we may want the enemies to perform actions that are somehow related to the goal of converging or diverging from a single point or area of interest. For example, Figure 7-3 shows a top view of a battleground with a collection of aliens and a single player. If the aliens were to group together, they might have a better chance of defeating the player. So, how can we tell them to do this?

Convergence

Given a set of game objects or creatures, we can easily devise an algorithm to select a proper heading for each object that will bring all the objects toward a central meeting place. For example, say there were 20 mechs in a 3D robotic battle game and the player was getting the best of them on one-to-one terms. It might be wise to direct a subset of the mechs to converge upon the player or converge upon their own center of mass–that is, the average position among them–to better defeat the player.

If the mechs are using a complex intelligence model, they may all decide to do their own thing and stray too far from each other. However, by coupling some convergence logic with their standard logic every now and then, the mechs can be kept in close formation. This may be desirable when pitting them against a far superior human mind. The question is, how do we compute headings for the mechs or objects so they move toward a central meeting place?

Well, a bit of vector algebra is needed, but not too much. We can compute a direction vector by subtracting the terminal point (convergence position) from the initial point (center of the object). Referring to Figure 7-3, we see that each object or creature that is to be moved can be thought of as an initial point. And the terminal point can be thought of as the convergence point. Then to compute the trajectory vectors, all we need to do is subtract the initial points from the terminal points one by one and come up with a set of direction vectors. Hence, if an object is at (*object_x,object_y*) and the point that we wish the object to move toward is at (*center_x, center_y*), the direction vector is computed by:

```
heading = <center_x - object_x, center_y - object_y>
```

The result of the computation is a vector that originates from the object, points in the direction of the center point, and has length equal to the distance between

FIGURE 7-4

◎ ◎ ◎ ◎ ◎ ◎

Relationship between a heading vector and its unit vector

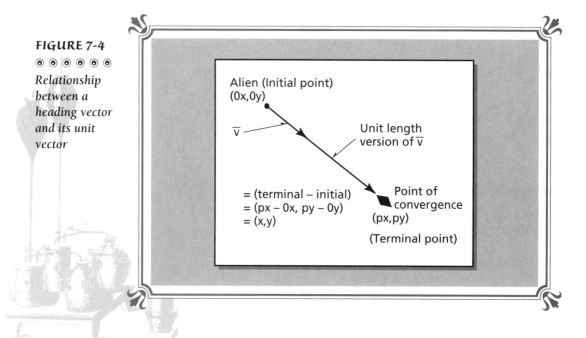

the object and center point. Figure 7-3 shows this graphically. If we were to use the heading vector to translate the object, it would work, but it would only take one frame for the object to reach the center point! To rectify this, we must normalize the heading vector to a length of 1.0 and then translate the object toward the center point by a multiple of the normalized heading. A vector is normalized by scaling its magnitude to 1.0, where magnitude means its overall length. Take a look at Figure 7-4 to see these concepts graphically.

Somehow we must shrink the heading vector so that when we compute its magnitude the result is 1. This can be accomplished by dividing each component of the heading vector by the length of the original heading vector. Let's take a look at the whole process. First, we compute the heading vector between each object and the center point at which we want all the objects to converge. This is done by subtracting each object's position from the center position a coordinate at a time. The result of this computation is a direction vector, which we'll call $V = <x,y>$, where $<x,y>$ are the x and y components of the previous subtraction. Then we'll compute the length of V with the following equation:

vector magnitude of $V = sqrt(x^2 + y^2) = |V|$

The vertical bars around V mean "magnitude."

Then we divide V by its own length, like this:

Unit vector of $V = \dfrac{V}{|V|} = v$

FIGURE 7-5

◎ ◎ ◎ ◎ ◎ ◎

Relationship between a vector and its scalar multiples

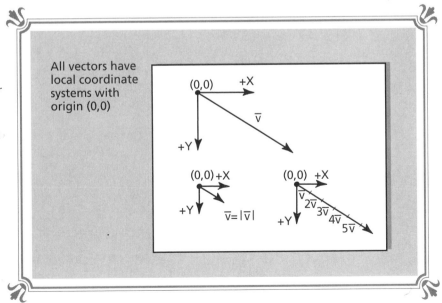

Now if we were to compute the length of **v** with the length equation, we would find that it has a length of 1. Thus, if we use **v** to translate the object toward the center point, it will move one pixel per frame. Therefore, to speed this up, we can multiply **v** by a constant (which is a scaling factor) such as (*speed*∗**v**.) If *speed* were equal to 5, then **v** would be scaled to a length of 5, but it would still be in the direction of the center point. Figure 7-5 shows the relationship between **V**, **v**, and 5∗**v**.

The selection of a center point can be anything we wish, such as the player, the center of mass of all the enemies, a fuel dump, a launch pad, or whatever. Moreover, if the center point moves as a function of time, the heading vectors will have to be recomputed each frame (which can be time consuming). The final caveat on computing heading vectors and vector math in general concerns the precision needed to accomplish it. The demo that follows shortly uses floating point computations. Unfortunately, floating point calculations are slow on the PC even with a math coprocessor, 486, or 586. Thus, when we finally delve into 3D graphics and write a high-speed library, we'll cover fixed point math (which we'll learn about later on in the book). But for now, just keep in mind that floating point calculations should be avoided during run time.

As an example of convergence (otherwise known as *flocking*), the program named CRITTERS.EXE forces a group of green dots (critters) to converge about a single point. The point they converge upon is their own centroid, but could just as easily be any point we wish. If you're not familiar with the term *centroid*, it is simply the average position. It can be computed by summing all the X components of the critters and calling that *center_x*, and doing the same for the Y components and calling that *center_y*. Mathematically, given that a set of N objects are defined by position vectors P_i , then the centroid position is,

$$Cp = (1/n) * \sum_{i=0}^{n} P_i$$

which simply says, "add up all the points and divide the result by the number of points."

Before we fall off the deep end with a bunch of math, let's take a look at the program. It's much easier to understand. The source is named CRITTERS.C and is shown in Listing 7-3.

LISTING 7-3 Demo of convergence

```
// CRITTERS.C - A demo of convergence or flocking

// I N C L U D E S ////////////////////////////////////////////////////////////

#include <io.h>
#include <conio.h>
```

```c
#include <stdio.h>
#include <stdlib.h>
#include <dos.h>
#include <bios.h>
#include <fcntl.h>
#include <memory.h>
#include <malloc.h>
#include <math.h>
#include <string.h>

#include "black3.h"
#include "black4.h"

// D E F I N E S ///////////////////////////////////////////////////////////

#define NUM_CRITTERS  200

// S T R U C T U R E S ///////////////////////////////////////////////////////

typedef struct critter_typ
        {
        float x,y,     // position of critter
              xv,yv;   // velocity of critter

        int back;      // the background color under the critter
        } critter, *critter_ptr;

// G L O B A L S /////////////////////////////////////////////////////////////

pcx_picture image_pcx;  // general PCX image used to load background and
                        // imagery

critter critters[NUM_CRITTERS];  // the array that holds all the critters

// M A I N ///////////////////////////////////////////////////////////////////

void main(int argc, char **argv)
{
int index;   // loop variable

float speed,         // used to scale velocity vector of trajectory
      dx,dy,         // used to compute trajectory vectors
      length,        // length of trajectory vector, used to normalize
      centroid_x,    // center of mass of all critters
      centroid_y;

// set the graphics mode to mode 13h
Set_Graphics_Mode(GRAPHICS_MODE13);

// create the double buffer
Create_Double_Buffer(200);
```

continued on next page

continued from previous page

```
// now load the background image
PCX_Init((pcx_picture_ptr)&image_pcx);
PCX_Load("critback.pcx",(pcx_picture_ptr)&image_pcx,1);

// copy PCX image to double buffer
PCX_Copy_To_Buffer((pcx_picture_ptr)&image_pcx,double_buffer);
PCX_Delete((pcx_picture_ptr)&image_pcx);

// put up exit instructions
Print_String_DB(80,2,9,"Hit any key to exit",1);

// create the arrays of little critters
for (index=0; index<NUM_CRITTERS; index++)
    {
    // select a random position for critter
    critters[index].x = rand()%320;
    critters[index].y = rand()%200;
    } // end for index

// now compute the meeting place for the critters. This could be any point
// you wish, but in this case we'll use their centroid, but in many cases you
// may want them to converge upon a player or specific spot

centroid_x = 0;
centroid_y = 0;

for (index=0; index<NUM_CRITTERS; index++)
    {
    // average in next critter position
    centroid_x+=critters[index].x;
    centroid_y+=critters[index].y;
    } // end for index

// compute final average
centroid_x/=(float)NUM_CRITTERS;
centroid_y/=(float)NUM_CRITTERS;

// mark centroid
Print_String_DB(centroid_x,centroid_y,15,"C",1);

// now vector each critter toward centroid on a straight line trajectory
for (index=0; index<NUM_CRITTERS; index++)
    {
    // compute deltas
    dx = centroid_x-critters[index].x;
    dy = centroid_y-critters[index].y;

    // compute a unit vector pointing toward centroid for this critter
    length = sqrt(dx*dx+dy*dy);
    dx = dx/length;
    dy = dy/length;

    // now scale the vector by some factor to synthesize velocity
```

```
        speed = 2 + rand()%3;

        // compute trajectory vector
        critters[index].xv = dx*speed;
        critters[index].yv = dy*speed;

        } // end for index

// scan under all critters
for (index=0; index<NUM_CRITTERS; index++)
    critters[index].back = Read_Pixel_DB((int)critters[index].x,
                                         (int)critters[index].y);

// main event loop, process until keyboard hit

while(!kbhit())
    {
    // do animation cycle, erase, move draw...

    // erase all critters by replacing what was under them
    for (index=0; index<NUM_CRITTERS; index++)
        Write_Pixel_DB((int)critters[index].x,
                       (int)critters[index].y,
                       critters[index].back);

// BEGIN CONVERGENCE CODE ///////////////////////////////////////////////////

    // move critters toward centroid if they are far enough away
    for (index=0; index<NUM_CRITTERS; index++)
        {
        // test if critter is far enough away from centroid use
        // manhattan distance

        if ((abs(critters[index].x-centroid_x)+
             abs(critters[index].y-centroid_y)) > 20)
         {
         critters[index].x+=critters[index].xv;
         critters[index].y+=critters[index].yv;

         } // end if critter is far enough
        } // end for index

// END CONVERGENCE CODE ///////////////////////////////////////////////////

        // scan under critters
        for (index=0; index<NUM_CRITTERS; index++)
            critters[index].back=Read_Pixel_DB((int)critters[index].x,
                                               (int)critters[index].y);

        // draw critters
        for (index=0; index<NUM_CRITTERS; index++)
            Write_Pixel_DB((int)critters[index].x,
```

continued on next page

continued from previous page

```
                          (int)critters[index].y,10);

    // display double buffer
    Display_Double_Buffer(double_buffer,0);

    // lock onto 9 frames per second max
    Time_Delay(2);
    } // end while

// exit in a very cool way
Screen_Transition(SCREEN_SWIPE_X);

// free up all resources
Delete_Double_Buffer();
Set_Graphics_Mode(TEXT_MODE);

} // end main
```

The program begins as usual by creating a double buffer and loading the graphics. However, in this case there is only a background, since all the critters are drawn with green dots instead of sprites. Then the *critters[]* array is generated by randomly selecting a position on the screen for each critter. Once all the critters have been randomly positioned, their centroid is computed by averaging all their positions. At this point, the centroid is used as the center meeting point to compute all of their heading vectors. The heading vectors are all computed and then placed in the critter structure fields *xv* and *yv*, which are the velocity or translation factors of the critter.

Notice that both the position and velocity fields of the critter structure are floating point. This is necessary for accuracy. However, we could use other techniques, such as fixed point math, if this were a real game. For instructional purposes floating point will suffice for now. Finally, the main event loop is entered and the convergence begins. The interesting thing to note about this program is that it is the first program that supports *replication,* in other words, there are many copies of the same object. This is implemented with multiple data sets that use the same logic. This is a very important concept to grasp. When we write a game that has 100 aliens in it, we don't create separate code for each alien, but a set of functions that work on a set of data (usually elements in an array) that represent the 100 aliens. In the case of CRITTERS.EXE, the array *critters[]* contains all the critters, and *for* loops are used to process each critter in the same way.

The critters are first erased by replacing the pixels previously under them. Then the convergence logic is executed, which moves each critter toward the centroid. The motion of each critter stops once the critter has moved within a specific radius of the centroid (so they don't bunch up too much). However, instead of using the standard distance calculation, sqrt(x^2+y^2), which is slow, the Manhattan distance is used, which is also known as the 1-norm. It's calculated as the sum of components (x+y) instead of the square root of the squares. The results, of course, are in incorrect, but they will be close enough for our purposes. The interesting thing about Manhattan distance is the shape of the boundary that is generated by the tests. Figure 7-6 shows the results of using the standard distance equation and that of the Manhattan distance. Notice that the shape of the Manhattan distance bounding box is a diamond or square on its side! Manhattan distance can be used to speed up collision detection if you're willing to lose the accuracy of the standard 2-norm or $sqrt(x^2 + y^2)$ calculation.

The next phase of the program scans under the critters, making use of the *Read_Pixel_DB()* function, and then draws the critters as green dots. The program executes until a key is pressed. Pay close attention to the final resting place of each critter. They will actually outline the region defined by a (x+y) distance decision variable (very cool!).

FIGURE 7-6

Manhattan distance compared to the standard 2-norm

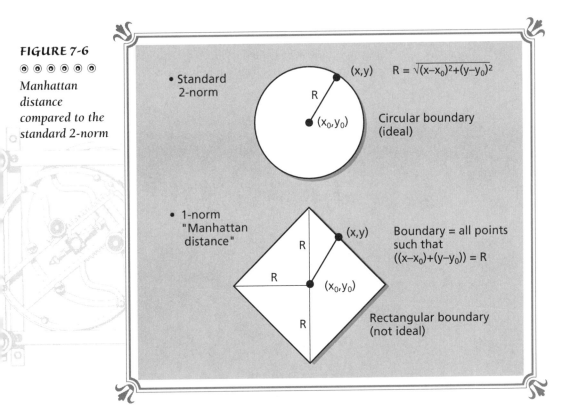

Divergence

Before moving on to the next topic, patterns, we should at least touch upon the opposite of convergence, which is divergence. Similar to evasion, divergence is accomplished by selecting a point of divergence and then computing the negative heading vectors and using these to move the objects. Therefore, all the calculations are performed as before except that the vector **V** is negated with (-1∗**V**) to arrive at the opposite direction vector. Then the vector is normalized, and so forth, as before.

The beauty of convergence and divergence is that once the heading vectors are computed, the objects can be made to converge or diverge during run time simply by multiplying the heading vectors by -1 to toggle the direction. As an exercise, try adding this ability to the CRITTERS.C program, but be careful to test for each critter moving off the screen since there is no such test as the program stands. Otherwise, the critters might get into memory!

Moving in Patterns

We have seen how random variables and conditional logic can be used to drive the motion of a game object; however, there is another classic technique that was and still is very popular in action games. This technique is based on the use of prere-

FIGURE 7-7

◎ ◎ ◎ ◎ ◎ ◎

Using a retreat pattern to minimize damage

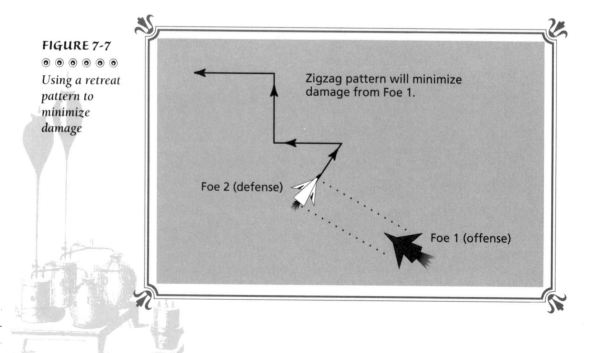

Zigzag pattern will minimize damage from Foe 1.

Foe 2 (defense)

Foe 1 (offense)

FIGURE 7-8

◎ ◎ ◎ ◎ ◎ ◎

*Typical patterns
used in a game*

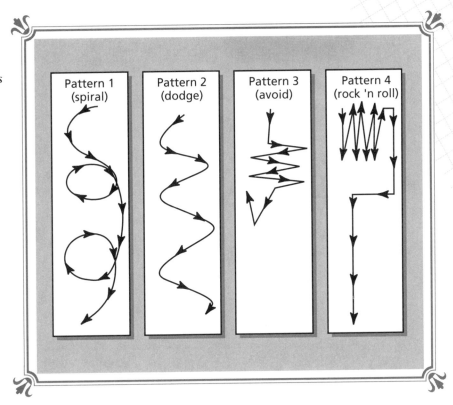

Pattern 1
(spiral)

Pattern 2
(dodge)

Pattern 3
(avoid)

Pattern 4
(rock 'n roll)

corded *patterns*. Patterns are a way of mimicking complex strategies without any underlying logic. For example, when two foes are engaging each other and one of them starts to take the upper hand, the defensive foe might back off in a zigzag pattern to minimize the number of hits he takes during his retreat. Figure 7-7 shows this scenario graphically.

Conditional logic and probability could be used to generate movements with much the same effect, but using patterns is easier to implement. As another example, take a look at Figure 7-8. Here we see four patterns, each of differing length and complexity. If we encode these patterns into some data structure (possibly an array or linked list), we can select one of the patterns based on the state of the game, a random variable, or a combination of the two. Then the data in the pattern is used to control the motion or other aspects of an object in the game.

The demo that we will see shortly uses a very simple encoding system. A pattern is defined as a string of characters that consists of the language r, l, u, d, . (period), and x. Table 7-1 defines the meaning of each character.

TABLE 7-1

◇◇◇◇◇◇

Interpretation of characters in a pattern logic system

ASCII Character	Meaning
r	Move right
l	Move left
u	Move up
d	Move down
x	Do nothing
.	End of pattern

As you can see, by concatenating strings of the pattern commands, complete sequences can be made. For example, if we wanted to encode a pattern of a square, the following string would work:

"rrrrrrrrrrrruuuuuuuuuuuuuuullllllllllllllllllldddddddddddddddd."

FIGURE 7-9

⊙ ⊙ ⊙ ⊙ ⊙ ⊙

Using random variables to select patterns

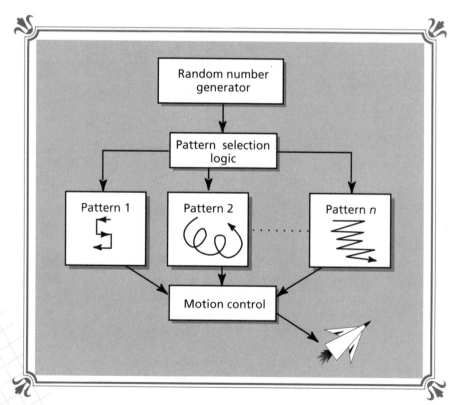

Notice the "." at the end of the pattern to signify that pattern data is complete. Other methods can be used to terminate the sequence, but an end-of-pattern character is fine for our discussions. So how would we implement the use of patterns in a game? Well, we could store a set of patterns in arrays, then a pattern could be selected by a random variable, and an object would then use the pattern data to control its movement. Figure 7-9 shows this process schematically. A random number selects one of four patterns, then the selected pattern is fed into the motion control logic of an object (a ship in this case), and the object moves as commanded by the pattern.

When the pattern data is exhausted, a new pattern can be selected, or possibly the object can use a different AI logic such as random motion or something else. In general, you may want to mix techniques to create an overall thinking model.

As an example of using patterns to control a game object, the following program, JUMPER.EXE, uses patterns to control the motion of a juicy spider. The spider will randomly select a pattern and then execute it until the pattern is complete. At this time a new pattern is selected and the process repeats. The program also displays a small information area at the bottom indicating the current pattern and data being interpreted. The source for the program is called JUMPER.C and is shown in Listing 7-4 for your review.

LISTING 7-4 Demo of using patterns to control motion

```c
// JUMPER.C - A demo of spider jumping around using patterns

// I N C L U D E S ///////////////////////////////////////////////////////////

#include <io.h>
#include <conio.h>
#include <stdio.h>
#include <stdlib.h>
#include <dos.h>
#include <bios.h>
#include <fcntl.h>
#include <memory.h>
#include <malloc.h>
#include <math.h>
#include <string.h>

#include "black3.h"
#include "black4.h"

// D E F I N E S ///////////////////////////////////////////////////////////

#define NUM_PATTERNS 6

// G L O B A L S ///////////////////////////////////////////////////////////

pcx_picture image_pcx;   // general PCX image used to load background and imagery
```

continued on next page

continued from previous page
```
sprite spider;                // the jumping spider

// these are the patterns encoded as strings, with a max of 64 commands
// kinda like DNA patterns

char *patterns[NUM_PATTERNS] = {

"rrrrrrrrrrrrruuuuuuuuuuuuulllllllllllllllllddddddddddddddlllllllll.",
"urururururururururrrrrrrrrdrdrdrdrdrdrdrdrlllllllllllllllddddlllddd.",
"rrrrurrrrurrrruururururururuulululululululdldldldldrdrdrdrdrdrdrd.",
"xxxxxxxxxxuuuuuuuuuuddddduuuudddduuudddduuuddduuuddduuulll.",
"rrrrrrrrrrrrrrrrrrrrrrrrrrrrrruuuuuuuuuuuuuuuuuuuuuuuuuuuu.",
"lllllllllllllllrrrrrrrrrrrrrrrddddddddddddddddxxxxxxxrrrrruu.", };


// M A I N //////////////////////////////////////////////////////////////

void main(int argc, char **argv)
{

int index;              // loop variable

char buffer[64];    // used to print strings

// set the graphics mode to mode 13h
Set_Graphics_Mode(GRAPHICS_MODE13);

// create the double buffer
Create_Double_Buffer(200);

// load the imagery for the spider
PCX_Init((pcx_picture_ptr)&image_pcx);
PCX_Load("jumpspd.pcx", (pcx_picture_ptr)&image_pcx,1);

// initialize the spider
Sprite_Init((sprite_ptr)&spider,160,100,30,24,0,0,0,0,0,0);
spider.state     = 0;   // select pattern one
spider.counter_1 = 0;

// extract the bitmaps for the spider, there are 4 animation cells
for (index=0; index<4; index++)
    PCX_Get_Sprite((pcx_picture_ptr)&image_pcx,(sprite_ptr)&spider,index,index,0);

// done with this PCX file so delete memory associated with it
PCX_Delete((pcx_picture_ptr)&image_pcx);

// now load the background image
PCX_Init((pcx_picture_ptr)&image_pcx);
PCX_Load("jumpbak.pcx",(pcx_picture_ptr)&image_pcx,1);

// copy PCX image to double buffer
PCX_Copy_To_Buffer((pcx_picture_ptr)&image_pcx,double_buffer);
```

```
PCX_Delete((pcx_picture_ptr)&image_pcx);

// scan background before entering event loop
Sprite_Under_Clip((sprite_ptr)&spider,double_buffer);

// put up exit instructions
Print_String_DB(80,2,9,"Hit any key to exit",1);

// main event loop, process until keyboard hit
while(!kbhit())
    {
    // do animation cycle, erase, move draw...
    // erase all objects by replacing what was under them
    Sprite_Erase_Clip((sprite_ptr)&spider,double_buffer);

// BEGIN PATTERN MOTION LOGIC ///////////////////////////////////////////////

    // move spider, test if there is still data commands in current pattern

    if (patterns[spider.state][spider.counter_1]!='.')
       {
       // what is the command

       switch(patterns[spider.state][spider.counter_1])
            {
            case 'r': // right
                  {
                  // move spider
                  spider.x+=4;

                  // test if off edge
                  if (spider.x > 320)
                     spider.x=-30;

                  } break;

            case 'l': // left
                  {
                  // move spider

                  spider.x-=4;

                  // test if off edge
                  if (spider.x < -30)
                     spider.x=320;

                  } break;

            case 'u': // up
                  {
                  // move spider
```

continued on next page

continued from previous page

```
                        spider.y-=4;

                        // test if off edge
                        if (spider.y <-24)
                           spider.y=200;

                        } break;

                case 'd': // down
                        {
                        // move spider
                        spider.y+=4;

                        // test if off edge
                        if (spider.y > 200)
                           spider.y=-24;

                        } break;

                case 'x': // do nothing
                        {
                        } break;

                default:break;

                } // end switch
        // increment pattern index

        spider.counter_1++;

        } // end if pattern data hasn't been consumed
     else
        {
        // select a new pattern and reset pattern index
        spider.state    = rand()%NUM_PATTERNS;
        spider.counter_1 = 0;

        } // end else pattern done

// END PATTERN MOTION LOGIC ////////////////////////////////////////////////////

    // animate spider
    if (++spider.curr_frame == 4)
       spider.curr_frame = 0;

    // display current pattern and data
    sprintf(buffer,"Pattern #%d, data=%c",spider.state,
                            patterns[spider.state][spider.counter_1]);

    Print_String_DB(88,190,15,buffer,0);

    // ready to draw spider, but first scan background under it
```

```
      Sprite_Under_Clip((sprite_ptr)&spider,double_buffer);
      Sprite_Draw_Clip((sprite_ptr)&spider,double_buffer,1);

      // display double buffer
      Display_Double_Buffer(double_buffer,0);

      // lock onto 18 frames per second max
      Time_Delay(1);

      } // end while
// exit in a very cool way
Screen_Transition(SCREEN_DARKNESS);

// free up all resources
Sprite_Delete((sprite_ptr)&spider);
Delete_Double_Buffer();
Set_Graphics_Mode(TEXT_MODE);

} // end main
```

The program does all the usual stuff: allocate the double buffer, load the imagery, initialize the sprite, and so forth. The action begins in the main event loop with the test to see if the current pattern is complete by means of a "." character being read. If this is true, then one of the six patterns is randomly selected and started up. Notice the use of the sprite elements *counter_1* and *state*. The *state* is used to hold the index of the currently active pattern, and *counter_1* is used to hold the current element being processed of the current pattern. Again, we see that the extra elements of the sprite structure come in handy for tracking and counting. As a matter of fact, I wish I had added a couple more variables such as velocity and a scratch pad area, but, oh well!

Moving right along in the code, the next section following the pattern logic is the animation code, which simply increments the current frame and tests whether all the frames have been displayed. If so, the current frame number is reset and the animation cycle repeats. Finally, the spider is drawn and the double buffer is displayed. I hope you are becoming very comfortable with the animation cycle. By the end of this chapter, you will have the necessary tools to write simple 2D games, and by the end of the next chapter, I bet you could start your own shareware enterprise! We are definitely making a lot of progress. Next, let's talk about the techniques used to move objects in unison.

Synchronous Motion

Synchronous motion simply means a group of objects moving together as a single entity. This is very simple to accomplish if we look at the way we implement multiple objects in a game. As mentioned before, multiple objects are nothing more than multiple data structures that are each processed by the same logic (see Figure 7-10).

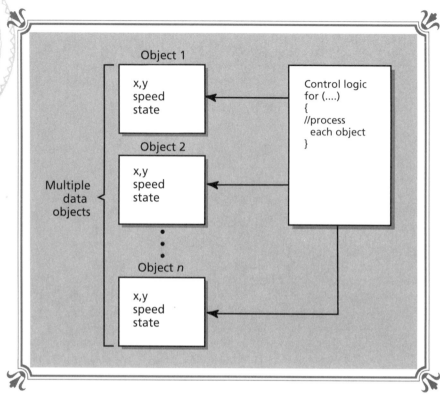

Each object may move in a different way depending on its position and current state, but we can move all the objects together if the situation calls for it.

There is no reason why we can't select one object as the *controller*. This object would do its own thing based on its position and state, but the other objects wouldn't perform any of their own calculations, they would simply mimic the leader's motions for a period of time and break off after some premise was met. This technique is very common in 3D combat games: a group of enemies makes an attack run in formation and then at some point, each breaks away from the pattern and attacks on its own.

State Machines

Thus far the thinking models we have covered lack two main attributes: memory and rules. To create a robust thinking model, the model must have some kind of

FIGURE 7-11

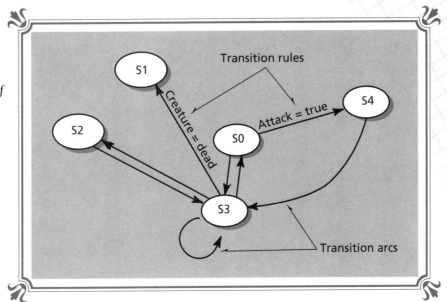

*Abstract
representation of
a state machine*

memory to remember its past, along with a set of rules or premises to guide its logic. The tracking algorithms, random motion, and patterns can be thought of as the resulting action that a high-level thought process might select, but how was the selection made in the first place? In other words, the final motion or action of a game object is a "motor" operation. We are interested in modeling the thought process that selected the motor operation in the first place.

State machines can bring us closer to the goal of an autonomous thinking model. State machines are machines (software, hardware, or biological) that have a set of states and a set of transition arcs. Take a look at Figure 7-11. Here we see a general state machine diagram. There are five states, labeled S0 through S4. Also, we see that there are *transition arcs* from one state to another. These transition arcs are the events that must occur for the state machine to move into the state at the terminal end of any transition arc. For example, we see that for the system to move from S0 to S4, *attack* must equal true. Whatever that means is relevant to the context of the game the state machine runs in, but nevertheless is a rule that must be followed.

State machines are used widely in the control of synthetic game creatures to make them perform in certain ways based on the environment of the game, state of other game objects, and the current state of the machine. As an example, imagine that we create a monster that can be in one of the states listed in Table 7-2.

TABLE 7-2
◇◇◇◇◇◇

*Some possible
states for a monster*

Name of State	Numeric Representation
MORPHING	S0
EATING	S1
HUNTING	S2
MOVING_RANDOMLY	S3
CONVERGING	S4
DYING	S5
DEAD	S6

Using the state table as a foundation, a state diagram can be generated, as seen in Figure 7-12. The transition arcs and associated rules are only for illustrative purposes, but you get the picture. The notion of "state" and software versions of a state machine can easily be implemented in software. For example, the *state* field of the

FIGURE 7-12
◉ ◉ ◉ ◉ ◉ ◉

*A possible
implementation
of the states in
Table 7-2*

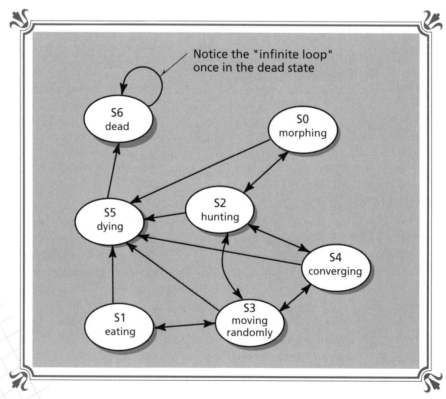

sprite structure is for just such a purpose. To create a software state machine that drives a sprite, we might place one of the possible state constants in the *state* field of a sprite. Then we would use the counter variables along with the threshold variables to control how long the software state machine would remain in a specific state. We could further embellish this with some extra conditional logic that took into consideration other aspects of the game.

The transition arcs are implemented as conditional statements in software. For example, if the creature is in any of the states and is hit by a torpedo, it moves into the *DYING* state. The *DYING* state will execute for a number of cycles and then move into the *DEAD* state. The fragment of code that implements this follows:

```
// make sure the creature is alive
if (creature.state!=DEAD)
{
// process each possible state of the creature
if (creature.state==MORPHING)
    {
    // perform next iteration of morphing logic
    } // end if in morphing state
else
if (creature.state==EATING)
    {
    // perform next iteration eating logic
    } // end if in eating state
else
if (creature.state==HUNTING)
    {
    // perform next iteration of hunting logic
    } // end if in hunting state
else
if (creature.state==MOVING_RANDOMLY)
    {
    // perform next iteration of random logic
    } // end if in random state
else
if (creature.state==CONVERGING)
    {
    // perform next iteration of convergence sequence
    } // end if in convergence state

// test if creature is hit

if (creature.state!=DYING && creature.state!=DEAD && Creature_Hit())
    {
    // set state of creature to dying
    creature.state = DYING;
    // set up all other auxiliary variables
    //....
    } // end if hit

if (creature.state==DYING)
```

continued on next page

continued from previous page

```
    {
    // perform next iteration of death sequence

    if (death_sequence_complete)
        creature.state=DEAD;

    } // end if in dying state

} // end if creature is not dead
```

As you can see, the software implementation of a state machine consists of a series of *if* statements (usually one for each state) coupled with other supporting logic within each state that determines if a state transition is to be made. There are other structures that can be used to implement state machines, such as *switch()* statements and look-up tables, but the *if* version is the clearest. Most of the logic is missing (since it would take pages to complete), but we do see some of the implementation of the dying test sequence. The test is made to see if the creature has been hit; if so, the state of the creature is set to *DYING*, and then the code continues. Next time around the main event loop, the state machine will fall into the

FIGURE 7-13

◉ ◉ ◉ ◉ ◉ ◉

Using a probability distribution to select states

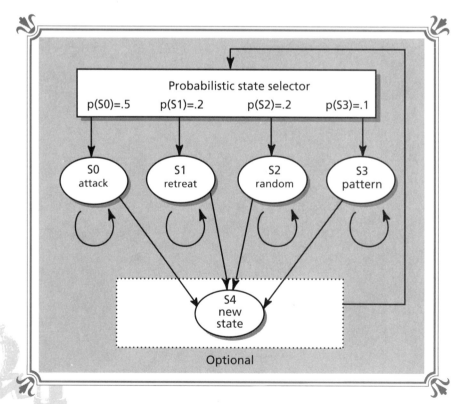

DYING state, which will continue until the dying sequence is complete, at which point the state of the creature is set to *DEAD*, and the creature is no longer processed.

Once we have designed the possible states that a creature or game object may take on, we must decide how the states are to be selected. We can use a strict decision system that is deterministic, but a better way would be to allow some probability into the equation so that the creatures aren't predictable.

Probabilistic State Selection

Take a look at Figure 7-13. Here we see a state machine that is driven by a probability density function. The probability density function directs the control logic to select a new state based on a set of probabilities. The sum of the probabilities should equal 1.0 so that the probability selection makes sense. For example, Table 7-3 lists the four possible states.

TABLE 7-3
◇◇◇◇◇◇
Some possible action states

State Name	Value
ATTACK	S0
RETREAT	S1
RANDOM	S2
PATTERN	S3

Of course, there may be other states, such as *DYING* and *DEAD*, but these are the only states that are going to be selected by random probability. Then we could assign a probability to each state, as shown in Table 7-4.

TABLE 7-4
◇◇◇◇◇◇
A probability density for a set of action states

State Name	Probability of Occurrence
ATTACK	.5
RETREAT	.2
RANDOM	.2
PATTERN	.1

$$\sum = .5 + .2 + .2 + .1 = 1.0$$

Now if we write some logic that takes these probabilities into consideration to select a new action state, the results would be a game object or creature that has a

"personality." This personality is defined by the probability of each state occurring. The implementation of selection is as simple as:

```
// this table has elements which are the states themselves

int state_table[0,0,0,0,0,1,1,2,2,3];

new_state = state_table[rand()%10];
```

Since each state is in the *state_table[]* a number of times equal to the probability of the state multiplied by 10, each state will be selected, on average, the proper number of times as a function of time. For example, the *ATTACK* state is supposed to have a .5 probability. Since 0 is in the *state_table[]* five times and there are a total of ten elements, when the following line is executed,

```
new_state = state_table[rand()%10];
```

the *ATTACK* state will be selected 50 percent of the time. The other states are selected in the same way. Hence, we use a look-up table to convert probabilities into final states. There are other ways to do this, but this way is very clean and works well. Moreover, it avoids floating point calculations, which are an absolute no-no in AI algorithms. We can't select new states at random all the time; that defeats the whole purpose of a state machine. Sometimes we want to select the next state based on some conditions. Let's talk about that now.

Rule-Based State Selection

The whole idea behind state machines is to make state transitions based on the current state and a set of rules or conditions that are met. However, we have learned that sometimes an initial state can be selected at random using probability. In any case, what rules should we use to make state transitions and how do we derive them? This is a complex question and there is no single correct answer. The answer is…shall we say…fuzzy. In general, use common sense when you model your state machines that drive the game objects. For example, if a state machine is controlling the flight path of a ship, the determination of the next state should use relevant information such as the environment, what the other ships are doing, and what the current objective of the ship is.

If we look at real ecosystems and study the results of their interactions without trying to understand the mechanism of their reactions, we can come up with a lot of useful information that we can use to help model state machines in games. For instance, instinctive rules and reactions are very easy to model. If a creature in a game is being shot at, then it should simply transition into the retreat state; on the other hand, if a creature is low on fuel, then it might transition into the fuel searching state (if there are no higher priority tasks at the moment). Hence, state transition rules themselves should have an element of randomness in them.

FIGURE 7-14

◎ ◎ ◎ ◎ ◎ ◎

Human avoiding
an object

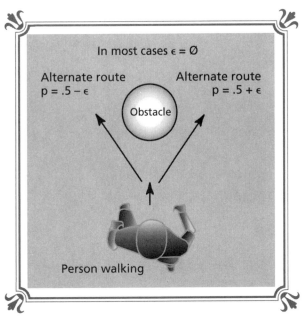

A perfect example of randomness in human decision making is the following: you are walking and an obstacle is directly in front of you. You can avoid it by altering your course either to the left or to the right (see Figure 7-14). So which one do you pick, and why? The answer is, you will pick the one that is most convenient. However, if both are equally convenient, then the decision is usually random. Of course, we should temper this statement by noting that if you had a previous experience of avoiding the obstacle to the right, then there is a high probability that you will use the same tactic, since you have learned and performed it once before with success.

This brings us to the final aspect of state machine design: local memory systems that update state transition probability tables.

State Machine Probability Tables

We have seen how probability tables can be used to select the next state of a state machine, and how random variables can be used to select directions of motions, and so forth. However, the probabilities are always fixed. Agreed, they are random, but the distributions themselves never change. Hence, an opportunity for learning is possible. What if we were to record a specific subset of events that occur as the game runs? In essence, we keep track of the environment of the game in some way as a function of time.

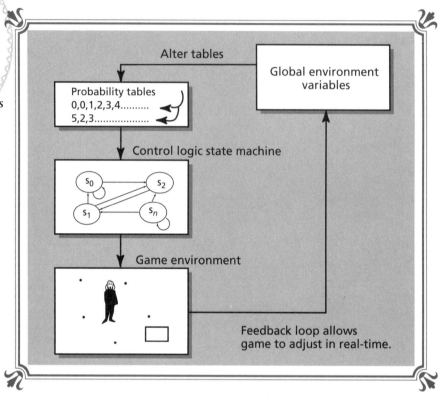

Take a look at Figure 7-15. Here we see probability tables being used as driving inputs into a state machine. However, there is an added property: the probability tables themselves are driven by a set of game variables that are derived from the game itself. We can think of this as an interpretation of environment. Just as humans may change their actions and behaviors based on environmental conditions, we can use the environment of a game to alter the probability distributions and decision making that is done by the state machines controlling the game objects. As a solid example of this, imagine that a game uses a random variable to decide whether or not to attack or retreat from the player with the following probability distribution:

ATTACK 60%
RETREAT 40%

However, the state machine logic will never "look" at the state of the game and decide if this probability distribution should be altered. A simple way of altering this static probability distribution would be to use the current health of the creature versus the player. If the creature was very strong with little damage and the player was weak and ready to fall, then the probability of attacking should be increased. On the other hand, if the creature was weak, then it should retreat more often. This type of information can easily be modeled into the system via altering probability distributions.

Terrain Following

The next topic of discussion, although a bit off the subject of pure intelligence modeling, is that of *terrain following*. If we're going to write games that have objects flying around in the air and driving on the ground, then some means of control must be thought up so the objects don't crash! Since we're primarily still discussing 2D implementations at this point, we will use terrain following as the illustrative example instead of the more general 3D case of flying through a collection of objects, but the fundamental concepts are the same. We must derive a technique to keep the game object on the game surface and away from collisions.

Although terrain following can be done using AI or synthetic intelligence, a much simpler implementation can be achieved by looking at the geometry of the problem in two dimensions. Take a look at Figure 7-16. Here we see a mountain range and a ship. The idea of the game is to fly the ship as close as possible to the terrain without hitting it. Many solutions come to mind. We could have a database

FIGURE 7-16

The terrain following setup

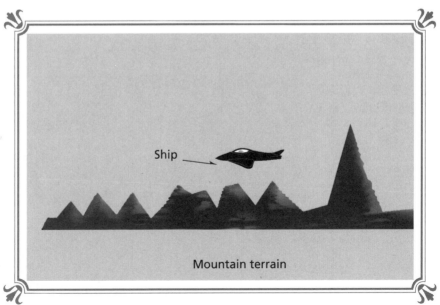

Ship

Mountain terrain

of the heights of each vertical strip of the terrain and then, depending on the position of the ship, we could index into a table and modify the vertical position of the ship as a function of time. Another solution would be to maintain a rough vector map of the terrain that has the main topology in it without all the detail, as shown in Figure 7-17. We could then compute the normal vectors or perpendicular vector to each segment and make sure that the ship flies in a way that is parallel to the normal vectors of each segment while staying above the segments themselves.

The method of using segments and normals is very important in 3D systems and is usually used for terrain following. But as an example of simple tactics, we are going to implement a terrain follower using image space techniques. Or in other words, we're going to make the ship "look down" at the pixels under it to see if the mountaintop is too close, and if so, the ship will gain altitude, otherwise, it will descend. To accomplish this crude vision, we will simply scan the pixels under the midsection of the ship using the *Read_Pixel()* function. If the pixel read isn't black, there must be land there; hence, the ship should remain at its current altitude. However, if the scanning probe doesn't report any solid pixels, the altitude can be dropped. By performing this process each frame, the ship will track the terrain, but its orientation will never change. To accomplish that, we need to use the normal segmented method.

Unfortunately, image space algorithms–that is, algorithms that function in the frame buffer itself–don't work very well in 3D. Most of the time 3D algorithms must work in object space, or in other words, the 3D mathematical space that the

FIGURE 7-17

◉ ◉ ◉ ◉ ◉ ◉

A vector contour map of the detailed terrain in Figure 7-16

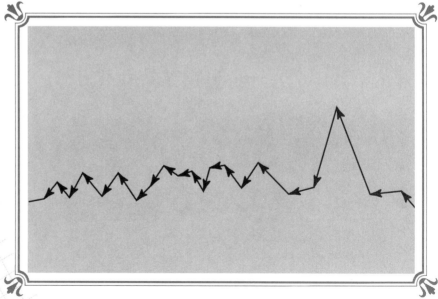

objects exist in. However, as a simple example of 2D image-space terrain following, the program below, named FLOATER.EXE, will show how it's done. The program begins by querying you to enter the roughness of the terrain and the tracking distance the ship will fly above the terrain. The roughness of the terrain is 1 to 10, where 10 is the roughest. The minimum height at which the ship can track is 1 pixel, but I suggest you don't go lower than 2. Anyway, the name of the source is FLOATER.C and it's shown in Listing 7-5.

LISTING 7-5 *Demonstration of 2D image-space terrain following*

```c
// FLOATER.C - A demo of 2D terrain following

// I N C L U D E S ///////////////////////////////////////////////////////////

#include <io.h>
#include <conio.h>
#include <stdio.h>
#include <stdlib.h>
#include <dos.h>
#include <bios.h>
#include <fcntl.h>
#include <memory.h>
#include <malloc.h>
#include <math.h>
#include <string.h>

#include "black3.h"
#include "black4.h"

// G L O B A L S ///////////////////////////////////////////////////////////

pcx_picture image_pcx;  // general PCX image used to load background and imagery

sprite speeder;         // the floating speeder

// M A I N ///////////////////////////////////////////////////////////

void main(int argc, char **argv)
{
int index,             // loop variable
    terr_y=160,        // these are used to draw random terrain
    terr_draw=1,
    rough,             // roughness of terrain ,input by user
    x,y,
    hover_height = 2;  // minimum terrain following height

// query user about terrain roughness and terrain following height
printf("\nEnter the roughness of terrain from 1-10?");
scanf("%d",&rough);
```

continued on next page

continued from previous page

```
printf("\nEnter the terrain following height from 1-50?");
scanf("%d",&hover_height);

// set the graphics mode to mode 13h
Set_Graphics_Mode(GRAPHICS_MODE13);

// create the double buffer
Create_Double_Buffer(200);

// load the imagery for the speeder
PCX_Init((pcx_picture_ptr)&image_pcx);
PCX_Load("floatspd.pcx", (pcx_picture_ptr)&image_pcx,1);

// initialize the speeder
Sprite_Init((sprite_ptr)&speeder,320,100,40,10,0,0,0,0,0,0);

// extract the bitmaps for the speeder, there are 4 animation cells
for (index=0; index<4; index++)
    PCX_Get_Sprite((pcx_picture_ptr)&image_pcx,(sprite_ptr)&speeder,index,index,0);

// done with this PCX file so delete memory associated with it
PCX_Delete((pcx_picture_ptr)&image_pcx);

// draw the terrain one vertical strip at a time
// seed the random number generator with current time
srand(*(int far *)0x0000046CL);

for (x=0; x<320; x++)
    {
    // test if its time to change directions
    if (--terr_draw<=0)
       {
       terr_draw=rand()%(20/rough);
       terr_y = terr_y - 1 + rand()%3;
       } // end if time to select new direction

    // draw a vertical strip at current x location
    Write_Pixel_DB(x,terr_y,15);

    for (y=terr_y+1; y<200 ;y++)
        Write_Pixel_DB(x,y,200+rand()%16);

    } // end for index

// scan background before entering event loop
Sprite_Under_Clip((sprite_ptr)&speeder,double_buffer);

// put up exit instructions
Print_String_DB(80,2,9,"Hit any key to exit",1);

// main event loop, process until keyboard hit
while(!kbhit())
     {
```

```
              // do animation cycle, erase, move, draw...

              // erase all objects by replacing what was under them
              Sprite_Erase_Clip((sprite_ptr)&speeder,double_buffer);

              // move speeder

              // if there is no terrain under speeder then apply downward thrust
              // at constant velocity
              if (!Read_Pixel_DB(speeder.x+4,speeder.y+12+hover_height))
                speeder.y+=2;

              // now horizontal thrust
              speeder.x-=6;

              // now probe under speeder for terrain and apply upward thrust
              // if crust is found
              if (Read_Pixel_DB(speeder.x+4,speeder.y+12+hover_height))
                speeder.y-=2;

              // test if speeder has moved off screen
              if (speeder.x <-40)
                speeder.x = 320;

              // this should never happen, but just in case
              if (speeder.y > 200)
                 speeder.y=200;

              // animate speeder
              if (++speeder.curr_frame == 4)
                speeder.curr_frame = 0;

              // ready to draw speeder, but first scan background under it
              Sprite_Under_Clip((sprite_ptr)&speeder,double_buffer);
              Sprite_Draw_Clip((sprite_ptr)&speeder,double_buffer,1);

              // display double buffer
              Display_Double_Buffer(double_buffer,0);

              // lock onto 18 frames per second max
              Time_Delay(1);

              } // end while

// exit in a very cool way
Screen_Transition(SCREEN_DARKNESS);

// free up all resources
Sprite_Delete((sprite_ptr)&speeder);
Delete_Double_Buffer();
Set_Graphics_Mode(TEXT_MODE);

} // end main
```

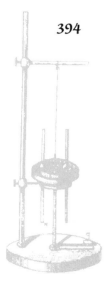

The floater program has a couple of neat effects other than the terrain following itself. The program draws a fractal 2D terrain using a random variable. The terrain is drawn by using a random variable to select whether or not the next pixel of the terrain should be above or below the previous pixel. The number of times these changes are made as a function of horizontal position is related to the "jaggedness" of the mountain. Also, note how the random number generator is seeded with the current time by the following line, which extracts the current time from the real-time clock in seconds.

```
srand(*(int far *)0x0000046CL);
```

Since the time will always be different, it is a good number to use as a seed for the random number generator so that the random sequences will be different every time the program is run. Remember, the random number generator does *not* produce random numbers. It only produces a sequence of numbers that seem to be random and exhibit the proper distribution and noncorrelation that random numbers must have. If the random number generator isn't seeded with a different number at program startup, the sequence of random numbers will always be the same. Thus, by seeding the random number generator with the time (as one example), a new set of random numbers will be generated each time the program is run. This is a very important fact to know when writing games. If you use random numbers, seed the random number generator at the beginning of the game, otherwise, the computer will select the same moves every game!

Anyway, after the terrain is drawn on the screen, the main event loop is entered and the ship sprite appears at the right edge of the screen. It will then start descending until it "sees" the mountain terrain under it via its vision probe, which is nothing more than this single line:

```
if (Read_Pixel_DB(speeder.x+4,speeder.y+12+hover_height))
       speeder.y-=2;
```

Depending on the results of the vision probe, the ship will be translated either up or down to follow the contour of the terrain. After this, the sprite is drawn and the cycle repeats. As an addition to the program, try creating two more animation frames depicting the ship climbing and falling, as in Figure 7-18. Then rewrite the program so the ship logic scans forward and if an ascent is going to occur, the ship tilts upward, and if a descent is inevitable, then the ship tilts downward.

Implementing Vision

Once we have designed a rudimentary thinking model that will drive some object or creature in a game, another enhancement to the model can be realized using simulated sensory organs. The creatures in a video game can't really see because

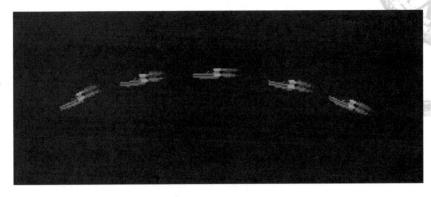

they are only projections. However, since we know the position and state of every object in a game, we can simulate all the senses if we wish. Vision, for example, is the most important of the senses, so let's concentrate on how we can implement simulated vision.

Take a look at Figure 7-19, where we see a top view of a battleground. There are a few tanks and the player. The tanks are all trying to find the player. Obviously, we

FIGURE 7-19
⊙ ⊙ ⊙ ⊙ ⊙ ⊙
A battleground where vision is a must!

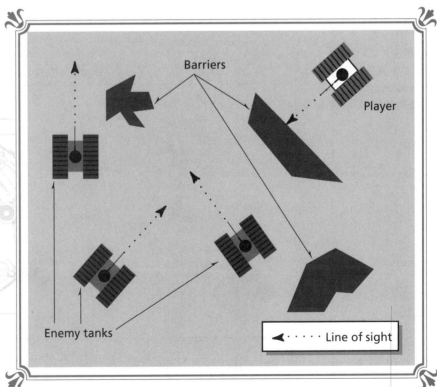

know the position of the player and the tanks and we can simply use one of the tracking algorithms to lock the tanks onto the player. But wait a minute, is this really fair? The answer is no. Paying close attention to the position of the tanks and that of the player, we see that if the tanks had eyes they wouldn't be able to see the player and therefore, they shouldn't be able to "cheat" by looking at his coordinates.

A more realistic solution to controlling the tank logic would be to implement a vision probe or scan from the viewpoint of a tank. The probe would scan out a certain distance and a certain angle, as shown in Figure 7-20. During the scan, if any objects were detected, they would be marked, inserted into a list, and processed as "visible" by the tank logic. Using this technique, the tanks will act in a more realistic manner, since they will use vision as feedback into their logic controls instead of cheating. Admittedly, the player has a big advantage since he can see the tanks when they can't see him because of the 2D aspect of this example. However, if the game were 3D and the viewpoint of the player were first person, then the player couldn't see the tanks through a wall, so the tanks shouldn't be able to see the player through a wall either!

The question is, how do we implement this scanning process? Well, it depends on the situation. In a top-down 2D game, we can divide the game grid into squares,

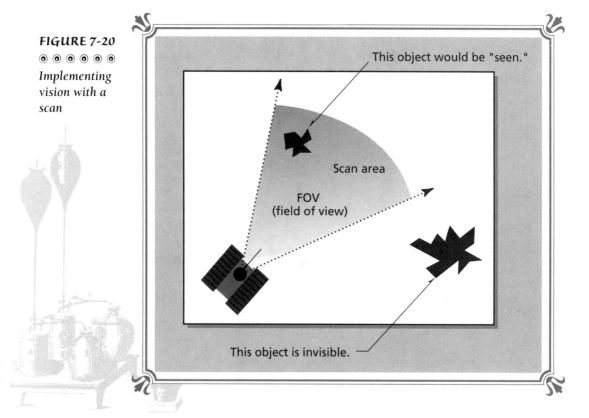

FIGURE 7-20

◎ ◎ ◎ ◎ ◎ ◎

*Implementing
vision with a
scan*

FIGURE 7-21
◎ ◎ ◎ ◎ ◎ ◎

Scanning an area by breaking it down into cells

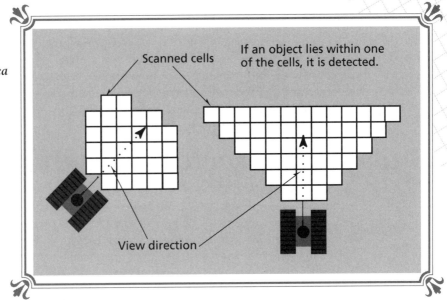

as shown in Figure 7-21. Then for each tank, a small pyramid shape of squares would be scanned, and any objects in the squares would be processed. In essence, we are only scanning the field of view of the object. On the other hand, a 3D game would need a more complex scanning method. Maybe instead of using a 2D scan of squares, 3D cubes would be the scanning primitive, as shown in Figure 7-22. Or

FIGURE 7-22
◎ ◎ ◎ ◎ ◎ ◎

Scanning a volume in 3D with cubes

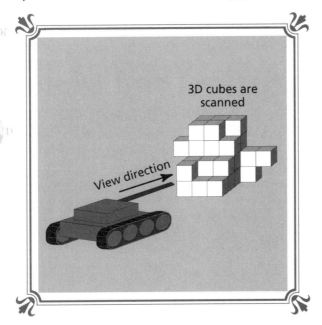

rays might be cast out from the object's viewpoint. The technique is up to you, but the main idea is to simulate vision in some way (as inaccurate as it may be) and use the data for feedback into the thinking logic of the game objects.

Vision systems are very important when a game object is trying to navigate in an area that has a lot of solid objects and obstacles. In this case, having an idea of what's in front of the moving game object can be used to make course changes before it's too late.

Building the Perfect Predator

We now have all the elements needed to create reasonably complex thinking models for our games. The question is, what do we use and when? Every game has creatures and objects that are of varying intelligence. I suggest that objects and creatures that aren't the main attraction in a game use simple methods to implement their intelligence such as tracking algorithms, random variables, and patterns. Game elements that the player will be interacting with that are supposed to be challenging should use state machines with probabilistic state selection and maybe even environmental feedback via global indicators.

The main objects in the game that really are supposed to have brains should add vision and memory systems. The memory systems should record simple indicators of the player's actions and reactions to try to learn strategies to beat the player. In general, building thinking models is an art form and it will take time for you to get the hang of it, but by using the techniques outlined here, you have more than enough information to create game opponents that can match or beat their human counterparts!

Extending to the Third Dimension

Although we have focused mainly on 2D representations during this chapter, all the concepts translate to 3D, in most cases, simply by adding another variable—the Z coordinate. For example, the chasing algorithm we covered can be altered to function in 3D with the addition of a couple lines:

```
// test X axis position

if (player_x > creature_x)
   creature_x+=dx;
else
if (player_x < creature_x)
   creature_x-=dx;

// test Y axis position
```

```
if (player_y > creature_y)
    creature_y+=dy;
else
if (player_y < creature_y)
    creature_y-=dy;

// added code!

// test Z axis position
if (player_z > creature_z)
    creature_z+=dz;
else
if (player_z < creature_z)
    creature_z-=dz;
```

The material on state machines is dimensionally invariant so there won't be many changes in there. In general, once we have covered all the aspects of 3D space, math, and transformations, all the topics discussed here will be easily convertible to their 3D counterparts, in most cases with a couple lines of code.

Summary

Within this chapter we have discussed and detailed the main techniques used to create thinking models for video games. We have in fact learned to bring the images on the screen to life to do as we command. Remember, the goal of a Cybersorcerer is to create a real universe within the computer, not just to mimic one. Thus, the algorithms and techniques we have learned, such as tracking algorithms, state machines, probability distributions, and sensory simulation, are only the starting point for more complex research. Who knows, maybe a video game programmer will create the world's first living machine. Hmmm, while you're thinking about that, get ready for the next step in our training, and that's possession.

8

The Art of Possession

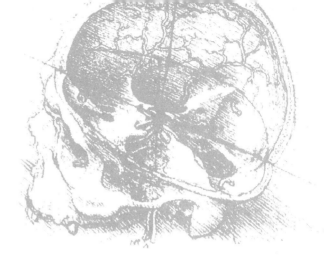

8

The Art
of Possession

Video game programming is like no other programming on Earth (or any other planet). Video games are so complex and use so much of the PC's resources that they must control every aspect of the computer. In this chapter, we're going to sharpen our skills as Cybersorcerers by learning about some of the low-level aspects of game programming, such as multitasking, the interrupt controller, the internal timer, and general real-time programming techniques.

Multitasking Fundamentals

A video game is a perfect example of a multitasking single-processor program. The word *multitasking* means to process many tasks at the same time. This definition is a bit loose, but the fact is that a single-processor computer can only process a single task at a single time. However, by virtue of the sheer speed of the PC, the PC can execute tasks sequentially so quickly that it seems as if they are all being executed at once. Figure 8-1 shows a representation of many tasks being executed in a sequential manner on the PC. A true multitasking computer would have multiple processors and hence be called a *multiprocessor* computer. In fact, multiprocessor computers do exist and are common in the workstation arena of computing. As an

FIGURE 8-1

A multitasking
single-processor
computer

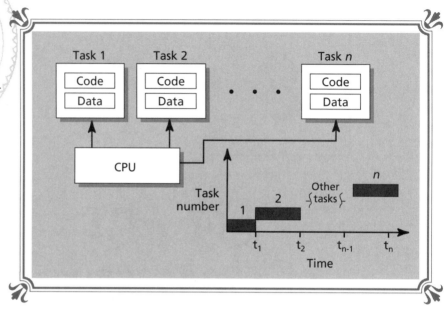

extreme example, the Connection Machine (Thinking Machines Inc.) has up to 64,000 processing elements!

A multiprocessor computer *can* execute more than one process at a time since a single processor can be allocated to each task, as shown in Figure 8-2. This is the ultimate video game machine. Alas, since the price tag is upwards of $100,000, we'll have to stick with the single-processor PC. But this isn't too bad, when we consider that a single 486 or Pentium processor is equivalent to a few dozen 8086s! Therefore, by time-multiplexing the resources of these advanced processors, we can achieve the same performance as a slow multiprocessor computer. Anyway, that's all academic. We need to stick to reality–well, at least Virtual Reality.

The PC under DOS has no means to accomplish multitasking. There is a form of crude multitasking that takes place when an interrupt occurs, but this doesn't really allow us to perform general multitasking. However, we don't care that DOS doesn't do multitasking, since we'll write our games in such a way that they are themselves multitasking on a functional level. Take a look at Figure 8-3. Here we see a diagram of a typical game event loop calling many subfunctions. These subfunctions are the elements that make up the game. There are calls to draw the objects, move them, process the input devices, and so forth. Moreover, since each of these tasks is repeated every game cycle, the game itself is acting like a small multitasking kernel.

This is the first concept to learn about game programming: the multitasking or real-time aspect of the game is synthesized by means of an event loop that repeats a sequence of tasks every cycle. Of course, the PC's ability to be interrupted by some

FIGURE 8-2

◉ ◉ ◉ ◉ ◉ ◉

*A multiprocessor-
multitasking
computer*

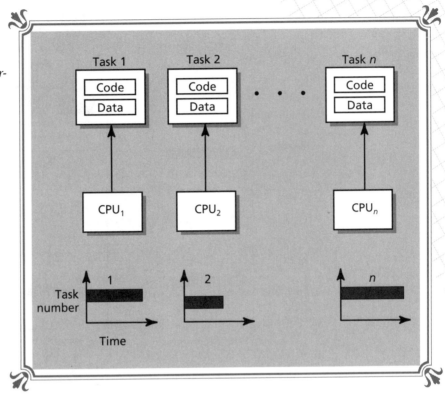
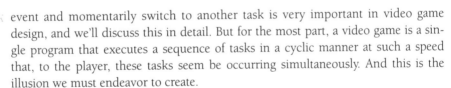

event and momentarily switch to another task is very important in video game design, and we'll discuss this in detail. But for the most part, a video game is a single program that executes a sequence of tasks in a cyclic manner at such a speed that, to the player, these tasks seem be occurring simultaneously. And this is the illusion we must endeavor to create.

Even though we'll process most of the game logic within the main event loop via calls to subfunctions, there are nevertheless times when some aspects of a game must be triggered by events either physical or temporal. For this reason, we must understand the interrupt structure of the PC and how to interface with it. By mastering this incantation, we can wield the full power of the PC and use it as a weapon against the competition!

PC Interrupts

The PC is equipped to handle interrupts as part of its normal processing stream. Interrupts can be generated either by a hardware event, such as a serial communi-

FIGURE 8-3

⊙ ⊙ ⊙ ⊙ ⊙ ⊙

*Multitasking
aspects of an
event loop*

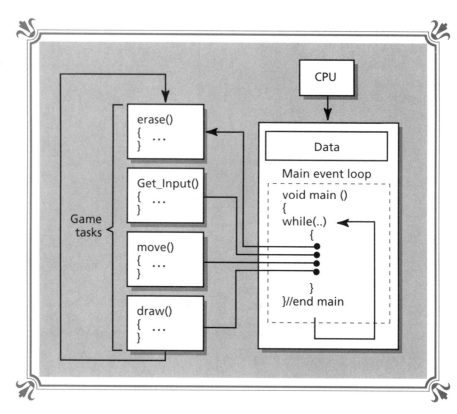

cations signal, or a software event, such as a call to *INT 21h*. In either case, the sequence of events is similar, as shown in Figure 8-4. An interrupt begins with the CPU pushing the flags register along with the address of the next instruction onto the stack. Then the CPU indexes into the interrupt table and vectors to the address of the appropriate *interrupt service routine* (ISR).

The ISR then processes the interrupt and performs its work. On completion, an *IRET* instruction is used to return to the interrupted program. The *IRET* instruction differs from *RET* in only one way–*IRET* restores the flags register from the stack, whereas *RET* doesn't. In reality, the only reason the flags register is saved by an interrupt is that this is the bare minimum that is needed to make a "context switch." However, it is up to your ISR to save any registers on the stack that may be altered by the ISR itself. This is necessary because the interrupted program has no idea that an interrupt occurred; and if the program was performing a calculation with the *AX* register and the contents of the register are modified by the ISR, then the resulting calculation will be in error. Thus, ISRs must save any CPU registers that they use and restore them on exit.

Now that we have a general idea of what interrupts are and how they are generated, let's focus on the two origins of interrupts–software and hardware.

FIGURE 8-4

◎ ◎ ◎ ◎ ◎ ◎

*Sequence of
events when an
interrupt occurs*

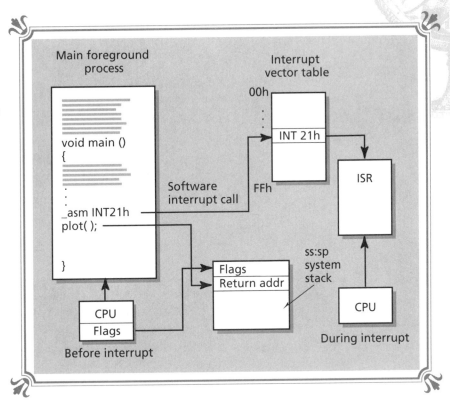

Software Interrupts

Software interrupts are generated by program calls on the PC. The interrupts themselves are initiated by a call with the *INT XXh* instruction. When the CPU comes
across an *INT XXh* instruction, the *XXh* is used as an index into the *interrupt vector
table*. This table holds the address of all the interrupt service routines within the
PC. Even though software interrupts aren't very useful for timing purposes or physical event tracking, they're a good way of creating a layer between the application
programs and the operating system. This extra layer allows future versions of the
operating system to add functions onto these interrupts without changing previous
software, since the interface can stay the same while the underlying code within
each interrupt routine can change radically.

For example, *INT 10h* is the video BIOS software interrupt, and regardless of
whether you wrote a program five years ago, yesterday, or today, the interface to the
interrupt is the same and the general functionality is the same. However, options
and features can be added to the ISR by the BIOS engineers without our being too
concerned, since in most cases the routines are kept downward compatible.

Basically, software interrupts are a good way to add functionality to the operating system at a system level rather than an application level such as the run-time library for C or the DLLs for Visual Basic. All programs have the ability to use the standard software interrupts.

Hardware Interrupts

Hardware interrupts are much more interesting than software interrupts, but amazingly enough, they work in the same way (from a programmer's point of view). The major difference is that hardware interrupts are generated by some physical event, such as another character in the communications buffer, a keyboard press, a DMA transfer request, and so forth. Hardware interrupts allow the CPU and system software to respond to real-world events. The implementation of hardware interrupts is rather interesting and worth a bit of explanation, so let's take a look.

The Programmable Interrupt Controller (PIC)

The PC is equipped with a chip called a *programmable interrupt controller* or PIC. The numerical designation of this chip is 8259A, which probably is completely arbitrary. Anyway, the PIC has a series of external connections. These connections are physically connected to devices on the PC, as shown in Figure 8-5. When one of the devices "pulls" on one of the PIC interrupt lines, the PIC sends a hardware interrupt request, along with the index number of the interrupt, to the CPU. The CPU uses this information to index into the interrupt table, and the appropriate ISR is called to service the hardware processed.

If you recall, we have already used a hardware interrupt to control the keyboard. The keyboard has a processor in it named the 8048, and when the keyboard senses a keypress (or release), this causes a scan code to be sent to the PC. When the PC receives the scan code, an interrupt is generated by the PIC, which causes the CPU to vector to the proper ISR (the address of which is located at location 09h of the interrupt table). The PIC is rather complex, but there are a couple aspects of it we need to understand. First, whenever an interrupt occurs, the PIC is inhibited so that it won't generate another interrupt. This state can be cleared by writing to one of the registers in the PIC called the *interrupt control register* or ICR. This register can be found at I/O port 20h. To reset the PIC and enable interrupts again, the ISR should write a 20h to the ICR. The value 20h is the *end of interrupt* (EOI) command that instructs the PIC to reenable interrupt processing.

The second register of interest on the PIC is the *interrupt mask register* or IMR. This register is located at I/O port 21h and has the bit assignments shown in Table 8-1.

FIGURE 8-5

The program-
mable interrupt
controller

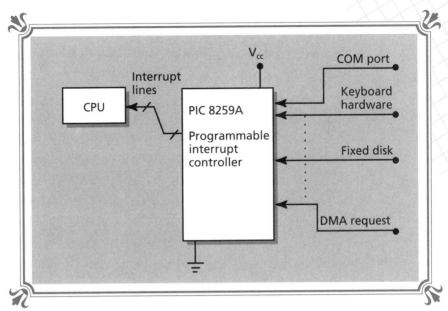

TABLE 8-1

The PIC interrupt
mask register at
I/O port 21h

Bit Number	Assignment
0	IRQ 0—Timekeeper interrupt
1	IRQ 1—Keyboard interrupt
2	IRQ 2—Reserved (used by vertical blank)
3	IRQ 3—COM2 or COM4 interrupts
4	IRQ 4—COM1 or COM3 interrupts
5	IRQ 5—Fixed disk interrupt (XT); 2nd parallel port in AT class
6	IRQ 6—Floppy disk interrupt
7	IRQ 7—Printer interrupt

Granted, the PC hasn't nearly the number of hardware interrupts that it has software interrupts, but these have sufficed for years and probably will suffice in the
future. Although there are other hardware interrupts that are not listed in Table 8-1,
called *non-maskable interrupts* or NMIs, we aren't going to cover them since they are
for more advanced operating system-related functions.

When the PC starts, the BIOS programs the IMR with the proper pattern depending on the PC's configuration. To enable an interrupt, the desired bit is cleared, and

to disable an interrupt, the desired bit is set. This is a bit backwards, but that's life. For example, if we wanted to turn the keyboard off, we could write this:

```
unsigned char data;  // used to read and write the data

// read the IMR register
data = _inp(0x21);

// clear the keyboard bit d1
data = data & 0xFD;

// write the new mask data back to IMR
_outp(0x21,data);
```

If you were to run this program, the keyboard wouldn't function anymore and you would have to reboot!

In general, the only thing we need to worry about with the PIC is enabling interrupts and sending the EOI command to the PIC when an ISR is complete. We have been referring to this phantom interrupt vector table for a while, so let's see where it is and how it works.

FIGURE 8-6

◎ ◎ ◎ ◎ ◎ ◎

The PC's interrupt vector table

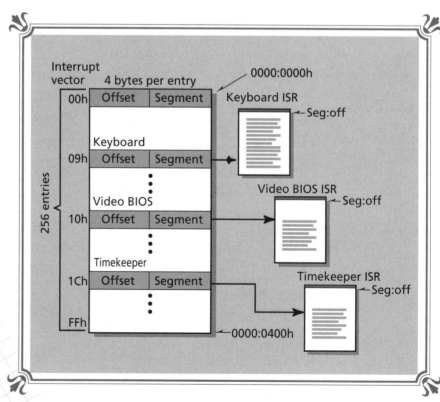

The Interrupt Vector Table

The interrupt vector table is located at 0000:0000 to 0000:0400 of the PC's memory map. The table consists of 256 entries (each entry is 4 bytes long) that are addresses to each ISR, 0 to 255. Each entry is in the form offset:segment; thus, each 4-byte entry is simply a pointer to an ISR. Figure 8-6 shows a graphic of the interrupt vector table with a few of the more important ISRs labeled. This table is the key to everything, and by manipulating it, we can totally control the PC. We can literally throw the operating system out and take complete control of every aspect of the PC. Although we don't need to do this, it's nice to know we can! Each of the 256 interrupt vectors has a function, and they are listed in Table 8-2.

TABLE 8-2
◇◇◇◇◇◇

Interrupt vector table

Interrupt Number	Address	Function
0H	**000-003H**	**Divide by zero**
1H	004-007H	Single step
2H	**008-00BH**	**Non-maskable interrupt**
3H	00C-00FH	Breakpoint
4H	**010-013H**	**Overflow**
5H	014-017H	Print screen
6H	018-01BH	Reserved on PC/XT; Invalid OPCode on 80286 and up
7H	01C-01FH	Math coprocessor not present
8H	**020-023H**	**Timer 18.2** (IRQ0)
9H	**024-027H**	**Keyboard**
AH	028-02BH	Cascaded IRQ2
BH	**02C-02FH**	**RS-232 Port 1**
CH	**030-033H**	**RS-232 Port 0**
DH	034-037H	Hard disk (XT class) LPT2 AT class
EH	038-03BH	Diskette
FH	03C-03FH	Parallel printer LPT1
10H	040-043H	Video I/O call
11H	044-047H	Equipment check call
12H	048-04BH	Memory check call

continued on next page

continued from previous page

Interrupt Number	Address	Function
13H	04C-04FH	Diskette I/O call
14H	050-053H	Serial I/O call
15H	54-057H	System services I/O call
16H	58-05BH	Keyboard I/O call
17H	05C-05FH	Parallel printer I/O call
18H	060-063H	Process boot failure
19H	064-067H	Bootstrap loader
1AH	068-06BH	Time of day call
1BH	**06C-06FH**	**Get control on break**
1CH	**070-073H**	**Get control on timer**
1DH	074-077H	Video initialization table
1EH	078-07BH	Diskette parameter table
1FH	07C-07FH	Graphics CHAR table
20H	080-083H	DOS program terminate
21H	084-087H	DOS universal function
22H	088-08BH	DOS terminate address
23H	08C-08FH	DOS CTRL BREAK
24H	090-093H	DOS fatal error vector
25H	094-097H	DOS absolute disk read
26H	098-09BH	DOS absolute disk write
27H	**09C-09FH**	**DOS terminate and stay resident**
28-3FH	A0-0FFH	Reserved for DOS
40-7FH	00-1FFH	Not used for normal processing
80-F0H	00-3C3H	Reserved by BASIC
F1-FFH	C4-3FFH	Not used for normal processing

Note: **INT 66h** is used by MIDPAK and DIGPAK when installed.

We only need to take control of a few of the PC's interrupts, such as the keyboard, internal timer, and the serial ports. However, I have highlighted a few others that might come in handy. So how does the table work? Whenever a software or hardware interrupt occurs, the CPU looks up the appropriate ISR vector in the table and vectors to it. For example, if a divide by zero occurs, the CPU saves the flags register on the stack along with the next instruction to be executed (the return address), and a jump is made to the address located in ISR vector 0000:0000-0000:0003. Hopefully, the address in these bytes points to a valid ISR routine that processes the divide by zero interrupt. And the ISR had better end with an *IRET* or a call to another ISR that does.

What we want to do as Cybersorcerers is change the entries in the table to point to our own ISRs rather than those that belong to DOS. We do this by accessing the interrupt vector table with a pointer and changing the ISR vectors. However, performing this seemingly simple operation can be dangerous since an interrupt could occur as we are making the change. The result would be a half-updated interrupt vector that would then be used, causing a jump to a random location in memory, resulting in an error or crash. Hence, a cleaner method must be used to perform these updates using operating system calls, but before we study them, let's talk about how an ISR is written in C.

Writing an Interrupt Service Routine in C

Luckily for us, we won't need to resort to pure assembly language to write interrupt service routines. Although in many cases we will write portions of a particular ISR using the inline assembler, there is support for ISRs within C itself. An ISR is no more than a function that performs a particular task and then returns. However, ISRs have a few special properties that must be observed:

* The ISR code must execute quickly and release control back to the foreground process as soon as possible.

* The ISR code must be *re-entrant*, meaning that the interrupt itself must be able to be interrupted by itself (which may occur in special cases) without crashing.

* The ISR must restore any data structures that it modifies.

* The ISR must issue an end of interrupt command 20h to the PIC at the exit of the ISR (in most cases–but, better safe than sorry).

In general, ISRs should be short and to the point. The whole idea of an ISR is to perform its task without the main foreground process being affected by its execution. The C language has a new keyword (_interrupt) which, when placed in a function declaration, takes care of the prolog and epilog code that an ISR must have (such as saving the CPU registers and using an *IRET* instead of a standard *RET* to terminate the ISR function). The shell for an ISR in the C language is shown in Listing 8-1.

LISTING 8-1 Minimum C implementation of an ISR

```
void far _interrupt ISR_Function(void)
{

_asm sti    ; re-enable interrupts

// ISR code goes here


// end of ISR code

// re-enable hardware interrupts by sending an EOI command to the PIC
_outp(PIC_ICR,PIC_EOI);

} // end ISR_Function
```

You will notice the function begins with a *STI* instruction. This tells the CPU to reenable interrupts. However, if we wish, we can inhibit interrupts while processing the ISR. This can be dangerous if an important interrupt occurs and isn't serviced, but is sometimes necessary in time-critical code that can't be interrupted. The disabling of interrupts can be accomplished through the use of the assembly language instruction *CLI*. Interrupts can then be reenabled with the *STI* instruction. Adding this to our ISR shell, the results are shown in Listing 8-2.

LISTING 8-2 The C ISR with interrupt disabling

```
void far _interrupt ISR_Function(void)
{

_asm cli    ; clear interrupt flag

// ISR code goes here
// end of ISR code

_asm sti    ; set interrupt flag

// re-enable hardware interrupts by sending an EOI command to the PIC
_outp(PIC_ICR,PIC_EOI);

} // end ISR_Function
```

Using one of the two shells shown in Listings 8-1 and 8-2, most interrupts can be written as if they were normal C functions. For example, the keyboard handler we created in Chapter 5 uses a shell similar to the first. By the way, the defines used in the shells are declared in BLACK8.H as:

```
#define PIC_ICR  0x20 // the interrupt control register
#define PIC_IMR  0x21 // the interrupt mask register
#define PIC_EOI  0x20 // end of interrupt command
```

All right, now we know how to write an ISR function. How can we install it into the interrupt vector table?

Installing an Interrupt Service Routine

Let's refresh our memories a little about the problems with manually changing interrupt vectors ourselves. The interrupt vector table is nothing more than a collection of 4-byte entries that spans 0000:0000 to 0000:0400 in the PC's memory. Thus, we can alias a pointer to this region and manipulate any of the interrupt vectors that we wish. However, there is a problem with this. If the PC is interrupted while the update is taking place and the interrupt happens to be the interrupt that we are updating, a system crash can occur. Hence, the update to the table must occur in a single instruction. There is no single instruction to do this, but there is a C function (based on a DOS call) that can install an interrupt service routine without danger of being interrupted by the PC.

The DOS-based C function accomplishes this by inhibiting all interrupts and using a clever method to update the interrupt vector. In any case, we will use the C function to install our ISRs. The name of the function is _dos_setvect() and has the following syntax:

```
_dos_setvect(unsigned interrupt_number, void (_interrupt _far
         *ISR_Function)());
```

If the syntax is a bit confusing, it basically reads, "send the interrupt number along with a pointer to the ISR function." For example, to install one of our ISR shells at interrupt 1Ch (the timekeeper), we can write:

```
_dos_setvect(0x1C, ISR_Function);
```

Once the ISR is installed, the old ISR vector will be lost, as shown in Figure 8-7. This isn't acceptable; we must find a way to save the old ISR. This can be done with the C function _dos_getvect(). It works in the opposite way that _dos_setvect() does. That is, instead of setting an interrupt vector, _dos_getvect() retrieves one. The syntax is,

```
void (_interrupt _far *_dos_getvect(unsigned interrupt_number))();
```

which simply returns a *FAR* pointer to the current ISR installed at location *interrupt_number*. For example, continuing with our previous example of redirecting the

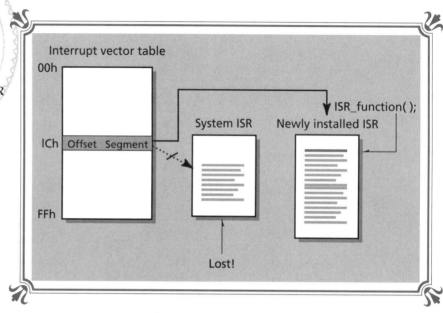

FIGURE 8-7

◎ ◎ ◎ ◎ ◎ ◎

Effect of installing an ISR without saving the old one

timekeeper interrupt, we can first save the old timekeeper ISR with the following code fragment:

```
void (_interrupt _far *Old_Time_ISR)();  // we'll place the old isr in here

// save old ISR
Old_Time_ISR = _dos_getvect(0x1C);

// install new ISR
_dos_setvect(0x1C, ISR_Function);
```

Finally, when a game or application exits back to DOS, we'll need to replace all of the old interrupt vectors that we changed. Let's see how.

Restoring an Interrupt Service Routine

As long as we save any ISRs that we update with new ones, we can restore the old ISR by using _dos_setvect() once again. However, this time instead of installing our own ISR, we reinstall the old DOS ISR that was originally there. Figure 8-8 shows this process graphically. First, the DOS ISR is saved in a variable. Then our new ISR is installed. Then when the game terminates, the old DOS ISR is reinstalled and the system is back to normal.

Again continuing with the ongoing example, we can reinstall the saved DOS timekeeper ISR with the following code:

```
_dos_setvect(0x1C,Old_Time_ISR);
```

FIGURE 8-8

Replacing an old system ISR

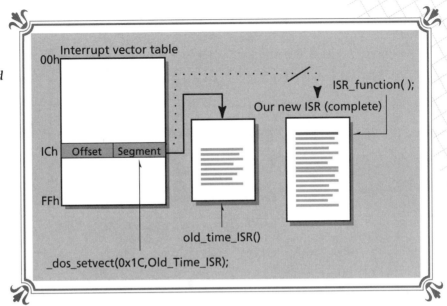

That's it! As a solid example of creating an ISR and installing it into the interrupt table, the following program, JELLY.C (Listing 8-3), installs a new timekeeper ISR at interrupt vector 1Ch. This interrupt will be called every 1/18 second. The ISR itself simply updates a pair of global variables that are used in the *main()* function of the program to move a creature on the screen. The executable of the code is called JELLY.EXE.

LISTING 8-3 Program that installs a new timekeeper ISR

```c
// JELLY.C - A demo of latching onto the timer interrupt 0x1C

// I N C L U D E S ///////////////////////////////////////////////////////////

#include <io.h>
#include <conio.h>
#include <stdio.h>
#include <stdlib.h>
#include <dos.h>
#include <bios.h>
#include <fcntl.h>
#include <memory.h>
#include <malloc.h>
#include <math.h>
#include <string.h>

#include "black3.h"
#include "black4.h"
```

continued on next page

continued from previous page

```c
#include "black8.h"


// G L O B A L S //////////////////////////////////////////////////////////////

pcx_picture image_pcx;  // general PCX image used to load background and imagery

sprite jelly;               // the jelly fish

int ISR_jelly_x = -20,  // global variables that track the position of the
    ISR_jelly_y = 100;  // jelly fish and are updated by the ISR

// this holds the old timer keeper isr

void (_interrupt _far *Old_Timer_ISR)();

///////////////////////////////////////////////////////////////////////////////

void _interrupt _far Jelly_ISR(void)
{
// this function will update the global jelly fish position variables and
// test if the jelly fish has moved off the screen, this function will be
// called once every timer tick

_asm sti  ; re-enable interrupts

///////////////////////////////////////////////////////

// move the jelly fish
if (++ISR_jelly_x > 320)
   ISR_jelly_x = -20;
ISR_jelly_y = ISR_jelly_y - 1 + rand()%3;

// test y bounds
if (ISR_jelly_y > 200)
    ISR_jelly_y=-20;
else
if (ISR_jelly_y < -20)
    ISR_jelly_y=200;

//////////////////////////////////////////////////

// re-enable pic
_outp(PIC_ICR,PIC_EOI);

} // end Jelly_ISR

// M A I N ///////////////////////////////////////////////////////////////////

void main(int argc, char **argv)
{
int index;          // loop variable
```

```
// set the graphics mode to mode 13h

Set_Graphics_Mode(GRAPHICS_MODE13);

// create the double buffer
Create_Double_Buffer(200);

// load the imagery for the jelly fish
PCX_Init((pcx_picture_ptr)&image_pcx);
PCX_Load("jelly.pcx", (pcx_picture_ptr)&image_pcx,1);

// initialize the jelly fish
Sprite_Init((sprite_ptr)&jelly,-20,100,16,16,0,0,0,0,0,0);

// extract the bitmaps for the speeder, there are 4 animation cells
for (index=0; index<4; index++)
    PCX_Get_Sprite((pcx_picture_ptr)&image_pcx,(sprite_ptr)&jelly,index,index,0);

// done with this PCX file so delete memory associated with it
PCX_Delete((pcx_picture_ptr)&image_pcx);

// install the jelly fish motion interrupt
Old_Timer_ISR = _dos_getvect(TIME_KEEPER_INT);
_dos_setvect(TIME_KEEPER_INT,Jelly_ISR);

// scan background before entering event loop
Sprite_Under_Clip((sprite_ptr)&jelly,double_buffer);

// put up exit instructions
Print_String_DB(80,2,9,"Hit any key to exit",1);

// main event loop, process until keyboard hit
while(!kbhit())
    {

    // do animation cycle

    // erase the jelly fish
    Sprite_Erase_Clip((sprite_ptr)&jelly,double_buffer);

    // move the jelly fish, note that we only copy global variables here
    // the variables themselves are modified by the ISR
    jelly.x = ISR_jelly_x;
    jelly.y = ISR_jelly_y;

    // animate the jelly fish
    if (++jelly.curr_frame == 4)
        jelly.curr_frame = 0;

    // ready to draw speeder, but first scan background under it
    Sprite_Under_Clip((sprite_ptr)&jelly,double_buffer);
    Sprite_Draw_Clip((sprite_ptr)&jelly,double_buffer,1);
```

continued on next page

continued from previous page

```
    // display double buffer
    Display_Double_Buffer(double_buffer,0);

    // lock onto 18 frames per second max
    Time_Delay(1);

    } // end while

// exit in a very cool way
Screen_Transition(SCREEN_DARKNESS);

// free up all resources

Sprite_Delete((sprite_ptr)&jelly);
Delete_Double_Buffer();

// restore the old isr
_dos_setvect(TIME_KEEPER_INT,Old_Timer_ISR);
Set_Graphics_Mode(TEXT_MODE);

} // end main
```

The program is rather simple, but we can do a lot with it. The beginning sets up the graphics and loads the imagery. Then the old timekeeper interrupt is saved, and the new ISR named *Jelly_ISR()* is installed in its place. Then the program falls into the main event loop. The event loop does nothing except draw the creature on the screen and animate it. However, the creature moves even though the position variables (*jelly.x,jelly.y*) are not explicitly updated by *main()*. This is because *Jelly_ISR()* is being called by the timekeeper interrupt, which itself is updating the global variables *ISR_jelly_x* and *ISR_jelly_y*. Then these variables are copied into the sprite's position variables at the correct time. Hence, we have created a crude form of multitasking: the main event loop is responsible for rendering the creature, while the ISR is responsible for moving it. An important detail to be learned from this demo that may not be apparent is that the precise moment of the interrupt isn't known relative to the program execution; thus, we can't guarantee that the interrupt will occur when the sprite is being erased, drawn, or animated. Consequently, we must buffer the position in a pair of global variables and, when the time is right, move them into the position variables of the creature's sprite structure. Figure 8-9 shows this process graphically. Notice that no matter when the global variables are updated, the "effect" of the update isn't propagated to the logic until the logic makes use of them.

The timer interrupt is one of the most important and useful interrupts in video games. In many cases, it's the only way to perform some task at a specific time with any precision. The timekeeper interrupt is used for such things as music systems, color palette updates, I/O device polling, and other similar operations that must be done on a regular basis. The only drawback to the timer interrupt is that it occurs once every 1/18.2 seconds or 55ms, which may not be fast enough. However, since

FIGURE 8-9

Use of message passing to nullify temporal invariances

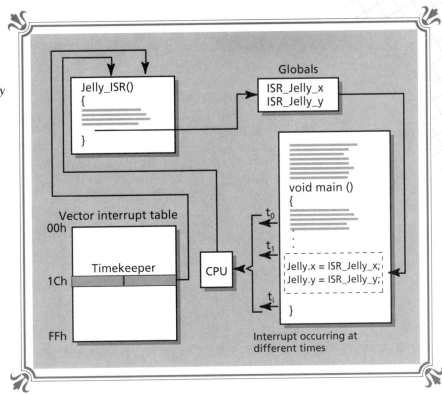

the timer interrupt is generated by a timer chip (the 8255), this rate can be changed by software. But we'll cover that a bit later.

The only problem with installing a new ISR is that many times the new ISR doesn't perform the tasks that the original ISR was meant to do. There are two solutions to this. The first solution is to make sure that any new ISR that is installed has the functionality of the old ISR in addition to performing any special tasks. The second and more common solution is to install the new ISR and chain it to the old one, so the menial tasks are performed by the old ISR. This is a common practice for the keyboard and timekeeper ISRs.

Chaining Interrupt Service Routines

The timer and keyboard are two of the most common interrupts that are latched onto when the game needs tight control of these resources. However, the way we've learned to latch onto these resources is quite brutal. In fact, we completely took them over without considering other programs or the responsibilities that the system interrupt handlers may have had. In the case of the keyboard ISR that we installed to create the keyboard driver in Chapter 5, completely taking over the

keyboard didn't have too much effect since that was the main goal. However, if the user had installed a TSR that installed its own ISR into the keyboard interrupt vector, then it wouldn't work anymore. Granted, we probably don't want or need TSRs we don't know about lurking around, but on the other hand, we should learn how to play nice with the other children.

The solution to the problem is to chain ISRs when applicable. Take a look at Figure 8-10, where we see two possible scenarios of installing an ISR. In one case, the old ISR is suspended in hyperspace while the newly installed one takes over. However, the second case depicted installs the new ISR on top of the old ISR. This allows the old ISR to be called after the newly installed ISR completes its tasks, performing any menial tasks that the new ISR doesn't. As Cybersorcerers, we aren't always that nice; we'll usually take over all the interrupts of interest and let the old system ISRs hang out to dry. But if we need to chain ISRs, it's nice to know how.

Chaining ISRs is very simple. Nothing more than a call to the previously saved ISR's address is needed at the end of the newly installed ISR. For example, let's see how we can create a chained timer ISR. First, we need to save the old timer ISR address, like this:

```
void (_interrupt _far *Old_ISR)();    // pointer to old ISR

// extract vector of timer interrupt 0x1C
Old_ISR = _dos_getvect(TIME_KEEPER_INT);
```

Also, assume that the new timer interrupt is called *Timer_ISR()*. To install it we would do the following:

```
_dos_setvect(TIME_KEEPER_INT, Timer_ISR());
```

That's it! You're probably saying, "What's the difference between the chained ISR and the standard one?" The difference is in the ISR itself. The definition of *Timer_ISR()* would look something like this:

```
void _interrupt _far Timer_ISR(void)
{

_asm sti ; re-enable interrupts
// do work

// end of work

// re-enable PIC

_outp(PIC_ICR,PIC_EOI);

// now call old interrupt and chain!

Old_ISR();

} // end Timer_ISR
```

FIGURE 8-10

◎ ◎ ◎ ◎ ◎ ◎

Chaining
interrupts

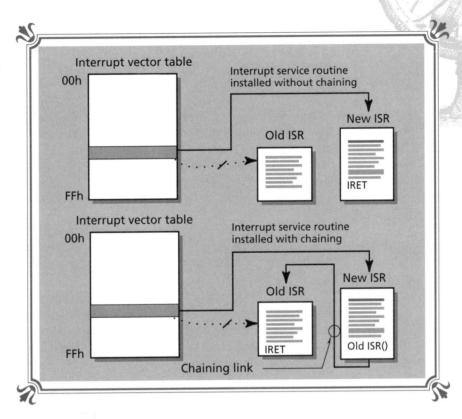

In essence, all we need to do is call the old ISR by creating a function invocation with the saved function pointer. The first ISR is called by the interrupt itself, and then at the tail end of the newly installed ISR, the old ISR is called. There is one interesting detail to note though. After the old ISR executes, it returns to the newly installed ISR, and the new ISR performs the final return to the operating system. If you do not wish this to occur, you can use the C function *_chain_intr()*, which will modify the stack such that the old ISR will directly return to the operating system when complete. Hence, if the ISR shell above were to take this into consideration, it would look like this:

```
void _interrupt _far Timer_ISR(void)
{
_asm sti ; re-enable interrupts

// do work

// end of work

// re-enable PIC
```

continued on next page

continued from previous page
```
_outp(PIC_ICR,PIC_EOI);

// now call old interrupt and chain!
_chain_intr(Old_ISR);

} // end Timer_ISR
```

Basically, _chain_intr() changes the stack so that the second ISR won't return to its calling point in the new ISR, but to the place where the original interrupt was issued in the game application. The actual stack manipulation is too low level, so we won't concern ourselves with it. Pretend it's magick! Reflecting upon this new information about interrupt chaining, we'll only need it in special cases. Most of the time, we'll want total control of the PC.

The Issues of Re-Entrancy and DOS Calls

We've mentioned that interrupt service routines must be re-entrant. This isn't totally true, especially if the newly installed ISR inhibits all interrupts while performing its task. However, for an ISR to be nonabusive to the system, it should be re-entrant or, in other words, be able to be interrupted by itself without a problem. Writing re-entrant functions can be easy and it can be hard. Fortunately for us, the problem of

FIGURE 8-11

⊙ ⊙ ⊙ ⊙ ⊙ ⊙

Interrupt being interrupted while executing a DOS call

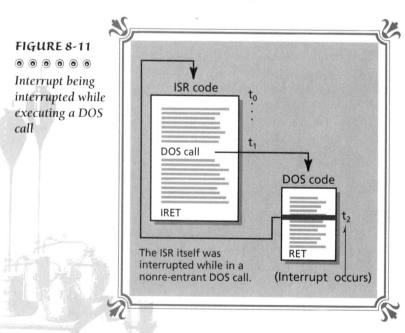

The ISR itself was interrupted while in a nonre-entrant DOS call.

(Interrupt occurs)

an interrupt interrupting itself seldom occurs (if at all). So we don't need to concern ourselves too much with re-entrant programming techniques, but as a caution, DOS calls should be avoided if at all possible within ISRs.

DOS calls are very slow and in general are not re-entrant. The combination of these two factors increases the probability of the same interrupt occurring while it's being processed. For example, say we wrote an ISR that took over the timekeeper interrupt. We basically have a maximum of 1/18 second to do something and exit. But imagine that we make a few DOS calls that are slow. They may take more than 1/18 second, and it's possible that the timekeeper interrupt itself could be reissued (see Figure 8-11).

Referring to the figure, we see that during the processing of the timekeeper interrupt on the first generated interrupt, it was again interrupted in the middle of a nonre-entrant DOS call. Therefore, not only did the interrupt routine take much too long, a DOS call has been reentered and chaos is bound to occur. The moral of the story is: stay away from DOS calls in ISRs, and write ISR code that is as fast and efficient as possible.

The Vertical Blank Interrupt

Even though the keyboard and timer interrupts are the most popular interrupts to latch onto, there is another that is even better (when it works). This interrupt is called the *vertical blank interrupt* or Vblank. The problem is that it isn't supported on all VGA cards and assuming that it exists is a gamble. However, the concept of it is so important that we are going to discuss it and see an implementation of it.

The vertical blanking period or interval occurs when the raster is retracing after drawing the entire screen (see Figure 8-12). The time it takes the raster to perform the retrace is about 5 to 10 percent of the time it takes to draw the screen. Thus, this is an opportune time to update the video buffer, since the VGA hardware isn't accessing the video RAM. Moreover, an interrupt that is connected to the vertical blank will occur precisely every 1/70 second (if the VGA is in mode 13h), which is a great time base for games.

So which interrupt in the interrupt vector table is the vertical blank interrupt? It's number 0x0A, which is reserved for IRQ 2. This means that any device attached to IRQ 2 will generate an interrupt, and the ISR installed at 0x0A will be called. Of course, the PIC's interrupt mask register would have to be enabled, but that's as easy as clearing a bit. The problem is forcing the VGA to generate the interrupt in the first place! To instruct the VGA to generate a vertical blank interrupt takes a bit of trickery but can be done in a few lines of code. Unfortunately, some VGAs work one way and others work another way. The ramifications of this fact are that some bits must be on or off depending on the manufacturer. Alas, there is a bit of hardware dependence. But don't be too intimidated; most of the time the Vblank will

FIGURE 8-12
◎ ◎ ◎ ◎ ◎ ◎

*The vertical
retrace period*

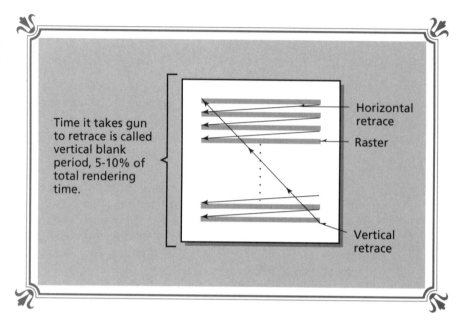

Time it takes gun
to retrace is called
vertical blank
period, 5-10% of
total rendering
time.

Horizontal
retrace

Raster

Vertical
retrace

work the way we're going to learn it does. Only in a few cases do the code and bit settings need tweaking.

All right, here we go. To enable a vertical blank interrupt, we must do three things:

1. Install a vertical blank interrupt handler at location 0x0A in the interrupt vector table.

2. Enable the interrupt on the PIC by clearing bit d2 (the third bit from the right) of the PIC interrupt mask register (IMR).

3. Clear the d4 (vertical blank interrupt latch) and d5 (vertical blank interrupt enable) bits of the VGAs Vertical Retrace End Register (in the CRT controller). The bit designations are shown in Table 8-3.

TABLE 8-3
◇ ◇ ◇ ◇ ◇ ◇

*Bit designations of
the Vertical Retrace
End Register at
index 0x11 of the
CRT controller*

Bit Number	Function
d7	Write protect index
d6	Alternate refresh rate
d5	Enable vertical blank interrupt (0 = Enable)
d4	Clear vertical blank interrupt latch (0 = Clear)
d3–d0	Vertical retrace end

When the vertical blank interrupt occurs, the system calls the ISR pointed to in the interrupt vector table. The ISR has to perform two tasks. First, it should make sure that the interrupt that caused it to be called was in fact the vertical blank interrupt. This is a safety precaution, since other devices may also be connected to IRQ 2, causing phantom interrupts. This test can be performed by looking at bit d7 of the VGA's input status register 0 at I/O port 0x3C2. If you remember, the *Wait_For_Vertical_Retrace()* function uses this very register. The second part of processing a vertical blank interrupt is resetting the vertical interrupt latch at bit d4 of the Vertical Retrace End Register in the CRT controller. This is done by writing a 0 to the bit.

Before we delve into writing a vertical blank interrupt program, there is one detail that we must adhere to. This detail is that during the manipulations of the bits in the various registers, we only modify the bits that we are interested in while leaving the others alone. This is of great importance, especially when manipulating the PIC's interrupt mask register. One false move with those bits and the whole computer can be locked up! For that reason, we will be using the *SET_BITS()* and *RESET_BITS()* macros in the program so that only the bits we wish altered are in fact changed. In general, this is a good programming practice. If you aren't sure what will happen if you inadvertently change bits in a register, then don't do it!

The program in Listing 8-4 demonstrates the vertical blank interrupt. The name of the program is VBLANK.EXE and the source code is called VBLANK.C. The program does nothing more than install a vertical blank interrupt handler that increments a counter and prints the number of times the vertical blank has been called. The program only works on one of my two VGA cards, so it might not work on yours at all. If it doesn't, make sure to at least understand the process of installing the interrupt. To create your own executable, include the library modules BLACK3.C and BLACK8.C. The source code is shown here for review.

LISTING 8-4 *Demo of the vertical blank interrupt*

```
// VBLANK.C - demo of the vertical blank interrupt supported by a few VGA cards

// I N C L U D E S ///////////////////////////////////////////////////////////////

#include <io.h>
#include <conio.h>
#include <stdio.h>
#include <stdlib.h>
#include <dos.h>
#include <bios.h>
#include <fcntl.h>
#include <memory.h>
#include <malloc.h>
#include <math.h>
#include <string.h>
```

continued on next page

continued from previous page

```c
#include "black3.h"
#include "black8.h"

// D E F I N E S ////////////////////////////////////////////////////////////

#define VERTICAL_BLANK_INTERRUPT    0x0A   // index of vblank in vector table
#define CRT_VERTICAL_END            0x11   // register with vblank enable bits

// G L O B A L S ////////////////////////////////////////////////////////////

void (_interrupt far *Old_Vertical)();
// F U N C T I O N S ////////////////////////////////////////////////////////

void _interrupt _far Vertical_Blank(void)
{
// this function is the vertical blank handler
static int count = 0; // used to count the vertical blanks
char buffer[64];      // used to print a string
unsigned char data;   // used to read data

_asm sti ; // re-enable interrupts

// reset latch on VGA
_outp(CRT_CONTROLLER,CRT_VERTICAL_END);
data = _inp(CRT_CONTROLLER+1);
data = RESET_BITS(data,0x10);
_outp(CRT_CONTROLLER+1,data);

// do whatever you want here, but make it quick!
sprintf(buffer,"Number of vertical blanks is %d",count++);
Print_String(0,0,10,buffer,1);

// end process vertical blank

// re-enable interrupts on PIC, send end of interrupt command EOI, 20h
_outp(PIC_ICR, PIC_EOI);

} // end Vertical_Blank

// M A I N ///////////////////////////////////////////////////////////////////

void main(void)
{
unsigned char data;

// set the graphics mode to mode 13h
Set_Graphics_Mode(GRAPHICS_MODE13);

// save old vertical blank interrupt
Old_Vertical = _dos_getvect(VERTICAL_BLANK_INTERRUPT);

// set new interrupt
_dos_setvect(VERTICAL_BLANK_INTERRUPT,Vertical_Blank);
```

```
// enable interrupt on VGA
_outp(CRT_CONTROLLER,CRT_VERTICAL_END);
data = (unsigned char)_inp(CRT_CONTROLLER+1);

data = RESET_BITS(data,0x20);    // for your VGA you may need to SET this bit
_outp(CRT_CONTROLLER+1,data);

data = RESET_BITS(data,0x10);
_outp(CRT_CONTROLLER+1,data);

// enable interrupt on PIC, i.e. enable IRQ 2

data = (unsigned char)_inp(PIC_IMR);
data = RESET_BITS(data,0x40);
_outp(PIC_IMR,data);

while(!kbhit());

// disable interrupts from VGA
_outp(CRT_CONTROLLER,CRT_VERTICAL_END);
data =(unsigned char)_inp(CRT_CONTROLLER+1);

data = SET_BITS(data,0x20);     // for your VGA you may need to reset this bit
_outp(CRT_CONTROLLER+1,data);

// disable vertical blank interrupt on PIC

data =(unsigned char)_inp(PIC_IMR);
data = SET_BITS(data,0x04);
_outp(PIC_IMR,data);

// restore old vector
_dos_setvect(VERTICAL_BLANK_INTERRUPT,Old_Vertical);

Set_Graphics_Mode(TEXT_MODE);

} // end main
```

The program begins by setting the graphics mode to 13h and then saving the old VBI vector at 0x0A (which is probably NULL). At this point the vertical blank interrupt is enabled on the VGA, and the proper bit is cleared in the PIC's interrupt mask register to allow the hardware interrupt IRQ 2 to occur. Then the program sits in the tight loop,

```
while(!kbhit());
```

until a key is pressed. However, if your VGA supports vertical blanks, you will see a green line of text displaying a real-time count of the number of vertical blanks that have occurred. Thus, the PC is again performing a crude form of multitasking. Finally, when a key is hit, the program resets both the VGA and the PIC and reinstalls the old ISR that was originally in the interrupt vector table.

It is truly a shame that the vertical blank interrupt doesn't work on all VGA cards. I admit I haven't tried it on new cards, but I hope it works, since this interrupt can be a vital help in the video updating and synchronization aspects of a game.

The Internal Timer

The PC has come a long way, but much of its design still looks like something you would find in an old issue of BYTE magazine! One of its flaws is the lack of onboard timers. Video games are extremely time-critical applications. We must time a great many events in a game–something the PC doesn't lend itself to easily. For example, we have been placing the function call,

```
Time_Delay(1);
```

at the end of most of the demos so far. This has the effect of locking the demo at a frame rate of no higher than 18 FPS. We do this because the timer function is based on the PC's internal timer, which is itself running at 18.2 clicks per second or 18.2 Hz. The only problem with this is that 18.2 clicks per second is an eternity in computer time. We need something with a higher resolution, at least 30 or 60 Hz. The question is, how do we manipulate the PC's internal timer? And are there extra timers so we can have multiple time bases? The answer to the second question is yes and no. Yes, there are other timers, but we can't modify them because they are being used for system control. The answer to the first question takes a bit of explaining, so let's start from the beginning.

The PC has a chip in it called the 8253 (or at least there is a chunk of silicon that emulates this chip in new board designs). The 8253 has, among other things, three counters numbered 0, 1, and 2 and a control register. The designations and I/O ports of these counters are shown in Table 8-4.

TABLE 8-4
✧✧✧✧✧✧
The PC's counters

Counter Number	I/O Port	Function
0	40h	System timer
1	41h	Dynamic memory refresh
2	42h	Tape drive rate controller/speaker driver

The control port is located at I/O port 43h.

With a paltry three counters at our disposal, there's not a lot we can do. First, counters 1 and 2 are already in use (especially counter 1). The only counter we can really use is counter 0, which is already being used to generate the system timer interrupt. Currently, the counter is counting at a rate of 18.2 Hz. Changing this rate is a matter of understanding how the 8253 is programmed to generate this rate. It turns out that with a bit of work and an Intel chip guide, we can figure out how to program the chip's counters for any rate. Moreover, the counters not only count but can be used to generate interrupts and other interesting timing structures.

We won't be interested in all the neat things that can be done with the counters. We only want to know how to reprogram the rate of counter 0. To accomplish this, take a look at Table 8-5, which describes the bit designations of the control register.

TABLE 8-5
❖❖❖❖❖

Bit designations of the 8253's control register at I/O port 43h

Bit Number(s)	Function
d7-d6	Counter select
	00—Counter 0
	01—Counter 1
	10—Counter 2
	11—Invalid!
d5-d4	Read/write mode
	00—Counter latch operation
	01—Read/write least significant byte of counter
	10—Read/write most significant byte of counter
	11—Read/write least then most significant byte
d3-d1	Counter operation mode
	000—Interrupt on terminal count
	001—Hardware retriggerable one-shot
	X10—Rate generator
	X11—Square wave output
	100—Software retriggerable strobe
	101—Hardware retriggerable strobe
d0	Counting base
	0—Count in binary
	1—Count using binary coded decimal (BCD)

Most of the information in Table 8-5 will only make sense to an electrical engineer, so don't worry about things like strobes and one-shots. We only need to understand how to program counter 0 for a different rate. This is done in the following sequence of steps. First the new rate is computed as a 16-bit value (a pair of bytes, high and low). These bytes are derived by taking the desired frequency and dividing into 1.19318 MHz. This is the frequency of the oscillator input into the 8253. Figure 8-13 shows the frequency division graphically. The value in the counter register is used to divide down the input frequency of 1.19318 MHz. The result of this division is used as the output of the 8253. Hence, if we wanted to find the proper value to program the 8253 so it would generate an output of 100 Hz, we would compute the following quotient (notice that we truncate the decimal portion):

$$\text{16 bit counter value} = \frac{1.19318 \times 10^6}{100 \text{ Hz}} = 11931 = \text{2E9Bh}$$

Using the above technique, we can come up with a set of 16-bit values that can be used to program the counters at different rates. If you look in BLACK8.H, you will find the following values already defined:

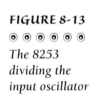

FIGURE 8-13

◎ ◎ ◎ ◎ ◎ ◎

The 8253 dividing the input oscillator

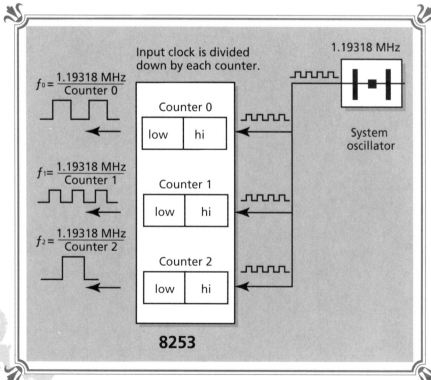

Input clock is divided down by each counter.

$f_0 = \dfrac{1.19318 \text{ MHz}}{\text{Counter 0}}$

Counter 0

| low | hi |

$f_1 = \dfrac{1.19318 \text{ MHz}}{\text{Counter 1}}$

Counter 1

| low | hi |

$f_2 = \dfrac{1.19318 \text{ MHz}}{\text{Counter 2}}$

Counter 2

| low | hi |

1.19318 MHz

System oscillator

8253

```
#define TIMER_120HZ    0x26D7  // 120 hz
#define TIMER_100HZ    0x2E9B  // 100 hz
#define TIMER_60HZ     0x4DAE  // 60 hz
#define TIMER_50HZ     0x5D37  // 50 hz
#define TIMER_40HZ     0x7486  // 40 hz
#define TIMER_30HZ     0x965C  // 30 hz
#define TIMER_20HZ     0xE90B  // 20 hz
#define TIMER_18HZ     0xFFFF  // 18.2 hz (slowest possible)
```

So how do we program these values into the 8253? It is a two-step process. The 8253 can only accept one byte at a time; therefore, the 16-bit values are sent as a pair of bytes: first the low byte then the high byte. If you take a look at bits d5 and d4 of the 8253's control register, they are used to select the exact way that bytes will be written to the counters. We are going to use the method of "least then most significant byte" sequence or mode 11. The next aspect of programming a timer is setting the rest of the bits, and to make a long story short, the bits should be set for binary counting/rate generator. Before we move on to writing the function that reprograms the counters, let's see the remaining defines that are declared in BLACK8.H, so we are on the same page!

```
#define TIMER_CONTROL  0x43  // the 8253's control register
#define TIMER_SET_BITS 0x3C  // the bit pattern that will place the timer into
                             // binary counting with counter load sequence of
                             // low byte then high byte

#define TIMER_COUNTER_0  0x40  // counter 0
#define TIMER_COUNTER_1  0x41  // counter 1
#define TIMER_COUNTER_2  0x42  // counter 2
```

As you see, the defines are simply the I/O ports and some constants to make the cryptic work of bit manipulating easier to see. We're now ready to write a function to reprogram the timer chip. To be general, we'll write it so that any counter can be programmed, even though we won't program any counter but 0 (right?). Listing 8-5 contains the function.

LISTING 8-5 Function to reprogram the 8253's counters

```
void Timer_Program(int timer,unsigned int rate)
{
// this function re-programs the internal timer

// first program the timer to mode 2 - binary and data loading sequence of
// low byte then high byte
_outp(TIMER_CONTROL, TIMER_SET_BITS);
// write least significant byte of the new rate to the counter register
_outp(timer,LOW_BYTE(rate));

// and now the most significant byte
_outp(timer,HI_BYTE(rate));

} // end Timer_Program
```

The function takes two parameters. The first is the counter to be programmed and the second is the new rate. For example, to reprogram counter 0 to 100 Hz, we can write:

```
Timer_Program(TIMER_COUNTER_0,TIMER_100HZ);
```

And instantly time will start moving very quickly. In fact, if you use a utility to watch the time on the PC, you will notice that it has been sped up about five times or, to be exact:

100/18.2 = 5.49 times

This is because the newly programmed rate of 100 Hz is causing the timer interrupt to occur more frequently, and thus the PC's time is moving faster than normal. This is the side effect of reprogramming the internal timer at counter 0. The system time will get out of whack. The solution to this is to keep track of time ourselves when we reprogram the timer and restore the proper time when our application exits.

Programming the Timer

Most of the time (pun intended) we'll reprogram the internal timer to run at a rate that is more conducive to some time-critical element of the video game, such as the frame rate or some event that occurs periodically. For example, MIDPAK reprograms the timer to a rate of 120h or 288 Hz (which in my opinion is a bit much). The reason 288 Hz is necessary for music is to keep up with the subtle changes in the MIDI music that is generating the sound. The only problem with such a high rate is that the PC is being interrupted 288 times a second, and this can be quite a strain on the application. The Creative Labs sound driver SBFMDRV.COM only runs at 60h or 96 Hz, which is much easier on the system.

As an example of programming the internal timer, the following program, TIMER.EXE, allows you to select one of the defined counter rates and reprogram the internal timer. The source code is named TIMER.C and is shown in Listing 8-6.

LISTING 8-6 Program that allows you to change the timer rate

```
// TIMER.C - A demo of reprogramming the PC's internal timer

// I N C L U D E S ////////////////////////////////////////////////////////////

#include <io.h>
#include <conio.h>
#include <stdio.h>
#include <stdlib.h>
#include <dos.h>
#include <bios.h>
```

```c
#include <fcntl.h>
#include <memory.h>
#include <malloc.h>
#include <math.h>
#include <string.h>

#include "black8.h"

// M A I N ///////////////////////////////////////////////////////////////////

void main(void)
{

int done=0,      // exit flag
    selection;   // user input variable

// main event loop

while(!done)
    {
    // display menu

    printf("\nPC Timer Re-Programming Utility\n");
    printf("\n1 - Program timer to 120HZ.");
    printf("\n2 - Program timer to 100HZ.");
    printf("\n3 - Program timer to 60HZ.");
    printf("\n4 - Program timer to 50HZ.");
    printf("\n5 - Program timer to 40HZ.");
    printf("\n6 - Program timer to 30HZ.");
    printf("\n7 - Program timer to 20HZ.");
    printf("\n8 - Program timer to 18HZ.");
    printf("\n9 - Exit program.");
    printf("\n\nSelect one?");

    // get input
    scanf("%d",&selection);

    // what rate did user select?
    switch(selection)
        {
        case 1: // set timer to 120hz
            {
            Timer_Program(TIMER_COUNTER_0,TIMER_120HZ);
            } break;
        case 2: // set timer to 100hz
            {
            Timer_Program(TIMER_COUNTER_0,TIMER_100HZ);
            } break;

        case 3: // set timer to 60hz
            {
            Timer_Program(TIMER_COUNTER_0,TIMER_60HZ);
```

continued on next page

continued from previous page

```
                    } break;

            case 4: // set timer to 50hz
                    {
                    Timer_Program(TIMER_COUNTER_0,TIMER_50HZ);
                    } break;

            case 5: // set timer to 40hz
                    {
                    Timer_Program(TIMER_COUNTER_0,TIMER_40HZ);
                    } break;

            case 6: // set timer to 30hz
                    {
                    Timer_Program(TIMER_COUNTER_0,TIMER_30HZ);
                    } break;

            case 7: // set timer to 20hz
                    {
                    Timer_Program(TIMER_COUNTER_0,TIMER_20HZ);
                    } break;

            case 8: // set timer to 18hz
                    {
                    Timer_Program(TIMER_COUNTER_0,TIMER_18HZ);
                    } break;

            case 9: // exit program
                    {
                    done=1;

                    } break;

            default:
                    {
                    printf("\nInvalid Selection!\n");
                    } break;

            } // end switch

        } // end while

} // end main
```

The program is so simple it's not worth reviewing. About the only thing the program does is obtain user input and use it to select the rate at which to program counter 0. Just one caution: when this program exits, the timer will run at the last rate you programmed; hence, if you want the system to run at its standard rate of 18.2 Hz, select command 8 before exiting.

Time Tracking

We have mentioned event timing from time to time, but we haven't written any specific software to implement it. In many situations we may need to compute the amount of time a process has taken or allow some process to execute for a specific amount of time. For example, we use the function *Time_Delay()* at the end of most of our demos to lock the demos at a frame rate of no more than 18 FPS. However, the downfall to this approach is that if the game processing takes 50 milliseconds (ms), and then at the end of the game loop another 55 milliseconds is taken up during the call to *Time_Delay()* with a parameter of 1, then the maximum frame rate will be:

$$\frac{1}{50 \text{ ms} + 55 \text{ ms}} = 9 \text{ FPS}$$

Again, this occurs because the game logic and rendering takes some amount of time, and this time must be added onto the time delay at the end of the game. A better solution is to lock a game at a specific frame rate by timing the events from the start of the event loop to the end of it, and if the elapsed time is greater than or equal to the desired delay time (which results in a specific frame rate), the next cycle of the event loop is processed. However, if less than the required time has elapsed, a *while()* or similar structure waits until the specified amount of time has passed. As an example, take a look at the following fragment:

```
// main event loop

while(!done)
     {
     // obtain starting time

     start_time = Timer_Query();

     // do the standard operations in a game loop

     Erase_Objects();
     Move_Objects();
     Draw_Objects();
     Draw_Screen();
     // end main portion of game loop

     // now determine if a clock tick has passed

     while ((Timer_Query() - start_time)<WAIT_TIME);

     } // end main event loop
```

The above fragment functions by first saving the current time with the function *Timer_Query()*, and then the main game logic is executed. Now the timing aspect of the program comes into play. Instead of simply making a call to *Time_Delay()* (with the desired number of ticks), the starting time is continually subtracted from the current time until the desired number of ticks has passed. Thus, if during the execution of the logic portion of the event loop the desired execution time of the program was already used up, the waiting loop would evaluate as true and the event loop would continue.

On the other hand, if the logic portion of the code only took up a few milliseconds and we had set *WAIT_TIME* to 3 clicks (3*55 ms), which is roughly 165 ms, then the *while()* loop would wait until the time expired. If you are getting a bit confused by the use of the constant 55 ms, remember that it is the amount of time it takes for one clock tick with the default setting of the system timer–that is, 1/18.2 = 55 ms when rounded up.

Of course, if we had programmed the PC's timer with a rate of 100 Hz using the *Timer_Program()* function, the resolution of the timer becomes 10 ms; thus, a delay of 3 system clicks would equal 30 ms, and if this were used to control the frame rate at the end of an event loop, the frame rate would be roughly 33 FPS.

Another use of time tracking is "timing out." As noted, there are many processes that we may want to time in a video game. For example, we may want to give a player only a certain amount of time to solve a puzzle, or maybe we want to allot only a certain amount of time to make a MODEM connection. It's up to you, but time tracking and the software to implement it is a necessity in a video game. Luckily, the software to track time is nothing more than a single variable lookup. The function *Time_Delay()* uses a memory location in the PC at 0000:046Ch, which contains a 32-bit value of the number of ticks from 1970 (don't ask me why). We don't care about the absolute meaning of the data, just the relative meaning. We know, for instance, if the value increments by 10, then 10 clock ticks must have passed since the last time we read it. Furthermore, since we know a clock tick is roughly 55 ms, then we can deduce that 550 ms have passed since the last reading.

With this information, all we really need to do is dereference a pointer aliased to 0000:046Ch whenever we want to know the current time in clicks. Although this works, a bit cleaner interface would be to use a function (in case that variable location changes some day). The *Timer_Query()* function is shown in Listing 8-7.

LISTING 8-7 Function to query the current time of the PC in clicks

```
long Timer_Query(void)
{
// this function is used to record the current time

long far *clock = (long far *)0x0000046CL; // address of timer
```

```
return(*clock);

} // end Timer_Query
```

The function takes no parameters and simply returns the current value in the system time variable. There is one important detail that must not be overlooked. The system timer variable will change at a rate that is equal to the value programmed into the timer chip at counter 0. Hence, if we change the counter, we had better take note of it when using the *Timer_Query()* or *Time_Delay()* functions in our code, since they will be operating in a different time scale than the default of 18.2 clicks per second.

Background Processing

One of the main goals of this chapter is to learn the fundamental techniques to gain temporal control of the PC. And I think that we are starting to learn why interrupts and reprogramming the timer are important, but let's discuss briefly a few applications of all this sorcery.

We learned that a video game can be thought of as an entire environment unto itself. This environment is responsible for one thing, and that's running a game. The game consists of a set of modules that are each executed for a period of time in a cyclic manner, as shown in Figure 8-14. Thus, the game is a form of a multitasking kernel, and the tasks that are processed make up the game itself. However, the sin-

FIGURE 8-14

◉ ◉ ◉ ◉ ◉ ◉

Cyclic execution of tasks

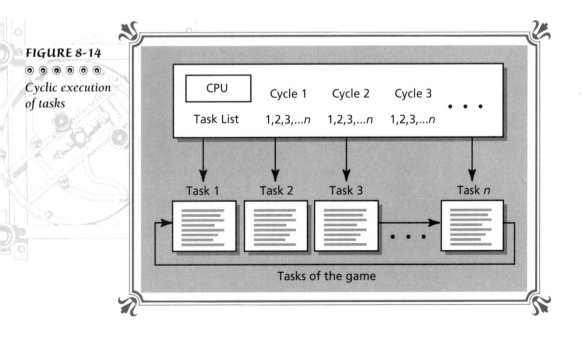

gle drawback to this setup is that the game logic doesn't have a good grasp on time. For example, if a light is supposed to blink every 20 seconds, it's hard for the program to make this happen since the game logic may be processing an explosion at the time the light is supposed to blink.

Of course, the solution to the problem is to have an interrupt with enough resolution to process all of the events that must occur at regular intervals regardless of the state of the game. For example, the music system that we're using, MIDPAK, uses the timer interrupt to process the MIDI music. If MIDPAK didn't do this, the game program would have to do the processing. And if the game started slowing down because of complex graphics or lots of explosions, then so would the sound. However, if the sound system is attached to an interrupt, the speed of the game is irrelevant. The interrupt will occur like clockwork no matter what the CPU is doing. This is because the interrupt by definition will interrupt anything that is occurring. That's a brutal statement!

As another example, imagine we have a game with a lot of color palette animation. This animation can and should be done by an interrupt (as long as the animation is passive). Figure 8-15 shows two possible situations the same game can get

FIGURE 8-15

⊙ ⊙ ⊙ ⊙ ⊙ ⊙

*Interrupts
occurring on cue*

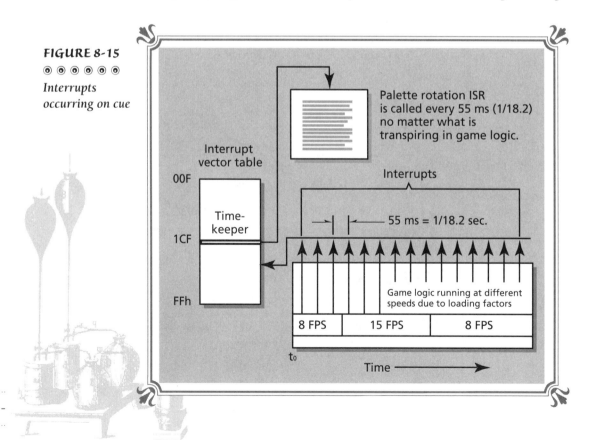

Palette rotation ISR
is called every 55 ms (1/18.2)
no matter what is
transpiring in game logic.

Interrupt
vector table

00F

Time-
keeper

1CF

FFh

Interrupts

55 ms = 1/18.2 sec.

Game logic running at different
speeds due to loading factors

| 8 FPS | 15 FPS | 8 FPS |

t_0

Time ⟶

into at different times. Due to the current state of the game, in one case it has slowed down to 8 FPS, while in the other case it has slowed to 15 FPS. In both cases if the palette animation were done by the main game logic itself, these updates would also occur at 8 or 15 FPS, which may be unacceptable and visually bothersome. However, if we have reprogrammed the timer for 60 Hz and latched the color animation ISR onto it, at least the color animation will occur at 60 Hz no matter what is happening to the game. Of course, we must realize that we don't want to make interrupt functions too complex or long. The idea of background tasks using ISRs is to keep them relatively simple and short.

In conclusion, background processes that are based on interrupts should be used for tasks that we never want to see slow down or for tasks that must occur at some specific interval no matter how much the game logic is loading the system and CPU. I use background tasks in my games for animations that aren't part of the game logic, such as shooting stars, birds, color changes, screen shakes, and so forth. Try to keep your background tasks at the same level of complexity. For example, don't try to render a 3D view in an ISR!

We have almost completed our discussion of interrupts and timing; now we are going to change gears a little and talk about some techniques that are necessary evils in game programming. The first is writing self-contained or autonomous functions.

Autonomous Functions and Programming Techniques

You're probably getting pretty excited about writing your first game, even though we haven't begun the 3D portion of our studies. However, before we bury ourselves in a full game (which we will do in the next chapter), let's take a look at some programming techniques that will make life easier during the creation of game code.

In general, writing games isn't like writing other pieces of software. As Cybersorcerers we must break a lot of rules and make up some as we go. This is because we must squeeze every particle of power from the PC. The result: we may use some questionable programming techniques. But their performance won't be! I'm going to give you a list of dos and don'ts when writing game software and functions.

✤ Don't add error detection logic unless an error is going to occur. You don't have time to test for errors in a game. The only error checking should be done during initialization and user input if possible.

✤ Use global variables freely. Passing parameters to a function that simply plots a pixel will probably take more time than plotting the pixel!

✣ Use 32-bit fixed point math instead of floating point where possible. Even on 486 and Pentium processors, 32-bit fixed point is faster than floating point in most cases. We will learn about the mechanics of fixed point math in later chapters.

✣ Try to use look-up tables with precomputed values where possible, especially for mathematically intensive computations such as trigonometric tables and square root functions.

✣ Use inline assembly language for time-critical operations such as graphics and I/O. However, shy away from assembly language for AI and general game logic.

✣ Try to use the smallest memory model possible. The MEDIUM memory model is the best choice in most cases, but if you can squeeze your code into 64K, by all means use the SMALL model.

✣ Most of the time in a game is spent in rendering graphics. Take the time to optimize these sections. Don't waste effort optimizing AI algorithms and general game logic; these won't give you large enough returns for the time investment.

✣ Finally, stay away from complex data structures such as binary trees and linked lists. Use them only when necessary. Arrays and simple variables are much faster.

If you pay attention to these dos and don'ts, you'll avoid many headaches, but game programming takes a lot of effort and experience. There aren't any magickal techniques, but there are a few standard methodologies for writing some of the more common functions in a game. One of these methodologies I refer to as *autonomous functions*. Really this is nothing more than a function that can take a command and has one or more local static variables so the function can track its own state. This feature relieves the main game logic from having to know everything.

In essence, autonomous functions are like game objects. They take care of themselves and do their own thing. If there is one mistake that a game programmer can make, it's writing all of a game's control logic into the *main()* function of the program. Instead, we must think of all the subsystems of the game–the explosions, the rendering engine, the I/O system, and so forth–as independent autonomous entities that we direct to do work. But we don't have to stand over them like the MCP to make sure they do the work. To start your thinking along these lines, take a look at the function in Listing 8-8.

LISTING 8-8 Shell for an autonomous function

```
int Auto_Function(int command)
{
```

```
static int times_executed = 0; // this tracks the number of times the
                               // function is called

// test if this is the first time the function has been called

if (!times_executed)
   {

   //..initialize any data structures and perform any start up tasks

   } // end if first time

// we have executed this function once more

times_executed++;

// what command has caller issued

switch(command)
      {
      case COMMAND_1:
           {
           // process command
           } // break;

      // other commands

      default:break;

      } // end switch

} // end Auto_Function
```

This function is simple in appearance, but it has much power to offer. Notice that the function is aware of the number of times it's called; moreover, during its first call, the function will execute a section of code that initializes any data structures. Thus, we have seen that using a static variable, a function can remember its own local state. Improvements can of course be made on the function shell (based on what the function is doing). For example, we could add more local static variables and some parameters.

The model of computation for a game must have some air of object orientation within it, meaning that functions should be thought of as objects composed of functions and their data, as shown in Figure 8-16. Using this technique consistently (when applicable), a video game becomes very object-oriented, and each function or module can be updated, debugged, and so forth, without knowing how the rest of the system works.

Now that we have mastered the art of writing efficient functions for our game objects (hopefully), the next logical step in our evolution is to learn how to replicate our work to create many of the same objects.

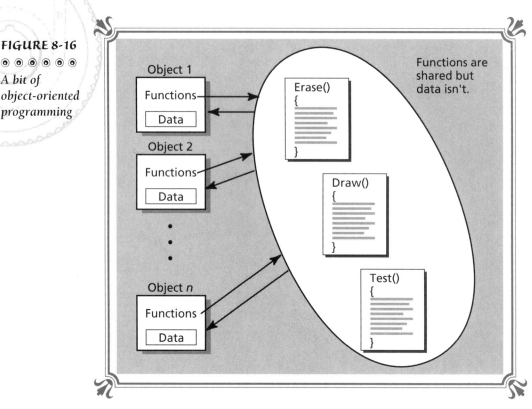

FIGURE 8-16

◉ ◉ ◉ ◉ ◉ ◉

A bit of object-oriented programming

Processing Multiple Data Objects

In the previous chapter, we saw how many objects can be created from one template by using multiple data sets with the same code, but we didn't know all that we know now to really appreciate the technique. And since being able to replicate or make multiple copies of objects in a game is so important, we are going to see another example of it here.

The example is based on a system that is commonly modeled in games called *particle systems*, which is a system of relatively simple game objects that follow a specific set of rules. We're going to simulate hot chunks of molten rock (cinders) spewing out of the mouth of a volcano on an alien world. Let's begin with the data structure of the particles. The structure needs to track the position, velocity, and color, and have a few timing variables to track the particle's progress. Here is such a data structure:

```
typedef struct cinder_typ
        {
        int x,y;                // position of cinder
```

```
        int xv,yv;          // velocity of cinder
        int color;          // color of cinder
        int lifetime;       // total number of frames cinder will live for
        int counter_1;      // tracks when cinder color will change
        int threshold_1;
        int counter_2;      // tracks when gravity will be applied
        int threshold_2;
        int col;            // the current color of the cinder
        int under;          // this holds the pixel under the cinder

        } cinder, *cinder_ptr;
```

About the only fields that aren't obvious from their names are the counter fields. They are used to "granulate" time. To avoid floating point calculations, we use integers, but mathematical operations are only performed every few frames. The result of this technique (which is important in itself) is that objects move as if they had decimal accuracy. For example, say that we wanted to move a pixel .25 pixel per frame. This would be impossible with standard integers, but if we use a counter that counts frames, then it can be done. When the counter reaches 4, the pixel is moved 1.0, which is equivalent to 4*.25. Anyway, this technique is used to simulate the gravity and the rate at which the volcanic cinders lose their red-hot glow.

So how do we write a single set of functions that can process a number of cinders? It's actually very simple–the cinders can be located in an array (a linked list could be used alternatively). This array would hold the data for each cinder. Something like this would work,

```
cinder cinders[MAX_CINDERS];  // this holds all the cinders
```

where *MAX_CINDERS* is the maximum number of cinders in the simulation.

With the array in hand, all that is needed are the functions that erase, move, draw, scan under, and initialize all the cinders. The trick is understanding that each function really works on one cinder at a time, but the functions are written so that a *for* loop processes all the cinders in the array. Abstractly put, if a function operates on a game object named *game_object*, then an algorithm to process a collection of *game_objects* would look like this:

```
for (index=0; index<number_of_objects; index++)
    {
    Process(game_object[index]);
    } // end for
```

This technique is all that is needed to transform any function into a function that works on an array of base types. Using this technique, we can write all the functions we need. I don't want to list every function of the volcano program since the complete program follows in a couple of pages, but let's take a look at one of the volcano functions and see what's in it. Listing 8-9 contains the *Erase_Cinders()* function for analysis.

LISTING 8-9 The cinder erasure function

```
void Erase_Cinders(void)
{
// this function replaces the pixel that was under a cinder

int index; // looping variable

for (index=0; index<active_cinders; index++)
    if (cinders[index].y >=0)

Write_Pixel_DB(cinders[index].x,cinders[index].y,cinders[index].under);

} // end Erase_Cinders
```

The function is rather simple, but it is derived using the techniques just discussed. The cinders are contained in the array *cinders[]*. The function retrieves the pixel that was under the current cinder within its own data structure and places it at the proper (x, y) coordinates. This is done for each cinder in the array. If our program only had one cinder, the *Erase_Cinders()* function would be called *Erase_Cinder()* and it might look like Listing 8-10.

LISTING 8-10 A single cinder eraser

```
void Erase_Cinder(void)
{

if (cinders.y >=0)
        Write_Pixel_DB(cinders.x,cinders.y,cinders.under);

} // end Erase_Cinder
```

The only difference between the two functions is that the *Erase_Cinder()* logic lacks the array indexing! Therefore, 90 percent of the functions we write to control a single object can be transformed with a text editor in minutes to handle multiple objects. The only functions that we have to write more carefully are collision detection and the initialization functions that set up the data structures, since we may want to have some data dependencies between each data object. Anyway, the other functions, *Draw_Cinders()*, *Move_Cinders()*, and *Scan_Cinders()* are all written similarly to *Erase_Cinders()*. The function *Init_Cinders()* generates all the random positions and velocities of the cinders during startup. It works in much the same way (each cinder is processed in a loop), except that it takes a pair of parameters that indicate which subset of cinders to initialize. This is a general practice. You should write your functions so that a subset of the objects can be called upon for work.

At this point I think the best thing to do is look at the short program and see it in action. The name of the program is VOLCANO.EXE and the source is VOLCANO.C. When you run the program, you will see an alien landscape with a volcano in the middle (well, it's supposed to look like a volcano). Anyway, the volcano spews out cinders at different velocities and temperatures (indicated by color), and the cinders fall back to the surface and die out. To build this program, you'll need the library modules BLACK3, BLACK4, and BLACK8. Listing 8-11 contains the code.

LISTING 8-11 Program that replicates a single cinder to simulate an active volcano

```c
// VOLCANO.C - A demo of multiple data single logic programming

// I N C L U D E S /////////////////////////////////////////////////////////

#include <io.h>
#include <conio.h>
#include <stdio.h>
#include <stdlib.h>
#include <dos.h>
#include <bios.h>
#include <fcntl.h>
#include <memory.h>
#include <malloc.h>
#include <math.h>
#include <string.h>

#include "black3.h"
#include "black4.h"
#include "black8.h"


// D E F I N E S /////////////////////////////////////////////////////////

#define MAX_CINDERS          100   // maximum number of cinders in the simulation

#define VOLCANO_MOUTH_X      145   // position where cinders will be emitted
#define VOLCANO_MOUTH_Y      102

#define CINDER_START_COLOR 48      // starting cinder color
#define CINDER_END_COLOR   48+15   // ending cinder color

// S T R U C T U R E S /////////////////////////////////////////////////////////

typedef struct cinder_typ
        {
        int x,y;           // position of cinder
        int xv,yv;         // velocity of cinder
        int color;         // color of cinder
        int lifetime;      // total number of frames cinder will live for
        int counter_1;     // tracks when cinder color will change
        int threshold_1;
        int counter_2;     // tracks when gravity will be applied
        int threshold_2;
```

continued on next page

continued from previous page

```
        int col;            // the current color of the cinder
        int under;          // this holds the pixel under the cinder

        } cinder, *cinder_ptr;

// G L O B A L S //////////////////////////////////////////////////////////////

pcx_picture image_pcx;  // general PCX image used to load background and imagery

cinder cinders[MAX_CINDERS];  // this holds all the cinders
int active_cinders;           // number of active cinders in the world

// F U N C T I O N S ////////////////////////////////////////////////////////////

void Init_Cinders(int starting_cinder, int ending_cinder)
{
// this function initializes cinders, it can initialize a sequence of cinders,
// or a single cinder

int index; // looping variable

// initialize each cinder or restart a single cinder
for (index=starting_cinder; index<=ending_cinder; index++)
    {
    // fill in position, velocity and color of cinder
    cinders[index].x = VOLCANO_MOUTH_X - 5 + rand() % 11;
    cinders[index].y = VOLCANO_MOUTH_Y - rand() % 3;

    cinders[index].xv = - 2 + rand() % 5;
    cinders[index].yv = - 5 - rand() % 5;

    cinders[index].col = CINDER_START_COLOR;

    // scan under cinder
    cinders[index].under = Read_Pixel_DB(cinders[index].x,cinders[index].y);

    // set timing fields
    cinders[index].lifetime = 20 + rand()%100;

    cinders[index].counter_1 = 0;
    cinders[index].counter_2 = 0;

    // set how long it will take for cinder to cool
    cinders[index].threshold_1 = 2 + rand()%6;

    // set how long it will take for gravity to take effect
    cinders[index].threshold_2 = 1+rand()%3;

    } // end for index

} // end Init_Cinders
```

```c
/////////////////////////////////////////////////////////////////////////

void Erase_Cinders(void)
{
// this function replaces the pixel that was under a cinder

int index; // looping variable

for (index=0; index<active_cinders; index++)
    if (cinders[index].y >=0)
        Write_Pixel_DB(cinders[index].x,cinders[index].y,cinders[index].under);

} // end Erase_Cinders

/////////////////////////////////////////////////////////////////////////

void Scan_Cinders(void)
{
// this function scans under the cinders

int index; // looping variable

for (index=0; index<active_cinders; index++)
    if (cinders[index].y >=0)
        cinders[index].under = Read_Pixel_DB(cinders[index].x,cinders[index].y);

} // end Scan_Cinders

/////////////////////////////////////////////////////////////////////////

void Draw_Cinders(void)
{
// this function draws the cinders

int index; // looping variable

for (index=0; index<active_cinders; index++)
    if (cinders[index].y >=0)
        Write_Pixel_DB(cinders[index].x,cinders[index].y,cinders[index].col);

} // end Draw_Cinders

/////////////////////////////////////////////////////////////////////////

void Move_Cinders(void)
{
// this function moves and updates all the timing fields of the cinder
// it also applies gravity to the cinders

int index, // looping variable
    pixel; // used to read the pixels under the cinder
```

continued on next page

continued from previous page

```
// process each cinder
for (index=0; index<active_cinders; index++)
    {
    // move the cinder
    cinders[index].x+=cinders[index].xv;
    cinders[index].y+=cinders[index].yv;

    // apply gravity
    if (++cinders[index].counter_2 >= cinders[index].threshold_2)
       {
       // apply a downward velocity of 1
       cinders[index].yv++;

       // reset gravity counter
       cinders[index].counter_2 = 0;

       } // end if time to update gravity

    // test if it's time to update cinder color

    if (++cinders[index].counter_1 >=cinders[index].threshold_1)
       {
       // reset counter
       cinders[index].counter_1 = 0;

       // test if cinder is already out
       if (cinders[index].col < CINDER_END_COLOR)
          cinders[index].col++;

       } // end if time for color change

    // test if cinder is dead, off screen, lifetime over, or hit mountain
    pixel = Read_Pixel_DB(cinders[index].x,cinders[index].y);

    // test if the pixel is part of the mountain

    if (pixel!=0 && (pixel < CINDER_START_COLOR || pixel > CINDER_END_COLOR))
       {
       // restart this cinder

       Init_Cinders(index,index);

       } // end if cinder hit mountain
    else
    if (--cinders[index].lifetime <= 0)
       {
       // restart this cinder
       Init_Cinders(index,index);

       } // end if cinders lifetime expired
    else
```

```
        if (cinders[index].x > 320 || cinders[index].x < 0)
           {
           // restart this cinder
           Init_Cinders(index,index);

           } // end if cinder is off screen

        } // end for index

} // end Move_Cinders

// M A I N //////////////////////////////////////////////////////////////

void main(int argc, char **argv)
{

// set the graphics mode to mode 13h
Set_Graphics_Mode(GRAPHICS_MODE13);

// create the double buffer
Create_Double_Buffer(200);

// now load the background image
PCX_Init((pcx_picture_ptr)&image_pcx);
PCX_Load("volcano.pcx",(pcx_picture_ptr)&image_pcx,1);

// copy PCX image to double buffer
PCX_Copy_To_Buffer((pcx_picture_ptr)&image_pcx,double_buffer);
PCX_Delete((pcx_picture_ptr)&image_pcx);

// draw instructions
Print_String_DB(80,2,9,"Hit any key to exit",1);

// intialize all the cinders
Init_Cinders(0,19);
active_cinders = 20;

// main event loop, process until keyboard hit
while(!kbhit())
    {
    // erase all the cinders coming out of the volcano
    Erase_Cinders();

    // move all the cinders
    Move_Cinders();

    // scan under and draw the cinders
    Scan_Cinders();
    Draw_Cinders();

    // display double buffer
```

continued on next page

continued from previous page

```
        Display_Double_Buffer(double_buffer,0);

        // lock onto 18 frames per second max
        Time_Delay(1);

        } // end while

// exit in a very cool way
Screen_Transition(SCREEN_DARKNESS);

// free up all resources
Delete_Double_Buffer();
Set_Graphics_Mode(TEXT_MODE);

} // end main
```

The *main()* function of the program is surprisingly simple, but this is an illusion since most of the work is done in the cinder functions. In fact, the most complex of the functions is *Move_Cinders()*, which updates all the positions of the cinders and updates the colors of the cinders. In addition to moving and transforming the cinders, *Move_Cinders()* tests them to see if their life cycle is complete. This occurs in a few cases: the cinder has burnt out, the cinder has hit the surface, the cinder has gone off a screen edge. In any of these cases, the cinder is recycled and restarted from the mouth of the volcano with another call to *Init_Cinders()*, but with a pair of parameters that are the index of the cinder that just died.

For a small exercise, I want you to add to the program the ability to change the gravity and the number of active cinders by keyboard input.

Summary

This chapter is probably one of the most important of the whole book. We learned the lowest forms of alchemy that are needed to take control of the PC. We learned about multitasking, the timer, autonomous functions, and standard game programming techniques used to optimize game code. But the most important thing of all to gain from this chapter is that a video game is a little world, a self-contained universe that is generated within the PC. Making this world seem alive and functioning in real-time is one of the Black Arts we so much desire.

Now it's time to learn how to pull more than yourself into the Cyberspace abyss, with multiplayer game techniques.

9

Multiplayer Game Techniques

come tuoli per le manouelle .... de quali primo uano e lalza
ro e gira piu ...ur le mini ... o ... fa oppe ano di one
oro a ... ... per mag nel ... manuelle pui quiri
a forca ... pu i uomo ... ...

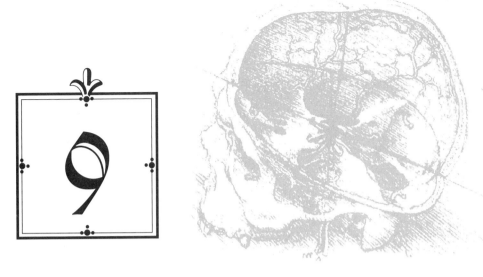

9

Multiplayer Game Techniques

Up to this point, we have assumed that our games will run on a single machine and support only a single player. But what if we want to support multiple players on two or more machines? Well, things get a bit complicated. Many of the functions (graphics, logic, sound) work in the same way, but the game from a high-level point of view must be rethought taking into consideration the new model. Aspects such as separate display partitions, collision detection, input device control, and so forth, must all be written to support two or more players. Admittedly, supporting two or more players on a single computer is fairly easy to track and understand. However, if the multiplayer game is built upon two or more computers, the complexity of the game logic (relating to the players) increases an order of magnitude. These issues and more are what we need to understand if we are ever going to put more than one player in our games. Hence, in this chapter we will use our powers of Cybersorcery to construct various models of multiplayer games and summon the images from Cyberspace into two machines at the same time.

Introduction to Multiplayer Games

Any game can be made into a multiplayer game. However, for some games multiple players aren't easy to implement due to interfaces, game play, input devices, and other game-specific aspects. Most of the game loops we've seen thus far have had a section that moves the objects and a section that moves the player. Figure 9-1 shows a typical single-player game event loop. The figure includes the standard cycle of a game loop and, as usual, there is only one section that moves and draws the player. But what if we wanted to have two players? How would the game loop change?

FIGURE 9-1

ⓞ ⓞ ⓞ ⓞ ⓞ ⓞ

Video game with a single-player loop

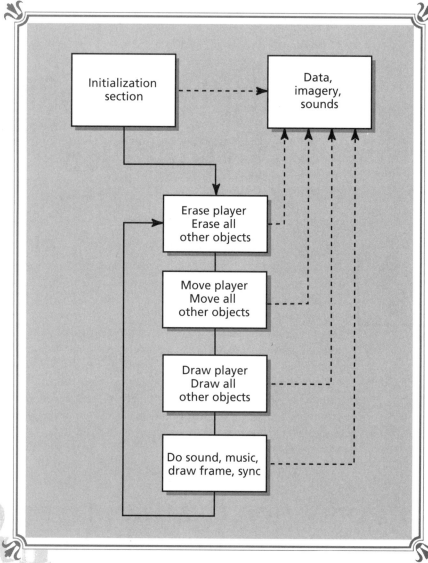

The revised game loop would replace the section that erases, moves, and draws the single player with code that erases, moves, and draws both players (in a specific order). Figure 9-2 shows the new setup of a game loop with support for two players. The second player can be thought of as a copy of the first player with its own local set of variables that the first player has. As far as the game logic is concerned, additions have to be made to take into consideration that there are two players now.

FIGURE 9-2

Two-player event loop

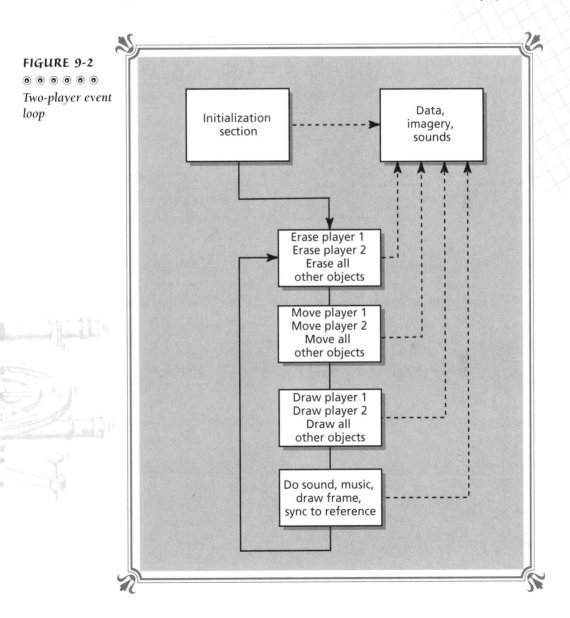

If there is collision code that tests for collisions between floating mines and the player, now the code must test the collisions between the floating mines and both players, one and two.

If both players work in roughly the same way, implementing these additions to the game code isn't too complex; however, if each player works differently (player 1 is a human and player 2 is an airplane), we'll have to write more code. Since the functionality of the players is so different, many functions that worked on the original single player version of the game won't work in the two-player version even with appropriate modifications.

In general, adding players (on a single machine) is like adding more game objects, but instead of these new players being controlled by AI algorithms, they are controlled by another player via some input device. All this is a bit loose–we need to be a bit more specific about what kinds of multiplayer games there are and how they are implemented. Let's take a look at some of the specific models of multiplayer games.

Multiple Players—One at a Time

A multiplayer game that allows player 1 to play for a while and then player 2 to play after player 1 has completed his task is probably the easiest to implement. This is true since the main game loop is very similar to that of the standard single-player game except that there may be conditional logic to change the color or appearance of the second player's ship or character. Also, when each player takes his turn, the appropriate variables and data structures that belong to each player are used. Hence, only one player plays at a time, but the data that is associated with each player may be very different.

As an oversimplified example, imagine that a game has two players and the only variables that need to be tracked are the X and Y positions of each player and the current level. We might define these variables like this:

```
int player_1_x, player_1_y, player_1_level;  // holds player 1
int player_2_x, player_2_y, player_2_level;  // holds player 2

int current_x, current_y, current_level;     // used during run-time
```

The "current" variables would be set with the player's specific variables depending on which player is currently playing. Then at the end of that player's turn, the "current" variables are stored back into the player they represent, and the other player's local variables are moved into the "current" variables. Of course, this can be done more elegantly with arrays, structures, or whatever, but the main idea is that each player has his own data set, and when the player gets his turn, the data set is copied into the active or current variables that are used in the game logic. Using this technique coupled with arrays, literally dozens of players can be implemented (if they are willing to wait their turn).

Multiple Players—Same Time, Same Screen

Taking turns in a game is fine, but it's much more exciting if two or more players can play at the same time on the same screen. However, implementing this is much harder than multiple players taking turns. In the case of multiple players on the same screen at the same time, there must be logic for both players in the game loop and in all other subfunctions of the game. This means that if a player can be hit by an asteroid, each player must be tested to see if an asteroid has made contact. Again, all of this can be implemented in arrays and structures, but the main point here is that regardless of the underlying data structure, each player must be processed during each game loop. Moreover, if there are going to be player-to-player interactions, then tests for these interactions must also be performed.

We must consider many factors when designing a game for multiple players playing on a single screen at the same time. One of the most important is input device allocation. If you've written a game designed for a keyboard, how will both players use the keyboard at the same time? Alas, if a game is to be made a multiplayer game, each player must be able to use a different input device, such as the keyboard, mouse, and joystick. Although I have seen games that share the keyboard, it is awkward to say the least!

In addition, the technicalities of what happens when one player dies or one tries to move off the screen in one direction while the other player is moving in another direction, must all be taken into consideration. What if one player wants to go his own way? Well, there is a solution to this, as you'll see in the next section.

Multiple Players—Split Screen

In a scrolling or adventure-type game, one of the main reasons for having two or more players in the game world is to allow them to stick together or split up if they wish. This can be implemented using a split screen or multiple-window technique. Figure 9-3 shows the difference between a two-player single-screen game and a two-player split-screen game. As you can see, the split-screen game is similar to having two computers that are sharing the same monitor since each player has his own view. If the players want to work together they can, but if they want to split up and each move to different parts of the game world, it's not a problem.

There are some drawbacks to split-screen games. First, it only is reasonable for two players. If you try to support more than two players, it becomes confusing for each player to track his screen area. Second, the added rendering time to draw two or more screens may become a bottleneck if the graphics being rendered are too complex. This is especially true for 3D games in which drawing one view is hard enough and drawing two views is a strain on the system.

FIGURE 9-3

◉ ◉ ◉ ◉ ◉ ◉

*Single-screen vs.
split-screen
setups*

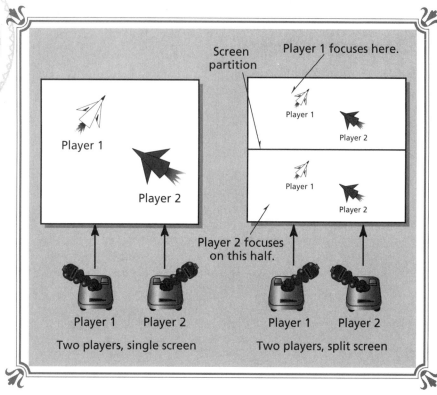

There is nothing really magickal about writing a game that supports two or more players on a single machine. For the most part, it means adding more functions, more tests, and allocating the resources among the players. But the main detail that makes it easy is that each player is really a section of code that is executing, one after the other, in the main event loop on the same machine. Thus, there is nothing to get out of synchronization since there is only one PC running the whole game.

However, this picture-perfect world falls apart once we link two or more PCs and create a networked multiplayer game.

Linking Two PCs

When two or more PCs are linked through some kind of communications medium to create a multiplayer game, everything becomes very complex. This is because each machine must stay in synchronization with each other machine. If any machine gets as much as a single frame out of synchronization with the other machines, one or more players will be playing a different game than everyone else, which is definitely not desirable. For our discussions, we are going to stick to a simple model of multiplayer games that consists of two PCs, each running the video game and connected by a modem. Larger models are for the most part a generalization of this system. Figure 9-4 shows the details of our model.

There are so many details necessary to create the simple model in Figure 9-4 that it's hard to know where to begin, but we will begin with the most important aspect of the model, and that is the communications interface. This, as we shall see, is also one of the most complex aspects to implement. It's not that the concepts of serial communications or modem connections are hard to grasp, but there are so many standards, details, and little problems that if not addressed will make the simple act of writing and reading a single character to and from the modem almost insurmountable. So, for a while we're going to talk about serial communications and modem connections.

We know that we need to create a communications channel between each PC via the serial system and the modem. To do this, we must learn how to control, configure, and take over the serial ports of the PC as well as understand how modems work. Our goals are as follows:

✦ Figure out the serial ports.

✦ Learn to write and read characters to and from the serial ports.

✦ Learn how to command the modem (attached to a serial port or internal) to make a call and answer a call.

FIGURE 9-4
◉ ◉ ◉ ◉ ◉ ◉
Basic two-player game model

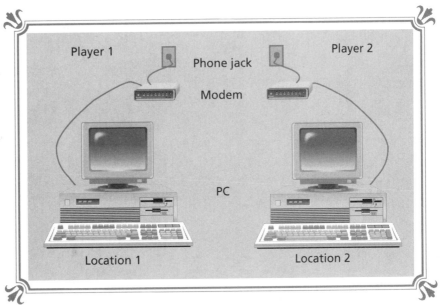

Once we can make a modem-to-modem connection, we must learn how to send game packet information back and forth to keep each machine apprised of the remote player. The following material is long and tedious, but that's the way communications is. However, it's something we have to do, just like taking political science in school! But after we cover all this stuff, we'll use it to write a killer two-player modem game called Starblazer. If you feel very comfortable with serial and modem communications, feel free to skim this section, only slowing down to look at the functions we'll write along the way.

First, we'll add a couple of words to our multiplayer vocabulary. Take a look at Figure 9-5. Here we see two PCs connected by a modem and two players represented by icons on each screen. Moreover, each player is labeled *local* or *remote*. However, if you look at the figure for a minute, you'll realize that both players are local and remote relative to which machine you're playing on. This can be a very confusing concept. In essence, if you and I were playing a game, you would be the remote player on my machine and I would be the local player on my machine. By the same token, I would be the remote player on your machine and you would be the local player on your machine. It's a bit like time travel; just say it a few times and you'll get it!

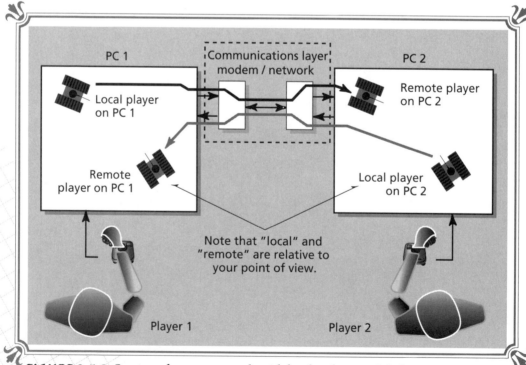

FIGURE 9-5 ◎ *Our two-player game mode with local and remote labeling*

The Serial Communications System

The PC contains a chip called a UART (universal asynchronous receiver/transmitter), which is responsible for the serial communications of the computer. On the market today are three versions of this chip that your specific computer may have (depending on age and manufacturer). The low-end UART is the 8250. For the most part, the 8250 has been replaced by the 16450 high-performance UART, which itself has been replaced by the 16550 UART. All of the chips are register-compatible with the 8250; the 16450 and 16550 are high-speed versions. Furthermore, the 16550 has an internal FIFO (first in-first out) software buffer.

As far as programming the chips, they are all the same to us. We'll use the 8250 registers as the base model. If a PC has a 16450 or 16550, the software will work fine but won't take advantage of the extra goodies. So, what does the UART do? Well, it does a lot, but the main thing it does is send and receive characters to and from the serial port. Thus, our first goal is to learn how to control the UART and send and receive characters. To do this, it helps if we have an understanding of what's in the UART as far as registers go. Table 9-1 lists the registers and their bitmapping for the UART.

TABLE 9-1 ◇ *UART registers and their meanings*

Register	Description
Register 0	Receiver Buffer Register (RBR) and Transmitter Holding Register (THR). This dual-purpose register is used both to send data and to receive data. If a byte of data is received by the UART, it will be received and placed in this register. However, if you wish to write data, the data is written here.

Bit Number	Meaning
0	Bit 0 of data.
1	Bit 1 of data.
2	Bit 2 of data.
3	Bit 3 of data.
4	Bit 4 of data.
5	Bit 5 of data, may be undefined if using a 5-bit word.
6	Bit 6 of data, may be undefined if using a 6-bit word.

continued on next page

continued from previous page

Register	Description	
	Bit Number	**Meaning**
	7	Bit 7 of data, may be undefined if using a 7-bit word.

Note: We are going to use all 8 bits of data.

Register 1	Interrupt Enable Register (IER). This register is used to direct the UART to generate interrupts based on different events. In our case we are only interested in generating an interrupt when a character has been received by the UART in the Receiver Buffer Register.	
	Bit Number	**Meaning**
	0	RxRDY: If set to 1, the UART will generate an interrupt whenever a character is received in the RBR.
	1	TBE: If set to 1, the UART will generate an interrupt whenever a character is moved from the THR into the UART's Internal Shift Register.
	2	ERROR: If set to 1, the UART will generate an interrupt whenever a parity error, an overrun error, a framing error, or a BREAK conditions detected.
	3	DELTA: If set to 1, the UART will generate an interrupt whenever any of the RS-232 lines change state.
	4	Always set to 0.
	5	Always set to 0
	6	Always set to 0.
	7	Always set to 0.

Register 2	Interrupt Identification Register (IIR). This register is read to determine what event has caused a UART interrupt. This is necessary since setting the bits in the IER enables specific interrupts, but the application's ISR must know the exact cause of the interrupt.

Register	Description	
	Bit Number	**Meaning**
	0	If this bit is 0, an interrupt has occurred.
	1-2	If an interrupt has occurred, bits 1 and 2 indicate what caused it.

	Bit 2	Bit 1	Interrupt Cause
	0	0	Modem RS-232 line change.
	0	1	THR empty.
	1	0	RBR full.
	1	1	There has been an error.

	Bit Number	Meaning
	3	Always 0.
	4	Always 0.
	5	Always 0.
	6	Always 0.
	7	Always 0.

Register 3	Line Control Register (LCR). This register is used to configure the UART settings, such as number of data bits, parity, and stop bits. This register is also used to force register 0,1 into a second mode of operation, that is, the Divisor Latch Register (16 bit). We will discuss this in greater detail later; for now the main points to understand about this register are the setting of the data word parameters.

Bit Number	**Meaning**
0-1	Used to set the number of data bits per serial word.

Bit 1	Bit 0	Data Bits
0	0	5
0	1	1
1	0	7
1	1	8

2	Number of stop bits. If set to 0, one stop bit will be sent per word; if set to 1, two stop bits will be sent per word.

continued on next page

continued from previous page

Register	Description

Bit Number	Meaning
3-5	Parity setting.

Bit 5	Bit 4	Bit 3	Setting
0	0	0	NONE
0	0	1	ODD
0	1	1	EVEN
1	0	1	MARK
1	1	1	SPACE

Bit Number	Meaning
6	BREAK control. If this bit is set to 1 for one character clock, the receiver will detect a BREAK condition.
7	Divisor latch access enable. If this bit is set to 1, register 0 (RBR/THR) will act as the low word of the baud rate divisor and register 1 (IER) will act as the high byte of the divisor. The value programmed into the Divisor Latch Register will be used to compute the final baud rate of the UART.

Register 4	Modem Control Register (MCR). This register is used to control the lines on the RS-232 interface, such as DTR (Data Terminal Ready), in addition to controlling the General Purpose Output (GPO) hardware lines within the PC. One of these, GPO2, is needed to enable interrupts to the PIC from the UART (a hardware bug in the PC's design!).

Bit Number	Meaning
0	This bit will be reflected on the RS-232's serial interface DTR line. It is used as an overall modem communications enable and a way to place the modem back in command mode once a connection has been made.
1	This bit will be reflected by the RS-232's serial interface Request To Send (RTS) line. Basically, RTS is used to tell the other data terminal that the PC is willing to take information.

Register	Description	
	Bit Number	**Meaning**
	2	General Purpose Output 1. This is user-defined and if set to 1, can reset some internal modems, but don't count on it.
	3	General Purpose Output 2. This is used to enable a tri-state buffer within the PC that transmits interrupts from the UART. Hence, it must be set to 1 if interrupts are to be sent from the UART to the programmable interrupt controller (PIC).
	4	Local loop back test. If set to 1, all characters sent out the serial port will be echoed back. Normally, this bit is set to 0.
	5	Always 0.
	6	Always 0.
	7	Always 0.
Register 5	Line Status Register (LSR). This register is a general-purpose status register for the UART. It reports such things as errors and state of the receive and transmit buffers. When this register is read, all the error detection bits will be reset.	
	Bit Number	**Meaning**
	0	RXRDY: If this bit is 1, a character is ready in the RBR.
	1	If this bit is 1, an input data overrun has occurred. In general, a character overwrote the last character in the RBR.
	2	If this bit is 1, a parity error has occurred.
	3	If this bit is set, a framing error has occurred, which means that a character's stop bit was a 0 instead of a 1.
	4	If this bit is 1, a BREAK has occurred, meaning the sender has sent a BREAK signal for more than one character cycle.

continued on next page

continued from previous page

Register	Description	
	Bit Number	**Meaning**
	5	Transmitter buffer empty (TBE). If this bit is set to 1, the UART has sent the data from the THR into the output shift register and another character may be written. Always look in this bit and test if it's 1 before writing into the THR, otherwise, data may be lost.
	6	Transmitter empty (TXE). If this bit is set to 1, both the THR and the UART shift register are empty. Hence, the character has been sent.
	7	Always 0.
Register 6	Modem Status Register (MSR). This register is tied directly to the modem control lines, such as Data Set Ready (DSR), Ring Indicator (RI), Clear To Send (CTS), and so forth. This register may be polled by the application program to determine what state the modem interface is in. When the register is read, all of the "delta" indicators are reset.	
	Bit Number	**Meaning**
	0	Delta CTS. If this bit is 1, the state of the Clear To Send line has changed state since the MSR was last read.
	1	Delta DSR. If this bit is 1, the state of the Data Set Ready line has changed state since the last time the MSR was read.
	2	Delta Ring Indicator. If this bit is 1, the Ring Indicator has made a low to high transition since the last time the MSR was read.
	3	Delta Carrier Detect. If this bit is set to 1, the state of the modem Carrier Detect line has changed state since the MSR was last read.
	4	Status of CTS.

Register	Description	
	Bit Number	*Meaning*
	5	Status DSR.
	6	Status of RI.
	7	Status of Data Carrier Detect.
Register 7	Scratch Pad Register. This register is used as a scratch pad data area and isn't implemented on all UARTs.	
Register 8	Baud Rate LSB Divisor Latch Register (DLL). This register contains the low-order byte of the baud rate divisor word. Together with register 9 (the high-order byte), the baud rate divisor controls the final baud rate of the serial communications port. However, there is one detail that must be considered when accessing this register. The address of the DLL is *not* at offset 0x08 from the base COM port address, but is at offset 0x00. In other words, register 8 is accessed at the same location as register 0 (RBR/THR). Of course, this wouldn't normally work since two I/O ports can't exist at the same location; however, when bit 7 of the Line Control Register is set to 1, register 0 becomes register 8. I just love hardware engineers, don't you?	
Register 9	Baud Rate MSB Divisor Latch Register (DLM).The high-order byte of the baud rate divisor is placed in this register. Again, this register is mirrored. It exists at register 1 (IER) when bit 7 of the LCR is set to 1. Hence, to set the baud rate divisor, we simply set bit 7 in the LCR to 1 and then use register 0 and 1 as if they were the low and high byte of the baud rate divisor latch. Don't worry, it sounds more complex than it is. The question is, what is the baud rate divisor's relationship to the desired baud rate? The relationship is simple. The baud rate divisor is programmed using the results from the following formula: baud rate divisor (16-bit result) = 115,200/desired baud rate Once the calculation is complete, the low byte and high byte of the baud rate divisor are placed into their respective registers, and the serial system will function at the proper rate.	

Now we know what all the registers of the UART do, but where are these registers located? And moreover, since a PC typically has four COM ports, how do we differentiate among them? The answer to the first and second questions can be answered at once. The UART has a separate set of identical registers for each COM port, and the base address of these registers can be found in Table 9-2.

Using Table 9-2 as a base I/O address accessing any of the COM ports is easy. For example, if we wanted to access the Line Status Register (register 5) of COM2, we would write the following:

```
status = _inp(0x2F8 + 0x05);
```

TABLE 9-2

◇◇◇◇◇◇

Base addresses of all the COM ports

Serial Port	Base I/O Address
COM1	3F8H
COM2	2F8H
COM3	3E8H
COM4	2E8H

In general, any register at a specific COM port can be accessed with the base address of the COM port along with the register number, for example, if reading a register,

```
data = _inp(base_address + register_number);
```

and if writing data:

```
_outp(base_address + register_number, data);
```

That's all there is to accessing the UART registers. Now that we have the tools to program the registers in the UART, we must define exactly what must be done to open a serial port and then read and write characters.

Overview of the Serial System

The first thing that must be done to create a serial communications channel using one of the COM ports is to configure the COM port with the appropriate settings. This is done via the Line Control Register (LCR at register 3). The number of data bits, parity, and stop bits can be programmed using this single register. Then the baud rate should be programmed, which is accomplished by computing the desired baud rate divisor, as shown in Table 9-1. For example, Table 9-3 lists the low and high byte components that must be placed into the baud rate divisor registers for some popular baud rates.

TABLE 9-3
◇◇◇◇◇

*Baud rate
divisors for
popular baud
rates*

Baud Rate	Low Byte of Divisor	High Byte of Divisor
1200	96	0
2400	48	0
4800	24	0
9600	12	0
19200	6	0

Note: In all cases the high-order byte is 0. That's convenient!

Using the values in Table 9-3, we can select a baud rate and then, after setting bit 7 of register 3 (the Line Control Register) to 1, we write the low byte of the divisor into register 0 and then the high byte of the divisor into register 1 (which in essence is writing to registers 8 and 9). After these steps, we reset bit 7 in the LCR to 0 so that registers 0 and 1 can be accessed normally as the Transmitter Holding Register (THR) and Receiver Buffer Register (RBR).

At this point, we would actually be able to send characters out the serial port. This can be accomplished simply by writing the character to register 0, which is the Transmitter Holding Register. However, reception of characters is done in a different way. The problem with receiving characters is that we don't want to poll the RxRDY bit of the LSR (register 5) to determine whether a character has been received by the hardware. Instead, the more common approach is to enable the UART to generate an interrupt when a character is received. Then an interrupt service routine (ISR) is installed to process the interrupt.

Figure 9-6 shows the setup of the ISR in relation to the serial system and the application program. Notice that the serial receiver ISR simply places the received data into an internal software buffer, so the application program can refer to the buffer at its leisure. Hence, a hundred characters could be received by the serial ISR before the application felt like checking the input receiver buffer. However, since the characters are buffered, nothing is lost.

Of course, if the serial application program doesn't access the input serial buffer within a reasonable amount of time, the input buffer will overflow and data will be lost. Therefore, it is wise when using an interrupt-driven serial receiver ISR for the application program to consume the data in the input buffer at regular intervals. In the case of a modem-to-modem game, this consumption will occur every frame and there won't be the chance of overflow. In fact, the application will want to consume data faster than the modems will be able to transfer it!

If we refer again to Figure 9-6, we also note that the serial interrupts cause the PC to vector to the ISR attached to interrupt vectors 0x0B for COM2 and 0x0C for

FIGURE 9-6

◎ ◎ ◎ ◎ ◎ ◎

*Serial system
and its
relationship to
the application*

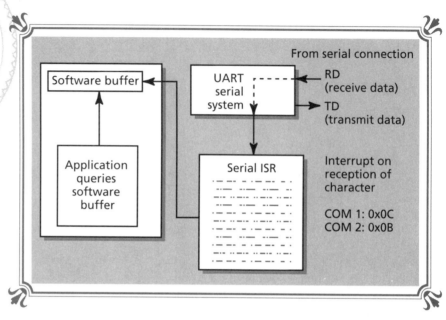

COM1. This is a little backward, but that's life. So the next question is, how do we enable the UART to generate an interrupt when a character has been received? Well, get ready for a long, drawn-out mystery, because when I first went through this and finally figured it out, I felt as if I just solved one!

Here are the steps that must be performed to enable the UART to generate a receive character interrupt:

1. Bit 3 of the Modem Control Register (register 4) must be set to 1. This controls the General Purpose Output control line 2 (GP02), which enables the output interrupt line on the UART and takes it out of TRI-STATE (high impedance mode).

2. Bit 0 of the Interrupt Enable Register (register 1) must be set to 1. This enables the UART's interrupt mask and lets it generate an interrupt.

3. The proper bit(s) must be set in the PIC's Interrupt Mask Register (I/O port 21h). We saw this register in the previous chapter, but here it is again for review:

Bit Number	Meaning
0	IRQ0 - Timekeeper interrupt
1	IRQ1 - Keyboard interrupt

Bit Number	Meaning
2	IRQ2 - Vertical retrace (reserved). Cascaded IRQ2 on AT class
3	**IRQ3 - COM2 or COM4 interrupt**
4	**IRQ4 - COM1 or COM3 interrupt**
5	IRQ5 - Fixed disk interrupt (XT class) Parallel port #2 (AT class)
6	IRQ6 - Floppy disk interrupt. Parallel port #1 (AT class)
7	IRQ7 - Printer interrupt

Note: The highlighted bits control the COM interrupts.

So, to receive characters we would enable the COM interrupts by resetting bits 3 and 4 depending on which COM ports we were trying to control. Remember, the Interrupt Mask Register uses inverse logic; hence, we use 0's to enable and 1's to disable. Moreover, when manipulating bits in this register, be sure to first read its contents and manipulate only the bits of interest; then write the original settings along with the changed bit(s) back out to the mask register. This way, the floppy drive or other interrupts won't inadvertently be disabled! (Note that this is a very good way to implement a very hard disk-crashing virus.)

4. Install an ISR to service the serial interrupt at interrupt vector 0x0B or 0x0C (depending on COM port). This ISR should test bit 0 of the Line Status Register (register 5) to determine whether the interrupt really was caused by the COM port receive buffer (this is a precaution). Then the ISR function should read the character from the Receiver Buffer Register (register 0) and place it into some kind of ring or recirculating global buffer that the game application has access to.

Granted, there are about a million little details that must be considered to get this all to work, but once it works, it works perfectly. So with all that in mind, let's write an entire serial communications library, on top of which we'll place the modem communications layer. But first things first!

Writing a Serial Communications Library

Since the goal of this book is to write 3D games and not a communications program, the serial communications library we're going to create won't be as complete as a commercial library, but it will have more than enough for our needs.

Furthermore, we'll have a firm understanding of it, since we've written it instead of blindly using someone else's software.

This brings me to an important philosophical point about video game programming and Cybersorcery: Video game programming is a Black Art because many people no longer care to understand how everything works. Programmers and engineers today would rather use OPT (other people's technology). True Cybersorcerers use other technology only when they fully understand the technology and could recreate it if necessary. Using software and techniques we don't understand breeds laziness, which is the root of poor programming. So, the moral of the story is to be a master of all trades and a jack of none. Enough of that, let's begin with the serial library.

First, all the C source and header information is contained in the modules BLACK9.C and BLACK9.H. To make writing the functions easier and more readable, I have defined many useful constants in the header file. Here are the most important ones to know for the functions:

```
// register indices in 16450/16550 UART

#define SERIAL_RBF          0       // the read buffer
#define SERIAL_THR          0       // the write buffer
#define SERIAL_IER          1       // the int. enable register
#define SERIAL_IIR          2       // the int. identification register
#define SERIAL_LCR          3       // control data config. and divisor latch
#define SERIAL_MCR          4       // modem control reg.
#define SERIAL_LSR          5       // line status reg.
#define SERIAL_MSR          6       // modem status of cts, ring etc.
#define SERIAL_DLL          0       // the low byte of baud rate divisor
#define SERIAL_DLH          1       // the hi byte of divisor latch

// baud rate divisors

#define SERIAL_BAUD_1200    96      // baud rate divisors for 1200 baud - 19200
#define SERIAL_BAUD_2400    48
#define SERIAL_BAUD_4800    24
#define SERIAL_BAUD_9600    12
#define SERIAL_BAUD_19200   6

// bit masks for different comm settings

#define SERIAL_STOP_1       0       // 1 stop bit per character
#define SERIAL_STOP_2       4       // 2 stop bits per character

#define SERIAL_BITS_5       0       // send 5 bit characters
#define SERIAL_BITS_6       1       // send 6 bit characters
#define SERIAL_BITS_7       2       // send 7 bit characters
#define SERIAL_BITS_8       3       // send 8 bit characters

#define SERIAL_PARITY_NONE  0       // no parity
#define SERIAL_PARITY_ODD   8       // odd parity
#define SERIAL_PARITY_EVEN  24      // even parity
```

```
#define SERIAL_DIV_LATCH_ON 128    // used to turn reg 0,1 into divisor latch

#define SERIAL_GPO2         8      // enable interrupt

// comm port I/O port base addresses

#define COM_1                      0x3F8 // base port address of port 0
#define COM_2                      0x2F8 // base port address of port 1

#define INT_SERIAL_PORT_0   0x0C // port 0 interrupt com 1 & 3
#define INT_SERIAL_PORT_1   0x0B // port 1 interrupt com 2 & 4

#define SERIAL_BUFF_SIZE 1024      // size of re-circulating receive buffer
```

Let's begin the serial functions with the ISR since it is the basis for the whole library. The serial ISR only needs to do a couple of things. First, it should extract the character from the Receiver Buffer Register of the UART and then insert the character into a recirculating buffer. But before we write the function, let's briefly discuss what a *ring* or *recirculating* buffer is.

In any kind of communications system, whether it be phone services, networks, or lines at the DMV, there are going to be times when the rate of production is greater than that of the rate of consumption. When this happens, data is lost. Thus, many communications systems have an input buffer that holds the input data until it can be serviced. Figure 9-7 shows such a buffer. The incoming data is placed into the buffer, and the consumer or application using the data feeds from the buffer instead of the communications channel. The idea of a buffer is a good one, but a

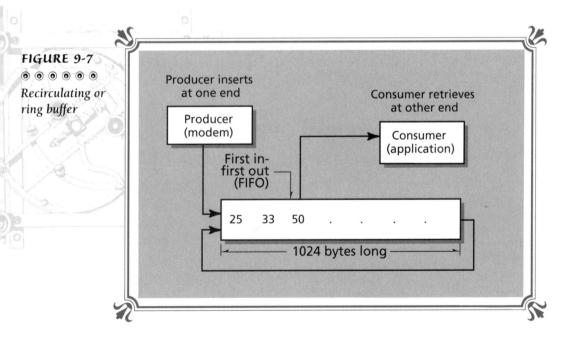

FIGURE 9-7

Recirculating or ring buffer

type of buffer must be selected that is most efficient. One such buffer, called a *FIFO* (first in-first out) buffer, has the property that the order of the incoming data is kept even though the data itself may be buffered. In addition, the time that a data item is finally processed and consumed by the application may be far in the future from the time the data was sent.

The next design decision we must make with an input communications buffer is, what happens when the buffer overflows? There are many solutions to this, but the most common and most successful solution is to make the buffer circular in design. In other words, make it recirculate. Referring to Figure 9-7, we see that the buffer receives data at one point while data is removed at another, but these two points may "wrap around" and be reset to the beginning of the buffer; thus, the name ring or recirculating buffer. In the case of our serial communications library, the size of the ring buffer will be set to 1024 bytes (more than enough), and it is defined like this:

```
char serial_buffer[SERIAL_BUFF_SIZE];  // the receive buffer
```

As we discussed, characters will be inserted at a certain point, which we will refer to as *serial_end*, and characters will be removed from a point referred to as *serial_start*. Moreover, as characters are removed, *serial_start* will be incremented, and as characters are inserted, *serial_end* will be incremented. If either index reaches the end of the input buffer, it is reset to point to the beginning of the buffer. The serial ISR is shown in Listing 9-1.

LISTING 9-1 Serial communications receive character ISR

```
void _interrupt _far Serial_ISR(void)
{
// this is the serial ISR that is installed. It is called whenever a character
// is received. The received character is then placed into the next position
// in the input ring buffer

_asm sti

serial_ch = _inp(open_port + SERIAL_RBF);

// wrap buffer index around

if (++serial_end > SERIAL_BUFF_SIZE-1)
    serial_end = 0;

// move character into buffer

serial_buffer[serial_end] = serial_ch;

++char_ready;

// restore PIC
```

```
_outp(PIC_ICR,0x20);

} // end Serial_ISR
```

The function reads the characters out of the RBR and then inserts them into the recirculating input buffer. Notice that the base COM port is referred to as *open_port*. This is made global throughout the serial system so that all references to the serial communications system are made to the same port. Thus, the next function we're going to write will be responsible for opening the COM port, configuring it, and setting this global variable, among other things.

Now that we have a serial ISR, let's write a function that will open a serial port of choice. To keep things simple, we will only support COM1 and COM2, which should suffice for 99 percent of all applications. Anyway, the function that opens up a COM channel should set the number of data bits, parity, and stop bits, along with enabling the serial interrupt by setting (or resetting) the appropriate bits in both the UART and programmable interrupt controller. Finally, the open function should install the serial ISR and save the old DOS ISR (if there is one) in a pointer, so it may be replaced later. Listing 9-2 shows the function to open, configure, and set up a serial communications port.

LISTING 9-2 Function to open a serial COM port

```
int Serial_Open(int port_base, int baud, int configuration)
{

// this function will open up the serial port, set its configuration, turn
// on all the little flags and bits to make interrupts happen and load the ISR

unsigned char data;

// save the port I/O address for other functions
open_port = port_base;

// first set the baud rate
// turn on divisor latch registers
_outp(port_base + SERIAL_LCR, SERIAL_DIV_LATCH_ON);

// send low and high bytes to divisor latches
_outp(port_base + SERIAL_DLL, baud);
_outp(port_base + SERIAL_DLH, 0);

// set the configuration for the port
_outp(port_base + SERIAL_LCR, configuration);

// enable the interrupts
data = _inp(port_base + SERIAL_MCR);
data = SET_BITS(data,SERIAL_GPO2);
_outp(port_base + SERIAL_MCR, data);
```

continued on next page

continued from previous page

```
_outp(port_base + SERIAL_IER, 1);

// hold off on enabling PIC until we have the ISR installed
if (port_base == COM_1)
   {
   Old_Serial_ISR = _dos_getvect(INT_SERIAL_PORT_0);
   _dos_setvect(INT_SERIAL_PORT_0, Serial_ISR);

   }
else
   {
   Old_Serial_ISR = _dos_getvect(INT_SERIAL_PORT_1);
   _dos_setvect(INT_SERIAL_PORT_1, Serial_ISR);
   }

// enable the receive character interrupt on PIC for selected comm port
old_int_mask = _inp(PIC_IMR);

_outp(PIC_IMR, (port_base==COM_1) ? (old_int_mask & 0xEF) :
     (old_int_mask & 0xF7 ));

return(1);

} // Serial_Open
```

The function basically takes three parameters: the base COM port address, the baud rate, and the configuration bits. However, the defines in BLACK9.H must be used as the parameters to set up the COM port properly. Furthermore, the configuration parameter can be generated as a combination of settings by logically ORing the desired setting together. For example, to set up the serial system for COM1 at 2400 baud with 8 data bits, no parity, and 1 stop bit, the following parameterization would be used:

```
Serial_Open(COM_2,SERIAL_BAUD_2400,SERIAL_PARITY_NONE |
           SERIAL_BITS_8 | SERIAL_STOP_1);
```

That's all there is to it! At this point, the ISR will take care of any incoming characters and place them into the input buffer. To read a character from the input buffer, we don't need much. It can be done in a couple of lines. First, let's write a function that tests whether a character has been received, as shown in Listing 9-3.

LISTING 9-3 Function that tests whether a character has been received

```
int Serial_Ready(void)
{
// this function returns true if there are any characters waiting and 0
// if the buffer is empty

return(char_ready);

} // end Serial_Ready
```

There's not much to it other than a test of the variable *char_ready*. But how is this going to help us determine if a character is ready? If we look carefully at the serial ISR, we see that it updates *char_ready* when it receives a character. Hence, the ISR sends a "signal" to the global variable space that records whether a character has been received. And all the application has to do is test this variable.

Once we have determined that a character is ready, we can read it by accessing the global input buffer and extracting it. Listing 9-4 contains the function to do that.

LISTING 9-4 *Extracting the next character from the input buffer*

```
int Serial_Read(void)
{
// this function reads a character from the circulating buffer and returns it
// to the caller, if there is no character waiting then the function returns 0

int ch;

// test if there is a character(s) ready in buffer

if (serial_end != serial_start)
   {
   // wrap buffer index if needed

   if (++serial_start > SERIAL_BUFF_SIZE-1)
      serial_start = 0;

   // get the character out of buffer
   ch = serial_buffer[serial_start];

   // one less character in buffer now
   if (char_ready > 0)
      --char_ready;

   // send data back to caller
   return(ch);

   } // end if a character is in buffer
else
   // buffer was empty return a NULL i.e. 0
   return(0);

} // end Serial_Read
```

The *Serial_Read()* function accesses the global input array serial buffer, and if *serial_end* is not equal to *serial_start*, then *Serial_Read()* reads the character out of the position indexed by *serial_start*. Then the function updates the *serial_start* variable. If a character isn't ready, the function returns a 0. Actually, this may cause a problem later since a 0 could be interpreted as a data word; hence, we may change this to -1, but it is fine for now.

Now that we can read characters, it's time to write them. To do this, we write the value we wish transmitted out to the Transmitter Holding Register (register 0) of the UART. However, before we do this, we must make sure that the THR is empty–that is, the last character has been shifted out. This can be done by testing bit 5 of the Line Status Register (register 5) of the UART to see if the transmitter buffer is empty. If it is, then another character can be placed in it for transmission; otherwise, we must wait until this bit is true before placing the next character. Listing 9-5 contains the function to write a character to the open serial port.

LISTING 9-5 Function to write a character

```
void Serial_Write(char ch)
{
// this function writes a character to the transmit buffer, but first it
// waits for the transmit buffer to be empty.  note: it is not interrupt
// driven and it turns off interrupts while it's working

// wait for transmit buffer to be empty
while(!(_inp(open_port + SERIAL_LSR) & 0x20)){}

// turn off interrupts for a bit
_asm cli

// send the character
_outp(open_port + SERIAL_THR, ch);

// turn interrupts back on
_asm sti

} // end Serial_Write
```

The *Serial_Write()* function simply tests the empty bit with *while()* and then proceeds to blast the next character out when the buffer is clear.

The next function we need is more of a utility than a building block, but we'll find it useful later. It is a function to write a string of characters out to the serial port with a carriage return appended to the end of the string. This function will be used when sending packets or communicating with modems. Listing 9-6 contains the code to write an entire string out to the serial port.

LISTING 9-6 Function to write a string to the serial port

```
void Serial_Print(char *string,int cr)
{
// this function is used to print a string to the serial port

int index,       // looping variable
    length;      // used for length of string
```

```
length = strlen(string);

// write each character
for (index=0; index<length; index++)
    Serial_Write(string[index]);
// send a carriage return if requested
if (cr)
    Serial_Write(13);

} // end Serial_Print
```

The *Serial_Write()* function has nothing new; it is just a higher level version based on the *Serial_Write()* function. I added it since I found myself using multiple *Serial_Write()*'s all the time. The next function is the converse of the *Serial_Print()* function, that is, a function to read a sequence of characters out of the serial system and flush the buffer. Buffer flushing is necessary in any communications program to help place the system in a known state and get rid of any unwanted garbage. The flushing function should flush the whole buffer, which is 1024 bytes; however, 32 characters will suffice in most cases since our games should not buffer up any more than a character or two. But if you want to, go ahead and change it for different applications. The flushing function is shown in Listing 9-7.

LISTING 9-7 Function to flush the serial system

```
void Serial_Flush(void)
{
// this function flushes out the serial buffer

int index; // looping index

// read up to 32 characters

for (index=0; index<32; index++)
    {
    Serial_Read();
    Time_Delay(1);
    } // end for index

} // end Serial_Flush
```

Of course, we could have reset the *serial_start* and *serial_end* indices, but that's not the desired effect. Instead, we want to flush the next 32 characters for a period of a second or two and make sure that any incoming transmission is thrown away.

That about wraps up all the functions we need for the serial communications system. The only function left is one to shut everything down and close the serial port. The function in Listing 9-8 does just that.

LISTING 9-8 Function to close a previously opened serial port

```
int Serial_Close(void)
{
// this function closes the port which entails turning off interrupts and
// restoring the old interrupt vector
unsigned char data; // used to hold data

// disable the comm port interrupts
data = _inp(open_port + SERIAL_MCR);
data = RESET_BITS(data,SERIAL_GPO2);

_outp(open_port + SERIAL_MCR, data);

_outp(open_port + SERIAL_IER, 0);
_outp(PIC_IMR, old_int_mask );

// replace old comm port isr

if (open_port == COM_1)
    {
    _dos_setvect(INT_SERIAL_PORT_0, Old_Serial_ISR);
    }
else
    {
    _dos_setvect(INT_SERIAL_PORT_1, Old_Serial_ISR);
    }

return(1);

} // end Serial_Close
```

The main tasks of *Serial_Close()* are to disable the interrupts in both the UART and the programmable interrupt controller and to remove the serial ISR and replace it with the old serial ISR that was saved in the pointer *Old_Serial_ISR()*.

An Example of Serial Communications

In a while we are going to see a full modem example of the COM ports, but for now let's briefly cover the steps to open a serial port, process data, and close the port. First, we open the serial port with the desired configuration using the *Serial_Open()* function:

```
Serial_Open(COM_2,SERIAL_BAUD_2400,SERIAL_PARITY_NONE |
          SERIAL_BITS_8 | SERIAL_STOP_1);
```

Then we would have a main loop of some kind that tests whether any characters are ready, and if so, they are processed. The loop also might write characters to the serial port:

```
while(!done)
    {
```

```
          // test if a character is ready

          if (Serial_Ready())
             {
             ch = Serial_Read();
          // print character to display
          printf("%c",ch);

             // do any further processing of character
             } // end if ready

         // test if user is trying to send output

      if (kbhit())
          {
          // get the key
          ch = getch();

          // send the character to the COM port
          Serial_Write(ch);

          // print the key to the screen
         Serial_Write(ch);

        // test if user is trying to exit
        if (ch==27) // escape
           done=1;

          } // end if keyboard hit

      } // end while
```

The above loop fragment is almost a complete terminal program that will print any characters received by the open COM port and send any characters typed by the user. Finally, when the user presses ESC, the *while()* loop is exited. After that the serial port should be closed with a call to:

```
Serial_Close();
```

This is too easy! If you hook a NULL modem from computer to computer (a cable with lines 2–3, 3–2, and 7–7), you can actually have a conversation between two computers. However, this is crude. We need to figure out how to interface with a modem so that we can use a modem-to-modem connection to carry on our serial conversations. Let's see how that works.

Making Contact with Modems

We should begin our quest by asking the question, what is a modem? A *modem* is a device that is capable of transmitting and receiving encoded data over a phone line. Figure 9-8 depicts the basic communications model between two PCs using

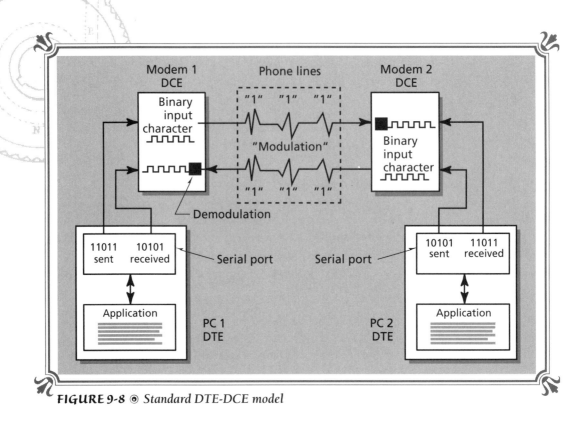

FIGURE 9-8 ⊙ *Standard DTE-DCE model*

modems as the communications devices. As we see from the figure, the PCs are called data terminal equipment (DTE) and the modems are called data communications equipment (DCE). The single task of the modem is to take care of all the details of managing the phone line, modulating the transmitter data, and demodulating the incoming receiver data. That's where the name modem comes from—*mod*ulator-*demo*dulator.

Today there are many types of modems and many new standards of transmission that are supported. Since modems use the phone lines for transmission, only so much information can be transferred over them. The original designers of the phone system never dreamed that computers would be talking over the phone lines some day. Thus, phone lines are designed to have only enough bandwidth to send and receive human voices. With the advent of personal computers in the 1970s and the resulting use of modems, the phone lines have been continually pushed to their limits. However, the bandwidth of run-of-the-mill phone lines hasn't changed much in the past 25 years. Of course, there are special high-speed phone lines that can be purchased, such as T1 lines, but the general public still must use the standard phone network, which is slow to say the least.

Today's modems can operate at 57.6K baud, and 14.4K baud is common. However, these rates are far more than can be supported by the phone lines' bandwidth. How are these high-speed transmissions possible? They are made possible using protocols, data compression, and error correction schemes. Some of the popular protocols are CCITT V.32bis/V.32/V.22bis and Bell 103/212A. Some popular data compression schemes are CCITT V.42bis and MNP–5. And finally, most modems use the CCITT V.42/MNP–4 error correction systems. Alas, as you can see, the acronyms themselves are forbidding, let alone how they actually work! Hence, we are not going to use data compression, error correction, or any protocols at all. We are simply going to use our modems at a slow enough rate that none of the above is necessary.

This maximum rate at which modem transmissions can be performed on a standard phone line without problems is 2400 baud. And this is what we're going to use. Even if you have a 57.6K baud modem, trying to send data using protocols, compression, and error checking would take a whole book to explain! Furthermore, 2400 baud will suffice as a starting point to grasp the game-related concepts that we are more interested in. Once you understand these concepts, feel free to write libraries to support every modem speed and protocol that your heart desires!

Let's reiterate our plan. We are going to use a pair of modems to allow two PCs to communicate. The information communicated will be data that is sent back and forth to control and play a multiplayer game. We don't want to use modem speeds greater than 2400 baud since setting the communications up at higher speeds is too complex. Instead, we will stick to 2400 baud and use the Hayes Smartmodem AT command set, which is the industry standard. This command set is a set of ASCII character strings that can be sent to the modem to direct it to do things such as dial, answer, go off hook, and so forth. Once we make a connection with the modems using the AT command set, we can forget that there are modems connected to the PCs and use the serial communications library to send and receive characters through the COM ports, which are connected to the modems.

Before we delve into the AT command set, let's be absolutely sure we understand the communications model that we are trying to implement. The modems are linked to the serial ports on the PCs (actually the serial ports are in the modems if the modems are internal). Thus, by opening a serial port that the modem is listening to, we can send and receive data to and from the modem. The data is sent and received by use of the serial communications library, but the modems are responsible for modulating and demodulating the data.

Now, the trick is to instruct the modems to make a connection between the two computers. This is done by sending commands (ASCII strings) through the COM ports to the modems. The modems will then listen and interpret these commands. If we send the right commands, we can instruct one modem to call the remote modem and make a connection. Once the modem-to-modem connection has been made, then as far as we are concerned, the communications model looks like Figure 9-9. As you see, modems no longer appear in the abstract model, only a serial-to-serial communications channel. This is the result we are looking for. Let's see how to make this connection.

FIGURE 9-9

ⓞ ⓞ ⓞ ⓞ ⓞ ⓞ

Communications model from a programmer's point of view (after a connection has been made)

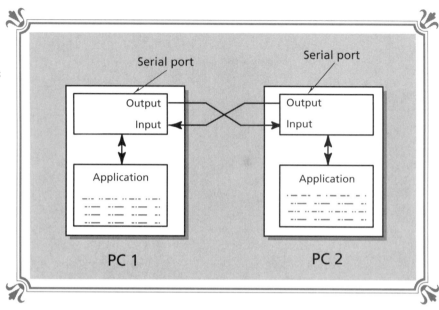

The AT Command Set

From a programmer's point of view, the modem is no more than a gateway that enables a PC to communicate over a phone line. However, to instruct the modem to perform tasks or to query its state, some form of protocol must be used. For modems that are 2400 baud and below, this protocol is called the AT command set and was originally standardized by the Hayes Corporation. This set of simple commands instructs a modem to do different things. You see, whenever a modem starts up, it is in what is called the *command state*. After the modem has made a connection, it is in the *online state*. Figure 9-10 shows the possible state transitions that a modem can make.

Notice that once a modem is in the online state it can only be placed back into the command state by hanging up the phone line and losing the carrier (the carrier is the base tone that modems use to communicate). The problem with the online state is that once a modem is in this state, it will no longer listen to commands. The modem will simply pass any data received through the serial port out to the phone line for transmission. This situation is usually acceptable unless we want to fall back to the command state (we will learn how this is done later). So, all we need the AT command set for is to control and configure the modem and make a connection. Once the connection is made, the data sent and received through the serial port (which is connected to the modem internally or externally) will flow through the modem transparently. Unfortunately, the complete AT command set is too big to list, so we are only going to look at the commands that are the most important for us along with their parameterizations. They are listed in Table 9-4. Notice that all commands sent to the modem are preceded by AT followed by the command.

FIGURE 9-10

◎ ◎ ◎ ◎ ◎ ◎

States of a
modem

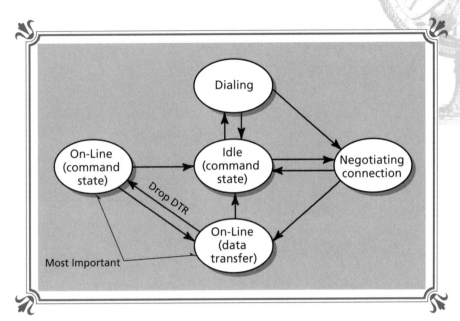

TABLE 9-4 ◇ *AT command set for Hayes-compatible modems*

Command Syntax	Description
ATA - Answer	This command instructs the modem to answer an incoming call. Normally the modem will take the phone off the hook and listen for a carrier.
AT - Attention	This command is used as the prefix for most commands. If sent alone (without a suffix), it directs the modem to pay attention.
ATB - Compatibility	This command instructs the modem to use specific compatibility modes. It can be followed by a single digit with the following meanings: ATB0 - Instructs the modem to use CCITT V.22/V.22bis (default). ATB1 - Instructs the modem to use Bell 103/212A.
ATC - Carrier Control	This command is used to control the carrier generation of the modem. The forms are: ATC0 - Carrier always off. ATC1 - Carrier controlled by modem.

continued on next page

continued from previous page

Command Syntax	Description
ATD - Dial	This command is used to dial a number. The command can be followed by these characters:

0-9,#,*	Dial the digit.
P	Use pulse dialing.
R	Send answer tones instead of originate tones.
T	Use Touch-Tone dialing.
W	Wait for a second dial tone.
@	Wait for one or more rings and five seconds of silence.
,	Pause.
!	Flash (hang up).
;	Return to command mode after dialing.

Note: For example, to dial my phone number, you would use the command ATDT408-555-1234.

ATE - Echo	This command is used to instruct the modem to echo commands back or not. It has the following forms:

ATE0 - Turn command echo off.

ATE1 - Turn command echo on (default).

Note: Normally, when a character is sent to the modem in command mode, the character is echoed back. The ATE command is used to enable or disable this feature.

ATH - Switch Hook Control	This command is used to instruct the modem to go on or off the hook. It can be used to close the connection in some cases. It has the following forms:

ATH0 - Go off hook.

ATH1 - Go on hook.

ATQ - Quiet	This command is used to instruct the modem to send responses or be silent. Normally, when an AT command is sent to the modem, the modem will respond with a string such as "OK","CONNECT", and so forth. We will cover these responses in detail later; however, the ATQ command is used to control the sending of these responses and has the following forms:

Command Syntax	Description
	ATQ0 - Enable command responses (default).
	ATQ1 - Disable command responses.
ATV - Verbosity	This command is used to instruct the modem whether to return digit codes or ASCII strings. It has the following forms:
	ATV0 - Send single-digit codes.
	ATV1 - Send ASCII string responses (default).
ATX - Response Code Sets	This command instructs the modem to send certain types of response strings and codes. By selecting a specific setting, the modem will only respond with a specific set of the total response codes. Here are the various forms of ATX:

Digit Code	ASCII String	ATX0	ATX1	ATX2	ATX3	ATX4
0	OK	*	*	*	*	*
1	CONNECT	*	*	*	*	*
2	RING	*	*	*	*	*
3	NO CARRIER	*	*	*	*	*
4	ERROR	*	*	*	*	*
5	CONNECT 1200		*	*	*	*
6	NO DIALTONE		*		*	
7	BUSY			*	*	
8	NO ANSWER	*	*	*	*	*
9	reserved for future					
10	CONNECT 2400		*	*	*	*

Note: In most cases the default is ATX4, which instructs the modem to support all responses.

ATZ - Reset	This command instructs the modem to perform a full reset and should be sent first since it will wipe out all previous programming and reset the modem to the standard factory defaults.

The next set of commands are prefixed by the & character, which must be in the ASCII command string.

continued on next page

continued from previous page

Command Syntax	Description
AT&D - Data Terminal Ready Line Control	This command instructs the modem on how the DTR line should be handled by the modem. In most cases the only way to place the modem back into command mode once it is in the online mode is to toggle the DTR line on the RS-232 interface using the UART. The AT&D command qualifies this functionality. Here are the forms of the command:
	AT&D0 - Ignore DTR line completely.
	AT&D1 - Return to command state if DTR is toggled.
	AT&D2 - Hang up the phone, return to the command state (default).
	AT&D3 - Reset the line using hardware.
AT&Q - Protocol Enable (used on protocol modems only)	This command is used to enable protocols for modems capable of rates higher than 2400 baud. Since we are only interested in 2400 baud modems, we will use the command to instruct the modem to use direct mode without any protocol. Here are the forms of the command:
	AT&Q0 - Direct asynchronous, no protocol.
	AT&Q1 - Synchronous.
	AT&Q2 - Synchronous.
	AT&Q3 - Synchronous.
	AT&Q4 - Synchronous.
	AT&Q5 - Enable error correction.
	AT&Q6 - Hybrid mode.

Note: We are only interested in mode 0 - Direct asynchronous mode.

AT&C - DCD Control	This command informs the modem when a carrier should be sent. The forms are:
	AT&C0 - Carrier always on.
	AT&C1 - DCD enabled after carrier linkage (default).

Table 9-4 details the more commonly used commands out of the 60 or so in the AT command set. If you need a more complete listing, your modem's manual should have one. As we see in the table, the modem sends response codes to AT commands. It is by these response codes that we determine the status of the modem and the connection. Table 9-5 lists the response codes in order of their numerical definitions.

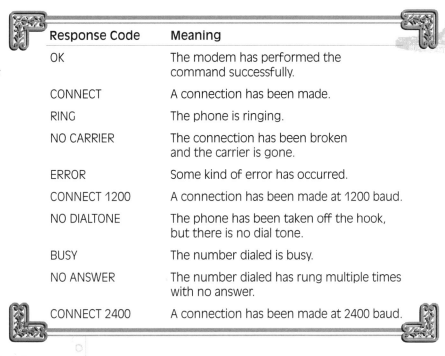

TABLE 9-5
❖❖❖❖❖❖
Modem response codes and their meanings

Response Code	Meaning
OK	The modem has performed the command successfully.
CONNECT	A connection has been made.
RING	The phone is ringing.
NO CARRIER	The connection has been broken and the carrier is gone.
ERROR	Some kind of error has occurred.
CONNECT 1200	A connection has been made at 1200 baud.
NO DIALTONE	The phone has been taken off the hook, but there is no dial tone.
BUSY	The number dialed is busy.
NO ANSWER	The number dialed has rung multiple times with no answer.
CONNECT 2400	A connection has been made at 2400 baud.

As an example of using the AT command set, I have taken our serial communications library and written a small terminal program. When the program starts it will ask which COM port your modem is attached to, and then it will open that serial port. At this point, the modem will be listening to your input since all the keypresses are being sent to the modem. The name of the program is TERM1.C and the executable is TERM1.EXE. The source code is shown in Listing 9-9.

LISTING 9-9 Simple terminal program that allows commands and data to be sent and received to and from the modem

```
// TERM1.C - A simple serial communications program.

// I N C L U D E S ///////////////////////////////////////////////////////

#include <io.h>
#include <conio.h>
#include <stdio.h>
#include <stdlib.h>
#include <dos.h>
```

continued on next page

continued from previous page

```
#include <bios.h>
#include <fcntl.h>
#include <memory.h>
#include <malloc.h>
#include <math.h>
#include <string.h>

#include "black9.h"
#include "black3.h"

// G L O B A L S ///////////////////////////////////////////////////////

// M A I N ///////////////////////////////////////////////////////

void main(void)
{

char ch;            // input character

int done    = 0,   // global exit flag
    sel,            // user menu input
    com_port;       // the com port to open

printf("\nSerial Communications Program Version 1.0\n\n");

// ask the user for the com port
printf("\nWhich COM port is your modem attached to 1 or 2?");
scanf("%d",&com_port);

// depending on users selection open COM 1 or 2

if (com_port==1)
    Serial_Open(COM_1,SERIAL_BAUD_2400,SERIAL_PARITY_NONE |
                SERIAL_BITS_8 | SERIAL_STOP_1);
else
    Serial_Open(COM_2,SERIAL_BAUD_2400,SERIAL_PARITY_NONE |
                SERIAL_BITS_8 | SERIAL_STOP_1);

// main loop
// flush serial port
Serial_Flush();

printf("\n");
// enter event loop
while(!done)
    {
    // try and get a character from local machine
    if (kbhit())
        {
        // get the character from keyboard
        ch = getch();
```

```
        printf("%c",ch);

        // send the character to other machine
        Serial_Write(ch);

        // has user pressed ESC ? if so bail.
        if (ch==27)
           {
           Serial_Flush();
           done=1;
           } // end if esc

        // test for CR, if so add a line feed
        if (ch==13)
             printf("\n");

        } // end if kbhit

   // try and get a character from remote
   if (ch = Serial_Read())
       {
       // print the character to the screen
       printf("%c",ch);

       // if it's a carriage return add a line feed
       if (ch==13)
             printf("\n");

       // if a esc character is sent from remote then close down
       if (ch==27)
           {
           printf("\nRemote Machine Closing Connection.");
           Serial_Flush();
           done=1;

           } // end if remote close

       } // end if serial read

    } // end if not done

// close the connection and blaze
Serial_Close();

} // end main
```

When the program executes, the first thing it does is ask for the COM port that your modem is attached to (in most cases this will be COM2). Then the program uses the *Serial_Open()* command to open up the COM port at 2400 baud with 8 data bits, 1 stop bit, and no parity. At this point, the program enters the main event loop. The event loop does two things. First, it tests whether a key has been pressed and if so, retrieves the character and sends it to the COM port, which in turn is connected to the modem. The remaining logic of the event loop tests whether there is a character ready at the serial port and if so, the program prints the character to the screen. The interesting thing about the program is that characters sent to the modem through the serial port are reflected or echoed by the modem. This can be disabled by using the command ATE0.

In any case, just to get an idea of controlling the modem from the terminal program, let's type in the following commands:

ATZ [ENTER]	Reset the modem.
AT&D2 [ENTER]	Instruct modem to allow UART to control DTR line.
AT&Q0 [ENTER]	Instruct modem to use direct non-protocol mode.

After we have entered the above sequence, the modem can be instructed to dial up another modem with this command:

ATDT phone number [ENTER]

The modem would then take the phone off the hook and dial the number. When the other end answers, the other modem will send a CONNECT message, which you should see on your terminal. So, how would we make the other modem answer? Well, the same initial configuration commands would be used:

ATZ [ENTER]	Reset the modem.
AT&D2 [ENTER]	Instruct modem to allow UART to control DTR line.
AT&Q0 [ENTER]	Instruct modem to use direct non-protocol mode.

But to make the receiving modem answer the phone, it would wait for a ring and the ATA would be sent, which instructs the modem to answer the phone. But how can we detect a ring? The answer is simple. When the modem is in the command state, it will send a response string if an incoming call is made, which will look like this:

RING

Thus, if we program our terminal program to look for the string "RING" coming from the serial port, then when the string is detected, we would instruct the modem to answer using the ATA (answer phone) command. Hence, making a connection between two modems can be done by sending a few initialization commands to each modem and then instructing one modem to dial while the other modem listens to the COM port until it receives a "RING" response. Then the receiver sends the ATA command to the modem, and the receiving computer will answer the phone.

Once a connection has been made, both modems will send a "CONNECT" response followed by the connection baud rate. In our case the response string would be "CONNECT 2400". Therefore, once each terminal program has detected the final "CONNECT 2400" response, both modems (the sender and receiver) have connected, and the serial ports are now basically a full-duplex connection. However, the modem will no longer listen to commands. So, if an AT command is sent, the ASCII characters of the commands will simply be sent over the phone line to the remote machine without any interpretation.

Once a connection has been made between the two PCs, the only way to break the connection (at least the simplest way) is to drop the DTR line. The DTR or Data Terminal Ready line can be thought of as the overall communications enable. If it is inhibited, communications will cease and the modem(s) will be placed back into command mode and will again respond to AT commands. How do we control the DTR and enable and disable it? If you recall, the Modem Control Register (MCR, register 4) of the UART controls, among other things, the DTR line. So all we need to do is write a program that can set or reset the 0 bit in the MCR, and we can break the connection if there is one.

Sending Multiple AT Commands

Before moving on to the interface library, there is one aspect of the AT command set and sending AT commands to the modem that comes in handy. This is the ability to send a string of AT commands following a single "AT" string. For example, if we wanted to reset the modem, place it in verbose mode, and enable DTR control, we would normally do the following:

ATZ ENTER
ATV1 ENTER
AT&D2 ENTER

However, the same results can be achieved with:

ATZV1&D2 ENTER

The only drawback to this method is that if there is an error, it's not possible to figure out which part of the command string caused it, but being able to send large strings is very useful. For example, in the game Starblazer, I have created a file called BLAZE.MOD that contains any modem initialization string that your particular modem may need in addition to the standard initialization that is performed on the modem. Having the ability to send entire concatenated command strings allows the BLAZE.MOD file to consist of a single ASCII line with the AT commands on it. (I'm sure you've seen modem initialization strings if you've ever tried to get modem-DOOM to work.)

The Modem Interface Library

As we have seen, controlling the modem means nothing more than sending ASCII strings that begin with "AT" followed by the appropriate command sequence through the serial port. Using these commands and a couple functions to read the response strings back through the modem, we could stop here. However, since we have gone this far, we may as well add a few more functions to make calling up another player as simple as possible.

Since we aren't trying to do anything spectacular with the modem, we don't need many functions. Here is a list of the main functions we are going to implement:

  ✛ A function to initialize the modem

  ✛ A function to control the handshaking lines on the modem, such as DTR (Data Terminal Ready)

  ✛ A function to send a command string to the modem

  ✛ A function to parse the result string from the modem

  ✛ A function to dial another modem and make a connection

  ✛ A function to wait for a call and then make a connection

Let's begin by implementing the simple functions first. To make things easier, we'll use the defines shown here (found in BLACK9.H):

```
// modem responses

#define MODEM_USER_ABORT      -1
#define MODEM_OK              0
#define MODEM_CONNECT         1
#define MODEM_RING            2
#define MODEM_NO_CARRIER      3
#define MODEM_ERROR           4
#define MODEM_CONNECT_1200    5
#define MODEM_NO_DIALTONE     6
#define MODEM_BUSY            7
#define MODEM_NO_ANSWER       8
#define MODEM_CONNECT_0600    9
#define MODEM_CONNECT_2400    10

// these are non-standard, but added for fun

#define MODEM_CARRIER_2400    11
#define MODEM_CONNECT_4800    12
#define MODEM_CONNECT_9600    13

#define NUM_MODEM_RESPONSES   14

// standard delay times
```

```
#define DELAY_1_SECOND        18
#define DELAY_2_SECOND        38
#define DELAY_3_SECOND        48

// modem control commands

#define MODEM_DTR_ON          0
#define MODEM_DTR_OFF         1
```

The first function we are going to write is the one that will enable or disable the DTR line on the modem. The DTR line allows a connection to be made (when enabled) or to be broken if a connection is in progress. Remember, once a connection has been made and the modem is in the online mode, it is very difficult to place the modem back into the command mode. Our function, shown in Listing 9-10, will allow this transition to be made by means of the hardware and the DTR line.

LISTING 9-10 Function to control different hardware aspects of the modem interface

```
void Modem_Control(int command)
{
// this function is used to control specific aspects of the modem hardware

unsigned char data;

// which command is being issued?
switch(command)
    {
    case MODEM_DTR_ON:
        {
        // read modem control register
        data = _inp(open_port + SERIAL_MCR);
        data = SET_BITS(data,1);
        _outp(open_port + SERIAL_MCR,data);

        } break;

    case MODEM_DTR_OFF:
        {
        // read modem control register

        data = _inp(open_port + SERIAL_MCR);
        data = RESET_BITS(data,1);
        _outp(open_port + SERIAL_MCR,data);

        } break;

    default: break;

    } // end switch
```

continued on next page

continued from previous page

```
// wait a sec for it to take effect

Time_Delay(DELAY_1_SECOND);

} // end Modem_Control
```

The function takes a single parameter, which is a flag that requests the DTR line to be enabled or disabled. We can add more commands to the function in the future if we wish, but for now the DTR control suffices. Anyway, depending on the value of the command flag, the function will either set or reset the DTR control bit in the Modem Control Register (MCR). Then the function waits a second to make sure the DTR transition has taken place. This will be a common theme in many of the functions; that is, we will add a small time delay at the tail end of the function to make sure the operation has completed. Remember, modems are hardware and they contain relays and other slow devices, so it's a good idea to place delays in key functions.

The next function we're going to write, shown in Listing 9-11, is one that hangs up the phone line. This is a bit redundant since the *Modem_Control()* function can do this, but it's nice to have a separate function, called *Hang_Up()*, that does the job. Actually, the function could have been implemented with a macro, but no one's perfect!

LISTING 9-11 Function to hang up the phone line

```
int Hang_Up(void)
{
// this function hangs up the phone and places the modem back into its
// command state

// drop dtr line

Modem_Control(MODEM_DTR_OFF);

return(MODEM_OK);

} // end Hang_Up
```

The function simply makes a call to *Modem_Control()* with the DTR off command and then returns *MODEM_OK*, which is a bit synthetic, but helps maintain a common exit response.

Moving on, the next function we need is one that will send a command string to the modem. This can be done by sending the characters of an AT-prefixed command out to one of the serial ports followed by a carriage return. The code is shown in Listing 9-12.

LISTING 9-12 Function to send command strings to the modem

```
void Modem_Send_Command(char *buffer)
{
```

```
// this function sends a command string to the modem

int index,     // looping variable
    length;    // length of command

// write the string out
length = strlen(buffer);

for (index=0; index<length; index++)
    Serial_Write(buffer[index]);

// uncomment the next line if you want to see what's being sent
// printf("\nSending:%s",buffer);

// send a carriage return
Serial_Write(13);

Time_Delay(DELAY_1_SECOND);

} // end Modem_Send_Command
```

The function takes a single parameter–the command string. The function then sends each character of the command string to the modem's COM port followed by a carriage return. It waits a second to make sure the command has been processed and then returns. For example, if we wanted to send the reset modem command "ATZ" using this function, we could write:

```
Modem_Send_Command("ATZ");
```

The *Modem_Send_Command()* function is very similar to the *Serial_Print()* function except that a carriage return and delay is added. Similarities like this are common in serial communications packages. There are a lot of functions, each with a little twist in them.

The next function we need is something to parse the response string that will be emitted by the modem. Figure 9-11 shows the process in action. When a command string is sent to the modem, the modem returns a response code. Most of the time the response code will be "OK", but in other cases, such as dialing another modem, it may be "CONNECT 2400", and so forth. Therefore, we need a function that can parse the response code coming back from the modem while filtering out any garbage or echoed command strings.

Filtering out the response code isn't a simple task. There are two things to consider. First, if the command echo is enabled, the echoed command string mustn't be interpreted as a response code; second, the response code is embedded within a prefix and suffix string. The prefix string is ASCII values 13,10 and the suffix is 13,10. If you look on an ASCII chart, 13 is a carriage return and 10 is a line feed. Therefore, all response strings look like this:

13,10,"response string in ASCII",13,10

FIGURE 9-11

◉ ◉ ◉ ◉ ◉ ◉

*Sending and
receiving
commands to and
from the modem*

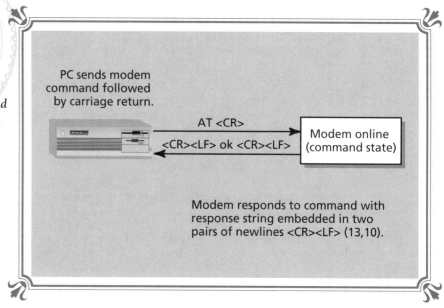

So the response string for "OK" would look like this:

13,10,79,75,13,10

With this information in hand, we can come up with an algorithm to parse response strings. The algorithm goes something like this:

1. Scan for the ASCII pair 13,10.

2. If 13,10 is found, then consume them and copy the following characters into a buffer until the value of 13 is found, then consume the 13 and 10 and return the response code.

Of course, if you have ever written parsing functions, you know they always seem to be messy, and they just don't look right! But I have tried to make the function clear. There are three main parts that accomplish the scan and extraction of the response string, as shown in Listing 9-13.

LISTING 9-13 Function to retrieve the results of a modem command

```
int Modem_Result(char *output,int exit_enable)
{
// this function is a bit messy (as are all parsing functions), it is used
// to retrieve a response from the modem, however, it will disregard any
// echoed commands, also, the last parameter exit_enable is used as a flag
// to allow the keyboard to force an exit, this is useful in a situation
```

```
// such as waiting for an answer or waiting to be called, in any case, this
// gives the function an exit avenue, the exit is enabled by pressing a key
// on the keyboard, however, the keyboard handler must be installed for
// this to work!

int index=0,          // looping variable
    start=0;

char ch,              // working character
     buffer[64];      // working buffer

// hunt for start of response
while(1)
    {
    // is a character ready?

    if (Serial_Ready())
       {
       if (Serial_Read()==10)
          break;
       } // end if a character is ready

    // test if user is trying to abort
    if (exit_enable && (kbhit() || keys_active))
       return(MODEM_USER_ABORT);

    } // end while

// read the response
while(1)
    {
    // is a character ready?
    if (Serial_Ready())
       {
       ch = Serial_Read();

       if (ch==10)
          break;
       buffer[index++] = ch;

       } // end if a character is ready

    // test if user is trying to abort
    if (exit_enable && (kbhit() || keys_active))
       return(MODEM_USER_ABORT);

    } // end while

// terminate response
buffer[index-1] = 0;

// uncomment the next line if you want to see what's being received
```

continued on next page

continued from previous page

```
// printf("\nReceived:%s",buffer);

// copy the result into the output string
if (output!=NULL)
   strcpy(output,buffer);

// compute which response has been given

for (index=0; index<NUM_MODEM_RESPONSES; index++)
   {
   // test the response to next response string
   if (strcmp(modem_strings[index],buffer)==0)
      return(index);

   } // end for index

// there must be some kind of error
return(MODEM_ERROR);

} // end Modem_Result
```

The function takes a pair of parameters. The first is the destination space in which to place the response code and the second is an exit enable flag. The exit enable flag is needed for the following reason. Once the *Modem_Result()* function is called, it will wait forever for a response string. In most cases, forever will only be a few milliseconds since this function will be called immediately after a *Modem_Send_Command()* call. But in some cases the result from the *Modem_Send_Command()* call may take seconds to minutes. For example, if a number was dialed with,

```
Modem_Send_Command("ATDT 555-1234");
```

then the response could take awhile, since this number is only listed in the movies! Alas, the user may not want to wait and will want to exit from the application. However, the *Modem_Result()* function would be trapped in a tight loop; therefore, the exit enable allows a keypress to be used to bail out of the function. The keypress logic will work with standard C I/O and with our new keyboard handler since the conditional is of the form *(kbhit() || keys_active)*. In essence, we just need a way to get out of the function.

As I said, the function has three main parts. The first part hunts for the 13,10 sequence. Once found, the second part extracts the response string, and then NULL terminates it. Finally, a look-up table of response strings is used to compare the returned response string, and the string is converted into a digit response code so that conditional logic can be performed more easily.

We are almost done! The next few functions are based on ones we have already written and simply make calls to them. Let's take a look at Listing 9-14, the modem initialization function that resets the modem and sends a couple commands to it.

LISTING 9-14 Function to initialize the modem

```c
int Initialize_Modem(char *extra_init)
{
// this function will initialize the modem and prepare it for use
// if your modem has some specific sequence that must be sent to reset
// it then send it in the extra string, otherwise set extra equal to NULL

int result;

// send reset command

Modem_Send_Command("ATZ");

result = Modem_Result(NULL,0);

if (result!=MODEM_OK)
    return(result);


// allow dtr line to be controlled, uncomment this if you want
// the function to perform the DTR set, otherwise, leave it
// commented and send AT&D2 in the extra string. This
// is commented out because it causes problems with some external modems

// Modem_Send_Command("AT&D2");

// result = Modem_Result(NULL,0);

// if (result!=MODEM_OK)
//     return(result);

// place modem in direct asynchronous mode

Modem_Send_Command("AT&Q0");

result = Modem_Result(NULL,0);

if (result!=MODEM_OK)
    return(result);

// send hardware specific modem command

if (extra_init && strlen(extra_init)>=2)
    {
    // this is where the modem will be given most of its
    // correct initialization information
    Modem_Send_Command(extra_init);

    result=Modem_Result(NULL,0);

    } // end if
```

continued on next page

continued from previous page
```
return(result);

} // end Initialize_Modem
```

The *Initialize_Modem()* function does nothing more than send a few AT commands to the modem, which puts it into a known state. I have sent the reset command, DTR control (you may or may not want this), and enabled direct mode of operation (no protocol). You may have to add a couple more AT commands to get your specific modem into the standard Hayes Smartmodem 2400 mode. This is what the *extra_init* parameter is for. If you find that the function just doesn't initialize the modem properly, you can add some more commands in this parameter.

For example, maybe you have to enable the verbose mode of the modem with the ATV1 command, and so forth. However, my testing shows that most modems (protocol or not) seem to default to a fairly standard setting that, along with the above initialization strings, does what we want. If you have trouble making a connection, pull out your modem manual and look for the standard initialization string that it likes.

In any case, the AT commands are sent to the modem and each of the responses are tested. If there is a problem, an error is returned and the function exits. The next pair of functions are going to make life very easy on us because making a connection between two modems takes a bit of legerdemain and encapsulating the sorcery into a pair of functions is a good idea! The first of the functions to make a connection allows the game application to be the originator (the caller). It's shown in Listing 9-15.

LISTING 9-15 Function to make a call and then make a connection

```
int Make_Connection(char *number)
{
// this function calls up the sent phone number and returns true if the
// connection was made or false if it wasn't

int result;
char command[64];
// flush serial buffers
Serial_Flush();

// enable the DTR line
Modem_Control(MODEM_DTR_ON);

Time_Delay(DELAY_1_SECOND);

// dial number
sprintf(command,"ATDT%s",number);

// make the call
Modem_Send_Command(command);
```

```
result = Modem_Result(NULL,1);

// test the result
if (result==MODEM_CONNECT       ||
    result==MODEM_CONNECT_1200 ||
    result==MODEM_CONNECT_2400)
    {
    // a successful connection has been made

    return(result);

    } // end if connection made
else
    {
    // there must be a problem, hang up the phone
    Hang_Up();

    // return the error
    return(result);

    } // end else

} // end Make_Connection
```

The function takes a single parameter, which is the phone number to call. In general, the phone number can have white space and/or single hyphens (-) between the area code, prefix, and number, but don't add any parentheses! For example, the following are valid phone numbers:

408-555-1234
777-2000
1 408 234 9000

This one's invalid:

1(408) 555-1200

If you want to be able to use parentheses and other syntactic niceties, I suggest a pre-parser that strips the extraneous characters before they are sent to the *Make_Connection()* function.

Anyway, let's talk about the function. It begins by enabling the DTR line. This is necessary to indicate to the modem hardware that everything is a go. Then the phone number is dialed using the "ATDT" command followed by the number. The function then makes the call and waits in the *Modem_Result()* function, which will return in a few seconds with the response of a connection, busy, no answer, or other appropriate string. If one of the connect messages is returned, such as "CON-NECT 2400", the function returns the response code and exits. However, if a connection wasn't made, the function hangs up the phone line (a precaution) and then returns the response code, whatever it may be.

You will also notice a *Serial_Flush()* at the beginning of the function. This is just a precaution to make sure there is no garbage in the serial buffer when the connection process begins.

Our next function, *Wait_For_Connection()*, is the converse of the *Make_Connection()* function. This function does almost the same thing as *Make_Connection()* except that *Wait_For_Connection()* waits for a response code of "RING". Once this is found, the modem is instructed to answer via the "ATA" command and a connection will be made (we hope). The implementation of *Wait_For_Connection()* is shown in Listing 9-16.

LISTING 9-16 *Function that waits for an incoming call and then makes a connection*

```
int Wait_For_Connection(void)
{
// this function will wait for a connection to be made and return true
// when this occurs. the function will return false if a connection isn't
// made or in a specific amount of time or if a key is pressed

int result;

char command[64];

// flush serial buffers
Serial_Flush();

// make sure modem is hung up
Hang_Up();

Modem_Control(MODEM_DTR_ON);

// wait for phone to ring...
result =  Modem_Result(NULL,1);

// was that a ring?

if (result == MODEM_RING)
   {
   // tell modem to answer
   Modem_Send_Command("ATA");

   result = Modem_Result(NULL,1);

   // test the result
   if (result==MODEM_CONNECT ||
     result==MODEM_CONNECT_1200 ||
     result==MODEM_CONNECT_2400)
     {
     // a successful connection has been made
     return(result);

     } // end if connection made
```

```
    else
       {
       // there must be a problem, hang up the phone
       Hang_Up();

       // return the error
       return(result);

       } // end else

    } // end if ringing

} // end Wait_For_Connection
```

The *Wait_For_Connection()* function doesn't take any parameters since its sole purpose is to wait for the phone to ring. When this happens, the modem will send a "RING" response code to the serial port. The response code can then be used as the initiator of the "ATA" command, which instructs the modem to take the phone off the hook and answer. This sequence is more or less what the function does. The function starts by flushing the serial buffer and then disabling the DTR line (making sure the phone is hung up). Then the function waits for a response. When a response arrives, it is tested to see if it's the "RING" response. If so, the "ATA" answer command is sent to the modem and the function again waits for a response.

When a response arrives the second time, it is tested to see if it is the desired response code for a connection—"CONNECT 2400." If so, the result code is returned and a connection is made. Otherwise, the phone is hung up and the function returns the response code, whatever it may be.

Using the *Make_Connection()* and *Wait_For_Connection()* functions along with our other calls, we're now ready to make a modem-to-modem connection. As an example, I have written another terminal program that has a nice little menu system. The name of the program is TERM2.EXE and the source code is TERM2.C. The program allows you to make a call, wait for a call, hang up the line, and exit. Load the program onto two different machines that have modems and give it a try. As in the TERM1.EXE program, TERM2.EXE will query you for the COM port that your modem is attached to. The source code for the program is shown in Listing 9-17.

LISTING 9-17 *A complete terminal program*

```
// TERM2.C - A menu driven modem terminal program.

// I N C L U D E S /////////////////////////////////////////////////////////

#include <io.h>
#include <conio.h>
#include <stdio.h>
#include <stdlib.h>
#include <dos.h>
#include <bios.h>
```

continued on next page

continued from previous page

```c
#include <fcntl.h>
#include <memory.h>
#include <malloc.h>
#include <math.h>
#include <string.h>

#include "black9.h"
#include "black3.h"

// G L O B A L S /////////////////////////////////////////////////////////////

// M A I N ////////////////////////////////////////////////////////////////////

void main(void)
{

char ch,          // input character
     number[64];  // the phone number that is dialed

int done   = 0,   // global exit flag
    sel,          // user menu input
    linked = 0,   // has a connection been made
    result,       // result of modem commands
    com_port;     // the com port to open

printf("\nModem Terminal Communications Program Version 2.0\n\n");

// ask the user for the com port
printf("\nWhich COM port is your modem attached to 1 or 2?");

scanf("%d",&com_port);

// depending on users selection open COM 1 or 2
if (com_port==1)
    Serial_Open(COM_1,SERIAL_BAUD_2400,SERIAL_PARITY_NONE |
                SERIAL_BITS_8 | SERIAL_STOP_1);
else
    Serial_Open(COM_2,SERIAL_BAUD_2400,SERIAL_PARITY_NONE |
                SERIAL_BITS_8 | SERIAL_STOP_1);

// main loop

// flush modem and serial port
Serial_Flush();

Initialize_Modem("AT&D2"); // make this NULL if you have a problem with
                           // an external modem

printf("\n");

// enter event loop

while(!done)
```

```
{
// if a connection hasn't been made then enter into menu

if (!linked)
   {
   printf("\nMain Menu\n");
   printf("\n1 - Make a Call");
   printf("\n2 - Wait for Call");
   printf("\n3 - Hang Up");
   printf("\n4 - Exit");
   printf("\n\nSelect ?");

   // get input from user
   scanf("%d",&sel);

   // what is user trying to do
   switch(sel)
        {

        case 1:  // make a call
             {
             printf("\nNumber to dial?");
             scanf("%s",number);

             // try and make the connection
             result = Make_Connection(number);

             // was the response code a connect message
             if (result==MODEM_CONNECT_1200 || result==MODEM_CONNECT_2400 ||
                 result==MODEM_CONNECT || result==MODEM_CARRIER_2400)
                {
                linked=1;
                printf("\nEntering Terminal Mode...\n");
                }
             else
             if (result==MODEM_USER_ABORT)
                {
                printf("\nUser Aborted!\n");
                Hang_Up();
                Serial_Flush();
                } // end else

             } break;

        case 2:  // wait for call
             {
             printf("\nWaiting...");

             // wait for a call
             result = Wait_For_Connection();

             // was the response code a connection
```

continued on next page

continued from previous page

```
                   if (result==MODEM_CONNECT_1200 ||
                       result==MODEM_CONNECT_2400 ||
                        result==MODEM_CONNECT ||
                       result==MODEM_CARRIER_2400)
                       {
                       linked=1;
                       printf("\nEntering Terminal Mode...\n");
                       }
                   else
                   if (result==MODEM_USER_ABORT)
                       {
                       printf("\nUser Aborted!\n");
                       Hang_Up();
                       Serial_Flush();
                       } // end else

                   } break;

              case 3: // hang up
                   {
                   // drop DTR and flush serial buffer

                   Hang_Up();
                   Serial_Flush();

                   } break;

              case 4: // exit
                   {
                   // set global exit flag
                   done=1;

                   } break;

              default:break;

              } // end switch

          } // end if not linked


          // once machines are linked, allow bi-directional communication

          while(linked==1)
              {
              // try and get a character from local machine
              if (kbhit())
                  {
                  // get the character from keyboard
                  ch = getch();

                  printf("%c",ch);
```

```
                    // send the character to other machine
                    Serial_Write(ch);

                    // has user pressed ESC ? if so bail.
                    if (ch==27)
                       {
                       linked=0;
                       Hang_Up();
                       Serial_Flush();
                       } // end if esc

                    // test for CR, if so add a line feed
                    if (ch==13)
                        printf("\n");

                    } // end if kbhit

              // try and get a character from remote

              if (ch = Serial_Read())
                 {
                 // print the character to the screen
                 printf("%c",ch);

                 // if it's a carriage return add a line feed
                 if (ch==13)
                     printf("\n");

                 // if an esc character is sent from remote then close down
                 if (ch==27)
                    {
                    printf("\nRemote Machine Closing Connection.");
                    linked=0;
                    Hang_Up();
                    Serial_Flush();

                    } // end if remote close

                 } // end if serial read

           } // end while linked

       } // end if not done

   // close the connection and blaze

   // break connection just in case
   Hang_Up();

   Serial_Close();

   } // end main
```

The program is easy to follow, as it is basically TERM1.C with the added menu system and modem functions implemented. However, once the connection is made, the data retrieved from the keyboard is sent to the other machine transparently, and incoming data is printed to the screen from the remote machine.

We have completed our study of serial communications and modems. Although there is much more to be learned, we have the fundamentals needed to use the modems and serial ports as a transparent communications channel. Now let's continue our studies by learning how two computers are kept in synchronization.

Game Synchronization Techniques

Alrighty then! Finally, we can create a bidirectional full-duplex connection between two PCs. And to send and receive data we will use two functions:

```
Serial_Write(...);
Serial_Read();
```

The question is, how do we keep two games that are running on two PCs in synchronization with each other? The answer to this question is not an easy one. As usual there are many constraints in flux, such as baud rate, errors, bandwidth, and so forth, which will force us to stick to a very simple model. Even though we have chosen 2400 baud as the maximum transmission rate (to avoid protocols), the same issues will emerge at any baud rate. Thus, we need to define some basic strategies to keep two games in synchronization.

There are a multitude of techniques to accomplish this, each with their pros and cons. But the name of the game is to keep both games doing the same thing, so that each player stays within the same universe. Of course, some things don't need to be kept in synchronization. For example, anything in a game that is totally passive, such as background animation or maybe even music, isn't going to make a big difference if it's not in synchronization on each machine. On the other hand, if the player on one machine is at a specific position in the game universe, he had better be at the same position in the remote universe; otherwise, there are going to be problems. So, let's discuss some of the synchronization techniques and models that are used. With this information we can create models that suit our needs for our specific applications.

Input Device Reflection

The simplest way to write a two-player, two-computer game is to use *input device reflection*. This is a technique whereby each remote PC treats the communications channel like a long cable that sends the player's input device changes through the channel. Figure 9-12 shows this setup. We see that PC 1 sends its joystick movements to PC 2 and vice versa. We also see that the remote on PC 1 is the local on PC

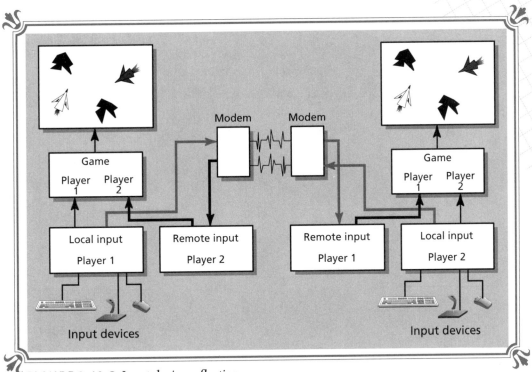

FIGURE 9-12 ◉ *Input device reflection*

2. In essence, the phone line becomes a really long keyboard, mouse, or joystick cable. And it's through this cable that the other player's data is sent to the remote PC.

However, sending the motion of each player to the remote machine isn't enough. What if one machine is faster than the other? In this case, PC 1 may be on frame 504 while PC 2 is on frame 505 (since PC 2 is slightly faster). It may not seem that this could happen since most of our demos use a timer synchronization at the end of the game loop. However, if you recall, the timer synchronization only forces the game loop to execute at no more than some specific frame rate, such as 18 FPS. If the logic takes longer than an 18th of a second during a particular iteration of the game loop, this could cause the games to get out of sync.

To illustrate this point, take a look at Figure 9-13. Here, two PCs are executing the same game, but one PC is a 386 and the other is a 586 Pentium. The 386 can barely keep up the 18 FPS rate, but the Pentium spends most of its time waiting in the delay section at the end of the game loop since the game logic is executing so quickly. If we assume that the two PCs are in sync, they will stay in sync until the 18 FPS is not kept up.

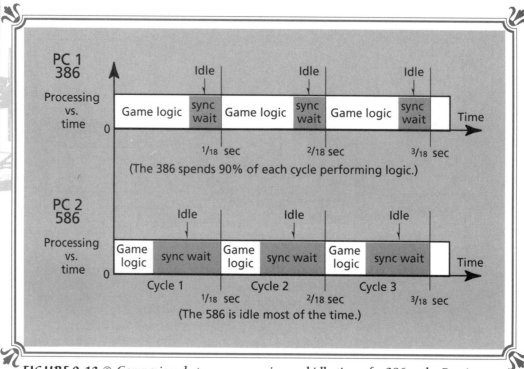

FIGURE 9-13 ⊙ *Comparison between processing and idle time of a 386 and a Pentium*

In Figure 9-14, possibly as a result of a large number of explosions, PC 1 has taken longer than an 18th of a second to process the game logic, and for an instant the frame rate dropped to 5 FPS. But PC 2, with the Pentium processor, didn't flinch and stayed locked to 18 FPS. The result is that PC 1 and 2 are now at least one frame out of sync. Therefore, in addition to sending information about the state of the remote machine, there must be some method of temporal synchronization to keep both machines on the same frame.

I have seen and written games that didn't have temporal synchronization, but the games must perform a "relocking" cycle every 30 frames or so. Basically, the two machines are allowed to run free, but after a certain number of frames, the machines send a ton of information back and forth to make sure that everything is in synchronization. This method, while valid, is a bit too cavalier for our use. We are going to use a token message passing scheme to keep temporal synchronization. But we'll get to that in a bit, after we discuss the second popular method of universe synchronization.

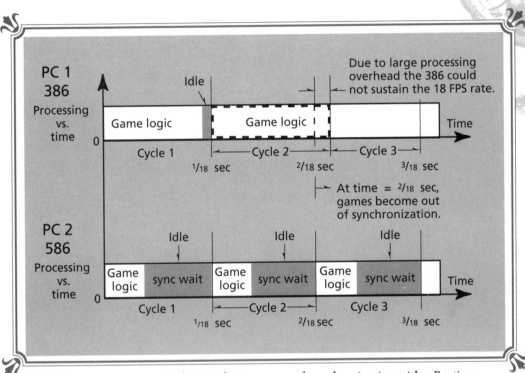

FIGURE 9-14 ◉ *Overworked 386 is losing temporal synchronization with a Pentium*

Universe Reflection

Sending the input device states back and forth between machines works great, but there are times when we may want to have slightly different events happening on both machines. You see, normally the two games that are running on each machine must be almost identical. This means that any event that occurs on one machine must occur on the other. For example, if an alien randomly enters into one game, it had better enter into the other at the exact same time and position. This brings us to the concept of *deterministic processes*. Simply put, there can be no random events on either machine unless the random events are pseudorandom and occur on both machines.

For example, assume the same game is running on two PCs, and at time t0 both machines are in synchronization, but then at time t1, PC 2 decides to add an alien, but PC 1 doesn't do this. The only way that this could happen is that a random number was used in the game code somewhere. We already know that PCs can't generate random numbers; they only generate random sequences that exhibit the proper distributions to be called random. These sequences are *seeded* with a seed that starts the sequence. Hence, if we seed the random number generator (which is a fairly simple function) with a 13,

```
srand(13);
```

then the random sequence will always be the same. Therefore, random numbers aren't really random. But if both PCs don't use the same seed number, the sequences will be out of order. The whole point of all this is that all sections of the game that are dependent on the player's interaction must be exactly the same! So, what if we don't want the two games to be exactly the same, and we want random events to occur on both machines? Well, the only way to deal with this is to send a message to the remote PC describing the event(s) to make sure that both machines know what's going on within each other. This is where the term *universe reflection* comes from.

Universe reflection is the brute-force method of game synchronization. As each frame displays, data from each remote machine is used to make any updates that are necessary to each local machine. Figure 9-15 shows this in action. The position

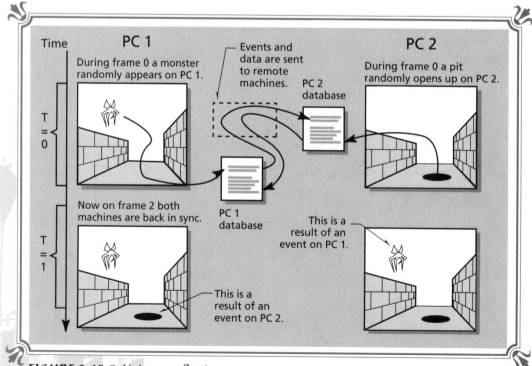

FIGURE 9-15 ☉ *Universe reflection*

and state of the pit that opens up on PC 2 is sent to PC 1 at some point within the same frame, and a pit opens up on PC 1. And if any nondeterministic events occur on PC 1, they would likewise be sent to PC 2.

Universe reflection is widely used in high-end military simulations. Basically, there is a global database, and each machine has a local copy of the database (see Figure 9-16). Any change that occurs on any machine is sent to the database, and any change that occurs in the database is sent to the remote machines. Our model is a bit simpler since there are only two machines, but the concept is the same. This is actually the technique used for many online games.

The major problem with universe reflection is the amount of data that must be sent back and forth every frame. For example, say the positions, directions, and states of ten objects must be sent to the remote machine during one frame. Assuming that each object uses 16 bytes to define it, that's a total of 160 bytes. But this is doubled since both machines may have to do this at the same time and the transmissions may be, at worst case, in series—hence, the total amount of data time will be 320 bytes. This is a lot of information to be sending over a modem. In general, the number of bytes per second that can be transmitted over a modem is only 70 to 80 percent of the baud rate because each character must be sent with a start bit, stop bit(s), and possibly, parity. Thus, our simple example of 320 bytes is a total impossibility, since even at 9600 baud that would mean (if we were lucky) 960 characters per second or 50 characters per frame at 18 FPS, which is only a fraction of the 320 bytes we need!

FIGURE 9-16
◎ ◎ ◎ ◎ ◎ ◎
*High-end
universe
reflection setup*

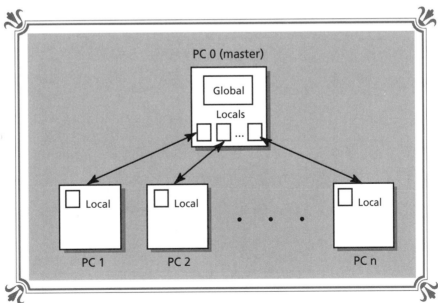

If nondeterministic events occur infrequently, universe reflection can be used as a resynchronization method performed every now and then. Under normal conditions a game may use input device reflection and occasionally, a bit of universal reflection if something really big happens.

Now that we know the two main methods for keeping the objects in the games synchronized, we have to make sure that the PCs stay synchronized in the case of a slow frame and a pair of PCs running at different speeds.

Sending Tokens to Stay Locked

A 386 slowing to 5 FPS while a Pentium stays locked at 18 FPS is the perfect example of why some sort of temporal synchronization is necessary. Somehow, we must make sure that each PC waits for the other to process one frame. Only when both PCs are complete with the current frame can each move to the next. This can be implemented by using a "wait" function when requesting the remote machine's data (which could be input device changes or universe changes). Figure 9-17 shows this

FIGURE 9-17

◉ ◉ ◉ ◉ ◉ ◉

The "send and wait" synchronization technique

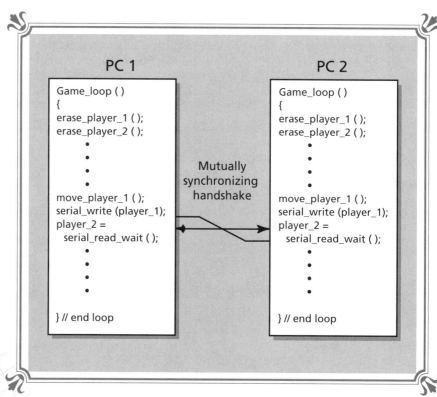

concept graphically. PC 1 processes its local player and then sends the local information to the remote with a call to *Serial_Write()*; then PC 1 waits for the response from the remote by using the variant of *Serial_Read()* named *Serial_Read_Wait()*.

By using *Serial_Read_Wait()*, PC 1 will wait as long as it takes for PC 2 to send its local information. But since both PCs are running the same game, this waiting structure will force both machines to lock to the slower machine and wait for it. Hence, if PC 1 slows to 5 FPS, then so will PC 2 since PC 2's game loop will have to wait for a character to be ready at the serial port. But this will occur at the frame rate of PC 1, which is 5 FPS, therefore, both machines will keep in synchronization.

This technique can be abstracted to sending a token back and forth, even though the token itself is data. The only drawback to this scheme is that the game will slow to the slower machine's rate. Furthermore, the bandwidth of the communications port can also become a bottleneck. For example, if the communications line can only support a rate of 10 CPS (characters per second) and each machine sends a single byte each frame, then the games are going to be stuck at 10 FPS even if they are running on supercomputers!

We have been using a model of a multiplayer game that has two PCs, each running the exact same program, so that the local player on one machine becomes the remote on the other and vice versa. Although this is almost true, it needs a bit of modification.

The Master-Slave Setup

Imagine that we write a game called GAME.EXE, which supports two players. One player is controlled by the local keyboard and the other is controlled by the remote keyboard via a modem connection. Let's say that the game is quite simple, something like Figure 9-18: a barren game grid with two tanks. Here's the problem: on PC 1 there will be two tanks named tank 1 and tank 2. Tank 1 is the local tank and tank 2 is supposed to be the remote tank. Moreover, tank 1 is located at (0,0) and tank 2 is located at (100,100). But this is a paradox because on the second computer, PC 2, tank 1 is supposed to be the local player and tank 2 is supposed to be the remote player. But tank 1 from PC 1's point of view is supposed to be the remote at position (100,100), but on PC 2 tank 1 is the local player at (0,0)! See the problem? We need to differentiate slightly between each PC so that the remote on PC 1 is the local on PC 2, but is placed at the same position, and so forth.

One method of dealing with this problem is the *master-slave* setup. Referring to Figure 9-19, we see that PC 1 is now called the *master* and PC 2 is the *slave*. Depending on whether or not a PC is the master or slave, the game executables will be slightly different. For example, using tank 1 and tank 2 to name the tanks on both master and slave machines, we could place the tanks in the following way:

FIGURE 9-18

ⓞ ⓞ ⓞ ⓞ ⓞ ⓞ

*The problem
with running the
exact same game
on two linked
machines*

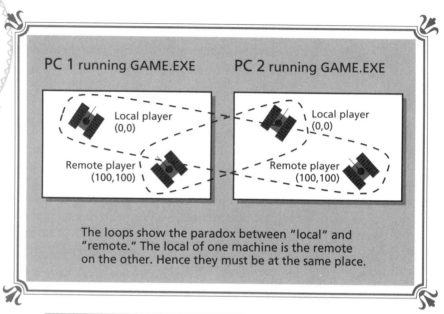

The loops show the paradox between "local" and "remote." The local of one machine is the remote on the other. Hence they must be at the same place.

Master (PC 1)	Slave (PC 2)
Tank 1 at (0,0)	Tank 1 at (100,100)
Tank 2 at (100,100)	Tank 2 at (0,0)

Now the tanks are placed correctly because PC 1 becomes the ringmaster and PC 2 is the performer. From PC 1's point of view, the remote should be at (100,100), and it will be since PC 2 takes on a subservient role. The master-slave concept can be taken even further. It is possible to make one machine perform all the logic and game algorithms and only send visual and sound information to the slave. This is the epitome of the master-slave setup–the slave becomes a client of the master.

Most two-player games are written using the first version of the master-slave setup rather than the full client-server version. However, I know of many new companies that are trying to create networks to support the client-server architecture. One such company is Challenge Net here in Silicon Valley. Challenge Net's new network will primarily support games that use a set of servers that are the master(s), and the players calling up the network are clients, or slaves.

Anyway, implementing a master-slave setup with two versions of the game on a disk in which player 1 must use version 1 (master) and player 2 uses version 2 (slave) isn't such a good idea. It would be better if the exact same piece of software could be used on both machines as either master or slave, but the software would use some method to decide who is master and who is slave. Then this information would be used by both machines to make sure the game starts off correctly.

FIGURE 9-19

◎ ◎ ◎ ◎ ◎ ◎

Using a master-slave setup to place objects

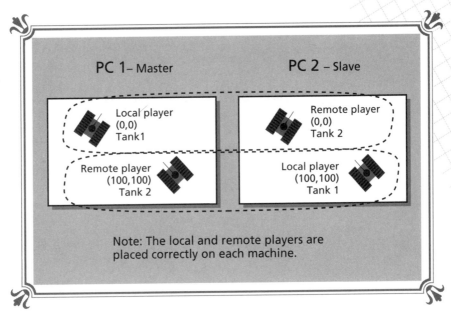

Note: The local and remote players are placed correctly on each machine.

The Master-Master Setup

Using a separate version of a game that must be used on each PC is fine for classroom examples and even a book like this, but let's see if we can't use a bit of Cybersorcery to come up with a plan that in effect creates a virtual master-slave setup for purposes of object placement and general who's who synchronization. The final model that we are going to use throughout the book is called the *master-master* model, and it is implemented like this: The same game is loaded on both machines; however, when a connection is made between the PCs, the originator is called the master and the receiver is called the slave. This might be recorded in a single variable like this:

```
if (dialing)
    master=1;
else
if (answering)
    master=0;
```

Then by testing *master*, a determination can be made on each local machine whether the game should take the point of view of being a master or a slave. This detail is used throughout the game to select starting positions of objects and order of operations within functions. We have already seen the example in which each tank must be placed in the proper position so that the remote tank of PC 1 is the

local tank of PC 2 and is placed correctly on both machines, but what about game logic? Let's take a look at a piece of code that normally runs fine on a single machine, but can cause problems on a modem to modem game:

```
While(!done)
        {
        // erase both the local player and remote player
        Erase_Local();
        Erase_Remote();

        // perform logic

        Move_Local();
        Move_Remote();

        // Draw objects

        Draw_Local();
        Draw_Remote();

        // show the frame

        Display_Next_Frame();

        // wait for time synchronization

        Wait();

        } // end main game loop
```

The problem lies in the highlighted area. You see, the order of execution of these two functions may make a difference since the local player on one machine is the remote on the other. The functions will be reversed on the other machine and in essence look like this:

```
Move_Remote();
Move_Local();
```

This may or may not cause a problem. For example, if there was only one missile in the game universe shared by both players and each player fired it at the same time, then there would be a *deadlock*, or in other words a finite resource would be allocated to both players incorrectly. We can fix this problem by using the master flag to force the functions to be called in the same order on both machines. Take a look below:

```
if (master)
    {
    Move_Local();
    Move_Remote();
    }
else
```

```
{
Move_Remote();
Move_Local();
} // end else must be slave
```

With the above logic structure, each machine–master and slave–will execute the functions in the same order, resulting in only one missile being fired. This gives us another layer of sanity checking to further ensure that each game is running the same way. You will notice that this test isn't done for the drawing or erasing sections. This is because we don't really care which object gets drawn or erased first since the results will almost always look the same. Basically, the local player will always be on top or under the remote player as drawn on the screen, but this isn't a big deal. Nevertheless, if you don't like it, you can use the same logic structure to force each machine to execute the rendering functions in the same order also.

That's about all there is to making modem-to-modem games. You will no doubt come across little details and problems during your own research, but you have the fundamentals. To make sure, I have written a modem-to-modem game called Starblazer that supports a master-master connection using input device reflection. But before we get to that (the fun part), let's touch upon a couple more esoteric topics to complete our studies.

Protocol Modems

We have spoken briefly about protocol modems and decided not to use them. The main reason for this is that protocol modems use all kinds of data formats, compression techniques, and error correction, and we just don't have the time to cover all of it. Moreover, there are so many standards in flux, to make a working library to transmit data would be a miracle! However, in real life a modem-to-modem game needs more than 2400 baud to function at a reasonable frame rate. Thus, after you get a solid grasp on the standard Hayes 2400 baud AT command set, you should move on to protocol modems and higher rates.

When using protocols, you must compose the data that is going to be sent each frame very carefully so that it can fit into a packet and be sent at a high enough rate. Also, you may have to deal with a lot of software handshaking to acknowledge transmissions, and so forth. This means that there are a lot of details to consider. There is a way out of all this though. You could buy a standard modem communications software library and use it (which is probably a good idea), but as Cybersorcerers our creed is "use nothing that we can't make ourselves." So, try not to use anything if you don't understand how it works! Don't get me wrong, I don't expect you to reinvent the wheel continually, but make sure that if you did have to reinvent the wheel, you would know how.

On-Line Games

The final topic we are going to discuss is the generalization of a two-player game to an infinite number of players. This genre of gaming is referred to as *On-Line*. An On-Line game is basically a collection of terminals or computers that are interlinked by means of some communication layer to a central master or server, as shown in Figure 9-20. Each player has his own local game environment, and the master computer has a complete database of all players in the universe. Even though most multiplayer Online games today are implemented through modem networks such as CompuServe, America Online, Prodigy, Imagination Network, and other similar service providers, the games are usually not what we would refer to as real-time.

Since there are so many players in the game, the games aren't usually drawn frame by frame at 15 to 30 FPS. Instead, the games are more of the strategy type. Each player takes a turn, the global database is updated, and then all the players are updated. The main reason for the lack of real-time is the communications bandwidth. If there

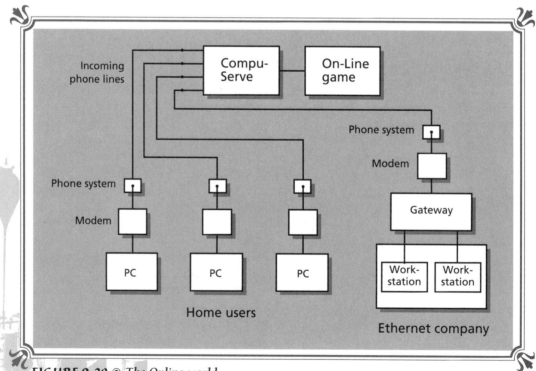

FIGURE 9-20 ☉ *The Online world*

are 100 players in an On-Line game, the computer master must update all 100 players each cycle in most cases. Of course, there are variants of this, and there are some On-Line games that come close to real-time, but most of them are quasi-interactive–meaning that each player has to wait a bit to see the results of his actions. Anyway, let's cover some fundamental aspects of On-Line game programming.

Common Games

In the beginning of On-Line games, the whole idea was to allow people using some sort of network to play games with each other and interact at some level. Thus, the first games were simple implementations of common board games, such as Dungeons & Dragons (D&D), Axis & Allies, and other similar role-playing games. The beauty of implementing these kinds of games on the PC was that the games, by their very nature, were sequential. In D&D, for example, there is a group of players. Each player roles the dice, makes his move, and then the DM (Dungeon Master) decides on the result. This cycle is repeated ad infinitum until the dungeon is solved or everybody is dead. (At least that's what I have read–of course, I've never played D&D myself.)

These sequential games became popular, but players didn't like waiting around for each player to take his turn, especially with 100 players in the game! Alas, new ways of thinking were needed to bring the response of the On-Line games closer to real-time. The result of this was to think of each player as a node that could send orders at any time (asynchronously).

The Basic Model

There are as many models of On-Line games as there are sequels to *Friday the 13th*, but they all have basic elements in common. Take a look at Figure 9-21, which shows an abstraction of the On-Line game model. A global database on the server knows everything about everything. In addition, the smaller local databases on each local machine reflect the state of the game on that machine. Now, if a command is given on the local machine to do something that can be done without communication to the master, the command is carried out without any message passing. For example, a player may want to know how many game pieces he has or what the damage is to his shields. These kinds of queries can be answered by the local data set.

However, if a player wants to move a piece (which may have global effects), this action is sent to the master, the master then updates the global database, the update trickles down to all the local databases, and after a second or so, all players are updated. The key to this system is asynchronous communication. During every cycle, the master tests all the input ports representing each player or, possibly, each player may cause an interrupt to occur that the master would process. In either

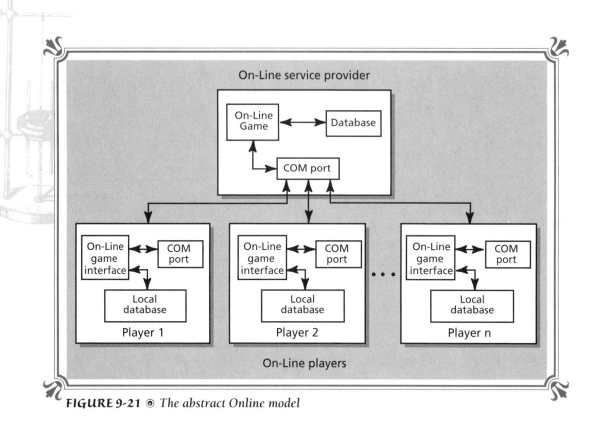

FIGURE 9-21 ⊙ *The abstract Online model*

case, the master interprets the actions and decides whether the other players need to be updated. If a global update is needed, the master may do it at the time the change occurred, or, to be efficient, the master may wait awhile for other changes so that the global update reflects as many player commands as possible in the next cycle.

For example, a game may listen to all commands within a one second period and then update all machines with the results. Thus, the time resolution on a game may be one second. This means that when a player does something, a maximum of one second will pass before all the other players "see" the result.

The Master and the Database

We haven't discussed data structures too often because I prefer to use simple constructs such as arrays and linked lists for most games. However, for an On-Line game, more complex structures may be needed. For example, the master database must have a structure that contains master-only information that the master needs for operation. Under this structure will be all the local states of all the players.

Hence, a tree structure may be in order, with pointers to all the player's structures. When a player is added or deleted, a pointer from the main structure is added or deleted.

Furthermore, many actions may be from player to player, and possibly the other players don't need to "see" the results of these actions. Therefore, there may be some communications between local structures within the database on a peer-to-peer basis. Whichever way you do it, remember one thing, keep it simple!

Keeping in Sync

Most On-Line games are not real-time, but you may come across some that are. For example, if a game has access to a high-speed network like Ethernet (10 megabit bandwidth), real-time isn't a problem. In this case, an On-Line game can be written similarly to a two-player modem-to-modem game–each game would have to be almost identical, and the order of operations would have to be very close in each game. However, there is the added stipulation that if there are more than two players, the best way to run the game is with a single master and multiple slaves.

The *single master-multiple slaves* or SMMS model is implemented using the same techniques already described except that when the game begins, the first machine on the network becomes the master (or the players simply agree to designate one machine as the master). The SMMS model is loose in that the master doesn't run the whole game and simply send the visuals to all the slaves. The only thing the master is responsible for in the SMMS model is forcing each player to take his turn in sequence. Then when all players have taken their turns, the master sends each player's changes to each of the other players, and the cycle is complete. Figure 9-22 shows this process in action. Player 1 through player n send their actions to the master, then the master, after waiting for each player's response, sends out a global state back to each player. Thus, the global state is used by each player to update all the remote players in the local game. Then each PC's game can move to the next cycle, and the process is repeated.

Writing On-Line games, real-time or not, is still a relatively new area because not many game developers have access to networks to try their designs on! Therefore, there are a lot of ways to do it, but the basic methods we have described are a good starting point.

Starblazer

We're ready to take what we've learned and apply it to a real game. The game I have created is called Starblazer (see Figure 9-23). Starblazer is a modem-to-modem space combat simulator that pits two players against each other in the cold vacuum of space. I like the sound of that...Each player is equipped with a craft of his choice

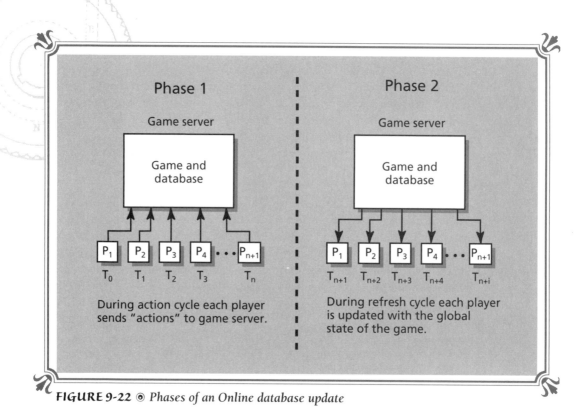

FIGURE 9-22 ◉ *Phases of an Online database update*

(Raptor or Gryfon). The object of the game is to defeat your opponent while avoiding the various objects floating around in the universe, such as asteroids, wormholes, and aliens. To make things more interesting, each player's ship is equipped with shields, a cloaking device, long-range scanners, and rapid fire photon cannons.

FIGURE 9-23

◉ ◉ ◉ ◉ ◉ ◉

Screen shot of Starblazer

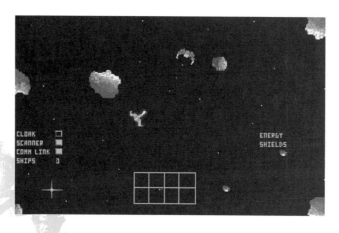

The game uses most of the graphics library and software that we have created thus far as well as this chapter's modules (for the communications). The entire game is roughly 7,500 lines of C code (plus all our libraries) and was written in about ten days. Normally, a game even as simple as Starblazer would take much longer, but with our graphics, sound, and communications library it was a snap! Even though it would be nice if we could discuss the game line by line, it would take a few hundred pages of explanation, not to mention that listing the game in the book would take another few hundred pages. Therefore, the explanations that follow are "high level."

At this point in the game, we are sophisticated enough that there shouldn't be any technical questions, such as "how was the ship drawn," and so forth. The only questions that need be answered are those of conceptualization and general design. In short, there is nothing in Starblazer that you haven't seen before. It's just that this is the first time everything has been put together in a single game. Anyway, let's start the analysis and hurry up and finish. I'm sure that you will want to try obliterating your best friend!

The Idea

The idea behind a game is always important. All games begin with an idea, so if the idea is bad, the game (no matter how good the graphics and sound) will also be bad. The idea behind Starblazer was generated from a list of needs. I wanted to do a pseudo-3D game (since we haven't covered true 3D) that was fun, simple, and allowed two people to use their skills to try and defeat each other. I'll always have a weak spot for space games, and I had just watched *Aliens* and *Star Trek VI* for the millionth time, so I decided to do a simple scrolling space game that allowed two players to fly around and shoot at each other. Then for good measure, I thought that it would be nice to add some asteroids, fuel pods, a wormhole, and a lot of neat gadgets for the ships, such as cloaks and shields.

The resulting game is fun, and when played with the music and digital FX, it can be quite excellent. I played my friend Mark Bell for about four hours and we both actually worked up a sweat! I'll never forget the look on his face when I de-cloaked, engaged shields, and blew him out of the stars! However, I have to admit he did that to me a few times also.

Playing the Game

Starblazer can be played in Solo or Modem-2-Modem mode. The game is started by running the executable named BLAZER.EXE. The game can run with both music and sound effects enabled or disabled. This is done with command line parameters. Here are the parameters and their meanings:

s - Enable sound FX

m - Enable music

For example, if you want to play Starblazer with both music and sound effects, type

BLAZER.EXE m s

at the DOS command prompt. If you don't add any command line parameters, the game defaults to no sound and no music. But to hear the music or the sound FX, the MIDPAK and DIGPAK drivers MIDPAK.COM and SOUNDRV.COM must be loaded. Once the game is running, the main menu will be displayed. It allows you to select the game options shown in Table 9-6.

TABLE 9-6

◇◇◇◇◇◇

Main menu selections for Starblazer

Menu Item	Description
Play Solo	This will enter you into the game alone for practice.
Make Connection	This is used to make a call to another computer.
Wait for Connection	This is used to wait for a call from another computer.
Select Ship	This is used to select the Raptor or Gryfon ship.
Set Comm Port	This is used to select the COM port your modem is attached to if you are going to play Modem-2-Modem.
Mission Briefing	This enters you into the instruction system.
Exit to DOS	This exits Starblazer and returns to DOS.

You navigate the menu with the arrow keys and press (ENTER) to make a selection. If there's a problem during one of the menu selections or you decide that you don't want to continue, pressing (ESC) will usually exit the submenu (if there is one).

Once you have configured the game's COM port and selected a ship, you can play alone or make a connection with another computer and play a friend. You control the ship the same way in either case, so let's cover that first. The control keys and how they function are shown in Table 9-7.

TABLE 9-7

◇◇◇◇◇◇

Controls for Starblazer

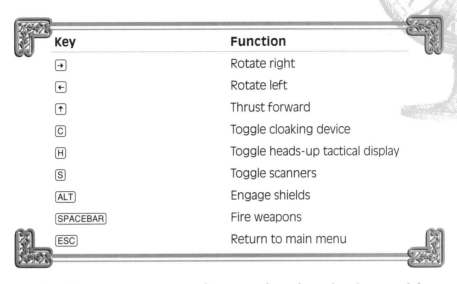

Key	Function
→	Rotate right
←	Rotate left
↑	Thrust forward
C	Toggle cloaking device
H	Toggle heads-up tactical display
S	Toggle scanners
ALT	Engage shields
SPACEBAR	Fire weapons
ESC	Return to main menu

When playing, your current coordinates are always located in the upper-left corner of the screen. The game universe is 2500x2500 units; if you go beyond these bounds in any direction, your ship will be warped to the other edge.

Minimum Requirements

For Starblazer to run in its full mode with music and sound FX, it needs about 580K of conventional memory, but 600K is safer. If you have DOS 5.0 or greater, this shouldn't be a problem. If you are finding it hard to run the game in full mode, either remove all TSRs, load DOS high, or play without music or sound.

Loading MIDPAK and DIGPAK

The game relies on both MIDPAK and DIGPAK for sound support. Hence, you must first use the SETM.EXE, SETD.EXE, or the general SETUP.EXE program that comes with the MIDPAK/DIGPAK development system to generate the files:

    SOUNDRV.COM

    MIDPAK.COM
    MIDPAK.ADV
    MIDPAK.AD

Then you must install both MIDPAK and DIGPAK by loading them at the DOS prompt with the following commands:

    SOUNDRV.COM
    MIDPAK.COM

If the music sounds really bad, try replacing MIDPAK.AD with my special instrument patches in the PATCHES directory. They are specifically designed for OPL2 and OPL3 sound cards, such as the Sound Blaster, Sound Blaster 16, and Sound Blaster PRO. In any case, if you enable music and/or sound in the command line parameters for BLAZER.EXE, and you haven't loaded the patches, Starblazer will hang! Finally, if the volume of the sound FX or music isn't strong enough or the base and treble are weak, try using the configuration utility that came with your sound card to manually set these features. Sound Blaster products are shipped with a mixer program that allows all the output settings of the card to be set. For example, Sound Blaster 16 comes with a program called SB16MIX.COM that loads as a TSR. If you have a SB16, load the mixer program, make your changes, and then unload it (to save memory) with the /U (unload) option. Other sound cards and manufacturers should have similar software and capabilities.

Making a Modem-2-Modem Connection

Linking up two PCs to play head to head is easy. Each player should select the ship and COM port of his choice. Then one player uses the Wait for Connection option on the main menu, and the other player uses the Make Connection option. The player using Make Connection will be the caller. The PC will call the second waiting PC (with the number entered by the calling player), negotiate a connection, and then the game will enter into space and the two ships will be sitting right next to each other! The game is terminated and the connection broken either after a player has won or the (ESC) key is pressed. In either case, this will hang up the phone line, so you can call your friend and gloat!

The communications system sets the rate of the modems to 2400 baud, so everybody should be able to play. If you have trouble making a connection with another computer, try the following:

1. Let your friend call you instead.

2. Edit the file named BLAZE.MOD, which contains the extra initialization string used for the modem. Change it as needed to make your modem and your opponent's setup as similar as possible. In general, the modems should be set for verbose mode, direct asynchronous transmission, no protocol, and DTR control enabled. However, some modems may need the DCD line and the RTS/CTS line controls tweaked. Use the AT&C, ATC, and ATR commands for these options.

3. As a final solution, use the TERM1.EXE program and send the AT&V command to the modem. This will extract the default profile from the modem, and this data can be used to compare each modem's setting and arrive at a happy medium. Then set up each PC's modem initialization string in the BLAZE.COM file to reflect the differences.

4. Make sure there are no TSRs or other programs that may be interfering with serial communications.

5. Buy a new modem.

That's about it for "user" discussions. Let's talk about the actual game design now and some of the major elements of the software.

The Game Universe

The game is played in a 2D universe that is 2500x2500, as shown in Figure 9-24. The background is simply a 3D parallax scrolling star field. The ship always stays in the center of the screen and the game elements move relative to it. This is accomplished by remapping all the game objects to screen coordinates that are always centered about the player's ship. Thus, the player becomes the center of the universe. The only downside to this is that the player never moves; instead, the whole universe is moved to the player. This is inefficient in that if there are 1,000 objects in the game and the player moves one time, then all 1,000 objects must be moved during the rendering process.

In addition to the star field, there is an asteroid belt that consists of large, medium, and small asteroids. The asteroids move in random directions. To replenish the player's fuel supplies, there also are fuel cells floating freely in the game from left to right. They are completely passive, and the only thing they do is animate through a few frames of animation and translate each frame. Finally, there is a wormhole at

FIGURE 9-24

◉ ◉ ◉ ◉ ◉ ◉

The Starblazer universe

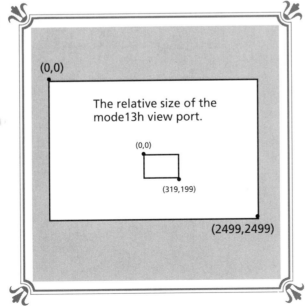

(0,0)

The relative size of the mode13h view port.

(0,0)

(319,199)

(2499,2499)

position (1250,1250). The wormhole was added to solve a problem. Whenever an object entered into the game, it was difficult to choose a random position beyond the game boundaries along with a random trajectory, since it's possible that the object may never come into view. Therefore, the wormhole is the perfect place to start objects. Objects can simply be emitted out of the wormhole.

Introduction and Control Panel

The introduction consists of the Waite Group Press artwork file followed by an initialization phase that loads images, allocates memory, and so forth. But to make this loading phase exciting, a font engine prints out each operation on the screen in a high-tech font. When everything has been loaded, the main Starblazer title screen is displayed for a couple seconds. Then randomly placed star-burst or twinkle effects are drawn every now and then for that added touch. These simple sprites were drawn as crosses that get bigger and smaller. When animated quickly, they look like reflections.

After the main title screen, the menu pops up and the user is free to navigate the menu with the keyboard. The keyboard interface is the interrupt driven one that we constructed in Chapter 5. When the menu system is active, the main event loop of the game is in the setup mode. Figure 9-25 shows the different states that the main event loop can be in. As you can see, the setup phase is the first state. The system will remain in the setup state until the user selects the Play Solo command or a connection is made. All of this logic is performed with simple *switch()* statements.

The entire game runs in real-time, meaning the game will never wait for input. Hence, even while the user is in the setup stage of the game, there is another simple process going on. This process is the scrolling red lights on the controller. During every cycle of the setup loop, a function is called that scrolls the lights (color rotation). However, if the setup loop waited for user input, this wouldn't be possible. There is an important point to learn here, and that is, no process should completely lock up the PC and force a "waiting" situation.

The Star Field

When the game arena is entered, the first thing you will see is a collection of stars. There are 50 to be exact. However, all 50 of these stars are placed in one of three star planes. And each of these star planes is rendered in a different shade of grey to show depth. Moreover, each of the star fields moves at a different velocity to simulate parallax. Together, both of these effects make for a realistic looking star background.

The stars are implemented as single pixels and are rendered with screen coordinates only. In other words, the star field logic has no idea that the universe is

FIGURE 9-25

◎ ◎ ◎ ◎ ◎ ◎

The states of Starblazer

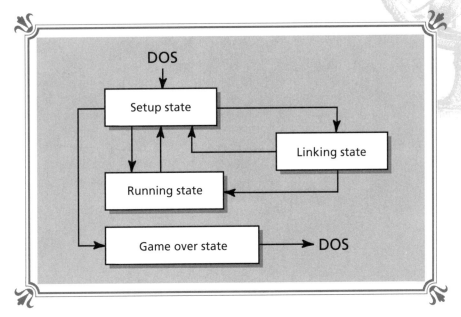

2500x2500. The star field logic thinks that the universe is 320x200. Hence, as the ship moves around, the same stars will scroll over and over. Most people won't even notice this little imperfection.

The Asteroid Belt

The asteroids are one of the coolest aspects of the game. The asteroid system consists of a set of functions that erase, move, and draw an asteroid object. However, each asteroid object can have one of three different sizes: small, medium, and large. This allows larger asteroids to break into smaller pieces, which is a bit more realistic. The structure for the asteroids is fairly simple, and a sprite might have sufficed if the extra variables such as velocity and universe coordinates didn't need to be tracked. Here's the structure for review:

```
// this is the structure for the asteroids

typedef struct asteroid_typ
        {
        int xv;                 // x velocity of asteroid
        int yv;                 // y velocity of asteroid
        int x,y;                // universe coordinates

        int type;               // type of asteroid, big, medium, small
```

continued on next page

continued from previous page

```
    sprite rock;            // the asteroid sprite

} asteroid, *asteroid_ptr;
```

As you can see, there isn't much to it. The asteroids of the game are all contained in a single array called *asteroids[]*. Other than moving around in random directions, the only other thing that the asteroid logic does is perform collision tests with the players in the game. Simple bounding box tests are used for these calculations.

The Alien

Even with the asteroids, the game needed something that could possibly attack the player(s), so I added an alien. The alien emanates from the wormhole and will move around randomly until a boundary is hit, at which point the alien is restarted at the wormhole. Currently, the alien has no aggressive logic installed, but this is one of the things you get to add!

The Wormhole

The wormhole is nothing more than a sprite that is stationary and animated every frame. The code that runs the wormhole isn't more than 100 or so lines. And if you get time, please redraw the animation cells for the wormhole; they are terrible, I just couldn't draw what I was thinking.

The Ship and Its Equipment

The ship is the focus of the game and the instrument of destruction. The game supports two ships, the Raptor and Gryfon, which the user selects in the main menu. The ships are 22x18 pixels and were generated with Deluxe Animation from Electronic Arts and a lot of Mountain Dew. The only thing interesting about the artwork for the ships is that all the rotations of the ships were prerotated using Deluxe Animation. This is a common technique used in games. Bitmaps are so hard to rotate that most games use prerotated bitmaps (if the memory is available).

Since the ships are the main instruments that the players use to fight each other, they needed to have some interesting equipment on board.

Shields

The shields are implemented using a pair of color registers and palette animation. Each ship is bordered with these color registers, and when the shields are engaged, a flag is set and the color registers are animated to make the ship(s) look like it's generating a shield. Then any collision detection consults the shield flag before making any decisions.

Photon Cannon

The player can fire a green photon cannon. These photons are nothing more than single pixels that are fired from the center of the ship in the direction of the ship. The photon logic moves the photons for a number of frames and then they die out. The other task that the photon missile logic performs is collision detection between the missiles and asteroids and the missiles and ships. Finally, there is an interesting aspect of how the velocity is computed for the photon missiles. When an object is moving and fires a projectile, the projectile is fired with a velocity relative to that of the moving object. Thus, if an object is moving in space at 50,000 kph and fires a missile that is moving at 100,000 kph, the missile will really be moving 150,000 kph relative to a stationary object (if the missile is fired in the direction the ship is traveling). Thus, relative motion is taken into consideration in the photon missile logic, and the missiles are always moved at a velocity equal to the sum of the ship's velocity (at the time of firing) and that of the missiles.

Cloaking Device

The cloaking device was one of the easiest effects to implement. When the Ⓒ key is pressed, a variable is toggled. If the variable becomes 1, then during the rendering logic the ship isn't drawn. When the cloaking variable becomes –1, the rendering logic draws the ship. That's all there is to cloaking. Of course, an eerie sound is played when the ship cloaks or de-cloaks, but for the most part the effect was very easy to implement.

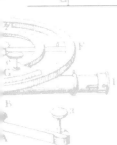

Scanners

The scanners are represented by a rectangular grid at the bottom of the screen when the Ⓢ key is pressed. When the scanners are engaged, the idea of them is to show the player's position and the position of his opponent along with all the asteroids, fuel cells, and alien ship. Currently, the only things shown on the scanner are the player's ship and the opponent's ship. The other objects are left for you to implement.

Scanners are very easy to make. In general, if you want to represent an object on a scanner, you divide down the position of the object relative to the size of the scanner and plot a pixel at the resulting location. For example, in Starblazer the scanner is 64x32 pixels in size and the universe is 2500x2500. Therefore, to convert an object's position to scanner coordinates for plotting, a simple division is needed, such as:

```
scanner_x = 64*object_x / 2500;
scanner_y = 32*object_y / 2500;
```

As an example, if the game object was at (2500,2500), then on the scanner it would be at 64*2500/2500, 32*2500/2500) = (64,32), which is correct. Of course, the constants can be precomputed, and the final scanner blip positions must be translated to the position of the scanner itself on the screen.

Heads-Up Display

The heads-up display or HUD is a collection of indicators that detail the state of the player at all times. The state of the cloaking device, communications link, energy, shield strength, and number of ships left are all displayed in real-time. The heads-up display is implemented by drawing the icons for the display on the screen whenever there is a change in the display status. This way the game doesn't need to redraw the heads-up information every cycle. To facilitate this, a variable named *refresh_heads* is used in the game. And if any function changes the state of any of the elements that are reported on the heads-up display, then it is redrawn during the next animation cycle.

Making the Music

The music for Starblazer was created by the gifted Dean Hudson of Eclipse Productions using an Ensonique EPS sequencer along with Cake Walk Professional by Twelve Tone Systems for Windows. After we had all the sequences sounding great on Cake Walk, we had the joy of converting all the sequences to sound right using MIDPAK. This is not easy and can be very time-consuming. You see, MIDPAK uses a different instrument patch set than general MIDI does, resulting in sounds being different–transposed and so forth. Anyway, with a bit of help from Rob Wallace of Wallace Music And Sound, we finally got the music to sound exactly like it did when it was composed. This conversion is such a pain that I suggest you simply pay for it to be done. Most composers charge from $25 to $100 to convert a general MIDI song over to the MIDPAK instrument patches.

The music system for Starblazer is nothing more than a single layer on top of the functions we already wrote to play MIDI music under MIDPAK, except that a single array contains within it the sequences that should be played as a function of time. Here is the array:

```
int game_sequence[] = {0+5,1+5,4+5,5+5,4+5,2+5,1+5,3+5,1+5,5+5,5+5,4+5,
                       1+5,2+5,3+5,2+5,4+5,4+5};
```

Disregard the 5's–they are irrelevant. Basically, the array is used in conjunction with the *Music_Status()* call. When a sequence is complete, the next sequence in the array is started. When all the sequences have been played, the whole thing starts over. All the music for Starblazer is contained in the single XMI file named BLAZEMUS.XMI. There are a total of 12 sequences contained within it. Five of the sequences are for the introduction music and the remaining 7 are used during game play.

The Digital FX System

The digital sound FX system is a bit more complex than the music system. The problem is that most sound cards only have a single digital channel. Although it's possible to synthesize a set of virtual channels from a single channel, I didn't take that approach for Starblazer. Instead, a simple priority-based preemptive scheduler was used. All sounds to be played are requested through the scheduler. If a sound is playing, the priority of the sound requested is compared to that of the currently playing sound. If the requested sound has a higher priority, the currently playing sound is stopped and the new sound is played. If there isn't a sound playing, the requested sound is played regardless of its priority.

The sound FX function is fairly short and worth taking a look at. It's shown in Listing 9-18.

LISTING 9-18 Sound scheduler function used in Starblazer

```
int Digital_FX_Play(int the_effect, int priority)
{
// this function is used to play a digital effect using a pre-emptive priority
// scheme. The algorithm works like this: if a sound is playing then its
// priority is compared to the sound that is being requested to be played
// if the new sound has higher priority (a smaller number) then the currently
// playing sound is pre-empted for the new sound and the global FX priority
// is set to the new sound. If there is no sound playing then the new sound
// is simply played and the global priority is set

// is the digital fx system Online?

if (!digital_enabled)
   return(0);

// is there a sound playing?
if (!Sound_Status() || (priority <= digital_FX_priority))
   {
   // start new sound
   Sound_Stop();
   Sound_Play((sound_ptr)&digital_FX[the_effect]);

   // set the priority
   digital_FX_priority = priority;

   return(1);

   } // end if
```

continued on next page

continued from previous page

```
else // the current sound is of higher priority
  return(0);

} // end Digital_FX_Play
```

To use the function, an identifier of the sound to be played is sent along with its priority. Lower numeric priorities have the highest priorities.

The Explosions

There are two explosions in Starblazer. One is a standard bitmapped explosion that lasts about a second and sequences through a set of animation cells, and the other is a particle explosion referred to as a *supernova* in the game code. The supernova explosion is created with a collection of "particles," each with its own color, speed, position, and lifetime. The supernova explosion starts by generating the velocities and directions of all the particles and then the explosion is started. The supernova logic moves the particles and modulates the color of the particles for a number of frames and then terminates the explosion.

The supernova is used when one of the ships is destroyed either by another player or an asteroid. This adds a bit of variety to the game. In general, if a game supports only simple bitmapped explosions, then there should be at least three different sets of artwork for the explosions.

Modem Communications Strategy

The modem communications technique used for Starblazer is input device reflection. During each cycle, both PCs create a single byte that contains all the possible keys pressed; then this byte is sent to the remote and interpreted. This way, each PC thinks of the remote player as another keyboard or input stream. The synchronization is sustained using a token passing scheme. PC 1 can't progress to the next frame until PC 2 sends its input information and vice versa. This forces both PCs to wait for each other, and they will never get out of frame synchronization. However, if one machine slows down, the other will track to the slower machine; but this is acceptable in most cases.

End of Game Sequence

When the game ends, the computer stops both machines (if there is a connection) and informs each player whether they were victorious or defeated. This is done visually and by voice FX. Then the game is sent back to the setup stage. This sequence could use some work–maybe some kind of cinematic sequence, such as blood and guts for the loser and fireworks and warp drive for the winner?

The Game Loop

Now that we have touched upon the main elements of the game, let's take a look at the overall game loop and logic. Referring to Figure 9-25, the game loop is entered after the initialization section of Starblazer takes place. Once entered, the game loop will never be exited until the game ends. There are four main states that the game loop can be in:

✥ Setup state

✥ Linking state

✥ Running state

✥ Game over state

The setup state consists of a tight real-time loop that updates the introduction music and the scrolling red lights on the controller, and consumes player input, updates, and data structures. Also, the setup state is responsible for making a modem-to-modem connection.

The linking state is entered after the game has made a connection to another machine. The linking state is very important because it's here that both machines are synchronized and the master sends a "magic cookie," which is a random number seed for the remote machine. After the linking state is complete, the running state is entered.

The running state of the game has two portions, the initialization and event loop. You see, if the game is played more than once without exiting and restarting the game, there are a lot of variables that must be reset, and so forth. Thus, the beginning of the running state resets the whole game, and then the actual game event loop is entered. The game event loop is a standard one that consists of erase, move, draw. However, since there are two players, much of the code is replicated to support the other player. Also, I decided to place almost all of the logic for the players in *main()* so you could follow it easily. It may be a good idea to move some of this code out into functions once you understand how everything works. The running state of the game can only be exited if the player hits ESC or the player wins or loses. Then the game moves back into the setup state.

The game over state is moved into from the setup state when the user selects the Exit to DOS menu item. At this point the game is exited and all resources are released back to the operating system.

The Cybersorcerer Contest

You've seen the game and had a peek at its insides, now it's up to you to make it better. As you know, there is a contest (detailed in Appendix A), which you can

enter either as a Cybersorcerer or Cyberwizard. Cybersorcerers should use Starblazer as the foundation and improve upon it. Then send in the finished product for judging. I'll give you a few hints for things that will make me happy:

✛ More sound FX.

✛ The alien shoots at the ships.

✛ When ships cloak, it would be cool if the space around them distorted.

✛ The scanner must be completed.

✛ Players should be able to enter through the wormhole and pop out somewhere else in the game.

✛ Ships should be able to be damaged instead of destroyed with a single shot.

✛ Players should be able to pick up the energy cells.

✛ Maybe just a little bit of cinematic sequences here and there.

✛ Anything else you can think of!

Summary

We have covered so much information about modems in this chapter, I forgot this was a video game book! But this was necessary since we need to know how things work. We learned about the serial communications system, the AT command set, and modems. We also wrote software to implement an entire modem-to-modem communications system. But the main point of the chapter was to learn the techniques used for multiplayer games, such as master-slave, master-master setups, servers, and synchronization techniques, and methods such as input device reflection and universe reflection to keep each computer running the same game. Finally, we ended the chapter with a description of Starblazer, a complete modem-to-modem video game that is a conglomeration of not only this chapter, but all the others up until now.

Well, it's been nice while it lasted, but prepare to see the most evil writings you have ever seen–the math for 3D graphics!

10

3D Fundamentals

come trutti fiore se manote lle . . . . se quali permobano . . . l alga
e . gra . p . si . iure . commati e . gone . s . sa . goy . rano . de . bo . ne .
er . g . are . nella . ma . e . l . a . per . ma . nella . della . ma . della . pegi . quer
sforga . et . pib . i . omo . pib . ville .

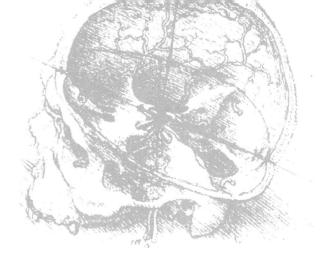

10

3D Fundamentals

We now have the knowledge and power to cast many spells. However, all of our magick is still trapped in the two-dimensional space called the *Cartesian plane*. It's time to put away our toys and become real Cybersorcerers! This chapter is an introduction to basic 3D concepts, jargon, and mathematics needed to cast the most wicked of 3D spells. Then during the remaining chapters of the book, we'll focus more on each of these topics and generate the proper computer code for a complete 3D graphics engine, much like the 2D engine used to make Starblazer.

This chapter is full of trigonometry and linear algebra. However, we're going to move through the material very slowly and make sure that we understand the origin and derivation of all of it. Keep in mind that we're going to cover all of these concepts in detail many more times, so if something doesn't click, don't worry too much–it will become clearer down the line. The main point of this chapter is to acquire a new vocabulary along with getting a grip on 3D fundamentals and the mathematics used throughout the remainder of the book.

Starting with the Flatlands

Before we begin studying 3D systems, let's review the simpler 2D plane and the basic concepts and operations that relate to it. Figure 10-1 shows the standard 2D

FIGURE 10-1

◎ ◎ ◎ ◎ ◎ ◎

The Cartesian plane

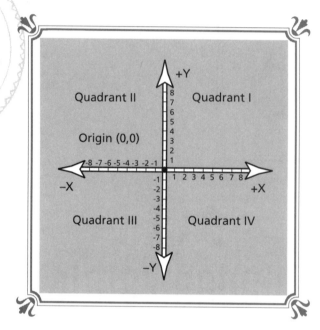

plane. There are two axes, labeled X and Y. The X axis runs horizontally and the Y axis runs vertically. Furthermore, the X and Y axes intersect at a 90 degree angle–in other words, they are perpendicular.

Up to this point, we have been performing graphics on the 2D plane, except that the Y axis on the computer screen is inverted, and the origin of the computer screen is located at the upper-left corner of the screen. Thus, to transform any coordinate from a standard 2D Cartesian plane to screen coordinates, we would use the following formulas:

```
x_screen = x + SCREEN_WIDTH/2;
y_screen = -y + SCREEN_HEIGHT/2;
```

Basically, the above fragment translates the origin to the center of the screen and inverts the Y component. Anyway, let's see what the 2D plane has to offer as far as geometrical primitives.

Points, Lines, and Polygons in 2D

Since the 2D plane is flat, not many primitives can be defined in this rather limited space. However, there are a few primitives, each based on the previous one, that we can discuss. The first geometric primitive is the *point*. A point is a single location on the 2D plane located by its coordinates (x,y). For example, Figure 10-2 shows a collection of points labeled on a 2D plane. A point has a very interesting attribute–it has no dimension! That's right. Even though a point locates a particular

FIGURE 10-2
◎ ◎ ◎ ◎ ◎ ◎
*Some points in
the plane*

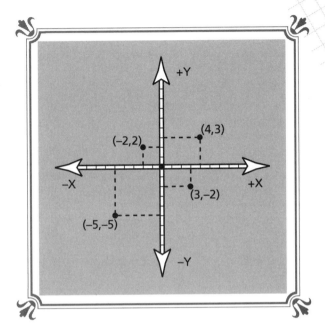

location in the 2D plane, the point itself has no dimension. That's because a point has no size. It is infinitely small.

The next geometrical entity is the *line*. A line is a collection of points that span from some starting location to some ending location. Figure 10-3 shows a couple of

FIGURE 10-3
◎ ◎ ◎ ◎ ◎ ◎
*Lines in the
plane*

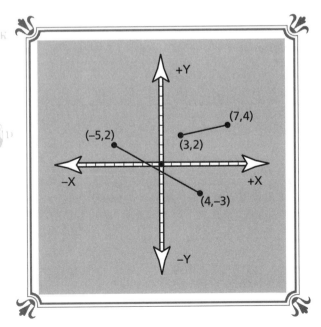

lines drawn between points. Referring to the figure, we see that to define a line in a 2D plane, we simply need two points: the starting point and the ending point.

The final geometrical primitive is the *polygon*, which means "many-sided object." For our purposes, a polygon is a collection of lines that make up a closed shape. Figure 10-4 depicts a few familiar polygons, including a triangle (three sides), a square (four sides), and a multisided polygon that is irregular. This brings us to the concept of *regular* and *irregular* polygons.

A regular polygon is a polygon that has interior angles that are similar. An irregular polygon has interior angles that have no such restraint. Figure 10-5 illustrates the difference between regular and irregular polygons. Finally, a polygon, by nature of its composition (a group of lines), can be defined by either a set of line segments or by a set of points. We will use the latter definition since it will make many of our future calculations simpler. Therefore, a polygon will be thought of as a collection of points that are connected by line segments that make up the closed polygon.

FIGURE 10-4
◎ ◎ ◎ ◎ ◎ ◎
Polygons in the plane

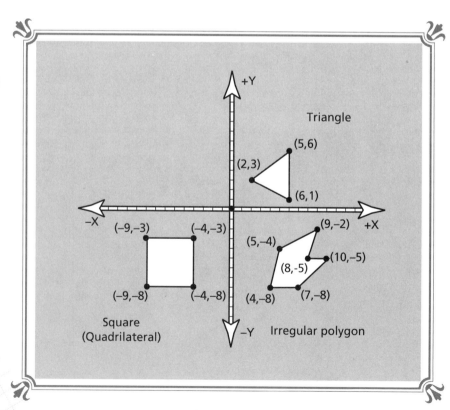

FIGURE 10-5

◎ ◎ ◎ ◎ ◎ ◎

*Regular vs.
irregular
polygons*

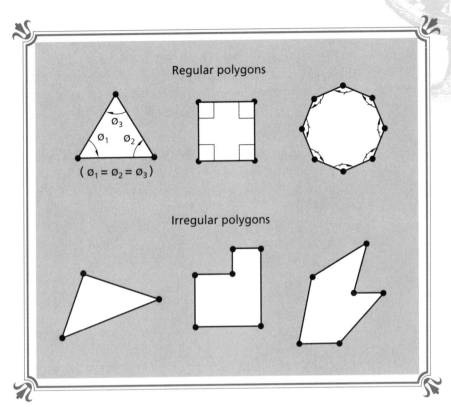

Transformations in the 2D Plane

Now that we have a little ammo to work with, let's learn to manipulate 2D objects. Since all the 2D primitives we have spoken of are based on a single point, it makes sense to learn how to manipulate a single point and use the results as the foundation to manipulate more complex objects, such as lines and polygons. With that in mind, the three basic transformations that can be performed in the 2D plane are *translation, scaling,* and *rotation.* Translation and rotation make sense on single points, but scaling really only works on lines and polygons. We'll get to that in a minute; for now let's see how translation works.

Translation

Given that an object (which in our case is a single point) is located at the position (x,y), the object is translated or moved by an amount *tx* in the X direction and *ty* in the Y direction by the following transformation:

```
x = x+tx;  // x translation
y = y+ty;  // y translation
```

Figure 10-6 shows this process in action. If an object were made up of more than one point, then each point of the object would be transformed in the same way. For example, if an object is defined by a set of points like this,

```
int x[NUM_POINTS],y[NUM_POINTS];
```

and the arrays *x[]* and *y[]* are initialized with a set of points that make up the object, then the object can be translated with the following variation of the translation transformation:

```
for (index=0; index<NUM_POINTS; index++)
    {
    // translate the ith point
    x[index] = x[index] + tx;
    y[index] = y[index] + ty;
    } // end for index
```

Therefore, if an object is defined by a set of points, in order to translate the object, each point is translated separately.

Scaling

Scaling simply means "to change the size of." However, since a single point has no dimension, the simplest object that we can scale is a line segment, which can be

FIGURE 10-6

◎ ◎ ◎ ◎ ◎ ◎

A point being translated

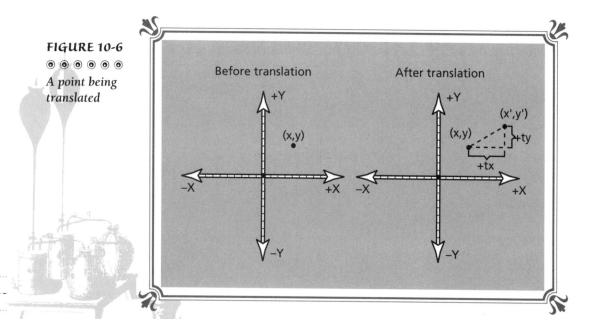

thought of as an object constructed of two points. But let's take this idea a little further and talk about scaling a real object that is made of three or more points (three points is the minimum number of points that can define a polygon).

Take a look at Figure 10-7, which shows two triangles. The leftmost triangle is defined as the points (0,2), (–2,–2), and (2,–2). If the triangle is scaled by a factor of 2, then the result is shown on the right of Figure 10-7. Analyzing the new points that make up the triangle, we see that they are (0,4), (–4,–4), and (4,–4). Amazingly enough, they are all exactly two times each of the original triangle's points. Well, it's not that amazing…they'd better be!

Mathematically, the X and Y components of each of the points that make up the first triangle are multiplied by the scaling factor, which in this case is 2. Thus, to scale an object that is composed of a set of points, the following algorithm can be used:

```
for (index=0; index<NUM_POINTS; index++)
    {
    // multiply each component by the scaling factor
    x[index] = x[index] * scaling_factor;
    y[index] = y[index] * scaling_factor;
    } // end for index
```

There is one caveat about scaling that we must take into consideration: Any object that we scale must be defined by a set of points such that its center is located at the origin, that is, (0,0). Otherwise, scaling will also produce translation. Take a look at Figure 10-8 to see this happening. The problem is that the object has no

FIGURE 10-7

◎ ◎ ◎ ◎ ◎ ◎

Scaling a triangle

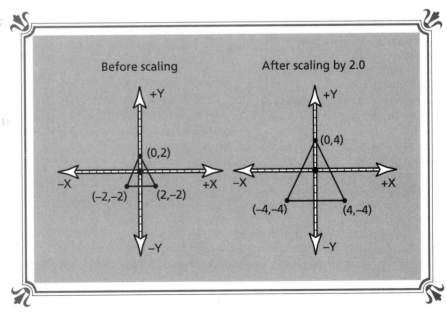

FIGURE 10-8

◉ ◉ ◉ ◉ ◉ ◉

Scaling an object not centered at the origin

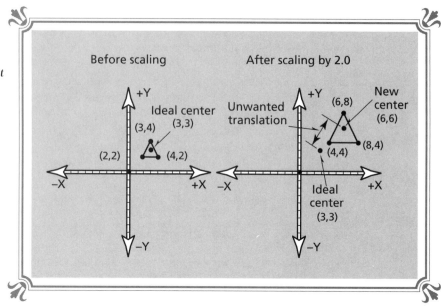

"anchor." When the object is defined such that its origin is (0,0), the object scales about the origin. When the object isn't defined relative to the origin, the object will scale *and* translate about its local origin, and the result will be a properly scaled object but at the wrong location.

One final detail about scaling is, we can scale an object up or down. In other words, the scaling factor can be less than 1.0. For instance, if we wanted to make an object half its current size, we would multiply by a scaling factor of 0.5. Negative scaling factors will work also, but the results are called *reflections* and aren't that useful, at least in our work.

Rotation

This is the big one. Rotation has always been a complicated transformation to nail down mathematically. Therefore, we are going to derive the rotation equations ourselves, and if there is one thing that you get out of this chapter, it will be how to rotate something! We are going to begin our rotation derivation with the following setup. We want to rotate a single point an angle θ (theta) in the counterclockwise direction (see Figure 10-9).

There are many ways to derive the rotation equations, but I think the following method is the easiest to grasp. All right, here's how it works. Given any point (x,y), if we want to rotate it by an angle theta, then the result will be a new point (x',y') that is a linear combination of the old point (x,y) and some functions of theta, such as

FIGURE 10-9

◎ ◎ ◎ ◎ ◎ ◎

*Rotating a point
in the plane*

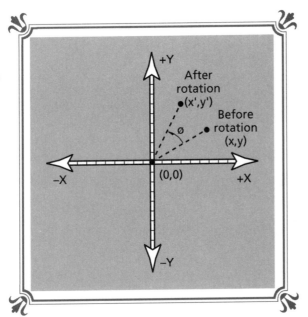

$$x' = x*f_1(\theta) + y*f_2(\theta)$$
$$y' = y*f_3(\theta) + y*f_4(\theta)$$

We have (x,y) and θ, but we need to know the functions $f_1(\theta)$, $f_2(\theta)$, $f_3(\theta)$, and $f_4(\theta)$. Well, most people know that they have something to do with SIN and COSINE, but the question is, what is the relationship? The answer can be found by rotating the points (0,1) and (1,0) and then using the results to solve for the unknown functions $f_1(\theta)$, $f_2(\theta)$, $f_3(\theta)$, and $f_4(\theta)$. First, let's take the point (1,0) and rotate an angle θ in the counterclockwise direction. This is shown in Figure 10-10. The result of this rotation is a point (x,y), but what are x and y in terms of θ? The answer can be found by breaking down the resulting triangle that is formed by the X axis and the point (x,y).

We'll use the *Pythagorean theorem*, which states that the sum of the squares of the sides of a right triangle is equal to the square of the hypotenuse. Thus, the hypotenuse in Figure 10-10 is $(x^2 + y^2)^{1/2}$. Now, recalling that SIN and COSINE of any angle are defined as

$$\text{SIN } \theta = \frac{\text{opposite side}}{\text{hypotenuse}}$$

and

$$\text{COS } \theta = \frac{\text{adjacent side}}{\text{hypotenuse}}$$

FIGURE 10-10

◎ ◎ ◎ ◎ ◎ ◎

*Rotating the first
test point (1,0)*

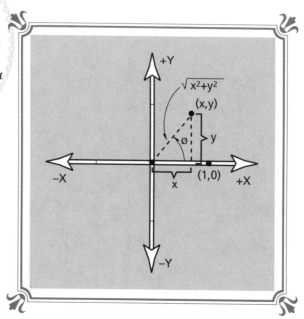

then SIN θ and COS θ in Figure 10-10 must be equal to

$$SIN\ \theta = \frac{y}{(x^2+y^2)^{1/2}}$$

and

$$COS\ \theta = \frac{x}{(x^2+y^2)^{1/2}}$$

which for a line that has length 1.0, the denominators also become 1.0, and the results are

COS θ = x and SIN θ = y

Therefore, we can deduce that if the point (1,0) is rotated by an angle θ in the counterclockwise direction, then (1,0) becomes (COS θ, SIN θ), or in other words, the functions $f_1(\theta)$ = COS θ and $f_3(\theta)$ = SIN θ since COS θ = x and SIN θ = y. We're halfway there!

To find the remaining two unknown functions, we must rotate another test point that will give us the other two desired functions. And of course, the logical selection is the point (0,1). Take a look at Figure 10-11. Here, we see the point (0,1) being rotated an angle θ in the counterclockwise direction. The resulting point we again label (x,y). And using the same reasoning as before, we deduce that COS θ and SIN θ have the following formulas

COS θ = y and SIN θ = −x

or

COS θ = y and −SIN θ = x

Therefore, the point (0,1) when rotated an angle θ in the counterclockwise direction, becomes (−SIN θ, COS θ). Hence, the final functions are $f_2(\theta) = $ −SIN θ and $f_4(\theta) = $ COS θ. If we take our results and plug them back into our original linear transformations, the resulting rotation equations are

x′ = x*(COS θ) − y*(SIN θ)
y′ = x*(SIN θ) + y*(COS θ)

Although the above derivation is one of the simplest (there are much harder ways to derive the equations, right Dr. Mitchem?), it would be a lot simpler if we did it with matrices–but don't worry, that's on our hit list!

So how do we use the rotation equations now that we have them? We use the rotation equations similarly to how we use the translation or scaling equations. However, there is one detail that we need to keep in mind when performing the calculation, and that's the interdependence of the equations. Basically, both x′ and y′ are functions of the old point (x,y). This means that during the rotation calculations, the old (x,y) can't change. For example, we might be tempted to do something like this:

FIGURE 10-11

◎ ◎ ◎ ◎ ◎ ◎

*Rotating the
second test point
(0,1)*

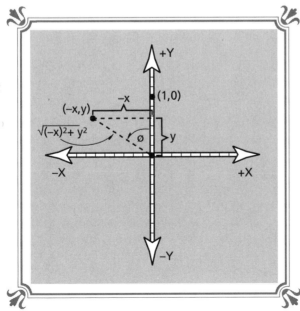

```
for (index=0; index<NUM_POINTS; index++)
    {
    x[index] = x[index] * cos(theta) - y[index] * sin(theta);
    y[index] = x[index] * sin(theta) + y[index] * cos(theta);
    } // end for index
```

The problem with the above fragment is that after *x[index]* has been computed, it's used in the computation of *y[index]*! This will result in an error. The solution is to use temporary variables during the rotation process, as shown in the next fragment:

```
for (index=0; index<NUM_POINTS; index++)
    {
    // rotate the point and save in temporary variables
    x_rot = x[index] * cos(theta) - y[index] * sin(theta);
    y_rot = x[index] * sin(theta) + y[index] * cos(theta);

    // restore results back into array
    x[index] = x_rot;
    y[index] = y_rot;
    } // end for index
```

The above fragment would result in the proper rotation of the points defined in the arrays *x[]* and *y[]* by an angle theta in the counterclockwise direction. Of course, all calculations are done in floating point and theta is in radians, since C/C++ math libraries like radians instead of degrees. If you have forgotten the relationship between radians and degrees, here it is:

360 degrees = 2Π radians

The beauty about all the transformations we have just discussed is that they can all be performed using matrices. Moreover, by using matrices, multiple operations can be concatenated into a single transformation matrix, allowing an object to be scaled, translated, and rotated in a single pass. But we will get to this a bit later. At this point, let's take a look at 3D space and see what we're dealing with.

Introduction to 3D Space

Three-dimensional space should be very familiar to you since we live in one! The question is, how are points and objects located in 3D space? The answer is, the same way they are located in 2D space—with coordinates. Any point in 3D space can be located with three coordinates: x, y, and z. The new z coordinate relates to the new axis that must be added to describe a 3D space. There is a single catch with this z coordinate, and that is the relationship between the positive Z axis and the X and Y axes we are used to. The catch is that given a standard X-Y plane or Cartesian coordinate system, the new Z axis can either point into or out of the paper. For this reason there are two popular systems in use for locating points and objects. They are called the *left-handed system* and the *right-handed system*.

The Left-Handed System

Figure 10-12 shows the left-handed system for locating points and objects. As you can see, the X and Y axes are where we would expect, but the new Z axis is pointing into the paper. It's called the left-handed system because if you roll your left hand from X-Y, your thumb points in the positive Z-axis direction. This system is commonly used in computer graphics, while the right-handed system is more popular in mathematics. Let's see why.

The Right-Handed System

As shown in Figure 10-13, the right-handed system is almost the same as the left-handed system except that the Z axis is mirrored. This really doesn't mean much as far as calculations are concerned, but it does make diagrams a bit easier to draw and analyze. This is why many math and physics books prefer the right-handed system to the left-handed system.

As an example, imagine that we wanted to plot the point (1,1,1) on a right-handed coordinate system. The result would look like Figure 10-14. The point is

FIGURE 10-12

◉ ◉ ◉ ◉ ◉ ◉

The left-handed system for locating points and objects

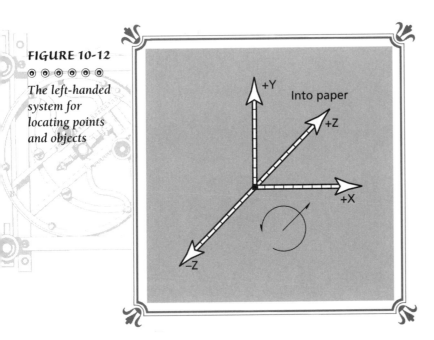

FIGURE 10-13

⊙ ⊙ ⊙ ⊙ ⊙ ⊙

The right-handed system

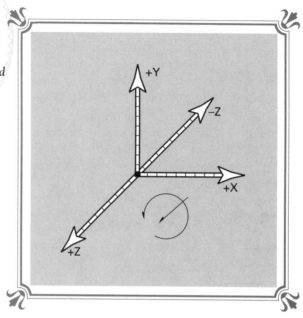

"in front" of the paper, if you will. However, if we plot the same point on a left-handed system, as shown in Figure 10-15, the point is behind the X-Y plane, or behind the paper. It's just a bit weird.

FIGURE 10-14

⊙ ⊙ ⊙ ⊙ ⊙ ⊙

The point (1,1,1) plotted in the right-handed system

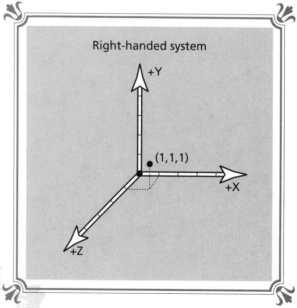

FIGURE 10-15

◎ ◎ ◎ ◎ ◎ ◎

The point (1,1,1) plotted in the left-handed system

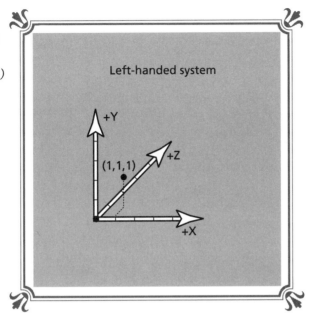

Anyway, the moral of the story is that either system works fine, it's really a matter of taste. We use both systems in this book. Our final graphics engine will use a left-handed system, but when we are diagramming and so forth, we will tend to use the right-handed system since it makes figures easier to visualize.

Now that we have that down, it's time for a crash course in vector math.

Vectors and Vector Operations

Vectors are mathematical entities that describe both magnitude and direction. For example, the number 100 is a *scalar* value. It describes a magnitude, but no direction. A vector, on the other hand, has both a magnitude and direction that are in a compact form. For example, take a look at Figure 10-16. Here we see a 2D plane with a vector drawn in it. The name of the vector is **u** (we will always use lowercase bold to denote vectors), and it points in the northeast direction. Moreover, **u** has a length associated with it, which relates to its magnitude. But let's see if we can be a little more precise about these quantities.

The vector **u** is said to have components. In the case of Figure 10-16, the vector **u** is a 2D vector and thus has two components. The components are the x and y values associated with the tip of the vector, which are <3,5>. This means that the vector **u** has an X component of 3 and a Y component of 5. Figure 10-17 shows a

FIGURE 10-16

◉ ◉ ◉ ◉ ◉ ◉

A vector in the 2D plane

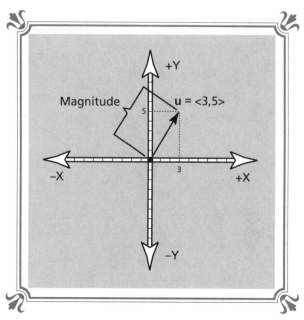

few more vectors and their components. As you see, some vectors can have the same direction, but have different lengths or magnitudes.

So, how do we compute the magnitude of a vector? The answer is that we use a triangle along with a bit of geometry. All vectors by definition have their initial

FIGURE 10-17

◉ ◉ ◉ ◉ ◉ ◉

More vectors

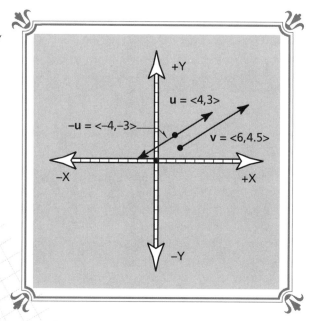

points at the origin, which is (0,0) in a 2D space or (0,0,0) in a 3D space. Therefore, the magnitude of a vector can be found by dropping down a perpendicular and then solving for the hypotenuse. This process is shown in Figure 10-18. The vector **v**, which has components <3,4>, is really the hypotenuse of the triangle. Therefore, the length of **v**, denoted |**v**|, can be computed with this equation:

length of $\mathbf{v} = |\mathbf{v}| = (x^2 + y^2)^{1/2} = (3^2 + 4^2)^{1/2} = 5$.

Amazingly enough, the above calculation is simply the Pythagorean theorem again.

Vectors are very useful in computer graphics, as they help simplify much of the complex calculations. Since computer graphics deals with 2D or 3D points, and a point itself is a vector, it makes sense to make up a set of rules to manipulate vectors. But before we do that, let's reiterate what a vector is. A vector is a mathematical entity that contains both magnitude and direction. Vectors are especially useful in 2D and 3D graphics, where they are represented by arrows with a certain direction and length. The tip of a vector is called the *terminal point* and the start of a vector is called the *initial point*. Also, each vector is really composed of a set of components. These components are made up of the x, y, and z (if the vector is in 3D) contributions of the vector as drawn from the origin.

Now let's talk about the operations that can be performed on vectors and what they mean mathematically and geometrically.

FIGURE 10-18

◉ ◉ ◉ ◉ ◉ ◉

Computing the magnitude of a vector

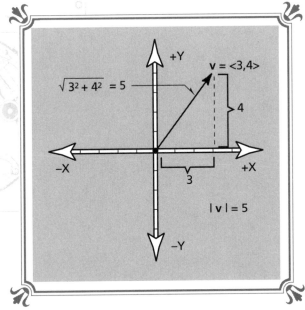

Addition of Vectors

Vectors can be added just as scalars can, except that we must be careful adding vectors since they are made up of one or more components. For example, suppose we have two vectors in a 2D space, as shown in Figure 10-19, and we want to add them. This can be done by adding the components of each of the vectors. If we refer to Figure 10-19, we see that vector $u=<4,2>$ and vector $v=<1,2>$. To add the vectors, we must separately add the X and Y components of the vectors, like this:

$u + v = <4,2> + <1,2> = <4+1,2+2> = <5,4>$

The geometrical addition of **u** and **v** is shown in Figure 10-20. Basically, to add two vectors together, we can take one vector and attach it to the terminal point of the other vector. Then we draw a third vector, which starts from the origin, to the resulting geometrically added vectors. You might be wondering how this works? Well, if you think about it in another way, it makes sense. The first vector **u** can be thought of as a *locator*. Then vector **v** can be thought of as another locator that is relative to **u**. Thus, we walk to the end of **u**, and then we walk in the direction of **v** for the length of **v**. The result will be a position that is the sum of the two vectors.

Subtraction of Vectors

Subtraction of vectors is done in the same way as addition. For example, Figure 10-21 shows two vectors **u** and **v**. If we want to subtract them, we simply subtract

FIGURE 10-19

◎ ◎ ◎ ◎ ◎ ◎

Two vectors to be added

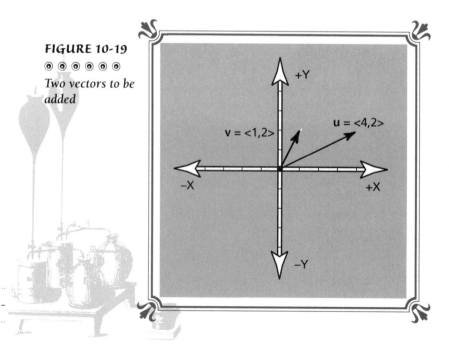

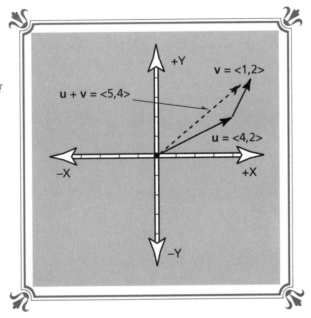

components, just as we added components to add vectors. Thus, to compute **u–v**, we use the following math:

$$\mathbf{u} - \mathbf{v} = <4,1> - <1.5,4> = <4-1.5, 1-4> = <2.5, -3>.$$

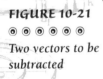

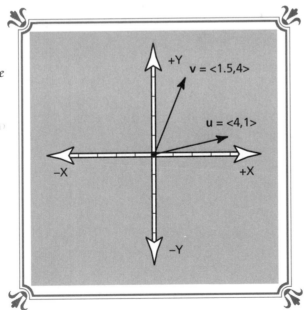

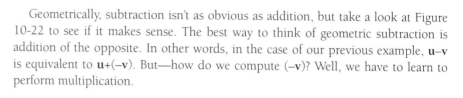

Geometrically, subtraction isn't as obvious as addition, but take a look at Figure 10-22 to see if it makes sense. The best way to think of geometric subtraction is addition of the opposite. In other words, in the case of our previous example, **u–v** is equivalent to **u**+(**–v**). But—how do we compute (**–v**)? Well, we have to learn to perform multiplication.

Scalar Multiplication

Just as scalar numbers can be multiplied by one another, vectors can also be multiplied by a scalar. However, the scalar multiplier must be multiplied by each component of the vector. Figure 10-23 shows the vector **u** being multiplied by 3. You will notice that the direction of **u** does not change, but its length does. This operation can be illustrated by the following math:

$3*\mathbf{u} = 3*<2,4> = <3*2,3*4> = <6,12>.$

Or, in general, a vector **u** times a scalar S is equal to

$S*\mathbf{u} = S*<u1,u2,...un> = <S*u1, S*u2,...S*un>.$

which in the case of a 3D vector would look like

$S*\mathbf{u} = S*<ux,uy,uz> = <S*ux,S*uy,S*uz>.$

where u1, u2, and u3 are the x, y, and z components of the vector, respectively.

FIGURE 10-22

◉ ◉ ◉ ◉ ◉ ◉

The geometrical interpretation of vector subtraction

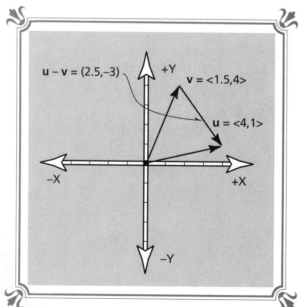

FIGURE 10-23

◎ ◎ ◎ ◎ ◎ ◎

*Scalar
multiplication*

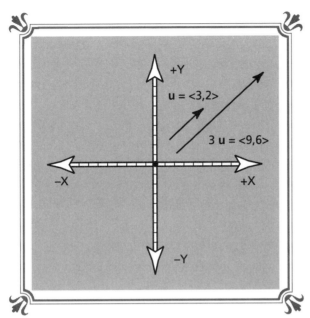

Scalar multiplication has many uses. We can shrink or stretch vectors by multi-plying scaling factors smaller or larger than 1.0. Also, we can flip or invert a vector by multiplying by −1, as shown in Figure 10-24. An important fact to remember is that vectors can have from one to a number of components. Of course, in computer

FIGURE 10-24

◎ ◎ ◎ ◎ ◎ ◎

*Inverting a
vector by
multiplying by -1*

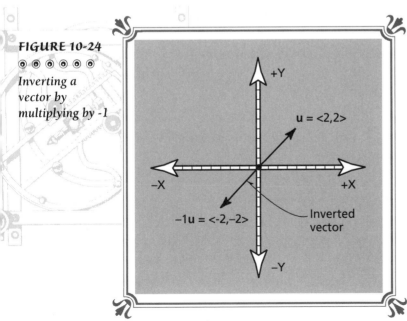

graphics most of the vectors are 2D or 3D and thus have two or three components. But if we wish, we can have vectors of any dimension. Nevertheless, the same operations can be performed on all vectors. We must simply make sure to process each element or component of each vector.

The Dot Product

We've seen how to multiply a scalar and a vector. But can we multiply two vectors, and if we can, what does the result mean? The truth is, in general, multiplying the components of two vectors doesn't do much. However, there is a special vector product that is useful, and it is called the *dot product* or *Euclidean inner product*. The dot product is used to extract the angular relationship between two vectors. Take a look at Figure 10-25. Here we see two vectors **u** and **v**. What if we wanted to know the angle between them? This is a trivial question, but it is an important one. Luckily for us, we aren't going to derive this one, we are simply going to look at the results. The dot product is denoted by the "·" symbol and is computed as follows:

$$\mathbf{u} \cdot \mathbf{v} = |\mathbf{u}| * |\mathbf{v}| * \cos \theta$$

where $|\mathbf{u}|$ and $|\mathbf{v}|$ are the magnitudes of **u** and **v**, and θ is the angle between them.

FIGURE 10-25

◉ ◉ ◉ ◉ ◉ ◉

Vectors have interior angles between them

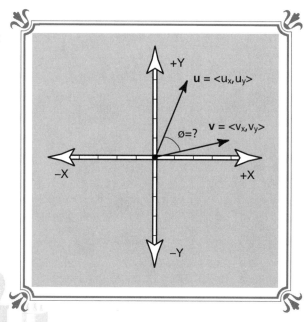

If we use a bit of algebraic manipulation, we see that θ can be found with the following formula,

$$\theta = \cos^{-1} \frac{(\mathbf{u} \cdot \mathbf{v})}{|\mathbf{u}| * |\mathbf{v}|}$$

which states that θ is the inverse COSINE of $\mathbf{u}$ dot $\mathbf{v}$ divided by the magnitude of $\mathbf{u}$ and the magnitude of $\mathbf{v}$. However, there is a bit of a problem here. How do we compute $(\mathbf{u} \cdot \mathbf{v})$? The answer is that $(\mathbf{u} \cdot \mathbf{v})$ is the sum of the products of the components of the vectors $\mathbf{u}$ and $\mathbf{v}$. In the case of vectors that have two components $(\mathbf{u} \cdot \mathbf{v})$ looks like this:

Given $\mathbf{u}$=<ux,uy>, $\mathbf{v}$=<vx,vy>

$\mathbf{u} \cdot \mathbf{v}$ = ux*vx + uy*vy

In the case of 3D vectors then, $(\mathbf{u} \cdot \mathbf{v})$ is computed with:

Given $\mathbf{u}$=<ux,uy,uz>, $\mathbf{v}$=<vx,vy,vz>

$\mathbf{u} \cdot \mathbf{v}$ = ux*vx + uy*vy + uz*vz

Now, $(\mathbf{u} \cdot \mathbf{v})$ has some interesting properties. If we don't want to go through the pain of finding the actual angle θ between the vectors $\mathbf{u}$ and $\mathbf{v}$, but instead are only interested in the gross relationship between them, we can simply compute $(\mathbf{u} \cdot \mathbf{v})$ and refer to the following:

If $(\mathbf{u} \cdot \mathbf{v})$ is
> 0, then the angle between $\mathbf{u}$ and $\mathbf{v}$ is acute, as shown in Figure 10-26 (A).
< 0, then the angle between $\mathbf{u}$ and $\mathbf{v}$ is obtuse, as shown in Figure 10-26 (B).
= 0, then $\mathbf{u}$ and $\mathbf{v}$ are perpendicular, as in Figure 10-26 (C).

The dot product is very important in 3D graphics during hidden surface removal and lighting calculations, so make sure your tractor beam has a lock on it before moving on!

The Cross Product and Normal Vectors

Many times in 3D graphics, a pair of vectors exist that we would like the *normal* to—in other words, we would like a vector that is perpendicular to both of the vectors in question. Figure 10-27 shows this situation. The vectors $\mathbf{u}$ and $\mathbf{v}$ form a base for the vector $\mathbf{n}$ that is perpendicular to both $\mathbf{u}$ and $\mathbf{v}$. But how can we compute such a vector? We compute the normal vector using a computation called the *cross product*.

FIGURE 10-26

Results of the dot product

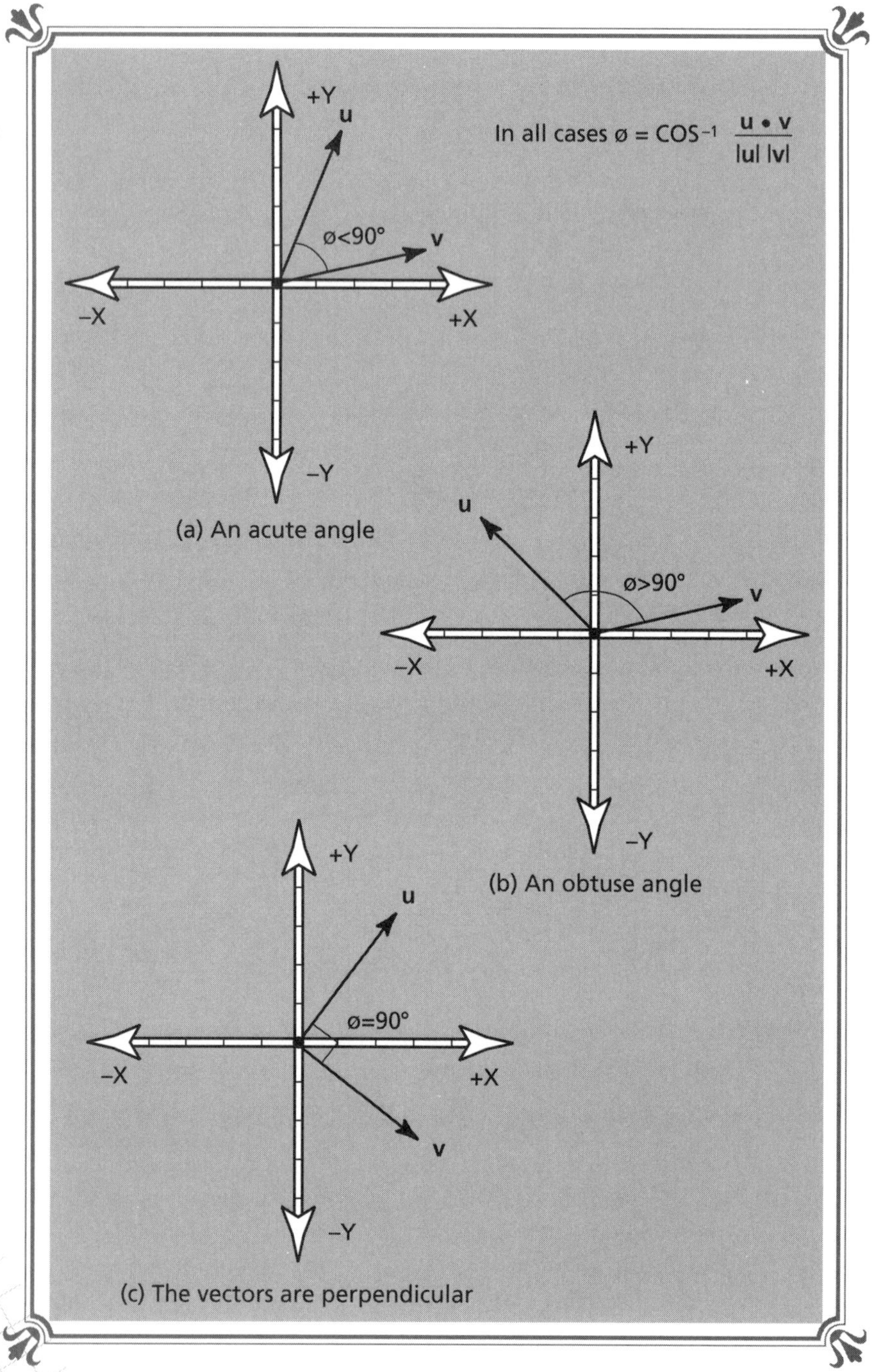

+Y
u
In all cases ø = COS-1 u • v / |u| |v|
ø<90°
v
–X
+X
–Y
(a) An acute angle
+Y
u
ø>90°
v
–X
+X
–Y
(b) An obtuse angle
+Y
u
ø=90°
–X
+X
v
–Y
(c) The vectors are perpendicular

FIGURE 10-27

◎ ◎ ◎ ◎ ◎ ◎

A vector normal to both u and v

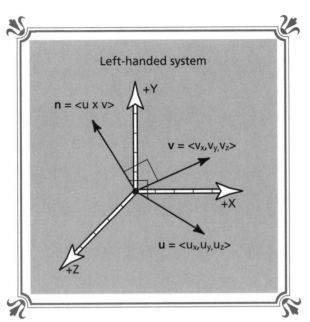

Again, we aren't going to derive the cross product since it is rather complex and tedious. We simply want the final results. The cross product operation is denoted by *x* and is computed as follows:

Given **u** = <ux,uy,uz>, **v** = <vx,vy,vz>

uxv =<ux,uy,uz>x<vx,vy,vz>=<uy*vz − uz*vy, ux*vz − uz*vx,ux*vy − uy*vx>
  = <nx, ny, nz>

In most cases, when a normal vector is computed, the resulting vector is *normalized.* Normalization is the process of resizing a vector so that its length is equal to 1.0. This operation can be performed on any vector, but it's almost always performed on normal vectors. Let's see how to do it.

Unit Vectors

The concept of normalization is a common one. In general, normalization is the scaling of a data set such that all the elements in the set have values relative to some specific baseline value. In most cases, this baseline value is selected to be 1.0. This is also the case in vector mathematics. *Unit vectors* are vectors that have been scaled down such that their resulting magnitude is 1.0. The direction of the vector isn't changed, only its length. Figure 10-28 shows the results of normalizing a vector to length 1.0. Obviously, we must multiply the components of the vector by some

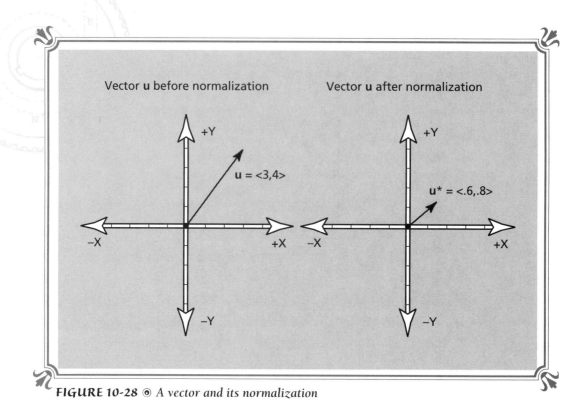

FIGURE 10-28 ⊚ *A vector and its normalization*

magic number such that the resulting components, when used in a magnitude calculation, will result in a magnitude of 1.0.

The magic number we're looking for is the magnitude of the vector! For example, if we want to create a unit vector from the vector **u**, then we simply divide each component of **u** by its own magnitude, denoted by |**u**|. If we again refer to Figure 10-28, we see that **u**=<3,4>; therefore, to compute a unit vector version of **u**, we would perform the following calculations:

First compute the length of **u**, that is, |**u**|:

$|\mathbf{u}| = (3^2+4^2)1/2 = 5$

Then divide each component of the original **u** by 5:

$\mathbf{u}^* = 1/5*<3,4> = <3/5,4/5>$

Now, if we were to calculate the magnitude of **u***, we would find it to be 1.0. Give it a try and see what you get.

In general, to compute a unit vector, the following formula can be used:

$$u^* = \frac{u}{|u|}$$

where the * character denotes unit vector.

Generating Vectors from Points

We have been speaking of vectors in a rather cavalier way thus far. Let's stop a moment and look at a real-world example of computing and using vectors productively. First, a vector can always be generated from any two points P1 and P2 in any space, 2D or 3D. Take a look at Figure 10-29. It shows the two points P1 and P2 in a 3D space. If we wanted to compute a vector from P1 to P2, we would use the following formula:

$\mathbf{u}$ = P2 − P1 = (3,4,5) − (1,1,1) = <2,3,4>

We see that a vector that starts from a point and ends at another point is computed by subtracting the tail or terminal end from the start or initial point. Figure 10-29 shows the vector $\mathbf{u}$. Now, if we wanted the vector from P2 to P1, we would reverse the operation, resulting in the following calculation:

$\mathbf{v}$ = P1 − P2 = (1,1,1) − (3,4,5) = <−2,−3,−4>

FIGURE 10-29

◎ ◎ ◎ ◎ ◎ ◎

Computing vectors based on points

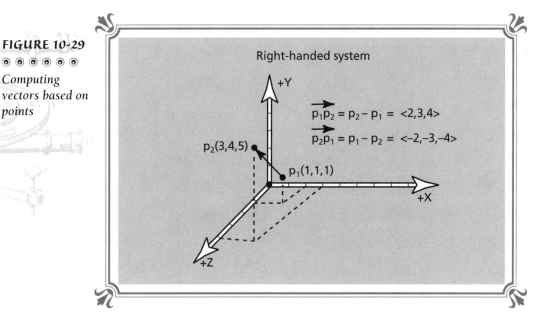

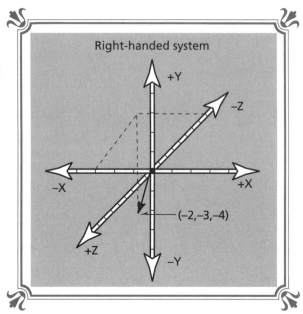

FIGURE 10-30

◎ ◎ ◎ ◎ ◎ ◎

*A vector with all
negative
components*

Right-handed system

+Y

−Z

−X

+X

(−2,−3,−4)

+Z

−Y

Don't be alarmed by the negative signs, they are perfectly legal and make sense when we look at the resulting vector **v** in Figure 10-30.

Now, as a hard-core example of using vectors, let's make up a quick problem to get the hang of it. Take a look at Figure 10-31, which depicts a triangle in 3D made

FIGURE 10-31

◎ ◎ ◎ ◎ ◎ ◎

*Constructions
based on points*

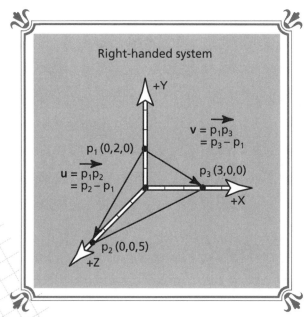

Right-handed system

+Y

$\mathbf{v} = \overrightarrow{p_1 p_3}$
$= p_3 - p_1$

$p_1\,(0,2,0)$

$\mathbf{u} = \overrightarrow{p_1 p_2}$
$= p_2 - p_1$

$p_3\,(3,0,0)$

+X

$p_2\,(0,0,5)$

+Z

up of the points P1, P2, P3. Let's see if we can compute a normal to this triangle. Let's begin by computing the two vectors **u** and **v**, as shown in the figure, with the following calculations:

u = P2 − P1 = (0,0,5) − (0,2,0) = <0,−2,5>
v = P3 − P1 = (3,0,0) − (0,2,0) = <3,−2,0>

Now if we compute the cross product between **u** and **v**—that is, **u** x **v**—then the resulting normal vector will be perpendicular to the triangle. The dot product is computed as follows:

u x **v** = <−2*0 − (−10), −(0*0 − 3*5), 0*(−2) − (−2)*3> = <10,15,6> = **n**

The result is shown in Figure 10-32; but **n** should be normalized, so let's make it a unit vector. Here's the final calculation:

$$\mathbf{n}^* = \frac{\mathbf{n}}{|\mathbf{n}|} = \frac{<10,15,6>}{(10^2 + 15^2 + 6^2)^{1/2}} = \frac{<10,15,6>}{19} = <10/19,\ 15/19,\ 6/19> = <.526,\ .789,\ .315>$$

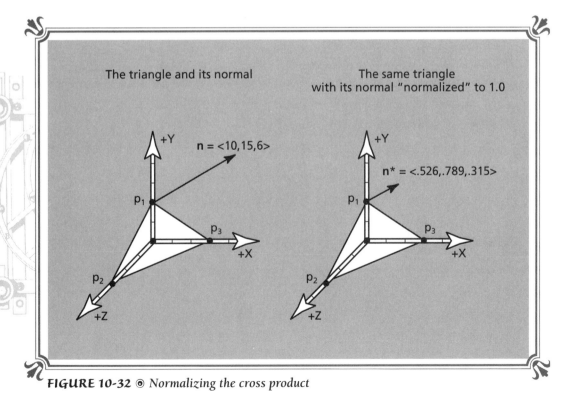

The triangle and its normal

n = <10,15,6>

+Y

p₁

p₃

+X

p₂

+Z

The same triangle with its normal "normalized" to 1.0

+Y

n* = <.526,.789,.315>

p₁

p₃

+X

p₂

+Z

FIGURE 10-32 ⊚ *Normalizing the cross product*

The original triangle with **n**∗ as its normal is also shown in Figure 10-32.

Luckily, that's all we need to know about vectors to get started on the 3D graphics engine. However, we will pick up little bits here and there as we progress. The next mathematical topic we must discuss is matrices. Maybe it's time for a colorful metaphor?

Matrices and Matrix Operations

Matrices are mathematical tools that were invented mainly to manipulate systems of linear equations, such as:

$$3x + 2y + 5z = 10$$
$$10x - 4y + 7z = 20$$
$$30x + 10y - z = 30$$

If you recall, to solve the system, we need to find an x, y, and z such that all the equations are simultaneously satisfied. This can be accomplished in myriad ways, including substitutions, adding multiples of one row to another, and so forth. However, when a system of equations has 50 or 100 variables, writing them out can be quite unnerving, and solving them is next to impossible for creatures as frail and slow as humans. Consequently, mathematicians came up with a shorthand form to write systems of linear equations, called matrices. Then an entire area of mathematical study was born, called *linear algebra*. In any case, we're only interested in using matrices to simplify our operations rather than to solve systems of linear equations. However, just to be complete, let's see what the previous system of linear equations looks like in matrix form:

$$AX=B$$

That's pretty simple! But what are A, X, and B? They are matrices formed by taking specific components of the original system of equations. For example, A is called the *coefficient matrix* and is generated by taking the coefficients of x, y, and z row-by-row and placing them in a matrix like this:

$$A = \begin{bmatrix} 3 & 2 & 5 \\ 10 & -4 & 7 \\ 30 & 10 & -1 \end{bmatrix}$$

The variable X is called the *variable matrix* and is simply the variable involved in the linear system of equations. In our case, X looks like this:

$$X = \begin{bmatrix} x \\ y \\ z \end{bmatrix}$$

Note: It is just a coincidence that one of the variables in the problem is called X.

Finally, the last matrix in the matrix equation is B. This is called the *constant matrix* and is another single-column matrix, which contains the right side or constants of the problem, such as:

$$B = \begin{bmatrix} 10 \\ 20 \\ 30 \end{bmatrix}$$

Thus, the entire linear system of equations can be written as:

AX=B, which is equivalent to:

$$T = \begin{bmatrix} 3 & 2 & 5 \\ 10 & -4 & 7 \\ 30 & 10 & -1 \end{bmatrix} * \begin{bmatrix} x \\ y \\ z \end{bmatrix} = \begin{bmatrix} 10 \\ 20 \\ 30 \end{bmatrix}$$

Although it looks a little nicer, it doesn't seem to help the situation at hand, which is the solution of the original set of linear equations. Actually, it does, because if we forget about the matrices for a minute and manipulate the original matrix equation AX=B, then we can solve for X like this:

$$X = A^{-1} B$$

This states that the variable matrix X is equal to the product of the inverse of the coefficient matrix and the constant matrix. Exciting, huh! Well, if you're not that impressed, don't worry about it. We aren't interested in finding the solutions to linear systems of equations, but we are interested in using some of the concepts and techniques from matrix mathematics and linear algebra to make our 3D manipulations easier to perform and more efficient. Let's begin with some definitions, shall we?

A matrix is defined as a collection of numbers, *mxn* (the x doesn't mean cross product, it means "by"), where *m* is the number of rows and *n* is the number of columns. For example, here are a few matrices of different sizes:

$$A = \begin{bmatrix} 3 & 4 & 5 \\ 2 & 6 & -1 \\ 6 & 0 & 9 \end{bmatrix}$$

3 rows by 3 columns, 3 x 3

$$B = \begin{bmatrix} 4 & 6 \\ 3 & 4 \\ 1 & 3 \end{bmatrix}$$

3 rows by 2 columns, 3 x 2

$$C = \begin{bmatrix} 1 & 4 & 5 \end{bmatrix}$$

1 row by 3 columns, 1 x 3

$$D = \begin{bmatrix} 1 \end{bmatrix}$$

1 row by 1 column, 1 x 1

As you can see, matrices can be of any size. For a moment let's not worry about the significance of the numbers in the matrices and learn to manipulate matrices as algebraic entities.

Matrix Addition and Subtraction

You can add and subtract matrices in much the same way you add and subtract numbers and vectors. However, to add or subtract a pair of matrices, they must be the same size, or in other words, they must be the same dimension. For example, none of the preceding matrices A, B, C, nor D can be added together, since all of their dimensions are different. However, if we have two matrices with the same dimensions mxn, where m and n can be any whole number greater than 1, the two matrices can be added.

So, how do we add matrices? Simple—we just add the elements and then place the sums in the proper positions in the result matrix. Take a look at the following example.

Given that,

$$A = \begin{bmatrix} 2 & 3 \\ 1 & 4 \end{bmatrix} \qquad B = \begin{bmatrix} 3 & -1 \\ 5 & 6 \end{bmatrix}$$

2 x 2   2 x 2

$$A+B = \begin{bmatrix} 2 & 3 \\ 1 & 4 \end{bmatrix} + \begin{bmatrix} 3 & -1 \\ 5 & 6 \end{bmatrix} = \begin{bmatrix} 2+3 & 3+(-1) \\ 1+5 & 4+6 \end{bmatrix} = \begin{bmatrix} 5 & 2 \\ 6 & 10 \end{bmatrix}$$

Notice that the result matrix has the same dimensions as both A and B. In C/C++, matrices are nothing more than 2D arrays. For example, we might define a matrix type that is 3x3 with the following code structure:

```
typedef struct matrix_typ
        {
        int matrix_1[3][3]; // an integer 3x3 matrix
        } matrix, *matrix_ptr;
```

Then we can define a couple of matrices like this:

```
matrix mat_1 = {3,4,5,
                2,6,9,
                3,0,-6};

matrix mat_2 = {1,2,0,
                2,45,10,
                -9,3,4};

matrix sum;
```

Then if we wanted to write a function to add matrices, something like this would be at the core of it:

```
for (row=0; row<3; row++)
        for (column=0; column<3; column++)
          sum[row][column] = mat_1[row][column] + mat_2[row][column];
```

And that's all there is to it! Of course, subtraction is performed exactly as addition is except the elements of the second matrix are subtracted from the first rather than added. Now that we can add and subtract, let's see if we can multiply matrices in some way that makes a bit of sense.

Matrix Multiplying

Unfortunately, matrix multiplying isn't as simple as multiplying each element of the two matrices together. The algorithm used to perform matrix multiplying has a mathematical basis, which we aren't going to delve into. We are simply going to learn how to do it since we'll need it to perform 3D graphics (as we will learn later).

For the matrix multiplication of A*B to make sense, the inner dimension of the two matrices must be the same, or in other words, if A is mxn, then B must be nxr. This means that the number of rows of A can be anything and the number of columns in B can also be anything, but the number of columns in A must be the same as the number of rows in B. This is shown graphically in Figure 10-33. The result of multiplying the matrices A and B will be a matrix that is mxr, which are the outer dimensions of A and B.

So if we wanted to multiply matrix A, which is 3x2, by matrix B, which is 2x4, we could do it. However, if A was 3x2 and B was 3x3, this wouldn't work since A and B don't have the same inner dimension.

Now that we know what we can and can't multiply, let's see how the actual multiplication is performed. Refer to Figure 10-34 for the following discussion. In general, to multiply a matrix A by B, we must multiply rows of A by columns of B, and the resulting sum of products are used as the elements of the resulting product matrix. Or, to put it more precisely, the (i,j)th element of the result matrix is computed by taking ith row of A and multiplying each element of it with the jth column of B (which is actually nothing more than a dot product).

The result of this multiplication is placed in the (i,j)th position of the result matrix. Therefore, with a bit of thought, one can deduce that multiplying a matrix that is mxn by a matrix that is nxr takes $(m*r*n)$ multiplications and $(m*r*(n-1))$ additions. Most of the matrices we are going to deal with will be 3x3 and 4x4, so this isn't too much of a problem. As a quick exercise, figure out how many multiplications and additions are needed to compute the product shown below:

$$\begin{bmatrix} 2 & 3 \\ 1 & 2 \end{bmatrix} * \begin{bmatrix} 5 & 6 \\ 3 & 0 \end{bmatrix} = \begin{bmatrix} (2*5 + 3*3) & (2*6 + 3*0) \\ (1*5 + 5*3) & (1*6 + 2*0) \end{bmatrix} = \begin{bmatrix} 19 & 12 \\ 11 & 6 \end{bmatrix}$$

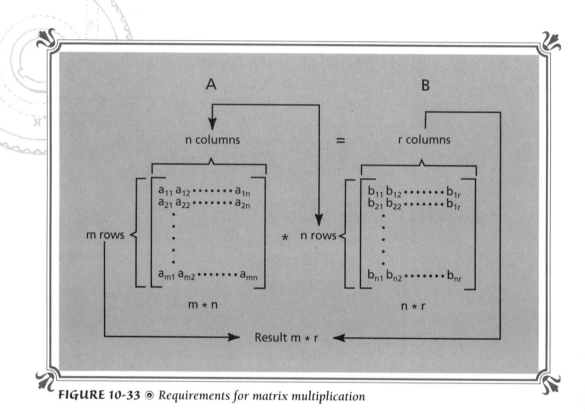

FIGURE 10-33 ◉ *Requirements for matrix multiplication*

Answer: Eight multiplications and four additions, which is correct since $(m*r*n)=(2*2*2)$ and $(m*r*(n-1))=(2*2*(2-1))=4$.

We need to learn matrix multiplication because it allows us to transform 3D points very easily by multiplying them by matrices. Moreover, we will shortly learn that matrices can be concatenated, resulting in a single matrix that can perform scaling, rotation, and translation (among other things) in a single shot! But before we get to all that fun stuff, let's talk about the identity matrix, since it's nice to know what the equivalent of 1.0 is in any mathematical space.

The Identity Matrix

The *identity matrix* is the *multiplicative identity* of matrices. This means that any matrix multiplied by the identity matrix (if the dimensions are correct) will result in the original matrix. To put it explicitly in matrix notation:

$$A*I = A = I*A = A$$

This states that any matrix A that is multiplied by the identity matrix I is equal to A; moreover, the order of multiplication doesn't matter.

FIGURE 10-34

◎ ◎ ◎ ◎ ◎ ◎

*Mechanics of
matrix
multiplication*

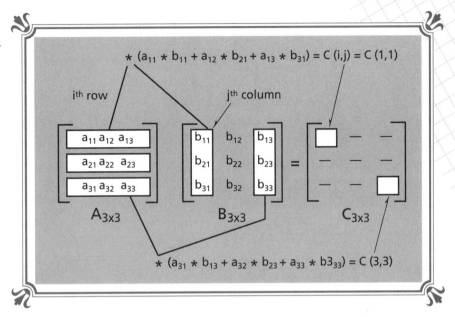

This brings us to an important point in matrix multiplying: The order of multiplication of two matrices in general is not commutative; in other words, order *does* matter. Take a look below:

A*B is not generally equal to B*A

The only reason that A*I=I*A is that the identity matrix is a special matrix, and because of its properties, the order of multiplication is irrelevant. But what does an identity matrix look like? Well, an identity matrix must be *nxn* or square. Thus, the only matrices that can be multiplied by an identity matrix are square matrices that have the same number of rows and columns.

The second property of an identity matrix is that the main diagonal consists of all 1's and the remaining elements are 0's. For example, if we wanted a 3x3 identity matrix, we would construct the following matrix:

$$I_{3x3} = \begin{bmatrix} 1 & 0 & 0 \\ 0 & 1 & 0 \\ 0 & 0 & 1 \end{bmatrix}$$

And a 2x2 identity matrix would look like this:

$$I_{2x2} = \begin{bmatrix} 1 & 0 \\ 0 & 1 \end{bmatrix}$$

Now let's see if the identity matrix does what it's supposed to do when we multiply it by another matrix. Here is the multiplication between a 2x2 matrix and a 2x2 identity matrix:

$$\begin{bmatrix} a & b \\ c & d \end{bmatrix} * \begin{bmatrix} 1 & 0 \\ 0 & 1 \end{bmatrix} = \begin{bmatrix} a*1 + b*0 & a*0 + b*1 \\ c*1 + d*0 & c*0 + d*1 \end{bmatrix} = \begin{bmatrix} a & b \\ c & d \end{bmatrix}$$

As you can see, the result is the original matrix no matter what order we perform the matrix multiplication.

The identity matrix is useful for many operations in matrix math, but in 3D graphics it is commonly used as a blank or starting matrix that can be multiplied with other matrices to arrive at a final transformation matrix. But remember, all identity matrices are square; therefore, it is impossible to compute an identity matrix that is non-square.

Computing the Inverse

In the beginning of the section on matrices we saw a bit of black magick performed with the matrix equation:

AX=B

The results were a series of manipulations to compute the variable matrix X. Here are the manipulations in more detail:

$A^{-1}AX = A^{-1}B$
$IX = A^{-1}B$
$X = A^{-1}B$

The final result states that the variable matrix, which is the x, y, and z of the linear system of equations, can be found by multiplying the inverse of A by the constant matrix B. However, what exactly is an inverse and what is the importance of inverses? An *inverse* is a matrix such that when multiplied by the original matrix, results in the identity matrix. For example, in standard real numbers, the inverse of any number can be found by taking one over the number. Or, more precisely, the inverse of i is:

$i^{-1} = 1/i$

Therefore:

$i * i^{-1} = i * 1/i = 1 = i^{-1} * i = 1$

And similarly to ordinary numbers, matrices also have inverses. However, computing these inverses is beyond the scope of this book for the general case. We will need to compute the inverses of some specific matrices that have to do with graphical transformations such as translation, scaling, and rotation. However, we will cross that bridge when we come to it.

For now, let's take a look at a simple example that illustrates the multiplication of a matrix A by its own inverse, resulting in the identity matrix. Of course, I am going to pull the inverse out of a hat (since I know how to compute them in general), but don't tweak too much—just watch how the result of the multiplication is the identity matrix.

Given the matrix,

$$A = \begin{bmatrix} 2 & 3 \\ -1 & 4 \end{bmatrix}$$

its inverse is equal to:

$$A^{-1} = \begin{bmatrix} 4/12 & -3/12 \\ 1/12 & 2/12 \end{bmatrix}$$

And if we multiply $A*A^{-1}$, then the result is:

$$A*A^{-1} = \begin{bmatrix} 2 & 3 \\ -1 & 4 \end{bmatrix} * \begin{bmatrix} 4/12 & -3/12 \\ 1/12 & 2/12 \end{bmatrix} = \begin{bmatrix} (8/12 + 3/12) & (-6/12 + 6/12) \\ (-4/12 + 4/12) & (3/12 + 8/12) \end{bmatrix} = \begin{bmatrix} 1 & 0 \\ 0 & 1 \end{bmatrix} = I$$

Of course, we just as well could have multiplied $A^{-1}*A$, and the result also would have been the identity matrix I.

Concatenation

The final topic we are going to touch upon is one of the coolest things about matrices, and that's the property of *concatenation*. Concatenation means that a single matrix can be generated by multiplying a set of matrices together:

$$C = A_1 * A_2 * A_3 * ... * A_n$$

The interesting thing is that now the single matrix C holds all of the transformation information that the other matrices contained. This is a very useful tool when performing multiple transformations to all the points that make up the objects of the game. We can use the single concatenated matrix, which is the product of all of the desired transformations, instead of multiplying each point by two or three different matrices that each perform a single operation such as translation, scaling, and rotation.

Using this technique speeds up the game calculations by about 300 percent! So this is a good thing to know. However, as we learned earlier, the order of multiplication is very important. When we concatenate matrices, we must multiply them in the order in which we wish them to operate, so make sure that translation is performed first or rotation is done last (or whatever).

Fixed Point Mathematics

The last purely mathematical topic we must discuss is *fixed point mathematics*. If you know anything about 3D graphics, you're sure to know something about fixed point math. Fixed point math is a form of mathematics that is based on the use of integers to approximate decimals and fractions. Normally, we do calculations using floating point numbers. However, there is a problem with floating point numbers and microprocessors–they don't get along. Floating point math is very complex and slow, mainly because of the format of a floating point number as it is represented in the computer.

Floating point numbers use a format called IEEE, which is based on representing any number by its *mantissa* and *exponent*. For example, the number 432324.23123 in floating point is represented like this,

4.3232423123E+5

which might be more familiar as:

4.3232423123×10^5

In either case, the IEEE format stores the mantissa and the exponent in a way that is a computational hazard to say the least. The results of this format are that multiplication and division are slow, but addition and subtraction are really slow! Doesn't that seem a bit backward? Fortunately, as time has marched on, most CPUs, including the 486DX and 586 Pentium, have on-chip math coprocessors. However, only the latest Pentium processor has floating point performance that exceeds integer performance (sometimes). Thus, we have to make a decision–whether or not to assume that everybody has a Pentium. That would be a mistake, since it will be two to three years before the majority of people have converted. Hence, we must assume that most users have a 486DX (even that is pushing it).

The floating point performance of a 486DX is good, but it's still not as good as integer performance (especially for addition and subtraction). Moreover, since graphics are performed on an integral pixel matrix, at some point, floating point numbers must be converted to integers, and this is a real performance hit. The moral to the story is that we are going to avoid math as much as possible, but we *are* going to use floating point numbers for the majority of our calculations during the prototyping phase of our graphics engine. Then when we are ready to make the engine really rock, we will convert all the floating point math to fixed point math to get the best possible speed.

Another reason to use floating point math during the prototype phase of our 3D graphics engine is that the graphics are hard enough to understand without a ton of confusing fixed point calculations getting in the way of the purity of everything. And many people might just want to keep the floating point library and forget the final fixed point version, so this gives everyone the best options.

So what exactly is fixed point math? Fixed point math is a form of computer math that uses an integer to represent both the whole part and fractional part of a decimal number by means of *scaling*. The main premise is that all numbers are represented in binary; therefore, if we use a large integer representation such as a LONG, which is 32 bits, we can play a little game. The game has the rules that the whole part of a number will be placed in the upper 16 bits and the decimal part will be placed in the lower 16 bits. Figure 10-35 shows this breakdown. Although

FIGURE 10-35

◎ ◎ ◎ ◎ ◎ ◎

Typical fixed point representation

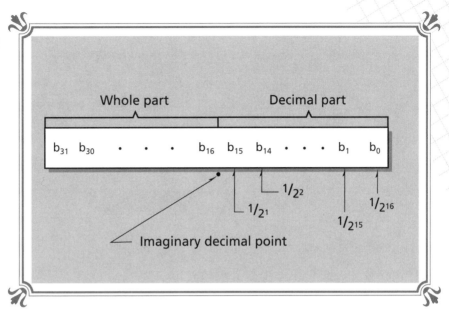

we can place the "fixed point" anywhere, most implementations place it smack in the middle for simplicity.

The lower 16 bits are called the *decimal part* and the upper 16 bits are called the *whole part*. All we need is to come up with a set of rules so that we can assign numbers to fixed point numbers. Well, it turns out to be quite easy. First, let's define a fixed point type:

```
typedef long fixedpoint;
```

We know that the whole part is supposed to be in the upper 16 bits and the decimal part in the lower 16 bits; therefore, if we want to convert the simple integer 10 into a fixed point number, we can do something like this:

```
fixedpoint f1;
```

```
f1 = (fixedpoint)(10 << 16);
```

What's happening is, we are scaling or shifting the 10 by 16 bits (which is equivalent to multiplying by 65536) to place it into the upper half of the fixed point number where it belongs. But how can we place a decimal number into a fixed point number? That's easy—instead of shifting the number, we must multiply it by 65536, like this:

```
f1 = (fixedpoint)(34.23432 * 65536);
```

The reason for this is that the compiler represents all decimal numbers as floating point numbers and shifting doesn't make sense, but multiplying does. Now that

we can assign a fixed point number with a standard integer or a decimal number, how do we perform addition, subtraction, multiplication, and division? Addition and subtraction are simple. Given two fixed point numbers f1 and f2, to add them we use the following code:

```
f3 =f1+f2;
```

And to subtract them we use:

```
f3 = f1-f2;
```

Isn't that easy! The problem occurs when we try to multiply or divide fixed point numbers. Let's begin with multiplication. When two fixed point numbers are multiplied, there is an overscaling because each fixed point number is really multiplied internally by 65536 (in our format); therefore, when we try to multiply two fixed point numbers, like this,

```
f3 = f1*f2;
```

the result is overscaled. To solve the problem, we can do one of two things. We can shift the result back to the right by 16 bits after the multiplication, or shift one of the multiplicands to the right by 16 bits before the multiplication. This will result in an answer that is scaled correctly. So, we could do this

```
f3 = (f1*f2)>>16;
```

or this:

```
f3 = ((f1>>16) * f2);
```

However, now we have a problem. Take a look at Figure 10-36. If we shift the results after the multiplication, it's possible that we may get an overflow since, in the worst case, two 32-bit numbers can result in a 64-bit product (actually, in this particular 16.16 representation, whenever numbers greater than 1.0 are multiplied there will be an overflow). On the other hand, if we shift one of the numbers to the right before the multiplication, we diminish our accuracy since we are in essence throwing away the decimal portion of one of the numbers. This can be remedied a bit by shifting each number by 8 bits and symmetrically decreasing their accuracy. However, the best solution to the problem is to use 64-bit math.

Using 64-bit math is possible, but it isn't easy to do with a 16-bit C/C++ compiler. Even with the in-line assembler that most C/C++ compilers come with, performing 64-bit math may not be possible if the compiler doesn't support 32-bit instructions. But we will deal with all these problems later. If worse comes to worst, we can always link in external assembly language functions that perform full 64-bit integer fixed point mathematics. Don't miss the little hidden lesson here, which is this: fixed point math performed with 32-bit numbers on a 16-bit compiler is slower than floating point on 486DXs and Pentiums! This is because the compiler turns simple operations like

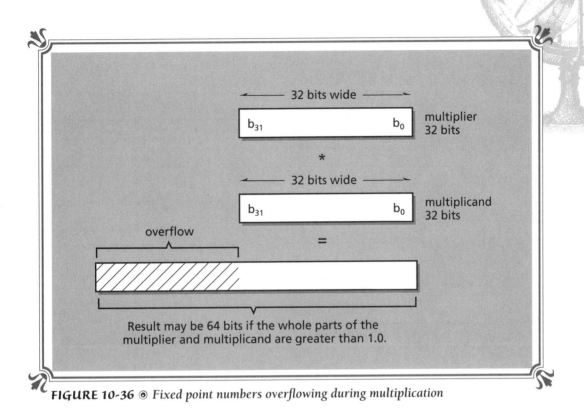

FIGURE 10-36 ◉ *Fixed point numbers overflowing during multiplication*

```
long a,b;
a=a+b;
```

into multiple 16-bit operations, killing the speed gained from the whole fixed point format.

Finally, division is performed much the same way as multiplication, but the numbers after division are underscaled! This occurs since there is a factor of 65536 in each dividend and divisor, and this factor will be divided out during the division. Thus, before the division is performed, the dividend must be scaled by another 16 bits–that is shifted to the left, for example

```
f3 = ((f1 <<16) / f2);
```

Once again this poses a problem, since during the shift to the left of the dividend, the 32-bit fixed point number may overflow, as shown in Figure 10-37. We can come up with a "best of the worst" solution by scaling each number up 8 bits and then hoping for the best, but the best way to solve the problem is to use 64-bit math again. Therefore, our final library, to be totally accurate, must use 64-bit fixed point math to hold the overflows and underflows. However, if all the math we per-

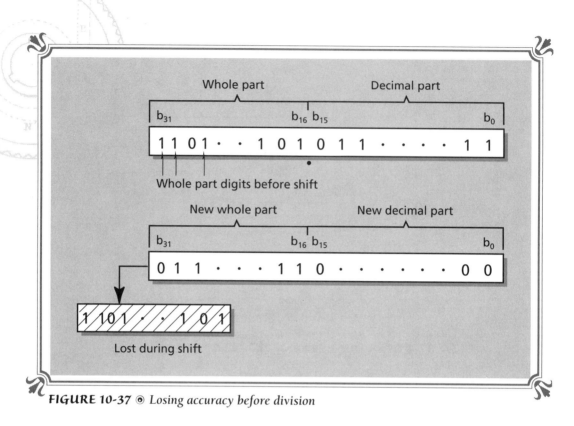

FIGURE 10-37 ⊚ *Losing accuracy before division*

form can't possibly overflow or underflow in 32 bits, we can get away with 32-bit math. These are decisions that we will make as we design the 3D graphics engine.

Finally, to convert a fixed point number back to an integer, all we need to do is shift it back to the right 16 bits, as in:

```
int number;

number = (f1>>16);
```

Making the Quantum Leap to 3D

Now that we have laid the mathematical foundation necessary to discuss 3D graphics, let's begin by realizing that 3D graphics is not hard, not beyond comprehension. However, there are many details that we have to consider. As long as we take it slow and understand all the material and concepts, we'll have no trouble at all. The remaining material in this chapter is going to be an overall coverage of 3D graphics. Rather than describing any single topic in detail, we are going to see how it all fits together.

Understanding the interrelationships in a 3D graphics system is probably the most important thing. Once we have a top-down view of all the workings of a 3D graphics engine, we can break each system down and implement it. Learning each system one by one without knowing how they all fit together can be frustrating. Therefore, think of the rest of this material as an outline for the following chapters, which will focus on each separate aspect.

Points, Lines, and Polygons in 3D

As we know, all objects in 3D space can be defined by a collection of points. Points are in fact the basic building block of 3D objects. Some 3D graphics systems like to think of objects as sets of lines and some like to think of objects as sets of polygons. We are going to take the latter point of view. Thus, a 3D object in our graphics engine is going to be nothing more than a set of polygons defined by a set of points. Take a look at Figure 10-38. The figure depicts a cube made of a set of points, and each face of the cube is made up of a specific set of points.

So a polygon is a set of points in 3D space. This is true, but we need to add one more premise, and that is that the points are coplanar. This means that a plane exists containing all the points. Otherwise, the polygon isn't flat. Take a look at Figure 10-39 to see this. The left side of the figure shows a polygon that is coplanar, and the right side of the figure shows a polygon that isn't coplanar. It's also interest-

FIGURE 10-38

◎ ◎ ◎ ◎ ◎ ◎

A cube defined in 3D

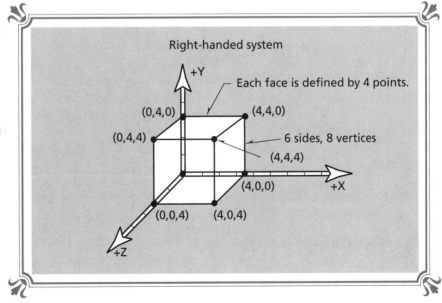

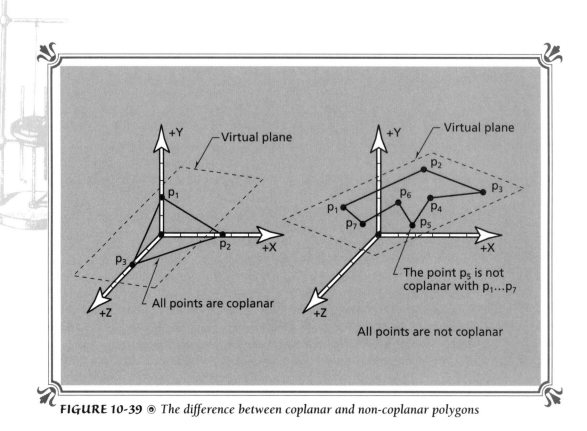

FIGURE 10-39 ⊚ *The difference between coplanar and non-coplanar polygons*

ing to notice that all triangles are coplanar. Or in other words, all polygons with exactly three vertices, by definition, lie in a single plane, since three points is the absolute minimum number of points needed to describe a plane in 3D.

We know that our graphics engine is going to use polygons. But are we going to allow polygons of any shape? The answer is no! We are only going to support triangles and quadrilaterals (four-sided polygons–we'll call them quads). The reason for this is that triangles are the easiest and fastest objects to draw and are very easy to model with. Quads, on the other hand, aren't as easy to draw, but are nice for modeling. Luckily, we can always convert a quad into a pair of triangles by a method called *triangulation*. Then we can render each of the triangles separately (see Figure 10-40). In fact, any polygon can be triangulated, but let's keep things simple!

Data Structures

Let's talk a bit about data structures now. How should we represent the objects in our game world? Well, this is actually a very important detail, and we're going to evolve it as we go; but for now, let's rough out a possible data structure graphically.

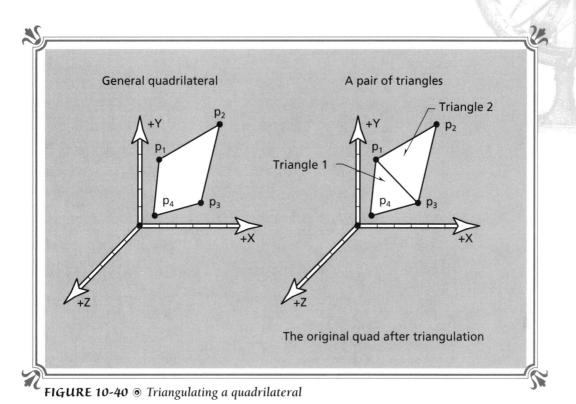

FIGURE 10-40 ⊙ *Triangulating a quadrilateral*

Figure 10-41 shows the objects in a game universe. Each object consists of a set of polygons, which themselves consist of a set of points.

Since many polygons in an object will have points in common, it would be inefficient to have multiple copies of vertices, so each polygon definition will be based on a common set of vertices. Thus, Figure 10-42 is a more realistic picture of what we are going to end up with. The end result is still going to have the single point as the basic building block. This means that all of our functions are at some point going to transform to each point that makes up an object. Hence, we are going to concentrate on learning how to transform single points and then use that technology to transform entire objects, and in the end, the whole universe.

With all that in mind, let's make up some data structures so we have something to reference in the remaining examples of the chapter. These data structures aren't going to be the final ones we use, but just something that we can plug into any code fragments that we might want to write. First is the single point or vertex:

```
typedef struct point_typ
        {
        float x,y,z;  // notice they are floating point values
        } point, *point_ptr, vertex, *vertex_ptr;
```

Now let's define a polygon as a list of vertices:

```
typedef struct polygon_typ
        {
        int num_vertices;    // number of vertices in this polygon (3
                             // or 4 in our case)
        int vertex_list[4]; // the list of vertices, 4 or less
        } polygon, *polygon_ptr;
```

Finally, let's define an object as a collection of polygon faces made of vertices:

```
typedef struct object_typ
        {
        int num_vertices;                  // total number of vertices
                                           // that make up object
        vertex vertices[MAX_VERTICES];     // the vertices of the object
        int num_polygons;                  // the total number of poly-
                                           // gons that make up the object

        polygon faces[MAX_FACES];          // the faces of the object

        float world_x,world_y,world_z;     // the position of the object
                                           // in the universe

        } object, *object_ptr;
```

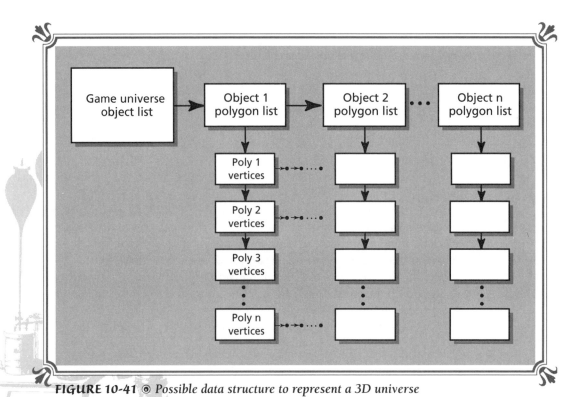

FIGURE 10-41 ⊙ *Possible data structure to represent a 3D universe*

You will notice that I have used static arrays to hold the vertices and polygons. A more elegant and memory-efficient solution would be to use linked lists, but for illustrative purposes, arrays are easier to manipulate. However, I doubt that any object will have more than 16 or 32 vertices and a dozen or so faces–otherwise, our graphics engine is going to have a hard time running in real-time!

Coordinate Systems

When we worked with 2D graphics and sprites in the previous chapter, we had two different coordinate systems. Each sprite had its own (x,y) location, and the sprite image was defined relative to this (x,y) location as a rectangle that extended some width and some height from the (x,y) position of the sprite. This can be thought of as the sprite's local coordinate system. Then when we drew the sprite on the screen, we used its (x,y) location as a position relative to the upper corner of the screen (0,0) to position and draw the sprite. This is the coordinate system we refer to as screen coordinates.

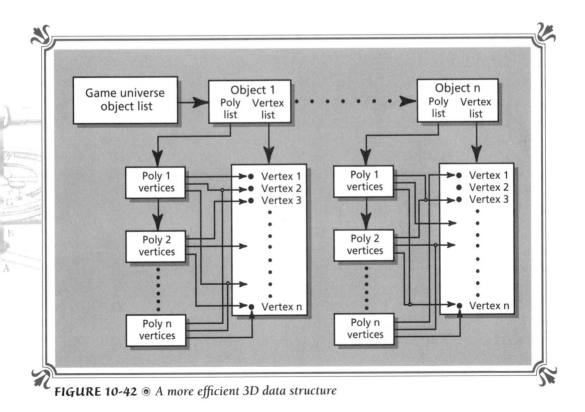

FIGURE 10-42 ⊙ *A more efficient 3D data structure*

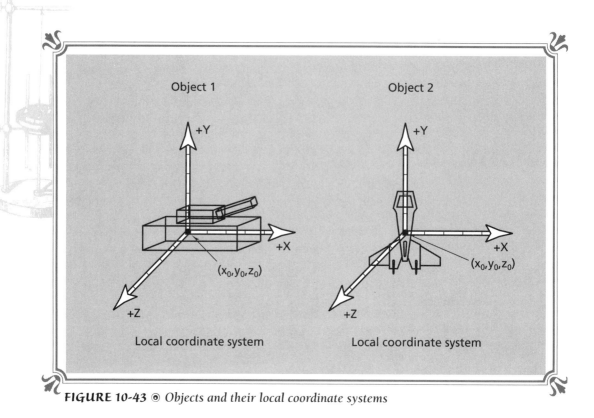

FIGURE 10-43 ⊙ *Objects and their local coordinate systems*

Three-dimensional computer graphics also has multiple coordinate systems. Many coordinate systems are necessary because each object must be defined relative to its own local origin, as shown in Figure 10-43. Then each object needs to be placed somewhere in the world relative to a universal origin (see Figure 10-44), and finally, the objects have to be drawn or projected onto the screen. Let's take a look at all these systems in detail.

Local Coordinates

All the objects in our 3D graphics engine are going to be defined as a set of vertices or points that are relative to a local origin of (0,0,0). This means that when we model our objects, we are always going to assume that they are centered about the origin. However, during game play, they are of course going to move around, but the vertices of the object won't be altered such that they are adjusted to move the object to another location. The vertices will be translated and projected only during the rendering process. Take a look at the cube in Figure 10-45 to see this graphically.

The figure shows the cube moving 20 units in the positive X direction. However, this is not what happens in the data structures. Within the data structures, all we

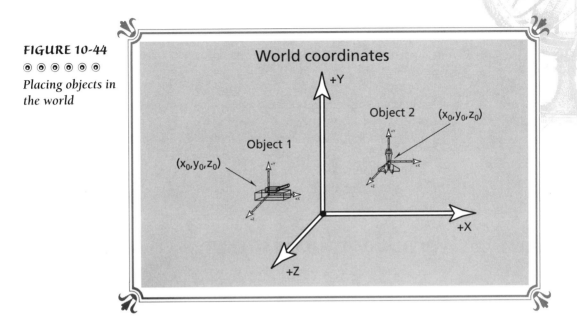

FIGURE 10-44

◎ ◎ ◎ ◎ ◎ ◎

Placing objects in the world

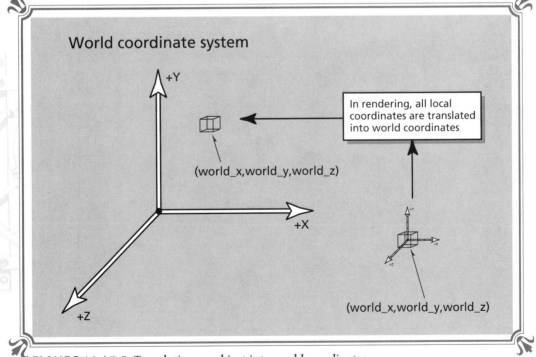

FIGURE 10-45 ◎ *Translating an object into world coordinates*

will update is the position of the cube or its *world_x*, *world_y*, and *world_z*. Just as we translated sprites by updating their (x,y) position in the structure, we are going to manipulate 3D objects by moving their position instead of manipulating their vertices. One of the reasons for this is that once an object has been moved, its vertices are changed and its center is no longer (0,0,0). This creates a problem with both scaling and rotation; since the new center of the object isn't (0,0,0), the object will scale and rotate incorrectly.

Summing up, each object in our 3D database will be defined relative to the point (0,0,0). Then when we want to move an object, we are only going to update its world position, not its vertices. This keeps the object centered at (0,0,0) mathematically as far as the vertices are concerned and allows us to scale and rotate without problems.

World Coordinates

The world coordinate system is like the universe. It has a center (0,0,0) and extends out to infinity in all the directions X, Y, and Z, as shown in Figure 10-46. In a 3D game, we are going to move around and place game objects in this world coordinate system. Now in a real game, the world coordinate system may have finite limitations due to the underlying implementation. For example, our worlds may only be 32,000x32,000x32,000, as shown in Figure 10-47. But whatever size the world coordinate system is, all the objects are contained within it and manipulated within it.

FIGURE 10-46

◎ ◎ ◎ ◎ ◎ ◎

The mathematically correct world coordinate system

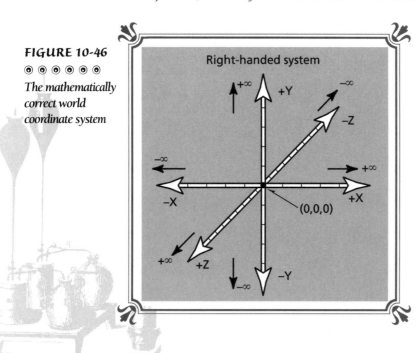

FIGURE 10-47

◎ ◎ ◎ ◎ ◎ ◎

The real world coordinate system

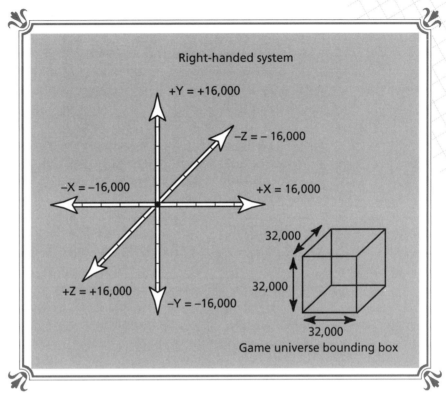

For example, imagine that we have defined an object named *jet_fighter*. The object might look like Figure 10-48. We could place the object in the world coordinate system by setting the *world_x, world_y,* and *world_z* components of the object structure like this:

```
world_x = 1000;
world_y = 50;
world_z = -10000;
```

The jet would then be placed in the world as shown in Figure 10-49. As you can see, because the scale of jet is so small to the size of the world coordinate system, it is nothing more than a dot!

Let's recapitulate the relationship between local coordinates and world coordinates. Local coordinates are used to define an object with a set of vertices that are relative to (0,0,0). This allows rotation and scaling to be performed properly. The position of the object in world coordinates is held in a set of variables called *world_x, world_y,* and *world_z*. These coordinates define where the center of the object should be placed in the game universe. For example, if an object was a cube defined by 8 vertices, the local vertex coordinates are added to the *world_x, world_y,*

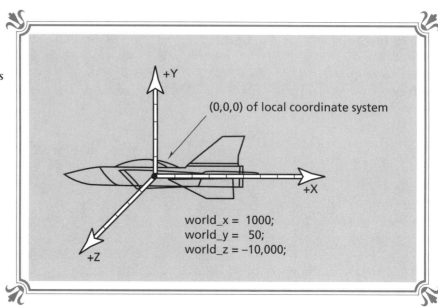

FIGURE 10-48

⊚ ⊚ ⊚ ⊚ ⊚ ⊚

Jet fighter and its local coordinate system

and *world_z* position coordinates to position the object for rendering. However, that is the extent of the contact between local coordinates and world coordinates. The vertices that make up an object are only temporarily modified by the position of the object during rendering, otherwise, they stay the same unless the object is scaled or rotated.

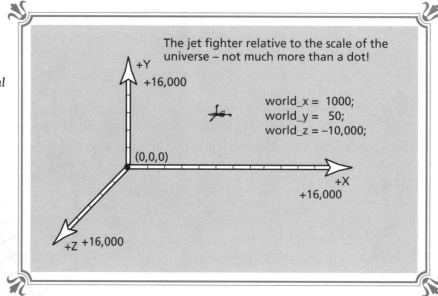

FIGURE 10-49

⊚ ⊚ ⊚ ⊚ ⊚ ⊚

Jet fighter being placed in the real world

Camera Coordinates

The final coordinate system that we need to consider is called the *camera coordinate system*, which is really the view that the user sees. Take a look at Figure 10-50. Here we see a game universe with the user looking in a certain direction. Based on the user's field of view, he should see a specific amount of imagery within the 3D universe. Therefore, the camera coordinate system needs to know two things: the position of the viewpoint and the view direction in which the user is looking.

The viewpoint is easy enough to understand. It is simply a point in world coordinates at which the user or player is positioned. The view direction is a bit harder to grasp. Let's give it a try. Given that the user is positioned at a view position, imagine that position has a local coordinate system mapped on top of it, as shown in Figure 10-51. Thus, relative to the world coordinate system, the view direction is made up of the angles relative to the world axes that the user is pointing toward. Or to put it another way, imagine that the user is standing at the origin of the world coordinate system, as shown in Figure 10-52, so that the viewpoint is (0,0,0). Further imagine that the user is looking straight down the positive Z axis. We might call this "the neutral position." Then when the user turns parallel to either the X, Y, or Z axis, we record these changes as a set of angles: *angle_x*, *angle_y*, and *angle_z*.

These angles are in essence the *pitch*, *yaw*, and *roll* of the player. They are used along with the view position to compute the final image viewed by the user in Cyberspace. For example, imagine that a universe has the objects in it as shown in

FIGURE 10-50

◎ ◎ ◎ ◎ ◎ ◎

Camera coordinate system

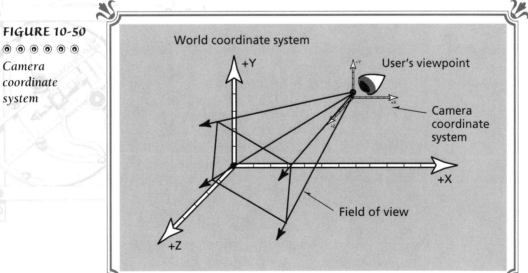

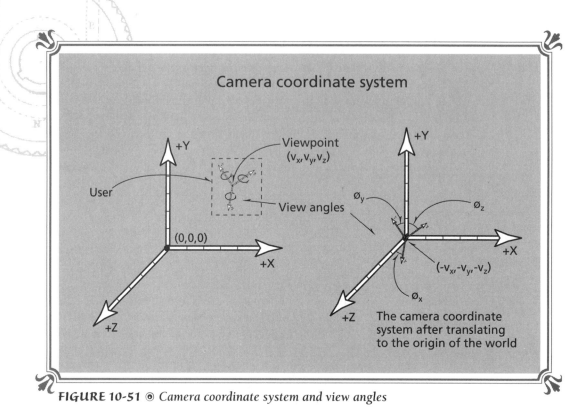

FIGURE 10-51 ⊙ *Camera coordinate system and view angles*

FIGURE 10-52

⊙ ⊙ ⊙ ⊙ ⊙ ⊙

The user in a neutral position

Figure 10-53 (which is an X-Z top-down view of a battleground). You will note that the player has *angle_y* of 180 degrees, that is, he is looking down the negative Z axis. Thus, all the objects shouldn't be visible since the player is looking the other way. This is the whole idea of the camera coordinate system. Think of the player's position and viewing angle literally as a camera that is the window on the scene. The trick is to render the scene that the camera is looking at on the screen. This is called the *viewing transformation* and *projection*. One of the first steps in projection is to translate all the objects relative to the viewpoint and then rotate them relative to the view direction. What's visible is what's drawn. This may seem a bit confusing, but hang in there. We'll talk more about projection and the viewing transformation a bit later, but now let's see how to transform 3D objects.

Transformations in 3D

Earlier we saw how to manipulate 2D points with simple equations. We learned how to translate, rotate, and even scale objects in two dimensions. All these techniques

FIGURE 10-53

◉ ◉ ◉ ◉ ◉ ◉

Battleground view to illustrate view angle

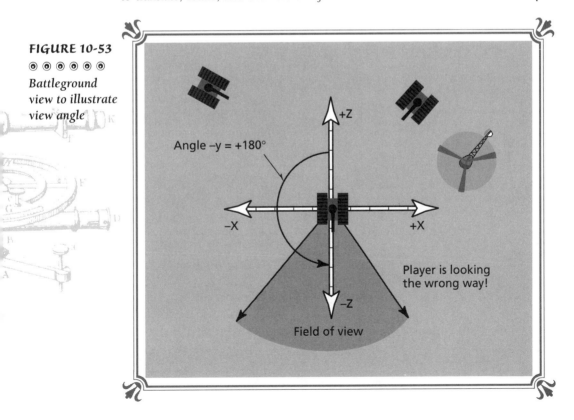

can be accomplished in 3D in much the same way. We simply need to add one more coordinate and a few more equations. However, instead of using explicit equations to perform the manipulations, we are going to use matrices. That is the whole reason we studied them in the previous pages. Three-dimensional transformations can be quite long, and it's nice to be able to write them in a short form and perform them efficiently–hence, the use of matrices.

This brings us to the question, how are we going to do this? Well, we're going to pretend that all the points in our 3D world are really little matrices that each consist of a single row, such as:

$$[x \quad y \quad z]$$

Then we are going to multiply the points by transformation matrices that are of the correct size and contain the proper elements to perform the required transformation. However, we are going to have to add a little bit to our definition of a point. All points must be defined not by three components but by four. This fourth component is called the *normalizing factor*. The normalizing factor is more of a mathematical need than an implementational need. By adding a fourth coordinate, the 3D coordinates become *homogeneous*, which simply means they are scaled relative to the normalizing factor. The only reason we need to use homogeneous coordinates is that they allow us to perform translation with a matrix. You see, to translate a 3D point, a 4x4 matrix is needed. Try to perform translation with a 3x3 matrix and you'll see what I mean. Anyway, homogeneous coordinates look like this:

$$[xw \quad yw \quad zw \quad w]$$

The fourth component is the normalizing factor. Thus, if we want to recover the original point (x,y,z), we perform the following transformation:

x=x/w;
y=y/w;
z=z/w;

Doing three divisions to extract a point that we already have isn't too smart, so we are going to let w=1; therefore, our new homogeneous coordinates look like this:

$$[x \quad y \quad z \quad 1]$$

We need not perform any division to extract the original point. The whole idea of all this is to be able to multiply our original homogeneous point by a transformation matrix that results in a new transformed point. Therefore, we want to multiply a 1x4 matrix by some *nxm* matrix that results in another 1x4 matrix. Therefore, all the transformation matrices must be 4x4 because 1x4*4x4=4x4. So let's start by learning to translate a single point.

Translation

To translate a single point (x,y,z), we need three translation factors tx, ty, and tz. The operation we wish to perform is shown in Figure 10-54. The point (x,y,z) is moved to a location (x+tx,y+ty,z+tz). Therefore, translation is simply,

```
x=x+tx;
y=y+ty;
z=z+tz;
```

and we must convert this into matrix form using homogeneous coordinates. OK, here's how we do it. First, let's represent our input point by the matrix:

$$\begin{bmatrix} x & y & z & 1 \end{bmatrix}$$

Then we need to come up with a 4x4 transformation matrix that results in

$$\begin{bmatrix} (x + tx) & (y + ty) & (z + tz) & 1 \end{bmatrix}$$

when multiplied by the input point. With a little thought and a lot of experience in matrix multiplication, you could deduce that the matrix we need looks like this:

$$T = \begin{bmatrix} 1 & 0 & 0 & 0 \\ 0 & 1 & 0 & 0 \\ 0 & 0 & 1 & 0 \\ tx & ty & tz & 1 \end{bmatrix}$$

FIGURE 10-54

◎ ◎ ◎ ◎ ◎ ◎

Translating a point in 3D

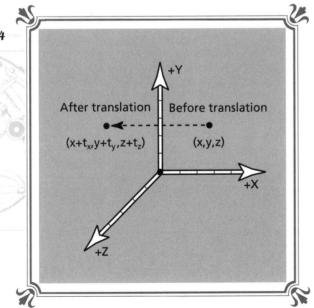

Therefore, to translate a point, the following multiplication is used, and the end result is what we desired.

$$
\begin{bmatrix} x & y & z & 1 \end{bmatrix} * \begin{bmatrix} 1 & 0 & 0 & 0 \\ 0 & 1 & 0 & 0 \\ 0 & 0 & 1 & 0 \\ tx & ty & tz & 1 \end{bmatrix}
$$

Scaling

Scaling is the next operation that we may want to perform on a 3D object. Given that an object is defined with a local origin of (0,0,0), we want to derive a scaling matrix such that the object will scale relative to (0,0,0) without translation. Such an operation is shown in Figure 10-55. The object (a cube) is scaled in the X, Y, and Z directions by the scaling factors sx, sy, and sz. Note that objects need not be uniformly scaled in all directions. Anyway, we want to perform the following operation:

```
x=x*sx;
y=y*sy;
z=z*sz;
```

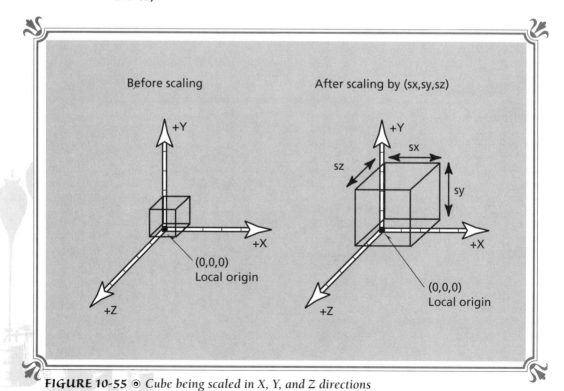

FIGURE 10-55 ⊙ *Cube being scaled in X, Y, and Z directions*

So we need a 4x4 transformation matrix that will do this without adding or subtracting any other factors to the original point. See if you can come up with such a matrix without looking below.

We need to find a 4x4 matrix such that the homogeneous point,

$$\begin{bmatrix} x & y & z & 1 \end{bmatrix}$$

when multiplied by some 4x4 matrix, results in the new transformed point of:

$$\begin{bmatrix} x*sx & y*sy & z*sz & 1 \end{bmatrix}$$

Do you give up? Here's the answer:

$$S = \begin{bmatrix} sx & 0 & 0 & 0 \\ 0 & sy & 0 & 0 \\ 0 & 0 & sz & 0 \\ 0 & 0 & 0 & 1 \end{bmatrix}$$

Using the above matrix and the input point, the following multiplication will perform the scale, which gives the correct result.

$$\begin{bmatrix} x & y & z & 1 \end{bmatrix} * \begin{bmatrix} sx & 0 & 0 & 0 \\ 0 & sy & 0 & 0 \\ 0 & 0 & sz & 0 \\ 0 & 0 & 0 & 1 \end{bmatrix} = \begin{bmatrix} x*sx & y*sy & z*sz & 1 \end{bmatrix}$$

Rotation

Unlike rotation in 2D, rotation in 3D has a bit more variety since we are no longer trapped in a single plane. On the contrary, we can rotate in three different planes. Figure 10-56 shows the possible directions of rotation for a left-handed system. As you can see, rotation can be parallel to the Z axis (similar to the 2D rotation) or it can be parallel to either the X or Y axis. Actually, it can be around all of them simultaneously if we really want to get crazy. But for now, we'll stick to one axis at a time.

The first detail that we must note is that the rotation equations (unlike the translation and scaling equations) work differently on right-handed and left-handed systems. This is because the positive Z axis is in the opposite direction between the right- and left-handed systems. A rotation in one direction in the right-handed system will result in the same rotation but in the other direction in the left-handed system. Take a look at Figure 10-57. This isn't a big deal, but it's nice to know when you are trying to rotate something and it keeps turning the wrong way.

With that in mind, we are going to derive the rotation matrices for the left-handed system. The right-handed derivation is exactly the same except for a sign change here and there. Let's begin with rotation parallel to the Z axis similar to the flat 2D rotation. The rotation equations we derived for 2D can be used. They state that

FIGURE 10-56

⊙ ⊙ ⊙ ⊙ ⊙ ⊙

*Possible axes of
rotation in 3D*

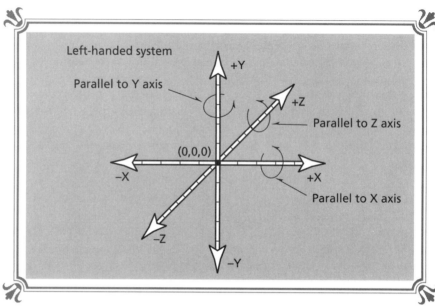

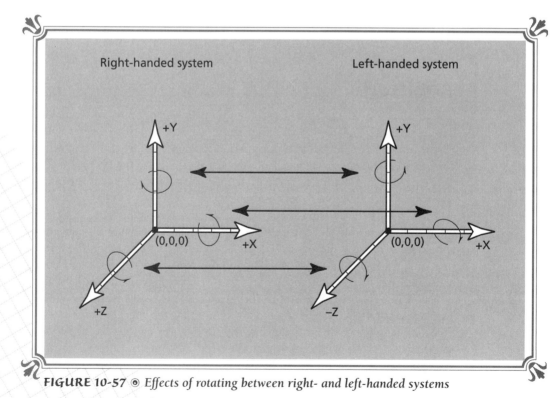

FIGURE 10-57 ⊙ *Effects of rotating between right- and left-handed systems*

given a point (x,y), to rotate the point by an angle theta, the following formulas can be used:

$$x' = x*(COS\ \theta) - y*(SIN\ \theta)$$
$$y' = x*(SIN\ \theta) + y*(COS\ \theta)$$

Using the above information and noting that rotation parallel to the Z axis doesn't affect the Z axis, we can add the following equation to the transformation:

$$z' = z$$

Therefore, we need to derive a matrix that will perform the overall transformation:

$$x' = x*(COS\ \theta) - y*(SIN\ \theta)$$
$$y' = x*(SIN\ \theta) + y*(COS\ \theta)$$
$$z' = z$$

The desired matrix is shown here:

$$R_z = \begin{bmatrix} COS\ \theta & SIN\ \theta & 0 & 0 \\ -SIN\ \theta & COS\ \theta & 0 & 0 \\ 0 & 0 & 1 & 0 \\ 0 & 0 & 0 & 1 \end{bmatrix}$$

Let's try it out with the standard input point and an angle theta and see if it works:

$$\begin{bmatrix} x & y & z & 1 \end{bmatrix} * \begin{bmatrix} COS\ \theta & SIN\ \theta & 0 & 0 \\ -SIN\ \theta & COS\ \theta & 0 & 0 \\ 0 & 0 & 1 & 0 \\ 0 & 0 & 0 & 1 \end{bmatrix}$$

$$= [(x*COS\ \theta - y*SIN\ \theta)\quad (x*SIN\ \theta + y*COS\ \theta)\quad z\quad 1]$$

If you stare at it a minute, you will see this is the result we wanted. Rotations parallel to the X and Y axes are similarly derived by swapping variables. Here are the rotation matrices:

$$R_x = \begin{bmatrix} 1 & 0 & 0 & 0 \\ 0 & COS\ \theta & SIN\ \theta & 0 \\ 0 & -SIN\ \theta & COS\ \theta & 0 \\ 0 & 0 & 0 & 1 \end{bmatrix}$$

And the Y-axis rotation matrix is:

$$R_y = \begin{bmatrix} COS\ \theta & 0 & -SIN\ \theta & 0 \\ 0 & 1 & 0 & 0 \\ SIN\ \theta & 0 & COS\ \theta & 0 \\ 0 & 0 & 0 & 1 \end{bmatrix}$$

I hope you have noticed that all these matrices are rather sparse—that is, they are mostly 0's. We can take advantage of this since there is no reason to multiply a number by 0 if we know the result will be 0! This is actually one of the optimizations we'll implement in the final 3D engine.

Projecting the Image

Once we have defined a set of objects and the user is positioned at a given viewpoint with a specific view direction, the image must be rendered on the screen. But before we can render (draw) the objects, we must project them from 3D to 2D. This is called *projection*. But before the projection can be accomplished, the objects must be transformed by the world to camera transformation, which is done by translating each object to the viewpoint and rotating each object by the inverse of the view direction. This is done to normalize the projection so that it is always in relation to the X-Y plane, which is parallel to the video screen with the positive Z axis pointing into the screen.

We'll talk more about the viewing transformation that brings all the objects into the proper position, but for now, let's assume that the objects are ready to be displayed and we want to draw them on the screen. The question is, how do we do this? As an example, let's take the simple case shown in Figure 10-58. Here we see the user looking at a simple cube, and we would like to project this image on the screen. Since the screen is only 2D, we must somehow take into consideration all the Z components of the object before we map the object onto the 2D video screen. This "consideration" is called projection and is used to display a reasonable image of a 3D object onto a 2D plane. Let's see what techniques we can propose to do this.

Parallel Projections

The simplest technique used to project a 3D image on a 2D plane is to throw away the z component of each vertex. This is called a *parallel projection*. The following transformation will accomplish this.

Given the point (x,y,z) in 3D:

```
x_par = x;
y_par = y;
```

Of course, we might need to center the image with translation factors and scale one of the axes to take into consideration aspect ratio, so the actual transformation will end up looking like this:

```
x_screen = x_par + SCREEN_WIDTH/2;
y_screen = y_par*aspect_ratio + SCREEN_HEIGHT/2;
```

In either case, all lines are projecting in parallel. This means that no matter how far away an object is from the view screen, it will always be projected as the same

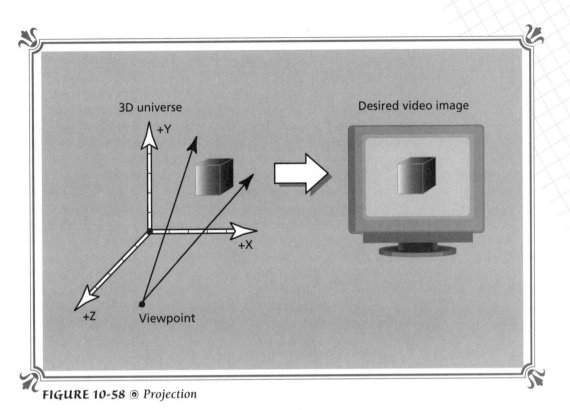

FIGURE 10-58 ◉ *Projection*

size. Although parallel projections are very useful in mechanical imaging and so forth, for a video game, it's not going to cut it. The whole idea of a 3D video game is the 3D part! Thus we need a projection that takes into consideration the z component and scales the x and y in some manner to make the object look bigger as it gets closer and smaller as it moves farther away.

Perspective Projections

Perspective projection is the ultimate in realism that can be achieved with a 2D video screen. Perspective projection is based on the premise that light rays converge to the user's viewpoint. This is shown in Figure 10-59. Basically, we use the user's viewpoint as a projection reference and then compute where a straight line (a ray) would intersect the view plane (video screen) if it were projected to the user's viewpoint. This type of projection has the effect of scaling objects down as they move away and scaling them up as they get closer to the user's viewpoint. But what is the transformation that will accomplish this? With a bit of geometry, it can be deduced that the perspective screen coordinates (x_per, y_per) are simply:

```
x_per = x*viewing_distance/z;
y_per = y*viewing_distance/z;
```

FIGURE 10-59

◎ ◎ ◎ ◎ ◎ ◎

Projection techniques

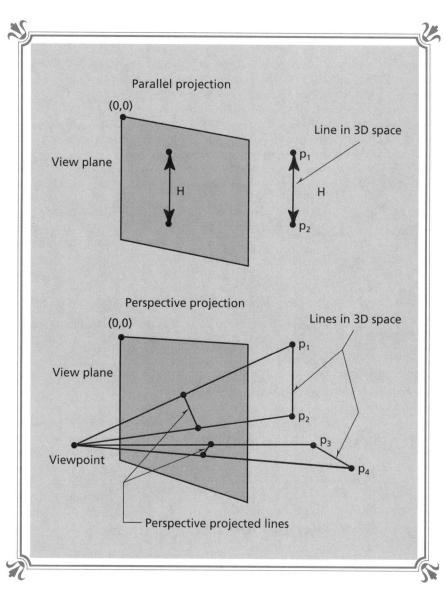

where (x,y,z) is the point being projected. Again, (*x_per,y_per*) should be taken with a grain of salt since they need to be slightly modified to be used as physical screen coordinates. But once we have them, we use the same technique as we did in the parallel projection. Thus:

```
x_screen = x_per + SCREEN_WIDTH/2;
y_screen = y_per*aspect_ratio + SCREEN_HEIGHT/2;
```

Hence, we see that the final physical screen transformation is invariant of the type of projection, which is as we would expect since the physical screen coordinate system doesn't care which projection was used to arrive at the screen coordinates.

Since we are using matrices to do everything, let's create a perspective transformation matrix with which we can multiply a point (x,y,z) with which to arrive at the point (x_per, y_per). The transformation matrix needs only one value in it and that is the position of the view plane, which is really the *viewing_distance*. Here is the perspective transformation matrix,

$$
T_{per} = \begin{bmatrix} 1 & 0 & 0 & 0 \\ 0 & 1 & 0 & 0 \\ 0 & 0 & 1 & 1d \\ 0 & 0 & 0 & 0 \end{bmatrix}
$$

where d is the *viewing_distance* or the positive z position of the viewing plane. As an example, let's project the point (x,y,z) using the perspective transformation matrix:

$$
\begin{bmatrix} x & y & z & 1 \end{bmatrix} * \begin{bmatrix} 1 & 0 & 0 & 0 \\ 0 & 1 & 0 & 0 \\ 0 & 0 & 1 & 1/d \\ 0 & 0 & 0 & 0 \end{bmatrix}
$$

$$
= \begin{bmatrix} x & y & z & z/d \end{bmatrix}
$$

We must divide by the normalizing factor since it is not 1; thus, the final result is

$$
= \begin{bmatrix} x*d/z & y*d/z & d & 1 \end{bmatrix}
$$

Then we throw away the third and fourth components, leaving us with the projected point (x*d/z,y*d/z), which is what we wanted. Yuk!

Using a matrix to do this is a bit of overkill since it would be a lot easier just to divide x and y by z and then multiply by the viewing distance. This is what we are actually going to do in the engine, but it's important to know how to do it with matrices since they are more general.

Clipping the Image

The next part of the viewing transformation is called *clipping*. Clipping can be done before or after the perspective transformation depending on what kind of clipping is performed. But in general, we don't want to project any objects that lie outside the viewing volume of the player. This viewing volume is shown in Figure 10-60. It consists of six sides. The top and bottom of the viewing volume are called the *hither*

FIGURE 10-60

◎ ◎ ◎ ◎ ◎ ◎

The viewing volume

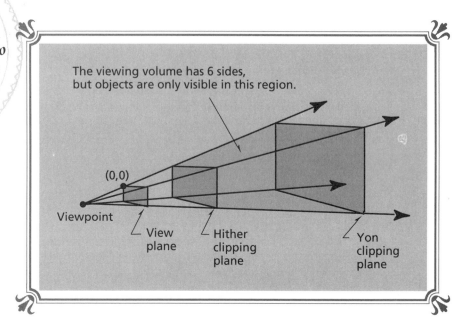

The viewing volume has 6 sides, but objects are only visible in this region.

(0,0)

Viewpoint

View plane

Hither clipping plane

Yon clipping plane

and *yon* or *near* and *far* clipping planes. The remaining sides are just called sides! The idea of clipping is to remove components of the final 3D image that can't possibly be seen before they are projected.

As an example, take a look at Figure 10-61, which shows the viewing volume along with an object that is totally outside of it. This object can't possibly be visible; therefore, there is no reason to project and render it. In fact, trying to project it might result in a floating point error! The second (more common) clipping case is also shown in Figure 10-61. Here we have an object that is partially clipped. This is the hard case. There are a number of ways to approach this. First, we might try to partition the polygons into sets that are totally invisible, partially clipped, and totally visible. Then the polygons that are totally invisible are thrown away and only the partially visible and totally visible polygons are rendered.

Normally, the partially clipped polygons would be clipped to the viewing volume and a new polygon might be generated. However, with the system we are going to use, this isn't going to be efficient since the only polygons we are going to support are triangles and quads. Thus during clipping, we may end up with a five-sided polygon, which won't work. Hence, once we have clipped objects that aren't visible at all, we will project all the polygons that are partially or totally visible, and while we are drawing them on the screen, we will clip them in 2D against the screen boundaries. This is called *image space clipping*, and the clipping done on the object level is called *object space clipping*.

The final plan of attack is listed below in steps:

FIGURE 10-61

◎ ◎ ◎ ◎ ◎ ◎

Visibility of objects

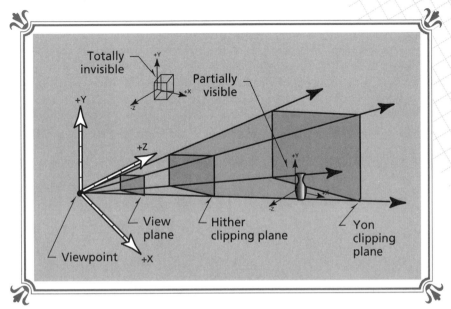

1. Determine which objects are totally invisible and throw them away.

2. Break up objects that are partially visible into polygons.

3. Project polygons that are partially visible or totally visible on the screen and throw away the invisible polygons.

4. As the polygons are being *scan-converted* (drawn on the screen line-by-line), clip them using a pixel-based image space clipper that operates in 2D.

Now that we have the gist of the overall process, let's see exactly how object space and image space clipping are performed.

Object Space Clipping

Object space clipping is a bit of an unfortunate name because it really has nothing to do with objects. Instead, object space clipping means to perform clipping in a pure mathematical space without concern for physical rendering. For example, imagine that we have translated and rotated all the objects in the universe so that from the user's viewpoint it is as if he is located at the projection point or viewpoint looking down the positive Z axis into the view plane, as shown in Figure 10-62.

Object space clipping is basically a method that filters out polygons and/or objects that lie outside the viewing volume. This is achieved mathematically by comparing the points that make up objects against the six clipping planes defined by the viewing volume of Figure 10-62. The easiest of the calculations are the tests

FIGURE 10-62

Rotating the world relative to the viewpoint

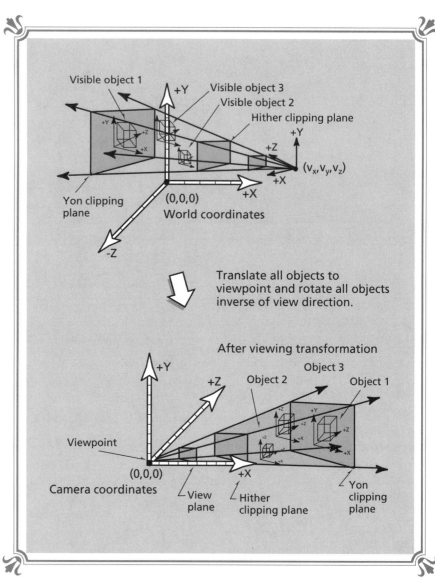

for the yon and hither clipping planes. These tests are performed by examining the z coordinates of each object, polygon, or point depending on the level at which the clipping is performed.

For example, Figure 10-63 shows a top view of the clipping volume—that is, a view looking down the Y axis onto the X-Z plane. Anyway, the figure depicts a pair of objects. One of the objects is within the Z extents of the clipping volume and the other is not, and thus would summarily be discarded. However, the object that is

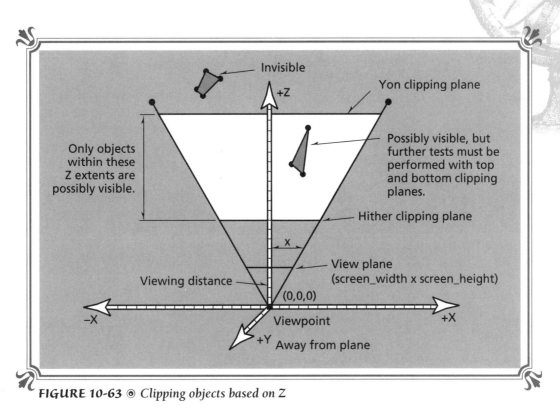

FIGURE 10-63 ◉ *Clipping objects based on Z*

within the Z extents of the clipping volume might possibly be outside the X and Y extents of the clipping volume. Determining this is the main difficulty with object space clipping.

The solution to the problem can be derived by looking at the geometry of the viewing volume one plane at a time and then using the results to solve both the X-Y and X-Z planar cases (since the Z clipping is trivial). The main reason for the difficulty is that unlike the hither and yon Z clipping planes, the other four sides of the clipping volume are not parallel to the view plane. In fact, they are at angles and are general planes. To solve this, we need to come up with a test function that for any given z distance from the view plane, the function will determine whether or not the point (x,y,z) lies within the clipping volume. Referring to Figure 10-63 and using similar triangles, we can deduce that:

$$\frac{x}{z} = \frac{\text{SCREEN\_WIDTH}}{2 * \text{viewing\_distance}}$$

Therefore:

$$x = \frac{\text{SCREEN\_WIDTH}*z}{2 * \text{viewing\_distance}}$$

And if we think of x and z as the x and z components of a general point (x,y,z), then the point is within the X-Z clipping region if and only if

$$x <= \frac{SCREEN\_WIDTH*z}{2*viewing\_distance}$$

and

$$x >= \frac{-SCREEN\_WIDTH*z}{2*viewing\_distance}$$

That takes care of the two clipping planes that bound the clipping region on the right and left. The top and bottom plane testing equations are computed in the same way with similar triangles, and the results are

$$y <= \frac{SCREEN\_HEIGHT*z}{2*viewing\_distance}$$

and

$$y >= \frac{-SCREEN\_HEIGHT*z}{2*viewing\_distance}$$

Notice the only differences between the x and y equations is that the constant in the numerator has to do with the height of the viewing plane instead of its width. Using the above four equations along with the trivial z equations,

z >hither_plane

and,

z <yon_plane

we can come up with a simple algorithm that clips objects, polygons, or points in 3D. The algorithm can use either positive logic or negative logic. This means it can either test if the point is within the clipping region, or it can test if the point is outside the clipping region. At this point, it doesn't really matter which way we do it, but later when we optimize the engine, it might. Basically in computer programs, it's sometimes more efficient to test if something is false rather than if it's true. Anyway, the entire object space clipping algorithm is just a long conditional statement based on the formulas we have derived. Figure 10-64 shows this process as a pipeline.

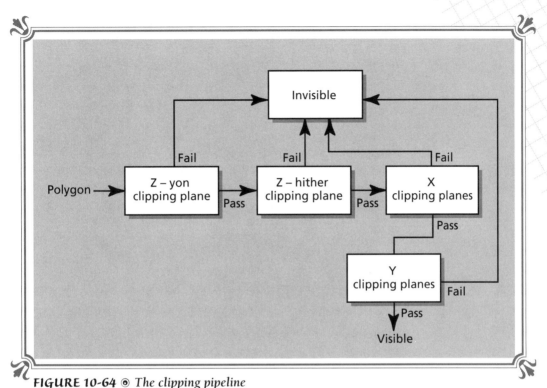

FIGURE 10-64 ⊙ *The clipping pipeline*

Image Space Clipping

Although object space clipping is elegant mathematically, sometimes (especially in the realm of video games) it's more efficient to use image space clipping. Image space clipping is a form of clipping that disregards the 3D geometrical aspects of an object and simply looks at the 2D rasterization of the object as it appears on the display device (which in our case is the video screen).

For example, assume that object space clipping is not performed at all. Then polygons that are really rows of pixels (see Figure 10-65) might be passed to the rendering engine that can't possibly be drawn on the finite extents of mode 13h. So an image space clipper would test each pixel to see if it is within the screen bounds. For example, Listing 10-1 shows our function *Write_Pixel()*, which we wrote many chapters ago.

LISTING 10-1 The old Write_Pixel() function

```
void Write_Pixel(int x,int y,int color)
{
```

continued on next page

continued from previous page

```
// plots the pixel in the desired color a little quicker using binary shifting
// to accomplish the multiplications

// use the fact that 320*y = 256*y + 64*y = y<<8 + y<<6

video_buffer[((y<<8) + (y<<6)) + x] = (unsigned char )color;

} // end Write_Pixel
```

Notice that the function blindly computes the offset into memory and plots the pixel. But what if the sent parameters don't make sense? What if x and y are beyond the mode 13h screen bounds of 320x200? This is what image space clipping takes care of. Image space clipping is accomplished by putting the clipping code into the actual rendering function (or maybe in a filter in front of it that only passes valid coordinates to the final pixel plotting code). For example, if we want to keep the *Write_Pixel()* function and add an image space filter, we can do something like what's shown in Listing 10-2.

LISTING 10-2 An image space pixel clipping filter

```
void Write_Pixel_Clip(int x,int y, int color)
{
// test if pixel coordinates are within range of mode 13h

if (x>=0 && x<319 && y>=0 && y<=199)

    Write_Pixel(x,y,color);

} // end Write_Pixel_Clip
```

FIGURE 10-65

⊚ ⊚ ⊚ ⊚ ⊚ ⊚

Polygons are scan-converted into rows of pixels

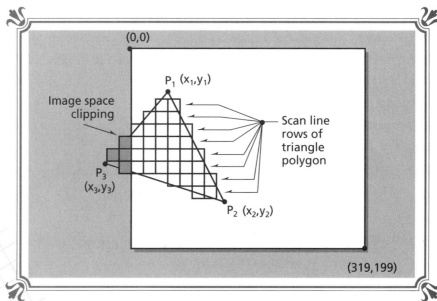

So instead of an application calling *Write_Pixel()*, all the calls are changed to *Write_Pixel_Clip()*, and the filter function only sends valid pixel coordinates to the *Write_Pixel()* function. On the other hand, we might want to make a slightly faster version by getting rid of the second function call, as shown in Listing 10-3.

LISTING 10-3 A second version of the image space clipping pixel plotter with the plot in-line

```
void Write_Pixel_Clip(int x,int y, int color)
{
// test if pixel coordinates are within range of mode 13h and if so plot the pixel

if (x>=0 && x<319 && y>=0 && y<=199)
   video_buffer[((y<<8) + (y<<6)) + x] = (unsigned char )color;

} // end Write_Pixel_Clip
```

This version of the pixel plotter doesn't make a separate call to the *Write_Pixel()* function since the code for it is in-line. Using image space clipping for everything is usually too slow for software implementations, although many hardware graphics engines use this method. We are going to use a hybrid of both object space and image space clipping for our systems. We are going to use object space clipping for objects and polygons. Then, once we have surmised that a polygon is visible or partially visible, we are going to render it line-by-line using an image space clipper to draw only the visible portions of it.

Hidden Surface Removal and Rendering

Hidden surface removal is probably the most complex aspect of 3D graphics and is the number one bottleneck that slows down 3D games. The problem is, when the player is positioned at some viewpoint with a given view direction, many of the objects will be clipped, but the ones that aren't must be drawn in such a way that the order of polygons is correct. Moreover, since most objects in a 3D game are solid, many of the back-facing polygons shouldn't be visible to the player and hence need not be rendered. This brings us to the concept of *hidden surface removal.*

Hidden surface removal is a bit of a fuzzy area and is sometimes mixed up with rendering. However, since we are Cybersorcerers, we aren't too interested in a bunch of critical definitions, we are simply interested in the facts! And the fact is that hidden surface removal ultimately means drawing 3D objects in the right order. And to do this, there are two distinct phases. The first phase is called *back-face culling*, which basically removes polygons that are facing away from the player's viewpoint and need not be processed.

This might be a bit confusing, so let's use Figure 10-66 as a reference to clear it up. Figure 10-66 shows a solid cube with the player's viewpoint situated on one side of the cube looking at it. From the player's viewpoint, the far side of the cube is totally invisible; thus, we shouldn't process those faces since they can't possibly be seen. Therefore, the back-face culling process should throw these faces away before further useless computations are performed on them.

But how is back-face removal done? We do it with a bit of vector math. Again referring to Figure 10-66, we see a line-of-sight vector **v** along with a set of normal vectors to some of the faces of the cube. The trick is to take the dot product between the normal vectors and the line-of-sight vector. Then the sign of the result is used to determine if the face is visible. If you recall, the sign of the dot product will be positive if the angle between the two vectors being dotted is less than or equal to 90 degrees. Therefore, if the results of the dot product are positive, the face must be visible and hence should be rendered. On the other hand, if the sign of the dot product is negative, the angle between the player's view direction and the face is greater than 90 degrees, and the face can't possibly be visible. To sum up:

if **v** · **n** >=0 then the face is visible
else the face is invisible and should be culled

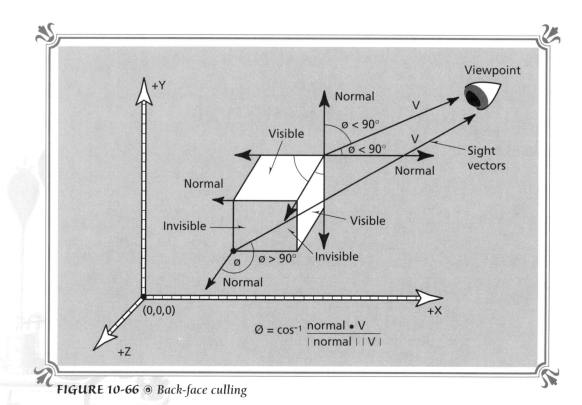

FIGURE 10-66 ⊚ *Back-face culling*

This calculation is performed on all polygon faces that make up the objects in the universe. Then, once a list of visible polygons has been determined, the rendering process begins, which is the second phase of hidden surface removal (in a roundabout, cavalier way). The whole reason we perform the back-face culling is that it usually cuts scene complexity down by 50 percent, since in any given scene, half the faces that make up the objects are usually invisible (facing the other way). This speeds up the rendering by a factor of 2!

Now that we have pruned away the back faces, the next step is to render the polygons. This step can be harder than you may think since the order that the polygons are drawn in is very important.

Depth Sorting and the Painter's Algorithm

Given a set of polygons that are not parallel to the view plane, as shown in Figure 10-67, it isn't obvious what order they should be drawn in so that the final scene looks 3D. This is the function of hidden surface determination, or ordering, algorithms such as the *Painter's algorithm* and the *Z-buffer algorithm*. These algorithms are responsible for rendering a 3D set of polygons that are drawn in such a way that they occlude each other properly.

Let's say we wish to render the two polygons that are shown in Figure 10-68, which is a top-down X-Z plane view. We see that polygon A looks like it should be drawn first if the polygons are viewed straight on from the Z axis. However, we came

FIGURE 10-67
◉ ◉ ◉ ◉ ◉ ◉
In what order should the polygons be drawn?

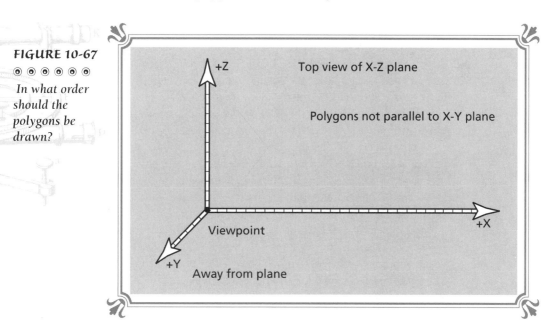

+Z   Top view of X-Z plane

Polygons not parallel to X-Y plane

Viewpoint   +X

+Y   Away from plane

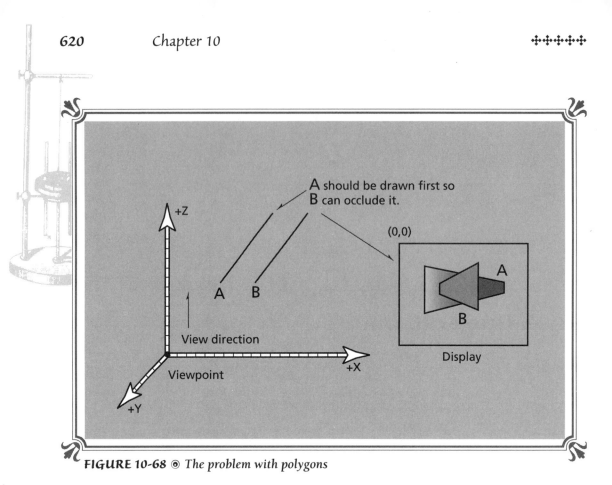

FIGURE 10-68 ⊚ *The problem with polygons*

to this conclusion using our own vision systems and about 100 billion brain cells. The computer doesn't have that luxury. Instead, we supply it with a set of rules to produce the correct image. One possible set of rules would be to take the Z extents of the polygons and draw the polygons with farthest Z extents first, then the polygons with closer Z extents last, so they will overlap and obscure the farther polygons.

This technique actually works, but not in all cases. If all the polygons are parallel to the view plane, this algorithm works perfectly since the farther polygons are rendered first and then occluded by the nearer polygons. The name Painter's algorithm originated from the fact that painters use a technique much like this when painting on a canvas. The painter paints the distant objects first followed by the nearer ones; hence, the nearer objects obscure the more distant ones.

The problem with the Painter's algorithm is that it falls apart when the polygons are not all parallel to the view plane. For example, if we take a look at Figure 10-69, we see another example of two polygons. This time polygon A extends farther than polygon B does; so using our same line of thought as before, we would draw polygon A first, but this would result in an error! As we can see by looking at the figure,

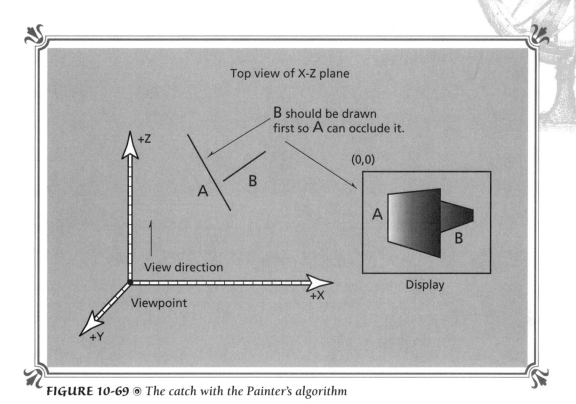

FIGURE 10-69 ⊙ *The catch with the Painter's algorithm*

we should really draw polygon B first. Therefore, we need to add more rules to our algorithm to solve this problem. Well, it turns out that there are about five rules that need to be implemented along with a lot of special case code. The end result is an algorithm that is crude, slow, and a mess to implement.

So what do we do? Well, if we are willing to be imperfect, we can partially solve the problem by using a subset of the Painter's algorithm that works reasonably well. For example, if we sort all the polygons in a scene by their average Z values and then draw the polygons with farther Z values first and smaller Z values last, the final image will be reasonably correct most of the time. The algorithm can further be improved by making the polygons very small and using only *convex* objects in the universe. Convex objects are objects that don't have dents in them. Figure 10-70 shows a convex object in comparison to a non-convex or *concave* object.

In reality, many 3D games use only a depth sort to compute the order to draw polygons. Although this will result in incorrect displays from time to time, it is acceptable. The question is, are there other rendering algorithms that create a perfect image all the time and are easier to implement? The answer, of course, is yes!

FIGURE 10-70
◎ ◎ ◎ ◎ ◎ ◎

*Convex vs.
concave objects*

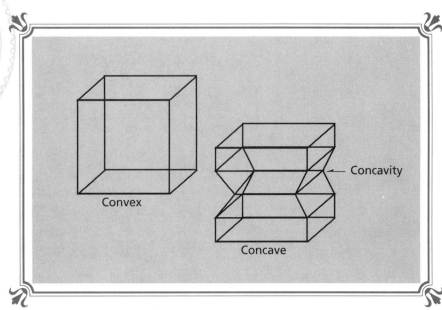

Z-Buffer Algorithms

Since all polygons in a 3D scene have vertices that are coplanar, all polygons lie in some plane. Therefore, using the vertices of the polygon, it is possible to compute the plane equation of the plane that the polygon lies in, as shown in Figure 10-71. With the plane equation in hand, we can compute the z component of every point on the polygon. Using this information, we can then compare the z components of all the polygons pixel-by-pixel and draw the pixels in the proper order. This is called the Z-buffer algorithm and is by far the simplest and most reliable hidden surface rendering technique available.

Let's try and pin down exactly how a Z-buffer system works. First, there is the Z-buffer, which is simply a 2D matrix that has the same resolution as the display screen except that instead of holding colors, it holds the z coordinate of every pixel of the final image. Since a Z-buffer might contain wildly varying values, most high-performance Z-buffers are 32 bits deep; however, we don't have that luxury, so our hypothetical Z-buffer is going to be only 16 bits deep (see Figure 10-72). Therefore, our Z-buffer can record z values in the range of 0 to 65535 or −32768 to 32767, which will suffice for our purposes.

Once a Z-buffer has been allocated, it is initialized with the maximum value that can be recorded, which in our case is 65535. Then the Z-buffer is ready to process all the polygons. But to do this, we must compute the plane equation of each polygon, and then for each (x,y) screen location that makes up a polygon, the z component must be computed and tested against the Z-buffer. So how do we compute the

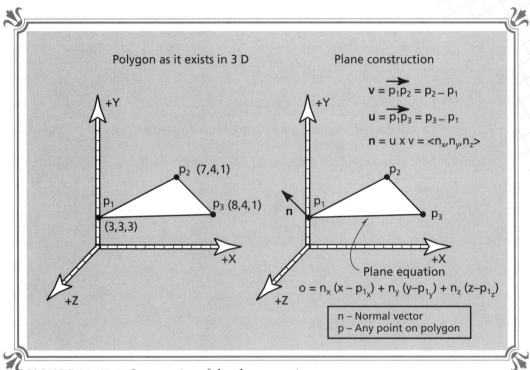

FIGURE 10-71 ⊙ *Construction of the plane equation*

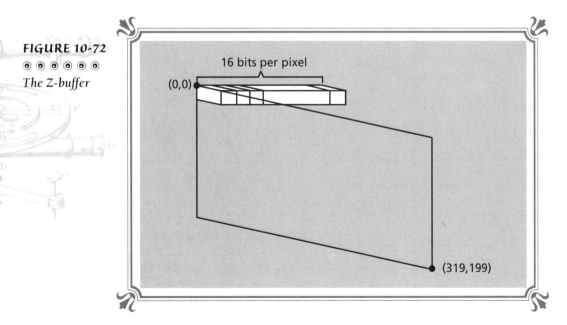

FIGURE 10-72

◎ ◎ ◎ ◎ ◎ ◎

The Z-buffer

plane equation of a general polygon? First, all the polygons in our engine are going to be either triangles or quads, so that makes things easier. In general, all we need to do is compute the normal vector to the polygon and select a single point from the polygon. Using that information, we can construct the point normal form of the plane equation shown below,

$$nx*(x-xo) + ny*(y-yo) + nz*(z-zo) = 0$$

where the point (xo,yo,zo) is any point on the polygon and the vector <nx,ny,nz> is the normal to the vector.

As an example, let's compute the plane equation of the triangle in Figure 10-71. The vectors are

$$v1 = P2-P1 = (7,4,1) - (3,3,3) = <4,1,-2>$$
$$v2 = P3-P1 = (8,1,3) - (3,3,3) = <5,-2,0>$$

The normal vector **n** is found by taking the cross product between **v1** and **v2**:

$$n = v2 \times v1 = <-11,13,25>$$

Therefore, using point P1 on the triangle, we can write the point normal form of the equation as:

$$nx*(x-xo) + ny*(y-yo) + nz*(z-zo) = -11*(x-3) + 13*(y-13) + 25*(z-3) = 0$$

And collecting terms, we get,

$$-11*x + 13*y + 25*z = 81$$

which is the general form of a plane. Then we can take this equation and solve for z, resulting in:

$$z = \frac{81+11*x - 13*y}{25}$$

Then as we scan-convert the polygon values, we can solve for z. Using the above formulation or a variation, you can see that it is possible to compute the z values for a polygon as it is being scan-converted. Therefore, the final Z-buffer algorithm is shown as follows:

Initialize the Z-buffer.
    For each polygon in the scene, compute the plane equation of the polygon.
        {
        Scan-convert the polygon, and for each point (x,y) compute the z value. If the z value is nearer than the current z value in the Z-buffer, then place the color of the polygon into the frame buffer, overwriting the old color.
        }
Display the frame buffer.

Of course, we have left out a few details, but this captures the essence of the Z-buffer algorithm. The question is, how fast is it? Well, to tell you the truth, as it stands, it would be very difficult to implement in software with reasonable performance. Moreover, we can't waste 128K of memory for a Z-buffer in a standard DOS application. Therefore, most 3D engines use a modified version of the Z-buffer called the *Scanline Z-buffer*, which is similar to the standard Z-buffer shown above except that it operates on a scanline at a time. That, along with some clever optimizations, will result in a very slick hidden surface rendering algorithm, but we'll get to that in Chapter 15. Now, let's talk a little about light and color.

Illumination

Now that we have an idea of how we're going to create a 3D universe and display it on the video screen, it's time to discuss lighting and illumination. In a standard 2D game, the objects are simply colored with static colors. These colors stay the same regardless of the position of the game objects relative to the synthetic lights that may exist in the game.

Granted, some 2D games may have simulated lighting and color palette rotation effects; however, these effects have no mathematical or physical basis. They simply look good. Within a real 3D game, there usually exist real light sources. These light sources are used to shade and render each polygon face in an appropriate way based on a mathematical model that is usually an approximation. We aren't going to delve too deeply into lighting in this chapter, but let's at least take a look at the different light models and their general implementation.

Ambient Lighting

Ambient lighting is the lighting that exists due to the average light level in a room or area. For example, the room you're in right now may have a lamp or two in it. However, these lamps(s) usually have shades on them and point up toward the ceiling. The result of this is that the light (photons) is diffused and reflected in all directions. This creates an average light level in the room. This average is called the ambient light level.

Three-dimensional graphics engines usually model ambient light by simply coloring the polygon faces with an intensity relative to the ambient light level. For instance, if we allowed the ambient light level to range from 0 to 15, then based on the color of a polygon, we would select a shade to color the polygon based on the ambient light level. In a mathematical way, we would use the following rule,

$I_a = k*(ambient\_light\_level)$

where k is a constant that scales the ambient level to make it fit with our color palette.

Using the above equation, how would we implement an ambient lighting system? One way would be to divide the color palette into 16 shades of 16 colors. Then when defining an object, we only select the color of the object's faces. However, when the objects are drawn, the ambient light level is used to compute the final color register value to use. For example, if the color palette was of the format

color 0
shade 1, shade 2,…shade 15

color 1
shade 1, shade 2,…shade 15

.

.

.

color 15
shade 1, shade 2,…shade 15

and we defined the colors as being in the range 0 to 15, then given that a polygon face was given by the variable color, we might find the final color register to use by the following formula:

Given that I_a ranges from 0 to 15,

final_color = color*16 + I_a

Nothing more than a simple calculation and a proper color palette are needed to implement ambient lighting. But ambient lighting can be a bit boring. More 3D realism can be achieved by using point light sources.

Point Light Sources

Point light sources are like lightbulbs (see Figure 10-73). The light from them radiates out in all directions like a spherical energy wave. Point light sources are more of what we are used to in everyday life. They have the property that objects illuminated by them reflect more or less light off their faces based on the angles the faces make with the point light source. Furthermore, the farther an object is from the point light source, the weaker the overall light intensity becomes (this is an effect of the inverse square law).

Although both of the aforementioned effects occur with point light sources, most implementations only consider the first or the angular variance. The distance falloff is so infinitesimal that it really doesn't help the realism very much and isn't worth the trouble of implementing. With that in mind, let's briefly take a look at how point light sources are used to compute light intensity.

Figure 10-74 shows the relationship between a point light source and a polygon face. Similarly to the back-face visibility computations, the normal vector of the

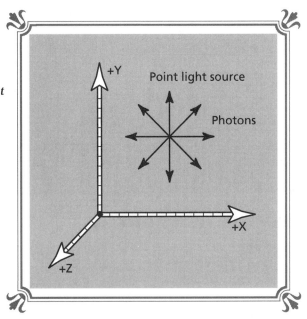

FIGURE 10-73
◎ ◎ ◎ ◎ ◎ ◎
Radiation pattern of a point light source

polygon is computed along with the light source vector **l**. Then the dot product is computed between them solving for the COSINE of the angle theta:

$$COS\ \theta = \frac{u \cdot v}{|u||v|}$$

FIGURE 10-74
◎ ◎ ◎ ◎ ◎ ◎
Computing the intensity of light due to a point light source

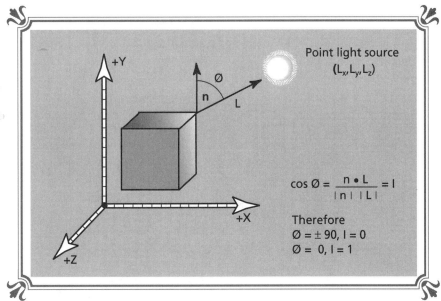

Since the COS θ varies from −1 to 1, this information is used to compute the intensity of incident light on the polygon face. For example, when COS θ = 0, the incident light is grazing and its intensity should be 0. However, when the COS θ becomes |1|, the light source is perpendicular to the polygon face and the incident light will be the highest. As an example, the incident light on a polygon face, as a function of θ, is shown in Figure 10-75. Basically, the curve is nothing more than a COSINE curve.

To add point light sources is very simple. After the ambient light computation is complete, the point light source computation is performed and added to the ambient light to arrive at an overall intensity level. Again, this intensity is used to index into a color table and select the appropriate shade of color.

Directional Light Sources

The final type of light source we are going to discuss is directional lights. Figure 10-76 shows the physics of a directional light source. As you can see, all the light rays are parallel and reflect off the polygon face at an angle opposite to the angle at which the light rays were incident. This type of reflection model creates specular effects or highlights. However, implementing specular effects and highlights is rather complex and time-consuming. This is true since not only the direction of the light source is needed along with the polygon normals, but the view direction of the player is also needed to compute the final angle that the reflected light makes with the viewing direction.

FIGURE 10-75

◉ ◉ ◉ ◉ ◉ ◉

Light intensity as a function of theta

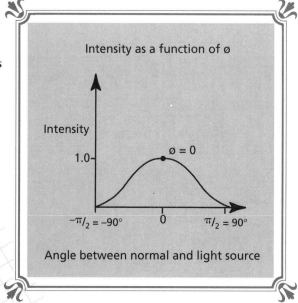

FIGURE 10-76

◎ ◎ ◎ ◎ ◎ ◎

Directional light in action

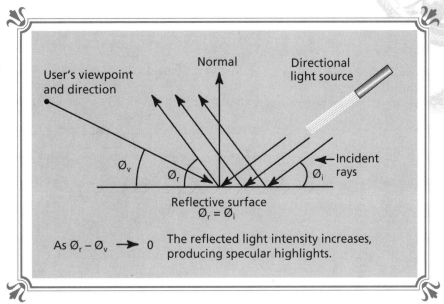

This final angle is then used to compute the intensity of the light as seen by the player. However, in reality the relationship isn't linear, and a more complex exponential model is employed many times. Hence, specular effects aren't going to be part of our final graphics engine, but it's nice to know how they are computed.

The Graphics Pipeline

We have covered all the main aspects of 3D computer graphics. Admittedly, we have glazed over a few topics, but they will all be covered in depth in the following chapters, along with the software implementations. The main goal of the preceding material is to give you an overall idea of the order of operations that must be performed to create a 3D scene. Having even a loose grasp on this will help immensely during the following chapters. As I said before, one of the most important concepts to grasp about 3D graphics is not the individual algorithms or mathematics so much, but how everything fits together. With that in mind, let's take a final look at a possible 3D graphics pipeline. Figure 10-77 shows one such pipeline.

As you can see from the figure, the system does both object space clipping and image space clipping. Moreover, the clipping is done after the viewing transformation. If we wanted to, we could place the clipping before the viewing transformation, but the math is a bit harder since we would have to use general plane equations. In any case, the idea of all of this is to minimize the amount of computations and the number of polygons processed per frame.

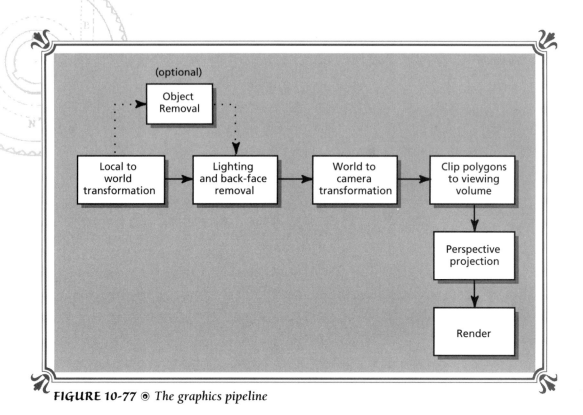

FIGURE 10-77 ⊚ *The graphics pipeline*

It's possible that one pipeline may be very efficient for a flight simulator, but terrible for an architectural walk-through. As Cybersorcerers, we must find the right combinations, tricks, and methods to extract as much 3D performance as possible out of our engine, even if it means some things aren't done correctly all the time. For example, we might use a primitive depth sort to compute the rendering order of polygons instead of a more precise Z-buffer.

Summary

Without a doubt, this chapter has been the most complex so far. We began by learning the language of 3D graphics, which is vectors, matrices, and fixed point math. Then we learned about 3D transformations, coordinate systems, clipping, and hidden surface removal and rendering techniques. Finally, we touched upon lighting models used to make the 3D images more realistic, and ended with a final look at the graphics pipeline.

If you have a good understanding of the general topics in this chapter, the following chapters that focus on each subject should make everything crystal clear.

11

Building a 3D Graphics Engine

ome uiti bono cemanoleuf li e lequali pueubano e llaiga
e igropli curre comenti e roni o lasogramo dibono
uyari nellamano e la pumagolla della manobella pegi quon
aforga e pio isomo prebiuat.

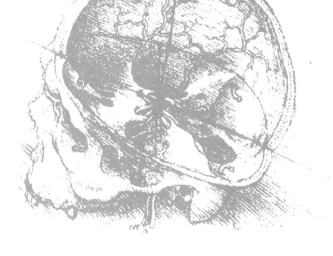

11

Building a 3D Graphics Engine

One of the primary goals of this book is to create a *3D graphics engine*. A 3D graphics engine is basically a set of data structures and functions to load 3D objects into a database, manipulate them, and render them in real-time. Of course, the engine should support additional features, such as lighting models, object culling, 3D clipping, collision detection, and various rendering techniques. Creating such a 3D engine is no simple task. However, if written correctly, the engine will be understandable and in modular form. This modularity will allow us to change different pipeline structures and various other aspects depending on the task at hand.

Any program, whether it is a video game or a word processor, begins with the selection of some reasonable data structures and functions to manipulate them. This is one of the main goals of this chapter. We're going to design the data structures used by the 3D engine and use them in simple wireframe examples to see their use.

To accomplish the goals we have set forth requires the utmost concentration and power. We must be one with the computer; we must allow the sorcerous forces to flow through and around us, and to guide us as we write this most excellent piece of software. So put your scepter aside, dim the lights, and read on.

Engine Data Structures

Most of the work performed by any 3D graphics engine is mathematical in nature. Only the final step of rendering the 3D image is graphical. Hence, we will begin writing the 3D engine by creating a collection of data structures to represent vectors, points, polygons, objects, and so forth. The definitions we select at this point are more or less what we'll use in the final 3D engine, but they are by no means the "best" selections of data structures. However, for illustrative purposes they will suffice.

Before we begin analyzing each data structure, let's touch on something we spoke of earlier in the book—optimization. The first version of the engine isn't going to be very optimized, as this isn't a priority at this point in our studies. Instead, we simply want to learn how to write a general 3D polygon engine. Optimization will come later. This philosophy will allow us to move at a much faster pace than if we had to understand new concepts while at the same time reviewing code that was unreadable due to optimizations! So let's get 3D, shall we?

Many of the computations performed by the engine will use matrices as the basic data type. These matrices will represent transformations such as rotation, scaling, translation, and so forth. Since translation is one of the transformations we wish to include, all matrices must be 4x4—that is, they need to be homogeneous. This allows the last row to be used for translation. Here is the simple data structure for a 4x4 matrix for our engine:

```
typedef float matrix_4x4[4][4];        // the standard 4x4 homogeneous matrix
```

What if we want to represent a single homogeneous point in 3D as a matrix? Well, we can define the point along with its homogenizing factor w (which we have set to 1) as a 1x4 matrix defined as:

```
typedef float matrix_1x4[4];           // a 1x4 matrix or a row vector
```

Now, the name of the game in a 3D graphics engine is to draw 3D objects and scenery. However, these objects and scenery must be based on some simple elementary data type, such as a face, line, or point. We are going to select the single 3D point as the basic building block of our objects. Thus, the data structure that holds a point is:

```
typedef struct vector_3d_typ
    {

    float x,y,z,w;      // a 3D vector along with normalization factor
                        // if needed

    } point_3d,vector_3d,*point_3d_ptr,*vector_3d_ptr;
```

Notice that the structure has many different aliases. This is simply because a 3D vector and a 3D point are very similar as far as the computer is concerned, so we have used the same general data structure to contain both. Also, notice w, the homogenizing factor. It is added to be complete, but in 99 percent of the cases, it won't be used.

The next data structure that we will need from time to time is an angular orientation structure. In many cases, it's nice to know the angles that an object is making with the principle axes, as shown in Figure 11-1. The following structure is used for just such a purpose:

```
typedef struct dir_3d_typ
       {

       int ang_x,    // angle relative to x axis
           ang_y,    // angle relative to y axis
           ang_z;    // angle relative to z axis

       } dir_3d, *dir_3d_ptr;
```

Notice that the angles are integers. This is because all trigonometric functions in the engine will be performed using look-up tables, so floating point angles won't be necessary. Of course, this will limit us to integral angles, but believe me, no one will notice the difference between 1.0 and 1.25 degrees!

The main goal of our final 3D graphics engine is to render solid objects that are shaded. Therefore, instead of objects being defined by a collection of points alone, we must somehow define polygon faces with these points. The following data structure is for that purpose:

FIGURE 11-1
◎ ◎ ◎ ◎ ◎ ◎
An object with its angular orientation

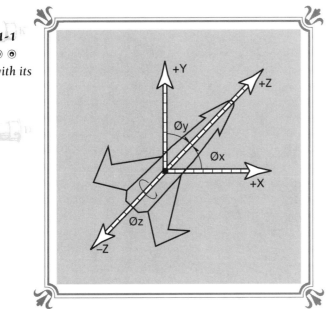

```
typedef struct polygon_typ
        {

        int num_points;    // number of points in polygon (usually 3 or 4)
        int vertex_list[MAX_POINTS_PER_POLY];   // the index number of
                                                // vertices
        int color;         // color of polygon
        int shade;         // the final shade of color after lighting
        int shading;       // type of lighting, flat or constant shading
        int two_sided;     // flags if the polygon is two sided
        int visible;       // used to remove backfaces
        int active;        // used to turn faces on and off
        int clipped;       // flags that polygon has been clipped or removed
        float normal_length; // pre-computed magnitude of normal

        } polygon, *polygon_ptr;
```

The above polygon structure is rather interesting. Recall Chapter 10's discussion of efficient data structures in which we came to the conclusion that it's best to use a list of vertices or points to define an object; then each polygon in the object is defined by a list of pointers or indices into the list of vertices. Using this technique, points aren't defined twice. For example, imagine that we want to define a simple 3D cube, as shown in Figure 11-2. Using a set of points to define the cube, we quickly come to the conclusion that 8 points are needed. However, if we were to use a polygon-based representation of the same cube, as shown in Figure 11-3, then there are 6 faces each, with 4 points, for a total of 24 points! This means that

FIGURE 11-2

◉ ◉ ◉ ◉ ◉ ◉

A cube can be defined by 8 points

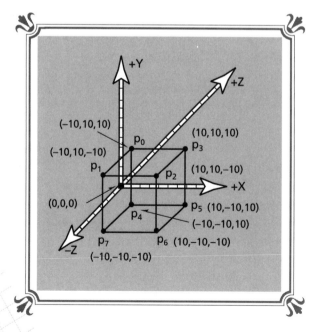

FIGURE 11-3

When polygon faces are used to define objects, the number of points goes up

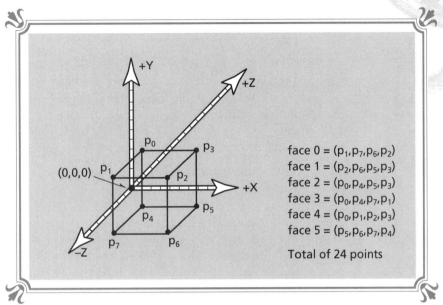

each point would be transformed two extra times relative to the vertex method of definition. So, it's much better to define objects as sets of points and then polygons as lists of pointers or indices naming off these points.

The only problem with the preceding data structure is that it relies on a second data structure (the object definition) as a source of the actual vertex points. This is fine, but there may be cases when we need a completely self-contained version of a polygon that also includes the vertices. This type of data structure comes in handy when the final polygon display list is being generated by the engine (which we will get to much later). Hence, another useful polygon definition that is self-contained should contain actual vertices instead of a list of them. Here is the structure that fits this need:

```
typedef struct facet_typ
        {

        int num_points;   // number of vertices
        int color;        // color of polygon
        int shade;        // the final shade of color after lighting
        int shading;      // type of shading to use
        int two_sided;    // is the facet two sided
        int visible;      // is the facet transparent
        int clipped;      // has this poly been clipped
        int active;       // used to turn faces on and off
        point_3d vertex_list[MAX_POINTS_PER_POLY]; // the points that make
                                                   // up the polygon facet
```

continued on next page

continued from previous page

```
float normal_length;  // holds pre-computed length of normal

} facet, *facet_ptr;
```

I named the structure *facet* for no particular reason other than I didn't want to call it *polygon_2* or something corny like that! If you are paying attention to these structures, you have undoubtedly noticed some of the other fields of the data structures. Most of these fields' purposes are understandable by reading the comments, but then again, some aren't. To be complete, let's take a quick look at the questionable ones.

num_points	Our engine is only going to support triangles or quadrilaterals; thus, this field holds the number of vertices, which will be either 3 or 4.
color	This field holds the raw color for the polygon, but depending on the type of shading used, the color will be altered during run time.
shade	After the shading calculations have been performed (if any), this field holds the final color, from 0 to 255, that the polygon should be rendered with.
shading	This field holds the type of shading to be used on the polygon. We're only going to support constant shading and flat shading. Constant shading means the color stays the same no matter what the lights are doing, and flat shading means that the color changes intensity based on the lights.
two_sided	A polygon has two sides; however, many times we may know ahead of time that only one side of the polygon can possibly be visible. The six faces that make a cube are such an example. The user will never be able to see the faces from inside the cube, so the polygons should be one-sided. However, in the case that a single polygon is used to create a wing on a jet, both sides should be visible. This is the function of the *two_sided* field.
visible	This field holds the results of back-face removal, which we will learn about later. Briefly, back-face removal is a preprocessing step performed in a 3D universe, which removes polygon faces that couldn't possibly be seen from the user's viewpoint and angle.
clipped	This field is similar to the visible field except that it is set by the clipping functions when a polygon has been totally clipped from the viewing volume.
active	This field acts like a switch to enable or disable polygons from being processed. For example, you might have a spaceship with shields on it. By setting the *active* switch to *FALSE*, the shields wouldn't be processed by the engine and would become invisible for all intents and purposes.

Now that we have defined points and polygons, let's put together a complete object with them. Here's that structure:

```
typedef struct object_typ
        {
        int id;              // identification number of object
        int num_vertices;    // total number of vertices in object
        point_3d vertices_local[MAX_VERTICES_PER_OBJECT];  // local ver-
                                                           // tices
        point_3d vertices_world[MAX_VERTICES_PER_OBJECT];  // world ver-
                                                           // tices
        point_3d vertices_camera[MAX_VERTICES_PER_OBJECT]; // camera ver-
                                                           // tices
        int num_polys;       // the number of polygons in the object
        polygon polys[MAX_POLYS_PER_OBJECT]; // the polygons of the object

        float radius;        // the average radius of object
        int state;           // state of object
        point_3d world_pos; // position of object in world coordinates

        } object, *object_ptr;
```

The object structure isn't too complex except for three arrays, *vertices_local[]*, *vertices_world[]*, and *vertices_camera[]*. These arrays are used to contain the vertices of the object at different points in the graphics pipeline. For example, the *vertices_local[]* array holds the definition of the object relative to its own local origin of (0,0,0). However, when the object is transformed into world coordinates with the rest of the objects, the array *vertices_world[]* holds the results. And finally, when the object is projected into camera coordinates (so that the user can view it), the world coordinates contained in *vertices_world[]* are transformed into the camera coordinates and stored in *vertices_camera[]*. We don't really need three arrays. We can actually get by with two, or maybe even a single array. But three arrays aid in our discussions and make everything easier to track through the graphics pipeline.

So how do we define an object with the preceding data structure? Good question. We could use brute force and set up all the fields ourselves, but this would be a bit sadistic. A better solution would be to use a function to load an object off disk that's in some standard format, such as DXF, PLG, or NFF. This is exactly what we will do. But before we get to that, let's take a look at the math component of our 3D engine since many calls will be made to these functions.

Math Functions

The mathematics portion of the engine is used to perform calculations such as matrix multiplications, cross products, dot products, and vector magnitudes. Of course, we could add dozens if not hundreds more functions to this list; but in most cases, the above functionality, along with a few more functions to create vectors and matrices, will suffice for much of the computation needed for a 3D engine. So let's begin with Listing 11-1, a function that creates a vector from two points.

LISTING 11-1 Function that creates a vector from two points

```
void Make_Vector_3D(point_3d_ptr init,
                    point_3d_ptr term,
                    vector_3d_ptr result)
{
// this function creates a vector from two points in 3D space

result->x = term->x - init->x;
result->y = term->y - init->y;
result->z = term->z - init->z;

} // end Make_Vector
```

The function *Make_Vector()* takes two points and returns a vector. The vector is computed by subtracting the initial point from the terminal point a component at a time. The next function, shown in Listing 11-2, will be useful from time to time when the magnitude or length of a vector is needed.

LISTING 11-2 Function that computes the length of a vector

```
float Vector_Mag_3D(vector_3d_ptr v)
{
// computes the magnitude of a vector

return((float)sqrt(v->x*v->x + v->y*v->y + v->z*v->z));

} // end Vector_Mag_3D
```

The function takes a single vector as a parameter and computes its length. Notice that the function uses the *sqrt()* function, which is to be avoided in a real-time 3D engine. Therefore, vector magnitudes should only be computed during initialization or only when absolutely necessary. The next function we need is the dot product. The dot product is needed during shading and hidden surface removal, so it's a must. A function to do this is shown in Listing 11-3. Notice that the dot product is nothing more than a sum of products.

LISTING 11-3 Function that computes the dot product between two vectors

```
float Dot_Product_3D(vector_3d_ptr u,vector_3d_ptr v)
{
// this function computes the dot product of two vectors
```

```
return( (u->x * v->x) + (u->y * v->y) + (u->z * v->z));

} // end Dot_Product
```

The *Dot_Product()* function takes two vectors as parameters and computes their dot product. Notice that the result is a scalar and *not* a vector. This is the definition of dot product, which is mathematically equivalent to:

$$u \cdot v = |u|*|v|*\cos \theta$$

The next function we need is one to compute the cross product between two vectors. This comes in handy when trying to find a perpendicular to two vectors. The code to compute the cross product is shown in Listing 11-4.

LISTING 11-4 *Function that computes the cross product between two vectors*

```
void Cross_Product_3D(vector_3d_ptr u,
                      vector_3d_ptr v,
                      vector_3d_ptr normal)
{
// this function computes the cross product between two vectors

normal->x =  (u->y*v->z - u->z*v->y);
normal->y = -(u->x*v->z - u->z*v->x);
normal->z =  (u->x*v->y - u->y*v->x);

} // end Cross_Product_3D
```

We need to be careful when using the above function because the result of the computation will be a vector that is perpendicular to both **u** and **v**, but if we take a look at Figure 11-4, we see there are two such vectors! The one that results from the cross product is computed by using the right-hand or left-hand rule, depending on the coordinate system that is used. In our case, we are going to use the left-hand system; hence, the result of **u**x**v** will be **n1**. Note the following formula:

$$u \times v = -v \times u$$

This formula can be used to reverse the orientation of the cross product between different coordinate systems with a simple scalar multiplication. Anyway, the cross product, like the dot product, is most useful in shading and hidden surface removal, so it's something we need.

We could write a function to add and subtract vectors, but that would be unnecessary and a waste of a function call. In most cases, we will simply add or subtract vectors manually in the context of the functions where the computations need to be done. However, an inline macro might be cleaner (but that's just a thought). The

FIGURE 11-4

◎ ◎ ◎ ◎ ◎ ◎

The cross product

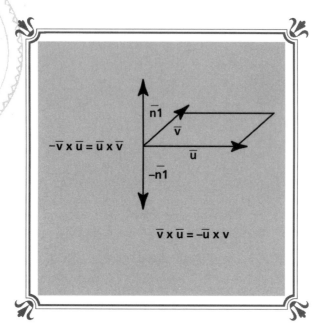

next mathematical objects that we must consider are matrices. Let's see what we need in order to support them.

A matrix can be defined using the 4x4 matrix *typedef* with something like this:

```
matrix_4x4 mat_1;
```

But we need some means to initialize the matrix. Granted, we could perform the initialization during the declaration, but writing down 16 numbers is a bit of a pain. A better solution is to write a function that initializes the matrix for us. Actually, we should write two functions, one to set a matrix to 1 and one to set the matrix to 0. However, recall from Chapter 10 that the concept of 1 and 0 has a different meaning in the context of matrices. The 1 is really the identity matrix, which is created by zeroing the matrix and then setting all elements in the main diagonal to 1. This is done by the function in Listing 11-5.

LISTING 11-5 Function to make a matrix equal to the identity matrix

```
void Mat_Identity_4x4(matrix_4x4 a)
{
// this function creates a 4x4 identity matrix

a[0][1] = a[0][2] = a[0][3] = 0;
a[1][0] = a[1][2] = a[1][3] = 0;
a[2][0] = a[2][1] = a[2][3] = 0;
a[3][0] = a[3][1] = a[3][2] = 0;
```

```
// set main diagonal to 1's

a[0][0] = a[1][1] = a[2][2] = a[3][3] = 1;

} // end Mat_Identity_4x4
```

Although zeroing out a matrix is seldom done, we may need it for some reason or other; so to be complete, Listing 11-6 is a function to zero out a matrix.

LISTING 11-6 Function to zero out a matrix

```
void Mat_Zero_4x4(matrix_4x4 a)
{
// this function zeros out a 4x4 matrix

a[0][0] = a[0][1] = a[0][2] = a[0][3] = 0;
a[1][0] = a[1][1] = a[1][2] = a[1][3] = 0;
a[2][0] = a[2][1] = a[2][2] = a[2][3] = 0;
a[3][0] = a[3][1] = a[3][2] = a[3][3] = 0;

} // end Mat_Zero_4x4
```

Since we aren't using C++ (which sometimes would be nice), we can't really assign matrices to each other and expect the compiler to copy them correctly (some do, some don't). Alas, we must write a function to do this. Therefore, if we wanted to copy one matrix into another, Listing 11-7 shows how.

LISTING 11-7 Function to copy one matrix into another

```
void Mat_Copy_4x4(matrix_4x4 source, matrix_4x4 destination)
{
// this function copies one 4x4 matrix to another

int index_i,
    index_j; // looping vars

// copy the matrix row by row

for (index_i=0; index_i<4; index_i++)
    for (index_j=0; index_j<4; index_j++)
        destination[index_i][index_j] = source[index_i][index_j];

} // end Mat_Copy_4x4
```

The function takes two matrices: a source and a destination. The function simply uses a pair of *for* loops to copy the elements of the source matrix into the destination matrix. Note that we don't need to use pointers here. The matrices themselves are really arrays of pointers. The next function is a diagnostic function and not really part of the engine, but it comes in handy from time to time when the elements of a matrix need analysis. The function shown in Listing 11-8 is called *Mat_Print_4x4()* and simply prints the elements of a 4x4 matrix to the standard output stream.

LISTING 11-8 Function that prints out a 4x4 matrix

```
void Mat_Print_4x4(matrix_4x4 a)
{
// this function prints out a 4x4 matrix

int row,       // looping variables
    column;

// iterate through all elements
for (row=0; row<4; row++)
    {
    printf("\n");
    for (column=0; column<4; column++)
        printf("%f ",a[row][column]);

    } // end for row

printf("\n");

} // end Mat_Print_4x4
```

And its little brother, listed in Listing 11-9, prints out a 1x4 matrix.

LISTING 11-9 Function that prints out a row vector

```
void Mat_Print_1x4(matrix_1x4 a)
{
// this function prints out a 1x4 matrix

int column;     // looping variable

printf("\n");

// iterate through elements
for (column=0; column<4; column++)
    printf("%f ",a[column]);

printf("\n");

} // end Mat_Print_1x4
```

Finally, we come to the most complex of all the math functions, which is about ten lines long. So it can't be that hard! It's a function to multiply two 4x4 matrices together and store the result in an output matrix. The matrix multiplication is performed just as we defined it in Chapter 10; that is, each element of the result matrix is computed by summing the products of one row of the first matrix by a column of the second matrix. The code to do this is shown in Listing 11-10.

LISTING 11-10 Function that multiplies two 4x4 matrices together

```
void Mat_Mul_4x4_4x4(matrix_4x4 a,
                     matrix_4x4 b,
                     matrix_4x4 result)
{
// this function multiplies a 4x4 by a 4x4 and stores the result in a 4x4

int index_i,  // row and column looping vars
    index_j,
    index_k;

float sum;     // temp used to hold sum of products

// loop thru rows of a
for (index_i=0; index_i<4; index_i++)
    {
    // loop thru columns of b

    for (index_j=0; index_j<4; index_j++)
        {
        // multiply ith row of a by jth column of b and store the sum
        // of products in the position i,j of result

        sum=0;

        for (index_k=0; index_k<4; index_k++)
            sum+=a[index_i][index_k]*b[index_k][index_j];

        // store result
        result[index_i][index_j] = sum;

        } // end for index_j

    } // end for index_i

} // end Mat_Mul_4x4_4x4
```

The function *Mat_Mul_4x4_4x4()* is rather simple, but it hides a very important fact: to perform a general 4x4 matrix multiply takes 64 multiplications and 48 additions! That's quite a bit when we realize that down the line, this must be done for every point in the 3D universe. Hence, we must come up with ways to perform the multiplication with fewer computations, and we will when we cover optimizations in Chapter 17.

The main reason to include a matrix multiplication function is so that we may concatenate matrices into a single transformation matrix. For example, by concatenating three matrices into a single matrix, such as

```
Mat_Mul_4x4_4x4(a,b,result_1);
Mat_Mul_4x4_4x4(result_1,c,result_2);
```

the matrix *result_2* will hold the entire transformation of *a*∗*b*∗*c*. Thus, if *a* was a rotation matrix, *b* a scale matrix, and *c* a translation matrix, then by multiplying a point by *result_2*, all of these transformations would be achieved in a single matrix multiply instead of three!

Although we probably won't use it much, we should write a function to multiply a row vector—that is, a 1x4 matrix by a 4x4 matrix. Listing 11-11 shows such a function.

LISTING 11-11 Function that multiplies a row vector by a matrix

```
void Mat_Mul_1x4_4x4(matrix_1x4 a,
                     matrix_4x4 b,
                     matrix_1x4 result)
{
// this function multiplies a 1x4 by a 4x4 and stores the result in a 1x4

int index_j,    // column index
    index_k;    // row index

float sum;      // temp used to hold sum of products

// loop thru columns of b
for (index_j=0; index_j<4; index_j++)
    {
    // multiply ith row of a by jth column of b and store the sum
    // of products in the position i,j of result

    sum=0;

    for (index_k=0; index_k<4; index_k++)
        sum+=a[index_k]*b[index_k][index_j];

    // store result
    result[index_j] = sum;

    } // end for index_j

} // end Mat_Mul_1x4_4x4
```

This function is almost identical to the 4x4 version except that the *for* loop responsible for iterating through the rows of the first matrix is no longer needed since the first matrix has a single row.

Now that we have our math functions down, let's switch gears back to defining and loading objects.

Defining Objects

For the most part, our 3D graphics engine is going to work on objects that are themselves defined by polygons and, ultimately, points. However, when we write a

3D game, we are going to be thinking in terms of tanks, starbases, and buildings; thus, the primary element of the 3D engine should be at the level of abstraction of the object. With that in mind, let's take another look at the data structure we have defined to hold an object along with the actual assignments for the cube shown in Figure 11-2.

As we can see, the object consists of 8 points and 6 polygon faces. Moreover, each face is one-sided and is made up of 4 points. The other fields, such as color and shade, aren't as important, but the main bulk of the data structure for the cube in Figure 11-2 is shown in Figure 11-5. Well, that's all very pretty, but how do we get the cube into the data structure?

The answer is to write a 3D modeler (or use someone else's) and import the files of the 3D objects as input to a function that extracts the information about the model that our system needs. That's a bold statement! Let's see if there's any hope.

DXF Files

One of the most popular file formats is called DXF, which is used by Autodesk's Autocad and 3D Studio. Even though DXF files are very complete and one of the

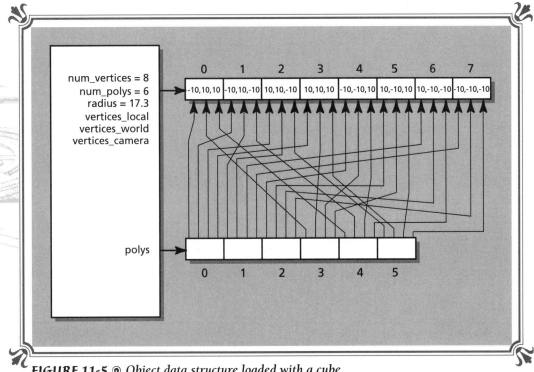

FIGURE 11-5 ◉ *Object data structure loaded with a cube*

best ways to describe 3D objects, it would probably take a whole book to describe the file format and another book to write the parser! So we won't be using that format, but there are simpler formats. One such format is called PLG.

PLG Files

The PLG file format was invented by the people who made REND386, one of whom is Bernie Roehl (author of Waite Group Press' *Playing God*). The format is simple and to the point. Unfortunately, it lacks a bit in the texturing and two-sided polygon area, but it will suffice with a bit of finesse. The main reason to use it is that there are 3D modelers that generate PLG files and utilities that convert DXF files to PLG files. But most of all, writing a parser to read the files only takes an hour or two instead of a week like it would for a DXF reader! Anyway, let's take a look at the PLG file format.

PLG Header Line

A PLG file starts off with the name of the object and the number of vertices and polygon faces:

```
pyramid 5 5
```

This says that the data to follow is for the object "pyramid," which has 5 vertices and 5 faces.

PLG Vertex List

The next part of a PLG file are the vertices ordered from 0 to n. Each vertex should be separated by white space and be in X, Y, Z order. For the pyramid shown in Figure 11-6, the vertex data is:

```
 0    20   0
 30  -10   30
 30  -10  -30
-30  -10  -30
-30  -10   30
```

PLG Polygon List

The last elements in the PLG file are the *polygon descriptors*, which are a series of text lines that describe the color of the polygon, the number of vertices in the polygon, and the index number of the vertices. In our example, they look like this:

```
10  3 0 2 1
10  3 0 3 2
```

FIGURE 11-6

◎ ◎ ◎ ◎ ◎ ◎

A pyramid

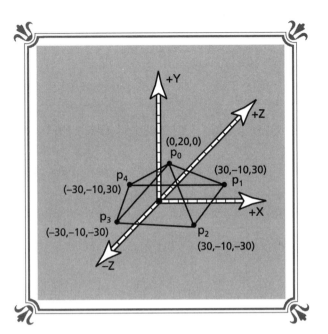

```
10  3 0 4 3
10  3 0 1 4
10  4 1 2 3 4
```

This says that there are 5 polygon faces (5 lines). The first number on each row is called the *color descriptor* (which we'll get to in a moment), and the next number is the number of vertices in that particular polygon. For example, the polygon in the second row has 3 vertices (0,3,2), and the polygon in the fifth row has 4 vertices (1,2,3,4). Now let's take a look at those mysterious 10s, which are the color descriptors.

PLG Color Descriptor

The first number in each of the polygon definitions is called the color descriptor and is really a 16-bit number. It's best if we look at the number in a hexadecimal representation, such as $0xh_3h_2h_1h_0$. The 4-bit nibble h_3 is the important one. It has the following bitmapping:

Given that,

$h_3 = b_3\,b_2\,b_1\,b_0$

then,

b3	b2	b1	b0	Color type
1	X	X	X	Mapped color; the remaining 15 bits are an index into color table.
0	0	0	0	Simple unshaded color.
0	0	0	1	A flat shaded color.
0	0	1	0	A pseudo-metallic color.
0	0	1	1	A special effect, such as glass.

Since we are only going to be using simple shading and flat shading, the first hex digit of any color descriptor should be either 0 or 1. Hence, if we wanted simple shaded red, we would use the following color descriptor:

0x000C

If we wanted the surface to be flat shaded, we would change the first nibble to 1. However, we must also change the last hex digits. This is because our engine is going to use a special palette and a couple of tricks to make things easier. So here are the rules:

1. If you want a polygon to be "simple shaded" or a constant color, make the first hex digit of the color descriptor a 0 and the last two hex digits the index number of the color register that you wish to use for the surface.

2. If you want the surface to be flat shaded, make the first hex digit of the color descriptor a 1, and the last two digits should be one of these:

```
#define SHADE_GREY          31    // hex value = 1F
#define SHADE_GREEN         111   // hex value = 6F
#define SHADE_BLUE          159   // hex value = 9F
#define SHADE_RED           47    // hex value = 2F
#define SHADE_YELLOW        79    // hex value = 4F
#define SHADE_BROWN         223   // hex value = DF
#define SHADE_LIGHT_BROWN   207   // hex value = CF
#define SHADE_PURPLE        175   // hex value = AF
#define SHADE_CYAN          127   // hex value = 7F
#define SHADE_LAVENDER      191   // hex value = BF
```

The reason for the above table is that the VGA isn't a full 24-bit color card and we only have 256 colors to choose from. So I have created 16 shades of some of the most popular colors, and these shades are partitioned into banks within the color registers. For example, to make a surface a flat shaded blue, we would use the following color descriptor:

0x109F

And to make a surface a flat shaded yellow, use this color descriptor:

    0x104F

The reason that we have to diverge a bit from the original PLG color descriptor format is that in general, 16-bit numbers don't make a lot of sense in the context of the 256-color VGA card—unless of course, we interpret them as RGB values and hunt for the nearest match (which we aren't going to do). The bottom line is this: if you want a surface to be flat shaded, you must use one of the constants listed under rule 2, along with setting the upper nibble to 1. If you want the surface to have a constant color, simply use a number from 0 to 255 as the color, and the upper nibble should be 0.

Now that we are both totally confused, let's write a function to load one of these PLG files, parse it, and set our object data structure up correctly. Let's see…where did I put my compiler design book?

Importing Objects with PLG Files

Loading a PLG file isn't too much trouble. Basically, PLGs are standard ASCII files with one or more lines of text in a specific format. The only thing that makes reading PLG files a bit complicated is that color descriptors can be in either hex or decimal format depending on a leading 0x, and the files can have comments in them, which can begin with the # character (actually, I also added the ; character as a comment initiator). Let's take a look at our original pyramid PLG file and see if we can come up with a simple plan to read in a PLG file and set up the object data structure correctly.

The complete pyramid PLG file is as follows:

```
pyramid 5 5

; vertex list
  0    20   0
 30  -10   30
 30  -10  -30
-30  -10  -30
-30  -10   30

; polygon list

10   3 0 2 1
10   3 0 3 2
10   3 0 4 3
10   3 0 1 4
10   4 1 2 3 4
```

A rough plan of attack would be to do the following:

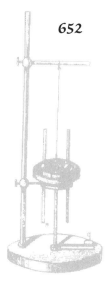

⊹ Read in the first line and parse the object name, number of vertices, and number of faces; then store the number of vertices and number of polygons in the object data structure.

⊹ Read the vertices in as triples and store them in the object data structure.

⊹ Read in each polygon as a color descriptor, number of vertices, and vertex list, but be careful to read the color descriptor in a way that takes into consideration that it can be either a hex number led by 0x or a standard decimal number.

⊹ As each polygon descriptor line is being read, the polygon list in the object structure is being fed with vertex numbers, number of vertices, shading type, and primary color.

And as all this is being done, the parser is looking out for the # or ; character. If either of these characters is found in the input stream, the remainder of the line is regarded as a comment. Amazingly enough, the simple tasks just listed aren't as simple as you might think, but they can be done with patience.

Anyway, before we write the function, let's add the ability to scale the object as the PLG reader loads it. It's always nice to be able to scale an object as it's loaded so we don't have to do it during run time. Taking all that into consideration, let's look at Listings 11-12 and 11-13. Listing 11-13 is the *PLG_Load_Object()* function, and its support function (Listing 11-12) is used to read each line of the PLG file.

LISTING 11-12 The line-parsing function used to read in a PLG file

```
char *PLG_Get_Line(char *string, int max_length, FILE *fp)
{
// this function gets a line from a PLG file and strips comments
// just pretend it's a black box!

char buffer[80]; // temporary string storage

int length,      // length of line read
    index=0,     // looping variables
    index_2=0,
    parsed=0;    // has the current input line been parsed

// get the next line of input, make sure there is something on the line

while(1)
    {
    // get the line

    if (!fgets(buffer,max_length,fp))
        return(NULL);
```

```
// get length of line
length = strlen(buffer);

// kill the carriage return
buffer[length-1] = 0;

// reset index
index = 0;

// eat leading white space
while(buffer[index]==' ')
      index++;

// read line into buffer, if "#" arrives in data stream then disregard
// rest of line
parsed=0;
index_2=0;

while(!parsed)
    {
    if (buffer[index]!='#' && buffer[index]!=';')
       {
       // insert character into output string
       string[index_2] = buffer[index];

       // test if this is a null terminator
       if (string[index_2]==0)
          parsed=1;

       // move to next character
       index++;
       index_2++;

       } // end if not comment
    else
       {
       // insert a null termination since this is the end of the
       // string for all intense purposes
       string[index_2] = 0;
       parsed=1;

       } // end else

    } // end while parsing string

    // make sure we got a string and not a blank line
    if (strlen(string))
       return(string);

    } // end while

} // end PLG_Get_Line
```

LISTING 11-13 Function to load a PLG file from disk

```
int PLG_Load_Object(object_ptr the_object,char *filename,float scale)
{
// this function loads an object off disk and allows it to be scaled

FILE *fp; // disk file

static int id_number = 0; // used to set object id's

char buffer[80],        // holds input string
     object_name[32],   // name of 3D object
     *token;            // current parsing token


unsigned int total_vertices,   // total vertices in object
             total_polys,      // total polygons per object
             num_vertices,     // number of vertices on a polygon
             color_des,        // the color descriptor of a polygon
             logical_color,    // the final color of polygon
             shading,          // the type of shading used on polygon
             index,            // looping variables
             index_2,
             vertex_num,       // vertex numbers
             vertex_0,
             vertex_1,
             vertex_2;

float x,y,z;                   // a single vertex

vector_3d u,v,normal;          // working vectors

// open the disk file
if ((fp=fopen(filename,"r"))==NULL)
   {
   printf("\nCouldn't open file %s",filename);
   return(0);

   } // end if
// first we are looking for the header line that has the object name and
// the number of vertices and polygons

if (!PLG_Get_Line(buffer, 80,fp))
   {
   printf("\nError with PLG file %s",filename);
   fclose(fp);
   return(0);
   } // end if error

// extract object name and number of vertices and polygons
sscanf(buffer,"%s %d %d",object_name, &total_vertices, &total_polys);
```

```
                // set proper fields in object
                the_object->num_vertices = total_vertices;
                the_object->num_polys    = total_polys;
                the_object->state        = 1;

                the_object->world_pos.x  = 0;
                the_object->world_pos.y  = 0;
                the_object->world_pos.z  = 0;

                // set id number, maybe later also add the name of object in the
                // structure???
                the_object->id = id_number++;

                // based on number of vertices, read vertex list into object
                for (index=0; index<total_vertices; index++)
                    {
                    // read in vertex
                    if (!PLG_Get_Line(buffer, 80,fp))
                       {
                       printf("\nError with PLG file %s",filename);
                       fclose(fp);
                       return(0);
                       } // end if error

                    sscanf(buffer,"%f %f %f",&x,&y,&z);

                    // insert vertex into object
                    the_object->vertices_local[index].x = x*scale;
                    the_object->vertices_local[index].y = y*scale;
                    the_object->vertices_local[index].z = z*scale;

                    } // end for index

                // now read in polygon list
                for (index=0; index<total_polys; index++)
                    {
                    // read in color and number of vertices for next polygon

                    if (!PLG_Get_Line(buffer, 80,fp))
                       {
                       printf("\nError with PLG file %s",filename);
                       fclose(fp);
                       return(0);
                       } // end if error

                    // intialize token getter and get first token which is color descriptor
                    if (!(token = strtok(buffer," ")) )
                       {
                       printf("\nError with PLG file %s",filename);
                       fclose(fp);
                       return(0);
```

continued on next page

continued from previous page

```
          } // end if problem

    // test if number is hexadecimal

    if (token[0]=='0' && (token[1]=='x' || token[1]=='X'))
       {
       sscanf(&token[2],"%x",&color_des);
       } // end if hex color specifier
    else
       {
       color_des = atoi(token);
       } // end if decimal

    // extract base color and type of shading
    logical_color = color_des & 0x00ff;
    shading       = color_des >> 12;

    // read number of vertices in polygon

    if (!(token = strtok(NULL," ")))
       {
       printf("\nError with PLG file %s",filename);
       fclose(fp);
       return(0);
       } // end if problem

    if ((num_vertices = atoi(token))<=0)
       {
       printf("\nError with PLG file (number of vertices) %s",filename);
       fclose(fp);
       return(0);
       } // end if no vertices or error

    // set fields in polygon structure

    the_object->polys[index].num_points = num_vertices;
    the_object->polys[index].color      = logical_color;
    the_object->polys[index].shading    = shading;
    the_object->polys[index].two_sided  = 0;
    the_object->polys[index].visible    = 1;
    the_object->polys[index].clipped    = 0;
    the_object->polys[index].active     = 1;

    // now read in polygon vertex list

    for (index_2=0; index_2<num_vertices; index_2++)
       {
       // read in next vertex number
       if (!(token = strtok(NULL," ")) )
          {
          printf("\nError with PLG file %s",filename);
          fclose(fp);
```

```
              return(0);
              } // end if problem

        vertex_num = atoi(token);

        // insert vertex number into polygon
        the_object->polys[index].vertex_list[index_2] = vertex_num;

        } // end for index_2

    // compute length of the two co-planar edges of the polygon, since they
    // will be used in the computation of the dot-product later

    vertex_0 = the_object->polys[index].vertex_list[0];
    vertex_1 = the_object->polys[index].vertex_list[1];
    vertex_2 = the_object->polys[index].vertex_list[2];

    // the vector u = vo->v1
    Make_Vector_3D((point_3d_ptr)&the_object->vertices_local[vertex_0],
                   (point_3d_ptr)&the_object->vertices_local[vertex_1],
                   (vector_3d_ptr)&u);

    // the vector v = vo->v2
    Make_Vector_3D((point_3d_ptr)&the_object->vertices_local[vertex_0],
                   (point_3d_ptr)&the_object->vertices_local[vertex_2],
                   (vector_3d_ptr)&v);

    Cross_Product_3D((vector_3d_ptr)&v,
                     (vector_3d_ptr)&u,
                     (vector_3d_ptr)&normal);

    // compute magnitude of normal and store in polygon structure
    the_object->polys[index].normal_length = Vector_Mag_3D((vector_3d_ptr)&normal);

    } // end for index

// close the file
fclose(fp);

// compute object radius
Compute_Object_Radius(the_object);

// return success
return(1);

} // end PLG_Load_Object
```

The *PLG_Load_Object()* function takes three parameters: a pointer to the object that the PLG should be loaded into, the file name of the PLG file to load, and finally, a scaling factor to scale the PLG object as it's loaded (set this to 1 if you don't want to scale). After running the function with a valid PLG file and object, the object will be ready to go; that is, all of its internal structures and fields will be set up and ready to be processed by the 3D engine. As an example, say that the pyramid PLG file is on disk and it is named PYRAMID.PLG. To load it into an object structure, we could write something like this:

```
object stargate; // the object
```

```
PLG_Load_Object(&stargate,"pyramid.plg",1.0);
```

That's all there is to it!

If you have taken more than a fleeting glance at the *PLG_Load_Object()* function, you've probably noticed that it does a few tricks, such as compute normal vectors, vector magnitudes, and the radius of the object. What does all this mean?

When doing 3D graphics and animation, there are some things that we like to precompute so that during run time we don't need to perform expensive computations. An example of this is precomputing the surface normals to each polygon in order to speed up the shading and back-face removal. A second example is precomputing the average radius of an object for use in collision detection and object culling. Figure 11-7 shows a typical object and its bounding sphere. Just as we used

FIGURE 11-7

⊙ ⊙ ⊙ ⊙ ⊙ ⊙

A bounding sphere around a spaceship

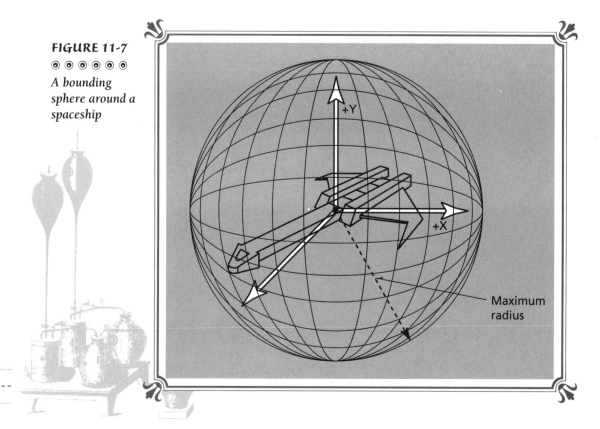

bounding for collision detection in our 2D examples such as Starblazer, we can use bounding spheres in much the same way in 3D games. The function that computes the bounding sphere of an object simply computes the distance between the origin of the object to each vertex and takes the maximum value. The bounding sphere function is shown in Listing 11-14.

LISTING 11-14 *Function that computes the bounding sphere of a 3D object*

```
float Compute_Object_Radius(object_ptr the_object)
{

// this function computes maximum radius of object, maybe a better method would
// use average radius? Note that this function shouldn't be used during
// runtime but when an object is created
float new_radius,   // used in average radius calculation of object
      x,y,z;        // a single vertex

int index;          // looping variable

// reset object radius

the_object->radius=0;

for (index=0; index<the_object->num_vertices; index++)
    {
    x = the_object->vertices_local[index].x;
    y = the_object->vertices_local[index].y;
    z = the_object->vertices_local[index].z;

    // compute distance to point
    new_radius = (float)sqrt(x*x + y*y + z*z);

    // is this radius bigger than last?
    if (new_radius > the_object->radius)
       the_object->radius = new_radius;

    } // end for index

// return radius just in case
return(the_object->radius);

} // end Compute_Object_Radius
```

The function takes a single parameter, which is the object to compute the radius of, and then performs the bounding sphere computations on the vertex list. The largest radius is returned from the function and stored in the radius field of the object's data structure. Later, when we write the 3D game (Chapter 18), we may find that using the average radius instead of the maximum radius is a better choice, but we'll see about that.

Wireframe Graphics—Drawing Lines

Now that we have a collection of data structures, software to perform mathematical operations, and routines to load an object, we are almost in a position to render a simple 3D object on the screen just to see the overall process. However, rendering a full 3D shaded object is going to take more than a few pages of explanation, so let's try something simpler to begin with, such as a *wireframe* image.

Wireframe 3D graphics are one step below standard shaded 3D graphics. Instead of filled polygons, we use lines to represent objects—hence the name wireframe. This is a good place to start, so let's try to draw a 3D object using wires, something like that shown in Figure 11-7. However, before we can begin, we need to write some software that will draw lines. In essence, we need a wireframe engine. Unfortunately, we don't have one! We have been concentrating on bitmapped graphics so far in the book and haven't stopped to write a line-drawing function. But line-drawing algorithms are a dime a dozen, so we shouldn't have too much trouble finding one.

We aren't going to completely re-derive the line-drawing algorithm since it has been derived in so many books and articles. We simply need it for a demo and not for the final 3D engine. If we did use it for the final 3D engine, we would definitely need to know how it works so we could optimize it. We simply need a function that draws a line between two given endpoints (xo,yo) and (x1,y1). Let's see how we can do this.

Drawing a line between two points on the screen seems as if it wouldn't be much trouble. Actually, it's very simple, if we recall that lines have many mathematical forms. One such form is called the *point slope form*, which states: Given a point on a line and the slope of the line, the points along the line as a function of either x or y can be computed. The equation looks like this,

$$(y-yo) = M*(x-xo)$$

where M is the slope of the line, which is equal to:

$$\frac{dy}{dx} = \frac{(y1-yo)}{(x1-xo)} = M$$

With a bit of algebraic manipulation, we can rewrite the point slope equation in one of the two forms,

$$y = M*(x-xo) + yo$$

or

$$x = M^{-1}*(y-yo) + xo$$

Since we know the values of (xo,yo) and (x1,y1), we can use either of these equations in a *for* loop to compute values of x or y as a function of the other variable. For example, if we wanted to solve for y, we could use the following algorithm to draw a line:

```
// pre-compute the slope
m = (y1-yo)/(x1-xo);

// draw the line
for (x=xo; x<=x1; x++)
    {
    // compute the next y value
     y = m*(x-xo) + yo;

    // plot the pixel
    Write_Pixel((int)x,(int)y,color);

    } // end for x
```

Of course, we could optimize this little program by noting that x increases by 1 every iteration, allowing us to remove the multiply m*(x–xo) and replace it with an incremental technique such as:

y+=m;

The problem with this approach is that the computations are done in floating point and, because of this, they are slow. Furthermore, we must make sure to handle each quadrant correctly and take into consideration infinite slopes, and so forth. Figure 11-8 shows the ranges of the different slopes. In any case, it would be nice if there was another way to draw a line that didn't use floating point math and brute force math based on the definition of a line.

Bresenham's Algorithm

In the mid-sixties a researcher at IBM came up with a new way to draw lines that was very fast. The researcher's name was, of course, Bresenham, and the most popular line-drawing algorithm we have today is either a version of his algorithm or in some way based on it. Figure 11-9 shows a typical line drawn on an integer matrix. The problem is that computer screens have finite resolutions, and we are trying to draw something that has infinite resolution. Thus, we can't draw any true lines except perfectly horizontal and vertical ones without error.

In any case, Bresenham stared at a figure something like Figure 11-9 for a while and realized that a line as it's drawn must illuminate pixels either above or below the "true line." Normally, the pixels selected for illumination are derived from the point slope form or *y-intercept form* of the line, and hence, the final pixel locations are computed as rounded off or truncated versions of the mathematically correct ones.

FIGURE 11-8

⊙ ⊙ ⊙ ⊙ ⊙ ⊙

The slopes of lines

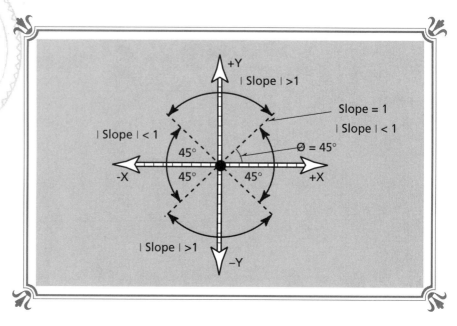

Basically, the insight Bresenham had was that instead of using an equation to draw the line, why not come up with a decision variable that determines the closest pixel to the "true line" on the finite resolution video screen as the line is being drawn. And that is the basis of the algorithm. Therefore, a decision variable is used

FIGURE 11-9

⊙ ⊙ ⊙ ⊙ ⊙ ⊙

A true line drawn on an integer matrix along with a possible approximation

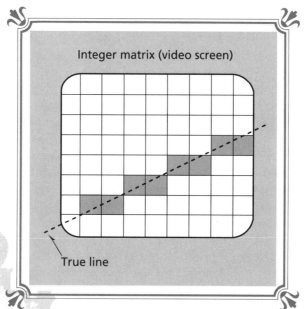

to select points above or below the true line if the |slope| (the vertical bars mean absolute value) is less than 1, and another decision variable is used to select a point to the left or right of the true line for |slopes| that are greater than 1. (Remember, we have to be careful about the handling of slopes that are less than and greater than 1.)

The derivation of the decision variable is extremely complex and not something we're going to do, but we will think of it as something like an "error term." Instead of a static computation that is performed, think of the decision variable as an error term that somehow relates how much the current pixel location being plotted is "close" to the true line and, when the closeness is in range, the proper pixel is selected. Anyway, that's the basis of all this line-drawing stuff, and the best thing to do at this point is to see the function that draws a line. However, be warned—the function is optimized to work directly in screen coordinates and memory to gain speed, but the concept of an error term is readily visible. Listing 11-15 is the line-drawing function we are going to use to render 3D objects.

LISTING 11-15 Line-drawing function based on Bresenham's algorithm

```
void Draw_Line(int xo, int yo, int x1,int y1, unsigned char color)
{
// this function draws a line from xo,yo to x1,y1 using differential error
// terms (based on Bresenham's work)

int dx,            // difference in x's
    dy,            // difference in y's
    x_inc,         // amount in pixel space to move during drawing
    y_inc,         // amount in pixel space to move during drawing
    error=0,       // the discriminant i.e. error i.e. decision variable
    index;         // used for looping

unsigned char far *vb_start = double_buffer; // directly access the video
                                             // buffer for speed

// pre-compute first pixel address in video buffer
vb_start = vb_start + ((unsigned int)yo<<6) +
                      ((unsigned int)yo<<8) +
                      (unsigned int)xo;

// compute horizontal and vertical deltas
dx = x1-xo;
dy = y1-yo;

// test which direction the line is going in i.e. slope angle
if (dx>=0)
   {
   x_inc = 1;
   } // end if line is moving right
else
```

continued on next page

continued from previous page

```
    {
    x_inc = -1;
    dx    = -dx;  // need absolute value
    } // end else moving left

// test y component of slope
if (dy>=0)
    {
    y_inc = 320; // 320 bytes per line
    } // end if line is moving down
else
    {
    y_inc = -320;
    dy    = -dy;  // need absolute value
    } // end else moving up

// now based on which delta is greater we can draw the line
if (dx>dy)
    {
    // draw the line
    for (index=0; index<=dx; index++)
        {
        // set the pixel
        *vb_start = color;

        // adjust the error term
        error+=dy;

        // test if error has overflowed
        if (error>dx)
            {
            error-=dx;

            // move to next line
            vb_start+=y_inc;

            } // end if error overflowed

        // move to the next pixel
        vb_start+=x_inc;

        } // end for

    } // end if |slope| <= 1
else
    {
    // draw the line
    for (index=0; index<=dy; index++)
        {
        // set the pixel
        *vb_start = color;

        // adjust the error term
```

```
error+=dx;

// test if error overflowed
if (error>0)
   {
   error-=dy;

   // move to next line
   vb_start+=x_inc;

   } // end if error overflowed

// move to the next pixel
vb_start+=y_inc;

} // end for

} // end else |slope| > 1

} // end Draw_Line
```

The function is divided into three parts. The first part computes the deltas and initializes the pixel increments and error terms. The next two parts each handle lines that have |slope| > 1 and |slope| < 1, respectively. This logic is necessary since each case results in lines that are either x dominant or y dominant, and different *for* loops and pixel increments must be used. However, regardless of which part of the function draws the line, the function simply draws a pixel and updates the error term with the appropriate delta. If the error overflows, it's time to move up or down, right or left, and when this is done, the error term is reset. This continues until the line is drawn.

Speeding Up Line Drawing

Bresenham's algorithm surely isn't the only available line algorithm, and many twists on the algorithm have been invented. For example, since all lines are symmetric about their centers, only half the pixels need to be computed, and the other half of the line is simply a reflection, as shown in Figure 11-10. Further optimizations can be made by noting that only so many pixel patterns are used in short spans of a line. This is the basis of the *Symmetric Double Step algorithm* by Wu. It uses precomputed patterns and selects one of the patterns to draw the line (see Figure 11-11). This, coupled with symmetry, can speed up Bresenham's algorithm three to four times! But we aren't really interested in speed or lines, we simply need a function to draw lines to write a demo with. And while we're on the subject of demos, we might as well throw one in for good measure.

The program in Listing 11-16, LINEDEMO.EXE, and its source, LINEDEMO.C, demonstrate the line-drawing function. To build the program, compile and link it to the game library BLACKLIB.LIB. Before you do that, you will have to compile the

FIGURE 11-10
◎ ◎ ◎ ◎ ◎ ◎

Using symmetry to speed up line drawing

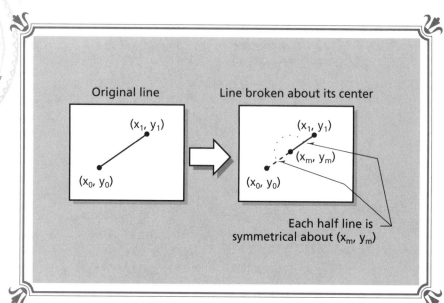

Original line

Line broken about its center

Each half line is
symmetrical about (x_m, y_m)

FIGURE 11-11
◎ ◎ ◎ ◎ ◎ ◎

The pixel patterns that are the foundation of the Symmetric Double Step algorithm

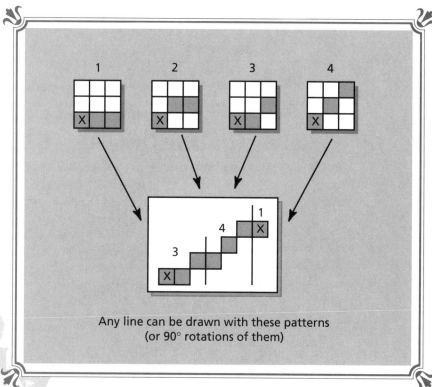

Any line can be drawn with these patterns
(or 90° rotations of them)

library module for this chapter, BLACK11.C, and add it to the library. If you are using a project-based environment, add BLACK11.C and BLACK11.H to the project import files.

Try not to peek too much at BLACK11.C and BLACK11.H because they contain many more functions that we are going to talk about in this chapter. In fact, within the single file BLACK11.C is the entire 3D graphics engine (almost). Anyway, if you don't feel like compiling the program yourself, as always, the CD that comes with the book contains a precompiled version. To run the program, simply type **LINEDEMO.EXE** at the DOS prompt.

LISTING 11-16 Line-drawing demo based on the Draw_Line() function

```
// I N C L U D E S ////////////////////////////////////////////////////////////

#include <io.h>
#include <conio.h>
#include <stdio.h>
#include <stdlib.h>
#include <dos.h>
#include <bios.h>
#include <fcntl.h>
#include <memory.h>
#include <malloc.h>
#include <math.h>
#include <string.h>
#include <search.h>                    // this one is needed for qsort()

// include all of our stuff

#include "black3.h"
#include "black4.h"
#include "black5.h"
#include "black6.h"
#include "black8.h"
#include "black9.h"
#include "black11.h"

// M A I N ////////////////////////////////////////////////////////////////////

void main(void)
{
// set graphics mode to mode 13h
Set_Graphics_Mode(GRAPHICS_MODE13);

// draw randomly positioned lines until user hits a key
while(!kbhit())
    {
    // draw the line with random (xo,yo) - (x1,y1) with a random color
    Draw_Line(rand()%320,rand()%200,
            rand()%320,rand()%200,
            rand()%256,video_buffer);
```

continued on next page

continued from previous page
```
        } // end while
```

```
// restore graphics mode back to text
Set_Graphics_Mode(TEXT_MODE);
```

```
} // end main
```

The demo doesn't have much meat to it! Basically, all it does is select two random endpoints and then draw a colored line between them. This process continues until a key is hit.

Using Projection to Draw Lines in 3D

Drawing lines in 3D space isn't possible since we only have a 2D display device. Hence, we first must project the 3D lines (which exist in mathematical space) into 2D lines (which we can draw) and then render them on the screen. To accomplish this, we need to somehow reduce the dimension of the lines to two dimensions. We have already seen this process in Chapter 10, namely, projection. Since we want to see an entire object, we need to write a function that takes an object definition and projects the object as a set of lines on the video screen.

FIGURE 11-12

◎ ◎ ◎ ◎ ◎ ◎

A simple polygon to draw

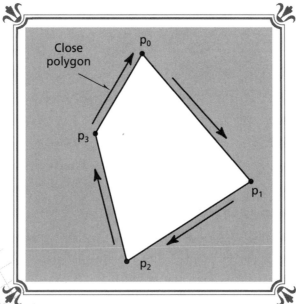

We've already seen the mathematics necessary to project a 3D image onto a 2D plane, but now it's time to implement the math with code. The plan of attack is to take the object definition (which in essence is a collection of polygons made of points) and then draw the polygon edges with lines. For example, if we wanted to draw the polygon shown in Figure 11-12, we would draw a line from point p0 to p1, then from p1 to p2, p2 to p3, and finally, to close the polygon, a line from p3 to p0. This can be done with nothing more than a loop that iterates through the object data structure and extracts the vertices that make up each polygon.

However, we must remember two things. First, the wireframe objects are 3D and must be projected onto the 2D screen, either using a parallel or perspective projection. Second, since we are drawing the objects with lines and not removing hidden surfaces or performing any kind of hidden line removal, the objects will be see-through—that is, wireframe. Let's review the two methods of projection: parallel and perspective.

Parallel Projection

Parallel projection is the easiest of the two projection types and can be implemented simply by throwing away the z component of every vertex. Figure 11-13 shows the standard parallel projection, which can be done with the following transformation:

FIGURE 11-13
◎ ◎ ◎ ◎ ◎ ◎
Parallel projection

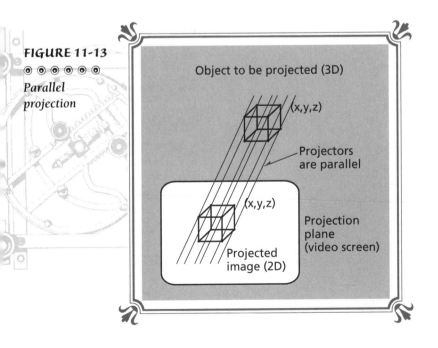

FIGURE 11-13

Parallel projection

Object to be projected (3D)

(x,y,z)

Projectors are parallel

(x,y,z)

Projection plane (video screen)

Projected image (2D)

Given a point (x,y,z)

The parallel projected point (x′,y′) is equal to:

x′ = x;

y′ = y;

As you can see, the z component is completely disregarded. Although this transform is simple and in some cases useful (such as in mechanical imaging), it lacks the proper *foreshortening* or perspective. Foreshortening means that as an object moves away from the viewpoint, it becomes smaller and migrates toward the centerline of projection. Without this feature, a 3D game will hardly look 3D. Hence, we must forego the simpler parallel projection for the much more realistic perspective projection!

Perspective Projection

The perspective projection is the one that we are going to use throughout the remainder of the book. Even though we have seen the math for it, let's briefly review the transformation. A perspective projection has the property that objects nearer to the viewpoint become larger, and objects farther from the viewpoint become smaller. This action was implemented by analyzing the geometry of the sit-

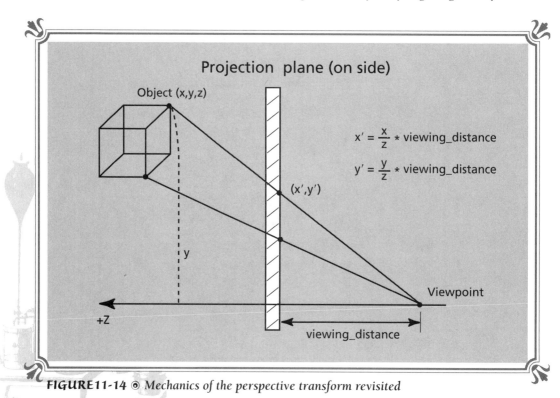

FIGURE 11-14 ⊚ *Mechanics of the perspective transform revisited*

uation as shown in Figure 11-14. Using similar triangles, we came up with the result that the perspective projected point (x,y,z) is equal to x and y divided by the z component and then multiplied by the viewing distance, or specifically,

$$x' = \text{viewing\_distance} * x/z$$
$$y' = \text{viewing\_distance} * y/z$$

where (x',y') are the final perspective projection of (x,y,z) at a given viewing distance.

Although that's all we need to know to write the function that draws a perspective projected object, it's also nice to know a little about the *viewing_distance* parameter and what its real meaning is. This is a bit difficult since within the computer there is no sense of inches, millimeters, or any other kind of physical distances. Granted, it's possible to compute scaling factors and make statements that a single screen pixel equals an inch, or centimeter, or mile, but this isn't what we are going to do. Instead, we are going to look at something called *field of view*.

Field of view means the angular displacement within which our vision functions, in both the X and Y axes. For example, most humans have a horizontal field of view of 110 to 140 degrees and a vertical field of view of 80 to 110 degrees. Figure 11-15 shows this graphically. In essence, our field of view (or FOV) defines a viewing cone within which we can see objects. Beyond this cone the objects are

FIGURE 11-15

◎ ◎ ◎ ◎ ◎ ◎

Meaning of field of view

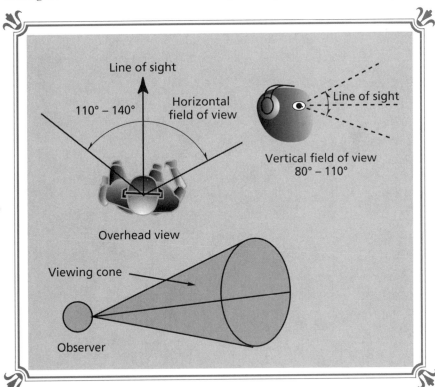

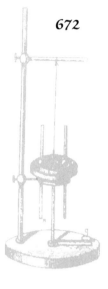

clipped or invisible to us. Taking this into consideration, we can derive mathematically the virtual field of view that our viewing volume exhibits given the viewing distance and the size of the view plane (which is the computer screen in this case). Figure 11-16 shows the setup for the FOV calculations.

Referring to Figure 11-16, we see that the FOV is basically two times the angle that each of the sides of the viewing volume makes with the line of sight as defined by the viewpoint and *viewing_distance*. Thus, formulas can be derived for both the horizontal and vertical fields of view for a given *viewing_distance* and screen size.

Horizontal Field of View (HFOV)

To calculate the HFOV, we begin by using the TANGENT function and noting that the field of view is two times the angle theta, as shown in Figure 11-16. Here are the calculations:

TAN θ = SCREEN_WIDTH/2*viewing_distance

Solving for θ,
θ = TAN $^{-1}$ (SCREEN_WIDTH/2*viewing_distance)

Therefore,
HFOV = 2*θ = 2* TAN $^{-1}$ (SCREEN_WIDTH/2*viewing_distance)

As an example, assume that we are using mode 13h, which has a width of 320. If we let the *viewing_distance* be 200, then the horizontal field of view is:

HFOV = 2* TAN $^{-1}$ (320/2*200) = 77.3 degrees

FIGURE 11-16

◎ ◎ ◎ ◎ ◎ ◎

Computing the field of view for a given viewing distance

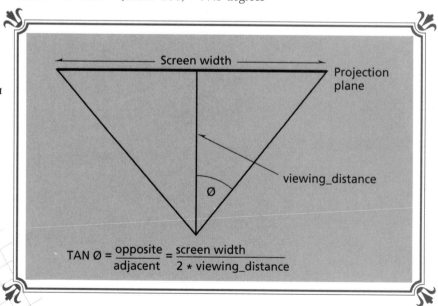

Vertical Field of View (VFOV)

The vertical field of view is calculated in much the same way except that instead of using the width of the projection plane, the height is used. Thus:

TAN θ = SCREEN_HEIGHT/2*viewing_distance

Solving for θ,
θ = TAN $^{-1}$ (SCREEN_HEIGHT/2*viewing_distance)

Therefore,
VFOV = 2*θ = 2* TAN $^{-1}$ (SCREEN_HEIGHT/2*viewing_distance)

Continuing with our mode 13h example (which has a height of 200), if we again set *viewing_distance* to 200, the vertical field of view is:

VFOV = 2* TAN $^{-1}$ (200/2*200) = 53.13 degrees

This is closer to the actual VFOV for humans than the HFOV we calculated for a distance of 200.

The moral of the story is to select a *viewing_distance* that both looks good and causes a minimal amount of perspective distortion (too much perspective caused by an impossibly large field of view) without being so small that objects are beyond the cone of vision most of the time. As a rule of thumb, I suggest values from 100 to 300 when using mode 13h as the projection plane.

2D Clipping to the Viewport

We are just about ready to write a function to draw a wireframe 3D object on the screen, but before we do, let's talk about clipping. We saw in Chapter 10 how to clip objects against the 3D viewing volume using the following equations:

$$x <= \frac{SCREEN\_WIDTH * z}{2 * viewing\_distance}$$

$$x >= \frac{- SCREEN\_WIDTH * z}{2 * viewing\_distance}$$

$$y <= \frac{SCREEN\_HEIGHT * z}{2 * viewing\_distance}$$

$$y >= \frac{- SCREEN\_HEIGHT * z}{2 * viewing\_distance}$$

z >hither_plane

z <yon_plane

However, these equations operate in object space on the mathematical level using the viewing volume as the clipping frustum. At some point we will actually use full 3D clipping, but for now a simpler 2D object space version will be employed. Again, the reason for this is that we are simply trying to draw a 3D object made of wires; we aren't yet ready for a full-blown shaded polygon engine. Therefore, the best thing to do is simply to project the lines that make up each polygon and look at their (x,y) components; and if the endpoints of the line extend beyond the viewing plane (which is going to be mode 13h's screen), then clip the lines.

Basically, we need to write a 2D object space clipper that takes a line to be clipped as a parameter and returns a line that is clipped to fit into the 320x200 resolution of mode 13h. OK, great! So how do we clip lines in 2D space? The answer is, we look at the geometry of the problem and come up with an answer. And since we aren't trying to do things at warp speed (yet), we don't have to optimize the line clipper.

Figure 11-17 shows the different cases we must consider when writing a line clipper. There are basically four different classes of lines that we need to deal with:

✛ Lines that are totally within the clipping region can be passed directly through to the line-drawing algorithm.

FIGURE 11-17

◎ ◎ ◎ ◎ ◎ ◎

Cases that must be considered by a 2D line clipper

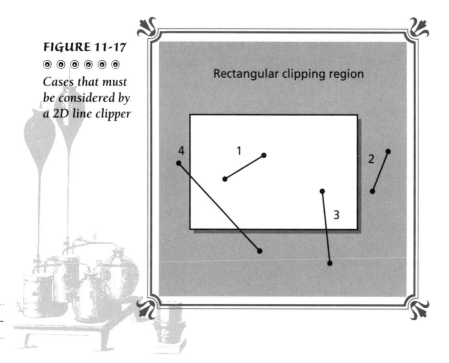

✣ Lines that are totally outside the clipping region need not be drawn.

✣ Lines that have one vertex within the clipping region and one vertex outside the clipping region must be clipped by computing the point at which the line exits the clipping region and then drawing the new line based on the intersection point.

✣ Lines that begin outside the clipping region, enter the clipping region, and then exit the clipping region must be drawn by computing two new intersection points—the point of entry and the point of exit. Then the line is drawn between them.

Reviewing the four cases, it looks like a few *if* statements and some math to compute intersection is all we need. For the most part this is true; but actually implementing a 2D line clipper is quite involved because the four cases seem to explode into four million subcases if you're not careful. However, the final function we'll write to perform the clipping works pretty well. But, I'm sure there is a better way to do it. Before we look at the function, let's see what's involved with computing a general intersection.

Let's assume we have the situation shown in Figure 11-18. A line is drawn from (xo,yo) to (x1,y1). However, the point (xo,yo) is outside the clipping region, and we must clip this line so that a new line is computed that is totally within the clipping region, as shown in Figure 11-19. Thus, we must find the values of (x′,y′). This is rather easy to do. First, x′ is simply equal to the left edge of the clipping

FIGURE 11-18

◉ ◉ ◉ ◉ ◉ ◉

Line to be clipped

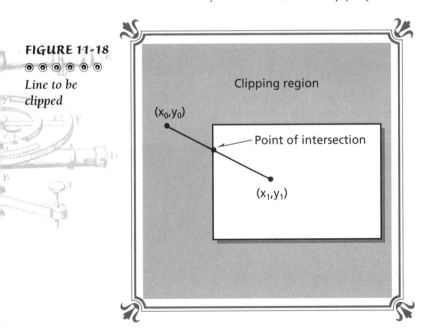

FIGURE 11-19

◎ ◎ ◎ ◎ ◎ ◎

Line after
clipping

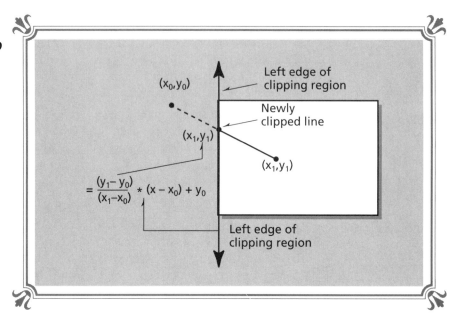

region or, if we are using mode 13h, x'=0. The computation of y' is the only hard part, but with the equation of the line, it's a snap. Here is the calculation to find y':

$$y' = \frac{(y1-yo)}{(x1-xo)} * (x-xo) + yo$$

Analyzing the above formula, we see that there are four additions and two multiplies (normally in math analysis, additions and subtractions are simply called additions and multiplies and divides are called multiplies—this makes accounting easier). This isn't too bad, since we are going to use this technique for a demo that we hope won't need many lines clipped in real-time.

Using the techniques just described, along with the appropriate conditional logic to filter out the trivial cases, the following function (Listing 11-17) accepts two endpoints as pointers and writes new values into the endpoints after clipping them to the clipping region (which is kept as a set of variables we'll see in a moment).

LISTING 11-17 Function that clips lines in 2D

```
int Clip_Line(int *x1,int *y1,int *x2, int *y2)
{
// this function clips the sent line using the globally defined clipping
// region

int point_1 = 0, point_2 = 0; // tracks if each end point is visible or invisible
```

```
int clip_always = 0;            // used for clipping override

int xi,yi;                      // point of intersection

int right_edge=0,               // which edges are the endpoints beyond
    left_edge=0,
    top_edge=0,
    bottom_edge=0;


int success = 0;                // was there a successful clipping

float dx,dy;                    // used to hold slope deltas

// test if line is completely visible
if ( (*x1>=poly_clip_min_x) && (*x1<=poly_clip_max_x) &&
     (*y1>=poly_clip_min_y) && (*y1<=poly_clip_max_y) )
     point_1 = 1;

if ( (*x2>=poly_clip_min_x) && (*x2<=poly_clip_max_x) &&
     (*y2>=poly_clip_min_y) && (*y2<=poly_clip_max_y) )
     point_2 = 1;

// test endpoints
if (point_1==1 && point_2==1)
   return(1);

// test if line is completely invisible
if (point_1==0 && point_2==0)
   {
   // must test to see if each endpoint is on the same side of one of
   // the bounding planes created by each clipping region boundary

   if ( ((*x1<poly_clip_min_x) && (*x2<poly_clip_min_x)) || // to the left
        ((*x1>poly_clip_max_x) && (*x2>poly_clip_max_x)) || // to the right

        ((*y1<poly_clip_min_y) && (*y2<poly_clip_min_y)) || // above
        ((*y1>poly_clip_max_y) && (*y2>poly_clip_max_y)) )  // below
        {
        // no need to draw line
        return(0);

        } // end if invisible

   // if we got here we have the special case where the line cuts into and
   // out of the clipping region
   clip_always = 1;

   } // end if test for invisibility

// take care of case where either endpoint is in clipping region
if (( point_1==1) || (point_1==0 && point_2==0) )
```

continued on next page

continued from previous page

```
{
// compute deltas
dx = *x2 - *x1;
dy = *y2 - *y1;

// compute what boundary lines need to be clipped against
if (*x2 > poly_clip_max_x)
   {
   // flag right edge
   right_edge = 1;

   // compute intersection with right edge
   if (dx!=0)
      yi = (int)(.5 + (dy/dx) * (poly_clip_max_x - *x1) + *y1);
   else
      yi = -1;  // invalidate intersection

   } // end if to right
else
if (*x2 < poly_clip_min_x)
   {
   // flag left edge
   left_edge = 1;

   // compute intersection with left edge
   if (dx!=0)
      yi = (int)(.5 + (dy/dx) * (poly_clip_min_x - *x1) + *y1);
   else
      yi = -1;  // invalidate intersection

   } // end if to left

// horizontal intersections

if (*y2 > poly_clip_max_y)
   {
   // flag bottom edge
   bottom_edge = 1;

   // compute intersection with right edge
   if (dy!=0)
      xi = (int)(.5 + (dx/dy) * (poly_clip_max_y - *y1) + *x1);
   else
      xi = -1;  // invalidate intersection

   } // end if bottom
else
if (*y2 < poly_clip_min_y)
   {
   // flag top edge
   top_edge = 1;
```

```
        // compute intersection with top edge
        if (dy!=0)
           xi = (int)(.5 + (dx/dy) * (poly_clip_min_y - *y1) + *x1);
        else
           xi = -1;  // invalidate intersection

        } // end if top

    // now we know where the line passed thru
    // compute which edge is the proper intersection

    if (right_edge==1 && (yi>=poly_clip_min_y && yi<=poly_clip_max_y) )
       {
       *x2 = poly_clip_max_x;
       *y2 = yi;

       success = 1;

       } // end if intersected right edge
    else
    if (left_edge==1 && (yi>=poly_clip_min_y && yi<=poly_clip_max_y) )
       {
       *x2 = poly_clip_min_x;
       *y2 = yi;

       success = 1;

       } // end if intersected left edge

    if (bottom_edge==1 && (xi>=poly_clip_min_x && xi<=poly_clip_max_x) )
       {
       *x2 = xi;
       *y2 = poly_clip_max_y;

       success = 1;

       } // end if intersected bottom edge
    else
    if (top_edge==1 && (xi>=poly_clip_min_x && xi<=poly_clip_max_x) )
       {
       *x2 = xi;
       *y2 = poly_clip_min_y;

       success = 1;

       } // end if intersected top edge

    } // end if point_1 is visible

// reset edge flags
right_edge = left_edge= top_edge = bottom_edge = 0;
```

continued on next page

continued from previous page

```
// test second endpoint
if ( (point_2==1) || (point_1==0 && point_2==0))
   {
   // compute deltas
   dx = *x1 - *x2;
   dy = *y1 - *y2;

   // compute what boundary line needs to be clipped against
   if (*x1 > poly_clip_max_x)
      {
      // flag right edge

      right_edge = 1;

      // compute intersection with right edge
      if (dx!=0)
         yi = (int)(.5 + (dy/dx) * (poly_clip_max_x - *x2) + *y2);
      else
         yi = -1;  // invalidate intersection

      } // end if to right
   else
   if (*x1 < poly_clip_min_x)
      {
      // flag left edge

      left_edge = 1;

      // compute intersection with left edge
      if (dx!=0)
         yi = (int)(.5 + (dy/dx) * (poly_clip_min_x - *x2) + *y2);
      else
         yi = -1;  // invalidate intersection

      } // end if to left

   // horizontal intersections
   if (*y1 > poly_clip_max_y)
      {
      // flag bottom edge

      bottom_edge = 1;

      // compute intersection with right edge
      if (dy!=0)
         xi = (int)(.5 + (dx/dy) * (poly_clip_max_y - *y2) + *x2);
      else
         xi = -1;  // invalidate inntersection

      } // end if bottom
   else
   if (*y1 < poly_clip_min_y)
      {
      // flag top edge
```

```
          top_edge = 1;

          // compute intersection with top edge
          if (dy!=0)
             xi = (int)(.5 + (dx/dy) * (poly_clip_min_y - *y2) + *x2);
          else
             xi = -1;  // invalidate inntersection

          } // end if top

       // now we know where the line passed thru
       // compute which edge is the proper intersection
       if (right_edge==1 && (yi>=poly_clip_min_y && yi<=poly_clip_max_y) )
          {
          *x1 = poly_clip_max_x;
          *y1 = yi;

          success = 1;

          } // end if intersected right edge
       else
       if (left_edge==1 && (yi>=poly_clip_min_y && yi<=poly_clip_max_y) )
          {
          *x1 = poly_clip_min_x;
          *y1 = yi;

          success = 1;

          } // end if intersected left edge

       if (bottom_edge==1 && (xi>=poly_clip_min_x && xi<=poly_clip_max_x) )
          {
          *x1 = xi;
          *y1 = poly_clip_max_y;

          success = 1;

          } // end if intersected bottom edge
       else
       if (top_edge==1 && (xi>=poly_clip_min_x && xi<=poly_clip_max_x) )
          {
          *x1 = xi;
          *y1 = poly_clip_min_y;

          success = 1;

          } // end if intersected top edge


       } // end if point_2 is visible

   return(success);

   } // end Clip_Line
```

As I warned you, the function is a bit long, not because of its complexity, but because of all the special cases. A better way of implementing all the special cases would be to use a bit code or look-up table, and this is actually a technique used by the *Sutherland-Cohen algorithm*—but sometimes I like to reinvent the wheel! Anyway, the function takes four parameters, which are the (x,y) endpoints of the line to be drawn. Instead of sending the parameters by value, they are sent by reference so the function can alter them with the clipped values. Hence, the variables used to send the endpoints can be modified, so the caller should place them in temporaries if this side effect is going to be a problem.

You will notice that the *Clip_Line()* function also uses four clipping variables. These are

```
// the clipping region, set it to default on start up

int poly_clip_min_x = POLY_CLIP_MIN_X,
    poly_clip_min_y = POLY_CLIP_MIN_Y,

    poly_clip_max_x = POLY_CLIP_MAX_X,
    poly_clip_max_y = POLY_CLIP_MAX_Y;
```

where the constants are defined as:

```
#define POLY_CLIP_MIN_X          0  // minimum x,y clip values
#define POLY_CLIP_MIN_Y          0

#define POLY_CLIP_MAX_X          319 // maximum x,y clip values
#define POLY_CLIP_MAX_Y          199
```

These will be used throughout the engine as the 2D clipping rectangle.

In most cases, the clipping region is set to the size of mode 13h, but in others, we will want to make the clipping region smaller so that the objects are only drawn in a small window in the middle of the screen. This might be used to implement a screen partition, with the top half being 3D graphics, while the bottom half is bitmapped instrumentation.

Now that we can draw a 3D object (hopefully), we would like to be able to move it around and transform it. This is the whole idea of a 3D graphics engine— to see things move around and interact in 3D. Let's see what's involved from a programming point of view.

Transforming Objects

As we learned in Chapter 10 on 3D fundamentals, the primary transformations performed on 3D objects are translation, scaling, and rotation. Of course, we can perform more exotic transforms, such as sheering, non-uniform scaling, inversion, and so on, but translation, scaling, and rotation are the most common. Now, we need to be careful right from the beginning about coordinate systems so we don't confuse ourselves and dig a hole too deep to climb out of!

We must consider some rules when transforming objects, such as what the transformations mean in the 3D world as opposed to what we think they mean. First, all objects that we import as PLG files are loaded into an object data structure and fill up the local coordinate array of the structure. This means that each object is defined relative to its own local origin of (0,0,0), as shown in Figure 11-20. When we perform rotation or scaling, these local coordinates should be modified and stored back into the local coordinate array, as shown in Figure 11-21. However, when we perform translation to an object, we need to stop for a moment and think, what do we want this to mean?

Within the object data structure, there is a field called *world_pos*, which holds the (x,y,z) position of the object in the universe—that is, world position. This is used to position the object in world coordinates with the rest of the objects in the universe. This facilitates computations such as viewing or determination of the relationship to other objects. This is what the *world_pos* is for. Even though we might rotate and scale the object in local coordinates, at some point we must convert the object into world coordinates using *world_pos*.

So to translate an object, all we need to do is translate the point found in *world_pos*, since it holds the final position of the object. We spoke before about the

FIGURE 11-20

◉ ◉ ◉ ◉ ◉ ◉

Objects in their local coordinate systems

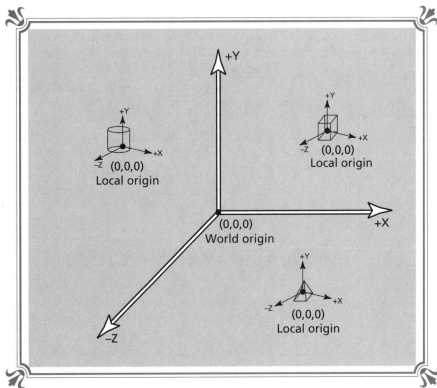

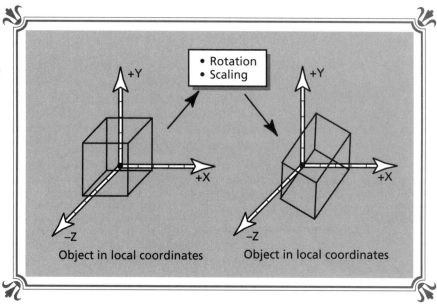

transformations from local coordinates to world coordinates and from world to camera coordinates for viewing. This is all necessary, but can be avoided for special cases. For example, if the viewpoint is located at (0,0,0) and the view angles are also (0,0,0), then there is no need to perform a world-to-camera transformation. All we need to compute are the world coordinates of any object in order to project it. This can be done by adding *world_pos* to each vertex of the local coordinates. The resulting coordinates are stored in the *vertices_world[]* array and can be used for a simple projection. This is the technique we are going to use to create the wireframe demo at the end of the chapter.

The point of all this is that each object is mathematically defined by its local coordinates at an origin of (0,0,0), which doesn't do us any good since we must position the object at some point in the universe—that is, world coordinates, at the very least—to obtain an image. With all that in mind, let's see the code needed to translate, scale, and rotate an object.

Positioning and Translation

Since each object in our 3D world is located in world coordinates by the variable *world_pos*, all we need to do to move an object is translate the single point contained within *world_pos*. The reason for this is that during the local-to-world transformation, *world_pos* will be used to move the entire vertex list of the local coordinates into world coordinates. But that process is handled by the code that performs the local-to-world transformation. As far as translation goes, we simply need to update the variable *world_pos* with x, y, and z translation factors.

We learned that translation can be performed by a matrix multiplication with a matrix of the form:

$$T = \begin{bmatrix} 1 & 0 & 0 & 0 \\ 0 & 1 & 0 & 0 \\ 0 & 0 & 1 & 0 \\ tx & ty & tz & 1 \end{bmatrix}$$

However, this is a bit of overkill. A better way would be simply to add the translation factors manually to each of the components of the *world_pos* in the object's structure with the function in Listing 11-18.

LISTING 11-18 Function that translates an object

```
void Translate_Object(object_ptr the_object,int x_trans,int y_trans,int z_trans)
{
// this function translates an object relative to its own local
// coordinate system

the_object->world_pos.x+=x_trans;
the_object->world_pos.y+=y_trans;
the_object->world_pos.z+=z_trans;

} // end Translate_Object
```

The function takes a pointer to the object to translate along with the x, y, and z translation factors and performs the requested translation.

Now when an object is loaded or created, its position is (0,0,0). We can position the object with some code like this:

```
object.world_x = x;
object.world_y = y;
object.world_z = z;
```

Or, to keep things orthogonal, maybe we should write a simple positioning function just to be complete. Listing 11-19 contains such a function.

LISTING 11-19 Function to position an object at a specific set of coordinates

```
void Position_Object(object_ptr the_object,int x,int y,int z)
{
// this function positions an object in the world

the_object->world_pos.x = x;
the_object->world_pos.y = y;
the_object->world_pos.z = z;

} // end Position_Object
```

As you can see, the *Position_Object()* function is almost identical to the *Translate_Object()* function except that the position is initialized instead of added.

Scaling Objects

The next transformation that we want to implement is scaling or, in other words, changing the size of an object. As we discussed, this transformation must be performed in local coordinates unless you wish to get all kinds of weird translations. To scale an object by some scaling factor, each local vertex component must be multiplied by the scaling factor and stored back into the local vertices array. Listing 11-20 will do the job.

LISTING 11-20 Function that scales an object

```
void Scale_Object(object_ptr the_object,float scale_factor)
{
// this function scales an object relative to its own local coordinate system
// equally in x,y and z

int curr_poly,    // the current polygon being processed
    curr_vertex;  // the current vertex being processed

float scale_2;    // holds the square of the scaling factor, needed to
                  // resize the surface normal for lighting calculations

// multiply each vertex in the object definition by the scaling factor

for (curr_vertex=0; curr_vertex<the_object->num_vertices; curr_vertex++)
    {
    the_object->vertices_local[curr_vertex].x*=scale_factor;
    the_object->vertices_local[curr_vertex].y*=scale_factor;
    the_object->vertices_local[curr_vertex].z*=scale_factor;

    } // end for curr_vertex

// compute scaling factor squared

scale_2 = scale_factor*scale_factor;

// now scale all pre-computed normals
for (curr_poly=0; curr_poly<the_object->num_polys; curr_poly++)
    the_object->polys[curr_poly].normal_length*=scale_2;

// finally scale the radius up
the_object->radius*=scale_factor;

} // end Scale_Object
```

It doesn't take a rocket scientist to see that the scaling function is doing a bit more than scaling the vertices! I admit there is a bit of trickery going on here, but at this point, it's not that important. Still, let's at least take a quick look at it. Remember that each object has a precomputed radius? And also remember that the *PLG_Load_Object()* function computes some normals and vectors to help with the back-face removal and shading? Well, that's what the extra code is for. The length of the surface normal must be scaled (since it isn't 1.0) by the scaling factor, and the radius of the object must also be scaled by the scaling factor. However, with a bit of math, you can see that the new scaled radius of the object is simply the old radius times the scaling factor, but the length of surface normals is not. We must multiply the normal length by the scaling factor squared since the normal length itself has the length of the product of two sides of a polygon, which themselves both contribute to the length of the surface normal.

This will get clearer down the line, as we start using the precomputed surface normal length data. In fact, the final engine may precompute the entire surface normal to speed things up, but we'll see about that later.

Rotation and Matrix Concatenation

Rotation is another transformation that must be performed in local coordinates. If an object is not rotated about its center (0,0,0), it will rotate *and* translate. Figure 11-22 shows this. There are two ways we can perform rotation in local coordinates: we can write separate functions to rotate an object in the X, Y, and Z axes, or we can write a single function that performs all the rotations at the same time.

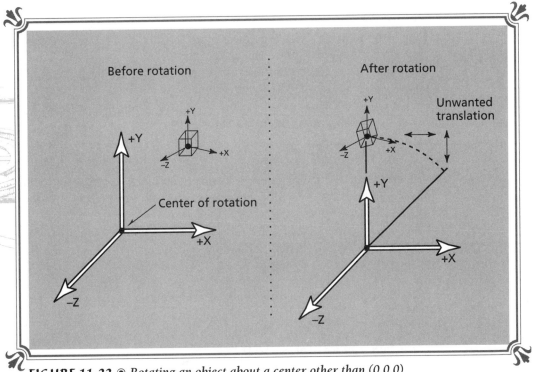

FIGURE 11-22 ◉ *Rotating an object about a center other than (0,0,0)*

Although it may be more efficient to write separate functions (especially if objects are rotated on one axis most of the time), this is a good opportunity to see matrix concatenation at work. Hence, we will write a function that can perform all rotations at once.

Here's how we are going to do it. Each object consists of a set of vertices, and if we rotate each of these vertices, the entire object will itself be rotated. However, if we want to rotate an object some angle in X, then in Y, and finally in Z, this can be a bit time-consuming. Can we perform the X, Y, Z rotation in a single transaction using a single matrix? The answer is yes! If you recall our discussion about matrices and their concatenation property, it should be apparent that all we need to do to rotate an entire object in all three axes at the same time is compute a single rotation matrix that is the product of each of the single axis rotation matrices.

To put it mathematically, if R_x is the matrix that performs X-axis rotation, R_y is the matrix that performs Y-axis rotation, and R_z is the matrix that performs Z-axis rotation, the product R is computed as:

$$R = R_x * R_y * R_z$$

The resulting matrix R contains all the rotations in a single matrix. Thus, R can then be multiplied with each vertex to accomplish the complete X, Y, Z rotation with a single matrix multiply! Before we write the function, let's take a quick detour to trigonometric calculations.

The rotation equations and matrices make use of both the SIN and COSINE trigonometric functions. However, these functions take about a million years in computer time to calculate; therefore, our rotation equations (and any function that uses SIN and COSINE) are going to use look-up tables instead of calls to the actual functions. However, to simplify things even more, the look-up tables are going to be in the form of degrees instead of radians as the C library calls are. Hence, the graphics engine will have access to two tables, named

```
float sin_look[360+1],                    // SIN from 0 to 360
      cos_look[360+1];                    // COSINE from 0 to 360
```

which each contain the precomputed floating point values for SIN and COSINE from 0 to 360 degrees. And the function that generates these tables is shown in Listing 11-21.

LISTING 11-21 The look-up table generator

```
void Build_Look_Up_Tables(void)
{
// this function builds all the look up tables for the engine
int angle;
float rad;

   // generate sin/cos look up tables
```

```
for (angle=0; angle<=360; angle++)
    {
    // convert degrees to radians
    rad = (float) (3.14159*(float)angle/(float)180);

    cos_look[angle] = (float)cos(rad);
    sin_look[angle] = (float)sin(rad);

    } // end for angle

} // end Build_Look_Up_Tables
```

After the tables are built, it's easy to compute the SIN or COSINE of an angle. For example, if we wanted to know the COSINE of 21 degrees, we would write:

```
cos_look[21];
```

If we use the new look-up tables in place of the standard trigonometric functions, along with the rotation formulas from Chapter 10, we can write a complete 3D rotation function. Listing 11-22 shows the source that will rotate an object in X, Y, or Z simultaneously by means of concatenation.

LISTING 11-22 Function that rotates an object on any or all of the axes

```
void Rotate_Object(object_ptr the_object,int angle_x,int angle_y,int angle_z)
{
// this function rotates an object relative to its own local coordinate system
// and allows simultaneous rotations

int index,        //  looping variable
    product=0;    // used to determine which matrices need multiplying

matrix_4x4 rotate_x,    // the x,y and z rotation matrices
           rotate_y,
           rotate_z,
           rotate,      // the final rotation matrix
           temp;        // temporary working matrix

float temp_x, // used to hold intermediate results during rotation
      temp_y,
      temp_z;

// test if we need to rotate at all
if (angle_x==0 && angle_y==0 && angle_z==0)
    return;

// create identity matrix
Mat_Identity_4x4(rotate);

// create X rotation matrix
```

continued on next page

continued from previous page

```
if (angle_x)
   {
   // x matrix
   Mat_Identity_4x4(rotate_x);

   rotate_x[1][1] = ( cos_look[angle_x]);
   rotate_x[1][2] = ( sin_look[angle_x]);
   rotate_x[2][1] = (-sin_look[angle_x]);
   rotate_x[2][2] = ( cos_look[angle_x]);

   } // end if any X rotation

// create Y rotation matrix
if (angle_y)
   {
   Mat_Identity_4x4(rotate_y);

   rotate_y[0][0] = ( cos_look[angle_y]);
   rotate_y[0][2] = (-sin_look[angle_y]);
   rotate_y[2][0] = ( sin_look[angle_y]);
   rotate_y[2][2] = ( cos_look[angle_y]);

   } // end if any Y rotation

// create Z rotation matrix

if (angle_z)
   {
   Mat_Identity_4x4(rotate_z);

   rotate_z[0][0] = ( cos_look[angle_z]);
   rotate_z[0][1] = ( sin_look[angle_z]);
   rotate_z[1][0] = (-sin_look[angle_z]);
   rotate_z[1][1] = ( cos_look[angle_z]);

   } // end if any Z rotation

// compute final rotation matrix, determine the proper product of matrices
// use a switch statement along with a bit pattern to determine which
// matrices need multiplying, this is worth the time it would take
// to concatenate matrices together that don't have any effect

// if bit 2 of product is 1 then there is an x rotation
// if bit 1 of product is 1 then there is an y rotation
// if bit 0 of product is 1 then there is an z rotation

if (angle_x)
   product|=4;

if (angle_y)
   product|=2;

if (angle_z)
```

```
    product|=1;

// compute proper final rotation matrix

switch(product)
    {
    case 0: // do nothing there isn't any rotation
        {
        // this shouldn't happen
        } break;

    case 1: // final matrix = z
        {
        Mat_Copy_4x4(rotate_z,rotate);
        } break;

    case 2: // final matrix = y
        {
        Mat_Copy_4x4(rotate_y,rotate);

        } break;

    case 3: // final matrix = y*z
        {
        Mat_Mul_4x4_4x4(rotate_y,rotate_z,rotate);
        } break;

    case 4: // final matrix = x
        {
        Mat_Copy_4x4(rotate_x,rotate);
        } break;

    case 5: // final matrix = x*z
        {
        Mat_Mul_4x4_4x4(rotate_x,rotate_z,rotate);
        } break;

    case 6: // final matrix = x*y
        {
        Mat_Mul_4x4_4x4(rotate_x,rotate_y,rotate);
        } break;

    case 7: // final matrix = x*y*z
        {
        Mat_Mul_4x4_4x4(rotate_x,rotate_y,temp);
        Mat_Mul_4x4_4x4(temp,rotate_z,rotate);
        } break;

    default:break;

    } // end switch

// now multiply each point in object by transformation matrix
```

continued on next page

continued from previous page

```
for (index=0; index<the_object->num_vertices; index++)
    {
    // x component
    temp_x = the_object->vertices_local[index].x * rotate[0][0] +
             the_object->vertices_local[index].y * rotate[1][0] +
             the_object->vertices_local[index].z * rotate[2][0];

    // y component
    temp_y = the_object->vertices_local[index].x * rotate[0][1] +
             the_object->vertices_local[index].y * rotate[1][1] +
             the_object->vertices_local[index].z * rotate[2][1];

    // z component
    temp_z = the_object->vertices_local[index].x * rotate[0][2] +
             the_object->vertices_local[index].y * rotate[1][2] +
             the_object->vertices_local[index].z * rotate[2][2];

    // store rotated point back into local array
    the_object->vertices_local[index].x = temp_x;
    the_object->vertices_local[index].y = temp_y;
    the_object->vertices_local[index].z = temp_z;

    } // end for index

} // end Rotate_Object
```

The *Rotate_Object()* function takes as parameters the object to rotate along with the X, Y, and Z angles of rotation. The function works by creating an identity matrix and then concatenating each of the axial rotation matrices to the final rotation matrix. The function also endeavors to minimize matrix multiplication by only concatenating matrices to the final rotation matrix that are non-zero. Once the final matrix has been computed, each point is multiplied by the matrix manually (for speed), and the resulting vertices are stored back into the *vertices_local[]* array of the object structure. The function also supports negative angles by using the formula:

$$-\theta = 360 - \theta$$

Hence, if we wanted to rotate an object named "car" 10 degrees in the X axis and 5 degrees in the Y axis, we could use the following code:

```
Rotate_Object((object_ptr)&car,10,5,0);
```

This would result in rotating the car 10 degrees parallel to the X axis and 5 degrees parallel to the Y axis.

Before we move on, let's talk about the direction of rotation. Since we are using a left-handed coordinate system, all rotations performed by the functions in the engine are clockwise when looking toward the origin, as shown in Figure 11-23. This is good to remember when jets are turning left instead of right!

Viewing a 3D Wireframe Object

We're finally ready to see a 3D demo of an object being projected on the screen, so let's write a small program to do this based on the functions we have written thus far. All we need to do is this:

+ Place the PC into mode 13h.

+ Create a double buffer.

+ Load an object off disk.

+ Position the object at some distance out on the Z axis.

+ Enter the main event loop and erase the double buffer.

+ Allow the user to enter keyboard commands to translate the object in X, Y, or Z directions.

+ Rotate the object at a constant rate to make things exciting.

+ Convert the local coordinates into camera coordinates and project the object on the screen by drawing all the lines that make up the polygons.

+ Copy the double buffer to the video screen.

+ Synchronize the system to 18.2 hertz.

+ Loop back to the beginning of the event loop.

FIGURE 11-23

◎ ◎ ◎ ◎ ◎ ◎

Directions of rotation for positive angles using our system

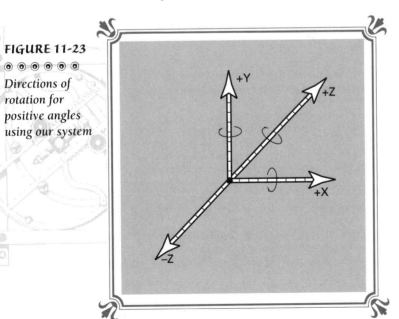

It may seem like quite a bit, but it really isn't. We have the code to do everything except draw the image into the double buffer with perspective projection. Let's take a look at the function that does this. Actually, we will probably never use it again, but I made it just for this demo, so it's worth looking at. The name of the function is *Draw_Object_Wire()* (Listing 11-23) and can be found in BLACK11.C.

LISTING 11-23 Function that draws a wireframe 3D object with perspective

```
void Draw_Object_Wire(object_ptr the_object)
{
// this function draws an object out of wires

int curr_poly,        // the current polygon
    curr_vertex,      // the current vertex
    vertex;           // vertex index

float x1,y1,z1,       // working variables
      x2,y2,z2;

int ix1,iy1,          // integers used to hold screen coordinates
    ix2,iy2;

// compute position of object in world
for (curr_poly=0; curr_poly<the_object->num_polys; curr_poly++)
    {
    // is this polygon visible?
    if (the_object->polys[curr_poly].visible==0 ||
        the_object->polys[curr_poly].clipped )
        continue;

    // printf("\npolygon #%d",curr_poly);
    for (curr_vertex=0; curr_vertex<the_object->polys[curr_poly].num_points-1; curr_vertex++)
        {
        // extract two endpoints
        vertex=the_object->polys[curr_poly].vertex_list[curr_vertex];

        x1 = the_object->vertices_camera[vertex].x;
        y1 = the_object->vertices_camera[vertex].y;
        z1 = the_object->vertices_camera[vertex].z;

        vertex=the_object->polys[curr_poly].vertex_list[curr_vertex+1];

        x2 = the_object->vertices_camera[vertex].x;
        y2 = the_object->vertices_camera[vertex].y;
        z2 = the_object->vertices_camera[vertex].z;

        // convert to screen ccordinates
        x1=(HALF_SCREEN_WIDTH  + x1*viewing_distance/z1);
        y1=(HALF_SCREEN_HEIGHT - ASPECT_RATIO*y1*viewing_distance/z1);

        x2=(HALF_SCREEN_WIDTH  + x2*viewing_distance/z2);
```

```
        y2=(HALF_SCREEN_HEIGHT - ASPECT_RATIO*y2*viewing_distance/z2);

        // convert floats to integers for line clipper
        ix1=(int)x1;
        iy1=(int)y1;
        ix2=(int)x2;
        iy2=(int)y2;


        // draw clipped lines
        if (Clip_Line(&ix1,&iy1,&ix2,&iy2))
           {
           Draw_Line((int)ix1,(int)iy1,(int)ix2,(int)iy2,
                     (unsigned char)the_object->polys[curr_poly].color,
                     double_buffer);

           } // end if clip

        } // end for vertex

    // close polygon

    ix1=(int)x2;
    iy1=(int)y2;

    // extract starting point again to close polygon
    vertex=the_object->polys[curr_poly].vertex_list[0];

    x2 = the_object->vertices_camera[vertex].x;
    y2 = the_object->vertices_camera[vertex].y;
    z2 = the_object->vertices_camera[vertex].z;

    // compute screen coordinates
    x2=(HALF_SCREEN_WIDTH  + x2*viewing_distance/z2);
    y2=(HALF_SCREEN_HEIGHT - ASPECT_RATIO*y2*viewing_distance/z2);

    // convert floats to integers

    ix2=(int)x2;
    iy2=(int)y2;

    // draw clipped lines

    if (Clip_Line(&ix1,&iy1,&ix2,&iy2))
       {
       Draw_Line((int)ix1,(int)iy1,(int)ix2,(int)iy2,
                 (unsigned char)the_object->polys[curr_poly].color,
                 double_buffer);

       } // end if clip

    } // end for curr_poly

} // end Draw_Object_Wire
```

The *Draw_Object_Wire()* function is the heart of our simple display system. It loops through all the polygons of the object and then draws each polygon with lines. As the lines are drawn, they are clipped using the *Clip_Line()* function. The only interesting thing about the function is the final screen projection code, which looks like this:

```
x1=(HALF_SCREEN_WIDTH  + x1*viewing_distance/z1);
y1=(HALF_SCREEN_HEIGHT - ASPECT_RATIO*y1*viewing_distance/z1);
```

What are the constants *HALF_SCREEN_WIDTH*, *HALF_SCREEN_HEIGHT*, and *ASPECT_RATIO* all for? Well, first off, we must project the image as if the user is looking straight down the positive Z axis, and the origin is right in the middle of the screen, as shown in Figure 11-24. This is why we translate each point to the center of the screen. Second, in mode 13h, the X and Y axes aren't equal pixel-for-pixel, so we must multiply all y components by a scaling factor to make changes in x equal to changes in y. This factor is typically called the *aspect ratio*. Finally, you may have also noticed the negative sign in front of *ASPECT_RATIO*. This is because the positive Y axis is downward on the VGA, but we want it upward, as shown in Figure 11-24.

Now that we have everything in perspective (pun not intended), let's see a demo that will load an object from disk, display the object in real-time with perspective, rotate it, and allow the user to move it around the screen using the arrow keys. The name of the demo is WIREDEMO.C, shown in Listing 11-24, and the executable is WIREDEMO.EXE. Again, if you wish to make your own EXE, you must of course link in BLACK11.C and include BLACK11.H.

LISTING 11-24 Wireframe 3D demo

```
// I N C L U D E S ///////////////////////////////////////////////////////

#include <io.h>
#include <conio.h>
#include <stdio.h>
#include <stdlib.h>
#include <dos.h>
#include <bios.h>
#include <fcntl.h>
#include <memory.h>
#include <malloc.h>
#include <math.h>
#include <string.h>
#include <search.h>                    // this one is needed for qsort()

// include all of our stuff
#include "black3.h"
#include "black4.h"
#include "black5.h"
#include "black6.h"
```

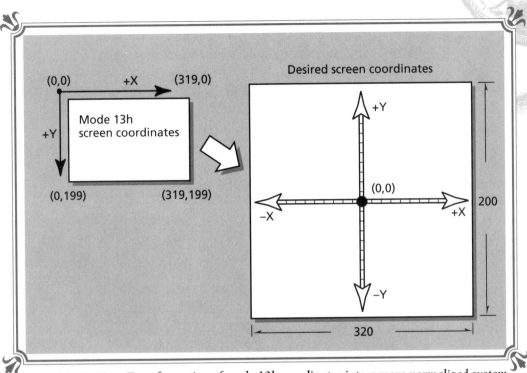

FIGURE 11-24 ⊙ *Transformation of mode 13h coordinates into a more normalized system*

```
#include "black8.h"
#include "black9.h"
#include "black11.h"


// G L O B A L S ///////////////////////////////////////////////////////////

object test_object;   // the test object

// M A I N ///////////////////////////////////////////////////////////////////

void main(int argc,char **argv)
{

int index,   // looping variable
    done=0;  // exit flag

char buffer[80]; // used to print strings

// load in the object from the command line
if (!PLG_Load_Object(&test_object,argv[1],1))
   {
   printf("\nCouldn't find file %s",argv[1]);
```

continued on next page

continued from previous page

```
    return;

    } // end if

// position the object
test_object.world_pos.x = 0;
test_object.world_pos.y = 0;
test_object.world_pos.z = 300;

// create the sin/cos lookup tables used for the rotation function
Build_Look_Up_Tables();

// set graphics to mode 13h
Set_Graphics_Mode(GRAPHICS_MODE13);

// allocate double buffer
Create_Double_Buffer(200);

// install the isr keyboard driver
Keyboard_Install_Driver();

// set viewing distance
viewing_distance = 250;

// main event loop
while(!done)
    {
    // compute starting time of this frame
    starting_time = Timer_Query();

    // erase the screen
    Fill_Double_Buffer(0);

    // test what key(s) user is pressing

    // test if user is moving object to right
    if (keyboard_state[MAKE_RIGHT])
       test_object.world_pos.x+=5;

    // test if user is moving object to left
    if (keyboard_state[MAKE_LEFT])
       test_object.world_pos.x-=5;

    // test if user is moving object up

    if (keyboard_state[MAKE_UP])
       test_object.world_pos.y-=5;

    // test if user is moving object down
    if (keyboard_state[MAKE_DOWN])
       test_object.world_pos.y+=5;
```

```
        // test if user is moving object farther
        if (keyboard_state[MAKE_PGUP])
          test_object.world_pos.z+=15;

        // test if user is moving object nearer
        if (keyboard_state[MAKE_PGDWN])
          test_object.world_pos.z-=15;

        // test for exit key
        if (keyboard_state[MAKE_ESC])
          done=1;

        // rotate the object on all three axes
        Rotate_Object((object_ptr)&test_object,2,4,6);

//////////////////////////////////////////////////////////////////////////////

        // convert the local coordinates into camera coordinates for projection
        // note the viewer is at (0,0,0) with angles 0,0,0 so the transformation
        // is simply to add the world position to each local vertex

        for (index=0; index<test_object.num_vertices; index++)
            {
            test_object.vertices_camera[index].x =
                    test_object.vertices_local[index].x+test_object.world_pos.x;

            test_object.vertices_camera[index].y =
                    test_object.vertices_local[index].y+test_object.world_pos.y;

            test_object.vertices_camera[index].z =
                    test_object.vertices_local[index].z+test_object.world_pos.z;

            } // end for index

//////////////////////////////////////////////////////////////////////////////

        // draw the object
        Draw_Object_Wire((object_ptr)&test_object);

        // print out position of object
        sprintf(buffer,"Object is at (%d,%d,%d)      ",(int)test_object.world_pos.x,
                                                       (int)test_object.world_pos.y,
                                                       (int)test_object.world_pos.z);

        Print_String_DB(0,0,9,buffer,0);

        // display double buffer
        Display_Double_Buffer(double_buffer,0);

        // lock onto 18 frames per second max
        while((Timer_Query()-starting_time)<1);
```

continued on next page

continued from previous page

```
      } // end while

// restore graphics mode back to text
Set_Graphics_Mode(TEXT_MODE);

// restore the old keyboard driver
Keyboard_Remove_Driver();

} // end main
```

When you execute the program, you must supply it with the name of a PLG file to load as the object. Within the directory for this chapter, you will find two such files:

CUBEW.PLG
PYRAMIDW.PLG

To load the demo with the cube, you would type:

WIREDEMO CUBEW.PLG

You will be presented with a spinning 3D wireframe cube. To move the cube around, use the arrow keys: the ➡ and ⬅ keys move the cube in the X axis; the ⬆ and ⬇ keys move the cube in the Y axis, and (PAGE UP) and (PAGE DOWN) move the cube in the Z axis. To exit, press (ESC). Notice how the object is clipped at the edges, and also notice how sometimes your brain gets confused and distorts the cube. If this occurs, close your eyes and then look at it again. This occurs because there aren't any depth cues going to your brain, such as shading and so forth, and sometimes your brain inverts the cube's geometry. This occurs less with the pyramid.

Positioning the Viewer

Other than being wireframe, the demo only lacks one thing—the ability to move the user's viewpoint and change the view angle. This will come later, as we learn to convert world coordinates into camera coordinates for any camera position and orientation. For now, just assume that the camera is always fixed at (0,0,0) with angles (0,0,0).

Summary

This chapter has taken us from the theoretical to the practical. We have seen the math and functions involved in loading, transforming, and viewing 3D wireframe objects. In fact, we have enough information to write a simple 3D game at this point. But we aren't satisfied with hollow objects void of soul and dimension; we want solid 3D shaded objects! So turn the page and let's see how to do this.

12

Solid Modeling and Shading

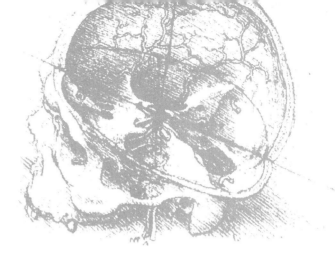

Solid Modeling and Shading

In Chapter 11 we learned how to represent and display 3D wireframe models of objects loaded as PLG files. Even though this is a great achievement, we must strive for more realism. Thus, within this chapter, we're going to turn our hollow wireframe models into solid 3D shaded representations. Now, so we don't get too carried away, most of our discussions will be on rendering. We aren't going to cover motion and the complex world to camera transformation yet. But we are going to learn how to render solid objects using basic geometric objects such as triangles and quadrilaterals.

Be warned—by creating models that are more realistic, we are pushing the integrity of the subspace barrier that separates our universe from Cyberspace, and as we all know, if this barrier is breached, darkness will fall upon us.

Introduction to Solid Modeling

Solid modeling is performed in much the same way as wireframe modeling—an object is constructed from a set of vertices that are used to represent polygons. However, instead of rendering the object as a set of lines, the polygons are filled as if they were solid facets. Figure 12-1 shows the difference between a wireframe representation and a solid representation.

703

FIGURE 12-1

ⓞ ⓞ ⓞ ⓞ ⓞ ⓞ

*Wireframe vs.
solid object*

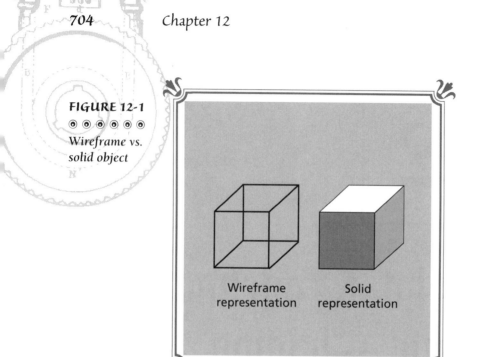

Wireframe
representation

Solid
representation

As far as data structures are concerned, the solid cube in Figure 12-1 is no different than the wireframe cube. The difference lies in the way the cube is rendered. Well, that's not totally true. The objects that are to be drawn as solids also need the structure fields, such as *two_sided*, set properly. Furthermore, we must adhere to some conventions when labeling vertices and polygons so that hidden surface removal and shading can be performed properly.

Vertex Ordering

Probably the most important thing to stabilize right from the beginning is a standard vertex order for all polygons. In other words, when an object is defined by a set of vertices, the polygons that make up the object are generated by listing the vertices in some order. Thus far we haven't really considered the ordering as being important. But in fact, it is. We must select either a *clockwise* or *counterclockwise* order and continue to use this convention throughout the book.

For example, take a look at Figure 12-2, where we see two quadrilaterals in a left-handed system. The quad on the left has its vertices labeled in clockwise order, while the quad on the right has its vertices labeled in counterclockwise order. Both labelings are acceptable, but we are going to stick to the labeling on the right or the counterclockwise ordering. Most 3D modelers use this ordering, so we might as well use it to be as standard as possible.

FIGURE 12-2

◎ ◎ ◎ ◎ ◎ ◎

Different polygon labelings

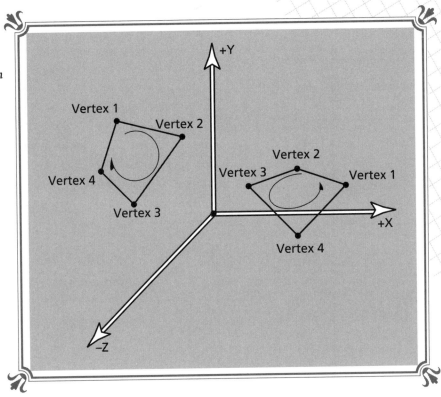

Let's start by modeling a 3D solid on paper and labeling each vertex. Then we'll create a vertex list for each polygon such that the vertices are in counterclockwise order. Take a look at Figure 12-3. Here we see a cylinder made of five faces along with a top and bottom. The vertices are labeled p0 to p9 in a convenient order, and the polygons are all labeled in such a way that the vertices are in counterclockwise order. There is a subtle point here that we need to understand: as long as the vertices are in counterclockwise order, it doesn't matter which order we numerically list them in the PLG file. For example, polygon 0 in Figure 12-3 is defined by the vertex list:

0,1,2,3,4

However, the vertex list

2,3,4,0,1

would work just as well, since the counterclockwise ordering is still in flux. Hence, the counterclockwise property of a vertex list is invariant to rotation of vertex numbers.

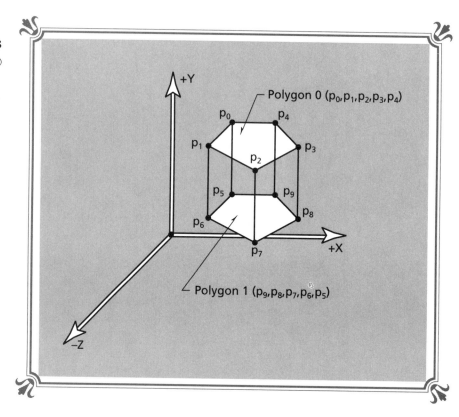

FIGURE 12-3

Vertex numbering an object

Polygon 0 (p_0,p_1,p_2,p_3,p_4)

Polygon 1 (p_9,p_8,p_7,p_6,p_5)

Two-Sided Polygons

We have mentioned the two-sided aspect of a polygon when in a 3D world and have even allocated a field for this case in the object data structure. It's now time to nail down this concept.

The simple cube that we continually use as an example is a perfect illustration of an object that is composed of one-sided polygons. Basically, we don't ever expect to be able to fly into the cube, so the interior sides of the polygons that make up the cube are for all intents and purposes invisible. Thus, if we actually loaded a PLG file that represented a cube, we would probably want to set all the *two_sided* fields of each polygon to *false*. By doing this, fewer calculations must be performed by the 3D engine.

It's easy enough to set the *two_sided* field in each polygon structure to *true* or *false*, but it would be nice if this was part of the PLG file description. To my knowledge it's not; however, this can be easily remedied. We can use one of the bits in the color descriptor to flag whether a polygon is one or two sided and then set the *two_sided* field appropriately in the *PLG_Load_Object()* function. To do this, we would have to rewrite the *PLG_Load_Object()* function and redefine the PLG format to something like "PLX." Hence, we aren't going to do this yet because we may find that there are more details of an object that we will want to include in the modified PLG format. For now the *PLG_Load_Object()* function simply sets all polygons to one-sided by setting the *two_sided* flag to *false*. The bottom line is that I didn't want to show you the standard PLG file format and then change it before you even knew why! However, when we construct the final 3D engine for the game, we will probably add a few tidbits to the PLG format.

At this point, with all polygons defaulting to one-sided, how do we determine which side will be visible?

The Surface Normal of a Polygon and Visibility

Each polygon has an imaginary surface normal that is perpendicular to the plane in which the vertices lie. With a counterclockwise ordering, all surface normals will have the orientation shown in Figure 12-4. This is obtained by using the left-hand rule, which states: if you take your left hand and roll your fingers from vertex to vertex in counterclockwise order, your thumb will point in a direction perpendicular to the plane of the vertices and in the direction of the "outward" normal. Thus, each polygon that is one-sided will only be visible from the outward direction—that is, looking toward the initial point of the "outward" normal.

FIGURE 12-4
◉ ◉ ◉ ◉ ◉ ◉

The normal of a polygon in a left-handed system

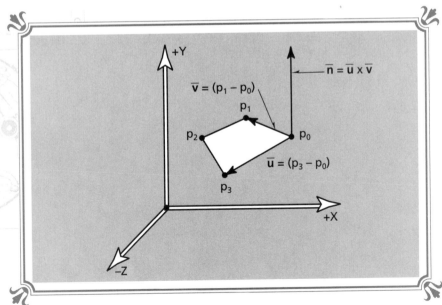

Later when we fully implement two-sided polygons, this won't matter, and the polygon will be visible from both the outward normal direction and the opposite direction (inward normal). However, we must still order the polygon's vertices in the correct manner because the shading engine will count on the specific counter-clockwise ordering.

Concave and Convex Polygons

Before we move on to defining some more mathematical properties of polygons, let's stop for a moment and review the concepts of concave and convex. Figure 12-5 shows two polygons, one convex and one concave. The convex polygon has no dents, while the concave polygon does. This difference is extremely important when rendering polygons. Concave polygons are much more difficult to draw than convex ones. Moreover, concave polygons can actually turn in on themselves and become almost impossible to interpret.

For these reasons and others, such as speed, we are only going to allow convex polygons in representations of objects for our engine. And this has already been implied by the *MAX_POINTS_PER_POLY* constant in the BLACK11.H header file. As a matter of fact, there are a few constraints that have already been put on the engine at this early time. Here are some important constants that we should review:

```
#define MAX_POINTS_PER_POLY      4    // a maximum of four points per poly
#define MAX_VERTICES_PER_OBJECT 32    // this should be enough
#define MAX_POLYS_PER_OBJECT    16    // this will have to do!
```

FIGURE 12-5

◉ ◉ ◉ ◉ ◉ ◉

Concave and convex polygons

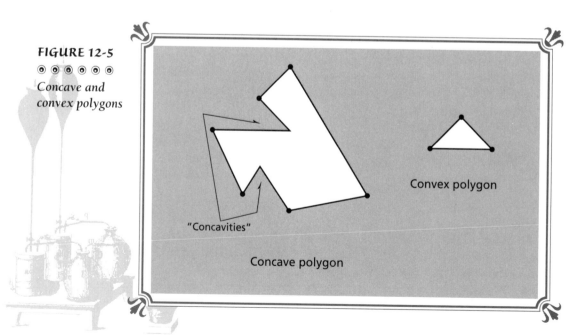

"Concavities"

Convex polygon

Concave polygon

```
#define MAX_OBJECTS            32   // maximum number of objects in world
#define MAX_POLYS_PER_FRAME    128  // maximum number of polys in a single
                                    // animation frame
```

In general, all objects can have up to 32 vertices and 16 polygons. Of course, we can change this simply by changing these constants, but then more memory will be used by each object since the arrays are statically allocated no matter how big or small the objects are. A more memory efficient method would be to use pointers, but at this time let's not make the engine more complex than it needs to be.

Anyway, with three or four vertices per polygon, the only possible shapes are triangles and quadrilaterals, which by definition are always convex, so we have satisfied our convexity requirement.

The Plane Equation of a Polygon

Many of the computations performed by a 3D graphics engine need to know something about the *plane equation* of each polygon or, to be more precise, the plane in which the vertices of any given polygon lie. In Figure 12-6, for example, the poly-

FIGURE 12-6

◉ ◉ ◉ ◉ ◉ ◉

Polygons that have coplanar vertices lie in a single plane

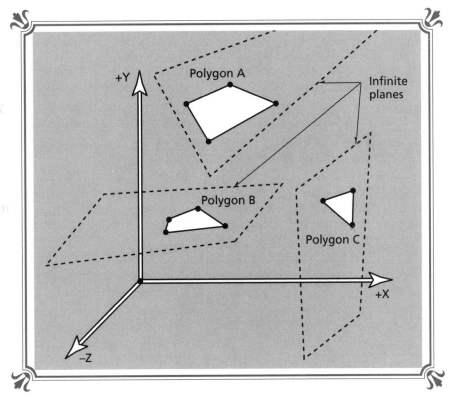

gons a, b, and c all lie in specific planes. We have already seen that the surface normal of a polygon is necessary for back-face removal and shading. Moreover, the plane equation can be useful for advanced rendering and more exotic hidden surface ordering algorithms such as the *Binary Space Partition*. Therefore, let's review how to obtain the plane equation of any polygon.

The general plane equation looks like this:

Ax+By+Cz+D=0

One way to obtain an equation of this form is to use the dot product, which states: if any two vectors are perpendicular, then their dot product must be zero. So, here's the trick—we are going to find a vector that lies in the plane of the polygon that we are trying to determine, and then we are going to compute the dot product of that vector with the normal vector of the polygon. The result will have the form of the above equation, and presto, we are done!

As an example, take a look at Figure 12-7. It depicts a polygon made of four vertices. The normal to the polygon is computed by computing the cross product of **u** and **v**. At this point we have all we need to define a plane. We are going to obtain the plane equation by means of a preliminary form called the point-normal form, which is based on the dot product we spoke of. The equation looks like

Nx*(x–xo)+Ny*(y–yo)+Nz*(z–zo)=0

where <Nx,Ny,Nz> is normal to the polygon or plane and (xo,yo,zo) is a point on the plane. Multiplying the equation out, we get:

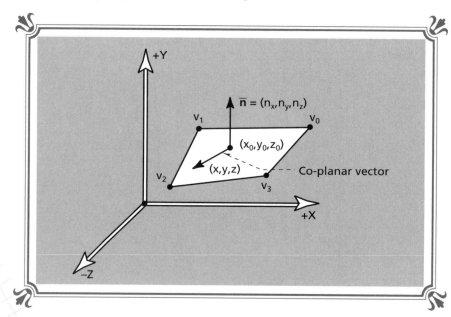

$$Nx*x+Ny*y+Nz*z+(-Nx*xo-Ny*yo-Nz*zp)=0$$

Hence, A=Nx, B=Ny, C=Nz, and D=(-Nx*xo-Ny*yo-Nz*zp).

Once we have derived the plane equation (in either of the forms), we can use it for many different things. One use is in computing the z value for any given (x,y) coordinate pair within the polygon. This is part of the hidden surface removal technique (actually a rendering technique) called the Z-buffer. In any case, the plane equation of a polygon is just about all we need, along with the vertices of the polygon, to perform all the tasks necessary in a 3D engine.

Building Objects from Triangles and Quadrilaterals

Creating 3D solid models is difficult to say the least. First off, 2D paper and tools are always cumbersome and hard to work with. You might think that limiting ourselves to triangles and quadrilaterals makes this difficult task even harder. For example, the object shown in Figure 12-8 is a six-sided cylinder or a hexagonal solid. The natural selection for the sides is quadrilaterals, and the top and bottom face would be easily defined as hexagons, but this is an impossibility since we don't support them. So what can we do to solve this little problem?

FIGURE 12-8

◉ ◉ ◉ ◉ ◉ ◉

An object that contains polygons with more than four sides

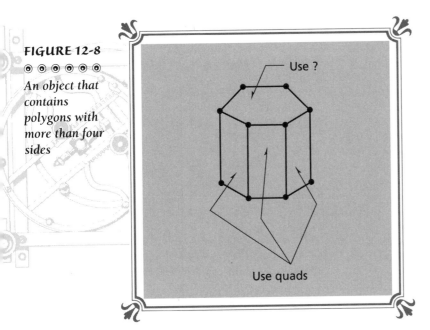

Use ?

Use quads

The answer is to use triangles, as shown in Figure 12-9. The figure uses quads for the sides, but the top and bottom of the hexagonal cylinder are made of triangles. This may seem inefficient, but trust me, in the end, triangles are the most efficient primitives to use for modeling and rendering. Furthermore, modeling with triangles keeps you out of trouble and avoids many pitfalls that occur when modeling with higher sided primitives. This tip comes from one of the world's foremost 3D modeling experts, Josh White, so it's as good as law!

Of course, if your modeling package supports multisided polygons, and you just can't live without it, then you can always write a preprocessor that triangulates your models for you. For example, a triangulator program may take as input an object or stream of polygons and output another object or polygon stream that is composed solely of triangles. Figure 12-10 shows such a filter. Using a technique like this, the polygon engine will always be presented with triangles even though the modeling was done with general N-sided polygons.

Filled Polygons

We are just about ready to rewrite the object drawing function and render solid objects instead of wireframe ones. However, one thing stands between us and total domination of Cyberspace, and that's filling the polygons! We have seen how to draw bitmaps, but we haven't even attempted to fill a polygon, even simple polygons such as triangles and quads. This filling process can be done in a number of

FIGURE 12-9

The cylinder after triangulation

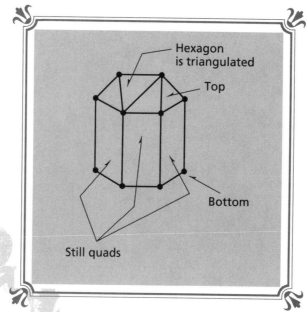

FIGURE 12-10
◉ ◉ ◉ ◉ ◉ ◉
*Polygon
triangulation
software filter*

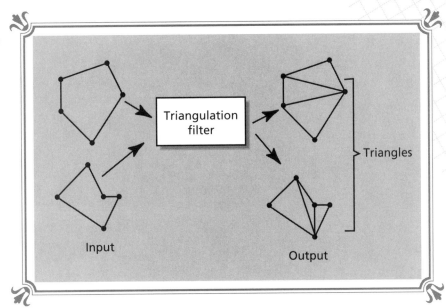

ways. The first way is to use a method called *flood filling*, which uses recursion to "flood" a polygon with color.

Flood filling is commonly used in painting programs to fill a region. However, it is far too slow and memory intensive for a real-time polygon engine. The second method of polygon filling is called *scan conversion* and is intimately connected to the raster architecture of the video screen. It works on the premise that at some point the final rendered polygon (triangle or quad) is going to be drawn on the actual raster video screen. However, if we analyze the polygon on the screen, we quickly come to the conclusion that it is nothing more than a vertical series of lines, each of some given width. This is the basis of scan conversion, which uses this insight to draw polygons as a series of horizontal strips.

Scan Conversion

Scan conversion is a mathematical method of breaking down a polygon into a set of rows of pixels that can be easily rendered on the video screen (see Figure 12-11). The question is, how do we scan-convert a polygon? Scan conversion is accomplished by orienting the polygon to be scan-converted in such a way that the vertices are in order of increasing y. Figure 12-12 shows a typical triangle to be scan-converted. Notice that the triangle has two distinct regions to be filled: the upper half and the lower half.

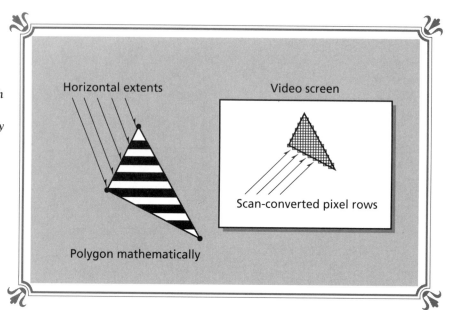

Let's begin with the upper half. All we need to do is compute the pixel coordinates for the left edge and right edge of the two lines emanating from the topmost vertex. Then if we draw horizontal lines between the points along the edges, the triangle will be filled from top to bottom. How do we find these points along the edges? The key is to use the line equations of the edges of the triangle. Referring to Figure 12-12, we see that there are line equations for the left and right edges of the triangle.

We want to use these formulas in a way that is both efficient and fast. In addition, we would like to manipulate them into a form that is incremental or, in other words, is based on some prior knowledge that y is going to change by a constant amount every iteration (one scan line). Let's begin our manipulations and see if we can't satisfy all of these requirements. The equations for the left and right lines of the triangle in Figure 12-12 are as follows:

For the leftmost line:
$m\_left * (x\_left - xo) = (y\_left - yo)$
$m_left = $ slope of left line $ = (y_left - yo)/(x_left - xo)$

For the rightmost line:
$m\_right * (x\_right - xo) = (y\_right - yo)$
$m_right = $ slope of right line $ = (y2 - yo)/(x2 - xo)$

Let's analyze the leftmost line equations and see what they mean. The equation reads in English, "the slope of the line times the change in x is equal to the change in y." However, since we want to draw lines in a scan-line order, that is, row by row, we would much rather have an equation that is in the form:

FIGURE 12-12

⊙ ⊙ ⊙ ⊙ ⊙ ⊙

Computing the line equations of a triangle

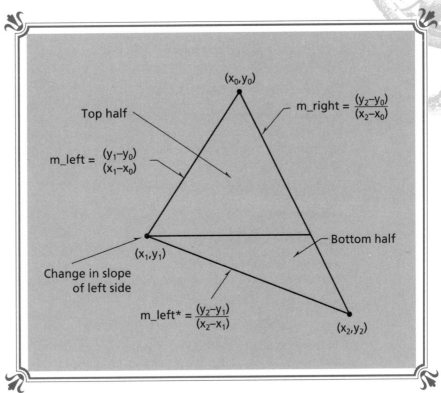

$$(x\_left - xo) = m\_left^{-1} * (y\_left - yo)$$

This states that the change in x is equal to the inverse of the slope times the change in y. Now we are getting somewhere. If we wrote a piece of code that had a *for* loop in y, then we could solve for the x of the line each iteration, like this:

$$x\_left = m\_left^{-1} * (y\_left - yo) + xo$$

Placing this into a loop and performing the same logic to the right line, we would end up with something like this:

```
for (y=yo; y<=y1; y++)
    {
    x_left  = m_left_inv*(y yo) + xo
    x_right = m_right_inv*(y yo) + xo

    // Draw a horizontal line from x_left to x_right at the vertical position of y

    } // end for y
```

That is basically the technique used to draw a triangle. However, there are optimizations we can make. First, we might be tempted to use fixed point math.

However, we are going to forego that optimization to keep things simple. The main optimization we are interested in is determining an incremental method of computing x_left and x_right each iteration. Here's how we do that.

Let's begin with the equation for x_left:

$$x\_left = m\_left^{-1}*(y-yo)+xo$$

Now let's compute the forward difference for y+1. In other words, since we know that y only changes by 1 each iteration, let's see what the difference is in the equation from vertical line to vertical line. To do this, we simply replace y by y+1 and simplify:

$$x\_left = m\_left^{-1}*((y+1)-yo)+xo$$

After simplifying, we get:

$$x\_left = m\_left^{-1}*(y-yo)+xo+m\_left^{-1}$$

Interesting! It looks like the left portion of the simplified equation is the same as we would find for y. Thus, we can conclude that each time we change y by 1 (that is, increment y), the x_left changes by m_left^{-1} or, mathematically,

$$x\_left_{i+1} = x\_left_i + m\_left^{-1}$$

which states that the i+1th value of x_left is equal to the ith + the inverse of the slope. Hence, we have derived an incremental algorithm to compute the values of x_left as a function of y. The same logic can be performed on x_right, and the results are:

$$x\_right = m\_right^{-1}*(y-yo)+xo+m\_right^{-1}$$
$$x\_right_{i+1} = x\_right_i + m\_right^{-1}$$

In essence, we can perform two additions each iteration of y to recompute the position of x_left and x_right and then draw the horizontal line between them. Using this technique, we can scan-convert the triangles at warp speed, and that's what we want!

Drawing Triangles

Although the preceding mathematical analysis is perfectly correct and works, the fact is that implementing algorithms and deriving them are two different ball games. To actually draw a triangle, we must take a lot of factors into consideration that we assumed for the analysis. For example, we assumed that the vertices were in a nice order from top to bottom and in a counterclockwise order. This may not always be true; thus, we may have to sort them to make sure that the vertices are in a known state.

Also, triangles may look simple enough, but there are a few details that we must consider in order to be complete. Figure 12-13 shows three cases of triangles. The first triangle is called *flat top* since the top of it is flat; the second type of triangle is called *flat bottom*; and the third is called *general*. The first and second types must be handled by separate sections of code. And the third type of triangle must be handled by breaking it into a flat top and flat bottom triangle.

Of course, we can simply write one all-encompassing triangle function that processes any triangle, but there are pros and cons to this. The main disadvantage can be seen in Figure 12-14. Here we have a general triangle. Imagine that we have scan-converted the portion that is filled in. Now we must continue to scan-convert the remainder of the triangle, but there is a bit of a problem. We see that the left edge of the triangle changes slope during the scan. So, what do we do? Should we place an *if* statement that tests for this as the triangle is being drawn? Should we break the triangle into two loops? Performing the first test is too slow, and if we do the latter, we are back to drawing two triangles.

Also, we must consider rendering details such as clipping, which we haven't even spoken about. In the end, breaking triangles into a top and bottom half seems to work the best, so we'll stick to that. It looks like we should write a function with the following properties:

1. The function is sent a raw triangle as input and sorts the vertices in the y direction.

FIGURE 12-13

Three cases of triangles

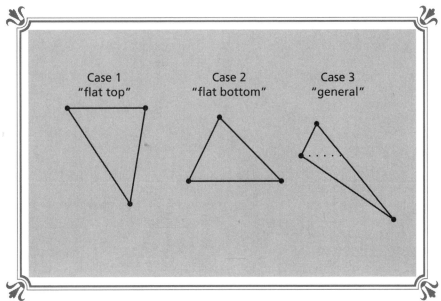

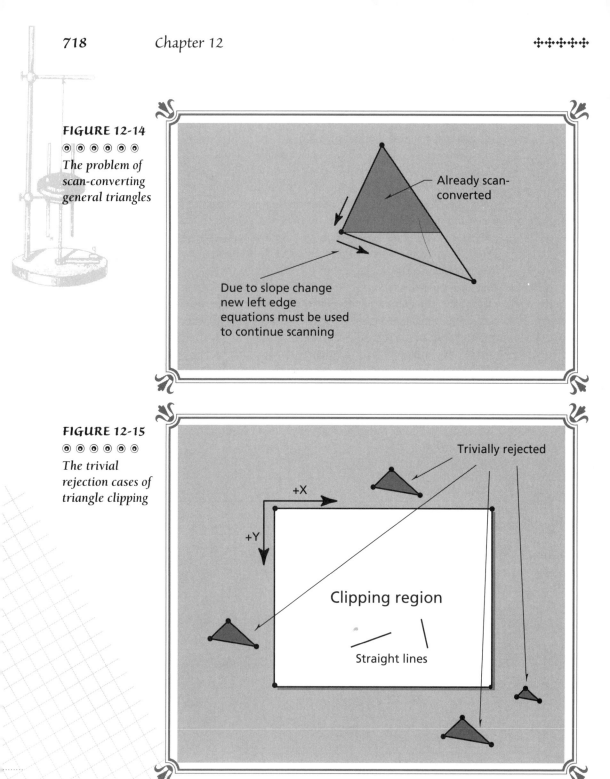

FIGURE 12-14

◉ ◉ ◉ ◉ ◉ ◉

The problem of scan-converting general triangles

Already scan-converted

Due to slope change new left edge equations must be used to continue scanning

FIGURE 12-15

◉ ◉ ◉ ◉ ◉ ◉

The trivial rejection cases of triangle clipping

Trivially rejected

+X

+Y

Clipping region

Straight lines

2. The function then performs a bit of object space clipping and determines if all the vertices are beyond the clipping region, as shown in Figure 12-15. This is called *trivial rejection*.

3. Next, the function determines if the triangle has a flat top or bottom and calls the appropriate subfunction.

4. Finally, if the triangle is general—that is, lacking a flat top or bottom—then the triangle is broken into two halves, one that has a flat top and one that has a flat bottom. Then each half is drawn with a call to each of the subfunctions.

Clipping should also be performed somewhere, but we'll get to that a bit later. At this point, let's take a look at Listing 12-1, the master triangle function that performs the above tasks.

LISTING 12-1 The main triangle rendering function

```
void Draw_Triangle_2D(int x1,int y1, int x2,int y2,int x3,int y3,int color)
{
// this function draws a triangle on the screen

int temp_x, // temporaries used for sorting
    temp_y,
    new_x;

// test for h lines and v lines
if ((x1==x2 && x2==x3)  ||  (y1==y2 && y2==y3))
    return;

// sort p1,p2,p3 in ascending y order
if (y2<y1)
    {
    temp_x = x2;
    temp_y = y2;
    x2     = x1;
    y2     = y1;
    x1     = temp_x;
    y1     = temp_y;
    } // end if

// now we know that p1 and p2 are in order
if (y3<y1)
    {
    temp_x = x3;
    temp_y = y3;
    x3     = x1;
    y3     = y1;
    x1     = temp_x;
    y1     = temp_y;
    } // end if
```

continued on next page

continued from previous page

```
// finally test y3 against y2
if (y3<y2)
   {
   temp_x = x3;
   temp_y = y3;
   x3     = x2;
   y3     = y2;
   x2     = temp_x;
   y2     = temp_y;
   } // end if

// do trivial rejection tests
if ( y3<poly_clip_min_y || y1>poly_clip_max_y ||
    (x1<poly_clip_min_x && x2<poly_clip_min_x && x3<poly_clip_min_x) ||
    (x1>poly_clip_max_x && x2>poly_clip_max_x && x3>poly_clip_max_x) )
   return;

// test if top of triangle is flat
if (y1==y2)
   {
   Draw_Top_Triangle(x1,y1,x2,y2,x3,y3,color);
   } // end if
else
if (y2==y3)
   {
   Draw_Bottom_Triangle(x1,y1,x2,y2,x3,y3,color);
   } // end if bottom is flat
else
   {
   // general triangle that needs to be broken up along long edge
   new_x = x1 + (int)((float)(y2-y1)*(float)(x3-x1)/(float)(y3-y1));

   // draw each sub-triangle
   Draw_Bottom_Triangle(x1,y1,new_x,y2,x2,y2,color);
   Draw_Top_Triangle(x2,y2,new_x,y2,x3,y3,color);

   } // end else

} // end Draw_Triangle_2D
```

The function *Draw_Triangle_2D()* takes as parameters the (x,y) coordinates of the three points that make up the triangle to be rendered along with the color of the triangle. Note that the order of the vertices isn't important since the function sorts them in y ascending order. The function performs the tasks that we outlined almost verbatim. The only part of the code that may seem a bit mysterious is the triangle splitter at the end of the function. In general, the splitter simply uses the three slopes of the triangle, along with the knowledge of the triangle's vertical extents, to compute the points of the subtriangles. Then these points are passed to the rendering functions, and two simpler triangles are drawn that compose the larger, more complex one.

The code for each function that draws the flat top triangle and flat bottom triangle is almost identical except for the computation of the initial left and right edge slopes. The version that draws a flat bottom triangle uses the same initial point, whereas the code that draws triangles with flat tops uses the same terminal points for each line. Anyway, Listings 12-2 and 12-3 contain the triangle scan converters.

LISTING 12-2 Flat top triangle drawing function

```
void Draw_Top_Triangle(int x1,int y1, int x2,int y2, int x3,int y3,int color)
{
// this function draws a triangle that has a flat top

float dx_right,      // the dx/dy ratio of the right edge of line
      dx_left,       // the dx/dy ratio of the left edge of line
      xs,xe,         // the starting and ending points of the edges
      height;        // the height of the triangle

int temp_x,         // used during sorting as temps
    temp_y,
    right,          // used by clipping
    left;

unsigned char far *dest_addr;

// test order of x1 and x2
if (x2 < x1)
   {
   temp_x = x2;
   x2     = x1;
   x1     = temp_x;

   } // end if swap

// compute delta's
height = y3-y1;

dx_left  = (x3-x1)/height;
dx_right = (x3-x2)/height;

// set starting points
xs = (float)x1;
xe = (float)x2+(float)0.5;

// perform y clipping
if (y1<poly_clip_min_y)
   {
   // compute new xs and ys
   xs = xs+dx_left*(float)(-y1+poly_clip_min_y);
   xe = xe+dx_right*(float)(-y1+poly_clip_min_y);

   // reset y1
```

continued on next page

continued from previous page

```c
        y1=poly_clip_min_y;

    } // end if top is off screen

if (y3>poly_clip_max_y)
    y3=poly_clip_max_y;

// compute starting address in video memory
dest_addr = double_buffer+(y1<<8)+(y1<<6);

// test if x clipping is needed
if (x1>=poly_clip_min_x && x1<=poly_clip_max_x &&
    x2>=poly_clip_min_x && x2<=poly_clip_max_x &&
    x3>=poly_clip_min_x && x3<=poly_clip_max_x)
    {
    // draw the triangle
    for (temp_y=y1; temp_y<=y3; temp_y++,dest_addr+=320)
        {
         Triangle_Line(dest_addr,(unsigned int)xs,
                    (unsigned int)xe,color);

         //_fmemset((unsigned char far *)dest_addr+(unsigned int)xs,
         //         color,
         //         (unsigned int)(xe-xs));

         // adjust starting point and ending point
         xs+=dx_left;
         xe+=dx_right;

         } // end for

    } // end if no x clipping needed
else
    {
    // clip x axis with slower version

    // draw the triangle
    for (temp_y=y1; temp_y<=y3; temp_y++,dest_addr+=320)
        {
        // do x clip
        left  = (int)xs;
        right = (int)xe;

        // adjust starting point and ending point
        xs+=dx_left;
        xe+=dx_right;

        // clip line
        if (left < poly_clip_min_x)
            {
            left = poly_clip_min_x;
```

```
         if (right < poly_clip_min_x)
            continue;
         }

      if (right > poly_clip_max_x)
         {
         right = poly_clip_max_x;

         if (left > poly_clip_max_x)
            continue;
         }

       Triangle_Line(dest_addr,(unsigned int)left,(unsigned int)right,color);

      //_fmemset((unsigned char far *)dest_addr+(unsigned int)left,
      //         color,
      //         (unsigned int)(right-left));

      } // end for

   } // end else x clipping needed

} // end Draw_Top_Triangle
```

LISTING 12-3 Flat bottom triangle drawing function

```
void Draw_Bottom_Triangle(int x1,int y1, int x2,int y2, int x3,int y3,int color)
{
// this function draws a triangle that has a flat bottom

float dx_right,    // the dx/dy ratio of the right edge of line
      dx_left,     // the dx/dy ratio of the left edge of line
      xs,xe,       // the starting and ending points of the edges
      height;      // the height of the triangle

int temp_x,        // used during sorting as temps
    temp_y,
    right,         // used by clipping
    left;

unsigned char far *dest_addr;

// test order of x1 and x2
if (x3 < x2)
   {
   temp_x = x2;
   x2     = x3;
   x3     = temp_x;

   } // end if swap
```

continued on next page

continued from previous page

```
// compute delta's
height = y3-y1;

dx_left  = (x2-x1)/height;
dx_right = (x3-x1)/height;

// set starting points
xs = (float)x1;
xe = (float)x1+(float)0.5;

// perform y clipping
if (y1<poly_clip_min_y)
   {
   // compute new xs and ys
   xs = xs+dx_left*(float)(-y1+poly_clip_min_y);
   xe = xe+dx_right*(float)(-y1+poly_clip_min_y);

   // reset y1
   y1=poly_clip_min_y;

   } // end if top is off screen

if (y3>poly_clip_max_y)
   y3=poly_clip_max_y;

// compute starting address in video memory
dest_addr = double_buffer+(y1<<8)+(y1<<6);

// test if x clipping is needed
if (x1>=poly_clip_min_x && x1<=poly_clip_max_x &&
    x2>=poly_clip_min_x && x2<=poly_clip_max_x &&
    x3>=poly_clip_min_x && x3<=poly_clip_max_x)
   {
   // draw the triangle
   for (temp_y=y1; temp_y<=y3; temp_y++,dest_addr+=320)
      {
      Triangle_Line(dest_addr,(unsigned int)xs,(unsigned int)xe,color);

      //_fmemset((unsigned char far *)dest_addr+(unsigned int)xs,
      //         color,
      //         (unsigned int)(xe-xs));

      // adjust starting point and ending point
      xs+=dx_left;
      xe+=dx_right;

      } // end for

   } // end if no x clipping needed
else
   {
   // clip x axis with slower version
```

```
// draw the triangle
for (temp_y=y1; temp_y<=y3; temp_y++,dest_addr+=320)
    {
    // do x clip

    left  = (int)xs;
    right = (int)xe;

    // adjust starting point and ending point
    xs+=dx_left;
    xe+=dx_right;

    // clip line
    if (left < poly_clip_min_x)
        {
        left = poly_clip_min_x;

        if (right < poly_clip_min_x)
            continue;
        }

    if (right > poly_clip_max_x)
        {
        right = poly_clip_max_x;

        if (left > poly_clip_max_x)
            continue;
        }

    Triangle_Line(dest_addr,(unsigned int)left,(unsigned int)right,color);

    //_fmemset((unsigned char far *)dest_addr+(unsigned int)left,
    //          color,
    //          (unsigned int)(right-left));

    } // end for

} // end else x clipping needed

} // end Draw_Bottom_Triangle
```

Notice that both functions have identical interfaces to the master function *Draw_Triangle_2D()*. You might think that this is overkill since we know that the y coordinate of two of the vertices is the same, and hence, there is no need to send it twice. This is true, but in the pursuit of simplicity for illustrative purposes, I decided to keep the interfaces the same. So sue me!

Both functions use the incremental technique that we spoke of earlier and basically draw the triangle by iterating on y and updating the left and right points of the next horizontal line to be drawn. The code that performs the update is simply:

```
// adjust starting point and ending point

        xs+=dx_left;
        xe+=dx_right;
```

Then each horizontal line is drawn at y between xs and xe. Now if you take a look at the code, you will notice that there is a piece of it commented out in a few places. This piece looks like,

```
//_fmemset((unsigned char far *)dest_addr+(unsigned int)xs,
//          color,
//          (unsigned int)(xe-xs));
```

which is how the horizontal lines are drawn for the most part.

However, as we know, the *memset()* functions only work on bytes; therefore, nearly a 100 percent speed increase can be made by writing WORDS. To do this, we must use inline assembly language. This is exactly what the function *Triangle_Line()* is for. Basically, it is a very fast horizontal line renderer that draws two pixels at a time. Although this may seem simple to implement, there are a few pitfalls that we must watch out for. For example, if we simply use a *STOSW* command and blast out a horizontal line, what if the line is a single pixel? What if the line doesn't have an even number of pixels?

These kinds of questions must be addressed in a preprocessing section of the code that takes care of those cases. Once those cases have been handled, the function should compute the longest stretch of the line that can be drawn with *WORD*s and then draw it. The source to the *Triangle_Line()* is shown in Listing 12-4.

LISTING 12-4 A fast horizontal line renderer used for scan-converting triangles

```
void Triangle_Line(unsigned char far *dest_addr,
                   unsigned int xs,
                   unsigned int xe,
                   int color)
{
// this function draws a fast horizontal line by using WORD size writes
// its speed can be doubled by use of an external 32 bit DWORD version in
// assembly...

// plot pixels at ends of line first
if (xs & 0x0001)
   {
   // plot a single starting pixel and move xs to an even boundary
   dest_addr[xs++] = (unsigned char)color;
   } // end if

if (!(xe & 0x0001))
   {
```

```
    // plot a single terminating pixel and move xe back to an odd boundary
    dest_addr[xe--] = (unsigned char)color;
    } // end if

// now plot the line
dest_addr+=xs;

// now blast the middle part of the line a WORD at a time, later use
// an external assembly program to do it a DOUBLE WORD at a time!

_asm
    {
    les di,dest_addr        ; point es:di at data area
    mov al,BYTE PTR color   ; move into al and ah the color
    mov ah,al

    mov cx,xe               ; compute number of words to move  (xe-xs+1)/2
    sub cx,xs
    inc cx
    shr cx,1                ; divide by 2

    rep stosw               ; draw the line

    } // end asm

} // end Triangle_Line
```

As you can see, the initial overhead of the function is due to the determination of the endpoints of the line. Once that has been taken care of, inline assembly is used to blast the rest of the line. Of course, you might ask, why not use double *WORD* writes to the double buffer? We can, but the inline assemblers don't support it, so we will have to either manually insert opcodes into the C code or use external assembler modules. We will take up these issues at the end of the book, when we perform the final optimizations on the 3D engine.

Clipping the Triangles

Now that we have all the components of the triangle scan converter, let's take a look at exactly how and when the clipping is performed. The clipping that is implemented by the triangle functions is really a mixture of object space and image space clipping. If you recall, object space clipping means to clip an object in mathematical space at the geometric level. Image space clipping means to filter out portions of the image (usually at the pixel level) from the final rendered image. Our triangle functions do a bit of both.

The first and most important clipping is performed in the main *Draw_Triangle_2D()* function. Here, triangles that have degenerated into straight lines, along with triangles that are completely beyond the 2D clipping region, are rejected. This was shown in Figure 12-15. Then as the triangles are drawn, the following tests are made. First, the y extents of the triangle are used to recompute the portion of the triangle that is visible. For example, if a triangle is to be drawn from –20 to 50 on the Y axis, then this is clipped so that the y loop that iterates through the horizontal lines only processes lines 0 to 50.

The horizontal clipping is done in two phases. Take a look at Figure 12-16. Here we see two possible triangles. Regardless of their y position or generality, obviously, the one on the left must be clipped to the left edge of the clipping region, while the rightmost triangle needs no clipping at all. Therefore, in the quest for speed and efficiency, the triangle drawing functions test to see if a triangle is partially visible. If it is, then one portion of the code draws the triangle and clips the x coordinates during rasterization a line at a time. On the other hand, if the triangle is totally visible as far as the x extents are concerned, then yet another portion of the code draws the triangle without any horizontal clipping at all. This way we get the best of both worlds—clipping is only performed when necessary.

Testing for all these cases results in more code to do the rendering, but it's well worth the speed (many times, longer programs are faster because of special casing). If we always clipped and didn't take any of the geometric qualities of the triangle into consideration, then triangles that didn't need clipping at all would pay the same price as triangles that did need clipping. And considering that only 20 to 30 percent of the polygons rendered at any time will be clipped, this isn't worth it.

FIGURE 12-16

◎ ◎ ◎ ◎ ◎ ◎

Two cases of horizontal clipping

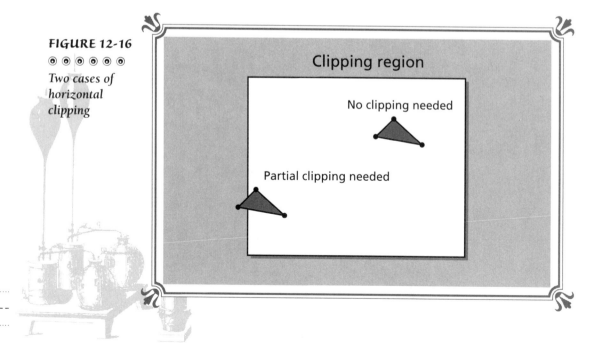

Clipping region

No clipping needed

Partial clipping needed

As a demonstration of the triangle drawing functions, the following demo, TRIDEMO.EXE, draws triangles onto the video screen at random locations with random colors. The source code for TRIDEMO.EXE is TRIDEMO.C and is shown in Listing 12-5.

LISTING 12-5 Demo of the triangle functions

```
// I N C L U D E S ///////////////////////////////////////////////////////////

#include <io.h>
#include <conio.h>
#include <stdio.h>
#include <stdlib.h>
#include <dos.h>
#include <bios.h>
#include <fcntl.h>
#include <memory.h>
#include <malloc.h>
#include <math.h>
#include <string.h>

// include all of our stuff

#include "black3.h"
#include "black4.h"
#include "black5.h"
#include "black6.h"
#include "black8.h"
#include "black9.h"
#include "black11.h"

// M A I N ////////////////////////////////////////////////////////////////////

void main(void)
{
int done=0;            // exit flag

// set graphics mode to 13h
Set_Graphics_Mode(GRAPHICS_MODE13);

// point double buffer to video buffer since the triangle function
// only writes to the double buffer and we want to see it doing the
// writing
double_buffer = video_buffer;

// main loop
while(!kbhit())
    {
    // draw a triangle somewhere on the screen

    Draw_Triangle_2D(rand()%320,rand()%200,
```

continued on next page

continued from previous page

```
                          rand()%320,rand()%200,
                          rand()%320,rand()%200,
                          rand()%256);

        } // end while

// restore text mode
Set_Graphics_Mode(TEXT_MODE);

} // end main
```

The demo consists of no more than a call to the *Draw_Triangle_2D()* function with some random values for the vertices. If you wish to create your own EXE, make sure to include the module BLACK11.C from the previous chapter.

Drawing Quads

We have also agreed to support quadrilaterals or "quads" as primitives used in our models; however, how are we going to draw these? The answer is, we are going to manually triangulate them at run time. This means that whenever we want to draw a quad that is made up of vertices p0,p1,p2,p3, we are simply going to make two calls to the *Draw_Triangle_2D()* function: one call with the vertices p0,p1,p2 and one call with p0,p2,p3. This is shown in Figure 12-17.

Using this technique, we can easily support quads. In fact, we could support multisided objects, but then the efficiency of the triangle primitive would be lost. Quads are important for modeling buildings and related structures that have square facets. The only question may be, why not preprocess each quad into a pair of triangles? Because then we would have to perform shading and hidden surface removal on two polygons instead of one! It's better to keep a quad intact until the last moment before it's drawn. Therefore, we aren't going to supply a quad drawing function, we will simply test for a quad in whatever function is drawing the 3D object and make two calls to the triangle function when the time is right.

Lighting Models

We've already discussed lighting, but now it's time to cover exactly how lighting will be implemented in our engine. Before we do this, let's quickly review the different types of lighting models that are available.

Ambient Light

Ambient light is the average lighting or photon energy that exists in a region of space. This is due to light sources, diffuse reflectors, and so on. Usually, ambient lighting is implemented with a single variable in the light model that controls the

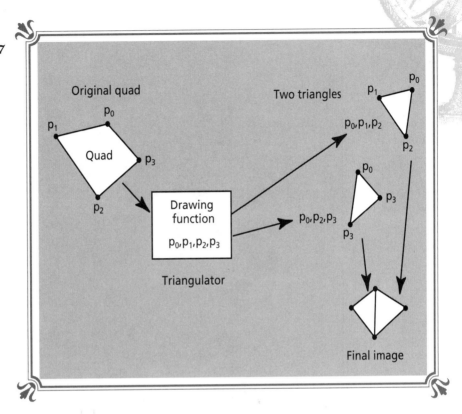

average brightness of all polygons before other light sources are applied. For example, if *final_intensity* is a variable that describes the final intensity of some surface, the ambient light term may be included as follows:

final_intensity=ambient_light_intensity+(intensity due to light sources)

And that's it! Ambient lighting is the easiest light term to include in a lighting model.

Directional Light

Directional light is much like what the sun provides. Take a look at Figure 12-18. The sun is so far away that the rays that strike the Earth are all parallel. Thus, directional lights have rays that are all parallel. Although the rays may have different wavelengths (colors), the rays will all be traveling in the same direction.

Directional lights result in two kinds of reflections: *diffuse* and *specular*. If a surface is totally reflective (like a mirror), then a surface will reflect light in only one direction, which is opposite to the angle of incidence (specular). On the other hand, if a surface is rough, or matte, then the light will scatter in all directions (dif-

FIGURE 12-18

◎ ◎ ◎ ◎ ◎ ◎

Directional lighting

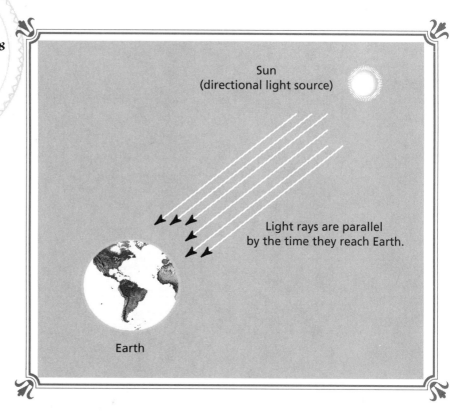

fuse). However, the intensity of the scattered light is still proportional to the angle of incidence. Figure 12-19 shows a directional light source and the properties of the reflected light for both a totally reflective and diffuse reflector.

Our engine is going to use directional lighting, but we aren't going to model the specular components of the light. To minimize calculations, we're only going to model the diffuse component. This component is calculated in the following way: the angle between each surface to be shaded and the light source vector is computed using the dot product, which states that

light_source · normal=|light_source| * |normal| * cos θ

where *light_source* and *normal* are the vectors shown in Figure 12-19.

From the above equation, the amount of light reflecting diffusely from the surface is proportional to the angle; thus, an equation can be derived something like

directional_diffuse_intensity=(cos θ+1)/2.

which results in a range from 0.0 to 1.0, depending on the incident light angle. Then the range of 0.0 to 1.0 can be scaled to 64 shades, or 256 shades, or whatever, using a multiplier.

FIGURE 12-19

⊙ ⊙ ⊙ ⊙ ⊙ ⊙

Reflections of light

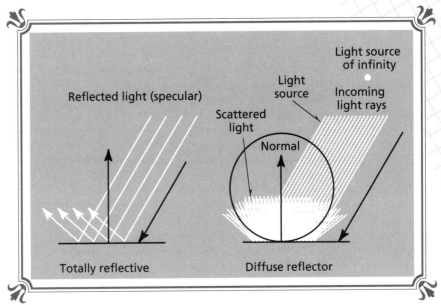

We have been foregoing the wavelength aspect or color of the lights in the model. The reason for this is that we are going to assume that all objects are mathematically white surfaces. The shading calculations will only tell us intensities. These intensities will be used to select a shade of a desired color. This makes the mathematics much easier because, in reality, each material reflects and absorbs each wavelength of light differently. Hence, each of the lighting calculations would have to be performed for red, green, and blue to take into consideration the material properties of the reflector, which we're not going to do!

Moving along, and taking the diffuse intensity into consideration along with the ambient term, we can rewrite the final light intensity for a surface as:

final_intensity = ambient_light_intensity+directional_diffuse_intensity
    + (point light sources)

We will get to the point light sources in a minute, but let's discuss the computational difficulties in finding the directional component of the light. We see that we must compute something like this in the end:

$$\cos \theta = \frac{light\_source \cdot normal}{|light\_source| * |normal|}$$

Computing the normal of the surface is a necessity. However, we can save a little time by precomputing the normals to all surfaces and normalizing them so their length is 1.0. Then the above equation simplifies to:

$$\cos \theta = \frac{\text{light\_source} \cdot \text{normal}}{|\text{light\_source}|}$$

Since the *light_source* is simply a vector such as <lx,ly,lz>, we can normalize it during creation and forget about its length (unless we move the lights). Therefore, the light source vector also will have unit length. Plugging this into the above equation, the final results are:

$$\cos \theta = \frac{\text{light\_source} \cdot \text{normal}}{1} = <lx,ly,lz> \cdot <nx,ny,nz>$$

It looks like all we need to do is compute the dot product between the light source and the normal (which is equivalent to three multiplies) to compute cos θ. That's about as good as it's going to get without resorting to serious tricks. However, that's not bad considering we only need to shade surfaces that are visible, and there will usually only be a few dozen visible surfaces in each frame of our worlds.

It looks like directional lights are very simple to implement, but they aren't as dramatic as point light sources. Let's see what's involved in implementing a point light source.

Point Light Sources

Directional lights are similar to point light sources at infinity. But as a point light source is brought nearer to the object it is illuminating, the directionality of the light source becomes spherical, and we need to perform another step during the shading calculations to compute the intensity of the light falling on the surface. The extra step is a direct result of the fact that the vector from the object's surface to the light source is no longer a constant direction vector. Figure 12-20 shows this situation.

The normal vector of the surface being illuminated is computed in the usual way (or precomputed), but the vector from the surface to the light source and its magnitude must be computed each frame (unless both the light source and the surface are static). Let's take a look at the new process by beginning with computing the vector from the surface being illuminated to the light source. Given that the point light source is at (plx,ply,plz) and a point on the surface being lit is (xo,yo,zo), then the vector from the surface to the light source is:

light_source=<plx–xo, ply–yp, plz–zo>

The problem is that, in order to compute cos θ, we need the length of *light_source* to plug into the denominator of the equation:

$$\cos \theta = \frac{\text{light\_source} \cdot \text{normal}}{|\text{light\_source}|}$$

FIGURE 12-20

◎ ◎ ◎ ◎ ◎ ◎

Point light source calculations

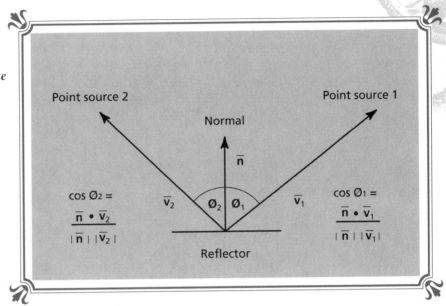

And finding the length of *light_source* means using a square root function, since the length of a vector is equal to the square of the sum of the squares of its components. In this case, we would have to compute:

$$|\text{light\_source}| = \text{sqrt}(\,(plx-xo)^2 + (ply-yp)^2 + (plz-zo)^2\,)$$

And taking a *sqrt()* is like taking a vacation in computer time!

Fortunately, there are mathematical tricks and methods to perform fast square roots and even approximations to the square root. But we're going to keep things simple and stick to directional lights or point light sources at infinity for our engine.

Building a Flat Shader

To tell you the truth, there's not much to building a flat shader. We have already seen the individual components more than once. It's just a matter of putting everything together. Let's begin by recalling a few points that might be a source of confusion. First, when the function *PLG_Load_Object()* (from Chapter 11) loads an object, each polygon is processed and the normal is computed. However, instead of storing the normal, only its length is stored. This length can be found in the *normal_length* field of the polygon structure. The precomputed *normal_length* will be used during the calculation of light reflecting off each polygon due to the directional light source.

Now, for proper shading to take place, we must have a reasonable palette to shade with! This is one of those little details that has to be taken care of, so I generated one. The palette is named STANDARD.PAL and consists of 16 shades of various colors along with the standard EGA palette in the first 16 positions of the palette. My palette is loaded from disk with the function *Load_Palette_Disk()*, which is shown in Listing 12-6.

LISTING 12-6 Function that loads a color palette from disk

```c
int Load_Palette_Disk(char *filename, RGB_palette_ptr the_palette)
{
// this function loads a color palette from disk
int index; // used for looping
RGB_color color;
FILE *fp;

// open the disk file
if (!(fp = fopen(filename,"r")))
   return(0);

// load in all the colors
for (index=0; index<=255; index++)
   {
   // get the next color
   fscanf(fp,"%d %d %d",&color.red,&color.green,&color.blue);

   // store the color in next element of palette
   the_palette->colors[index].red   = color.red;
   the_palette->colors[index].green = color.green;
   the_palette->colors[index].blue  = color.blue;

   } // end for index

// set palette size to a full palette
the_palette->start_reg = 0;
the_palette->end_reg   = 255;

// close the file and return success
fclose(fp);

return(1);

} // end Load_Palette_Disk
```

The function takes as a parameter the name of the disk file that contains the color palette to load along with a pointer to an *RGB_palette* structure to store it in. The file format for the palette is:

$$R_0 \ G_0 \ B_0$$
$$R_1 \ G_1 \ B_1$$

$$.$$
$$.$$
$$.$$

$$R_{255} \ G_{255} \ B_{255}$$

Note that there are no commas. Also, the system does not perform scaling; thus, the values must each range from 0 to 63.

To be consistent and orthogonal, there is also a function that saves an *RGB_palette* to disk. It is called *Save_Palette_Disk()* and is shown in Listing 12-7.

LISTING 12-7 Function that saves a color palette to disk

```
int Save_Palette_Disk(char *filename, RGB_palette_ptr the_palette)
{
// this function saves a palette to disk

int index; // used for looping
RGB_color color;
FILE *fp;

// open the disk file
if (!(fp = fopen(filename,"w")))
   return(0);

// write 255 lines of r g b

for (index=0; index<=255; index++)
    {
    // get the next color

    // store the color in next element of palette
    color.red   = the_palette->colors[index].red;
    color.green = the_palette->colors[index].green;
    color.blue  = the_palette->colors[index].blue;

    // write the color to disk file
    fprintf(fp,"\n%d %d %d",color.red, color.green, color.blue);

    } // end for index

// close the file and return success
fclose(fp);

return(1);

} // end Save_Palette_Disk
```

The function takes as parameters a file name to the destination disk file along with a pointer to an *RGB_palette* structure that has been previously loaded with the system palette. The function then opens the disk file and writes the RGB triples out line-by-line. Hence, you can use this function to store algorithmically generated palettes on disk.

Once we have loaded the palette, we are ready to draw shaded polygons. Now we are getting to the point where the design details of the 3D engine are important, and the decisions we make are going to haunt us forever—so let's make good

decisions! The first decision is that both shading and back-face removal will be performed in the same routine. The reason for this is that we can't recompute surface normals and perform two dot products just to make the code more modular. Hence, the function we're going to see shortly will test whether a surface is visible and shade it if it is.

Since we haven't really discussed back-face removal yet, try to disregard the back-face removal aspect of the function and focus on the shading portion. The light source we're going to use is a single directional light that is normalized. We'll define it as:

```
vector_3d light_source = {-0.913913,0.389759,-0.113369};
```

The values used to initialize it are simply chosen to look good for the demos. They can be changed during run time as long as the resulting *light_source* vector is normalized (that is, its length remains 1.0). Also, there is a little detail that we must consider. The *light_source* vector actually points toward the light source instead of from the light source. This is because when we perform the dot product to compute the light intensity, both vectors (the normal of the surface and the light source vector) must be pointing outward. Of course, we could flip the sign in the computations, but pointing the vector toward the light source is just as good. Figure 12-21 shows the orientation of the actual *light_source* vector.

Now that we have the directional light source defined, let's add the ambient term to the lighting model. We'll use a variable to hold the intensity of the ambient light; then during the shading process, we'll add this value to the final intensity computed due to the directional light. The ambient term is defined as:

```
float ambient_light = 6;          // ambient light level
```

Notice that it's a floating point value. We will probably change this in the final optimized engine, but for now it will suffice.

Next, we might ask ourselves, what units are both the ambient and directional sources in? Well, that's a bit arbitrary, but we are going to follow this convention: All polygon surfaces can have 16 different intensities. Intensity 0 is totally black and intensity 15 is totally white. The intensities within the range are different shades of the color of the polygon. So by setting the ambient term to 6, we have in essence set the average light level of the universe to about 37 percent of full intensity, which will give objects a nice look as they move around in the directional light. Of course, we can change this term at will during run time to change the ambient light level. For example, when an explosion goes off, we might crank it up to 12 or 13 for a few frames to simulate the blast energy.

We have talked enough about the shader function. It's now time to implement the function and focus on the code that makes it happen. The function is going to operate at the object level using world coordinates. This means that before an object is passed to the shader the world coordinates stored in *vertices_world[]* must

FIGURE 12-21

The exact vector orientations used in our 3D shading engine

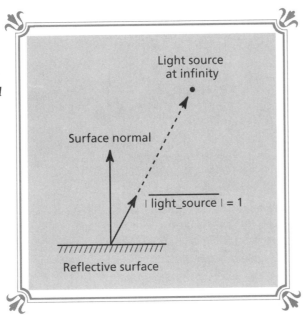

be initialized, but we'll pretend this step has been done for us. The final shading function is shown in Listing 12-8.

LISTING 12-8 Function to perform lighting along with back-face removal for objects

```
void Remove_Backfaces_And_Shade(object_ptr the_object)
{
// this function removes all the backfaces of an object by setting the removed
// flag. This function assumes that the object has been transformed into
// camera coordinates. Also, the function computes the flat shading of the
// object

int vertex_0,         // vertex indices
    vertex_1,
    vertex_2,
    curr_poly;        // current polygon

float dp,             // the result of the dot product
      intensity;      // the final intensity of the surface

vector_3d u,v,        // general working vectors
          normal,     // the normal to the surface being processed
          sight;      // line of sight vector

// for each polygon in the object determine if it is pointing away from the
```

continued on next page

continued from previous page

```
// viewpoint and direction

for (curr_poly=0; curr_poly<the_object->num_polys; curr_poly++)
    {
    // compute two vectors on polygon that have the same initial points
    vertex_0 = the_object->polys[curr_poly].vertex_list[0];
    vertex_1 = the_object->polys[curr_poly].vertex_list[1];
    vertex_2 = the_object->polys[curr_poly].vertex_list[2];

    // the vector u = vo->v1
    Make_Vector_3D((point_3d_ptr)&the_object->vertices_world[vertex_0],
                  (point_3d_ptr)&the_object->vertices_world[vertex_1],
                  (vector_3d_ptr)&u);

    // the vector v = vo-v2
    Make_Vector_3D((point_3d_ptr)&the_object->vertices_world[vertex_0],
                  (point_3d_ptr)&the_object->vertices_world[vertex_2],
                  (vector_3d_ptr)&v);

    // compute the normal to polygon v x u
    Cross_Product_3D((vector_3d_ptr)&v,
                    (vector_3d_ptr)&u,
                    (vector_3d_ptr)&normal);

    // compute the line of sight vector, since all coordinates are world all
    // object vertices are already relative to (0,0,0), thus
    sight.x = view_point.x-the_object->vertices_world[vertex_0].x;
    sight.y = view_point.y-the_object->vertices_world[vertex_0].y;
    sight.z = view_point.z-the_object->vertices_world[vertex_0].z;

    // compute the dot product between line of sight vector and normal to surface
    dp = Dot_Product_3D((vector_3d_ptr)&normal,(vector_3d_ptr)&sight);

    // set the clip flagged appropriately
    if (dp>0)
       {
       // set visibility
       the_object->polys[curr_poly].visible = 1;

       // compute light intensity if needed
       if (the_object->polys[curr_poly].shading==FLAT_SHADING)
          {
          // compute the dot product between the light source vector
          // and normal vector to surface
          dp = Dot_Product_3D((vector_3d_ptr)&normal,
                              (vector_3d_ptr)&light_source);

          // test if light ray is reflecting off surface
          if (dp>0)
             {
             // now cos 0 = (u.v)/|u||v| or
             intensity = ambient_light + (15*dp/(the_object->
                         polys[curr_poly].normal_length));
```

```
            // test if intensity has overflowed
            if (intensity >15)
                intensity = 15;

            // intensity now varies from 0-1, 0 being black or grazing and 1 being
            // totally illuminated. use the value to index into color table

            the_object->polys[curr_poly].shade =
                        the_object->polys[curr_poly].color - (int)intensity;

            // printf("\nintensity of polygon %d is %f",curr_poly,intensity);

            } // end if light is reflecting off surface
          else
            the_object->polys[curr_poly].shade =
            the_object->polys[curr_poly].color - (int)ambient_light;

        } // end if use flat shading
      else
        {
        // assume constant shading and simply assign color to shade
        the_object->polys[curr_poly].shade = the_object->polys[curr_poly].color;

        } // end else constant shading

      } // end if face is visible
    else
        the_object->polys[curr_poly].visible = 0; // set invisible flag

    } // end for curr_poly

} // end Remove_Backfaces_And_Shade
```

The function takes a single parameter, and that's the object to be shaded and tested for back-face removal. When the function returns, both the visibility fields and the shade fields of the polygons that make up the object will be set appropriately. However, let's focus on the shade field and how it's computed.

The function iterates through each polygon of the object and performs both the shading and back-face test. Both tests begin by computing the surface normal of the polygon in question. Figure 12-22 shows how the surface normal is computed. Regardless of whether the polygon is a triangle or quad, the function selects vertices p0, p1, and p2 to create two vectors that emanate from p0. Then the cross product between these vectors is computed, and the resulting surface normal is ready for use by both the back-face removal and shader logic.

The only difficulty lies in the length of the normal. Back-face removal can be accomplished by testing the sign of the dot product, but shading needs the cos θ term to be computed, and thus the length of the normal vector is needed. However, we have already computed this during the *PLG_Load_Object()* function, and we simply need to look it up. You may be asking, won't the length of the normal

FIGURE 12-22

◎ ◎ ◎ ◎ ◎ ◎

*How
PLG_Load_Object()
computes surface
normals*

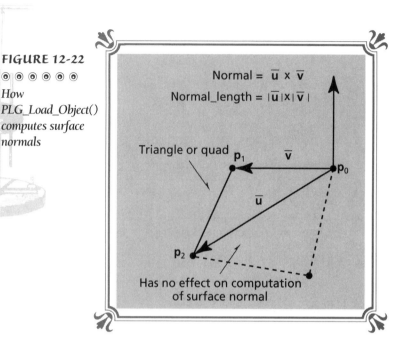

change as the object is rotated? The answer is no! Normal lengths are invariant to rotation and translation, but not to scaling. That is why the *Scale_Object()* function (Chapter 11) has an extra bit of code to scale the normal.

Anyway, the normal vector is used along with the *light_source* vector to compute the intensity of light that is falling on the polygon surface. Then this value is added to the ambient term, and the result is clipped to stay within the range of 0 to 15. The value of the intensity is used as an offset into the color palette at some base value that is the desired color of the polygon. However, there is a little twist. The way I made the color palette has higher intensities of each color in descending order; hence, the intensity is inverted and then added to the base color. The final result is stored in the shade field of each polygon.

In the case that a polygon is supposed to be *constant* shaded, the color field of the polygon is simply copied into the shade field and no look-up or translation is performed. It's really a lot simpler than it seems, maybe?

Now we are getting somewhere. We have a function that can remove hidden surfaces (which we'll just pretend we understand) along with a shader that supports directional and ambient lighting. Moreover, we have software to draw triangles and quads. I wonder if we have enough to rewrite that boring wireframe demo and make something a little more exciting? The answer is yes! And that is exactly what we are going to do. In fact, we are going to copy the wireframe demo almost verbatim; except before we draw the object, we are going to make a call to the *Remove_Backfaces_And_Shade()* function to compute the intensities of all the polygons along with removing unwanted back faces.

We still need a function to draw the object—that is, to make calls to the *Draw_Triangle_2D()* function. Well, it turns out that the *Draw_Object_Wire()* function can be used as a basis for a *Draw_Object_Solid()* function that makes calls to the triangle engine instead of the line drawing function. Listing 12-9 shows the code.

LISTING 12-9 *Function that can draw a solid object*

```
void Draw_Object_Solid(object_ptr the_object)
{

// this function draws an object shaded solid and can perform
// simple z extent clipping

int curr_poly,      // the current polygon
    vertex_1,       // vertex index numbers
    vertex_2,
    vertex_3,
    vertex_4,
    is_quad=0;      // quadrilateral flag

float x1,y1,z1,     // working variables
      x2,y2,z2,
      x3,y3,z3,
      x4,y4,z4;

// compute position of object in world
for (curr_poly=0; curr_poly<the_object->num_polys; curr_poly++)
    {
    // is this polygon visible?
    if (the_object->polys[curr_poly].visible==0 ||
        the_object->polys[curr_poly].clipped )
       continue;

    // extract the vertex numbers
    vertex_1=the_object->polys[curr_poly].vertex_list[0];
    vertex_2=the_object->polys[curr_poly].vertex_list[1];
    vertex_3=the_object->polys[curr_poly].vertex_list[2];

    // do Z clipping first before projection
    z1=the_object->vertices_camera[vertex_1].z;
    z2=the_object->vertices_camera[vertex_2].z;
    z3=the_object->vertices_camera[vertex_3].z;

    // test if this is a quad

    if (the_object->polys[curr_poly].num_points==4)
        {
        // extract vertex number and z component for clipping and projection
        vertex_4=the_object->polys[curr_poly].vertex_list[3];
        z4=the_object->vertices_camera[vertex_4].z;

        // set quad flag
```

continued on next page

continued from previous page

```
            is_quad=1;

            } // end if quad
        else
          z4=z3;

#if 0
        // perform z clipping test

        if ( (z1<clip_near_z && z2<clip_near_z && z3<clip_near_z &&
             z4<clip_near_z) ||
             (z1>clip_far_z && z2>clip_far_z && z3>clip_far_z &&
             z4>clip_far_z) )
          continue;
#endif

            // extract points of polygon
            x1 = the_object->vertices_camera[vertex_1].x;
            y1 = the_object->vertices_camera[vertex_1].y;

            x2 = the_object->vertices_camera[vertex_2].x;
            y2 = the_object->vertices_camera[vertex_2].y;

            x3 = the_object->vertices_camera[vertex_3].x;
            y3 = the_object->vertices_camera[vertex_3].y;


            // compute screen position of points
            x1=(HALF_SCREEN_WIDTH  + x1*viewing_distance/z1);
            y1=(HALF_SCREEN_HEIGHT - ASPECT_RATIO*y1*viewing_distance/z1);

            x2=(HALF_SCREEN_WIDTH  + x2*viewing_distance/z2);
            y2=(HALF_SCREEN_HEIGHT - ASPECT_RATIO*y2*viewing_distance/z2);

            x3=(HALF_SCREEN_WIDTH  + x3*viewing_distance/z3);
            y3=(HALF_SCREEN_HEIGHT - ASPECT_RATIO*y3*viewing_distance/z3);

            // draw triangle

            Draw_Triangle_2D((int)x1,(int)y1,(int)x2,(int)y2,(int)x3,(int)y3,
                        the_object->polys[curr_poly].shade);

            // draw second poly if this is a quad
            if (is_quad)
               {
               // extract the point
               x4 = the_object->vertices_camera[vertex_4].x;
               y4 = the_object->vertices_camera[vertex_4].y;

               // project to screen
               x4=(HALF_SCREEN_WIDTH  + x4*viewing_distance/z4);
               y4=(HALF_SCREEN_HEIGHT - ASPECT_RATIO*y4*viewing_distance/z4);
```

```
                // draw triangle
                Draw_Triangle_2D((int)x1,(int)y1,(int)x3,(int)y3,(int)x4,(int)y4,
                                 the_object->polys[curr_poly].shade);

                } // end if quad

            } // end for curr_poly

        } // end Draw_Object_Solid
```

The function works almost identically to the wireframe version except that it draws triangles and tests whether each surface should be drawn by referring to the visibility field of each polygon. You will also notice that the function has a section commented out that seems to perform a clipping of sorts. This section can be uncommented if you wish the function to perform Z clipping. Remember the viewing volume we spoke of in Chapter 10? Well, we aren't ready to implement complete 3D clipping yet, but we can do a bit of it. At least we can clip to the near and far clipping planes, as shown in Figure 12-23. Simple Z clipping makes sure that objects that should be behind us or far in the distance aren't projected.

You will also notice that the rendering is performed in camera coordinates. Remember, we are assuming that the viewpoint is at (0,0,0) and the view angles are equal to (0,0,0). In this case, the camera coordinates will be identical to the world coordinates, which are simply computed by adding the *world_pos* to each vertex

FIGURE 12-23

◉ ◉ ◉ ◉ ◉ ◉

Simple clipping to the near and far Z planes

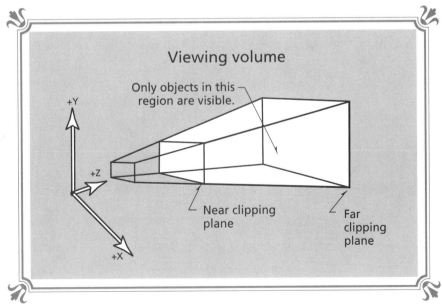

Viewing volume

Only objects in this region are visible.

+Y

+Z

+X

Near clipping plane

Far clipping plane

and storing the results in the camera coordinates array before calling the *Draw_Object_Solid()*. It may seem as though we should simply let the function do the conversion, but I'm trying to get you in the habit of thinking in terms of using different coordinate systems for different aspects of the graphics pipeline. Again, we probably won't use the *Draw_Object_Solid()* function for anything more than a demo, but that's life.

The demo of a solid rotating cube is called SOLIDEMO.EXE and the source is called SOLIDEMO.C. The controls are the same as for the WIREDEMO.EXE program. But run the program with the PLG file named CUBE.PLG instead of CUBEW.PLG; it has been modified to look better as a solid object. Experiment with moving the object close to the view plane and see what happens (remember to use the arrow keys along with the page up and down keys to move the object). The source is shown in Listing 12-10 and, as usual, if you wish to make an executable, you must link to BLACK11.C and include BLACK11.H from the previous chapter.

LISTING 12-10 A solid version of WIREDEMO.EXE

```
// I N C L U D E S /////////////////////////////////////////////////////////////

#include <io.h>
#include <conio.h>
#include <stdio.h>
#include <stdlib.h>
#include <dos.h>
#include <bios.h>
#include <fcntl.h>
#include <memory.h>
#include <malloc.h>
#include <math.h>
#include <string.h>
#include <search.h>                 // this one is needed for qsort()

// include all of our stuff

#include "black3.h"
#include "black4.h"
#include "black5.h"
#include "black6.h"
#include "black8.h"
#include "black9.h"
#include "black11.h"

// G L O B A L S /////////////////////////////////////////////////////////////

object test_object;   // the test object

// M A I N /////////////////////////////////////////////////////////////

void main(int argc,char **argv)
```

```
{
int index,   // looping variable
    done=0;  // exit flag

char buffer[80]; // used to print strings

// load in the object from the command line
if (!PLG_Load_Object(&test_object,argv[1],1))
   {
   printf("\nCouldn't find file %s",argv[1]);
   return;

   } // end if

// position the object

Position_Object((object_ptr)&test_object,0,0,300);

// set the viewpoint
view_point.x = 0;
view_point.y = 0;
view_point.z = 0;

// create the sin/cos lookup tables used for the rotation function
Build_Look_Up_Tables();

// set graphics to mode 13h
Set_Graphics_Mode(GRAPHICS_MODE13);

// allocate double buffer
Create_Double_Buffer(200);

// read the 3d color palette off disk
Load_Palette_Disk("standard.pal",(RGB_palette_ptr)&color_palette_3d);
Write_Palette(0,255,(RGB_palette_ptr)&color_palette_3d);

// install the isr keyboard driver
Keyboard_Install_Driver();

// set viewing distance
viewing_distance = 250;

// main event loop

while(!done)
     {
     // compute starting time of this frame
     starting_time = Timer_Query();

     // erase the screen
     Fill_Double_Buffer(0);
```

continued on next page

continued from previous page

```
// test what key(s) user is pressing

// test if user is moving object to right
if (keyboard_state[MAKE_RIGHT])
   test_object.world_pos.x+=5;

// test if user is moving object to left
if (keyboard_state[MAKE_LEFT])
   test_object.world_pos.x-=5;

// test if user is moving object up
if (keyboard_state[MAKE_UP])
   test_object.world_pos.y-=5;

// test if user is moving object down
if (keyboard_state[MAKE_DOWN])
   test_object.world_pos.y+=5;

// test if user is moving object farther
if (keyboard_state[MAKE_PGUP])
   test_object.world_pos.z+=15;

// test if user is moving object nearer

if (keyboard_state[MAKE_PGDWN])
   test_object.world_pos.z-=15;

// test for exit key
if (keyboard_state[MAKE_ESC])
   done=1;

// rotate the object on all three axes
Rotate_Object((object_ptr)&test_object,2,4,6);

////////////////////////////////////////////////////////////////////////////

// convert the local coordinates into world and camera coordinates for shading
// and projection. note the viewer is at (0,0,0) with angles 0,0,0
// so the transformation is simply to add the world position to each
// local vertex

for (index=0; index<test_object.num_vertices; index++)
   {
   test_object.vertices_camera[index].x =
   test_object.vertices_world[index].x  =
         test_object.vertices_local[index].x+test_object.world_pos.x;

   test_object.vertices_camera[index].y =
   test_object.vertices_world[index].y  =
         test_object.vertices_local[index].y+test_object.world_pos.y;

   test_object.vertices_camera[index].z =
```

```
        test_object.vertices_world[index].z =
                test_object.vertices_local[index].z+test_object.world_pos.z;

        } // end for index

///////////////////////////////////////////////////////////////////////////

        // shade and remove backfaces, ignore the backface part for now
        Remove_Backfaces_And_Shade((object_ptr)&test_object);

        // draw the object
        Draw_Object_Solid((object_ptr)&test_object);

        // print out position of object
        sprintf(buffer,"Object is at (%d,%d,%d)      ",(int)test_object.world_pos.x,
                                                        (int)test_object.world_pos.y,
                                                        (int)test_object.world_pos.z);

        Print_String_DB(0,0,9,buffer,0);

        // display double buffer
        Display_Double_Buffer(double_buffer,0);

        // lock onto 18 frames per second max
        while((Timer_Query()-starting_time)<1);

        } // end while

// restore graphics mode back to text
Set_Graphics_Mode(TEXT_MODE);

// restore the old keyboard driver
Keyboard_Remove_Driver();

} // end main
```

You have to admit that's pretty cool! We are getting close to having all the pieces necessary for a complete 3D graphics engine. Hey, don't get too excited, I said close, I didn't say how close! Now let's talk about some advanced topics that we aren't going to implement in our engine, but you may wish to implement in your own engine.

Gouraud Shading

First, it's pronounced "garow." That's probably the hardest thing about *Gouraud shading*. So what is Gouraud shading? It's a method of shading that attempts to make 3D solid objects look more realistic, and it is based on the following observation: as the number of polygons in a polygonal approximation increases, the

resulting models look more realistic. Figure 12-24 shows two cylinders. The one on the right has many more polygons and thus looks more like a cylinder.

However, by increasing the number of polygons in a model, the amount of computation needed is also increased. So what Gouraud shading tries to do is make the model look like it has more polygon faces by shading each face not with a single shade or intensity, but with a number of intensities so that the flat polygon surface looks as if it's curved. Figure 12-25 shows a Gouraud shaded object versus a flat shaded object. Notice how your eyes instantly smooth the Gouraud shaded object, while the flat shaded object just sits there.

Gouraud shading works by interpolating the intensity of the polygon as a function of each pixel within the polygon. Basically, each polygon has a surface normal, and during a flat shade the surface normal is used to compute the light reflecting off the surface. However, Gouraud shading goes a little further by first computing vertex normals for each polygon being rendered, as shown in Figure 12-26.

You may ask, how can a flat polygon have multiple normals? Actually, it can't. But the Gouraud method computes an average surface normal at each vertex of a polygon by averaging the surface normals of the polygons that share the vertex. Figure 12-27 shows this graphically. Referring to the figure, we see that normal **na** is the average of the normals of polygons 1, 2, and 3, while **nb** is the average of the normals of polygons 1, 3, and 4. Finally, **nc** is the average of the normals for polygons 2, 3, and 4.

FIGURE 12-24

⊙ ⊙ ⊙ ⊙ ⊙ ⊙

Increasing the number of polygons in a 3D model to increase realism

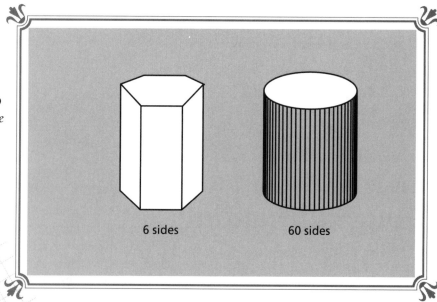

6 sides   60 sides

FIGURE 12-25

FIGURE 12-25

*Gouraud shading
makes polygon
mesh models
smoother and
more realistic*

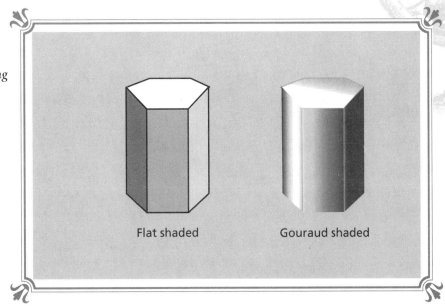

Flat shaded   Gouraud shaded

Once each vertex has an associated normal computed for it, the standard flat shading reflection computation is performed on each normal just as it's done for the flat shading model. That is, the light source is dotted with each of the vertex nor-

FIGURE 12-26

*The first step in
Gouraud shading
is to compute the
vertex normals*

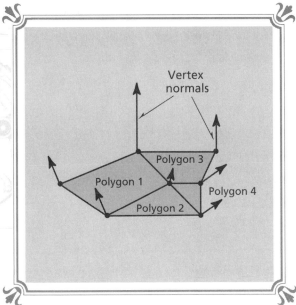

Vertex
normals

Polygon 3

Polygon 1

Polygon 4

Polygon 2

FIGURE 12-27

◎ ◎ ◎ ◎ ◎ ◎

*Computation of
vertex normals*

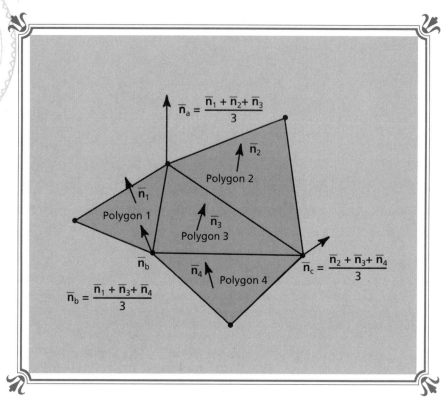

mals, and the resulting intensity is computed for each vertex. To recapitulate, the
first steps of Gouraud shading are as follows:

1. For each polygon, we compute the vertex normals by averaging the surface
   normals of all polygons that have the vertex in common.

2. We use the dot product calculation to compute the light intensity incident
   on each vertex as if it were a *micro facet* (a polygon with width and height
   equal to one pixel).

3. Once we compute all the vertex intensities, the actual shading can be done
   by interpolation.

How is the shading performed and what will be the results of it? Let's answer the
second question first. The Gouraud shading technique will tend to average surface
normals out along the surface of an object, making it look smooth and rounded
even though it's not. For example, if a cube is Gouraud shaded, it actually looks a
bit like a sphere! Anyway, the shading is performed by using *linear interpolation*. We
know the vertex intensities; all we need to do is ask the question, what is the inten-

sity of any pixel within the polygon being rendered if the vertices have these intensities?

If you haven't seen linear interpolation before, here's a one-dimensional example. Let's say that we have a situation as shown in Figure 12-28. A fighter jet is stationed on a carrier and has to bomb a target designated by the position s. Also, imagine that the statisticians of the Pentagon have computed the probability of the jet being destroyed while sitting on the carrier and at the final target site s. The probability of being destroyed while sitting on the friendly carrier is 20 percent, and the probability of being shot down and destroyed at the target site is 70 percent. But they are stumped when the fighter pilot asks, what is the probability of my being shot down while flying?

The answer to this question can be found by using linear interpolation, as long as the data being interpolated is linear (which you can assume or determine). In our case, we are going to assume that the probability of the pilot being destroyed is linear and a function of distance from the carrier, so if the pilot is at a location x where 0<x<s, what is the probability of the pilot being shot down? Here is the interpolation equation:

probability of being shot down (x)=(p_carrier * (s–x)+p_site * x)/s

Let's test the equation. If the pilot is sitting on the carrier, then x=0 and the probability of being destroyed should be 20 percent. Evaluating the equation, we get:

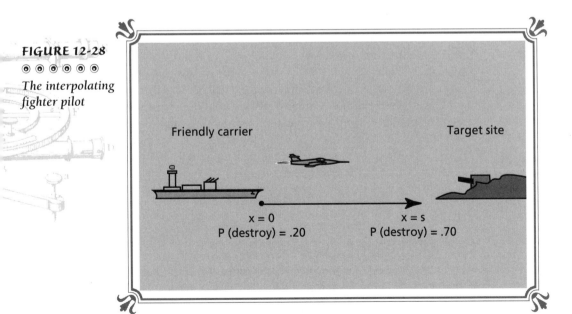

FIGURE 12-28

◎ ◎ ◎ ◎ ◎ ◎

The interpolating fighter pilot

Friendly carrier   Target site

x = 0   x = s
P (destroy) = .20   P (destroy) = .70

probability of being shot down (x=0)=(p_carrier * (s–0)+p_site * 0)/s

=p_carrier

=20%

This is correct! On the other hand, if the pilot is at the target site, the probability of being shot down is 70 percent. Let's see if the equation works:

probability of being shot down (x=s)=(p_carrier * (s–s)+p_site * s)/s

=p_site

=70%

So the interpolation equation works at both ends of the spectrum, but here's the big test. What is the probability of the pilot being shot down, say, at x=.5*s or, in other words, halfway between the carrier and the target site? We would expect it to be something like 50 percent or so. Let's see what the interpolation equation results are:

probability of being shot down (x=.5*s)=(p_carrier * (s–.5*s)+p_site * .5s)/s

=(p_carrier*.5*s + p_site*.5*s)/s

=(p_carrier*.5 + p_site*.5)

=(10% + 35%)

=(45%)

This is in the range of what we expected. Of course, we have been a bit cavalier about percents, but we have shown how interpolation works. Hence, interpolation is a very important part of computing values in ranges where only the extremes of the range are known.

Getting back to the Gouraud shading problem, it seems that all we need to do is interpolate the vertex intensities as a function of x and y as the polygon (usually a triangle) is being drawn. This is exactly what we are going to do. Take a look at Figure 12-29. Here we see a sample triangle that has already had its vertex normals and final light intensities computed. All we need to do is scan-convert the triangle and compute the intensity of each pixel within the triangle during the scan conversion process using the vertex intensities and the position of the vertices to control the interpolation. As you can see from the figure, the intensity of the light along the left edge of the triangle is:

I_left=((y2 – y)*I1+(y–y1)*I2)/(y2–y1);

And, similarly, the right edge is:

I_right=((y3–y1)*I1+(y–y1)*I3)/(y3–y1);

Once *I_left* and *I_right* have been computed, we need to interpolate them as well in the X axis. This is done with the final interpolation equation:

I_middle=((x_right – x)*I_left+(x – x_left)*I_right)/(x_right – x_left);

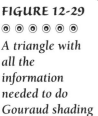

FIGURE 12-29
◎ ◎ ◎ ◎ ◎ ◎
A triangle with all the information needed to do Gouraud shading

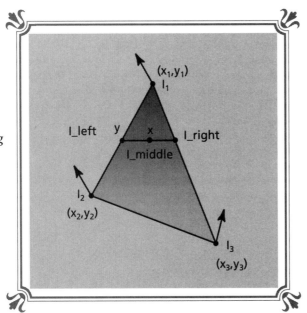

Although the equations look complex, they aren't that bad since they can be forward differenced, and incremental versions can be obtained for a more efficient scan conversion. For example, we see that once *I_left* and *I_right* have been computed, they don't change as a function of x; therefore, they only need to be computed once per line. The final interpolation equation does change as a function of x, but with a bit of algebra, an incremental version of the *I_middle* equation can be derived. Take a look below:

$$I\_middle_{i+1} = ((x\_right-(x+1))*I\_left+(x+1-x\_left)*I\_right)/(x\_right- x\_left);$$

$$= ((x\_right-x)*I\_left+(x-x\_left)*I\_right+I\_right-I\_left)/(x\_right-x\_left);$$

$$= I\_middle_i+(I\_right-I\_left)/(x\_right-x\_left);$$

We see that the rightmost part of the final result is a constant as long as the change in x remains 1.0 each iteration (which it does). Thus, we can precompute this each line and simply use a single addition each cycle to draw the row of pixels. For demonstration purposes, I have written a Gouraud shading function called *Draw_Triangle_2D_Gouraud()*. The function is totally un-optimized so you can follow its operation. In fact, it doesn't even have the incremental optimization we just spoke of. However, it is very clear, and you should be able to get a good grasp of Gouraud shading by studying it. It is shown in Listing 12-11 for review.

LISTING 12-11 A Gouraud shading function

```c
void Draw_Triangle_2D_Gouraud(int x1,int y1,
                              int x2,int y2,
                              int x3,int y3,
                              unsigned char far *buffer,
                              int intensity_1,
                              int intensity_2,
                              int intensity_3)
{
// this function draws a Gouraud shaded triangle, but doesn't perform any clipping
// and is very slow (mostly for demonstrative purposes)

int x,y,            // looping variables
    x_index,        // integer texture coordinates
    y_index,
    bottom_1,       // distance from top to middle of triangle on y axis
    bottom_2;       // distance from middle to bottom triangle on y axis

float dx_right,     // the dx/dy ratio of the right edge of line
      dx_left,      // the dx/dy ratio of the left edge of line
      xs,xe,        // the starting and ending points of the edges
      height_left,  // the heights of the triangle
      height_right;


float intensity_right,    // the intensity of the right edge of the triangle
      intensity_left,     // the intensity of the left edge of the triangle
      intensity_mid,      // the average between the right and left
      delta_y21,delta_y31;  // the y delta's

unsigned char far *dest_addr; // pointer to memory space of video write

// compute height of sub triangles
height_left  = y2-y1;
height_right = y3-y1;

// compute distances from starting y vertex
if (y2>y3)
   {
   bottom_1 = y3;
   bottom_2 = y2;
   }
else
   {
   bottom_1 = y2;
   bottom_2 = y3;
   } // end else

// compute edge deltas
dx_left  = (float)(x2-x1)/height_left;
```

```
dx_right = (float)(x3-x1)/height_right;

// set starting points
xs = (float)x1;
xe = (float)x1+(float)0.5;

// compute shading constants
delta_y21 = (float)1/(float)(y2-y1);
delta_y31 = (float)1/(float)(y3-y1);

// compute starting address in video memory
dest_addr = buffer+(y1<<8)+(y1<<6);

// draw the triangle using Gouraud shading
for (y=y1; y<=bottom_1; y++,dest_addr+=320)
    {
    // compute left and right edge intensities as a function of y
    intensity_left  = delta_y21*(float)((y2-y)*intensity_1 +
                                 (y-y1)*intensity_2);
    intensity_right = delta_y31*(float)((y3-y)*intensity_1 +
                                 (y-y1)*intensity_3);

    // draw line

    for (x=(int)xs; x<=(int)xe; x++)
        {
        // compute x axis intensity interpolant
        intensity_mid = ((xe-x)*intensity_left +
                     (x-xs)*intensity_right)/(xe-xs);

        // plot pixel on screen
        dest_addr[x] = (unsigned char)(16+intensity_mid);

        } // end for x

    // adjust starting point and ending point
    xs+=dx_left;
    xe+=dx_right;

    } // end for

// now recompute slope of shorter edge to make it complete triangle

if (y3>y2)
    {
    // recompute left edge slope
    dx_left = (float)(x3-x2)/(float)(y3-y2);

    }
else
```

continued on next page

continued from previous page

```
    {
    // y2>y3, recompute right edge slope
    dx_right = (float)(x2-x3)/(float)(y2-y3);

    } // end else

// draw remainder of triangle

for (y--; y<=bottom_2; y++,dest_addr+=320)
    {
    // compute left and right edge intensities as a function of y
    intensity_left  = (float)((y3-y)*intensity_2 +
                        (y-y2)*intensity_3)/(float)(y3-y2);
    intensity_right = delta_y31*(float)((y3-y)*intensity_1 +
                        (y-y1)*intensity_3);

    // draw line
    for (x=(int)xs; x<=(int)xe; x++)
        {
        // compute x axis intensity interpolant
        intensity_mid = ((xe-x)*intensity_left +
                        (x-xs)*intensity_right)/(xe-xs);

        // plot pixel on screen
        dest_addr[x] = (unsigned char)(16+intensity_mid);

        } // end for x

    // adjust starting point and ending point
    xs+=dx_left;
    xe+=dx_right;

    } // end for

} // end Draw_Triangle_2D_Gouraud
```

The Gouraud shading function takes as parameters the coordinates of the three triangle vertices along with their respective intensities. Notice that the intensities must be within the range of 0 to 63. This is because there are only 64 possible shades of a single color, and that limits the value of intensities. Of course, the standard VGA palette doesn't come with 64 shades of any color, so we need to write a function to set 64 of the color registers to 64 shades of a color (such as gray). The function that generates the palette is shown in Listing 12-12.

LISTING 12-12 The Gouraud palette function

```
void Make_Gray_Palette(void)
{
// this function generates 64 shades of gray and places them in the palette
// at locations 16 to 96
```

```
int index;

RGB_color color;

// generate 64 shades of gray
for (index=0; index<64; index++)
    {
    // gray equals equal percentage of Red, Green and Blue
    color.red   = index;
    color.green = index;
    color.blue  = index;

    // write the color in the palette starting at location 16, so as not to
    // fry the EGA palette

    Write_Color_Reg(index+16,(RGB_color_ptr)&color);

    } // end for index

} // end Make_Gray_Palette
```

The *Make_Gray_Palette()* function is fairly straightforward. It simply increments each RGB value by one and then sets the next color register in the range that has been chosen, which in this case is 16 to 95 for the grays.

Getting back to the Gouraud shader—other than the computation of the intensities along the triangle edges, the function has much the same architecture of the *Draw_Triangle_2D()* function used to draw standard flat shaded polygons. Of course, the Gouraud version is totally slow and un-optimized, but I don't expect that we are actually going to use it for our games! It is just for educational purposes.

As an example of Gouraud shading, I have written a little demo. The demo draws a Gouraud shaded triangle on the screen and allows you to increase or decrease the vertex intensities using the numeric keypad. The name of the demo is GOURDEMO.EXE and the source is named GOURDEMO.C, shown in Listing 12-13. If you wish to compile it yourself, remember to link in GRAPH11.C. Use the following keys to change the vertex intensities:

Keypress	Description
7	Increase vertex one's intensity.
4	Decrease vertex one's intensity.
8	Increase vertex two's intensity.
5	Decrease vertex two's intensity.
9	Increase vertex three's intensity.
6	Decrease vertex three's intensity.

LISTING 12-13 Demo of Gouraud shading

```c
// I N C L U D E S /////////////////////////////////////////////////////////

#include <io.h>
#include <conio.h>
#include <stdio.h>
#include <stdlib.h>
#include <dos.h>
#include <bios.h>
#include <fcntl.h>
#include <memory.h>
#include <malloc.h>
#include <math.h>
#include <string.h>

// include all of our stuff

#include "black3.h"
#include "black4.h"
#include "black5.h"
#include "black6.h"
#include "black8.h"
#include "black9.h"
#include "black11.h"

// M A I N /////////////////////////////////////////////////////////////////

void main(void)
{
int done=0,          // exit flag
    x=140,y=60,      // position of triangle

    intensity_1=15,
    intensity_2=50,
    intensity_3=5;

char buffer[80]; // output string buffer

// set graphics mode to 13h
Set_Graphics_Mode(GRAPHICS_MODE13);

// alter the palette and introduce some grays
Make_Gray_Palette();

// draw gouraud shaded triangle

Draw_Triangle_2D_Gouraud(x,y,x-50,y+60,x+30,y+80,video_buffer,
                         intensity_1,intensity_2,intensity_3);

// label vertices
Print_String(x,y-10,9,"1",1);
```

```
Print_String(x-60,y+60,9,"2",1);
Print_String(x+40,y+80,9,"3",1);

// main loop

while(!done)
    {
    // test for key
    if (kbhit())
        {
        // get the key
        switch(getch())
            {
            case 27: // escape key
                {
                // exit system
                done=1;

                } break;

            case '7': // increase vertex 1 intensity
                {
                if (++intensity_1>63)
                    intensity_1=63;
                } break;

            case '4': // decrease vertex 1 intensity
                {
                if (--intensity_1<0)
                    intensity_1=0;
                } break;

            case '8': // increase vertex 2 intensity
                {
                if (++intensity_2>63)
                    intensity_2=63;
                } break;

            case '5': // decrease vertex 2 intensity
                {
                if (--intensity_2<0)
                    intensity_2=0;
                } break;

            case '9': // increase vertex 3 intensity
                {
                if (++intensity_3>63)
                    intensity_3=63;
                } break;

            case '6': // decrease vertex 3 intensity
                {
```

continued on next page

continued from previous page

```
                    if (--intensity_3<0)
                        intensity_3=0;
                    } break;

                default:break;

                } // end switch

        // draw Gouraud shaded triangle
        Draw_Triangle_2D_Gouraud(x,y,x-50,y+60,x+30,y+80,video_buffer,
                                    intensity_1,intensity_2,intensity_3);

        } // end kbhit

    // print out vertex intensities
    sprintf(buffer,"Vertex 1 = %d  ",intensity_1);
    Print_String(0,0,12,buffer,0);

    sprintf(buffer,"Vertex 2 = %d  ",intensity_2);
    Print_String(0,10,12,buffer,0);

    sprintf(buffer,"Vertex 3 = %d  ",intensity_3);
    Print_String(0,20,12,buffer,0);

    } // end while

// restore text mode
Set_Graphics_Mode(TEXT_MODE);

} // end main
```

If you play with the demo, you'll notice how Gouraud shading seems to "pull" the light toward the strongest vertex. This is the property that makes the resulting polygons look more rounded and less faceted as with flat shading.

Before moving to the next topic, there is one little mathematical detail that we should at least consider: the interpolating of vertex intensities was performed using linear interpolation when in fact the interpolation is not linear! This is because we projected a 3D triangle into a 2D space; thus, the interpolation was carried out without considering the depth of the triangles. This fact was overlooked for many years by graphics researchers. So remember, when you project a 3D polygon onto a 2D plane and then perform some calculation such as interpolation, you have lost the 3D aspect of the geometry.

Texture Mapping

Texture mapping adds the ultimate in realism to a 3D solid object. Figure 12-30 shows a texture-mapped environment. The only drawbacks to texture mapping are its computational expense (on the order of Gouraud shading) and use of memory.

FIGURE 12-30

◎ ◎ ◎ ◎ ◎ ◎

*Texture-
mapped
environment*

However, the computational complexity is definitely more prohibitive than the memory!

Texture mapping can be done relatively easily in real-time for special cases such as those you see in Doom (id) and Dark Forces (Lucas Arts). But performing texture mapping within worlds that allow the viewpoint to rotate in all axes, such as Descent (Interplay), is rather complex. This is a job for 32-bit programming and a DOS extender such as Tenberry Software's (formerly Rational Systems) DOS4G. Even with optimizations it takes at least a couple of additions per pixel and quite a few multiplications per polygon to set up the texture mapping.

Granted, a couple of additions per pixel isn't bad, but when you compare this to the simple assembly language memory fill used for flat shading, there is an order of magnitude of difference! In any case, with advanced programming techniques such as CPU cache utilization and 32-bit programming, texture mapping can be done at lightning speeds.

Our engine isn't going to support texture mapping in real-time, but we are going to step through the mathematics of one texture mapping method to see how it's done. Then if you're feeling lucky, you can try to implement a real-time texture mapper that allows a reasonable number of polygons to be drawn per second. So let's begin by stating the problem: given a 2D texture defined in texture space, as seen in Figure 12-31, map this image onto a polygon in 3D space.

This is quite a challenge, but it can be done with a lot of vector math and some patience. First, since our engine only renders triangles, we're only going to consider texture mapping on a triangle. Quads can be texture mapped by texture mapping each of the subtriangles. To texture map a rectangular shaped texture bitmap on a triangle doesn't seem to make sense; however, we will derive the math so only half the texture map is mapped down on the triangle, as shown in Figure 12-32. A slightly different version of the math can be used to map the other half of the tex-

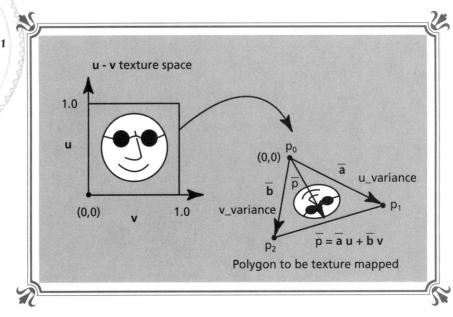

Polygon to be texture mapped

ture onto another triangle. Anyway, let's begin by referring to Figure 12-31 for the analysis. The figure shows the texture map in U-V space (texture map coordinates) and the triangle to be texture mapped in 2D Cartesian space. The range of both u and v in texture space are from 0.0 to 1.0.

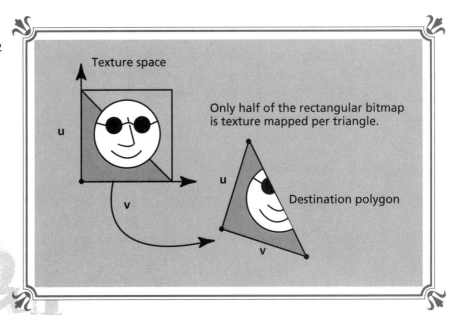

Also on Figure 12-31, we see that there are two vectors labeled **a** and **b**. These vectors both originate from the vertex p0 of the triangle and terminate at p1 and p2. The vectors have the value:

a=p1−p0=<x1−x0,y1−y0>
b=p2−p0=<x2−x0,y2−y0>

The position vector labeled at (x,y) is called **p** and is found by subtracting the point p0 from (x,y). However, for simplicity, we will assume that p0=(0,0) for the moment, and thus **p**=<x,y>. This is just to make the math easier. Later, during the actual texture mapping, we must recall that we made this assumption and think of **p**=<x,y> relative to the point p0, but forget it for now. Here's the hard part. Assuming that we are trying to texture map the pixel located at (x,y), then what U-V coordinates should we use to select the proper *textel* (texture pixel) from the texture map? This can be answered by the following vector equation:

p=**a**∗u+**b**∗v;

This means that the vector **p** is a linear combination of **a** and **b**, moreover, as u and v change so does **p**. So what does that help? Well, if we break the vector equation down into its components, we will see something. Here is the breakdown:

$p_x = a_x * u + b_x * v;$
$p_y = a_y * u + b_y * v;$

You have probably caught something by now, which is that we are working in 2D not 3D. Why? The answer is that 3D texture mapping—that is, taking the Z dimension into consideration—is more complex and much more computationally expensive. Furthermore, the perspective foreshortening that it adds isn't worth the trouble when we're trying to learn; so we will stick to projecting 2D texture maps onto the polygons after they have been projected on the screen.

Continuing with the analysis, we know that:

$p_x = a_x * u + b_x * v = x$
$p_y = a_y * u + b_y * v = y;$

or,

$a_x * u + b_x * v = x$
$a_y * u + b_y * v = y;$

where

$a_x = x1 - x0$
$b_x = y1 - y0$
$a_y = x2 - x0$
$b_y = y2 - y0$

Now we know everything except u and v. That's what we are trying to find, because we want to know the U-V texture coordinates for any (x,y) position, not the other way around. So we need to perform a bit of math to solve for u and v. First, let's place the linear equations into matrix form,

$$\begin{bmatrix} a_x & b_x \\ a_y & b_y \end{bmatrix} * \begin{bmatrix} u \\ v \end{bmatrix} = \begin{bmatrix} x \\ y \end{bmatrix}$$

$$A \quad * \quad X \quad = \quad B$$

which is of the form AX=B, and we are interested in the X part! So what we need to do is compute the inverse of A and premultiply it by B, and the results are u and v. In matrix form we have:

$$\begin{bmatrix} u \\ v \end{bmatrix} = \begin{bmatrix} a_x & b_x \\ a_y & b_y \end{bmatrix}^{-1} * \begin{bmatrix} x \\ y \end{bmatrix}$$

The problem is, how do we invert A or, in other words, find the inverse of the coefficient matrix? The answer is, we look it up in a book such as Antons' *Elementary Linear Algebra*, which states that the inverse of a 2x2 matrix is as follows:

Given,

$$A = \begin{bmatrix} a & b \\ c & d \end{bmatrix} \text{ then, } A^{-1} = \frac{1}{(a*d - b*c)} * \begin{bmatrix} d & -b \\ -c & a \end{bmatrix} = \begin{bmatrix} a' & b' \\ c' & d' \end{bmatrix}$$

Therefore, to find the inverse of a 2x2, we compute the determinate (that's the part under the division bar) and then flip a couple of signs and swap a couple of elements. Once we have the results, we can carry out the final calculation and find u and v. Then with u and v, we can index into the texture and find the pixel color that we have been trying to find for the last half hour or so! You may be thinking, with all that math, how can texture mapping be done at all in real-time? The answer lies in using incremental techniques again. If we forget about all the math used to derive the final texture space coordinates u and v and look at the final results, there isn't that much per pixel.

To illustrate the point, let's analyze the computations. First, we have to compute a_x, a_y, b_x, and b_y. This takes 4 additions (remember we group both additions and subtractions into additions and multiplies and divides into multiplies when benchmarking). Then we need to compute the determinate (a*d–b*c) and invert it, so 3 more multiplies and 1 more add, for a total of 3 multiplies and 5 adds so far. Now if we let the constants a', b', c', and d' be

a'=d/(a*d – b*c);

b'=–b/(a*d – b*c);

c'=–c/(a*d – b*c);

d'=a/(a*d − b*c);

then we have 4 more multiplications, and that's it, since we don't need to keep recomputing the denominator.

Therefore, here are the final totals for the setup phase, per triangle to be texture mapped:

Multiplications: 7
Additions: 5

This isn't bad; however, we are more interested in the per pixel computation. Let's take a look at that. To do this, we need to multiply A^{-1} by the $[xy]^t$ column matrix, resulting in:

u=a'*x+b'*y
v=c'*x+c'*y

And we can again use forward differencing to arrive at an incremental formula. Let's analyze the formula's x variation for a delta x of 1.0. Since triangles are scanned horizontally, it makes sense to first come up with an x variation incremental formula, so

u_{i+1}=a'*(x+1)+b'*y
v_{i+1}=c'*(x+1)+d'*y

which when simplified results in:

u_{i+1}=u_i+a';
v_{i+1}=v_i+c';

Therefore, as the horizontal strips of the triangle are scanned, only two additions need to be performed per pixel. The same logic and calculations can be performed for the Y axis, but since the x starting position changes on each line, the best that can be achieved is something of the form

u_{i+1}=u_i+b'+a'*dx;
v_{i+1}=v_i+d'+c'*dx;

where dx is the slope of the left edge of the triangle being scan-converted. However, the products a'*dx and c'*dx can be precomputed as part of the polygon overhead calculation and summed with b' and d', arriving at secondary constants b_dx and d_dx. Based on these y values, we can use the following incrementals,

u_{i+1}=u_i+b_dx;
v_{i+1}=v_i+d_dx;

which results in 2 additions each scan line. Therefore, the final texture mapper has the final performance shown in Table 12-1.

TABLE 12-1

◇◇◇◇◇◇

The performance of our texture mapper

	Multiplications	Additions
Initial setup per polygon	9	5
Incremental calculation per y	0	2
Incremental calculation per x	0	2

Overall, that's not bad. We've had enough of theory. It's time to see the actual texture mapping function. The texture mapping is based on a triangle. The texture that is mapped must be 64x64 and loaded into a *char* array. We'll use a sprite to hold all the textures; hence, the sprite must be initialized and loaded with at least one texture before calling the texture mapper. The texture mapping function takes as parameters the three vertices of the triangle to be textured along with a pointer to the destination buffer, such as the video buffer or double buffer, and finally, an index of which texture to map. So if more than one texture is loaded into the sprite, it can be displayed, but if only one texture is loaded into the sprite, the index should always be zero. The triangle texture mapper is shown in Listing 12-14.

LISTING 12-14 Function that texture maps a triangle

```
void Draw_Triangle_2D_Text(int x1,int y1,
                           int x2,int y2,
                           int x3,int y3,
                           unsigned char far *buffer,
                           int texture_index)
{
// this function draws a textured triangle, but doesn't perform any clipping
// and is very slow (mostly for demonstrative purposes)

int x,y,          // looping variables
    x_index,      // integer texture coordinates
    y_index,
    bottom_1,     // distance from top to middle of triangle on y axis
    bottom_2;     // distance from middle to bottom triangle on y axis

float dx_right,   // the dx/dy ratio of the right edge of line
      dx_left,    // the dx/dy ratio of the left edge of line
      xs,xe,      // the starting and ending points of the edges
      height_left, // the heights of the triangle
      height_right;

float a,b,c,d,det,       // texture mapping inverse matrix elements
      ix,iy,jx,jy,       // texture vectors
      delta_uy,delta_vy, // pre-computed deltas of texture
                         // coordinates on y axis
```

```
        u_start,v_start,      // the starting u,v coordinates on each line
        u_curr,v_curr;        // the current u,v texture coordinates

unsigned char far *dest_addr;    // final destination address of memory write

unsigned char far *text;         // texture memory

// assign text pointer to current texture map
text = textures.frames[texture_index];

// compute height of sub-triangles

height_left  = y2-y1;
height_right = y3-y1;

// compute distances from starting y vertex
if (y2>y3)
   {
   bottom_1 = y3;
   bottom_2 = y2;
   }
else
   {
   bottom_1 = y2;
   bottom_2 = y3;
   } // end else

// compute edge deltas
dx_left  = (float)(x2-x1)/height_left;
dx_right = (float)(x3-x1)/height_right;

// set starting points
xs = (float)x1;
xe = (float)x1+(float)0.5;

// compute vector components for texture calculations
ix = (float)(x3-x1);
iy = (float)(y3-y1);

jx = (float)(x2-x1);
jy = (float)(y2-y1);

// compute determinant
det = (ix*jy - iy*jx);

// compute inverse matrix
a =  jy/det;
b = -jx/det;
c = -iy/det;
d =  ix/det;

// compute starting texture coordinates
```

continued on next page

continued from previous page

```
u_start = 0;
v_start = 0;

// compute delta texture coordinates for unit change in y
delta_uy=(a*dx_left + b);
delta_vy=(c*dx_left + d);

// compute starting address in video memory
dest_addr = buffer+(y1<<8)+(y1<<6);

// draw the triangle
for (y=y1; y<=bottom_1; y++,dest_addr+=320)
    {
    // start off working texture coordinates for current row
    u_curr = u_start;
    v_curr = v_start;

    // draw line
    for (x=(int)xs; x<=(int)xe; x++)
        {
        x_index = abs((int)(u_curr*63+0.5));
        y_index = abs((int)(v_curr*63+0.5));

        // printf("\nu=%d v=%d  ",x_index, y_index);
        dest_addr[x] = text[y_index*64 + x_index];

        // adjust x texture coordinates
        u_curr+=a;
        v_curr+=c;

        } // end for x

    // adjust starting point and ending point
    xs+=dx_left;
    xe+=dx_right;

    // adjust texture coordinates based on y change
    u_start += delta_uy;
    v_start += delta_vy;

    } // end for

// now recompute slope of shorter edge to make it complete triangle
if (y3>y2)
    {
    // recompute left edge slope
    dx_left = (float)(x3-x2)/(float)(y3-y2);

    }
else
    {
    // y2>y3, recompute right edge slope
    dx_right = (float)(x2-x3)/(float)(y2-y3);
```

```
    } // end else

// recompute texture space coordinate increments for y changes
delta_uy=(a*dx_left + b);
delta_vy=(c*dx_left + d);

// draw remainder of triangle

for (y--; y<=bottom_2; y++,dest_addr+=320)
    {
    // start off working texture coordinates for current row
    u_curr = u_start;
    v_curr = v_start;

    // draw line
    for (x=(int)xs; x<=(int)xe; x++)
        {
        // scale each texture coordinate by 64 since textures are 64x64
        x_index = (int)(u_curr*63);
        y_index = (int)(v_curr*63);

        // plot textel on screen
        dest_addr[x] = text[y_index*64 + x_index];

        // adjust x texture coordinates
        u_curr+=a;
        v_curr+=c;

        } // end for x

    // adjust starting point and ending point
    xs+=dx_left;
    xe+=dx_right;

    // adjust texture coordinates based on y change
    u_start += delta_uy;
    v_start += delta_vy;

    } // end for

} // end Draw_Triangle_2D_Text
```

The code almost implements our theoretical results exactly, except some of the variable names have been changed. The code is broken into three parts: the first part computes all of the constants, part two draws the top half of the triangle, and part three draws the bottom half of the triangle. Thus, the function assumes that the triangle hasn't a flat top or bottom. This is different from our standard triangle renderer that needs a flat top or bottom—however, for the case of texture mapping, this function is a bit easier to write this way. Moreover, it's just a demo and that's why we can impose such restraints on the geometry of the triangle.

As for a complete example of the texture mapper in action, I have written a program similar to the Gouraud demo that draws a textured triangle on the screen and allows you to toggle through the texture maps by pressing the [SPACEBAR]. The name of the program is TEXTDEMO.EXE and the source is called TEXTDEMO.C, which is shown in Listing 12-15.

LISTING 12-15 Demo of the texture-mapping function

```
// I N C L U D E S /////////////////////////////////////////////////////////

#include <io.h>
#include <conio.h>
#include <stdio.h>
#include <stdlib.h>
#include <dos.h>
#include <bios.h>
#include <fcntl.h>
#include <memory.h>
#include <malloc.h>
#include <math.h>
#include <string.h>

// include all of our stuff

#include "black3.h"
#include "black4.h"
#include "black5.h"
#include "black6.h"
#include "black8.h"
#include "black9.h"
#include "black11.h"


// G L O B A L S ///////////////////////////////////////////////////////////

pcx_picture image_pcx;  // general PCX image used to load background and
                        // imagery

////////////////////////////////////////////////////////////////////////////

void main(void)
{

int done=0,          // exit flag
    index,           // looping variable
    x=140,y=100,     // position of triangle
    curr_texture=0;  // current texture

// set graphics mode to 13h
Set_Graphics_Mode(GRAPHICS_MODE13);

// load in the text textures 64x64
```

```
            PCX_Init((pcx_picture_ptr)&image_pcx);
            PCX_Load("textures.pcx", (pcx_picture_ptr)&image_pcx,1);

            // initialize the texture sprite
            Sprite_Init((sprite_ptr)&textures,0,0,64,64,0,0,0,0,0,0);

            // extract the bitmaps for the textures(four of them:stone, wood, slime, lava)
            for (index=0; index<4; index++)
                PCX_Get_Sprite((pcx_picture_ptr)&image_pcx,(sprite_ptr)&textures,index,index,0);

            // done with this PCX file so delete memory associated with it
            PCX_Delete((pcx_picture_ptr)&image_pcx);

            // draw textures on screen so user can see what is going on
            Sprite_Draw((sprite_ptr)&textures,video_buffer,1);
            textures.x+=64;
            textures.curr_frame++;

            Sprite_Draw((sprite_ptr)&textures,video_buffer,1);
            textures.x+=64;
            textures.curr_frame++;

            Sprite_Draw((sprite_ptr)&textures,video_buffer,1);
            textures.x+=64;
            textures.curr_frame++;

            Sprite_Draw((sprite_ptr)&textures,video_buffer,1);
            textures.x+=64;
            textures.curr_frame++;

            // draw textured triangle
            Draw_Triangle_2D_Text(x,y,x-50,y+60,x+30,y+80,video_buffer,curr_texture);

            // main loop

            while(!done)
                {
                // test for key
                if (kbhit())
                    {
                    // get the key

                    switch(getch())
                        {
                        case ' ': // space bar to select next texture
                            {
                            if (++curr_texture>3)
                                curr_texture=0;

                            } break;

                        case 27: // escape key
```

continued on next page

continued from previous page

```
                    {
                    // exit system
                    done=1;

                    } break;

                default:break;

                } // end switch

            // draw textured triangle
            Draw_Triangle_2D_Text(x,y,x-50,y+60,x+30,y+80,
                                  video_buffer,curr_texture);

            } // end kbhit

        } // end while

// restore text mode
Set_Graphics_Mode(TEXT_MODE);

} // end main
```

As you can see, the demo runs fairly slowly, and only half the texture is shown. The slowness is due to the floating point calculations, but the half-visible texture is due to the fact that we are trying to map a rectangular texture on a triangle, and it's better to map only half the texture on the triangle than to map a rectangle on a triangle!

Modeling Special FX

Our 3D engine is hardly going to have enough horsepower to do the things you see in movies. However, it's possible to simulate some of these effects with a few simple models, a lot of approximation, and a bit of luck. Our engine isn't going to support any of the following FX, but with a bit of work and the proper optimizations, you should be able to achieve many of these FX in special cases.

Transparency

Physically speaking, transparency is the transmission of light through one medium into another and back out again (possibly). This is shown in Figure 12-33. During the transmission, different physical effects—such as refraction, reflection, and absorption—occur to the light as it passes from one medium to another. As game programmers, we aren't interested in the mathematical origins of transparency and transmission physics because we aren't going to use the math. Instead, we're going to look more at the end results and see how we might implement them.

FIGURE 12-33

◎ ◎ ◎ ◎ ◎ ◎

The physics of
transparency

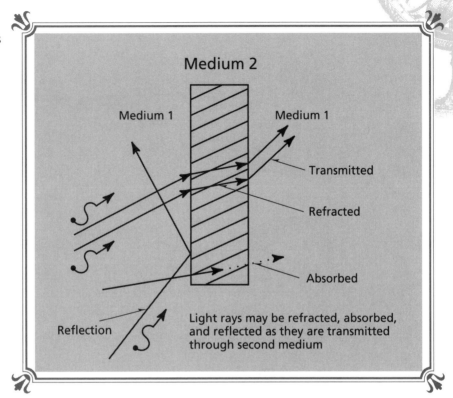

Light rays may be refracted, absorbed, and reflected as they are transmitted through second medium

Imagine that we have drawn a 3D solid object made of facets, and let's assume that the object is made from a transparent blue glass. If we draw this object on top of a region of space that is monochrome, we won't really be able to tell that the object is transparent. On the other hand, if we draw the object on top of one or more different colored objects, then we'll see them through the transparent object, as shown in Figure 12-34.

In essence, if an object is transparent, then objects behind it are shown, but their colors are filtered in some way as seen through the transparent object. So, can we take this simple observation and come up with an algorithm to draw transparent polygon facets or pixels? The answer is yes! Remember, we are Cybersorcerers and we can do anything! Anyway, let's try to make a first approximation at drawing a single transparent pixel. Then, with this primitive, we can always draw lines, triangles, and more complex geometrical entities, but the transparent pixel is the basis of all of them.

Let's assume that the background pixel has RGB components (R_b, G_b, B_b), and the foreground pixel has the RGB components (R_f, G_f, B_f). Furthermore, we'll refer to some value as the transparency that can range from 0.0 to 1.0, where 0.0 is totally

FIGURE 12-34
◉ ◉ ◉ ◉ ◉ ◉

A transparent object obscuring objects in the background

opaque and 1.0 is totally transparent, like glass. We are going to derive an algorithm that operates in image space (the frame buffer) that can successfully plot the foreground transparent pixel on top of the background pixel such that it looks like the foreground pixel is actually transparent.

As a first attempt, we might do something like this: given the RGB values for each of the pixels, mix the pixel values together using the transparency value as the amount of mixing. This can be done using a linear interpolation as we have seen before. The interpolation equations must be done for each component and have the following form:

$$R_{final} = (R_b * transparency + R_f * (1 - transparency))$$
$$G_{final} = (G_b * transparency + G_f * (1 - transparency))$$
$$B_{final} = (B_b * transparency + B_f * (1 - transparency))$$

With the above equations and a transparency setting of 1.0, the final pixel color would be that of the background pixel, which is correct. This is true because we are assuming that a transparency of 1.0 means the foreground pixel is like glass. On the other hand, if we plug in a value of 0.0, which means that the foreground pixel is totally opaque, then the equations result in (R_f, G_f, B_f), which again is correct—that is, an object that is totally opaque shouldn't be transparent. And, of course, all the values in between will be linearly interpolated from the background pixel to the foreground pixel.

The preceding equations are great, but performing all those calculations for each pixel is too much, and what if the results of the calculation aren't in the color look-up table? The solution to the problem is to precompute transparency look-up tables that contain all possible values for any given color palette and a value of transparency. The table is made in the following way. For each color register, the RGB values are extracted, and the preceding equations are solved with every other color register; so a double *for* loop is required. Basically, the *for* loops compute the results of all possible combinations of the 256 color registers (which is 65,536 combinations). As the computations are being performed, the resulting perfect RGB result is used to select a result that most closely matches in the current color look-up table; then a giant 2D array is updated with this information. The array might look like this:

```
unsigned char transparent_array[256][256];
```

Then the current background pixel value might be used as the row, and the foreground pixel might be used as the column. The output of the array would be the precomputed transparent pixel value that best matches the results of mixing the transparent foreground pixel with the background pixel.

About the only question is, how do we select the closest color to the desired color in each iteration? The best way to do this is to use the *Least-Squares-Method*, which, basically, finds the closest match by using a variation of the distance equation. Say that all the RGB values of the VGA color palette have been loaded into the arrays:

```
float red[256],
      green[256],
      blue[256];
```

Now imagine that we want to see what color best matches a color that has RGB values *r_test*, *g_test*, and *b_test*. A technique can be employed that performs an RGB distance formula in color space, comparing the test color to all the candidates. Then the candidate with the smallest error—that is, shortest distance—is selected. Here is a rough algorithm:

```
float error=256000, // this will track the error, set it to an impossibly large error
      test_error;        // temp error variable

int best_match = 0,      // this will track the best match
    index;

// hunt for best match

for (index=0; index<=255; index++)
    {
    // compute distance in color space between test color and candidate

    test_error = sqrt( (r_test - red[index])  * (r_test - red[index]) +
                       (g_test - green[index]) * (g_test - green[index]) +
                       (b_test - blue[index])  * (b_test - blue[index]));

    // test if this is a better match
```

continued on next page

continued from previous page

```
        if (test_error < error)
            {
            // update current best match and error
            best_match = index;
            error=temp_error;
            } // end if

    } // end for index
```

By the end of the algorithm, the variable *best_match* will hold the RGB index of the closest match to the desired color that the VGA color look-up table has to offer. Now we might ask ourselves, are there better color schemes to use? Yes—for the best results, a color scheme that has an equal distribution of all colors in the spectrum is the best. So the palette registers should be programmed appropriately before the algorithm is run, and that same palette must of course be used for the game.

Before we move on, we might want to consider whether the method we have used can be improved? Well, this depends on what improvement means. Since we are using a precomputed transparency look-up table, the computations don't really matter, but the results of the computations do. Maybe there is a better way to arrive at the values for a transparent pixel? Actually, there is, and I'll briefly review it. Transparency has to do with the transmission of different wavelengths of light. And therefore, if an object is totally blue and the transparent object to be drawn on top of it is totally red—that is, only transmits red wavelengths—then the object behind it shouldn't be visible. Therefore, a better model might be based on filtering instead of mixing, as ours is. Now let's talk about the basis of T2.

Morphing

One of the hottest techniques in computer graphics is called *morphing*—the transformation of one object into another. In our case, morphing would mean the transformation of a solid 3D object into another. How would we go about doing something like this? Figure 12-35 shows the general case of morphing in a wireframe form. As you can see, object one has 4 vertices, object two has 8 vertices, and object three has 12 vertices. The problem is, we must be able to transform each object in the figure into each of the other objects so the results look believable. This may seem almost impossible, but it can be done with the right math.

The problem is actually doing it. First, there are three cases to consider when morphing an object:

Case 1: The source and target objects have the same number of vertices.
Case 2: The source object has fewer vertices than the target object.
Case 3: The source object has more vertices than the target object.

If you think case 1 is the simplest, you're correct. We can simply map each vertex of the source object to each vertex of the target object and then linearly interpo-

FIGURE 12-35

◎ ◎ ◎ ◎ ◎ ◎

Some typical objects that may be morphed

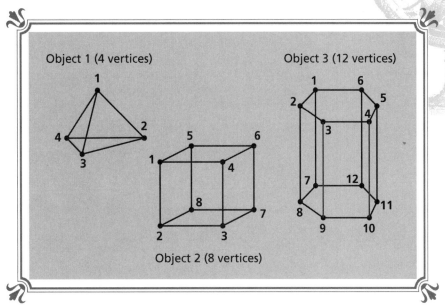

late the position of the source vertices frame after frame until they match that of the target objects' vertices. The problem lies in cases 2 and 3.

Cases 2 and 3 need an intermediate preprocessing step that reconfigures the source object to make it more "morphable" into the target object. For example, the situation of case 2 might be solved by selecting pairs of vertices on the source object and then inserting new vertices on the line between them until the number of vertices in the source and target objects matches. In essence, synthetic vertices are added to the source object to force it into a case 1 configuration. This is shown in Figure 12-36. In the third case, the problem is that the source object has too many vertices. The best thing to do is to select sets of vertices in the source object and map them into the same vertex on the target object. This is shown in Figure 12-37.

Although these techniques will work, and the objects will morph, the problem is usually selecting the best vertices to add (case 2) and the best vertices to group (case 3). Both of these decisions are usually performed with a heuristic algorithm that tries to distribute things equally. However, as a first try, you might simply use random variables.

So how can we use morphing in our game? Well, it might be cool to see a cube change into a tank or vice versa. Effects like this aren't impossible with the engine we are making since we have access to the vertex list of each object. The trick is performing the computations fast enough during real-time.

FIGURE 12-36

*Adding vertices
to make
morphing easier*

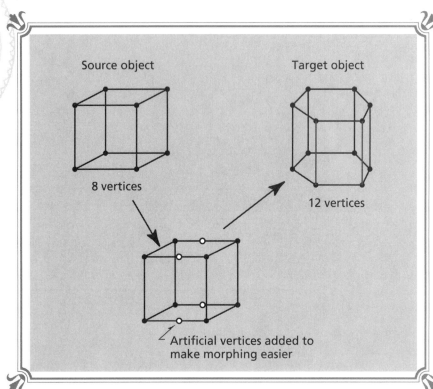

Source object   Target object

8 vertices

12 vertices

Artificial vertices added to
make morphing easier

FIGURE 12-37

*The degenerative
case of morphing*

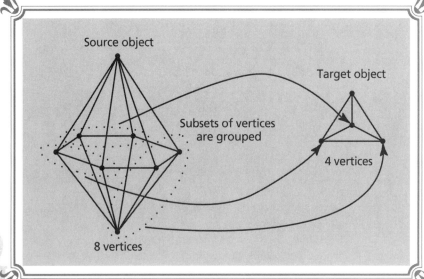

Source object

Target object

Subsets of vertices
are grouped

4 vertices

8 vertices

Summary

Within this chapter we learned how to make our wireframe objects into solid ones. We discussed scan conversion, different shading techniques, and how to do texture mapping. We also covered some topics a bit off the beaten path, such as transparency and morphing. Finally, we have taken a few steps further toward our final 3D engine. During these few steps, we have generated more questions, but that's the idea.

Now let's learn to move around in these 3D universes. As Bruce Lee said, "Hit me; you heard me; hit me!!!"

13

Universal Transformations

come trib[...] fame [...] manu[...] lla [...] li quali [...] obano [...] a[...]
[...] gra p[...] [...] ur [...] o[...] [...] e [...] o [...] gen[...] l [...] la [...] g[...] ano [...] fe ba ne
[...] y a[...] [...] la [...] [...] p[...] [...] a[...] manu be[...] li p[...] gi [...] ni [...]
[...] forga [...] o p[...] i[...] omo p[...] b [...] bal.

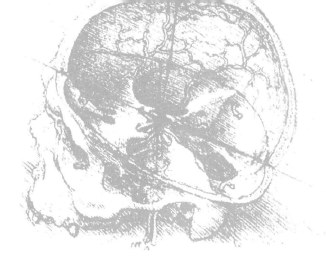

13

Universal Transformations

We have learned how to create 3D and how to display 3D objects. It's now time to bring our static objects to life. Within this chapter, we are going to breach all the barriers of time and space and learn how to move around in the 3D virtual worlds that we have created. We are going to cover in detail the complex chain of transformations necessary to move the player's viewpoint anywhere in the universe and then project the images from Cyberspace onto the video screen. By the end of this chapter, you'll be able to traverse and explore the parallel dimension of Cyberspace as if you were there.

The Player and the Universe

Thus far, we have thought of the player as being located at some specific viewpoint in the universe with a specific set of viewing angles. This is shown in Figure 13-1. However, due to limitations in our current graphics engine, we haven't had much control over the position and orientation of the player. We have been fixing the position of the player at the origin (0,0,0) and setting the view angles at (0,0,0). Hence, the player has been sitting at the origin of the world coordinate system looking down the positive Z axis, as shown in Figure 13-2.

FIGURE 13-1

ⓞ ⓞ ⓞ ⓞ ⓞ ⓞ

*The viewing
vector*

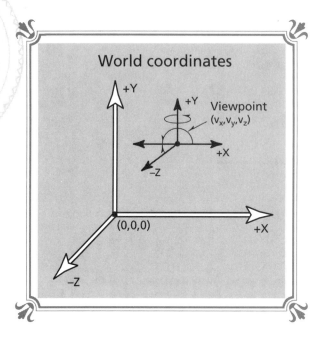

The reason we have kept the player's viewpoint at (0,0,0) and set the view angles to (0,0,0) is that it makes the world to camera transformation easy. Basically, camera coordinates are equal to world coordinates in this case; hence, the transformation is nothing more than a simple assignment. However, that's all about to change. The

FIGURE 13-2

ⓞ ⓞ ⓞ ⓞ ⓞ ⓞ

*Our simple
viewpoint at the
origin*

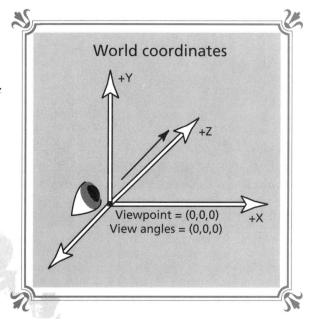

main point of a 3D game is to allow the player to move around in the universe while at the same time changing the angles of his viewing direction. To do this, we must convert world coordinates into camera coordinates. In other words, we must manipulate the positions and orientation of all the objects in the universe such that the final image seen on the video screen is that of the player's current view in Cyberspace at whatever position and orientation his virtual eyes are looking at the time. To accomplish this Cybersorcery, we must perform the following:

1. The local to world transformation.

2. The world to camera transformation.

3. The final perspective projection to screen coordinates.

Actually, we have already spoken of all of these concepts in the theoretical discussions in Chapter 10, and we've even implemented much of the transformations in the previous two chapters. Now we are going to formally write functions that perform these operations at the object level.

Moving the Player and the Camera

The first thing we need to be able to do is move the player's viewpoint and change the orientation of the viewing angles. This is accomplished by setting the viewpoint to the desired position in world coordinates and the view angle to the desired X, Y, Z view angles in degrees (relative to the axes). For example, we know that the viewpoint of the engine is contained in the global variable *view_point*, which is simply a point in 3D space, along with the homogenizing component *w*, which is usually set to 1.0. Therefore, if we wanted to position the camera at (1000,2000,3000) in world coordinates, we would perform the following assignment:

```
view_point.x = 1000;
view_point.y = 2000;
view_point.z = 3000;
view_point.w = 1;
```

Then the viewpoint or camera position would be that shown in Figure 13-3. Positioning the viewpoint is not enough. We must also set the view direction. Normally, the view direction is along the positive Z axis. However, we may want to change this. Making this change is as simple as changing another triplet of data–that is, the view angles stored in the global variable *view_angle*. As an example, say we wanted to set the view angles equal to the view direction of (45,45,45), as shown in Figure 13-4. The assignments would be:

```
view_angle.ang_x = 45;
view_angle.ang_y = 45;
view_angle.ang_z = 45;
```

FIGURE 13-3

Positioning the
viewpoint at an
arbitrary
location

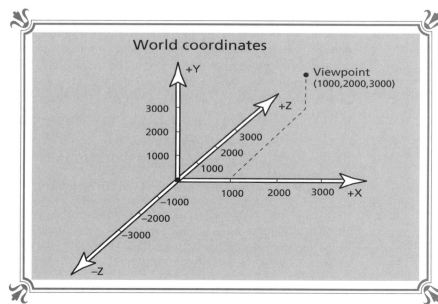

Notice that the angles are in degrees rather than radians. This is because we aren't using the built-in transcendental functions. We are instead using precomputed look-up tables that are stored as linear arrays of 360 elements, one element for each value of SIN and COSINE from 0 to 360 degrees (we have used these before

FIGURE 13-4

The transformed
viewing vector

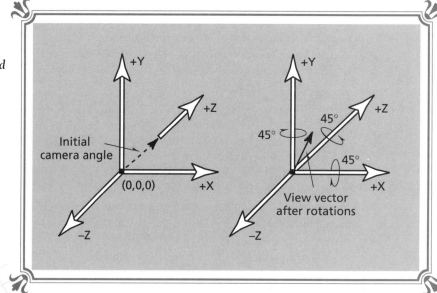

for the object rotations in Chapter 11). Negative values are also legal, but a preprocessing filter must be used to convert the negative angle to a positive one via the formula:

```
if (angle<0)
   angle+=360;
```

Finally, no one said that the camera had to be attached to the player. For example, we might want to make a 3D game that has a second person's view, so we can see ourselves in front of the view screen. Thus, the camera viewpoint and view angles need not be the same as the player's, if that's what we wish. Furthermore, we can implement multiple cameras and switch amongst them by creating an array or similar structure and then assigning the desired virtual camera position and orientation to the global variables *view_point* and *view_angles* whenever a different camera angle is desired. An example of this might be a 3D sports game, or maybe a combat game, in which the player has a team on his side and from time to time may want to see out of each of his teammate's eyes.

Positioning the Virtual Viewpoint at the Origin

Now that we have the technology to move the viewpoint around and change the view angles, how do we take this into account to generate the final image on the screen? Well, we have already seen a form of this during both of the demos WIREDEMO.EXE and SOLIDEMO.EXE. Both of these have a bit of code that transforms the local coordinates of each object into world coordinates, but they lack the world to camera transform. The local to world transformation is the only step necessary because the viewpoint is at the origin and the view angles are all zero; that is, the camera is looking down the positive Z axis. Basically, it is in a neutral position. This is a must!

To perform a 3D projection, we must position and rotate the objects such that the camera is located at (0,0,0) with view angles of (0,0,0), as shown in Figure 13-5. How can this be done? Well, it's accomplished by moving the entire universe relative to the camera position and rotating the entire universe relative to the view angles. After the transformation, all the objects will have been transformed so that they are all located in positions such that the camera seems to be at (0,0,0) with view angles (0,0,0). This is called the *camera transformation* and is the one we have been leaving out. Once we have figured out how to perform this transformation, our viewing system is complete. We can then fly around in our virtual game universe and explore it at will. But before we do this, let's formally write out the local to world transformation function for an object.

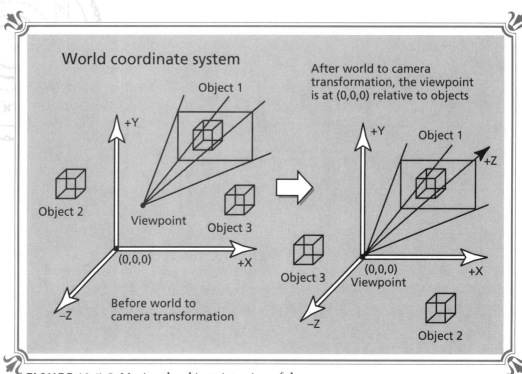

FIGURE 13-5 ◉ *Moving the objects into view of the camera*

The Local to World Transformation

When each object is loaded into the computer, it is relative to its own *local coordinate space*, as shown in Figure 13-6. This is to facilitate local transformations such as rotation and scaling. However, when we want to view an object, we must move it into position in the game universe. This is accomplished by adding to each vertex of the local vertex list the position of the object in world coordinates. This world position is recorded in the *world_pos* field of each object. So a function that converts local coordinates to world coordinates should simply loop through all the vertices of the local vertex list and add the *world_pos* to each vertex. The results should then be stored in the world vertex list of the object. Listing 13-1 does just that.

LISTING 13-1 *Function that converts local coordinates of an object into world coordinates and stores the results in the world vertex list of the object*

```
void Local_To_World_Object(object_ptr the_object)
{
// this function converts an object's local coordinates to world coordinates
```

FIGURE 13-6

◉ ◉ ◉ ◉ ◉ ◉

*Each object has
its own local
coordinate
system*

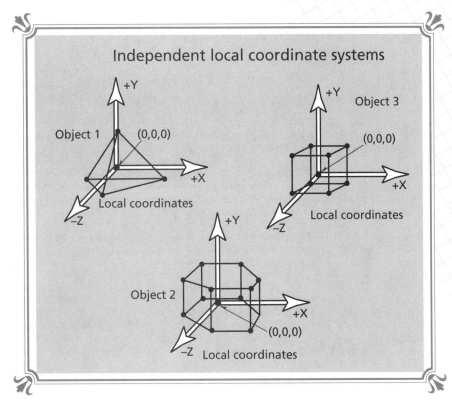

```
// by translating each point in the object by the objects current position

int index;  // looping variable

// move object from local position to world position

for (index=0; index<the_object->num_vertices; index++)
    {
    the_object->vertices_world[index].x = the_object->vertices_local[index].x +
                                    the_object->world_pos.x;

    the_object->vertices_world[index].y = the_object->vertices_local[index].y +
                                    the_object->world_pos.y;

    the_object->vertices_world[index].z = the_object->vertices_local[index].z +
                                    the_object->world_pos.z;

    } // end for index

// reset visibility flags for all polys
for (index=0; index<the_object->num_polys; index++)
```

continued on next page

continued from previous page

```
    {
    the_object->polys[index].visible = 1;
    the_object->polys[index].clipped = 0;
    } // end for

} // end Local_To_World_Object
```

The function *Local_To_World_Object()* takes a single parameter, which is the object to be transformed. The function computes the world coordinates of the object and then resets the visibility and clipped flags of each polygon (just as a precaution). You may or may not want this reset to be performed, so keep it in mind. After processing an object with the above function, the previous *vertices_world[]* array will become invalidated and refreshed with the current world coordinates of the object.

The next step is to convert the world coordinates into camera coordinates relative to the viewpoint and view angles. Therefore, we need a world to camera transformation.

The World to Camera Transformation

The world to camera transformation is probably the most complex thing to understand of all this material, so once we've got it, it's all downhill! What we want to do is move all the objects in such a way that the viewpoint seems to be at (0,0,0), and rotate all the objects in such a way that the view angles seem to be at (0,0,0). We will do this in two steps. The first step is the translation. During this step we take the position of the viewpoint or camera and subtract it from each object in world coordinates. In other words, we multiply each object by a translation matrix that is the inverse of the viewpoint translation matrix.

For example, if the viewpoint was at (10,50,−30), we would want to translate each object by the amounts (−10,−50,30) or, in matrix form, we would multiply each object's world vertex list by:

$$
T^{-1} = \begin{bmatrix} 1 & 0 & 0 & 0 \\ 0 & 1 & 0 & 0 \\ 0 & 0 & 1 & 0 \\ -10 & -50 & 30 & 1 \end{bmatrix} = \text{the inverse of the viewpoint translation matrix}
$$

The next step is a bit more complex. We must rotate the objects in world coordinates in such a way that the camera is positioned so that its view angles are (0,0,0). This may seem hard, but it is achieved in a similar way as the translation: the inverse of the view angle rotation is computed and applied to each vertex of each object in world coordinates. Thus, if the view angles are (5,10,–5), which means 5 degrees around the X axis, 10 degrees around the Y axis, and –5 degrees around the Z axis, then the inverse of this would be (–5,–10,5). In other words, to rotate the objects into the camera position, we rotate them the opposite of the camera angles. In matrix form, this is a bit easier to see. We must perform three separate operations, one for each axis. Then if we wish, we can concatenate them. Thus, we must compute:

$$\text{The world to camera transformation} = T^{-1} * R_x^{-1} * R_y^{-1} * R_z^{-1} = WC$$

This states that the final world to camera transformation is the result of multiplying the inverse of the player's translation matrix along with the inverse of the player's X, Y, and Z rotation matrices. The final result, WC (world to camera), can then be multiplied by each vertex of each object's world coordinate, and the results will be camera coordinates ready for projection.

Therefore, assuming we have computed WC, the function to perform the world to camera transformation is shown in Listing 13-2.

LISTING 13-2 Function that converts world coordinates to camera coordinates

```
void World_To_Camera_Object(object_ptr the_object)
{
// this function converts an object's world coordinates to camera coordinates
// by multiplying each point of the object by the inverse viewing transformation
// matrix which is generated by concatenating the inverse of the view position
// and the view angles the result of which is in global_view

int index; // looping variable

// iterate thru all vertices of object and transform them into camera coordinates
for (index=0; index<=the_object->num_vertices; index++)
    {
    // multiply the point by the viewing transformation matrix

    // x component

    the_object->vertices_camera[index].x =

            the_object->vertices_world[index].x * global_view[0][0] +
            the_object->vertices_world[index].y * global_view[1][0] +
            the_object->vertices_world[index].z * global_view[2][0] +
                                                  global_view[3][0];

    // y component

    the_object->vertices_camera[index].y =
```

continued on next page

continued from previous page

```
                    the_object->vertices_world[index].x * global_view[0][1] +
                    the_object->vertices_world[index].y * global_view[1][1] +
                    the_object->vertices_world[index].z * global_view[2][1] +
                                                          global_view[3][1];

    // z component

    the_object->vertices_camera[index].z =

                    the_object->vertices_world[index].x * global_view[0][2] +
                    the_object->vertices_world[index].y * global_view[1][2] +
                    the_object->vertices_world[index].z * global_view[2][2] +
                                                          global_view[3][2];

    } // end for index

} // end World_To_Camera_Object
```

Similarly to the *Local_To_World_Object()* function, the *World_To_Camera_Object()* function takes as a single parameter a pointer to the object to be transformed. The results of the transformation are placed into the *vertices_camera[]* array of the object's data structure. The function needs the global world to camera transformation *global_view* matrix to be precomputed. Also, note that instead of making a separate call to one of the matrix multiplying functions, the function manually performs the matrix multiplication a component at a time, solving for x, y, and then z of each transformed point. This is for speed.

The question is, where are we going to get the global world to camera transformation matrix? Well, we need to write a function that computes it.

Implementing the Global Transformation Matrix

The global transformation matrix is named *global_view*, and it contains the product of the inverses of the viewing position and viewing angle rotation matrices. Computing this matrix can be done in five steps:

1. Compute the inverse of the translation matrix of the viewpoint.

2. Compute the inverse of the X rotation matrix of the view angles.

3. Compute the inverse of the Y rotation matrix of the view angles.

4. Compute the inverse of the Z rotation matrix of the view angles.

5. Compute the product of all of them and store the result in *global_view*.

The function shown in Listing 13-3 does just that.

LISTING 13-3 Function that creates the global_view world to camera transformation matrix

```
void Create_World_To_Camera(void)
{
// this function creates the global inverse transformation matrix
// used to transform world coordinates to camera coordinates

matrix_4x4 translate,    // the translation matrix

            rotate_x,    // the x,y and z rotation matrices
            rotate_y,
            rotate_z,
            result_1,
            result_2;

// create identity matrices

Mat_Identity_4x4(translate);
Mat_Identity_4x4(rotate_x);
Mat_Identity_4x4(rotate_y);
Mat_Identity_4x4(rotate_z);

// make a translation matrix based on the inverse of the viewpoint

translate[3][0] = -view_point.x;
translate[3][1] = -view_point.y;
translate[3][2] = -view_point.z;

// make rotation matrices based on the inverse of the view angles
// note that since we use lookup tables for sin and cosine, it's hard to
// use negative angles, so we will use the fact that cos(-x) = cos(x)
// and sin(-x) = -sin(x) to implement the inverse instead of using
// an offset in the lookup table or using the technique that
// a rotation of -x = 360-x. note the original rotation formulas will be
// kept in parentheses, so you can better see the inversion

// x matrix

rotate_x[1][1] =  ( cos_look[view_angle.ang_x]);
rotate_x[1][2] = -( sin_look[view_angle.ang_x]);
rotate_x[2][1] = -(-sin_look[view_angle.ang_x]);
rotate_x[2][2] =  ( cos_look[view_angle.ang_x]);

// y matrix

rotate_y[0][0] =  ( cos_look[view_angle.ang_y]);
rotate_y[0][2] = -(-sin_look[view_angle.ang_y]);
rotate_y[2][0] = -( sin_look[view_angle.ang_y]);
rotate_y[2][2] =  ( cos_look[view_angle.ang_y]);

// z matrix
```

continued on next page

continued from previous page

```
rotate_z[0][0] =  ( cos_look[view_angle.ang_z]);
rotate_z[0][1] = -( sin_look[view_angle.ang_z]);
rotate_z[1][0] = -(-sin_look[view_angle.ang_z]);
rotate_z[1][1] =  ( cos_look[view_angle.ang_z]);

// multiply all the matrices together to obtain a final world to camera
// viewing transformation matrix i.e.
// translation * rotate_x * rotate_y * rotate_z

Mat_Mul_4x4_4x4(translate,rotate_x,result_1);
Mat_Mul_4x4_4x4(result_1,rotate_y,result_2);
Mat_Mul_4x4_4x4(result_2,rotate_z,global_view);

} // end Create_World_To_Camera
```

The function is fairly straightforward except maybe for a little trick. You may notice that the rotation equation seems a bit reversed. You may think that we would use negative angles to obtain the inverse, and we could, but I decided to use identities along with negative angles. For example, if we wanted the

$\cos(-x)$

then this is equivalent to:

$\cos(x)$

Furthermore, the $\sin(-x)$ is equivalent to:

$-\sin(x)$

Therefore, we can plug these rules into the rotation equations and save a few sign inversions, and so forth.

We are almost ready to go! Assuming that we have defined and loaded an object named *obj_1*, we could transform it into camera coordinates and prepare it for projection with the following calls:

```
Local_To_World_Object((object_ptr)&obj_1);
Create_World_To_Camera
Local_To_World_Object((object_ptr)&obj_1);
```

That's it!

Now that we have a camera-ready object(s), let's take a look at how to project it to make sure we really understand it.

Projecting the Universe on the Screen

We have already seen the functions that can draw objects on the screen; however, later we will want to remodel our little engine a bit to break each object down into polygons and then project them on the screen. But let's stick to objects for now. As an example of using our new functions, let's once again rewrite the demo program so that it allows us to move the viewpoint and change the view angles in real-time while viewing a solid object. The only real changes to the SOLIDEMO.C program are going to be calls to the new transformation functions along with some keyboard support to change both the viewing position and viewing angles. Moreover, we are going to remove the code that moves the object and simply fix it in space.

The name of the demo program that does all this is SOL2DEMO.EXE and the source is called SOL2DEMO.C. To generate your own executable, you will have to link in the module BLACK11.C if it isn't already in your library. This chapter as well as the last chapter haven't added any new library modules—we are still exploring the large set of functions from BLACK11.C and BLACK11.H. Anyway, let's take a look at the control and execution of the program. Table 13-1 lists the keys we will use to move the viewpoint and orientation.

TABLE 13-1
❖❖❖❖❖❖

Viewpoint controls for SOL2DEMO.EXE

Keypress	Movement
→	Move the viewpoint in the positive X direction.
←	Move the viewpoint in the negative X direction.
↑	Move the viewpoint in the positive Y direction.
↓	Move the viewpoint in the negative Y direction.
PAGE ↑	Move the viewpoint in the positive Z direction.
PAGE ↓	Move the viewpoint in the negative Z direction.
A	Rotate the view angle in the positive X direction.
Z	Rotate the view angle in the negative X direction.
S	Rotate the view angle in the positive Y direction.
X	Rotate the view angle in the negative Y direction.
D	Rotate the view angle in the positive Z direction.
C	Rotate the view angle in the negative Z direction.
ESC	Exit program.

To run the program, you must feed it a PLG file. Within this chapter's directory, you will find:

CUBE.PLG - A cube
PYRAMID.PLG - A four-sided pyramid
CRYSTAL.PLG - A crystal-looking object (sorta!)

For example, to load the cube, you would type:

SOL2DEMO CUBE.PLG

The source for the program is shown in Listing 13-4.

LISTING 13-4 Demo of the complete local to camera transformation pipeline

```c
// I N C L U D E S ////////////////////////////////////////////////////////////

#include <io.h>
#include <conio.h>
#include <stdio.h>
#include <stdlib.h>
#include <dos.h>
#include <bios.h>
#include <fcntl.h>
#include <memory.h>
#include <malloc.h>
#include <math.h>
#include <string.h>
#include <search.h>            // this one is needed for qsort()

// include all of our stuff

#include "black3.h"
#include "black4.h"
#include "black5.h"
#include "black6.h"
#include "black8.h"
#include "black9.h"
#include "black11.h"

// G L O B A L S ////////////////////////////////////////////////////////////

object test_object;   // the test object

// M A I N ////////////////////////////////////////////////////////////

void main(int argc,char **argv)
{
int index,    // looping variable
    done=0;  // exit flag

char buffer[80]; // used to print strings

// load in the object from the command line
if (!PLG_Load_Object(&test_object,argv[1],1))
    {
    printf("\nCouldn't find file %s",argv[1]);
```

```
        return;

    } // end if

// position the object 300 units in front of user
Position_Object((object_ptr)&test_object,0,0,300);

// set the viewpoint
view_point.x = 0;
view_point.y = 0;
view_point.z = 0;

// create the sin/cos lookup tables used for the rotation function
Build_Look_Up_Tables();

// set graphics to mode 13h
Set_Graphics_Mode(GRAPHICS_MODE13);

// allocate double buffer
Create_Double_Buffer(200);

// read the 3d color palette off disk
Load_Palette_Disk("standard.pal",(RGB_palette_ptr)&color_palette_3d);
Write_Palette(0,255,(RGB_palette_ptr)&color_palette_3d);

// install the isr keyboard driver
Keyboard_Install_Driver();

// set viewing distance
viewing_distance = 250;

// main event loop
while(!done)
    {
    // compute starting time of this frame
    starting_time = Timer_Query();

    // erase the screen
    Fill_Double_Buffer(0);

    // test what key(s) user is pressing

    // test if user is moving viewpoint in positive X
    if (keyboard_state[MAKE_RIGHT])
       view_point.x+=5;

    // test if user is moving viewpoint in negative X
    if (keyboard_state[MAKE_LEFT])
       view_point.x-=5;

    // test if user is moving viewpoint in positive Y
    if (keyboard_state[MAKE_UP])
```

continued on next page

continued from previous page

```
                    view_point.y+=5;

        // test if user is moving viewpoint in negative Y
        if (keyboard_state[MAKE_DOWN])
           view_point.y-=5;

        // test if user is moving viewpoint in positive Z
        if (keyboard_state[MAKE_PGUP])
           view_point.z+=5;

        // test if user is moving viewpoint in negative Z
        if (keyboard_state[MAKE_PGDWN])
           view_point.z-=5;

        // this section takes care of view angle rotation
        if (keyboard_state[MAKE_Z])
           {
           if ((view_angle.ang_x+=10)>360)
              view_angle.ang_x = 0;

           } // end if

        if (keyboard_state[MAKE_A])
           {
           if ((view_angle.ang_x-=10)<0)
              view_angle.ang_x = 360;
           } // end if

        if (keyboard_state[MAKE_X])
           {
           if ((view_angle.ang_y+=10)>360)
              view_angle.ang_y = 0;
           } // end if

        if (keyboard_state[MAKE_S])
           {
           if ((view_angle.ang_y-=5)<0)
              view_angle.ang_y = 360;

           } // end if

        if (keyboard_state[MAKE_C])
           {
           if ((view_angle.ang_z+=5)>360)
              view_angle.ang_z = 0;

           } // end if


        if (keyboard_state[MAKE_D])
           {
           if ((view_angle.ang_z-=5)<0)
              view_angle.ang_z = 360;
```

```
          } // end if

      // test for exit key
      if (keyboard_state[MAKE_ESC])
         done=1;

      // rotate the object on all three axes
      Rotate_Object((object_ptr)&test_object,2,4,6);

      // convert to world coordinates
      Local_To_World_Object((object_ptr)&test_object);

      // shade and remove backfaces, ignore the backface part for now
      // notice that shading and backface removal is done in world coordinates
      Remove_Backfaces_And_Shade((object_ptr)&test_object);

      // create the global world to camera transformation matrix
      Create_World_To_Camera();

      // convert to camera coordinates
      World_To_Camera_Object((object_ptr)&test_object);

      // draw the object
      Draw_Object_Solid((object_ptr)&test_object);

      // print out viewpoint
      sprintf(buffer,"Viewpoint is at (%d,%d,%d)        ",(int)view_point.x,
                                                          (int)view_point.y,
                                                          (int)view_point.z);

      Print_String_DB(0,0,9,buffer,0);

      sprintf(buffer,"Viewangle is at (%d,%d,%d)          ",(int)view_angle.ang_x,
                                                          (int)view_angle.ang_y,
                                                          (int)view_angle.ang_z);

      Print_String_DB(0,10,9,buffer,0);

      // display double buffer
      Display_Double_Buffer(double_buffer,0);

      // lock onto 18 fra,mes per second max
      while((Timer_Query()-starting_time)<1);

      } // end while

   // restore graphics mode back to text
   Set_Graphics_Mode(TEXT_MODE);

   // restore the old keyboard driver
   Keyboard_Remove_Driver();

   } // end main
```

Visually, the program doesn't seem to do much more than the SOLIDEMO.EXE program. But internally, as we know, it is doing far more.

We actually have enough software at this point to fly freely in a 3D universe. Of course, we are still lacking the knowledge about hidden surface removal and 3D clipping, but we're getting there!

Order of Operations

We are reaching a point of sophistication and complexity in our software where we need to start thinking about the order that we are performing various operations. We have talked about the graphics pipeline a few times now, and it's becoming clear that as we learned, the pipeline can be executed in more than one order depending on the situation. We already have software for local to world transformations, world to camera transformations, shading, back-face culling (even though we are going to cover it in the next chapter), and 2D screen projections. We should start asking ourselves, do we need to perform all of these operations in the order we have been performing them? And, do we need to perform all of them all of the time?

The answer to both questions is no! In fact, as long as the final results are the desired picture, the less we have to do, the better. So, keep this in mind as we cover the material. By fully understanding each component of the pipeline, you may find ways to improve and make it faster that aren't shown in this book!

Summary

This chapter has been a nice break from the complexity of the others. Basically, we formalized some concepts such as local to world and world to camera transformations. We also pinned down the difference between the camera and the player and how they can be separate.

The demi-gods of Cyberspace are getting worried–soon we will master their universe and control their minds... ha ha ha! Sorry about that; I get carried away sometimes. Anyway, now it's time to learn how to remove the unwanted polygons from our displays; otherwise known as hidden surface removal.

14

Hidden Surfaces and Object Removal

...ome ...ti ...one le manovelle ... le quali si mob ano ... la ...
... gra p si ... tutti le m...n...e o ...gen...so sag o grano di bo ne
... r ... a r... nella ...o ... si o per ma ...la a...la mano bella p...gi anor
a fonga o più ... omo p...b...bal.

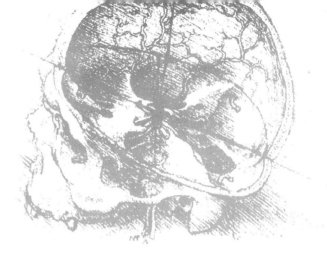

hidden Surface and Object Removal

We almost have all the pieces to our 3D puzzle! Although we have seen and used the code that removes hidden surfaces, it's time to understand the why, what, and how of it a little better. Furthermore, we're going to take the concept of hidden surface removal and extend it to entire objects. This will give us the ability to remove entire objects from the graphics pipeline.

We'll round out the chapter with some optimization ideas to get our "wet-ware" optimizing compilers in the habit of thinking about ways to improve something even before it's written. And by the way, funny things are starting to happen around here… there are dark forces trying to keep this information from being viewed by mortal eyes. So be careful.

The Hidden Surface Removal Problem

The phrase *hidden surface removal* has been totally confused in the computer lexicon to mean something that it doesn't really mean. Hidden surface removal simply means to remove surfaces that aren't visible from the viewer's viewpoint. It has nothing to do with the final rendering of the image; it is a preprocessing step to

speed up the graphics pipeline by minimizing the number of polygons that must be transformed, projected, and scan-converted.

Hidden surface removal can be performed in either world coordinates or camera coordinates. However, the calculation is more efficient if performed in world coordinates, since invisible surfaces will not be transformed during the world to camera transformation step. Figure 14-1 shows the two different approaches to testing for back faces.

At this point, we are still using objects as the primary element for calculations since objects themselves are sets of vertices, and performing transformations on the vertices that make up an object is more efficient in most cases than the same calculation on polygons that make up the object. For example, there are 8 vertices in a cube using the vertex definition of an object, but 24 vertices if polygons are used to define the same cube. Therefore, we're going to perform the hidden surface removal at an object level for the most part. What I'm trying to say is, we are going to remove hidden surfaces from an object *before* the object has been converted into a polygon list and mixed with other polygons.

Back-Face Culling

The actual process of removing hidden surfaces is called back-face culling. Even though we have covered the math, and even performed the process within the *Remove_Backfaces_And_Shade()* function in Chapter 11, let's review exactly how the

FIGURE 14-1

◉ ◉ ◉ ◉ ◉ ◉

Two ways to perform hidden surface removal

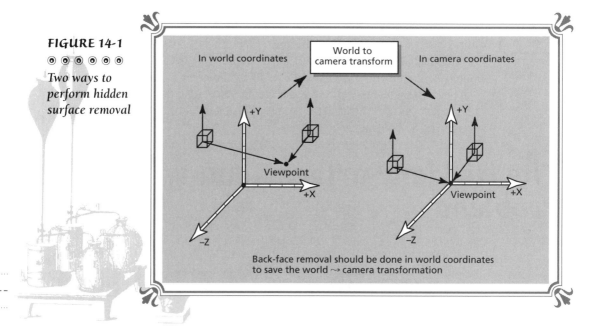

function and mathematics work. The idea is to determine for each polygon face that makes up an object whether the face is visible from the viewpoint. This is done by creating a normal to the polygon surface that is being tested and then computing the interior angle of the normal with a vector that extends from the polygon surface to the viewpoint. This is shown in Figure 14-2.

To accomplish this task, we need to compute the cross product of two vectors lying within the plane of the polygon being tested; compute a line of sight vector with the viewpoint; and finally, compute the dot product to determine whether the angle between the normal vector and the line of sight vector is less than or greater than 90 degrees. This is shown in Figure 14-3.

Computing the Normal

Our engine works (at this point) by using the first three vertices of each polygon to create two coplanar vectors, as shown in Figure 14-4. Even if the polygon is a quad, it doesn't matter, since the normal that is computed based on these two coplanar vectors will be the same if there are four vertices, such as in a quad. Once the two vectors **u** and **v** are computed, the cross product is computed as **vxu** instead of **uxv**. Since the vertices are in counterclockwise order, and we are using a left-handed coordinate system, we must compute **vxu** rather than **uxv** to guarantee that the outward normal points in the correct direction, as shown in Figure 14-2. Granted, we could compute **uxv** and simply invert the vector by multiplying by -1.0, but this is an extra step that can be avoided.

FIGURE 14-2
◉ ◉ ◉ ◉ ◉ ◉

Determining visibility of a surface

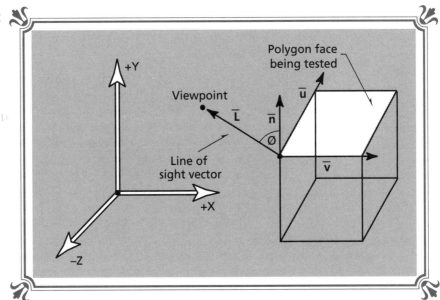

FIGURE 14-3

◎ ◎ ◎ ◎ ◎ ◎

Results of the dot product

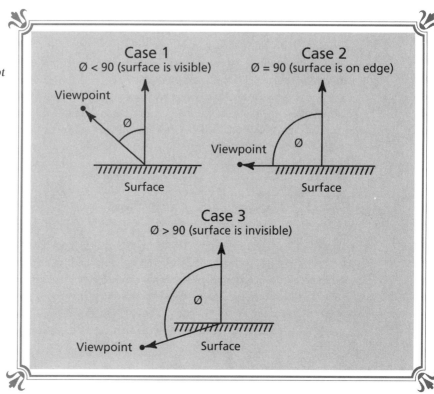

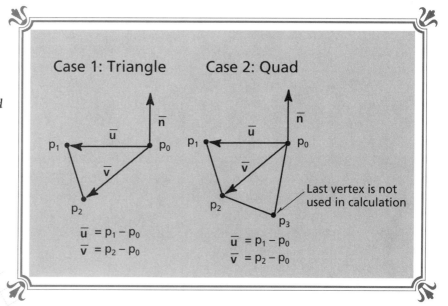

The previous paragraph illustrates a very important detail. Many times when beginners are trying to implement 3D graphics, they use a formula that works in a left-handed system within a right-handed system, and the results are not expected! Even though they verify the equations in their references, it just won't work. The reason for this is that everything matters in 3D graphics. We must be certain of the coordinate system we are using and make sure that the formulas and equations we're using are of the correct form, which in most cases can be fixed with a sign change or two, but it is still a factor to consider.

Crossing the Edges

To compute the surface normal, given that we have computed the vectors **u** and **v** from the polygon vertices, we simply use the formula:

Given $\mathbf{u}=<u_x,u_y,u_z>$ and $\mathbf{v}=<v_x,v_y,v_z>$
$\mathbf{v} \times \mathbf{u} = <(u_z*v_y - u_y*v_z), -(u_z*v_x - u_x*v_z), (u_y*v_x - u_x*v_y)> = \mathbf{n}$

The only glitch is that the length of **n** may be very long or very short; however, since we are only interested in the dot product and not the angle between the vectors, this doesn't matter. Hence, we don't need to normalize the vector, which would take a very long time.

Finding the Angle

As we just learned, we really don't need to find the actual value of the angle; we just need to find its relationship to 90 degrees. This is determined by looking at the sign of the results of the dot product between the normal vector of the test polygon and the line of sight vector, which is computed by subtracting a point on the polygon from the viewpoint, as shown in Figure 14-2. The calculation we must perform is:

$\mathbf{n} \cdot \mathbf{l}=n_x*l_x+n_y*l_y+n_z*l_z=\alpha$

Then we perform the following test:

If ($\alpha<0$), then the angle between the vectors is *obtuse* or greater than 90 degrees, therefore, the surface can't possibly be visible.

Although this test works correctly, it doesn't take into consideration the viewing angles of the camera. Don't they have anything to do with this? The answer is yes, but taking the angles of the viewpoint into consideration can only make the surface invisible, not the other way around. In other words, if the dot product says that the surface is invisible, then the surface is invisible no matter what the view angles are. However, if the dot product indicates that the surface is visible, then it is still possible that the surface is invisible or clipped because the viewer could be looking the other way. As an example of this, take a look at Figure 14-5.

FIGURE 14-5

◎ ◎ ◎ ◎ ◎ ◎

*A visible surface
that's really
hidden*

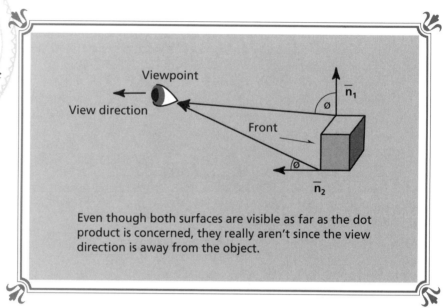

Even though both surfaces are visible as far as the dot product is concerned, they really aren't since the view direction is away from the object.

The figure depicts a cube and the viewpoint. The face labeled "front" will be computed as "visible" from the dot product's point of view, but we can see that the player is looking the other way and couldn't possibly see the face. Therefore, the back-face culling phase actually doesn't remove all back faces; some may slip through and have to be removed by the clipping phase.

Removing the Surface

Once we have computed that a surface is invisible using the dot product and back-face culling technique, we definitely don't need to draw it. Therefore, the *visible* flag in the polygon structure is set to *false*, so that during the rendering process the polygon is not scan-converted. However, this doesn't help us much in the world to camera transformation department since the polygon vertices will still be transformed; it does help us to minimize the number of polygons that are scan-converted.

Precomputing the Normal

Even though we are going to implement most of the optimizations to our 3D engine in one fell swoop, it's nice to hint at them once in a while to keep them on our minds. One such optimization that we have spoken of before and now could make a big difference is precomputing the normals to each surface. But how can we do this if the objects can move and rotate? We can do it by adding a single vertex to each polygon, which lies at the tip of a unit normal vector that is precomputed when objects are loaded. Figure 14-6 shows the added normal vertex. Then to compute the normal, all we have to do is subtract P0 from Pn to obtain **n**.

The only downside to this is that during rotations and transformations we must also rotate and transform the added point Pn, which might not be worth it in the long run. But on the other hand, we saw how important the surface normal was for computing the light intensity for flat shading. We also saw that it's nice if normals have length 1.0, so we don't have to divide by the magnitude of the normal during the lighting calculation. Anyway, these are all issues we should continually investigate as we are building the engine. It's important to realize that no engine works the best in all cases. We must try to find optimizations that help in most cases, while hindering the least.

The Limits of Back-Face Removal

Now we are going to talk a bit about *rendering*. Rendering is the process of drawing the polygons on the screen. Actually, we already have software to do this. The problem is, we haven't addressed the issue of the order in which the polygons of an object or set of objects should be rendered such that the resulting image will be properly drawn and faces that should occlude others will in fact do so. The main

FIGURE 14-6
◎ ◎ ◎ ◎ ◎ ◎
Adding a surface normal point

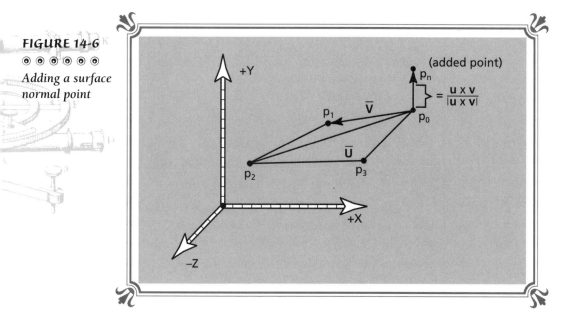

course of this topic will be presented in Chapter 15, but as an appetizer, let's see what we can do with our current tools.

It turns out that back-face removal alone can provide all that is needed to render objects in the proper order. However, one rule must be followed: The objects must be convex and not concave. Furthermore, if there is more than one object in the scene, the objects must not overlap; and they must be sorted based on Z, so that the farther objects are drawn first. Let's begin by analyzing the first premise, that is, convexity.

Convex Objects

Just as 2D polygons can be convex, so can 3D objects. The computation and determination of this mathematically is very difficult, but it's a fairly simple concept to grasp visually. As an example, Figure 14-7 shows two sets of objects. The objects on the left are convex, and the objects on the right are concave. The first thing that comes to mind, if we had to state some overall quality of convex objects, is that they have no dents, while the concave objects do.

FIGURE 14-7

⊚ ⊚ ⊚ ⊚ ⊚ ⊚

Convex vs.
concave objects

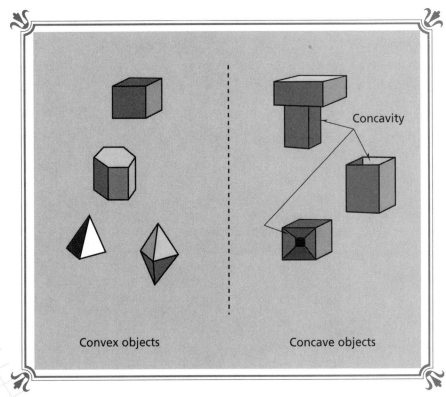

Concavity

Convex objects   Concave objects

Basically, if we create a 3D game and keep the objects as convex as possible, all we need to do to take care of multiple objects and then render the polygons, is remove back faces along with a bit of sorting (which we'll discuss in more detail in Chapter 15). This, in fact, is one of the easiest rendering techniques and works well for simple objects that are non-overlapping and intersecting.

Concave Objects

How can we render concave objects properly? This is a bit of a problem. There are many techniques, such as the Painter's algorithm and Z-buffer, along with other more exotic techniques, such as the Binary Space Partition and Quad Trees. However, we will see more of this in the next chapter because the restraint of convexity on all objects is a bit strict for most 3D games.

Object Level Culling

Switching gears back to removing unwanted polygons, I propose something a little more ambitious. What about removing entire objects from the graphics pipeline? For example, take a look at Figure 14-8. Here we see a top view of a battleground. The player is looking toward the objects, but due to his field of view, only some of

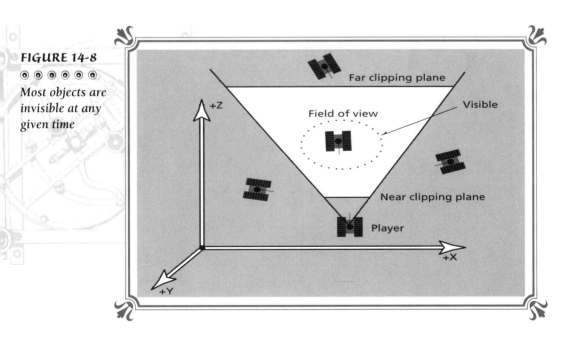

FIGURE 14-8

◉ ◉ ◉ ◉ ◉ ◉

Most objects are invisible at any given time

the objects are visible. Even though back-face removal will remove most of the polygons, we see that all but one object should be totally invisible!

We can take advantage of this fact using a technique called *object level culling*. But how can we achieve this? Well, the trick is, we need to somehow take into consideration the viewing volume of the player. In essence, we are going to perform 3D clipping on an object-to-object basis. However, instead of clipping the polygons that make up an object, we are going to clip the bounding sphere of each object with the viewing volume. Although this may seem like we are about to encroach on mathematical purgatory, we aren't.

Projecting the Object's Sphere

This is what we are going to do: first, we are going to project each of the objects' world positions into camera coordinates. We aren't going to do anything with all the vertices that make up an object, only its center point, which is called *world_pos*. To do this, we are going to perform the following world to camera transformation on the single point *world_pos* for each object:

Given that an object is located at *world_pos* and *global_view* has been computed, then:

```
x_bsphere = the_object->world_pos.x * global_view[0][0] +
                the_object->world_pos.y * global_view[1][0] +
                the_object->world_pos.z * global_view[2][0] +
                                          global_view[3][0];

// compute y component

y_bsphere = the_object->world_pos.x * global_view[0][1] +
                the_object->world_pos.y * global_view[1][1] +
                the_object->world_pos.z * global_view[2][1] +
                                          global_view[3][1];
// compute z component

z_bsphere = the_object->world_pos.x * global_view[0][2] +
                the_object->world_pos.y * global_view[1][2] +
                the_object->world_pos.z * global_view[2][2] +
                                          global_view[3][2];
```

where *x_bsphere*, *y_sphere*, and *z_sphere* are the camera coordinates of the object's center if it were to be transformed into camera coordinates.

Figure 14-9 shows the results of the above equations on a test object. Now, here comes the fun part. We know that there are 6 planes that we must test the sphere against. They are the near and far Z clipping planes, the top and bottom Y clipping planes, and finally the right and left X clipping planes. These are all shown in Figure 14-10.

So what do we do? First we have to generate a sphere from the single point. This is accomplished by setting out 6 points from the center of the object on radii that

FIGURE 14-9
◉ ◉ ◉ ◉ ◉ ◉

Projecting an object's bounding sphere to camera coordinates to test for visibility

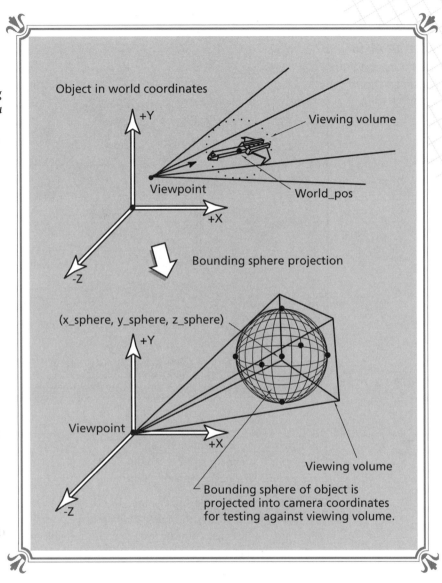

Object in world coordinates

+Y

Viewing volume

Viewpoint

World_pos

-Z

+X

Bounding sphere projection

(x_sphere, y_sphere, z_sphere)

+Y

Viewpoint

+X

Viewing volume

-Z

Bounding sphere of object is projected into camera coordinates for testing against viewing volume.

are each at a position equal to a single object radius, as shown in Figure 14-11. The list of points that make up the bounding sphere are:

P1:(x_sphere+radius,y_sphere,z_sphere)
P2:(x_sphere–radius,y_sphere,z_sphere)
P3:(x_sphere,y_sphere+radius,z_sphere)

FIGURE 14-10

◉ ◉ ◉ ◉ ◉ ◉

Clipping objects to the viewing volume

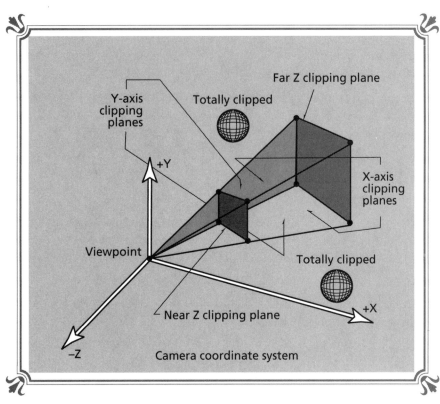

P4:(x_sphere,y_sphere−radius,z_sphere)
P5:(x_sphere,y_sphere,z_sphere+radius)
P6:(x_sphere,y_sphere,z_sphere−radius)

Of course, we could pick other points, but these all lie on one of the major axes of X, Y, and Z, which makes the calculations much easier. Now the trick is to test if the above points that make up the sphere could possibly be within or beyond the viewing volume defined by the 6 planes. However, this is a bit of a problem since the viewing volume is a pyramid and not a rectangular solid. This is a result of the perspective transform that is applied to the final objects; thus, we must take this into consideration when performing the object clipping.

The Trivial Rejection Tests

With that in mind, let's take care of the simple cases first, which are objects beyond the far Z clipping plane and objects beyond the near Z clipping plane. These cases are shown in Figure 14-12. We see that the simple tests of the two Z-axis sphere

FIGURE 14-11

◎ ◎ ◎ ◎ ◎ ◎

The points that make up the bounding sphere of an object

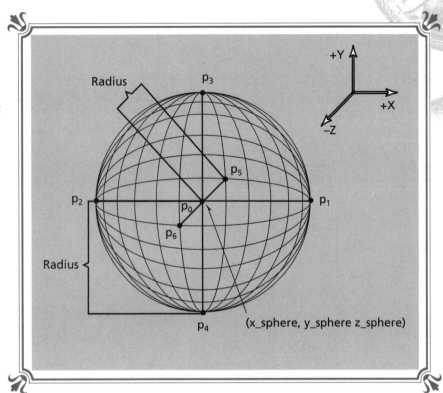

points against the near and far clipping planes will suffice. The actual tests look something like this:

```
if ( ((z_bsphere-radius) > clip_far_z) ||
     ((z_bsphere+radius) < clip_near_z) )
{
 // then object is beyond one of the Z axis clipping planes.
}
```

The test for the other clipping planes is much more complex because we need to project the bounding sphere in perspective and see what the results of the projection are. Then the results are used along with the standard 3D clipping rules for the X and Y axes that we derived earlier in Chapter 10, which are:

A point x,y is within the viewing volume if and only if:

$$x <= \frac{SCREEN\_WIDTH * z}{2 * viewing\_distance}$$

FIGURE 14-12

ⓞ ⓞ ⓞ ⓞ ⓞ ⓞ

*The Z object
tests*

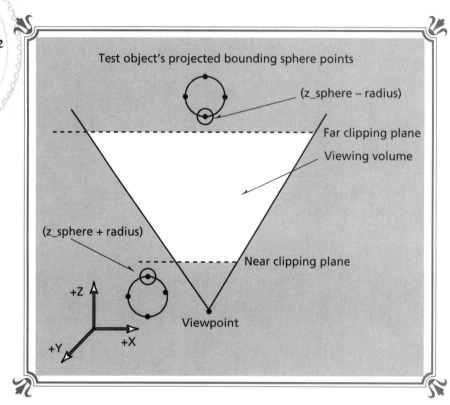

$$x \geq \frac{- \text{SCREEN\_WIDTH} * z}{2 * \text{viewing\_distance}}$$

$$y \leq \frac{\text{SCREEN\_HEIGHT} * z}{2 * \text{viewing\_distance}}$$

$$y \geq \frac{- \text{SCREEN\_HEIGHT} * z}{2 * \text{viewing\_distance}}$$

Therefore, to compute whether the object's bounding sphere when perspectively projected is within or outside the viewing volume, we must use derivatives of the above formulas. Taking all that into consideration, the function shown in Listing 14-1 removes an entire object from the pipeline by means of returning a Boolean that states whether the object is visible or not from the current viewpoint.

LISTING 14-1 *An object removal function*

```
int Remove_Object(object_ptr the_object, int mode)
{
// this function determines if an entire object is within the viewing volume
// or not by testing if the bounding sphere of the object in question
// is within the viewing volume. In essence, this function "culls" entire objects

float x_bsphere,    // the x,y and z components of the projected center of object
      y_bsphere,
      z_bsphere,
      radius,       // the radius of object
      x_compare,    // the extents of the clipping volume in x and y at the
      y_compare;    // bounding spheres current z

// first transform world position of object into camera coordinates

// compute x component

x_bsphere = the_object->world_pos.x * global_view[0][0] +
            the_object->world_pos.y * global_view[1][0] +
            the_object->world_pos.z * global_view[2][0] +
                                      global_view[3][0];

// compute y component

y_bsphere = the_object->world_pos.x * global_view[0][1] +
            the_object->world_pos.y * global_view[1][1] +
            the_object->world_pos.z * global_view[2][1] +
                                      global_view[3][1];
// compute z component

z_bsphere = the_object->world_pos.x * global_view[0][2] +
            the_object->world_pos.y * global_view[1][2] +
            the_object->world_pos.z * global_view[2][2] +
                                      global_view[3][2];

// extract radius of object

radius = the_object->radius;

if (mode==OBJECT_CULL_Z_MODE)
   {
   // first test against near and far z planes

   if ( ((z_bsphere-radius) > clip_far_z) ||
        ((z_bsphere+radius) < clip_near_z) )
        return(1);
   else
        return(0);

   } // end if z only
```

continued on next page

continued from previous page

```
else
    {
    // perform full x,y,z test

    if ( ((z_bsphere-radius) > clip_far_z) ||
         ((z_bsphere+radius) < clip_near_z) )
        return(1);

    // test against x right and left planes, first compute viewing volume
    // extents at position z position of bounding sphere

    x_compare = (HALF_SCREEN_WIDTH*z_bsphere)/viewing_distance;

    if ( ((x_bsphere-radius) > x_compare) ||
         ((x_bsphere+radius) < -x_compare) )
       return(1);

    // finally test against y top and bottom planes

    y_compare = (INVERSE_ASPECT_RATIO*HALF_SCREEN_HEIGHT*z_bsphere)/viewing_distance;

    if ( ((y_bsphere-radius) > y_compare) ||
         ((y_bsphere+radius) < -y_compare) )
       return(1);

    // else it just can't be removed!!!

    return(0);

    } // end else

} // end Remove_Object
```

The function simply performs the algorithm we have outlined. First, the bounding sphere is converted to camera coordinates and projected. Then, based on the *mode* parameter, either the simple Z tests are performed or the entire suite of tests on all the X, Y, and Z axes are performed to try to remove the object. Selection of the tests is controlled via the *mode* variable, which can take one of the two values:

```
OBJECT_CULL_Z_MODE              - simple Z tests only.
OBJECT_CULL_XYZ_MODE            - full X,Y and Z tests.
```

We can use the function in Listing 14-1 to help prune objects out before displaying them. To do this, we call the function before performing any other transformations that might fill up the graphics pipeline with objects that can't possibly be seen from the current viewpoint. Using object culling along with back-face removal, we decrease the image complexity to the point that only the polygons that are visible (in most cases) are processed by the graphics pipeline. Of course, the final step is to implement 3D clipping, but we'll get to that in the next chapter.

As an example of back-face removal coupled with object removal, I have created yet another demo called OBJECTS.EXE, and the source is OBJECTS.C. The demo loads four objects from the command line as PLG files and then proceeds to render them on the screen. For example, to load in the cube you would type:

OBJECTS CUBE.PLG

The controls are the same as for the SOL2DEMO.EXE in Chapter 13, but the program is doing a bit more. First off, there are four objects; second, as the object removal code is being called, and as objects are removed from the pipeline, a message is printed on the screen notifying you of the objects that are being clipped. As you run the demo, notice how the 3D objects are drawn correctly, but in some cases the objects are not drawn relative to each other correctly. This is because we haven't sorted the objects in proper order so that when they are rendered they are rendered in back-to-front order. Anyway, Listing 14-2 shows the code.

LISTING 14-2 *Demo of back-face removal, multiple objects, and object removal*

```c
// I N C L U D E S ///////////////////////////////////////////////////////////

#include <io.h>
#include <conio.h>
#include <stdio.h>
#include <stdlib.h>
#include <dos.h>
#include <bios.h>
#include <fcntl.h>
#include <memory.h>
#include <malloc.h>
#include <math.h>
#include <string.h>
#include <search.h>              // this one is needed for qsort()

// include all of our stuff

#include "black3.h"
#include "black4.h"
#include "black5.h"
#include "black6.h"
#include "black8.h"
#include "black9.h"
#include "black11.h"

// G L O B A L S ///////////////////////////////////////////////////////////

object test_object[4];   // the test objects
```

continued on next page

continued from previous page

```
// M A I N ///////////////////////////////////////////////////////////////////////////

void main(int argc,char **argv)
{
int index,    // looping variable
    done=0;   // exit flag

char buffer[80]; // used to print strings

// load in the objects from the command line
for (index=0; index<4; index++)
    {
    if (!PLG_Load_Object((object_ptr)&test_object[index],argv[1],1))
       {
       printf("\nCouldn't find file %s",argv[1]);
       return;

       } // end if

    } // end for index

// position the objects 300 units in front of user
for (index=0; index<4; index++)
    Position_Object((object_ptr)&test_object[index],-150+index*100,0,300);

// set the viewpoint
view_point.x = 0;
view_point.y = 0;
view_point.z = 0;

// create the sin/cos lookup tables used for the rotation function
Build_Look_Up_Tables();

// set graphics to mode 13h
Set_Graphics_Mode(GRAPHICS_MODE13);

// allocate double buffer
Create_Double_Buffer(200);

// read the 3d color palette off disk
Load_Palette_Disk("standard.pal",(RGB_palette_ptr)&color_palette_3d);
Write_Palette(0,255,(RGB_palette_ptr)&color_palette_3d);

// install the isr keyboard driver
Keyboard_Install_Driver();

// set viewing distance
viewing_distance = 250;

// main event loop

while(!done)
    {
```

```
// compute starting time of this frame
starting_time = Timer_Query();

// erase the screen
Fill_Double_Buffer(0);

// test what key(s) user is pressing

// test if user is moving viewpoint in positive X
if (keyboard_state[MAKE_RIGHT])
   view_point.x+=5;

// test if user is moving viewpoint in negative X
if (keyboard_state[MAKE_LEFT])
   view_point.x-=5;

// test if user is moving viewpoint in positive Y
if (keyboard_state[MAKE_UP])
   view_point.y+=5;

// test if user is moving viewpoint in negative Y
if (keyboard_state[MAKE_DOWN])
   view_point.y-=5;

// test if user is moving viewpoint in positive Z
if (keyboard_state[MAKE_PGUP])
   view_point.z+=5;

// test if user is moving viewpoint in negative Z
if (keyboard_state[MAKE_PGDWN])
   view_point.z-=5;

// this section takes care of view angle rotation
if (keyboard_state[MAKE_Z])
   {
   if ((view_angle.ang_x+=10)>360)
     view_angle.ang_x = 0;

   } // end if

if (keyboard_state[MAKE_A])
   {
   if ((view_angle.ang_x-=10)<0)
     view_angle.ang_x = 360;

   } // end if

if (keyboard_state[MAKE_X])
   {
   if ((view_angle.ang_y+=10)>360)
     view_angle.ang_y = 0;

   } // end if
```

continued on next page

continued from previous page

```
        if (keyboard_state[MAKE_S])
           {
           if ((view_angle.ang_y-=5)<0)
              view_angle.ang_y = 360;

           } // end if

        if (keyboard_state[MAKE_C])
           {
           if ((view_angle.ang_z+=5)>360)
              view_angle.ang_z = 0;

           } // end if

        if (keyboard_state[MAKE_D])
           {
           if ((view_angle.ang_z-=5)<0)
              view_angle.ang_z = 360;

           } // end if

        // test for exit key
        if (keyboard_state[MAKE_ESC])
           done=1;


        // create the global world to camera transformation matrix
        Create_World_To_Camera();

        // blank object removal message area
        sprintf(buffer,"Objects Removed                    ");
        Print_String_DB(0,180,10,buffer,0);

        // process each object
        for (index=0; index<4; index++)
        {
        // test if this object should be processed

        if (!Remove_Object(&test_object[index],OBJECT_CULL_XYZ_MODE))
           {
           // convert to world coordinates
           Local_To_World_Object((object_ptr)&test_object[index]);

           // shade and remove backfaces
           // notice that shading and backface removal is done in
           // world coordinates
           Remove_Backfaces_And_Shade((object_ptr)&test_object[index]);

           // convert to camera coordinates
           World_To_Camera_Object((object_ptr)&test_object[index]);

           // draw the object
           Draw_Object_Solid((object_ptr)&test_object[index]);
```

```
        } // end if object is visible
    else
        {
        sprintf(buffer,"%d, ",index);
        Print_String_DB(128+index*16,180,10,buffer,0);
        }

    } // end for index

    // print out viewpoint
    sprintf(buffer,"Viewpoint is at (%d,%d,%d)      ",(int)view_point.x,
                                                       (int)view_point.y,
                                                       (int)view_point.z);

    Print_String_DB(0,0,10,buffer,0);

    sprintf(buffer,"Viewangle is at (%d,%d,%d)       ",(int)view_angle.ang_x,
                                                        (int)view_angle.ang_y,
                                                        (int)view_angle.ang_z);
    Print_String_DB(0,10,10,buffer,0);

    // display double buffer
    Display_Double_Buffer(double_buffer,0);

    // lock onto 18 frames per second max
    while((Timer_Query()-starting_time)<1);

    } // end while

// restore graphics mode back to text
Set_Graphics_Mode(TEXT_MODE);

// restore the old keyboard driver
Keyboard_Remove_Driver();

} // end main
```

As usual, if you want to create an executable, all you need is BLACK11.C and BLACK11.H and all the previous modules. This chapter doesn't add to our library.

Summary

We are about to start our own little enterprise here! In this chapter we learned the details of back-face removal—why it works and how it works. Also, we implemented a very slick trick called object culling to remove entire objects from the graphics pipeline. We are definitely becoming worthy of the title Cybersorcerer!

Well, the fun's over, and the easy material in this and the previous chapter is going to be a fond memory in a moment! Turn the page and get ready to complete the first version of the 3D graphics engine.

15

Clipping
and Rendering
the Final
View

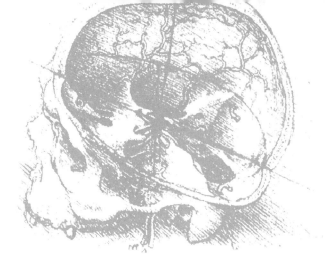

Clipping and Rendering the Final View

Total control of Cyberspace is almost ours! This chapter is the final piece of the puzzle that will solidify our knowledge and bring it together to create a complete 3D graphics engine. Although the engine is not yet optimized, it is of a form that we have been endeavoring to capture since the beginning of our magickal journey. Within this chapter we are finally going to learn the details of 3D clipping along with some of the most popular methods of rendering 3D polygonal representations. Also, as a treat, we are going to devour the technology used to create Doom and other similar games—that is, the Binary Space Partition.

The power that flows within these pages is not meant for mortal eyes. If you dare to read on, then may your soul be spared!

Clipping to the 3D Viewing Volume

Clipping is the process of determining whether a polygon or object is within some finite space. In the introductory 3D material of Chapter 10, we learned the mathematics of clipping in 3D. In essence, the 3D clipping volume is a pyramid or *frustum* that is defined by six sides, as shown in Figure 15-1. We learned how to determine if a point is inside or outside the viewing volume by testing it against a set of equations that model the sides of the viewing volume and the Z extents of the volume. Furthermore, we implemented forms of 2D clipping within the triangle rendering functions. We even used a form of clipping to remove entire objects. But we still haven't performed clipping of an object at the polygon level. This is the next step to complete the clipping process.

The question is, how do we clip the polygons of an object? Well, the answer to this question must be based on a design decision that we are going to make a little later; thus, we need to look into the future for a moment to see the best way to attack this problem. In the end, we are going to convert each object that is completely or partially within the viewing volume into a set of polygons and then add this set of polygons to a master polygon list. Then the master polygon list is going to be scan-converted to the screen. Hence, we would like to filter any polygons that are entirely clipped from being added to the master polygon list so they don't clutter up the graphics pipeline. To do this, we're going to write a function that takes an object as input and then sets the *clipped* flags for each polygon within the object based on the viewing volume.

If you recall, there are a few extra fields for each polygon in an object. One of them is the *clipped* flag, which was added for just this purpose. So the 3D clipping function is going to process each object and set the *clipped* flags appropriately for each polygon. Then, when the final polygon list is generated, not only will we look at the *visible* flag (which was set or reset during the back-face culling), but the *clipped* flag for each polygon will be checked to see if the polygon has been *clipped* against the 3D volume.

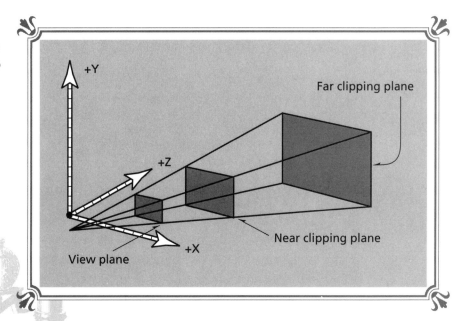

FIGURE 15-1
◉ ◉ ◉ ◉ ◉ ◉
The viewing volume once again

FIGURE 15-2

◎ ◎ ◎ ◎ ◎ ◎

The bare minimum Z clipping

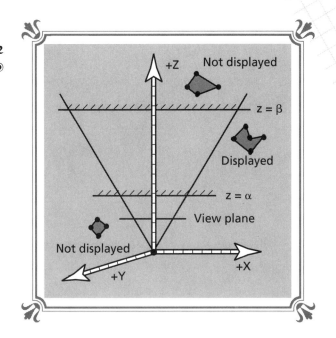

Now before we begin writing a 3D polygon clipping function, do we really need one? Well, that's a hard question to answer. Many graphics engines do not perform full 3D clipping. However, this can be dangerous. For example, if polygons that have negative Z values or zero Z values are perspectively projected, then divide-by-zero errors and bizarre distortions will occur. Therefore, we must at least clip polygons against the far and near Z clipping planes, as shown in Figure 15-2. But clipping polygons to the other four sides of the viewing volume can help cut down the number of polygons needlessly passed to the scan converter.

If the majority of the polygons in the world are never clipped and they all stay in view most of the time, then performing a 3D clipping phase isn't worth the overhead. But whether it's better or not, we're going to implement it, so at the very least, we are familiar with full 3D clipping and the mathematics behind it. Before we write the function, let's clarify a possible misunderstanding. In general terms, *clipping* means to intersect a polygon with a bounding plane and compute the visible polygon that would result from the intersection. Figure 15-3 shows an example of this. As you can see, the image on the left shows a polygon (a quad in this case) that is supposed to be clipped against a boundary.

However, instead of recomputing a new polygon, as shown on the right of the figure, we simply make a note that the polygon is partially visible and need not be clipped at this time. We will let the scan converter clip the polygon in image space a scan line at a time. Although this might not seem like the best approach, it will have to do, because if we allow polygons to intersect with multiple planes, then the

FIGURE 15-3

◎ ◎ ◎ ◎ ◎ ◎

Clipping
polygons can add
vertices as well
as many
calculations

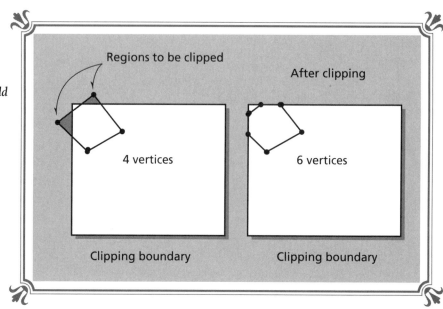

resulting visible portion of the polygon after clipping might not have a maximum of four sides. This isn't an option since we can't deal with polygons with more than four sides.

Let's take a look at the function that performs full 3D clipping of an object's polygons. The function has been lurking in BLACK11.C, so it's not part of this chapter's library. The name of the function is *Clip_Object_3D()* and is shown in Listing 15-1.

LISTING 15-1 *Function that performs full 3D clipping on the polygon level*

```
void Clip_Object_3D(object_ptr the_object, int mode)
{
// this function clips an object in camera coordinates against the 3D viewing
// volume. the function has two modes of operation. In CLIP_Z_MODE the
// function performs only a simple z extend clip with the near and far clipping
// planes. In CLIP_XYZ_MODE mode the function performs a full 3D clip

int curr_poly;   // the current polygon being processed

float x1,y1,z1,
      x2,y2,z2,
      x3,y3,z3,
```

```
            x4,y4,z4,   // working variables used to hold vertices

            x1_compare, // used to hold clipping points on x and y
            y1_compare,
            x2_compare,
            y2_compare,
            x3_compare,
            y3_compare,
            x4_compare,
            y4_compare;


// test if trivial z clipping is being requested
if (mode==CLIP_Z_MODE)
   {
   // attempt to clip each polygon against viewing volume
   for (curr_poly=0; curr_poly<the_object->num_polys; curr_poly++)
       {
       // extract z components

       z1=the_object->vertices_camera[the_object->polys[curr_poly].vertex_list[0]].z;
       z2=the_object->vertices_camera[the_object->polys[curr_poly].vertex_list[1]].z;
       z3=the_object->vertices_camera[the_object->polys[curr_poly].vertex_list[2]].z;

         // test if this is a quad
         if (the_object->polys[curr_poly].num_points==4)
            {
            // extract 4th z component
            z4=the_object->vertices_camera[the_object->polys[curr_poly].vertex_list[3]].z;

            } // end if quad
         else
           z4=z3;

         // perform near and far z clipping test
         if ( (z1<clip_near_z && z2<clip_near_z && z3<clip_near_z && z4<clip_near_z) ||
             (z1>clip_far_z && z2>clip_far_z && z3>clip_far_z && z4>clip_far_z) )
             {
             // set clipped flag
             the_object->polys[curr_poly].clipped=1;

             } // end if clipped

         } // end for curr_poly

     } // end if CLIP_Z_MODE
else
    {
    // CLIP_XYZ_MODE, perform full 3D viewing volume clip
    for (curr_poly=0; curr_poly<the_object->num_polys; curr_poly++)
       {
```

continued on next page

continued from previous page

```
// extract x,y and z components

x1=the_object->vertices_camera[the_object->polys[curr_poly].vertex_list[0]].x;
y1=the_object->vertices_camera[the_object->polys[curr_poly].vertex_list[0]].y;
z1=the_object->vertices_camera[the_object->polys[curr_poly].vertex_list[0]].z;

x2=the_object->vertices_camera[the_object->polys[curr_poly].vertex_list[1]].x;
y2=the_object->vertices_camera[the_object->polys[curr_poly].vertex_list[1]].y;
z2=the_object->vertices_camera[the_object->polys[curr_poly].vertex_list[1]].z;

x3=the_object->vertices_camera[the_object->polys[curr_poly].vertex_list[2]].x;
y3=the_object->vertices_camera[the_object->polys[curr_poly].vertex_list[2]].y;
z3=the_object->vertices_camera[the_object->polys[curr_poly].vertex_list[2]].z;

// test if this is a quad
if (the_object->polys[curr_poly].num_points==4)
   {
   // extract 4th vertex
   x4=the_object->vertices_camera[the_object->polys[curr_poly].vertex_list[3]].x;
   y4=the_object->vertices_camera[the_object->polys[curr_poly].vertex_list[3]].y;
   z4=the_object->vertices_camera[the_object->polys[curr_poly].vertex_list[3]].z;

   // do clipping tests

   // perform near and far z clipping test first
   if (!((z1>clip_near_z || z2>clip_near_z || z3>clip_near_z || z4>clip_near_z) &&
       (z1<clip_far_z || z2<clip_far_z || z3<clip_far_z || z4<clip_far_z)) )
      {
      // set clipped flag

      the_object->polys[curr_poly].clipped=1;
      continue;

      } // end if clipped

   // pre-compute x comparison ranges
   x1_compare = (HALF_SCREEN_WIDTH*z1)/viewing_distance;
   x2_compare = (HALF_SCREEN_WIDTH*z2)/viewing_distance;
   x3_compare = (HALF_SCREEN_WIDTH*z3)/viewing_distance;
   x4_compare = (HALF_SCREEN_WIDTH*z4)/viewing_distance;

   // perform x test
   if (!((x1>x1_compare || x2>x1_compare || x3>x3_compare || x4>x4_compare) &&
       (x1<x1_compare || x2<x2_compare || x3<x3_compare || x4<x4_compare)) )
      {
      // set clipped flag
      the_object->polys[curr_poly].clipped=1;
      continue;

      } // end if clipped

   // pre-compute x comparison ranges
   y1_compare = (HALF_SCREEN_HEIGHT*z1)/viewing_distance;
```

```
        y2_compare = (HALF_SCREEN_HEIGHT*z2)/viewing_distance;
        y3_compare = (HALF_SCREEN_HEIGHT*z3)/viewing_distance;
        y4_compare = (HALF_SCREEN_HEIGHT*z4)/viewing_distance;

        // perform x test

        if (!((y1>-y1_compare || y2>-y1_compare || y3>-y3_compare || y4>-y4_compare) &&
             (y1<y1_compare || y2<y2_compare || y3<y3_compare || y4<y4_compare))  )
           {
           // set clipped flag

           the_object->polys[curr_poly].clipped=1;
           continue;

           } // end if clipped

        } // end if quad
   else
      {
      // must be triangle, perform clipping tests on only 3 vertices

      // do clipping tests

      // perform near and far z clipping test first
      if (!((z1>clip_near_z || z2>clip_near_z || z3>clip_near_z) &&
            (z1<clip_far_z || z2<clip_far_z || z3<clip_far_z))  )
         {
         // set clipped flag

         the_object->polys[curr_poly].clipped=1;
         continue;

         } // end if clipped

      // pre-compute x comparison ranges
      x1_compare = (HALF_SCREEN_WIDTH*z1)/viewing_distance;
      x2_compare = (HALF_SCREEN_WIDTH*z2)/viewing_distance;
      x3_compare = (HALF_SCREEN_WIDTH*z3)/viewing_distance;

      // perform x test

      if (!((x1>-x1_compare || x2>-x1_compare || x3>-x3_compare ) &&
            (x1<x1_compare || x2<x2_compare || x3<x3_compare ))   )
         {
         // set clipped flag

         the_object->polys[curr_poly].clipped=1;
         continue;

         } // end if clipped

      // pre-compute x comparison ranges
      y1_compare = (HALF_SCREEN_HEIGHT*z1)/viewing_distance;
```

continued on next page

continued from previous page

```
            y2_compare = (HALF_SCREEN_HEIGHT*z2)/viewing_distance;
            y3_compare = (HALF_SCREEN_HEIGHT*z3)/viewing_distance;

            // perform x test
            if (!((y1>-y1_compare || y2>-y1_compare || y3>-y3_compare) &&
                (y1<y1_compare || y2<y2_compare || y3<y3_compare ))   )
                {
                // set clipped flag
                the_object->polys[curr_poly].clipped=1;
                continue;

                } // end if clipped

            } // end else triangle

        } // end for curr_poly

    } // end else clip everything

} // end Clip_Object_3D
```

The function takes two parameters—the first is a pointer to the object to process and the second is the method of processing. The two methods of processing are:

CLIP_Z_MODE   Clips only the Z extents of the object's polygons.

CLIP_XYZ_MODE   Clips each polygon against the full 3D viewing volume.

The constants are defined in BLACK11.H. The simpler of the two modes is *CLIP_Z_MODE*, which simply tests the Z components of each polygon to determine whether they are inside or outside the viewing volume's near and far Z clipping planes. Then the *clipped* flag for each polygon is set based on the results of the test. The more complex, and hence slower, clipping mode is *CLIP_XYZ_MODE*, which performs a full X, Y, and Z viewing volume test of all six containment planes that make up the viewing volume. The results of the test are again recorded in the *clipped* flag for each polygon.

The *Clip_Object_3D()* function should be used after the call to *Remove_Object()* to further prune the number of polygons that will be entered into the master polygon list for the current animation frame. For example, say that we have defined an object named *car*, and we have already removed back faces and tried to remove the whole object. The next call might be

```
Clip_Object_3D((object_ptr)&car,CLIP_XYZ_MODE);
```

which would proceed to set the *clipped* flags for the remaining polygons that make up the *car* that wasn't removed by the back-face culling step. Moreover, a full 3D clip is performed instead of the simple Z plane clip that the function supports as well.

Now we are finally ready to talk about this mysterious polygon list!

Generating the Polygon List

Most graphics engines use objects as the basic graphics element, but at some point the engine creates a polygon list based on the polygons that make up each object (see Figure 15-4). This single list is much easier to deal with than a conglomeration of objects when it comes down to the final rendering and scan conversion. This sounds like a good plan to me, so we're going to jump on the bandwagon and use a similar technique. It's true we have seen demos that draw 3D objects and even multiple objects, but the rendering was done by a function that only draws single objects; that is, the function has no idea that other objects are in the game universe. This is a bit of a problem since the other objects might be drawn in an order that is not correct compared to the proper 3D view that should be displayed.

Anyway, that alone is the major reason we need to create a polygon list. Granted, we could sort objects based on their Z values and then draw the distant ones first, followed by the nearer ones, but this won't work if the objects get too close and begin to overlap. Furthermore, supporting a general polygon list allows us more flexibility with further additions to the 3D engine and different rendering techniques, as we are going to see.

So how should we construct this polygon list? Well, in a high-performance, memory-efficient graphics system, the list would usually be implemented as a linked list of polygons. However, if you haven't already noticed, I like to stay away from data structures since they don't add much to the techniques and make things

FIGURE 15-4

◉ ◉ ◉ ◉ ◉ ◉

Creating a polygon list from objects

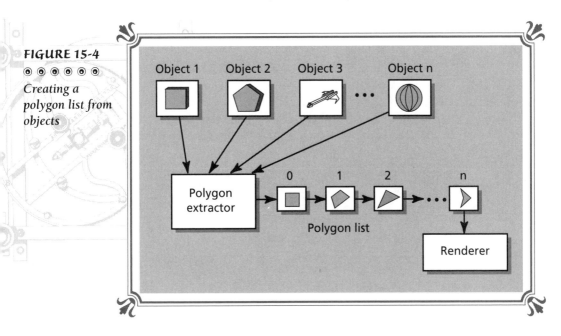

much more confusing. We're simply going to use an array to hold the polygons. And we will make the array large enough to hold a number of polygons that will be sufficient for any single frame. But before we create this array, we need to stop a minute and think about how we are going to represent a polygon.

In the object definition of a polygon, each polygon is defined as an array of indices into a general vertex list. This data structure won't do now. A simpler data structure is actually better; thus, the polygon list will contain a list of polygons where each polygon structure has storage for up to four vertices. Here is the data structure we are going to use to hold a polygon:

```
// this structure holds a final polygon facet and is self contained

typedef struct facet_typ
        {

        int num_points;   // number of vertices
        int color;        // color of polygon
        int shade;        // the final shade of color after lighting
        int shading;      // type of shading to use
        int two_sided;    // is the facet two sided
        int visible;      // is the facet transparent
        int clipped;      // has this poly been clipped
        int active;       // used to turn faces on and off

        point_3d vertex_list[MAX_POINTS_PER_POLY]; // the points that make
                                                   // up the polygon facet

        float normal_length;  // holds pre-computed length of normal

        } facet, *facet_ptr;
```

You will notice that the data structure is almost identical to the *polygon* data structure except that it is completely self-contained and doesn't require an external vertex list to exist somewhere else. Also, the name of the structure is *facet*, which is as good as any since we already used up the word *polygon*. Now that we know what the elements of the polygon array look like, let's make a global array to put them in. Here it is:

```
facet world_poly_storage[MAX_POLYS_PER_FRAME];  // the storage for the visible
                                                // polygons is pre-allocated
                                                // so it doesn't need to be
                                                // allocated frame by frame
```

And *MAX_POLYS_PER_FRAME* is defined in BLACK11.H as,

```
#define MAX_POLYS_PER_FRAME     128 // maximum number of polys in a single
                                    // animation frame
```

which should be more than enough. Actually, if there are this many visible polygons in a single frame, our engine is going to start bailing, if you know what I mean!

Next, we need to write a function that takes an object as input and then traverses the object looking for polygons that haven't been removed by the back-face culler or clipped and adds them to the polygon list. However, there is one little detail that, again, we must look into the future to deal with. One of the most popular rendering algorithms, the Painter's algorithm, is based on sorting the polygons in the polygon list and then performing a suite of tests (among other things); however, if we try to sort the polygon list, the overhead of moving all the data around will kill us!

The solution to this is to create a level of indirection by creating yet another array that contains pointers to the storage array. Then by simply sorting the pointers to the storage array and then referencing the pointer array, we can manipulate the polygons much quicker than accessing the physical storage. This indirection is shown in Figure 15-5. As you can see, the second array simply contains a list of pointers, and there is a one-to-one correspondence from each element in the pointer array to the physical storage array. The name of the pointer array is *world_polys[]* and is defined as follows:

```
facet_ptr world_polys[MAX_POLYS_PER_FRAME]; // the visible polygons for
                                            // this frame
```

Again, this array is defined in BLACK11.C.

Now let's write the function that creates the polygon list. Remember, this list is generated each frame, so we need to have a way to reset and create it each frame.

FIGURE 15-5

◎ ◎ ◎ ◎ ◎ ◎

The polygon list data structures

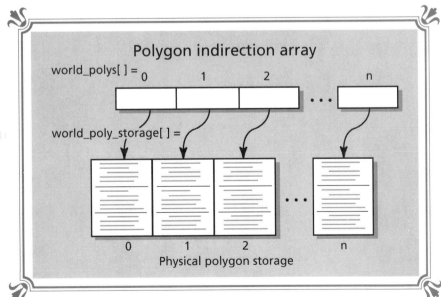

Since the storage for the array is preallocated at startup, this resetting boils down to using a variable to track the number of polygons in the list. To reset the list, we simply set this variable back to zero. It just so happens that a variable with this exact use in mind is defined in BLACK11.C and is called:

```
int num_polys_frame;                    // the number of polys in
                                        // this frame
```

All we need to do is update this variable within the function that generates the polygon list so that other functions know how many polygons have been added to the list.

We're now ready to write the polygon list function. Listing 15-2 contains the completed function.

LISTING 15-2 Function that creates the polygon list from objects

```
void Generate_Poly_List(object_ptr the_object,int mode)
{
// this function is used to generate the final polygon list that will be
// rendered. Object by object the list is built up


int vertex,
    curr_vertex,
    curr_poly;

// test if this is the first object to be inserted
if (mode==RESET_POLY_LIST)
    {
    // reset number of polys to zero
    num_polys_frame=0;
    return;

    } // end if first

// insert all visible polygons into polygon list
for (curr_poly=0; curr_poly<the_object->num_polys; curr_poly++)
    {
    // test if this poly is visible, if so add it to poly list
    if (the_object->polys[curr_poly].visible &&
       !the_object->polys[curr_poly].clipped)
        {
        // add this poly to poly list

        // first copy data and vertices into an open slot in storage area

        world_poly_storage[num_polys_frame].num_points
                    =the_object->polys[curr_poly].num_points;
        world_poly_storage[num_polys_frame].color
                    =the_object->polys[curr_poly].color;
```

```
world_poly_storage[num_polys_frame].shade
                    = the_object->polys[curr_poly].shade;
world_poly_storage[num_polys_frame].shading
                    = the_object->polys[curr_poly].shading;
world_poly_storage[num_polys_frame].two_sided
                    = the_object->polys[curr_poly].two_sided;
world_poly_storage[num_polys_frame].visible
                    = the_object->polys[curr_poly].visible;
world_poly_storage[num_polys_frame].clipped
                    = the_object->polys[curr_poly].clipped;
world_poly_storage[num_polys_frame].active
                    = the_object->polys[curr_poly].active;

// now copy vertices

for (curr_vertex=0; curr_vertex<the_object->polys[curr_poly].num_points;
    curr_vertex++)
    {
    // extract vertex number
    vertex=the_object->polys[curr_poly].vertex_list[curr_vertex];

    // extract x,y and z
    world_poly_storage[num_polys_frame].vertex_list[curr_vertex].x
                        = the_object->vertices_camera[vertex].x;

    world_poly_storage[num_polys_frame].vertex_list[curr_vertex].y
                        = the_object->vertices_camera[vertex].y;

    world_poly_storage[num_polys_frame].vertex_list[curr_vertex].z
                        = the_object->vertices_camera[vertex].z;


    } // end for curr_vertex

// assign pointer to it
world_polys[num_polys_frame] = &world_poly_storage[num_polys_frame];

// increment number of polys
num_polys_frame++;

} // end if poly visible

} // end for curr_poly

} // end Generate_Poly_List
```

The function takes as parameters the object to add to the polygon list along with a mode of operation. The mode is used to reset the polygon list or add the polygons of the object to the list. For example, to reset the polygon list for the next frame, the function would be called like this:

```
Generate_Poly_List(NULL,RESET_POLY_LIST);
```

And to add the polygons of an object to the polygon list, the function is called like this:

```
Generate_Poly_List((object_ptr)&object, ADD_TO_POLY_LIST);
```

Again, the constants are defined in BLACK11.H.

To use the function, we would first remove back faces, shade, remove objects, and clip. After all those steps are complete, a call is made to *Generate_Poly_List()* with each object that has survived all the previous perils, and the final polygon list will reflect only those polygons that are visible or partially visible for the current camera position and animation frame. The only problem is, even with a polygon list, we still have one burning problem—in what order should we draw the polygons? This is called the "rendering problem" and is the next incantation to be mastered.

Rendering vs. Hidden Surface Removal

The concepts of rendering and hidden surface removal often are confused and intertwined. *Rendering* has to do with how the polygons are drawn, and hidden surface removal simply means removing hidden surfaces! It's true that during rendering, some portions of some polygons may be obscured by other polygons, but the surfaces are definitely not removed; they are omitted or obscured during the rendering process. Anyway, we need to figure out some ways to draw the polygons in the proper order, so they look correct and the 3D universe looks 3D!

There are more 3D rendering algorithms than sequels to *Friday the 13th*, so we're going to concentrate on three of my favorites that are prevalent in most 3D graphics engines. Although our final game engine implementation is going to use a very simplified version of the Painter's algorithm, the other techniques are equally important and have been used successfully in many games.

The Painter's Algorithm and Depth Sorting

The Painter's algorithm is the simplest conceptually to understand of all the rendering techniques. It is based on how a painter paints on a canvas (well, at least the name is). When a painter is painting a picture, he or she paints objects in the distance first and then draws the objects that are nearer to obscure these farther objects, as shown in Figure 15-6. In essence, the painter is performing a mental Z sort on the images and drawing the farther Z images first.

FIGURE 15-6

◎ ◎ ◎ ◎ ◎ ◎

A painter paints distant objects first

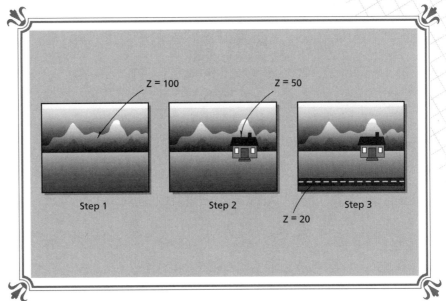

We can use a similar technique to draw the polygons in the polygon list; however, there are some problems with the technique as it stands. The main problem is that polygons, unlike painting, exist within 3D space and have three or four vertices; these vertices can have different Z values. So, when we sort the polygons, which Z value should we use for the sort? Figure 15-7 shows this dilemma. The first case uses the minimum Z, the second case uses the maximum Z, and the third case uses the average Z. We quickly realize that all the methods fall short in some case, as Figure 15-7 points out. Using the average Z yields the best results in most cases, so we'll choose it as the lesser of all the evils.

We must recognize that sometimes the polygons are going to be sorted incorrectly and, hence, displayed wrong. Can we fix this problem? The answer is yes, but to fix it takes a lot of work, and the final algorithm has a run-time performance of $O(n^2)$. This means that in the worst case, not only do we have to perform very complex tests, but we may have to reorder the polygons and perform n^2 swaps. Thus, we aren't going to use a full Painter's algorithm; instead, we're going to limit ourselves to the depth sort version only.

If you're interested in implementing a full Painter's algorithm, here are the tests that you must perform on each polygon pair to determine if they are in the correct or incorrect order:

1. **The Z Extents Test:** This test determines whether the Z extents of the polygons overlap, as shown in Figure 15-8. Note that polygon A is the nearer one—this will be important in further tests. If the Z extents do overlap, it's

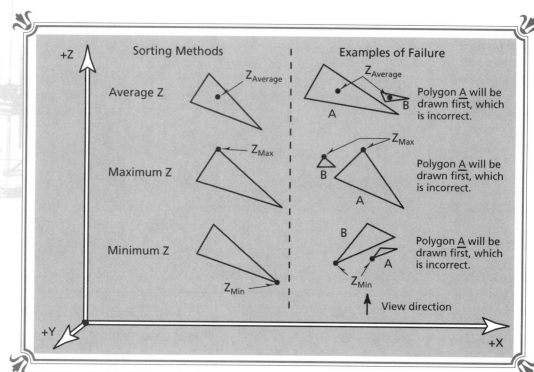

FIGURE 15-7 ⊚ *Different depth sorting tactics*

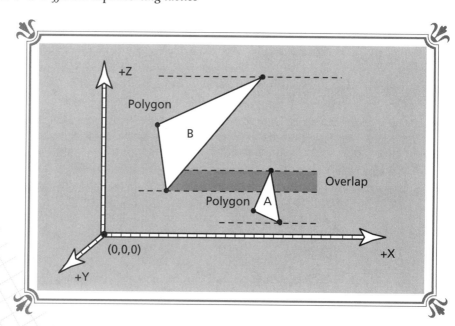

FIGURE 15-8
⊚ ⊚ ⊚ ⊚ ⊚ ⊚
*The Z extents
overlap test*

FIGURE 15-9
◎ ◎ ◎ ◎ ◎ ◎
The X extents
test

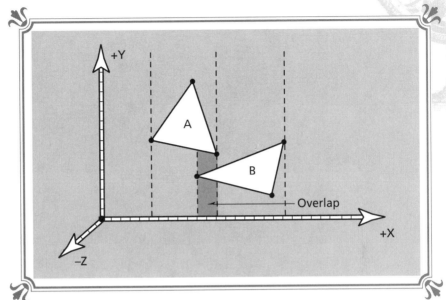

possible that the polygons must be swapped, so the next test must be performed. On the other hand, if the Z extents do not overlap, the polygons
can't possibly be in the incorrect order, and the next pair of polygons can be
processed.

2. **The X Extents Test:** This test is similar to the first one, but tests whether
   the X extents of the test polygons overlap. This is shown in Figure 15-9. If
   the X extents overlap, it's possible that the polygons might need to be
   swapped; therefore, the next test must be performed. If the polygon's X
   extents do not overlap, the polygons are in the correct order, and the next
   pair of polygons can be processed.

3. **The Y Extents Test:** By now, you can guess that this test is similar to the
   second one, but tests whether the Y extents of the test polygons overlap.
   This is shown in Figure 15-10. If the Y extents overlap, it's possible that the
   polygons might need to be swapped; therefore, the next test must be performed. If the polygon's Y extents do not overlap, the polygons are in the
   correct order, and the next pair of polygons can be processed.

4. **The Far Side Test:** This test determines if polygon B is on the far side of
   polygon A (which is the one with the nearer Z coordinate in Figure 15-8).
   This can be calculated by testing each point of polygon B against the plane
   equation of polygon A and testing the sign of the result. Depending on the
   direction of the surface normal of A, the signs should be all positive or

FIGURE 15-10

◎ ◎ ◎ ◎ ◎ ◎

The Y extents test

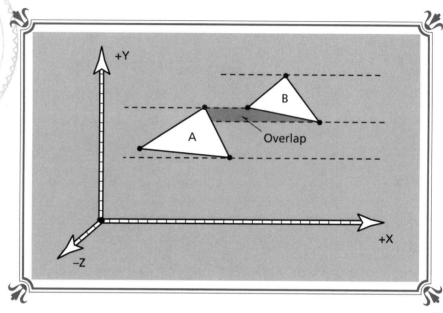

negative. If this test passes, the polygons are in correct order. If the test fails, the next test must be performed.

5. **The Near Side Test:** This test determines if polygon A is on the near side of polygon B (which is the one with the farther Z coordinate in Figure 15-8). This can be calculated by testing each point of polygon A against the plane equation of polygon B and testing the sign of the result. Depending on the direction of the surface normal of B, the signs should be all positive or negative. If this test passes, the polygons are in correct order. If this test fails, the polygons are definitely ordered incorrectly and should be swapped.

Of course, there is always a "but." And the "but" is that even if the polygons fail all the tests, it's possible they don't overlap if they are concave (have dents). This is shown in Figure 15-11. However, since all our polygons are triangles or squares, we don't need to go this far.

Although the tests seem simple enough to implement, the truth is, they're not. There are a lot of special cases and "fudges" that must be used to get them to work. Because of that, along with the fact that techniques such as the Z-buffer are becoming more common due to increasing PC speed and memory availability, we're going to leave well enough alone and simply use a depth Z sort for now. (Later, for the final game engine, we may add a test or two to help the Z sort a little.) Of course, using a simple Z sort is going to result in incorrect polygon orders now and then. But this isn't going to kill us in a game since the game is in motion and the speed of

FIGURE 15-11

⊚ ⊚ ⊚ ⊚ ⊚ ⊚

The special concave situation in testing for overlap

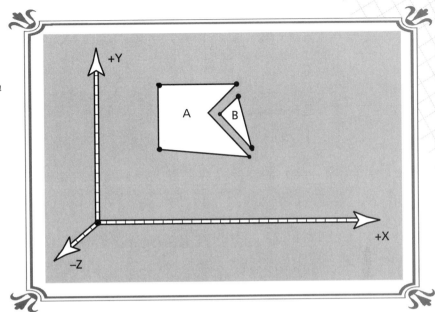

using a simple Z sort outweighs the slowdown incurred by performing all the tests to obtain the correct order.

To perform the Z sort, we need to sort the polygons in the polygon list. And remember, this is fairly easy since we have pointers to the polygons. Thus, all we need to do is swap pointers around to perform the actual sort. So how do we sort a collection of objects on some key such as average Z? Well, we need a sorting algorithm, and one of the fastest is called Quick Sort. It has run-time behavior of $O(n*log_2 n)$, which is just about optimal. However, using hardware and special memories, sorting can be performed in a single cycle, but that's a fantasy on the PC! Luckily for us, Quick Sort has become so popular that it is a standard call in the C/C++ languages. All we need to do is supply the function with the data to be sorted along with a comparison function, and Quick Sort will sort the data for us.

The header for the Quick Sort function can be found in the SEARCH.H C/C++ header file and looks like this:

```
void qsort(void *base, size_t num, size_t width,
           int (_cdecl *compare)(const void *elem_1,const void *elem2));
```

Wow, that's a syntactic nightmare! Let's break this down a piece at a time. Here's what each parameter does:

base   Starting address of array to be sorted.

num   Number of elements in array to be sorted.

> width   Size of a single array element in bytes.
> compare A pointer to a comparison function that we must
>   supply and that takes two pointers and returns a
>   result of the form shown in Table 15-1.

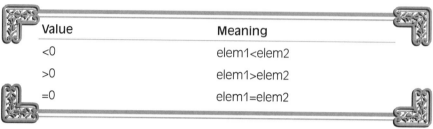

Value	Meaning
<0	elem1<elem2
>0	elem1>elem2
=0	elem1=elem2

Using the return codes in Table 15-1, the array will be sorted in ascending order. If we want to reverse this, we would return the opposite return codes. It looks like the only thing that's a bit complex is the *compare* function. If you've never used function pointers, or are a little rusty, it probably looks like a syntax error, but it's not! All it means is that we must write a function that takes a pair of pointers to array elements, performs the comparison (however it's done), and then returns the proper return code as defined in Table 15-1. So we need to write a function that averages the Z values of the polygons and then performs the comparison. Listing 15-3 fills the requirements.

LISTING 15-3 Z value comparison function to be used by qsort()

```
int Poly_Compare(facet **arg1, facet **arg2)
{
// this function compares the average z's of two polygons and is used by the
// depth sort surface ordering algorithm

float z1,z2;
facet_ptr poly_1,poly_2;

// dereference the poly pointers
poly_1 = (facet_ptr)*arg1;
poly_2 = (facet_ptr)*arg2;

// compute z average of each polygon
if (poly_1->num_points==3)
   {
   // compute average of 3 point polygon
   z1 = (float)0.33333*(poly_1->vertex_list[0].z+
                        poly_1->vertex_list[1].z+
                        poly_1->vertex_list[2].z);
   }
else
   {
```

```
// compute average of 4 point polygon
z1 = (float)0.25*(poly_1->vertex_list[0].z+
                  poly_1->vertex_list[1].z+
                  poly_1->vertex_list[2].z+
                  poly_1->vertex_list[3].z);

} // end else

// now polygon 2

if (poly_2->num_points==3)
   {
   // compute average of 3 point polygon
   z2 =(float)0.33333*(poly_2->vertex_list[0].z+
                       poly_2->vertex_list[1].z+
                       poly_2->vertex_list[2].z);
   }
else
   {
   // compute average of 4 point polygon
   z2 = (float)0.25*(poly_2->vertex_list[0].z+
                     poly_2->vertex_list[1].z+
                     poly_2->vertex_list[2].z+
                     poly_2->vertex_list[3].z);

   } // end else

// compare z1 and z2, such that polys will be sorted in descending Z order
if (z1>z2)
   return(-1);
else
if (z1<z2)
   return(1);
else
   return(0);

} // end Poly_Compare
```

The *Poly_Compare()* function is of the correct form and performs the proper calculation by averaging together the Z values of each polygon. Note that the average is computed correctly regardless of whether the polygon has three or four vertices. At this point, we're ready to write the polygon depth sorting function. The function will simply call *qsort()* with the correct parameter list. Listing 15-4 contains the final sorting function.

LISTING 15-4 The final depth sorting function

```
void Sort_Poly_List(void)
{
// this function does a simple z sort on the poly list to order surfaces
// the list is sorted in descending order, i.e. farther polygons first
```

continued on next page

continued from previous page

```
qsort((void *)world_polys,num_polys_frame, sizeof(facet_ptr), Poly_Compare);

} // end Sort_Poly_List
```

If that isn't easy, then I don't know what is! However, we are being insulated from the hideous *qsort()* function, which isn't too hard to write, but not something we want to do (unless you like recursion, binary sorting, and asymptotic analysis). Let's see if the parameters make sense. The first should be a pointer to the beginning of the array to be sorted, and it is. The second is the number of elements in the array, which is correct again, but the third is the size of an element, and it looks wrong. Shouldn't it be *sizeof(facet)*? No! Remember, the whole reason we created a second level of indirection using an array of pointers is for just this reason—so we could sort the pointers, not the actual polygon data. So that's OK. The final parameter is a pointer to the comparison function, which could use a bit of a cast, but let's let the compiler complain a little, shall we.

We could defer the last step, which is a function to draw the polygon list, but let's skip right to it so we can see a demo of all that we've learned so far.

Rendering the Final Image with Perspective

We need to draw the polygons in the polygon list with perspective. And we have done this many times during the implementation of all the *Draw_Object()* functions. However, this time, instead of breaking an object down into polygons, we're simply going to traverse the global polygon list and draw the polygons one at a time using the perspective projection equations that we have memorized by now (right!). Listing 15-5 shows the polygon list rendering function.

LISTING 15-5 Function that draws the polygons in the polygon list

```
void Draw_Poly_List(void)
{

// this function draws the global polygon list generated by calls to
// Generate_Poly_List

int curr_poly,          // the current polygon
    is_quad=0;          // quadrilateral flag

float x1,y1,z1,         // working variables
      x2,y2,z2,
      x3,y3,z3,
      x4,y4,z4;

// draw each polygon in list
for (curr_poly=0; curr_poly<num_polys_frame; curr_poly++)
```

```
        {
        // do Z clipping first before projection
        z1=world_polys[curr_poly]->vertex_list[0].z;
        z2=world_polys[curr_poly]->vertex_list[1].z;
        z3=world_polys[curr_poly]->vertex_list[2].z;

        // test if this is a quad

        if (world_polys[curr_poly]->num_points==4)
           {
           // extract vertex number and z component for clipping and projection
           z4=world_polys[curr_poly]->vertex_list[3].z;

           // set quad flag
           is_quad=1;

           } // end if quad
        else
          z4=z3;

#if 0
        // perform z clipping test
        if ( (z1<clip_near_z && z2<clip_near_z && z3<clip_near_z && z4<clip_near_z) ||
             (z1>clip_far_z && z2>clip_far_z && z3>clip_far_z && z4>clip_far_z) )
           continue;
#endif

           // extract points of polygon

           x1 = world_polys[curr_poly]->vertex_list[0].x;
           y1 = world_polys[curr_poly]->vertex_list[0].y;

           x2 = world_polys[curr_poly]->vertex_list[1].x;
           y2 = world_polys[curr_poly]->vertex_list[1].y;

           x3 = world_polys[curr_poly]->vertex_list[2].x;
           y3 = world_polys[curr_poly]->vertex_list[2].y;

           // compute screen position of points

           x1=(HALF_SCREEN_WIDTH  + x1*viewing_distance/z1);
           y1=(HALF_SCREEN_HEIGHT - ASPECT_RATIO*y1*viewing_distance/z1);

           x2=(HALF_SCREEN_WIDTH  + x2*viewing_distance/z2);
           y2=(HALF_SCREEN_HEIGHT - ASPECT_RATIO*y2*viewing_distance/z2);

           x3=(HALF_SCREEN_WIDTH  + x3*viewing_distance/z3);
           y3=(HALF_SCREEN_HEIGHT - ASPECT_RATIO*y3*viewing_distance/z3);

           // draw triangle

           Draw_Triangle_2D((int)x1,(int)y1,(int)x2,(int)y2,(int)x3,(int)y3,
                       world_polys[curr_poly]->shade);
```

continued on next page

continued from previous page

```
                // draw second poly if this is a quad
                if (is_quad)
                    {
                    // extract the point

                    x4 = world_polys[curr_poly]->vertex_list[3].x;
                    y4 = world_polys[curr_poly]->vertex_list[3].y;

                    // project to screen

                    x4=(HALF_SCREEN_WIDTH  + x4*viewing_distance/z4);
                    y4=(HALF_SCREEN_HEIGHT - ASPECT_RATIO*y4*viewing_distance/z4);

                    // draw triangle

Draw_Triangle_2D((int)x1,(int)y1,(int)x3,(int)y3,(int)x4,(int)y4,
                            world_polys[curr_poly]->shade);

                    } // end if quad

            } // end for curr_poly

    } // end Draw_Poly_List
```

The function doesn't take any parameters since it refers to the global polygon arrays and the variable *num_polys_frame*. The function works by traversing the polygon pointer list, dereferencing the next polygon in the list, extracting the vertices of it, and then sending the appropriate perspective projected 2D coordinates to the triangle rendering functions. You should also notice that there is a chunk of code conditionally compiled out of the function. This is the Z clipping code and you can reenable it to be compiled if you wish the function to perform Z clipping (in the event that you don't want to call *Clip_Object_3D()* for some reason). This is a good example of different pipeline structures. We can perform different operations at different times depending on design considerations; that is, the pipeline doesn't have to have one specific order to work right.

Now it's time to see some Cybersorcery, don't you think? Let's put everything we have learned together and write a demo that loads multiple objects and displays them using the depth sort rendering algorithm. The name of the demo is SORTDE-MO.EXE and the source is called SORTDEMO.C. To create an executable, you'll need to link in all the graphics modules, including BLACK15.C. The demo works like the other 3D demos in that it takes as input the name of a PLG file to use as the test object. So to run the demo with the standard cube, you would type:

```
SORTDEMO CUBE.PLG
```

When the program runs, it loads the object and creates a game field with 16 test objects staggered in a regular grid. Then, using the standard keyboard commands along with some extras to move the light source, the user can manipulate the universe. To refresh your memory, Table 15-2 lists the keyboard commands (once again).

TABLE 15-2
✧✧✧✧✧✧
Keyboard commands for SORTDEMO.EXE

Keypress	Movement
→	Move the viewpoint in the positive X direction.
←	Move the viewpoint in the negative X direction.
↑	Move the viewpoint in the positive Y direction.
↓	Move the viewpoint in the negative Y direction.
PAGE ↑	Move the viewpoint in the positive Z direction.
PAGE ↓	Move the viewpoint in the negative Z direction.
A	Rotate the view angle in the positive X direction.
Z	Rotate the view angle in the negative X direction.
S	Rotate the view angle in the positive Y direction.
X	Rotate the view angle in the negative Y direction.
D	Rotate the view angle in the positive Z direction.
C	Rotate the view angle in the negative Z direction.
T	Rotate the light source direction parallel to the positive X axis.
G	Rotate the light source direction parallel to the positive Y axis.
B	Rotate the light source direction parallel to the positive Z axis.
Y	Rotate the light source direction parallel to the negative X axis.
H	Rotate the light source direction parallel to the negative Y axis.
N	Rotate the light source direction parallel to the negative Z axis.
ESC	Exit program.

Listing 15-6 contains the source for the demo.

LISTING 15-6 The summation of our 3D knowledge

```
// I N C L U D E S ///////////////////////////////////////////////////////////

#include <io.h>
#include <conio.h>
#include <stdio.h>
#include <stdlib.h>
#include <dos.h>
#include <bios.h>
#include <fcntl.h>
#include <memory.h>
#include <malloc.h>
#include <math.h>
#include <string.h>
#include <search.h>                    // this one is needed for qsort()

// include all of our stuff

#include "black3.h"
#include "black4.h"
#include "black5.h"
#include "black6.h"
#include "black8.h"
#include "black9.h"
#include "black11.h"
#include "black15.h"

// G L O B A L S ///////////////////////////////////////////////////////////

object test_objects[16];                    // objects in universe

// M A I N ///////////////////////////////////////////////////////////////////

void main(int argc,char **argv)
{
int done=0, // exit flag
    index;  // looping variable

char buffer[80]; // output string buffer

float x,y,z;     // working variables

// build all look up tables
Build_Look_Up_Tables();

// load in the test object
for (index=0; index<16; index++)
    {
    if (PLG_Load_Object(&test_objects[index],argv[1],1))
```

```
           printf("\nplg loaded.");
        else
           printf("\nCouldn't load file");

     } // end for index

// set the position of the object
for (index=0; index<16; index++)
    {
    test_objects[index].world_pos.x=-200 + (index%4)*100;
    test_objects[index].world_pos.y=0;
    test_objects[index].world_pos.z=200 + 300*(index>>2);
    } // end index

// set graphics to mode 13h
Set_Graphics_Mode(GRAPHICS_MODE13);

// read the 3D color palette off disk
Load_Palette_Disk("standard.pal",(RGB_palette_ptr)&color_palette_3d);
Write_Palette(0,255,(RGB_palette_ptr)&color_palette_3d);

// allocate double buffer
Create_Double_Buffer(200);

// install the isr keyboard driver
Keyboard_Install_Driver();

// main event loop
while(!done)
    {
    // compute starting time of this frame
    starting_time = Timer_Query();

    // erase all objects
    Fill_Double_Buffer(0);

    // test what user is doing

    // move the light source

    if (keyboard_state[MAKE_T])
       {
       x = light_source.x;
       y = cos(.2)*light_source.y - sin(.2) * light_source.z;
       z = sin(.2)*light_source.y + cos(.2) * light_source.z;
       light_source.y = y;
       light_source.z = z;
       }

       if (keyboard_state[MAKE_G])
          {
          y = light_source.y;
```

continued on next page

continued from previous page

```
        x = cos(.2)*light_source.x + sin(.2) * light_source.z;
        z = -sin(.2)*light_source.x + cos(.2) * light_source.z;
        light_source.x = x;
        light_source.z = z;
        }

    if (keyboard_state[MAKE_B])
        {
        z = light_source.z;
        x = cos(.2)*light_source.x - sin(.2) * light_source.y;
        y = sin(.2)*light_source.x + cos(.2) * light_source.y;
        light_source.x = x;
        light_source.y = y;
        }

    if (keyboard_state[MAKE_Y])
        {
        x = light_source.x;
        y = cos(-.2)*light_source.y - sin(-.2) * light_source.z;
        z = sin(-.2)*light_source.y + cos(-.2) * light_source.z;
        light_source.y = y;
        light_source.z = z;
        }

    if (keyboard_state[MAKE_H])
        {
        y = light_source.y;
        x = cos(-.2)*light_source.x + sin(-.2) * light_source.z;
        z = -sin(-.2)*light_source.x + cos(-.2) * light_source.z;
        light_source.x = x;
        light_source.z = z;
        }

    if (keyboard_state[MAKE_N])
        {
        z = light_source.z;
        x = cos(-.2)*light_source.x - sin(-.2) * light_source.y;
        y = sin(-.2)*light_source.x + cos(-.2) * light_source.y;
        light_source.x = x;
        light_source.y = y;
        }

    // move the viewpoint

    if (keyboard_state[MAKE_UP])
        view_point.y+=20;

    if (keyboard_state[MAKE_DOWN])
        view_point.y-=20;

    if (keyboard_state[MAKE_RIGHT])
```

```
            view_point.x+=20;

if (keyboard_state[MAKE_LEFT])
   view_point.x-=20;

if (keyboard_state[MAKE_KEYPAD_PLUS])
   view_point.z+=20;

if (keyboard_state[MAKE_KEYPAD_MINUS])
   view_point.z-=20;


// change the viewangles

if (keyboard_state[MAKE_Z])
   if ((view_angle.ang_x+=10)>360)
      view_angle.ang_x = 0;

if (keyboard_state[MAKE_A])
   if ((view_angle.ang_x-=10)<0)
      view_angle.ang_x = 360;

if (keyboard_state[MAKE_X])
   if ((view_angle.ang_y+=10)>360)
      view_angle.ang_y = 0;

if (keyboard_state[MAKE_S])
   if ((view_angle.ang_y-=10)<0)
      view_angle.ang_y = 360;

if (keyboard_state[MAKE_C])
   if ((view_angle.ang_z+=10)>360)
      view_angle.ang_z = 0;

if (keyboard_state[MAKE_D])
   if ((view_angle.ang_z-=10)<0)
      view_angle.ang_z = 360;

if (keyboard_state[MAKE_ESC])
   done=1;

// rotate one of the objects
Rotate_Object(&test_objects[0],3,6,9);

// now that user has possible moved viewpoint, create the global
// world to camera transformation matrix
Create_World_To_Camera();

// reset polygon list
sprintf(buffer,"                            ");
Print_String_DB(0,0,10,buffer,0);
```

continued on next page

continued from previous page

```
// BEGIN 3D RENDERING SECTION

    Generate_Poly_List(NULL,RESET_POLY_LIST);

    for (index=0; index<16; index++)
        {
        // test if object is visible

        if (!Remove_Object(&test_objects[index],OBJECT_CULL_XYZ_MODE))
            {
            // convert object local coordinates to world coordinate
            Local_To_World_Object(&test_objects[index]);

            // remove the backfaces and shade object
            Remove_Backfaces_And_Shade(&test_objects[index]);

            // convert world coordinates to camera coordinate
            World_To_Camera_Object(&test_objects[index]);

            // clip the objects polygons against viewing volume
            Clip_Object_3D(&test_objects[index],CLIP_Z_MODE);

            // generate the final polygon list
            Generate_Poly_List(&test_objects[index],ADD_TO_POLY_LIST);
            }
        else
            {
            sprintf(buffer,"%d, ",index);
            Print_String_DB(0+index*26,0,10,buffer,0);
            }
        } // end for

    // sort the polygons
    Sort_Poly_List();

    // draw the polygon list
    Draw_Poly_List();

// END 3D RENDERING SECTION

    // display double buffer
    Display_Double_Buffer(double_buffer,0);

    // lock onto 18 frames per second max
    while((Timer_Query()-starting_time)<1);

    } // end while

// restore graphics mode back to text
Set_Graphics_Mode(TEXT_MODE);

// restore the old keyboard driver
Keyboard_Remove_Driver();
```

```
// print out some stats
printf("\nSettings...\n");
printf("\nview point x=%f, y=%f, z=%f",view_point.x,view_point.y,view_point.z);
printf("\nview angle x=%d, y=%d, z=%d",view_angle.ang_x,view_angle.ang_y,view_angle.ang_z);
printf("\nlight source x=%f, y=%f, z=%f",light_source.x,light_source.y,light_source.z);

} // end main
```

Not bad, huh? We are definitely getting somewhere. Granted, the engine uses floating point, and it could be optimized about ten times, but what we have now isn't too bad. The final engine that we are going to use for the game is going to blaze! So don't worry if you still think what we have now isn't going to cut it. Let's move on to the next method of rendering—the Z-buffer.

The Z-Buffer Algorithm

The Z-buffer algorithm (which we're going to refer to as Z-buffer from now on) is becoming the most popular and widely used rendering technique in both hardware and software. In fact, most of the hardware-based 3D graphics engines on the market use a Z-buffer, and many software engines are implementing Z-buffers also. Hence, with the Pentium processor taking a strong hold and the new P6 around the corner, software Z-buffers are very feasible and can perform fast enough to get the job done. Moreover, Z-buffering is just about the best way to render 3D polygons from a mathematical point of view because of the purity and simplicity of the algorithm, so let's see what exactly it is!

The Z-buffer is a method of rendering polygons that functions on the following premise: if the Z coordinate of every pixel of every polygon is determined, we can perform a sort on the pixel level. And for each pixel in the frame buffer, the pixel that is nearest to the viewer or has the minimum Z is the one that should be displayed. In essence, the Z-buffer is a depth sort at the pixel level, and hence, always gives the correct rendering order of the polygons since they can't be broken down any further than individual pixels.

So how do we do it? Well, to begin with, we need a Z-buffer that has the same dimensions as the screen buffer. However, instead of each element in the Z-buffer being a pixel, each element contains a Z value. Therefore, the elements must have enough accuracy to represent Z values that range from decimals to large numbers. In most cases, Z-buffers are implemented with a minimum of 16 bits, and many are 32 bits. Figure 15-12 shows a typical Z-buffer that might be used for mode 13h of 320x200 resolution. The only problem is that the Z-buffer needs 64,000 elements that are each 2 bytes. The result is an array that is 128,000 bytes long! This is a problem for standard real mode DOS programs since segments are only 64K. We can deal with this with a bit of a trick that we will learn later, but it's definitely a problem that needs to be overcome for a real implementation. Anyway, once we

FIGURE 15-12

◎ ◎ ◎ ◎ ◎ ◎

The Z-buffer

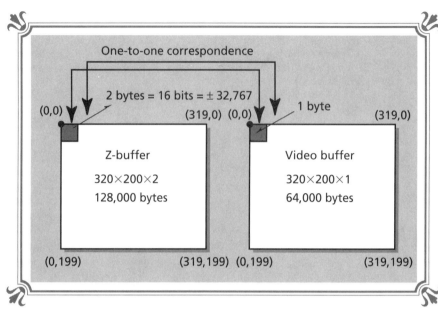

have the Z-buffer allocated and we can access it, the next step is to compute the Z value of each pixel of each polygon and insert the data into the Z-buffer. This is where things get a bit difficult.

In essence, we need to write a triangle scan converter that not only scan-converts the triangle, but as it's doing that, computes all the Z values of the pixels along

FIGURE 15-13

◎ ◎ ◎ ◎ ◎ ◎

Initializing the Z-buffer

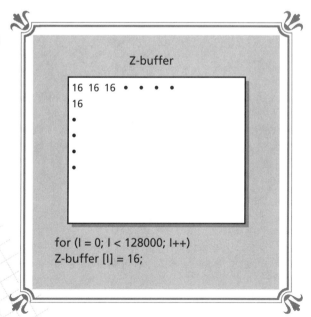

FIGURE 15-14

◎ ◎ ◎ ◎ ◎ ◎

Updating the Z-buffer with the Z values of scan-converted triangles

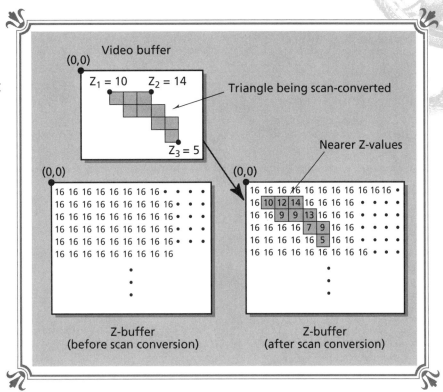

the way. For example, imagine that we first initialize the Z-buffer with a Z value of 16.0, as shown in Figure 15-13. Then imagine that the triangle in Figure 15-14 is scan-converted and its Z values are inserted into the Z-buffer, as shown in the figure. Since all the values of the triangle are nearer to the viewer—that is, smaller than the earlier initialized values—the Z-buffer reflects the triangle's Z values, and the Z-buffer itself looks like there is a triangle made of the actual Z values of each pixel of the scan-converted triangle.

The interesting part comes when we scan-convert another triangle into the Z-buffer and see what results. Imagine that another triangle is scan-converted into our little Z-buffer, but this one is nearer to the viewer than the previous one where the two triangles overlap. Therefore, as the second triangle is scan-converted, the closer Z values in the area of overlap will overwrite the previous ones in the Z-buffer. Thus, the Z-buffer reflects the nearer pixels of each triangle that is scan-converted into it. In the end, this results in a pixel-level Z sort. This is all great, but where are the actual pixels being drawn for the image if all we have is a Z-buffer version of the data? The answer is that while the Z-buffer is being updated, so is the frame buffer. Basically, when the scan converter is ready to draw a pixel at (x,y) and it has the Z value of the pixel, the algorithm tests if the Z value in the Z buffer is greater or farther away. If it is, then the actual pixel color is drawn in the frame buffer and the Z-buffer is updated with the new Z value. We have skipped ahead a bit, but that's all right—it's better to have an idea where things are going sometimes.

Now, how do we compute the Z value of each pixel as we are scan-converting each polygon? There are a few ways, but we're going to look at two of the simplest. The first method is to simply use the definition of a plane during the scan conversion. We know that each polygon's vertices lie in a single plane—this is a requirement of all the polygons in our system and a physical constant of all triangles. Therefore, if we are scan-converting a triangle, for example, we could first compute the plane equation of the plane in which the triangle lies. This can be done by finding the normal to the polygon and then using it in the point normal form of the plane equation, which looks like

$$Nx*(x-xo)+Ny*(y-yo)+Nz*(z-zo)=0$$

where $<Nx,Ny,Nz>$ is the normal to the polygon being scan-converted, and (xo,yo,zo) is a point on the polygon. This can then be converted into the form

$$A*x+B*y+C*z+D=0$$

where $A=Nx$, $B=Ny$, $C=Nz$ and $D=-(Nx*xo+Ny*yo+Nz*zo)$.

Then it's easy to see that Z can be found with the following formula:

$$z=-(A*x+B*y+D)/C$$

And this can be computed from the (x,y) coordinates of every pixel, which we know because the scan converter is generating them during the whole process.

The only drawback to the above method is that the plane equation and constants must be computed, and there are two multiplies, one division, and two additions per pixel to find z. But of course, we can trim this down. First off, we can use a precomputed surface normal that is part of each polygon (and we will do this in the final engine). This will save us the time of computing the surface normal. Second, we can totally simplify the Z calculation by using forward differencing and incremental calculations, just as we did for the Gouraud shading and the standard triangle scan converter. To do this first, let's start by realizing that the change in x each pixel is exactly 1.0; therefore, we can come up with the following incremental calculations.

Z as a function of X:

$$\begin{aligned}
z_{i+1} &= -(A*(x+1)+B*y + D)/C \\
&= -(A*x + A + B*y + D)/C \\
&= -(A*x + B*y + D)/C + (-A/C) \\
&= z_i + (-A/C)
\end{aligned}$$

We see that the next z value on a horizontal run is simply the previous z value plus the constant term (–A/C). This cuts down the z interpolation to a single addition per pixel. Of course, we still need to compute the very first z value of each line, but again, this can be done incrementally since the change in y in each line is 1.0. Therefore, carrying out the same incremental calculations on z, we get:

Z as a function of Y:

$$z_{i+1} = -(A*x+B*(y+1) + D)/C$$
$$= -(A*x + B*y +B+ D)/C$$
$$= -(A*x + B*y + D)/C + (-B/C)$$
$$= z_i + (-B/C)$$

This states that as y is incremented down one line, the new value of z is equal to the old value at the beginning of the last line plus the constant (–B/C).

Figure 15-15 shows the relationship between both of the incremental calculations and the scan conversion of a polygon.

Unfortunately, our current engine doesn't have the precomputed normal we need to efficiently compute the plane equation, so we are going to look at yet another way of computing the Z values as a polygon is being scan-converted.

FIGURE 15-15

◎ ◎ ◎ ◎ ◎ ◎

The planar-based incremental calculations

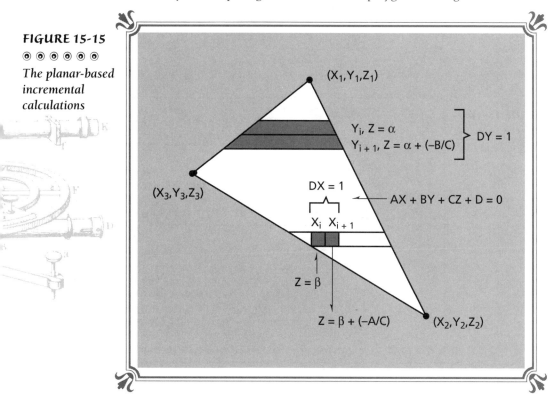

This method is based on interpolation. Just as we interpolated the intensity levels of the three corners of a triangle to Gouraud shade it, we can do the same thing with the Z values! Take a look at Figure 15-16, which shows the setup we're going to work from. You will notice that the triangle has a flat top. The calculations are similar for the flat bottom triangle, so we will only derive the flat top version, and the final software implementation will handle both.

The interpolation equations for the values of *z_left*, *z_right*, and *z_middle* are complex to say the least:

z_left=((y3–y)*z1+(y–y1)*z3)/(y3–y1)
z_right=((y3–y)*z2+(y–y1)*z3)/(y3–y1)
z_middle=((xe – x)*z_left+(x–xs)*z_right)/(xe–xs)

But since we are forward differencing experts by now, we can derive versions of these equations that are incremental.

First, let's find an incremental version of *z_middle* for changes in x:

z_middle $_{i+1}$ =((xe–x–1)*z_left+(x+1–xs)*z_right)/(xe–xs)
         =((xe–x)*z_left –z_left + (x–xs)*z_right + z_right)/(xe–xs)
         =((xe–x)*z_left + (x–xs)*z_right + z_right–z_left)/(xe–xs)
         =((xe–x)*z_left+(x–xs)*z_right)/(xe–xs)+(z_right–z_left)/(xe–xs)
         =z_middle $_i$+(z_right–z_left)/(xe–xs)

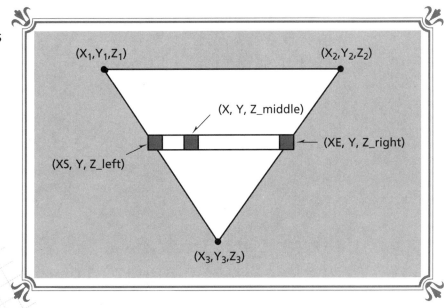

Therefore, if we let Bx be equal to the constant $(z\_right-z\_left)/(xe-xs)$, then the next z value pixel to the right of the previously scan-converted pixel is simply the last z value plus Bx. In other words:

$$z\_middle_{i+1}=z\_middle_i+Bx$$

We have once again succeeded in finding an algorithm that yields the next value with a single addition. We still have the problem of determining z_right and z_left for each scan line, but again, we can apply the forward differencing and come up with an incremental algorithm based on the fact that each scan line differs by a change in y of 1.0. Foregoing the long version of the derivation, the results of the calculations are as follows:

$$z\_left_{i+1}=z\_left_i +(z3-z1)/(y3-y1)$$
$$z\_right_{i+1}=z\_right_i+(z3-z2)/(y3-y1)$$

Furthermore, if we let the constants $B1x=(z3-z1)/(y3-y1)$ and $B2x=(z3-z2)/(y3-y1)$, then the incremental formulas for z_right and z_left simplify to,

$$z\_left_{i+1}=z\_left_i+B1x$$
$$z\_right_{i+1} = z\_right_i + B2x$$

which states that the new values of z_right and z_left can be found with a single addition each per scan line. Pretty cool, huh?

All right, now that we have the interpolation equations, all we need to do is work them into a new triangle scan converter along with the physical Z-buffer, and we're in business. We're going to need a few functions to create, destroy, and initialize the Z-buffer, along with some global variables to track everything and allow other functions access to the Z-buffer. So let's begin with the implementation of the Z-buffer and talk about how we're going to do it.

If you have been a PC programmer for long, you know that DOS and 16-bit C/C++ compilers don't like arrays larger than 64K. This, of course, is a limitation due to the segmented architecture of the original 8086 (wash your mouth out now) PC. Fortunately, the compiler companies, such as Microsoft and Borland, created a new type of memory model called HUGE that allows arrays to be larger than 64K. However, there is a catch. Accessing the arrays is about as slow as computing SIN and COSINE because of the primitive 16-bit compiler code used! Therefore, we're going to use a "memory bank" method that uses two banks of integers to hold the entire Z-buffer. Each bank will exist in a different segment and represent one half of the screen, as shown in Figure 15-17. Of course, we will have to perform a bit of logic to determine which bank a pixel should go into, but it's much faster than using a C/C++ built-in HUGE model, believe me. So let's define some global variables first and then write some Z-buffer support functions.

FIGURE 15-17

⊙ ⊙ ⊙ ⊙ ⊙ ⊙

Z-buffer memory bank system

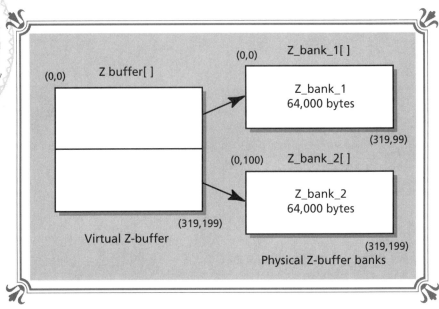

Here are the globals we will need:

```
int far *z_buffer,    // the current z buffer memory
    far *z_bank_1,    // memory bank 1 of z buffer
    far *z_bank_2;    // memory bank 2 of z buffer

unsigned int z_height   = 200,    // the height of the z buffer
             z_height_2 = 100,    // the height of half the z buffer
             z_bank_size = 64000L; // size of a z buffer bank in bytes
```

The variables should make sense, but here's their meaning to make sure: *z_buffer* points to the current active Z-buffer memory bank, which is either *z_bank_1* or *z_bank_2*. The variable *z_height* is the total height of the Z-buffer in scan lines, and *z_height_2* is the size of each bank (a bit redundant, but oh well). Finally, *z_bank_size* is the size in bytes of each Z-buffer memory bank.

Now let's write a function (Listing 15-7) that allocates each of the Z-buffer memory banks given the total size of the Z-buffer as a parameter.

LISTING 15-7 Function that allocates the memory for the Z-buffer

```
int Create_Z_Buffer(unsigned int height)
{
// this function allocates the z buffer in two banks

// set global z buffer values

z_height   = height;
z_height_2 = height/2;
```

```
z_bank_size = (height/2)*(unsigned int)640;

// allocate the memory

z_bank_1 = (int far *)_fmalloc(z_bank_size);
z_bank_2 = (int far *)_fmalloc(z_bank_size);

// return success or failure

if (z_bank_1 && z_bank_2)
   return(1);
else
   return(0);

} // end Create_Z_Buffer
```

Basically, the *Create_Z_Buffer()* function sets the global variables and allocates the Z-buffer memory from the FAR heap. Notice that the function has no error detection. (If you want error detection, buy a Windows book.) When the function exits, both of the pointers *z_bank_1* and *z_bank_2* will point to the allocated Z-buffer memory.

The next function we need is a way to release the memory back to DOS when we're done with it. This can be accomplished in a couple lines, but it's best to encapsulate it in a function, as shown in Listing 15-8.

LISTING 15-8 Function to delete the Z-buffer memory

```
void Delete_Z_Buffer(void)
{
// this function frees up the memory used by the z buffer memory banks

_ffree(z_bank_1);
_ffree(z_bank_2);

} // end Delete_Z_Buffer
```

Finally, we need a way to initialize the Z-buffer memory each frame to a value that is far in the distance. This is simple to do and can be performed with a *for* loop or *memset()* function. But since there is so much memory that needs to be cleared, we're going to use the inline assembler and *WORD*-size moves to get some speed. The function is shown in Listing 15-9.

LISTING 15-9 Function that initializes the Z-buffer memory banks with a value

```
void Fill_Z_Buffer(int value)
{
// this function fills the entire z buffer (both banks) with the sent value
_asm
```

continued on next page

continued from previous page

```
{
; bank 1

les di,z_bank_1          ; point es:di to z buffer bank 1
mov ax,value             ; move the value into ax
mov cx,z_bank_size       ; number of bytes to fill
shr cx,1                 ; convert to number of words
rep stosw                ; move the value into z buffer

; bank 2

les di,z_bank_2          ; point es:di to z buffer bank 1
mov ax,value             ; move the value into ax (redundant)
mov cx,z_bank_size       ; number of bytes to fill  (so is this)
shr cx,1                 ; convert to number of words
rep stosw                ; move the value into z buffer

} // end asm

} // end Fill_Z_Buffer
```

If we wanted to, we could double the speed of the function by using 32-bit instructions and memory moves. But then we would have to link in an external assembly module because most inline assemblers only support up to 286 instructions, and hence, quad byte memory operations are illegal. Anyway, the function has two sections that do the same thing but with different banks, so let's concentrate on the first bank initialization since the second one is similar.

The inline assembly simply sets up a memory fill using *ES:DI* as the destination, which is equated to the memory bank area *z_bank_1*. The number of bytes to transfer is placed in *CX*, and then this is divided by two since we are going to use a *WORD* fill instead of a *BYTE* fill. Then the line *REP STOSW* performs the memory fill with the value that is in *AX*, which is the initial Z value. The second part of the function does the exact same thing except the memory destination in *ES:DI* is changed to *z_bank_2*.

So to start up the Z-buffer system, we would make the call:

```
Create_Z_Buffer(200); // a 200 line high z buffer
```

And then at the beginning of each frame, a call would be made to *Fill_Z_Buffer()*, like this:

```
Fill_Z_Buffer(8000);   // a large z value that will never occur during the
                       // polygon scan conversion.
```

The next element of the Z-buffer system is the actual new polygon scan converter function that will draw Z-buffered triangles. To do this, we will follow the same architecture we have been using except that we are going to combine the flat top and flat bottom functions in one (for a bit more speed), and the function interfaces are going to change a bit since we need to send the Z components of each triangle in addition to (x,y). Let's begin with the high-level function that sorts the vertices and then makes calls to draw the two subtriangles that make up the sent triangle. The function is shown in Listing 15-10.

LISTING 15-10 *The high-level 3D triangle drawing function*

```
void Draw_Tri_3D_Z(int x1,int y1,int z1,
                   int x2,int y2,int z2,
                   int x3,int y3,int z3,
                   int color)
{
// this function sorts the vertices, and splits the triangle into two
halves and draws them

int temp_x,    // used for sorting
    temp_y,
    temp_z,
    new_x,     // used to compute new x and z at triangle splitting point
    new_z;

// test for h lines and v lines
if ((x1==x2 && x2==x3)  ||  (y1==y2 && y2==y3))
    return;

// sort p1,p2,p3 in ascending y order

if (y2<y1)
    {
    temp_x = x2;
    temp_y = y2;
    temp_z = z2;

    x2     = x1;
    y2     = y1;
    z2     = z1;

    x1     = temp_x;
    y1     = temp_y;
    z1     = temp_z;

    } // end if

// now we know that p1 and p2 are in order

if (y3<y1)
    {
    temp_x = x3;
    temp_y = y3;
    temp_z = y3;
```

continued on next page

continued from previous page

```
x3      = x1;
y3      = y1;
z3      = z1;

x1      = temp_x;
y1      = temp_y;
z1      = temp_z;

} // end if

// finally test y3 against y2

if (y3<y2)
   {
   temp_x = x3;
   temp_y = y3;
   temp_z = z3;

   x3      = x2;
   y3      = y2;
   z3      = z2;

   x2      = temp_x;
   y2      = temp_y;
   z2      = temp_z;

   } // end if

// do trivial rejection tests

if ( y3<poly_clip_min_y || y1>poly_clip_max_y ||
   (x1<poly_clip_min_x && x2<poly_clip_min_x && x3<poly_clip_min_x) ||
   (x1>poly_clip_max_x && x2>poly_clip_max_x && x3>poly_clip_max_x) )
   return;

// test if top of triangle is flat

if (y1==y2 || y2==y3)
   {
   Draw_TB_Tri_3D_Z(x1,y1,z1,x2,y2,z2,x3,y3,z3,color);
   } // end if
else
   {
   // general triangle that needs to be broken up along long edge
   // compute new x,z at split point

   new_x = x1 + (int)((float)(y2-y1)*(float)(x3-x1)/(float)(y3-y1));
   new_z = z1 + (int)((float)(y2-y1)*(float)(z3-z1)/(float)(y3-y1));

   // draw each sub-triangle

   if (y2>=poly_clip_min_y && y1<poly_clip_max_y)
```

```
        Draw_TB_Tri_3D_Z(x1,y1,z1,new_x,y2,new_z,x2,y2,z2,color);

  if (y3>=poly_clip_min_y && y1<poly_clip_max_y)
        Draw_TB_Tri_3D_Z(x2,y2,z2,new_x,y2,new_z,x3,y3,z3,color);

  } // end else

} // end Draw_Tri_3D_Z
```

The *Draw_Tri_3D_Z()* function is virtually the same as its 2D cousin except for the following points:

1. The interface to the function requires the Z components of the triangle's vertices.

2. During the vertex sort, the Z components are swapped also.

3. When the triangle is split, not only a new X value is computed but a Z value as well. This is shown in Figure 15-18.

Of course, the new function makes calls to a different triangle scan converter named *Draw_TB_Tri_3D_Z()*, which stands for "draw a triangle with either a flat top or bottom using 3D coordinates into the Z-buffer." So, let's look at this workhorse function (Listing 15-11) that performs the actual scan conversion and Z interpolation.

FIGURE 15-18
◉ ◉ ◉ ◉ ◉ ◉

When triangles are split, both the X and Z split values must be computed

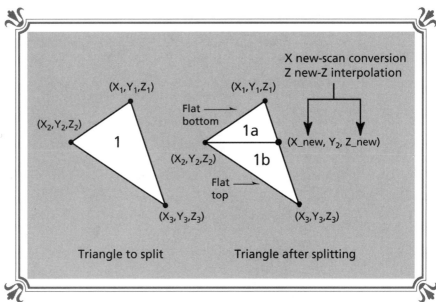

LISTING 15-11 Z-buffer triangle scan converter

```
void Draw_TB_Tri_3D_Z(int x1,int y1, int z1,
                      int x2,int y2, int z2,
                      int x3,int y3, int z3,
                      int color)

{
// this function draws a triangle that has a flat top

float dx_right,    // the dx/dy ratio of the right edge of line
      dx_left,     // the dx/dy ratio of the left edge of line
      xs,xe,       // the starting and ending points of the edges
      height,      // the height of the triangle

      dx,          // general delta's
      dy,
      z_left,      // the z value of the left edge of current line
      z_right,     // the z value for the right edge of current line
      ay,          // interpolator constant
      b1y,         // the change of z with respect to y on the left edge
      b2y;         // the change of z with respect to y on the right edge

int temp_x,        // used during sorting as temps
    temp_y,
    temp_z,
    xs_clip,       // used by clipping
    xe_clip,
    x,
    x_index,       // used as looping vars
    y_index;

// change these two back to float and remove all *32 and >>5
// if you don't want to use fixed point during horizontal z interpolation

int z_middle,  // the z value of the middle between the left and right
    bx;        // the change of z with respect to x

unsigned char far *dest_addr; // current image destination

// test order of x1 and x2, note y1=y2.

// test if top or bottom is flat and set constants appropriately
if (y1==y2)
   {
   // perform computations for a triangle with a flat top

   if (x2 < x1)
      {
      temp_x = x2;
      temp_z = z2;

      x2    = x1;
```

```
    z2      = z1;

    x1      = temp_x;
    z1      = temp_z;

    } // end if swap

// compute deltas for scan conversion

height = y3-y1;

dx_left  = (x3-x1)/height;
dx_right = (x3-x2)/height;

// compute deltas for z interpolation
z_left  = z1;
z_right = z2;

// vertical interpolants
ay  = 1/height;

b1y = ay*(z3-z1);
b2y = ay*(z3-z2);

// set starting points

xs = (float)x1;
xe = (float)x2;

    } // end top is flat
else
    { // bottom must be flat

// test order of x3 and x2, note y2=y3.
if (x3 < x2)
    {
    temp_x = x2;
    temp_z = z2;

    x2      = x3;
    z2      = z3;

    x3      = temp_x;
    z3      = temp_z;

    } // end if swap

// compute deltas for scan conversion

height = y3-y1;

dx_left  = (x2-x1)/height;
dx_right = (x3-x1)/height;
```

continued on next page

continued from previous page

```
        // compute deltas for z interpolation

        z_left  = z1;
        z_right = z1;

        // vertical interpolants

        ay  = 1/height;

        b1y = ay*(z2-z1);
        b2y = ay*(z3-z1);

        // set starting points
        xs = (float)x1;
        xe = (float)x1;

        } // end else bottom is flat

    // perform y clipping

    // clip top

    if (y1<poly_clip_min_y)
        {
        // compute new xs and ys

        dy = (float)(-y1+poly_clip_min_y);

        xs = xs+dx_left*dy;
        xe = xe+dx_right*dy;

        // re-compute z_left and z_right to take into consideration
        // vertical shift down

        z_left  += b1y*dy;
        z_right += b2y*dy;

        // reset y1

        y1=poly_clip_min_y;

        } // end if top is off screen

    // clip bottom

    if (y3>poly_clip_max_y)
        y3=poly_clip_max_y;

    // compute starting address in video memory

    dest_addr = double_buffer+(y1<<8)+(y1<<6);
```

```
        // start z buffer at proper bank

        if (y1<z_height_2)
           z_buffer = z_bank_1+(y1<<8)+(y1<<6);
        else
           {
           temp_y = y1-z_height_2;

           z_buffer = z_bank_2+(temp_y<<8)+(temp_y<<6);

           } // end else

        // test if x clipping is needed

        if (x1>=poly_clip_min_x && x1<=poly_clip_max_x &&
            x2>=poly_clip_min_x && x2<=poly_clip_max_x &&
            x3>=poly_clip_min_x && x3<=poly_clip_max_x)
           {
           // draw the triangle

           for (y_index=y1; y_index<=y3; y_index++)
               {
               // test if we need to switch to z buffer bank two

               if (y_index==z_height_2)
                  z_buffer = z_bank_2;

///////////////////////////////////////////////////////////////////////////////

        // this section uses a bit of 16 bit fixed math point for the horizontal
        // interpolation. The format is 11:5 i.e 11 whole places and 5 decimal places
        // Also, notice the use of >>5 and *32 to convert to fixed point and back to
        // simple integer, also the old version of each line is commented out under each
        // fixed point calculation, so you can see what was originally done...

               // compute horizontal z interpolant

               z_middle = 32*z_left;
               // z_middle = z_left;

               bx = 32*(z_right - z_left)/(1+xe-xs);
               // bx = (z_right - z_left)/(1+xe-xs);

               // draw the line

               for (x_index=xs; x_index<=xe; x_index++)
                   {
                   // if current z_middle is less than z-buffer then replace
                   // and update image buffer

                   if (z_middle>>5 < z_buffer[x_index])
```

continued on next page

continued from previous page

```
                      // if (z_middle < z_buffer[x_index])
                         {
                         // update z buffer

                         z_buffer[x_index]=(int)z_middle>>5;
                         // z_buffer[x_index]=(int)z_middle;

                         // write to image buffer

                         dest_addr[x_index] = color;

                         // update video buffer

                         } // end if update buffer

                      // update current z value

                      z_middle += bx;

// END FIXED POINT DEMO SECTION //////////////////////////////////////////////////////////

                  } // end draw z buffered line

            // adjust starting point and ending point for scan conversion

            xs+=dx_left;
            xe+=dx_right;

            // adjust vertical z interpolants

            z_left  += b1y;
            z_right += b2y;

            // adjust video and z buffer offsets

            dest_addr += 320;
            z_buffer  += 320;

            } // end for

    } // end if no x clipping needed
else
   {
   // clip x axis with slower version

   // draw the triangle

   for (y_index=y1; y_index<=y3; y_index++)
      {

      // test if we need to switch to z buffer bank two
```

```
            if (y_index==z_height_2)
               z_buffer = z_bank_2;

        // do x clip

        xs_clip  = (int)xs;
        xe_clip  = (int)xe;
```

///

```
// this section uses a bit of 16 bit fixed point math for the horizontal
// interpolation. The format is 11:5 i.e 11 whole places and 5 decimal places
// Also, notice the use of >>5 and *32 to convert to fixed point and back to
// simple integer, also the old version of each line is commented out under each
// fixed point calculation.

        // compute horizontal z interpolant

        z_middle = 32*z_left;
        // z_middle = z_left;

        bx = 32*(z_right - z_left)/(1+xe-xs);
        // bx = 32*(z_right - z_left)/(1+xe-xs);

        // adjust starting point and ending point

        xs+=dx_left;
        xe+=dx_right;

        // adjust vertical z interpolants

        z_left  += b1y;
        z_right += b2y;

        // clip line

        if (xs_clip < poly_clip_min_x)
           {
           dx = (-xs_clip + poly_clip_min_x);

           xs_clip = poly_clip_min_x;

           // re-compute z_middle to take into consideration horizontal shift

           z_middle += 32*bx*dx;
           // z_middle += bx*dx;

           } // end if line is clipped on left

        if (xe_clip > poly_clip_max_x)
           {
```

continued on next page

continued from previous page

```
                    xe_clip = poly_clip_max_x;

                    } // end if line is clipped on right

                // draw the line

                for (x_index=xs_clip; x_index<=xe_clip; x_index++)
                    {
                    // if current z_middle is less than z-buffer then replace
                    // and update image buffer

                    if (z_middle>>5 < z_buffer[x_index])
                    // if (z_middle < z_buffer[x_index])
                        {
                        // update z buffer

                        z_buffer[x_index]=(int)z_middle>>5;
                    // z_buffer[x_index]=(int)z_middle;

                        // write to image buffer

                        dest_addr[x_index] = color;

                        // update video buffer

                        } // end if update z buffer

                    // update current z value

                    z_middle += bx;

// END FIXED POINT DEMO SECTION ////////////////////////////////////////////////////////

                    } // end draw z buffered line

                // adjust video and z buffer offsets

                dest_addr += 320;
                z_buffer  += 320;

                } // end for y_index

        } // end else x clipping needed

} // end Draw_TB_Tri_3D_Z
```

The *Draw_TB_Tri_3D_Z()* function is based on the standard 2D triangle function with added logic to perform the Z interpolation along with combining both the flat top and flat bottom triangles into one function. I think we have a handle on the scan conversion part of the function since we've seen it before, so let's concentrate on the Z-buffer aspect of the function.

The function begins by determining whether the triangle has a flat top or bottom, then it calculates the various constants needed for both the scan conversion and the Z interpolation. The constants are identical to the mathematical derivation shown in the preceding pages. The first interesting piece of code is the section that aliases the *z_buffer* to the proper Z-buffer bank based on the starting Y scan line. Here's that code:

```
if (y1<z_height_2)
    z_buffer = z_bank_1+(y1<<8)+(y1<<6);
else
    {
    temp_y = y1-z_height_2;
    z_buffer = z_bank_2+(temp_y<<8)+(temp_y<<6);
    } // end else
```

This is really the only overhead needed to select the proper memory bank. Once this is done, the Z-buffer is accessed efficiently as a normal FAR array with the simple dereferencing:

```
value =z_buffer[index];
```

The next section of the program then determines if X-axis clipping is needed and, based on this, executes similar blocks of code as far as the Z interpolation is concerned. Therefore, we will concentrate on the section that is executed when X clipping is not needed. The code begins by computing the vertical interpolation constant for Z, then it enters into the main scan conversion *for* loop. The *for* loop tests each pixel that is currently being scan-converted against the current value in the Z-buffer. If the current Z value of the pixel being scan-converted is less than the Z-buffer's, the Z-buffer is updated and the pixel is rendered in the double buffer or target image buffer. Here's the main conditional that performs this update:

```
if (z_middle < z_buffer[x_index])
    {
    // update z buffer
    // z_buffer[x_index]=(int)z_middle;

    // write to image buffer
    dest_addr[x_index] = color;

    // update video buffer
    } // end if update buffer
```

If you're awake, you should notice that this code is a bit different from the version in the function. In fact, there are lines that are commented out in the function's code, and these are those lines. Basically, the final version in the function uses fixed point 16-bit math for speed, but this severely limits the Z depth resolution of the buffer. However, it was the only way I could get real-time performance out of it without resorting to assembly (or giving up my best secrets). But we'll get to the

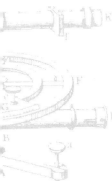

fixed point stuff in a moment; for now realize that the conditional logic is performing the preceding test, more or less.

After one scan line is scan-converted, the *z_left* and *z_right* constants are properly updated, and the process continues until, finally, the entire triangle has been scan-converted and Z interpolated. Therefore, at the exit of the function, the image buffer will reflect portions of the triangle that are nearer to the viewer, and the Z-buffer will reflect Z values that are nearer to the viewer. That's all there is to it. We simply draw all the polygons with this function, and when all the polygons are drawn, the results will be properly rendered in the image buffer, and the Z-buffer will contain the Z values of all the pixels. Then we simply display the image buffer (which will be the double buffer in most cases).

Now let's back up to the fixed point stuff for a moment. We have already seen how fixed point math works, so I won't belabor it again in this simple case. Basically, we should use 32-bit fixed point math if we want to have any accuracy, but if you recall, to make this work right, we need to use 32-bit instructions for the multiplication and division (if we want the math to perform better than floating point). This means that we need to use an external assembler, which we don't want to do just yet. The question is, can we get away with 16-bit math, which is very fast on the PC with a 16-bit compiler? The answer is, sort of, if we're willing to really cut the accuracy of the computations.

It turns out that this isn't going to be too much of a problem, at least for a demo. Here's the plan: we know that the near and far clipping planes are about 3000 units apart, which means that it would take 12 bits of accuracy to track this (2^{12} is 4096). That would leave us with 4 bits to represent the decimal portion, which is an accuracy of 1/16. This is not quite enough on the small scale of things, so I decided to fudge it a little and go with a 11:5 representation. This works reasonably well for demo purposes, but better yet, allows real-time frame rates to be achieved with multiple objects. So when you see the >>5 and <<5 in the code, it's simply converting back and forth between fixed point and whole representations. If you're confused, note that each fixed point instruction line in the program has the original floating point version commented out below it.

We are almost ready to write a full 3D Z-buffered demo that we can plug into our polygon engine. But first, let's write a quick demo that simply draws a couple of overlapping triangles, as shown in Figure 15-19. Referring to the figure, we see that the two triangles actually cut through or pierce one another. Our depth sort can't even begin to do something like this, but with the Z-buffer, it's a snap. Just render each triangle and if they intersect, overlap, or whatever, the Z-buffer will draw them correctly. As a demo, the program in Listing 15-12 does just that. It's called ZDEMO.EXE and its source is called ZDEMO.C. If you wish to build it, you will have to link in BLACK15.C and BLACK15.H, which make up this chapter's library module. The program has no controls—just run it and look at the display.

FIGURE 15-19

FIGURE 15-19

◉ ◉ ◉ ◉ ◉ ◉

The Z-buffer handles cases like this with ease

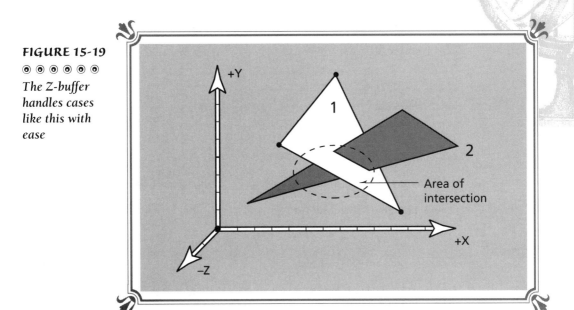

Area of intersection

LISTING 15-12 Demo of the Z-buffer system and two intersecting triangles

```
// I N C L U D E S ///////////////////////////////////////////////////////

#include <io.h>
#include <conio.h>
#include <stdio.h>
#include <stdlib.h>
#include <dos.h>
#include <bios.h>
#include <fcntl.h>
#include <memory.h>
#include <malloc.h>
#include <math.h>
#include <string.h>
#include <search.h>              // this one is needed for qsort()

// include all of our stuff

#include "black3.h"
#include "black4.h"
#include "black5.h"
#include "black6.h"
#include "black8.h"
#include "black9.h"
#include "black11.h"
#include "black15.h"
```

continued on next page

continued from previous page
//

```c
void main(void)
{

int x=160,   // local position of object
    y=100,
    z=100;

// set graphics to mode 13h
Set_Graphics_Mode(GRAPHICS_MODE13);

// point double buffer at video buffer, so we can see output without an
// animation loop
double_buffer = video_buffer;

// create a 200 line z buffer (128k)

Create_Z_Buffer(200);

// initialize the z buffer with an impossibly distant value
Fill_Z_Buffer(16000);

// draw two intersecting triangles
Draw_Tri_3D_Z(x,y,z,
              x-30,y+40,z,
              x+40,y+50,z,
              10);

Draw_Tri_3D_Z(x+10,y+10,z-5,
              x-50,y+60,z+5,
              x+30,y+20,z-2,
              1);

// wait for keyboard hit
while(!kbhit());

// restore graphics mode back to text
Set_Graphics_Mode(TEXT_MODE);

// release the z buffer memory
Delete_Z_Buffer();

} // end main
```

The program is short and to the point. It simply allocates the Z-buffer, draws a couple of triangles in it, and that's it. Also, notice the little trick with the double buffer. Normally, all output of the Z-buffer triangle scan converter goes to the double buffer, but if we alias this to the *video_buffer*, we can see the output directly without allocating the double buffer and displaying it. Of course, we wouldn't use this technique if we wanted animation, but for a quick-and-dirty display, it works fine. You see, already we are using the graphics engine in ways we're not supposed to. That's exactly how Cybersorcerers think!

At this point let's complete the Z-buffer system and make it work with the polygon system. To do this, we only need to write a single function, and that's a new *Draw_Poly_List()* function. Take a look at Figure 15-20(a), which shows the current graphics pipeline. After the polygons are added to the polygon list, they are sorted

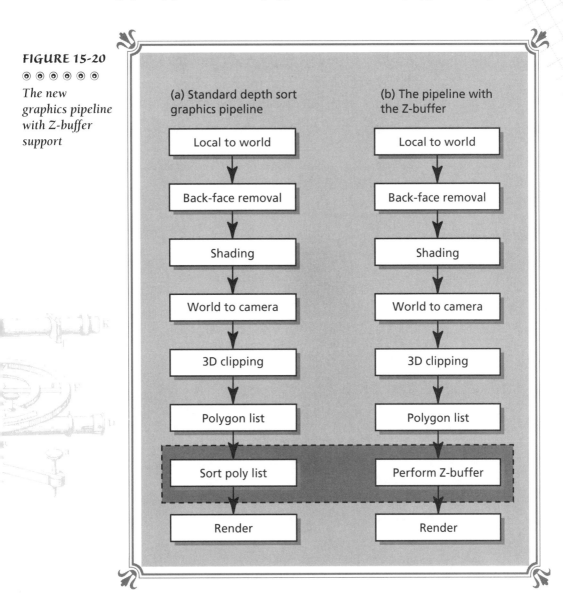

FIGURE 15-20

◉ ◉ ◉ ◉ ◉ ◉

The new graphics pipeline with Z-buffer support

and presented to the *Draw_Poly_List()* function. All we need to do is intervene a bit and remove the sorting step; and instead of using the standard *Draw_Poly_List()* function that blindly blasts the polygons to the image buffer, we are going to write a new Z-buffer version of the function that passes all the polygons in the polygon list to the Z-buffer system. Then when the new polygon Z-buffer function completes, we can display the double buffer since it now reflects the polygons for the current frame. Figure 15-20(b) shows the modified graphics pipeline with the Z-buffer installed. The code for new polygon list drawing function is shown in Listing 15-13.

LISTING 15-13 Polygon list-drawing function that uses the Z-buffer system

```
void Draw_Poly_List_Z(void)
{
// this function draws the global polygon list generated by calls to
// Generate_Poly_List using the z buffer triangle system

int curr_poly,          // the current polygon
    is_quad=0;          // quadrilateral flag

float x1,y1,z1,         // working variables
      x2,y2,z2,
      x3,y3,z3,
      x4,y4,z4;

// draw each polygon in list

for (curr_poly=0; curr_poly<num_polys_frame; curr_poly++)
    {
    // do Z clipping first before projection

    z1=world_polys[curr_poly]->vertex_list[0].z;
    z2=world_polys[curr_poly]->vertex_list[1].z;
    z3=world_polys[curr_poly]->vertex_list[2].z;

    // test if this is a quad

    if (world_polys[curr_poly]->num_points==4)
        {
        // extract vertex number and z component for clipping and projection
        z4=world_polys[curr_poly]->vertex_list[3].z;

        // set quad flag
        is_quad=1;

        } // end if quad
    else
      z4=z3;

#if 0
    // perform z clipping test
```

```
        if ( (z1<clip_near_z && z2<clip_near_z && z3<clip_near_z && z4<clip_near_z) ||
             (z1>clip_far_z && z2>clip_far_z && z3>clip_far_z && z4>clip_far_z) )
          continue;
#endif

        // extract points of polygon

        x1 = world_polys[curr_poly]->vertex_list[0].x;
        y1 = world_polys[curr_poly]->vertex_list[0].y;

        x2 = world_polys[curr_poly]->vertex_list[1].x;
        y2 = world_polys[curr_poly]->vertex_list[1].y;

        x3 = world_polys[curr_poly]->vertex_list[2].x;
        y3 = world_polys[curr_poly]->vertex_list[2].y;

        // compute screen position of points

        x1=(HALF_SCREEN_WIDTH  + x1*viewing_distance/z1);
        y1=(HALF_SCREEN_HEIGHT - ASPECT_RATIO*y1*viewing_distance/z1);

        x2=(HALF_SCREEN_WIDTH  + x2*viewing_distance/z2);
        y2=(HALF_SCREEN_HEIGHT - ASPECT_RATIO*y2*viewing_distance/z2);

        x3=(HALF_SCREEN_WIDTH  + x3*viewing_distance/z3);
        y3=(HALF_SCREEN_HEIGHT - ASPECT_RATIO*y3*viewing_distance/z3);

        // draw triangle

        Draw_Tri_3D_Z((int)x1,(int)y1,(int)z1,
                      (int)x2,(int)y2,(int)z2,
                      (int)x3,(int)y3,(int)z3,
                      world_polys[curr_poly]->shade);

        // draw second poly if this is a quad
        if (is_quad)
           {
           // extract the point

           x4 = world_polys[curr_poly]->vertex_list[3].x;
           y4 = world_polys[curr_poly]->vertex_list[3].y;

           // project to screen

           x4=(HALF_SCREEN_WIDTH  + x4*viewing_distance/z4);
           y4=(HALF_SCREEN_HEIGHT - ASPECT_RATIO*y4*viewing_distance/z4);

           // draw triangle

           Draw_Tri_3D_Z((int)x1,(int)y1,(int)z1,
                         (int)x3,(int)y3,(int)z3,
                         (int)x4,(int)y4,(int)z4,
```

continued on next page

continued from previous page

```
                              world_polys[curr_poly]->shade);

        } // end if quad

    } // end for curr_poly

} // end Draw_Poly_List_Z
```

The function is almost identical to the standard *Draw_Poly_List()* function except that the new Z-buffered triangle functions are used instead of the 2D ones. Well, that's it. We can take the last demo, SORTDEMO.C, and make a few changes to it to create a full Z-buffered real-time display. The name of this program is SOLZDEMO.EXE and the source is SOLZDEMO.C. The control interface is identical to SORTDEMO.EXE except that you can move the rotating cube with the Q and W keys. This way you can see what happens when two objects overlap. As usual, the program must be fed with a PLG file for the test object, and I suggest you use CUBE.PLG, as in:

SOLZDEMO CUBE.PLG

Listing 15-14 contains the source to the demo program for your analysis.

LISTING 15-14 A full Z-buffered, real-time, multiple object demo

```
// I N C L U D E S /////////////////////////////////////////////////////////

#include <io.h>
#include <conio.h>
#include <stdio.h>
#include <stdlib.h>
#include <dos.h>
#include <bios.h>
#include <fcntl.h>
#include <memory.h>
#include <malloc.h>
#include <math.h>
#include <string.h>
#include <search.h>              // this one is needed for qsort()

// include all of our stuff

#include "black3.h"
#include "black4.h"
#include "black5.h"
#include "black6.h"
#include "black8.h"
#include "black9.h"
#include "black11.h"
#include "black15.h"
```

```
// G L O B A L S ///////////////////////////////////////////////////////////////

object test_objects[4];                     // objects in universe

// M A I N ///////////////////////////////////////////////////////////////////

void main(int argc,char **argv)
{

int done=0,
    z1=0,
    index;

char buffer[80];
float x,y,z;

// build all look up tables
Build_Look_Up_Tables();

// load in the test object
for (index=0; index<4; index++)
    {
    if (PLG_Load_Object(&test_objects[index],argv[1],1))
       printf("\nplg loaded.");
    else
       printf("\nCouldn't load file");

    } // end for index

// set the position of the object
for (index=0; index<4; index++)
    {
    test_objects[index].world_pos.x=-200 + (index%4)*100;
    test_objects[index].world_pos.y=0;
    test_objects[index].world_pos.z=200 + 300*(index>>2);
    } // end index


// set graphics to mode 13h
Set_Graphics_Mode(GRAPHICS_MODE13);

// read the 3d color palette off disk
Load_Palette_Disk("standard.pal",(RGB_palette_ptr)&color_palette_3d);
Write_Palette(0,255,(RGB_palette_ptr)&color_palette_3d);

// allocate double buffer
Create_Double_Buffer(200);

// create a 200 line z buffer (128k)
Create_Z_Buffer(200);

// initialize the z buffer with a distant value
```

continued on next page

continued from previous page

```
Fill_Z_Buffer(16000);

// install the isr keyboard driver
Keyboard_Install_Driver();

// main event loop

while(!done)
    {

    // compute starting time of this frame
    starting_time = Timer_Query();

    // erase all objects
    Fill_Double_Buffer(0);

    // initialize z buffer
    Fill_Z_Buffer(16000);

    // test what user is doing
    if (keyboard_state[MAKE_T])
       {
       x = light_source.x;
       y = cos(.2)*light_source.y - sin(.2) * light_source.z;
       z = sin(.2)*light_source.y + cos(.2) * light_source.z;

       light_source.y = y;
       light_source.z = z;

       }

    if (keyboard_state[MAKE_G])
       {
       y = light_source.y;

       x = cos(.2)*light_source.x + sin(.2) * light_source.z;
       z = -sin(.2)*light_source.x + cos(.2) * light_source.z;

       light_source.x = x;
       light_source.z = z;

       }

    if (keyboard_state[MAKE_B])
       {
       z = light_source.z;

       x = cos(.2)*light_source.x - sin(.2) * light_source.y;
       y = sin(.2)*light_source.x + cos(.2) * light_source.y;

       light_source.x = x;
       light_source.y = y;
```

```
         }

      if (keyboard_state[MAKE_Y])
         {
         x = light_source.x;

         y = cos(-.2)*light_source.y - sin(-.2) * light_source.z;
         z = sin(-.2)*light_source.y + cos(-.2) * light_source.z;

         light_source.y = y;
         light_source.z = z;

         }

      if (keyboard_state[MAKE_H])
         {

         y = light_source.y;

         x = cos(-.2)*light_source.x + sin(-.2) * light_source.z;
         z = -sin(-.2)*light_source.x + cos(-.2) * light_source.z;

         light_source.x = x;
         light_source.z = z;

         }

      if (keyboard_state[MAKE_N])
         {
         z = light_source.z;

         x = cos(-.2)*light_source.x - sin(-.2) * light_source.y;
         y = sin(-.2)*light_source.x + cos(-.2) * light_source.y;

         light_source.x = x;
         light_source.y = y;

         }

      if (keyboard_state[MAKE_UP])
         view_point.y+=20;

      if (keyboard_state[MAKE_DOWN])
         view_point.y-=20;

      if (keyboard_state[MAKE_RIGHT])
         view_point.x+=20;

      if (keyboard_state[MAKE_LEFT])
         view_point.x-=20;

      if (keyboard_state[MAKE_KEYPAD_PLUS])
```

continued on next page

continued from previous page

```
                view_point.z+=20;

        if (keyboard_state[MAKE_KEYPAD_MINUS])
            view_point.z-=20;

        if (keyboard_state[MAKE_LFT_BRACKET])
            Scale_Object(&test_objects[0],1.1);

    if (keyboard_state[MAKE_RGT_BRACKET])
        Scale_Object(&test_objects[0],.9);

        if (keyboard_state[MAKE_Z])
            if ((view_angle.ang_x+=10)>360)
                view_angle.ang_x = 0;

        if (keyboard_state[MAKE_A])
            if ((view_angle.ang_x-=10)<0)
                view_angle.ang_x = 360;

        if (keyboard_state[MAKE_X])
            if ((view_angle.ang_y+=10)>360)
                view_angle.ang_y = 0;

        if (keyboard_state[MAKE_S])
            if ((view_angle.ang_y-=10)<0)
                view_angle.ang_y = 360;

        if (keyboard_state[MAKE_C])
            if ((view_angle.ang_z+=10)>360)
                view_angle.ang_z = 0;

        if (keyboard_state[MAKE_D])
            if ((view_angle.ang_z-=10)<0)
                view_angle.ang_z = 360;

        if (keyboard_state[MAKE_ESC])
            done=1;

        if (keyboard_state[MAKE_Q])
            test_objects[0].world_pos.x-=2;

        if (keyboard_state[MAKE_W])
            test_objects[0].world_pos.x+=2;

        Rotate_Object(&test_objects[0],3,6,9);

        // now that user has possible moved viewpoint, create the global
        // world to camera transformation matrix

        Create_World_To_Camera();

        // reset polygon list
        sprintf(buffer,"                              ");
        Print_String_DB(0,0,10,buffer,0);
```

```
Generate_Poly_List(NULL,RESET_POLY_LIST);

for (index=0; index<4; index++)
    {
    // test if object is visible

    if (!Remove_Object(&test_objects[index],OBJECT_CULL_XYZ_MODE))
        {
        // convert object local coordinates to world coordinates
        Local_To_World_Object(&test_objects[index]);

        // remove the backfaces and shade object
        Remove_Backfaces_And_Shade(&test_objects[index]);

        // convert world coordinates to camera coordinates
        World_To_Camera_Object(&test_objects[index]);

        // clip the objects polygons against viewing volume
        Clip_Object_3D(&test_objects[index],CLIP_Z_MODE);

        // generate the final polygon list
        Generate_Poly_List(&test_objects[index],ADD_TO_POLY_LIST);
        }
    else
        {
        sprintf(buffer,"%d, ",index);
        Print_String_DB(0+index*26,0,10,buffer,0);
        }
    } // end for object

// draw the polygon list using z-buffer, notice the call to sort the
//   polys has been removed
Draw_Poly_List_Z();

// display double buffer
Display_Double_Buffer(double_buffer,0);

// lock onto 18 frames per second max
while((Timer_Query()-starting_time)<1);

} // end while

// restore graphics mode back to text
Set_Graphics_Mode(TEXT_MODE);

// release the z buffer memory
Delete_Z_Buffer();

// restore the old keyboard driver
Keyboard_Remove_Driver();

// print out some stats
printf("\nSettings...\n");

printf("\nview point x=%f, y=%f,
```

continued on next page

continued from previous page

```
        z=%f",view_point.x,view_point.y,view_point.z);
printf("\nview angle x=%d, y=%d,
        z=%d",view_angle.ang_x,view_angle.ang_y,view_angle.ang_z);
printf("\nlight source x=%f, y=%f,
        z=%f",light_source.x,light_source.y,light_source.z);

} // end main
```

Even though properly optimized, the Z-buffer technology we've covered can be used in 3D games. The question is, do we need this much generality? The answer is no. For example, games like Doom and Dark Forces are "hallway" games. In other words, all the polygons that make up the world are either perpendicular to the floor or parallel. Thus, there is an opportunity for optimization. The optimization is called the *vertical scan line Z-buffer*. Let's take a quick look at it.

The Vertical Scan Line Z-Buffer

The vertical scan line Z-buffer algorithm is from a class of Z-buffer algorithms that process entire lines at a time instead of pixels. For example, in the case of a Dark Forces or Doom-type engine, all the walls are running up and down. Therefore, the Z value of each pixel in a vertical column is constant. Figure 15-21 shows this graphically. The Z values only change as a function of X, not Y. Hence, an algorithm can be derived based on the Z-buffer that only computes the Z value for every vertical scan line. Then the Z-buffer only needs to be large enough to hold a number of elements equal to the width of the screen (see Figure 15-22).

FIGURE 15-21

The vertical scan line Z-buffer case

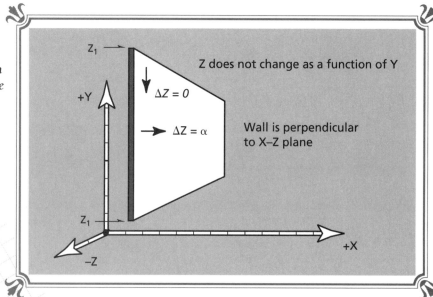

FIGURE 15-22

◎ ◎ ◎ ◎ ◎ ◎

*A vertical scan
line Z-buffer*

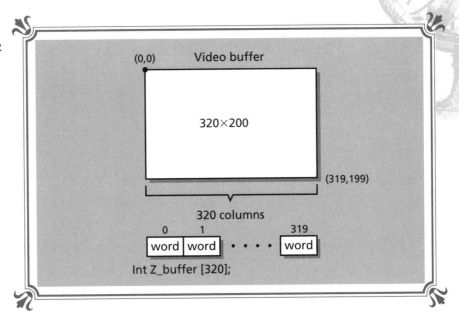

The only problem with this method is that it becomes necessary to draw polygons using vertical scan lines instead of horizontal ones. However, as it turns out, this is better since most 3D "hallway" games use texture mapping, which can be done very quickly a vertical scan line at a time. Therefore, using a vertical scan line Z-buffer along with vertical scan conversion, a special case of a Z-buffer renderer can be made that is orders of magnitude faster than the general Z-buffer, but it is simple to implement texture mapping with since all the polygons are drawn with vertical scan lines.

That's about enough Z-buffering for one lifetime. Now let's move onto the Doom of all games—the Binary Space Partition.

The Binary Space Partition

The Binary Space Partition, or BSP, is a technique that belongs to the class of 3D rendering algorithms that trade initial space and computation along with some geometrical constraints for faster run-time performance. Basically, the BSP is a method that takes as input a collection of polygons and then, through a fairly complex recursive algorithm, creates a binary tree structure. This BSP tree can then be used during run time as a map of how to draw the polygons from any viewpoint at lightning speeds. Take a look at the aerial view shown in Figure 15-23 as you read the following explanation of how the BSP works.

The figure depicts a set of polygons that might make up the walls of a game universe. As you can see, if we were to place the viewer in any position within the figure, it wouldn't be too hard to determine manually the order of polygons to be

FIGURE 15-23
◎ ◎ ◎ ◎ ◎ ◎

*The basic
problem for the
BSP to solve*

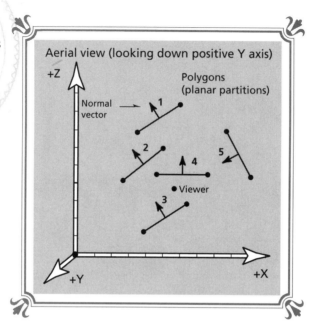

drawn. The BSP works based on this premise—that is, at any point in the universe, it should be possible to compute the order of polygons to be rendered and create an efficient data structure to contain these orderings.

It turns out that a method called *space partitioning* can be used to figure out this little problem. Space partitioning works like this: the BSP algorithm selects one of the polygons in the scene as the partitioning plane (it doesn't really matter which). This partitioning plane then cuts space into two half spaces, as shown in Figure 15-24. Then the algorithm tests each polygon in the scene against the partitioning plane and determines which half space the polygon lies in. If the partitioning plane happens to cut a polygon in half, then the polygon is split, as shown in Figure 15-25.

Once the algorithm has processed this first step, each of the lists that were generated—that is, the list of polygons on each side of the partitioning plane—are recursively processed in a similar way. This continues until all the polygons have been processed and the BSP tree has been built. As an example, Figure 15-26 shows the construction of two small BSP trees from a scene consisting of five polygons using two different partitioning planes for the starting selections. The first step is to create a single node that contains the partitioning plane. The children of this node are two lists; one is the front plane list, and the other is the back plane list. Then each of these lists is processed in the same way. The front list has a partitioning plane selected (again, any will work), and then the polygons in the front list are partitioned. This process continues until trees of the form in Figure 15-26b and 15-26e are obtained. Once the BSP tree is constructed, a special algorithm can be used to traverse the tree in a modified *inorder* traversal to display the polygons in the BSP tree from any viewpoint.

FIGURE 15-24

◎ ◎ ◎ ◎ ◎ ◎

A polygon cutting space in half

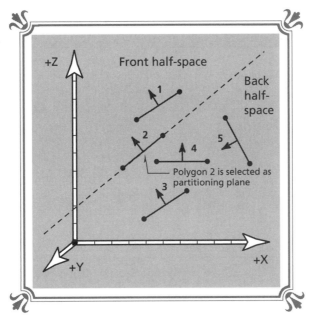

Polygon 2 is selected as partitioning plane

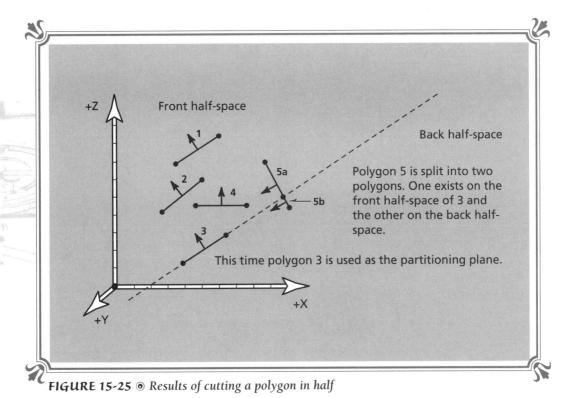

Polygon 5 is split into two polygons. One exists on the front half-space of 3 and the other on the back half-space.

This time polygon 3 is used as the partitioning plane.

FIGURE 15-25 ◎ *Results of cutting a polygon in half*

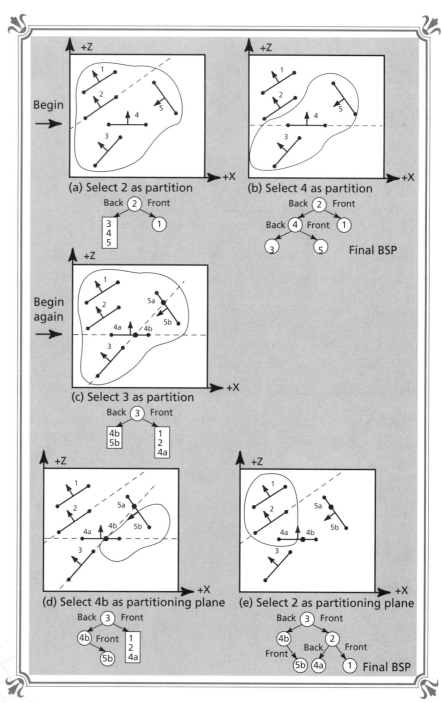

FIGURE 15-26
◎ ◎ ◎ ◎ ◎ ◎
*Creation of a
BSP tree*

Assuming that a linked list of polygons that make up the universe to be partitioned has been created and the head of it is called *root*, a rough algorithm of creating the BSP tree is as follows:

1. Select a polygon in the list and use it as a partitioning plane. If there are none left in the list, then exit.

2. Create two sublists, each attached to the front and back pointer of the partitioning plane. This list will be filled with the polygons in front of and behind the parent node, which is the partitioning plane. This is shown in Figure 15-27.

3. Process the front list recursively.

4. Process the back list recursively.

Of course, there are a million details to attend to, such as: How do we determine which side a polygon is on relative to the partitioning plane? Which plane should be selected as the partitioning plane each cycle? What are the best data structures to use? And on and on. But that's why we are going to write a complete set of

FIGURE 15-27

◎ ◎ ◎ ◎ ◎ ◎

A closer look at the BSP data structure

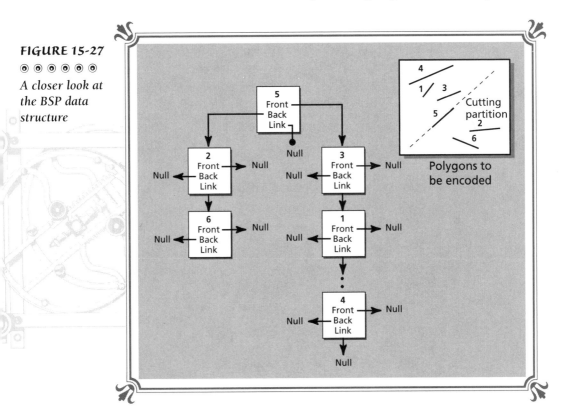

functions along with a demo program that has a simple CAD interface to allow you to draw some walls, create a BSP tree, and then fly through the universe.

Now let's talk about how we display the BSP tree. Displaying the BSP tree is much easier than building it. All we need to do is write an algorithm that uses a modified inorder binary tree traversal algorithm along with a traversal condition that guides the branches taken, based on which side the viewer is of each test polygon. Basically, the algorithm works like this: We begin at the root of the BSP, as shown in Figure 15-28. Then the viewpoint is tested against the plane equation of the root. If the viewpoint is on the front side of the root, the algorithm recursively searches the back branch, displays the polygon, and then recursively traverses the front branch. On the other hand, if the viewpoint is on the back side of the partitioning plane, the opposite is done. The front branch is traversed recursively, the polygon is drawn, and finally, the back branch is recursively traversed.

This may all seem rather confusing, and recursion is definitely one of those confusing things in computer science. But if it helps, don't think of it as a function calling itself, but as another function that does the exact same thing with the same name (I wonder if that helped?). Anyway, why does this algorithm work? This is best illustrated by an example. Using the BSP tree from Figure 15-28, assume the viewpoint is located as shown in Figure 15-28 also. Let's see if the algorithm works correctly.

1. Begin at polygon 2. The viewpoint is within the back half space, therefore, traverse the front half space of polygon 2.

2. Since polygon 1 has no children, it is rendered and the stack is popped back to polygon 2.

3. Polygon 2 is rendered and the back half space is traversed.

4. The viewpoint is within the front half space of polygon 4, therefore, traverse the back half space of polygon 4.

5. Since polygon 3 has no children, it is rendered and the stack is popped back to polygon 4.

6. Polygon 4 is rendered.

7. The front half space of polygon 4 is traversed.

8. Since polygon 5 has no children, it is rendered and the stack is popped all the way out.

Thus, the polygons are drawn in the following sequence: 1, 2, 3, 4, 5. How convenient! And I didn't even plan that!

The algorithm will work all the time regardless of the polygons selected as the partitioning planes and regardless of the view angles. And just to be complete, let's see the traversal algorithm in pseudo-C code this time instead of step-by-step. (Assume each node has both a *front* and a *back* pointer.)

FIGURE 15-28

◎ ◎ ◎ ◎ ◎ ◎

Polygons and BSP tree used for the example traversal

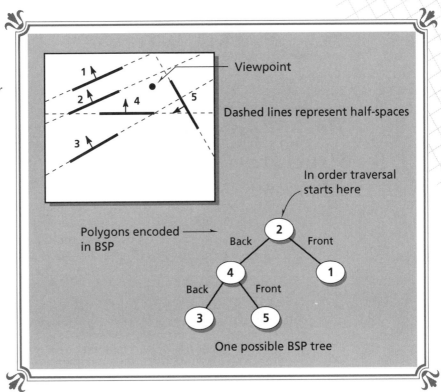

```
if (root==NULL)
   return;

if (viewpoint is on front side of root)
   {
   // perform an inorder traversal
   Bsp_Traverse(root->back, viewpoint);
   Display_Polygon(root->poly);
   Bsp_Traverse(root->front, viewpoint);
   }
else
   {
   // perform an inorder traversal
   Bsp_Traverse(root->front, viewpoint);
   Display_Polygon(root->poly);
   Bsp_Traverse(root->back, viewpoint);
   }

   } // end else

} // end Bsp_Traverse
```

Simple, huh! But the little detail of figuring out which side the viewpoint is relative to each polygon isn't a single line of code, as we'll see when we implement the actual BSP code.

The BSP Tree Functions and Data Structures

Implementing a BSP tree and supporting functions isn't as simple as it may seem. There are many decisions to make. Even though we are only interested in a demo of the technique, creating such a demo isn't an easy task. Anyway, in the end, I have tried to make everything as simple as possible so you can understand the ideas. Let's begin with the data structure used to hold a wall. Here it is:

```
typedef struct wall_typ
        {
        int id;                      // used for debugging
        int color;                   // color of wall
        point_3d wall_world[4];      // the points that make up the wall
        point_3d wall_camera[4];     // the final camera coordinates of the wall
        vector_3d normal;            // the outward normal to the wall used during
                                     // creation of BSP only, after that it becomes
                                     // invalid

        struct wall_typ *link;       // pointer to next wall
        struct wall_typ *front;      // pointer to walls in front
        struct wall_typ *back;       // pointer to walls behind

        } wall, *wall_ptr;
```

The wall is the basic unit that will be contained within the BSP tree. Each node consists of four vertices (both world and local versions) along with the normal to the wall, its color, an identification number for debugging, and finally, three pointers. We have already discussed two of these—they are the front and back pointers. The last pointer is called *link* and is used to link all the walls together in a linked list. This is the raw input format for the walls to the binary space partitioner. Therefore, any program can create the linked list of walls that make up the universe, and the list is then presented to the binary space partitioner for processing. So let's assume for a moment that we have generated the wall list with another program, and a linked list using the link elements to connect each wall has been generated, as shown in Figure 15-29. We'll write a program that takes this as the input and creates the final BSP tree.

FIGURE 15-29

◎ ◎ ◎ ◎ ◎ ◎

The wall list before being processed into a BSP

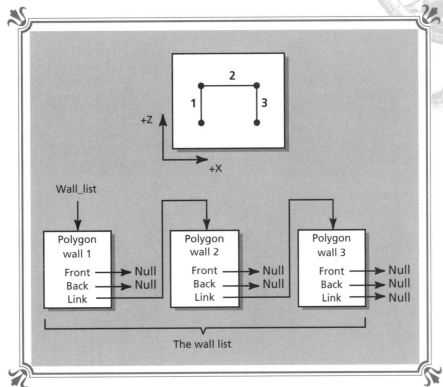

Creating the BSP Tree

Theoretically, building the BSP isn't too hard, but things get a bit complex when the pointers start flying, memory is being allocated, and we start dealing with the little details of two walls having a point in common, partitioning planes cutting walls in half, and so forth. In spite of that, I have tried to make the function as clean as possible. Abstractly, the function works like this: the wall list is presented to the function; then the first element in the list is used as the partitioning plane, and the walls on the front and back of the plane are put into two lists that lead from the front and back pointers of the first node. Furthermore, the individual lists are linked together using the *link* field of the wall structure. Then each of these lists is used as input to recursive calls to the BSP creation function again. This process continues until each of the front and back lists has only one or zero polygons. At this point the BSP tree is complete.

There are a couple of major difficulties during this process and some special cases that must be considered. First, let's talk about the difficulties. Problem number one is how to determine which side a polygon is on of the partitioning plane. Figure 15-30 shows the three cases.

FIGURE 15-30

⊙ ⊙ ⊙ ⊙ ⊙ ⊙

Three cases of walls

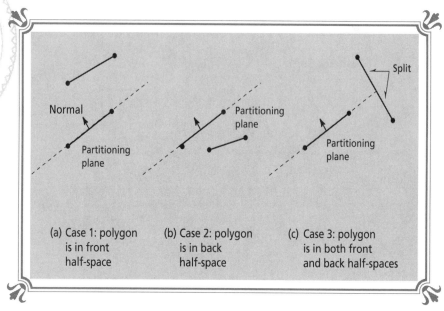

(a) Case 1: polygon is in front half-space

(b) Case 2: polygon is in back half-space

(c) Case 3: polygon is in both front and back half-spaces

Case 1: Both endpoints are on the front side, as shown in Figure 15-30(a).

Case 2: Both endpoints are on the back side, as shown in Figure 15-30(b).

Case 3: One endpoint is on the front side and one is on the back side; therefore, the polygon must be split, as shown in Figure 15-30(c).

FIGURE 15-31

⊙ ⊙ ⊙ ⊙ ⊙ ⊙

Two intersecting lines

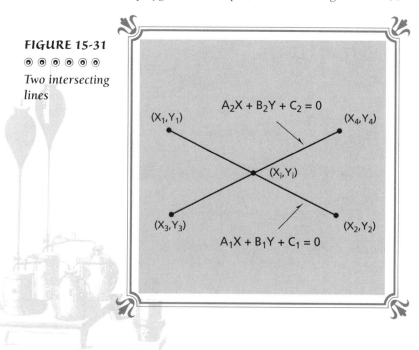

Cases 1 and 2 are easy to test and easy to deal with. The surface normal of the partitioning plane, along with the dot products, are used to determine which side each of the endpoints of the test wall is on. Then walls that are on the front side are added to the front list of the partitioning wall, and walls on the back side of the partitioning wall are added to the back linked list. Case 3 is the problem. What we need to do is extend the partitioning plane and determine where it intersects the test wall. This is easy to do since the walls are vertical and we can perform the calculations in 2D. To compute the point of intersection between two walls thus becomes the same as determining the point of intersection between two 2D lines, as shown in Figure 15-31.

There are about a million ways to do this, but we are going to use one of the more straightforward and brute force methods. Creating the BSP isn't time critical (only displaying it is) since once we have the BSP, we can just load it from a disk and use it. Anyway, let's refer to Figure 15-31 for the derivation of the intersection equations. What we want are two equations of the form:

A1*x+B1*y=C1
A2*x+B2*y=C2

Then we can solve these using Cramer's rule, matrix multiplying, or substitution. I prefer Cramer's rule, which states in a nutshell that the variables in a system of linear equations can be computed by replacing the column in the coefficient matrix of the desired variable with the constant column vector and then computing the determinant of the matrix. The results of this calculation are then divided by the determinant of the original coefficient matrix. This is done for each variable to be computed. The coefficient matrix of the above system is as follows:

$$C = \begin{bmatrix} A1 & B1 \\ A2 & B2 \end{bmatrix}$$

and Det(C)=(A1*B2–A2*B1)

To find x, we would compute this:

$$x = \frac{Det\ of\ \begin{bmatrix} C1 & B1 \\ C2 & B2 \end{bmatrix}}{(A1*B2 - A2*B1)} = \frac{(B2*C1 - B1*C2)}{(A1*B2 - A2*B1)}$$

And y can be found with:

$$y = \frac{Det\ of\ \begin{bmatrix} A1 & C1 \\ A2 & C2 \end{bmatrix}}{(A1*B2 - A2*B1)} = \frac{(A1*C2 - A2*C1)}{(A1*B2 - A2*B1)}$$

The only problem is, how do we get the lines into linear equation form? Simple—we can use the point-slope form of a line, which states,

m*(x–xo)=(y–yo)

where m is the slope (y1–yo)/(x1–xo). And if we rearrange the equation, the results are what we desire,

(m)*x+(–1)* y=(m*xo–yo)

which is of the form:

A*x+B*y=C

Anyway, Listing 15-15 shows the function that uses the preceding math to find the intersection between two lines.

LISTING 15-15 General intersection function

```
void Intersect_Lines(float x0,float y0,float x1,float y1,
                      float x2,float y2,float x3,float y3,
                      float *xi,float *yi)
{
// this function computes the intersection of the sent lines
// and returns the intersection point, note that the function assumes
// the lines intersect. the function can handle vertical as well
// as horizontal lines. note the function isn't very clever, it simply applies
// the math, but we don't need speed since this is a pre-processing step

float a1,b1,c1, // constants of linear equations
      a2,b2,c2,
      det_inv,  // the inverse of the determinant of the coefficient matrix
      m1,m2;    // the slopes of each line

// compute slopes, note the cludge for infinity, however, this will
// be close enough

if ((x1-x0)!=0)
   m1 = (y1-y0)/(x1-x0);
else
   m1 = (float)1e+10;   // close enough to infinity

if ((x3-x2)!=0)
   m2 = (y3-y2)/(x3-x2);
else
   m2 = (float)1e+10;   // close enough to infinity

// compute constants

a1 = m1;
a2 = m2;
```

```
b1 = -1;
b2 = -1;

c1 = (y0-m1*x0);
c2 = (y2-m2*x2);

// compute the inverse of the determinate

det_inv = 1/(a1*b2 - a2*b1);

// use Cramers rule to compute xi and yi

*xi=((b1*c2 - b2*c1)*det_inv);
*yi=((a2*c1 - a1*c2)*det_inv);

} // end Intersect_Lines
```

The function takes as parameters the endpoints of two lines and a pair of pointers to floats in which the function will return the intersection point. Note that the function assumes that the lines are not parallel—that is, they must intersect. Now that we know how to find the intersection of the partitioning plane with the test wall, we can surmise that when a wall is cut in half, it is simply made into two walls. One wall is in the front half space of the partitioning plane, and the other is

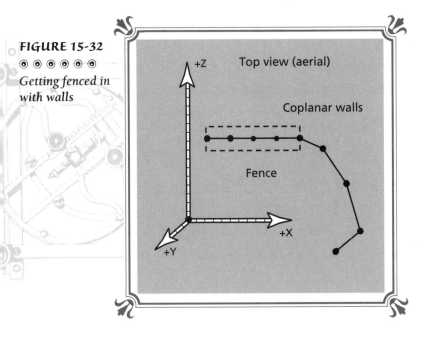

FIGURE 15-32

◎ ◎ ◎ ◎ ◎ ◎

Getting fenced in with walls

within the back half space, and they are thus appropriately inserted onto the front and back linked list of the partitioning plane's node.

Now let's talk about special cases, because they always exist. First, we're going to assume that no two walls intersect. This isn't much of a constraint since if we want a wall to intersect another, we can always use two walls, one on each side of the cutting wall. But two walls having a point in common is unavoidable and has to be dealt with. Take a look at Figure 15-32. Here we see a fence; but the problem is that during our calculation, the points in common can neither be classified as on the front side or on the back side of the partitioning planes, so what should we do? We ask, what exactly does it mean when two walls have an edge in common, and then we use this as the key to determine what to do in this case.

Here goes. When two walls have an edge in common, or from the aerial view, they have common endpoints, all it means is that the point is neither on the front nor on the back side. In essence, the common point is on the plane itself; therefore, we must decide which half space the test wall is by looking at the second endpoint. Once it has been determined that the partitioning plane and the test wall have a common edge or point (however you want to think of it), the second point of the test wall is used to clear it up. Alas, there seems to be one little problem. What if the second endpoint or edge is also on the plane of the partitioning plane! Well, this isn't a problem. In fact, in this case, it doesn't matter which side we put the test wall on; the front or the back will both do equally well.

Now that we have an outline of the algorithm in implementational terms, let's see the actual function that creates the BSP tree given a linked list of walls generated by some other source. Listing 15-16 creates the BSP tree.

LISTING 15-16 The magickal BSP tree creation function

```
void Build_Bsp_Tree(wall_ptr root)
{
// this function recursively builds the bsp tree from the sent wall list
// note the function has some calls to Draw_Line() and a Time_Delay() at
// the end, these are for illustrative purposes only for the demo interface
// and should be removed if you wish to use this function in a real
// application

static wall_ptr next_wall,     // pointer to next wall to be processed
                front_wall,    // the front wall
                back_wall,     // the back wall
                temp_wall;     // a temporary wall

static float

        dot_wall_1,                // dot products for test wall
        dot_wall_2,
        wall_x0,wall_y0,wall_z0,   // working vars for test wall
        wall_x1,wall_y1,wall_z1,
```

```
             pp_x0,pp_y0,pp_z0,            // working vars for partitioning plane
             pp_x1,pp_y1,pp_z1,
             xi,zi;                        // points of intersection when the partitioning
                                           // plane cuts a wall in two

   static vector_3d test_vector_1,         // test vectors from the partitioning plane
                    test_vector_2;         // to the test wall to test the side
                                           // of the partitioning plane the test wall
                                           // lies on

   static int front_flag =0,               // flags if a wall is on the front or back
              back_flag = 0,               // of the partitioning plane
              index;                       // looping index

   // SECTION 1 /////////////////////////////////////////////////////////////////

   // test if this tree is complete

   if (root==NULL)
      return;

   // the root is the partitioning plane, partition the polygons using it

   next_wall  = root->link;
   root->link = NULL;

   // extract top two vertices of partitioning plane wall for ease of calculations

   pp_x0 = root->wall_world[0].x;
   pp_y0 = root->wall_world[0].y;
   pp_z0 = root->wall_world[0].z;


   pp_x1 = root->wall_world[1].x;
   pp_y1 = root->wall_world[1].y;
   pp_z1 = root->wall_world[1].z;

   // highlight space partition green

   Draw_Line(pp_x0/WORLD_SCALE_X-SCREEN_TO_WORLD_X,
             pp_z0/WORLD_SCALE_Z-SCREEN_TO_WORLD_Z,
             pp_x1/WORLD_SCALE_X-SCREEN_TO_WORLD_X,
             pp_z1/WORLD_SCALE_Z-SCREEN_TO_WORLD_Z,
             10,
             video_buffer);

   // SECTION 2  /////////////////////////////////////////////////////////////////

   // test if all walls have been partitioned

   while(next_wall)
       {
       // test which side test wall is relative to partitioning plane
```

continued on next page

continued from previous page

```
          // defined by root

          // first compute vectors from point on partitioning plane to point on
          // test wall

          Make_Vector_3D((point_3d_ptr)&root->wall_world[0],
                         (point_3d_ptr)&next_wall->wall_world[0],
                         (vector_3d_ptr)&test_vector_1);

          Make_Vector_3D((point_3d_ptr)&root->wall_world[0],
                         (point_3d_ptr)&next_wall->wall_world[1],
                         (vector_3d_ptr)&test_vector_2);

          // now dot each test vector with the surface normal and analyze signs

          dot_wall_1 = Dot_Product_3D((vector_3d_ptr)&test_vector_1,
                                      (vector_3d_ptr)&root->normal);

          dot_wall_2 = Dot_Product_3D((vector_3d_ptr)&test_vector_2,
                                      (vector_3d_ptr)&root->normal);


// SECTION 3 /////////////////////////////////////////////////////////////////

          // perform the tests

          // case 0, the partitioning plane and the test wall have a point in common
          // this is a special case and must be accounted for, in the code
          // we will set a pair of flags and then the next case will handle
          // the actual insertion of the wall into BSP

          // reset flags

          front_flag = back_flag = 0;

          // determine if wall is tangent to endpoints of partitioning wall

          if (POINTS_EQUAL_3D(root->wall_world[0],next_wall->wall_world[0]) )
             {
             // p0 of partitioning plane is the same at p0 of test wall
             // we only need to see what side p1 of test wall is on

             if (dot_wall_2 > 0)
                front_flag = 1;
             else
                back_flag = 1;

             } // end if
          else
          if (POINTS_EQUAL_3D(root->wall_world[0],next_wall->wall_world[1]) )
             {
             // p0 of partitioning plane is the same at p1 of test wall
```

```
              // we only need to see what side p0 of test wall is on

              if (dot_wall_1 > 0)
                 front_flag = 1;
              else
                 back_flag = 1;


              } // end if
          else
          if (POINTS_EQUAL_3D(root->wall_world[1],next_wall->wall_world[0]) )
             {
             // p1 of partitioning plane is the same at p0 of test wall
             // we only need to see what side p1 of test wall is on

             if (dot_wall_2 > 0)
                front_flag = 1;
             else
                back_flag = 1;

             } // end if
          else
          if (POINTS_EQUAL_3D(root->wall_world[1],next_wall->wall_world[1]) )
             {
             // p1 of partitioning plane is the same at p1 of test wall
             // we only need to see what side p0 of test wall is on

             if (dot_wall_1 > 0)
                front_flag = 1;
             else
                back_flag = 1;

             } // end if

// SECTION 4 ///////////////////////////////////////////////////////////////

// case 1 both signs are the same or the front or back flag has been set

if ( (dot_wall_1 >= 0 && dot_wall_2 >= 0) || front_flag )
   {

   // highlight the wall blue

   Draw_Line(next_wall->wall_world[0].x/WORLD_SCALE_X-SCREEN_TO_WORLD_X,
             next_wall->wall_world[0].z/WORLD_SCALE_Z-SCREEN_TO_WORLD_Z,
             next_wall->wall_world[1].x/WORLD_SCALE_X-SCREEN_TO_WORLD_X,
             next_wall->wall_world[1].z/WORLD_SCALE_Z-SCREEN_TO_WORLD_Z,
             9,
             video_buffer);

   // place this wall on the front list
```

continued on next page

continued from previous page

```
            if (root->front==NULL)
               {
               // this is the first node

               root->front     = next_wall;
               next_wall       = next_wall->link;
               front_wall      = root->front;
               front_wall->link = NULL;

               } // end if
            else
               {
               // this is the nth node

               front_wall->link = next_wall;
               next_wall       = next_wall->link;
               front_wall      = front_wall->link;
               front_wall->link = NULL;

               } // end else

            } // end if both positive

// SECTION 5 ///////////////////////////////////////////////////////////////

        else
        if ( (dot_wall_1 < 0 && dot_wall_2 < 0) || back_flag)
           {

           // highlight the wall red

           Draw_Line(next_wall->wall_world[0].x/WORLD_SCALE_X-SCREEN_TO_WORLD_X,
                     next_wall->wall_world[0].z/WORLD_SCALE_Z-SCREEN_TO_WORLD_Z,
                     next_wall->wall_world[1].x/WORLD_SCALE_X-SCREEN_TO_WORLD_X,
                     next_wall->wall_world[1].z/WORLD_SCALE_Z-SCREEN_TO_WORLD_Z,
                     12,
                     video_buffer);

           // place this wall on the back list

           if (root->back==NULL)
              {
              // this is the first node

              root->back     = next_wall;
              next_wall      = next_wall->link;
              back_wall      = root->back;
              back_wall->link = NULL;

              } // end if
           else
```

```
                {
                // this is the nth node

                back_wall->link = next_wall;
                next_wall       = next_wall->link;
                back_wall       = back_wall->link;
                back_wall->link = NULL;

                } // end else

            } // end if both negative

        // case 2 both signs are different

// SECTION 6 ///////////////////////////////////////////////////////////////////

            else
            if ( (dot_wall_1 < 0 && dot_wall_2 >= 0) ||
                 (dot_wall_1 >= 0 && dot_wall_2 < 0))

                {
                // the partitioning plane cuts the wall in half, the wall
                // must be split into two walls

                // extract top two vertices of test wall for ease of calculations

                wall_x0 = next_wall->wall_world[0].x;
                wall_y0 = next_wall->wall_world[0].y;
                wall_z0 = next_wall->wall_world[0].z;

                wall_x1 = next_wall->wall_world[1].x;
                wall_y1 = next_wall->wall_world[1].y;
                wall_z1 = next_wall->wall_world[1].z;

                // compute the point of intersection between the walls
                // note that x and z are the plane that the intersection takes place in

                Intersect_Lines(wall_x0,wall_z0,wall_x1,wall_z1,
                                pp_x0,pp_z0,pp_x1,pp_z1,
                                &xi,&zi);

                // here comes the tricky part, we need to split the wall in half and
                // create two walls. We'll do this by creating two new walls,
                // placing them on the appropriate front and back lists and
                // then deleting the original wall

                // process first wall

                // allocate the memory for the wall

                temp_wall = (wall_ptr)malloc(sizeof(wall));
```

continued on next page

continued from previous page

```
                temp_wall->front = NULL;
                temp_wall->back  = NULL;
                temp_wall->link  = NULL;

                temp_wall->normal = next_wall->normal;
                temp_wall->id       = next_wall->id+1000; // add 1000 to denote a split

                // compute wall vertices

                for (index=0; index<4; index++)
                    {
                    temp_wall->wall_world[index].x = next_wall->wall_world[index].x;
                    temp_wall->wall_world[index].y = next_wall->wall_world[index].y;
                    temp_wall->wall_world[index].z = next_wall->wall_world[index].z;
                    } // end for index

                // now modify vertices 1 and 2 to reflect intersection point
                // but leave y alone since it's invariant for the wall splitting

                temp_wall->wall_world[1].x = xi;
                temp_wall->wall_world[1].z = zi;

                temp_wall->wall_world[2].x = xi;
                temp_wall->wall_world[2].z = zi;

// SECTION 7 ///////////////////////////////////////////////////////////

                // insert new wall into front or back of root

                if (dot_wall_1 >= 0)
                    {

                    // highlight the wall blue

                    Draw_Line(temp_wall->wall_world[0].x/WORLD_SCALE_X-SCREEN_TO_WORLD_X,
                              temp_wall->wall_world[0].z/WORLD_SCALE_Z-SCREEN_TO_WORLD_Z,
                              temp_wall->wall_world[1].x/WORLD_SCALE_X-SCREEN_TO_WORLD_X,
                              temp_wall->wall_world[1].z/WORLD_SCALE_Z-SCREEN_TO_WORLD_Z,
                              9,
                              video_buffer);


                    // place this wall on the front list

                    if (root->front==NULL)
                        {
                        // this is the first node

                        root->front       = temp_wall;
                        front_wall        = root->front;
                        front_wall->link  = NULL;
```

```
                } // end if
            else
                {
                // this is the nth node

                front_wall->link = temp_wall;
                front_wall       = front_wall->link;
                front_wall->link = NULL;

                } // end else

            } // end if positive
        else
        if (dot_wall_1 < 0)
            {
            // highlight the wall red

            Draw_Line(temp_wall->wall_world[0].x/WORLD_SCALE_X-SCREEN_TO_WORLD_X,
                      temp_wall->wall_world[0].z/WORLD_SCALE_Z-SCREEN_TO_WORLD_Z,
                      temp_wall->wall_world[1].x/WORLD_SCALE_X-SCREEN_TO_WORLD_X,
                      temp_wall->wall_world[1].z/WORLD_SCALE_Z-SCREEN_TO_WORLD_Z,
                      12,
                      video_buffer);

            // place this wall on the back list

            if (root->back==NULL)
                {
                // this is the first node

                root->back       = temp_wall;
                back_wall        = root->back;
                back_wall->link = NULL;

                } // end if
            else
                {
                // this is the nth node

                back_wall->link = temp_wall;
                back_wall       = back_wall->link;
                back_wall->link = NULL;

                } // end else

            } // end if negative

// SECTION 8 //////////////////////////////////////////////////////////////////

        // process second wall

        // allocate the memory for the wall
```

continued on next page

continued from previous page

```
                temp_wall = (wall_ptr)malloc(sizeof(wall));

                temp_wall->front = NULL;
                temp_wall->back  = NULL;
                temp_wall->link  = NULL;

                temp_wall->normal = next_wall->normal;
                temp_wall->id     = next_wall->id+1000;

                // compute wall vertices

                for (index=0; index<4; index++)
                    {
                    temp_wall->wall_world[index].x = next_wall->wall_world[index].x;
                    temp_wall->wall_world[index].y = next_wall->wall_world[index].y;
                    temp_wall->wall_world[index].z = next_wall->wall_world[index].z;
                    } // end for index

                // now modify vertices 0 and 0 to reflect intersection point
                // but leave y alone since it's invariant for the wall splitting

                temp_wall->wall_world[0].x = xi;
                temp_wall->wall_world[0].z = zi;

                temp_wall->wall_world[3].x = xi;
                temp_wall->wall_world[3].z = zi;

                // insert new wall into front or back of root

                if (dot_wall_2 >= 0)
                    {
                    // highlight the wall blue

                    Draw_Line(temp_wall->wall_world[0].x/WORLD_SCALE_X-SCREEN_TO_WORLD_X,
                              temp_wall->wall_world[0].z/WORLD_SCALE_Z-SCREEN_TO_WORLD_Z,
                              temp_wall->wall_world[1].x/WORLD_SCALE_X-SCREEN_TO_WORLD_X,
                              temp_wall->wall_world[1].z/WORLD_SCALE_Z-SCREEN_TO_WORLD_Z,
                              9,
                              video_buffer);

                    // place this wall on the front list

                    if (root->front==NULL)
                        {
                        // this is the first node

                        root->front       = temp_wall;
                        front_wall        = root->front;
                        front_wall->link  = NULL;

                        } // end if
                    else
```

```
        {
        // this is the nth node

        front_wall->link = temp_wall;
        front_wall        = front_wall->link;
        front_wall->link = NULL;

        } // end else


    } // end if positive
else
if (dot_wall_2 < 0)
    {
    // highlight the wall red

    Draw_Line(temp_wall->wall_world[0].x/WORLD_SCALE_X-SCREEN_TO_WORLD_X,
              temp_wall->wall_world[0].z/WORLD_SCALE_Z-SCREEN_TO_WORLD_Z,
              temp_wall->wall_world[1].x/WORLD_SCALE_X-SCREEN_TO_WORLD_X,
              temp_wall->wall_world[1].z/WORLD_SCALE_Z-SCREEN_TO_WORLD_Z,
              12,
              video_buffer);

    // place this wall on the back list

    if (root->back==NULL)
        {
        // this is the first node

        root->back       = temp_wall;
        back_wall        = root->back;
        back_wall->link = NULL;

        } // end if
    else
        {
        // this is the nth node

        back_wall->link = temp_wall;
        back_wall        = back_wall->link;
        back_wall->link = NULL;

        } // end else

    } // end if negative

// SECTION 9 //////////////////////////////////////////////////////////////

    // we are now done splitting the wall, so we can delete it

    temp_wall = next_wall;
    next_wall = next_wall->link;
```

continued on next page

continued from previous page

```
            free(temp_wall);

        } // end else

    } // end while

// SECTION 10 //////////////////////////////////////////////////////////////

// delay a bit so user can see BSP being created

Time_Delay(5);

// recursively process front and back walls

Build_Bsp_Tree(root->front);

Build_Bsp_Tree(root->back);

} // end Build_Bsp_Tree
```

The function has a few calls to *Draw_Line()* and a *Time_Delay()* call at the end just for illustrative purposes of the demo. They can be taken out without fear. The function is sectioned off for ease of explanation, so let's take a quick look at what each section does.

Section 1: This tests whether the current wall pointer is *NULL*; if not, then the vertices of the partitioning plane are extracted and the partitioning plane is highlighted.

Section 2: The two endpoints of the first wall below the partitioning plane are used to determine their relative positions to the partitioning wall by use of dot products.

Section 3: The special case of common endpoints is processed and flags are set to track it into the next phase.

Section 4: Based on the signs of the dot products, the test wall is determined to be on the front side of the partitioning plane, and the test wall is added to the front linked list.

Section 5: Based on the signs of the dot products, the test wall is determined to be on the back side of the partitioning plane, and the test wall is added to the back linked list.

Section 6: The test wall must have been cut in half by the partitioning plane; therefore, the coordinates of the two halves are computed.

Section 7: If section 6 is executed, the first half of the wall is inserted into either the front or back linked list.

Section 8: If section 6 is executed, the second half of the wall is inserted into either the front or back linked list.

Section 9: The next wall to be processed is accessed and the process continues.

Section 10: When all the walls of the list have been processed, the front and back wall lists are recursively processed, and the whole thing starts again.

When the function exits, the BSP tree will have been generated and the original wall list will be mangled. The memory won't be lost, but we can't use the links anymore to traverse the wall list. Now that we have the BSP tree, let's see how to display it.

Traversing the BSP Tree

We have already seen the algorithm to traverse the BSP tree, but how can we work this into our graphics engine? The answer is that we will traverse the BSP tree and, during the traversal, place the polygons to be drawn on the global polygon list, then simply draw the polygons. The ordering of them will be correct since they will be inserted into the polygon list during the modified recursive inorder traversal of the BSP tree, which is guaranteed to generate the proper order for any viewpoint. Listing 15-17 contains the function that will traverse the BSP tree and add the polygons to the global polygon list.

LISTING 15-17 *The BSP traversal function*

```
void Bsp_Traverse(wall_ptr root)
{
// this function traverses the BSP tree and generates the polygon list used
// by Draw_Polys() for the current global viewpoint (note the view angle is
// irrelevant), also as the polygon list is being generated, only polygons
// that are within the z extents are added to the polygon, in essence, the
// function is performing Z clipping also, this is to minimize the amount
// of polygons in the graphics pipeline that will have to be processed during
// rendering

// this function works by testing the viewpoint against the current wall
// in the bsp, then depending on the side the viewpoint is the algorithm
// proceeds. the search takes place as the rest using an "inorder" method
// with hooks to process and add each node into the polygon list at the
// right time

static vector_3d test_vector;

static float dot_wall,
             z1,z2,z3,z4;

// SECTION 1 ///////////////////////////////////////////////////////////////

// is this a dead end?

if (root==NULL)
   return;

// test which side viewpoint is on relative to the current wall
```

continued on next page

continued from previous page

```
Make_Vector_3D((point_3d_ptr)&root->wall_world[0],
               (point_3d_ptr)&view_point,
               (vector_3d_ptr)&test_vector);

// now dot test vector with the surface normal and analyze signs

dot_wall = Dot_Product_3D((vector_3d_ptr)&test_vector,
                          (vector_3d_ptr)&root->normal);

// SECTION 2 ///////////////////////////////////////////////////////////////

// if the sign of the dot product is positive then the viewer is on the
// front side of current wall, so recursively process the walls behind then
// in front of this wall, else do the opposite

if (dot_wall>0)
   {
   // viewer is in front of this wall

   // process the back wall sub tree
   Bsp_Traverse(root->back);

   // try to add this wall to the polygon list if it's within the Z extents

   z1=root->wall_camera[0].z;
   z2=root->wall_camera[1].z;
   z3=root->wall_camera[2].z;
   z4=root->wall_camera[3].z;

   // perform the z extents clipping test

   if ( (z1>clip_near_z && z1<clip_far_z ) || (z2>clip_near_z && z2<clip_far_z ) ||
        (z3>clip_near_z && z3<clip_far_z ) || (z4>clip_near_z && z4<clip_far_z ))
      {
      // first copy data and vertices into an open slot in storage area

      world_poly_storage[num_polys_frame].num_points = 4;
      world_poly_storage[num_polys_frame].color      = BSP_WALL_COLOR;
      world_poly_storage[num_polys_frame].shade      = root->color;
      world_poly_storage[num_polys_frame].shading    = 0;
      world_poly_storage[num_polys_frame].two_sided  = 1;
      world_poly_storage[num_polys_frame].visible    = 1;
      world_poly_storage[num_polys_frame].clipped    = 0;
      world_poly_storage[num_polys_frame].active      = 1;

      // now copy vertices

      world_poly_storage[num_polys_frame].vertex_list[0].x = root->wall_camera[0].x;
      world_poly_storage[num_polys_frame].vertex_list[0].y = root->wall_camera[0].y;
      world_poly_storage[num_polys_frame].vertex_list[0].z = root->wall_camera[0].z;

      world_poly_storage[num_polys_frame].vertex_list[1].x = root->wall_camera[1].x;
```

```
world_poly_storage[num_polys_frame].vertex_list[1].y = root->wall_camera[1].y;
world_poly_storage[num_polys_frame].vertex_list[1].z = root->wall_camera[1].z;

world_poly_storage[num_polys_frame].vertex_list[2].x = root->wall_camera[2].x;
world_poly_storage[num_polys_frame].vertex_list[2].y = root->wall_camera[2].y;
world_poly_storage[num_polys_frame].vertex_list[2].z = root->wall_camera[2].z;

world_poly_storage[num_polys_frame].vertex_list[3].x = root->wall_camera[3].x;
world_poly_storage[num_polys_frame].vertex_list[3].y = root->wall_camera[3].y;
world_poly_storage[num_polys_frame].vertex_list[3].z = root->wall_camera[3].z;


// assign poly list pointer to it
world_polys[num_polys_frame] = &world_poly_storage[num_polys_frame];

// increment number of polys in this frame
num_polys_frame++;

} // end if polygon is visible

// now process the front walls sub tree
Bsp_Traverse(root->front);

} // end if

// SECTION 3 ////////////////////////////////////////////////////////////////////

else
   {
   // viewer is behind this wall

   // process the front wall sub tree
   Bsp_Traverse(root->front);

   // try to add this wall to the polygon list if it's within the Z extents

   z1=root->wall_camera[0].z;
   z2=root->wall_camera[1].z;
   z3=root->wall_camera[2].z;
   z4=root->wall_camera[3].z;

   // perform the z extents clipping test

   if ( (z1>clip_near_z && z1<clip_far_z ) || (z2>clip_near_z && z2<clip_far_z )  ||
        (z3>clip_near_z && z3<clip_far_z ) || (z4>clip_near_z && z4<clip_far_z ))
      {

      // first copy data and vertices into an open slot in storage area

      world_poly_storage[num_polys_frame].num_points = 4;
      world_poly_storage[num_polys_frame].color       = BSP_WALL_COLOR;
      world_poly_storage[num_polys_frame].shade       = root->color;
```

continued on next page

continued from previous page

```
world_poly_storage[num_polys_frame].shading    = 0;
world_poly_storage[num_polys_frame].two_sided  = 1;
world_poly_storage[num_polys_frame].visible    = 1;
world_poly_storage[num_polys_frame].clipped    = 0;
world_poly_storage[num_polys_frame].active     = 1;

// now copy vertices, note that we don't use a structure copy, it's
// not dependable

world_poly_storage[num_polys_frame].vertex_list[0].x = root->wall_camera[0].x;
world_poly_storage[num_polys_frame].vertex_list[0].y = root->wall_camera[0].y;
world_poly_storage[num_polys_frame].vertex_list[0].z = root->wall_camera[0].z;

world_poly_storage[num_polys_frame].vertex_list[1].x = root->wall_camera[1].x;
world_poly_storage[num_polys_frame].vertex_list[1].y = root->wall_camera[1].y;
world_poly_storage[num_polys_frame].vertex_list[1].z = root->wall_camera[1].z;

world_poly_storage[num_polys_frame].vertex_list[2].x = root->wall_camera[2].x;
world_poly_storage[num_polys_frame].vertex_list[2].y = root->wall_camera[2].y;
world_poly_storage[num_polys_frame].vertex_list[2].z = root->wall_camera[2].z;

world_poly_storage[num_polys_frame].vertex_list[3].x = root->wall_camera[3].x;
world_poly_storage[num_polys_frame].vertex_list[3].y = root->wall_camera[3].y;
world_poly_storage[num_polys_frame].vertex_list[3].z = root->wall_camera[3].z;

// assign poly list pointer to it
world_polys[num_polys_frame] = &world_poly_storage[num_polys_frame];

// increment number of polys in this frame
num_polys_frame++;

} // end if polygon is visible

// now process the front walls sub tree
Bsp_Traverse(root->back);

} // end else

} // end Bsp_Traverse
```

As usual, the reality of implementing a function is much different from the theoretical version. As you can see, the above function is much more complex than the pseudocode version we saw a while ago. Let's take a look at the sections.

Section 1: This tests whether the current node is *NULL*; if so, exit. If it is not, it computes the viewpoint position relative to the current node using a dot product.

Section 2: The sign of the dot product from section 1 is used to determine which side the viewpoint (and hence the viewer) is. Based on this, one of two different traversal methods is selected, which are identical except for the recursive calls.

Section 3: First, a recursive call to process the back walls is made. Second, the polygon is tested to see if it's within the Z extents of the viewing volume. If it is, then it is added to the polygon list and the necessary pointers and data structures are updated. Finally, a recursive call is made to process the back walls.

The second block of code works in a similar way except the order of the recursive calls is reversed.

So once the call is made to *Bsp_Traverse()*, the global polygon list is generated, and we can simply use the *Draw_Poly_List()* function to draw the scene. However, there still are a couple issues we need to deal with. First, you should have noticed that the *Bsp_Traverse()* function uses the *wall_camera[]* vertices during the insertion of the wall into the polygon list. Therefore, we need some method to fill in these values. This can be done by traversing the BSP tree and then multiplying the *wall_world[]* vertices by the global world to camera transformation matrix and storing the results in the *wall_camera[]* array in the BSP tree. Listing 15-18 shows such a function.

LISTING 15-18 Function that computes the camera coordinates for all the walls in the BSP tree

```
void Bsp_World_To_Camera(wall_ptr root)
{
// this function traverses the bsp tree and converts the world coordinates
// to camera coordinates using the global transformation matrix. note the
// function is recursive and uses an inorder traversal, other traversals
// such as preorder and postorder will work just as well...

static int index; // looping variable

// test if we have hit a dead end

if (root==NULL)
   return;

// transform back most sub-tree

Bsp_World_To_Camera(root->back);

// iterate thru all vertices of current wall and transform them into
// camera coordinates

for (index=0; index<4; index++)
    {
    // multiply the point by the viewing transformation matrix

    // x component

    root->wall_camera[index].x =

            root->wall_world[index].x * global_view[0][0] +
            root->wall_world[index].y * global_view[1][0] +
```

continued on next page

continued from previous page

```
                         root->wall_world[index].z * global_view[2][0] +
                                             global_view[3][0];

    // y component

    root->wall_camera[index].y =

                 root->wall_world[index].x * global_view[0][1] +
                 root->wall_world[index].y * global_view[1][1] +
                 root->wall_world[index].z * global_view[2][1] +
                                     global_view[3][1];
    // z component

    root->wall_camera[index].z =

                 root->wall_world[index].x * global_view[0][2] +
                 root->wall_world[index].y * global_view[1][2] +
                 root->wall_world[index].z * global_view[2][2] +
                                     global_view[3][2];

    } // end for index

// transform front most sub-tree

Bsp_World_To_Camera(root->front);

} // end Bsp_World_To_Camera
```

The function simply multiplies the global world to camera transformation matrix by each point in each wall that makes up the BSP tree. The only weird thing about the function is the recursion, but it's kinda cool, don't you think? Also, note that I used an inorder traversal. A preorder or postorder will work just as well as long as each node is visited exactly once.

Now, to make the BSP walls look semi-real, we are going to write a shading function that need only be called if the light source changes direction. That is, since the walls never move, there is no need to recompute the light intensities falling on them unless the light source changes. Thus, a single call can be made to shade the walls at the beginning of the display program. Anyway, the shading is almost identical to the flat shader used to shade standard general polygons of our objects, with the recursive twist. The code is shown in Listing 15-19.

LISTING 15-19 Recursive flat shader for the walls in the BSP tree

```
void Bsp_Shade(wall_ptr root)
{
// this function shades the bsp tree and need only be called if the global
// lightsource changes position

static int index; // looping variable
```

```
static float normal_length, // length of surface normal
             intensity,     // intensity of light falling on surface being processed
             dp;            // result of dot product

// test if we have hit a dead end

if (root==NULL)
   return;

// shade the back most sub-tree

Bsp_Shade(root->back);

// compute the dot product between line of sight vector and normal to surface

dp = Dot_Product_3D((vector_3d_ptr)&root->normal,(vector_3d_ptr)&light_source);

// compute length of normal of surface normal, remember this function
// doesn't need to be time critical since it is only called once at startup
// or whenever the light source moves

normal_length = Vector_Mag_3D((vector_3d_ptr)&root->normal);

// cos 0 = (u.v)/|u||v| or

intensity = ambient_light + (15*dp/normal_length);

// test if intensity has overflowed

if (intensity >15)
    intensity = 15;

// intensity now varies from 0-1, 0 being black or grazing and 1 being
// totally illuminated. use the value to index into color table

root->color = BSP_WALL_SHADE - (int)(fabs(intensity));

// shade the front most sub-tree

Bsp_Shade(root->front);

} // end Bsp_Shade
```

Notice that the interface to all these functions is very simple. Basically, all we need is the root to the BSP and maybe a parameter, and that's it. To complete the functions and show how to do simpler things, Listing 15-20 translates the entire BSP tree into world coordinates.

LISTING 15-20 BSP tree translator

```
void Bsp_Translate(wall_ptr root,int x_trans,int y_trans,int z_trans)
{
```

continued on next page

continued from previous page

```
// this function translates all the walls that make up the bsp world
// note function is recursive, we don't really need this function, but
// it's a good example of how we might perform transformations on the BSP
// tree and similar tree like structures using recursion

static int index; // looping variable

// test if we have hit a dead end

if (root==NULL)
   return;

// translate back most sub-tree

Bsp_Translate(root->back,x_trans,y_trans,z_trans);

// iterate thru all vertices of current wall and translate them

for (index=0; index<4; index++)
    {
    // perform translation

    root->wall_world[index].x+=x_trans;
    root->wall_world[index].y+=y_trans;
    root->wall_world[index].z+=z_trans;

    } // end for index

// translate front most sub-tree

Bsp_Translate(root->front,x_trans,y_trans,z_trans);

} // end Bsp_Translate
```

The *Bsp_Translate()* function has the most complex interface so far. The root along with the x, y, and z translation factors must be sent. The interesting thing about translation is that it doesn't affect the ordering of the BSP tree. In other words, the structure of the BSP tree is invariant to translation. Is this correct? Well, if you move your house, do the walls still occlude each other? Yes, as long as you move the entire house the same amount. And the same holds for BSP trees. Finally, Listing 15-21 shows the code to delete or release all the memory allocated by the BSP tree.

LISTING 15-21 Function that releases all the memory used by the BSP tree

```
void Bsp_Delete(wall_ptr root)
{
// this function recursively deletes all the nodes in the bsp tree and frees
// the memory back to the OS.

wall_ptr temp_wall; // a temporary wall
```

```
// test if we have hit a dead end

if (root==NULL)
   return;

// delete back sub tree
Bsp_Delete(root->back);

// delete this node, but first save the front sub-tree
temp_wall = root->front;

// delete the memory
free(root);

// assign the root to the saved front most sub-tree
root = temp_wall;

// delete front sub tree
Bsp_Delete(root);

} // end Bsp_Delete
```

Just make a call to the *Bsp_Delete()* function with the root of the BSP tree and the tree will be recursively deallocated. That's about all there is to a complete BSP system. Now let's see how we're going to add it to our graphics pipeline.

Adding the BSP Tree to the Graphics Pipeline

Adding the BSP tree to the graphics pipeline shouldn't be that hard—the procedure is similar to the way we added the Z-buffer system. All we have to do is this: Since the BSP tree contains all the geometry for the universe, we don't need to worry about objects anymore. Each animation cycle, we need to compute the global world to camera transformation matrix, transform the BSP tree, traverse it to create the polygon list, and finally, make a call to the *Draw_Poly_List()* function. That's about it.

Here are the main code elements we need to perform each cycle:

```
Create_World_To_Camera();
Bsp_World_To_Camera(bsp_root);
num_polys_frame = 0;
Bsp_Traverse(bsp_root);
Draw_Poly_List();
Display_Double_Buffer(double_buffer,0);
```

This code fragment is the heart of the BSP display function called *Bsp_View()*, which is a self-contained function that the demo program calls when the BSP tree is viewed. Listing 15-22 contains the code for *Bsp_View()*.

LISTING 15-22 BSP display function used in BSPDEMO

```
void Bsp_View(wall_ptr bsp_root)
{
// this function is a self contained viewing processor that has its own event
// loop, the display will continue to be generated until the ESC key is pressed

int done=0;

// install the isr keyboard driver
Keyboard_Install_Driver();

// change the light source direction
light_source.x =(float)0.398636;
light_source.y =(float)-0.374248;
light_source.z =(float)0.8372275;

// reset viewpoint to (0,0,0)
view_point.x = 0;
view_point.y = 0;
view_point.z = 0;

// main event loop

while(!done)
    {
    // compute starting time of this frame
    starting_time = Timer_Query();

    // erase all objects
    Fill_Double_Buffer(0);

    // move viewpoint

    if (keyboard_state[MAKE_UP])
       view_point.y+=20;

    if (keyboard_state[MAKE_DOWN])
       view_point.y-=20;

    if (keyboard_state[MAKE_RIGHT])
       view_point.x+=20;

    if (keyboard_state[MAKE_LEFT])
       view_point.x-=20;

    if (keyboard_state[MAKE_KEYPAD_PLUS])
       view_point.z+=20;

    if (keyboard_state[MAKE_KEYPAD_MINUS])
       view_point.z-=20;

    if (keyboard_state[MAKE_Z])
       if ((view_angle.ang_x+=10)>360)
```

```
                    view_angle.ang_x = 0;

         if (keyboard_state[MAKE_A])
            if ((view_angle.ang_x-=10)<0)
               view_angle.ang_x = 360;

         if (keyboard_state[MAKE_X])
            if ((view_angle.ang_y+=10)>360)
               view_angle.ang_y = 0;

         if (keyboard_state[MAKE_S])
            if ((view_angle.ang_y-=10)<0)
               view_angle.ang_y = 360;

         if (keyboard_state[MAKE_C])
            if ((view_angle.ang_z+=10)>360)
               view_angle.ang_z = 0;

         if (keyboard_state[MAKE_D])
            if ((view_angle.ang_z-=10)<0)
               view_angle.ang_z = 360;

         if (keyboard_state[MAKE_ESC])
            done=1;

         // now that user has possible moved viewpoint, create the global
         // world to camera transformation matrix

         Create_World_To_Camera();

         // now convert the bsp tree world coordinates into camera coordinates
         Bsp_World_To_Camera(bsp_root);

         // reset number of polygons in polygon list
         num_polys_frame = 0;

         // traverse the BSP tree and generate the polygon list
         Bsp_Traverse(bsp_root);

         // draw the polygon list generated by traversing the BSP tree
         Draw_Poly_List();

         // display double buffer
         Display_Double_Buffer(double_buffer,0);

         // lock onto 18 frames per second max
         while((Timer_Query()-starting_time)<1);

         } // end while

    // restore the old keyboard driver
    Keyboard_Remove_Driver();

    } // end Bsp_View
```

The *Bsp_View()* function is very similar to many of the *main()*s of the 3D demos that we have been writing except that it is a function. This is because it had to be called from the demo program, which contains all the interface code to draw the universe and manipulate the BSP. Study the viewing function and compare it to SORTDEMO.C and SOLZDEMO.C so that you see how simple it is to implement a multitude of rendering techniques with a well-designed engine.

Let's get to what we've been building up to, and that's a full BSP demo program complete with a user interface.

The BSP Demo

The BSP demo program is about 90 percent interface code with a few calls to all the BSP functions. This is a perfect example of how complex it is to write interfaces. Most of the time the interface code is ten times bigger than the program it encapsulates. Anyway, the BSPDEMO.EXE program allows us to use the mouse to draw a top view of a universe made of walls. Figure 15-33 shows a screen shot of the program.

As you can see, there are two main areas of interest. The area on the right is the control area and the area on the left is the editor area. To draw a wall, simply move the mouse cursor to the desired location and click the left button. Then move to the endpoint of the wall and click the left button again, and a line representing a wall will be drawn. If you don't want to complete a wall, click the right mouse button. Unfortunately, the editor doesn't have "rubber banding," so you'll have to bear with it.

Here are the rules:

1. You can't have more than 64 lines (walls).

2. Lines can't intersect.

3. Lines *can* have common endpoints.

FIGURE15-33

Screen shot of BSPDEMO.EXE

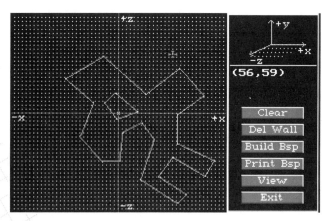

Deleting a wall: If you want to delete a wall, select Del Wall, and the cursor will change into a red circle with a slash. Simply move the mouse cursor over the line you wish deleted and click the left button.

Clearing the whole editor: To clear all the walls, click the Clear button.

Creating the BSP tree data structure in memory: To create the BSP from the 2D view, press Build BSP and you will see a slowed down version of the process on the screen. When it's complete, hit [SPACEBAR] to continue.

Printing out the BSP tree data structure: If you wish to see the BSP tree in printed form, click Print BSP, and the program will print all the nodes in the BSP fully annotated using an inorder search. The output will be fed to the file BSPDEMO.OUT, which will be created by the program. You can then edit this file with any ASCII editor after exiting the program.

Viewing the 3D BSP tree-based universe: Once you have built the BSP, you may fly through the universe in real-time by clicking the View button. Once into the viewing mode, use the same control interface as all the other 3D programs to move the viewpoint and view angles. To exit, press [ESC], and the program will return to the interface.

Exiting the program: To exit the program, press the Exit button on the interface, and you will be returned to DOS.

After playing with the program for a while, you might want to look at the demo source called BSPDEMO.C. I'm not going to list it since it's mostly interface code and is too long, but it has some coding techniques for interfaces that you might be interested in. It might even be the start of a new book, titled "Tricks of the GUI Gurus"!

Limitations of the BSP

Although the BSP tree is an incredibly fast way to determine polygon rendering orders during run time, it isn't without its limitations. The first limitation is that the universe must be semistatic. This means polygons can't rotate, but they can translate in cases. For example, take a look at Figure 15-34, where we see a view of two walls. If we slide one of the walls upward, as in Figure 15-34(b), the order remains the same; thus, a BSP tree can be used if there are polygon translations in the plane that the polygon exists on, but that's it. This isn't bad if we're making Doom or Dark Forces-type engines, since walls usually don't move much, and if they do, it's because they are doors, which can be supported using this technique.

The second main limitation is that BSP trees are definitely not the way to go for simulators or games with a lot of motion since the BSP would have to be regenerated each frame. But, all in all, the BSP tree is a very elegant solution to the rendering

FIGURE 15-34
◎ ◎ ◎ ◎ ◎ ◎

The BSP tree is invariant for Y-axis translations of the walls

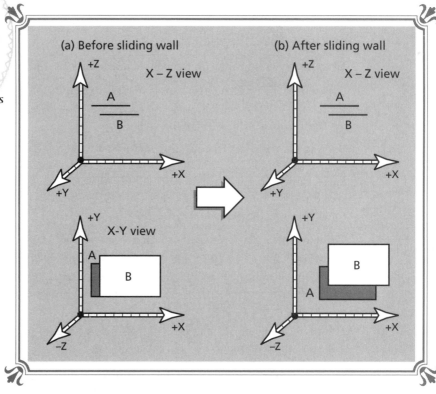

problem and can be used in situations where the player is moving through a generally static environment.

Comparative Analysis of Techniques

After studying the techniques in this chapter, implementing demos of them, and seeing the results, which one(s) should we use in our games? This isn't a simple question, and therefore, there is no simple answer. However, we can at least make some general statements. First, the Painter's algorithm and the simpler depth sort should be used for games that have objects and geometry that are mostly convex. Moreover, the Painter's algorithm and depth sort are good techniques to be used by beginners and during your first implementation of a 3D engine.

The second technique of Z-buffering is probably the best overall 3D rendering technique as far as handling extremely complex geometry and intersections; however, it is memory intensive and computationally intensive in software. Therefore, it really only makes sense in a 32-bit environment such as DOS protected mode. Nevertheless, versions of the Z-buffer, such as the vertical scan line Z-buffer, can be successfully implemented in 16-bit DOS, and they actually perform extremely well. But of course, this technique limits the types of geometry that can be modeled.

The final method we studied, the Binary Space Partition, is applicable to static universes and "walkthrough" games. It trades initial computational time and overhead for extremely fast run-time behavior; but again, it suffers from certain geometric constraints, such as the fact that intersecting polygons must be split. Furthermore, placing movable objects in a BSP universe is hard to implement since the BSP tree must be regenerated or manipulated in real-time to make sure that the objects are visited in the correct order with the background imagery.

Adding Other Entities to the 3D World

Thus far our 3D engine has been totally polygon based. However, most 3D games have other types of geometry in the 3D universe that is of a simpler nature—for example, points, lines, and even 2D sprites. Can we add these to our engine without too much trouble?

Adding Points

Adding points to our 3D engine is very easy. All we need to do is add a new point type to the engine. Then we can either load the points or generate them algorithmically at run time. In any case, after we have performed the manipulations to the 3D objects, we can apply the same manipulations to the points. The world to camera and clipping transformations would be performed just as they are for the polygons of each object. However, the tricky part comes when we wish to render the points. Ideally, we can think of each point as an infinitesimally small polygon—that is, a polygon whose vertices are all equal. Using this point of view, it's not hard to see how to mix the single-point polygons into the engine.

The only problem with this technique is that we are probably going to use points for only a few effects, such as environmental effects, weapons fire, explosion shrapnel, and so forth. So, do we really need to place each point into the rendering pipeline and slow it down? Not really—if we want to use points for explosions, for instance, we can probably get away with drawing them last after performing the complex rendering operation for all the points in the polygon. Even though many times the points should be occluded by some object(s), the player probably isn't going to care too much for the short duration that the visual error occurs.

Adding Lines

Lines can be added in much the same way that points are, but we can't be so cavalier about displaying them since we might actually use lines for geometry of the world or of objects. Therefore, lines will have to be transformed in the same way objects are and then entered into the polygon list with a special flag that marks them as being lines. Then they will be sorted, Z-buffered, or whatever, and finally, scan-converted using a special filter in the *Draw_Poly_List()* function that tests for polygons with only two endpoints.

The 3D Animation Model for Games

We have seen all there is to see about basic 3D graphics and animation, and we have studied many 3D animation loops during the process. The following general structure is all we need for a 3D game:

```
while(1)
        {
 Erase Screen();
 Transform_3D_Objects();
 Draw_Frame();
 } // that's it baby!
```

Of course, the transform objects part consists of many of the 3D calls, but the same structure of erase-move-draw that we used for the 2D game portion of the book remains in flux.

Summary

This chapter has been the culmination of everything that we have learned so far, and we have put it all to use and then some. We learned about some of the most popular rendering techniques, including the Painter's algorithm, depth sorting, Z-buffering, and the Binary Space Partition. We also saw demos of all of them and learned how easy it is to add rendering techniques to our 3D graphics pipeline with only the addition of a couple functions each time. Finally, we decided that the depth sort and Painter's algorithm are probably the best choice for us on our first 3D game endeavors.

Now it's time to learn a bit about voxel graphics and terrain modeling.

16

Voxel Graphics

come tucti fanci lo manouelle . . di quali pino obano . l aiga
. i gra pi . i . luor lo mio di o . i . goni . fo . i a go p rano fi bo no
or . . . . i . nella moto . . o . o p . . . i . . . lla . . lla mano bi . . . p . gi . . .
a forca . . o . pio . i . o . o . p . b . i . o . .

. . l p . . . .
. . l . . . .
. . . .

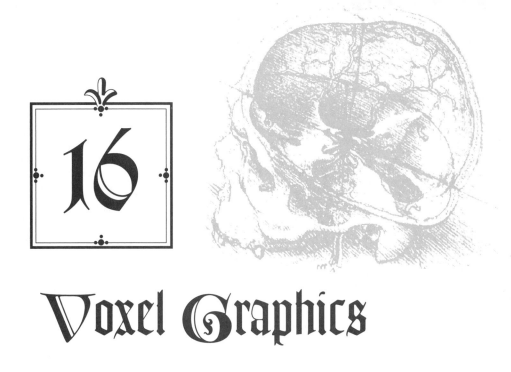

16

Voxel Graphics

Have you had enough polygons yet? I know I have! Let's take a little break in this chapter and look at the new and powerful technology of voxel graphics. Although we briefly discussed the subject in the first chapter of the book, it would be nice to try generating a simple voxel display just to get some idea of how it's done. This is exactly what we are going to do in this chapter. We're going to write a simple, near real-time voxel engine that will create a recognizable voxel display. Of course, it would take a whole book to really learn voxel graphics and generate a real-time voxel engine (such as those seen in Nova Logic's Commanche and Armored Fist). However, we will at least cover one method of generating a voxel display based on the technique of ray casting. We'll also learn to speed things up a little and how to add sprites and other objects to the voxel world.

Voxel Primer

Voxel graphics is basically a technique of generating terrain-type data for mountains, ocean floors, and so forth. Figure 16-1 is a typical voxel display. Voxel means "volume pixel"; hence, voxel graphics is the science of rendering objects that have volume and can be broken up into little cubes or volume elements.

FIGURE 16-1

◎ ◎ ◎ ◎ ◎ ◎

*Typical voxel
display*

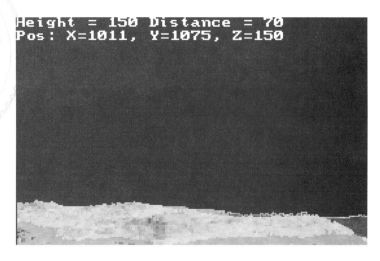

As Cybersorcerers, we really don't care too much about what voxel graphics is supposed to be used for, we just want to abuse the technique for our needs, which of course, are games. We want to find a simple way to generate 3D terrain based on some kind of data set. The data might be contour maps, simple 2D textures, or whatever, but somehow we want to turn the data into a 3D image. We will generate this image in a completely new way; that is, instead of using polygons and transformations, we are going to use other techniques that are more adapted for the type of "rough" data set we are trying to render.

It turns out that the technique of ray casting (which you may be familiar with) can be used. Ray casting is the method used by Wolfenstein 3D and Blake Stone to generate the realistic displays for the games. We'll talk more about ray casting later in the chapter, but now let's take a look at exactly what we are going to use as data for our voxel engine.

Generating the Voxel Database

Voxel data consists of height data along with color data. For example, Figure 16-2 shows a contour map of some region of the planet. The different contours are marked with heights. This is one example of a data set that we might want to look at with a voxel engine. Another example of possible voxel data is shown in Figure 16-3. Here we see an infrared satellite scan of some area of Earth. Even though this data is 2D in nature, we can interpret the different intensities as the height of each region and thus extrapolate a 3D image from the 2D color image. In essence, the type of voxel data we are going to be using is called height data in a 2D array. The

FIGURE 16-2

◎ ◎ ◎ ◎ ◎ ◎

*Topological
contour map*

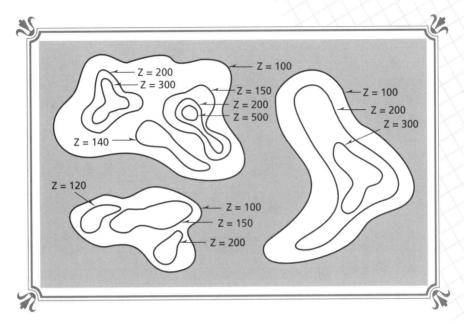

2D array holds a bird's-eye view of the data, and each element of the array contains a height and color of the terrain at the element's location.

Figure 16-4 shows a simple 8x8 height array. Each element of the array holds the height above sea level of the voxel element and its color. So the question is, where can we obtain voxel data? There are two basic sources of data: scanned data and algorithmically generated data. Let's take a look at both.

FIGURE 16-3

◎ ◎ ◎ ◎ ◎ ◎

*Infrared
satellite scan*

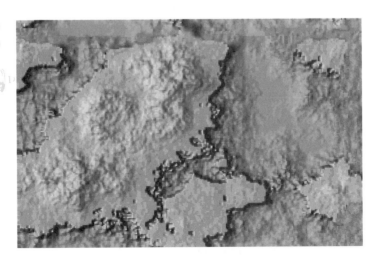

FIGURE 16-4

An 8x8 height map

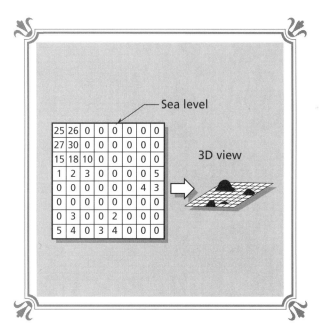

Using Scanned Terrain Maps

Our voxel engine is going to use 2D bitmaps for the voxel data. The 2D bitmaps will be interpreted in such a way that the color of each pixel is not only the color of the voxel data at that point, but the height from 0 to 255. For example, Figure 16-5 shows a voxel data set that originally was an earthquake intensity satellite scan. I took the image and tweaked it with Adobe Photoshop to make the scan more colorful. If we wanted to, we could support both a height and color map. For example, we could use the image of Figure 16-5 as just the color map, and a second 2D array of the same dimensions would be used as a height map. This gives a bit more free-

FIGURE 16-5

2D color map

dom, but we are going to keep things simple and use a single 2D bitmap for both the color and height. Of course, this means that the largest variance in height and color can range from 0 to 255 using 8 bits per pixel, but this will do.

The only problem with using a 2D image as both the color information and the height information is that the relationship between color indices and heights may not be a good one. For example, say that we have an aerial picture of an island surrounded by water. There would be blue around the island, browns and whites around the beach, and browns and greens near the more inland parts of the island. We would naturally want the blues to have small heights, while the browns and greens have larger heights since they should be at a higher level than sea level. Unfortunately, this may not be true based on the palette used to scan the image. It may, in fact, be that the blues have very high color index numbers and the greens have very low numbers, which would make the terrain look inverted when rendered using the color indices as both the height and color of each voxel. Thus, care must be taken in palette selection so that there is a one-to-one correspondence between colors and desired heights. We could use a look-up table to map the colors to the proper heights, but this added look-up would slow things down. Anyway, before learning how to actually draw the voxel terrain, let's take a quick look at totally algorithmic ways of generating the data.

Fractal and Random Terrain Maps

Using scanned images is great for voxel data, but sometimes it's nice to be able to parametrically generate the data. This can be accomplished with various algorithms that can process a 2D array and set the elements of the array up in such a way that they look like a terrain or whatever the desired height distribution was. There are many ways to do this, such as with fractals, random numbers, or scripts. For example, we have all seen fractals and fractal mountainscapes. We could use the data generated by a fractal program as the heights of a 2D array. A typical fractal technique used to generate fractal mountains is called a *plasma fractal* and is very simple to implement.

Plasma fractals are usually based on some geometric primitive such as a triangle. The triangle is recursively subdivided, and during each subdivision, the smaller triangles have a bit of randomness added to them. Figure 16-6 shows this process in action. The only problem with this is that we don't really have polygons, but single points, and it's a bit harder to implement a plasma fractal with this type of data. Having tried it, the results didn't look as good as the scanned data, so I threw it out. But let's take a quick look at how it's done.

We begin with a 2D terrain array, say 256x256 elements, as shown in Figure 16-7. We initialize the terrain heights to some value and subdivide the array into four smaller arrays in which the endpoints are distorted a bit up or down, as shown in Figure 16-8. Then we recursively call the algorithm again with the four smaller subquadrants. This is repeated until the size of each subquadrant is a single pixel. The results of this will be a plasma fractal terrain.

FIGURE 16-6

⊙ ⊙ ⊙ ⊙ ⊙ ⊙

Fractalization of a triangle

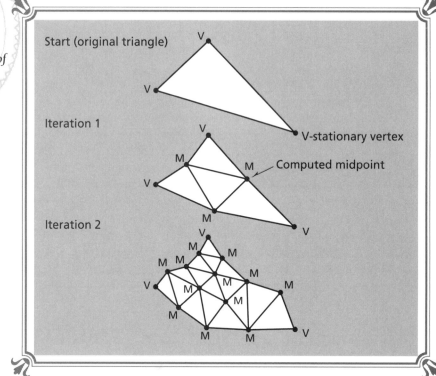

FIGURE 16-7

⊙ ⊙ ⊙ ⊙ ⊙ ⊙

Phase one of recursive subdivision

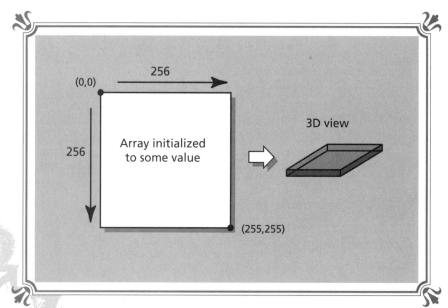

FIGURE 16-8
◎ ◎ ◎ ◎ ◎ ◎
*Recursively
subdividing a 2D
height map*

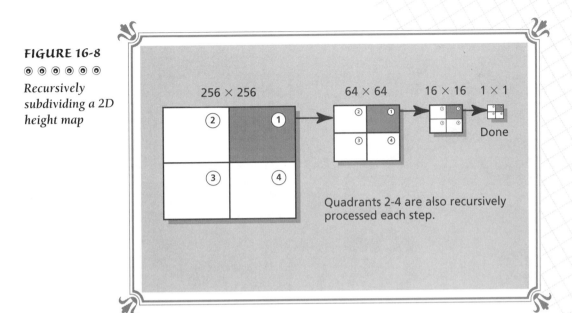

Finally, the second way to generate a terrain is simply to use random numbers and fill the 2D terrain array with these numbers. However, there must be some kind of logic to make sure that the random values vary smoothly or else the data will look like noise when rendered, or like "grass."

That's about it for the data part of the voxel engine—let's see how we actually draw the voxel data.

Ray Casting

There are two methods used in computer graphics to generate scenery. The first and most common method is synthesis, using math and simple models to generate 3D images. This is the method we have been using in the previous chapters of the book—that is, polygons. The second method is more natural and is based on the physical interactions of light and energy in an environment or, more precisely, ray tracing and radiosity. Ray tracing is a method of tracing the rays of light from the light sources in a scene off the objects in the scene, keeping track of their color, and testing whether they intersect the view plane of the viewer. Figure 16-9 shows a simple ray-tracing diagram. Ray tracing is nice because in one stroke it removes hidden surfaces and performs lighting, shadows, transparency, and rendering. But it's very slow and tends to look synthetic. A relatively new technique is called *radiosity*, which deals with the radiant heat transfer of *phonons* (heat particles) in a closed system. It works by assuming that each object in a scene gives off energy,

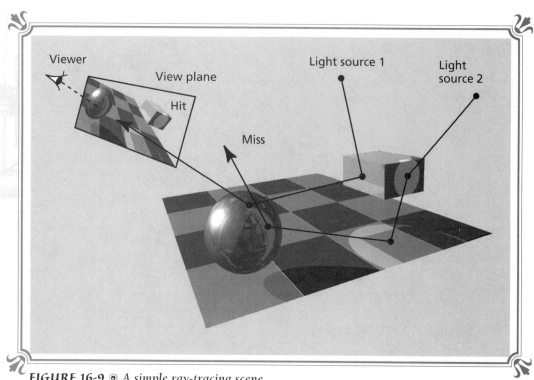

FIGURE 16-9 ⊙ *A simple ray-tracing scene*

reflects energy, and absorbs energy. By tracking the energy transfer from object to object and waiting for a steady state, hyper-realistic lighting can be achieved. However, that's about all radiosity does for us. It is not a rendering technique, it is simply a lighting technique. But once the radiosity has been computed, the renderer can render any view of the room or environment.

Well, that's all great, but what is ray casting? Ray casting is the little brother of ray tracing. First, ray casting is forward ray tracing, and it traces rays from the viewpoint out into the viewing volume, as shown in Figure 16-10. Second, ray casters usually are written for special cases based on geometric constraints. For example, if you have played *Wolfenstein 3D* by id, I'm sure you realized that the world is made of cubes. This is entirely true. However, computing the intersections between cubes and rays is very easy since cubes lie on a regular array. For example, Figure 16-11 shows a series of rays casted out from the viewer into a regular grid. Furthermore, the points of intersection are marked. Computing these intersection points is very easy. As a matter of fact, we don't actually need to compute them! All we need to do is step the ray one block at time and look at the square it is in. If there is a solid

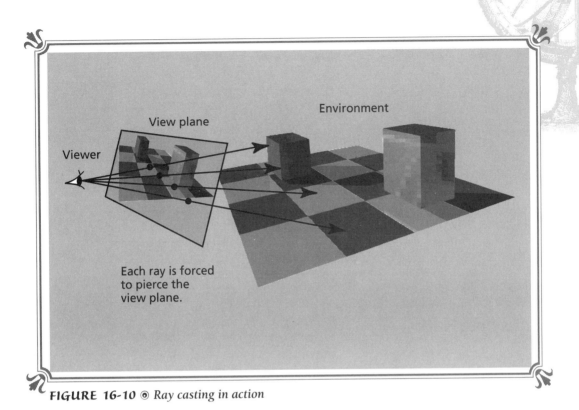

FIGURE 16-10 ◉ *Ray casting in action*

cube there, then there must have been an intersection. Using this technique, a full 3D textured image can be drawn by simply casting 320 rays (one for each column of the screen) and testing their intersections with the cubic regular environment.

If you are interested in learning more about ray casting, I suggest you pick up The Waite Group's *Gardens of Imagination* by Christopher Lampton. It covers everything about the topic you might want to know.

Anyway, we aren't going to use ray casting to draw walls, but we are going to use it to draw the slivers of voxel terrain. What we're going to do is called height mapping. Let's check it out.

Height Mapping

Height mapping is a technique of casting rays out from a viewpoint and seeing where they intersect the ground or terrain being scanned. Then from this information, a 3D display can be generated. Take a look at Figure 16-12. Here we see a side

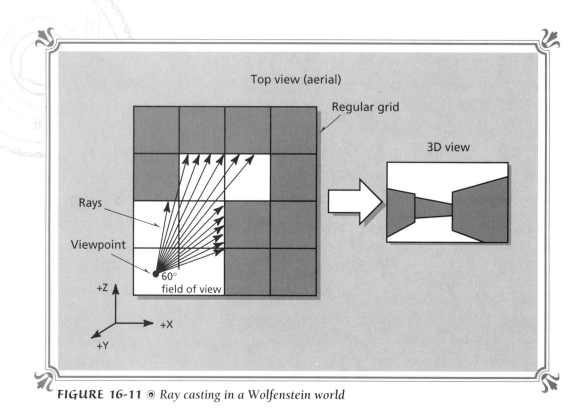

FIGURE 16-11 ⊙ *Ray casting in a Wolfenstein world*

view or cross section of a mountain or terrain of some sort along with a view plane and viewer at a given viewing position. As you see, some of the terrain will be visible to some rays, while other portions won't be. This is the key to using height mapping to generate a voxel display. All we need to do is cast a series of rays from the viewpoint and scan along a single direction. Then we rotate a little and perform the scan again until we have scanned our entire field of view. We then use the results of the scan to draw the proper display.

In case this is a little confusing, let's make sure we understand what we're going to do. We are going to use the 2D terrain data as the ground under us. Then we are going to place the viewing plane, which is the mode 13h screen of 320x200, somewhere above the terrain. Then we are going to place the viewpoint somewhere in front of the view plane. Now for the interesting part: For each of the 320 columns of the screen, we are going to cast 50 to 100 rays, one through each row (depending on the viewing angle). Each of the rays is aligned to the current column, but pierces the view plane at rows 50, 51, 52, 53 intersecting the terrain. The intersection points will be used to compute the color and height of each voxel strip. For example, if we hit an element that has a height of 30, it will have some perspective-

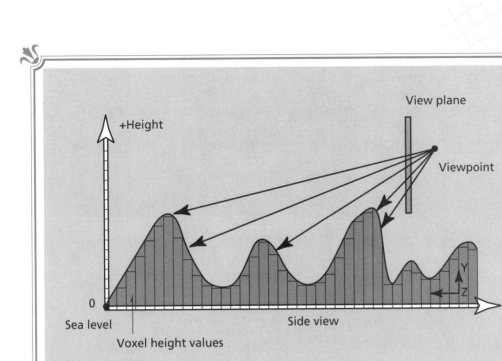

FIGURE 16-12 ⊚ *Casting rays to generate a voxel display*

adjusted height when displayed. The key to understanding the process is that we must perform two *for* loops like this:

```
for (column=0; column<320; column++)
    for (row=150; row<200; row++)
        {
        // 1. cast a ray from the viewpoint thru the current column and row
        //    and test its intersection with the terrain

        // 2. record the height and color of the voxel intersected with

        // 3. draw the voxel strip

        } // end for row
```

Steps 2 and 3 may be merged, but you get the idea. Now, how should we generate each ray? This can be a problem because of a few factors. First, the player's viewpoint may be anywhere in the universe. Second, the player must be able to turn and rotate, so this means that there is a viewing angle or yaw. Take a look at Figure 16-13 to see this. Referring to the figure, we see that the player can be any-

FIGURE 16-13

ⓞ ⓞ ⓞ ⓞ ⓞ ⓞ

*Moving around
the voxel
landscape*

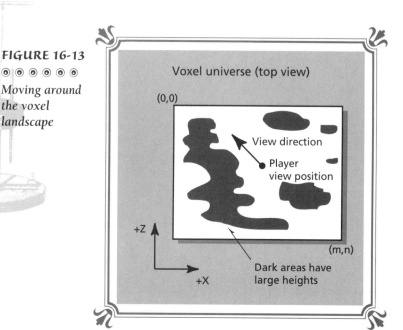

where within the bounds of the universe while looking in any direction. The position in the universe isn't that hard to deal with, but the angle can be. Let's take a look at a trick to make this easier.

Rotating the Ray

One of the biggest problems with ray tracing, ray casting, and height mapping is generating the scanning rays quickly enough; but luckily there are tricks to do this. One of them is to use look-up tables. Before we do that, we need to talk about field of view again. If you recall, field of view is the angular displacement from looking straight that you can see to the sides and above and below; in other words, your peripheral vision. In computer graphics, we don't have the luxury of physics, so we have to simulate everything. And just as we computed how to implement various fields of view for a polygon engine, we must do the same in the context of voxel graphics.

I have found that 60 degree fields of view work pretty well, so that's what we are going to use. However, in our voxel engine, we'll only get control of the horizontal field of view; the vertical field of view is a function of viewing distance, height, and row per screen. If we want a 60 degree field of view to be drawn within the extents of 320 columns, this means that there are 320 columns per 60 degrees, or 1920 columns for 360 degrees, since 360/60=6 and 6*320 is 1920. As a result, we need to make a look-up table that has all the rotations of a ray in 1920 little angular increments. Figure 16-14 shows this graphically. We must subdivide a circle into 1920 subarcs, and then create look-up tables such that each element represents the value of a function that can be used to rotate a ray to any direction within the 1920 positions of the subdivided circle. Since I'm trying to make things easy, I decided to create both a SIN and COSINE table that are each 1920 elements long.

Using these tables, we forget about the normal 360 degrees in a circle and pretend that there are 1920 degrees, based on look-up table degrees. There are now 1920 degrees in a complete circle. If we need to rotate a ray to 690 degrees, we simply access the SIN and COSINE arrays and do the following:

```
ray_x = cos_look[690];
ray_y = sin_look[690];
```

Then *(ray_x,ray_y)* would contain a unit vector pointing in the desired direction. We could then scale this by any factor that we wish, and the resulting point can be used as the scanning tip into the terrain data relative to the viewer's position. Figure 16-15 shows this graphically. So we spray out a series of rays for each of the 320 columns based on a circular scan to do the height mapping, but unfortunately, this will introduce a type of distortion. Let's take a look at it.

FIGURE 16-14
◉ ◉ ◉ ◉ ◉ ◉
Dividing a circle unit

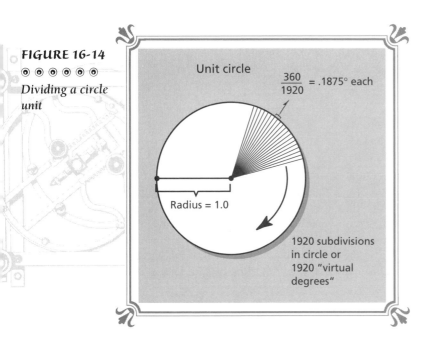

Unit circle

$$\frac{360}{1920} = .1875° \text{ each}$$

Radius = 1.0

1920 subdivisions in circle or 1920 "virtual degrees"

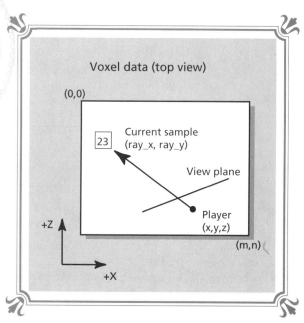

FIGURE 16-15

ⓞ ⓞ ⓞ ⓞ ⓞ ⓞ

*Rotating a ray
into position for
scanning*

Fixing the Distortion

Figure 16-16 shows a typical sequence of scanning positions from a top view. As you can see, the scanning positions follow a circular path. The results of this will be that the view, when rendered, will look as if it's seen through a spherical lens. To remove this distortion, we must multiply by some factor. This factor can be derived as follows: when we cast out the ray for each column from 0 to 319, column 160 is basically our view direction. Since we are casting out a 60 degree field of view, there are 30 degrees to the left and 30 degrees to the right of the center column. This is shown in Figure 16-17. Since we know that the distortion is spherical, we can deduce that multiplication by the inverse of a sin or cosine wave should cancel it out. And in fact this is what we must do. As the rays are casted from column 0 to 319, we multiply the length of each ray by the inverse cosine (secant) of the angle relative to the center. In other words, the rays from 0 to 159 are multiplied by the values of 1/cosine(-30...0 degrees), and the lengths from 160 to 319 are multiplied by the values of 1/cosine(0...30 degrees).

So I think we understand how we cast each ray for each column, but how do we cast through all the rows of each column? We'll cover that next.

FIGURE 16-16

⊙ ⊙ ⊙ ⊙ ⊙ ⊙

Casting along a circular path

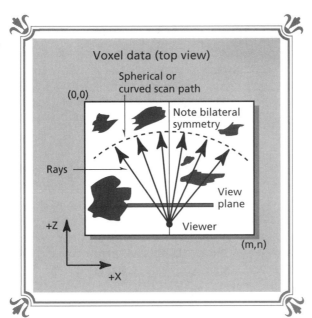

FIGURE 16-17

⊙ ⊙ ⊙ ⊙ ⊙ ⊙

The details to uncover the actual distortion

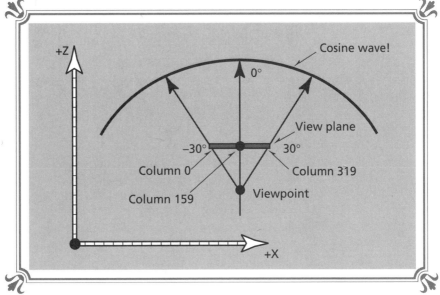

Finding the Height of the Voxel

For any given column of the video display, a series of rays must be casted through each row, and their intersections with the terrain must be found. We could do this just as we casted the rays through the column, but there is a simpler way. What we are going to do is this: For each of the 320 columns in the display, we will rotate a ray into position. Then we will use similar triangles to compute where this ray would intersect the terrain if it were forced to pierce each of the rows of the particular column of interest. Figure 16-18 shows this. The question is, how can we compute the base of each of the triangles so that we can use this point to inquire into the terrain data to see the color and height of the voxel? The key is to use the geometry of the system to our advantage. Take a look at Figure 16-19. Here we see a typical ray being casted through a given row (the column is irrelevant). All we are interested in is computing the length of the base of the triangle labeled *ray_length*.

We know the height of the viewer above the terrain (*height*), and we know the distance of the viewer from the viewing plane (*distance*). We indeed have enough information to compute the value of *ray_length*. But how? We are going to use the

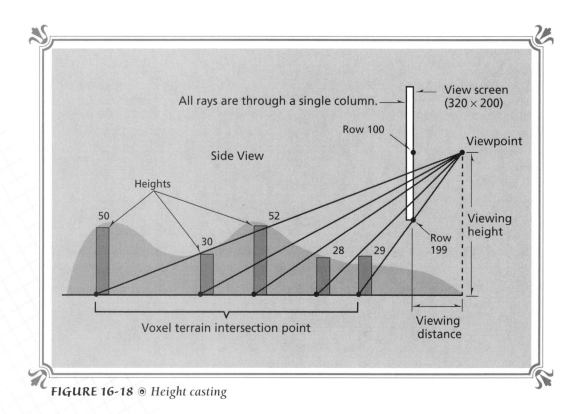

FIGURE 16-18 ⊙ *Height casting*

FIGURE 16-19

◎ ◎ ◎ ◎ ◎ ◎

Casting a ray down

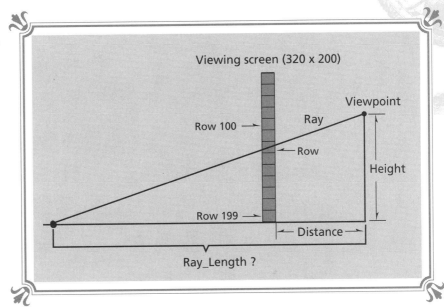

method of *Similar Triangles*, a geometry rule that states: If the angles of a pair of triangles are equal, then the lengths of the sides are either all equal or all proportional. For example, in Figure 16-20, we see that there are actually two triangles in the diagram. One is labeled A and the other B. We also see that A and B are similar,

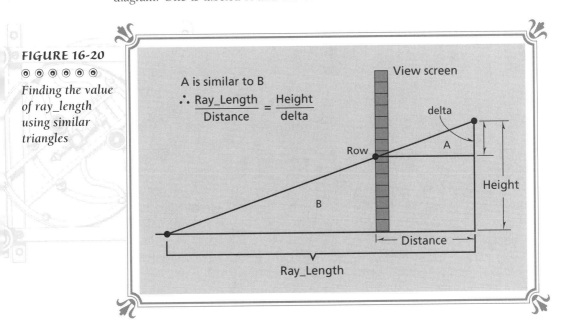

therefore, we can deduce the following relationship. The length of the base on the larger triangle B divided by the length of the base of the smaller triangle A is proportional to the height of the larger triangle B divided by the height of the smaller triangle A. Or, mathematically we have

$$\frac{ray\_length}{distance} = \frac{height}{delta}$$

or:

ray_length = distance * height / delta

What exactly is *delta*? The value of *delta* can be computed in terms of other variables, such as the height of the viewing plane and the height of the player. It turns out that *delta* is

delta = height - (SCREEN_HEIGHT - row)

All these minus signs are due to the fact that the Y axis is inverted in mode 13h; that is, positive Y is downward instead of upward. In any case, once we have the proper *ray_length* for the current row, we can multiply it by the current columns *ray_x* and *ray_y*, along with the distortion compensation, to compute the final scanning point in the terrain, something like this,

```
ray_length = sphere_cancel[column] * (distance*height)/(height-(SCREEN_HEIGHT - row));

xr = player_x + ray_length * cos_look[curr_ang];
yr = player_y -   ray_length * sin_look[curr_ang];
```

where *curr_angle* varies from -30 to 30 degrees over the 320 columns of the ray cast.

Notice the multiplication of *sphere_cancel[]* to compensate for the spherical distortion we spoke of earlier. Once the values of *xr* and *yr* have been computed, we can then use these to access the 2D terrain data, and we finally have the voxel that we are looking for. At this point, we simply need to compute the height of the strip and render it.

Scaling the Strips

If we wanted to, we could cast two rays for each voxel; one to find the bottom and one to find the top, as shown in Figure 16-21. However, since we know the height of each voxel strip, we need only find its bottom and then draw the voxel strip with the proper scale based on the distance of the voxel from the player's point of view. Remember the perspective equations we have been using to project 3D polygons onto the 2D viewing plane of the screen? Well, if we analyze the math a bit, we come up with an interesting little tidbit: the scale of an object is inversely proportional to its distance from the viewing plane. Mathematically, we have

scale = k/object(z)

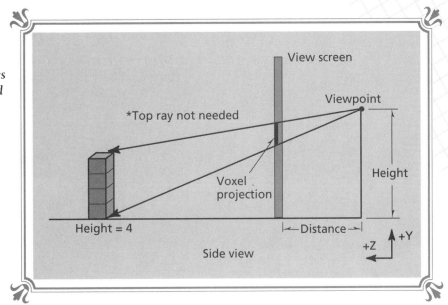

where *k* is simply a scaling factor and *object(z)* means the Z distance of the object from the viewing plane. Hence, in our system, *object(z)* would simply be *ray_length*.

Putting It All to Work

Let's see if we can't write a simple voxel display demo using the knowledge and techniques outlined so far. Let's begin by loading a 320x200 PCX file and using it as the height and color data. The heights will range from 0 to 255 and so will the colors. The PCX image should be of some kind of terrain data or contour map. Luckily, I found one; then, using Adobe Photoshop, I played with the colors and made multiple versions of the map that look like terrain of Earth, Mars, and other exotic places.

Once we have the terrain map loaded, we will enter into a simple event loop that queries the keyboard and allows us to change the view position, height, and distance from the virtual viewing plane. These variables will then be fed into the terrain generator, and the voxel display will be rendered in order of farther voxels to nearer voxels. Since we will be using a single bitmap, we will have to wrap around the bitmap in both the X and Y directions, but this can be achieved with the *MOD* operator or logical *AND*ing. The complete terrain generator program is called VOXEL.C and the executable is named VOXEL.EXE. The source is shown in Listing 16-1.

LISTING 16-1 Demo of single bitmap voxel

```c
// VOXEL.C - Single texture based, ray casted voxel engine

// I N C L U D E S //////////////////////////////////////////////////////////

#include <io.h>
#include <conio.h>
#include <stdio.h>
#include <stdlib.h>
#include <dos.h>
#include <bios.h>
#include <fcntl.h>
#include <memory.h>
#include <malloc.h>
#include <math.h>
#include <string.h>

#include "black3.h"
#include "black4.h"
#include "black5.h"


// D E F I N E S ////////////////////////////////////////////////////////////

#define WORLD_X_SIZE    320   // width of universe
#define WORLD_Y_SIZE    200   // height of universe

// constants used to represent angles for the ray casting a 60 degree field of view

#define ANGLE_0         0
#define ANGLE_1         5
#define ANGLE_2         10
#define ANGLE_4         20
#define ANGLE_5         25
#define ANGLE_6         30
#define ANGLE_15        80
#define ANGLE_30        160
#define ANGLE_45        240
#define ANGLE_60        320
#define ANGLE_90        480
#define ANGLE_135       720
#define ANGLE_180       960
#define ANGLE_225       1200
#define ANGLE_270       1440
#define ANGLE_315       1680
#define ANGLE_360       1920

// there are 1920 degrees in our circle or 360/1920 is the conversion factor
// from real degrees to our degrees

#define ANGULAR_INCREMENT   ((float)0.1875)
```

```
// conversion constants from radians to degrees and viceversa

#define DEG_TO_RAD          ((float)3.1415926/(float)180)
#define RAD_TO_DEG          ((float)180/(float)3.1415926)

// G L O B A L S ///////////////////////////////////////////////////////

pcx_picture image_pcx;          // general pcx image

int play_x=1000,                // the current world x of player
    play_y=1000,                // the current world y of player
    play_z=150,
    play_ang=ANGLE_90,          // the current viewing angle of player
    play_dist = 70,
    mountain_scale=10;          // scaling factor for mountains

float play_dir_x,               // the direction the player is pointing in
      play_dir_y,
      play_dir_z,
      cos_look[ANGLE_360],      // cosine look up table
      sin_look[ANGLE_360],      // sin look up table
      sphere_cancel[ANGLE_60];  // cancels fish eye distortion

// F U N C T I O N S ///////////////////////////////////////////////////

void Line_VDB(int y1,int y2,int x,int color)
{
// draw a vertical line, note that a memset function can no longer be
// used since the pixel addresses are no longer contiguous in memory
// note that the end points of the line must be on the screen

unsigned char far *start_offset; // starting memory offset of line

int index, // loop index
    temp;  // used for temporary storage during swap

// make sure y2 > y1

if (y1>y2)
    {
    temp = y1;
    y1    = y2;
    y2    = temp;
    } // end swap

// compute starting position

start_offset = double_buffer + ((y1<<8) + (y1<<6)) + x;

for (index=0; index<=y2-y1; index++)
    {
```

continued on next page

continued from previous page

```
    // set the pixel

    *start_offset = (unsigned char)color;

    // move downward to next line

    start_offset+=320;

    } // end for index

} // end Line_VDB

////////////////////////////////////////////////////////////////////////

int Initialize(char *filename)
{
// this function builds all the look up tables for the terrain generator and
// loads in the terrain texture map

int ang;             // looping variable

float rad_angle;     // current angle in radians

// create sin and cos look up first

for (ang=0; ang<ANGLE_360; ang++)
    {
    // compute current angle in radians

    rad_angle = (float)ang*ANGULAR_INCREMENT*DEG_TO_RAD;

    // now compute the sin and cos

    sin_look[ang] = sin(rad_angle);
    cos_look[ang] = cos(rad_angle);

    } // end for ang

// create inverse cosine viewing distortion filter

for (ang=0; ang<ANGLE_30; ang++)
    {
    // compute current angle in radians

    rad_angle = (float)ang*ANGULAR_INCREMENT*DEG_TO_RAD;

    // now compute the sin and cos

    sphere_cancel[ang+ANGLE_30] = 1/cos(rad_angle);
    sphere_cancel[ANGLE_30-ang] = 1/cos(rad_angle);

    } // end for ang
```

```
// initialize the pcx structure

PCX_Init((pcx_picture_ptr)&image_pcx);

// load in the textures

return(PCX_Load(filename, (pcx_picture_ptr)&image_pcx,1));

} // end Initialize

//////////////////////////////////////////////////////////////////////////////

void Draw_Terrain(int play_x,
                  int play_y,
                  int play_z,
                  int play_ang,
                  int play_dist)
{
// this function draws the entire terrain based on the location and orientation
// of the player's viewpoint

int curr_ang,        // current angle being processed
    xr,yr,           // location of ray in world coords
    x_fine,y_fine,   // the texture coordinates the ray hit
    pixel_color,     // the color of textel
    ray,             // looping variable
    row,             // the current video row being processed
    row_inv,         // the inverted row to make upward positive
    scale,           // the scale of the current strip

    top,             // top of strip
    bottom;          // bottom of strip

float ray_length;    // the length of the ray after distortion compensation

// start the current angle off -30 degrees to the left of the player's
// current viewing direction

curr_ang = play_ang - ANGLE_30;

// test for underflow

if (curr_ang < 0)
   curr_ang+=ANGLE_360;

// cast a series of rays for every column of the screen

for (ray=1; ray<320; ray++)
    {

    // for each column compute the pixels that should be displayed
    // for each screen pixel, process from top to bottom
```

continued on next page

continued from previous page

```
    for (row = 100; row<150; row++)
        {

        // compute length of ray

        row_inv = 200-row;

        // use the current height and distance to compute length of ray.

        ray_length = sphere_cancel[ray] * ((float)(play_dist*play_z)/
                                    (float)(play_z-row_inv));

        // rotate ray into position of sample

        xr = (int)((float)play_x + ray_length * cos_look[curr_ang]);
        yr = (int)((float)play_y - ray_length * sin_look[curr_ang]);

        // compute texture coords

        x_fine = xr % WORLD_X_SIZE;
        y_fine = yr % WORLD_Y_SIZE;

        // using texture index locate texture pixel in textures

        pixel_color = image_pcx.buffer[x_fine + (y_fine*320)];

        // draw the strip

        scale = (int)mountain_scale*pixel_color/(int)(ray_length+1);

        top       = 50+row-scale;

        bottom    = top + scale;

        Line_VDB(top,bottom,ray,pixel_color);

        //  Write_Pixel_DB(ray,50+row,pixel_color);

        } // end for row

    // move to next angle

    if (++curr_ang >= ANGLE_360)
        curr_ang=ANGLE_0;

    } // end for ray

} // end Draw_Terrain

// M A I N ////////////////////////////////////////////////////////////////////

void main(int argc, char **argv)
```

```
{
char buffer[80];

int done=0; // exit flag

float speed=0;   // speed of player

// check to see if command line parms are correct

if (argc<=2)
   {
   // not enough parms

   printf("\nUsage: voxopt.exe filename.pcx height");
   printf("\nExample: voxopt voxterr3.pcx 10\n");

   // return to DOS

   exit(1);

   } // end if

// set the graphics mode to mode 13h

Set_Graphics_Mode(GRAPHICS_MODE13);

// create a double buffer

Create_Double_Buffer(200);

// create look up tables and load textures

if (!Initialize(argv[1]))
   {

   printf("\nError loading file %s",argv[1]);
   exit(1);

   } // end if


// install keyboard driver

Keyboard_Install_Driver();

// set scale of mountains

mountain_scale = atoi(argv[2]);

// draw the first frame

Draw_Terrain(play_x,
```

continued on next page

continued from previous page

```
                play_y,
                play_z,
                play_ang,
                play_dist);

Display_Double_Buffer(double_buffer,0);

// main event loop

while(!done)
    {

    // reset velocity

    speed = 0;

    // test if user is hitting keyboard

    if (keys_active)
        {
        // what is user trying to do

        // change viewing distance

        if (keyboard_state[MAKE_F])
            play_dist+=10;

        if (keyboard_state[MAKE_C])
            play_dist-=10;

        // change viewing height

        if (keyboard_state[MAKE_U])
            play_z+=10;

        if (keyboard_state[MAKE_D])
            play_z-=10;


        // change viewing position

        if (keyboard_state[MAKE_RIGHT])
            if ((play_ang+=ANGLE_5) >= ANGLE_360)
                play_ang-=ANGLE_360;

        if (keyboard_state[MAKE_LEFT])
            if ((play_ang-=ANGLE_5) < 0)
                play_ang+=ANGLE_360;

        // move forward

        if (keyboard_state[MAKE_UP])
            speed=20;
```

```
            // move backward

            if (keyboard_state[MAKE_DOWN])
               speed=-20;

            // exit demo

            if (keyboard_state[MAKE_ESC])
               done=1;

            // compute trajectory vector for this view angle

            play_dir_x = cos_look[play_ang];
            play_dir_y = -sin_look[play_ang];
            play_dir_z = 0;

            // translate viewpoint

            play_x+=speed*play_dir_x;
            play_y+=speed*play_dir_y;
            play_z+=speed*play_dir_z;

            // draw the terrain

            Fill_Double_Buffer(0);

            Draw_Terrain(play_x,
                         play_y,
                         play_z,
                         play_ang,
                         play_dist);

            // draw tactical

            sprintf(buffer,"Height = %d Distance = %d      ",play_z,play_dist);
            Print_String_DB(0,0,10,buffer,0);

            sprintf(buffer,"Pos: X=%d, Y=%d, Z=%d      ",play_x,play_y,play_z);
            Print_String_DB(0,10,10,buffer,0);

            Display_Double_Buffer(double_buffer,0);

            } // end if

      } // end while

// reset back to text mode
Set_Graphics_Mode(TEXT_MODE);

// remove the keyboard handler
Keyboard_Remove_Driver();

} // end main
```

The main function that does all the work is called *Draw_Terrain()*. It is responsible for rendering the current view into the double buffer. You will also notice, if you review the *Draw_Terrain()* function, a call to the function *Line_VDB()*, which is just a version of the vertical line function that writes to the double buffer.

To run the program, you must supply it with two things: the file name of the 320x200x256 PCX file to use as the height map along with a scaling factor for the rendering. On the directory for this chapter, I have supplied the following PCX files:

VOXTERR1.PCX	Colorful satellite scan
VOXTERR2.PCX	Colorful satellite scan
VOXTERR3.PCX	Colorful satellite scan
VOXTERR4.PCX	Colorful satellite scan
VOXTERR5.PCX	Colorful satellite scan
VOXTERR6.PCX	Colorful satellite scan
VOXTERR7.PCX	Colorful satellite scan
QUAKE.PCX	Earthquake intensity map

If you want to see VOXTERR4.PCX at a scale of 10, for example, at the command line type:

VOXEL VOXTERR4.PCX 10

You will see the display shown in Figure 16-22. To move around the world, use the following controls:

Keypress	Description
UP ARROW	Turns right
DOWN ARROW	Turns left
RIGHT ARROW	Moves forward
LEFT ARROW	Moves backward
U	Increases height
D	Decreases height
F	Moves farther from view plane
C	Moves closer to view plane
ESC	Exits demo

The demo is cool, but it is very limited by the size of the bitmap used for the height map. This can be a major problem in a real game, so what can we do? Well, we can use a tile system along with small texture maps.

FIGURE 16-22
◎ ◎ ◎ ◎ ◎ ◎
Screen shot of
VOXEL.EXE

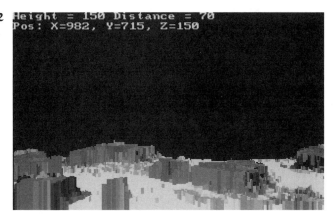

A Tile-Based Voxel Engine

The source for VOXEL.C assumes that there is a single height map for the voxel data, but what if we want a really large world that is bigger than a paltry 320x200? We could load a height map that was, say, 10,000x10,000, but that would take a whopping 100,000,000 bytes of memory! Just a bit too much for today's computers. A better solution is to use cells, or tiles, that represent specific textures, as shown in Figure 16-23. Using this technique, we can design a tile world that has, say, 100x100 tiles, but each tile is 64x64 pixels; therefore, we have a 6400x6400 world that uses only 10K of memory. Not bad. Of course, the tile bitmaps will cost 64x64=4096 bytes each, but that's reasonable since we shouldn't need that many bitmaps.

To implement a tile-based world takes about an extra five lines of code in the terrain generator function *Draw_Terrain()* along with some extra code to load the bitmaps for the tiles. And, of course, an area of storage must be initialized with the tile map. As an example, let's assume that we have a tile-based world of 32x32. Furthermore, let's assume that there are a total of four height/color bitmaps that are numbered 0 to 3 and have size 64x64 pixels. We will define the tile map as a simple 2D array with the numbers 0 to 3 entered in it at the location we wish to see those tiles. The array would look something like this:

```
// this map holds the terrain texture cells
// each cell is really a bitmap texture, so by using cells and tiling much
// larger worlds can be constructed

char terrain_texture[] =
```

continued on next page

continued from previous page

```
{ 1,1,1,1,1,1,1,1,1,1,1,1,1,1,1,1,1,1,1,1,1,1,1,1,1,1,1,1,1,1,1,1,
  1,0,0,0,0,0,0,0,0,0,0,0,0,0,0,0,0,0,0,0,0,0,0,0,0,0,0,0,0,0,0,1,
  1,0,0,0,0,0,0,0,0,0,0,0,0,0,0,0,0,1,0,0,0,0,0,0,0,0,0,0,0,0,0,1,
  1,0,0,3,3,0,0,0,0,0,0,1,1,1,0,0,0,1,0,0,3,0,0,0,0,0,0,0,3,0,0,1,
  1,0,0,3,3,0,0,0,0,0,0,0,1,0,0,0,0,0,0,0,3,0,0,0,0,0,0,0,3,3,0,1,
  1,0,0,3,3,0,0,0,0,0,2,2,1,0,0,0,0,0,3,0,0,3,3,0,0,0,3,3,0,0,1,
  1,0,0,0,3,0,0,2,0,0,0,0,0,0,0,0,3,0,0,0,3,3,0,0,0,0,3,0,0,1,
  1,0,0,0,0,0,0,2,0,2,2,2,0,0,3,0,3,3,3,0,0,0,3,3,0,0,0,0,0,1,
  1,0,0,0,0,0,2,0,0,0,0,0,3,0,3,3,3,0,0,0,3,0,0,0,0,0,0,0,0,1,
  1,0,0,2,0,0,0,2,0,0,0,0,0,3,0,3,3,0,0,0,0,0,0,2,0,0,2,0,0,1,
  1,0,0,2,0,0,0,0,0,0,0,0,0,0,0,0,0,0,0,2,2,0,0,0,0,0,0,0,0,1,
  1,0,0,2,0,0,1,1,1,0,0,2,0,2,0,0,1,0,0,0,2,2,2,0,0,0,0,0,0,1,
  1,0,0,0,0,2,1,1,1,0,0,0,0,0,0,1,0,0,0,2,0,2,0,0,0,0,0,0,0,1,
  1,0,0,0,0,0,0,1,3,3,0,0,0,0,0,0,0,0,0,0,0,0,0,0,0,0,0,0,0,1,
  1,0,0,0,0,2,0,0,0,3,0,0,0,2,0,2,0,2,0,0,0,0,0,0,0,0,0,0,0,1,
  1,0,0,0,0,0,0,0,0,3,0,0,0,0,0,0,0,0,0,0,0,0,0,0,0,0,0,0,0,1,
  1,0,2,0,0,0,0,0,3,0,0,0,0,3,0,0,0,0,1,0,3,0,0,0,0,0,0,0,0,1,
  1,0,0,0,0,0,2,0,0,0,0,0,0,0,0,2,0,0,1,0,3,0,0,0,2,0,0,0,0,1,
  1,0,0,0,0,2,0,2,0,0,2,0,3,0,0,0,0,2,2,0,1,0,0,0,0,2,0,0,0,0,1,
  1,0,2,0,0,2,0,0,0,0,2,0,0,0,3,0,0,2,0,0,0,0,3,3,0,2,2,2,0,0,1,
  1,0,0,0,0,2,0,0,0,0,2,0,0,0,3,0,0,0,0,2,0,0,0,0,0,2,0,2,0,0,1,
```

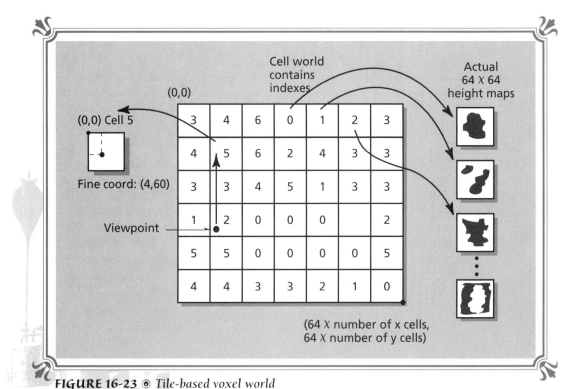

FIGURE 16-23 ⊙ *Tile-based voxel world*

```
1,0,0,0,0,2,0,0,0,0,0,3,0,0,0,0,0,0,2,2,0,0,0,3,0,0,2,2,0,0,0,1,
1,0,0,0,0,0,2,2,2,2,0,0,0,0,3,0,0,0,0,0,0,0,0,0,0,2,0,0,0,0,0,1,
1,0,0,2,0,0,0,0,0,0,0,0,0,0,0,0,2,0,0,0,0,0,0,0,0,0,0,0,0,0,0,1,
1,0,2,2,0,0,0,0,0,1,1,1,1,0,0,0,0,2,2,0,0,0,0,0,0,2,0,0,0,0,0,1,
1,0,2,2,0,0,0,0,0,0,0,0,0,0,0,0,0,2,0,0,0,0,0,0,0,0,0,0,0,0,0,1,
1,0,2,0,0,2,2,0,0,0,3,0,0,3,3,3,0,0,0,2,0,0,0,0,0,0,0,0,0,0,0,1,
1,0,0,2,0,2,2,0,0,0,3,0,0,3,3,3,0,0,0,0,0,3,3,3,0,0,0,0,0,0,0,1,
1,0,0,0,0,2,2,0,0,0,0,0,3,0,0,0,0,0,0,0,3,3,3,0,0,0,0,0,0,0,0,1,
1,0,0,0,0,0,0,0,0,1,1,0,0,0,0,0,0,0,0,0,0,3,3,3,0,0,0,0,0,0,0,1,
1,0,0,0,0,0,0,0,0,0,0,0,0,0,0,0,0,0,0,0,0,0,0,0,0,0,0,0,0,0,0,1,
1,1,1,1,1,1,1,1,1,1,1,1,1,1,1,1,1,1,1,1,1,1,1,1,1,1,1,1,1,1,1,1,
```

```
};
```

If you blur your eyes, you will be able to see the different areas a little better. After the 2D tile map is defined as shown above, we need to load the four height/color bitmaps. We will use a sprite to do this. We will simply load each of the 64x64 bitmaps into the first four animation cells of the sprite. It would probably be better to use the simpler bitmap structure, but what's done is done! Anyway, once we have the data loaded, the problem boils down to this: at the position (*xr,yr*) found during the voxel height cast, which cell does the scan fall in, and which exact pixel does the scan fall in within the cell?

We will answer both of these questions in a moment, but first, since we know that the tile map is 32x32 and each texture is 64x64, this means that the virtual world is really 2048x2048. Thus (*xr,yr*) will range anywhere within these bounds.

Finding the Correct Cell

To find the correct cell, all we need to do is divide the point (*xr,yr*) by the number of cells in the X and Y direction (which is 32). Therefore:

```
x_cell = xr / 32;
y_cell = yr / 32;
```

Then, using this information, we can index into the *terrain_texture[]* array and extract the proper bitmap index.

Finding the Exact Pixel

Once we have the proper bitmap index, the next step is to find the exact pixel within that bitmap of the voxel in question. This is done by using the *MOD* operator. Basically, we want to divide the position (*xr,yr*) by 64 and look at the remainder of both the X and Y division. This is in fact the *MOD* operation. The remainders can then be used to index into the bitmap. Here's the code to do it:

```
x_fine = xr % 64;
y_fine = yr % 64;
```

Once both the cell location and the pixel location have been computed, the proper bitmap and pixel within the bitmap can be found with the following code or equivalent,

```
// locate proper texture in tile map

texture_index = terrain_texture[x_cell + (y_cell*32)];

// use texture index to locate texture pixel in texture

pixel_color = text_spr.frames[texture_index][x_fine + (y_fine*64)];
```

where *text_spr* is the sprite containing the height/color bitmaps. And that's about all there is to adding tile support to the voxel engine.

The Tile-Based Demo

As a demo, I have taken the VOXEL.C source and tweaked it into a tile-based version named VOXTILE.C. The source is shown in Listing 16-2, and the executable is named VOXTILE.EXE.

LISTING 16-2 Tile-based version of the voxel engine

```
// VOXTILE.C - CELL based, ray casted voxel engine

// I N C L U D E S ///////////////////////////////////////////////////////

#include <io.h>
#include <conio.h>
#include <stdio.h>
#include <stdlib.h>
#include <dos.h>
#include <bios.h>
#include <fcntl.h>
#include <memory.h>
#include <malloc.h>
#include <math.h>
#include <string.h>

#include "black3.h"
#include "black4.h"
#include "black5.h"

// D E F I N E S ///////////////////////////////////////////////////////

#define NUM_X_CELLS    32    // number of cells in x direction
#define NUM_Y_CELLS    32    // number of cells in y direction

#define CELL_WIDTH     64    // width of a cell in pixels
#define CELL_HEIGHT    64    // height of a cell in pixels

#define WORLD_X_SIZE   (NUM_X_CELLS*CELL_WIDTH)    // width of universe in pixels
#define WORLD_Y_SIZE   (NUM_Y_CELLS*CELL_HEIGHT)   // height of universe in pixels
```

```
// constants used to represent angles for the ray casting a 60 degree field of
// view

#define ANGLE_0          0
#define ANGLE_1          5
#define ANGLE_2          10
#define ANGLE_4          20
#define ANGLE_5          25
#define ANGLE_6          30
#define ANGLE_15         80
#define ANGLE_30         160
#define ANGLE_45         240
#define ANGLE_60         320
#define ANGLE_90         480
#define ANGLE_135        720
#define ANGLE_180        960
#define ANGLE_225        1200
#define ANGLE_270        1440
#define ANGLE_315        1680
#define ANGLE_360        1920


// there are 1920 degrees in our circle or 360/1920 is the conversion factor
// from real degrees to our degrees

#define ANGULAR_INCREMENT  ((float)0.1875)

// conversion constants from radians to degrees and viceversa

#define DEG_TO_RAD         ((float)3.1415926/(float)180)
#define RAD_TO_DEG         ((float)180/(float)3.1415926)

#define NUM_TEXTURES  4    // holds the number of textures in the system

// G L O B A L S  /////////////////////////////////////////////////////////

pcx_picture image_pcx;        // general pcx image

sprite text_spr;              // this sprite holds the bitmap textures
                              // to drape over each cell

int play_x=1000,              // the current world x of player
    play_y=1000,              // the current world y of player
    play_z=150,               // the current world z of player, same as height
    play_ang=ANGLE_90,        // the current viewing angle of player
    play_dist = 70,
    mountain_scale=10;        // scaling factor for mountains


float play_dir_x,             // the direction the player is pointing in
      play_dir_y,
      play_dir_z,
      cos_look[ANGLE_360],    // cosine look up table
```

continued on next page

continued from previous page

```
      sin_look[ANGLE_360],        // sin look up table
      sphere_cancel[ANGLE_60]; // cancels fish eye distortion


// this map holds the terrain texture cells
// each cell is really a bitmap texture, so by using cells and tiling much
// larger worlds can be constructed

char terrain_texture[] =

     { 1,1,1,1,1,1,1,1,1,1,1,1,1,1,1,1,1,1,1,1,1,1,1,1,1,1,1,1,1,1,1,1,
       1,0,0,0,0,0,0,0,0,0,0,0,0,0,0,0,0,0,0,0,0,0,0,0,0,0,0,0,0,0,0,1,
       1,0,0,0,0,0,0,0,0,0,0,0,0,0,0,0,0,1,0,0,0,0,0,0,0,0,0,0,0,0,0,1,
       1,0,0,3,3,0,0,0,0,0,0,1,1,1,0,0,0,1,0,0,3,0,0,0,0,0,0,0,3,0,0,1,
       1,0,0,3,3,0,0,0,0,0,0,0,1,0,0,0,0,0,0,0,3,0,0,0,0,0,0,3,3,0,0,1,
       1,0,0,3,3,0,0,0,0,0,0,2,2,1,0,0,0,0,0,0,3,0,0,3,3,0,0,0,3,3,0,1,
       1,0,0,0,3,0,0,2,0,0,0,0,0,0,0,0,0,3,0,0,0,0,0,3,3,0,0,0,0,3,0,1,
       1,0,0,0,0,0,0,2,0,2,2,2,0,0,3,0,3,3,3,0,0,0,3,3,0,0,0,0,0,0,0,1,
       1,0,0,0,0,0,0,2,0,0,0,0,0,0,3,0,3,3,3,0,0,0,0,3,0,0,0,0,0,0,0,1,
       1,0,0,2,0,0,0,2,0,0,0,0,0,3,0,3,3,3,0,0,0,0,0,0,2,0,0,2,0,0,1,
       1,0,0,2,0,0,0,0,0,0,0,0,0,0,0,0,0,0,0,2,2,0,0,0,0,0,0,0,0,0,0,1,
       1,0,0,2,0,0,1,1,1,0,0,2,0,2,0,0,1,0,0,0,2,2,2,0,0,0,0,0,0,0,0,1,
       1,0,0,0,0,2,1,1,1,0,0,0,0,0,0,1,0,0,0,2,0,2,0,0,0,0,0,0,0,0,0,1,
       1,0,0,0,0,0,0,1,3,3,0,0,0,0,0,0,0,0,0,0,0,0,0,0,0,0,0,0,0,0,0,1,
       1,0,0,0,0,2,0,0,0,3,0,0,0,2,0,2,0,2,0,0,0,0,0,0,0,0,0,0,0,0,0,1,
       1,0,0,0,0,0,3,0,0,0,0,0,0,0,0,0,0,0,0,0,0,0,0,0,0,0,0,0,0,0,0,1,
       1,0,2,0,0,0,0,3,0,0,0,0,0,3,0,0,0,0,0,1,0,3,0,0,0,0,0,0,0,0,0,1,
       1,0,0,0,0,0,0,2,0,0,0,0,0,0,0,0,2,0,0,1,0,3,0,0,0,2,0,0,0,0,0,1,
       1,0,0,0,2,0,2,0,0,2,0,3,0,0,0,0,2,2,0,1,0,0,0,0,2,0,0,0,0,0,0,1,
       1,0,2,0,0,2,0,0,0,2,0,0,0,3,0,0,2,0,0,0,0,3,3,0,2,2,2,0,0,0,0,1,
       1,0,0,0,0,2,0,0,0,0,2,0,0,0,3,0,0,0,0,2,0,0,0,0,0,2,0,2,0,0,0,1,
       1,0,0,0,0,2,0,0,0,0,0,3,0,0,0,0,0,0,2,2,0,0,0,3,0,0,2,2,0,0,0,1,
       1,0,0,0,0,0,2,2,2,2,0,0,0,0,3,0,0,0,0,2,0,0,0,0,0,0,0,2,0,0,0,1,
       1,0,0,2,0,0,0,0,0,0,0,0,0,0,0,0,0,0,2,0,0,0,0,0,0,0,0,0,0,0,0,1,
       1,0,2,2,0,0,0,0,0,1,1,1,1,1,0,0,0,0,2,2,0,0,0,0,0,0,2,0,0,0,0,1,
       1,0,2,2,0,0,0,0,0,0,0,0,0,0,0,0,0,0,2,0,0,0,0,0,0,0,0,0,0,0,0,1,
       1,0,2,0,0,2,2,0,0,0,3,0,0,3,3,3,0,0,0,2,0,0,0,0,0,0,0,0,0,0,0,1,
       1,0,0,2,0,2,2,0,0,0,3,0,0,3,3,3,0,0,0,0,0,0,3,3,3,0,0,0,0,0,0,1,
       1,0,0,0,0,2,2,0,0,0,0,0,0,3,0,0,0,0,0,0,0,0,3,3,3,0,0,0,0,0,0,1,
       1,0,0,0,0,0,0,0,0,1,1,0,0,0,0,0,0,0,0,0,0,0,3,3,3,0,0,0,0,0,0,1,
       1,0,0,0,0,0,0,0,0,0,0,0,0,0,0,0,0,0,0,0,0,0,0,0,0,0,0,0,0,0,0,1,
       1,1,1,1,1,1,1,1,1,1,1,1,1,1,1,1,1,1,1,1,1,1,1,1,1,1,1,1,1,1,1,1,

     };

// F U N C T I O N S ///////////////////////////////////////////////////////

void Line_VDB(int y1,int y2,int x,int color)
{
// draw a vertical line, note that a memset function can no longer be
// used since the pixel addresses are no longer contiguous in memory
// note that the end points of the line must be on the screen
```

```
unsigned char far *start_offset; // starting memory offset of line

int index, // loop index
    temp;  // used for temporary storage during swap

// make sure y2 > y1

if (y1>y2)
   {
   temp = y1;
   y1   = y2;
   y2   = temp;
   } // end swap

// compute starting position

start_offset = double_buffer + ((y1<<8) + (y1<<6)) + x;

for (index=0; index<=y2-y1; index++)
    {
    // set the pixel

    *start_offset = (unsigned char)color;

    // move downward to next line

    start_offset+=320;

    } // end for index

} // end Line_VDB

/////////////////////////////////////////////////////////////////////////////

void Initialize(void)
{
// this function builds all the look up tables for the terrain generator

int ang,          // looping variable
    index;        // looping variable

float rad_angle;   // current angle in radians

// create sin and cos look up first

for (ang=0; ang<ANGLE_360; ang++)
    {
    // compute current angle in radians

    rad_angle = (float)ang*ANGULAR_INCREMENT*DEG_TO_RAD;

    // now compute the sin and cos
```

continued on next page

continued from previous page

```
      sin_look[ang] = sin(rad_angle);
      cos_look[ang] = cos(rad_angle);

      } // end for ang

// create inverse cosine viewing distortion filter

for (ang=0; ang<ANGLE_30; ang++)
    {
    // compute current angle in radians

    rad_angle = (float)ang*ANGULAR_INCREMENT*DEG_TO_RAD;

    // now compute the sin and cos

    sphere_cancel[ang+ANGLE_30] = 1/cos(rad_angle);
    sphere_cancel[ANGLE_30-ang] = 1/cos(rad_angle);

    } // end for ang


// load the texture tiles into memory

// intialize the pcx structure

PCX_Init((pcx_picture_ptr)&image_pcx);

// load in the textures

PCX_Load("voxtext.pcx", (pcx_picture_ptr)&image_pcx,1);

// initialize the texture sprite

Sprite_Init((sprite_ptr)&text_spr,0,0,64,64,0,0,0,0,0,0);

// extract the bitmaps for the textures

for (index=0; index<NUM_TEXTURES; index++)
    PCX_Get_Sprite((pcx_picture_ptr)&image_pcx,(sprite_ptr)&text_spr,index,index,0);

// done with this PCX file so delete memory associated with it

PCX_Delete((pcx_picture_ptr)&image_pcx);


} // end Initialize

/////////////////////////////////////////////////////////////////////////////

void Draw_Terrain(int play_x,
                  int play_y,
                  int play_z,
                  int play_ang,
```

```
                    int play_dist)
{
// this function draws the entire terrain based on the location and orientation
// of the player's viewpoint

int curr_ang,              // current angle being processed
    xr,yr,                 // location of ray in world coords
    x_cell,y_cell,         // the cell the ray hit
    x_fine,y_fine,         // the texture coordinates the ray hit
    texture_index,         // which texture
    pixel_color,           // the color of textel
    ray,                   // looping variable
    row,                   // the current video row being processed
    row_inv,               // the inverted row to make upward positive
    scale,                 // the scale of the current strip
    top,                   // top of strip
    bottom;                // bottom of strip


float ray_length;          // the length of the ray after distortion compensation

// start the current angle off -30 degrees to the left of the player's
// current viewing direction

curr_ang = play_ang - ANGLE_30;

// test for underflow

if (curr_ang < 0)
   curr_ang+=ANGLE_360;

// cast a series of rays for every column of the screen

for (ray=1; ray<320; ray++)
    {

    // for each column compute the pixels that should be displayed
    // for each screen pixel, process from top to bottom

    for (row = 100; row<150; row++)
        {
        // compute length of ray

        row_inv = 200-row;

        // use the current height and distance to compute length of ray.

        ray_length = sphere_cancel[ray] * ((float)(play_dist*play_z)/
                                    (float)(play_z-row_inv));

        // rotate ray into position of sample

        xr = (int)((float)play_x + ray_length * cos_look[curr_ang]);
```

continued on next page

continued from previous page

```
            yr = (int)((float)play_y - ray_length * sin_look[curr_ang]);

            // compute cell of sampling tip

            x_cell = xr >> 5; //  / NUM_X_CELLS;
            y_cell = yr >> 5; //  / NUM_Y_CELLS;

            // compute texture coords

            x_fine = xr & 0x003F; // % CELL_WIDTH;
            y_fine = yr & 0x003F; // % CELL_HEIGHT;

            // locate texture index

            texture_index = terrain_texture[x_cell + (y_cell<<5)];
// *NUM_X_CELLS];

            // using texture index locate texture pixel in textures

            pixel_color = text_spr.frames[texture_index][x_fine + (y_fine<<6)];
// *CELL_WIDTH];

            // draw the strip

            scale = (int)mountain_scale*pixel_color/(int)(ray_length+1);

            top        = 50+row-scale;

            bottom     = top + scale;

            Line_VDB(top,bottom,ray,pixel_color);

            } // end for row

        // move to next angle

        if (++curr_ang >= ANGLE_360)
           curr_ang=ANGLE_0;

        } // end for ray

} // end Draw_Terrain

// M A I N ///////////////////////////////////////////////////////////////////

void main(int argc, char **argv)
{

char buffer[80]; // text output buffer

int done=0;      // exit flag
```

```
float speed=0;    // speed of player

// check to see if command line parms are correct

if (argc<=1)
   {
   // not enough parms

   printf("\nUsage: voxtile.exe height");
   printf("\nExample: voxtile 15\n");

   // return to DOS

   exit(1);

   } // end if

// set scale of mountains

mountain_scale = atoi(argv[1]);

// set the graphics mode to mode 13h

Set_Graphics_Mode(GRAPHICS_MODE13);

// install keyboard driver

Keyboard_Install_Driver();

// build the look up tables and load textures

Initialize();

// create a double buffer

Create_Double_Buffer(200);

// display terrain manually first time

Draw_Terrain(play_x,
             play_y,
             play_z,
             play_ang,
             play_dist);

Display_Double_Buffer(double_buffer,0);

// main event loop

while(!done)
   {
```

continued on next page

continued from previous page

```
// reset velocity

speed = 0;

// test if user is hitting keyboard

if (keys_active)
   {
   // what is user trying to do


   // change viewing distance

   if (keyboard_state[MAKE_F])
      play_dist+=10;

   if (keyboard_state[MAKE_C])
      play_dist-=10;

   // change viewing height

   if (keyboard_state[MAKE_U])
      play_z+=10;

   if (keyboard_state[MAKE_D])
      play_z-=10;


   // change viewing position

   if (keyboard_state[MAKE_RIGHT])
      if ((play_ang+=ANGLE_5) >= ANGLE_360)
         play_ang-=ANGLE_360;

   if (keyboard_state[MAKE_LEFT])
      if ((play_ang-=ANGLE_5) < 0)
         play_ang+=ANGLE_360;

   // move forward

   if (keyboard_state[MAKE_UP])
      speed=20;

   // move backward

   if (keyboard_state[MAKE_DOWN])
      speed=-20;

   // exit demo

   if (keyboard_state[MAKE_ESC])
```

```c
        done=1;

      // compute trajectory vector for this view angle

      play_dir_x = cos_look[play_ang];
      play_dir_y = -sin_look[play_ang];
      play_dir_z = 0;

      // translate viewpoint

      play_x+=speed*play_dir_x;
      play_y+=speed*play_dir_y;
      play_z+=speed*play_dir_z;


      // draw the terrain

      Fill_Double_Buffer(0);

      Draw_Terrain(play_x,
                   play_y,
                   play_z,
                   play_ang,
                   play_dist);


      // print out tactical

      sprintf(buffer,"Height = %d Distance = %d     ",play_z,play_dist);
      Print_String_DB(0,0,10,buffer,0);

      sprintf(buffer,"Pos: X=%d, Y=%d, Z=%d     ",play_x,play_y,play_z);
      Print_String_DB(0,10,10,buffer,0);

      // show buffer

      Display_Double_Buffer(double_buffer,0);

      } // end if

   } // end while

// reset back to text mode

Set_Graphics_Mode(TEXT_MODE);

// remove the keyboard handler

Keyboard_Remove_Driver();

} // end main
```

FIGURE 16-24

ⓞ ⓞ ⓞ ⓞ ⓞ ⓞ

Screen shot of
VOXTILE.EXE

```
Height = 150 Distance = 70
Pos: X=1003, Y=980, Z=150
```

To run VOXTILE.EXE, you need only send the height scaling factor on the command line. For example, to scale the terrain by a factor of 15, type:

VOXTILE 15

The resulting display looks like Figure 16-24. To move around in the world, the controls are the same as for VOXEL.EXE. Other than the added data structures and the subtle changes to *Draw_Terrain()*, both voxel demos are identical.

Now you might be asking, why aren't these demos and the underlying engines in real-time? The answer is that the optimizations needed to make the engine run in real-time just about turn the code to mush, and it wouldn't be clear; so I thought it would be better to give you unoptimized code in this case. However, in the next section we'll talk about some of the optimizations that can be made to speed things up. You can then implement them at your own pace. You may come up with some better ways to make it go faster!

Optimizations

In the next chapter we're going to optimize the 3D polygon engine and learn a lot of cool tricks, but for now let's take a quick look at some ways to get a little more pow out of our voxel engine. We are going to begin by performing a simple analysis, followed by some classic optimizations and insights that are fairly obvious. Nevertheless, these optimizations should speed up the voxel engine by at least a factor of two. So, let's get with the program!

Code Analysis

The voxel engine function *Draw_Terrain()* is basically two nested loops. The outer loop controls the casting of the 320 rays, and the inner loop processes the walking of the ray through all of the 50 or so rows of the current column. Hence, we have a looping structure like this:

```
for (ray=1; ray<320; ray++)
    {

    for (row=100; row<150; row++)
        {

        // do X amount of compute cycles here

        } // end for row

    // do Y amount of compute cycles here

    } // end for ray
```

If we stare at this looping structure, we can quickly conclude that the total compute cycles of the structure is

Outer Loop		Inner Loop
320*Y	+	320*(50*X)

You see, the inner loop is being executed a total of 320*50=16,000, taking a total of 16,000*X compute cycles, while the outer loop only executes 320 times, taking a total of 320*Y compute cycles.

The main point of this analysis is to realize that we must focus on the inner loop, not the outer loop. Therefore, even if we were to make Y approach 0 compute cycles, it would still be drowned out by the 16,000*X compute cycles of the inner loop. So the moral of the story is, let's not waste time with the outer loop. What we have just performed is a bit of asymptotic analysis, and it is an entire branch of computer science that was formulated just for such problems. Anyway, now that we know to optimize the inner loop, let's see what we can do with it.

Inlining Everything

Let's begin optimizing the inner loop by looking at what's inside it. Here is the code that lies within the inner *for* loop of the voxel engine, along with some numeric place holders so we can refer to it in the discussion that follows.

```
// Step 1. compute length of ray
row_inv = 200-row;

// Step 2. use the current height and distance to compute length of ray.
ray_length = sphere_cancel[ray] * ((float)(play_dist*play_z)/
                                    (float)(play_z-row_inv));

// Step 3. rotate ray into position of sample
```

continued on next page

continued from previous page

```
xr = (int)((float)play_x + ray_length * cos_look[curr_ang]);
yr = (int)((float)play_y - ray_length * sin_look[curr_ang]);

// Step 4. compute texture coords
x_fine = xr % WORLD_X_SIZE;
y_fine = yr % WORLD_Y_SIZE;

// Step 5. using texture index locate texture pixel in textures
pixel_color = image_pcx.buffer[x_fine + (y_fine*320)];

// Step 6. draw the strip
scale = (int)mountain_scale*pixel_color/(int)(ray_length+1);

// Step 7. compute the top and bottom of strip
top        = 50+row-scale;
bottom     = top + scale;
// Step 8. draw the strip
Line_VDB(top,bottom,ray,pixel_color);
```

The first thing that jumps out at me is step 8, the call to *Line_VDB()*. This call is made 16,000 times. This means there are 16,000 stack frames created and destroyed! To remedy this, we can simply inline the *Line_VDB()* function by taking the code for it and replacing the call to *Line_VDB()* with the raw code. This alone should speed up the rendering quite a bit.

Drawing Less Is More

The next optimization will probably be the one that gives us the best performance increase. The optimization is very simple: draw every pixel once and only once. Currently, we are drawing the voxel terrain from back to front and letting the nearer strips occlude the more distant ones. In essence, we are performing a vertical scan line Painter's algorithm. However, if we draw the terrain from front to back instead, we can make a very aggressive optimization, which is this: if the current vertical strip's scale is larger than that of the last vertical strip, then we should only draw the portion of the strip that wouldn't be occluded by the last strip.

For example, say the last strip drawn had a scale of 50, and the new strip has a scale of 60. Then we know that the new strip towers over the last one by only 10 pixels; thus, that's all we need to draw. Figure 16-25 shows an example of this for both cases in which the current strip is drawn and isn't drawn based on the scale of the last strip. This "smart" rendering can be implemented with a variable that tracks the scale of the last strip along with a little conditional logic.

Using Shifts and Logical Operations

Looking at the various steps in the rendering algorithm, we quickly notice quite a few multiplications and divisions. The question is, can we remove these and replace

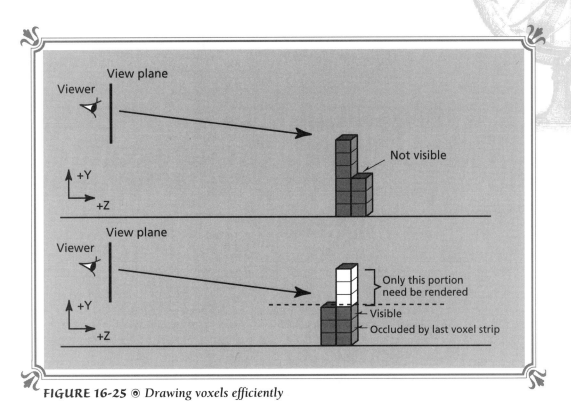

FIGURE 16-25 ⊙ *Drawing voxels efficiently*

them with shift and/or logical operations? The answer is yes. Let's take a look at our first victim below:

```
// Step 4. compute texture coords
x_fine = xr % WORLD_X_SIZE;
y_fine = yr % WORLD_Y_SIZE;
```

Basically, *x_fine* and *y_fine* are the remainder or residue of division of the world dimensions into *xr* and *yr*. However, if these dimensions were a power of 2, say 256x256 instead of 320x200, then we could use a trick. The trick would look like this:

```
x_fine = ((int)xr) & 0x00ff;
y_fine = ((int)yr) & 0x00ff;
```

We see that logically *AND*ing the values of *xr* and *yr* with 255 or 0xffh, is equivalent to *MOD*ing them by 256. This is only true for powers of 2. So if we are willing to alter the dimensions of our universe so that they are powers of 2, we can use this optimization.

The next optimization has to do with using binary shifts to achieve multiplication. Actually, we have seen it before. Take a look at the look-up table below:

```
// Step 5. using texture index locate texture pixel in textures
pixel_color = image_pcx.buffer[x_fine + (y_fine*320)];
```

Do you see the multiplication by 320? This can be rewritten as *(y_fine << 8+y_fine << 6)*. We used this same insight when writing the fast version of the pixel plotter. However, an even faster version can be made with the use of look-up tables. Let's see if we can't add a few more look-up tables to get some more speed.

Using Look-Up Tables

When analyzing the program, we see that there are quite a few areas that are good candidates for look-ups. The first one is the last topic we just spoke of—the multiplication by 320. We could simply create a table that contained the product of 320 with all possible *y_fine* values (which would be 0 to 199) for the particular setup. Then step 5 could be rewritten as:

```
// Step 5*. using texture index locate texture pixel in textures
pixel_color = image_pcx.buffer[x_fine + y_320_fine_look[y_fine]];
```

The next place we can use a look-up is in the calculation of *ray_length*. Take a look at step 2 below:

```
// Step 2. use the current height and distance to compute length of ray.
ray_length = sphere_cancel[ray] * ((float)(play_dist*play_z)/
                                    (float)(play_z-row_inv));
```

The boldfaced code can be precomputed for all values of *row_inv*, or in other words, a table that is 50 to 100 elements long could remove one multiplication, one division, and one subtraction. However, the only downside to using a table is that it fixes the values of *play_dist* and *play_z*; but if moving the viewpoint distance and height isn't important, then this is a good area to use a table.

Finally, we could probably also use a table for the scale calculation. Take a look at step 6 below:

```
// Step 6. draw the strip
scale = (int)mountain_scale*pixel_color/(int)(ray_length+1);
```

We see that the only variable that varies is *ray_length,* so if we create a table that is indexed by both the pixel color and the *ray_length*, we could remove the multiplication and division of step 6. However, this table might be quite large since we know that *pixel_color* can range from 0 to 255, and *ray_length* might range even larger!

The Optimized Voxel Engine

Those should at least get you started on your way to optimizing the voxel engine, but just to be complete, here is a version of the single-texture version of VOXEL.C with some of the optimizations we just reviewed. The new source is called VOXOPT.C and the executable is VOXOPT.EXE. The code is shown in Listing 16-3.

LISTING 16-3 Optimized voxel engine

```c
// VOXOPT.C - Single texture based, ray casted voxel engine

// I N C L U D E S ////////////////////////////////////////////////////

#include <io.h>
#include <conio.h>
#include <stdio.h>
#include <stdlib.h>
#include <dos.h>
#include <bios.h>
#include <fcntl.h>
#include <memory.h>
#include <malloc.h>
#include <math.h>
#include <string.h>

#include "black3.h"
#include "black4.h"
#include "black5.h"

// D E F I N E S ////////////////////////////////////////////////////

#define WORLD_X_SIZE    320  // width of universe
#define WORLD_Y_SIZE    200  // height of universe

// constants used to represent angles for the ray casting a 60 degree field of view

#define ANGLE_0         0
#define ANGLE_1         5
#define ANGLE_2         10
#define ANGLE_4         20
#define ANGLE_5         25
#define ANGLE_10        50
#define ANGLE_6         30
#define ANGLE_15        80
#define ANGLE_30        160
#define ANGLE_45        240
#define ANGLE_60        320
#define ANGLE_90        480
#define ANGLE_135       720
#define ANGLE_180       960
#define ANGLE_225       1200
#define ANGLE_270       1440
#define ANGLE_315       1680
#define ANGLE_360       1920

// there are 1920 degrees in our circle or 360/1920 is the conversion factor
// from real degrees to our degrees

#define ANGULAR_INCREMENT   ((float)0.1875)
```

continued on next page

continued from previous page

```
// conversion constants from radians to degrees and viceversa

#define DEG_TO_RAD          ((float)3.1415926/(float)180)
#define RAD_TO_DEG          ((float)180/(float)3.1415926)

// G L O B A L S  ///////////////////////////////////////////////////////////

pcx_picture image_pcx;          // general pcx image

int play_x=1000,                // the current world x of player
    play_y=1000,                // the current world y of player
    play_z=150,
    play_ang=ANGLE_90,          // the current viewing angle of player
    play_dist = 70,
    mountain_scale=10;          // scaling factor for mountains

float play_dir_x,               // the direction the player is pointing in
      play_dir_y,
      play_dir_z,
      cos_look[ANGLE_360],      // cosine look up table
      sin_look[ANGLE_360],      // sin look up table
      sphere_cancel[ANGLE_60],  // cancels fish eye distortion
      ray_length[100];          // holds ray length look up

// F U N C T I O N S ////////////////////////////////////////////////////////

int Initialize(char *filename)
{
// this function builds all the look up tables for the terrain generator and
// loads in the terrain texture map

int ang,              // looping variable
    row,
    row_inv;

float rad_angle;      // current angle in radians

// create sin and cos look up first

for (ang=0; ang<ANGLE_360; ang++)
    {
    // compute current angle in radians

    rad_angle = (float)ang*ANGULAR_INCREMENT*DEG_TO_RAD;

    // now compute the sin and cos

    sin_look[ang] = sin(rad_angle);
    cos_look[ang] = cos(rad_angle);

    } // end for ang
```

```
// create inverse cosine viewing distortion filter

for (ang=0; ang<ANGLE_30; ang++)
    {
    // compute current angle in radians

    rad_angle = (float)ang*ANGULAR_INCREMENT*DEG_TO_RAD;

    // now compute the sin and cos

    sphere_cancel[ang+ANGLE_30] = 1/cos(rad_angle);
    sphere_cancel[ANGLE_30-ang] = 1/cos(rad_angle);

    } // end for ang

// create the pre-computed ray length array

for (row = 100; row<150; row++)
    {

    // compute length of ray

    row_inv = 200-row;

    // use the current height and distance to compute length of ray.

    ray_length[row-100] = ((float)(play_dist*play_z)/(float)(play_z-row_inv));

    } // end for row

// initialize the pcx structure

PCX_Init((pcx_picture_ptr)&image_pcx);

// load in the textures

return(PCX_Load(filename, (pcx_picture_ptr)&image_pcx,1));

} // end Initialize

/////////////////////////////////////////////////////////////////////////////

void Draw_Terrain(int play_x,
                  int play_y,
                  int play_z,
                  int play_ang,
                  int play_dist)
{
// this function draws the entire terrain based on the location and orientation
// of the player's viewpoint
```

continued on next page

continued from previous page

```
int curr_ang,        // current angle being processed
    xr,yr,           // location of ray in world coords
    x_fine,y_fine,   // the texture coordinates the ray hit
    pixel_color,     // the color of textel
    ray,             // looping variable
    row,             // the current video row being processed
    scale,           // the scale of the current strip
    top,             // top of strip
    last_scale,
    last_top,
    diff,
    index;           // looping variable

float ray_length_final;   // the length of the ray after distortion compensation

unsigned char far *start_offset;  // used by inline line drawer

// start the current angle off -30 degrees to the left of the player's
// current viewing direction

curr_ang = play_ang - ANGLE_30;

// test for underflow

if (curr_ang < 0)
   curr_ang+=ANGLE_360;

// cast a series of rays for every column of the screen

for (ray=1; ray<320; ray++)
   {

   // reset last top and scale

   last_scale = 0;

   last_top = 0;

   // for each column compute the pixels that should be displayed
   // for each screen pixel, process from top to bottom

   for (row = 149; row>=100; row--)
      {

      // use the current height and distance to compute length of ray.

      ray_length_final = sphere_cancel[ray] * ray_length[row-100];

      // rotate ray into position of sample

      xr = (int)((float)play_x + ray_length_final * cos_look[curr_ang]);
      yr = (int)((float)play_y - ray_length_final * sin_look[curr_ang]);
```

```
        // compute texture coords

        x_fine = xr % WORLD_X_SIZE;
        y_fine = yr % WORLD_Y_SIZE;

        // using texture index locate texture pixel in textures

        pixel_color = image_pcx.buffer[x_fine + (y_fine<<8) + (y_fine<<6)];

        // draw the strip

        scale = (int)mountain_scale*pixel_color/(int)(ray_length_final+1);

        // test if we need to draw this segment

        if (scale>=last_scale)
           {

           diff = scale-last_scale;

           top  = 50+row-scale;

           // compute starting position

           start_offset = double_buffer + ((top<<8) + (top<<6)) + ray;

           for (index=0; index<=diff; index++)
               {
               // set the pixel

               *start_offset = (unsigned char)pixel_color;

               // move downward to next line

               start_offset+=320;

               } // end for index

           } // end if scale

        last_scale = scale;

        } // end for row

    // move to next angle

    if (++curr_ang >= ANGLE_360)
       curr_ang=ANGLE_0;

    } // end for ray

} // end Draw_Terrain
```

continued on next page

continued from previous page

```
// M A I N //////////////////////////////////////////////////////////////////////

void main(int argc, char **argv)
{
char buffer[80];

int done=0; // exit flag

float speed=0;  // speed of player

// check to see if command line parms are correct

if (argc<=2)
   {
   // not enough parms

   printf("\nUsage: voxel.exe filename.pcx height");
   printf("\nExample: voxel voxterr4.pcx 10\n");

   // return to DOS

   exit(1);

   } // end if

// set the graphics mode to mode 13h

Set_Graphics_Mode(GRAPHICS_MODE13);

// create a double buffer

Create_Double_Buffer(200);

// create look up tables and load textures

if (!Initialize(argv[1]))
   {

   printf("\nError loading file %s",argv[1]);
   exit(1);

   } // end if

// install keyboard driver

Keyboard_Install_Driver();

// set scale of mountains

mountain_scale = atoi(argv[2]);

// draw the first frame
```

```
Draw_Terrain(play_x,
             play_y,
             play_z,
             play_ang,
             play_dist);

Display_Double_Buffer(double_buffer,0);

// main event loop

while(!done)
    {

    // reset velocity

    speed = 0;

    // test if user is hitting keyboard

    if (keys_active)
       {
       // what is user trying to do

       // change viewing distance

       if (keyboard_state[MAKE_F])
          play_dist+=10;

       if (keyboard_state[MAKE_C])
          play_dist-=10;

       // change viewing height

       if (keyboard_state[MAKE_U])
          play_z+=10;

       if (keyboard_state[MAKE_D])
          play_z-=10;

       // change viewing position

       if (keyboard_state[MAKE_RIGHT])
          if ((play_ang+=ANGLE_10) >= ANGLE_360)
             play_ang-=ANGLE_360;

       if (keyboard_state[MAKE_LEFT])
          if ((play_ang-=ANGLE_10) < 0)
             play_ang+=ANGLE_360;

       // move forward

       if (keyboard_state[MAKE_UP])
```

continued on next page

continued from previous page

```
            speed=20;

    // move backward

    if (keyboard_state[MAKE_DOWN])
        speed=-20;

    // exit demo

    if (keyboard_state[MAKE_ESC])
        done=1;


    // compute trajectory vector for this view angle

    play_dir_x = cos_look[play_ang];
    play_dir_y = -sin_look[play_ang];
    play_dir_z = 0;

    // translate viewpoint

    play_x+=speed*play_dir_x;
    play_y+=speed*play_dir_y;
    play_z+=speed*play_dir_z;

    // draw the terrain

    Fill_Double_Buffer(0);

    Draw_Terrain(play_x,
                 play_y,
                 play_z,
                 play_ang,
                 play_dist);

    // draw tactical

    sprintf(buffer,"Height = %d Distance = %d      ",play_z,play_dist);
    Print_String_DB(0,0,10,buffer,0);

    sprintf(buffer,"Pos: X=%d, Y=%d, Z=%d     ",play_x,play_y,play_z);
    Print_String_DB(0,10,10,buffer,0);

    Display_Double_Buffer(double_buffer,0);

    } // end if

    } // end while

// reset back to text mode

Set_Graphics_Mode(TEXT_MODE);
```

```
// remove the keyboard handler

Keyboard_Remove_Driver();

} // end main
```

The controls and command line parameter for VOXOPT.EXE are the same as those for VOXEL.EXE except that due to the use of look-up tables, you can't change the height or the viewing distance. In any case, the optimizations made were as follows:

1. Inlining of the line-drawing function
2. Using a look-up table for the precomputed ray lengths
3. Using shifts for multiplication where possible
4. Drawing each pixel only once in a front-to-back order

Adding Foreground Objects

Finally, you might be asking, how do I add objects to the voxel display? The answer is that objects must be added using a Z-buffer technique, that is, as the voxel display is being rendered from back to front. Sprite objects that you wish to be some distance from the view plane should be rendered at the appropriate time so that the remainder of the voxel terrain occludes appropriate portions of the sprite.

Summary

Within this chapter we learned about a totally new and, for the most part, unexplored type of computer graphics commonly referred to as voxel graphics. We created a simple voxel engine based on ray casting and experimented with a few optimizations. These optimizations are a good primer for the next chapter, because this chapter has been a vacation in the Caribbean compared to what we are going to tackle next.

Part III

Spells

17

Optimizing the 3D Engine

ome tutti fiori e manubelli e de quali pino brano e l'asa
e gra pese auere le mani si e gente se sa qo grano de Bone
eryare nella mano e la permazzella asia manobesta pegi gnon
aforza se pib isomo pib dual.

17

Optimizing the 3D Engine

In the dark chasm that separates time and space, thought and reason, lies infinite knowledge. This is the place that we're going to visit today. Optimization is the final step needed to control the parallel dimension of Cyberspace and become true Cybersorcerers.

The 3D engine that we have created thus far really isn't anything that takes too many brain cells to comprehend. Granted, it's complex, and we have mastered many concepts and details to create it. However, now that we have created it, there's not really that much to it—just a lot of code. The engine uses standard textbook mathematics and performs the transformations and processes using well-known techniques. In essence, the engine isn't mysterious. Hence, the goal of this chapter is to look at things in another way—to look at them through the eyes of a true Cybersorcerer and not those of a mortal. Thus equipped, we will optimize the engine in a myriad of ways. The final result will be a set of routines that can support a full 3D video game in real-time and a collection of spells that can be used for 3D graphics, game programming, and anything else that we might wish to conjure up.

Updating the PLG File Format

We should begin our optimizations with the very first component of the 3D engine, that is, the functions used to load 3D objects. When we first wrote the PLG file loader, we realized that the final engine might need a more descriptive file format to take care of two-sided polygons, texture mapping, and other more advanced attributes. I'll leave the texture mapping to you, but the two-sided polygon idea is something we need to implement, because without it, we're going to have a hard time modeling objects that have wings or other single polygon protrusions.

If we recall the format of the color descriptor from Chapter 11, we know that the color descriptor for each polygon is a 16-bit number divided into 4 nibbles, $n_3 n_2 n_1 n_0$. The nibble n_3 selects the type of shading, nibble n_2 is used for mapped colors, and nibbles n_1 and n_0 are used as the final color to be used, from 0 to 255. Since we are only using a couple of the PLG shading types—simple shading and flat shading—we can assume that nibble n_2 is unused. Therefore, we can use nibble n_2 for extra attributes that we want to add to the PLG file format, such as a *two-sided* flag. Table 17-1 shows the bit encoding for the shading types.

TABLE 17-1
❖❖❖❖❖❖
*PLG color
descriptor format
(upper four bits)*

b3	b2	b1	b0	Color type
1	X	X	X	Mapped color; the remaining 15 bits are an index into color table
0	0	0	0	Simple unshaded color
0	0	0	1	A flat shaded color
0	0	1	0	A pseudometallic color
0	0	1	1	A special effect, such as glass

We're going to use bit number 0 as a flag that selects how many sides a polygon has. If bit 0 is 0, there is one side; hence, all our current PLG files will work without change. However, if we wish to indicate that a polygon has two sides, we simply set bit 0 of nibble n_2 to 1 in the PLG file. Then this information can be tracked in a new PLG load object function, and the function can set the appropriate field in the 3D object structure.

So what do we need in order to add this functionality? Not much really. We already have everything set up to handle two sides. The polygon data structure already has a *two_sided* field, as shown here:

```
typedef struct polygon_typ
        {

        int num_points; // number of points in polygon (usually 3 or 4)
        int vertex_list[MAX_POINTS_PER_POLY];  // the index number of vertices
        int color;                  // color of polygon
        int shade;                  // the final shade of color after lighting
        int shading;                // type of lighting, flat or constant shading
```

```
      int two_sided;          // flags if the polygon is two sided
      int visible;            // used to remove backfaces
      int active;             // used to turn faces on and off
      int clipped;            // flags that polygon has been clipped or removed
      float normal_length;    // pre-computed magnitude of normal

} polygon, *polygon_ptr;
```

So all we need to do is test the rightmost bit of the second nibble of the color descriptor word and set the *two_sided* field appropriately in each polygon. Listing 17-1 is a new *PLG_Load_Object()* function that does just that.

LISTING 17-1 New PLG file loader that supports two-sided polygons

```
int PLG_Load_Object(object_ptr the_object,char *filename,float scale)
{
// this function loads an object off disk and allows it to be scaled, the files
// are in a slightly enhanced PLG format that allows polygons to be defined
// as one or two sided, this helps the hidden surface removal system. This
// extra functionality has been encoded in the 2nd nibble from the left of the
// color descriptor

FILE *fp; // disk file

static int id_number = 0; // used to set object id's

char buffer[80],         // holds input string
     object_name[32],    // name of 3D object
     *token;             // current parsing token


unsigned int total_vertices,   // total vertices in object
             total_polys,      // total polygons per object
             num_vertices,     // number of vertices on a polygon
             color_des,        // the color descriptor of a polygon
             logical_color,    // the final color of polygon
             shading,          // the type of shading used on polygon
             two_sided,        // flags if poly has two sides
             index,            // looping variables
             index_2,
             vertex_num,       // vertex numbers
             vertex_0,
             vertex_1,
             vertex_2;

float x,y,z;                   // a single vertex

vector_3d u,v,normal;          // working vectors

// open the disk file

if ((fp=fopen(filename,"r"))==NULL)
```

continued on next page

continued from previous page

```
    {
    printf("\nCouldn't open file %s",filename);
    return(0);

    } // end if

// first we are looking for the header line that has the object name and
// the number of vertices and polygons

if (!PLG_Get_Line(buffer, 80,fp))
    {
    printf("\nError with PLG file %s",filename);
    fclose(fp);
    return(0);
    } // end if error

// extract object name and number of vertices and polygons

sscanf(buffer,"%s %d %d",object_name, &total_vertices, &total_polys);

// set proper fields in object

the_object->num_vertices = total_vertices;
the_object->num_polys    = total_polys;
the_object->state        = 1;

the_object->world_pos.x  = 0;
the_object->world_pos.y  = 0;
the_object->world_pos.z  = 0;

// set id number, maybe later also add the name of object in the
// structure???

the_object->id = id_number++;

// based on number of vertices, read vertex list into object

for (index=0; index<total_vertices; index++)
    {

    // read in vertex

    if (!PLG_Get_Line(buffer, 80,fp))
        {
        printf("\nError with PLG file %s",filename);
        fclose(fp);
        return(0);
        } // end if error

    sscanf(buffer,"%f %f %f",&x,&y,&z);

    // insert vertex into object
```

```
                the_object->vertices_local[index].x = x*scale;
                the_object->vertices_local[index].y = y*scale;
                the_object->vertices_local[index].z = z*scale;

                } // end for index

// now read in polygon list

for (index=0; index<total_polys; index++)
    {
    // read in color and number of vertices for next polygon

    if (!PLG_Get_Line(buffer, 80,fp))
        {
        printf("\nError with PLG file %s",filename);
        fclose(fp);
        return(0);
        } // end if error

    // initialize token getter and get first token which is color descriptor

    if (!(token = strtok(buffer," ")) )
        {
        printf("\nError with PLG file %s",filename);
        fclose(fp);
        return(0);
        } // end if problem

    // test if number is hexadecimal

    if (token[0]=='0' && (token[1]=='x' || token[1]=='X'))
        {

        sscanf(&token[2],"%x",&color_des);

        } // end if hex color specifier
    else
        {

        color_des = atoi(token);

        } // end if decimal

    // extract base color and type of shading

    logical_color = color_des & 0x00ff;
    shading       = color_des >> 12;
    two_sided     = ((color_des >> 8) & 0x0f);

    // read number of vertices in polygon

    if (!(token = strtok(NULL," ")))
```

continued on next page

continued from previous page

```
       {
       printf("\nError with PLG file %s",filename);
       fclose(fp);
       return(0);
       } // end if problem

    if ((num_vertices = atoi(token))<=0)
       {
       printf("\nError with PLG file (number of vertices) %s",filename);
       fclose(fp);
       return(0);
       } // end if no vertices or error

    // set fields in polygon structure

    the_object->polys[index].num_points = num_vertices;
    the_object->polys[index].color      = logical_color;
    the_object->polys[index].shading    = shading;
    the_object->polys[index].two_sided  = two_sided;
    the_object->polys[index].visible    = 1;
    the_object->polys[index].clipped    = 0;
    the_object->polys[index].active     = 1;

    // now read in polygon vertex list

    for (index_2=0; index_2<num_vertices; index_2++)
       {

       // read in next vertex number

       if (!(token = strtok(NULL," ")) )
          {
          printf("\nError with PLG file %s",filename);
          fclose(fp);
          return(0);
          } // end if problem

       vertex_num = atoi(token);

       // insert vertex number into polygon

       the_object->polys[index].vertex_list[index_2] = vertex_num;

       } // end for index_2

    // compute length of the two co-planar edges of the polygon, since they
    // will be used in the computation of the dot-product later

    vertex_0 = the_object->polys[index].vertex_list[0];
    vertex_1 = the_object->polys[index].vertex_list[1];
    vertex_2 = the_object->polys[index].vertex_list[2];
```

```
// the vector u = vo->v1

Make_Vector_3D((point_3d_ptr)&the_object->vertices_local[vertex_0],
               (point_3d_ptr)&the_object->vertices_local[vertex_1],
               (vector_3d_ptr)&u);

// the vector v = vo->v2

Make_Vector_3D((point_3d_ptr)&the_object->vertices_local[vertex_0],
               (point_3d_ptr)&the_object->vertices_local[vertex_2],
               (vector_3d_ptr)&v);

Cross_Product_3D((vector_3d_ptr)&v,
                 (vector_3d_ptr)&u,
                 (vector_3d_ptr)&normal);


// compute magnitude of normal, take its inverse and multiply it by
// 15, this will change the shading calculation of 15*dp/normal into
// dp*normal_length, removing one division

the_object->polys[index].normal_length = 15.0/Vector_Mag_3D
                 ((vector_3d_ptr)&normal);

} // end for index

// close the file

fclose(fp);

// compute object radius

Compute_Object_Radius(the_object);

// return success

return(1);

} // end PLG_Load_Object
```

Before we get too carried away, I have decided to make all the function names the same as before (for the most part). So the module BLACK17.C and BLACK17.H will replace BLACK11.C and BLACK11.H. If you have BLACK11.OBJ in a library or have the .C and .H files in your project, you should remove them since they're outdated!

Back to the function now. If you take a look at the code, it's almost identical to the previous version of *PLG_Load_Object()*. The only differences are in the decomposition of the color descriptor to extract the two-sided information and in the calculation of the normal length (which we'll discuss later during the back-face removal and shading optimizations).

Let's take a quick look at how we would use the new extended PLG file format. Imagine that we wanted to create an object that was basically a dart, something like what is shown in Figure 17-1. Normally, we couldn't do this, but with the new two-sided flag it's a snap. We still should order polygon vertices in a counterclockwise order to be consistent, but there will not be a back-face removal phase. This will speed up the engine considerably. Anyway, a PLG file for the dart depicted in Figure 17-1 looks like this:.

```
; Three-sided dart
DART 5 3
; vertex list
0 0 25
0 0 –20
0 10 –25
–5 –5 –25
5 –5 –25
; polygons
0x119f 3 0 2 1
0x119f 3 0 1 3
0x119f 3 0 1 4
; end of DART
```

FIGURE 17-1

◎ ◎ ◎ ◎ ◎ ◎

A dart consisting of two-sided polygons

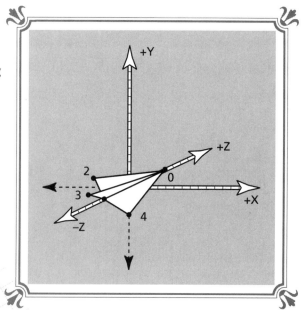

That's it! So if you know that a polygon is going to be visible from both sides (or you wish it to be), set the *two_sided* field. Of course, we have to rewrite the back-face removal and shading function, but we'll do that later in the chapter—one thing at a time.

More Efficient Data Structures

We have been working with the object-based data structure for quite some time now, so it's time we examined it to see whether we can do better or if it's going to suffice in most cases. Let's begin with memory consumption. Obviously, pre-allocating static arrays for vertices and polygons is inefficient, but we can always define the array sizes such that they are made large enough to hold the average number of vertices and polygons per object. However, it would definitely be better to use dynamically allocated arrays in future drafts of the engine if memory is at a premium. But for small games and reasonably complex objects, setting the number of polygons per object and the number of vertices per object to be equal to 16 should suffice and isn't going to eat up too much memory.

The big question is, should we continue defining objects as sets of polygons based on vertices that are in common? The answer seems to be yes. I have tried different structures, but I keep returning to the common vertex list, with polygons being defined as vertex lists into the data set. However, we should definitely get rid of the three sets of vertices—local, world, and camera—for each object. We can get away with only local and another array that holds world and camera, depending on the position of the object in the graphics pipeline. The next question we should ask is, can we use more pointers in the object or polygon structures to make them more efficient? The answer is probably no. We might be able to make the structures a bit cleaner and more abstract, but when it comes time to dereference them, we would have a nightmare!

The final data structure aspect we should discuss is how to create single polygon objects or even single points. Well, we will have to add these depending on the situation. The rendering engine surely can handle them since it is based on polygons, but all the transformation logic is based on objects, not polygons. Hence, we will have to write separate functions to deal with single polygons and points. We may or may not do this for the final version of the engine, but basically all the functions that perform shading, back-face removal, local to world transformations, world to camera transformations, and 3D clipping must be rewritten to handle polygons and single points. This can probably be done with a lot of text copying (using the object-based versions as the foundation) along with some simplification. Hence, we have all the raw code needed to support these simpler data types that might find use for projectiles, star fields, and explosions.

Multiple Levels of Detail

The next "global" optimization that we can implement is called *level of detail switching*. Based on the distance that the viewpoint is from an object, different objects are selected with varying numbers of polygons. Figure 17-2 shows this graphically. Here we see that at a distance of 100 units, *object_1* is used; at a distance of 101 to 499, the model of *object_2* is used; and finally, for distances of 500 to infinity, the model named *object_3* is used. The trick is that each object's model has a different number of polygons. *Object_1* is the closest version and thus should have the highest number of polygons (maybe 16). *Object_2* on the other hand, is going to be out there a little, so it should have maybe 10 polygons. Finally, the third model, *object_3*, will look like a little dot, so 4 to 6 polygons might be in order.

The whole idea of multiple levels of detail is to select polygon models that are good enough for the size and distance of the object they represent. How would we implement this in software? Well, our engine at this point isn't really set up for it, but a crude attempt would look something like this:

```
object tank_lod[3];  // three levels of details


//  load the highest resolution tank model with 24 polygons

PLG_Load_Object((object_ptr)&tank_lod[0],"TANK_24",1.0);
```

FIGURE 17-2

◉ ◉ ◉ ◉ ◉ ◉

Levels of detail based on distance

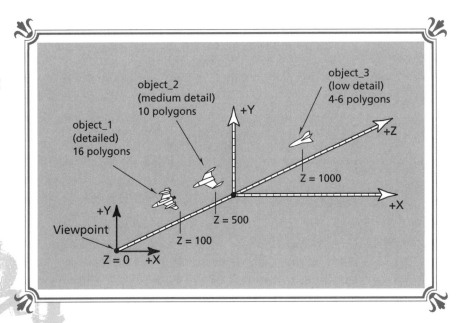

```
//  load the medium resolution tank model with 16 polygons

PLG_Load_Object((object_ptr)&tank_lod[1],"TANK_16",1.0);

//  load the lowest resolution tank model with 12 polygons

PLG_Load_Object((object_ptr)&tank_lod[2],"TANK_12",1.0);


// main game loop

while(1)
        {
        // process game logic

        // here is where the objects are ready to be processed by the graphics engine
        if (distance_from_viewer < 250)
           {
           // process tank_lod[0]
           } // end if
        else
        if (distance_from_viewer >250 && distance_from_viewer <500)
           {
           // process tank_lod[1]
           } // end if
        else
        if (distance_from_viewer > 500)
           {
           // process tank_lod[2]
           } // end if

        } // end main
```

Of course, we have left out about a million details, but you get the idea. By using multiple level of detail models, we give less attention to the number of polygons processed for objects that aren't close to the player (and are far from the immediate action) than those that are central to the action. Hence, the number of polygons sent to the graphics pipeline is minimized.

Revised Matrix Mathematics

Even though much of the mathematics performed by the 3D engine use general 4x4 matrices, this isn't an absolute necessity. In fact, the only reason we used matrices was to use them as tools to understand translation, scaling, rotation, concatenation, and other related operations. We don't need to perform matrix math in the standard way nor do we need to perform complete calculations in most cases. This is one of the main areas where we can extract more performance. By the end of this chapter, we will have practically eradicated almost every matrix multiplication in the engine and trimmed the matrix multiplies down to a bare minimum.

Let's start the optimization analysis by taking a look at matrix multiplication itself.

Matrix Multiplication Analysis
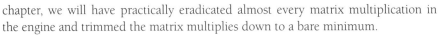

Since we're using homogeneous coordinates to support translation, we need to use 4x4 matrices and 4x4 matrix multiplication. There are two times that we perform a matrix multiplication. We can multiply a 1x4 row vector (a point) by a matrix, and we can perform a full-blown 4x4 matrix multiplied by another 4x4 to concatenate them. For example, if you've been paying attention to the engine functions, you will notice that even though there is a function to perform 1x4 by 4x4 matrix multiplication, this operation has usually been done inline with explicit code for the functions in which it was needed. As a matter of fact, I don't think there has been one call to the *Mat_Mul_1x4_4x4()* function! On the other hand, there are many calls to the *Mat_Mul_4x4_4x4()* function, so we should try to optimize this function at the very least.

To accomplish the optimization, we need to look at the math and see why optimization is so important. To perform a matrix multiplication between a 1x4 matrix and 4x4 matrix takes 4 multiplications per element and 3 additions per element. Since the result of a 1x4 multiplied by a 4x4 is a 1x4 row matrix, that means there is a total of:

Multiplications: 4*4=16
Additions: 4*3=12

That's a lot when you consider that each point of the database must be matrix multiplied at least once to transform it from world to camera coordinates, and yet another matrix multiplication is needed every time an object is rotated!

Now, based on our knowledge of a 1x4 times a 4x4, we can deduce that a 4x4 times a 4x4 should have four times as many calculations. Therefore, there will be a total of:

Multiplications: 16*4=64
Additions: 12*4=48

Wow! This means that when we concatenate three matrices, a total of 128 multiplications and 96 additions are performed. Hence, you see why it's important to make these matrix operations as fast and efficient as possible.

Manual Matrix Multiplication

The first thing we can do to make matrix multiplication faster is to unroll the matrix multiplication loops. For example, the code for the 4x4 by 4x4 multiply is shown in Listing 17-2.

LISTING 17-2 The old 4x4 matrix multiply

```
void Mat_Mul_4x4_4x4(matrix_4x4 a,
                     matrix_4x4 b,
                     matrix_4x4 result)
{
// this function multiplies a 4x4 by a 4x4 and stores the result in a 4x4

int index_i,  // row and column looping vars
    index_j,
    index_k;

float sum;     // temp used to hold sum of products

// loop thru rows of a
for (index_i=0; index_i<4; index_i++)
    {
    // loop thru columns of b
    for (index_j=0; index_j<4; index_j++)
        {
        // multiply ith row of a by jth column of b and store the sum
        // of products in the position i,j of result

        sum=0;

        for (index_k=0; index_k<4; index_k++)
            sum+=a[index_i][index_k]*b[index_k][index_j];

        // store result
        result[index_i][index_j] = sum;

        } // end for index_j
    } // end for index_i

} // end Mat_Mul_4x4_4x4
```

As you can see, there are two loops and temporary variables. These things aren't for free. Loops need counters, logic, and jumps. And temporary variables need to be created on the stack, initialized, and reset. So, what if we manually performed all 64 multiplications and 48 additions? This is exactly what we're going to do. Therefore, we can rewrite the core of the function as shown in Listing 17-3.

LISTING 17-3 A 4x4 matrix multiply with the loops unrolled

```
void Mat_Mul_4x4_4x4 (matrix_4x4 a,
                      matrix_4x4 b,
                      matrix_4x4 result)
{
// this function multiplies a 4x4 by a 4x4 and stores the result in a 4x4

// first row
```

continued on next page

continued from previous page

```
result[0][0]=a[0][0]*b[0][0]+a[0][1]*b[1][0]+a[0][2]*b[2][0]+a[0][3]*b[3][0];
result[0][1]=a[0][0]*b[0][1]+a[0][1]*b[1][1]+a[0][2]*b[2][1]+a[0][3]*b[3][1];
result[0][2]=a[0][0]*b[0][2]+a[0][1]*b[1][2]+a[0][2]*b[2][2]+a[0][3]*b[3][2];
result[0][3]=a[0][0]*b[0][3]+a[0][1]*b[1][3]+a[0][2]*b[2][3]+a[0][3]*b[3][3];

// second row

result[1][0]=a[1][0]*b[0][0]+a[1][1]*b[1][0]+a[1][2]*b[2][0]+a[1][3]*b[3][0];
result[1][1]=a[1][0]*b[0][1]+a[1][1]*b[1][1]+a[1][2]*b[2][1]+a[1][3]*b[3][1];
result[1][2]=a[1][0]*b[0][2]+a[1][1]*b[1][2]+a[1][2]*b[2][2]+a[1][3]*b[3][2];
result[1][3]=a[1][0]*b[0][3]+a[1][1]*b[1][3]+a[1][2]*b[2][3]+a[1][3]*b[3][3];

// third row

result[2][0]=a[2][0]*b[0][0]+a[2][1]*b[1][0]+a[2][2]*b[2][0] +a[2][3]*b[3][0];
result[2][1]=a[2][0]*b[0][1]+a[2][1]*b[1][1]+a[2][2]*b[2][1] +a[2][3]*b[3][1];
result[2][2]=a[2][0]*b[0][2]+a[2][1]*b[1][2]+a[2][2]*b[2][2] +a[2][3]*b[3][2];
result[2][3]=a[2][0]*b[0][3]+a[2][1]*b[1][3]+a[2][2]*b[2][3] +a[2][3]*b[3][3];

// fourth row

result[3][0]=a[3][0]*b[0][0]+a[3][1]*b[1][0]+a[3][2]*b[2][0]+a[3][2]*b[3][0];
result[3][1]=a[3][0]*b[0][1]+a[3][1]*b[1][1]+a[3][2]*b[2][1]+a[3][2]*b[3][1];
result[3][2]=a[3][0]*b[0][2]+a[3][1]*b[1][2]+a[3][2]*b[2][2]+a[3][2]*b[3][2];
result[3][3]=a[3][0]*b[0][3]+a[3][1]*b[1][3]+a[3][2]*b[2][3]+a[3][2]*b[3][3];

} // end Mat_Mul_4x4_4x4
```

Even though it's a bit drawn out, it's about 50 percent faster than the previous version, which is definitely worth it. But the question is, can we totally remove some of the multiplications based on our knowledge of the kinds of matrices that we might be multiplying? The answer is yes.

Sparse Matrices and Zeros

In linear algebra and matrix mathematics, there are matrices that have special properties, such as being upper triangular, lower triangular, singular, and so on. But the class of matrices that interests us is called *sparse*. Sparse matrices are matrices with a majority of their entries equal to 0, as shown here:

$$\begin{bmatrix} a & 0 & 0 & b \\ 0 & 0 & c & d \\ e & 0 & 0 & 0 \\ 0 & 0 & f & g \end{bmatrix}$$

This means that a product with any zero element will always be zero. Well, that seems obvious enough; but how can we tell if our matrices are sparse, and how can we rewrite the matrix multiply routine to take this into consideration? Let's begin with the first question relating to the determination of *sparsity*. The matrices we are going to be multiplying are translation and rotation. The translation matrix looks like this:

$$T = \begin{bmatrix} 1 & 0 & 0 & 0 \\ 0 & 1 & 0 & 0 \\ 0 & 0 & 1 & 0 \\ tx & ty & tz & 1 \end{bmatrix}$$

And the rotation matrices look like this:

$$R_x = \begin{bmatrix} 1 & 0 & 0 & 0 \\ 0 & \cos\theta & \sin\theta & 0 \\ 0 & -\sin\theta & \cos\theta & 0 \\ 0 & 0 & 0 & 1 \end{bmatrix}$$

$$R_y = \begin{bmatrix} \cos\theta & 0 & -\sin\theta & 0 \\ 0 & 1 & 0 & 0 \\ \sin\theta & 0 & \cos\theta & 0 \\ 0 & 0 & 0 & 1 \end{bmatrix}$$

$$R_z = \begin{bmatrix} \cos\theta & \sin\theta & 0 & 0 \\ -\sin\theta & \cos\theta & 0 & 0 \\ 0 & 0 & 1 & 0 \\ 0 & 0 & 0 & 1 \end{bmatrix}$$

If you sit and stare at these matrices and imagine multiplying them all out (worst case), you will realize that the fourth column is always:

$$\begin{bmatrix} 0 & 0 & 0 & 1 \end{bmatrix}^t$$

Therefore, the matrix multiplication can be optimized to take two factors into consideration:

Elements [0][3], [1][3], [2][3] always equal 0.
Element [3][3] always equals 1.

We can use this information to our advantage now by looking at the unrolled matrix multiply function, and everywhere we see elements [0][3], [1][3], and [2][3], we can deduce that the product is 0 and not needed. Furthermore, everywhere we see element [3][3], we can deduce that [3][3] can be replaced by 1. So our next and final 4x4 by 4x4 matrix multiply function is shown in Listing 17-4.

LISTING 17-4 *The final sparse-aware matrix multiply*

```
void Mat_Mul_4x4_4x4 (matrix_4x4 a,
                      matrix_4x4 b,
                      matrix_4x4 result)
```

continued on next page

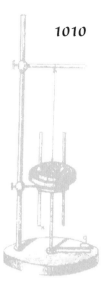

continued from previous page

```
{
// this function multiplies a 4x4 by a 4x4 and stores the result in a 4x4

// first row

result[0][0]=a[0][0]*b[0][0]+a[0][1]*b[1][0]+a[0][2]*b[2][0];
result[0][1]=a[0][0]*b[0][1]+a[0][1]*b[1][1]+a[0][2]*b[2][1];
result[0][2]=a[0][0]*b[0][2]+a[0][1]*b[1][2]+a[0][2]*b[2][2];
result[0][3]=0;  // can probably get rid of this too, it's always 0

// second row

result[1][0]=a[1][0]*b[0][0]+a[1][1]*b[1][0]+a[1][2]*b[2][0];
result[1][1]=a[1][0]*b[0][1]+a[1][1]*b[1][1]+a[1][2]*b[2][1];
result[1][2]=a[1][0]*b[0][2]+a[1][1]*b[1][2]+a[1][2]*b[2][2];
result[1][3]=0; // can probably get rid of this too, it's always 0

// third row

result[2][0]=a[2][0]*b[0][0]+a[2][1]*b[1][0]+a[2][2]*b[2][0];
result[2][1]=a[2][0]*b[0][1]+a[2][1]*b[1][1]+a[2][2]*b[2][1];
result[2][2]=a[2][0]*b[0][2]+a[2][1]*b[1][2]+a[2][2]*b[2][2];
result[2][3]=0; // can probably get rid of this too, it's always 0

// fourth row

result[3][0]=a[3][0]*b[0][0]+a[3][1]*b[1][0]+a[3][2]*b[2][0]+b[3][0];
result[3][1]=a[3][0]*b[0][1]+a[3][1]*b[1][1]+a[3][2]*b[2][1]+b[3][1];
result[3][2]=a[3][0]*b[0][2]+a[3][1]*b[1][2]+a[3][2]*b[2][2]+b[3][2];
result[3][3]=1; // can probably get rid of this too, it's always 0

} // end Mat_Mul_4x4_4x4
```

Cool, huh! We have reduced the number of multiplications from 64 to 36 and the number of additions from 48 to 27. We cut the math almost in half by simply noticing that all of our products and transform matrices have the last column equal to:

$$[0 \quad 0 \quad 0 \quad 1]^t$$

Can we do better? Yes and no. We could write matrix multiply functions that are optimized for certain inputs, but at this point it's not worth optimizing anymore. The only times we are going to multiply two or more 4x4 matrices is during the creation of the world to camera transformation matrix and the creation of the rotation matrix to rotate an object. Furthermore, the world to camera transformation matrix only needs to be created once per frame and the rotation matrix once per object. So I think we're OK.

I think we are going to stick to floating point calculation for most of the engine since, by the time this book is published, the 486DX should be common and the Pentium will have a large market, and both processors have very good floating point support. Hence, assuming that most of the matrix math is going to be done using *floats,* are there any other simple optimizations we can do to speed up the matrix operations? Yes, one of them is variable assignment.

Floating Point Data Assignments via Memory Movements

As I was trying to optimize the 3D engine and performing code profiling, I found that simple floating point assignments were slow. For example, I found that the code shown in Listing 17-5 to create an identity matrix was taking a bit of time.

LISTING 17-5 The 4x4 identity matrix function

```
void Mat_Identity_4x4(matrix_4x4 a)
{
// this function creates a 4x4 identity matrix

a[0][1] = a[0][2] = a[0][3] = 0;
a[1][0] = a[1][2] = a[1][3] = 0;
a[2][0] = a[2][1] = a[2][3] = 0;
a[3][0] = a[3][1] = a[3][2] = 0;

// set main diagonal to 1's

a[0][0] = a[1][1] = a[2][2] = a[3][3] = 1;

} // end Mat_Identity_4x4
```

The reason for this is that the compiler uses the floating point processor to convert the 0's into temporary reals and then assigns them to the array elements, which is slow. A better way to do this would be to simply fill the array memory with 0's. But there's a catch! Remember, floating point numbers are not in standard binary integer format, they are in IEEE format. This means that a 23 in binary looks nothing like a 23 in IEEE format. However, luckily for us, 0's do look the same in both formats. Therefore, if we perform a memory fill with binary 0's (4 for each float), we can place a 0 into a floating point value. Furthermore, since we know that 2D matrices in C are in *row-major* form, as shown in Figure 17-3, we can simply fill 64 bytes with 0's to zero out a matrix. Then to make the matrix and identity matrix, we simply place 1's into the main diagonal. This turns out to be almost twice as fast, so it's all good, baby! Listing 17-6 shows our new function to create a 4x4 identity matrix.

LISTING 17-6 Memory move-based identity matrix function

```
void Mat_Identity_4x4(matrix_4x4 a)
{
```

continued on next page

continued from previous page

```
// this function creates a 4x4 identity matrix

memset((void *)a,0,sizeof(float)*16);

// set main diagonal to 1's

a[0][0] = a[1][1] = a[2][2] = a[3][3] = 1;

} // end Mat_Identity_4x4
```

We could actually speed the function up another two times by using the *fword-cpy()* function. But I'll leave that to you. Remember, don't continue to optimize sections of code that aren't a major bottleneck. For example, making fast identity matrices is good, but we only need it a few times each frame. However, rotating points is done hundreds if not thousands of times per frame, so we should concentrate on that operation more. Get it? The theory of *diminishing returns* is in flux, especially in software optimization.

FIGURE 17-3

◎ ◎ ◎ ◎ ◎ ◎

Internal memory layout of a 2D array

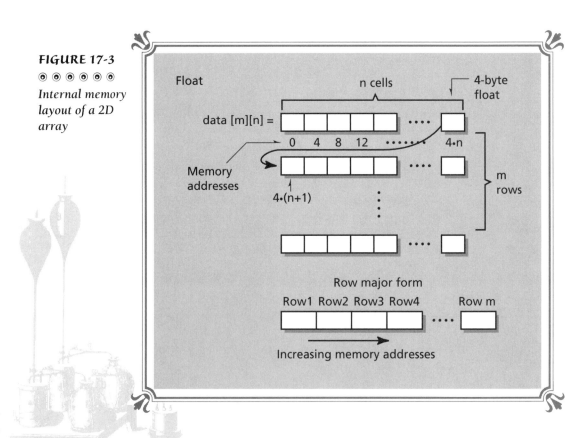

Minimizing the Degrees of Freedom

Now that we see how matrix multiplication can be optimized, let's see if we can totally remove matrix multiplication. Again, all we need to do is make a list of the times we must perform matrix multiplication.

❖ When preparing to rotate an object, the X, Y, and Z rotation matrices are concatenated—in essence performing 4x4 by 4x4 matrix multiplies.

❖ When rotating objects point by point, a 1x4 by 4x4 matrix multiplication is performed.

❖ When the world to camera transformation matrix is generated, the viewpoint along with the view angles are used to create a final concatenated transformation matrix from world coordinates to camera coordinates. Again, this is simply a series of 4x4 by 4x4 matrix multiplies.

❖ When each point of each object is transformed from world coordinates to camera coordinates using the global transformation matrix, 1x4 by 4x4 matrix multiplies are performed.

Based on the preceding material, we can deduce that there are only a few areas that we need to optimize. If we can make optimizations in these areas, the engine will be much faster since the above transformations are one of the largest 3D graphics engine bottlenecks. Hence, let's begin with the first two cases.

Faster Object Rotation

Basically, an object can be rotated in all axes simultaneously. That is, the *Rotate_Object()* function allows an X, Y, and Z rotation angle to be sent along with the object to be rotated. The function then proceeds to compute X, Y, and Z rotation matrices, concatenate them, and then multiply each vertex point of the object by the matrix. This is great, but it is a total waste of time. First off, most games only rotate an object on two axes at a time and sometimes even one. This means that there is no reason to perform a complete concatenation of

$$R' = R_x^{-1} * R_y^{-1} * R_z^{-1}$$

to arrive at a final rotation matrix. This is true, and we even took this into consideration in our current version of *Rotate_Object()*. If you recall, the function performs some conditional logic to determine what subset of matrices should be concatenated, and then the matrix is used to transform and rotate the object. For example, if the X rotation angle is 5, and the Y rotation angle is 13, but Z is equal to 0, the rotation matrix is computed with:

$$R' = R_x^{-1} * R_y^{-1}$$

However, this can be further optimized by realizing that the matrix multiplication can be precomputed! That's right, we can perform the matrix multiplication on paper and then simply create a matrix that has the right elements in the proper positions based on our results. Hence, we need to compute the product of $R_x^{-1} * R_y^{-1}$. This is a bit tedious, but worth it. Here's the calculation:

$$R_x^{-1} * R_y^{-1} = \begin{bmatrix} 1 & 0 & 0 & 0 \\ 0 & Cx & Sx & 0 \\ 0 & -Sx & Cx & 0 \\ 0 & 0 & 0 & 1 \end{bmatrix} * \begin{bmatrix} Cy & 0 & -Sy & 0 \\ 0 & 1 & 0 & 0 \\ Sy & 0 & Cy & 0 \\ 0 & 0 & 0 & 1 \end{bmatrix}$$

$$R' = \begin{bmatrix} Cy & 0 & -Sy & 0 \\ SxCy & Cx & CySx & 0 \\ CxSy & -Sx & CxCy & 0 \\ 0 & 0 & 0 & 1 \end{bmatrix}$$

Note: Cx stands for the COS of angle X, Cy stands for the COS of angle y, Sx stands for the SIN of angle X, and Sy stands for the SIN of angle y.

Now if we analyze R', there are many interesting things to note about it. First, there are only four products in it, namely $SxCy$, $CySx$, $CxSy$, and $CxCy$. Therefore, by manually performing the math, we have cut down our already optimized matrix multiplication operation from 36 multiplies to 4. Furthermore, there are no additions at all! That's pretty good. So all we need to do is create a matrix, place the values into the elements, and we're done. And to use the matrix, we perform the standard multiplication of each vertex of the object by the matrix like this:

$$\begin{bmatrix} x' & y' & z' & 1 \end{bmatrix} =$$

$$\begin{bmatrix} x & y & z & 1 \end{bmatrix} * \begin{bmatrix} Cy & 0 & -Sy & 0 \\ SxCy & Cx & CySx & 0 \\ CxSy & -Sx & CxCy & 0 \\ 0 & 0 & 0 & 1 \end{bmatrix}$$

Therefore:

$$x' = (x*Cy + y*(SxCy) + z*(CxSy))$$
$$y' = (x*0 + y*Cx - z*Sy)$$
$$z' = (-x*Sy + y*(CySx) + z*(CxCy))$$

Counting multiplications and additions, we arrive at 9 multiplies and 6 additions per vertex. That's not bad—but do you see the 0 that's multiplying x in the equation for y? We don't need it; therefore, here are the final rotation equations for rotations parallel to both the X and Y axes:

$$x'=(x*Cy+y*(SxCy)+z*(CxSy))$$
$$y'=(y*Cx-z*Sy)$$
$$z'=(-x*Sy+y*(CySx)+z*(CxCy))$$

We now have 8 multiplies and 5 additions per vertex. Not bad.

The same logic can be performed to compute all the single axis rotation cases and the remaining pairs. Hence, we should perform a similar analysis for:

✛ $R_x^{-1} * R_z^{-1}$

✛ $R_y^{-1} * R_z^{-1}$

✛ R_x^{-1}

✛ R_y^{-1}

✛ R_z^{-1}

✛ $R_x^{-1} * R_y^{-1} * R_z^{-1}$ (Note: this case is practically unoptimizable.)

Then, using the results, we can rewrite the object rotation function to really blaze—especially in the single axis rotation cases. Listing 17-7 shows the revised *Rotate_Object()* function.

LISTING 17-7 New and improved object rotation function

```
void Rotate_Object(object_ptr the_object,int angle_x,int angle_y,int angle_z)
{
// this function rotates an object relative to its own local coordinate system
// and allows simultaneous rotations

int index,        //  looping variable
    product=0;    // used to determine which matrices need multiplying

matrix_4x4 rotate_x,    // the x,y and z rotation matrices
           rotate_y,
           rotate_z,
           rotate,      // the final rotation matrix
           temp;        // temporary working matrix

float temp_x, // used to hold intermediate results during rotation
      temp_y,
      temp_z;

// test if we need to rotate at all

if (angle_x==0 && angle_y==0 && angle_z==0)
   return;

// create identity matrix

Mat_Identity_4x4(rotate);
```

continued on next page

continued from previous page

```
// figure out which axes are active

if (angle_x)
   product+=4;

if (angle_y)
   product+=2;

if (angle_z)
   product+=1;

// compute final rotation matrix and perform rotation all in one!

switch(product)
     {

     case 1: // final matrix = z
          {
          // set up matrix

          rotate[0][0] = ( cos_look[angle_z]);
          rotate[0][1] = ( sin_look[angle_z]);
          rotate[1][0] = (-sin_look[angle_z]);
          rotate[1][1] = ( cos_look[angle_z]);

          // matrix is of the form

          // | cos   sin  0    0 |
          // | -sin  cos  0    0 |
          // | 0     0    1    0 |
          // | 0     0    0    1 |

          // hence we can remove a number of multiplications during the
          // computations of x,y and z since many times each variable
          // isn't a function of the other two


          // perform rotation

          // now multiply each point in object by transformation matrix

          for (index=0; index<the_object->num_vertices; index++)
             {

             // x component

             temp_x = the_object->vertices_local[index].x * rotate[0][0] +
                      the_object->vertices_local[index].y * rotate[1][0];
                   // the_object->vertices_local[index].z * rotate[2][0];

             // y component
```

```
        temp_y = the_object->vertices_local[index].x * rotate[0][1] +
                 the_object->vertices_local[index].y * rotate[1][1];
                 // the_object->vertices_local[index].z * rotate[2][1];

        // z component

        temp_z =

                 the_object->vertices_local[index].z;

        // store rotated point back into local array

        the_object->vertices_local[index].x = temp_x;
        the_object->vertices_local[index].y = temp_y;
        the_object->vertices_local[index].z = temp_z;

        } // end for index


    } break;

case 2: // final matrix = y
    {

    rotate[0][0] = ( cos_look[angle_y]);
    rotate[0][2] = (-sin_look[angle_y]);
    rotate[2][0] = ( sin_look[angle_y]);
    rotate[2][2] = ( cos_look[angle_y]);

    // matrix is of the form

    // | cos   0    -sin   0 |
    // | 0     1     0     0 |
    // | sin   0     cos   0 |
    // | 0     0     0     1 |

    // hence we can remove a number of multiplications during the
    // computations of x,y and z since many times each variable
    // isn't a function of the other two


    // now multiply each point in object by transformation matrix

    for (index=0; index<the_object->num_vertices; index++)
        {

        // x component

        temp_x = the_object->vertices_local[index].x * rotate[0][0] +
                 // the_object->vertices_local[index].y * rotate[1][0] +
                 the_object->vertices_local[index].z * rotate[2][0];
```

continued on next page

continued from previous page

```
                    // y component

                    temp_y =
                            the_object->vertices_local[index].y;

                    // z component

                    temp_z = the_object->vertices_local[index].x * rotate[0][2] +
                            // the_object->vertices_local[index].y * rotate[1][2] +
                            the_object->vertices_local[index].z * rotate[2][2];

                    // store rotated point back into local array

                    the_object->vertices_local[index].x = temp_x;
                    the_object->vertices_local[index].y = temp_y;
                    the_object->vertices_local[index].z = temp_z;

                    } // end for index

                } break;

        case 3: // final matrix = y*z
                {

                // take advantage of the fact that the product of Ry*Rz is
                //
                // | (cos angy)*(cos angz)   (cos angy)*(sin angz)  -sin angy 0|
                // | -sin angz               cos angz                     0   0|
                // | (sin angy)*(cos angz)   (sin angy)*(sin angz)  cos angy  0|
                // | 0                       0                            0    1|

                // also notice the 0 in the 3rd column, we can use it to get
                // rid of one multiplication in the for loop below per point

                rotate[0][0] = cos_look[angle_y]*cos_look[angle_z];
                rotate[0][1] = cos_look[angle_y]*sin_look[angle_z];
                rotate[0][2] = -sin_look[angle_y];

                rotate[1][0] = -sin_look[angle_z];
                rotate[1][1] = cos_look[angle_z];

                rotate[2][0] = sin_look[angle_y]*cos_look[angle_z];
                rotate[2][1] = sin_look[angle_y]*sin_look[angle_z];
                rotate[2][2] = cos_look[angle_y];

                // now multiply each point in object by transformation matrix

                for (index=0; index<the_object->num_vertices; index++)
                    {

                    // x component
```

```
        temp_x = the_object->vertices_local[index].x * rotate[0][0] +
                 the_object->vertices_local[index].y * rotate[1][0] +
                 the_object->vertices_local[index].z * rotate[2][0];

        // y component

        temp_y = the_object->vertices_local[index].x * rotate[0][1] +
                 the_object->vertices_local[index].y * rotate[1][1] +
                 the_object->vertices_local[index].z * rotate[2][1];

        // z component

        temp_z = the_object->vertices_local[index].x * rotate[0][2] +
                 // the_object->vertices_local[index].y * rotate[1][2] +
                 the_object->vertices_local[index].z * rotate[2][2];

        // store rotated point back into local array

        the_object->vertices_local[index].x = temp_x;
        the_object->vertices_local[index].y = temp_y;
        the_object->vertices_local[index].z = temp_z;

        } // end for index

    } break;

case 4: // final matrix = x
    {

    rotate[1][1] = ( cos_look[angle_x]);
    rotate[1][2] = ( sin_look[angle_x]);
    rotate[2][1] = (-sin_look[angle_x]);
    rotate[2][2] = ( cos_look[angle_x]);

    // matrix is of the form

    // | 1     s    0     0 |
    // | 0     cos  sin   0 |
    // | 0     -sin cos   0 |
    // | 0     0    0     1 |

    // hence we can remove a number of multiplications during the
    // computations of x,y and z since many times each variable
    // isn't a function of the other two



    // now multiply each point in object by transformation matrix

    for (index=0; index<the_object->num_vertices; index++)
```

continued on next page

continued from previous page

```
                            {

                            // x component

                            temp_x =

                                    the_object->vertices_local[index].x;

                            // y component

                            temp_y = // the_object->vertices_local[index].x * rotate[0][1] +
                                    the_object->vertices_local[index].y * rotate[1][1] +
                                    the_object->vertices_local[index].z * rotate[2][1];

                            // z component

                            temp_z = // the_object->vertices_local[index].x * rotate[0][2] +
                                    the_object->vertices_local[index].y * rotate[1][2] +
                                    the_object->vertices_local[index].z * rotate[2][2];

                            // store rotated point back into local array

                            the_object->vertices_local[index].x = temp_x;
                            the_object->vertices_local[index].y = temp_y;
                            the_object->vertices_local[index].z = temp_z;

                            } // end for index

                    } break;

            case 5: // final matrix = x*z
                    {

                    // take advantage of the fact that the product of Rx*Rz is
                    //
                    // | cos angz                    sin angz                 0         0|
                    // | -(cos angx)*(sin angz)  (cos angx)*(cos angz)  sin angx  0|
                    // | (sin angx)*(sin angz)   -(sin angx)*(cos angz)  cos angx  0|
                    // | 0                           0                        0         1|

                    // also notice the 0 in the 3rd column, we can use it to get
                    // rid of one multiplication in the for loop below per point

                    rotate[0][0] = cos_look[angle_z];
                    rotate[0][1] = sin_look[angle_z];

                    rotate[1][0] = -cos_look[angle_x]*sin_look[angle_z];
                    rotate[1][1] = cos_look[angle_x]*cos_look[angle_z];
                    rotate[1][2] = sin_look[angle_x];

                    rotate[2][0] = sin_look[angle_x]*sin_look[angle_z];
                    rotate[2][1] = -sin_look[angle_x]*cos_look[angle_z];
```

```
        rotate[2][2] = cos_look[angle_x];

        // now multiply each point in object by transformation matrix

        for (index=0; index<the_object->num_vertices; index++)
            {

            // x component

            temp_x = the_object->vertices_local[index].x * rotate[0][0] +
                     the_object->vertices_local[index].y * rotate[1][0] +
                     the_object->vertices_local[index].z * rotate[2][0];

            // y component

            temp_y = the_object->vertices_local[index].x * rotate[0][1] +
                     the_object->vertices_local[index].y * rotate[1][1] +
                     the_object->vertices_local[index].z * rotate[2][1];

            // z component

            temp_z = // the_object->vertices_local[index].x * rotate[0][2] +
                     the_object->vertices_local[index].y * rotate[1][2] +
                     the_object->vertices_local[index].z * rotate[2][2];

            // store rotated point back into local array

            the_object->vertices_local[index].x = temp_x;
            the_object->vertices_local[index].y = temp_y;
            the_object->vertices_local[index].z = temp_z;

            } // end for index

        } break;

    case 6: // final matrix = x*y
        {

        // take advantage of the fact that the product of Rx*Ry is
        //
        // | cos angy               0            -sin angy            0|
        // | (sin angx)*(sin angy)  cos angx     (sin angx)*(cos angy) 0|
        // | (cos angx)*(sin angy)  -sin angx    (cos angx)*(cos angy) 0|
        // | 0                      0            0                    1|

        // also notice the 0 in the 2nd column, we can use it to get
        // rid of one multiplication in the for loop below per point

        rotate[0][0] = cos_look[angle_y];
        rotate[0][2] = -sin_look[angle_y];

        rotate[1][0] = sin_look[angle_x]*sin_look[angle_y];
        rotate[1][1] = cos_look[angle_x];
```

continued on next page

continued from previous page

```
            rotate[1][2] = sin_look[angle_x]*cos_look[angle_y];

            rotate[2][0] = cos_look[angle_x]*sin_look[angle_y];
            rotate[2][1] = -sin_look[angle_x];
            rotate[2][2] = cos_look[angle_x]*cos_look[angle_y];

            // now multiply each point in object by transformation matrix

            for (index=0; index<the_object->num_vertices; index++)
                {

                // x component

                temp_x = the_object->vertices_local[index].x * rotate[0][0] +
                         the_object->vertices_local[index].y * rotate[1][0] +
                         the_object->vertices_local[index].z * rotate[2][0];

                // y component

                temp_y = // the_object->vertices_local[index].x * rotate[0][1] +
                         the_object->vertices_local[index].y * rotate[1][1] +
                         the_object->vertices_local[index].z * rotate[2][1];

                // z component

                temp_z = the_object->vertices_local[index].x * rotate[0][2] +
                         the_object->vertices_local[index].y * rotate[1][2] +
                         the_object->vertices_local[index].z * rotate[2][2];

                // store rotated point back into local array

                the_object->vertices_local[index].x = temp_x;
                the_object->vertices_local[index].y = temp_y;
                the_object->vertices_local[index].z = temp_z;

                } // end for index

            } break;

    case 7: // final matrix = x*y*z, do it the hard way
            {
            Mat_Identity_4x4(rotate_x);

            rotate_x[1][1] = ( cos_look[angle_x]);
            rotate_x[1][2] = ( sin_look[angle_x]);
            rotate_x[2][1] = (-sin_look[angle_x]);
            rotate_x[2][2] = ( cos_look[angle_x]);

            Mat_Identity_4x4(rotate_y);

            rotate_y[0][0] = ( cos_look[angle_y]);
            rotate_y[0][2] = (-sin_look[angle_y]);
            rotate_y[2][0] = ( sin_look[angle_y]);
```

```
            rotate_y[2][2] = ( cos_look[angle_y]);

            Mat_Identity_4x4(rotate_z);

            rotate_z[0][0] = ( cos_look[angle_z]);
            rotate_z[0][1] = ( sin_look[angle_z]);
            rotate_z[1][0] = (-sin_look[angle_z]);
            rotate_z[1][1] = ( cos_look[angle_z]);

            Mat_Mul_4x4_4x4(rotate_x,rotate_y,temp);
            Mat_Mul_4x4_4x4(temp,rotate_z,rotate);

            // now multiply each point in object by transformation matrix

            for (index=0; index<the_object->num_vertices; index++)
                {

                // x component

                temp_x = the_object->vertices_local[index].x * rotate[0][0] +
                         the_object->vertices_local[index].y * rotate[1][0] +
                         the_object->vertices_local[index].z * rotate[2][0];

                // y component

                temp_y = the_object->vertices_local[index].x * rotate[0][1] +
                         the_object->vertices_local[index].y * rotate[1][1] +
                         the_object->vertices_local[index].z * rotate[2][1];

                // z component

                temp_z = the_object->vertices_local[index].x * rotate[0][2] +
                         the_object->vertices_local[index].y * rotate[1][2] +
                         the_object->vertices_local[index].z * rotate[2][2];

                // store rotated point back into local array

                the_object->vertices_local[index].x = temp_x;
                the_object->vertices_local[index].y = temp_y;
                the_object->vertices_local[index].z = temp_z;

                } // end for index

            } break;

        default:break;

        } // end switch

} // end Rotate_Object
```

The function is quite long, and it special-cases everything it can for speed. The result is a rotation function that can be an order of magnitude faster than our previous one for certain cases and at least twice as fast for most cases. Notice that the interface to the function is the same. This is very important. We should always try to change the inside of the function and leave the interface alone.

Speeding Up the World to Camera Transformation

The next thing that we want to optimize is the world to camera transformation. This is really a two-part optimization. First, we would like to speed up the creation of the global world to camera transformation matrix and then speed up the actual multiplication of each object's world coordinates by the matrix. Let's begin with the global world to camera transformation matrix.

The current world to camera transformation matrix function simply generates the inverses of the player's translation matrix and viewpoint rotation matrices. This results in a total of 3 matrix multiplies and a total of 3*64=192 multiplications and 3*48=144 additions with our old matrix multiplier, and 3*36=108 multiplications and 3*27=81 additions with our new matrix multiplier. Either way you look at it, there are too many multiplications and additions going on!

To eliminate these operations, we're going to do the same thing we did with the rotation function—that is, figure out all the possible products of matrices, multiply them manually, and create a set of special cases in the code. So let's take a look at what we're dealing with as far as computing the global world to camera transformation matrix products. There are quite a few cases that we must figure out since there can be translation and rotation on all three axes. However, to minimize the number of cases a bit, we are always going to take translation into consideration, since it's doubtful that the viewpoint will remain at (0,0,0) for very long. Here are the possible situations:

Case 1: Translation only: T^{-1} (no matrix multiplication needed)
Case 2: Translation and X rotation: $T^{-1}*R_x^{-1}$ (1 matrix multiply)
Case 3: Translation and Y rotation: $T^{-1}*R_y^{-1}$ (1 matrix multiply)
Case 4: Translation and Z rotation: $T^{-1}*R_z^{-1}$ (1 matrix multiply)
Case 5: Translation and X,Y rotation: $T^{-1}*R_x^{-1}*R_y^{-1}$ (2 matrix multiplies)
Case 6: Translation and X,Z rotation: $T^{-1}*R_x^{-1}*R_z^{-1}$ (2 matrix multiplies)
Case 7: Translation and Y,Z rotation: $T^{-1}*R_y^{-1}*R_z^{-1}$ (2 matrix multiplies)
Case 8: Translation and X,Y,Z rotation: $T^{-1}*R_x^{-1}*R_y^{-1}*R_z^{-1}$ (3 matrix multiplies)

So here's the plan: cases 1 through 4 are the most common in the game we are going to create in Chapter 18, so we are only going to manually multiply these cases. The remaining cases (5 through 8) are left as an exercise to you.

Alrighty then, let's take a look at what we would do to compute cases 2 and 3. We simply need to multiply out the player's inverse translation matrix and rotation

matrix. Let's use case 3 as an example, since the game in Chapter 18 is predominant-
ly a ground-based game and the player will mostly be turning right or left—that is,
parallel to the Y axis. Given that the player's viewpoint is located at (tx,ty,tz) with
view angles (θx,θy,θz), the product of the inverse matrices $T^{-1}*R_y^{-1}$ looks like this:

$$T^{-1} * R_y^{-1} =$$

$$\begin{bmatrix} 1 & 0 & 0 & 0 \\ 0 & 1 & 0 & 0 \\ 0 & 0 & 1 & 0 \\ -Tx & -Ty & -Tz & 1 \end{bmatrix} * \begin{bmatrix} \text{Cos } \theta y & 0 & \text{Sin } \theta y & 0 \\ 0 & 1 & 0 & 0 \\ -\text{Sin } \theta y & 1 & \text{Cos } \theta y & 0 \\ 0 & 0 & 0 & 1 \end{bmatrix}$$

$$\begin{bmatrix} \text{Cos } \theta y & 0 & \text{Sin } \theta y & 0 \\ 0 & 1 & 0 & 0 \\ -\text{Sin } \theta y & 0 & \text{Cos } \theta y & 0 \\ (tx*\text{Cos } \theta y + tz*\text{Sin } \theta y) & (-ty) & (-tx*\text{Sin } \theta y - tz*\text{Cos } \theta y) & 1 \end{bmatrix}$$

Therefore, we only need to perform 4 multiplications and 2 additions to find the
world to camera transformation matrix! Of course, this will get about three times
worse when we try to figure out the results of something like $T^{-1}*R_x^{-1}*R_y^{-1}$; but even
then, there will be less than a dozen multiplications and additions in comparison to
the worst case of 108 multiplications and 81 additions, so we are doing pretty well.

Once a similar analysis has been performed for each of the cases, further optimization can be performed by realizing that the product of a single vertex,

$$\begin{bmatrix} x & y & z & 1 \end{bmatrix}$$

and the preceding matrix has a lot of zeros; that is, the preceding matrix and the
others relating to X and Z rotation are fairly sparse. Hence, the final vertex point
transformation loop that uses the global transformation matrix need only have 4
multiplications and 5 additions. As an example, let's replace the elements of the
preceding matrix with dummy variables to simplify the example and then multiply
a generic point with the matrix and discuss the form of the result.

$$\begin{bmatrix} x & y & z & 1 \end{bmatrix} * \begin{bmatrix} C & 0 & S & 0 \\ 0 & 1 & 0 & 0 \\ -S & 0 & C & 0 \\ a & b & c & 1 \end{bmatrix}$$

$$=$$

$$x' = x*C - z*S + a$$
$$y' = y + b$$
$$z' = x*S + z*C + c$$

As you can see, we have not only cut the matrix multiplication totally out of the creation of the world to camera transformation matrix, we have cut the per point calculations down to half! Not bad, huh? Using all the nifty tricks we just learned, Listing 17-8 is a new version of the function that creates the world to camera transformation.

LISTING 17-8 New world to camera transformation function

```
void Create_World_To_Camera(void)
{
// this function creates the global inverse transformation matrix
// used to transform world coordinates to camera coordinates

matrix_4x4 translate,    // the translation matrix

            rotate_x,    // the x,y and z rotation matrices
            rotate_y,
            rotate_z,
            result_1,
            result_2;

int active_axes=0;

// create identity matrices

Mat_Identity_4x4(translate);

// make a translation matrix based on the inverse of the viewpoint

translate[3][0] = -view_point.x;
translate[3][1] = -view_point.y;
translate[3][2] = -view_point.z;

// test if there is any X rotation in view angles

if (view_angle.ang_x)
   {
   Mat_Identity_4x4(rotate_x);

   // x matrix

   rotate_x[1][1] =  ( cos_look[view_angle.ang_x]);
   rotate_x[1][2] = -( sin_look[view_angle.ang_x]);
   rotate_x[2][1] = -(-sin_look[view_angle.ang_x]);
   rotate_x[2][2] =  ( cos_look[view_angle.ang_x]);

   active_axes += 1;

   } // end if

if (view_angle.ang_y)
```

```
         {
         Mat_Identity_4x4(rotate_y);

         // y matrix

         rotate_y[0][0] =  ( cos_look[view_angle.ang_y]);
         rotate_y[0][2] = -(-sin_look[view_angle.ang_y]);
         rotate_y[2][0] = -( sin_look[view_angle.ang_y]);
         rotate_y[2][2] =  ( cos_look[view_angle.ang_y]);

         active_axes += 2;

         } // end if


     if (view_angle.ang_z)
         {
         Mat_Identity_4x4(rotate_z);

         // z matrix

         rotate_z[0][0] =  ( cos_look[view_angle.ang_z]);
         rotate_z[0][1] = -( sin_look[view_angle.ang_z]);
         rotate_z[1][0] = -(-sin_look[view_angle.ang_z]);
         rotate_z[1][1] =  ( cos_look[view_angle.ang_z]);

         active_axes += 4;

         } // end if

     // multiply all the matrices together to obtain a final world to camera
     // viewing transformation matrix i.e.
     // translation * rotate_x * rotate_y * rotate_z, however, only, multiply
     // matrices that can possibly add to the final view

     switch(active_axes)
         {

         case 0: // translation only
             {
             Mat_Copy_4x4(translate,global_view);
             } break;

         case 1: // translation and X axis
             {
             // since only a single axis is active manually set up the matrix

             // Mat_Mul_4x4_4x4(translate,rotate_x,global_view);

             // manually create matrix using knowledge that final product is
             // of the form
```

continued on next page

continued from previous page

```
// | 1              0             0            0|
// | 0              c            -s            0|
// | 0              s             c            0|
// |(-tx)          (-ty*c-tz*s) (ty*s-tz*c)   1|

Mat_Copy_4x4(rotate_x,global_view);

// now copy last row into global_view


global_view[3][0] = (-view_point.x);

global_view[3][1] = (-view_point.y*cos_look[view_angle.ang_y] -
                      view_point.z*sin_look[view_angle.ang_y]);

global_view[3][2] = (view_point.y*sin_look[view_angle.ang_y] -
                      view_point.z*cos_look[view_angle.ang_y]);


} break;


case 2: // translation and Y axis
    {
    // Mat_Mul_4x4_4x4(translate,rotate_y,global_view);

    // manually create matrix using knowledge that final product is
    // of the form

    // | c              0             s            0|
    // | 0              1             0            0|
    // | -s             0             c            0|
    // |(tx*c+tz*s) (-ty)        (-tx*s-tz*c) 1|

    Mat_Copy_4x4(rotate_y,global_view);

    // now copy last row into global_view

    global_view[3][0] = (-view_point.x*cos_look[view_angle.ang_y] +
                          view_point.z*sin_look[view_angle.ang_y]);

    global_view[3][1] = (-view_point.y);

    global_view[3][2] = (-view_point.x*sin_look[view_angle.ang_y] -
                          view_point.z*cos_look[view_angle.ang_y]);


    } break;


case 3: // translation and X and Y
    {
```

```
        Mat_Mul_4x4_4x4(translate,rotate_x,result_1);
        Mat_Mul_4x4_4x4(result_1,rotate_y,global_view);
        } break;

    case 4: // translation and Z
        {
         // Mat_Mul_4x4_4x4(translate,rotate_z,global_view);

        // manually create matrix using knowledge that final product is
        // of the form

        // | c                -s              0             0|
        // | s                 c              0             0|
        // | 0                 s              c             0|
        // |(-tx*c-ty*s)  (tx*s-ty*c)   (-tz)          1|

        Mat_Copy_4x4(rotate_z,global_view);

        // now copy last row into global_view

        global_view[3][0] = (-view_point.x*cos_look[view_angle.ang_z] -
                            view_point.y*sin_look[view_angle.ang_z]);

        global_view[3][1] = (view_point.x*sin_look[view_angle.ang_z] -
                            view_point.y*cos_look[view_angle.ang_z]);

        global_view[3][2] = (-view_point.z);

        } break;


    case 5: // translation and X and Z
        {
        Mat_Mul_4x4_4x4(translate,rotate_x,result_1);
        Mat_Mul_4x4_4x4(result_1,rotate_z,global_view);
        } break;

    case 6: // translation and Y and Z
        {
        Mat_Mul_4x4_4x4(translate,rotate_y,result_1);
        Mat_Mul_4x4_4x4(result_1,rotate_z,global_view);
        } break;

    case 7: // translation and X and Y and Z

        {

        Mat_Mul_4x4_4x4(translate,rotate_x,result_1);
        Mat_Mul_4x4_4x4(result_1,rotate_y,result_2);
```

continued on next page

continued from previous page

```
                Mat_Mul_4x4_4x4(result_2,rotate_z,global_view);

            } break;

        default:break;

        } // end switch

} // end Create_World_To_Camera
```

To speed up the function even more, try using the same technique on cases 3, 5, 6, and 7.

Now, once we have the world to camera transformation matrix built, we will want to transform all the points of the objects. Therefore, Listing 17-9 shows the optimized *World_To_Camera_Object()* function.

LISTING 17-9 New, optimized world to camera transformation function

```
void World_To_Camera_Object(object_ptr the_object)
{
// this function converts an object's world coordinates to camera coordinates
// by multiplying each point of the object by the inverse viewing transformation
// matrix which is generated by concatenating the inverse of the view position
// and the view angles the result of which is in global_view

int index; // looping variable

int active_axes = 0;

if (view_angle.ang_x)
    active_axes+=1;

if (view_angle.ang_y)
    active_axes+=2;

if (view_angle.ang_z)
    active_axes+=4;

// based on active angles only compute what's neccessary

switch(active_axes)
    {
    case 0:    // T-1
        {

            for (index=0; index<=the_object->num_vertices; index++)
                {
                // multiply the point by the viewing transformation matrix
```

```
                // x component

                the_object->vertices_camera[index].x =

                            the_object->vertices_world[index].x +
                                                    global_view[3][0];
                // y component

                the_object->vertices_camera[index].y =

                            the_object->vertices_world[index].y +
                                                    global_view[3][1];
                // z component

                the_object->vertices_camera[index].z =

                            the_object->vertices_world[index].z +
                                                    global_view[3][2];
                } // end for index

            } break;

        case 1:    // T-1 * Rx-1
            {
            for (index=0; index<=the_object->num_vertices; index++)
                {
                // multiply the point by the viewing transformation matrix
                // x component

                the_object->vertices_camera[index].x =

                            the_object->vertices_world[index].x +
                                                    global_view[3][0];
                // y component

                the_object->vertices_camera[index].y =

                            the_object->vertices_world[index].y *
                                                    global_view[1][1] +
                            the_object->vertices_world[index].z *
                                                    global_view[2][1] +
                                                    global_view[3][1];
                // z component

                the_object->vertices_camera[index].z =

                            the_object->vertices_world[index].y *
                                                    global_view[1][2] +
                            the_object->vertices_world[index].z *
                                                    global_view[2][2] +
                                                    global_view[3][2];
                } // end for index
```

continued on next page

continued from previous page

```
                } break;

        case 2:  // T-1 * Ry-1 , this is the standard rotation in a plane
                {

                for (index=0; index<=the_object->num_vertices; index++)
                    {
                    // multiply the point by the viewing transformation matrix

                    // x component
                    the_object->vertices_camera[index].x =

                                    the_object->vertices_world[index].x *
                                                    global_view[0][0] +
                                    the_object->vertices_world[index].z *
                                                    global_view[2][0] +
                                                    global_view[3][0];
                    // y component
                    the_object->vertices_camera[index].y =

                                    the_object->vertices_world[index].y +
                                                    global_view[3][1];
                    // z component
                    the_object->vertices_camera[index].z =

                                    the_object->vertices_world[index].x *
                                                    global_view[0][2] +
                                    the_object->vertices_world[index].z *
                                                    global_view[2][2] +
                                                    global_view[3][2];
                    } // end for index



                } break;

        case 4:   // T-1 * Rz-1
                {

                for (index=0; index<=the_object->num_vertices; index++)
                    {
                    // multiply the point by the viewing transformation matrix

                    // x component

                    the_object->vertices_camera[index].x =

                                    the_object->vertices_world[index].x *
                                                    global_view[0][0] +
                                    the_object->vertices_world[index].y *
                                                    global_view[1][0] +
                                                    global_view[3][0];
                    // y component
```

```
            the_object->vertices_camera[index].y =

                        the_object->vertices_world[index].x *
                                                global_view[0][1] +
                        the_object->vertices_world[index].y *
                                                global_view[1][1] +
                                                global_view[3][1];
            // z component

            the_object->vertices_camera[index].z =

                        the_object->vertices_world[index].z +
                                                global_view[3][2];
            } // end for index


        } break;


    // these can all be optimized by pre-computing the form of the world
    // to camera matrix and using the same logic as the cases above

    case 3:  // T-1 * Rx-1 * Ry-1
    case 5:  // T-1 * Rx-1 * Rz-1
    case 6:  // T-1 * Ry-1 * Rz-1
    case 7:  // T-1 * Rx-1 * Ry-1 * Rz-1
        {

        for (index=0; index<=the_object->num_vertices; index++)
            {
            // multiply the point by the viewing transformation matrix

            // x component

            the_object->vertices_camera[index].x =

                        the_object->vertices_world[index].x *
                                                global_view[0][0] +
                        the_object->vertices_world[index].y *
                                                global_view[1][0] +
                        the_object->vertices_world[index].z *
                                                global_view[2][0] +
                                                global_view[3][0];
            // y component

            the_object->vertices_camera[index].y =

                        the_object->vertices_world[index].x *
                                                global_view[0][1] +
                        the_object->vertices_world[index].y *
                                                global_view[1][1] +
                        the_object->vertices_world[index].z *
                                                global_view[2][1] +
```

continued on next page

continued from previous page

```
                                                          global_view[3][1];
            // z component

            the_object->vertices_camera[index].z =

                        the_object->vertices_world[index].x *
                                          global_view[0][2] +
                        the_object->vertices_world[index].y *
                                          global_view[1][2] +
                        the_object->vertices_world[index].z *
                                          global_view[2][2] +
                                          global_view[3][2];

            } // end for index


            } break;

        default: break;

        } // end switch

} // end World_To_Camera_Object
```

You will notice that I am leaving out all the cases of optimization. There are two reasons for this: I want you to do some yourself, and I am making optimizations based on what we'll need for the final game. Actually, when we finally write the game, we may make further optimizations, but we should wait because they may be so game-specific that the engine will be useless for anything else. However, all the optimizations in this chapter will be totally transparent; the engine will simply work faster but will still have all the generality that it did before we started optimizing.

Now let's move on to another step of the graphics engine that is fairly hard to optimize: the 3D clipper.

Clipping Time from the 3D Clipper

As I said before, we don't want to waste too much time on optimizations that aren't going to give us big gains. In the context of a 3D engine, this means that any operation that is performed on each vertex should definitely be scrutinized (optimizations of the first kind), operations done on a per object basis should be looked at (optimizations of the second kind), and finally, operations that occur once a frame should be cleaned up if possible (optimizations of the third kind). The 3D clipping operation is definitely an optimization of the first kind, so let's see if we can speed it up.

If you take a look in BLACK11.C and review the *Clip_Object_3D()* function, you will find that, all in all, it's fairly clean. There are no overwhelmingly obvious optimizations that can be done. About all we can hope for is maybe to remove a couple of multiplications per vertex and rewrite some of the logic to make it faster, perhaps by using negative logic. Upon inspecting the following code fragment, it turns out that we can indeed remove some multiplications.

```
x1_compare = (HALF_SCREEN_WIDTH*z1)/viewing_distance;
x2_compare = (HALF_SCREEN_WIDTH*z2)/viewing_distance;
x3_compare = (HALF_SCREEN_WIDTH*z3)/viewing_distance;
x4_compare = (HALF_SCREEN_WIDTH*z4)/viewing_distance;
```

Since *HALF_SCREEN_WIDTH* is a constant and *viewing_distance* will definitely stay constant on a frame-by-frame basis, we can compute a new constant that is equal to:

```
fov_width = HALF_SCREEN_WIDTH/viewing_distance;
```

Then we can simply perform one multiplication per vertex instead of a multiplication and a division (probably equal to 2 multiplications). The same technique can be used on the Y-axis compares to yield a similar result. Therefore, taking both of these simple optimizations into account, we can remove 4 multiplications per polygon and totally remove the division (which is very slow). As far as optimizing the conditional logic and the data structure access, we can probably speed it up by 10 percent, but it's really not worth our time since we have already made our best gains by pre-multiplying to compute the constants in the computation of the X and Y compare values. Anyway, to be complete, the Y compare value's new constant would be equal to:

```
fov_height = HALF_SCREEN_HEIGHT/viewing_distance;
```

Hence, our new function should compute these values during its entrance and then use them during the main vertex transformation and test loop. Listing 17-10 shows the *Clip_Object_3D()* function with the new optimizations.

LISTING 17-10 New clipping function that uses pre-multiplication to speed things up

```
void Clip_Object_3D(object_ptr the_object, int mode)
{
// this function clips an object in camera coordinates against the 3D viewing
// volume. the function has two modes of operation. In CLIP_Z_MODE the
// function performs only a simple z extend clip with the near and far clipping
// planes. In CLIP_XYZ_MODE mode the function performs a full 3D clip

int curr_poly;    // the current polygon being processed

float x1,y1,z1,
      x2,y2,z2,
      x3,y3,z3,
      x4,y4,z4,    // working variables used to hold vertices
```

continued on next page

continued from previous page

```
            x1_compare, // used to hold clipping points on x and y
            y1_compare,
            x2_compare,
            y2_compare,
            x3_compare,
            y3_compare,
            x4_compare,
            y4_compare,
            fov_width,  // width and height of projected viewing plane
            fov_height; // used to speed up computations, since it's constant
                        // for any frame


// test if trivial z clipping is being requested

if (mode==CLIP_Z_MODE)
   {
   // attempt to clip each polygon against viewing volume

   for (curr_poly=0; curr_poly<the_object->num_polys; curr_poly++)
      {

      // extract z components

      z1=the_object->vertices_camera[the_object->polys[curr_poly].vertex_list[0]].z;
      z2=the_object->vertices_camera[the_object->polys[curr_poly].vertex_list[1]].z;
      z3=the_object->vertices_camera[the_object->polys[curr_poly].vertex_list[2]].z;

      // test if this is a quad

      if (the_object->polys[curr_poly].num_points==4)
         {
         // extract 4th z component

         z4=the_object->vertices_camera[the_object->polys[curr_poly].vertex_list[3]].z;

         } // end if quad
      else
        z4=z3;

      // perform near and far z clipping test

      if ( (z1<clip_near_z && z2<clip_near_z && z3<clip_near_z && z4<clip_near_z) ||
           (z1>clip_far_z && z2>clip_far_z && z3>clip_far_z && z4>clip_far_z) )
         {
         // set clipped flag

         the_object->polys[curr_poly].clipped=1;

         } // end if clipped

      } // end for curr_poly
```

```
        } // end if CLIP_Z_MODE
else
    {
    // CLIP_XYZ_MODE, perform full 3D viewing volume clip

    // compute dimensions of clipping extents at current viewing distance

    fov_width  = ((float)HALF_SCREEN_WIDTH/viewing_distance);
    fov_height = ((float)HALF_SCREEN_HEIGHT/viewing_distance);

    // process each polygon

    for (curr_poly=0; curr_poly<the_object->num_polys; curr_poly++)
        {

        // extract x,y and z components

        x1=the_object->vertices_camera[the_object->polys[curr_poly].vertex_list[0]].x;
        y1=the_object->vertices_camera[the_object->polys[curr_poly].vertex_list[0]].y;
        z1=the_object->vertices_camera[the_object->polys[curr_poly].vertex_list[0]].z;

        x2=the_object->vertices_camera[the_object->polys[curr_poly].vertex_list[1]].x;
        y2=the_object->vertices_camera[the_object->polys[curr_poly].vertex_list[1]].y;
        z2=the_object->vertices_camera[the_object->polys[curr_poly].vertex_list[1]].z;

        x3=the_object->vertices_camera[the_object->polys[curr_poly].vertex_list[2]].x;
        y3=the_object->vertices_camera[the_object->polys[curr_poly].vertex_list[2]].y;
        z3=the_object->vertices_camera[the_object->polys[curr_poly].vertex_list[2]].z;

        // test if this is a quad

        if (the_object->polys[curr_poly].num_points==4)
            {
            // extract 4th vertex

            x4=the_object->vertices_camera[the_object->polys[curr_poly].vertex_list[3]].x;
            y4=the_object->vertices_camera[the_object->polys[curr_poly].vertex_list[3]].y;
            z4=the_object->vertices_camera[the_object->polys[curr_poly].vertex_list[3]].z;

            // do clipping tests

            // perform near and far z clipping test first

            if (!((z1>clip_near_z || z2>clip_near_z || z3>clip_near_z || z4>clip_near_z) &&
                (z1<clip_far_z || z2<clip_far_z || z3<clip_far_z || z4<clip_far_z)) )
                {
                // set clipped flag

                the_object->polys[curr_poly].clipped=1;
                continue;

                } // end if clipped
```

continued on next page

continued from previous page

```
                   // pre-compute x comparison ranges

                   x1_compare = fov_width*z1;
                   x2_compare = fov_width*z2;
                   x3_compare = fov_width*z3;
                   x4_compare = fov_width*z4;

                   // perform x test

                   if (!((x1>-x1_compare || x2>-x1_compare || x3>-x3_compare || x4>-x4_compare) &&
                       (x1<x1_compare || x2<x2_compare || x3<x3_compare x4>-x4_compare))  )
                      {
                      // set clipped flag

                      the_object->polys[curr_poly].clipped=1;
                      continue;

                      } // end if clipped

                   // pre-compute x comparison ranges

                   y1_compare = fov_height*z1;
                   y2_compare = fov_height*z2;
                   y3_compare = fov_height*z3;
                   y4_compare = fov_height*z4;

                   // perform x test

                   if (!((y1>-y1_compare || y2>-y1_compare || y3>-y3_compare || y4>-y4_compare) &&
                       (y1<y1_compare || y2<y2_compare || y3<y3_compare || y4<y4_compare))  )
                      {
                      // set clipped flag

                      the_object->polys[curr_poly].clipped=1;
                      continue;

                      } // end if clipped

                   } // end if quad
                else
                   {
                   // must be triangle, perform clipping tests on only 3 vertices

                   // do clipping tests

                   // perform near and far z clipping test first

                   if (!((z1>clip_near_z || z2>clip_near_z || z3>clip_near_z) &&
                       (z1<clip_far_z || z2<clip_far_z || z3<clip_far_z))  )
                      {
                      // set clipped flag
```

```
            the_object->polys[curr_poly].clipped=1;
            continue;

            } // end if clipped

        // pre-compute x comparison ranges

        x1_compare = fov_width*z1;
        x2_compare = fov_width*z2;
        x3_compare = fov_width*z3;

        // perform x test

        if (!(((x1>-x1_compare || x2>-x1_compare || x3>-x3_compare ) &&
              (x1<x1_compare || x2<x2_compare || x3<x3_compare ))   )
            {
            // set clipped flag

            the_object->polys[curr_poly].clipped=1;
            continue;

            } // end if clipped

        // pre-compute x comparison ranges

        y1_compare = fov_height*z1;
(HALF_SCREEN_HEIGHT*z1)/viewing_distance;
        y2_compare = fov_height*z2;
(HALF_SCREEN_HEIGHT*z2)/viewing_distance;
        y3_compare = fov_height*z3;
(HALF_SCREEN_HEIGHT*z3)/viewing_distance;

        // perform x test

        if (!(((y1>-y1_compare || y2>-y1_compare || y3>-y3_compare) &&
              (y1<y1_compare || y2<y2_compare || y3<y3_compare ))   )
            {
            // set clipped flag

            the_object->polys[curr_poly].clipped=1;
            continue;

            } // end if clipped

        } // end else triangle

    } // end for curr_poly

  } // end else clip everything

} // end Clip_Object_3D
```

The next optimization we're going to make is to the Z depth sorter. It's not an obvious one, but nonetheless works well.

A Faster Z-Sort

I was almost finished optimizing the whole engine and had been concentrating so much on the rendering aspect of the engine that I was neglecting other areas. But luckily I caught myself, because I'm sure you would have seen this one if I hadn't. Here it is: we have been using a Z depth sort to order the polygons to be rendered each frame, and the comparison function we have written compares a pair of polygons by averaging their Z values. This is all fine and dandy, but there might be a total of n^2 comparisons using Quick Sort even though the average is $n*\log_2 n$. What this means is that it is very probable that many polygons are going to get tested more than once against other polygons, and hence, the average Z values are going to be computed many times!

How can we eliminate this step? Well, we can't totally get rid of the computation of average Z; but we should be able to precompute the average Z values, place them somewhere, and rewrite the comparison function to look at the precomputed values instead of computing average Z values on the fly. So what we're going to do is add a field to the polygon structure to hold the average Z value; then we'll write a function that takes the polygon list, computes the average Z of each polygon, and assigns the average Z field of each polygon. Then our new Z depth-sorting routine will make two calls: one to the average Z precomputation functions followed by the actual sort. Figure 17-4 shows this new setup graphically (it's been a while since we had a picture).

Before we write the function to precompute the average Z value of all the polygons in the polygon list, let's take a look at the new polygon facet structure (I've highlighted the new field):

```
// this structure holds a final polygon facet and is self contained

typedef struct facet_typ
        {
        int num_points;  // number of vertices
        int color;       // color of polygon
        int shade;       // the final shade of color after lighting
        int shading;     // type of shading to use
        int two_sided;   // is the facet two sided
        int visible;     // is the facet transparent
        int clipped;     // has this poly been clipped
        int active;      // used to turn faces on and off

        point_3d vertex_list[MAX_POINTS_PER_POLY]; // the points that make
                                                   // up the polygon facet
```

```
float normal_length;   // holds pre-computed length of normal
int average_z;         // holds average z, used in sorting

} facet, *facet_ptr;
```

Now let's see the new function to compute the average Z values of all the polygons in the polygon list. Listing 17-11 shows the code.

FIGURE 17-4

⊚ ⊚ ⊚ ⊚ ⊚ ⊚

New Z-sorting scheme

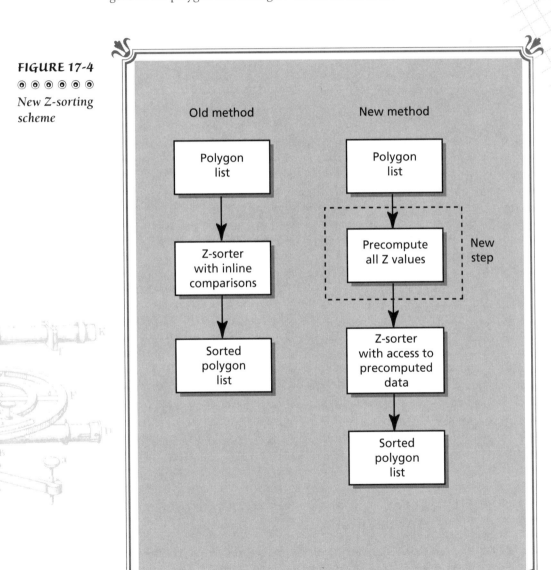

LISTING 17-11 Function to precompute the average Z value of each polygon

```
void Compute_Average_Z(void)
{
// this function pre-computes the average z of each polygon, so that the
// polygon sorter doesn't compute each z more than once

int index;

for (index=0; index<num_polys_frame; index++)
    {

    if (world_poly_storage[index].num_points==3)
        {
        world_poly_storage[index].average_z =

                (int)(0.3333*(world_poly_storage[index].vertex_list[0].z+
                             world_poly_storage[index].vertex_list[1].z+
                             world_poly_storage[index].vertex_list[2].z));

        } // end if
    else
        {
        world_poly_storage[index].average_z =

                    (int)(0.25*(world_poly_storage[index].vertex_list[0].z+
                               world_poly_storage[index].vertex_list[1].z+
                               world_poly_storage[index].vertex_list[2].z+
                               world_poly_storage[index].vertex_list[3].z));

        } // end if

    } // end for index

} // end Compute_Average_Z
```

As you can see, it's nothing more than the core code from the comparison function enclosed in a *for* loop.

The next step is to rewrite the sorting function so that it uses the new average Z field in the polygon facet structure for the comparison. Listing 17-12 shows the new code.

LISTING 17-12 New polygon comparison function

```
int Poly_Compare(facet **arg1, facet **arg2)
{
// this function compares the average z's of two polygons and is used by the
// depth sort surface ordering algorithm

facet_ptr poly_1,poly_2;
```

```
// dereference the poly pointers

poly_1 = (facet_ptr)*arg1;
poly_2 = (facet_ptr)*arg2;

if (poly_1->average_z>poly_2->average_z)
   return(-1);
else
if (poly_1->average_z<poly_2->average_z)
   return(1);
else
   return(0);

} // end Poly_Compare
```

Isn't that a lot better! No long floating point calculations, just simple comparisons. Also, note that the Z values are stored in integers rather than floating point numbers. This is to speed up the comparison and to save on data storage. The final function we need to rewrite is the actual depth-sorting function that calls the Quick Sort function. We don't really have to do this—we could simply call the Z averaging function first—but by placing the call to *Compute_Z_Average()* inline with the sorting function, the new functionality is transparent. Listing 17-13 contains the new sorting function code.

LISTING 17-13 A new sorter

```
void Sort_Poly_List(void)
{
// this function does a simple z sort on the poly list to order surfaces
// the list is sorted in descending order, i.e. farther polygons first

Compute_Average_Z();

qsort((void *)world_polys,num_polys_frame, sizeof(facet_ptr), Poly_Compare);

} // end Sort_Poly_List
```

That's all there is to the Z depth-sorting optimizations. Now let's move on to something that we can really sink our fangs into.

The 80387 Math Coprocessor

The 80387 and internal math coprocessors of the 486DX and Pentium are probably some of the most mysterious components of the PC's processing suite. To tell you the truth, it's next to impossible to find any references to the math coprocessor and its instructions set. However, that's all going to change right now. We are going to delve into the math coprocessor, at least to the point that we understand what's going on and how to actually program it using its own instruction set. Of course, the C/C++ compiler you are using generates coprocessor instructions when you compile code that uses floating point operations; however, this code can be optimized in many cases with external assembly language and full 32-bit instructions.

So how do the 80387 and internal math coprocessors of the 486DX and Pentium work? First, from a programming point of view, it doesn't matter whether you have an external 387 or a full-blown 486DX; the instruction sets are the same. Maybe the internal 486DX version is a bit faster, but as far as we're concerned, it doesn't matter. So from now on, I will refer to the math coprocessor as the 387 to make the explanations easier.

The 80387 Architecture

The 387 is a stack-based machine that has only one mission in life: to compute mathematical calculations for the 486 core. Figure 17-5 shows the abstract model of the 387 in relation to the 486. Basically, all instructions that the 486 encounters that are meant for the 387 are sent to the 387 where they are executed. Hence, 387 instructions don't directly affect the 486 or its internal registers. The 387 can perform the common mathematical operations of addition, subtraction, multiplication, and division. However, it is also equipped to handle logarithmic, transcendental, and numerical conversions, and more. Furthermore, the 387 can actually perform many operations faster than the equivalent integer fixed point math with much higher accuracy. Even in cases in which the 387 is slower than pure integer operations on the 486 core, it may be worth the extra accuracy, especially in 3D graphics.

Programming the 387 is actually very simple. It has its own instruction set, which we will cover shortly. Basically, whenever you want 387 instructions to be executed, you place them in your code along with the other assembly language instructions. This brings us to a little problem, which is that most 387 programming must be done using an external assembler. This is due to the 32-bit nature of floats and the 64-bit nature of doubles. As we know, most inline assemblers for 16-bit compilers barely support the standard 286 instruction set, let alone the 486 coupled with the 387! Therefore, we are going to use external assembly language when using the 387; but external assembly language with MASM and TASM are a snap.

Let's talk about the internal stack of the 387 since it's the basis of how everything works. There are 8 stack elements in the 387 and a status word, as shown in Figure 17-6. Each stack element is 80 bits wide with 64 bits for the decimal part, 14 bits for the exponent, and 1 bit for the sign bit. However, each stack element can hold different data types, as shown in Figure 17-7. We see that there are short, long, and 10-byte real numbers. The stack elements are used to hold inputs and return outputs; thus, they are the working registers, in a sense, for the 387. We can

FIGURE 17-5

◉ ◉ ◉ ◉ ◉ ◉

The floating point processor performs all floating point math

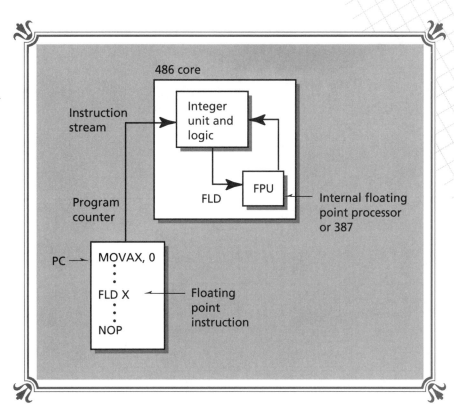

think of them as a register file, or we can think of them as a stack. In any case, the stack is referred to using the syntax ST(*n*), where *n* is the element. For example, take a look at Figure 17-8, which shows that:

ST is equivalent to the top of the stack.
ST(0) is equivalent to the top of the stack.
ST(1) is equivalent to the second element of the stack.
ST(7) is equivalent to the last element of the stack or element 8.

When programming the 387, many of the instructions take 0, 1, or 2 operands. This means that sometimes the operand(s) are implied. Also, the operands can either be constants, memory, or stack elements in most cases, so we have a bit of flexibility in defining what the data is for an operation. Furthermore, many of the instructions place the result on the top of the stack at ST(0). This is a good thing to know if you are expecting some piece of data to remain valid after an operation and it gets obliterated.

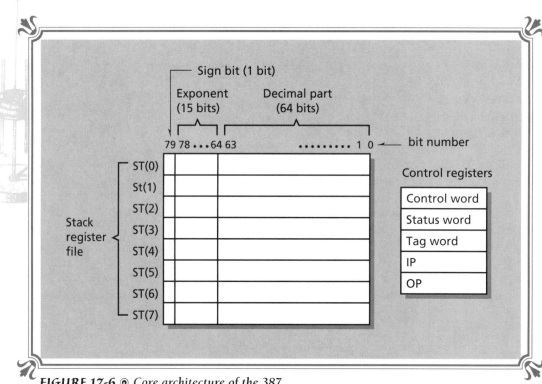

FIGURE 17-6 ⊙ *Core architecture of the 387*

FIGURE 17-7
⊙ ⊙ ⊙ ⊙ ⊙ ⊙
Data formats of the 387

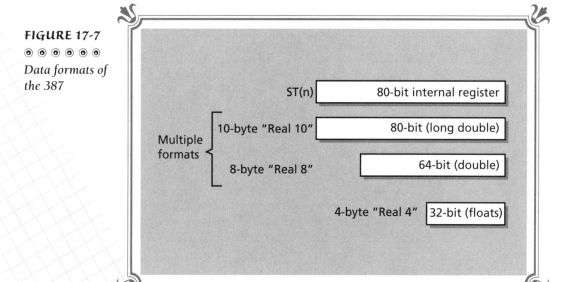

FIGURE 17-8

◎ ◎ ◎ ◎ ◎ ◎

Stack ordering and access in the 387

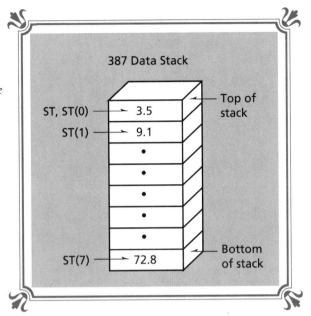

387 Data Stack

ST, ST(0) → 3.5 — Top of stack

ST(1) → 9.1

ST(7) → 72.8 — Bottom of stack

Now that we have a notion of what the 387 does and how it does it, let's take a look at the instruction set and see how to use it.

The 80387 Instruction Set

The 387 is a complete processor with a rather large instruction set. The instructions fall into the following categories:

Data transfer - Used to move data between the CPU and the 387.
Arithmetic - Used to perform standard arithmetic operations.
Transcendental - Used for nonlinear operations such as sin, cos, and so on.
Constants - Used to load commonly used constants, such as 1, pi, and so on.
Comparison - Used to compare floating point numbers.
Control - Used to control and set the state of the 387.

I don't know about you, but even if I don't know what a set of instructions does, I like to see them first before I learn about them just to get a feel for what's what! Therefore, Table 17-2 lists all of the 387 instructions available with a short description of what they do.

TABLE 17-2 ◇ *Instruction set for the 80387 processor*

Instruction Name	Description
Data Transfer	
FBLD	Loads a BCD number.
FBSTP	Stores and pops a BCD number.
FILD	Loads an integer.
FIST	Stores an integer.
FISTP	Stores an integer and pops the stack.
FLD	Loads a real number.
FSTP	Stores a real number and pops the stack.
FXCH	Exchanges two stack elements.
Arithmetic	
FABS	Computes the absolute value.
FADD	Adds real numbers.
FIADD	Adds integers.
FADDP	Adds real numbers and pops the stack.
FCHS	Changes the sign of a number.
FDIV	Divides real numbers.
FIDIV	Divides integers.
FDIVP	Divides real numbers and pops the stack.
FDIVR	Divides real numbers, but reverses which operand is dividend and divisor.
FIDIVR	Divides integers, but reverses which operand is dividend and divisor.
FDIVRP	Divides real numbers and pops the stack, but reverses which operand is dividend and divisor.
FMUL	Multiplies real numbers.
FIMUL	Multiplies integers.
FMULP	Multiplies real numbers and pops the stack.
FPREM	Computes partial remainder.
FPREM1	Computes partial remainder using IEEE format.
FRNDINT	Rounds the operand to an integer.

Instruction Name Data Transfer	Description
Arithmetic	
FSCALE	Scales by a power of two.
FSUB	Subtracts real numbers.
FISUB	Subtracts integers.
FSUBP	Subtracts real numbers and pops the stack.
FSUBR	Subtracts real numbers, but reverses which operand is minuend and subtrahend.
FISUBR	Subtracts integers, but reverses which operand is minuend and subtrahend.
FSUBRP	Subtracts real numbers and pops the stack, but reverses which operand is minuend and subtrahend.
FSQRT	Computes the square root.
FXTRACT	Extracts the exponents and significand from real number.
Transcendental (note: all angles must be in radians)	
F2XM1	Computes the value 2x–1.
FCOS	Computes the cosine.
FPATAN	Computes the partial arctangent.
FPTAN	Computes the partial tangent.
FSIN	Computes the sin.
FSINCOS	Computes both the sin and cosine.
FYL2X	Computes the expression $y*\log_2 x$.
FYL2XP1	Computes the expression $y*\log_2 (x+1)$.
Constants	
FLD1	Loads a 1.0.
FLDL2E	Loads $\log_2 e$.
FLDL2T	Loads $\log_2 10$.
FLDLG2	Loads $\log_{10} 2$.
FLDPI	Loads pi.
FLDZ	Loads zero.

continued on next page

continued from previous page

Instruction Name Data Transfer	Description

Comparison

FCOM	Compares reals.
FCOMP	Compares reals and pops the stack.
FCOMPP	Compares reals and pops the stack twice.
FICOM	Compares integers.
FICOMP	Compares integers and pops the stack.
FTST	Compares the top of the stack to zero.
FUCOM	Performs an unordered compare.
FUCOMP	Performs an unordered compare along with a pop.
FUCOMPP	Performs an unordered compare along with two pops.
FXAM	Sets condition bits for value at top of stack.

Control

FCLEX	Clears all unmasked floating point exceptions.
FNCLEX	Clears all exceptions.
FDECSTP	Decrements the stack pointer.
FFREE	Clears a stack element, making it seem as if it was popped.
FINCSTP	Increments stack pointer.
FINIT	Initializes 387 and checks for exceptions.
FNINIT	Initializes 387 without checking for exceptions.
FLDCW	Loads the control word.
FLDENV	Loads the 387 environment.
FNOP	Equivalent to NOP.
FRSTOR	Restores the state of the 387 with a given memory area.
FSAVE	Saves the state of the 387 into a memory area, but checks for exceptions.
FNSAVE	Saves the state of the 387 into a memory area without checking for exceptions.

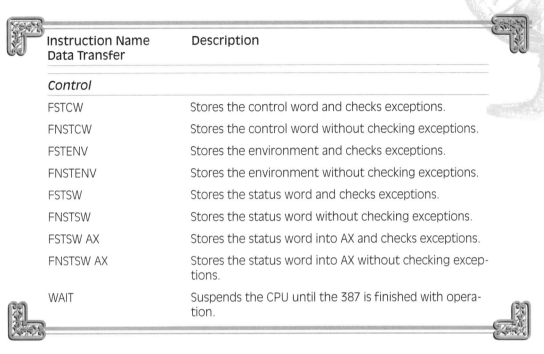

Instruction Name Data Transfer	Description
Control	
FSTCW	Stores the control word and checks exceptions.
FNSTCW	Stores the control word without checking exceptions.
FSTENV	Stores the environment and checks exceptions.
FNSTENV	Stores the environment without checking exceptions.
FSTSW	Stores the status word and checks exceptions.
FNSTSW	Stores the status word without checking exceptions.
FSTSW AX	Stores the status word into AX and checks exceptions.
FNSTSW AX	Stores the status word into AX without checking exceptions.
WAIT	Suspends the CPU until the 387 is finished with operation.

Because there are so many instructions, listing an example of each would take up too much space. Instead, Table 17-3 lists the general format of most instructions. Using this table, you should be able to deduce what the legal operands are for a particular instruction.

TABLE 17-3
❖❖❖❖❖
Operand formats for the 387

Instruction Format	Syntax	Implied Operands
Classical	F*instruction*	ST, ST(1)
Memory	F*instruction* memory operand	ST
Register	F*instruction* ST(n), ST	None
	F*instruction* ST, ST(n)	None
Register pop	F*instruction* P ST(n), ST	None

Notice that all the floating point processor instructions start with a leading *F*, and in the case of the register pop format, the instructions end with a *P*. Now let's discuss each of the instruction formats so we know how to use them in programs.

Classical Instruction Format

The classical format treats the 387's stack as if it were a classic stack. This means that all operations refer to the top of the stack ST(0) and the second element ST(1). For example, if we request an addition using the instruction,

FADD

the operation performed is ST(0)=ST(0)+ST(1). Therefore, the top of the stack is replaced by the sum of the topmost two items, as shown in Figure 17-9. In general, classical instructions use ST(0) and ST(1) if two operands are needed and ST(0) if only one operand is needed. If the instruction uses two operands, then typically, the source's topmost operand is popped off the stack and the result is placed at the top also.

Memory Instruction Format

The memory instruction format is similar to the classical format in that the stack is still treated like a stack. However, memory format allows memory items to be

FIGURE 17-9

◉ ◉ ◉ ◉ ◉ ◉

Example of a classical stack instruction

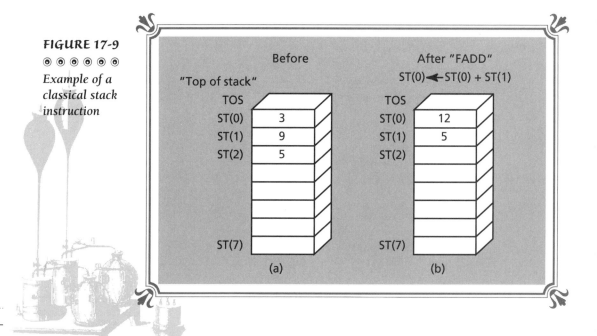

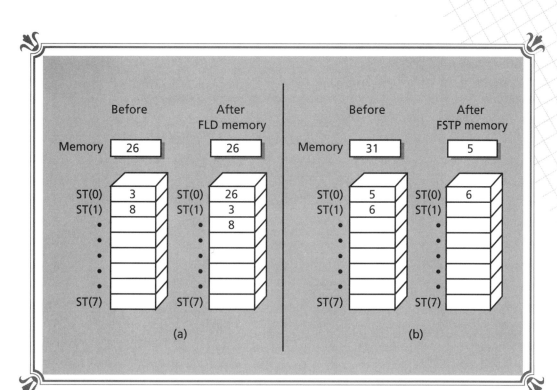

FIGURE 17-10 ◉ *Examples of memory instruction format*

pushed on the stack and popped off the stack into memory. For example, we might want to load the top of the stack with a memory operand like this:

```
FLD memory
```

And if we want to pop the top of the stack into a memory location, we can write:

```
FSTP memory
```

The results of both of these instructions are shown in Figure 17-10.

Register Instruction Format

The register instruction format simply allows the stack elements (registers) to be explicitly referred to. For example, say we want to add ST(0) and ST(4). We can write,

```
FADD ST(0), ST(4)
```

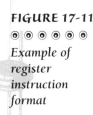

FIGURE 17-11

◉ ◉ ◉ ◉ ◉ ◉

Example of register instruction format

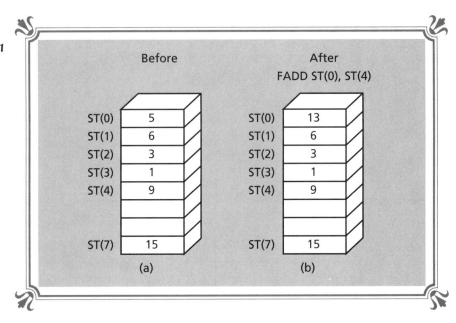

and the top of the stack will hold the sum of ST(0)+ST(4). This is shown in Figure 17-11. Also, when using register instruction format with two operand forms, one of the operands must be the top of the stack ST(0) or its abbreviation ST.

Register Pop Instruction Format

The register pop format is identical to the register instruction format except that after the result has been placed into the stack, the stack is popped once.

Popular 80387 Examples

Even though we aren't going to look at all the instructions the 387 has to offer, let's at least cover some of the basic ones that we will be using. We will be using the following instructions in all of their forms.

FLD
FST
FADD
FSUB
FMUL
FDIV

FLD Examples

The FLD instruction can be used to load reals (FLD), integers (FILD), and constants such as pi (FLDPI). The FLD instruction has the following formats:

FLD	op1	Loads a real number.
	32-bit short real	
	64-bit long real	
	80-bit temporary real	
	ST(n)	
FILD	op1	Loads an integer.
	16-bit word integer	
	32-bit short integer	
	64-bit long integer	
FLDcon		Loads a constant, where **con** is the suffix that determines the constant to load. (Refer to the section on constants in Table 17-2.)

Let's see some examples now. To load a real 32-bit number from memory, we can write:

```
FLD memory32
```

After the execution of the instruction, the top of the stack ST(0) will contain the value in *memory32*, as shown in Figure 17-12(a).

To load a standard binary 16-bit integer in the 387, we can write:

```
FILD memory16
```

After the instruction executes, the top of the stack will hold the 16-bit integer in IEEE format, as shown in Figure 17-12(b). This is an important point: all integers are converted to reals when processed by the floating point processor.

FST Examples

The FST instruction can be used to store reals (FST) and integers (FIST). Also, we can append a *P* to both instructions, and after the store, the top of the stack will be popped. In essence, the top of the stack, ST(0), is stored into the destination, and the stack pointer is adjusted when *P* is added to the instructions. The FST instruction has the following formats:

FST	op1	Stores a real number.
	32-bit short real	
	64-bit long real	
	ST(n)	
FSTP	op1	Stores a real number and pops the stack.
	32-bit short real	
	64-bit long real	
	ST(n)	
FIST	op1	Rounds the top of the stack and stores it.
	16-bit word integer	
	32-bit short integer	
	64-bit long integer	
FISTP	op1	Rounds the top of the stack, pops and stores it.
	16-bit word integer	
	32-bit short integer	
	64-bit long integer	

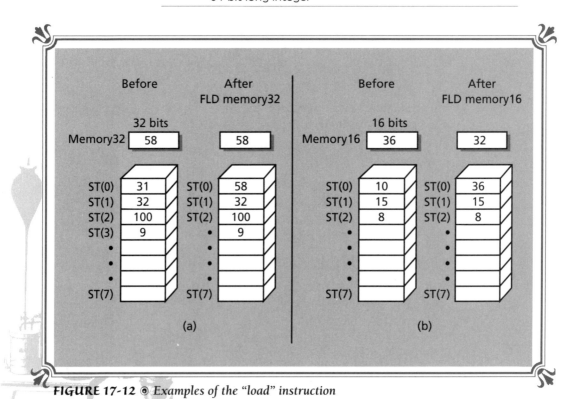

FIGURE 17-12 ⊙ *Examples of the "load" instruction*

Also, the top of the stack is always implied to be the source, hence, *op1* is the destination. Let's see some examples.

To store the top of the stack in a standard floating point location, we can write:

```
FST memory32
```

The results of this are shown in Figure 17-13(a). Notice that the top of the stack is not modified. On the other hand, if we were to execute this instruction,

```
FSTP memory32
```

the top of the stack would be popped into *memory32*.

Now let's try some integer examples. If we want to store the top of the stack into a 32-bit integer, we can write,

```
FIST memory32
```

and the value in the top of the stack will be converted to an integer by rounding and stored into *memory32*, as shown in Figure 17-13(b). FISTP works in the same way except the top of the stack is popped, as shown in Figure 17-13(c).

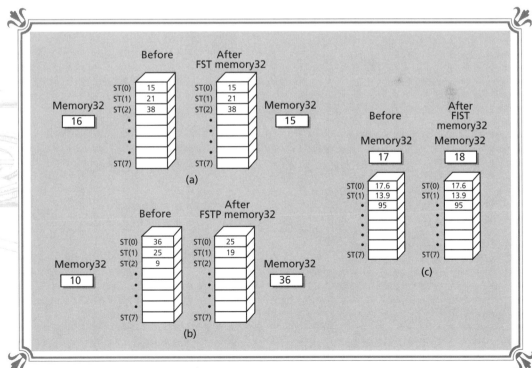

FIGURE 17-13 ⊙ *Examples of the "store" instructions*

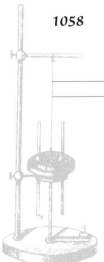

FADD Examples

The FADD instruction can add two reals (FADD) and two integers (FIADD). Also, we can add a *P* to the real version (FADDP) that pops the stack after the addition, but this isn't supported for the integer version. The FADD instruction has the following forms:

FADD		Implied operands are ST(0) and ST(1); also, the stack is popped after the addition.
FADD	op1	The top of the stack is implied as the destination and one of the operands.
	memory32	
	memory64	
	ST(n)	
FADD	op1, op2	One of the operands must still be the top of the stack, ST, but the destination need not be.
	ST, ST(n)	
	ST(n), ST	
FADDP	op1, op2	The operands are added and the result is popped off the top of the stack.
	ST, ST(n)	
	ST(n), ST	
FIADD	op1	The integer referred to by **op1** is converted to a real and added to the top of the stack.
	memory16	
	memory32	

Alrighty then! Seems easy enough. Let's try some examples. First, let's add the two topmost elements of the stack. The following instructions are equivalent:

```
FADD ST(1)
FADD ST,ST(1)
```

Figure 17-14(a) shows the results of executing either of the above instructions. As you can see, the top of the stack is obliterated with the sum. However, if we use this instruction,

```
FADD ST(2), ST
```

then the sum of ST(0) and ST(2) will be stored into ST(2), since it's the destination, and ST(0) will be unscathed. This is shown in Figure 17-14(b).

Next, let's try one of the integer forms. Say we want to add a 32-bit integer number from memory with the top of the stack ST(0). We can do the following:

```
FIADD memory32
```

The value within *memory32* will be converted to a real and then added to ST(0). The result is placed back into ST(0), as shown in Figure 17-14(c).

However, if we want to pop the top of the stack after the addition, we have to use a real addition, since popping isn't supported after integer addition; but we can pop the stack manually with the instruction:

```
FINCSTP
```

Now let's put together a little program that adds two reals and stores the result in a 32-bit integer. Here's the code:

```
FLD fvalue_1     ; load the first 4 byte real
FADD fvalue_2    ; load and add second 4 byte real
FISTP ivalue_1   ; store the top of stack into the 4 byte integer
```

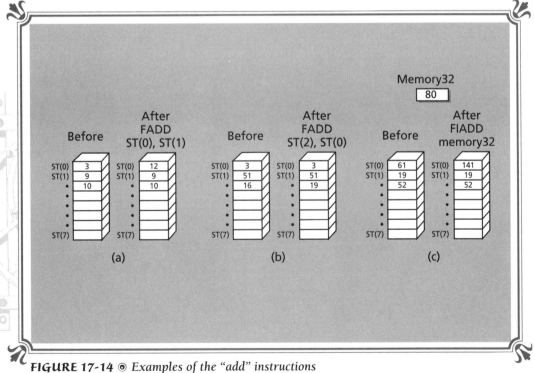

FIGURE 17-14 ⊙ *Examples of the "add" instructions*

Figure 17-15 shows the program executing step by step.

FSUB Examples

The FSUB instruction has the following forms:

FSUB		Implied operands are ST(1)-ST(0); also, the stack is popped after the addition.
FSUB	op1	The top of the stack is implied as the destination and one of the operands.
	memory32	
	memory64	
	ST(n)	
FSUB	op1, op2	One of the operands must still be the top of stack, ST, but the destination need not be.
	ST, ST(n)	
	ST(n), ST	

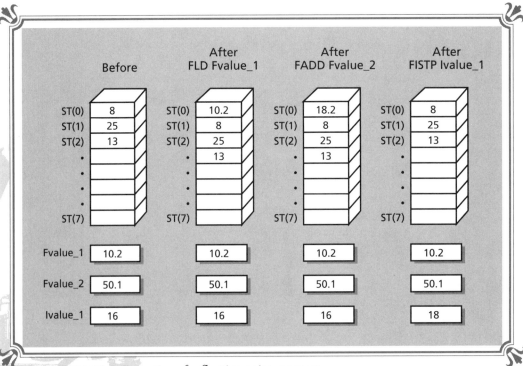

FIGURE 17-15 ⊙ *Execution of a floating point program*

FSUBP op1, op2   The operands **op1–op2** are subtracted and
                   the result is popped off the top of the stack.

ST, ST(n)

ST(n), ST

FISUB op1   The integer referred to by **op1** is converted
                   to a real and subtracted from the top of
                   the stack.

memory16

memory32

Subtraction works in the same way as addition except that the source and destination operands play a more important role. For example, the following instruction,

`FSUB memory32`

would subtract *memory32* from the top of the stack ST(0); that is, ST(0)=ST(0)–*memory32*. This is shown in Figure 17-16(a).

As another example, imagine that we want to subtract an integer from the top of the stack ST(0) (maybe to compute the decimal part). We can do this,

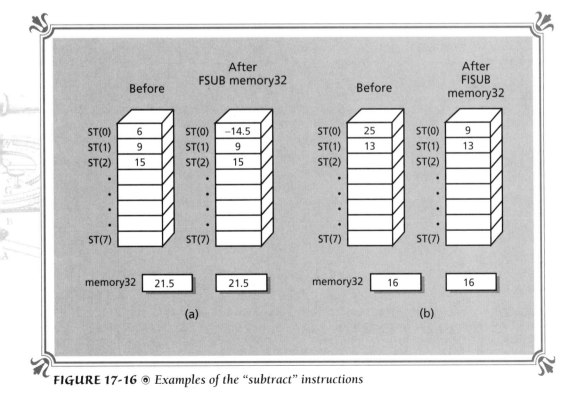

FIGURE 17-16 ◉ *Examples of the "subtract" instructions*

```
FISUB memory16
```

and the top of stack will have the results of ST(0)–(real)(*memory16*), as shown in Figure 17-16(b). Again, we see that all integers are converted into reals before they are used in calculations.

FMUL Examples

The FMUL instruction is very similar to the FADD instruction. It can multiply two reals (FMUL), an integer and a real (FIMUL); and as usual, a *P* can be added to the real version (FMULP) that pops the stack after the multiplication. The FMUL instruction has the following forms:

FMUL		Implied operands are ST(0)∗ST(1); also, the stack is popped after the multiplication.
FMUL	op1	The top of the stack is implied as the destination and one of the operands.
	memory32	
	memory64	
	ST(n)	
FMUL	op1, op2	One of the operands must still be the top of stack, ST, but the destination need not be.
	ST, ST(n)	
	ST(n), ST	
FMULP	op1, op2	The operands are multiplied and the result is popped off the top of the stack.
	ST, ST(n)	
	ST(n), ST	
FIMUL	op1	The integer referred to by **op1** is converted to a real and multiplied by the top of the stack.
	memory16	
	memory32	

I'm running out of examples! Let's say that we want to do something useful like compute 5!, which is read as "five factorial" and is equal to 5∗4∗3∗2∗1. This little program will do the trick:

```
FLD f_1    ; load 1.0 into stack
FLD f_2    ; load 2.0 into stack
```

```
FLD f_3    ; load 3.0 into stack
FLD f_4    ; load 4.0 into stack
FLD f_5    ; load 5.0 into stack

FMUL       ; 5*4
FMUL       ; 5*4*3
FMUL       ; 5*4*3*2
FMUL       ; 5*4*3*2*1

           ; top of stack ST(0) has 5*4*3*2*1 in it.
```

Figure 17-17 shows the factorial process and the stack, step by step.

FDIV Examples

The final instruction class we're going to look at is the division instruction FDIV. It is similar to the subtraction instruction in that the order of operands makes a difference. The instruction has all the forms—real, integer, and stack popping. Here are the formats for review:

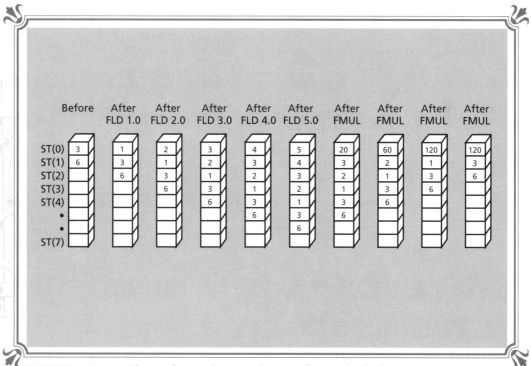

FIGURE 17-17 ⊙ *The stack, step-by-step, during a factorial calculation*

FDIV		Implied operands are ST(1)/ST(0); also, the stack is popped after the division.
FDIV	op1	The top of the stack is implied as the destination and one of the operands.
	memory32	
	memory64	
	ST(n)	
FDIV	op1, op2	One of the operands must still be the top of the stack, ST, but the destination need not be.
	ST, ST(n)	
	ST(n), ST	
FDIVP	op1, op2	The operands *op1–op2* are divided and the result is popped off the top of the stack.
	ST, ST(n)	
	ST(n), ST	
FIDIV	op1	The integer referred to by *op1* is converted to a real and divided into the top of the stack.
	memory16	
	memory32	

I'm all out of examples… how about, how long does it take to get from San Jose to San Francisco at 80mph?

```
FLD 45          ; SF is 45 miles from San Jose
FDIV f_80       ; divide 45 by 80
FSTP f_time     ; store the result into f_time and pop the stack
```

We have been using the instructions in a somewhat cavalier way—that is, we haven't really said how we can define *memory16*, *memory32*, *memory64*, reals, and constants. Let's see how to do all that and more with external assembly language programs.

Using an External Assembler and the 80387

To use external floating point modules, we need to do the following operations as a minimum:

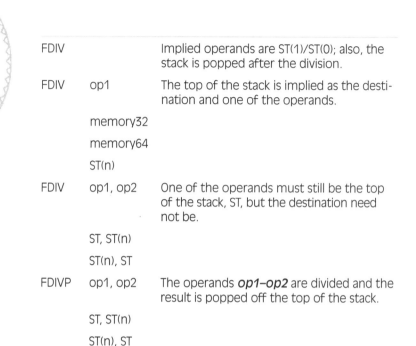

✤ Pass floating point values to an external assembly function.

✤ Return floating point values from an external assembly function.

✤ Define floating point constants within an external assembly function.

✤ Mix assembly language and C.

First off, even if you are a bit rusty on assembly language, you shouldn't have too much trouble because the following programs aren't going to be that complicated. However, I am going to be using the assembler directives for Microsoft MASM and not Borland's TASM. But they are similar, and you should at least get the gist of things even if you can't assemble the code. Let's begin by making the simple assembly language template called FOO.ASM shown in Listing 17-14.

LISTING 17-14 Sample assembly template for MASM 6.1

```
.MODEL MEDIUM, C          ; use medium memory model and C function
                          ; names
.386                      ; use the 386 instruction set

.CODE                     ; begin the code segment

PUBLIC Foo                ; export function name to linker

Foo PROC FAR C            ; function name, far visibility and pass variables
                          ; using C calling conventions

; begin code

; end code

Foo ENDP                  ; end foo

END                       ; end code
```

Now, using the list at the beginning of the section, let's see if we can figure out how to meet each of our needs.

Passing Floating Point Values to an External Assembly Function

The 16-bit C/C++ compilers we are using represent real numbers using three types: floats (4 bytes), doubles (8 bytes), and long doubles (10 bytes). These are synonymous with the 32-, 64-, and 80-bit real representations of the 387; they just have different names. Therefore, we can use two techniques: we can use the *DW, DQ,* and *DT* MASM directives to define reals, or we can use the new MASM directives

REAL4, REAL8, and REAL10. Let's use the new ones since they are easier to remember.

So, how do we pass values to an external assembly function? When we make a C/C++ call, the parameters are passed on the stack in a special order. And depending on the size of the parameters, different amounts of stack space will be used. For example, if we write a C/C++ header that reads,

```
float Fadd(float f1, float f2);
```

the compiler pushes *f2* and then *f1* on the stack (C pushes from right to left) and then makes the function call. Therefore, if we know that each *float* is 4 bytes and we know something about the stack pointer, we should be able to retrieve the floating point values in an external assembler routine. The fact is, we can and it's simple. MASM provides a mechanism for this. All we need to do is place the variables that we expect to be sent to our assembly function and their sizes in the right place. Listing 17-15 shows our template with the added ability to extract parameters passed to it.

LISTING 17-15 External assembly program that takes two floats

```
.MODEL MEDIUM, C          ; use medium memory model and C function
                          ; names
.386                      ; use the 386 instruction set

.CODE                     ; begin the code segment

PUBLIC Fadd               ; export function name to linker

; function name, far visibility and pass variables using C calling conventions
; there are two variables f1 and f2 both are 4 byte reals

Fadd PROC FAR C f1:REAL4, f2:REAL4

; begin code

; end code

Fadd ENDP                 ; end Fadd

END                       ; end code
```

As you can see, we have used the template to create a little shell that takes two parameters *f1* and *f2*. To use them, we simply use their names like any other variable. The reason for this is that they are really aliases for stack positions relative to the base pointer BP. That is, *f1* may really be translated to *[BP+12]*, but we can simply use the variable name without a problem. Now we did say that *Fadd(...)* returned a float, so how do we do this?

Returning Floating Point Values from an External Assembly Function

All values returned from C/C++ functions are placed in either *AX* or *DX:AX* depending on size. If the size is 2 bytes, the value is placed in *AX*. If the size is 4 bytes, the low part is placed in *AX* and the high part in *DX*. If the value is a far pointer, it is placed in *DX:AX*, and if it's a near pointer, it is placed in *AX*. Therefore, we need to place the results of our addition into *DX:AX* if we want to return the value to C/C++. To do this, we can use standard instructions along with the 387. So let's take what we know and complete the addition program. It should add the two parameters *f1+f2* and return the result in *DX:AX*. Listing 17-16 shows the complete code.

LISTING 17-16 External assembly program that adds two floats and returns the result

```
.MODEL MEDIUM, C            ; use medium memory model and C function
                           ; names
.386                       ; use the 386 instruction set

.CODE                      ; begin the code segment

PUBLIC Fadd                ; export function name to linker

; function name, far visibility and pass variables using C calling conventions
; there are two variables f1 and f2 both are 4 byte reals

Fadd PROC FAR C f1:REAL4, f2:REAL4

; LOCALS

LOCAL sum:REAL4

; begin code

FLD f1                     ; push the first number on the stack
FADD f2                    ; add the second number to the first
FSTP sum                   ; store result in sum

mov ax, WORD PTR sum       ; store low word of sum into ax
mov dx, WORD PTR sum[2]    ; store high word of sum into dx
ret                        ; return to caller

; end code

Fadd ENDP                  ; end Fadd

END                        ; end code
```

That's it. Listing 17-16 is a complete program that will add two floating point numbers together and return the result. Did you notice the curveballs I threw you? First, how does the local variable *sum* work? Well, MASM allows local variables to be defined as negative offsets in the stack. This can be done manually by using things like *[bp-12]*, or it can be done by using the *LOCAL* directive, which is much easier. The *LOCAL* directive has the following syntax:

```
LOCAL name1:type1, name2:type2,...
```

This is how we made *sum*. Anyway, the second trick is extracting the high and low words from *sum* and placing them into *DX:AX*. This is done using standard assembly tactics to access data at word boundaries.

Now let's see how to define and use floating point constants in our programs.

Defining Floating Point Constants Within an External Assembly Function

There are many times when a program may need some floating point constants, but how can we define these within an assembly language program? This is a good question, but again MASM (and I'm sure TASM) comes to the rescue. MASM allows constants to be defined using the "define data" directives such as *DW, DQ,* and so forth. However, there is no reason why we can't use *REAL4, REAL8,* or *REAL10*. For example, if we want to define a floating point variable that has the value of 100, we can write:

```
value_1 REAL4 100.0
```

Then the assembler will be able to access this memory storage and place the IEEE value for 100, and you can use it just like a memory operand in your programs, like this:

```
FLD value_1
```

The only catch is that you must be careful where you define memory-based constants in an assembly program, otherwise they might get executed like code. Therefore, I suggest that you place all constants at the end of your programs. For example, Listing 17-17 shows how we might add a constant to the addition program for later use.

LISTING 17-17 Floating point addition program with a floating point constant defined

```
MODEL MEDIUM, C        ; use medium memory model and C function
                       ; names
.386                   ;use the 386 instruction set
```

```
.CODE                       ; begin the code segment

PUBLIC Fadd                 ; export function name to linker

; function name, far visibility and pass variables using C calling conventions
; there are two variables f1 and f2 both are 4 byte reals

Fadd PROC FAR C f1:REAL4, f2:REAL4

; LOCALS

LOCAL sum:REAL4

; begin code

FLD f1                      ; push the first number on the stack
FADD f2                     ; add the second number to the first
FSTP sum                    ; store result in sum

mov ax, WORD PTR sum        ; store low word of sum into ax
mov dx, WORD PTR sum[2]     ; store high word of sum into dx
ret                         ; return to caller

; end code

value_1 REAL4 100.0         ; this will do since it's after the return

Fadd ENDP                   ; end Fadd

END                         ; end code
```

Mixing Assembly Language and C

The last thing we need to talk about is how to get the assembly language programs to work with C/C++. It's fairly simple—follow these steps (illustrated in Figure 17-18):

1. Write your external assembly module and assemble it into an object (.OBJ) file.

2. Based on the parameters the function takes or returns, create a C/C++ prototype and place the prototype in your C/C++ source or header file in which you wish to use the function.

3. During the linking process add the .OBJ file of your external assembly language program to the object's list.

If you follow these steps, everything should work, and there will be some examples later to solidify it more if you're a bit lost. Anyway, that's enough for floating point! We'd better stop before we end up with a book within a book. Let's move on to advanced fixed point math using assembly language.

FIGURE 17-18

◎ ◎ ◎ ◎ ◎ ◎

Inclusion of
external
assembly
language
functions

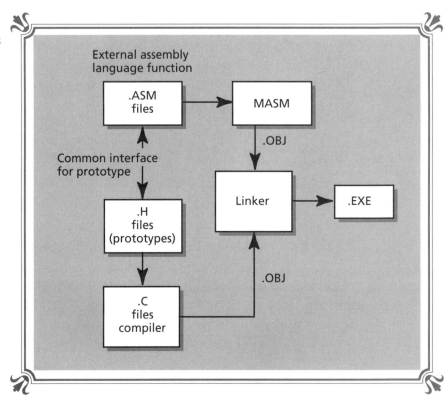

Advanced Fixed Point Math

In the beginning chapters of the book, now and then we hinted that we may keep the majority of the 3D engine using floating point math. Well, the fact is, the tests I have run show that the floating point version is more than fast enough for a simple game. Therefore, we are only going to use fixed point math for some of the graphics operations that are simple repetitive additions and so forth, but the bulk of the matrix math is going to stay in floating point.

On the other hand, if you don't have a 387, 486DX, or a Pentium, you are out of luck. Therefore, we're going to cover full 32-bit fixed point math and how it works so you can rewrite the entire engine if you need to. Just to refresh your memory, fixed point math is a method of performing mathematics on a computer that uses integers to represent fractional numbers. This is done by pretending that one portion of an integer represents the whole part while another portion represents the decimal part. For example, we are going to be using longs as our basic data type. We can use a definition such as:

```
typedef long fixed;
```

This gives us 32 bits of total precision; therefore, we can divide this up into two halves. The leftmost 16 bits will be the whole part and the rightmost 16 bits will be the decimal part. This is called a 16:16 representation and is shown in Figure 17-19. We have also learned that to convert a standard integer to a fixed point number in 16:16 format, we must shift it 16 times to the left, as shown here:

```
fixed x;
```

```
x = ((fixed)30 )<< 16);
```

And to convert a floating point number to fixed point, we multiply it by $2^{16}=65536$ and assign it to a fixed point type, such as:

```
fixed x1;
```

```
x1 = (fixed)(234.456 * 65536);
```

Finally, to convert a fixed point number back to an integer, we shift it 16 times to the right like this:

```
int i;
i = (int)(x1 >> 16);
```

Then we learned that addition and subtraction of fixed point numbers can be done just as if they weren't fixed point numbers. For example:

```
fixed f1,f2,f3;
```

continued on next page

FIGURE 17-19
◎ ◎ ◎ ◎ ◎ ◎
A 16:16 format fixed point number

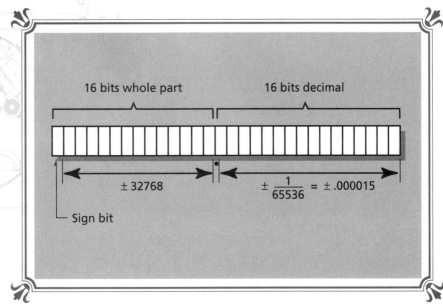

16 bits whole part   16 bits decimal

± 32768 $\pm \dfrac{1}{65536} = \pm .000015$

Sign bit

continued from previous page

```
f1 = ( (fixed)20) << 16);
f2 = ( (fixed)10) << 16);

f3=f1+f2; // add f1 and f2

f3=f1-f2;   // subtract f2 from f1
```

However, multiplication and division are much more troublesome since the results can be 64 bits long. But before we talk about that, let's look at something interesting. Remember how I said that fixed point math can be slower than floating point math on a 16-bit compiler even for addition and subtraction? The reason is that 16-bit compilers don't use 32-bit instructions. Instead they use 16-bit instructions, and a simple one-line addition (in 32-bit code) turns into multiple lines. For example, if we de-compile the above fragment of code, it looks something like this:

```
; main()
; {
; Line 29
                    _main:
            *** 000000      c8 00 00 00      enter    OFFSET L01477,
                                                      OFFSET 0
            *** 000004      56               push     si
            *** 000005      57               push     di
; f3 = fffa
; f1 = fff6
; f2 = fff2
;
; fixed f1,f2,f3;
; Line 31
;
;
; f1 = (((fixed)20) << 16);
; Line 34
            *** 000006      c7 46 f6 00 00   mov      WORD PTR
                                                      -10[bp],OFFSET 0
            *** 00000b      c7 46 f8 14 00   mov      WORD PTR
                                                      -8[bp],OFFSET 20
; f2 = (((fixed)20) << 16);
; Line 35
            *** 000010      c7 46 f2 00 00   mov      WORD PTR
                                                      -14[bp],OFFSET 0
            *** 000015      c7 46 f4 14 00   mov      WORD PTR
                                                      -12[bp],OFFSET 20
;
;
; f3 = f1+f2;
; Line 38
            *** 00001a      8b 46 f6         mov      ax,WORD PTR
                                                      -10[bp]
            *** 00001d      8b 56 f8         mov      dx,WORD PTR -8[bp]
```

```
        *** 000020      03 46 f2        add     ax,WORD PTR
                                                -14[bp]
        *** 000023      13 56 f4        adc     dx,WORD PTR
                                                -12[bp]
        *** 000026      89 46 fa        mov     WORD PTR -6[bp],ax
        *** 000029      89 56 fc        mov     WORD PTR -4[bp],dx
; f3 = f1-f2;
; Line 39
        *** 00002c      8b 46 f6        mov     ax,WORD PTR
                                                -10[bp]
        *** 00002f      8b 56 f8        mov     dx,WORD PTR -8[bp]
        *** 000032      2b 46 f2        sub     ax,WORD PTR
                                                -14[bp]
        *** 000035      1b 56 f4        sbb     dx,WORD PTR
                                                -12[bp]
        *** 000038      89 46 fa        mov     WORD PTR -6[bp],ax
        *** 00003b      89 56 fc        mov     WORD PTR -4[bp],dx
;
;
; } // end main
; Line 42
; Line 42
                L01473:
        *** 00003e      5f              pop     di
        *** 00003f      5e              pop     si
        *** 000040      c9              leave
        *** 000041      cb              ret     OFFSET 0
Local Size: 14
; Line 0
```

I have highlighted the addition and subtraction code. As you can see, there are six instructions each to perform the 32-bit long addition and subtraction. The problem with that is that it only takes three 32-bit instructions:

```
// f3=f1+f2

mov eax,f1
add eax,f2
mov f3,eax

// f3=f1-f2

mov eax,f1
sub eax,f2
mov f3,eax
```

Moreover, the 32-bit instructions are simpler to understand. However, there's not too much difference from three to six assembly instructions—other than six taking twice as long. The real nightmare occurs when we perform fixed point multiplication and division.

Multiplication of Fixed Point Numbers

The problem when multiplying fixed point numbers that are 32 bits long is that the results can be 64 bit. Hence, standard 16-bit compilers can't handle this. In essence, when two longs are multiplied, their product had better be able to fit into 32 bits, otherwise, there will be an overflow. We can remedy this with a couple of tricks. We can shift the multiplicand and multiplier to the right before the multiplication and lose accuracy. However, unless we totally shift out the decimal portion, we still might have an overflow since a product of two 16-bit numbers is 32 bits, and there are only 16 bits in our representation to hold the whole part. Finally, even if we do the shift to the right and perform multiplications that won't overflow, the 16-bit compiled code of a fixed point multiply is ugly. Take a look at this simple fixed point C version of multiplication:

```
fixed f1,f2,f3;

f3=f1*f2;
```

Although this seems simple enough, take a look at the decompiled code:

```
; main()
; {
; Line 29
                    _main:
          *** 000000      c8 00 00 00        enter     OFFSET L01477,
                                                       OFFSET 0
          *** 000004      56                 push      si
          *** 000005      57                 push      di
; f3 = fffa
; f1 = fff6
; f2 = fff2
;
; fixed f1,f2,f3;
; Line 31
;
;
; f3 = f1*f2;
; Line 34
          *** 000006      ff 76 f4           push      WORD PTR -12[bp]
          *** 000009      ff 76 f2           push      WORD PTR -14[bp]
          *** 00000c      ff 76 f8           push      WORD PTR -8[bp]
          *** 00000f      ff 76 f6           push      WORD PTR -10[bp]
          *** 000012      9a 00 00 00 00     call      FAR PTR __aFlmul
          *** 000017      89 46 fa           mov       WORD PTR -6[bp],ax
          *** 00001a      89 56 fc           mov       WORD PTR -4[bp],dx
;
;
; } // end main
; Line 37
; Line 37
```

```
              L01473:
      *** 00001d    5f              pop     di
      *** 00001e    5e              pop     si
      *** 00001f    c9              leave
      *** 000020    cb              ret     OFFSET 0
Local Size: 14
; Line 0
```

Gooooood night! You see that call to *__aFlmul*? That's one call too many and the straw that broke the camel's back. The fact is, 16-bit compilers are terrible at 32-bit fixed point operations. We need to use 32-bit instructions and external assembly programs. And since the compiled 16-bit code has a call in it, the overhead of the call to an external function to perform multiplication isn't that bad since, at worst, we would break even in comparison to the 16-bit code. However, with 32-bit code, we can beat the 16-bit compiler!

So how do we perform 64-bit multiplication? It turns out that the 486 performs 64-bit multiplication when using 32-bit instructions. Therefore, if we want to multiply two numbers together, we can write something like this:

```
mov eax, multiplicand
imul multiplier
```

The 64-bit result is stored in *EDX:EAX*. However, there is a little twist. The result is in the form 32:32. Take a look at Figure 17-20. The lower 16 bits of *EDX* have the low word of the whole part, but the most significant bits of the decimal portion

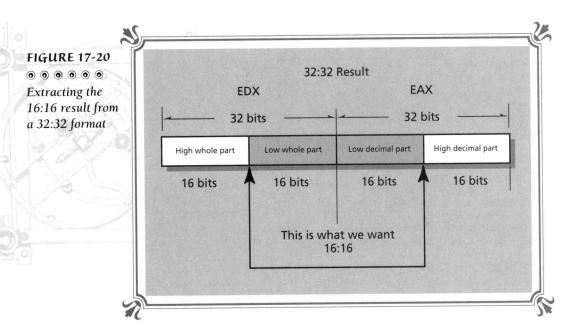

FIGURE 17-20

◉ ◉ ◉ ◉ ◉ ◉

Extracting the 16:16 result from a 32:32 format

are in the upper word of *EAX*. This means that when the function returns the result in *DX:AX*, which is 32 bits and composed of the lower 16 bits of *EDX* and the lower 16 bits of *EAX*, the decimal portion will be wrong. So what we need to do is shift the decimal portion in *EAX* over 16 bits with this instruction:

```
shr eax,16
```

Then the result in 32:32 format originally in *EDX:EAX* will be properly transferred to *DX:AX* in 16:16 format. An assembly language program that does all this nicely is shown in Listing 17-18.

LISTING 17-18 Assembly language program that multiplies two fixed point numbers together without overflowing

```
; this function uses 64 bit math to multiply two 32 bit fixed point numbers
; in 16:16 format

.MODEL MEDIUM,C              ; use medium memory model C function names

.386

.CODE                       ; begin the code segment

PUBLIC FP_Mul               ; export function name to linker


FP_Mul PROC FAR C multiplier:DWORD, multiplicand:DWORD

    mov eax,multiplicand     ; move into eax multiplicand
    imul multiplier          ; multiply by multiplier, result edx:eax
    shr eax,16               ; need to shift upper 16 bits of eax to right
                             ; so that result is in dx:ax instead of edx:eax
    ret                      ; return to caller

FP_Mul ENDP

END
```

The C prototype for the function looks like this:

```
fixed FP_Mul(fixed multiplier, fixed multiplicand);
```

To use the function, simply link the object FPMUL.OBJ into the game library and make a call like this:

```
fixed f1,f2,f3;

f3 = FP_Mul(f1,f2);
```

Before we go on, let's talk about these assembly object files for a second. Even if you don't have MASM, you can still use all the .OBJ files supplied on the CD-

ROM—you just can't make changes to the assembly files and reassemble them. Now let's move on to division.

Division of Fixed Point Numbers

Division is very similar to multiplication in that the resulting number can be prescaled so that the decimal portion of the fixed point numbers isn't shifted out. This is because each fixed point number has a scale of 65536. When two of these numbers are divided, the factor of 65536 is divided out. We can deal with this in two ways: we can shift the numbers to the left before the division (causing a possible overflow), or we can use 32-bit instructions and 64-bit math.

Let's use 32-bit instructions and see what we can come up with. First, we must look at how the division works. Using 32-bit instructions, the *IDIV* instruction will divide a 32-bit divisor into a 64-bit dividend in *EDX:EAX*. Therefore, we need to convert our 16:16 bit format into 32:32. How do we do this? We must first consider a very important point and that is that the fixed point number is signed. Therefore, we must be careful.

The trick to converting 32-bit signed numbers into 64-bit numbers is using sign extension. We begin by converting the 32-bit long into a double long with the instructions:

```
mov eax,dividend
cdq
```

The first instruction is easy enough to understand, but what about the *CDQ* instruction? Well, it stands for "convert signed number to quad word." And this is exactly what we want. After the above two instructions, our 16:16 number will be converted into a 32:32 number, but the data is in the wrong place. Figure 17-21 shows this. We need to center the decimal around the middle of the 64-bit dividend, not at the 16th position as it is now. To fix this, we need to perform a 16-bit shift to the left using the registers *EDX:EAX* as one register. But how can we do this? Luckily, there are two new 32-bit instructions used for double 64-bit shifting. The instructions are:

SHLD - Shift left double
SHRD - Shift right double

Basically, in the form we are going to use them, the double shift instructions have the following parameterization,

SHxD op1, op2, op3

or

SHLD reg32, reg32, immediate(0-31) or CL
SHRD reg32, reg32, immediate(0-31) or CL

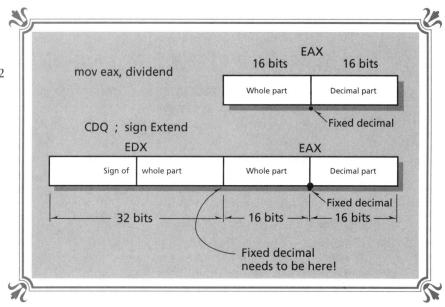

FIGURE 17-21

⊙ ⊙ ⊙ ⊙ ⊙ ⊙

Creating a 32:32 dividend for a full 64-bit division

The only strange thing about the instructions is how they do the shifting. In the case of *SHLD*, the instruction shifts the data in *op1:op2* to the left *op3* times with the low order bits of *op1* being filled by the high order bits of *op2*. However, during the shift, *op2* is not changed! Similarly, *SHRD* shifts *op1:op2* to the right. The high order bits of *op1* are filled in by the low order bits of *op2*, but *op2* is not changed. Figure 17-22 shows the shifting process for both instructions graphically.

What we're going to do is use the double shift to shift the 64-bit value in *EDX:EAX* 16 times to the left to align it properly. This can be done with the instruction:

```
shld edx,eax,16
```

However, the value in *EAX* still hasn't changed, so we need to move the lower 16 bits into position by shifting them to the left 16 bits. Finally, we will have a 32:32 number that has the whole portion of the fixed point number in the lower word of *EDX* and the decimal portion in the high word of *EAX*, which is what we desire. Now we're ready to divide the 32-bit divisor into the 64-bit number with:

```
idiv divisor
```

We're almost done. The problem now is that the result of the division is a 32-bit number in *EAX* and we need it in *DX:AX*. Bummer! We need to perform a very tricky shift so that the lower word of *EAX* is in *AX* and the upper word of *EAX* is in the lower word of *EDX*. Here's that instruction (again using the double shift instruction):

```
shld edx,eax, 16
```

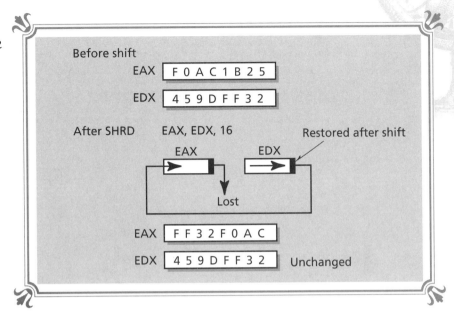

If you think about it for a while it's correct, but it may seem wrong. Here's what's going on: the lower word of *EDX* is replaced with the upper word of *EAX*. Therefore, the whole part of the 32-bit result is in *DX*. *EAX* still holds the upper and lower 16 bits of the resulting division, but the upper 16 bits holds the whole part and the lower 16 bits, which is *AX*, holds the decimal part. Therefore, when we return from the final division function, *DX:AX* will hold the result.

Now that we are both thoroughly and utterly confused with everything, let's take a look at the division function. Listing 17-19 shows the final fixed point division function.

LISTING 17-19 Fixed point division function

```
; this function uses 64 bit math to divide two numbers in 32 bit 16:16
; fixed point format

.MODEL MEDIUM,C          ; use medium memory model C function names

.386

.CODE                    ; begin the code segment

PUBLIC FP_Div            ; export function name to linker

FP_Div PROC FAR C dividend:DWORD, divisor:DWORD

    mov eax,dividend     ; move dividend into eax
```

continued on next page

continued from previous page

```
    cdq                       ; convert eax into edx:eax using sign extension
    shld edx,eax,16           ; shift edx:eax 16 bits to the left in so that
                              ; result is in fixed point
    sal eax,16                ; but manually shift eax since shld doesn't
                              ; change the source register (pretty stupid!)

    idiv divisor              ; perform divison

    shld edx,eax,16           ; move result into dx:ax since it's in eax
    ret                       ; return to caller

FP_Div ENDP

END
```

The function has the following C prototype:

```
fixed FP_Div(fixed divisor, fixed dividend);
```

To divide one fixed point number by another, we can write:

```
fixed f1,f2,f3;

f3 = FP_Div(f1,f2);
```

Don't forget to link the object FPDIV.OBJ to your final C program and include the prototype to make it work. By the way, I have placed the prototypes for these functions in BLACK17.H, so you only need to add the objects in your link phase.

Transcendental Functions

We can add, subtract, multiply, and divide, but what about transcendental functions like SIN and COS? To deal with these, we simply make tables, except the tables have fixed point numbers in them instead of floating point numbers. For example, to create a fixed point SIN and COSINE table, we can do something like this:

```
fixed sin_fp[360], cos_fp[360];

for (d=0; d<360; d++)
    {
    sin_fp[d] = (fixed)(65536*sin((double)d*(double)3.14159/(double)180);
    cos_fp[d] = (fixed)(65536*cos((double)d*(double)3.14159/(double)180);
    } // end for d
```

After the tables are created, the values in them can be used as if they were standard fixed point numbers.

Accuracy Analysis

Before we complete our discussion, we should talk briefly about how accurate fixed point numbers are. A floating point number based on the same number of bits is more accurate in most cases. The reason for this is that fixed point numbers allocate a specific number of bits to the whole part and a specific number of bits to the decimal part. For example, if our fixed point values were all between –1.0 and 1.0, why use 16 bits to hold 1.0! This is the beauty of floating point. The decimal moves around to give the accuracy where it's needed.

In any case, our format has a whole range of -2^{15} to $2^{15}- 1$, or –32768 to 32767, and a decimal accuracy of plus or minus $1/(2^{16})=1.5258\text{x}10^{-5}$, or roughly, one part in 10,000—not bad, but not good.

External 32-Bit Assembly Language Functions

Since we're on this assembly language kick, let's add a few 32-bit data movement functions just so we can use quad byte moves in some of our drawing and buffering functions. Basically, we want to be able to use the *STOSD* and *MOVSD* 32-bit instructions, but we can't with the inline assembler, so we'll just create a few simple external 32-bit functions and then make calls to them.

There are only two things we need to be able to do: fill a region of memory with a value 32 bits at a time and move data from one region to another 32 bits at a time. Let's take a look at these first and then see the functions we can rewrite based on them.

Data Filling

Filling a region with a constant value is a common operation during a game—for example, we might want to fill the screen with a solid color or clear the screen. Both of these operations can be done with a few lines of assembly language, but the problem is, we can only move words at a time using the inline assembler. To move quads at a time, we must resort to external assembly language. Anyway, the function we're about to look at works in much the same way as *memset()* except that it works with 4 bytes at a time. Listing 17-20 shows the fastest way to set data on a 486.

LISTING 17-20 *Quad byte memory fill function*

```
; this function fills a region of memory using 32 bit stores


.MODEL MEDIUM,C                    ; use medium memory model C function names

.CODE                              ; begin the code segment

PUBLIC fquadset                    ; export function name to linker


fquadset PROC FAR C dest:DWORD, data:DWORD, count:DWORD
```

continued on next page

continued from previous page

```
.386

cld                              ; clear the direction of movement

les di, dest                     ; point es:di at destination
mov ecx, count                   ; move into ecx number of quads
mov eax, data                    ; move the data into eax
rep stosd                        ; fill the region with data

ret                              ; return to caller

fquadset ENDP

END
```

The function takes as parameters the destination buffer to fill, the data to fill with, and the number of quads to be filled. The C prototype for the function is defined in BLACK17.H and looks like this:

```
void fquadset(void far *dest, long data, long count);
```

Here's how the function works: *ES:DI* is pointed to the destination, then the number of quads to be set is placed in *ECX*, and the data to fill is placed in *EAX*. This is the setup phase. Then the *REP STOSD* instruction is called, which performs the memory fill.

Data Movement

The next type of 4-byte transfer we would like to implement is movement of data similar to the standard *memcpy()* function, but using 4-byte moves. The assembly language version of this one is almost identical to the memory fill we just performed except that to perform a memory copy, *ES:DI* must point to the destination and *DS:SI* must point to the source. Therefore, the parameters need to be changed so that a source region is defined. Listing 17-21 shows the code for a quad byte memory move.

LISTING 17-21 Quad byte memory move

```
.MODEL MEDIUM,C                  ; use medium memory model C function names

.CODE                            ; begin the code segment

PUBLIC fquadcpy                  ; export function name to linker


fquadcpy PROC FAR C USES ds, source:DWORD, dest:DWORD, count:DWORD

.386
```

```
        cld                             ; clear the direction of movement

        lds si, source                  ; point ds:si at source
        les di, dest                    ; point es:di at destination

        mov ecx,count                   ; move into ecx number of words
        rep movsd                       ; move the data

        ret                             ; return to caller

        fquadcpy ENDP

        END
```

And, of course, the prototype for the function is defined in BLACK17.H as:

```
void fquadcpy(void far *dest, void far *source, long count);
```

Now that we have a couple tools to move and set memory quads at a time, let's use them to rewrite some video functions, making them twice as fast!

Clearing the Screen

Clearing the screen is an operation that must be done during each frame (in most cases) for a 3D game. The screen is either painted with black or a background color. In any case, we would like this operation to run as fast as possible since we are potentially clearing out 64,000 bytes or more (in higher resolution modes) of memory. So let's rewrite the clear screen function with a call to *fquadset()*. The new code is shown in Listing 17-22.

LISTING 17-22 New double buffer fill

```
void Fill_Double_Buffer_32(int icolor)
{
// this function fills in the double buffer with the sent color a QUAD at
// a time

long color;  // used to create a 4 byte color descriptor

color = icolor | (icolor << 8);

// replicate color into all four bytes of quad

color = color | (color<<16);

fquadset((void far *)double_buffer,color,(double_buffer_size >> 1));

} // end Fill_Double_Buffer_32
```

The function has the same interface as the word version *Fill_Double_Buffer()* except that, internally, a call is made to *fquadset()*. Also, the input color is replicated into a long data type before the call.

Copying the Double Buffer to the Video Buffer

The final function that we need is something to copy the double buffer to the video buffer 4 bytes at a time. So we're going to rewrite *Display_Double_Buffer()* using the new 32-bit quad byte memory move function. Listing 17-23 shows the code.

LISTING 17-23 New double buffer display function using the quad byte memory move function

```
void Display_Double_Buffer_32(unsigned char far *buffer,int y)
{
// this function copies the double buffer into the video buffer at the
// starting y location using quad byte transfers

fquadcpy((void far *)(video_buffer+y*320),
         (void far *)double_buffer,
         (double_buffer_size >> 1));

} // end Display_Double_Buffer_32
```

Do you see how easy it is to use external assembly functions? The key is to use a few short, simple functions that perform 32-bit tasks. Then these functions can be used by the 16-bit C code to perform 32-bit operations almost as fast as native 32-bit code.

Now we're ready to get back to work and find some of the bottlenecks in the display portion of the graphics pipeline. Let's start with the triangle renderer.

Faster Triangle Scan Conversion

Let's face it, our engine probably spends most of its time drawing to the double buffer or display memory. This is primarily what slows down a 3D engine. Currently, our triangle renderer works as follows: one function breaks the general triangle into two smaller triangles where one has a flat top and the other has a flat bottom. Then each of the smaller triangles is drawn separately using a simple floating point scan line algorithm that traces the edges of the triangles and draws lines between them. The entire loop that does this is of the form:

```
for (temp_y=y1; temp_y<=y3; temp_y++,dest_addr+=320)
    {
```

```
Triangle_Line(dest_addr,(unsigned int)xs,(unsigned int)xe,color);

// adjust starting point and ending point
xs+=dx_left;
xe+=dx_right;

} // end for
```

There just isn't much there. Basically there are two things that we would like to do: first, get rid of the call and make the line drawing inline and second, possibly use fixed point math. Well, I have to admit I played with this for a while before I came up with a simple, fast solution. First, I tried to rewrite the *Triangle_Line()* function inline and using quads along with external assembly language. The new function that drew the lines a quad at a time (instead of a word at a time) was faster for small lines, but for long lines it was only slightly faster. Then I tried converting the incrementals from floating point to fixed point, and the function actually became slower (this is probably due to the 16-bit compiler and the shifts to convert back and forth from fixed point and integers). Finally, I decided to try writing a completely external assembly program that would take as parameters *xs, xe, dx_left, dx_right*, and the starting address of the line in display memory. However, I decided to pass floating point numbers and perform the initial conversion to 32-bit fixed point within the function itself.

In the end, the new function is probably three to four times faster at drawing triangles and is very short. Interestingly enough, the function only draws lines a word at a time instead of a quad at a time. Although writing quads is faster (maybe 10 to 20 percent), it's just not worth the extra complexity of the assembler code for our purposes. Summing up, the new function draws an entire triangle itself using 32-bit 16:16 fixed point numbers and word writes to display memory. Listing 17-24 contains the function that does this.

LISTING 17-24 *The final triangle engine*

```
; this function draws a triangle from y1 to y2 using x1 and x2 as the starting
; x points along with deltas dx_right and dx_left. The function uses 32 bit
; fixed point math, notice the use of floating point instructions to convert
; the floating point values into fixed point values

.MODEL MEDIUM,C                    ; use medium memory model C function names

.386

.CODE                              ; begin the code segment

PUBLIC Triangle_Asm                ; export function name to linker


Triangle_Asm PROC FAR C dest:DWORD, y1:WORD, y2:WORD, x1:REAL4, x2:REAL4,
dx_left:REAL4, dx_right:REAL4, color:WORD
```

continued on next page

continued from previous page

```
; local variables

LOCAL xs_f:DWORD, xe_f:DWORD,dx_left_f:DWORD, dx_right_f:DWORD,xs:WORD,xe:WORD


        mov bx,0                        ; reset bx to 0, use for line increment

        mov dx,y1                       ; dx=y1

        fld  x1                         ; xs_f = (x1*65536)
        fmul FPSHIFT
        fistp xs_f

        fld  x2                         ; xe_f = (x2*65536)
        fmul FPSHIFT
        fistp xe_f

        fld  dx_left                    ; dx_left_f = (dx_left*65536)
        fmul FPSHIFT
        fistp dx_left_f

        fld  dx_right                   ; dx_right_f = (dx_right*65536)
        fmul FPSHIFT
        fistp dx_right_f


; for (dx=y1; dx<=y2; dx++)

begin_line:

        mov ax,WORD PTR xs_f[2]          ; get whole part of xs_f into xs
        mov xs,ax

        mov ax,WORD PTR xe_f[2]          ; get whole part of xe_f into xe
        mov xe,ax


        les di,dest                      ; point es:di to start of line
        add di,xs
        add di,bx                        ; add vertical offset

        mov cx, color                    ; cx = color | color << 8
        mov ch,cl

process_left_end:

        mov ax,WORD PTR xs_f[2]          ; ax=xs & 0x01
        and ax,01h

test_l1:

        cmp ax,1                         ; if (ax==1)
        jne process_right_end
```

```
        mov es:[di], cl              ; plot pixel
        inc xs                       ; xs++;

process_right_end:

    les di,dest                      ; point es:di to start of line
    add di,xe
    add di,bx                        ; add vertical offset

    mov ax,xe                        ; ax=xs & 0x01
    and ax,01h

test_r0:                             ; if (ax==0)

    cmp ax,0
    jne process_middle

    mov es:[di],cl                   ; plot pixel

    dec xe                           ; xe-=1

process_middle:

    les di,dest                      ; point es:di to start of line
    add di,xs
    add di,bx                        ; add vertical offset

    cld                              ; clear the direction of movement

    mov ax, cx                       ; move the color data into eax

    mov cx,xe                        ; compute number of words to move
                                     ; (xe-xs+1)/2
    sub cx,xs
    inc cx
    shr cx,1                         ; divide by 2

    rep stosw                        ; fill the region with data


end_line:
    mov eax,dx_left_f                ; perform fixed point addition of deltas
    add xs_f,eax                     ; xs_f+=dx_left_f

    mov eax,dx_right_f               ; xe_f+=dx_right_f
    add xe_f,eax

    add bx,320                       ; move to next line in destination buffer


    inc dx                           ; dx++
    cmp dx,y2
```

continued on next page

continued from previous page

```
        jle begin_line                    ; if (dx<=y2) process next line


        ret                               ; later!


; constants section, must be here so that processor doesn't try to execute
; data

FPSHIFT REAL4 65536.0 ; this is equivalent to FP_SCALE in the fixed point defines

Triangle_Asm ENDP

END
```

Although it may seem that the function is long, it's really not. Basically, the function is a conversion to assembly line-by-line from the original C version. I have even annotated the comments with their C equivalents to the right of each line. Anyway, let's take a look at how it works.

First the input parameters are all converted to fixed point by means of the floating point processor to convert floats to longs. This logic has been highlighted. Then the function enters into the main loop, which is basically the beginning of the old C *for* loop. The code in the loop extracts the ends of the line, which is very easy to do and does not require a shift. This is because when 16:16 format is used, the whole part is in the upper word and the decimal part is in the lower word, as shown in Figure 17-23. Therefore, a simple base pointer+offset addressing scheme can be

FIGURE 17-23

◉ ◉ ◉ ◉ ◉ ◉

Extracting the whole part and the decimal part of a fixed point number without shifting

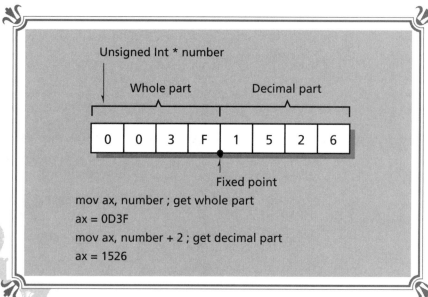

used to access the whole part and decimal part of a fixed point number without shifting.

Once the endpoints of the line have been extracted, they are tested to see whether they lie on a word boundary. Based on this, the ends of the line are drawn, which may be single pixels. Then the remainder of the line is computed and drawn using word moves. At the end of the loop, the endpoints are updated by adding the deltas, and a comparison is performed to see if the entire vertical extent of the line has been drawn. The updating of the fixed point deltas is also highlighted.

Now to make this new function work, we must replace the C code in each of the triangle rendering functions (flat top and flat bottom) with the new code. This has been done in the new functions within BLACK17.C, but I'm not going to list both of them, only the function that draws a flat top, since they are similar and we are running out of pages. Listing 17-25 shows the updated flat top triangle function that calls *Triangle_Asm* to draw the actual triangle.

LISTING 17-25 Updated triangle function with the new assembly call in it

```c
void Draw_Top_Triangle(int x1,int y1, int x2,int y2, int x3, int y3,int color)
{
// this function draws a triangle that has a flat top

float dx_right,    // the dx/dy ratio of the right edge of line
      dx_left,     // the dx/dy ratio of the left edge of line
      xs,xe,       // the starting and ending points of the edges
      height;      // the height of the triangle

int temp_x,        // used during sorting as temps
    temp_y,
    right,         // used by clipping
    left;

unsigned char far *dest_addr;

// test order of x1 and x2

if (x2 < x1)
   {
   temp_x = x2;
   x2     = x1;
   x1     = temp_x;

   } // end if swap

// compute delta's

height = y3-y1;

dx_left  = (x3-x1)/height;
```

continued on next page

continued from previous page

```
dx_right = (x3-x2)/height;

// set starting points

xs = (float)x1;
xe = (float)x2+(float)0.5;

// perform y clipping

if (y1<poly_clip_min_y)
    {
    // compute new xs and ys

    xs = xs+dx_left*(float)(-y1+poly_clip_min_y);
    xe = xe+dx_right*(float)(-y1+poly_clip_min_y);

    // reset y1

    y1=poly_clip_min_y;

    } // end if top is off screen

if (y3>poly_clip_max_y)
    y3=poly_clip_max_y;


// compute starting address in video memory

dest_addr = double_buffer+(y1<<8)+(y1<<6);

// test if x clipping is needed

if (x1>=poly_clip_min_x && x1<=poly_clip_max_x &&
    x2>=poly_clip_min_x && x2<=poly_clip_max_x &&
    x3>=poly_clip_min_x && x3<=poly_clip_max_x)
    {
    // draw the triangle

    // use the external assembly language triangle engine based on fixed point

    if (y3>y1)
       Triangle_Asm(dest_addr,y1,y3,xs,xe,dx_left,dx_right,color);

    } // end if no x clipping needed
else
   {
   // clip x axis with slower version

   // draw the triangle

   for (temp_y=y1; temp_y<=y3; temp_y++,dest_addr+=320)
       {
```

```
            // do x clip

            left  = (int)xs;
            right = (int)xe;

            // adjust starting point and ending point

            xs+=dx_left;
            xe+=dx_right;

            // clip line

            if (left < poly_clip_min_x)
               {
               left = poly_clip_min_x;

               if (right < poly_clip_min_x)
                  continue;

               }

            if (right > poly_clip_max_x)
               {
               right = poly_clip_max_x;

               if (left > poly_clip_max_x)
                  continue;

               }

            Triangle_16Line(dest_addr,(unsigned int)left,(unsigned int)right,color);

         } // end for

     } // end else x clipping needed

 } // end Draw_Top_Triangle
```

Also, if you're awake and you check out the code, you'll notice a call to a function *Triangle_16Line()* within the clipping section of the code. This is simply an external assembly version of the original *Triangle_Line()* C function. Listing 17-26 lists the code for the 16-bit version of the C line drawing code.

LISTING 17-26 External 16-bit version of *Triangle_Line()*

```
; this function draws a line from xs to xe using 16 bit data movement


.MODEL MEDIUM,C                  ; use medium memory model C function names

.CODE                            ; begin the code segment
```

continued on next page

continued from previous page

```
PUBLIC Triangle_16Line           ; export function name to linker


Triangle_16Line PROC FAR C dest:DWORD, xs:WORD, xe:WORD, color:WORD

.386

begin:

    les di,dest                  ; point es:di to start of line
    add di,xs

    mov cx, color                ; cx = color | color << 8
    mov ch,cl

process_left_end:

    mov ax,xs                    ; ax=xs & 0x01
    and ax,01h

test_l1:

    cmp ax,1                     ; if (ax==1)
    jne process_right_end

    mov es:[di], cl              ; plot pixel
    inc xs                       ; xs++

process_right_end:

    les di,dest                  ; point es:di to start of line
    add di,xe

    mov ax,xe                    ; ax=xs & 0x01
    and ax,01h

test_r0:                         ; if (ax==0)

    cmp ax,0
    jne process_middle

    mov es:[di],cl               ; plot pixel

    dec xe                       ; xe-=1

process_middle:

    les di,dest                  ; point es:di to start of line
    add di,xs

    cld                          ; clear the direction of movement
```

```
        mov ax, cx                      ; move the color data into eax

        mov cx,xe                       ; compute number of words to move  (xe-xs+1)/2
        sub cx,xs
        inc cx
        shr cx,1                        ; divide by 2

        rep stosw                       ; fill the region with data

        ret                             ; return to caller

Triangle_16Line ENDP

END
```

If you're interested, there is also a 32-bit version of the function. You can use it to draw horizontal lines extremely quickly. It is called *Triangle_32Line()* and its source is QLINE.ASM, but we aren't going to look at it.

Interestingly enough, our engine at this point is more than four times faster than when we started. Not bad! Let's see if we can squeeze out just a little bit more, so we can use the saved time to do AI or something constructive.

Back-Face Removal and Shading Tricks

The last area of the graphics pipeline that we can optimize is the back-face removal and shading section. If you recall, our new PLG file definition allows polygons to be made two-sided, and two-sided polygons are visible from both sides. We can use this fact to skip over the back-face removal step for two-sided polygons. Second, we can probably optimize the shading section of the code by checking it for any redundant calculations or constants that can be precomputed.

Let's begin by looking at how we can get rid of the back-face removal step.

Eliminating the Back-Face Removal Step

Back-face removal can be a complex process since a normal, a dot product, and various vectors must be computed to carry out the computation. However, when a polygon is defined to have two sides, the calculation is redundant since the polygon will always be visible and never removed. Therefore, we can implement this test with a simple conditional that tests the value of *two_sided*. If it's 1, the polygon is two-sided and we can avoid the back-face removal step. This test should be done on a polygon-by-polygon basis.

On the other hand, if the test must be performed, can we speed it up at all? Well of course, the answer is yes! We can inline all the function calls that compute vectors, dot products, and normals. However, I'll leave this one to you since the function of the code isn't clear when this is done. Furthermore, the gains are only a couple of percent and not worth the crypticness. (Is that a word?)

Faster Shading

If a polygon is determined to be visible and flat shading is enabled, we must shade the surface of the polygon by performing a dot product between the polygon normal and the direction of the light source. This really can't be avoided, but in the final calculation of the light intensity, we might be able to speed things up. Let's take a look at the core code that computes the light intensity and see what we can do:

```
if (the_object->polys[curr_poly].shading==FLAT_SHADING)
       {
       // compute the dot product between the light source vector
       // and normal vector to surface

       dp = Dot_Product_3D((vector_3d_ptr)&normal,
                           (vector_3d_ptr)&light_source);

       // test if light ray is reflecting off surface

       if (dp>0)
          {
          // now cos 0 = (u.v)/|u||v| or

          intensity = ambient_light + (15*dp/(the_object-
>polys[curr_poly].normal_length));

          // test if intensity has overflowed

          if (intensity >15)
             intensity = 15;

          // intensity now varies from 0-1, 0 being black or grazing and 1 being
          // totally illuminated. use the value to index into color table

          the_object->polys[curr_poly].shade =
                    the_object->polys[curr_poly].color - (int)intensity;

       } // end if light is reflecting off surface
       else
          the_object->polys[curr_poly].shade =
          the_object->polys[curr_poly].color - (int)ambient_light;
       } // end if use flat shading
     else
```

```
{
// assume constant shading and simply assign color to shade
the_object->polys[curr_poly].shade = the_object->polys[curr_poly].color;
} // end else constant shading
```

I have highlighted the only area that we have any hope of making faster. Let's take a look at it:

```
intensity = ambient_light + (15*dp/(the_object->polys[curr_poly].normal_length));
```

Basically, the function normalizes the light intensity with the precomputed normal length and then scales it by 15 (since there are 15 shades per color). The question is, can we simplify this? Let's rewrite the equation in a purer form as:

```
intensity = a + (c₁ * dp / c₂);
```

We know that a and dp can vary, but do c_1 and c_2 vary? The answer is no. So what we can do is pre-multiply them together into a single constant. This will not only get rid of the division but reduce the equation to

```
intensity = a + (c₁₂ * dp );
```

where c_{12} is the product of *(15*1/normal length)*. But how can we compute this constant ahead of time? The answer is that we will rewrite the *PLG_Load_Object()* function to compute the product of *(15*1/normal length)* and store it in *normal_length* instead of the actual normal length. This way we can simplify the intensity calculation down to a single multiply and addition.

Actually, I already slipped the code by you when you saw the new version of *PLG_Load_Object()*. Here is the fragment of code that performs the constant calculation:

```
// compute magnitude of normal, take its inverse and multiply it by
// 15, this will change the shading calculation of 15*dp/normal into
// dp*normal_length, removing one division

the_object->polys[index].normal_length = 15.0/Vector_Mag_3D((vector_3d_ptr)&normal);
```

Anyway, taking both the new back-face removal scheme and the faster shading calculation into consideration, the function shown in Listing 17-27 is an optimized version of *Remove_Backfaces_And_Shade()*.

LISTING 17-27 *New back-face removal and shading function*

```
void Remove_Backfaces_And_Shade(object_ptr the_object)
{
// this function removes all the backfaces of an object by setting the visibility
// flag. This function assumes that the object has been transformed into
// camera coordinates. Also, the function takes into consideration if the
// polygons are one or two sided and executes the minimum amount of code
// in addition to performing the shading calculations


int vertex_0,          // vertex indices
```

continued on next page

continued from previous page

```
        vertex_1,
        vertex_2,
        curr_poly;          // current polygon

float dp,                   // the result of the dot product
      intensity;            // the final intensity of the surface

vector_3d u,v,              // general working vectors
          normal,           // the normal to the surface being processed
          sight;            // line of sight vector

// for each polygon in the object determine if it is pointing away from the
// viewpoint and direction

for (curr_poly=0; curr_poly<the_object->num_polys; curr_poly++)
    {

    // is this polygon two-sided or one-sided

    if (the_object->polys[curr_poly].two_sided == ONE_SIDED)
        {

        // compute two vectors on polygon that have the same initial points

        vertex_0 = the_object->polys[curr_poly].vertex_list[0];
        vertex_1 = the_object->polys[curr_poly].vertex_list[1];
        vertex_2 = the_object->polys[curr_poly].vertex_list[2];

        // the vector u = vo->v1

        Make_Vector_3D((point_3d_ptr)&the_object->vertices_world[vertex_0],
                       (point_3d_ptr)&the_object->vertices_world[vertex_1],
                       (vector_3d_ptr)&u);

        // the vector v = vo-v2

        Make_Vector_3D((point_3d_ptr)&the_object->vertices_world[vertex_0],
                       (point_3d_ptr)&the_object->vertices_world[vertex_2],
                       (vector_3d_ptr)&v);

        // compute the normal to polygon v x u

        Cross_Product_3D((vector_3d_ptr)&v,
                         (vector_3d_ptr)&u,
                         (vector_3d_ptr)&normal);

        // compute the line of sight vector, since all coordinates are world all
        // object vertices are already relative to (0,0,0), thus

        sight.x = view_point.x-the_object->vertices_world[vertex_0].x;
        sight.y = view_point.y-the_object->vertices_world[vertex_0].y;
        sight.z = view_point.z-the_object->vertices_world[vertex_0].z;
```

```
// compute the dot product between line of sight vector and normal to surface

dp = Dot_Product_3D((vector_3d_ptr)&normal,(vector_3d_ptr)&sight);

// is surface visible

if (dp>0)
   {
   // set visible flag

   the_object->polys[curr_poly].visible = 1;

   // compute light intensity if needed

   if (the_object->polys[curr_poly].shading==FLAT_SHADING)
      {

      // compute the dot product between the light source vector
      // and normal vector to surface

      dp = Dot_Product_3D((vector_3d_ptr)&normal,
                          (vector_3d_ptr)&light_source);

      // test if light ray is reflecting off surface

      if (dp>0)
         {
         // now cos O = (u.v)/|u||v| or

         intensity = ambient_light + (dp*(the_object->
                     polys[curr_poly].normal_length));

         // test if intensity has overflowed

         if (intensity > 15)
            intensity = 15;

         // intensity now varies from 0-1, 0 being black or grazing and 1 being
         // totally illuminated. use the value to index into color table

         the_object->polys[curr_poly].shade =
                  the_object->polys[curr_poly].color -
                              (int)intensity;

         } // end if light is reflecting off surface
      else
         the_object->polys[curr_poly].shade =
         the_object->polys[curr_poly].color - (int)ambient_light;

      } // end if use flat shading
   else
      {
```

continued on next page

continued from previous page

```
                    // assume constant shading and simply assign color to shade

                    the_object->polys[curr_poly].shade =
                                    the_object->polys[curr_poly].color;

                    } // end else constant shading

                } // end if dp>0
            else
                the_object->polys[curr_poly].visible = 0;


            } // end if one sided
        else
            {
            // else polygon is always visible i.e. two sided, set visibility flag
            // so engine renders it

            // set visibility

            the_object->polys[curr_poly].visible = 1;

            // perform shading calculation

            if (the_object->polys[curr_poly].shading==FLAT_SHADING)
                {
                // compute normal

                // compute two vectors on polygon that have the same initial points

                vertex_0 = the_object->polys[curr_poly].vertex_list[0];
                vertex_1 = the_object->polys[curr_poly].vertex_list[1];
                vertex_2 = the_object->polys[curr_poly].vertex_list[2];

                // the vector u = vo->v1

                Make_Vector_3D((point_3d_ptr)&the_object->vertices_world[vertex_0],
                               (point_3d_ptr)&the_object->vertices_world[vertex_1],
                               (vector_3d_ptr)&u);

                // the vector v = vo-v2

                Make_Vector_3D((point_3d_ptr)&the_object->vertices_world[vertex_0],
                               (point_3d_ptr)&the_object->vertices_world[vertex_2],
                               (vector_3d_ptr)&v);

                // compute the normal to polygon v x u

                Cross_Product_3D((vector_3d_ptr)&v,
                                 (vector_3d_ptr)&u,
                                 (vector_3d_ptr)&normal);
```

```
// compute the dot product between the light source vector
// and normal vector to surface

dp = Dot_Product_3D((vector_3d_ptr)&normal,
                    (vector_3d_ptr)&light_source);

// test if light ray is reflecting off surface

if (dp>0)
   {
   // now cos 0 = (u.v)/|u||v| or

   intensity = ambient_light +
               (dp*(the_object->polys[curr_poly].normal_length));

   // test if intensity has overflowed

   if (intensity > 15)
       intensity = 15;

   // intensity now varies from 0-1, 0 being black or grazing and 1 being
   // totally illuminated. use the value to index into color table

   the_object->polys[curr_poly].shade =
               the_object->polys[curr_poly].color - (int)intensity;

   } // end if light is reflecting off surface
else
   the_object->polys[curr_poly].shade =
   the_object->polys[curr_poly].color - (int)ambient_light;

} // end if use flat shading
else
   {
   // assume constant shading and simply assign color to shade

   the_object->polys[curr_poly].shade =
               the_object->polys[curr_poly].color;

   } // end else constant shading

} // end else two sided

} // end for curr_poly


} // end Remove_Backfaces_And_Shade
```

As usual, you can use the new function as if it were the old—that is, the interface is still the same. Well, that's about it for optimizing our engine, let's briefly cover some advanced topics.

32-Bit Programming and DOS Extenders

I wish I had a whole book to explain this topic, but we're running out of time. Let's see if we can at least get an idea of what's going on. The 386, 486, and Pentium can all run in real mode, which basically means they are fast 8086s. However, all of these processors have another mode of operation called protected mode, which is their native mode. Basically, memory protection is on and the full 4 gigabyte memory space is available. The problem is that DOS isn't a 32-bit operating system and has no idea what protected mode is. Therefore, once the processor is placed into protected mode, all the functions, interrupts, and system software come to a halting crash!

To deal with this problem, a few standards have been created. One of them is called DPMI, which stands for DOS protected mode interface. There's another, but it's less popular and I can't remember the acronym, so… there we are. Anyway, DPMI is an interface for placing the PC into protected mode, performing operations such as accessing memory above 1 meg, and then returning to DOS. This is great, but it's not enough. We want to write full 32-bit programs and execute them in protected mode. This will allow us to use the full address space of the computer along with 32-bit instructions. But how can we do this? The answer is with a DOS Extender. A DOS Extender is a program that runs in protected mode most of the time, but when a DOS function or service is needed, it switches to real mode and then back again. To make our programs work, we need to obtain tools to write our programs for a protected mode 32-bit environment running under a DOS Extender.

It turns out that 99 percent of all game programmers use one DOS Extender and C/C++ compiler. The DOS Extender is Rational Systems' (Tenberry Software) DOS4G, and the compiler is Watcom's C/C++ compiler version 10.0. The cool thing about using Watcom's C/C++ compiler is that a version of Rational Systems' DOS Extender, called DOS4GW, is bundled with the compiler and has no runtime royalty. That means you can create full 32-bit protected mode games for free! That's the easy part. The hard part is learning protected mode programming, especially when it comes to implementing interrupts and system-level programs. In any case, if you're going to make games, I highly recommend that you purchase the Watcom 32-bit DOS compiler and write 32-bit protected mode games that use the 386, 486, and Pentium to their limits.

You will have a bit of a learning curve in understanding how to write interrupt handlers that can function in a protected mode environment, but once you have conquered that, there isn't much to it. A new memory model called *FLAT* is used, which allows near pointers to have access to 4 gigabytes. Therefore, virtually all segmentation is gone. Of course, there are some rules you must learn, such as, instead of simple addresses, there are local and global descriptor tables that are used to point to regions of memory, and the segment registers become look-ups or *selectors* into the descriptor tables. But even with all the little quirks of protected mode programming, it's worth it to be able to make something like Doom or Dark Forces.

Making More Optimizations

That's all she wrote! I am clean out of tricks...well, maybe tricks that I want to divulge. But here are a few ideas to get you going. It's possible to speed up the engine more by taking out all inline function calls. Also, some speed might be gained by creating some huge look-up tables in a very clever manner; but one of the best tricks is to do this: it's possible to create 32-bit inline assembly language to perform 32-bit fixed point math with an external assembler. This can be done using the technique of *self-modifying code.*

Here's what you do: write some assembly language functions and then look at the code that they generate. Then obtain a function pointer to areas in your C code that you want to modify on the fly. Write the new bytes into memory locations that have NOPS in them possibly (using the inline assembler). After the preprocessing step, your entire program will have been modified with 32-bit instructions even though the program was compiled with a 16-bit compiler. Good luck!

Starblazer 3D

As a final touch, let's write a little demo to show off the new optimized engine and its speed. How about a 3D asteroids demo that could possibly be expanded into a full 3D version of Starblazer? Sounds good to me! So how do we begin? First, we have already seen how to move and rotate objects, so all we need to do is write a game loop that moves a bunch of objects and bounds them in a giant 3D cube of space. The objects will be three different types: pyramids, diamonds, and cubes. Furthermore, each object will be given a different size, speed, and trajectory.

Finally, we will allow the player to fly around the asteroid field by moving the viewpoint and rotating the view angles. This is accomplished by creating a vector that's in the direction of view and translating the viewpoint along this vector. And for some last touches, let's throw in an instrument panel, a scanner, a digital speedometer, and an orientation indicator. The program that does all this is called BLAZE3D.EXE and its source is BLAZE3D.C. To run the program type

    BLAZE3D.EXE

The demo needs no parameters.

When the demo begins, you will see something like that shown in Figure 17-24. This is a first-person view of the space around you. On the upper instrument panel is your yaw, pitch, and roll, along with a digital speedometer that shows your velocity. Below, on your main instrument panel is a 2D scanner that depicts an X-Z top

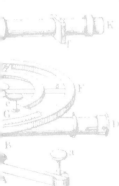

FIGURE 17-24
◎ ◎ ◎ ◎ ◎ ◎
Controls for
Starblazer 3D

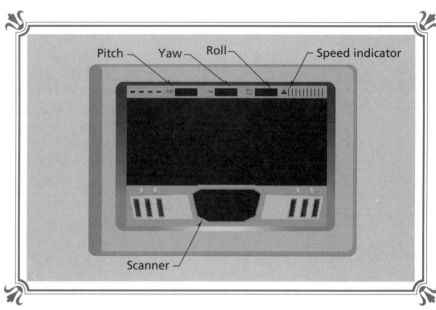

view of the universe. The asteroids above you are drawn as red dots, the asteroids below you are drawn as blue, and you are drawn as a green dot.

To play the demo, here are the controls:

Keypress	Description
→	Rotates or turns right
←	Rotates or turns left
↑	Dives down
↓	Climbs upward
[	Increases speed
]	Decreases speed
ESC	Exits demo

The source for the demo is shown in Listing 17-28; remember that it needs to be linked with BLACK17.C.

LISTING 17-28 Source for the 3D demo BLAZE3D.C

```
// Starblazer 3D

// I N C L U D E S ///////////////////////////////////////////////////////

#include <io.h>
```

```c
#include <conio.h>
#include <stdio.h>
#include <stdlib.h>
#include <dos.h>
#include <bios.h>
#include <fcntl.h>
#include <memory.h>
#include <malloc.h>
#include <math.h>
#include <string.h>
#include <search.h>                // this one is needed for qsort()

// include all of our stuff

#include "black3.h"
#include "black4.h"
#include "black5.h"
#include "black6.h"
#include "black8.h"
#include "black9.h"
#include "black17.h"


// D E F I N E S ///////////////////////////////////////////////////////////

#define NUM_ASTEROIDS   18         // total number of asteroids in demo

#define SCANNER_X       121        // position of scanner
#define SCANNER_Y       151

// T Y P E D E F S ///////////////////////////////////////////////////////////

typedef struct asteroid_typ
        {
        int state;              // state of asteroid
        int xv,yv,zv;           // velocity of asteroid
        int rx,ry,rz;           // rotation rate of asteroid

        } asteroid, *asteroid_ptr;

// G L O B A L S ///////////////////////////////////////////////////////////

object test_objects[NUM_ASTEROIDS]; // objects in universe, need to be in global
                                    // data segement to make things easier

// F U N C T I O N S ///////////////////////////////////////////////////////////

void Draw_Speedo(int speed)
{
// this function draws the digital speedometer

int mark_x=258, // starting tick mark
    index,      // looping variable
    color;      // color of tick mark
```

continued on next page

continued from previous page

```
// compute number of iterations

speed/=5;

if (speed>=0)
   {
   // select forward color

   color=10;
   }
else
   {
   // set color to backward

   color=12;

   // take abs of speed

   speed=-speed;

   } // end else

// draw the ticks

for (index=0; index<speed; index++,mark_x+=6)
   {
   // draw a vertical line

   Line_V(4,14,mark_x,color);

   } // end for index

// erase remaining tick marks

for (; index<10; index++,mark_x+=6)
   {
   // draw a vertical line

   Line_V(4,14,mark_x,0);

   } // end for index

} // end Draw_Speedo

/////////////////////////////////////////////////////////////////////////////

void Draw_Scanner(asteroid_ptr asteroids,int draw)
{
// this function erases or draws the blips on the scanner

int index, // looping variable
```

```
        xb,yb, // position of blip in screen coordinates on scanner
        cb;    // color of blip

static int blip_x[NUM_ASTEROIDS+1], // position 0 holds the ship
          blip_y[NUM_ASTEROIDS+1], // position 0 holds the ship
          active_blips;            // number of active blips this cycle

// should the scanner image be erased or drawn

if (!draw)
   {
   // erase all the blips

   for (index=0; index<=active_blips; index++)
       Write_Pixel(SCANNER_X+blip_x[index], SCANNER_Y+blip_y[index],0);

   } // end if erase
else
   {
   // draw the scanner blips

   // draw asteroids above player as red, below as blue and player as green
   // the asteroids exits in positions 1..n and the player at 0

   active_blips=0;

   for (index=0; index<NUM_ASTEROIDS; index++)
       {
       // test if asteroid is alive, if so, draw it, and save it in record

       if (asteroids[index].state)
          {
          // increase active number of blips

          active_blips++;

          // compute screen coordinates of blip

          xb = (test_objects[index].world_pos.x+2500)/63;
          yb = (2500-test_objects[index].world_pos.z)/139;

          // compute color

          if (test_objects[index].world_pos.y<view_point.y)
             cb = 12;
          else
             cb = 9;

          // save the blip

          blip_x[active_blips]=xb;
```

continued on next page

continued from previous page

```
                blip_y[active_blips]=yb;

                // draw the blip

                Write_Pixel(SCANNER_X+xb,SCANNER_Y+yb,cb);

                } // end if asteroid alive

            } // end for index

        // now process the ship blip

        blip_x[0]=(view_point.x+2500)/63;
        blip_y[0]=(2500-view_point.z)/139;

        Write_Pixel(SCANNER_X+blip_x[0],SCANNER_Y+blip_y[0],10);

        } // end else

} // end Draw_Scanner

// M A I N //////////////////////////////////////////////////////////////////

void main(int argc,char **argv)
{

int done=0,           // exit flag
    index,            // looping variable
    ship_pitch=0,     // current direction of ship
    ship_yaw=0,
    ship_roll=0,
    ship_speed = 0;

vector_3d unit_z        = {0,0,1,1},  // a unit vector in the Z
                                      // direction
          ship_direction = {0,0,1,1}; // the ships direction

asteroid asteroids[NUM_ASTEROIDS];   // the asteroid field
char buffer[80];                     // output string buffer
pcx_picture image_pcx;               // used to load in the background
                                     // imagery

matrix_4x4 rotate;                   // used to build up rotation matrix

// set 2D clipping region to take into consideration the instrument panels

poly_clip_min_y  = 0;
poly_clip_max_y  = 121;

// set up viewing and 3D clipping parameters

clip_near_z       = 100,
```

```
clip_far_z        = 4000,
viewing_distance = 250;

// turn the damn light up a bit!

ambient_light    = 8;

light_source.x    = 0.918926;
light_source.y    = 0.248436;
light_source.z    = -0.306359;

// build all look up tables
Build_Look_Up_Tables();

// load in small asteroids

for (index=0; index<6; index++)
    {
    if (PLG_Load_Object(&test_objects[index],"pyramid.plg",2))
       printf("\nplg loaded.");
    else
       printf("\nCouldn't load file");

    } // end for index

// load in medium asteroids

for (index=6; index<12; index++)
    {
    if (PLG_Load_Object(&test_objects[index],"diamond.plg",3))
       printf("\nplg loaded.");
    else
       printf("\nCouldn't load file");

    } // end for index

// load in large asteroids

for (index=12; index<18; index++)
    {
    if (PLG_Load_Object(&test_objects[index],"cube.plg",4))
       printf("\nplg loaded.");
    else
       printf("\nCouldn't load file");

    } // end for index

// position and set velocity of all asteroids

for (index=0; index<NUM_ASTEROIDS; index++)
    {
    // set position
```

continued on next page

continued from previous page

```
        test_objects[index].world_pos.x = -1000 + rand()%2000;
        test_objects[index].world_pos.y = -1000 + rand()%2000;
        test_objects[index].world_pos.z = -1000 + rand()%2000;

        // set velocity

        asteroids[index].xv = -20+rand()%40;
        asteroids[index].yv = -20+rand()%40;
        asteroids[index].zv = -20+rand()%40;

        // set angular rotation rate

        asteroids[index].rx = rand()%10;
        asteroids[index].ry = rand()%10;
        asteroids[index].rz = rand()%10;

        // set state to alive

        asteroids[index].state = 1;

        } // end for

// set graphics to mode 13h
Set_Graphics_Mode(GRAPHICS_MODE13);

// read the 3D color palette off disk

Load_Palette_Disk("standard.pal",(RGB_palette_ptr)&color_palette_3d);
Write_Palette(0,255,(RGB_palette_ptr)&color_palette_3d);

// allocate double buffer
Create_Double_Buffer(122);

// load in background image

PCX_Init((pcx_picture_ptr)&image_pcx);
PCX_Load("blz3dcoc.pcx", (pcx_picture_ptr)&image_pcx,1);
PCX_Show_Buffer((pcx_picture_ptr)&image_pcx);

// install the isr keyboard driver
Keyboard_Install_Driver();

// scan the asteroid field
Draw_Scanner((asteroid_ptr)&asteroids[0],1);

// main event loop

while(!done)
    {
    // compute starting time of this frame
    starting_time = Timer_Query();

    // erase all objects
```

```
        Fill_Double_Buffer_32(0);

// erase the scanner
Draw_Scanner((asteroid_ptr)&asteroids[0],0);

// test what user is doing

// change ship velocity
if (keyboard_state[MAKE_RGT_BRACKET])
   {
   // speed up

   if ((ship_speed+=5)>50)
      ship_speed=50;

   } // end if speed increase

if (keyboard_state[MAKE_LFT_BRACKET])
   {
   // slow down

   if ((ship_speed-=5)<-50)
      ship_speed=-50;

   } // end if speed decrease

// test for turns
if (keyboard_state[MAKE_RIGHT])
   {
   // rotate ship to right

   if ((ship_yaw+=4)>=360)
      ship_yaw-=360;

   } // end if

if (keyboard_state[MAKE_LEFT])
   {

   // rotate ship to left

   if ((ship_yaw-=4)<0)
      ship_yaw+=360;

   } // end if

// test for up and down
if (keyboard_state[MAKE_UP])
   {

   view_point.y-=25;

   } // end if
```

continued on next page

continued from previous page

```
if (keyboard_state[MAKE_DOWN])
   {

   view_point.y+=25;

   } // end if

// test for exit

if (keyboard_state[MAKE_ESC])
   done=1;

// rotate trajectory vector to align with view direction

Mat_Identity_4x4(rotate);

rotate[0][0] = ( cos_look[ship_yaw]);
rotate[0][2] = (-sin_look[ship_yaw]);
rotate[2][0] = ( sin_look[ship_yaw]);
rotate[2][2] = ( cos_look[ship_yaw]);

// x component

ship_direction.x =

         unit_z.x * rotate[0][0] +
         unit_z.z * rotate[2][0];

// y component

ship_direction.y =

         unit_z.y * rotate[1][1];

// z component

ship_direction.z =

         unit_z.x * rotate[0][2] +
         unit_z.z * rotate[2][2];

// move viewpoint based on ship trajectory
view_point.x+=ship_direction.x*ship_speed;
view_point.y+=ship_direction.y*ship_speed;
view_point.z+=ship_direction.z*ship_speed;

// test ship against universe boundaries
if (view_point.x>2500)
    view_point.x=-2500;
else
if (view_point.x<-2500)
    view_point.x=2500;
```

```
       if (view_point.y>2500)
           view_point.y=-2500;
       else
       if (view_point.y<-2500)
           view_point.y=2500;

       if (view_point.z>2500)
           view_point.z=-2500;
       else
       if (view_point.z<-2500)
           view_point.z=2500;

       // set view angles based on trajectory of ship
       view_angle.ang_x = ship_pitch;
       view_angle.ang_y = ship_yaw;
       view_angle.ang_z = ship_roll;

       // rotate asteroids
       for (index=0; index<NUM_ASTEROIDS; index++)
           {
           // rotate object based on rotation rates

           Rotate_Object(&test_objects[index],asteroids[index].rx,
                                               asteroids[index].ry,
                                               asteroids[index].rz);

           } // end for index

       // translate asteroids

       for (index=0; index<NUM_ASTEROIDS; index++)
           {

           // translate each asteroids world position

           test_objects[index].world_pos.x+=asteroids[index].xv;
           test_objects[index].world_pos.y+=asteroids[index].yv;
           test_objects[index].world_pos.z+=asteroids[index].zv;

           // test if the asteroid has gone off the screen anywhere

           if (test_objects[index].world_pos.x > 2500 ||
               test_objects[index].world_pos.x < -2500)
             asteroids[index].xv=-asteroids[index].xv;

           if (test_objects[index].world_pos.y > 2500 ||
               test_objects[index].world_pos.y < -2500)
             asteroids[index].yv=-asteroids[index].yv;

           if (test_objects[index].world_pos.z > 2500 ||
               test_objects[index].world_pos.z < -2500)
             asteroids[index].zv=-asteroids[index].zv;
```

continued on next page

continued from previous page

```
          }  // end motion

    // now that user has possible moved viewpoint, create the global
    // world to camera transformation matrix
    Create_World_To_Camera();

    // reset the polygon list
    Generate_Poly_List(NULL,RESET_POLY_LIST);

    // perform general 3D pipeline

    for (index=0; index<NUM_ASTEROIDS; index++)
        {
        // test if object is visible
        if (!Remove_Object(&test_objects[index],OBJECT_CULL_XYZ_MODE))
            {
            // convert object local coordinates to world coordinates
            Local_To_World_Object(&test_objects[index]);

            // remove the backfaces and shade object
            Remove_Backfaces_And_Shade(&test_objects[index]);

            // convert world coordinates to camera coordinates
            World_To_Camera_Object(&test_objects[index]);

            // clip the objects polygons against viewing volume
            Clip_Object_3D(&test_objects[index],CLIP_Z_MODE);

            // generate the final polygon list
            Generate_Poly_List(&test_objects[index],ADD_TO_POLY_LIST);
            }

        }  // end for

    // sort the polygons
    Sort_Poly_List();

    // draw the polygon list
    Draw_Poly_List();

    // display the pitch yaw and roll of ship
    sprintf(buffer,"%4d",ship_pitch);
    Print_String(80,6,10,buffer,0);

    sprintf(buffer,"%4d",ship_yaw);
    Print_String(144,6,10,buffer,0);

    sprintf(buffer,"%4d",ship_roll);
    Print_String(208,6,10,buffer,0);

    // draw speedo
    Draw_Speedo(ship_speed);
```

```
    // draw the scanner
    Draw_Scanner((asteroid_ptr)&asteroids[0],1);

    // display double buffer

    Display_Double_Buffer_32(double_buffer,18);

    // lock onto 18 frames per second max
    while((Timer_Query()-starting_time)<1);

    } // end while
// restore graphics mode back to text

Set_Graphics_Mode(TEXT_MODE);

// restore the old keyboard driver

Keyboard_Remove_Driver();

} // end main
```

The program is probably the first time we have used the 3D engine to make something that even remotely resembles a game. Study it carefully, but realize that other than the 3D aspect of it, the only difference compared to our other 2D programs is the graphics pipeline section that processes the 3D objects.

Summary

This chapter has become much larger than I thought it would! It's amazing that we covered so many topics, but we really put the engine through the ringer! We learned about more efficient data structures, 32-bit assembly language programming, a lot about optimizing matrix mathematics, and how to make the triangle engine much faster. We also learned that many calculations can be precomputed, such as the polygon sorting for the Z-sort and the shading calculations.

We diverged a bit to learn about the math coprocessor, which is very important since it is becoming more and more useful—especially with the Pentium's floating point performance. And somewhere in there we covered full 32-bit fixed point math using external assembly language, even learning how to do 64-bit math in some cases. Next, we got a bit philosophical and touched upon DOS Extenders and 32-bit compilers. Finally, we ended the chapter with a little demo of the 3D engine.

Now I want you to put this book down and think about all the optimizations we made and see if you can figure out a different way of looking at everything. Then pick up the book and read the next chapter.

18

Kill or Be Killed

come vedi foro le manobelle e di quali pivoberano i saja
e i gra pesi sum lommedio o pene o lato prano de Bone
orgare nella modo i fa permaziella della manobella pegi quon
forga o ppiv i tomo pib ivol.

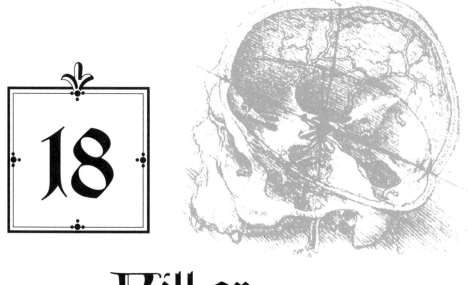

18

Kill or
Be Killed

This is it! We've made it through an incredible journey, and better yet, we are still in one piece—but not for long. Within this chapter, we're going to do two things: first, we're going to review the design and implementation of a full 3D game called Kill or Be Killed (KRK), and second, we're going to take a brief look at the future of PC games.

Since you are almost a full-fledged Cybersorcerer, this chapter isn't going to be highly technical; rather, we are going to converse at a high level, just as a couple game designers would. This is one of the last steps in your training—being able to forget about all the technology and math behind the games and look at them from a purely artistic standpoint. After we're done with the design of the game and some predictions about the future, it will be time for the final ceremony that will initiate you into the alliance of Cybersorcerers.

The Story

The story behind KRK goes something like this: Thousands of years in the future, humankind and other races within our galaxy have formed a federation of worlds. This federation governs the planets and helps resolve any disputes between worlds over territory or other various problems. If two or more worlds have a mutual disagreement, instead of their entering into a war, the CURR RAH TAK is performed. Basically, each world selects a champion to represent them. These champions are then sent to the world of Centari Alpha 3, beyond the second sun of the Rylon system.

Since no two races are equal physically, it would be unfair for the champions to battle against each other creature to creature. For example, Figure 18-1 shows a comparison between a typical Dylusion and Pilut. As you can see, the tiny Pilut would have no chance against the much larger Dylusion. Hence, each champion will be placed in a special neurally linked ground fighter, so that only cunning and tactics separate them. Figure 18-2(a) and 18-2(b) depict the original sketches of the two fighter ships that each champion may choose from.

Once the preliminary ceremonies are complete and the negotiators have defined the goals of the contest and the bounty to the winner, the contestants are instantly teleported to the planet's surface and the battle ensues! The battle must continue until there is only one champion alive. The rest must fall. Failure to terminate another opponent, or the blatant display of mercy, will result in termination. There are no exceptions!

FIGURE 18-1

⊙ ⊙ ⊙ ⊙ ⊙ ⊙

Typical Dylusion *compared to typical* Pilut

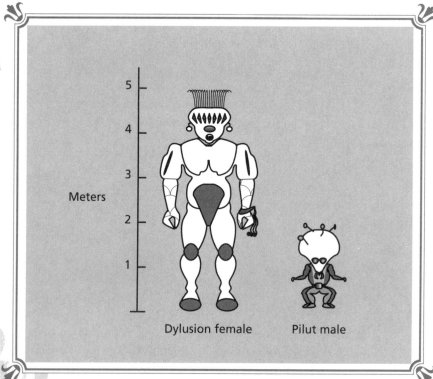

Dylusion female   Pilut male

FIGURE 18-2
⊙ ⊙ ⊙ ⊙ ⊙ ⊙
(a) The Tallon;
(b) The Slider

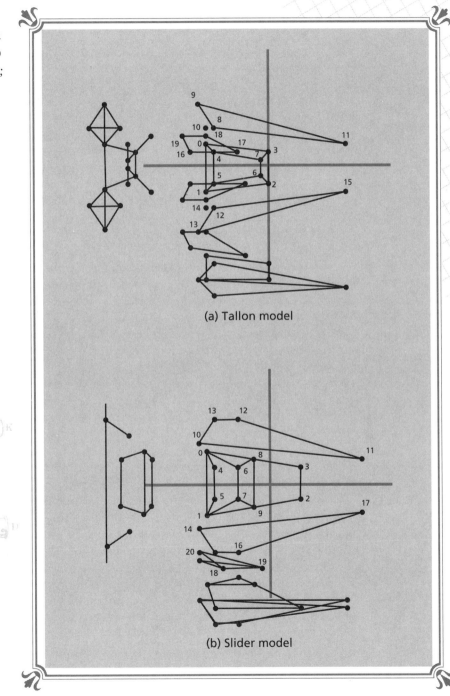

(a) Tallon model

(b) Slider model

The Design and Creation of KRK

The entire design and implementation of KRK took about two and a half weeks. My main goal was to show how to use the 3D engine that we have been working on and to create a reasonably simplistic 3D shooter that contained examples of everything we have covered, such as 2D, 3D, sound, music, color FX, and so on. Taking all this into consideration, I used Starblazer as a starting point. I wanted to follow the same kind of startup and selection interface, but with different artwork and maybe a screen or two more in the introduction. But that's as far as the resemblance goes. If you recall, Starblazer is a modem-to-modem game; hence, to support two players, the main event loop and even the control interface are much different. However, I was able to take the fundamental elements of the main game and set up event loops and use them as a basis for KRK.

After I did the code hijacking from Starblazer, instead of messing with the introduction and control interface, I dove straight into the design of the game portion of KRK. My basic vision was a red planet with various obstacles such as rocks and crystals growing out of the ground. Then to make the game a little more interesting, I thought it would be nice to place some telepods at the corners of the game grid so that the aliens and the player could teleport. In the final version, the telepods only work for the aliens, but they look pretty cool. Next, to let the player know that the game grid has bounds, I placed some large electronic laser barriers around the perimeter of the grid. The barriers have large blinking green beacons and are about 100 meters tall in scale size. Finally, I wanted to have a main court area that contained some observation towers along with a main power station. Figure 18-3 shows the sketch of the game grid from a bird's-eye view.

Now I had quite a few 3D objects that would be visible to the player, but still the game would look pretty dull without some kind of background, so I decided to put in a scrolling 2D mountainscape in the distance, using the layers system. And as the player turns, I thought it would be neat to scroll the background to make the game look more 3D, so I added this feature. At this point, I had most of the static portion of the game in place. I had background, objects, obstacles, and a large game area. Since the player isn't really an object, but just a view position and view angle, moving the player around is nothing more than moving the view position and rotating the camera parallel to the Y axis. The problem I was faced with was the alien ships!

I started out thinking that I was going to create weird insectlike walkers, but soon realized that two days (the time I had to implement the aliens) wasn't going to do. Not only would the actual 3D modeling of the walkers take days, but implementing the mechanics of walking would take too long. So I decided to use simple hovercraft-type ships based on sharp edges and lots of triangles. In the end, I was very happy with the look of the alien ships, and they served their purpose. Actually, I'm glad I used them instead of walkers. Anyway, I decided to use a maximum of

FIGURE 18-3

⊚ ⊚ ⊚ ⊚ ⊚ ⊚

*Aerial view of
the battleground*

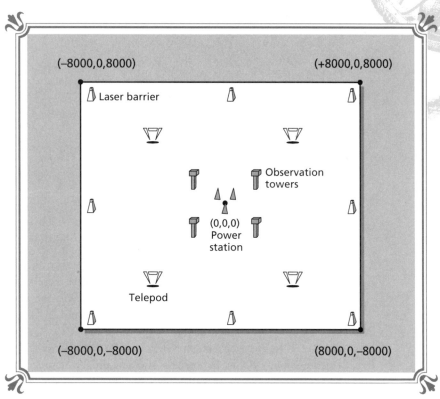

four aliens at any one time, and I gave them the basic state machine-probability intelligence system we have studied.

After I got the aliens working and the mechanics of their interactions with the player to a satisfactory point, I added the sound, music, and completed all the introductory stuff, such as the mech selection and Rules dialogs. Finally, I went through the game and tuned and cleaned it up as much as time permitted.

In a real game design you should take more than two or three weeks. Actually, I can't see anyone making even a low-end shareware game in less than a couple months, with the average being three months. And a real commercial game should take around a year to make. Anyway, that's how I did it.

Components of the Game

KRK is constructed of various code and data modules. The main code for KRK is KRK.C, which includes its own header information. The game itself depends on many of the modules we have already written throughout the preceding chapters of the book, as well as the ASM modules from Chapter 17.

I compiled it using:

KRK.C	BLACK9.C
BLACK3.C	BLACK18.C
BLACK4.C	QCPY.OBJ
BLACK5.C	QSET.OBJ
BLACK6.C	TRI_FP.OBJ
BLACK8.C	WLINE.OBJ

As far as data modules go, the game consists of a number of files—here's how to identify them:

KRK*.PCX: all the image files
KRK*.VOC: all the sound FX
KRKMUS.XMI: the music for KRK
Various PLG files with file names relating to what they represent in the game

I probably should have kept using the KRK prefix, but oh well! To create an executable, you simply do what you've been doing; that is, link in the various library modules included in the *includes* section of KRK and the assembly objects, and that's it. However, make sure to use BLACK18.C and BLACK18.H for this game, since some minor changes had to be made to BLACK17.C to implement the alien explosions. Nothing big, but nevertheless don't use BLACK17.C and BLACK17.H or there will be trouble. In any case, the new library module along with all the data files and the main KRK.C source file are all in the directory for this chapter, so you shouldn't have any trouble. I'm sure that by now you are a compiler expert anyhow! (I'm still trying to change the darn colors of the IDE.)

The New 3D Library Module

In the last chapter we optimized the 3D engine to a reasonable level of performance—at least enough to make some games with. However, the engine is based on objects and doesn't really work well with single polygons, points, or lines. This turns out to be a problem when trying to make something explode. My original idea was simply to rip apart the polygons of an object, but the problem is that once a 3D model is fried, it must be unfried, either by reloading it from disk or saving it before corrupting it. Both solutions are unacceptable, so I decided to do something a little less ambitious for explosions. Since both the aliens and the player fire plasma torpedoes (at least that's what we're going to pretend now), it seems to me that a ship hit by a torpedo should fission apart and disintegrate.

So I decided to make an alien that had been hit simply glow away. But there's a catch. How can we tell the graphics engine to always draw the polygons of a model using the same color or color register? Well, we can't. Granted, we could go into the model and reset all the polygon colors, but then the model would be corrupted. A better way to do this would be to force all the polygons to a specific color register during the lighting of an object. So what I did was rewrite the *Remove_Backfaces_And_Shade()* function to take one more parameter called *force_color*. This parameter, if non-negative, tells the shading portion of the code to use the *force_color* as the color register regardless of the shading settings, light source, and so on. This way, when an alien is disintegrating, the color register that is going to glow can simply be sent to the *Remove_Backfaces_And_Shade()* function and the polygons entered into the global polygon list will be colored appropriately, but the model itself won't be corrupted.

Listing 18-1 is the new, modified *Remove_Backfaces_And_Shade()* function that you will find in BLACK18.C.

LISTING 18-1 The new back-face removal and shading function

```
void Remove_Backfaces_And_Shade(object_ptr the_object, int force_color)
{
// this function removes all the backfaces of an object by setting the visibility
// flag. This function assumes that the object has been transformed into
// camera coordinates. Also, the function takes into consideration if the
// polygons are one or two sided and executes the minimum amount of code
// in addition to performing the shading calculations

// also, this function has been altered from the standard function found in
// black17.c by the addition of the parameter force_color, this is used
// to force all the polys to a specific color. this is needed for the
// explosion vaporization effect

int vertex_0,         // vertex indices
    vertex_1,
    vertex_2,
    curr_poly;        // current polygon

float dp,             // the result of the dot product
      intensity;      // the final intensity of the surface

vector_3d u,v,        // general working vectors
          normal,     // the normal to the surface being processed
          sight;      // line of sight vector

// for each polygon in the object determine if it is pointing away from the
// viewpoint and direction

for (curr_poly=0; curr_poly<the_object->num_polys; curr_poly++)
    {
    // is this polygon two-sided or one-sided

    if (the_object->polys[curr_poly].two_sided == ONE_SIDED)
        {

        // compute two vectors on polygon that have the same initial points
```
continued on next page

continued from previous page

```
vertex_0 = the_object->polys[curr_poly].vertex_list[0];
vertex_1 = the_object->polys[curr_poly].vertex_list[1];
vertex_2 = the_object->polys[curr_poly].vertex_list[2];

// the vector u = vo->v1

Make_Vector_3D((point_3d_ptr)&the_object->vertices_world[vertex_0],
               (point_3d_ptr)&the_object->vertices_world[vertex_1],
               (vector_3d_ptr)&u);

// the vector v = vo-v2

Make_Vector_3D((point_3d_ptr)&the_object->vertices_world[vertex_0],
               (point_3d_ptr)&the_object->vertices_world[vertex_2],
               (vector_3d_ptr)&v);

// compute the normal to polygon v x u

Cross_Product_3D((vector_3d_ptr)&v,
                 (vector_3d_ptr)&u,
                 (vector_3d_ptr)&normal);

// compute the line of sight vector, since all coordinates are world all
// object vertices are already relative to (0,0,0), thus

sight.x = view_point.x-the_object->vertices_world[vertex_0].x;
sight.y = view_point.y-the_object->vertices_world[vertex_0].y;
sight.z = view_point.z-the_object->vertices_world[vertex_0].z;

// compute the dot product between line of sight vector and normal to surface

dp = Dot_Product_3D((vector_3d_ptr)&normal,(vector_3d_ptr)&sight);

// is surface visible

if (dp>0)
   {
   // set visible flag

   the_object->polys[curr_poly].visible = 1;

// a little cludge

   // first test for a forced color
   if (force_color>-1)
      {
      the_object->polys[curr_poly].shade = force_color;
      continue;
      } // end if forced color

// end a little cludge
```

```
         // compute light intensity if needed

         if (the_object->polys[curr_poly].shading==FLAT_SHADING)
            {

            // compute the dot product between the light source vector
            // and normal vector to surface

            dp = Dot_Product_3D((vector_3d_ptr)&normal,
                                (vector_3d_ptr)&light_source);

            // test if light ray is reflecting off surface

            if (dp>0)
               {
               // now cos 0 = (u.v)/|u||v| or

               intensity = ambient_light + (dp*(the_object->polys
                                         [curr_poly].normal_length));

               // test if intensity has overflowed

               if (intensity > 15)
                  intensity = 15;

               // intensity now varies from 0-1, 0 being black or grazing and 1 being
               // totally illuminated. use the value to index into color table

               the_object->polys[curr_poly].shade =
                        the_object->polys[curr_poly].color - (int)intensity;

               } // end if light is reflecting off surface
            else
               the_object->polys[curr_poly].shade =
               the_object->polys[curr_poly].color - (int)ambient_light;

            } // end if use flat shading
         else
            {
            // assume constant shading and simply assign color to shade

            the_object->polys[curr_poly].shade =
                        the_object->polys[curr_poly].color;

            } // end else constant shading

         } // end if dp>0
      else
         the_object->polys[curr_poly].visible = 0;


      } // end if one sided
```

continued on next page

continued from previous page

```
    else
       {
       // else polygon is always visible i.e. two sided, set visibility flag
       // so engine renders it

       // set visibility

       the_object->polys[curr_poly].visible = 1;


// a little cludge

       // first test for a forced color
       if (force_color>-1)
          {
          the_object->polys[curr_poly].shade = force_color;
          continue;
          } // end if forced color

// end a little cludge

       // perform shading calculation

       if (the_object->polys[curr_poly].shading==FLAT_SHADING)
          {
          // compute normal

          // compute two vectors on polygon that have the same initial points

          vertex_0 = the_object->polys[curr_poly].vertex_list[0];
          vertex_1 = the_object->polys[curr_poly].vertex_list[1];
          vertex_2 = the_object->polys[curr_poly].vertex_list[2];

          // the vector u = vo->v1

          Make_Vector_3D((point_3d_ptr)&the_object->vertices_world[vertex_0],
                         (point_3d_ptr)&the_object->vertices_world[vertex_1],
                         (vector_3d_ptr)&u);

          // the vector v = vo-v2

          Make_Vector_3D((point_3d_ptr)&the_object->vertices_world[vertex_0],
                         (point_3d_ptr)&the_object->vertices_world[vertex_2],
                         (vector_3d_ptr)&v);

          // compute the normal to polygon v x u

          Cross_Product_3D((vector_3d_ptr)&v,
                           (vector_3d_ptr)&u,
                           (vector_3d_ptr)&normal);


          // compute the dot product between the light source vector
```

```
        // and normal vector to surface

        dp = Dot_Product_3D((vector_3d_ptr)&normal,
                            (vector_3d_ptr)&light_source);

        // test if light ray is reflecting off surface

        if (dp>0)
           {
           // now cos 0 = (u.v)/|u||v| or

           intensity = ambient_light + (dp*(the_object->polys
                                     [curr_poly].normal_length));

           // test if intensity has overflowed

           if (intensity > 15)
              intensity = 15;

           // intensity now varies from 0-1, 0 being black or grazing and 1 being
           // totally illuminated. use the value to index into color table

           the_object->polys[curr_poly].shade =
                     the_object->polys[curr_poly].color - (int)intensity;

           } // end if light is reflecting off surface
        else
           the_object->polys[curr_poly].shade =
           the_object->polys[curr_poly].color - (int)ambient_light;

        } // end if use flat shading
     else
        {
        // assume constant shading and simply assign color to shade

        the_object->polys[curr_poly].shade = the_object->polys
                        [curr_poly].color;

        } // end else constant shading

     } // end else two sided

  } // end for curr_poly

} // end Remove_Backfaces_And_Shade
```

I've highlighted the important changes. If the parameter *force_color* is set to -1, the function works exactly as before. Also, I've added a few old functions to BLACK18.C from BLACK11.C to help with one part of the introduction—the ship selection phase. I wanted to be able to draw wireframe versions of the ship, so I had to include the 2D line and clipping functions along with the old *Draw_Object_Wire()* function, but we have already seen these, so no need to check them out again.

Now let's step through some of the main elements of the game from a designer's view and see how everything is accomplished.

The Introductory Screens

Originally, I wanted to have a 3D Studio-modeled movie play for the introduction, and I actually had my friend (Joe Font) make one, but I didn't get time to put it in. You can find the FLC on the CD-ROM if you would like to add it yourself. Anyway, the introductory sequence for KRK is fairly standard. It begins by showing a PCX file that does a little advertising for Waite Group Press, followed by a nice rendering of the red planet Centari Alpha 3 made by Richard Benson. Then I call a screen fade, and the standard green teletypewriter text is drawn out that describes the different systems starting up. This is followed by another image of the red planet (I drew this in about five minutes with Deluxe Animation). Some text is printed that describes the mass, temperature, and so forth, of the planet. Then it instantly switches to the main menu screen, and the player can start navigating through menu items with the arrow keys.

The introductory process is rather simple, but it isn't bad considering that I drew the artwork, which resembles in some ways the work of a cabbage patch doll. However, with really good artwork and the simple screen transitions we've been using, a decent introductory sequence should be possible.

The Main Menu

The main menu has only four working items on it:

- ✤ Challenge
- ✤ Select Mech
- ✤ Rules
- ✤ Leave Planet

The Challenge selection sends the player down to the planet and the game begins. The Select Mech option allows the player to select either a Tallon or a Slider. The Rules menu item goes into a page-by-page description of the rules and controls of the game. Finally, the Leave Planet option exits the game and shows the extra credits.

The main menu is implemented as a real-time loop that does two things: it performs color animation on the borders of the currently selected menu item and tests for the [ENTER] key being pressed, which indicates a selection. Finally, the image for the main menu is loaded off disk each time it is displayed; that is, the main menu image is not kept in memory, but the few hundred milliseconds load time isn't noticeable.

Now let's take a closer look at how each menu item works.

Selecting a Mech

This is probably my favorite menu item that does just about nothing. When selected, the player is shown a rotating 3D model of the currently selected ship. This is totally 3D and not simulated with animation. The 3D engine is actually generating the view. However, instead of using the solid rendering engine, the old *Draw_Object_Wire()* function is used to draw the model of the ships. Since there are only two ships, there aren't that many models, but it's still a neat effect.

The player can select a new ship by pressing (ENTER) or exit the dialog with (ESC). If a new ship is selected, the player will see the new ship on his multifunction display (MFD) when in hull mode; however, it would be nice if each ship had its own characteristics, such as speed, shield strength, turning radius, and so on.

The Rules Dialog

The Rules dialog was lifted right out of Starblazer. I simply changed the artwork and the actual instructions, but the core code is the same. In fact, I took some out! Remember those scrolling lights at the top of the Starblazer briefing image? They're gone! This is because I was having palette problems, and it wasn't worth the time to figure out for some blinking lights.

Entering the Game

When the player enters the game, all the system variables are reset, the image for the instrumentation is loaded from disk and copied into the lower region of the video RAM, and the game music starts.

Leaving the Planet

When the player selects the Leave Planet menu option, the main menu is immediately exited and the screen is blanked out with black. Then, using the font engine, the extra credits are displayed one by one, followed by a vertical scroll (just like the movies). This is accomplished using a line-by-line memory move. Here's the code that smooth-scrolls the screen (notice that it uses the quad byte memory move for speed):

```
// scroll them away

for (index=0; index<135; index++)
    {
    // copy the video line to the line above it
    fquadcpy(video_buffer,video_buffer+320,16000-80);
```

continued on next page

continued from previous page

```
// test for exit
if (keys_active)
    return;

} // end for index
```

The Player's View

Once the game starts, the player is taken instantly to another world, a world that exists only in Cyberspace. The main elements of the world are real 3D objects; but other aspects, such as the instrumentation, the sky, ground, and mountain background, are all part of the illusion. Figure 18-4 shows a diagram of the screen layout. Let's take a look at how each region is implemented.

The Sky

The sky is drawn in vertical sections in three distinct shades of red. This is done to simulate a bit of perspective. The vertical extent of each shaded region was arrived at experimentally; however, the color of the last section had to match that of the sky color behind the mountainscape.

FIGURE 18-4

◎ ◎ ◎ ◎ ◎ ◎

Screen layout for KRK

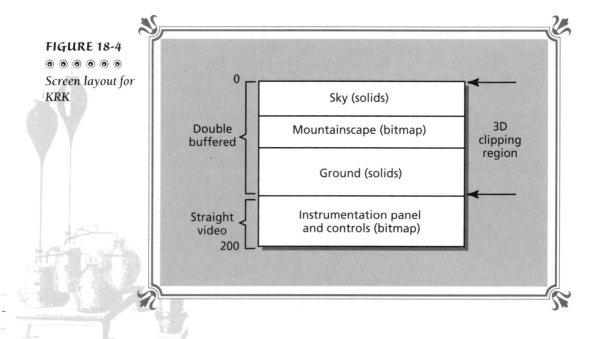

The Background Mountainscape

The background mountains are simply a single layer. I admit that I didn't try adding two or more layers because I was afraid that the speed wouldn't be there, but now I think that two layers might be possible. Anyway, the mountainscape uses the layers system from Chapter 4 and is a single rectangular region with width 320 and height 43 pixels, so it takes quite a bit of memory to move each frame. The 3D effect is achieved by using the current Y component of the view angle scaled by a constant as the amount to scroll the mountainscape. This gives the effect of the world rotating as the player does, which it should.

The Ground

The ground is drawn in the same way as the sky. The ground consists of three brown layers that become darker toward the horizon. This helps with depth perception. A little more realism could probably be achieved by adding a few more shades.

Next, let's talk about the player's instrument panel.

The Instrument Panel

The instrument panel was drawn using Deluxe Animation by Electronic Arts. Originally, I envisioned something a little more 3D, but the end result isn't bad. Figure 18-5 shows an actual screen shot of the game.

FIGURE 18-5

◎ ◎ ◎ ◎ ◎ ◎

Typical screen shot from KRK

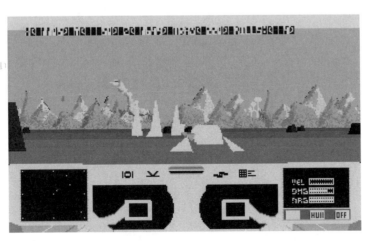

Before covering each area of the instrument panel, I want to explain an important design decision that I made for the control area. As you will notice from Figure 18-4, the control area is not double buffered. This is because, for the most part, not much of it changes as a function of time. This is always a hard decision to make—that is, what part of the video display to buffer. Ideally, we would like to buffer the whole screen, but redrawing a full 64,000 buffer or larger isn't cheap, and many times a full 64,000-byte double buffer isn't available. Luckily though, the only animation performed on the instrument panel is color animation and the scanner blips, so there isn't any perceivable erase-draw cycle. So in this case, we got the best of both worlds—more memory and faster video update by selecting not to buffer the instrumentation area.

The Scanner

The scanner is displayed on the leftmost virtual monitor and is toggled with the Ⓢ key. The scanner only displays the following items:

- ✣ Perimeter barriers
- ✣ Telepods
- ✣ The main power station
- ✣ Aliens
- ✣ The player

The scanner is nothing more than a top view of the world. During each frame, the positions of all the scanned objects are scaled down to fit in the scanner window and displayed in different colors. The player is blue, the aliens are red, and the other objects are various colors that I keep changing, so they could be anything by the time you read this. Also, the positions of the scanner blips are recorded in a static local array so that during erasure the positions need not be recomputed by the function. I was toying with the idea of adding the missiles to the scanner. Maybe you could add this? It would be cool to see torpedoes that are about to hit you, and it would help in shooting ahead of the enemies.

The Multifunction Display

The multifunction display, or MFD, is located on the right video screen of the instrument panel and is controlled by the Ⓣ key. By pressing Ⓣ, the player selects the different modes of the MFD. I originally envisioned a communications mode that would allow you to communicate with another player over the modem, but that idea got canned due to time limitations on the writing of this game. Anyway, the two displays that were implemented are system meters and a hull damage indicator.

System Meters

The system meters display shows three different line graphs. The first is the velocity of the ship (blue for forward and red for reverse), the second shows the damage to the ship, and the third shows the current energy level of the ship. Right now, only the first two work. They are implemented by referring to a set of variables. These variables are then scaled down so that their maximum lengths are 20. Then lines are drawn two pixels high within the meter bitmaps to indicate the current value of the data being shown. This works quite well for such a simple output device.

Hull Damage System

The hull damage system is supposed to work hand in hand with the overall damage indicator in the system meters display mode; however, what I was thinking is that there would be multiple bitmaps for each ship, each being more and more distorted or maybe showing red areas to indicate damage. Anyway, all that is displayed right now is the hull of the currently selected ship with predrawn bitmaps.

The Heads-Up Display

The heads-up display, or HUD, is always a favorite of mine. It's a nice way to add some extra information to a game that normally would clutter the screen if continually displayed. The HUD for KRK is toggled with the Ⓗ key and simply writes to the double buffer (after all the other imagery has been rendered, so it is on top). The HUD currently displays the X, Y, Z position of the player, his angular trajectory, and finally, the number of aliens he has dispatched. The HUD is drawn with standard text using the font engine function *Font_Engine_1()*.

The Objects in the Game

This is where I had the most trouble. The problem is that each model loaded into the computer takes up about 2.5K of memory. This means that after loading 20 objects, the *NEAR* data segment would be nearly full! But the question is, do we need to load multiple models of the same object? The answer is, of course, no. In fact, for any object we can get away with a single model, as long as we have a secondary data structure that holds the position and maybe the current angle of each replicated object.

Take a look at Figure 18-6, which depicts the data relationship between multiple models and the two necessary data structures. If we want 100 rocks, we load the PLG file for a single rock, and then we create a separate array or data structure that contains the positions of these 100 rocks. Then instead of simply processing the

FIGURE 18-6

◎ ◎ ◎ ◎ ◎ ◎

*Using a
secondary array
to replicate 3D
objects*

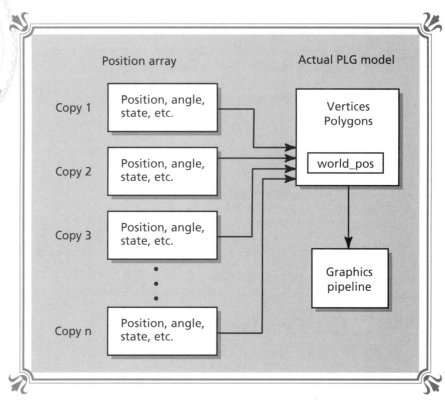

single rock model into the pipeline, we perform a little trick. We overwrite the
world_pos of the single rock model with the position of the first replica and send the
object down the pipeline; then we overwrite with the second replica's world position, and so on. This way the same model can be sent down the pipeline multiple
times with different positions (and possibly orientations). The graphics engine
doesn't know the difference though, and for all intents and purposes, we have replicated an object.

Just to make it clear how this is done, let's take a look at the secondary data
structure used for the static objects of the game. Static objects include everything
but the missiles and the aliens. Here's the data structure:

```
// this structure is used to replicate static similar objects based on the
// same model

typedef struct fixed_obj_typ
        {
        int state;          // state of object
        int rx,ry,rz;       // rotation rate of object
        float x,y,z;        // position of object

        } fixed_obj, *fixed_obj_ptr;
```

As you can see, this structure only takes a couple dozen bytes instead of 2.5K, but it serves the purpose of holding the position, orientation, and state of a replicated object. Now imagine that the following arrays have been allocated. These two arrays hold the actual models:

```
object static_obj[NUM_STATIONARY];         // there are six basic stationary
                                           // object types

object dynamic_obj[NUM_DYNAMIC];           // this array holds the models
                                           // for the dynamic game objects
```

These arrays hold the replication arrays:

```
fixed_obj obstacles_1[NUM_OBSTACLES_1];    // general obstacles, rocks etc.
fixed_obj obstacles_2[NUM_OBSTACLES_2];    // general obstacles, rocks etc.
fixed_obj barriers[NUM_BARRIERS];          // boundary universe boundaries
fixed_obj towers[NUM_TOWERS];              // the control towers
fixed_obj stations[NUM_STATIONS];          // the power stations
fixed_obj telepods[NUM_TELEPODS];          // the teleporters
```

Now let's imagine that we have initialized one of the elements of the *static_obj[]* array with the rock model and also initialized *fixed_obj obstacles_1[NUM_OBSTACLES_1]*. Then the following fragment of code would replicate the rock object through the graphics pipeline multiple times:

```
// phase 0: obstacle type one

for (index=0; index<NUM_OBSTACLES_1; index++)
    {
    // test if object is visible

    // now before we continue to process object, we must
    // move it to the proper world position

    static_obj[OBSTACLES_1_TEMPLATE].world_pos.x = obstacles_1[index].x;
    static_obj[OBSTACLES_1_TEMPLATE].world_pos.y = obstacles_1[index].y;
    static_obj[OBSTACLES_1_TEMPLATE].world_pos.z = obstacles_1[index].z;

    if (!Remove_Object(&static_obj[OBSTACLES_1_TEMPLATE],OBJECT_CULL_XYZ_MODE))
        {
        // convert object local coordinates to world coordinates
        Local_To_World_Object(&static_obj[OBSTACLES_1_TEMPLATE]);

        // remove the backfaces and shade object
        Remove_Backfaces_And_Shade(&static_obj[OBSTACLES_1_TEMPLATE],-1);

        // convert world coordinates to camera coordinates
        World_To_Camera_Object(&static_obj[OBSTACLES_1_TEMPLATE]);

        // clip the objects polygons against viewing volume
        Clip_Object_3D(&static_obj[OBSTACLES_1_TEMPLATE],CLIP_Z_MODE);

        // generate the final polygon list
```

continued on next page

continued from previous page

```
        Generate_Poly_List(&static_obj[OBSTACLES_1_TEMPLATE],ADD_TO_POLY_LIST);

        } // end if object visible

    }  // end for index
```

The highlighted section shows how the secondary data structure is used to update the single object model each time through the main rendering loop.

That's enough about how objects are replicated through the graphics pipeline, let's talk about each object type.

Static Objects

The static objects compose all of the background scenery that does not translate. Any object that translates is called a dynamic object. However, as we will see, some of the static objects, such as the power station and the telepods, do rotate. We have seen the array that holds the original models for all the static objects and the arrays that hold the positions or the replicated objects, so let's talk about the specific attributes of each object type.

Observation Towers

The observation towers are shown in Figure 18-7 and are basically two rectangular solids, one stacked on the other. They are positioned at the four points of a square that is centered at the center of the game universe at (0,0,0). Currently they do nothing. The PLG file that contains them is called TOWER.PLG.

FIGURE 18-7
⊙ ⊙ ⊙ ⊙ ⊙ ⊙
An observation tower

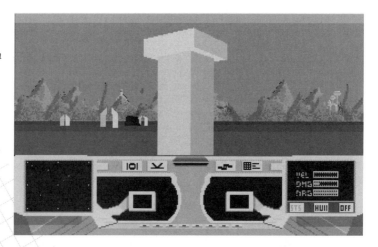

Power Station

The power station is located at the exact center of the game grid, and when the player is sent down to the planet, he will actually be within its radius. Figure 18-8 shows the power station. Unlike the towers, there is only a single power station, and it rotates. The rotation is performed as usual using the *Rotate_Object()* function.

This brings us to an important point that is both a pro and a con. When a single model is used to represent multiple objects and is replicated in the graphics pipeline, any transformation performed to the original model will be reflected in each replicated model. This means that if we replicate the power station 100 times through the pipeline at different locations and then rotate the original model, all 100 replicas will rotate! This may be desired, but if it's not, action must be taken so that before each replicated model is sent down the pipeline, the transformation(s) are done or undone to put the model into some known state.

Anyway, the purpose of the power station was going to be this (but I never got around to it): when the player was damaged and low on energy, he could drive over it and recharge. The name of the power station model is STATION.PLG.

Crystal Growths

The crystal growths were supposed to be the telepods, but when I saw them in 3D they looked too cool. Figure 18-9 shows what they look like. They almost look like ribs from some giant alien creature. Anyway, these are totally static and simply randomly placed on the game grid. There are 32 of them. The model name is PYLON.PLG.

FIGURE 18-8
◎ ◎ ◎ ◎ ◎ ◎
The main power station

FIGURE 18-9

ⓞ ⓞ ⓞ ⓞ ⓞ ⓞ

Typical crystal growth

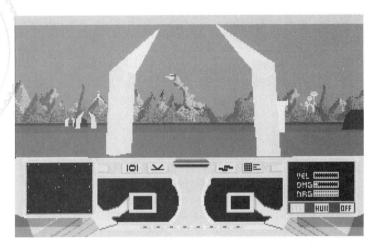

Rocks

The rocks could look a bit "rockier," but they do the job. One is shown in Figure 18-10. The rocks, like the crystals, are randomly positioned, and there are 32 of them in the entire universe. The file containing the model is ROCK.PLG.

Telepods

The telepods are probably the coolest of all the static objects. One is shown in Figure 18-11. As you can see, there is a shadow. How is this implemented? Well, I simply added a rectangular polygon that has a Y position of 0 to the basic model. This looks like a shadow when displayed. Also, the telepods are rotated. But as we learned, only one call is needed to rotate all four of the telepods, since the same model is replicated through the pipeline at different world coordinates.

FIGURE 18-10

ⓞ ⓞ ⓞ ⓞ ⓞ ⓞ

Typical rock

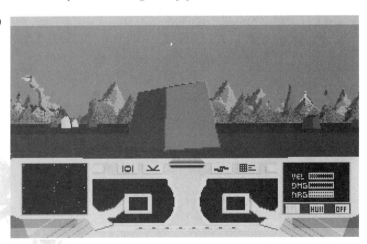

FIGURE 18-11

◎ ◎ ◎ ◎ ◎ ◎

A telepod

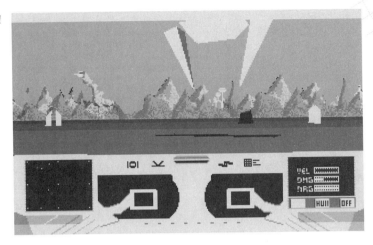

The telepods are located near the four corners of the game grid and are almost totally passive. They are used as entrance positions for regenerating dead aliens. You should definitely add teleportation ability for the player. When he drives under a telepod, maybe he sees a flash of light or a star field or something, and then he is teleported to another pod that is randomly selected. The model containing the telepod is called TELE.PLG.

Electronic Barriers

The electronic barriers are a nice touch. Take a look at Figure 18-12. As you can see, they look like monoliths. Actually, they are about 100 meters tall in game scale. There are eight of them located equidistant around the game perimeter, which is (16,000x16,000) units. On top of each barrier unit is a blinking beacon, which is

FIGURE 18-12

◎ ◎ ◎ ◎ ◎ ◎

One of the barriers that define the game area

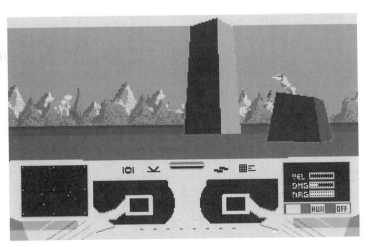

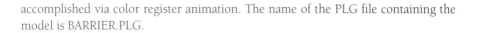

accomplished via color register animation. The name of the PLG file containing the model is BARRIER.PLG.

Alien Ships

The alien ships were probably the most complex of all the models in the game to deal with (Figures 18-13 and 18-14 are screen shots of both alien types). Since there can be more than one alien of each model type (Tallon and Slider), the replication technique had to be used. Unfortunately, this came back to bite me, because when I rotated the Tallon model to place it in the correct orientation for one of the replicated aliens, all of the replicated aliens rotated. This meant that every time through the replication pipeline, the desired direction of the replicated alien would

FIGURE 18-13

◎ ◎ ◎ ◎ ◎ ◎

A Tallon in action

FIGURE 18-14

◎ ◎ ◎ ◎ ◎ ◎

A Slider making a run for it

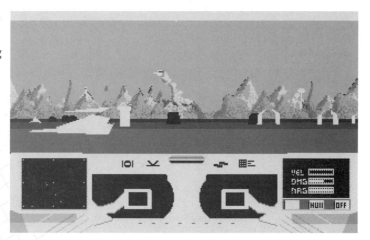

be compared to the actual direction of the single model. Then, based on the difference, the model would be rotated. Therefore, for each alien in the game, there is a rotation performed each frame. At worst, there can be four rotations per frame for the four aliens—still not bad!

The complete function that replicates the aliens and draws them is shown in Listing 18-2. Notice that it has separate sections for both the Tallon and the Slider models. These could have been merged, but this way it's a little faster and simpler to understand.

LISTING 18-2 *Alien rendering function*

```
void Draw_Aliens(void)
{
// this function simply draws the aliens

int index,       // looping variable
    diff_angle;  // used to track angular difference between virtual object
                 // and real object

// draw all the aliens (ya all four of them!)
for (index=0; index<NUM_ALIENS; index++)
    {
    // test if missile is alive before starting 3-D processing

    if (aliens[index].state!=ALIEN_DEAD)
       {

       // which kind of alien are we dealing with?

       if (aliens[index].type == ALIEN_TALLON)
          {
          dynamic_obj[TALLONS_TEMPLATE].world_pos.x = aliens[index].x;
          dynamic_obj[TALLONS_TEMPLATE].world_pos.y = aliens[index].y;
          dynamic_obj[TALLONS_TEMPLATE].world_pos.z = aliens[index].z;

          if (!Remove_Object(&dynamic_obj[TALLONS_TEMPLATE],OBJECT_CULL_XYZ_MODE))
             {
             // rotate tallon model to proper direction for this copy of it

             // look in state field of model to determine current angle and then
             // compare it to the desired angle, compute the difference and
             // use the result as the rotation angle to rotate the model
             // into the proper orientation for this copy of it

             diff_angle = aliens[index].angular_heading -
                          dynamic_obj[TALLONS_TEMPLATE].state;

             // fix the sign of the angle

             if (diff_angle<0)
                diff_angle+=360;
```

continued on next page

continued from previous page

```
                    // perform the rotation

                    Rotate_Object(&dynamic_obj[TALLONS_TEMPLATE],0,diff_angle,0);

                    // update object template with new heading

                    dynamic_obj[TALLONS_TEMPLATE].state = aliens[index].angular_heading;

                    // convert object local coordinates to world coordinates
                    Local_To_World_Object(&dynamic_obj[TALLONS_TEMPLATE]);

                    // remove the backfaces and shade object
                    if (aliens[index].state==ALIEN_DYING)
            Remove_Backfaces_And_Shade(&dynamic_obj[TALLONS_TEMPLATE],aliens[index].color_reg);
                    else
                       Remove_Backfaces_And_Shade(&dynamic_obj[TALLONS_TEMPLATE],-1);

                    // convert world coordinates to camera coordinates
                    World_To_Camera_Object(&dynamic_obj[TALLONS_TEMPLATE]);

                    // clip the objects polygons against viewing volume
                    Clip_Object_3D(&dynamic_obj[TALLONS_TEMPLATE],CLIP_Z_MODE);

                    // generate the final polygon list
                    Generate_Poly_List(&dynamic_obj[TALLONS_TEMPLATE],ADD_TO_POLY_LIST);

                    } // end if object is outside viewing volume

               } // end if tallon
            else
               {
               dynamic_obj[SLIDERS_TEMPLATE].world_pos.x = aliens[index].x;
               dynamic_obj[SLIDERS_TEMPLATE].world_pos.y = aliens[index].y;
               dynamic_obj[SLIDERS_TEMPLATE].world_pos.z = aliens[index].z;

               if (!Remove_Object(&dynamic_obj[SLIDERS_TEMPLATE],OBJECT_CULL_XYZ_MODE))
                  {
                  // rotate slider model to proper direction for this copy of it

                  // look in state field of model to determine current angle and then
                  // compare it to the desired angle, compute the difference and
                  // use the result as the rotation angle to rotate the model
                  // into the proper orientation for this copy of it

                  diff_angle = aliens[index].angular_heading -
                               dynamic_obj[SLIDERS_TEMPLATE].state;

                  // fix the sign of the angle

                  if (diff_angle<0)
                     diff_angle+=360;

                  // perform the rotation
```

```
        Rotate_Object(&dynamic_obj[SLIDERS_TEMPLATE],0,diff_angle,0);

        // update object template with new heading
        dynamic_obj[SLIDERS_TEMPLATE].state = aliens[index].angular_heading;

        // convert object local coordinates to world coordinates
        Local_To_World_Object(&dynamic_obj[SLIDERS_TEMPLATE]);

        // remove the backfaces and shade object
        if (aliens[index].state==ALIEN_DYING)
     Remove_Backfaces_And_Shade(&dynamic_obj[SLIDERS_TEMPLATE],
            aliens[index].color_reg);
        else
            Remove_Backfaces_And_Shade(&dynamic_obj[SLIDERS_TEMPLATE],-1);

        // convert world coordinates to camera coordinates
        World_To_Camera_Object(&dynamic_obj[SLIDERS_TEMPLATE]);

        // clip the objects polygons against viewing volume
        Clip_Object_3D(&dynamic_obj[SLIDERS_TEMPLATE],CLIP_Z_MODE);

        // generate the final polygon list
        Generate_Poly_List(&dynamic_obj[SLIDERS_TEMPLATE],ADD_TO_POLY_LIST);

        } // end if object is outside viewing volume

      } // end else slider

    } // end if alien alive

  } // end for index

} // end Draw_Aliens
```

I have highlighted the rotation aspect of the code. Basically, I used the *state* field of the model to hold its current angle—a bit of a kludge, but then beggars can't be choosers. As far as the logic goes for the aliens, their states and probabilities are shown in Table 18-1.

TABLE 18-1
◇◇◇◇◇◇
State table for the aliens

State Description	Probability of State
Attack	30%
Random	20%
Evade	10%
Stop	10%
Turn	20%

FIGURE 18-15

◉ ◉ ◉ ◉ ◉ ◉

Tracking the player

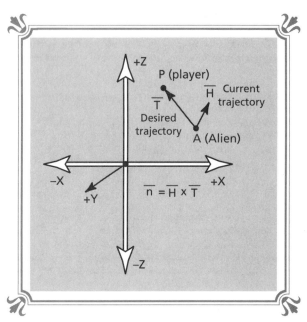

The aliens move in a very simple way. They are given an angular heading and a speed. The heading is used to compute a trajectory vector in the X-Z plane, and the speed is used as a scaling factor. The only interesting state is the attack state and how it is performed. Take a look at Figure 18-15. In the figure we see that the player is located at point P, and an alien who wishes to attack is located at point A. The question is, which way should the alien turn to drive toward the player?

This is not an easy question, and a bit of math is needed. Basically, the trick is this: A vector is computed from the alien to the player, and then the cross product is computed between the alien's current trajectory vector **h** and the desired trajectory vector **t**. Finally, the sign of the Y component of the result is tested, and based on this, we can deduce which way the alien needs to turn. If the alien is to the right of the player, then he will turn left, and if the alien is to the left of the player, then he will turn right. The logic that does this is rather simple, though, since we only need the sign of the result and not the whole cross product. Here it is for review:

```
case ALIEN_ATTACK:
                {
                // continue tracking player

                // test if it's time to adjust heading to track player

                if (++aliens[index].counter_2 > aliens[index].threshold_2)
                    {

                    // adjust heading toward player, use a heuristic approach
```

```
// that simply tries to keep turning the alien toward
// the player, later maybe we could add a bit of
// trajectory lookahead, so the alien could intercept
// the player???

// to determine which way the alien needs to turn we
// can use the following trick: based on the current
// trajectory of the alien and the vector from the
// alien to the player, we can compute a normal vector

// compute heading vector (happens to be a unit vector)

head_x = sin_look[aliens[index].angular_heading];
head_z = cos_look[aliens[index].angular_heading];

// compute target trajectory vector, players position
// minus aliens position

target_x = view_point.x - aliens[index].x;
target_z = view_point.z - aliens[index].z;

// now compute y component of normal

normal_y = (head_z*target_x - head_x*target_z);

// based on the sign of the result we can determine if
// we should turn the alien right or left, but be careful
// we are in a LEFT HANDED system!

if (normal_y>=0)
   aliens[index].angular_heading+=(10+rand()%10);
else
   aliens[index].angular_heading-=(10+rand()%10);

// check angle for overflow/underflow

if (aliens[index].angular_heading >=360)
   aliens[index].angular_heading-=360;
else
if (aliens[index].angular_heading < 0)
   aliens[index].angular_heading+=360;

// reset counter

aliens[index].counter_2 = 0;

} // end if

// test if attacking sequence is complete

if (++aliens[index].counter_1 > aliens[index].threshold_1)
   {
   // tell state machine to select a new state
```

continued on next page

continued from previous page

```
                                    aliens[index].state = ALIEN_NEW_STATE;

                                    } // end if

                            // try and fire a missile

                            distance = fabs(view_point.x - aliens[index].x) +
                                       fabs(view_point.z - aliens[index].z);

                            if ((rand()%15)==1 && distance<3500)
                               {
                               // create local vectors

                               // first position

                               alien_pos.x = aliens[index].x;
                               alien_pos.y = 45; // alien y centerline
                               alien_pos.z = aliens[index].z;

                               // now direction

                               alien_dir.x = sin_look[aliens[index].angular_heading];
                               alien_dir.y = 0;
                               alien_dir.z = cos_look[aliens[index].angular_heading];

                               // start the missile

                               Start_Missile(ALIEN_OWNER,
                                             &alien_pos,
                                             &alien_dir,
                                             aliens[index].speed+25,
                                             75);

                               } // end if fire a missile

                            } break;
```

As you can see, the *ALIEN_ATTACK* state is responsible for much of the action when we consider that there are timers running and weapon control is taking place. In any case, you should study it since most shooters use something like this to control the enemies.

Finally, if the player is lucky enough to hit an alien, the alien is regenerated at one of the telepods. The models used for the aliens are TALLON.PLG and SLIDER.PLG.

The Missiles

The missiles didn't turn out exactly like I wanted, but they look pretty cool nevertheless. I was trying for more of a *Star Trek*-style photon torpedo, but I just couldn't get it right. Anyway, the missiles' logic is similar to the logic in Starblazer. About the only difference is that the missiles are in 3D. They are basically 3D equilateral pyramids that rotate as they move. There are a total of 12 missiles available, and the player can shoot up to 6 at a time. The missiles have a finite range and will dissipate and be recycled after this range is reached.

The model for the missile is MISSILE.PLG. If you refer to the alien logic code, you will notice that the aliens only fire missiles when they are in attack mode.

Collision Detection

Collision detection in a 3D game is always hard. KRK doesn't perform player-to-environment or alien-to-environment collisions; it only performs missile-to-alien and missile-to-player collisions. The collisions are implemented using a bounding sphere technique. The maximum radius of each object loaded into the engine is recorded in the object structure, and this is used along with the position of the missiles to determine whether a hit has been made.

However, the problem is, how do we compute the distance between a missile and a possible target? We surely can't use the standard *sqrt()* function, since it is so slow. Instead, we are going to use an approximation that is based on a Taylor series for square root. If that doesn't mean anything to you, don't worry. Basically, in 2D we can approximate the distance between two points (x1,y1) and (x2,y2) within 10 percent with the following formula:

```
distance = abs(x1-x2) + abs(y1-y2) - minimum( abs(x1-x2), abs(y1-y2) )/2;
```

Of course, we can optimize this a bit, but the long form helps to show what's going on. The first section of the formula, *[abs(x1-x2) abs(y1-y2)]*, is called the Manhattan Distance, which will have quite a bit of error in some cases—that is, the distance will be too large. The second term helps to minimize this error. In any case, the final distance calculation is nothing more than a couple of subtractions, a comparison, and a shift—a definite improvement over a complex square root.

Once the distance between the missile being tested for collision and the object under test is computed, this value is compared to the radius of the object in question, and if the distance is less than or equal to the radius, then chances are there's been a collision. This is shown in Figure 18-16. You might think that combined errors of using the maximum radius (instead of average radius) along with the 10 percent distance calculation error would make for terrible collision detection, but in fact it works great!

Now let's move on to the effect of a collision between a missile and an object.

Explosions

If I had time, I was going to implement a full polygon explosion along with a scaled bitmap explosion overlay. This would be the best of both worlds. The player would see a collection of particles flying out from the explosion along with a blast of

FIGURE 18-16

◎ ◎ ◎ ◎ ◎ ◎

Using the bounding sphere technique for collision detection

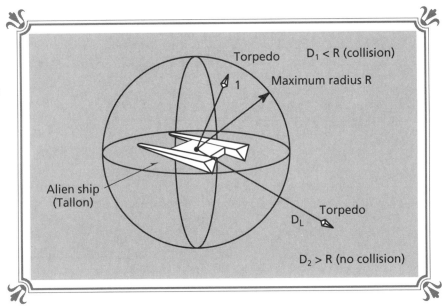

flames drawn or rendered and mapped onto a 2D surface, much like the objects in *Doom* or *Dark Forces*. However, I had to settle for something less. The little addition made to the *Remove_Backfaces_And_Shade()* function is now going to come into play. When a missile fired by the player hits an alien, the alien switches into the state *ALIEN_DYING*. In this state, the alien sends a non-negative parameter as the *force_color* parameter of the *Remove_Backfaces_And_Shade()* function, and hence, all the polygons of the alien model are added to the polygon list with the same color. Then the color register is cycled through shades of green, and the results are a vaporization. Figure 18-17 shows an alien being vaporized.

FIGURE 18-17

◎ ◎ ◎ ◎ ◎ ◎

One less alien in the world

The player doesn't really explode, but instead is knocked around, and the video system malfunctions when hit. The "screen-shake" effect is implemented by modulating the Y viewing position randomly for a few hundred milliseconds. Here is the actual screen-shaking code:

```
// test for ship hit message

            if (ship_message == SHIP_HIT)
               {
               // do screen shake
               view_point.y = 40+5*(rand()%10);

                // test if shake complete
               if (--ship_timer < 0)
                  {
                  // reset ships state
                  ship_message = SHIP_STABLE;
                  view_point.y = 40;

                  } // end if screen shake complete

               } // end if
```

Also, to add a little more realism, the video display or window into the world is garbled randomly with shades of green, as if the plasma energy of the torpedo hitting the player is dissipating over the hull. This is accomplished with this fragment:

```
// test if screen should be colored to simulate fire blast

             if (ship_message==SHIP_HIT)
               {
               // test for time intervals

               if (ship_timer>5 && (rand()%3)==1)
                  Fill_Double_Buffer_32(SHIP_FLAME_COLOR+rand()%16);

               } // end if ship hit
```

As you can see, these effects are easy to implement, but they look great. There is a lesson to be learned here: complex and amazing visual effects don't necessarily have to be hard to code.

Terrain Following

Although the surface of Centari Alpha 3 is rather flat (like the salt flats), there are some anomalies in the surface. To give the player some visual feedback, a little trick is used. The trick is based on the screen shake but to a much lesser degree. Basically, the current velocity of the player is used to scale a random number that only varies a few points, and then this result is used to modulate the Y or vertical position of the cockpit. The result is a bumpy terrain. Again, the code is so short, I can't resist showing it to you:

```
if (ship_speed)
    view_point.y = 40+rand()%(1+abs(ship_speed)/8);
else
    view_point.y = 40;
```

That's about it for the graphics and game play; let's take a quick look at the sound.

Music and Sound FX

The music and sound FX system are taken directly from Starblazer. There are two main sequences of music: the introduction sequence and the main game sequence. The introduction sequence was taken from Starblazer, but the main game sequence is totally new, which might take a little getting used to. At first you may not like it, but after a while the music "feels" right and it grows on you. The music was written by Dean Hudson of Eclipse Productions.

The sound FX system for KRK is the same preemptive system used in Starblazer without change. Most of the sound effects were made by my vocal cords, with the exception of a couple that were digitized from old sci-fi movies, but I'll never tell which. Now let's get to actually loading and playing the game.

Loading the Game

You load Kill or Be Killed with the single executable KRK.EXE. However, to support music and sound FX, the command line parameters "m" and "s" must be used, as in:

KRK.EXE m s [ENTER]

Of course, if you want the music and sound to play, you must load both MID-PAK and DIGPAK with the files,

MIDPAK.COM
SOUNDRV.COM

which are generated with the menu-driven programs SETM.EXE and SETD.EXE. I suggest that you make a batch file that looks something like this:

MIDPAK.COM
SOUNDRV.COM
KRK.EXE m s

The only reason I didn't do this is I'm not sure if you want music and sound all the time. Of course, a better way would be to allow the main menu in the game to turn music and sound on and off. Maybe your version of the game should have that? Whatever way you start the game, the game will go through the introductory sequence and drop you off in the main menu. Finally, KRK needs about 580K of memory to run after the sound and music drivers have been loaded.

Playing the Game

When you get to the main menu, you really don't need to do anything; you can simply select the Challenge menu item and start playing. But check out the Select Mech and Rules menu items, since I worked really hard on them! Once you enter into the game grid, the ship is controlled with the following keys:

Keypress	Description
→	Turns the ship right
←	Turns the ship left
↑	Increases throttle
↓	Decreases throttle
T	Selects tactical modes from the multi-function display
H	Toggles heads-up display
S	Toggles scanner
SPACEBAR	Fires missile
ESC	Exits back to main menu

The goal of the game: hunt down and kill everything!

Problems with the Game

About the only trouble you might have with the game is not enough memory to run it. If you do encounter sound, music, or lockup problems, unload all TSRs and drivers to free up as much conventional memory as possible. And remember, if you want sound and music, you must load MIDPAK.COM and SOUNDRV.COM.

The Cybersorcerer Contest

You've seen the game and had a peek at its insides; now it's up to you to make it better. As you know, there is a contest (detailed in Appendix A). You can enter

either as a Cybersorcerer or Cyberwizard. Cybersorcerers should use Starblazer as the foundation and improve upon it, and Cyberwizards should use KRK. Here are a few hints to get in good with the judges:

1. Add sound FX.

2. Add advanced alien logic.

3. Add cloaking.

4. Complete the instruments and make them all work.

5. Add modem support.

6. Ships should be able to be damaged instead of destroyed with a single shot.

7. Allow the player to be teleported.

8. Allow the player to fly for short distances.

9. Add a layer of clouds.

10. Add a judge that flies around on some kind of platform.

And any other cool stuff!

Looking Toward the Future

I think that we all feel a wind blowing and the wind is Windows. The question is, will Windows 95 and its successors be able to run games as well as 32-bit extended DOS? I think the answer is yes! By the time this book is published, Microsoft's new DirectDraw, DirectSound, and Direct everything else will be available, along with a multitude of hardware accelerators and 3D graphics libraries (which we'll talk about in a moment). I think that with direct access to video and sound hardware, game programmers will finally be happy. Now assuming that Windows 95 will be able to support high-speed 3D games, the next question is, will game programmers be willing to use Windows as a development platform? I think again the answer is yes. Most game programmers are already writing games in Windows, along with an IDE of some sort, so the transition won't be that bad.

The only downside to all of this is that there is a big learning curve for people new to Windows; so Windows is an option, but DOS will be around for some time to come. No one is not going to play a game just because it's written in DOS. However, as more and more games are written using the Windows 95 extensions, users are going to become more and more accustomed to plug-and-play technology without all the hassles of AUTOEXEC.BAT and CONFIG.SYS alterations. I think this is going to be the final blow to DOS games in the future.

As far as 3D libraries go, here is my opinion: Remember when PCs could do 2D graphics really well? There were a lot of 2D graphics libraries then, but many game programmers still wrote their own. The moral of the story is, although the technology is sufficiently high to write Doom-type games with standard libraries today, in order to push the limits, we're always going to need to do it ourselves! Anyway, I've actually played with a few of these new DOS and Windows-based 3D libraries, and for DOS games I think that BRENDER by Argonaut is the way to go. For Windows games, you can't beat the price of Intel's 3DR (free) or the performance of Microsoft's Rendermorphics, so there's a little bit of future for you.

Finally, as for the games of the future, I think the graphics will start to reach a visual limit and the game play will start to be embellished again. I see a lot more AI, fun factor, and game play coming back to the games, which has been lost for quite some time.

The Final Spell

Well, well, well—you made it! I knew you would. You have traveled far and long to reach this point, hazarding many obstacles, traversing many dark chasms. You have seen things few mortals will ever lay eyes upon. You have knowledge and powers that can be used to create other worlds and realities. You are now ready to become a Cybersorcerer! The final step in your training follows. Recite the ancient Latin words inscribed below and your training will be complete.

De Gratia Gaudeamus Igitur Tempus Fugit Carpe Diem Paz Vobiscum Vale!

May your life be filled with magick.

Cybersorcerer and Cyberwizard Contests

In Chapters 9 and 18, besides showing you how I created the Starblazer and Kill or Be Killed games, I said you'd get a chance to impress me by displaying your newly learned Cyber-chops by taking the games I created and making them better by adding the features I didn't have time to. Well, now it's time to get to work. If you apply everything you've learned so far, not only will you end up with a cool professional-quality video game of your own, you'll earn an opportunity to be crowned Cybersorcerer or Cyberwizard, and win a new computer system, professional, full-featured C++ compiler, or a library of Waite Group Press books.

The Contests

Cybersorcerer

In Chapter 9, I created Starblazer, a 2D modem-to-modem combat game. Your job as apprentice Cybersorcerer is to take my game and add the features and enhancements I suggested in the chapter (plus a few of your own!). Once again, these suggestions are:

- More sound FX.
- The alien shoots at the ships.

✣ When ships cloak, it would be cool if the space around them distorted.

✣ The scanner must be completed.

✣ Players should be able to enter through the wormhole and pop out somewhere else in the game.

✣ Ships should be able to be damaged instead of destroyed with a single shot.

✣ Players should be able to pick up the energy cells.

✣ Maybe just a little bit of cinematic sequences here and there.

✣ Anything else you can think of.

Remember, points are awarded for creativity and originality. Surprise and amaze me with your magick!

If you're the lucky person awarded the grand prize for reaching the level of Cybersorcerer, you will be awarded a Borland C++ 4.5 compiler for DOS, Windows, and Win32 (courtesy of Borland International). The runner-up Cybersorcerer will receive a library of 10 Waite Group Press books of his or her choice.

Cyberwizard

This is the big one! If you claim the title of Cyberwizard, look out world, because you'll be ready to take on all challengers in the video game pantheon. In Chapter 18, I introduced you to Kill or Be Killed, the futuristic battle game that is the culmination of all the techniques and know-how introduced in *Black Art of 3D Game Programming*. Your mission (if you choose to accept it) is to take the Kill or Be Killed game and make it even better. Some of the suggestions I made to do this:

✣ Add sound FX.

✣ Add advanced alien logic.

✣ Add cloaking.

✣ Complete the instruments and make them all work.

✣ Add modem support.

✣ Ships should be able to be damaged instead of destroyed with a single shot.

✣ Allow the player to be teleported.

✣ Allow the player to fly for short distances.

✣ Add a layer of clouds.

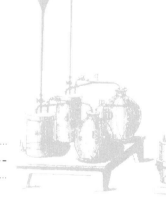

✦ Add a judge that flies around on some kind of platform.

✦ Any other cool stuff!

But those are just my suggestions—I want you to take the game places I never imagined. A true Cyberwizard will think of things no one else would even dream possible!

The grand prize for the ultimate Cyberwizard is a complete Pentium computer system. This system will include a CPU, color monitor, keyboard, mouse, and CD-ROM drive (exact specifications of hardware will be determined at a later date). The runner-up Cyberwizard will receive a library of 10 Waite Group Press books of his or her choice.

Rules and Regulations

By now, you're probably raring to get going. But hold on—even fledgling Cybersorcerers and Cyberwizards have to play by the rules. Here they are...

Eligibility

Your game must be submitted between September 1, 1995 and February 29, 1996, and it must utilize the programs and utilities provided in this book.

Dates and Deadlines

Entries must be received at the address provided by 5 P.M., February 29, 1996. Winners will be notified by August 31, 1996.

Preparation of Entries

Only one game may be submitted per entry, but you may enter both contests separately. Entries must be labeled with your name, phone number, and the name of the game. Waite Group Press is not responsible for lost or damaged entries. Waite Group Press will not return any entries unless entrants include a self-addressed stamped envelope designated for that purpose with their entry.

Media

Entries may be submitted on tape or disk. Entries submitted on tape should be sent in either QIC-80 or DAT compatible formats. Entries submitted on disk should be archived with the DOS backup command or as a self-extracting archive.

Judging

Games will be judged on the basis of technique, creativity, and presentation by the author and/or a panel of judges from Waite Group Press. Winners will be notified by August 31, 1996. For the names of the "Cybersorcerer Contest" or "Cyberwizard Contest" winners and their entries, send a self-addressed, stamped envelope after September 15, 1996, to Waite Group Press "Cybersorcerer Contest" or "Cyberwizard Contest" Winner, 200 Tamal Plaza, Suite 101, Corte Madera, CA 94925.

Miscellaneous

No purchase necessary. Waite Group Press "Cybersorcerer Contest" and "Cyberwizard Contest" are subject to all federal, state, local, and provincial laws and regulations and are void where prohibited. Waite Group Press "Cybersorcerer Contest" and "Cyberwizard Contest" are not open to employees of The Waite Group, Inc., Publishers Group West, participating promotional agencies, any WGP distributors, and the families of any of the above. By entering the "Cybersorcerer Contest" or "Cyberwizard Contest," each contestant warrants that he or she is the original author of the work submitted, non-exclusively licenses The Waite Group, Inc., to duplicate, modify, and distribute the game, and agrees to be bound by the above rules.

✂- -

Name _____   Daytime Phone _____

Address _____

City _____   State _____   Zip _____

I am entering:

❏ Cybersorcerer Contest   ❏ Cyberwizard Contest

Entry (name of game) _____

Comments/special instructions regarding game _____

_____

_____

Send entries to: "Cybersorcerer Contest" *or*
                     "Cyberwizard Contest" *(indicate contest entered on envelope)*
                     Waite Group Press
                     200 Tamal Plaza, Suite 101
                     Corte Madera, CA 94925

I signify that the enclosed is my own original work and that I abide by all rules described here.

Signature _____

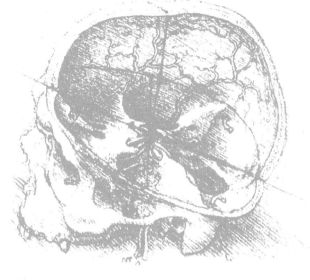

Index

; comment, 64
1-norm, 371
2-norm, 371
2D (Cartesian) plane, 57-59, 545-546
    primitives, 546-548
    transformations, 549-556
3D animation model, 932
3D fundamentals, 545
3D game library (Black Box), 18-20
3D games, future of, 1152-1153
3D games, history of, 6-13
3D graphics basics, 586-587, 629-630
3D graphics engine, 633, 995
3D graphics libraries, 1152-1153
3D motion, 398-399
3D palette animation, 193-197, 440-441
3D sound, 331-339
3D space, 556-559
4x4 matrix, 600-606, 634, 642-644, 1006
16-bit code, 1072, 1075
16-bit fixed point math, 879
16:16 format, 1071, 1075-1077, 1088
24-bit color, 134
32-bit code, 1072-1073, 1075, 1077
32-bit functions, 1081-1084
32-bit math, 442, 585, 586, 880, 1070, 1101. *See also* fixed
    point math

32-bit programming, 1100-1101
32:32 format, 1075-1077
64-bit math, 584-585, 1077. *See also* fixed point math
80387. *See* math coprocessor

A/D (analog-to-digital) converter, 275, 343
ADSR amplitude control, 279-280
algebra, linear, 574-575, 1008
alien world demo, 186-191
aliens, 1140-1146
amplitude, 270, 273, 279-280, 317-318
    amplification, 317-318
    control, 279-280
    resolution, 273, 317
ANDing, 979
angular orientation structure, 635
angular variance, 626
animation,
    3D model, 932
    ant, 263
    basics, 107-111
    color palette, 193-197, 440-441
    color register, 80, 229
    cycle, 108-111, 358, 379
    flicker-free, 91, 101, 111, 115, 117

animation (*continued*)
  jellyfish, 417-420
  and lighting effects, 193, 197
  nondestructive, 109-110
  palette, 193-197, 440-441
  spider, 375-379
  sprite, 155-160
array, objects, 445-446
artificial intelligence, 347-348
ASCII code, 208-211
asm keyword, 64
aspect ratio, 52-54, 91, 696
assembly language, 63-65, 118-121, 138-139, 288, 442
  and C, 1069
  external, 1044, 1064-1069, 1101
    functions, 1081-1084
  inline, 118-121, 138-139, 288, 442, 1101
asynchronous communication, 525
AT commands, 485-495
attack sequence, 1144-1146
attenuation, sound, 317-318
attribute controller, 56, 76
Audio Solution, The, 278, 280-284
audio. *See* sound
auto-logic, 40-41
autonomous functions, 40-41, 441-443

B

back-face culling, 617-618, 806-813, 820
back-face removal, 638, 738-741, 1093-1099
background processing, 439-441
background scanning, 151-152, 169-171
baud rate, 485, 523
baud rate divisor, 466, 469-471
binary counting, 433
binary shifting, 66-68, 71. *See also* shifts
Binary Space Partition, 710, 813, 893-931. *See also* BSP tree
BIOS, 57, 61-62, 74
BIOS input functions, 209-212, 237-238
BIOT (binary image overlap testing), 171-172
bit mask, 77, 84, 87
bitmap (defined), 122
bitmap drawing, 126-129
bitmap engine, 125-130
bitmap, prerotated, 536
bitmap scaling, 10-12
bitmap scanning, 129-130
bitmap structure, 126-127
bitmapped graphics, 122-125
  basics, 82-83
bitmapping, 82-83, 122
  functions, 125-130
Black Box game library, 18-20
BLACKLIB.LIB, 19-20

BLAZE3D.EXE, 1101
BLAZER.EXE, 529-541
bounding box, 160-163, 172-174, 371
bounding sphere, 658-659, 814, 1147
break code, 209, 214-216
Breakout game, xxiv-xxv
Bresenham's algorithm, 661-665
BSP (Binary Space Partition), 710, 813, 893-931. *See also* BSP tree
  BSPDEMO.C, 929
  traversal, 894, 898-900, 917-922
BSP tree, 893-931
  creation function, 901-917
  data structures, 900
  demo, 928-929
  display function, 925-928
  graphics pipeline, 925
  intersection, 903-906
  limitations, 929-930
  memory management, 924-925
  root, 897-898
  shading function, 922-923
  translation function, 923-924
  traversal function, 917-921
  world to camera function, 921-922
buffer
  double, 111, 115-122, 197-198, 204, 882, 1083-1084, 1132
  FIFO, 463, 476
  flushing, 481
  frame, 51, 61, 63, 65, 111, 115, 125, 1084
  offscreen, 115
  overflow, 471, 476
  recirculating, 473, 475-477
  ring, 473, 475-477
  Scanline Z-buffer, 625
    vertical, 892-893, 931
  video, 51, 61, 63, 65, 111, 115, 125, 1084
  Z-buffer. *See* Z-buffer
bus contingency, 42, 55, 75

C

C input functions, 209-213, 220
C interface, DIGPAK, 288-302
C interface, MIDPAK, 307-316
C library functions, 57
camera coordinates, 597-599, 639, 684, 786-787, 792-796, 806, 814, 921-922
camera position, 787-789
camera transformation, 789
carrier (modem), 486
Cartesian (2D) plane, 57-59, 545-546
  primitives, 546-548
  transformations, 549-556

Cartesian coordinate system, 52, 57-59, 546
case sensitivity, 210-211, 217
CD-ROM contents, xxviii-xxix, 20
CD-ROM installation, xxviii-xxix
cell coordinates, 145
cell location, 143-145
cells (tiles), 963-966
centroid, 366, 370
chaining, 226, 421-424
character set, 84-88
chasing, 349-358, 398-399
cinder functions, 445-452
cinder structure, 444-445
clear screen, 63-65, 98-99, 1083-1084
CLI instruction, 414, 480
client-server model, 521
clipping, 143, 160-171, 609-617, 673-682, 814-818, 829-
    836, 1034-1039
clipping algorithm, 162-163
clipping frustum, 674, 829
clipping planes, 609-610, 612, 614, 745, 814-818
clipping region, 161-163, 682, 727-728
clockwise order, 704-705
CMF music format, 277
code analysis, 976-977
code. *See* listings
collision detection, 39, 68, 171-175, 371, 389, 658-659,
    1147
color depth, 50
color descriptors, 649-652, 996, 1001
color, forced, 1122-1127
color indirection, 56, 65
color, and lighting, 625-628, 733
color lookup table, 56, 76-82. *See also* palette
color maps, 936-937
color palette, 735-737, 742. *See also* palette
color palette animation, 193-197, 440-441
color register, 77-80
color register animation, 80, 229
color rotation, 193-197
COM port, 477-478, 485. *See also* communications, serial
command state, 486
comment initiators, 64, 651-652
communications, serial, 461, 463-483
compiler options, 19-20
components, vector, 559, 561
compression, 131-133
concave object, 621, 708-709, 812-813, 846
concluding sequence, 26-27
conditional logic, 372-373
configuration, 24-25
constant shading, 638, 650-651, 742
contest, 541-542, 1151-1152, 1155-1158
controller, motion, 380
convergence, 363-371

convex object, 621, 708-709, 812-813, 930
coordinates
    camera, 597-599, 639, 684, 786-787, 792-796, 806,
        814, 921-922
    Cartesian, 52, 57-59, 546
    cell, 145
    homogeneous, 600-601
    image, 145
    integer, 59, 68
    local, 591-596, 639, 683-684, 790
    screen, 57-60, 65, 108, 546, 591
    systems, 591-599, 682-683, 807-808
    world, 594-596, 639, 683-684, 786-787, 790, 792-796,
        806, 814
    z coordinate, 398-399, 556
coplanar primitives, 587-588
COSINE look-up tables, 635, 688-689, 788, 947, 1080
cosine wave, 948
counter variables, 142, 362, 379, 383, 445
counterclockwise order, 704-705, 807, 1002
counters, 8253 chip, 430-434
Cramer's rule, 903
creativity, 18, 529. *See also* game design
cross product, 641
CRT controller, 56, 200-201
culling, back-face, 617-618, 638, 738-741, 806-813, 820,
    1093-1099
culling, object level, 813-821
Cybersorcerer, xxvii, 995, 1117, 1152-1153, 1155-1158
Cybersorcery, 5-6, 18, 20, 474
Cybersorcery contest, 541-542, 1151-1158
Cyberspace, 5-6, 995
Cyberwizard, 542, 1152, 1155-1158

D

D/A (digital-to-analog) converter, 325
data filling function, 1081-1082
data movement function, 1082-1083
data structures. *See* structures
_DB suffix, 117
deadlock, 522
debugger information, 19
decimal part, 583
decision variable, 662-663
degrees/radians, 556, 688-689, 788
demo mode, 25-26
demo programs
    3D engine, 1101-1113
    3D sound, 331-335
    alien world, 186-191
    back-face culling, 821-825
    Binary Space Partition, 928-929
    BSP tree, 928-929
    depth sort rendering, 852-859

demo programs (continued)
    digital sound, 297-302
    evasion, 351-358
    floater, 391-394
    Gouraud shading, 760-762
    interrupt service routine (ISR), 417-421
    joystick, 246-250
    keyboard, 227-229
    line drawing, 667-668
    MIDI music, 313-316
    mode 13h, 88-91
    mode Z, 102-103
    mouse, 258-264
    music, 313-316
    object removal, 821-825
    page flipping, 202-203
    parallax scrolling, 187-191
    patterns, 375-379
    PCX files, 139-140
    random motion, 359-363
    replication, 447-452
    serial communications, 491-495, 507-511
    solid modeling, 746-749, 798-801, 886-892
    sorting, 854-859, 886-892
    Starblazer 3D, 1101-1113
    terrain following, 391-394
    terrain generator, 953-963
    texture mapping, 772-774
    timer programming, 434-436
    tracking, 351-358
    triangle functions, 729-730
    vertical blank interrupt, 427-430
    view transformations, 798-801
    volcano, 444-452
    voxel engine, 953-963, 966-976, 980-989
    wireframe 3D, 693-700
    Z-buffer, 880-882, 886-892
depth illusion, 10
depth sort, 618-621, 843, 846-859, 930, 1040-1043
detail, multiple levels, 1004-1005
deterministic processes, 515
DIGIBLASTER, 323-335
digital concatenation, 297
DIGPAK driver, 281-303, 530-532
diminishing returns, 1012
display memory, 55-56
distance falloff, 626
distortion, spherical, 947-948, 952
divergence, 372
divide by zero, 413
DMPI (DOS protected mode interface), 1100
DOS calls, 424-425
DOS Extenders, 1100-1101
DOS games, 1152-1153
DOS protected mode interface, 1100
dot product, 566-567, 618, 640-641, 710, 732

double buffer, 111, 115-122, 197-198, 204, 882, 1083-
    1084, 1132
double sample rate, 274
DQ directive, 1065, 1068
DRIVERS directory, 283-285, 304
DSP (digital signal processer), 280, 340
DTR (Date Terminal Ready) line, 495, 497-498, 504-507
DW directive, 1065, 1068
DXF files, 647-648

E

ellipsoids, 16
EOI command, 408, 410, 413, 415
equations
    interpolation, 753-755, 776, 864-866
    intersection, 903-904
    line, 714-716
    plane, 622-624, 709-711, 862
    point slope, 660
    rotation, 553-556, 603-606, 688, 1014-1015, 1025
erase (redefined), 109
erasure function, 153-154, 168-169, 446
error checking, 148, 181, 441
error detection, 867
error term, 663
Euclidean inner product, 566
evading, 350-358
event driven programming, 30-40
event loops, 30-33
event timing, 437
event triggering, 306
exit enable flag, 502
explosions, 540, 1122, 1147-1149
exponent, 582

F

facet, micro, 752
facet structure, 637-638, 838, 1040-1041
facets, 13
factorial operation, 1062-1063
far (yon) clipping plane, 610, 612, 614, 674, 745, 814-818,
    831
field of view, 14-15, 396-398, 597, 671-673, 813, 946-947
FIFO buffer, 463, 476
filter function, 616-617
fish eye distortion, 947-948, 952
fixed point math, 366, 370, 442, 581-586, 879-880
    32-bit, 442, 585, 586, 880, 1070, 1101
    64-bit, 584-585, 1077
    advanced, 1070-1081
    defined, 1070
fixed point numbers, 1080-1081, 1088
flags register, 406, 413
flat shader, 735-749, 922-923
flat shading, 638, 650-651, 735-750, 1094

flicker, 111, 115, 117, 198
flicker-free animation, 91, 101, 111, 115, 117
flight simulators, 13
floater demo, 391-394
floating point math, 366, 370, 386, 442, 581-582, 661,
    1010-1011, 1070
flocking (convergence), 363-371
flood filling, 713
FM synthesis, 278-280
foreground objects, 989
foreshortening, 670. *See also* perspective
FOV. *See* field of view
fractal landscape, 939
frame (video) buffer, 51, 61, 63, 65, 111, 115, 125, 1084
frame rate, 26-29, 108
frequency (defined), 269
frequency modulation. *See* FM
frequency of fusion, 53
frequency resolution, 273
frequency response, 270
frequency spectrum, 343
function. *See also* functions *and* listings
    _bios_keybrd, 211, 217-218
    _chain_intr, 423-424
    _dos_freemem, 294
    _dos_getvect, 221-222, 415
    _dos_setvect, 222, 415-416
    abs, 173-174
    Clip_Line, 676-682, 696
    Display_Double_Buffer, 119-121, 1084
    Draw_Game_Grid, 39
    Draw_Object_Solid, 743-746
    Draw_Object_Wire, 694-696
    Draw_TB_Tri_3D_Z, 871-880
    Draw_Terrain, 957-958, 962-963, 970-972, 976,
        983-985
    Draw_Triangle_2D, 719-721, 725, 727-730
    free, 181
    getch, 209-210
    kbhit, 39, 210-211
    Keyboard_Driver, 221, 224-225
    Line_VDB, 955-956, 962, 968-969, 978
    MassageAudio, 293-294
    memcpy, 115, 117, 119
    memset, 69, 71, 726
    PLG_Load_Object, 654-657, 658, 686, 706-707, 735,
        997-1001, 1095
    Print_Char_DB, 204
    Print_String_DB, 204
    qsort, 847
    Read_Pixel_DB, 204
    Say_Number, 302
    Screen_Transition, 111-115
    Serial_Read_Wait, 519
    Set_Graphics_Mode, 62, 74-75
    Set_Mode_Z, 95-98

function (*continued*)
    Sound_Play_3D, 335
    SoundStatus, 295-296
    Sprite_Draw, 149-151
    sqrt, 640, 735, 1147
    StopSound, 296
    Time_Delay, 159, 191, 430, 437-439, 498
    Timer_Query, 437-439
    Triangle_Line, 726-727, 1085, 1091-1093
    Triangle_16Line, 1091-1093
    Triangle_32Line, 1093
    Write_Pixel, 68, 615-617
    Write_Pixel_DB, 116-117, 204
functions
    32-bit, 1081-1084
    assembly language, external, 1081-1084
    autonomous, 40-41, 441-443
    BIOS input, 209-212, 237-238
    bitmapping, 125-130
    BSP tree, 901-928
    C input, 209-213, 220
    C library, 57
    cinder, 445-452
    data filling, 1081-1082
    data movement, 1082-1083
    erasure, 153-154, 168-169, 446
    filter, 616-617
    interface, mouse, 254-258
    line drawing, 663-665, 667-668, 962
    line parsing, 652-653
    math, 3D graphics engine, 639-646
    memory allocation, PCX, 135-136
    memory filling, 1082-1083
    memory movement, 1082-1083
    parsing, 500-502, 652-653
    probability density, 385
    Quick Sort, 847-850, 1040, 1043
    sound effects, 539-540
    sprite deletion, 145-146
    sprite initialization, 145-146
    square root, 640, 735, 1147
    status, sound, 295, 312
    time delay, 40-42, 159, 191, 430, 437-439, 498
    transcendental, 1080
    triangles, demo, 729-730
    wait, 518-519
fuzzy logic, 348, 386

⑥

game design, 191, 529, 1120-1121, 1132
    creativity, 18, 529
    enemies, 398
    predator, 398
game library (Black Box), 18-20
game logic, 264-265

game loops, 26, 121-122
    multiplayer, 455-457
    Starblazer, 541
    typical, 34-40
game over state, 541
game sequence, 23-27
game synchronization, 512-523
games
    on CD-ROM, xxix
    future of, 1152-1153
    hallway, 892
    history of, 6-13
    Kill or Be Killed, 1117-1151, 1156
    multiplayer. See multiplayer games
    On-Line, 524-527
    Starblazer, 523, 527-542, 1101-1113, 1120, 1150, 1155
    video, xxvii
    and Windows, 1152-1153
genetic algorithms, 348
global state, 527
global transformation, 794-796, 1013, 1024-1034
global variables, 441
Gouraud shading, 749-762
graphics (video) modes, 62, 74-75, 91-100
graphics controller, 54-55
graphics files, 131
graphics libraries, 1152-1153
gray palette, 758-759

h

hallway games, 892
harmonics, 271
Hayes AT commands, 485-495
header files, CD-ROM, 63
heads-up display, 1133
height casting, 950-952
height mapping, 943-953
height maps, 936-937
hertz (Hz), 53, 269, 430
HFOV, 672
hidden surface removal, 14, 16, 617-625, 805-806, 842
high score screen, 26
highlights, 628
hither (near) clipping plane, 609-610, 612, 614, 674, 745,
        814-818, 831
homogeneous coordinates, 600-601
Hz (hertz), 53, 269, 430

I

IEEE format, 582, 1011, 1055
illumination. See lighting
image coordinates, 145
image loading, 131
image sources, 131

image space clipping, 610, 615-617, 727
image space techniques, 390-394
images, rendering, 65-74
initial point, 561
inline assembler. See assembly language
inlining, 977-978, 989, 1094
inorder traversal, 894, 898-900, 917-922
input channel, 27-29
input conditioning, 264-265
input device allocation, 459
input device reflection, 512-514, 540
input devices, 207-208
input driven event loops, 30-32
input event system, 264
input loss, 28-29
installation, CD-ROM, xxviii-xxix
installation phase, 24-25
instrument patches, 277, 280, 283, 532, 538
instruments. See MIDI
integer coordinate system, 59, 68
intelligence, 347-348
interface code, 928-929
interpolation, 752-755, 762, 776, 778-779
    equation, 753-755, 776, 864-866
    Z values, 864-866, 871-879
interrupt control register (ICR), 408, 415
interrupt controller (PIC), 221, 223, 408-410
interrupt disabling, 414, 480, 482
_interrupt keyword, 220, 414
interrupt mask register (IMR), 408-409, 415
interrupt service routine (ISR), 216, 218-223, 406, 413-425
    chaining, 421-424
    demo, 417-421
    installing, 415-416
    restoring, 416-417
    serial, 471-473, 475-477
    writing, 413-415
interrupt vectors, 219-221
    table, 407, 411-413, 415
interrupts, 61-62, 74-75
    end of interrupt (EOI), 408, 410, 413, 415
    hardware, 408
    joystick, 236-237
    keyboard, 209, 211-212, 216, 219-223, 408-410, 421
    mouse, 252-253
    non-maskable (NMI), 409
    PC, 405-406
    serial, 464-467, 471-473, 475-477
    software, 407-408
    sound, 281-285, 288, 303, 440
    timekeeper, 415-424
    timer, 44, 415-424
    UART, 464-467, 471-473, 475-477
    vertical blank, 425-430
    video, 61-62, 74-75
intersection equations, 903-904

intersection, line, 675
introductory sequence, 25-26, 1128
IRET instruction, 406, 413-414

J

joystick, 207-208, 230-250
    buttons, 232-234
    calibration, 235, 239-244
    demo, 246-250
    detection, 245-246
    hardware, 230-232
    interrupt, 236-237
    joystick port, 232-233
    position, 234-239
    strobe, 233-235

K

keyboard, 207-230
    demo, 227-229
    driver, 218-230
    interrupts, 209, 211-212, 216, 219-223, 408-410, 421
    key reading, 209-211
    layout, 208-209
    multiple keypresses, 218-219, 227
    programmable interrupt controller, 221, 223, 408
    scan codes, 208-216
    shift state, 216-218
    state table, 224-226
keypress, 208-209, 218-219, 227
Kill or Be Killed, 1117-1151, 1156

L

lag, sound, 322
lag, time, 28
layer structure, 180
layers, scrolling, 175-179
layers system, 179-186
Least-Squares-Method, 777
left-handed system, 557, 559, 807
level of detail switching, 1004-1005
lighting, 625-629, 730-735
    ambient, 625-626, 730-731
    directional, 628-629, 731-734
    incident, 628, 731-732
    and palette animation, 193, 197
    point light sources, 626-628, 734-735
    and radiosity, 941-942
    and shading, 738-739
line, 2D, 547-548, 674-682
line, 3D, 587, 660, 668-673
line clipper, 674-682
line drawing, 69-73
    algorithms, 661-665
    function, 663-665, 667-668, 962

line drawing *(continued)*
    wireframe, 660-668
line equations, 714-716
line, horizontal, 69, 71
line intersection, 903-905
line parsing function, 652-653
line renderer, 726-727
line, vertical, 69, 71-73
linear algebra, 574-575, 1008
linear interpolation, 752-755, 762, 776, 778-779
linear memory mapping, 51-52, 60-61
lines, 3D world, 932
linked games, 339-340
linked lists, 442, 445
linker, 19-20
linking PCs, 460-462
linking state, 541
listings. *See also* function
    3DIGI.C, 331-335
    ALIEN.C, 187-191
    Auto_Function, 442-443
    Bitmap_Get, 129-130
    Bitmap_Put, 127-128
    BLAZE3D.C, 1101-1113
    Bsp_Delete, 924-925
    Bsp_Shade, 922-923
    Bsp_Translate, 923-924
    Bsp_Traverse, 898-899, 917-920
    Bsp_View, 926-927
    Bsp_World_To_Camera, 921-922
    Build_Bsp_Tree, 906-916
    Build_Look_Up_Tables, 688-689
    Clip_Line, 676-682
    Clip_Object_3D, 832-836, 1035-1039
    Compute_Average_Z, 1042
    Compute_Object_Radius, 659
    Create_Double_Buffer, 117-118
    Create_World_To_Camera, 795-796, 1026-1030
    Create_Z_Buffer, 866-867
    CRITTERS.C, 366-370
    Cross_Product_3D, 641
    Delete_Double_Buffer, 121
    Delete_Z_Buffer, 867
    DIGIDEMO.C, 297-302
    Digital_FX_Play, 539-540
    Display_Double_Buffer, 119
    Display_Double_Buffer_32, 1084
    Dot_Product_3D, 640-641
    Draw_Aliens, 1141-1143
    Draw_Bottom_Triangle, 723-725
    Draw_Line, 663-665, 667-668
    Draw_Object_Solid, 743-745
    Draw_Object_Wire, 694-695
    Draw_Poly_List, 850-852
    Draw_Poly_List_Z, 884-885
    Draw_Rectangle, 73-74

listings *(continued)*

Draw_TB_Tri_3D_Z, 872-878
Draw_Terrain, 957-958, 970-972, 983-985
Draw_Top_Triangle, 721-723, 1089-1091
Draw_Tri_3D_Z, 869-871
Draw_Triangle_2D, 719-721
Draw_Triangle_2D_Gouraud, 756-758
Draw_Triangle_2D_Text, 768-771
Erase_Cinder, 446
Erase_Cinders, 446
Fadd, 1066-1069
Fill_Double_Buffer, 118-119
Fill_Double_Buffer_32, 1083
Fill_Screen, 64-65
Fill_Screen_Z, 99
Fill_Z_Buffer, 867-868
FLOATER.C, 391-393
Foo, 1065
FP_Div, 1079-1080
FP_Mul, 1076
fquadcpy, 1082-1084
fquadset, 1081-1083
fwordcpy, 154-155
Generate_Poly_List, 840-842
Get_Key, 211
Get_Scan_Code, 213
Get_Shift_State, 218
GOURDEMO.C, 760-762
GUESS.C, 31-32
Hang_Up, 498
Initialize_Modem, 503-504
Intersect_Lines, 904-905
ISR_Function, 414
JELLY.C, 417-420
Joystick, 235-236
Joystick_Available, 245
Joystick_Bios, 238
Joystick_Buttons, 234
Joystick_Calibrate, 240-243
JOYTEST.C, 246-250
JUMPER.C, 375-379
Keyboard_Driver, 224-225
Keyboard_Install_Driver, 222, 226
Keyboard_Remove_Driver, 222, 226
KEYTEST.C, 227-229
Layer_Build, 182
Layer_Create, 181
Layer_Delete, 181
Layer_Draw, 183-184
LIGHT.C, 35-38
Line_H, 71
Line_V, 72
Line_VDB, 955-956, 968-969
LINEDEMO.C, 667-668
Load_Palette_Disk, 736

listings *(continued)*

Local_To_World_Object, 790-792
LOCKON.C, 351-357
LOSTNSPC.C, 359-362
Make_Connection, 504-505
Make_Gray_Palette, 758-759
Make_Vector_3D, 640
Mat_Copy_4x4, 643
Mat_Identity_4x4, 642-643, 1011-1012
Mat_Mul_1x4_4x4, 646
Mat_Mul_4x4_4x4, 645, 1007-1010
Mat_Print_1x4, 644
Mat_Print_4x4, 644
Mat_Zero_4x4, 643
MIDIDEMO.C, 313-316
MODE13.C, 88-90
Modem_Control, 497-498
Modem_Result, 500-502
Modem_Send_Command, 498-499
MODEZ.C, 102-103
Mouse_Control, 255-258
MOUSETST.C, 258-263
Music_Load, 308-309
Music_Play, 311
Music_Register, 310
Music_Resume, 312
Music_Status, 312
Music_Stop, 311
Music_Unload, 311
OBJECTS.C, 821-825
PCX_Copy_To_Buffer, 154
PCX_Delete, 135
PCX_Get_Sprite, 146-147
PCX_Init, 135
PCX_Load, 136-138
PCX_Show_Buffer, 138-139
PCXDEMO.C, 139-140
PLG_Get_Line, 652-653
PLG_Load_Object, 654-657, 997-1001
Poly_Compare, 848-849, 1042-1043
Position_Object, 685
Print_Char, 86-87
Print_String, 87-88
Read_Color_Reg, 80
Read_Palette, 81
Read_Pixel, 68
Remove_Backfaces_And_Shade, 739-741, 1095-1099, 1123-1127
Remove_Object, 818-820
Rotate_Object, 689-692, 1015-1023
Save_Palette_Disk, 737
Scale_Object, 686
Screen_Transition, 112-114
Serial_Close, 482
Serial_Flush, 481

listings *(continued)*
    Serial_ISR, 476-477
    Serial_Open, 477-478
    Serial_Print, 480-481
    Serial_Read, 479
    Serial_Ready, 478
    Serial_Write, 480
    Set_Graphics_Mode, 62
    Set_Mode_Z, 97-98
    Set_Visual_Page_Mode_Z, 201
    Set_Working_Page_Mode_Z, 199-200
    SOL2DEMO.C, 798-801
    SOLIDEMO.C, 746-749
    SOLZDEMO.C, 886-892
    SORTDEMO.C, 854-859
    Sort_Poly_List, 849-850, 1043
    Sound_Load, 290-293
    Sound_Play, 295
    Sound_Status, 295-296
    Sound_Stop, 296
    Sound_Translate, 293-294
    Sound_Unload, 294
    SPEED.C, 194-197
    SPHERES.C, 202-203
    Sprite_Delete, 146
    Sprite_Draw, 149-150
    Sprite_Draw_Clip, 164-167
    Sprite_Erase, 153-154
    Sprite_Erase_Clip, 168
    Sprite_Init, 145-146
    Sprite_Under, 152
    Sprite_Under_Clip, 169-171
    TERM1.C, 491-493
    TERM2.C, 507-511
    TEXTDEMO.C, 772-774
    Time_Delay, 159, 191, 430, 437-439, 498
    TIMER.C, 434-436
    Timer_Program, 433-434
    Timer_Query, 438-439
    Translate_Object, 685
    Triangle_Asm, 1085-1088
    Triangle_Line, 726-727
    Triangle_16Line, 1091-1093
    TRIDEMO.C, 729-730
    VBLANK.C, 427-429
    Vector_Mag_3D, 640
    VOLCANO.C, 447-452
    VOXEL.C, 954-961
    VOXOPT.C, 981-989
    VOXTILE.C, 966-975
    Wait_For_Connection, 506-507
    Wait_For_Vertical_Retrace, 193
    WIREDEMO.C, 696-700
    World_To_Camera_Object, 793-794, 1030-1034
    WORMS.C, 156-159

listings *(continued)*
    Write_Color_Reg, 79
    Write_Palette, 82
    Write_Pixel, 68, 615-616
    Write_Pixel_Clip, 616-617
    Write_Pixel_DB, 116-117
    Write_Pixel_Z, 99-100
    ZDEMO.C, 881-882
local coordinate space, 790
local coordinates, 591-596, 639, 683-684, 790
local vs. remote, 462, 519, 522
locator, 562
logic unit, 54
logical operations, 978-979
look-up tables
    color, 56, 76-82. *See also* palette
    COSINE, 635, 688-689, 788, 947, 1080
    optimization and, 980, 989
    SIN, 635, 688-689, 788, 947, 1080
    transparency, 777-778
    trigonometric, 635, 688-689, 788, 947, 1080
loudness. *See* amplitude

M

macro, RESET_BITS, 96, 427
macro, SET_BITS, 96, 427
magnitude, vector, 365, 560-561, 640
make code, 209, 214-216
make files, 19
Manhattan Distance, 370-371, 1147
mantissa, 582
MASM, 1044, 1065-1066, 1068
master database, 526-527
master PC, 519-521
master-master setup, 521-523
master-slave setup, 517, 519-521
math
    factorial operation, 1062-1063
    fixed point. *See* fixed point math
    floating point. *See* floating point math
    functions, 3D engine, 639-646
    logical operations, 978-979
    matrix. *See under* matrix
    MOD operation, 965, 979
    order of operations, 802
    vector operations, 562-574
math coprocessor (80387), 1043-1069
    80387 architecture, 1044-1047
    80387 instruction set, 1047-1054
    and external assembler, 1064-1069
    instructions
        arithmetic, 1047-1049
        classical format, 1051-1052
        comparison, 1047, 1050

math coprocessor (80387) (*continued*)
    constants, 1047, 1049
    control, 1047, 1050-1051
    data transfer, 1047-1048
    examples, 1054-1064
    F prefix, 1052
    formats, 1051-1054
    memory format, 1051-1053
    P suffix, 1052, 1055, 1058, 1062
    register format, 1051, 1053-1054
    register pop format, 1051-1052, 1054
    transcendental, 1047, 1049
matrices, 574-581
matrix
    4x4, 600-606, 634, 642-644, 1006
    addition, 576-577
    coefficient, 574
    concatenation, 581, 687-692
    constant, 575
    copying, 643
    dimensions, 575-577
    global transformation, 794-796, 1013, 1025
    identity, 578-580, 642-643, 1011-1012
    inverse, 580-581
    math optimizations, 1005-1012
    multiplication, 577-578, 644-646, 1006-1012
    operations, 576-581
    printing, 644
    result, 576
    rotation, 603-606, 688, 1009, 1013-1015, 1024-1025
    sparse, 1008-1010, 1025
    subtraction, 576-577
    transformation, 600-606, 609, 1009-1010
    translation, 1009, 1024-1025
    variable, 574
    viewing transformation, 792-793
    world to camera transformation, 1013, 1024-1026
    zeroing out, 642-643, 1011
MEDIUM memory model, 19-20
memory allocation, 115, 118, 121, 181
    PCX file, 135-136
    sound, 293-294, 310
memory bank method, 865-866
memory consumption, sound, 302
memory deallocation, BSP, 924-925
memory filling function, 1082-1083
memory latches, 54-55
memory layout, 60-61
memory management, 1003
memory mapping, 51-52, 60-61, 92-95, 200-201
memory models, 19-20, 442
memory movement, 121, 154-155, 1011-1012, 1082-1083
memory planes, 94-95
memory, screen, 50
memory start address, 200-201
memory, state machines, 380-381

mickey (mouse unit), 252, 254
micro facet, 752
MIDI (Musical Instrument Digital Interface), 277
MIDI, Extended (XMI), 303-304
MIDI files, 277-278
MIDI, instrument patches, 277, 280, 283, 532, 538
MIDI music composing, 278, 538
MIDI music demo, 313-316
MIDPAK driver, 281-284, 303-316, 440, 530-532, 538
Miles, John, 281
mixing, sound, 317-320
MOD operation, 965, 979
mode 13h, 35, 39, 49, 60, 98, 101
    demo, 88-91
    palette, 76-77
mode 19. *See* mode 13h
mode, protected, 1100
mode, real, 1100
mode, video, 62, 74-75, 91-100
mode X, 91
mode Z, 49, 91-100
    demo, 102-103
    page flipping, 197-203
    synchronization, 191-193
modem (defined), 483
    AT commands, 485-495
    command responses, 488-491, 499
    command state, 486
    connections, 461, 483-512
    interface library, 496-512
    online state, 486
    programming, 483-512
    protocol, 523
    terminal program, 491-495, 507-511
morphing, 382-383, 778-779
motion control, patterns, 372-380
motion, random, 358-363, 394
motion, synchronous, 379-380
mouse, 207-208, 251-264
    demo, 258-264
    interface function, 254-258
    interrupt, 252-253
    mickey unit, 252, 254
    sensitivity, 252, 254
multifunction display, 1129, 1132-1133
multiplayer games
    basics, 455-458
    networked, 460-462
    On-Line games, 524-527
    split screen, 460
    synchronization, 460-462, 512-523, 527
    synchronous play, 459-460
    taking turns, 458, 527
multiplies, defined, 676
multiprocessor computer, 403-404
multitasking, 403-405, 420, 429, 439

music, 44, 277-284, 303-316, 538, 1150
    MIDPAK, 281-284, 303-316, 440, 530-532, 538
    structure, 307-308, 311
    See also sound
Musical Instrument Digital Interface. *See* MIDI

n

near (hither) clipping plane, 609-610, 612, 614, 674, 745,
    814-818, 831
negative angles, 796
neural networks, 348
normalization, 569, 738
normalizing factor, 600, 634-635
normals, 390, 567-569
    averaging, 750-752
    computing, 807-810
    inward, 708
    outward, 707, 807
    precomputing, 658, 686-687, 810-811, 862
    surface, 807-810
    vertex, 750-752
    and visibility, 707-708
Nyquist Frequency, 275

o

object (.OBJ) files, 1069, 1076-1077
object constants, 708-709
object level culling, 813-821
object oriented programming, 443
object rotation, 682, 687-692, 792, 1013-1024
object space clipping, 610-614, 617, 674, 727
object structure, 590, 639, 1134
objects
    defining, 647-651
    dynamic, 1136, 1140
    multiple (replication), 370, 379-380, 444, 1133-1136
    processing, 444-452
    static, 1136-1140
    transforming, 682-692
off-by-one error, 183
offscreen buffer, 115
On-Line games, 524-527
one-dimensional array, 122-124
opaque background, 87, 124. *See also* transparency
OPT (other people's technology), 474
optimization, 634
    3D engine, 995
    back-face removal, 1093-1099
    clipping, 1034-1039
    data structures, 1003
    depth sort, 1040-1043
    hints, 1101
    inlining, 977-978, 989
    logical operations, 978-979

optimization *(continued)*
    look-up tables, 980, 989
    matrix math, 1005-1012
    pixel drawing, 978, 989
    PLG file format, 995-1003
    rotation, objects, 1013-1024
    scan conversion, 1084-1093
    screen access, 75
    shading, 1093-1099
    shifts, 978-980, 989, 1071, 1077-1079
    transformations, 1013-1034
    triangle renderer, 1084-1093
    voxel engine, 976-989
    world to camera transformation, 1024-1034
    Z sort, 1040-1043
order, clockwise, 704-705
order, counterclockwise, 704-705, 807, 1002
order, operations, 802
order, rendering, 811-812, 893, 953
origin, 57-59, 108
origin as center, 551-552
oscillator, 432
overflow, 1074, 1077

p

page flipping, 91, 100-101, 111, 197-203
paint programs, 131
Painter's algorithm, 618-621, 813, 842-846, 930-931
palette, 76-77, 735-737, 742, 758-759
    animation, 193-197, 440-441
    restoring, 80-82
    saving, 80-82
    See also color
parallax scrolling, 10, 175-179, 187-191
parallel projection, 606-607, 669-670
parsing function, 500-502
particle systems, 444
partitioning. *See* BSP *and* BSP tree
patterns, motion, 372-380
PCX files, 953, 962
    demo, 139-140
    reading, 131-140
    sprite image, 146-147, 154
PCX format, 131
pcx_picture structure, 135, 138
perspective, 10-11, 15-16, 176, 179, 670
perspective projection, 607-609, 670-673, 694, 814-818,
    850
phone lines, 483-484
phonons, 941
PIC (programmable interrupt controller), 221, 223, 408-410
pitch, 597, 1101
pixel-level sort, 859, 861
pixels, 9, 49
    drawing, 978, 989

pixels *(continued)*
    plotting, 66-69, 99-100, 116-117, 616-617, 978, 989
    reading, 68
    text drawing, 84-88
    writing, 68, Z, 99-100
planar memory mapping, 52, 55, 61
plane enable register, 93-95, 100
plane equation, 622-624, 709-711, 862
plane select register, 93-95, 100
plane selection, 93
plasma fractal, 939
playback frequency, 289-290, 331
player position, 785-789
PLG files
    format, 648-651, 995-1003
    importing objects, 651-659
point, 2D, 546-547
point, 3D, 587, 600, 931
point normal form, 710, 862
point slope equation, 660
point slope form, 660-661, 904
point structure, 589
points, 3D world, 931
polygon, 2D, 548
polygon, 3D, 587-588
polygon clipping, 829-836
polygon descriptors, 648, 652
polygon, irregular, 548
polygon list, 648, 830, 837-842, 883-886, 1040, 1043
polygon, regular, 548
polygon rendering, 12-14
polygon structure, 590, 636, 996-997
polygons, filled, 13-14, 712-713
polygons, two-sided, 706-707, 1093
position, world. *See* world_pos
potentiometer, 230, 232, 234, 328
primitives, coplanar, 587-588
probability density function, 385
probability selection, 385-386
probability tables, state machine, 387-389
programmable interrupt controller (PIC), 221, 223, 408-410
projection, 599, 606-609
    and bounding sphere, 814-816
    and line drawing, 668-673
    objects, 796-802
    parallel, 606-607, 669-670
    perspective, 607-609, 670-673, 694, 814-818, 850
protected mode, 1100
protocol modems, 523
Pythagorean theorem, 553, 561

Q

Quad Trees, 813
quadrants, 57-59
quads (4 bytes), 1077, 1081-1084

quads (quadrilaterals), 588, 711-712, 730
Quick Sort function, 847-850, 1040, 1043

R

racing simulators, 13, 197
radians/degrees, 556, 688-689, 788
radiosity, 941-942
radius, precomputing, 658, 686-687
random motion, 358-363, 394
random number generator, 358-363, 394, 516
random number seed, 394, 516, 541
random number terrain, 941
random numbers, 515-516
random variables, 358-363, 394
raster graphics, 9, 12, 49-54
rasterization, 69
Ratcliff, John, 278, 281, 283, 285
ray casting, 14, 398, 935-936, 941-943
ray tracing, 14, 941-942
re-entrancy, 413, 424-425
real mode, 1100
real-time (defined), 32-33
real-time aspect, 30
real-time event loops, 32-33
recirculating buffer, 473, 475-477
rectangle filling, 73-74
reflection, diffuse, 731-732
reflection, negative scaling, 552
reflection, specular, 628-629, 731-732
refresh rate, 52-53
register file, 1045
remote vs. local, 462, 519, 522
rendering, 617-625, 811-812, 842
    algorithms, 619-625
    images, 65-74
    order of, 811-812, 893, 953
    polygon list, 850-852
    problem, 842
    smart, 978
    speed of, 978
    technique comparison, 930-931
replication, 370, 379-380, 444, 1133-1136
RESET_BITS macro, 96, 427
resistive ladder network, 325
resistors, 325
resolution, 50
resonation, 269
RET instruction, 406, 414
retrace period, 191-193
RGB_color structure, 78
RGB_palette structure, 80-81
right-handed system, 557-559
ring buffer, 473, 475-477
RLE (run length encoding), 132
roll, 597, 1101

ROM character set, 84-88
root, BSP tree, 897-898
rotation, 155
    2D, 549, 552-556
    3D, 559, 603-606
    direction, 692
    equations, 553-556, 603-606, 688, 1014-1015
    matrix, 603-606, 688, 1009, 1013-1015, 1024-1025
    objects, 682, 687-692, 792, 1013-1024
row major form, 1011
rules, state machines, 380, 386-387
run time phase, 26
running state, 541

S

sample rate (SR), 274, 289-290
sawtooth wave, 271
scalar, 559
scalar multiplication, 564-566
scale factor, 12, 551
scaling, 155
    2D, 549-552
    3D, 599, 602-603
    fixed point math, 582
    with loading, 652, 657
    objects, 682, 686-687
scan codes, 208-216
scan conversion, 611, 713-716, 871-879, 1084-1093
scan lines, 92-93
Scanline Z-buffer, 625
    vertical, 892-893, 931
scanner code, 152
scanning, 396-398
screen clearing, 63-65, 98-99, 1083-1084
screen coordinates, 57-60, 65, 108, 546, 591
screen filling, 63-65, 98-99
screen shake, 1149
screen transitions, 111-115, 194
scrolling games, 175
scrolling, parallax, 175-179, 187-191
seamless image, 178, 183
seed, random number, 394, 516, 541
segments, 390
self-modifying code, 1101
semicolon comment, 64
sensory simulation, 394-398
sequencer, 56-57, 93
sequences, 303
serial communications, 461, 463-483
    demo, 491-495, 507-511
serial interrupts, 464-467, 471-473, 475-477
serial transmission, 251
serializer, 56
SET_BITS macro, 96, 427
SETD.EXE, 283-284, 531

SETM.EXE, 283-284, 531
setup phase, 24-25, 541
shading, 996
    constant, 638, 650-651, 742
    flat, 638, 650-651, 735-750, 1094
    Gouraud, 749-762
    optimization, 1093-1099
Shannon's Theorem, 275
shift state, 216-218
shifts, 978-980, 989, 1071, 1077
    double shifting, 1077-1079
ships, 1140-1146
sign extension, 1077
signed numbers, 1077
Similar Triangles method, 951-952
SIN look-up tables, 635, 688-689, 788, 947, 1080
sine wave, 269-271, 274
single master-multiple slaves, 517
slave PC, 519-521
SMMS model, 527
SNDSTRUC structure, 285, 289
snow (screen), 229-230
solid modeling, basics, 703-709
sorting
    algorithms, 619-625
    demo (SORTDEMO.C), 854-859
    depth sort, 618-621, 843, 846-859, 930, 1040-1043
    depth sort rendering, 852-859
    optimization, 1040-1043
    pixel-level, 859, 861
    Quick Sort function, 847-850, 1040, 1043
    Sort_Poly_List, 849-850, 1043
    vertex, 74
    Z sort, 846-850, 1040-1043
sound
    aging, 321-322
    amplitude, 270, 273, 279-280, 317-318
        amplification, 317-318
    averaging, 342-343
    basics, 269-272
    cards, 44, 275
    digital recording, 303
    digital sound demo, 297-302
    digitized, 43-44, 273-277, 281-303, 539-540
    DIGPAK driver, 281-303, 530-532
    effects, 539-540, 1150
    formats, 276
    interrupts, 281-285, 288, 303, 440
    MIDPAK driver, 281-284, 303-316, 440, 530-532, 538
    mixing, 317-320
    music, 44, 277-284, 303-316, 538
    music demo, 313-316
    music structure, 307-308, 311
    phase shifting, 342
    preemption, 321-322
    priority, 321-322

sound (*continued*)
  processing, 316-320
  recording, 303
  remote FX, 339-340
  scheduling, 320-323, 539-540
  sound structure, 289
  temporal information, 342-343
  voice effects, 540
  voice recognition, 340-344
  volume control, 296, 325, 328, 532
space game. *See* Kill or Be Killed *and* Starblazer
space partitioning, 894. *See also* BSP
sparsity, 1008-1009
special effects, modeling, 774-779
specular reflection, 628-629, 731-732
speed, 26
spherical distortion, 947-948, 952
sprite, 122, 140
  animation, 155-160
  clipping, 160-171
  deletion function, 145-146
  drawing, 149-151, 164-167
  erasing, 145-146, 153-155
  initialization function, 145-146
  scanning under, 151-152, 169-171
  structure, 140-149
  transparency, 149, 151
square root function, 640, 735, 1147
square wave, 271
stack, 1044-1045
stack probes, 19
Star Trek, 529, 1146
Starblazer, 523, 527-542, 1101-1113, 1120, 1150, 1155
state field, 379, 382-383
state machines, 380-389
state tracking, 41, 142-143
static variables, 41, 442-443
status function, sound, 295, 312
STI instruction, 414, 480
structures, 588-591, 634-639, 1003
  bitmap, 126-127
  BSP tree, 900
  cinder_typ, 444-445
  dir_3d_typ, 635
  facet_typ, 637-638, 838, 1040-1041
  fixed_obj_typ, 1134
  layer, 180
  music, 307-308, 311
  object_typ, 590, 639, 1134
  pcx_picture, 135, 138
  point_typ, 589
  polygon_typ, 590, 636, 996-997
  RGB_color_typ, 78
  RGB_palette_typ, 80-81
  SNDSTRUC, 285, 289

structures (*continued*)
  sprite_typ, 141-142
  vector_3d_typ, 634
  wall_typ, 900
subharmonics, 271
Sutherland-Cohen algorithm, 682
Symmetric Double Step algorithm, 665
synchronization, 41-42, 159, 191-193
  game, 512-523
  temporal, 41-42, 513-514, 518, 527
synthesizer
  construction, 323-335
  DIGIBLASTER, 323-335
  FM, 278-280
  wave table, 280
SYSEX commands, 306

T

telephone lines, 483-484
teleportation, 1120, 1139
temporal synchronization, 41-42, 513-514, 518, 527
terminal point, 561
terrain, 3D, 935-936
terrain following, 389-394, 1149-1150
terrain generator demo, 953-963
terrain maps
  fractal, 939
  random, 939-941
  scanned, 937-939
  tiles, 963
text drawing, 84-88
textel, 765
texture mapping, 14, 762-774, 892-893
three dimensional. *See* 3D
threshold variables, 142, 362, 383, 445
tiles (cells), 963-966
tiling, 180
time delay function, 40-42, 159, 191, 430, 437-439, 498
time lag, 28
time source, high-resolution, 192-193
time synchronization, 41-42, 513-514, 518, 527
time tracking, 437-439
timekeeper interrupt, 415-424
timer, internal, 430-436
timer interrupt, 44, 415-424
timer, programming, 433-436
timer value, 42
timing, 191-193, 437
timing variables, 142, 444
token passing scheme, 514, 518-519, 540
tracking, 348-358
transcendental functions, 1080
transcendental instructions, 1047, 1049
transformation matrix, 600-606, 609, 1009-1010

transformation matrix (*continued*)
  global, 794-796, 1013, 1025
  viewing, 792-793
  world to camera, 1013, 1024-1026
transformations, 155
  2D, 549-556
  3D, 599-606
  camera, 789
  Cartesian, 549-556
  global, 794-796, 1013, 1024-1034
  local to world, 790-792
  objects, 682-692
  optimization, 1013-1034
  view, 798-801
  viewing, 599, 606-617, 607-609, 789-796
  world to camera, 792-794, 814, 921-922, 1013, 1024-
    1034
transition arcs, 381-383
translation, 155-156
  2D, 549-550
  3D, 599, 601-602
  BSP tree, 923-924
  matrix, 1009, 1024-1025
  objects, 682, 684-685, 792
  sound, 293-294
transparency, 83, 87, 124, 127, 129, 149, 151, 186, 774-778
traversal, inorder, 894, 898-900, 917-922
traversal methods, 920, 922
triangles, 711-712
  clipping, 717, 719, 727-728
  drawing, 716-727, 869-879, 1084-1093
  flat bottom, 717, 719, 723-725, 871, 878-879, 1084,
    1089
  flat top, 717, 719, 721-723, 871, 878-879, 1084, 1089
  functions demo, 729-730
  general, 717, 719
  intersecting, 880-882
  renderer, 716-727, 869-879, 1084-1093
  scan conversion, 713-716, 726-727
  texture mapping, 768-771
triangulation, 588, 711-712, 730
trigonometric look-up tables, 635, 688-689, 788, 947, 1080
trivial rejection, 719, 816-818
Truecolor, 134
TSRs, 44
two-sided polygons, 996, 1001-1003

U

UART interrupts, 464-467, 471-473, 475-477
UART registers, 463-470
universe reflection, 515-518

V

vapor trail, 362-363

vaporization, 1148
variables
  counter, 142, 362, 379, 383, 445
  decision, 662-663
  global, 441
  random, 358-363, 394
  static, 41, 442-443
  threshold, 142, 362, 383, 445
  timing, 142, 444
Vblank, 425-430
vector algebra, 364-366
vector graphics, 8
vector magnitude, 365, 560-561, 640
vector operations, 562-574
vector scaling, 365-366
vector structure, 634
vectors, 559-574
  addition, 562
  cross product, 567-569
  dot product, 566-567, 618
  generating, 571-574
  inversion, 565
  multiplication, 564-569
  normal, 567-569
  normalization, 569
  row, 644-646
  scalar multiplication, 564-566
  subtraction, 562-564
  unit, 569-571, 811
vertex list, 648, 705, 790
vertex normals, 750-752
vertex ordering, 704-705
vertex sorting, 74
vertical blank interrupt, 425-430
vertical blank period, 191-193, 229-230, 425-430
Vertical Retrace End Register, 426-427
vertical retrace flag, 192
vertical retrace period, 191-193, 229-230, 425-430
vertical scan line Z-buffer, 892-893, 931
VFOV, 673
VGA card, 49, 54-57
VGA input status register 1, 192
video access optimization, 75
video (frame) buffer, 51, 61, 63, 65, 111, 115, 125, 1084
video interrupt, 61-62, 74-75
video modes
  mode X, 91
  mode Z, 91-100
  restoring, 74-75
  table, 62
video synchronization, 42
view angles, 785-789
view direction, 597, 599, 606, 787
viewing distance, 671-673
viewing transformation, 599, 606-617, 607-609, 789-796

viewing volume, 609-610, 745, 814-816, 829-830
viewpoint, 396-398
    defined, 597
    field of view, 14-16, 671-673. *See also* field of view
    perspective, 10-11
    player, 785-789
    and projection, 599, 606
virtual reality, 6, 336
visibility, 707-708
visibility flag, 167
visibility, objects, 610-611, 617-618, 807-818
vision, simulated, 394-398
VOC file, 288-293
VOC format, 276
voice effects, 540
voice recognition, 340-344
voice wave, 271-272
volcano demo, 444-452
volume control, 296, 325, 328, 532
voxel (defined), 15, 935
voxel engine
    optimizations, 976-989
    texture-based, 953-963, 980-989
    tile-based, 963-976
voxel graphics, 15-16, 935
    basics, 935-936
    voxel data, 936-941
voxel height, 950-952
voxel strip scaling, 952-953
VRAM, 55

wait function, 518-519
wall structure, 900
warnings, 19
wave table synthesis, 278, 280
waveforms, 269-272
wetware, 348
white noise, 271-272
whole part, 583
Windows, and games, 1152-1153

wireframe 3D demo, 693-700
wireframe graphics, 660-668
wireframe models, 8, 12
word-size writes, 75, 117
world coordinates, 594-596, 639, 683-684, 786-787, 790,
    792-796, 806, 814
world to camera transformation, 792-794, 814, 921-922,
    1013, 1024-1034
world_pos, 683-685, 745, 790, 814, 1134
Wozniak, Steve, xxii, xxiv-xxvi
wrapping images, 178, 183

X mode, 91
XMI files, 303-304

y-intercept form, 661
yaw, 597, 945, 1101
yon (far) clipping plane, 610, 612, 614, 674, 745, 814-818,
    831

Z

Z-buffer, 711, 813, 930-931
    algorithm, 619, 622-625, 859-893
    demo, 880-882, 886-892
    foreground objects, 989
    memory, 865-868
    Scanline Z-buffer, 625
    vertical scan line, 892-893, 931
Z clipping, 745
z component, 669-671
z coordinate, 398-399, 556
Z interpolation, 864-866, 871-879
Z mode (mode Z), 49, 91-100
    demo, 102-103
    page flipping, 197-203
    synchronization, 191-193
Z sort, 846-850, 1040-1043. *See also* depth sort

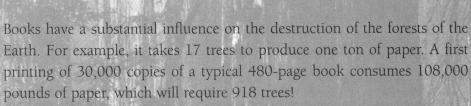

Books have a substantial influence on the destruction of the forests of the Earth. For example, it takes 17 trees to produce one ton of paper. A first printing of 30,000 copies of a typical 480-page book consumes 108,000 pounds of paper, which will require 918 trees!

Waite Group Press™ is against the clear-cutting of forests and supports reforestation of the Pacific Northwest of the United States and Canada, where most of this paper comes from. As a publisher with several hundred thousand books sold each year, we feel an obligation to give back to the planet. We will therefore support organizations which seek to preserve the forests of planet Earth.

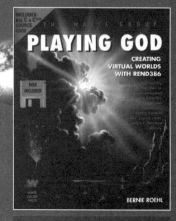
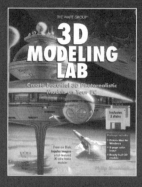